OCEAN AND COASTAL LAW

CASES AND MATERIALS

Fourth Edition

■ ■ ■

By

Alison Rieser

Dai Ho Chun Professor of Ocean Policy
University of Hawai'i at Manoa
Professor Emerita, University of Maine School of Law

Donna R. Christie

Elizabeth C. and Clyde W. Atkinson Professor of Law
Florida State University College of Law

Joseph J. Kalo

Graham Kenan Professor of Law Emeritus
University of North Carolina School of Law
Co-Director, North Carolina Coastal Resources
Law, Planning and Policy Center

Richard G. Hildreth

Professor of Law
Director, Ocean and Coastal Law Center
University of Oregon School of Law

AMERICAN CASEBOOK SERIES®

WEST.

Mat #41052003

American Casebook Series is a trademark registered in the U.S. Patent and Trademark Office.

© West, a Thomson business, 1998, 2002, 2007
© 2013 LEG, Inc. d/b/a West Academic Publishing
    610 Opperman Drive
    St. Paul, MN 55123
    1-800-313-9378

West, West Academic Publishing, and West Academic are trademarks of West Publishing Corporation, used under license.

Printed in the United States of America

ISBN: 978–0–314–26674–3

To the memories of our colleagues, Lindy S. Johnson and Jon M. Van Dyke, tireless advocates of justice for the oceans, and to our families

PREFACE TO THE FOURTH EDITION

So much has happened in our oceans and to our coasts since the last edition of this casebook that it seems an entirely new body of law is required, not just a new edition of a law casebook. From Hurricanes Katrina and Rita in 2005, to Superstorm Sandy on the eve of the federal elections in 2012, our cities and coastal communities have awoken to the 'new normal' of severe coastal flooding, rising sea levels and abnormally strong storms, all due to warmer oceans and changes in the climate. Coastal adaptation and planned retreat are now commonly heard terms in boardrooms and city halls. The legal and policy consequences of the oil spill disaster in the Gulf of Mexico in 2010 are still unfolding as are the long-term effects of the oil and dispersants on this already stressed ecosystem.

But these coastal storms and ocean disasters have made at least one thing clear: the time for developing offshore wind and other ocean renewable resources has arrived. With new legal authority, a reorganized Bureau of Ocean Energy Management now has an opportunity to be "smart from the start" about this new energy source, while states of the Atlantic seaboard compete to be the center of the promising new offshore wind industry. As this edition goes to press, oil drilling in the U.S. Arctic is on hold as agencies and companies acknowledge the unprecedented challenges, if not risks, of oil development in the retreating sea ice. An executive order has restructured the process for coordinating federal policies for the oceans and coasts, and a promising new tool, coastal and marine spatial planning, appears to be enjoying rapid uptake. But will these tools be up to the challenge of climate-changed coasts and marine ecosystems?

Species losing habitat to climate change are finding themselves on the endangered species list for the first time: species from Arctic ringed seals and polar bears, to reef-building coral species in the Atlantic and Pacific. Unprecedented organizational structures are being adopted for tradition-bound and overfished fisheries in New England. Some exploited species, however, have declined to levels that would be considered endangered if conservation and ecosystem norms were used to assess their populations rather than the shift-resistant paradigm of maximum sustainable yield. But several species of sharks are now listed under the Convention on International Trade in Endangered Species of Flora and Fauna, the international companion to the U.S. Endangered Species Act. And Chinese-Canadian couples in Vancouver are eschewing a wedding banquet of shark fin soup as a symbol of their love for each other and for the oceans of their children's future.

The field of ocean and coastal law has indeed come of age in interesting times. It remains to be seen if this is a curse or a blessing. We hope you find this revised edition suits our times and the challenges facing our students, our communities, and our oceans.

On behalf of my departed colleagues and co-authors, I wish you aloha.

ALISON RIESER

May 2013

ACKNOWLEDGMENTS

We are indebted to the following authors and publishers for generous permission to reprint excerpts from copyrighted materials:

Thomas T. Ankerson and Thomas Ruppert, Water-Dependent Use Definitions: A Tool to Protect and Preserve Recreational and Commercial Working Waterfronts (2010). Reprinted with permission.

Ernest R. Bartley, The Tidelands Oil Controversy (1953). Copyright © 1953, renewed 1981, University of Texas Press, reprinted with permission.

Neal D. Black, Note, Balancing the Advantages of Individual Transferable Quotas Against Their Redistributive Effects: The Case of Alliance Against IFQs v. Brown, 9 Georgetown Int'l Envt'l L. Rev. 727 (1998). Reprinted with permission of the publisher, Copyright © 1998.

Donna R. Christie and Richard Hildreth, Coastal and Ocean Management in a Nutshell (3rd ed. 2007). Copyright © 2007 West Publishing Co. Reprinted with permission of West Group.

Donna R. Christie, Of Beaches, Boundaries and SOBs, 25 J. Land Use & Envt'l L. 19 (2009). Reprinted with permission.

J. Firestone, W. Kempton, A. Kreuger, and C.E. Loper, Regulating Offshore Wind Power and Aquaculture: Messages from Land and Sea, 14 Cornell J. L. & Pub. Pol'y 71 (2004). Reprinted with permission.

K. Kimmel and D.S. Stalenhoef, The Cape Wind Offshore Wind Energy Project: A Case Study of the Difficult Transition to Renewable Energy, 5 Golden Gate U. Envt'l L.J. 197 (2011). Reprinted with permission.

John Warren Kindt, Ocean Dumping, 13 Denver J. Int'l L. & Pol'y 335 (1984). Reprinted with permission of the publisher.

Scott Kraus et al., North Atlantic Right Whales in Crisis, 309 Science 561 (July 22, 2005). Reprinted with permission.

Roger B. Krueger, The Background of the Continental Shelf and the Outer Continental Shelf Lands Act, 10 Nat. Resources Journal 442 (1970). Reprinted with permission of the Natural Resources Journal.

Frank E. Maloney and Richard C. Ausness, The Use and Legal Significance of the Mean High Tide Line in Coastal Boundary Mapping, 53 N. Carolina L. Rev. 185 (1974). Copyright © 1974 by the N.C. Law Review Association. Reprinted with permission.

Aaron L. Shalowitz, Boundary Problems Raised by the Submerged Lands Act, 54 Columbia Law Review 1021 (1954). Reprinted with permission of the Columbia Law Review.

William B. Stoebuck, Nontrespassory Takings in Eminent Domain (1977). Copyright© 1997 by Michie, a division of Reed Elsevier Inc. and Reed Elsevier Properties Inc. and reproduced with permission of Michie. Further reproduction is not authorized.

Ernest E. Smith and B.H. Diffen, Winds of Change: The Creation of Wind Law, 5 Texas Oil, Gas & Energy Law 65 (2009-10). Reprinted with permission.

James G. Titus, Rolling Easements Primer, U.S. Environmental Protection Agency (2011).

SUMMARY OF CONTENTS

TABLE OF CONTENTS

TABLE OF CASES

The principal cases are in bold type.

Bennett v. Spear ------------------535, 852
Bethlehem Steel Co. v. N.Y. State
   Labor Relations Bd. ---------------- 882
BFI Waste Sys. v. FAA--------------- 532
Biodiversity Legal Foundation v.
   Norton-------------------------------- 844
Biological Legal Found. v.
   Badgley ------------------------------- 905
Blackmer v. United States----------- 754
Blue Ocean Inst. v. Gutierrez------- 660
Blue Water Fishermen's Assoc. v.
   NMFS --------------------------------- 647
Board of Regents of State Colleges
   v. Roth-------------------------------- 371
Boca Ciega Hotel, Inc. v. Bouchard
   Transp. Co., Inc.--------------------- 482
Borax Consolidated Ltd. v. Los
   Angeles------------------------------- 164
Borough of Neptune City v. Borough
   of Avon–By–The–Sea ---------149, 222
Bostic v. United States--------------- 363
Boston Waterfront Dev. Corp. v.
   Commonwealth--- 144, 495, 498, 504
Bowes v. City of Chicago -------149, 151
Bowlby v. Shively---------------------- 185
Bowman, United States v. ----------- 755
Boynton, United States v.------------ 173
Bright, United States v. ------------- 119
Brower v. Evans---- 794, 796, 797, 798,
   799, 801, 846
Brown–Forman Distillers Corp. v.
   New York State Liquor Auth.----- 739
Building and Constr. Trades Council
   v. Associated Builders and
   Contractors -------------------------- 710
Building Indus. Ass'n of Superior
   Cal. v. Norton----------------------- 831
**Building Industry Ass'n of the
   Bay Area v. Commerce --------- 848**
Cabinet Mountains Wilderness v.
   Peterson ----------------------------- 402
Cal. ex rel. Lockyer v. U.S. Dep't
   of Agric. ----------------------------- 358
**California and State Lands
   Commission v. Deep Sea
   Research ----------------------117**, 119
California Coastal Comm'n v. U.S.
   Navy --------------------------------- 298
California Coastal Commission v.
   Granite Rock Company ------266, 309
California ex rel. State Lands
   Comm'n v. United States---------- 173
California Gillnetters Assoc. v.
   Dept. of Fish & Game -------876, 961
California v. ARC Am. Corp. -------- 883
California v. Mack--------------------- 269
California v. Norton---------------278, 400
California v. United States --------- 171
California v. Watt (Watt II) ---413, 414
California Wilderness Coalition v.
   U.S. Dept. of Energy --------------- 899

California, United States v. --- 77, 78,
   79, 80, 81, 82, 87, 88, 89, 97, 98, 500
Caminiti v. Boyle--------------144, **156**
Campo v. Department of
   Environmental Regulation--332, 335
Cape Hatteras Access Preservation
   Alliance v. U.S. Dept. of the
   Interior------------------------------ 854
Capune v. Robbins--------------------- 185
**Carol Severance v. Jerry
   Patterson ---------------------- 230**
Carolina Beach Fishing Pier, Inc. v.
   Town of Carolina Beach ----------- 344
Cartens v. California Coastal
   Commission--------------------160, 247
Cass v. Dicks ----------------------173, 174
Cayman Turtle Farm, Ltd. v.
   Andrus ------------------------------- 764
**Center for Biological Diversity
   v. Evans ----------------------- 840**
**Center for Biological Diversity
   v. U.S. Department of
   Interior ------------------------ 403**
Certain Parcels of Land Situated
   in City of Valdez, United States
   v. ------------------------------------- 208
Chevron U.S.A., Inc. v.
   Hammond----------------------------- 902
Chevron, U.S.A., Inc. v.
   Natural Resources Defense
   Council, Inc. ---- 623, 631, 632, 633,
   782, 837, 906
**Chinatown Neighborhood
   Association v. Brown------------ 731**
Choctaw Nation v. Oklahoma------- 154
Churchman v. Evans ----------------- 674
Cinque Bambini Partnership v.
   State --------------------------------- 129
City of Alameda v. Todd Shipyards
   Corp. --------------------------------- 155
City of Anchorage, United States
   v. ------------------------------------- 153
**City of Charleston, South Carolina
   v. A Fisherman's Best, Inc. --- 703**
City of Daytona Beach v.
   Toma–Rama, Inc. ------------------- 227
City of Houston v. Dep't of Hous.
   & Urban Dev. ----------------------- 409
City of Madison v. State ------------- 151
City of Milwaukee v. State---------- 151
City of New York v. U.S. E.P.A.---- 940
**City of Ocean City v.
   Maffucci ------------------------ 189**
City of Palmetto v. Katsch----------- 226
City of Sausalito v. O'Neill---------- 308
City of Shoreacres v.
   Waterworth--------------------543, 544
City of Tacoma, Washington v.
   F.E.R.C.------------------------------ 913
City of Waukesha v. EPA ----------- 532
Clean Ocean Action v. York --------- 939

TABLE OF STATUTES, REGULATIONS, AND TREATY PROVISIONS

OCEAN AND COASTAL LAW

CASES AND MATERIALS

Fourth Edition

CHAPTER 1

THE ORIGIN OF U.S. RIGHTS AND RESPONSIBILITIES IN THE OCEANS

■ ■ ■

1. INTRODUCTION

The oceans represent the interface of United States national sovereignty and jurisdiction with international waters and waters of other nations. Although the U.S. federal government shares jurisdiction over the marginal seas with the adjacent coastal states, the scope of U.S. jurisdiction, rights and responsibilities in the oceans derives in many respects from international law. State boundaries extend from the land into the marginal seas, but as one moves seaward from the coastline, state and local government prerogatives quickly become subordinate to federal constitutional interests in commerce, navigation and foreign affairs. Because these seas are bounded by international waters and waters of other countries, international law also circumscribes the limits and scope of United States sovereignty and jurisdiction.

When Congress in 1966 created the Commission on Marine Science, Engineering, and Resources, also known as the Stratton Commission, to investigate and make recommendations on United States marine law and policy, the Commission's report focused more on issues related to coastal land uses and how use of the oceans might alleviate the pressures on our highly developed coastlines. In recent decades, however, the oceans have become the focus of greater attention as the intensive use of oceans has depleted resources, led to serious pollution of the seas, and created conflicts in ocean uses. The oceans are the site for new kinds of renewable energy production and genetic resources. The oceans also play an important role in climate and global warming. In short, the economic and environmental importance of oceans is becoming an issue that can no longer be given a low priority in development of a coastal nation's policies, management and regulation.

This chapter deals with rights and jurisdiction over the ocean and its resources from the perspective of the United States as a coastal nation in the international community.

2. EVOLUTION OF THE INTERNATIONAL LAW OF THE SEA

A. A BRIEF HISTORY OF THE LAW OF THE SEA TO 1945

An historical perspective is necessary to understand the issues and problems of the modern law of the sea. For centuries before recorded history, the seas were freely used for navigation and trade before questions of access and control began to arise. The Age of Exploration and Discovery began in the fifteenth century and evolved as Europeans sought new trade routes and treasures. The era included expansive claims to the seas including Papal Bulls in 1493 and 1506 dividing most of the oceans between Portugal and Spain. England, too, extended the concept of closed seas to the "British Seas," a right which was espoused in John Selden's *Mare Clausem* (1635). The early 1600s also saw claims to the seas by Denmark, Genoa, Tuscany, Turkey, Venice and even the Papacy. Paradoxically, it was England that successfully challenged Spain's expansive claim and established freedom of the seas for navigation, trade and fishing—the concept that prevailed by the late seventeenth century.

The beginning of the era of the freedom of the seas is usually benchmarked by scholars to the publication in 1609 of *Mare Liberum* by Hugo Grotius, a young Dutch scholar who later came to be regarded as the "father of modern international law." *Mare Liberum* was a justification for the rights of the Dutch and the East India Company to participate in ocean navigation and commerce. Arguing that the oceans were limitless and could not be possessed, occupied or enclosed, Grotius concluded that the seas must be free and open to navigation, which did not harm or exhaust the sea to anyone's disadvantage. The ensuing debate among scholars, including Selden *supra*, provided unique insights into the state of the law of the sea at that time. Grotius's view ultimately prevailed and was reinforced by state practice and was solidified by the power of the British navy in the next two centuries.

The only encroachment on the rule of freedom of the high seas during the next three centuries was recognition of a territorial sea—a narrow belt of water and submerged lands extending seaward from a country's baselines. The development of this maritime zone was influenced by the work, *De Dominio Maris* (1702), by Bynkershoek, who argued that coastal waters within the range of a cannon were subject to the sovereignty of the adjacent state. This "cannon-shot rule" provided an argument for effective control and a basis for the authority to make a claim to the marginal sea, but did not provide a basis for a specific distance for the width of the territorial sea. Later in the century, the Italian jurist Galiani proposed three miles or one marine league as the breadth of the territorial sea to provide a continuous, uniform belt of coastal state sovereignty. By the early part of the nineteenth century, the notion of a three-mile territorial sea seemed to be "crystallizing" as customary practice. Although state practice was not completely uniform, by the beginning of the twentieth century, it seemed that a three-mile territorial sea was clearly the practice of a majority of coastal nations. In this zone, state sovereignty extended to the waters, the seabed, the living and non-living resources, as well as to the airspace over it. An important limitation on this sovereignty evolved, however, as the principle of the territorial sea developed—foreign ships retained a right of innocent passage through territorial waters. Passage that did not threaten the coastal state's peace and security could not be impeded by the coastal state. The right of innocent passage did not extend, however, to the later-developing kinds of passage by aircraft and submerged passage of submarines.

The beginning of the twentieth century, however, was a period of developing dissatisfaction with the three-mile limit. Numerous states extended claims to six or twelve miles, over the objection of major maritime countries who sought to preserve the greatest extent of freedoms of the high seas. In fact, the question of the breadth of territorial waters was hotly debated in the Preparatory Commission leading to the Hague Codification Conference of 1930, which was unable to reach agreement on the issue in its draft articles on the breadth of the territorial sea.

By the end of World War II, the United States had become aware of the vast oil and gas resources that existed off its coasts and the strategic importance of controlling those resources. But the United States also had a compelling interest, as a naval superpower, to assure the continuance of the broadest definitions and scope of the freedoms of the sea. In September 1945, President Truman issued two proclamations: one addressing conservation of high seas fisheries, and the second claiming exclusive United States jurisdiction and control over the natural resources of the country's adjacent continental shelf.

PROCLAMATION 2667 OF SEPTEMBER 28, 1945, POLICY OF THE UNITED STATES WITH RESPECT TO THE NATURAL RESOURCES OF THE SUBSOIL AND SEA BED OF THE CONTINENTAL SHELF

Executive Order 9633 of September 28, 1945
(The Truman Proclamation)

WHEREAS the Government of the United States of America, aware of the long range world-wide need for new sources of petroleum and other minerals holds the view that efforts to discover and make available new supplies of these resources should be encouraged; and

WHEREAS its competent experts are of the opinion that such resources underlie many parts of the continental shelf off the coasts of the United States of America, and the with modern technological progress their utilization is already practicable or will become so at an early date and;

WHEREAS recognized jurisdiction over these resources is required in the interest of their conservation and prudent utilization when and as development is undertaken; and

WHEREAS it is the view of the Government of the United States that the exercise of jurisdiction over the natural resources of the subsoil and sea bed of the continental shelf by the contiguous nation is reasonable and just, since the effectiveness of measures to utilize or conserve these resources would be contingent upon cooperation and protection from the shore, since the continental shelf may be regarded as an extension of the land-mass of the coastal nation and thus naturally appurtenant to it, since these resources frequently form a seaward extension of a pool or deposit lying within the territory, and since self-protection compels the coastal nation to keep close watch over activities off its shores which are of the nature necessary for utilization of these resources;

NOW THEREFORE. I, HARRY S. TRUMAN, President of the United States of America, do hereby proclaim the following policy of the United States of America with respect to the natural resources of the subsoil and sea bed of the continental shelf.

Having concern for the urgency of conserving and prudently utilizing its natural resources, the Government of the United States regards the natural resources of the subsoil and sea bed of the continental shelf beneath the high seas but contiguous to the coasts of the United States, subject to jurisdiction and control. In cases where the continental shelf extends to the shores of another State, or is shared with an adjacent State, the boundary shall be determined by the United States and the Sate concerned in accordance with equitable principles. The character as high seas of the waters above the continental shelf and the right to their free and unimpeded navigation are in no way thus affected.

QUESTIONS

1. The Truman Proclamation carefully excluded claims to any rights in water column over the continental shelf. Why?

2. What was the scope of the U.S. claim to the continental shelf—substantively and geographically?

3. While lacking any foundation in international law, the United States claim to the continental shelf was widely accepted. Why? For a history of the doctrine prior to the Truman proclamation, see Richard Young, Further Claims to Areas beneath the High Seas, 43 Amer. J. Int'l L. 790 (1949), cited

in Arbitration Between Petroleum Development (Trucial Coast) Ltd. and Sheikh of Abu Dhabi, 47 Amer. J. Int'l. L. 156 (1953) (legal doctrine of the continental shelf did not exist in 1939 when Abu Dhabi awarded exclusive oil drilling concession to British company).

4. President Truman's "other" proclamation claimed the right to establish "explicitly bounded conservation zones" in certain areas of the high seas contiguous to the U.S. coasts where fisheries of a substantial scale have or may be established. It provided that if the fisheries were conducted by U.S. nationals, they would be subject to U.S. regulation and control. If the fisheries were jointly maintained by the U.S. and other countries, the zones and regulations would be established by agreement. An accompanying executive order, No. 9634 (Sept. 28, 1945), provided for the establishment of fishery conservation zones pursuant to the proclamation. Why didn't the president declare a 200-mile fishery conservation zone of unilateral U.S. control and regulation?

B. UNCLOS I AND II: THE 1958 GENEVA CONVENTIONS

NOTE: THE MOVEMENT TOWARD CODIFICATION

In the second half of the twentieth century, nations were deeply divided by political and ideological issues in an era that now included the potential for nuclear warfare. The ability of submerged submarines to exercise freedom of navigation of the seas became the world's primary nuclear deterrent during the Cold War. New technologies developed during World War II, like sonar and monofilament line, led to increased efficiency of fishing vessels, dramatic increases in catch, and expansion of distant water fishing fleets. The world's reliance on petroleum also made control and development of newly discovered offshore oil fields a matter of crucial national state importance. Of equal importance was the transportation of that oil around the globe, and oil tankers became larger and larger to accommodate the world's immense appetite for oil.

The world was also changing geopolitically. With the end of the colonial era, the number of independent nations exploded. These nations were mostly poor and less developed, without extensive navies or technology for development of large-scale fisheries. Freedom of the high seas was much less important to these newly independent countries than to the maritime powers. To these nations, protection of the resources just off their coasts from distant water fishing fleets and the protection of their shores from pollution by intensifying traffic and increasingly larger oil tankers were the paramount concerns. Marine scientific research, a luxury affordable by a relative few of the richest countries of the world, was often viewed with suspicion when carried out off their shores. With protection of coastal resources more important to these nations than high seas freedoms, it is not surprising that the trend for newly independent and other less developed coastal nations was to claim 12-mile territorial seas.

The Truman Proclamation on the continental shelf provided an analogy for some nations that did not have extensive continental shelves—and therefore, no offshore oil reserves to protect—to make claims to protect other resources in the adjacent seas. In 1947, Chile and Peru made claims of jurisdiction to 200 miles to protect fisheries and other resources. Peru's claim has been characterized as a 200-mile territorial sea. In 1952, Ecuador extended its territorial sea to 200 miles. Unlike the virtually immediate and positive international response to the Truman Proclamation, however, the opposition to these claims was strong, especially from countries with navies and distant water fishing interests. In spite of this opposition, however, the number of Latin American and African countries making claims to 200-mile territorial seas or fishing zones gradually grew.

In the mid-1950s, the International Law Commission (ILC), a group of international law experts within the United Nations system charged with codifying and developing international law, took on the task of codifying the law of the sea. Four proposed law-making treaties developed by the ILC addressing the territorial sea, the continental shelf, the high seas and high seas fisheries were presented to the First United Nations Conference on the Law of the Sea (UNCLOS I) at Geneva and were adopted in 1958 following a few weeks of negotiations. The treaties were not viewed as radically changing the *status quo* of international law at the time, although the recognition of the doctrine of the continental shelf was rather remarkable in that it had evolved from a theory concocted in 1945 by the United States to something akin to a natural law right of coastal states by 1958. This was not the only indication that the law of the sea was rapidly evolving. In light of rapidly developing offshore technology, no agreement could be reached to establish the limit of the continental shelf either by depth or distance. In addition, the Conference could not agree on a maximum breadth for the territorial sea. Although there was a growing trend for claims to 6- or 12-mile territorial seas, the United States and other maritime powers staunchly defended the 3-mile limit. The Second United Nations Conference on the Law of the Sea (UNCLOS II) in 1960 again failed to resolve these issues.

* * *

NOTE: SOVEREIGNTY AND JURISDICTION

Sovereignty is one of the most basic principles of international law, but does not have a single meaning. The concept certainly embodies the principles of equality of states and nonintervention. Most fundamentally, however, sovereignty is the supreme authority over a territory and a population. Sovereignty also includes the right to acquire territory. International law historically allowed states to acquire territory through domination or conquest. Today, territory may be gained through voluntary cession by another nation, by prescription and by occupation of unclaimed land or resources. In modern times, unoccupied land is virtually non-existent, but until very recently the ocean and its resources were not the territory of or subject to the sovereignty of any state.

The supreme authority of a state over its territory includes legislative competency over the territory subject to its sovereignty. This is the related international law principle of jurisdiction. A nation has jurisdiction to proscribe and enforce its laws throughout its territory, and importantly for purposes of the law of the sea, it also has jurisdiction over its nationals and over ships and aircraft flying its flag even beyond national boundaries.

Sovereignty and jurisdiction of states is derived from and limited by international law, but states have a great deal of discretion on how to exercise that sovereignty and jurisdiction within their territories. For example, a state may claim a territorial sea of only three miles, even though international law recognizes the competence of states to claim up to twelve miles. International law takes on a special importance in the parts of the earth—the oceans—beyond any states' territory and sovereignty, because the law of the sea, a part of public international law, creates the applicable norms governing humanity's use of the sea and its resources. These norms developed extremely slowly since the earliest use of the sea for navigation and trade, until the second half of the twentieth century, when national security issues and technology development for resource exploitation (among other political, economic and social changes) combined to create an explosion in the development of the law.

Consider how sovereignty and jurisdiction are related in the following case. At the time of the foreign fishing vessel's arrest, the U.S. had an exclusive fishery zone of 9 miles contiguous to its territorial sea.

UNITED STATES V. F/V TAIYO MARU 28

D. Me., 1975
395 F.Supp. 413

GIGNOUX, DISTRICT JUDGE.

These two proceedings arise from the seizure of a Japanese fishing vessel, the F/V TAIYO MARU 28, by the United States Coast Guard for violation of United States fisheries law. On September 5, 1974, the Coast Guard sighted the TAIYO MARU 28 fishing at [a point] approximately 16.25 miles off the coast of the State of Maine and approximately 10.5 miles seaward from Monhegan Island. It is conceded to be within the contiguous fisheries zone of the United States. 16 U.S.C. § 1092. The Coast Guard signaled the TAIYO MARU 28 to stop, but the vessel attempted to escape by accelerating toward the high seas. The Coast Guard immediately pursued and seized the vessel on the high seas at . . . a point approximately 67.9 miles at sea from the mainland of the continental United States. The vessel was thereafter delivered to the port of Portland, and on

September 6, 1974, the United States filed in this Court a civil complaint for condemnation and forfeiture of the vessel and a criminal information against the master, Masatoshi Kawaguchi. Both actions charge violations of 16 U.S.C. §§ 1081 and 1091 and seek imposition of the sanctions for such violations provided by 16 U.S.C. § 1082.

On October 4, 1974, Miho Maguro Gyogyo Kabushiki Kaisha of Shimizi, Japan, a corporation, as the sole owner and party entitled to possesion of the TAIYO MARU 28, appeared through local counsel and filed its demand for restitution and right to defend, and an answer to the complaint, in the forfeiture action. On October 18, 1974, the master was arraigned and pleaded not guilty to the criminal information.[3] . . . Defendant seeks dismissal of all proceedings on the ground that the Court lacks jurisdiction, since the vessel, unlawfully, was seized on the high seas in violation of the territorial limitations imposed by international agreements on the power of the United States to pursue and seize foreign vessels and arrest foreign nationals for violation of its domestic fisheries law.

There is no dispute as to the events, recited above, which led to the seizure of the TAIYO MARU 28. For the purposes of the instant motions, the following undisputed facts are significant: (1) On September 5, 1974, the United States Coast Guard sighted the TAIYO MARU 28, a commercial Japanese fishing vessel, within waters which the United States claims as part of its contiguous fisheries zone, and had reasonable cause to believe that the vessel was fishing in the zone in violation of United States fisheries law; and (2) at that point, the Coast Guard signaled the TAIYO MARU 28 and, after giving immediate and continuous hot pursuit, effected seizure of the vessel on the high seas.

The United States contends that, by fishing in the contiguous fisheries zone, the TAIYO MARU 28 and her captain violated the Bartlett Act, 16 U.S.C. § 1081 et seq., and the Contiguous Fisheries Zone Act, 16 U.S.C. § 1091 et seq., and that international law permits, and United States law authorizes, the hot pursuit of a foreign vessel from the contiguous fisheries zone and the seizure of the vessel on the high seas for violation of domestic fisheries law. Defendant's position is that this Court lacks jurisdiction over the TAIYO MARU 28 and her master, because the vessel was seized on the high seas in violation of the 1958 Geneva Convention on the High Seas, opened for signature April 29, 1958, 13 U.S.T. 2312 (entered into force September 20, 1962), a multilateral treaty agreement to which both Japan and the United States are parties signatory.

---

[3] The vessel, its captain, and the crew have since been released upon posting a bond conditioned upon the payment of any penalty or fine which might be imposed in these proceedings.

II

By the Bartlett Act, enacted in 1964, Congress made it unlawful for any foreign vessel, or for the master of such a vessel, to engage in fishing within the territorial waters of the United States, or 'within any waters in which the United States has the same rights in respect to fisheries as it has in its territorial waters ... except ... as expressly provided by an international agreement to which the United States is a party.' 16 U.S.C. § 1081.[5] The Bartlett Act established criminal penalties for violators and provided for the seizure and forfeiture of any vessel and its catch found in violation. 16 U.S.C. § 1082.[6] In enacting the Bartlett Act, the intent of Congress was to fill a gap in existing law by making it clear that foreign vessels are denied the privilege of fishing within the territorial waters of the United States and by providing effective sanctions for unlawful fishing by foreign vessels within territorial waters. H.R.Rep. (Merchant Marine and Fisheries Committee) No. 1356 (1964), U.S.Cong. & Admin.News, 1964, pp. 2183, 2183–84. The Bartlett Act did not define the width of the territorial sea, 'thereby leaving the opportunity for the United States to follow the lead of Canada and other nations in establishing a limit beyond the present 3 miles for fishery purposes.' Id. at p. 2187. The words 'within any waters in which the United States has the same rights in respect to fisheries as it has in its territorial waters' were added in anticipation of the United States extending its fishery jurisdiction out to 12 miles. See H.R.Rep. (Merchant Marine and Fisheries Committee) No. 2086 (1966), U.S. Cong. & Admin.News, 1966, pp. 3282, 3289.

By the Contiguous Fisheries Zone Act, enacted in 1966, Congress established a fisheries zone contiguous to the territorial waters of the United States and provided with respect to such zone:

---

[5] 16 U.S.C. § 1081 provides in relevant part:

It is unlawful for any vessel, except a vessel of the United States, or for any master or other person in charge of such a vessel, to engage in the fisheries within the territorial waters of the United States, ... or within any waters in which the United States has the same rights in respect to fisheries as it has in its territorial waters or in such waters to engage in activities in support of a foreign fishery fleet or to engage in the taking of any Continental Shelf fishery resource which appertains to the United States except as provided in this chapter or as expressly provided by an international agreement to which the United States is a party.
* * *

[6] 16 U.S.C. § 1082(a) and (b) provide:

(a) Any person violating the provisions of this chapter shall be fined not more than $100,000, or imprisoned not more than one year, or both.

(b) Every vessel employed in any manner in connection with a violation of this chapter including its tackle, apparel, furniture, appurtenances, cargo, and stores shall be subject to forefeiture and all fish taken or retained in violation of this chapter or the monetary value thereof shall be forfeited. For the purposes of this chapter, it shall be a rebuttable presumption that all fish found aboard a vessel seized in connection with such violation of this chapter were taken or retained in violation of this chapter.

16 U.S.C. § 1082(c) makes applicable to such seizures and forfeitures the existing law relating to seizure, forfeiture and condemnation of a vessel for violations of the customs laws, except when inconsistent with the provisions of the Act.

The United States will exercise the same exclusive rights in respect to fisheries in the zone as it has in its territorial sea, subject to the continuation of traditional fishing by foreign states within this zone as may be recognized by the United States. 16 U.S.C. § 1091.[7]

The contiguous fisheries zone was defined by Congress in the Contiguous Fisheries Zone Act as having 'as its inner boundary the outer limits of the territorial sea and as its seaward boundary a line drawn so that each point on the line is nine nautical miles from the nearest point in the inner boundary.' 16 U.S.C. § 1092.[8] In so defining the contiguous zone, Congress recognized that the territorial sea of the United States extends three miles from the United States, which is where Thomas Jefferson set the outer limit in 1793 and where 'it has remained unaltered to this day.' H.R.Rep.No.2086, supra at pp. 3284–85. See Cunard Steamship Co. v. Mellon, 262 U.S. 100, 122–23 (1923).[9] It was the expressed intent of Congress in the 1966 legislation to 'unilaterally establish a fishery zone contiguous to the present 3-mile territorial sea of the United States by extending our exclusive fisheries rights to a distance of 12 miles from our shores.' H.R.Rep.No.2086, supra at p. 3285.

III

Defendant makes no contention that the contiguous fisheries zone created by the United States in the Contiguous Fisheries Zone Act violates customary international law. Defendant also recognizes that, within the three-mile territorial sea, the United States has the right to prohibit foreign fishing and that Article 23 of the Convention on the High Seas provides express authority for the United States to conduct hot pursuit from the territorial sea onto the high seas for the purpose of apprehending foreign ships which have violated domestic fisheries law within the territorial sea. And defendant does not contest that the Contiguous Fisheries Zone Act extended to a zone nine miles from the seaward limit of the territorial sea all the rights with respect to fisheries which the United States previously had in its territorial sea, and that, unless restricted by treaty, the United States has the right to conduct hot pursuit from a contiguous zone onto the high seas for violations of its domestic law. See The

---

[7] 16 U.S.C. § 1091 reads in full:

There is established a fisheries zone contiguous to the territorial sea of the United States. The United States will exercise the same exclusive rights in respect to fisheries in the zone as it has in its territorial sea, subject to the continuation of traditional fishing by foreign states within this zone as may be recognized by the United States.

[8] 16 U.S.C. § 1092 reads in full:

The fisheries zone has as its inner boundary the outer limits of the territorial sea and as its seaward boundary a line drawn so that each point on the line is nine nautical miles from the nearest point in the inner boundary.

[9] It is not disputed that the territorial sea extends a distance of three miles around Monhegan Island, as well as from the coastline of the mainland. See Convention on the Territorial Sea and the Contiguous Zone, infra, Art. 10(2).

Newton Bay, 36 F.2d 729, 731–32 (2d Cir. 1929); Gillam v. United States, 27 F.2d 296, 299–300 (4th Cir.), cert. denied, 278 U.S. 635 (1928); The Resolution, 30 F.2d 534, 537 (E.D.La.1929); The Pescawha, 45 F.2d 221, 222 (D.Ore.1928); The Vinces, 20 F.2d 164, 172–73 (E.D.S.C.1927). Defendant's sole contention is that the United States had no right to conduct hot pursuit from the contiguous zone and to effect seizure of the TAIYO MARU 28, because the vessel was seized on the high seas in violation of Article 23 of the 1958 Convention on the High Seas.

The Convention on the High Seas provides, in Article 2, that:

> The high seas being open to all nations, no State may validly purport to subject any part of them to its sovereignty. Freedom of the high seas ... comprises, inter alia, both for coastal and non-coastal States:
>
> .... as
>
> (2) Freedom of fishing; ...

Article 5 of the Convention vests 'exclusive jurisdiction' in each signatory over its vessels 'on the high seas.' Article 23 of the Convention, however, recognizes certain instances in which a State may seize a foreign vessel on the high seas, based on hot pursuit:

> The hot pursuit of a foreign ship may be undertaken when the competent authorities of the coastal State have good reason to believe that the ship has violated the laws and regulations of that State. Such pursuit must be commenced when the foreign ship or one of its boats is within the internal waters or the territorial sea or the contiguous zone of the pursuing State, and may only be continued outside the territorial sea or the contiguous zone if the pursuit has not been interrupted. ... If the foreign ship is within a contiguous zone, as defined in article 24 of the Convention on the Territorial Sea and the Contiguous Zone, the pursuit may only be undertaken if there has been a violation of the rights for the protection of which the zone was established.

Article 24 of the Convention on the Territorial Sea and the Contiguous Zone, opened for signature April 29, 1958, 15 U.S.T. 1607 (entered into force September 10, 1964), contains the following pertinent provisions:

> 1. In a zone of the high seas contiguous to its territorial sea, the coastal State may exercise the control necessary to:
>
>   a. prevent infringement of its customs, fiscal, immigration or sanitary regulations within its territory or territorial sea;
>
>   b. punish infringement of the above regulations committed within its territory or territorial sea.

2. The contiguous zone may not extend beyond twelve miles from the baseline from which the breadth of the territorial sea is measured.

Defendant asserts that Article 23 of the Convention on the High Seas must be read in conjunction with Article 24 of the Convention on the Territorial Sea and the Contiguous Zone. The argument is that since Article 24 only authorizes the establishment of a contiguous zone for the purposes of enforcing the coastal State's customs, fiscal, immigration or sanitary regulations, and since Article 23 permits hot pursuit of a foreign ship from such a contiguous zone only for the four purposes listed in Article 24, the United States was without authority to commence hot pursuit of the TAIYO MARU 28 from within the contiguous fisheries zone for the purpose of enforcing its fisheries regulations.

Both parties recognize that the general rule of law is that the power of the government to enforce a forfeiture or to prosecute a defendant is not impaired by the illegality of the method by which it has acquired control over the property or the defendant. Dodge v. United States, 272 U.S. 530, 532 (1926); The Caledonian, 17 U.S. 100 (1819); The Richmond, 13 U.S. 102 (1815) (unlawful seizure of property); Frisbie v. Collins, 342 U.S. 519, 522 (1952); Ker v. Illinois, 119 U.S. 436, 444 (1886); Lujan v. Gengler, 510 F.2d 62, 65–68 (2d Cir. 1975); but cf. United States v. Toscanino, 500 F.2d 267, 271–79 (2d Cir. 1974) (unlawful apprehension of defendant). Defendant relies upon the exception to this general rule established in Cook v. United States, 288 U.S. 102 (1933). In Cook, the United States Coast Guard seized a British vessel, the Mazel Tov, caught in rumrunning, on the high seas outside the American jurisdictional limits set by a British–American treaty covering the apprehension of prohibition law violators.[10] The Supreme Court held that the United States 'lacking power to seize, lacked power, because of the Treaty, to subject the vessel to our laws. To hold that adjudication may follow a wrongful seizure would go far to nullify the purpose and effect of the Treaty.' Id. at 121–22. . . . Mr. Justice Brandeis made clear, however, that the exception to the general rule recognized in Cook covers the particular situation where the United States has by treaty 'imposed a territorial limitation upon its own authority.' Cook v. United States, supra, 288 U.S. at 121. As stated in Autry v. Wiley, 440 F.2d 799 (1st Cir. 1971), the Cook doctrine is a 'narrow' exception to the general rule; it 'applies only to violations of a specific territorial jurisdictional circumscription set by treaty.' Id. at 802.

Defendant strenuously argues that the Cook exception destroys the jurisdiction of this Court in these proceedings because by Article 23 of the Convention on the High Seas, read together with Article 24 of the Con-

---

[10] The Mazel Tov was seized more than one hour's sail from the United States coastline. By prior treaty with Great Britain, the United States had limited its customs jurisdiction over British vessels to offenses which were discovered within one hour's sail from the coast.

vention of the Territorial Sea and the Contiguous Zone, the United States has undertaken a specific obligation not to institute hot pursuit of a foreign ship from the contiguous fisheries zone for violation of its fisheries law. Defendant's position is that Article 23 limits the government's right of hot pursuit from a contiguous zone to the four purposes for which Article 24 authorizes the establishment of such a zone, and the enforcement of domestic fisheries law is not one of the purposes recognized by Article 24. The Court is persuaded, however, that neither the language nor the history of the Conventions shows that the signatory parties intended to limit the right of a coastal State to exercise exclusive fishery jurisdiction within 12 miles of its coast, to establish a contiguous zone for such a purpose, or to conduct hot pursuit from such a zone.

Analysis of the text of Article 23 of the Convention on the High Seas shows that the Article provides general authority to undertake hot pursuit from a contiguous zone when the authorities of the coastal State have good reason to believe that a foreign vessel has violated the coastal State's laws and regulations. It is true that Article 23 permits hot pursuit from a contiguous zone, created for one of the four purposes enumerated in Article 24 of the Convention on the Territorial Sea and the Contiguous Zone, only if there has been a violation of the rights for the protection of which the zone was established. But Article 23 does not in terms deny a coastal State the right to commence hot pursuit from a contiguous zone established for a purpose other than one of the purposes listed in Article 24. Nor does Article 24 in terms prohibit the establishment of a contiguous zone for a purpose other than one of those specified in the Article. The language of Article 24, relating to the purposes for which a contiguous zone may be established, is permissive, rather than restrictive. It provides that a coastal State 'may' establish a contiguous zone for the purposes of enforcing its customs, fiscal, immigration or sanitary regulations. Although Article 24 only affirmatively recognizes the right of a coastal State to create a contiguous zone for one of the four enumerated purposes, nothing in the Article precludes the establishment of such a zone for other purposes, including the enforcement of domestic fisheries law. In short, unlike the British–American treaty in Cook, the Conventions in the case at bar contain no specific undertaking by the United States not to conduct hot pursuit from a contiguous fisheries zone extending 12 miles from its coast. The Cook exception, therefore, is not applicable, because the United States has not by treaty 'imposed a territorial limitation upon its own authority.'

The history of the 1958 Conventions confirms the conclusion that the United States did not specifically undertake to limit its authority to exercise exclusive fisheries jurisdiction within 12 miles of its coast, to establish a contiguous zone for such a purpose, or to conduct hot pursuit from such a zone. The Convention on the High Seas and the Convention on the

Territorial Sea and the Contiguous Zone were the product of the Conference on the Law of the Sea, convened at Geneva in 1958 pursuant to Resolution 1105 of the General Assembly of the United Nations. U.N. General Assembly, 11th Sess., Official Records, Supp. No. 17 (A/3572). Although the Conference was convened to resolve a variety of matters pertaining to the codification of the Law of the Sea, most commentators agree that the two principal issues presented for the Conference's consideration were the question of the breadth of the territorial sea, and the closely-related question of whether there should be an additional contiguous zone in which the coastal States could exercise exclusive jurisdiction over fishing. See, e.g., McDougal and Burke, The Public Order of the Oceans, 524–48 (1st ed. 1962); Fitzmaurice, Some Results of the Geneva Conference on the Law of the Sea, 8 International and Comparative Law Quarterly 73, 73–75 (1959); Dean, The Geneva Conference on the Law of the Sea: What Was Accomplished, 52 The American Journal of International Law 607, 607–08 (1958). See also Hearings on the Conventions on the Law of the Sea, Executives J, K, L, M, N, before the Committee on Foreign Relations, United States Senate, 86th Cong. 2nd Sess., p. 4 (January 20, 1960). The 1958 Geneva Conference was unable to achieve agreement on either issue, primarily because of the volatile political ramifications involved in setting a limit to the territorial sea.[12] In recommending that the Senate give its advice and consent to ratification of the Conventions, the Senate Report from the Committee on Foreign Relations made clear that the Convention on the Territorial Sea and the Contiguous Zone did not define the width of the territorial sea, or circumscribe the right of a coastal State to assert exclusive fisheries jurisdiction:

This convention does not fix the breadth of the territorial sea. This subject and the closely related one of the extent to which the coastal state

---

[12] The position of the United States at the Conference was that the territorial sea should be defined as narrowly as possible, preferably at the three-mile limit which it had traditionally recognized. In advocating this position, a major concern of the United States was to avoid undue limitation of its right to fish off the coasts of other nations. In this position, it was supported primarily by the maritime nations, which had traditionally engaged in fishing off foreign shores. Opposition to the American position was centered principally in the Soviet bloc countries and the newly-emerging and underdeveloped countries. When it became apparent that any proposal for a three-mile territorial sea would fail to attract the two-thirds vote necessary for adoption, the United States sponsored a compromise proposal which called for a six-mile territorial sea and a further six-mile contiguous fisheries zone. This proposal barely failed of passage, and since no other proposal was able to attract a two-thirds vote, the final Conventions do not define the breadth of the territorial sea, or the extent to which a coastal State may assert exclusive fisheries jurisdiction. See generally Dean, supra at 613–16; McDougal and Burke, supra at 529–48; Hearings, supra at 4–9, 21–22.

When the Law of the Sea Conference was reconvened at Geneva in 1960, the participants again were unable to agree on the width of the territorial sea or the extent to which a coastal State could exercise exclusive fishing jurisdiction in the waters off its coast. See generally Dean, Second Geneva Conference on the Law of the Sea: The Fight for Freedom of the Seas, 54 Am.J. Int'l L. 751, 779–81 (1960). A joint American–Canadian compromise proposal, in most respects similar to that made by the United States at the 1958 Conference, failed of passage by one vote. See McDougal and Burke, supra at 547.

should have exclusive fishing rights in the sea off its coast were hotly debated without any conclusion being reached. Exec. Rept. No. 5, Law of the Sea Conventions, to accompany Ex. J to N, inclusive, 86th Cong. 1st Sess., p. 4 (1960).

It is clear from the foregoing history that, in becoming a signatory to the 1958 Conventions, the United States could not have intended to accept any limitation on its right to conduct hot pursuit for violations of exclusive fishery rights occurring within 12 miles of its coast, since the Geneva Conference could not agree as to whether a contiguous zone could be established for the purpose of enforcing domestic fisheries law.

It is apparent that Congress was well aware of its obligations under the 1958 Conventions when the 1966 Contiguous Fisheries Zone Act was enacted, and that Congress perceived no conflict between the Act and the treaty provisions. This is evident from the House Report, which discusses the Conventions and their relationship to the proposed legislation:

In 1958, and again in 1960, the Law of the Sea Conferences held in Geneva, Switzerland, left unresolved the twin questions of the width of the territorial sea and to the extent to which a coastal state could claim exclusive fishing rights in the high seas off its coast. At the second conference in 1960, the United States and Canada put forward a compromise proposal for a 6-mile territorial sea, plus a 6-mile exclusive fisheries zone (12 miles of exclusive jurisdiction in all) subject to the continuation for 10 years of traditional fishing by other states in the outer 6 miles. This compromise proposal failed by one vote to obtain the two-thirds vote necessary for adoption.

Since the 1958 Law of the Sea Conference, there has been a trend toward the establishment of a 12-mile fisheries rule in international practice. Thirty-nine countries acting individually or in concert with other countries have extended their fisheries limits to 12 miles since 1958. H.R.Rep. No. 2086, supra at p. 3286.

The Report also notes that, as of July 1, 1966, of the 99 United Nations coastal nations, slightly more than 60 countries asserted a 12-mile exclusive fishery zone, either as territorial sea or as territorial sea plus a contiguous zone. Id.[13]

IV

Since the seizure of the TAIYO MARU 28 on the high seas following hot pursuit from the contiguous zone was not in violation of Article 23 of the 1958 Convention on the High Seas, and, moreover, was sanctioned by

---

[13] In this connection, it should also be noted that the Convention on the Territorial Sea and the Contiguous Zone does not define the breadth of the territorial sea. See Arts. 1, 3 and 6. Thus, nothing in the language of the Convention precludes the United States from claiming a territorial sea of 12 miles, in which it could exercise exclusive fishing rights.

domestic law and in conformity with the prevailing consensus of international law and practice, this Court has jurisdiction to decide the present

proceedings on their merits. Defendant's motions to dismiss for lack of jurisdiction are therefore denied.

It is so ordered.

* * *

NOTES AND QUESTIONS

1. By 1966, when the Contiguous Fishing Zone Act was enacted, the U.S. Congress had given up on the idea put forth in the Truman proclamation of relying on international agreement to regulate intensive foreign fisheries adjacent to the territorial sea. Judge Gignoux had to determine whether the 1966 zone was consistent with the 1958 Convention on the Territorial Sea and Contiguous Zone. From the defendant's argument, what do you think Japan's position was on exclusive fishing zones at the 1958 U.N. Geneva conference on the law of the sea, discussed in footnote 12? The conference adopted four conventions, discussed in the notes below.

2. The 1958 Convention on Fishing and Conservation of the Living Resources of the High Seas was not a codification of existing international law, but rather an attempt to deal with the growing tension between coastal countries and countries whose distant water fleets were a growing presence in the high seas just beyond territorial waters. The Fishing Convention would have created a mechanism for coastal states to initiate unilateral, non-discriminatory regulation of threatened fisheries in the high seas off their coasts if negotiations failed to result in an international agreement. Although the treaty was adopted and received enough ratifications to come into force, it was never effective because the major distant water fishing nations did not become parties and could not be bound by a coastal state's unilateral attempt to regulate high seas fishing. This resistance led coastal nations with domestic fishing industries to adopt exclusive fisheries zones, like the 1966 U.S. act discussed by Judge Gignoux. Then, less than a year after Judge Gignoux upheld the 9-mile contiguous fishery zone, the U.S. Congress adopted a 200-mile fishery conservation zone, Pub. L. No. 94-265 (April 13, 1976). The bill had been introduced in January 1975 by Representative Gerry E. Studds (D–Mass) with 24 co-sponsors as H.R. 200, the "Interim Fisheries Zone Extension and Management Act." Why do you think the House members called it an "interim" zone?

3. In its 1958 attempt at codification of the law of the sea, the International Law Commission dealt with each offshore jurisdictional zone in a separate treaty. Some concepts, however, were not ripe for codification. What issues remained controversial in regard to the territorial sea?

4. The Convention on the Territorial Sea and the Contiguous Zone codified the traditional sovereign rights of coastal states in the marginal territo-

rial sea, incorporating also the important exception for the right of innocent passage for foreign vessels transiting on the surface. The convention also set out the rules that had evolved to separate the territorial sea from internal waters, which are generally not the subject of international law, including the requirements for drawing ordinary baselines, straight baselines, and the closing of bays and rivers was set out.

The Convention also identified some exceptions to applying the standard rules for extension of sovereignty over areas and exercising the right of innocent passage. "Historic" bays or waters, for example, are not subject to the treaty's limitations on bays or baselines, expanding the possible scope of coastal sovereignty over offshore areas. International straits are also recognized as having a special status to protect international navigation from interference and even temporary closure.

5. Baselines are also often relevant when the offshore zones claimed by coastal nations overlap. Maritime delimitations by agreement or an international judgment that are based on equidistant or median lines are usually projected from the nations' territorial sea baselines. What happens if these baselines change significantly because of sea level rise? Do the international boundaries change? Should they? See "Climate Change, Sea Level Rise and the Coming Uncertainty in Oceanic Boundaries: A Proposal to Avoid Conflict," Maritime Boundary Disputes, Settlement Processes, and the Law of the Sea 1–17 (Seoung–Yong Hong and Jon M. Van Dyke, eds., Martinus Nijhof, 2009). See also Julia Lisztwan, Stability of Maritime Boundary Disputes, 37 Yale J. Int'l L. 153 (2012).

6. The Convention on the Territorial Sea and the Contiguous Zone introduced a new concept—the "contiguous zone"—which recognized the increasing practice of states to assert authority beyond a 3-mile territorial sea. The convention recognized only a limited enforcement jurisdiction in the contiguous zone, however, allowing a coastal state to prevent and punish violations of its customs, fiscal, immigration, and sanitary laws applicable to its territory or territorial sea. How did fisheries regulation relate to the contiguous zone? Consider the note on sources of international law following these questions when thinking about the relation of state practice and treaties.

7. The Convention on the Continental Shelf codified the continental shelf doctrine, adopting the 1945 Truman Proclamation's rationale that a coastal state's sovereign rights over the living and non-living resources of the adjacent seabed arise because the shelf is merely the "natural prolongation" of the land territory under the ocean. Consequently, the convention provides that these rights exist *ab initio*; that is, they are inherent and do not depend on any explicit claim by the coastal state. The coastal state's rights to explore and exploit the continental shelf and its resources are exclusive. How did the concept of the continental shelf evolve in such a short period of time from a rationale conjured up by the United States to justify extension of sovereignty over seabed resources to a right justified by something akin to natural law?

The limit of the continental shelf, like the breadth of the territorial sea, was a controversial issue within the 1958 negotiations. The continental shelf, as a geologic feature, is relatively easy to identify as the shallow submerged edge of the continental land mass that ends where the continental slope steepens to the deep seabed. The natural boundaries were not necessarily precise enough to provide a legal definition, however, and perhaps of more importance in the 1958 negotiations, the technology needed to exploit further offshore and deeper in the sea was developing rapidly. A limit based on depth, the 200-meter isobath, was chosen as a convenient approximation for the outer shelf limit, but the definition qualified this by adding "or, beyond that limit, to where the depth of the superjacent waters admits of the exploitation of the natural resources * * *." This exploitability test provided no real limit, and the many questions raised by it have been termed by some authors as "dangerously imprecise."

8. The Convention on the High Seas applied to the area seaward of the outer boundary of the territorial sea. The treaty codified the established principles that the high seas are open to all nations and that no nation may purport to subject any part of the high seas to its sovereignty. Four specific "freedoms of the high seas" were listed: (1) freedom of navigation (meaning both surface and submerged); (2) freedom to fish; (3) freedom of overflight; and (4) freedom to lay cables and pipelines on the sea floor. The list was not exhaustive, and the treaty provided room for other freedoms recognized by customary international law that would not involve appropriation of areas of the high seas, including marine scientific research.

The freedoms of the high seas are required to be exercised by nations "with reasonable regard to the interest of other states" in their exercise of the same freedoms. In general, no nation can unreasonably interfere with the flag vessels, aircraft or activities of other nations on the high seas. The High Seas Convention did list some limited exceptions, including control of piracy and boarding of ships engaged in slavery.

9. What is "hot pursuit"? What are the limitations of a coastal state in pursuing a vessel that has violated the state's laws? The1982 Law of the Sea Convention, art. 111, provides further details for exercise of hot pursuit:

Right of hot pursuit

1. The hot pursuit of a foreign ship may be undertaken when the competent authorities of the coastal State have good reason to believe that the ship has violated the laws and regulations of that State. Such pursuit must be commenced when the foreign ship or one of its boats is within the internal waters, the archipelagic waters, the territorial sea or the contiguous zone of the pursuing State, and may only be continued outside the territorial sea or the contiguous zone if the pursuit has not been interrupted. It is not necessary that, at the time when the foreign ship within the territorial sea or the contiguous zone receives the order to stop, the ship giving the order should likewise be within the territorial sea or the contiguous zone. If the foreign ship is within a contiguous

zone, as defined in article 33, the pursuit may only be undertaken if there has been a violation of the rights for the protection of which the zone was established.

* * *

3. The right of hot pursuit ceases as soon as the ship pursued enters the territorial sea of its own State or of a third State.

4. Hot pursuit is not deemed to have begun unless the pursuing ship has satisfied itself by such practicable means as may be available that the ship pursued or one of its boats or other craft working as a team and using the ship pursued as a mother ship is within the limits of the territorial sea, or, as the case may be, within the contiguous zone or the exclusive economic zone or above the continental shelf. The pursuit may only be commenced after a visual or auditory signal to stop has been given at a distance which enables it to be seen or heard by the foreign ship.

5. The right of hot pursuit may be exercised only by warships or military aircraft, or other ships or aircraft clearly marked and identifiable as being on government service and authorized to that effect.

6. Where hot pursuit is effected by an aircraft:

the provisions of paragraphs 1 to 4 shall apply mutatis mutandis, the aircraft giving the order to stop must itself actively pursue the ship until a ship or another aircraft of the coastal State, summoned by the aircraft, arrives to take over the pursuit, unless the aircraft is itself able to arrest the ship. It does not suffice to justify an arrest outside the territorial sea that the ship was merely sighted by the aircraft as an offender or suspected offender, if it was not both ordered to stop and pursued by the aircraft itself or other aircraft or ships which continue the pursuit without interruption.

NOTE: SOURCES OF INTERNATIONAL LAW

Public international law is the law that regulates the behavior of nations in their relations with one another. Most of the ocean was for many centuries considered beyond the jurisdiction of any coastal or maritime nation, so international law has played and plays a particularly important role in ocean jurisdiction and management.

But international law does not develop like the domestic law of modern legal systems. A fundamental understanding of how international law develops and the sources of international law is, therefore, necessary to comprehend how a legal system without statutes or binding court decisions works to regulate the behavior of nations concerning the jurisdiction, rights and duties of nations in regard to the seas.

The most often cited list of international law sources is found in Article 38 of the Statute of the International Court of Justice (ICJ). The Statute of the ICJ, a treaty to which almost all the world's nations are parties, requires the Court to apply international law in deciding the disputes before it. According to Article 38, the three primary sources of international law are (1) international agreements or treaties, (2) custom, and (3) general principles of law.

International agreements (treaties). Agreements between nation-states are frequently analogized to contracts between individuals in a domestic legal system. Although many international agreements or treaties are similar to contracts, most of the international agreements related to the law of the sea are in the category of "law making" treaties—treaties that attempt to codify the law of nations in regard to the oceans. Such treaties are typically negotiated at a conference called for that purpose by the interested states. In the case of the development of the law of the sea, three major conferences between 1958 and 1982, provided the fora for these negotiations.

"Law making" treaties are not, however, international legislation. Unlike a domestic statute, a treaty is binding only on those nations that have explicitly expressed their consent to be bound, *i.e.*, ratified the treaty. For a treaty to be an effective lawmaking instrument, therefore, it is essential that all directly concerned states, and not just a majority of states, become parties to it. The 1982 United Nations Convention on the Law of the Sea, currently with 162 parties, is one of the most prominent examples of a lawmaking treaty.

Custom. Custom or customary international law arises through general state practice that is accepted as law. In the *North Sea Continental Shelf Cases*, I.C.J. Reports (1969), the International Court of Justice (ICJ) described the elements of custom as follows:

> Not only must the acts concerned amount to a settled practice, but they must also be such, or be carried out in such a way, as to be evidence of a belief that this practice is rendered obligatory by the existence of a rule of law requiring it. The need for such a belief, the existence of a subjective element, is implicit in the very notion of the *opinio juris sive necessitatis*. The States concerned must therefore feel that they are conforming to what amounts to a legal obligation.

Substantial uniformity of practice is a required element, but even complete uniformity of practice does not suffice if the psychological element is lacking. A mere usage, with no sense of legal obligation, does not establish a legally binding custom.

How then is a customary norm created and how can one identify a rule of customary international law? The modern development of the law of sea provides two excellent examples. In 1945, President Truman claimed jurisdiction and control over the natural resources of the continental shelf off U.S. coasts for the United States. This claim of exclusive rights over resources extended far beyond the three mile territorial sea, to resources under the high seas.

Nothing in customary practice or treaty law supported such a unilateral assertion, and it most certainly violated international law at the time it was asserted. The response of the international community, however, was acquiescence and general approval—and the extension of such claims by other states. By no later than the mid-1950s the acceptance, approval and practice of states had clearly created a rule of international law granting sovereign rights to coastal nations over the living and non-living natural resources of their adjacent continental shelves. This "claim and response" process is a standard way for customary international law to arise. The rapid development of the doctrine regarding the exclusive rights of adjacent states to their continental shelf natural resources demonstrates that long duration is not a necessary element of custom in international law (in contrast to the "time immemorial" requirement for custom in the common law) if the primary elements of general practice and *opinio juris* are met.

Custom may also arise from a concept developed in context of a lawmaking treaty like the United Nations Convention on the Law of the Sea (UNCLOS). The Exclusive Economic Zone (EEZ), a 200-mile zone in which the adjacent coastal state has exclusive jurisdiction over the living and non-living resources and other economic uses of the water column and seabed, was conceived in the negotiation of this convention. In the *North Sea Continental Shelf Cases, supra*, the ICJ considered whether such a norm adopted in a treaty can be recognized also as customary law through subsequent practice and the impact of the treaty. The court noted that "[t]here is no doubt that this process is a perfectly possible one and does from time to time occur: it constitutes indeed one of the recognized methods by which new rules of customary international law may be formed." The court explained further, however, that for "conventional or contractual" provisions of a "norm-creating" character to become custom and binding even on countries that are not parties to the treaty and "even without the passage of any considerable period of time, a very widespread and representative participation in the convention might suffice of itself, provided it included that of States whose interests were specially affected." If a norm that first arises in a treaty passes into customary law, unlike treaty law, it will bind not only the parties to the treaty, but all members of the international community. An exception applies, however, to nations who have persistently objected to the formation of a rule of customary law while it is in the process of formation.

The provisions for the extension of the EEZ in UNCLOS are clearly of a "norm-creating character" and form a clearly defined basis for a general rule of law. Further, the principle has been widely accepted, with rapid, widespread adoption by states even before the UNCLOS negotiations had concluded. In fact, in both the *Libya–Malta* case, 1985 ICJ Reports at paras. 27–34, and the *Gulf of Maine* case, 1982 ICJ Reports at paras. 94–96, cases decided prior to the treaty entering into force, the ICJ recognized the impact of the EEZ concept on international law.

General principles of law. The scope of "general principles" is not a clear or rigid concept, but usually refers to those common principles that are recognized within domestic legal systems throughout the world. General principles that can be traced to state practice include res judicata, good faith, equality of states, laches, estoppel, and restitution based on unjust enrichment. General principles help fill in the gaps in the coverage of international treaty and customary law. For example, in the case of maritime boundary delimitation, the ICJ has used "equitable principles" to formulate ocean boundaries between states. While the Statute of the ICJ provides that the court may not decide a case *et aequo et bono*[1] without the agreement of the parties, the court has distinguished use of equitable principles as applying normative general principles of law recognized in all legal systems. *See North Sea Continental Shelf Cases* at para. 83.

General principles of law may also refer to general principles of international law. The doctrines of *pact sunt servanda* and *jus cogens* fall into this category.

Article 38 of the ICJ Statute provides two additional sources "as subsidiary means for the determination of rules of international law." The first of these secondary sources is *judicial decisions*. Because the Statute specifically states that an ICJ decision is not binding on any nation other than the parties to the case before it, there is no principal of precedent or *stare decisis*, and the Court is not bound to follow even its own prior judgments. Nevertheless, the ICJ treats its previous judgments as very persuasive, and reference to these earlier judgments contributes to creating a consistent body of international law. The judicial decisions referenced by Article 38 are not, however, limited to ICJ decisions. Other international and regional courts and international tribunals have proliferated, and the relevant decisions of these courts are within the scope of the sources of international law. It is also clear that Article 38's reference to judicial decisions includes decisions of national courts that analyze, interpret or apply rules of international law.

The writings of highly regarded publicists or scholars of all nations in the field of international law are the second category of subsidiary means of determining international law. In addition to looking to the most influential treatises and articles, one may also refer to such authorities as the International Law Commission (*e.g.*, Articles on State Responsibility) and the American Law Institute (*e.g.*, Restatement of Foreign Relations Law) as sources of evidence of international law.

The language of Article 38 actually dates back to the provisions for the Permanent Court of International Justice, the judicial arm of the League of Nations, so its scope may not adequately recognize the influence of the devel-

---

[1] *See* Ian Brownlie, Principles of Public International Law 25–26, 216 (Seventh Ed. 2008). Brownlie explains that *et aequo et bono* "involves elements of compromise and conciliation whereas equity in the English sense is applied as part of the normal judicial function." Equitable principles, on the other hand, are principles of "fairness, reasonableness and policy" that inhere in the court's "process of decision" to achieve an equitable result.

opment of international organizations in the creation of international law. For example, the resolutions or declarations of the United Nations General Assembly (UNGA) are not binding law, yet they have had an important role in the development of the law of the sea. In the case of the law of the sea, the pattern of voting and development of UNGA resolutions demonstrates that the resolutions can be important evidence of state practice in the development or "crystallizing" of customary law. Specialized international institutions have also arisen, primarily in the context of the League of Nations and later the United Nations. The administrative functions of these agencies have largely replaced *ad hoc* negotiations in development of the law in certain areas, for example, marine pollution or management of deep seabed resources. Conferences and publications of organizations like the International Maritime Organization and the UN Food and Agriculture Organization have also strongly influenced the development of the law of the sea.

International law of the sea developed primarily through custom during most its history, but treaties began to play the most important role as the law of the sea began to develop quickly after World War II. In addition, the ICJ and the International Tribunal for the Law of the Sea (ITLOS) have played an increasingly important role in interpreting and applying these law-making treaties.

3. LAW OF THE SEA: THE LATE TWENTIETH-CENTURY REVOLUTION

The Law of the Sea has developed over the many centuries that the oceans have been used for navigation, trade and its resources, but the rapid development and new directions since the last half of the twentieth century can truly be called a revolution.

A. THE AFTERMATH OF UNCLOS I AND II

During the ten years after the adoption of the four Geneva Conventions on the law of sea in 1958, the inadequacies of those treaties to meet the challenges created by even more intensive use of the oceans and their resources became apparent. The treaties' lack of clear limits on coastal state sovereignty and jurisdiction also failed to stifle the trend toward expanded jurisdictional claims. Not only were 12-mile territorial seas becoming the dominant state practice, but countries were also extending unilateral, exclusive fisheries zones beyond the territorial sea, and more Latin American and African countries were asserting claims to 200-mile zones or territorial seas. At the same time developed countries were enjoying expanding claims to continental shelf resources due to development of offshore technology, the United States and the Soviet Union, the major maritime powers, had grave concerns about "creeping jurisdiction" and the deterioration of the freedoms of the high seas. Their concern for maintaining broad definitions of the freedom of navigation and overflight led these two superpowers in 1970 to jointly call for a new international conference to reassess the ocean regime in a way that protected both coastal state interests and the freedom of navigation.

The event most often cited, however, as the tipping point for the initiation of a new regime for the oceans was the potential for the exploitation of manganese nodules—potato-sized polymetallic masses of manganese, copper, nickel and cobalt. The existence of these nodules had been known since the voyage of the H.M.S. *Challenger* in 1872–1876, one of the first marine scientific research expeditions and the foundation of modern oceanography. The *Challenger* discovered these nodules scattered on the deep seabed all around the globe. Not until the 1960s, however, would the development of technology and markets for minerals make the idea of commercial exploitation of the nodules at depths of over 3000 meters a possibility. Recently independent and other less developed countries, which by that time constituted a majority of the United Nations members, anticipated a new hegemony by a few technologically advanced countries as they appropriated the resources of the deep seabed beyond national jurisdiction in "land grab" that amounted to "neocolonialism" in the seas. Although the 1958 Conventions were less than a decade old, many of these new countries had had no opportunity to participate in the development of a regime that did not protect their interests, and they sought a new legal regime for the deep seabed. The fundamental issue that had to be decided to go forward was whether the seabed minerals were *res nullius*—belonging to no one and subject to appropriation and ownership as a high seas freedom—or *res communis*—belonging to everyone and not subject to appropriation by individuals to the detriment of the community.

Arvid Pardo, Malta's ambassador to the United Nations, became the voice of these states when he addressed the General Assembly in November 1967. Pardo proposed that the seabed beyond national jurisdiction be set aside for peaceful purposes and be declared the "common heritage of mankind" and exploited for the benefit of all mankind, particularly the least developed countries. He also called for an effective international regime to be established to regulate the seabed through an international treaty of universal character. The General Assembly moved quickly to establish an *ad hoc* seabed committee in 1967, which was replaced in 1968 by the permanent Committee on the Peaceful Uses of the Seabed the Ocean Floor beyond the Limits of National Jurisdiction (resolution 2467 A (XXIII) of 21 December 1968). In 1969, the General Assembly passed the Moratorium Resolution (over the 28 negative votes of the United States and most other developed states), calling for a prohibition on commercial exploitation of deep seabed minerals until an international regime could be put in place. By unanimous vote (including an affirmative U.S. vote), the General Assembly in 1970 passed the Declaration of Principles Governing the Seabed (resolution 2749 (XXV) of 17 December 1970), which declared the deep seabed beyond national jurisdiction "the common heritage of mankind" to be developed for the benefit of humankind as a whole. Finally, the General Assembly in 1970 passed the Conference Resolution (resolution 2750 C (XXV) of 17 December 1970), which called for the convening of a Third Conference on the Law of the Sea (UNCLOS III). The Conference Resolution took a broader view of the goals of the new negotiations, however, noting "that the problems of ocean space are closely interrelated and need to be considered as a whole."

B. THE UNCLOS III NEGOTIATIONS

The Third United Nations Conference on the Law of the Sea (UNCLOS III) began its deliberations in late 1973 with 160 national delegations participating. It was historic in many ways: It was the largest and most complex international law-making conference ever convened, and it continued for almost ten years. The negotiations addressed issues that were considered vital to virtually every nation on earth. Even land-locked countries were affected and sought to protect their access rights to new offshore zones that could be created in areas that had been high seas.

Developing countries were in a definite majority and were anxious to assert their role in a New International Economic Order. These nations realized, however, that their goals could not be achieved simply by a majority vote, but only through complex negotiations. This led to a unique process of negotiations, called "the package deal." The Conference put on the table virtually every issue dealing with the use of the oceans, providing a possibility for states to determine its priorities and what interests it might be willing to trade to protect those priorities. The Rules of Procedure for UNCLOS III, U.N. Doc. A/CONF.62/30/Rev. 3, included an agreement establishing the following principles for the negotiations: 1) the problems of the seabed are interrelated and need to be considered as a whole; 2) to be effective, the treaty must secure broad acceptance; 3) every effort should be made to reach agreement on substantive matters through consensus; and 4) there will be no voting until all consensus efforts are exhausted. The approach was one of attempting to reach an overall consensus on all issues, rather than on securing a majority vote on individual points within the treaty. This created an opportunity for trade-offs and political compromise across a broad spectrum of widely divergent issues, so that in the final text, the disposition of many seemingly unrelated matters were actually quite closely related.

As the world's preeminent naval power and the country with the world's second longest coastline, the United States had important interests to consider in regard to virtually every agenda item in UNCLOS III. The U.S. had both coastal fishermen and a distant water tuna fleet. The research of its renowned oceanographic institutions ranged around the globe. (During the UNCLOS III negotiations, scientists from Woods Hole Oceanographic Institution were discovering the completely new frontier of deep ocean hydrothermal vents.) With events like the infamous Santa Barbara oil platform blowout and major oil tanker spills in the very recent past, the protection of the marine environment was an important priority for the country. U.S. mining companies were preparing to mine the deep seabed. But the transcendent interest of the U.S. delegation was preserving freedoms of navigation and overflight for the naval and air forces.

UNCLOS III took place while the Cold War and the nuclear threat posed by the Soviet Union still dominated U.S. foreign policy. Free navigation and overflight of the oceans was viewed as essential to U.S. and world security. The United States needed to assure that there would be no interference with deployment of troops and ships to meet threats around the world, so restrictions on innocent passage of military vessels was not acceptable. In addition, nuclear-armed submarines had become the primary "nuclear deterrent" to a Soviet attack, but to be effective they had to ply the world's oceans submerged and undetected. The recognition of twelve-mile territorial seas compromised the ability of the United States to continue to use strategic international straits for overflight and submarine passage. The Department of Defense estimated that extension of territorial seas to twelve miles would result in up to 110 strategic straits, previously containing high seas passages, becoming incorporated in territorial seas. For example, the Strait of Gibraltar is slightly less than 8 miles wide; three mile territorial seas left a passage of high seas through the strait, but broader claims subsumed the Strait in the territorial seas of the bordering countries. There would be no right of innocent passage for aircraft or submerged vessels.

The work of the Conference was divided among three main committees and a number of specialized working groups: The First Committee dealt with the international regime for exploitation of the deep seabed; the Second Committee addressed traditional law of the sea issues concerning jurisdictional zones, maritime boundaries, and the rights and duties of nations; and the Third Committee dealt with marine scientific research and protection of the marine environment. By the mid-1970s, the negotiations had generally resolved most navigational and fisheries issues in ways that met the needs of both coastal states and the major maritime powers. But in the United States, Congress was frustrated with the slow pace of negotiations and was under pressure to take immediate action to prevent continued over-exploitation of fisheries off U.S. coasts. In 1976, the United States and, soon thereafter, Canada extended 200-mile exclusive fishery zones. By the close of the UNCLOS III negotiations in 1982, ninety nations had established 200-mile offshore jurisdictional zones. The concept of the 200-mile zone was quickly becoming state practice and accepted as customary international law.

By 1976, the negotiations were also headed for deadlock on complex deep seabed mining issues. While most developing countries wanted mining solely by an international mining institution charged with distributing profits consonant with the principle of the common heritage of mankind, a subset of this group, land-based producers of the same metals, had additional concerns. Mining for metals like manganese represented a large proportion of the GDP for these producing states, and they wanted production limits to protect their important export markets for the metals. The developed countries, with their companies already involved in technology development and prospecting, wanted access to be as open as possible, protection of technology and patents, and adequate compensation for the huge investment of these companies.

The United States was, of course, among the developed countries who wanted to assure that there was no monopolistic regime created barring opportunities for free enterprise to mine the deep seabed and receive an adequate return for the investment in research, technology and production. But like the United States, most developed countries were willing to compromise to protect the favorable arrangements that already had been negotiated concerning navigation. (Recall that all provisions remained open until consensus was reached on the entire "package.") The compromise reached involved the creation of a parallel mining regime, and by 1980, the treaty was nearing completion.

In 1981, however, this changed. The new president of the United States, Ronald Reagan, ordered a year-long reassessment of the treaty in light of the views of the new administration. Several last minute changes were made in the seabed provisions to try to meet new U.S. objections and demands for changes, but irreconcilable differences remained concerning the deep seabed mining regime. With the decision that all efforts at reaching consensus on those issues had been exhausted, the treaty was put to a vote and adopted on 30 April 1982 in New York with 130 States voting in favor, 4 against (including the United States) and 17 abstaining. In December of the same year, the treaty was opened for signature in the final session of UNCLOS III at Montego Bay, and received a record 119 signatures the first day.

The treaty provided that it would come into force one year after its sixtieth ratification, which occurred on November 16, 1993, with the ratification of Guyana. The problem was that almost all of those ratifications were by developing countries. In anticipation of the treaty coming into force without support from developed countries, the Secretary–General of the United Nations began negotiations in 1990 to address the defects and shortcomings of the seabed provisions and establish the "universality" of the treaty. Intense negotiations through the summer of 1994 resulted in the Agreement Relating to the Implementation of Part XI of the LOS Convention, commonly called the Boat Paper, which, although termed an implementation agreement, effectively amends the deep seabed provisions of the LOS Convention. The Agreement, which was co-sponsored by the United States, addressed many of the concerns of developed countries and received no negative votes. The changes to the seabed mining regime assured broad acceptance of the Convention by the time it came into force on November 16, 1994, with virtually all the major developed countries having signed or ratified the Convention at that point. The U.S. signing of the Agreement also served as signing the Convention. The Agreement relating to the implementation of Part XI of the Convention entered into force on 28 July 1996, thirty days after the deposit of the fortieth instrument of ratification. By 2012, 165 nations had become parties to the Convention by ratification, accession, or succession.

The United States is not, however, among those parties, nor has it yet ratified or acceded to the Convention. In late 1994 the Clinton Administration transmitted the Convention to the Senate and, as the U.S. Constitution requires, requested the Senate's consent to ratification. It was not until February 2004 that the Senate Foreign Relations Committee recommended, by unanimous vote, that the Senate give its advice and consent and transmitted the treaty to the Senate on October 7, 2004. At that point, however, significant opposition arose, and the Senate failed to act on the Convention. By 2012, the Convention has been supported by three presidents (Presidents Clinton, Bush and Obama) and has twice been favorably recommended by the Senate Foreign Relations Committee, but has yet to be subject to a vote of the U.S. Senate.

The United States thus remains outside the Convention and has no direct rights or duties under its provisions. Yet the 1982 Convention, together with the conference that brought it into being, has had a major impact on the customary international law of the sea, which does bind the United States. As early as 1983, President Reagan, while rejecting the deep seabed provisions of the Convention, announced that:

> the United States is prepared to accept and act in accordance with the balance of interests relating to traditional uses of the oceans— such as navigation and overflight. In this respect, the United States will recognize the rights of other states in the waters off their coasts, as reflected in the Convention, so long as the rights and freedoms of the United States and others under international law are recognized by such coastal states.

Statement by the President, 19 Weekly Comp. Pres. Doc. 383 (Mar. 10, 1983); U.S. Oceans Policy, 83 Dep't St. Bull., June 1983, at 70 (1983). On that same day, President Reagan signed Proclamation 5030. See Reagan's

EEZ proclamation on p. 36. In addition, international law requires that, as a signatory to the Agreement on Part XI and the Convention, the United States has an obligation not to take actions which may "defeat the object and purpose" of the LOS Convention. Through these actions the United States has to a great extent recognized the legitimacy of the LOS regime.

C. THE 1982 U.N. CONVENTION ON THE LAW OF THE SEA

The negotiation of the Law of the Sea Convention was a monumental accomplishment. The Convention is the most complex and far-reaching treaty ever concluded. It has 320 articles, set out in seventeen parts, and nine annexes and addresses virtually every aspect of ocean sovereignty, jurisdiction and use. Parts II—XI address maritime zones and jurisdiction: the territorial sea and contiguous zone, international straits, archipelagic waters, the EEZ, the continental shelf, the high seas, the International Seabed Area. Parts XII–XIV concern certain marine activities in all ocean areas: the protection of the environment, marine scientific research, and the development and transfer of marine technology. The settlement of disputes is addressed in Part XV (and annexes 5 to 8). Finally, Parts XVI and XVII set out general and final clauses. Further, the Convention sets up several new international institutions—the International Seabed Authority, the International Tribunal for the Law of the Sea, and the Commission on the Limits of the Continental Shelf (which will be discussed later in the chapter). An additional implementation agreement was concluded in 1995, and in 2001, the United Nations Agreement for the Implementation of the Provisions of the United Nations Convention on the Law of the Sea of 10 December 1982 relating to the Conservation and Management of Straddling Fish Stocks and Highly Migratory Fish Stocks entered into force on 11 December 2001, thirty days after the deposit of the thirtieth instrument of ratification.

Even before the Convention came into force in 1994, many of the normative provisions had passed into customary international law. Maritime boundary cases of the International Court of Justice and the writings of international law scholars provided evidence that not only state practice, but *opinio juris*, supported the proposition that most of the normative concepts of the Convention—like the 200-mile EEZ and 12-mile territorial seas—had become recognized as custom. The 1987 Restatement of Foreign Relations Law of the United States relied heavily on the 1982 Convention (which was not yet in force and which the United States had not yet even signed) to define the basic principles of the international law of the sea.

The provisions of the 1982 Convention are the best evidence of what the international law of the sea is today, either by treaty for the Convention's now 163 parties (as of November 2012) or by customary law for the few that have not become parties, including the United States. The new law of the sea is, in very significant respects, quite different from the 1958 attempt to codify its terms.

4. THE POLITICAL GEOGRAPHY OF THE OCEANS TODAY

This section will focus on the rights and obligations of coastal nations, such as the United States, currently recognized by the international law of the sea, principally as reflected in the 1982 U.N. Convention on the Law of the Sea (LOSC). The ocean zones within which coastal nations now have substantial governance rights are: (1) internal waters, (2) the territorial sea, (3) the contiguous zone, (4) the exclusive economic zone, and (5) the continental shelf. Table A provides an overview of maritime claims internationally. Figure 1–1 diagrams the scope of U.S. offshore jurisdictional claims.

Table A. Summary of National Claims to Maritime Zones

Distance (n.m.)	Territorial Sea	Contiguous Zone	EEZ	Fisheries Zones*
3	1			
6	1			
12	142			
24		83		
200 or to international boundary	5		134	
Other	1 (30)** 1 (by coordinates >12)	1 (14) 1 (15) 1 (18)		1 (100) 1 (25) 1 (32 or 52)

*Only indicated if no additional claim to an EEZ of the same distance.

**Distance of claim indicated in parentheses.

Source: Summarized from Table of Claims to Maritime Jurisdiction (as of 15 July 2011), available at http://www.un.org/Depts/los/ LEGISLATIONANDTREATIES/PDFFILES/table_summary_of_claims.pdf

Figure 1–1. United States Marine Jurisdictional Zones

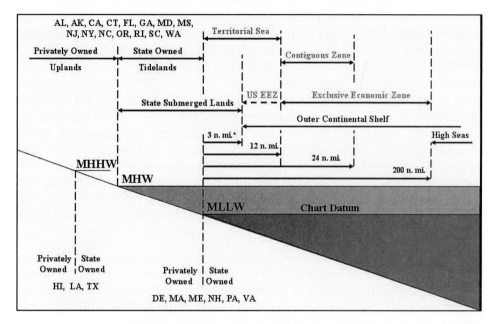

Source: Adapted from NOAA Office of the General Counsel, Maritime Zones and Boundaries

A. INTERNAL WATERS

The only zone of marine waters that was not changed by the LOSC was the jurisdictional zone of internal waters. Internal waters are those that lie landward of the inner boundary of the territorial sea. Most ports, harbors and estuarine areas are internal waters. As part of the nation's territory, these areas are subject to the complete sovereignty of the coastal nation.

The inner boundary of the territorial sea is referred to in the treaty as the baseline from which the breadth of the territorial sea is measured. The rules for drawing baselines are virtually unchanged from those found in the 1958 Geneva Convention on the Territorial Sea and Contiguous Zone. The normal baseline is the mean low-water line of the coast, but non-normal baselines can be drawn across river mouths, the openings of bays, and along the outer points of complex coastlines using the formulas set out in the treaty. The LOSC also added new provisions for drawing baselines around delta areas and certain fringing reefs.

The drawing of non-normal baselines has been one of the more controversial areas of the implementation of the LOSC. The areas enclosed by baselines as internal waters are not subject to the treaty's rules to protect international navigation rights, so illegal baselines greatly compromise the bargain struck in the negotiations to balance the rights of the coastal states and the maritime powers. Because the United States is not a party to the LOSC and its dispute resolution mechanisms, it must resort to other means to object to illegal baselines. Through the Freedom of Navigation Program, started in 1978 under President Carter, the United States uses both diplomatic notices and, in some instances, operational responses to demonstrate that the United States does not acquiesce to such illegal claims. To assert innocent passage or other navigation rights, operational responses involve sending ships and aircraft into areas claimed as internal or territorial waters based on illegal or excessive claims. The United States asserts that the Program is operated in accordance with principles of customary international law as codified in the LOSC. Ironically, the United States, the only non-party developed nation, is serving as the primary "policeman" for assuring compliance with the Treaty.

The LOSC also authorizes the use of special archipelagic baselines around the island groups of those nations composed entirely of islands, but since the United States is mainly a continental nation, this set of rather complicated rules and formulas does not apply to U.S. island groups, such as Hawaii, and therefore will not be discussed here.

B. THE TERRITORIAL SEA

The first notable change in the regime of the territorial sea instituted by the LOSC was the provision of a definite maximum breadth of the territorial sea. Article 3 of the convention provides a right of a coastal state to establish the breadth of its territorial sea up to a limit not exceeding 12 nautical miles.

The second change provided the crucial compromise for the acceptance of the treaty by the United States and the other maritime powers. The LOSC creates a special regime for transit through most straits used for international navigation incorporated in territorial seas. This special regime replaces the traditional right of innocent passage with a non-suspendable right of "transit passage" in most international straits. Importantly, the transit passage regime allows for submerged passage of submarines and a right of overflight—rights not included in innocent passage of other areas of territorial seas.

Except for the straits transit regime, which applies only to territorial seas in straits used for international navigation, the LOSC regime is essentially the same as the 1958 treaty. Coastal states exercise absolute sovereignty, subject only to the right of innocent passage by foreign vessels on the surface. To assure that the term was not interpreted in ways that unreasonably restrict navigation, the definition of innocent passage was substantially expanded to provide more explanation of the principle that passage is innocent so long as it is "not prejudicial to the peace, good order or security" of the coastal state.

President Reagan extended the U.S. territorial sea to 12 miles by presidential proclamation in 1988.

TERRITORIAL SEA OF THE UNITED STATES, PRESIDENTIAL PROCLAMATION 5928
December 27, 1988

International law recognizes that coastal nations may exercise sovereignty and jurisdiction over their territorial seas.

The territorial sea of the United States is a maritime zone extending beyond the land territory and internal waters of the United States over which the United States exercises sovereignty and jurisdiction, a sovereignty and jurisdiction that extend to the airspace over the territorial sea, as well as to its bed and subsoil.

Extension of the territorial sea by the United States to the limits permitted by international law will advance the national security and other significant interests of the United States.

Now, Therefore, I, Ronald Reagan, by the authority vested in me as President by the Constitution of the United States of America, and in accordance with international law, do hereby proclaim the extension of the territorial sea of the United States of America, the Commonwealth of Puerto Rico, Guam, American Samoa, the United States Virgin Islands, the Commonwealth of the Northern Mariana Islands, and any other territory or possession over which the United States exercises sovereignty.

The territorial sea of the United States henceforth extends to 12 nautical miles from the baselines of the United States determined in accordance with international law.

In accordance with international law, as reflected in the applicable provisions of the 1982 United Nations Convention on the Law of the Sea, within the territorial sea of the United States, the ships of all countries enjoy the right of innocent passage and the ships and aircraft of all countries enjoy the right of transit passage through international straits.

Nothing in this Proclamation:

    a. extends or otherwise alters existing Federal or State law or any jurisdiction, rights, legal interests, or obligations derived therefrom; or

b. impairs the determination, in accordance with international law, of any maritime boundary of the United States with a foreign jurisdiction.

QUESTIONS

1. President Reagan grounded the Territorial Sea Proclamation on customary international law as reflected in the 1982 U.N. Convention on the Law of the Sea. He made it clear, however, that the United States would recognize 12-mile territorial seas of other coastal nations only if they were consistent with the U.S. view of customary international law, including the right of transit passage through international straits. Could the United States "pick and choose" the provisions of the Convention it was willing to recognize as custom?

2. In extending the U.S. territorial sea from three to 12 miles, the proclamation limited its effect to U.S. international relations and specifically noted that the proclamation did not change the domestic law of the United States as it applied to its territorial sea. What kind of issues might be raised by this extension?

C. THE CONTIGUOUS ZONE

The LOSC, like the 1958 Geneva Convention on the Territorial Sea and the Contiguous Zone, authorizes coastal nations to exercise a limited enforcement jurisdiction, including drug interdiction and immigration laws, in a contiguous zone beyond the territorial sea. The 1982 Convention allows extension of the contiguous zone out to 24 miles from the baseline.

When President Ronald Reagan extended the U.S. territorial sea from three to 12 miles in 1988, he did not also assert a claim to extend the U.S. contiguous zone's outer boundary to 24 miles. The Reagan administration reasoned that the United States, as a party to the still-binding 1958 Geneva Convention on the Territorial Sea and the Contiguous Zone, could not validly claim a contiguous zone beyond the 12-mile line. In September 1999, however, President Clinton declared a contiguous zone to 24 miles from the U.S. baselines by Presidential Proclamation.

CONTIGUOUS ZONE OF THE UNITED STATES, PRESIDENTIAL PROCLAMATION 7219

September 2, 1999

A Proclamation

International law recognizes that coastal nations may establish zones contiguous to their territorial seas, known as contiguous zones.

The contiguous zone of the United States is a zone contiguous to the territorial sea of the United States, in which the United States may exercise the control necessary to prevent infringement of its customs, fiscal, immigration, or sanitary laws and regulations within its territory or territorial sea, and to punish infringement of the above laws and regulations committed within its territory or territorial sea.

Extension of the contiguous zone of the United States to the limits permitted by international law will advance the law enforcement and public health interests of the United States. Moreover, this extension is an important step in preventing the removal of cultural heritage found within 24 nautical miles of the baseline.

Now, Therefore, I, William J. Clinton, by the authority vested in me as President by the Constitution of the United States, and in accordance with international law, do hereby proclaim the extension of the contiguous zone of the United States of America, including the Commonwealth of Puerto Rico, Guam, American Samoa, the United States Virgin Islands, the Commonwealth of the Northern Mariana Islands, and any other territory or possession over which the United States exercises sovereignty, as follows:

The contiguous zone of the United States extends to 24 nautical miles from the baselines of the United States determined in accordance with international law, but in no case within the territorial sea of another nation. . . .

QUESTIONS

1. Is the U.S. 24-mile contiguous zone claim valid under international law? Why?

2. Can the U.S. Coast Guard arrest a foreign flag vessel and its crew for attempting to bring illegal drugs into the United States at a place nine nautical miles from the coast? What about a place at 20 nautical miles?

D. THE EXCLUSIVE ECONOMIC ZONE

In the 1970s, coastal nation claims to 200-mile exclusive economic zones (EEZs) or similar 200-mile zones proliferated at a rapid rate, due to UNCLOS III's unmistakable embrace of the 200-mile zone concept and the 1976 enactment by the U.S. Congress of a 200-mile exclusive fisheries conservation zone. Before the conclusion of the UNCLOS III negotiations, ninety nations had established 200-mile offshore jurisdictional zones.

The national rights and jurisdictions asserted by coastal nations usually, but not always, track those authorized by the 1982 U.N. Convention on the Law of the Sea's EEZ provisions. For example, the United Kingdom claims only a 200-mile fisheries zone.

LOSC, Article 56(1)

Rights, jurisdiction and duties of the coastal State
In the exclusive economic zone

In the exclusive economic zone, the coastal State has:

a. sovereign rights for the purpose of exploring and exploiting, conserving and managing the natural resources, whether living or non-living, of the waters superjacent to the sea-bed and of the sea-bed and its subsoil, and with regard to other activities for the economic exploitation and exploration of the zone, such as the production of energy from the water, currents and winds;

b. jurisdiction provided for in the relevant provisions of this Convention with regard to:

  i. the establishment and use of artificial islands, installations and structures;

  ii. marine scientific research;

  iii. the protection and preservation of the marine environment;

c. other rights and duties provided for in this Convention.

This summary list of EEZ rights and jurisdiction is fleshed out in other articles of the Convention. Although the Convention and the customary law it reflects do not grant to coastal nations full sovereignty in their EEZs, international law now permits an EEZ nation the primary governance role for nearly all types of activities that occur in the zone.

EXCLUSIVE ECONOMIC ZONE OF THE UNITED STATES, PRESIDENTIAL PROCLAMATION 5030

March 10, 1983

A Proclamation

Whereas the Government of the United States of America desires to facilitate the wise development and use of the oceans consistent with international law;

Whereas international law recognizes that, in a zone beyond its territory and adjacent to its territorial sea, known as the Exclusive Economic Zone, a coastal State may assert certain sovereign rights over natural resources and related jurisdiction; and

Whereas the establishment of an Exclusive Economic Zone by the United States will advance the development of ocean resources and promote the protection of the marine environment, while not affecting other lawful uses of the zone, including the freedoms of navigation and over-flight, by other States;

Now, Therefore, I, Ronald Reagan, by the authority vested in me as President by the Constitution and laws of the United States of America, do hereby proclaim the sovereign rights and jurisdiction of the United States of America and confirm also the rights and freedoms of all States within an Exclusive Economic Zone, as described herein.

The Exclusive Economic Zone of the United States is a zone contiguous to the territorial sea, including zones contiguous to the territorial sea of the United States, the Commonwealth of Puerto Rico, the Commonwealth of the Northern Mariana Islands (to the extent consistent with the Covenant and the United Nations Trusteeship Agreement), and United States overseas territories and possessions. The Exclusive Economic Zone extends to a distance 200 nautical miles from the baseline from which the breadth of the territorial sea is measured. In eases where the maritime boundary with a neighboring State remains to be determined, the boundary of the Exclusive Economic Zone shall be determined by the United States and other State concerned in accordance with equitable principles.

Within the Exclusive Economic Zone, the United States has, to the extent permitted by international law, (a) sovereign rights for the purpose of exploring, exploiting, conserving and managing natural resources, both living and non-living, of the seabed and subsoil and the superjacent waters and with regard to other activities for the economic exploitation and exploration of the zone, such as the production of energy from the water, currents and winds; and (b)jurisdiction with regard to the establishment and use of artificial islands, and installations and structures having economic purposes, and the protection and preservation of the marine environment.

This Proclamation does not change existing United States policies concerning the continental shelf, marine mammals and fisheries, including highly migratory species of tuna which are not subject to United States jurisdiction and require international agreements for effective management.

The United States will exercise these sovereign rights and jurisdiction in accordance with the rules of international law.

Without prejudice to the sovereign rights and jurisdiction of the United States, the Exclusive Economic Zone remains an area beyond the territory and territorial sea of the United States in which all States enjoy the high seas freedoms of navigation, overflight, the laying of submarine cables and pipelines, and other internationally lawful uses of the sea.

In Witness Whereof, I have hereunto set my hand this tenth day of March, in the year of our Lord nineteen hundred and eighty-three, and of the Independence of the United States of America the two hundred and seventh.

RONALD REAGAN

Figure 1–2. The United States' Exclusive Economic Zone

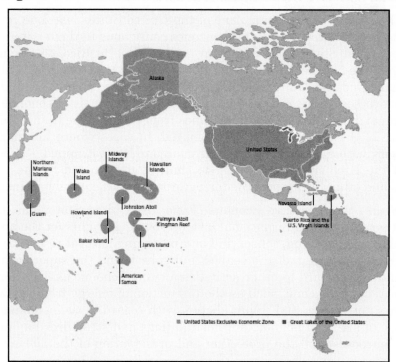

Source: U.S. Commission on Ocean Policy, An Ocean Blueprint

1. Fishing

Within its EEZ, a coastal nation has "sovereign rights" to the living resources, which includes the exclusive right to manage fisheries as well as a priority for the EEZ nation's fishermen to harvest the fish. The coastal nation can thus adopt and enforce laws regulating access to fishing and fishing within its EEZ. The coastal states have broad discretion in managing their fisheries resources and most of the process is not subject to the LOSC dispute resolution provisions. LOSC, art. 297(3)(a) provides that coastal states:

> [are not] obliged to accept the submission to [compulsory] settlement of any dispute relating to its sovereign rights with respect to the living resources in the [EEZ] or their exercise, including its discretion-

ary powers for determining the allowable catch, its harvesting capacity, the allocation of surpluses to other States and the terms and conditions established in its conservation and management laws and regulations.

The Convention does, however, in articles 61 and 62, impose some duties on the coastal state. The managing states are required to set an allowable catch that prevents overexploitation and achieves optimum utilization and maximum sustainable yield (MSY) taking into account the best available scientific information. The duty of optimum utilization requires that foreign fishing be allowed for the part of the allowable catch beyond the capacity of the coastal country's vessels to harvest. The concept of allowable catch is, however, so easily manipulated that most foreign fishing can be excluded by coastal nations. First, the allowable catch is determined by reference to MSY. The LOSC allows the coastal state discretion to qualify MSY by considering "relevant environmental and economic factors." Further, scholars and commentators agree that there is no obligation to set an allowable catch above zero or above domestic harvesting capacity. The vague management principles and unenforceability of the fisheries obligations make the treaty a weak vehicle for ensuring conservation of these marine resources.

The sovereign rights are also difficult for the coastal state to police, as the following case, decided more than thirty years after U.S. v. F/V Taiyo Maru 28, illustrates.

* * *

UNITED STATES V. MARSHALLS 201

D. Guam, 2008
Not rep'ted in F.Supp.2d, 2008 WL 2018299

TYDINGCO–GATEWOOD, CHIEF JUDGE.

FACTUAL BACKGROUND

An Exclusive Economic Zone ("EEZ") is a sea zone over which a state (including its territories) has special rights over the exploration and use of marine resources. The EEZ starts at the coastal baseline and extends 200 nautical miles out into the sea, perpendicular to the baseline. The outer boundary of the zone is a line drawn in such a manner that each point on it is 200 nautical miles from the baseline. United States EEZs were originally established by Presidential Proclamation in 1983. Even earlier, in 1976, the Fishery Conservation and Management Act of 1976 established a fishery conservation zone contiguous to the territorial sea of the United States, effective March 1, 1977. EEZs were designed to grant exclusive jurisdiction to the United States for the purposes of "exploring, exploiting, conserving, and managing natural resources." Presidential Proclamation No. 5030.

The controlling law governing the territorial seas, EEZs, and fisheries of the United States is the Magnuson–Stevens Fishery Conservation and Management Act ("Magnuson Act"). *See* 16 U. S. C. § 1857. The Magnuson Act provides for the conservation and management of United States fisheries. Since 1977, the United States has claimed an exclusive fishery zone around both Baker and Howland Islands. These Islands are undisputed territories of the United States, and are located on the equator, about 1,600 miles southwest of Hawaii. The Magnuson Act also codifies the EEZs of Baker and Howland Islands, and other United States territories in the Pacific.

On September 7, 2006, the United States Coast Guard ("USCG") performed a routine patrol of the EEZ of Baker and Howland Islands, and noticed a foreign flagged fishing vessel (Marshall Islands flagged) within the EEZ.[1] At the time, the boom was lowered and the fishing nets were not properly covered or stowed. This, in itself, is a violation of the Magnuson Act 16 U.S.C. § 1857(4)(A) and (B). According to the USCG, two other fishing vessels were detected inside the EEZ that day, the F/V KOO'S 101 and the F/V KOO'S 108.[2]

On September 9, 2006, the USCG again spotted the F/V MARSHALLS 201 while on patrol, and again it was located within the United States EEZ. When detected on this date, active fishing on the vessel was observed within the EEZ, a clear violation of the Magnuson Act. *See* 16 U.S.C. § 1857(2). The USCG contacted a nearby USCG cutter to intercept the fishing vessel and to determine whether the F/V MARSHALLS 201 was permitted to fish in the EEZ. The USCG Cutter WALNUT viewed F/V MARSHALLS 201 actively hauling nets, but the persons aboard the vessel refused to respond to repeated attempts at communication. The Cutter WALNUT tried to reach F/V MARSHALLS 201 by radio and by signal flag. After several minutes of effort by the USCG to make contact with F/V MARSHALLS 201, the vessel abruptly headed out of the EEZ, with her nets still hanging from the boom. The Cutter WALNUT pursued F/V MARSHALLS 201 out of the EEZ.

The vessel eventually stopped, and the USCG boarded and secured the F/V MARSHALLS 201 in order to investigate whether any illegal fishing activity had taken place. The USCG determined that the F/V MARSHALLS 201 did not possess a permit to fish in the EEZ, and it appeared that the vessel had a recent catch of 110 metric tons of tuna in its possession, from fishing in the United States EEZ on September 9, 2006.

---

[1] The vessel was later identified as F/V MARSHALLS 201.

[2] These fishing vessels were later determined to be partially owned by Marshall Islands Fishing Company ("MIFCO").

The next day, USCG law enforcement seized the F/V MARSHALLS 201 and her catch and escorted the vessel to Guam. On September 20, 2006, the F/V MARSHALLS 201 reached port in Apra Harbor, where the current market value of the F/V MARSHALLS 201 was determined to be $2,650,000.00, and the current market value of the tuna onboard was found to be $350,000.00.

PROCEDURAL BACKGROUND

On October 4, 2006, the United States filed a Complaint of Forfeiture of the vessel and its catch and appurtenances under 16 U.S.C. § 1860.[3] In the Complaint, the United States alleged violations of the Magnuson Act, for illegally fishing without a permit in the EEZ of the United States. On October 17, 2006, U.S. Magistrate Judge Manibusan granted a Stipulated Motion for Release of the vessel. Substituting for the vessel *in rem* was a bond in the amount of $2,950,000.00, which represented the value of the vessel and the catch. F/V MARSHALLS 201 left Guam soon after her release.

DISCUSSION

There are two main arguments on which the Defendant bases its Motion to Dismiss. The first argument is that Baker and Howland Islands are "rocks" under the Law of the Sea Treaty definition. The second argument is that the United States' enforcement of these EEZs is contrary to customary international law.

At the outset, the court notes that the United States addressed the issue of standing in its Opposition Brief and in oral arguments on April 3, 2008. The United States argued in its Opposition that the Defendant had no standing to dispute the EEZs of the United States because it believes the case is based on interpretations of international law. However, the court finds that because the legal premise of this case involves the seizure of the F/V MARSHALLS 201 by the United States, for allegedly being located in and engaged in fishing within the EEZ of the United States, the Defendant has standing to pursue its Motion to Dismiss in the District Court of Guam.

The court will now address the Defendant's Motion to Dismiss. The Defendant first argues that the United States lacks the legal authority to claim and enforce a 200-mile EEZ around Baker and Howland Islands. Specifically, the Defendant states that the complaint should be dismissed for lack of subject matter jurisdiction and *in rem* jurisdiction under Rule 12(b)(1),(2), and(3) of the Federal Rules of Civil Procedure. The Defendant

---

[3] This statute governs civil forfeitures, and states that "any fishing vessel (including its fishing gear, furniture, appurtenances, stores, and cargo) used, and any fish (or fair market value thereof) taken or retained, in any manner, in connection with or as a result of the commission of any act prohibited by section 1857 of this title . . . shall be subject to forfeiture to the United States." 16 U.S.C. § 1860(a).

claims that under international law, Baker and Howland Islands are not actually islands, but are considered "rocks" and therefore, do not provide a basis for claims of EEZs.

Article 121(3) of the United Nations Law of the Sea Convention ("Convention") states that "rocks which cannot sustain human habitation or economic life of their own shall have no exclusive economic zone or continental shelf." (*See* United Nations Law of the Sea Convention, Dec. 10, 1982, U.N. Doc. A/CONF.62/122). The Defendant argues that Baker and Howland Islands fit this definition, and more importantly, that the Convention is binding on the United States because it is a signatory to it. It should be noted though, that the United States has yet to ratify the Convention. . . . As a result, it is not yet legally enforceable on the United States.

Not only is the Convention not presently binding on the United States, the Defendant's argument is further weakened by the enactment of the Magnuson–Stevens Fishery Conservation and Management Act ("Magnuson Act") (*See* 16 U.S.C. § 1857) which specifically cites to "Pacific Insular Areas" as areas "contain[ing] unique historical, cultural, legal, political, and geographical circumstances which make fisheries resources important in sustaining their economic growth." 16 U.S.C. § 1801(a)(10). "Pacific Insular Area" is a term of art and is defined to mean "American Samoa, Guam, the Northern Mariana Islands, Baker Island, Howland Island . . . " 16 U.S.C. § 1802(30). The Magnuson Act also specifically and explicitly recognizes the EEZs off of Baker and Howland Islands. Section 1824(e)(8) of Title 16 (*as amended*) states that "[i]n the case of violations by foreign vessels occurring within the exclusive economic zones off . . . Howland, Baker, and Wake Islands, amounts received by the Secretary attributable to fines and penalties imposed under this Act, shall be deposited into" an account named for the action. (*See* 16 U.S.C. § 1824(e)(8), as amended by Magnuson–Stevens Fishery Conservation and Management Reauthorization Act of 2006, section 6, Pub.L. 109–479 (2007)).

Additionally, the Magnuson Act specifically recognizes jurisdiction for enforcement of the EEZs. It states that "in the case of Guam or any possession of the United States in the Pacific Ocean, the appropriate court is the United States District Court for the District of Guam . . . " 16 U.S.C. § 1861(d).

In sum, Congress has unequivocally established EEZs around its territories of Baker and Howland Islands, and has given justification for their protection, and jurisdictional relief for violations occurring within those EEZs, to the District Court of Guam.

The United States also suggests that even if Congress had not expressly declared EEZs around Baker and Howland Islands, these Islands do not fit the Convention definition of "rocks." In order to find that Baker and Howland Islands are "rocks" one must first determine that they "cannot sustain human habitation." The United States introduced evidence that both Islands can sustain human habitation and "have had periods of habitation in the relatively recent past and . . . have played a role in various economic ventures." (*See* Docket No. 121 at 13, Van Dyke Deposition 107–120, Exh. 8–15 (Attachment D)).

The Defendant argues that the principal determinant is whether a particular island or "islet" can sustain human habitation or economic life of its own. According to Professor Jon M. Van Dyke, a professor at University of Hawaii School of Law, the habitation must "exist for its own sake, as part of an ongoing community that sustains itself and continues through generations." (*See* Docket No. 98 at ¶ 5). Because Baker and Howland Islands "have no economic life of their own," they should be considered "rocks" under the Convention. (*See* Docket No. 98 at ¶ 2).

The court finds that the Defendant's argument misconstrues Article 121. The specific language of the statute reads that "rocks which *cannot* sustain human habitation *or* economic life on their own shall have no exclusive economic zone or continental shelf." (*See* United Nations Law of the Sea Convention, Dec. 10, 1982, U.N. Doc. A/CONF.62/122, *emphasis added*). In the present case, the United Sates has provided sufficient evidence in its pleadings to give the impression that Baker and Howland Islands are in fact islands as defined under the Convention.

Notwithstanding the arguments over the definition of an island under the Convention, Federal law makes clear that the United States may declare EEZs around its territories. As noted above, Baker and Howland Islands have been designated as two such territories. Jurisdiction regarding actions taking place in these EEZs is clearly set out in the Magnuson Act. As such, the Defendant has not met the burden of Rule 12(b)(1),(2), and (3) of the Federal Rules of Civil Procedure, and as such the Motion to Dismiss is DENIED.

* * *

NOTES AND QUESTIONS

1. Was the U.S. Coast Guard exercising the right of "hot pursuit" as defined in article 111, supra p. 18? Article 111(2) applies the right of hot pursuit to violations of the EEZ.

2. Why did the judge dismiss the defendant's argument that the U.S. is not entitled to an EEZ around Baker and Howland islands because they cannot sustain human habitation or an economic life of their own?

3. Can both rocks and islands generate 200 mile-EEZs? How are rocks and islands distinguished? Is a coral atoll a rock or an island? See LOSC, ar-

ticles 121 (islands); 6 (reefs). For an analysis of state practice, see Roger O'Keefe, Palm-Fringed Benefits: Island Dependencies in the New Law of the Sea, 45 Int'l & Comp. L.Q. 408 (1996).

4. If the U.S. becomes a party to the LOSC, will it lose its right to claim an EEZ around Baker and Howland islands? Will it have to amend the Magnuson-Stevens Act, 16 U.S.C. § 1824(e)(8), to "uncodify" the EEZs around these islets? What then becomes of the marine national monuments declared by President George W. Bush in 2009? Proclamation No. 8336 of Jan. 6, 2009, Establishment of the Pacific Remote Islands Marine National Monuments, 74 Fed. Reg. 1565 (Jan. 12, 2009). See generally Alison Rieser, The Papahanaumokuakea Precedent: Ecosystem-Scale Marine Protected Areas in the EEZ, 13 Asian-Pacific L. & Pol'y J. 210 (2011–12).

5. In President Reagan's Proclamation No. 5030, the U.S. declared EEZs around all of its island territories and dependencies. If the U.S. did not have EEZs around these features in the Pacific, which nations would enforce regulations governing Pacific tuna fisheries in those waters? See LOSC, art. 64. See also the Western and Central Pacific Fisheries Convention Implementation Act, Pub. L. No. 109-479, title V, § 502, Jan. 12, 2007, 120 Stat. 3635, codified at 16 U.S.C. §§ 6901–6910.

6. Can the captain of the illegally-fishing foreign-flag vessel be arrested for violations of U.S. EEZ fishing law? Do the U.S. statutory provisions meet the requirements of the LOSC for arrest and detention of vessels violating fisheries regulations in the U.S. EEZ?

7. On June 8, 2009, Judge Tydingco-Gatewood signed an order, dismissing the civil forfeiture action against the Marshall Islands Fishing Co. and its vessel, when the company agreed to forfeit $500,000 of the $2.95 million in funds being held in a Bank of Hawaii account. The civil penalty was transferred to NOAA. The consent decree required the fishing vessel, a tuna purse seiner, to stay within U.S. government radar and the company to give NOAA and the Coast Guard "near real-time access to the ship's Vessel Monitoring System tracking information in all areas of its fishing operations for three years." Because the vessel sets its nets around drifting buoys called "fish aggregating devices" the company is also required to deploy two satellite-tracked drifting buoys per fishing trip for five years. Given how difficult (and expensive) it is for coastal nations to patrol their EEZs for illegal fishing, was the agreed-to civil penalty too small relative to the value of the illegally caught tuna? Did these conditions make up for the small amount of the civil penalty? How does this fine and conditions compare to those approved by the law of the sea tribunal under the LOSC article 73 on prompt release? See materials below.

NOTE: LOSC ART. 73 AND PROMPT RELEASE PROVISIONS
LOSC, ARTICLE 73

Enforcement of Laws and Regulations of the Coastal State

1. The coastal State may, in the exercise of its sovereign rights to explore, exploit, conserve and manage the living resources in the exclusive economic zone, take such measures, including boarding, inspection, arrest and judicial proceedings, as may be necessary to ensure compliance with the laws and regulations adopted by it in conformity with this Convention.

2. Arrested vessels and their crews shall be promptly released upon the posting of reasonable bond or other security.

3. Coastal State penalties for violations of fisheries laws and regulations in the exclusive economic zone may not include imprisonment, in the absence of agreements to the contrary by the States concerned, or any other form of corporal punishment. . . .

––––––––

The judicial body created by the 1982 LOSC, the International Tribunal on the Law of the Sea (ITLOS), has jurisdiction to order the prompt release of vessels and crews under LOSC art. 292 upon application for release by the flag state of the vessel. The majority of the ITLOS cases have involved the issue of prompt release. The following excerpt outlines the primary issues that arise in such cases. The lucrative fishery for Patagonian toothfish, made infamous by the Australian arrest of the Viarsa I after a three-week hot pursuit, has attracted significant illegal fishing in the southern waters of the Atlantic and Indian oceans. See G. Bruce Knecht, Hooked: Pirates, Poaching, and the Perfect Fish (2007). ITLOS has heard several applications for prompt release of vessels arrested for EEZ violations while fishing for toothfish.

THE "CAMOUCO" CASE
(PANAMA V. FRANCE)
(Case No. 5, 7 February 2000)

* * *

57. In the view of the Tribunal, it is not logical to read the requirement of exhaustion of local remedies or any other analogous rule into article 292. Article 292 of the Convention is designed to free a ship and its crew from prolonged detention on account of the imposition of unreasonable bonds in municipal jurisdictions, or the failure of local law to provide for release on posting of a reasonable bond, inflicting thereby avoidable loss on a ship owner or other persons affected by such detention. Equally, it safeguards the interests of the coastal State by providing for release only upon the posting of a reasonable bond or other financial security de-

termined by a court or tribunal referred to in article 292, without preju-dice to the merits of the case in the domestic forum against the vessel, its owner or its crew.

58. Article 292 provides for an independent remedy and not an ap-peal against a decision of a national court. No limitation should be read into article 292 that would have the effect of defeating its very object and purpose. Indeed, article 292 permits the making of an application within a short period from the date of detention and it is not normally the case that local remedies could be exhausted in such a short period. * * *

66. In the M/V "SAIGA" Case, the Tribunal stated that "the criterion of reasonableness encompasses the amount, the nature and the form of the bond or financial security. The overall balance of the amount, form and nature of the bond or financial security must be reasonable." (Judg-ment of 4 December 1997, paragraph 82).

67. The Tribunal considers that a number of factors are relevant in an assessment of the reasonableness of bonds or other financial security. They include the gravity of the alleged offences, the penalties imposed or imposable under the laws of the detaining State, the value of the detained vessel and of the cargo seized, the amount of the bond imposed by the de-taining State and its form. * * *

71. That the Camouco has been in detention is not disputed. Howev-er, the parties are in disagreement whether the Master of the Camouco is also in detention. It is admitted that the Master is presently under court supervision, that his passport has also been taken away from him by the French authorities, and that, consequently, he is not in a position to leave Réunion. The Tribunal considers that, in the circumstances of this case, it is appropriate to order the release of the Master in accordance with arti-cle 292, paragraph 1, of the Convention.* * *

NOTES AND QUESTIONS

1. In the Camouco case, France required the vessel's owner to post a bond of 20 million French francs. The ITLOS found that the bond was not reasonable under the circumstances and reduced it to 8 million French francs. The bottom-fishing longline vessel was arrested with 6 tons of frozen Patagonian toothfish onboard, and the crew was seen jettisoning a 34-kg bag of fresh toothfish in the EEZ of the Crozet Islands. The vessel was fishing under license from Panama and had a Spanish master. Panama argued that a reasonable bond would be only 100,000 French francs (approximately US$15,000). See Erik Franckx, "Reasonable Bond" in the Practice of the IT-LOS, 32 Cal. W. Int'l L.J. 303 (2002).

2. After the Viarsa I arrest, the Australian federal court upheld the con-fiscation of the Uruguay-flagged vessel as forfeited, but the master's criminal prosecution resulted in a hung jury due to the circumstantial nature of the

evidence. After the vessel was forfeited, it was sent to India for dismantling and recycling. See Laurence Blakely, The End of the Viarsa Saga and the Legality of Australia's Vessel Forfeiture Penalty for Illegal Fishing in Its Exclusive Economic Zone, 17 Pac. Rim L.& Pol'y J. 677 (2008). An increasing number of coastal states are applying forfeiture sanctions to illegal fishing vessels. What would the ITLOS rule if a flag state challenged the validity of vessel forfeiture sanctions imposed by a coastal state?

3. In the 1976 Fishery Conservation and Management Act, the United States claimed exclusive "jurisdiction" over living resources within its new zone. Following the 1983 presidential proclamation of an EEZ, Congress changed "jurisdiction" to "sovereign rights" for living resources in the zone. The legislation also claims exclusive U.S. management authority, even beyond the EEZ, over anadromous stocks of U.S. origin, generally following the provision of LOSC art. 66 which gives the state in whose rivers the stock originates the "primary interest in and responsibility for such stocks." The EEZ provisions of the 1982 Convention do not apply to so-called sedentary species of the sea bottom. See LOSC, art. 68. These species—lobsters, for example—are treated as resources of the coastal nation's continental shelf and governed by that regime. LOSC, art. 77. See discussion of the continental shelf regime at p. 51. The 1982 Convention specially authorizes EEZ countries and international organizations to protect marine mammals to a greater degree than the general rules on optimum utilization of living resources would otherwise require. LOSC, articles 65, 120. Are the conservation duties for continental shelf sedentary species under article 77 different from those for the living resources of the EEZ under articles 61 and 62?

NOTE: TRANSBOUNDARY AND MIGRATORY FISHERIES AND STRADDLING STOCKS

Coastal nations must also cooperate with other affected nations in managing stocks of fish whose habitats or migratory ranges overlap the boundary between the EEZs of neighbor nations ("transboundary stocks") and stocks that migrate into the high seas beyond the EEZ ("straddling stocks"), where the vessels of other countries have the freedom to fish. In addition, all affected nations are obligated to cooperate in the management of "highly migratory species," such as tuna, which frequently migrate throughout broad areas of the high seas and several EEZs. The 1995 Agreement on Straddling Fish Stocks and Highly Migratory Fish Stocks is intended to implement articles 63–64 of the LOSC that require coordination of conservation and management measures for these stocks. The Agreement heightens the responsibility of coastal states over the requirements imposed by article 61 of the LOSC. Terms used in LOSC article 61, such as "take into account" and "consider," are generally replaced in the Agreement with "shall" adopt, ensure and protect. An important element of the Agreement is its adoption of the precautionary approach, an emerging principle of international environmental law that requires resource managers to exercise caution in the face of scientific uncertainty. The Agreement provides a detailed description of the elements of the precautionary approach, giving clear definition to the obligation of coastal states. Effective coastal state management is also encouraged by the "compatibility" provisions. Article 7(2)(a) of the Agreement requires compatible management of straddling stocks within *and beyond* national jurisdiction taking into account "the conservation and management measures adopted and applied . . . by the coastal States within areas under national jurisdiction and ensure that measures established in respect of such stocks for the high seas do not undermine the effectiveness of such measures."

The treaty received its 30th ratification and came into force in December 2001, and currently has 78 parties. The United States was among the first states to ratify it. The Agreement urges the creation of effective regional fisheries organizations (RFOs) to manage fisheries on the high seas. See generally Alison Reiser, International Fisheries Law, Overfishing and Marine Biodiversity, 9 Geo. Int'l. Envtl. L. Rev. 251 (1997); Donna Christie, It Don't Come EEZ: The Failure and Future of Coastal State Fisheries Management, 14 J. Transnat'l L. & Pol'y 1 (2004–05). Today, most of the high seas lies within jurisdiction of one or more of the more than 25 RFOs that now manage fisheries in particular areas of the high seas or a particular fishery throughout its migratory range. The Agreement also includes innovative enforcement provisions. These provisions were supplemented by the adoption in 2009 of the U.N. FAO Port State Measures Agreement, which enlists the aid of port states where illegally caught fish is often off-loaded, to help overcome any stalemate resulting from the balance struck by the LOSC between the authority of coastal states and flag states. In November 2011, President Obama submitted the agreement to the Senate for advice and consent to ratification.

––––––

2. Non-Living Resources

The 1982 U.N. Convention on the Law of the Sea recognizes the same "sovereign rights" of the EEZ nation in the zone's non-living natural resources as it does in the zone's living resources. This includes all kinds of economic exploitation and exploration of the zone, such as the production of energy from the water, currents and winds, not just extractive activities.

This sovereignty includes resources of the seabed and subsoil, as well as the water column. The law concerning exploration for and exploitation of offshore non-living resources, however, is set out much more completely in the articles on the continental shelf. Further, customary law's continental shelf doctrine, reflected in the Convention, is the traditional framework for addressing coastal nation rights and jurisdictions over the continental shelf. This redundancy contributes to a large, and sometimes confusing, overlap of EEZ and continental shelf law. U.S. law governing exploitation of the non-living resources of the continental shelf is examined in Chapter 5.

3. Marine Scientific Research

The LOSC creates a coastal nation consent regime for marine scientific research in the EEZ. LOSC, articles 245, 246. Researchers must apply for consent at least six months before the start of their proposed projects, but states are expected to give their consent "in normal circumstances," and to research projects that have as their purpose the expansion of scientific knowledge of the marine environment "for the benefit of all mankind." Consent is implied if the coastal nation does not respond to a research request within four months. A state may deny consent at its discretion for any research of direct significance to the exploration for or exploitation of the EEZ's or continental shelf's natural resources. The Convention subjects a researcher, who has been granted consent, to a long list of potentially costly obligations generally designed to assure that the coastal state is fully informed about the project as it progresses and to provide the opportunity for coastal state participation.

QUESTION

When the United States' EEZ was proclaimed by President Reagan in 1983, the president recognized that the Convention's consent regime for marine scientific research was part of customary law, but refused to assert the regime on behalf of the United States. Why? Today, the U.S. requires advance consent for marine research only if part of the research is conducted within the territorial sea, or if the research involves marine mammals or the taking of commercial quantities of marine resources, or if the research involves contact with the continental shelf.

－－－－－

4. Vessel Navigation and Overflight

The LOSC article 58 and current customary law continue to allow freedom of surface and submerged vessel navigation and freedom of overflight in the EEZ. The treaty's incorporation of these high seas freedoms into the EEZ was an important UNCLOS III victory for U.S. negotiators and those of other naval and maritime countries. However, some coastal nations, such as Brazil, contend that neither the Convention nor customary law permits military maneuvers in the EEZ without the consent of the coastal nation, especially if these maneuvers involve the use of weapons or explosives. The United States maintains that the freedoms of navigation and overflight, on the high seas and in the EEZ, encompass the freedom to conduct military exercises if done with reasonable regard for the rights and freedoms of other nations.

5. Protection of the Marine Environment

The protection of the marine environment is another area where the LOSC provides extensive new dimensions to the law of the sea. Collectively, the marine environment articles purport to impose an impressive array of duties on all nation states to prevent, reduce, and control ocean pollution from all sources subject to their jurisdiction, including land-based sources, vessels, and offshore installations. The treaty also requires nations to cooperate globally and regionally to establish rules and standards for protecting the marine environment.

The Convention allows different degrees of coastal state regulatory authority for vessels in ports, in the territorial sea and in the EEZ. Coastal states are given a great deal of authority to set standards for pollution prevention over vessels in their ports or territorial sea, so long as innocent passage is not impeded. The regime attempts to balance the rights of coastal nations to control vessel source pollution in their EEZs with recognition of freedom of navigation within EEZs. The Convention requires its parties to act through "the competent international organization" or general diplomatic conference to establish uniform rules and standards for protecting the marine environment from vessel-source pollution. The "competent international organization" is understood to mean the International Maritime Organization (IMO). Only in carefully restricted situations, in which a foreign flag vessel in the EEZ has clearly committed a violation that has caused or is threatening to cause serious damage, is the coastal nation authorized to interfere with the vessel's EEZ passage. The treaty continues to give primary jurisdiction for enforcing the vessel-source rules and standards to flag states and in certain circumstances, even where the offense is committed outside the waters of the port nation, to countries whose ports are visited by offending vessels.

The LOSC's frequent reference to and incorporation of "standards of competent international organizations" recognizes the extensive framework created by treaties like the 1970 London (Dumping) Convention, numerous regional seas treaties, MARPOL 73/78 and others. It also encourages other international agreements designed to protect and preserve the marine environment. Further, the 1992 U.N. Conference on Environment and Development (UNCED) referred to the marine environment articles of the Law of the Sea Convention as a basis or framework for further development of international rules for protecting and preserving the marine environment. As described in Chapter 8, the United States has not always followed the norm of giving primacy to international standards for marine pollution control, choosing instead to lead through the enactment of unilateral standards such as the oil-tanker double-hull requirement of the Oil Pollution Act of 1990.

E. THE CONTINENTAL SHELF

In general, the sovereign rights of coastal nations in the natural resources of the continental shelf remain the same today as the rights asserted in the 1945 Truman Proclamation and later codified in the 1958 Continental Shelf Convention. The most startling difference in the continental shelf in the LOSC regime is the physical extent of the legal continental shelf.

The 1958 Continental Shelf Convention began the process of distinguishing a coastal nation's *legal* continental shelf from the underwater geologic feature by defining the outer limit of the shelf as the 200-meter depth line or, beyond that, to the *limit of exploitability* of the natural resources. Although the 200-meter isobath in some locations lies hundreds of miles from the coast, the average is between 40 and 50 miles offshore. To be consistent with the development of the EEZ concept, the LOSC now establishes the minimum outer limit of the legal continental shelf, measured from the territorial sea baseline, at 200 miles. This means that the legal continental shelf may extend far beyond the geologic continental shelf and may encompass areas that would geologically be considered the deep seabed. Where the geologic continental margin (shelf, slope, and rise) extends farther than the 200-mile distance, the LOSC provides a choice of two complex formulas to allow a coastal state to claim a continental shelf beyond 200 miles: The boundary can be claimed along a line where the thickness of sediment on the seafloor is at least 1 percent of the distance to the foot of the slope (Formula 1), or the boundary can be asserted 60 nm beyond the foot of the slope (Formula 2). Such extended claims are limited to either 350 nautical miles seaward of the baseline, or 100 nautical miles seaward of the 2,500-meter depth contour. The coastal nation's rights are, however, somewhat qualified on the far "outer continental shelf." LOSC, articles 76–77, 82.

While it can be asserted that the 200-mile minimum continental shelf boundary is now part of customary international law, the LOS Convention's complicated formulas for delimiting the boundary of the outer shelf beyond 200 miles may not yet be part of custom. Because the delimitation of the extent of the continental shelf beyond 200 miles continues to be an indeterminate and complex process, the Convention provides for the establishment of an expert scientific and technical group, the Commission on the Limits of the Continental Shelf (CLCS), to review such claims. The Commission provides technical assistance, and when a country adopts a continental shelf limit based on the recommendations of the Commission, the limit of the shelf is "final and binding." LOSC, article 76(8). Because the provisions on the CLCS in LOSC Annex II, article 9 state that the Commission's actions "shall not prejudice matters relating to delimitation of boundaries between States with opposite or adjacent coasts," it seems relatively clear that the determination is intended to be "final and bind-ing" primarily in regard to the boundary between a coastal state's conti-nental shelf and the deep seabed administered under U.N. authority. This is not to say, however, that recognition by the CLCS of the legitimacy of a coastal state's claim to a submerged area as continental shelf would not carry significant weight in the resolution of a subsequent maritime boundary dispute with a country claiming the same area.

The United States has currently embarked on an "Extended Conti-nental Shelf Project * * * to establish the full extent of the continental shelf of the United States, consistent with international law." See Ex-tended Continental Shelf Project at http://continentalshelf.gov/. The pro-ject is described as the "largest and potentially most significant inter-agency marine survey ever undertaken by the U.S." The melting of the Arctic Ocean ice cover due to global warming is a primary impetus for this project. Arctic seabed resources, previously unrecoverable, may soon be exploitable due the diminished ice cover, and nations surrounding the Arctic Ocean have been submitting claims to extended continental shelves to the CLCS for several years. If the United States ever joins the treaty, it will have ten years to submit a claim.

The substance of coastal nation rights in the continental shelf are ex-pressed in both the 1958 and 1982 treaties as "sovereign rights for the purpose of exploring it and exploiting its natural resources." These rights exist without any declaration by the coastal state, and no one may under-take these activities without the consent of the coastal nation.

The non-living natural resources of the continental shelf continue to create the main economic value of continental shelves. Oil and gas depos-its are still the most valuable commercially exploited resources of the seabed and subsoil. With respect to any exploitation of non-living re-sources undertaken in a coastal nation's "outer continental shelf" beyond 200 miles, the 1982 Convention requires the coastal nation to contribute a small percentage, eventually a maximum of seven percent, of the value of the production to a fund to benefit developing countries. LOSC, article 82.

The resources of the continental shelf also include the living re-sources of the seabed and subsoil, so-called "sedentary species." Sedentary species are defined as those "organisms which, at the harvestable stage, either are immobile on or under the sea-bed or are unable to move except in constant physical contact with the sea-bed or the subsoil." This is a strange definition, with no basis in categories recognized by marine biolo-gy, created in the 1958 Convention to provide a basis for coastal state control over certain commercially important species. Although not even clearly within the definition of "sedentary species," the United States and many other countries include such creatures as lobsters and crabs in the category. A coastal nation's management of the continental shelf's sedentary species is not qualified by the duties to conserve and optimally utilize them found in the LOSC's EEZ articles. The 1958 Continental Shelf Convention did not impose any such obligations, and the 1982 treaty did not restrict these rights of coastal countries already recognized by international law.

NOTES AND QUESTIONS

1. Can the U.S. claim a 200-mile continental shelf where geology does not support the claim? As a non-party to the treaty, the U.S. will not be able to have the benefit of a CLCS validation of its claim to an extended continental shelf. How can the U.S. assert its rights? Can the U.S. object to claims of other nations that are recognized by the CLCS?

2. Are a coastal nation's continental shelf rights limited to *natural* resources of the seabed and subsoil? Are sunken ships or their cargoes, or submerged archaeological sites considered resources of the continental shelf? Rights in these objects have traditionally been governed by the law of salvage and other rules of admiralty law. The LOSC does include a section, however, oddly placed in a General Provisions near the end of the treaty that a coastal state may "presume that . . . removal [of objects of an archaeological and historical nature] from the seabed in the [contiguous] zone . . . without its approval would result in an infringement within its territory or territorial sea of the laws and regulations referred to in that article." LOSC art. 303 effectively extends coastal state jurisdiction through the contiguous zone to protect submerged cultural heritage, but beyond that, the continental shelf regime provides no basis for control or protection.

5. THE DEEP SEABED AND HIGH SEAS

A. THE DEEP SEABED MINING REGIME

Much time and energy was expended during the years of UNCLOS III in a largely successful attempt to compromise the often widely separated positions of the delegation blocs on the major topic that instigated the conference: the international mining regime for the deep seabed beyond national jurisdiction. Yet it is the part of the 1982 Convention, Part XI, devoted to that regime that caused the United States to vote against adoption of the treaty by the conference and to refuse to sign or ratify it after its adoption, over U.S. objection, by an overwhelming majority of nations. Considerations of length do not permit us to examine in detail the LOS Convention's complex provisions that make up Part XI and its Annexes. Many of the Convention's seabed mining provisions have been modified in response to U.S. objections, but it is, nevertheless, important to have a general understanding of the original provisions of Part XI in order to comprehend why the United States objected to them so strongly, rejecting a treaty that otherwise was quite favorable to other U.S. ocean interests.

In announcing his administration's decision in mid-1982 to refuse to sign or ratify the treaty, President Reagan did, indeed, recognize that the Convention's non-seabed parts were acceptable to the United States, but he went on to raise serious U.S. objections to Part XI. Basically, the objections of the United States to the 1982 Convention can be characterized as ideological. The Reagan administration strongly favored the free-enterprise system as a general tenet and viewed the Convention's deep seabed mining regime, which required private miners to compete with the semi-monopolistic Enterprise, as not sufficiently rewarding technological innovation and investment.

In addition, the Reagan administration took the position that the favorable non-seabed parts of the Convention had, by 1982, become customary international law, while the mining regime could be created only by the Convention and bind only the parties to it. According to this thinking, the United States could take advantage of the new customary law of the sea it liked and, by refusing to become a party to the Convention, renounce the deep-seabed mining provisions and the International Seabed Authority. Critics rejected the idea that a nation might accept piecemeal portions of the treaty. The argument was that the consensus negotiations led to a treaty with provisions that were based on complex bargaining and inter-relationships; the treaty could only be accepted as a "package deal."

In the waning days of the UNCLOS III negotiations, the U.S. Congress, with approval of the Executive Branch, enacted the Deep Seabed Hard Mineral Resources Act. Under this Act, the United States could issue licenses to its own nationals and companies to mine the deep seabed. The Act made no territorial claims to the seabed beyond the U.S. continental shelf and seemed to recognize the common heritage concept. It also encouraged other countries to enact similar legislation with the potential for reciprocal recognition of national licenses. The United States and other industrialized countries also pursued the potential for an international agreement among themselves to establish a seabed mining system.

Ironically, in the years since the United States took its position in opposition to the 1982 Convention's Part XI, changed circumstances reduced the significance of the Convention's deep seabed regime. First, world market prices for the important minerals of the seabed plummeted since UNCLOS III, making the expensive deep sea mining commercially impracticable in most cases. Second, the end of the Cold War and the current disrepute of centrally managed economies caused many nations to look more favorably at the principles of market driven systems and thus with increased empathy for the U.S. position. There was also a growing realization that the Convention could not succeed in achieving its hoped-for status as a constitution for the world ocean unless the most important ocean nations were parties.

As the treaty approached the submission of the 60th ratification needed for it to come into force, a series of efforts were made to make the seabed mining provisions of the Convention more palatable to the United States and other industrialized countries. These efforts led to the 1994 Implementation Agreement for Part XI and the ratification of the treaty by every developed country except the United States. Despite support for the treaty by the Clinton, Bush and Obama administrations, the Senate has not yet voted on the treaty. The United States remains outside the treaty.

The current seabed regime, the International Seabed Authority, has three principal organs—the Assembly, the Council, and the Secretariat. The Assembly is a representative body, but its decisions must be made in collaboration with a Council, the executive organ of the Authority. The Council has a more limited membership, elected according to a complex formula considering importing, exporting and producing countries, countries with most substantial investments, and geographical distribution. The Council establishes specific policies in conformity with the Convention and the general policies set by the Assembly. It supervises and coordinates implementation of the seabed regime and to date has concluded 11 contracts for exploration for deep seabed minerals. Each contractor has the exclusive right to explore an initial area of up to 150,000 square kilometers. Contractors include governments (India, the Republic of Korea and a consortium formed by Bulgaria, Cuba, Czech Republic, Poland, Russian Federation and Slovakia) and companies from countries that include Germany, China, Japan, Russia, Tonga and Nauru.

Seabed mining beyond national jurisdiction seems to be becoming a topic of interest again to mining companies. In addition to the manganese nodules that started the whole controversy over ownership of seabed resources, "massive-sulphide formations," occurring in areas only 1–2 km below the sea surface around deep sea vents, contain high concentrations of copper, gold, zinc and silver. Rare earths, elements crucial to electronics and currently exclusively controlled by China, have also reportedly been discovered offshore in relatively shallow seas.

B. JURISDICTION IN THE HIGH SEAS

In spite of the ocean enclosure movement of the past half century, sixty percent of the world's oceans still lie beyond coastal state jurisdiction. The traditional freedoms of the seas—the freedom of surface and submerged navigation, the freedom of overflight, the freedom to fish, and the freedom to lay submarine cables and pipelines—continue to be part of custom and treaty law. In addition, the 1982 LOSC, in article 87, specifically includes the freedom of scientific research and the "freedom to construct artificial islands and other installations permitted under international law." In general, no nation may interfere with any other nation's exercise of the freedoms of the high seas. However, most of the freedoms of the high seas are subject to certain qualifications. Most fundamentally, the LOSC codifies the principle that high seas "freedoms shall be exercised by all States with due regard for the interests of other States in their exercise of the freedom of the high seas." In addition to this rather vague limitation, certain other restrictions are set out in the treaty.

The freedom to fish is restricted in the Convention by the duty to conserve the living resources of the high seas and to cooperate with other nations to this end. The treaty also requires nations whose nationals fish the high seas to recognize the rights and duties of coastal nations with respect to straddling stocks, highly migratory species, anadromous stocks, and marine mammals. The 1995 Agreement on Straddling Fish Stocks and Highly Migratory Fish Stocks and the widespread development of regional high seas fisheries organizations are serving to flesh out the obligations of states whose nationals fish the high seas.

The high seas freedoms to lay submarine cables and pipelines and to construct artificial installations are subject to the treaty's provisions on the continental shelf. The freedom to conduct scientific research is subject to the "consent regime" applicable to the EEZ and to the exclusive right of the coastal nation to explore its continental shelf.

Vessels navigating the high seas are subject to the laws and regulations of their flag nations. Countries also have jurisdiction over nationals on the high seas. Therefore, persons and events occurring on U.S. flag vessels and aircraft are governed by U.S. law while on or over the high seas. This flag-state jurisdiction is somewhat like nationality jurisdiction, and it has also been analogized to territorial jurisdiction, with the ship or aircraft "assimilated to the territory" of the flag nation. A flag state has exclusive jurisdiction over its vessels on the high seas, except when it consents to the exercise of jurisdiction by another state or when the vessel has committed certain offenses enumerated in the LOSC.

The following case concerns one such offense, that of piracy, which, as a crime of universal jurisdiction, effectively preempts the principle of exclusive flag state jurisdiction.

UNITED STATES V. ABDI WALI DIRE

United States Court of Appeals for the Fourth Circuit, 2012
680 F.3d 446

KING, CIRCUIT JUDGE.

In the early morning hours of April 1, 2010, on the high seas between Somalia and the Seychelles (in the Indian Ocean off the east coast of Africa), the defendants—Abdi Wali Dire, Gabul Abdullahi Ali, Abdi Mohammed Umar, Abdi Mohammed Gurewardher, and Mohammed Modin Hasan—imprudently launched an attack on the USS Nicholas, having confused that mighty Navy frigate for a vulnerable merchant ship. The defendants, all Somalis, were swiftly apprehended and then transported to the Eastern District of Virginia, where they were convicted of the crime of piracy, as proscribed by *18 U.S.C. § 1651*, plus myriad other criminal offenses. In this appeal, the defendants challenge their convictions and life-plus-eighty-year sentences on several grounds, including that their fleeting and fruitless strike on the Nicholas did not, as a matter of law, amount to a *§ 1651* piracy offense. As explained below, we reject their contentions and affirm.

I.

A.

* * * The defendants' strike on the USS Nicholas was consistent with an accustomed pattern of Somali pirate attacks, designed to seize a merchant ship and then return with the vessel and its crew to Somalia, where a ransom would be negotiated and secured. Indeed, on April 4, 2010, during questioning aboard the Nicholas, the defendants separately confessed to participating willingly in a scheme to hijack a merchant vessel, and they provided details about their operation.

B.

The grand jury in the Eastern District of Virginia returned a six-count indictment against the defendants on April 20, 2010, and a fourteen-count superseding indictment (the operative "Indictment") on July 7, 2010. The Indictment, which alleged facts consistent with the subsequent trial evidence, [included]:

Count One—Piracy as defined by the law of nations (*18 U.S.C. § 1651*); * * *

The Indictment identified the Eastern District of Virginia as the proper venue under *18 U.S.C. § 3238*, which provides that "[t]he trial of all offenses begun or committed upon the high seas . . . shall be in the district in which the offender, or any one of two or more joint offenders, is arrested or is first brought."

At the conclusion of an eleven-day trial, conducted between November 9 and 24, 2010, the jury returned separate verdicts of guilty against all defendants on all counts. * * *

II.

In these consolidated appeals, the defendants first contend that their ill-fated attack on the USS Nicholas did not constitute piracy under *18 U.S.C. § 1651*, which provides in full:

> Whoever, on the high seas, commits the crime of piracy as defined by the law of nations, and is afterwards brought into or found in the United States, shall be imprisoned for life.

According to the defendants, the crime of piracy has been narrowly defined for purposes of *§ 1651* as robbery at sea, i.e., seizing or otherwise robbing a vessel. Because they boarded the Nicholas only as captives and indisputably took no property, the defendants contest their convictions on Count One, as well as the affixed life sentences.

A.

* * *

1. * * *[A]rticle I of the Constitution accords Congress the power "[t]o define and punish Piracies and Felonies committed on the high Seas, and Offences against the Law of Nations." *U.S. Const. art. I, § 8, cl. 10* (the "Define and Punish Clause"). In its present form, the language of *18 U.S.C. § 1651* can be traced to an 1819 act of Congress, which similarly provided, in pertinent part:

> That if any person or persons whatsoever, shall, on the high seas, commit the crime of piracy, as defined by the law of nations, and such offender or offenders, shall afterwards be brought into or found in the United States, every such offender or offenders shall, upon conviction thereof, . . . be punished. . . .

See Act of Mar. 3, 1819, ch. 77, § 5, 3 Stat. 510, 513–14 (the "Act of 1819"). Whereas today's mandatory penalty for piracy is life imprisonment, however, the Act of 1819 commanded punishment "with death." Id. at 514. Examining the Act of 1819 in its *United States v. Smith* decision of 1820, the Supreme Court recognized:

> There is scarcely a writer on the law of nations, who does not allude to piracy, as a crime of a settled and determinate nature; and whatever may be the diversity of definitions, in other respects, all writers concur, in holding, that robbery, or forcible depredations upon the sea, *animo furandi*, is piracy.

18 U.S. (5 Wheat.) 153, 161(1820). Accordingly, the *Smith* Court, through Justice Story, articulated "no hesitation in declaring, that piracy, by the law of nations, is robbery upon the sea." Id. at 162.

2. Here, the district court * * * focused on piracy's unusual status as a crime defined by the law of nations and subject to universal jurisdiction. * * * The district court began by recognizing that, "[f]or centuries, pirates have been universally condemned as *hostis humani generis*—enemies of all mankind—because they attack vessels on the high seas, and thus outside of any nation's territorial jurisdiction, . . . with devastating effect to global commerce and navigation." *Hasan I, 747 F.Supp.2d at 602.* * * *

a. * * * The court further recognized, however, that Congress encountered early difficulties in criminalizing "general piracy" (that is, piracy in contravention of the law of nations), rather than solely "municipal piracy" (i.e., piracy in violation of United States law). *See* id. at 606. On the one hand, "[w]hile municipal piracy is flexible enough to cover virtually any overt act Congress chooses to dub piracy, it is necessarily restricted to those acts that have a jurisdictional nexus with the United States." * * * On the other hand, "general piracy can be prosecuted by any nation, irrespective of the presence of a jurisdictional nexus." *Id.* (citing Sosa v. Alvarez–Machain, 542 U.S. 692, 762 (2004) (Breyer, J., concurring in part and concurring in the judgment) ("[I]n the 18th century, nations reached consensus not only on the substantive principle that acts of piracy were universally wrong but also on the jurisdictional principle that any nation that found a pirate could prosecute him.")). Importantly, though, "because it is created by international consensus, general piracy is restricted in substance to those offenses that the international community agrees constitute piracy." *Id.* * * *

b. The district court in *Hasan I* astutely traced the meaning of "piracy" under the law of nations, from the time of the Act of 1819 to the modern era and the crime's codification at *18 U.S.C. § 1651*. The court commenced with the Supreme Court's 1820 decision in *United States v. Smith*, relating that Justice Story easily concluded that "the Act of 1819 'sufficiently and constitutionally' defined piracy by expressly incorporating the definition of piracy under the law of nations." *See Hasan I, 747 F. Supp. 2d at 616* (quoting *Smith, 18 U.S. (5 Wheat.) at 162).* * * *

Having noted that "[n]o other Supreme Court decision since *Smith* has directly addressed the definition of general piracy," and recognizing the necessity of looking to foreign sources to determine the law of nations, the district court then focused on case law from other countries. *See Hasan I, 747 F. Supp. 2d at 614, 616 & n.16.* [The district court then reviewed the Privy Council of England's 1934 decision in *In re Piracy Jure Gentium*, [1934] A.C. 586 (P.C.), which it considered to be "[t]he most significant foreign case dealing with the question of how piracy is defined under international law." There the Privy Council concluded: "Actual robbery is not an essential element in the crime of piracy jure gentium. A frustrated attempt to commit a piratical robbery is equally piracy jure gentium." The district court also examined Kenya's 2006 *Republic v. Ahmed* prosecution of "ten Somali suspects captured by the United States Navy on the high seas"—"[t]he most recent case on [general piracy] outside the United States of which [the district court was] aware," which affirmed the defendants' convictions for piracy *jure gentium*, culling from international treaties a modern definition of piracy that encompasses acts of violence and detention.]

As detailed in *Hasan I*, "there are two prominent international agreements that have directly addressed, and defined, the crime of general piracy." *See 747 F. Supp. 2d at 618*. The first of those treaties is the Geneva Convention on the High Seas (the "High Seas Convention"), which was adopted in 1958 and ratified by the United States in 1961. . . . [and] the United Nations Convention on the Law of the Sea (the "UNCLOS"), which has amassed 162 parties since 1982—albeit not the United States, which has not ratified the UNCLOS "but has recognized that its baseline provisions reflect customary international law." *See* United States v. Alaska, 503 U.S. 569, 588 n.10 (1992) (internal quotation marks omitted). * * * Relevant here, the UNCLOS provides that

> [p]iracy consists of any of the following acts:
>
> a. any illegal acts of violence or detention, or any act of depredation, committed for private ends by the crew or the passengers of a private ship or a private aircraft, and directed:
>
>   i.   on the high seas, against another ship or aircraft, or against persons or property on board such ship or aircraft;
>
>   ii. against a ship, aircraft, persons or property in a place outside the jurisdiction of any State;
>
> b. any act of voluntary participation in the operation of a ship or of an aircraft with knowledge of facts making it a pirate-ship or aircraft;
>
> c. any act of inciting or of intentionally facilitating an act described in subparagraph (a) or (b).

UNCLOS, art. 101, *opened for signature* Dec. 10, 1982, 1833 U.N.T.S. 397 (entered into force Nov. 16, 1994). * * *

c. * * * First, the district court interpreted *18 U.S.C. § 1651* as an unequivocal demonstration of congressional intent "to incorporate . . . any subsequent developments in the definition of general piracy under the law of nations." *Hasan I, 747 F. Supp. 2d at 623*. The court rationalized:

The plain language of *18 U.S.C. § 1651* reveals that, in choosing to define the international crime of piracy by [reference to the "law of nations"], Congress made a conscious decision to adopt a flexible— but at all times sufficiently precise—definition of general piracy that would automatically incorporate developing international norms regarding piracy. Accordingly, Congress necessarily left it to the federal courts to determine the definition of piracy under the law of nations based on the international consensus at the time of the alleged offense.

Id. (citing Ex parte Quirin, 317 U.S. 1, 29–30 (1942), where the Supreme Court reiterated its 1820 ruling in *Smith* that "[a]n Act of Congress punishing 'the crime of piracy, as defined by the law of nations' is an appropriate exercise of its constitutional authority to 'define and punish' the offense, since it has adopted by reference the sufficiently precise definition of international law"). * * *

* * * Engaging in [an analysis of contemporary law to determine the definition of piracy], the court concluded:

As of April 1, 2010, the law of nations, also known as customary international law, defined piracy to *include* acts of violence committed on the high seas for private ends without an actual taking. More specifically, . . . the definition of general piracy under modern customary international law is, at the very least, reflected in Article 15 of the 1958 High Seas Convention and Article 101 of the 1982 UNCLOS.

Id. at 632–33 * * *. [The court relied on the UNCLOS definition of piracy as reflecting customary international law, the court chose the UNCLOS, which—in addition to "contain[-ing] a definition of general piracy that is, for all practical purposes, identical to that of the High Seas Convention"— "has many more states parties than the High Seas Convention" and "has been much more widely accepted by the international community than the High Seas Convention." Id. at 633.

In the course of its discussion of the High Seas Convention and the UNCLOS, the district court recognized that " '[t]reaties are proper evidence of customary international law because, and insofar as, they create legal obligations akin to contractual obligations on the States parties to them.' " *Hasan I, 747 F. Supp. 2d at 633* (quoting Kiobel v. Royal Dutch Petroleum Co., 621 F.3d 111, 137 (2d Cir. 2010)). According to the court, "[w]hile all treaties shed some light on the customs and practices of a state, 'a treaty will only constitute sufficient proof of a norm of customary international law if an overwhelming majority of States have ratified the treaty, and those States uniformly and consistently act in accordance with its principles.' " *Id.* (emphasis omitted) (quoting Kiobel, 621 F.3d at 137). "In this regard," the court emphasized, "it is also important to understand that a treaty can either 'embod[y] or create[ ] a rule of customary international law,' and such a rule 'applies beyond the limited subject matter of the treaty and *to nations that have not ratified it.*' " *Id.* (alterations in original) (quoting Kiobel, 621 F.3d at 138). With those principles in mind, the court recognized:

> There were 63 states parties to the High Seas Convention as of June 10, 2010, including the United States, and there were 161 states parties to UNCLOS (including the European Union) as of October 5, 2010, including Somalia. The 161 states parties to UNCLOS represent the "overwhelming majority" of the 192 Member States of the United Nations, and the 194 countries recognized by the United States Department of State. UNCLOS's definition of piracy therefore represents a widely accepted norm, followed out of a sense of agreement (or, in the case of the states parties, treaty obligation), that has been recognized by an overwhelming majority of the world.
>
> * * *Accordingly, UNCLOS's definition of general piracy has a norm-creating character and reflects an existing norm of customary international law that is binding on even those nations that are not a party to the Convention, including the United States.

Hasan I, 747 F. Supp. 2d at 633–34 (footnote and citations omitted).[12]

The district court further observed "that UNCLOS does not represent the first time that acts of violence have been included in the definition of general piracy." *Hasan I, 747 F. Supp. 2d at 635.* * * * The court took especial note of Kenya's recent reliance on the UNCLOS to define general piracy in the 2006 *Republic v. Ahmed* case, concluding:

---

[12] Expounding on the applicability of the UNCLOS herein, the district court observed:

The fact that the United States has not signed or ratified UNCLOS does not change the conclusion reached above regarding its binding nature. While the United States' failure to sign or ratify UNCLOS does bar the application of UNCLOS as treaty law against the United States, it is not dispositive of the question of whether UNCLOS constitutes customary international law, because such a determination relies not only on the practices and customs of the United States, but instead of the entire international community. In any event, while the United States has refused to sign UNCLOS because of . . . regulations related to deep seabed exploration and mining, in 1983, President Ronald Reagan announced that the United States would accede to those provisions of UNCLOS pertaining to "traditional uses" of the ocean. Schoenbaum, supra, § 2–2 ("With respect to the 'traditional uses' of the sea, therefore, the United States accepts [UNCLOS] as customary international law, binding upon the United States."). No succeeding Presidential Administration has taken a contrary position. Accordingly, with the exception of its deep seabed mining provisions, the United States has consistently accepted UNCLOS as customary international law for more than 25 years. [See Restatement (Third) of the Foreign Relations Law of the United States pt. 5, intro. note (1986) ("For purposes of this Restatement, [the UNCLOS] as such is not law of the United States. However, many of the provisions of the [UNCLOS] follow closely provisions in the [High Seas Convention] to which the United States is a party and which largely restated customary law as of that time. [Moreover], by express or tacit agreement accompanied by consistent practice, the United States, and states generally, have accepted the substantive provisions of the [UNCLOS], other than those addressing deep sea-bed mining, as statements of customary law binding upon them apart from the [UNCLOS].")].

This actual state practice by Kenya, the country currently most involved in prosecuting piracy, as well as the active support of such practice by other nations, which continue to bring other alleged pirates to Kenya for prosecution, is indicative of the fact that the definition of piracy contained in the High Seas Convention and UNCLOS have attained the status of a binding rule of customary international law.

Hasan I, 747 F. Supp. 2d at 636. Additionally, the court recognized that "[c]ontemporary scholarly sources . . . appear to agree that the definition of piracy in UNCLOS represents customary international law." Id. at 636 & *n.32* (citing pertinent works of scholars). "While writers on the issue do present disagreements regarding the definition of general piracy," the court acknowledged, "such disagreements do not implicate the core definition provided in UNCLOS." Id. at 637 (explaining that "writers [instead] disagree about the outer boundaries of the definition of general piracy, such as whether UNCLOS's requirement of 'private ends' prohibits its application to terrorist activities, or whether piracy can arise in situations involving just one ship rather than two").

* * *

The district court then reaffirmed that, as of the alleged offense date of April 2010, the definition of piracy under the law of nations was found in the substantively identical High Seas Convention and UNCLOS, the latter having "been accepted by the overwhelming majority of the world as reflecting customary international law." *Hasan I, 747 F. Supp. 2d at 640.* Mirroring those treaties, the court pronounced that "piracy within the meaning of *[§]1651* consists of any of the following acts and their elements:"

> (A)(1) any illegal act of violence or detention, or any act of depredation; (2) committed for private ends; (3) on the high seas or a place outside the jurisdiction of any state; (4) by the crew or the passengers of a private ship . . . ; (5) and directed against another ship . . . , or against persons or property on board such ship . . . ; or

> (B)(1) any act of voluntary participation in the operation of a ship . . . ; (2) with knowledge of the facts making it a pirate ship; or

> (C)(1) any act of inciting or of intentionally facilitating (2) an act described in subparagraph (A) or (B).

* * *

B.

On appeal, the defendants maintain that the district court erred with respect to Count One both by misinstructing the jury on the elements of the piracy offense, and in refusing to award post-trial judgments of acquittal. Each aspect of the defendants' position obliges us to assess whether the court took a mistaken view of *18 U.S.C. § 1651* and the incorporated law of nations. * * *

The crux of the defendants' position is now, as it was in the district court, that the definition of general piracy was fixed in the early Nineteenth Century, when Congress passed the Act of 1819 first authorizing the exercise of universal jurisdiction by United States courts to adjudicate charges of "piracy as defined by the law of nations." * * *

The defendants' view is thoroughly refuted, however, by a bevy of precedent, including the Supreme Court's 2004 decision in Sosa v. Alvarez–Machain. The *Sosa* Court was called upon to determine whether Alvarez could recover under the Alien Tort Statute, *28 U.S.C. § 1350* (the "ATS"). . . . Significantly, the ATS predates the criminalization of general piracy, in that it was passed by "[t]he first Congress . . . as part of the Judiciary Act of 1789." *See* Sosa, 542 U.S. at 712–13 (citing Act of Sept. 24, 1789, ch. 20, § 9, 1 Stat. 77 (authorizing federal district court jurisdiction over "all causes where an alien sues for a tort only in violation of the law of nations or a treaty of the United States")). Yet the *Sosa* Court did not regard the ATS as incorporating some stagnant notion of the law of nations. Rather, the Court concluded that, while the first Congress probably understood the ATS to confer jurisdiction over only the three paradigmatic law-of-nations torts of the time—including piracy—the door was open to ATS jurisdiction over additional "claim[s] based on the present-day law of nations," albeit in narrow circumstances. *See* id. at 724–25.* * *

* * * Moreover, in its 1820 *Smith* decision, the Supreme Court unhesitatingly approved of the piracy statute's incorporation of the law of nations, looking to various sources to ascertain how piracy was defined under the law of nations. *See Smith, 18 U.S. (5 Wheat.) at 159–61.*

The defendants would have us believe that, since the *Smith* era, the United States' proscription of general piracy has been limited to "robbery upon the sea." But that interpretation of our law would render it incongruous with the modern law of nations and prevent us from exercising universal jurisdiction in piracy cases. *See* Sosa, 542 U.S. at 761 (Breyer, J., concurring in part and concurring in the judgment) (explaining that universal jurisdiction requires, inter alia, "substantive uniformity among the laws of [the exercising] nations"). At bottom, then, the defendants' position is irreconcilable with the noncontroversial notion that Congress intended in *§ 1651* to define piracy as a universal jurisdiction crime. In these circumstances, we are constrained to agree with the district court that *§ 1651* incorporates a definition of piracy that changes with advancements in the law of nations.

We also agree with the district court that the definition of piracy under the law of nations, at the time of the defendants' attack on the USS Nicholas and continuing today, had for decades encompassed their violent conduct. That definition, spelled out in the UNCLOS, as well as the High Seas Convention before it, has only been reaffirmed in recent years as nations around the world have banded together to combat the escalating scourge of piracy. For example, in November 2011, the United Nations Security Council adopted Resolution 2020, recalling a series of prior resolutions approved between 2008 and 2011 "concerning the situation in Somalia"; expressing "grave[ ] concern[ ] [about] the ongoing threat that piracy and armed robbery at sea against vessels pose"; and emphasizing "the need for a comprehensive response by the international community to repress piracy and armed robbery at sea and tackle its underlying causes." Of the utmost significance, Resolution 2020 reaffirmed "that international law, as reflected in the [UNCLOS], sets out the legal framework applicable to combating piracy and armed robbery at sea."[15] Because the district court correctly applied the UNCLOS definition of piracy as customary international law, we reject the defendants' challenge to their Count One piracy convictions, as well as their mandatory life sentences.

IV.

Pursuant to the foregoing, we affirm the convictions and sentences of each of the defendants.

AFFIRMED

NOTES AND QUESTIONS

1. LOSC, art. 100 sets out the requirement that "[a]ll States shall cooperate to the fullest possible extent in the repression of piracy on the high seas …." If piracy is an international crime, what is the role of domestic law? Does the rise of modern piracy in the "sea lines of communication" reflect a breakdown of ocean governance? Has the new regime of the EEZ, ironically, contributed to this breakdown? Is Somalia able to exercise its sovereign rights and responsibilities in its EEZ?

2. In Institute for Cetacean Research v. Sea Shepherd Conservation Society, 860 F.Supp. 2d 1216 (W.D. Wash. 2012), a Japanese whaling company brought an action in federal court under the alien tort statute, alleging that the conservation organization's activities protesting the plaintiff's whaling violated international norms including the LOSC. The district court held that the alleged conduct did not violate international norms against piracy so as to support a claim for injunctive relief under the statute. The Ninth Circuit,

---

[15] Notably, as one of the permanent members of the Security Council, the United States supported the adoption of Resolution 2020, which was approved by a unanimous Security Council.

however, reversed, holding, inter alia: "You don't need a peg leg or an eye patch. When you ram ships; hurl glass containers of acid; drag metal-reinforced ropes in the water to damage propellers and rudders; launch smoke bombs and flares with hooks; and point high-powered lasers at other ships, you are, without a doubt, a pirate, no matter how high-minded you believe your purpose to be." 708 F.3d 1099 (9th Cir. 2013), 2013 WL 2278588 (May 24, 2013)(amending opinion supporting an injunction, denying petition for rehearing en banc; and ordering reassignment to another district court judge). Are the Society's protests for "private ends" under LOSC art. 100? If Captain Paul Watson is found in the U.S., can he be imprisoned for life under 18 U.S.C. § 1651? For background on Watson's activities and views, see R. Khatchadourian, A Reporter at Large: Neptune's Navy, The New Yorker (Nov. 5, 2007).

3. The U.N. Security Council's Resolution 2020 refers to "the need for a comprehensive response ... [to] tackle its underlying causes." What are these causes? See Emmanuel Kisiangani, Somali Pirates: Villains or Victims? 17 S. African J. Int'l. Aff. 361 (2010) (illegal fishing and dumping of toxic industrial wastes in Somalia's EEZ). Does Resolution 2020, which allows international forces to enter Somalia's territorial sea to apprehend pirates, constitute a comprehensive response?

4. Any country's warships can stop and board any ship if there is a reasonable basis for suspecting that the ship is engaged in the slave trade or that it is a ship without nationality, but the LOSC provides no universal jurisdiction for prosecution of slave traders. Is this a gap in the treaty?

5. Consider the question again following Section C on the Contiguous Zone on p. 35. Rights of non-flag countries do not extend to the high seas for illicit drug trafficking. See LOSC, art. 108. Can the U.S. interdict a vessel on the high seas if it is suspected of smuggling drugs intended to be taken into the country?

In U.S. v. Epifanio Matos–Luchi, 627 F.3d 1 (1st Cir. 2010), the U.S. Coast Guard interdicted a boat about 25 miles from Haiti. "No ensign, flag, registration, or other evidence of the vessel's nationality was found on board," and no one on board the vessel made a claim of nationality for the boat.

> Although enforcement jurisdiction presumptively lies with the flag state, 1 Oppenheim, supra, § 266, at 603, "[i]t is not enough that a vessel have a nationality; she must claim it and be in a position to provide evidence of it." Anderson, [Jurisdiction over Stateless Vessels on the High Seas: An Appraisal Under Domestic and International Law, 13 J. Mar. L. & Com. 323, 341 (1982)], pertinently quotes a Privy Council judgment:

>> [T]he freedom of the open sea, whatever those words may connote, is a freedom of ships which fly, and are entitled to fly, the flag of a State. . . . Their Lordships would accept as a valid statement of international law, the following passage from Oppenheim's Interna-

tional Law . . . : "In the interest of order on the open sea, a vessel not sailing under the maritime flag of a State enjoys no protection whatever. . . . "

Molvan v. Att'y–Gen. for Palestine, [1948] A.C. 351 (P.C.) 369–70; see also 1 Oppenheim, supra, § 261, at 595.

* * *

Practically every vessel, including the legendary Flying Dutchman, has links with some country; but the stateless vessel concept in the MDLEA [Maritime Drug Law Enforcement Act] and in international law is designed prudentially. The controlling question is whether at the point at which the authorities confront the vessel, it bears the insignia or papers of a national vessel or its master is prepared to make an affirmative and sustainable claim of nationality. To read the MDLEA more restrictively would mean that the master and crew need only carry no papers and jump overboard to avoid having their vessel classed as stateless.

The defendants are not entitled to raise a violation of international law as an objection, see 46 U.S.C. § 70505, but in any case the MDLEA does not conflict with international law. For international law too treats the "stateless vessel" concept as informed by the need for effective enforcement. Thus, a vessel may be deemed "stateless," and subject to the enforcement jurisdiction of any nation on the scene, if it fails to display or carry insignia of nationality and seeks to avoid national identification. This occurs

> if a "ship" repeatedly refuses, without reasonable excuse, to reveal its allocation [of nationality]. If no registration number is visible and no other indicator [of nationality] can be discerned, the cognoscibility is already demonstrably insufficient, and interference will then often be justifiable. . . . From the basic design of [the law of sea] and from the place the institution here called allocation occupies in it already it may be concluded that a "ship" which obscures the cognoscibility of its allocation repeatedly, deliberately, and successfully may be treated as stateless.

H. Meyers, The Nationality of Ships 322 (1967) (footnote omitted).

Id. at 6–7.

6. In the excerpt in note 5 above, the court notes that "[t]he defendants are not entitled to raise a violation of international law as an objection. . . . " If the international law obligation is to the flag state and not individuals, can a flag state waive the right, i.e., give permission to another state to board the vessel? Consider the following analysis:

Malta, under whose flag Suerte's vessel was registered, consented to the boarding and search of his vessel, as well as to the application of United States law. A flag nation's consent to a seizure on the high seas constitutes a waiver of that nation's rights under international law. See United States v. Williams, 617 F.2d 1063, 1090 (5th Cir. 1980) (en banc). "Interference with a ship that would otherwise be unlawful under international law is permissible if the flag state has consented". RESTATEMENT (THIRD) OF FOREIGN RELATIONS LAW OF THE UNITED STATES § 522 cmt. e (1987). . . .

Along this line, . . . the MDLEA provides: "[A] 'vessel subject to the jurisdiction of the United States' includes . . . a vessel registered in a foreign nation where the flag nation has consented or waived objection to the enforcement of United States law by the United States". 46 U.S.C. App. § 1903(c)(1)(C). This codifies the above-described generally accepted principle of international law: a flag nation may consent to another's jurisdiction. See RESTATEMENT (THIRD) § 522 reporters note 8 (the MDLEA *confirmed the practice*" of relying on informal grants of consent by flag nations (emphasis added)). . . .

U.S. v. Suerte, 291 F.3d 366, 375–76 (5th Cir. 2012). See also, Joseph E. Kramek, Bilateral Maritime Counter-Drug and Immigrant Interdiction Agreements: Is This the World of the Future?, 31 University of Miami Inter–American Law Review 121 (2000).

6. THE FUTURE OF U.S. OCEAN POLICY AND THE LAW OF THE SEA CONVENTION

The United States, whose coastal length and configuration give it the world's largest geographic area of offshore authority, is the chief beneficiary of the new ocean regime as a coastal nation. The United States has also benefitted from the protection of freedom of navigation rights, particularly through the provisions on transit passage and archipelagic sealanes passage that assure the continued ability of submarines to traverse international straits submerged and freedom of overflight. But customary law of the sea has been rapidly evolving in the last decade. Can the United States lead the direction of that evolution from outside the UNCLOS treaty regime?

In May and June 2012, the Senate Foreign Relations Committee once more held hearings concerning U.S. accession to the LOSC. The following excerpts from the testimony of Secretary of State Hillary Rodham Clinton set out the current U.S. interests at stake in remaining outside the treaty.

TESTIMONY OF HILLARY RODHAM CLINTON, SECRETARY OF STATE, BEFORE THE SENATE COMMITTEE ON FOREIGN RELATIONS

(May 23, 2012)

[O]ne could argue, that 20 years ago, 10 years ago, maybe even five years ago, joining the convention was important but not urgent. That is no longer the case today. Four new developments make our participation a matter of utmost security and economic urgency.

First, for years, American oil and gas companies were not technologically ready to take advantage of the convention's provisions regarding the extended U.S. continental shelf. Now they are. The convention allows countries to claim sovereignty over their continental shelf far out into the ocean, beyond 200 nautical miles from shore. The relevant area for the United States is probably more than 1.5 times the size of Texas. In fact, we believe it could be considerably larger.

U.S. oil and gas companies are now ready, willing, and able to explore this area. But they have made it clear to us that they need the maximum level of international legal certainty before they will or could make the substantial investments* * *. If we were a party to the convention, we would gain international recognition of our sovereign rights, including by using the convention's procedures, and therefore be able to give our oil and gas companies this legal certainty. Staying outside the convention, we simply cannot.

The second development concerns deep seabed mining, which takes place in that part of the ocean floor that is beyond any country's jurisdiction. Now for years, technological challenges meant that deep seabed mining was only theoretical; today's advances make it very real. But it's also very expensive, and before any company will explore a mine site, it will naturally insist on having a secure title to the site and the minerals that it will recover. The convention offers the only effective mechanism for gaining this title. But only a party to the convention can use this mechanism on behalf of its companies.

So as long as the United States is outside the convention, our companies are left with two bad choices—either take their deep sea mining business to another country or give up on the idea. Meanwhile, * * * China, Russia, and many other countries are already securing their licenses under the convention to begin mining for valuable metals and rare earth elements. And as you know, rare earth elements are essential for manufacturing high-tech products like cell phones and flat screen televisions. They are currently in tight supply and produced almost exclusively by China.* * * If we expect to be able to manage our own energy future and our need for rare earth minerals, we must be a party to the Law of the Sea Convention.

The third development that is now urgent is the emerging opportunities in the Arctic. As the area gets warmer, it is opening up to new activities such as fishing, oil and gas exploration, shipping, and tourism. This convention provides the international framework to deal with these new opportunities. We are the only Arctic nation outside the convention. Russia and the other Arctic states are advancing their continental shelf claims in the Arctic while we are on the outside looking in. As a party to the convention, we would have a much stronger basis to assert our interests throughout the entire Arctic region.

The fourth development is that the convention's bodies are now up and running. The body that makes recommendations regarding countries' continental shelves beyond 200 nautical miles is actively considering submissions from over 40 countries without the participation of a U.S. commissioner. The body addressing deep seabed mining is now drawing up the rules to govern the extraction of minerals of great interest to the United States and American industry. It simply should not be acceptable to us that the United States will be absent from either of those discussions.

Our negotiators obtained a permanent U.S. seat on the key decision-making body for deep seabed mining. I know of no other international body that accords one country and one country alone—us—a permanent seat on its decision making body. But until we join, that reserved seat remains empty.

So those are the stakes for our economy. * * * And * * * our security interests are intrinsically linked to freedom of navigation. We have much more to gain from legal certainty and public order in the world's oceans than any other country. U.S. Armed Forces rely on the navigational rights and freedoms reflected in the convention for worldwide access to get to combat areas, sustain our forces during conflict, and return home safely all without permission from other countries.

Now as a non-party to the convention, we rely—we have to rely—on what is called customary international law as a legal basis for invoking and enforcing these norms. But in no other situation at which—in which our security interests are at stake do we consider customary international law good enough to protect rights that are vital to the operation of the United States military. So far we've been fortunate, but our navigational rights and our ability to challenge other countries' behavior should stand on the firmest and most persuasive legal footing available, including in critical areas such as the South China Sea.

* * * The benefits of joining have always been significant, but today the costs of not joining are increasing. So much is at stake, and I therefore urge the Committee to listen to the experts, listen to our businesses,

listen to the Chamber of Commerce, listen to our military, and please give advice and consent to this treaty before the end of this year.

* * *

———

Recall the massive oil spill in 2010 in the Gulf of Mexico that resulted from the explosion of the semi-submersible oil drilling rig the Deepwater Horizon (flagged by the Republic of the Marshall Islands). Are you surprised that Secretary Clinton argued in 2012 that the U.S. should join the LOSC to give certainty to U.S. oil and gas companies to invest in the extended continental shelf? Is that the strongest reason for joining? Given the effects of global warming on the Arctic Ocean and the LOSC's emphasis on sovereign rights for marine resource development, is the LOSC a sufficient international framework for governance of this region?

CHAPTER 2

OFFSHORE FEDERALISM AND TRIBAL RIGHTS IN THE OCEANS

■ ■ ■

1. THE TIDELANDS CONTROVERSY, THE PARAMOUNT RIGHTS DOCTRINE, AND TRIBAL RIGHTS

When in 1988, President Reagan proclaimed a 12-mile territorial sea for the United States for international purposes, he specifically noted that the extension to 12 miles had no effect domestically. Neither state ocean boundaries nor the jurisdiction of state and federal laws were affected. But the extension created an interesting "void" in the area beyond the three- and nine-mile offshore limits of state waters out to 12 miles and raised a myriad of questions about the appropriate allocation of federal and state interests in the area. But that was just the latest round of a long controversy about federal "paramount rights" and the nature of federalism in the marginal seas, referred to (inappropriately) as the Tidelands Controversy.

A. PARAMOUNT RIGHTS AND THE STATES AND TERRITORIES

DONNA R. CHRISTIE, STATE HISTORIC INTERESTS IN THE MARGINAL SEAS
2 Terr. Sea. J. 151, 151–155 (1992)

A. Background of the Federal/State Offshore
Ownership Controversy

In Martin v. Waddell [1842], the United States Supreme Court articulated the basic principles governing the ownership of lands under navigable waters: When the Revolution took place, the people of each State became themselves sovereign; and in that character hold the absolute right to all their navigable waters and the soils under them for their common use, subject only to the rights surrendered by the Constitution to the general Government. The "equal footing doctrine" first explained in Pollard's Lessee v. Hagan and reiterated in Shively v. Bowlby stands for the principle that "new States admitted into the Union since the adoption

73

of the Constitution have the same rights as the original States in the tide waters, and in the lands under them, within their respective jurisdictions." Until the 1940s, little doubt seemed to exist that the coastal states "owned" the lands under their marginal seas, which were presumed to be encompassed within the definitions of navigable waters or tide waters.

Prior to 1940, most coastal states had legislation establishing offshore marine boundaries, and many state constitutions described state boundaries as extending a marine league or more offshore. Numerous state court cases had earlier concluded that the original colonies succeeded to the King's interest in the tidelands and adjacent seas, and, therefore, title vested in the original colonies. Decisions of federal courts, including the United States Supreme Court, impliedly, if not expressly, supported the presumption of state ownership of the seabed of the territorial sea. The Secretary of the Interior Harold L. Ickes, charged with administering United States public lands, stated that the federal government had "no authority to lease the seabed for mineral exploration." In the now famous 1933 Proctor Letter, Ickes explained to a lease applicant that "[t]itle to the soil under the ocean within the 3-mile limit is in the State of California, and the land may not be appropriated except by authority of the State."

In the late 1930s, controversies emerged within California concerning oil recovered from submerged lands by slant drilling from shore and ownership of mineral rights in submerged lands granted by the state to coastal cities for harbor and recreational development. Apparently instigated by Secretary Ickes and fueled by the oil industry and vocal individuals from California interested in settling the offshore ownership issue, Congress in 1938 began a series of hearings and attempted resolutions addressing federal interests in the tidelands. These efforts culminated in 1946 in House Joint Resolution 225, which quitclaimed any rights of the federal government in lands beneath tidelands and navigable waters to the states. President Truman vetoed the resolution on August 2, 1946, citing the fact that the issue was currently before the Supreme Court in United States v. California, President Truman stated in his veto message: * * * "[T]he issue * * * presents a legal question of great importance to the Nation, and one which should be decided by the [Supreme] Court. The Congress is not an appropriate forum to determine the legal issue * * *.

————

When a U.S. president makes an unequivocal statement regarding the allocation of powers between the branches of government, what do you think usually happens? The story of what happened is told in this case concerning a contemporary dispute over control of lands below the low water mark adjacent to the U.S.-affiliated Pacific islands known as the Commonwealth of the Northern Marianas.

COMMONWEALTH OF THE NORTHERN MARIANA ISLANDS v. U.S.

United States Court of Appeals, Ninth Circuit, 2005
399 F.3d 1057

BEEZER, CIRCUIT JUDGE.

I.

The CNMI is a commonwealth government comprised of sixteen islands in the West Pacific. Through a Covenant agreement with the United States, the CNMI is under the sovereignty of the United States but retains the "right of local self-government." Covenant to Establish a Commonwealth of the Northern Mariana Islands in Political Union with the United States of America §§ 101, 103, Pub.L. No. 94–241, 90 Stat. 263 (1976), reprinted in 48 U.S.C. § 1801 note [hereinafter "Covenant"]. * * *[W]e briefly summarize below the history of the relationship between the United States and the people of the islands included in the Commonwealth in order to provide the legal background for this lawsuit.

A

Following World War II, the United Nations established the "Trust Territory of the Pacific Islands" [hereinafter "TTPI"] over Micronesian islands in the Pacific. The United States "was not a sovereign over, but a trustee for the [TTPI]." Wabol v. Villacrusis, 958 F.2d 1450, 1458 (9th Cir.1992). The "paramount duty of the United States was to steward Micronesia to self-government." Temengil v. Trust Territory of the Pacific Islands, 881 F.2d 647, 649 (9th Cir.1989) (discussing Trusteeship Agreement for the Former Japanese Mandated Islands, July 18, 1947, United States–United Nations, art. 6, 61 Stat. 3301, T.I.A.S. No. 1665. * * * Representatives from one sub-group of islands, the Northern Marianas, favored establishing closer ties with the United States than representatives from the other islands. Ultimately, a delegation from the Northern Marianas entered into independent negotiations with the United States. The Covenant formed out of those talks. In 1975, the Northern Mariana Islands legislature unanimously approved the Covenant and 78.8% of voters in the Northern Marianas ratified the agreement in a plebiscite vote. See De Leon Guerrero, 4 F.3d at 751. Congress enacted the Covenant into law in 1976. Pub.L. No. 94–241, 90 Stat. 263 (1976).

The Covenant's ten articles detail the political relationship between the United States and the CNMI. Of particular relevance here is Article I. In addition to guaranteeing the Commonwealth the right of local self-government under the sovereignty of the United States, see Covenant §§ 101, 103, Article I provides that the Covenant, "together with those provisions of the Constitution, treaties, and laws of the United States applicable to the Northern Mariana Islands, will be the supreme law of the Northern Mariana Islands." Id. § 102. Article I also establishes that the

United States has "complete responsibility for and authority with respect to matters relating to foreign affairs and defense." Id. § 104.

Articles V, VIII and X of the Covenant also play central roles in this dispute. Pursuant to Article V, only certain provisions within the United States Constitution and other federal laws are applicable to the Commonwealth. See id. §§ 501, 502. Article VIII addresses distribution of "Property" within the Northern Marianas. In relevant part, Section 801 specifies that:

> All right, title, and interest of the Government of the Trust Territory of the Pacific Islands in and to real property in the Northern Mariana Islands on the date of the signing of this Covenant or thereafter acquired in any manner whatsoever will, no later than upon the termination of the Trusteeship Agreement, be transferred to the Government of the Northern Mariana Islands.

Finally, Article X controls how and when the provisions of the Covenant come into force. Id. § 1003. Some provisions, including Section 801's transfer of property, became effective immediately upon the Covenant's approval. See id. § 1003(a). Others, such as the right to local self-government, id. § 103, required the additional approval of the Covenant's Constitution, which occurred in 1978. See id. § 1003(b); Temengil, 881 F.2d at 650. The remainder became effective after the official termination of the trusteeship in 1986. See Sagana v. Tenorio, 384 F.3d 731, 733–34 (9th Cir.2004), cert. denied, 543 U.S. 1149 (2005) (No. 04–774). Included in this last category are the provisions establishing United States sovereignty and authority over foreign affairs and defense of the Commonwealth. Covenant §§ 101, 104.

B

The CNMI brought this action under the Quiet Title Act, 28 U.S.C. § 2409a, requesting a declaration that the Commonwealth holds title to, or for an order mandating that the United States quitclaim any interests in, the submerged lands "underlying the internal waters, archipelagic waters, and territorial waters adjacent to the Northern Mariana Islands." The CNMI further requested the court to enjoin the United States from claiming ownership of the submerged lands. The United States counter-claimed. * * *[B]oth parties filed for summary judgment. The district court granted the United States' motion, declaring that the "United States possesses paramount rights in and powers over the waters extending seaward of the ordinary low water mark of the Commonwealth Coast and the lands, minerals, and other things of value underlying such waters." The court also declared that the CNMI's Marine Sovereignty Act of 1980, 2 N. Mar. I.Code §§ 1101–1143 (1999), and Submerged Lands Act, 2 N. Mar. I.Code §§ 1201–1231 (1999), were preempted by federal law. This appeal followed.

II

We review de novo the district court's decision to grant or deny summary judgment. * * *

The district court properly granted summary judgment to the United States on the basis of the federal paramountcy doctrine. This doctrine instructs that the United States, as a "function of national external sovereignty," acquires "paramount rights" over seaward submerged lands. United States v. California, 332 U.S. 19, 34 (1947). Because the United States did not expressly cede its paramount rights to the submerged lands at issue here, summary judgment in favor of the United States was proper.

A

* * * We briefly review [the history of the paramountcy doctrine] here. The Supreme Court established the paramountcy doctrine through a series of cases between the federal government and shoreline states. In California, the Court held that the national government had paramount rights to submerged lands off the shores of states created from former United States territories. 332 U.S. at 38. The Court based its decision on theories of national interest and defense, concluding that because the sea had customarily been within the realm of international law, the federal government had an overriding interest in maintaining authority over these areas that were subject to international dispute and settlement. Id. at 34–36. As the Court explained a few years later in United States v. Louisiana, 339 U.S. 699 (1950):

> The marginal sea is a national, not a state concern. National interests, national responsibilities, national concerns are involved. The problems of commerce, national defense, relations with other powers, war and peace focus there. National rights must therefore be paramount in that area.

The Supreme Court has extended this doctrine to apply, presumably, to all coastal states. In United States v. Texas, 339 U.S. 707, 717–19 (1950), the Court held on the basis of "equal footing" and national interest principles that even a state previously possessing both "dominium" (ownership) and "imperium" (governmental powers and sovereignty) over its marginal sea as an independent sovereign lost that authority upon entry into the Union. See id. at 719 ("[A]lthough dominium and imperium are normally separable and separate, this is an instance where property interests are so subordinated to the rights of sovereignty as to follow sovereignty.") (footnote omitted). A quarter-century later, the Court again invoked national interest principles to establish in United States v. Maine, 420 U.S. 515, 519 (1975), that the federal government had paramount rights to submerged lands off the coasts of even Atlantic states that claimed to be successors in title to the original colonies.

Although the Supreme Court's paramountcy decisions all involved states as parties, "the paramountcy doctrine is not limited merely to disputes between the national and state governments." Eyak I, 154 F.3d at 1095. We held in Eyak I that a claim of exclusive aboriginal title to submerged lands was inconsistent with the paramountcy doctrine. We reasoned that "[a]ny claim of sovereign right or title over the ocean by any party other than the United States, including Indian tribes, is equally repugnant to the principles established in the paramountcy cases." Id.

The national interest principles that support the paramountcy doctrine do provide some limitation on its scope. The doctrine does not apply to land under "inland navigable waters such as rivers, harbors, and even tidelands down to the low water mark." California, 332 U.S. at 30 (discussing Pollard's Lessee v. Hagan, 44 U.S. (3 How.) 212 (1845)). This limitation reflects the different concerns present with "internal" and "external" submerged lands: the state interest diminishes, and the national interests increases, as the land in question moves further into the open sea. See id. at 29–35.

B

Allegiance to the paramountcy doctrine compels us to begin with the presumption that the United States acquired paramount rights to the disputed submerged lands off the CNMI's shores as a function of sovereignty. As we have held in Eyak I, the underlying principles of this doctrine apply "with equal force" to relationships other than that between states and the federal government. 154 F.3d at 1096. Through the Covenant, the Commonwealth agreed to United States sovereignty and received (among other benefits) protection and security in return. As the Court recognized in California, the United States' foreign affairs obligations demand that the national government have authority to control areas of national concern. See 332 U.S. at 35–36. Absent an express indication to the contrary, we will not presume the parties intended a different arrangement here.

The CNMI principally challenges the reliance on the paramountcy cases for two reasons. First, the Commonwealth contends that the paramountcy doctrine is inconsistent with the Covenant's limitations on the application of federal law to the CNMI. Second, the CNMI argues alternatively that the Covenant's transfer of real property creates a "recognized exception" to the paramountcy doctrine. We disagree on both counts.

1. The CNMI first asserts that the unique relationship between the United States and the CNMI makes the paramountcy doctrine inapplicable. According to the CNMI, federal law applies to the Commonwealth only to the extent that it is consistent with the Covenant. The CNMI argues that because the rationale for the paramountcy doctrine is based on foreign commerce, foreign affairs, and national defense powers found

within the United States Constitution, the doctrine cannot apply to the CNMI because the Covenant does not expressly provide the United States with this same constitutional authority over the Commonwealth.

We do not dispute that " 'the authority of the United States towards the CNMI arises solely under the Covenant.' " Sagana, 384 F.3d at 734 (quoting Hillblom v. United States, 896 F.2d 426, 429 (9th Cir.1990)). But the CNMI's argument wrongly assumes that the paramountcy doctrine and the Covenant are inconsistent. The paramountcy doctrine draws its authority from the inherent obligations placed on the sovereign governing entity to conduct international affairs and control matters of national concern. See California, 332 U.S. at 35–36; see also Eyak I, 154 F.3d at 1096 ("This principle applies with equal force to all entities claiming rights to the ocean[.]"). The Covenant unquestionably places these powers and obligations in the United States. See Covenant § 101 (establishing a Commonwealth "in political union with and under the sovereignty of the United States of America"); id. § 104 (providing the United States with "complete responsibility for and authority with respect to matters relating to foreign affairs and defense"). The CNMI's attempt to differentiate between a paramountcy doctrine based on powers found solely in the United States Constitution and one that is incorporated through the Covenant separates the doctrine from its rationale.

" '[O]nce low-water mark is passed the international domain is reached.' " Eyak I, 154 F.3d at 1094 (quoting Texas, 339 U.S. at 719). The submerged lands addressed by the district court's summary judgment fit this description. Because the Covenant places sovereignty and foreign affairs obligations in the United States, the paramountcy doctrine applies.

2. The CNMI next argues in the alternative that the Covenant transferred the submerged lands to the Northern Mariana Islands, thereby meeting a recognized exception to the paramountcy doctrine that allows Congress to cede its paramount authority over seaward submerged lands. The fact that the United States may provide the submerged lands to the CNMI does not mean it has done so here. Neither the text of the Covenant nor the actions taken by the parties during and after the negotiations lead to a conclusion that such a transaction took place.

The CNMI correctly asserts that, despite the national concerns underlying the paramountcy doctrine, Congress can transfer ownership of submerged lands to the states or other entities. Congress has done so in the past. See, e.g., Submerged Lands Act of 1953, 43 U.S.C. §§ 1301, 1311 (transferring submerged lands up to three miles from shore back to the states); see also Maine, 420 U.S. at 525–27 (observing that the Court held the Submerged Lands Act constitutional in Alabama v. Texas, 347 U.S. 272 (1954)).

The CNMI argues that the Covenant effected a similar transfer. The core of the CNMI's argument is that the transfer of "real property" in Section 801 of the Covenant includes seaward submerged lands. As noted above, Section 801 provides that "[a]ll right, title and interest of the Government of the [TTPI] in and to real property in the Northern Mariana Islands . . . will, no later than upon the termination of the Trusteeship Agreement, be transferred to the Government of the Northern Mariana Islands." Although the Covenant does not define real property, the Commonwealth notes that the Quiet Title Act itself specifically includes disputes over "tide and submerged lands." 28 U.S.C. §§ 2409a(i)–(l). If such lands were not "real property," the Commonwealth argues, such suits could not be brought under the Quiet Title Act.

We are hesitant to ascribe an implicit intent to cede paramount rights over seaward submerged lands on this basis. There is a significant distinction between the statutory transfers relied on by the CNMI and the alleged transfer in the Covenant: the statutes cited by the Commonwealth explicitly apply to submerged lands. See 43 U.S.C. § 1301 (defining submerged lands); 48 U.S.C. § 749 (defining and conveying submerged lands to Puerto Rico); 48 U.S.C. § 1705 (describing and conveying submerged lands to Guam, the Virgin Islands and American Samoa). The transfer found in Hawaii's Statehood Act is also informative. In addition to transferring to the new state all lands formerly held by the Territory as well as title to certain public lands held by the United States, this act also expressly made the Submerged Lands Act applicable to the new state. See Pub.L. No. 86–3, 73 Stat. 4 (1959). What these statutes demonstrate is that Congress knew how to grant submerged lands when it so desired. The fact no reference to submerged lands appears in the Covenant counsels against implying such a meaning here.

Ambiguity in drafting is far from novel, even within the limited universe of paramountcy cases. California raised an argument similar to the one the CNMI makes here, arguing that the state's Enabling Act ratified a territorial boundary that included a three-mile marginal sea. California, 332 U.S. at 29–30, 67 S.Ct. 1658. Although the Court's opinion did not focus on this assertion, judging from the Court's favorable decision for the United States, this argument apparently carried little weight.

A strong presumption of national authority over seaward submerged lands runs throughout the paramountcy doctrine cases, and we extend that same presumption to the case at hand. Absent express indication to the contrary, the ownership of seaward submerged lands accompanies United States sovereignty. The Covenant lacks such an expression.

The CNMI can point to no language in the Covenant that expressly addresses submerged lands. * * * We conclude that there exists no genuine issue of material fact because the evidence is not "such that a reasonable jury could return a verdict for the nonmoving party." Thrifty Oil Co. v. Bank of Am. Nat'l Trust & Sav. Ass'n, 322 F.3d 1039, 1046 (9th Cir.2003) (internal quotation marks omitted). The CNMI cannot overcome the paramountcy doctrine because there is no clear intention on the part of the United States to cede its authority off the shores of the Commonwealth that it is obligated to protect.

* * *

The official analysis to the CNMI Constitution does not help the Commonwealth's position, either. This document acknowledges that the United States "has a claim to the submerged lands off the coast of the Commonwealth" based on the paramountcy doctrine. It explains that the CNMI's Constitution "recognizes this claim and also recognizes that the Commonwealth is entitled to the same interest in the submerged lands off its coasts as the United States grants to the states." Analysis of the Constitution of the Commonwealth of the Northern Mariana Islands 144 (Dec. 6, 1976). We agree. Absent express language to the contrary, the CNMI is entitled to the same interest in the seaward submerged lands as that of the states when they submitted to the sovereignty of the United States. As the paramountcy cases established, that state interest is inferior to the federal rights. Although states have acquired greater control over submerged lands through congressional action, no similar legislation has provided analogous rights to the CNMI.

3. As the CNMI acknowledges, when the people of the Northern Mariana Islands and the United States entered into the Covenant agreement in 1975, "both parties had reason to seek a union." Both parties received benefits from this agreement. That the newly formed Commonwealth subsequently objected to the loss of title to submerged lands as result of agreeing to United States sovereignty is as unavailing to the CNMI as that same argument was to states in California, Texas, Louisiana and Maine. The CNMI's position is even less persuasive given that the Covenant was negotiated after the paramountcy doctrine had become well-settled law.

We recognize the importance of the submerged lands surrounding the CNMI to the culture, history and future of the Northern Mariana Islands. We also trust that the Supreme Court was cognizant of the similar importance of submerged lands to coastal states. See, e.g., California, 332 U.S. at 40, 67 S.Ct. 1658. The Supreme Court established the paramountcy doctrine in spite of these circumstances, leaving it to Congress to provide remedies for the states if it so chose. That same avenue is available here.

III.

The Commonwealth admits that its Submerged Lands Act, 2 N. Mar. I.Code §§ 1201–1231, and Marine Sovereignty Act of 1980, 2 N. Mar. I.Code §§ 1101–1143, "combine to assert the Commonwealth's ownership of the submerged lands" in dispute. Because we hold that the United States has paramount rights to the submerged lands at issue here, see supra, a declaration of ownership (or sovereignty) over these submerged lands is directly contrary to federal law. See Texas, 339 U.S. at 719 ("[T]his is an instance where property interests are so subordinated to the rights of sovereignty as to follow sovereignty."). The district court properly held that the Commonwealth's Submerged Lands Act and Marine Sovereignty Act of 1980 are preempted by federal law. * * *

IV.

We hold that the United States acquired paramount interest in the seaward submerged lands, as defined by the Supreme Court in California, found off the shores of the Commonwealth of the Northern Mariana Islands. Laws passed by the CNMI legislature to the contrary are inconsistent with the paramountcy doctrine and are preempted by federal law. The district court's grant of summary judgment for the United States is AFFIRMED.

NOTES AND QUESTIONS

1. United States v. California, relied upon in the case above, was a complex case. Ernest Bartley explained the unexpected legal twist in the Supreme Court's holding:

> The California pleadings were stated almost entirely in terms of property concepts. Since the case of the United States was premised on that line of reasoning, there was no reason for California to do otherwise.

> These were lawyers arguing, on the legal bases with which they were familiar, a concept of title and all that title implies. It appears that they saw no reason to argue the larger but ephemeral concept of "paramount rights," a doctrine of far greater importance to the general theory of federalism than the more prosaic and legalistic concept of title. Whether the outcome could or would have been different if the State of California had chosen to devote the bulk of its pleadings to this more inclusive theory is a matter for pure conjecture. * * * The fact remains that the case was argued entirely on one basis and decided on another.

Ernest Bartley, The Tidelands Oil Controversy 166 (1953).

Is the paramount rights doctrine of United States v. California suspect? Justice Frankfurter, in his California dissent, accused the majority of confusing the concepts of dominium and imperium. Dominium concerns ownership; imperium is the superior right of the federal government to act as sovereign in international affairs. See Donna Christie, State Historic Interests in the Marginal Seas, 2 Territorial Sea Journal 151 (1992); Note, States' Rights in the Outer Continental Shelf Denied by the United States Supreme Court, 30 U. Miami L. Rev. 203, 210 (1975).

2. The final outcome of United States v. California was ambiguous. At the following term, the government proposed a decree which would have given the United States proprietorship, as well as paramount rights, in the marginal sea. Therefore though neither California nor the United States had "title" to the area, the United States was entitled to an injunction to prevent further removal of oil under California leases. President Truman vetoed efforts by Congress to confirm ownership of the offshore in the adjacent coastal states because he viewed it as turning over to a few states, "as a free gift," valuable lands and mineral resources owned by the United States as a whole. See H.RJ. Res. 225, 79th Cong., 1st Sess. (1946) (veto message 92 CONG. REC. 10660 (1946)); S.J. Res. 20, 82d Cong., 2d Sess. (1952) (veto message 98 CONG. REc. 6251 (1952)).

————

DWIGHT D. EISENHOWER: STATEMENT BY THE PRESIDENT UPON SIGNING THE SUBMERGED LANDS ACT

May 22, 1953

I AM PLEASED to sign this measure into law recognizing the ancient rights of the States in the submerged lands within their historic boundaries. As I have said many times I deplore and I will always resist federal encroachment upon rights and affairs of the States. Recognizing the States' claim to these lands is in keeping with basic principles of honesty and fair play.

This measure also recognizes the interests of the Federal Government in the submerged lands outside of the historic boundaries of the States.

* * *

SELECTED PROVISIONS OF THE SUBMERGED LANDS ACT OF 1953

43 U.S.C. § 1301. Definitions

When used in this subchapter and subchapter II of this chapter—

(a) The term "lands beneath navigable waters" means—

(1) all lands within the boundaries of each of the respective States which are covered by nontidal waters that were navigable under the laws of the United States at the time such State became a member of the Union, or acquired sovereignty over such lands and waters thereafter, up to

the ordinary high water mark as heretofore or hereafter modified by accretion, erosion, and reliction;

(2) all lands permanently or periodically covered by tidal waters up to but not above the line of mean high tide and seaward to a line three geographical miles distant from the coast line of each such State and to the boundary line of each such State where in any case such boundary as it existed at the time such State became a member of the Union, or as heretofore approved by Congress, extends seaward (or into the Gulf of Mexico) beyond three geographical miles, and

(3) all filled in, made, or reclaimed lands which formerly were lands beneath navigable waters, as hereinabove defined; * * *

(c) The term "coast line" means the line of ordinary low water along that portion of the coast which is in direct contact with the open sea and the line marking the seaward limit of inland waters;

* * *

(e) The term "natural resources" includes, without limiting the generality thereof, oil, gas, and all other minerals, and fish, shrimp, oysters, clams, crabs, lobsters, sponges, kelp, and other marine animal and plant life but does not include water power, or the use of water for the production of power;

(f) The term "lands beneath navigable waters" does not include the beds of streams in lands now or heretofore constituting a part of the public lands of the United States if such streams were not meandered in connection with the public survey of such lands under the laws of the United States and if the title to the beds of such streams was lawfully patented or conveyed by the United States or any State to any person;

43 U.S.C. § 1311. Rights of the States

(a) Confirmation and establishment of title and ownership of lands and resources; management, administration, leasing, development, and use.

It is determined and declared to be in the public interest that (1) title to and ownership of the lands beneath navigable waters within the boundaries of the respective States, and the natural resources within such lands and waters, and (2) the right and power to manage, administer, lease, develop, and use the said lands and natural resources all in accordance with applicable State law be, and they are, subject to the provisions hereof, recognized, confirmed, established, and vested in and assigned to the respective States or the persons who were on June 5, 1950, entitled thereto under the law of the respective States in which the land is located, and the respective grantees, lessees, or successors in interest thereof;

(b) Release and relinquishment of title and claims of the United States; payment to States of moneys paid under leases

(1) The United States releases and relinquishes unto said States and persons aforesaid, except as otherwise reserved herein, all right, title, and interest of the United States, if any it has, in and to all said lands, improvements, and natural resources; (2) the United States releases and relinquishes all claims of the United States, if any it has, for money or damages arising out of any operations of said States or persons pursuant to State authority upon or within said lands and navigable waters; and (3) the Secretary of the Interior or the Secretary of the Navy or the Treasurer of the United States shall pay to the respective States or their grantees issuing leases covering such lands or natural resources all moneys paid thereunder to the Secretary of the Interior or to the Secretary of the Navy or to the Treasurer of the United States and subject to the control of any of them or to the control of the United States on May 22, 1953, except that portion of such moneys which (1) is required to be returned to a lessee; or (2) is deductible as provided by stipulation or agreement between the United States and any of said States; * * *.

43 U.S.C. § 1312. Seaward boundaries of States

The seaward boundary of each original coastal State is approved and confirmed as a line three geographical miles distant from its coast line or, in the case of the Great Lakes, to the international boundary. Any State admitted subsequent to the formation of the Union which has not already done so may extend its seaward boundaries to a line three geographical miles distant from its coast line, or to the international boundaries of the United States in the Great Lakes or any other body of water traversed by such boundaries. Any claim heretofore or hereafter asserted either by constitutional provision, statute, or otherwise, indicating the intent of a State so to extend its boundaries is hereby approved and confirmed, without prejudice to its claim, if any it has, that its boundaries extend beyond that line. Nothing in this section is to be construed as questioning or in any manner prejudicing the existence of any State's seaward boundary beyond three geographical miles if it was so provided by its constitution or laws prior to or at the time such State became a member of the Union, or if it has been heretofore approved by Congress.

43 U.S.C. § 1314. Rights and powers retained by the United States; purchase of natural resources; condemnation of lands

(a) The United States retains all its navigational servitude and rights in and power of regulation and control of said lands and navigable waters for the constitutional purposes of commerce, navigation, national defense, and international affairs, all of which shall be paramount to, but shall not be deemed to include, proprietary rights of ownership, or the rights of management, administration, leasing, use, and development of the lands and natural resources which are specifically recognized, confirmed, established and vested in and assigned to the respective States and others by Section 1311 of this title. * * *

* * *

The Submerged Lands Act (SLA), unfortunately, raised nearly as many questions as it answered. One of the most important unanswered questions was who owned or controlled lands and resources beyond the marginal sea. In the same year as the SLA, Congress passed the Outer Continental Shelf Lands Act of 1953 which ratified and codified the Truman Proclamation and asserted federal government jurisdiction over and ownership of the resources of the continental shelf. See R. Breeden, Federalism and the Development of Outer Continental Shelf Mineral Resources, 28 Stan. L. Rev. 1107, 1112–14 (1976).

Both federal and state interests found support for their positions in the SLA. States asserted that this Act was a congressional recognition that broad rights to these lands and waters had always existed in the states and that upon each states' entry into the Union the federal government had relinquished these broad rights to the states rather than retaining them in the federal government. (Note the quitclaim language in the statute.) The federal theory maintained that this Act merely granted limited authority over these lands back to the states, leaving most aspects of authority still vested in the hands of the federal government.

After the passage of the SLA, a number of coastal states, relying on 43 U.S.C. § 1312, asserted claims to submerged lands and resources extending beyond three miles from the coastline. Texas successfully claimed an historic boundary extending three marine leagues (nine nautical miles) into the Gulf of Mexico; but Louisiana's, Mississippi's, and Alabama's similar claims were rejected. United States v. Louisiana, 363 U.S. 1 (1960). See also United States v. Louisiana, 389 U.S. 155 (1967); United States v. Louisiana, 394 U.S. 1 (1969). It was also determined that Florida's Gulf of Mexico boundary was three marine leagues, but its Atlantic Ocean boundary was settled by consent decree at three geographical miles from shore. United States v. Florida, 363 U.S. 121 (1960); United States v. Florida, 420 U.S. 531 (1975). The other Atlantic and Pacific coast states' boundaries were also found to extend only three miles seaward from the coast. (Note that a nautical mile is synonymous with a geographical mile.)

NOTES AND QUESTIONS

1. The Submerged Lands Act also created a number of new boundary problems, the most serious of which was the definition of "inland waters." Coastlines, unfortunately for legal purposes, are rarely straight. Bays, estuaries, and shallow indentations make straight boundary lines impossible. In

its definition of "coast line," the SLA in Section 1301(c) mentioned "inland waters" but failed to provide a definition. At issue was whether the 3-mile marginal sea was to be measured from a line following the sinuosities of the coast, or a straight line drawn along the coast from headland to headland. Why would states with lots of bays or deeply indented coastlines favor the straight baseline method?

2. In 1963 the United States filed an amended complaint against the State of California and sought a supplemental decree defining "inland waters." The U.S. Supreme Court granted the supplemental decree in United States v. California, 381 U.S. 139 (1965). California, using the straight baseline method, claimed a huge offshore area as inland water. The Supreme Court ruled that by eliminating the definition of inland waters from the bill, Congress intended to leave the meaning of the term to the courts. The Court then held that the definition should conform to the one adopted by the 1958 Geneva Convention on the Territorial Sea and the Contiguous Zone. The Convention adopted a 24-mile closing line rule for bays and a semicircle test for the sufficiency of water enclosed as the definition of inland waters. Professor Aaron Shalowitz, in Boundary Problems Raised by the Submerged Lands Act, 54 Colum. L. Rev. 1021, 1031–32 (1954), explained the test:

> Since bays in nature are seldom exactly circular, recourse is had to the theory of equivalence and the rule adopted that if the area of a bay in nature is greater than the area of the semicircle formed with the distance between the headlands as a diameter, the bay is a closed bay, or intra-territorial, and the seaward boundary of inland waters is a headland-to-headland line. But if the area of the bay is less than the area of the semicircle, the bay is an open bay, or extra-territorial, and the boundary line of inland waters would be the ordinary low-water mark following the sinuosities of the coast.

When the Court applied the Convention's test to the California coast it found that only Monterey Bay qualified as inland water. The remainder of the huge expanse of ocean claimed by California, the Court held, was open sea and therefore measured by the low-water baseline method more favorable to the federal government.

3. In United States v. Louisiana, 394 U.S. 11 (1969), the Supreme Court defined the prerequisites for a claim of historic bay status. These were:

a. the exercise of authority over the area by the state claiming the historical right.
b. the continuity of this exercise of authority.
c. the attitude of foreign states.

United States v. Alaska, 422 U.S. 184 (1975) (lower Cook Inlet held not to be an "historic bay"); United States v. Louisiana, 470 U.S. 93 (1985) (Mississippi Sound is an historic bay). See generally Comment, The Doctrine of Historic Bays: Applying an Anachronism in the Alabama and Mississippi Boundary Case, 23 San Diego L. Rev. 763 (1986).

In United States v. Maine, 469 U.S. 504 (1985) (Rhode Island and New York boundary case), the Court determined that Long Island, although in reality an island, would be considered a peninsula attached to the New York mainland. The decision classified Long Island Sound as a closed bay and therefore part of the inland waters of New York and Connecticut. The baseline drawn from Long Island to Watch Hill on the mainland, however, defeated the Rhode Island claim to Block Island Sound as part of its territorial sea.

The Supreme Court in United States v. Maine, 475 U.S. 89 (1986), rejected Massachusetts' claim that Nantucket Sound is within the state's internal waters rather than partly territorial sea and partly high seas as the United States argued. The state claim rested entirely on the doctrine of "ancient title." Under that doctrine, occupation, as an original mode of territorial acquisition and an assertion of exclusive authority, vests the occupant with clear title if the "occupation" began before freedom of the high seas became part of international law. The doctrine is recognized by Juridical Regime of Historic Waters, Including Historic Bays, 2 Y.B. Int'l L. Comm'n 1 (1962), a United Nations study upon which the Supreme Court has relied in prior federal-state boundary determinations. See, e.g., United States v. Louisiana, 470 U.S. 93, 101 (1985). Assuming, arguendo, the legitimacy of claims based on "ancient title," Justice Stevens dismissed Massachusetts' claim on the grounds that the state failed to demonstrate the "existence of acts, attributable to the sovereign, manifesting an assertion of exclusive authority over the waters claimed." 475 U.S. at 98.

4. In United States v. Alaska, 521 U.S. 1 (1997), the Court rejected most of Alaska's claims to submerged lands in the Beaufort Sea off Alaska's Arctic coast. Alaska could not treat the alluvial formation known as Dinkum Sands as an island nor use straight baselines between barrier islands in Prudhoe Bay to extend its coastline seaward for Submerged Lands Act purposes.

5. Some (but not all) artificial coastline extensions, such as harbors and breakwaters, may extend state baselines. Compare United States v. California, 447 U.S. 1 (1980) with United States v. Alaska, 503 U.S. 569 (1992). For qualifying artificial extensions, the marginal sea is measured from their farthest seaward extent.

6. A further boundary problem under the Submerged Lands Act was the problem of ambulatory boundaries. Not only are ocean coastlines irregular, they are subject to change. In United States v. Louisiana, 394 U.S. 11 (1969), the U.S. Supreme Court held that if erosion takes place so that the historic boundary is more than three marine leagues from the present coastline, the present three-league line becomes the new boundary; in other words, the state loses territory. In places where accretion has extended the coastline, the historic seaward boundary of the state did not extend beyond three leagues. However, for most of the states, their SLA boundaries were ambulatory.

R. Krueger, in The Background of the Continental Shelf and the Outer Continental Shelf Lands Act, 10 Nat. Resources J. 442, 463 (1970), criticized the concept of ambulatory boundaries:

The concept of an ambulatory boundary is a sound one from an international standpoint. If the United States or any other country increases its land mass artificially, there are good reasons, such as national defense, for extending its territorial sea appropriately. It is not, however, a good rule of law with respect to federal-state relationships. It could lead to further federal-state litigation over boundaries and title and may have an inhibiting influence on beneficial coastal developments. It has been recommended that the federal government and the various states adopt appropriate legislation to fix their offshore boundaries.

As part of the Budget Reconciliation Act of 1985, P.L. 99–272, § 8005, Congress amended Section 2(b) of the Submerged Lands Act, 43 U.S.C. § 1301(b), to provide that once they are fixed by a decree of the Supreme Court, the coordinates delineating a federal-state offshore boundary "shall remain immobilized * * * and shall not be ambulatory." This provision does not appear to apply to lateral seaward boundaries between states, but a Supreme Court decree fixing such boundaries could itself provide that the decreed boundary shall be fixed rather than ambulatory with physical changes in the coastline. See generally New Jersey v. New York, 1998 WL 259994 (U.S. Sup. Ct. May 26, 1998); Texas v. Louisiana, 426 U.S. 465 (1976).

7. Section 1313 of the Submerged Lands Act led to the third supplemental decree granted in United States v. California, 436 U.S. 32 (1978). The last sentence of § 1313(a) exempted from the grant to the states "any rights the United States has in lands presently occupied by the United States under claim of right." The United States claimed dominion over the submerged lands and waters within the Channel Islands National Monument, situated inside the three-mile marginal sea off the southern California mainland. The United States had maintained and controlled the monument for decades and claimed that this was "actual occupation" under § 1313(a).

The Supreme Court held that the United States did not have dominion, and that title to the disputed area was in California. The Court noted that the entire purpose of the Submerged Lands Act would have been nullified if the "claim of right" exemption saved claims based solely on paramount rights obtained in the 1947 United States v. California decision. Thus, the exception in § 1313(a) applies only if the United States' claim rests on some basis other than paramount rights. The United States failed to show any other basis of ownership.

8. In Douglas v. Seacoast Products, Inc., 431 U.S. 265 (1977), the U.S. Supreme Court defined coastal state "ownership" under the Submerged Lands Act. Ownership consists of the right to exploit offshore resources subject to encumbrances previously created by the exercise of the commerce, navigation, national defense, and international affairs powers of the federal government. Justice Rehnquist, dissenting, preferred an alternative reading of the act—that the reservation of powers clause only gives fair warning of the

possibility that the government may, at some time in the future and in furtherance of the specifically enumerated powers, find it necessary to intrude
upon state ownership and control of coastal submerged lands. See T. Schoenbaum & F. Parker, Federalism in the Coastal Zone: Three Models of State
Jurisdiction and Control, 57 N.C. L. Rev. 231 (1979).

NOTE: MARITIME BOUNDARIES WITH CANADA AND MEXICO

Important maritime boundaries between the United States and neighboring countries have been resolved as well. On October 12, 1984, the International Court of Justice (ICJ) handed down its landmark decision delimiting
the U.S.–Canada maritime boundary in the Gulf of Maine. Delimitation of
the Maritime Boundary in the Gulf of Maine Area (Canada v. United States),
1984 ICJ 246. Pursuant to this decision, Canada is entitled to the lion's share
of Georges Bank's multimillion dollar scallop fishery located on its rich
Northeast Peak; both countries share several stocks of groundfish divided in
two by the new boundary. As a practical result, this decision profoundly affects optimum management of these resources and consequently mandates
international cooperation in conservation and management. Moreover, as the
delimitation marked the first single boundary ever drawn for both the continental shelf and the water column, this decision provided a significant mile-
stone in the law of international maritime boundaries. See, e.g., J. Bubier
and A. Rieser, U.S. and Canadian Groundfish Management in the Gulf of
Maine–Georges Bank Region, 10 Ocean Mgmt. 83 (1986); B. Shibles, Implications of an International Legal Standard for Transnational Management of
Gulf of Maine–Georges Bank Fishery Resources, 1 Ocean and Coastal L. J. 1
(1994).

Reflecting a century-old conflict, the dispute over Gulf of Maine resources began in earnest in 1977 when the U.S. and Canada simultaneously
expanded their fishery jurisdictions to 200 nautical miles. In the Gulf of
Maine, the new jurisdictions incorporated some of the world's richest fishing
grounds, including that of the prized Georges Bank, over which the claims
clashed irreconcilably. Bilateral negotiations failed to resolve the dispute,
forcing the two countries to seek outside binding settlement. In a Special
Agreement submitted November 1981, the two countries asked a five-
member Chamber of the ICJ to delimit by a single boundary both the continental shelf and the water column of the Gulf of Maine, pursuant to Article
26 of the Statute of the ICJ.

The ICJ based its delimitation almost exclusively on geography. Although the court consistently applied customary international law and its jurisprudence which requires that maritime boundary delimitations, in the absence of agreement, be based on equitable principles adjusted to account for
relevant circumstances in order to achieve an equitable result, it rejected the
application of any factors particularly related to the continental shelf or fisheries. See, e.g., Case Concerning the Continental Shelf (Tunisia v. Libya),
1982 ICJ 18. The court drew an initial boundary based on the equitable principle of coastline geography. The line bisecting the angle formed by the Nova

Scotia and North American continent coastal parallels provided the initial delimitation. In making this initial delimitation, the ICJ rejected application of the equidistance principle as defined in Article 6 of the 1958 Convention on the Continental Shelf even though both countries are parties to the treaty. The 1958 Convention governed only the continental shelf and was thus found inapplicable to the dual-purpose boundary. Furthermore, the court found that equidistance had not become a general rule of maritime boundary delimitation in customary international law and the court was under no obligation to follow it.

Relevant circumstances considered by the ICJ in making its initial delimitation equitable were again geographical: the boundary was adjusted by the proportional lengths of coastlines. In flatly refusing to consider certain nongeographical circumstances proposed by both parties, the court further emphasized the relationship of geography to equitable delimitations. Thus historical fishing patterns, socio-economic dependence on fishery resources, and naturally existing ecological boundaries delimiting fishery resources, were all deemed irrelevant to achieving an equitable result, purportedly because the parties asked for a single maritime boundary. Because of this, the case has been considered somewhat controversial, and perhaps not relevant to EEZ delimitations.

In 1978 the United States and Mexico were able to resolve their overlapping 200-mile claims in the Gulf of Mexico by a treaty (finally approved by the United States Senate in October 1997) utilizing the equidistant method of boundary line calculation. The EEZ boundaries completely surround a triangular "western gap" of high seas and continental shelf in the middle of the Gulf of Mexico, approximately 135 miles long. In 2000, the two countries adopted a treaty dividing the continental shelf beyond the EEZs with an equidistance line and reserving a buffer zone on each side of the boundary to deal with possible transboundary oil and gas deposits.

The United States maritime jurisdictional claims create over 30 areas where maritime jurisdictional zones overlap with the claims of other nations. Fewer than half of these have been finally resolved. For a list of the settled boundaries and copies of existing treaties and agreements, see the Department of State website at http://www.state.gov/e/oes/ocns/opa/c28187.htm.

PROBLEM

On December 27, 1988, President Ronald Reagan issued the Presidential Proclamation extending the territorial sea of the United States from three miles to twelve miles. The legislators in your state are interested in how this extension could affect state authority over offshore waters and resources. They have asked you to describe the division of state-federal authority over living and nonliving ocean resources as it existed before the issuance of the proclamation and after. What other kinds of jurisdictional issues could arise? If the proclamation has not changed the division, they wish to know what difficulties you perceive in persuading Congress to pass legislation extending state authority to the limits of the new territorial sea.

B. THE PARAMOUNT RIGHTS DOCTRINE AND TRIBAL RIGHTS

NATIVE VILLAGE OF EYAK V. BLANK
United States Court of Appeals, Ninth Circuit, 2012
688 F.3d 619

PER CURIAM.

The Alaskan Native Villages of Eyak, Tatitlek, Chenega, Nanwalek and Port Graham ("Villages") assert that, beginning thousands of years before European contact and continuing through modern times, their members fished, hunted and otherwise exploited portions of the Outer Continental Shelf ("OCS") in the Gulf of Alaska. Based on this history, the Villages claim they possess non-exclusive aboriginal hunting and fishing rights in the areas of the OCS they've traditionally used.

The OCS fisheries are regulated by the Secretary of Commerce. In 1993, the Secretary promulgated [Individual Fishing Quota (IFQ)] regulations limiting access to the halibut and sablefish fisheries * * *.

* * * The Villages claim that the Secretary's regulations fail to account for the Villages' non-exclusive aboriginal hunting and fishing rights, without Congress's consent in violation of the federal common law and the Indian Non–Intercourse Act, 25 U.S.C. § 177. The district court dismissed their complaint with prejudice. The Villages timely appealed.

At the heart of this dispute are the competing federal interests of honoring Native rights and preserving national fisheries. When this case was previously before us, we held that the Villages' claim to *exclusive* rights to hunt and fish on the OCS was barred by federal paramountcy. Native Village of Eyak v. Trawler Diane Marie, Inc. (Eyak I), 154 F.3d 1090, 1096–97 (9th Cir.1998). The paramountcy doctrine, as applied here, stands for the proposition that the national government has a paramount interest in ocean waters and submerged lands below the low-water mark. *See N.* Mariana Islands v. United States, 399 F.3d 1057, 1060–61 (9th Cir.2005). But the Villages point to Village of Gambell v. Hodel (Gambell III), 869 F.2d 1273 (9th Cir.1989), where we held that "aboriginal rights may exist concurrently with a paramount federal interest." Id. at 1277.

Gambell III holds that aboriginal rights and the doctrine of federal paramountcy can coexist, whereas *Eyak I* holds that the paramountcy doctrine trumps Native claims based on aboriginal title. We took this case en banc to resolve any conflict between *Gambell III* and *Eyak I. See* Eyak Native Village v. Daley, 364 F.3d 1057, 1057 (9th Cir.2004). But we do not reach that question because the Villages have failed to demonstrate the existence of aboriginal rights in the claimed area.

* * *

Aboriginal rights don't depend on a treaty or an act of Congress for their existence. *See* United States v. Santa Fe Pac. R.R., 314 U.S. 339, 347, 62 S.Ct. 248 (1941). Rather, the Villages have the burden of proving "actual, exclusive, and continuous use and occupancy 'for a long time' " of the claimed area. Sac & Fox Tribe of Indians of Okla. v. United States, 383 F.2d 991, 998 (Ct.Cl.1967). This use and occupancy requirement is measured "in accordance with the way of life, habits, customs and usages of the Indians who are its users and occupiers." *Id.*

* * *

* * * We adopt the district court's uncontested factual findings and conclude that the Villages have failed to prove their entitlement to aboriginal rights on the OCS. [The court found that although the Villages satisfied the "continuous use and occupancy" requirement, but failed to present sufficient evidence to establish "an exclusive and unchallenged claim to the disputed areas."]

* * *

Based on the uncontested factual findings of the district court, we affirm the district court's conclusion that the Villages failed to establish an entitlement to non-exclusive aboriginal rights on the OCS. Because the Villages haven't established aboriginal rights on the OCS, we have no occasion to consider whether there's a conflict with the federal paramountcy doctrine. We also need not consider whether the Secretary's actions violated the Indian Non–Intercourse Act.

AFFIRMED.

W. FLETCHER, Circuit Judge, with whom PREGERSON, THOMAS, and RAWLINSON, Circuit Judges, join, and with whom HAWKINS, Circuit Judge, joins as to Part I [Aboriginal Rights], dissenting:

I respectfully dissent.

[T]he majority concludes that Alaskan Native Villages of Eyak, Tatitlek, Chenega, Nanwalek, and Port Graham ("the Chugach") failed to establish aboriginal hunting and fishing rights on part of the Outer Continental Shelf ("OCS") in the Gulf of Alaska because they did not show exclusive use and occupancy of any part of the claimed area. In so doing, the majority misstates the law and misreads plain English.

I would hold, based on the district court's findings, that the Chugach have established aboriginal hunting and fishing rights in at least part of the claimed area of the OCS, and that these rights are consistent with federal paramountcy. I would reverse and remand with instructions to the district court to find, under the proper legal test, precisely where within the claimed area the Chugach have aboriginal rights.

I. Aboriginal Rights

* * *

The Chugach contend, and I agree, that the facts found by the district court are sufficient to establish their aboriginal rights under the *Sac & Fox* test. Based on the district court's findings, I conclude that the Chugach have established aboriginal rights in at least part of the claimed area of the OCS. I would remand to the district court for a determination, under the proper legal test, of precisely where within the claimed area they have aboriginal rights.

A. Continuous Use and Occupancy

The majority concludes that the Chugach have satisfied the "continuous use and occupancy" requirement of the *Sac & Fox* test. I agree.

Continuous use and occupancy are measured in accordance with the "way of life, habits, customs and usages of the Indians who are its users and occupiers." *Sac & Fox,* 383 F.2d at 998. The district court found that the Chugach were "skilled marine hunters and fishermen" who "found their sustenance largely in marine waters." They were "knowledgeable of ocean currents" and "entirely capable" of traversing the OCS in their boats. The Chugach navigated to Middleton Island, the Barren Islands, Cook Inlet, the Copper River Delta, and Wessels Reef to hunt and fish. They crossed portions of the OCS when traveling between these locations and fished along the way.

The district court found that such use and occupancy was "temporary and seasonal." The Chugach's seasonal use qualifies as "continuous" given their way of life as marine hunters and fishermen. *See* Confed. Tribes of the Warm Springs Reservation of Or. v. United States, 1966 WL 8893, at *5 (Ct.Cl. 1966); Spokane Tribe of Indians v. United States, 1963 WL 8583, at *5 (Ct.Cl.1963) ("[I]ntermittent or seasonal use has been accepted as showing Indian title." (collecting cases)).

B. Exclusive Use and Occupancy

The majority concludes that the Chugach have failed to satisfy the "exclusive . . . use and occupancy" requirement of the *Sac & Fox* test. I strongly disagree.

1. Governing Law

To carry its burden in establishing aboriginal rights, a plaintiff tribe "must show that it used and occupied the [claimed area] to the exclusion of other Indian groups." United States v. Pueblo of San Ildefonso, 513 F.2d 1383, 1394 (Ct.Cl.1975). Where there is no evidence of use or occupancy by others within the claimed area, the claimant tribe need only show its own use and occupancy. In such a case, a court "must conclude," without more, that the plaintiff tribe used and occupied the area exclusively. Zuni Tribe of N.M. v. United States, 12 Cl.Ct. 607, 617–20 & nn. 13–15 (1987); see also Caddo Tribe of Okla. v. United States, 35 Ind. Cl. Comm. 321, 358–60 (1975) (finding exclusivity where "[t]here is no evidence indicating that other tribes of Indians were using and occupying this [claimed] area at the same time").

Where there is evidence of use or occupancy by others within the claimed area, a claimant tribe must show that it had the ability to exclude those other groups, such that the use by the others was temporary or permissive. See Alabama–Coushatta Tribe of Tex. v. United States, 2000 WL 1013532, at *13 (Fed.Cl.2000) ("[W]here another tribe commonly uses the land with the claimant tribe, proof of the claimant tribe's dominance over the other tribe preserves its exclusive use of the land."). A tribe's exclusive use and occupancy "is called in question where the historical record of the region indicates that it was inhabited, controlled or wandered over by many tribes or groups." Pueblo of San Ildefonso, 513 F.2d at 1394; see also Strong v. United States, 518 F.2d 556, 561 (Ct.Cl.1975) (" 'Exclusiveness' becomes a problem to plaintiffs simply because the historical record . . . demonstrates clearly that . . . the area as a whole was 'inhabited, controlled or wandered over by many tribes or groups.' "). Evidence of use and occupancy by other groups "must be specific" to defeat a claim of exclusivity. Alabama–Coushatta Tribe, 2000 WL 1013532, at *17; Wichita Indian Tribe v. United States, 696 F.2d 1378, 1385 (Fed.Cir.1983).

* * *

Because of the "difficulty of obtaining the essential proof necessary to establish Indian title," courts take a "liberal approach" in weighing the limited historical evidence regarding exclusive use and occupancy. Nooksack Tribe of Indians v. United States, 3 Ind. Cl. Comm. 492, 499 (1955); see also Muckleshoot, 3 Ind. Cl. Comm. at 677 (because "it is extremely difficult to establish facts after the lapse of time involved in matters of Indian litigation," courts must "take a common sense approach" when evaluating exclusivity); Snake or Piute Indians v. United States, 112 F.Supp. 543, 552 (Ct.Cl.1953) (exclusivity "can only be inferred" because it is difficult to prove "as of a date too remote to admit of testimony of living witnesses").

In sum, the Sac & Fox test requires that the Chugach show that they used and occupied the claimed area exclusively. It does not require that the Chugach show that they could have repelled hypothetical intruders from the area. In the absence of evidence of use by others, the case law requires only that the Chugach show that they were the only group that used and occupied the area.

2. District Court Factual Findings

The factual findings of the district court establish that the Chugach used and occupied some areas exclusively, with no use or occupancy of those areas by others. * * *

* * *

Both parties' experts agreed that there is no evidence that other groups used or occupied Chugach territory. At trial, the Chugach introduced records of five eyewitness accounts from 18th-century explorers describing encounters with seafaring Chugach on the OCS more than three miles from shore. The Chugach's expert anthropologist, Matt Ganley, testified, "We don't see anybody else in the OCS when the first Russians come into that area. We don't see anybody else on Middleton Island. There's no mention of other groups, and from the descriptions that the people provided, these were clearly Chugach people." The Secretary's expert anthropologists gave similar testimony. Michael Yarborough and Christopher Wooley both testified that they were unaware of any evidence that groups other than the Chugach fished or hunted in the claimed area during the pre-contact period.

* * *

4. Summary

Based on the case law and the district court's factual findings, I would hold that the Chugach have established aboriginal hunting and fishing rights within at least part of the claimed area of the OCS. There is no evidence, and no finding by the district court, that other groups hunted or fished within the territory used and occupied by the Chugach. Evidence of use or occupancy by other tribes or groups "must be specific" to defeat a claim of exclusivity. Alabama–Coushatta Tribe, 2000 WL 1013532, at *17; *Wichita Indian Tribe,* 696 F.2d at 1385. As in Alabama–Coushatta Tribe, "we do not even have evidence that is too general" to defeat the claim of exclusivity. 2000 WL 1013532, at *17. In the case before us, there is no evidence whatsoever of use or occupancy by others.

II. Federal Paramountcy

Because I conclude that the Chugach have established aboriginal hunting and fishing rights in at least part of the claimed area of the OCS, I would reach the question whether aboriginal rights are consistent with federal paramountcy.

The Supreme Court articulated the federal paramountcy doctrine in a series of cases involving disputes between coastal states and the federal government over ownership and control of ocean resources. The Court repeatedly held that the federal government's paramount interest in "foreign commerce, foreign affairs and national defense" required that its control over the seabed be paramount to that of the states, regardless of the circumstances in which a state joined the Union. United States v. Maine, 420 U.S. 515, 522 (1975); United States v. Texas, 339 U.S. 707, 718–19 (1950); United States v. Louisiana, 339 U.S. 699, 704 (1950); United States v. California, 332 U.S. 19, 38–39 (1947). The federal government could grant ownership or control to the states to the degree that it wished, but control of the seabed belonged, "in the first instance," to the federal government. Maine, 420 U.S. at 522; California, 332 U.S. at 29. The Court explained:

> The marginal sea is a national, not a state concern. National interests, national responsibilities, national concerns are involved. The problems of commerce, national defense, relations with other powers, war and peace focus there. National rights must therefore be paramount in that area.

Louisiana, 339 U.S. at 704.

In Village of Gambell v. Hodel ("Gambell III"), 869 F.2d 1273, 1277 (9th Cir.1989), we held that federal paramountcy was consistent with aboriginal rights on the OCS because such rights "may exist concurrently with a paramount federal interest, without undermining that interest." However, nine years later in Native Village of Eyak v. Trawler Diane Marie, Inc. ("Eyak I"), 154 F.3d 1090, 1095–97 (9th Cir.1998), a different panel of this court held that the paramountcy doctrine barred plaintiff Villages from asserting exclusive rights on the OCS based on aboriginal title. We took this case en banc to reconcile our conflicting precedents.

Relying on *Eyak I,* the Secretary argues that the paramountcy doctrine automatically extinguishes aboriginal rights on the OCS. According to the Secretary, aboriginal rights exist on the OCS *only after they have been affirmatively recognized* by the federal government in a statute or treaty. The Secretary is correct that the federal government has ultimate control over aboriginal rights, but he has the doctrine backwards. Under long-established law, aboriginal rights exist *until affirmatively extinguished* by Congress. *See, e.g.,* Santa Fe Pac. R.R. Co., 314 U.S. at 347 (aboriginal rights need not "be based upon a treaty, statute, or other formal government action"). "[C]ongressional intent to extinguish Indian title must be plain and unambiguous and will not be lightly implied." Cnty. of Oneida v. Oneida Indian Nation of N.Y. ("Oneida II"), 470 U.S. 226, 247–48 (1985) (internal quotation and citations omitted). Here, neither the district court nor the Secretary has identified any plain and unambiguous intent by Congress to extinguish aboriginal rights of the Chugach on the OCS. *See* Gambell III, 869 F.2d at 1280 (finding it "clear" that the settlement provisions of the Alaska Native Claims Settlement Act "do not extinguish aboriginal subsistence rights that may exist in the OCS").

We manifestly erred in *Eyak I* by ignoring the "great difference" between asserted state ownership of the seabed, at issue in the federal paramountcy cases, and aboriginal use and occupancy rights, at issue in that case. *Sac & Fox,* 383 F.2d at 997 (aboriginal rights are "not the same as sovereign or legal title"); *see also* FELIX COHEN, COHEN'S HANDBOOK OF FEDERAL INDIAN LAW 998 (2005 ed.) ("[*Eyak I*] seems to be wrongly decided, given the differences between state title and Indian title."). In the paramountcy cases, states sought to lease the seabeds off their shores for oil and gas exploitation without the consent of, and to the exclusion of, the federal government. *See, e.g.,* California, 332 U.S. at 23, 38; Louisiana, 339 U.S. at 701. State control of the seabed posed a threat to national interests because the states, if they were owners of fee simple title, could sell or convey those rights without the federal government's consent. California, 332 U.S. at 29, 35; *see also N.* Mariana Islands v. United States, 399 F.3d 1057, 1062–63 (9th Cir.2005) (applying paramountcy doctrine to Commonwealth of the Northern Mariana Islands' claimed ownership of submerged lands off its coast).

In stark contrast to the states' asserted title as against the federal government in the paramountcy cases, aboriginal rights presume ultimate federal sovereignty and control. *See* Tee–Hit–Ton Indians v. United States, 348 U.S. 272, 279, 75 S.Ct. 313, 99 L.Ed. 314 (1955) ("[Aboriginal title] is not a property right but amounts to a right of occupancy which the sovereign grants and protects against intrusion by third parties. . . . "). Whereas the states sought to establish ownership exclusive of the federal government in the paramountcy cases, aboriginal rights prevail only against parties other than the federal government. *See* Oneida Indian Nation of N.Y. v. Oneida Cnty. ("Oneida I"), 414 U.S. 661, 667 (1974) (describing aboriginal title as "good against all but the sovereign"); Village of Gambell v. Clark ("Gambell I"), 746 F.2d 572, 574 (9th Cir.1984) ("[Aboriginal] rights are superior to those of third parties, including the states, but are subject to the paramount powers of Congress."). Unlike fee simple rights, aboriginal rights cannot be sold or leased to third parties without the federal government's consent. *See Oneida II,* 470 U.S. at 234; 25 U.S.C. § 177 ("No purchase, grant, lease, or other conveyance of lands, or of any title or claim thereto, from any Indian nation or tribe of Indians, shall be of any validity in law or equity, unless the same be made by treaty or convention entered into pursuant to the Constitution."). If aboriginal rights conflict with the national interest, Congress may extinguish those rights, even without paying compensation, so long as its intent is plain and unambiguous. *Tee–Hit–Ton,* 348 U.S. at 284–85; *Oneida II,* 470 U.S. at 247–48.

In *Eyak I,* we misconstrued the Chugach's claim as seeking "complete control over the OCS." 154 F.3d at 1096. The Chugach do not claim fee simple ownership in the OCS or a concomitant power to convey their interest to third parties. Rather, the Chugach seek only recognition of their aboriginal rights of use and occupancy in part of the OCS. We erred in *Eyak I* by stating that there was no "practical difference" between the relief sought by the Chugach and the relief sought by states in the paramountcy cases. Id. at 1095–96. The Chugach's asserted aboriginal rights are in no way comparable to the states' asserted right to fee simple ownership of offshore submerged land and a concomitant right to lease those lands to third parties without the consent of the federal government. As we wrote in *Gambell III,* the Chugach "are not asserting a claim of sovereign rights. Rather, they contend that they possess rights of occupancy and use that are subordinate to and consistent with national interests. This argument is persuasive." 869 F.2d at 1276.

I would overrule *Eyak I* insofar as it held that the paramountcy doctrine is inconsistent with the existence of aboriginal rights. I would reaffirm our holding in *Gambell III* that aboriginal rights may exist on the OCS without undermining the paramount federal interest.

III. Remand

The district court on remand from our en banc panel did not apply the test for aboriginal rights articulated in *Sac & Fox.* The court's conclusion that the Chugach's pre-contact hunting and fishing activities "did not give rise" to aboriginal rights on the OCS was premised on legal errors.

First, the district court assumed incorrectly that the law required the Chugach to show an ability to exclude others from the claimed area, even in the absence of evidence of use by others. It wrote:

> [N]one of the ancestral villages was in a position to control or dominate access to any part of the OCS. The area was too large; and the number of men of an age who would have been able to defend or control high seas marine areas were too few. . . . None of the ancestral villages was in a position to occupy or exercise exclusive control over any part of the OCS on a sustained basis.

The district court did not understand that, in the absence of evidence of use by other groups within the claimed area, the Chugach could establish exclusivity simply by showing their own use and occupancy. The Chugach did not need to show that they were able to exclude hypothetical intruders.

Second, as the singular "none" and "was" in the above passage illustrate, the court mistakenly analyzed the aboriginal rights of individual plaintiff Villages, as opposed to the Chugach as a whole. The district court found that the Chugach were culturally, ethnically, and linguistically related, and were "recognized by themselves and others as Chugach." The court's separate finding that the Villages were politically independent is immaterial. *See Northern Paiute Nation v. United States,* 7 Ind. Cl. Comm. 322, 416 (1959) (recognizing aboriginal rights for tribal group that lacked "political unity" but shared "similarities of language and culture"). The court's finding that the Villages had separate hunting and fishing "access" and did not regularly engage in joint hunting or fishing trips is similarly immaterial, so long as the Chugach commonly used hunting and fishing areas. Here, the Chugach "found their sustenance largely in marine waters" and traveled to the same areas of the OCS to hunt and fish. These findings are analogous to other cases that recognized aboriginal rights where autonomous villages shared hunting and fishing areas. *See, e.g.,* Upper Skagit Tribe v. United States, 8 Ind. Cl. Comm. 492, 497 (1960) (recognizing aboriginal rights where villages "extracted their principal sustenance from the same areas"); Suquamish Tribe v. United States, 5 Ind. Cl. Comm. 158, 164 (1957) (recognizing aboriginal rights where villages "shared gathering, fishing and hunting areas"); *Muckleshoot,* 3 Ind. Cl. Comm. at 674–75 (recognizing aboriginal rights where "fishing waters were used in common by the occupants of all the villages"). Accordingly, the district court should have analyzed the claimed aboriginal rights of the Chugach as a whole.

Because the district court concluded that the Chugach's pre-contact activities "did not give rise" to any aboriginal rights on the OCS, it did not make findings identifying the precise areas that the Chugach used and occupied exclusively. I would remand to allow the district court to make such findings.

Conclusion

The district court acknowledged that the Secretary's challenged regulations are "fatally arbitrary" if the Chugach have aboriginal fishing rights in the OCS that have not been preempted under the paramountcy doctrine. Because I would hold that the Chugach have established aboriginal rights in at least part of the claimed area of the OCS and that these rights do not conflict with federal paramountcy, I would reverse and remand with instructions to the district court to find precisely where within the claimed area the Chugach have such rights. Once it makes those findings, the district court would be in a position to deal appropriately with the challenged regulations.

NOTES AND QUESTIONS

1. Does acknowledgement of aboriginal rights interfere with the federal government's ability to protect the nation or regulate international trade? See Notes & Comments: Andrew P. Richards, Aboriginal Ttitle or the Paramountcy Doctrine? Johnson V. McIntosh Flounders in Federal Waters off Alaska in Native Village of Eyak V. Trawler Diane Marie, Inc., 78 Wash. L. Rev. 939 (2003).

2. Why didn't the Submerged Lands Act of 1953 address the issue of tribal or aboriginal rights in the foreshore or submerged lands? Is there another reason besides the fact that Alaska was still a territory?

3. How does ANILCA affect the rights of Native Alaskans to offshore fisheries? In People of Village of Gambell v. Clark, 746 F.2d 572 (9th Cir. 1984), Alaskan natives challenged OCS oil and gas development in Norton Sound because it would adversely affect their aboriginal right to subsistence hunting and fishing. The court found this claim to be without merit, stating (incorrectly as it turned out) that even if the natives did have an aboriginal right to hunt and fish, it had been extinguished by the Alaskan Native Claims Settlement Act, 43 U.S.C. §§ 1601–1628, 1603(b). See also Inupiat Community of Arctic Slope v. U.S., 746 F.2d 570 (9th Cir. 1984), cert. denied, 474 U.S. 820 (1985). The court (wrongly) accepted the second contention of the natives that the Alaska National Interest Land Conservation Act (ANILCA), 16 U.S.C. § 3120, applied to OCS lands and waters. In doing this, the court recognized that the Secretary of Interior had a duty to see that the utilization of the OCS for oil and gas development caused the least possible adverse impact upon rural Alaskan residents who depend upon subsistence resource uses for their survival. See Tribal Village of Akutan v. Hodel, 16 ELR 20245 (D. Ak. 1986), aff'd, 869 F.2d 1185 (9th Cir. 1988), in which the district court had enjoined the Bristol Bay OCS lease sale because the Interior Secretary had applied an incorrect standard under ANILCA in approving a lease sale "unlikely" to affect subsistence life styles.

In a unanimous 9–0 decision, the Supreme Court, in Amoco Production Co. v. Village of Gambell, 480 U.S. 531 (1987), lifted an injunction that had halted exploration in Norton Sound and the Navarin Basin of the Bering Sea in connection with a dispute over native Alaskan subsistence fishing and hunting rights. Several Alaskan native villages, including Gambell and Stebbins, brought suit to enjoin the Secretary of the Interior's sale of oil and gas leases for federal outer continental shelf land off Alaska. The villages claimed that the Secretary had failed to consider the possible adverse impacts of exploration on subsistence hunting and fishing as required by section 810(a) of ANILCA, 16 U.S.C. § 3120. The U.S. District Court for the District of Alaska granted the Secretary's motion for summary judgment and the villages appealed. The Ninth Circuit affirmed in part, reversed in part, and remanded, 746 F.2d 572 (1984), upon which the District Court denied the villages' consolidated motion for a preliminary injunction. The villages again appealed and the Ninth Circuit once more reversed and remanded, granting the injunction. 774 F.2d 1414 (1985).

In the majority opinion, Justice White held that the villages were not entitled to a preliminary injunction and that ANILCA, which sets forth procedures to be followed before allowing lease, occupancy, or disposition of public lands that would significantly restrict Alaskan natives' use of lands for subsistence, does not apply to the outer continental shelf. By ANILCA's plain language, section 810(a) applies only to federal lands within the State of Alaska's boundaries, and includes coastal waters only out to the three mile limit. The Court remanded to the Ninth Circuit native claims to aboriginal rights on the OCS.

The Ninth Circuit Court of Appeals then held that the federal government's paramount interest in oil and gas leasing on the Outer Continental Shelf subordinates, but does not extinguish, aboriginal subsistence hunting and fishing rights. People of the Village of Gambell v. Hodel, 869 F.2d 1273 (9th Cir. 1989). On remand, the Ninth Circuit said the district court must decide: first, whether the native villages possess aboriginal subsistence rights in the Outer Continental Shelf; second, if so, whether oil and gas drilling will significantly interfere with those rights; and, third, whether the Outer Continental Shelf Lands Act—which extended federal jurisdiction to the Outer Continental Shelf—extinguishes subsistence rights in the Outer Continental Shelf as a matter of law. The court did not rule out the possibility that Alaskan natives may have aboriginal rights to offshore resources. The court found that the United States had exerted sufficient control over the Outer Continental Shelf constituting sovereignty and requiring recognition of aboriginal rights. The court said the Alaska Native Claims Settlement Act, which extinguishes certain aboriginal titles, applies to the geographical boundaries of the state but, like ANILCA, also does not apply to the Outer Continental Shelf, contrary to its earlier ruling. See also Native Village of Eyak v. Trawler Diane Marie, Inc., 154 F.3d 1090 (9th Cir. 1998), cert. denied, 527 U.S. 1003 (1999), finding no exclusive aboriginal rights to groundfish off Alaska.

4. Should the Submerged Lands Act be amended to recognize state boundaries to twelve nautical miles? To address aboriginal rights to parts of the outer continental shelf or exclusive economic zone? How would you draft language to address these issues?

2. OFFSHORE FEDERALISM: OWNERSHIP VS. JURISDICTION

A. COASTAL STATE JURISDICTION AND FEDERAL PREEMPTION

The Submerged Lands Act of 1953, excerpted on pp. 83–86, undoubtedly delineated ownership of offshore land and resources and established the basis for boundaries between the states and federal government in the marginal seas. The boundaries established under the SLA, therefore, establish the limits of a state's dominium and, consequently, its territory and territorial jurisdiction. State jurisdiction over individuals and activities has not, however, traditionally been limited to territorial jurisdiction. For example, in Skiriotes v. Florida, 313 U.S. 69 (1941), the U.S. Supreme Court recognized that, like the United States, a state could regulate the conduct of its citizens on the high seas beyond its territorial waters "with respect to matters in which the State has a legitimate interest and where there is no conflict with acts of Congress." Effects within a state have also been a basis for state jurisdiction beyond its territory even in regard to non-citizens. Conversely, § 1314 of the SLA clearly preserves the paramount federal constitutional jurisdiction in state waters "for purposes of commerce, navigation, national defense, and international affairs." Federal admiralty law may also preempt state law even within state boundaries. An additional problem arising from the SLA, therefore, is that while it addresses issues of dominium, it leaves many questions unanswered about imperium, federalism, and the limits of state jurisdiction in the marginal seas both within and beyond state territorial waters. Does the following case provide clear tests for determining these limits?

TEN TAXPAYER CITIZENS GROUP V. CAPE WIND ASSOCIATES, LLC

U.S. Court of Appeals, 1st Circuit, 2004
373 F.3d 183

LYNCH, CIRCUIT JUDGE.

This appeal is an early round in the legal battle over whether a commercial wind energy farm may be built in Nantucket Sound.

In October 2002, Ten Taxpayer Citizens Group and several additional plaintiffs (together, Ten Taxpayer) filed a lawsuit in Massachusetts state court to prevent Cape Wind Associates from erecting a 197-foot data collection tower in Nantucket Sound. The complaint alleged that Massachusetts state courts had jurisdiction over the project and that Cape Wind had failed to obtain the necessary permits under state law. Cape Wind removed the action to federal court and Ten Taxpayer moved to remand. After denying the motion to remand, the district court dismissed the complaint on August 19, 2003.

On appeal, Ten Taxpayer argues that the district court was obligated to remand the case to state court for lack of federal subject-matter jurisdiction. Ten Taxpayer also challenges the court's dismissal of the complaint. We affirm.

I.

The facts underlying this case are essentially undisputed. Where the parties disagree, we accept as true the well-pleaded factual allegations in the plaintiffs' complaint, drawing all reasonable inferences in their favor. Soto–Negron v. Taber Partners I, 339 F.3d 35, 38 (1st Cir.2003).

Cape Wind is a limited liability corporation based in South Yarmouth, Massachusetts. Its goal is to construct a commercial windmill farm on Horseshoe Shoals, a shallow area of Nantucket Sound more than three miles offshore. The proposed windmill farm includes at least 130 industrial wind turbines, each 470 feet tall. If it is completed as presently envisioned, the facility will spread across 28 square miles of Nantucket Sound and will be visible from shore. The project is the first of its kind in North America.

To construct the wind farm, Cape Wind needs extensive meteorological and oceanographic data concerning conditions on Horseshoe Shoals. For that purpose, Cape Wind in late 2001 announced plans to build a "scientific measurement device station" (SMDS) on Horseshoe Shoals. Intended as a temporary facility, the SMDS was designed to collect data for five years. It would consist of a data tower rising approximately 200 feet in the air, supported by three steel pilings driven 100 feet into the seabed. Together with its tripodal support structure, the tower would occupy about 900 square feet of ocean surface.

On August 19, 2002, the United States Army Corps of Engineers issued a permit to Cape Wind under § 10 of the Rivers and Harbors Act of 1899, 33 U.S.C. § 401 et seq., for construction of the SMDS Cape Wind neither sought nor obtained permits for the SMDS project under Massachusetts law. A few weeks later, the Coast Guard issued a public notice that construction of the data tower would commence on or about October 11, 2002. Construction was briefly delayed when Ten Taxpayer obtained a temporary restraining order from a state court in a related lawsuit. Ten Taxpayer voluntarily dismissed that suit, however, and the temporary restraining order lapsed by its own terms. On October 27, 2002, Cape Wind began construction of the SMDS. It is now complete and in operation.

Ten Taxpayer filed this action in Barnstable Superior Court on October 16, 2002, shortly before construction of the data tower began. In its complaint, Ten Taxpayer acknowledged that the SMDS site is more than three miles from the nearest Massachusetts shoreline and that, accordingly, the location falls under the jurisdiction of the federal government. Nevertheless, Ten Taxpayer contended, Cape Wind could not build the SMDS without regulatory approval from Massachusetts because Congress has ceded to Massachusetts the power to regulate any activity affecting fishing in Nantucket Sound. Under the Massachusetts laws regulating fisheries and fish habitats, administrative approval is required for structures erected on the seabed. Because Cape Wind did not obtain such approval, Ten Taxpayer alleged, the SMDS project was in violation of Massachusetts law. Ten Taxpayer sought an injunction blocking construction of the SMDS or, if the court would not enjoin construction, a $25,000 fine for every day that the SMDS remained on Horseshoe Shoals. * * *

On November 14, 2002, the district court denied the motion to remand without opinion. Ten Taxpayer appealed that order, but this court dismissed the appeal on the ground that it was not a final judgment.

Meanwhile, on November 6, 2002, Cape Wind filed a motion in federal court to dismiss Ten Taxpayer's complaint. Cape Wind attached to its motion two letters from the Massachusetts Department of Environmental Management indicating that, at least under Mass. Gen. Laws ch. 132A, Massachusetts does not claim regulatory authority over activities on Horseshoe Shoals. Cape Wind also argued that Ten Taxpayer lacks standing to assert the Commonwealth's regulatory interest in offshore lands.

On August 19, 2003, the district court granted Cape Wind's motion to dismiss. Ten Taxpayers Citizen Group v. Cape Wind Assocs., LLC, 278 F.Supp.2d 98, 101 (D.Mass.2003). The court concluded that although Congress did delegate to Massachusetts the power to regulate fishing in Nantucket Sound, that grant did not confer on the Commonwealth a general warrant to "polic[e] the entire Nantucket Sound for environmental disturbances that could impact fishing." Id. Massachusetts had no authority over the construction of the SMDS, and thus no state permits were required. Id. * * *

II.

This case implicates the complex and rather obscure body of law that divides regulatory authority over Nantucket Sound between the state and federal governments. Because that body of law is essential to our disposition of this appeal, we summarize it briefly.

A. Regulation of the Seabed and Attached Structures

As a general rule, "paramount rights to the offshore seabed inhere in the Federal Government as an incident of national sovereignty." United States v. Maine (Maine I), 420 U.S. 515, 524 (1975). In a series of cases beginning in 1947, the Supreme Court established that the United States enjoys exclusive title in the lands underlying the sea, regardless of a state's historical claims to the waters off its coast. [citations omitted.] Together, those cases established that the "control and disposition" of the seabed is "the business of the Federal Government rather than the States." Maine I, 420 U.S. at 522, 95 S.Ct. 1155.

That background rule, however, has been modified by Congress in several significant respects. Most importantly, Congress in 1953 passed the Submerged Lands Act (SLA), 43 U.S.C. § 1301 et seq., which grants to the states full title to the seabed within three geographical miles of their shores. See 43 U.S.C. §§ 1301, 1311. Moreover, Congress expressly recognized that three-mile line as the official seaward boundary of the coastal states. Id. § 1312.

Shortly thereafter, however, Congress enacted the Outer Continental Shelf Lands Act of 1953 (OCSLA), 43 U.S.C. § 1331 et seq. A major purpose of the OCSLA was to specify that federal law governs on the "outer Continental Shelf"—defined as all submerged lands under U.S. sovereign control lying seaward of the three-mile boundary, see 43 U.S.C. § 1331(a)—and on any fixed structures attached to the outer Continental Shelf. Rodrigue v. Aetna Casualty & Surety Co., 395 U.S. 352, 355 (1969); see also 43 U.S.C. § 1332 (declaring it to be "the policy of the United States that . . . the subsoil and seabed of the outer Continental Shelf appertain to the United States and are subject to its jurisdiction, control, and power of disposition"). The OCSLA makes the Constitution, laws, and civil and political jurisdiction of the United States fully applicable to the outer Continental Shelf. 43 U.S.C. § 1333(a)(1). It also establishes nationwide rules for the leasing and development of natural resources in the seabed outside of state territory. Id. § 1337. Further, the OCSLA provides a federal cause of action for any person aggrieved by a violation of those rules, id. § 1349(a)(1), and grants the federal district courts jurisdiction to hear such cases, id. § 1349(b). It is, in short, a sweeping assertion of federal supremacy over the submerged lands outside of the three-mile SLA boundary. See id. § 1332 (declaring it to be "the policy of the United States that . . . the outer Continental Shelf is a vital national resource reserve held by the Federal Government for the public" (emphasis added)).

In 1975, the Supreme Court confirmed this broad understanding of the OCSLA in Maine I. The United States had brought an original complaint in the Supreme Court against thirteen states bordering the Atlantic Ocean, alleging that each state had claimed some right or title in the outer Continental Shelf that was inconsistent with federal interests. 420 U.S. at 516–17. * * * The Supreme Court ruled for the United States, reaffirming that "paramount rights" in the seabed belong to the federal government as national sovereign. Id. at 524. The SLA, the Court acknowledged, had transferred title to the states in a narrow band of the seabed. But that statute did not alter the federal government's rights outside of that narrow band. Id. at 526. On the contrary, the Court explained, Congress in the OCSLA had "emphatically implemented its view that the United States has paramount rights to the seabed beyond the three-mile limit." Id.

B. Regulation of Fishing and Marine Fisheries

With the framework for regulating the seabed thus settled, Congress in 1976 enacted the Magnuson (now Magnuson–Stevens) Fishery Conservation and Management Act, 16 U.S.C. § 1801 et seq.

Like the OCSLA, the Magnuson–Stevens Act asserts federal control over the waters outside of the three-mile limit of state jurisdiction. The Act creates a "national framework for conserving and managing marine fisheries." S.Rep. No. 104–276, at 2 (1996), U.S.Code Cong. & Admin.News 1996 at 4073, 4074 (describing the history and purposes of the Act). It claims for the federal government "exclusive fishery management authority" in outer Continental Shelf waters within and beyond the United States's "exclusive economic zone," which extends approximately 197 nautical miles seaward from the three-mile boundary of state jurisdiction. See 16 U.S.C. § 1811. Within that exclusive economic zone, the Act further claims for the United States "sovereign rights . . . over all fish, and all Continental Shelf fishery resources." Id. § 1811(a); see also id. § 1801(c)(1) (declaring Congress's intent "to maintain without change the existing territorial or other ocean jurisdiction of the United States for all purposes other than the conservation and management of fishery resources").

At the same time, the Magnuson–Stevens Act establishes that the states enjoy the power to regulate fishing activities within their borders, including within the three-mile SLA boundary: "[N]othing in this chapter shall be construed as extending or diminishing the jurisdiction or authority of any State within its boundaries." 16 U.S.C. § 1856(a)(1). By so providing, Congress "confirmed state jurisdiction over fisheries within a State's internal waters and, for coastal states, out to the three-mile limit." Davrod Corp. v. Coates, 971 F.2d 778, 786 (1st Cir.1992). . . .

C. Federal v. State Jurisdiction in Nantucket Sound

Nantucket Sound, where the disputed tower has been built, presents special difficulties in distinguishing the respective spheres of state and federal jurisdiction. Nantucket Sound is almost completely enclosed by Massachusetts's territorial sea; only at the extreme eastern end of the Sound does a channel of federal water approximately one mile wide connect it to the open ocean. But the Sound is a large body of water, and its center portion—including the site of Cape Wind's data tower on Horseshoe Shoal—is more than three miles from any coast.

* * * But there is a complication. In 1984 * * Congress passed a bill defining all of Nantucket Sound to be within the "jurisdiction and authority" of Massachusetts "[f]or the purposes of" the Magnuson–Stevens Act. See Pub.L. No. 98–623, § 404(4), 98 Stat. 3394, 3408 (Nov. 8, 1984) (codified at 16 U.S.C. § 1856(a)(2)(B)). * * *[T]his court held that § 1856(a)(2)(B) "expressly confirms" Massachusetts's power to regulate

the length of fishing vessels in Nantucket Sound. See 971 F.2d at 786. In this case, Ten Taxpayer contends that the same provision authorizes Massachusetts to regulate the construction of Cape Wind's data tower, which Ten Taxpayer claims has the potential to affect fishing and fish habitats. * * *

1. Scope of the Asserted Massachusetts Statutes

First, we are extremely doubtful that the Massachusetts statutes on which Ten Taxpayer relies apply to the SMDS site. Obviously, no permit was required for the SMDS if Massachusetts has not purported to regulate activities on that site. Ten Taxpayer asserts claims under three Massachusetts statutes: Mass. Gen. Laws chapters 91, 130, and 132A. On our reading of Massachusetts law, none of those statutes applies to the erection of a tower on Horseshoe Shoals.

In Count I of its complaint, Ten Taxpayer asserts that Cape Wind failed to comply with Mass. Gen. Laws ch. 130. Ten Taxpayer is correct that chapter 130, which regulates fishing and marine fisheries in Massachusetts, applies broadly to "all marine fisheries and fish within the jurisdiction of the commonwealth." Id. § 1. Ten Taxpayer's claim, however, arises under § 16, which is considerably more narrow: "Any occupation under this chapter of tide waters or any work done therein, shall be subject to the pertinent [permitting and licensing] provisions of chapter ninety-one."

Significantly, the term "tide waters" is not defined in chapter 130 or in the implementing regulations, and there are no published Massachusetts cases interpreting § 16. Ten Taxpayer argues that "tide waters" embraces all waters "subject to the rise and fall of the tides"—a definition that, it says, includes Horseshoe Shoals, where Coast Guard records indicate that the sea depth varies by as much as three feet between high and low tides.

In our view, that interpretation is too broad. Massachusetts cases referring to "tide waters," "tidal waters," "tidewaters," and the like invariably concern developments in harbors or along the shoreline. [Citations omitted]. At most, the term refers to the waters "belong[ing] to the Commonwealth." Trio Algarvio, 795 N.E.2d at 1153 n. 9. * * * We conclude that Mass. Gen. Laws ch. 130, § 16 is inapplicable to the SMDS site by its own terms.

In any event, even if § 16 were applicable on Horseshoe Shoals, we would still conclude that no permit was required.* * * The DEP's regulations . . . limit this licensing and permitting requirement to activities in "waterways" and "filled tidelands." Id. § 9.04. Neither of those terms, as defined in the regulations, embraces Horseshoe Shoals. Consequently, Cape Wind was not obligated to seek a permit for its data tower under Mass. Gen. Laws ch. 91.

Finally, Ten Taxpayer asserts in Count II of its complaint that Cape Wind was required to obtain approval for the SMDS under the Massachusetts Ocean Sanctuaries Act, Mass. Gen. Laws ch. 132A. Chapter 132A expressly provides that Nantucket Sound is within the Cape and Islands Ocean Sanctuary. See id. § 13(c). With few exceptions, the statute prohibits "the building of any structure on the seabed" in any ocean sanctuary. Id. § 15.* * *

The problem with this theory is that the Massachusetts Department of Environmental Management (DEM), which is charged with implementing the Ocean Sanctuaries Act, id. § 12C, including the "care, oversight and control" of ocean sanctuaries, id. § 14; Mass. Regs.Code tit. 302, § 5.09, has expressly disclaimed authority over Horseshoe Shoals. In a letter to counsel for Ten Taxpayer dated January 24, 2002, Myron Gildesgame, the DEM's director of the Office of Water Resources and the agency's official Ocean Sanctuaries Coordinator, explained that the Cape and Islands Ocean Sanctuary is not considered to include the Horseshoe Shoals area. Although chapter 132A purports to include Nantucket Sound in that sanctuary, that legislation was passed prior to the Supreme Court's decision [that all of Nantucket Sound was not state waters]. Now, he concluded, "jurisdiction over the central portion of the Sound, including Horseshoe Shoals, is with the federal government." * * *

2. Inconsistency with Federal Law

* * *

In our view, the OCSLA leaves no room for states to require licenses or permits for the erection of structures on the seabed on the outer Continental Shelf. Congress retained for the federal government the exclusive power to authorize or prohibit specific uses of the seabed beyond three miles from shore. See § 1333(a)(3) ("The provisions of this section for adoption of State law as the law of the United States shall never be interpreted as a basis for claiming any interest in or jurisdiction on behalf of any State for any purpose over the seabed and subsoil of the outer Continental Shelf. . . . "). If adopted and enforced on the outer Continental Shelf, statutes like Mass. Gen. Laws chs. 91 and 132A, which require the approval of state agencies prior to construction, would effectively grant state governments a veto power over the disposition of the national seabed. That result is fundamentally inconsistent with the OCSLA. See id. § 1332(3) (declaring it to be the policy of the United States that "the outer Continental Shelf is a vital *national* reserve held by the Federal Government for the public, which should be made available for expeditious and orderly development, subject to environmental safeguards, in a manner which is consistent with the maintenance of competition and other *national* needs" (emphasis added)).

Ten Taxpayer contends that the Magnuson–Stevens Act, which was enacted after the OCSLA, changed this calculus by defining the "body of water commonly known as Nantucket Sound" to be within the "jurisdiction and authority" of Massachusetts. See 16 U.S.C. § 1856(a)(2)(B). Yet nothing in the Magnuson–Stevens Act purports to repeal or amend the OCSLA. Cf. Passamaquoddy Tribe v. Maine, 75 F.3d 784, 790 (1st Cir.1996) (implied repeal of federal statutes is disfavored). On the contrary, the two statutes can readily coexist: the Magnuson–Stevens Act authorizes Massachusetts to regulate fishing-related conduct throughout Nantucket Sound, but "the subsoil and seabed of the outer Continental Shelf, and artificial islands and fixed structures erected thereon," 43 U.S.C. § 1333(a)(2)(A), remain the exclusive province of the federal government. Congress was perfectly clear in the Magnuson–Stevens Act that it did not intend to alter the rights of the United States in the outer Continental Shelf. See 16 U.S.C. § 1801(c)(1) (declaring it to be the policy of Congress in the Magnuson–Stevens Act "to maintain without change the existing territorial or other ocean jurisdiction of the United States for all purposes other than the conservation and management of fishery resources").

We conclude that any Massachusetts permit requirement that might apply to the SMDS project is inconsistent with federal law and thus inapplicable on Horseshoe Shoals under the OCSLA. The district court did not err in dismissing Ten Taxpayer's complaint.

IV.

The judgment of the district court is affirmed. Costs are awarded to Cape Wind.

NOTES AND QUESTIONS

1. The court in *Cape Wind* recognized that Congress had granted the state the right to regulate fisheries in the area beyond state waters. The court finds, however, that this grant of authority was not inconsistent with the exclusive jurisdiction of the federal government over the seabed and subsoil of the OCS for construction of structures. How would the analysis have changed if the state had brought an action asserting that the structures were to be constructed in areas designated for fisheries activities or habitat critical for specified fisheries?

2. The explicit or implicit exercise of exclusive control by the federal government is known as field preemption.

Field preemption arises when state law "regulates conduct in a field that Congress intended the Federal Government to occupy exclusively." English v. Gen. Elec. Co., 496 U.S. 72, 79 (1990). "We will find implicit preemption where the intent of Congress is clearly manifested, or implicit from a pervasive scheme of federal regulation that leaves no room for state and local supplementation, or implicit from the fact that the federal law touches a field (e.g. foreign affairs) in which 'the federal interest is so dominant that the federal system will be assumed to preclude enforcement of state laws on the same subject.' " Barber, 42 F.3d at 1189. In deciding whether a federal law preempts a state counterpart, our only task is to ascertain the intent of Congress. See, e.g., PMSA v. Aubry, 918 F.2d 1409, 1415 (9th Cir. 1990).

Pac. Merch. Shipping Ass'n v. Goldstene, 639 F.3d 11, 22–23 (2011).

Although there is a presumption against federal preemption of state law, "an 'assumption' of nonpreemption is not triggered when the State regulates in an area where there has been a history of significant federal presence." United States v. Locke, 529 U.S. 89 at 108 (2000). Are all regulated activities beyond state waters in this category?

3. Are regulations to protect state territory or citizens from pollution from activities outside state waters subject to the presumption against preemption? In Huron Portland Cement Co. v. City of Detroit, 362 U.S. 440 (1960), the Supreme Court observed that "[l]egislation designed to free from pollution the very air that people breathe clearly falls within the exercise of even the most traditional concept of what is compendiously known as the police power." Other courts have found that "[e]nvironmental regulation traditionally has been a matter of state authority." Exxon Mobil Corp. v. U.S. EPA, 217 F.3d 1246, 1255 (9th Cir. 2000). The Huron Portland Cement case involved the regulation air pollution from vessels in port. Compare this case to Goldstene at Chapter 8, where the state regulation purports to regulate air pollution from vessels up to 24 nautical miles offshore.

4. In a case involving sponge fisheries beyond state waters regulated by both the state of Florida (equipment used) and the federal government (size of sponges harvested), the Supreme Court stated: "According to familiar principles, Congress having occupied but a limited field, the authority of the State to protect its interests by additional or supplementary legislation otherwise valid is not impaired." Skiriotes v. Florida, 313 U.S. 69 (1941). What "interests" of a state are legally relevant to legitimacy of state regulations reaching beyond state waters: the state citizenship of the individual; the state registry of the vessel; the effects of fishing beyond state waters on the state's fishery; the ability of the state to enforce state laws effectively?

5. Because admiralty jurisdiction is vested in the federal government by the Constitution, cases involving maritime locations present particularly difficult questions.

IN RE OIL SPILL BY THE OIL RIG "DEEPWATER HORIZON"
United States District Court, E.D. Louisiana, 2011
808 F.Supp.2d 943

BARBIER, DISTRICT JUDGE.

* * *

D. Plaintiffs' state law claims

* * * Although Plaintiffs acknowledge that admiralty jurisdiction applies to this case, they insist that substantive maritime law does not preempt their state-law claims because state law can "supplement" general maritime law, either where there is a substantive gap in maritime law or where there is no conflict with maritime law. Plaintiffs also argue that OPA [Oil Pollution Act of 1990] contains a state-law savings provision, which preserves these claims. * * *

* * *

The focus turns, then, to the relationship between federal maritime law and state law. As mentioned, with the admiralty jurisdiction comes substantive maritime law. This means that general maritime law—an amalgam of traditional common law rules, modifications of those rules, and newly created rules—applies to this matter to the extent it is not displaced by federal statute. E. River S.S. Corp. v. Transamerica Delaval, Inc., 476 U.S. 858, 864 (1986). This framework, established by the Constitution,[6] intends that a consistent, uniform system will govern maritime commerce. See The Lottawanna, 88 U.S. 558, 575 (1874) ("It certainly could not have been the intention to place the rules and limits of maritime law under the disposal and regulation of the several States, as that would have defeated the uniformity and consistency at which the Constitution aimed on all subjects of a commercial character affecting the intercourse of the States with each other or with foreign states.").[7] Admiralty

---

[6] Article III, § 2 extends the judicial power to "all cases of admiralty and maritime jurisdiction." Congress legislates in this area by virtue of the Interstate Commerce Clause and Necessary and Proper Clause. U.S. Const. Art. I, § 8. The Supremacy Clause, Article VI, ensures federal maritime law supercedes state law. See 1 Thomas J. Schoenbaum, Admiralty and Maritime Law §§ 4–1 to 4–2 (4th ed.2004).

[7] See also Knickerbocker Ice Co. v. Stewart, 253 U.S. 149, 157 (1920) ("The Constitution itself adopted and established, as part of the laws of the United States, approved rules of the general maritime law and empowered Congress to legislate in respect of them and other matters within the admiralty and maritime jurisdiction. Moreover, it took from the states all power, by legislation or judicial decision, to contravene the essential purposes of, or to work material injury to, characteristic features of such law or to interfere with its proper harmony and uniformity in its international and interstate relations. To preserve adequate harmony and appropriate uniform rules relating to maritime matters and bring them within control of the federal government was the fundamental purpose; and to such definite end Congress was empowered to legislate within that sphere."); Schoenbaum, supra note 6, § 4–1 at 158 (stating that a desire for national uniformity drove the drafters to vest the federal courts with jurisdiction over admiralty cases). Although Knickerbocker Ice and its predecessor, Southern Pacific Co. v. Jensen, 244 U.S. 205

does not entirely exclude state law, however, and States may "create rights and liabilities with respect to conduct within their borders, when the state action does not run counter to federal laws or the essential features of an exclusive federal jurisdiction." Romero v. Int'l Terminal Operating Co., 358 U.S. 354, 375 n. 42 (1959) (emphasis added; internal quotations and citations omitted).

But this case does not concern conduct within state borders (waters). This casualty occurred over the Outer Continental Shelf—an area of "exclusive federal jurisdiction"—on waters deemed to be the "high seas." 43 U.S.C. §§ 1332(2), 1333(a)(1)(A). * * * While it is recognized that States have an interest to protect their citizens, property, and resources from oil pollution, to subject a discharger to the varying laws of each state into which its oil has flowed would contravene a fundamental purpose of maritime law: "[t]o preserve adequate harmony and appropriate uniform rules relating to maritime matters." Knickerbocker Ice Co., see supra note 7. Thus, to the extent state law could apply to conduct outside state waters, in this case it must "yield to the needs of a uniform federal maritime law." Romero, 358 U.S. at 373.

Plaintiffs argue that state law is not preempted in this instance because state law can supplement maritime law. Plaintiffs rely heavily on Yamaha Motor Corp. v. Calhoun, which involved a young girl killed in a jet ski accident in state territorial waters, where there is no federal statute providing a remedy for wrongful death. 516 U.S. 199 (1996). The decedent's parents attempted to sue under the state wrongful death statute. The question in Yamaha was whether general maritime law's wrongful death action, often called the "Moragne action" (named for the case that created it, Moragne v. States Marine Lines, Inc., 398 U.S. 375 (1970)), preempted state law.

The Court held that state law was not preempted. The Yamaha Court noted that before the Moragne action was created in 1970, courts permitted state wrongful death statutes to fill the substantive gap in the law. * * * Accordingly, Yamaha does not support using state law to supplement maritime law in this case, since there is no substantive gap for state law to fill . . . ; remedies are available under both OPA and general maritime law. * * *

* * *

Plaintiffs' contention that OPA's savings provisions preserve its state-law claims is also unavailing. These provisions state:

(1916), have certainly been limited by later decisions, they still retain "vitality." See Askew v. Am. Waterways Operators, Inc., 411 U.S. 325, 344 (1973).

(a) Preservation of State authorities; Solid Waste Disposal Act

Nothing in this Act or the Act of March 3, 1851 shall—

> (1) affect, or be construed or interpreted as preempting, the authority of any State or political subdivision thereof from imposing any additional liability or requirements with respect to—

(A) the discharge of oil or other pollution by oil within such State; or

(B) any removal activities in connection with such a discharge; or

> (2) affect, or be construed or interpreted to affect or modify in any way the obligations or liabilities of any person under the Solid Waste Disposal Act (42 U.S.C. 6901 et seq.) or State law, including common law.

* * *

(c) Additional requirements and liabilities; penalties

Nothing in this Act, the Act of March 3, 1851 (46 U.S.C. 183 et seq.), or section 9509 of title 26, shall in any way affect, or be construed to affect, the authority of the United States or any State or political subdivision thereof—

> (1) to impose additional liability or additional requirements; or

> (2) to impose, or to determine the amount of, any fine or penalty (whether criminal or civil in nature) for any violation of law;

relating to the discharge, or substantial threat of a discharge, of oil.

33 U.S.C. § 2718. These provisions evince Congress' intent to preserve the States' police power to govern pollution discharges within their territorial waters. The Court does not read as them giving States the power to govern out-of-state conduct affecting multiple states. "The usual function of a saving clause is to preserve something from immediate interference—not to create; and the rule is that expression by the Legislature of an erroneous opinion concerning the law does not alter it." Knickerbocker Ice, 253 U.S. at 162, 40 S.Ct. 438. In other words, although Congress has expressed its intent to not preempt state law, this intent does not delegate to the States a power that the Constitution vested in the federal government.

This conclusion is consistent with the Supreme Court's rationale in International Paper Co. v. Ouellette, 479 U.S. 481 (1987). There the Court addressed the question of "whether the [Clean Water] Act preempts a common-law nuisance suit filed in a Vermont court under Vermont law, when the source of the alleged injury is located in New York." Id. at 483.
* * *

Notwithstanding [the savings] provisions, the Ouellette Court determined that ". . . when a court considers a state-law claim concerning interstate water pollution that is subject to the CWA, the court must apply the law of the State in which the point source is located." Id. at 487. According to the Court, "[a]pplication of an affected State's law to an out-of-state source would . . . undermine the important goals of efficiency and predictability in the permit system." Id. at 496. The Court also noted that prohibiting an action under the affected State's laws did not leave the plaintiffs without a remedy, as they could avail themselves of either the source State's law or the CWA's citizen suit provision. Id. at 497–98 & n. 18. * * *[S]imilar goals exist in maritime law (uniformity), as discussed above. Thus, just as the Supreme Court limited the state-law claims preserved by the CWA savings clause, this Court finds it appropriate to limit state-law claims purportedly saved by OPA.

Plaintiffs' reliance on Askew v. American Waterways Operators, Inc. is unpersuasive despite that Court's observance that ship-to-shore pollution control is "historically within the reach of the police power of the States," and "not silently taken away from the States by the Admiralty Extension Act." 411 U.S. 325, 337 (1973). Askew involved a challenge to the constitutionality of the Florida Oil Spill Prevention and Pollution Control Act, which governed state and private damages incurred as a result of an oil spill in the State's territorial waters. The Court also noted that previous decisions "gave broad 'recognition of the authority of the States to create rights and liabilities with respect to conduct within their borders. . . .' " Id. at 340 (emphasis added). Thus, Askew does not suggest that state laws could apply to an out-of-state polluter. Askew is also distinguishable on the grounds that there was no overlap between the relevant federal and state statutes at issue, as there is with OPA. The federal statute in Askew addressed federal cleanup costs; the state statute addressed state and private damages. Thus, there was no available federal statutory remedy for the damages sought in Askew.

* * *

Accordingly, Plaintiffs' state common-law claims * * * are dismissed. Because the Court finds that state law is inapplicable to this case, Plaintiffs' arguments regarding the economic-loss doctrines of various states are moot.

B. SUBMERGED CULTURAL RESOURCES IN THE MARGINAL SEAS

New technologies and improved research techniques have led to the discovery of an increasing number of sunken and lost vessels in recent years, and conflicts concerning ownership and jurisdiction over these vessels have led to complex court cases. Both the federal government and the coastal states view ancient shipwrecks off the coasts of the United States as having significance beyond the monetary value of the recoverable cargo. The historic importance of such shipwrecks is illustrated by the designation of the site of the Civil War wreck of the USS Monitor as a national marine sanctuary. Marine archaeologists portray private salvage of historic wrecks as the equivalent of "looting" an archaeological or historic site. Private salvors do not perceive themselves as looters and point out that without their investment of resources and capital, historic wrecks would never be located.

During the last three decades, numerous shipwreck cases have addressed the appropriateness of the application of the maritime law of salvage or of finds, as well as issues of jurisdiction, preemption, ownership, and Eleventh amendment immunity of states from suit. The problem arises because the Submerged Lands Act of 1953 did not give states clear ownership of historic shipwrecks. See selected provisions on pp. 83–86. Prior to the passage of the Abandoned Shipwreck Act (ASA) of 1987, 43 U.S.C. § 2101 et seq., a split of opinion existed over whether the state received title or even the right to regulate ownership and recovery of abandoned shipwrecks situated on offshore submerged lands. Historically, such rights were governed by federal admiralty principles. According to the district court in Cobb Coin v. Unidentified Wrecked and Abandoned Sailing Vessel, 525 F. Supp. 186, 214–16 (S.D. Fla. 1981), the "paramount rights" ceded by the United States to the individual coastal states through the Submerged Lands Act included the right to determine the disposition of the natural resources in the area, not historic wreck sites that may be found there. However, in Subaqueous Exploration v. Unidentified Wrecked Vessel, 577 F. Supp. 597, 612–13 (D. Md. 1983), the district court held that the rights and powers granted to the states by the Submerged Lands Act included the right to regulate the ownership and recovery of abandoned shipwrecks situated on submerged lands within a state.

In the ASA, Congress resolved the issue in an interesting two-step process. First, Congress asserted title of the United States to all abandoned shipwrecks. 43 U.S.C. § 2105(a). Congress then transferred title to the state of ". . . any abandoned shipwreck that is—(1) embedded in submerged lands of a State; (2) embedded in coralline formations protected by a State on submerged lands of a State; or (3) on submerged lands of a State and is included in or determined eligible for inclusion in the National Register." Id. § 2105(c). Shipwrecks located on public lands of the United States remained the property of the United States and shipwrecks located on lands owned by Indian tribes became the property of the tribe. Id. § 2105(d).

The ASA did not define "abandoned" or totally clarify all the jurisdictional issues surrounding the shipwreck controversy. The U.S. Supreme

Court first addressed the application of the ASA in 1998, in a case known as The Brother Jonathan.

CALIFORNIA AND STATE LANDS COMMISSION V. DEEP SEA RESEARCH, INC.

Supreme Court of the United States, 1998
523 U.S. 491

JUSTICE O'CONNOR delivered the opinion of the Court.

* * *

The dispute before us arises out of respondent Deep Sea Research (DSR's) assertion of rights to both the vessel and cargo of the Brother Jonathan, a 220-foot, wooden-hulled, double side-wheeled steamship that struck a submerged rock in July 1865 during a voyage between San Francisco and Vancouver. It took less than an hour for the Brother Jonathan to sink, and most of the ship's passengers and crew perished. The ship's cargo, also lost in the accident, included a shipment of up to $2 million in gold and a United States Army payroll that some estimates place at $250,000. * * *

Shortly after the disaster, five insurance companies paid claims totaling $48,490 for the loss of certain cargo. It is unclear whether the remaining cargo and the ship itself were insured. Prior to DSR's location of the vessel, the only recovery of cargo from the shipwreck may have occurred in the 1930's, when a fisherman found 22 pounds of gold bars minted in 1865 and believed to have come from the Brother Jonathan. The fisherman died, however, without revealing the source of his treasure. There appears to be no evidence that either the State of California or the insurance companies that paid claims have attempted to locate or recover the wreckage.

In 1991, DSR filed an action in the United States District Court for the Northern District of California seeking rights to the wreck of the Brother Jonathan and its cargo under that court's in rem admiralty jurisdiction. California intervened, asserting an interest in the Brother Jonathan based on the Abandoned Shipwreck Act of 1987 (ASA) * * *. According to California, the ASA applies because the Brother Jonathan is abandoned and is both embedded on state land and eligible for inclusion in the National Register of Historic Places (National Register). California also laid claim to the Brother Jonathan under Cal. Pub. Res. Code Ann. § 6313 (hereinafter § 6313), which vests title in the Sate "to all abandoned shipwrecks . . . on or in the tide and submerged lands of California."

* * *

The District Court held two hearings on the motions. The first focused on whether the wreck is located within California's territorial waters, and the second concerned the possible abandonment, embeddedness, and historical significance of the shipwreck, issues relevant to California's claims to the res. For purposes of the pending motions, DSR stipulated that the Brother Jonathan is located upon submerged lands belonging to California.

After the hearings, the District Court concluded that the State failed to demonstrate a "colorable claim" to the Brother Jonathan under federal law, reasoning that the State had not established by a preponderance of the evidence that the ship is abandoned, embedded in the sea floor, or eligible for listing in the National Register as is required to establish title under the ASA. As for California's state law claim, the court determined that the ASA pre-empts § 6313. Accordingly, the court issued a warrant for the arrest of the Brother Jonathan, appointed DSR custodian of the shipwreck subject to further order of the court, and ordered DSR to take possession of the shipwreck as its exclusive salvor pending the court's determination of "the manner in which the wreck and its cargo, or the proceeds therefrom, should be distributed."

* * *

The Court of Appeals for the Ninth Circuit affirmed the District Court's orders. The court first concluded that § 6313 is pre-empted by the ASA because the state statute "takes title to shipwrecks that do not meet the requirements of the ASA and which are therefore within the exclusive admiralty jurisdiction of the federal courts." With respect to the State's claim under the ASA, the court presumed that "a federal court has both the power and duty to determine whether a case falls within its subject matter jurisdiction" * * *.

By concluding that the State must prove its claim to the Brother Jonathan by a preponderance of the evidence in order to invoke the immunity afforded by the Eleventh Amendment, the Ninth Circuit diverged from other Courts of Appeals that have held that a State need only make a bare assertion to ownership of a res. We granted certiorari to address whether a State's Eleventh Amendment immunity in an in rem admiralty action depends upon evidence of the State's ownership of the res, and to consider the related questions whether the Brother Jonathan is subject to the ASA and whether the ASA pre-empts § 6313.

II.

The judicial power of federal courts extends "to all Cases of admiralty and maritime Jurisdiction." Art. III, § 2, cl. 1. The federal courts have had a unique role in admiralty cases since the birth of this Nation, because "maritime commerce was . . . the jugular vein of the Thirteen States." F. Frankfurter & J. Landis, The Business of the Supreme Court 7 (1927). Accordingly, "the need for a body of law applicable throughout the nation was recognized by every shade of opinion in the Constitutional Convention." Ibid. * * * That jurisdiction encompasses "maritime causes of action begun and carried on as proceedings in rem, that is, where a vessel or thing is itself treated as the offender and made the defendant by name or description in order to enforce a lien."

The jurisdiction of the federal courts is constrained, however, by the Eleventh Amendment, under which "the Judicial power of the United States shall not be construed to extend to any suit in law or equity, commenced or prosecuted against one of the United States by Citizens of another State, or by Citizens or Subjects of any Foreign State." * * * According to this Court's precedents, a State may not be sued in federal court by one of its own citizens and a state official is immune from suit in federal court for actions taken in an official capacity.

The Court has not always charted a clear path in explaining the interaction between the Eleventh Amendment and the federal courts' in rem admiralty jurisdiction. Early cases involving the disposition of "prize" vessels captured during wartime appear to have assumed that federal courts could adjudicate the in rem disposition of the bounty even when state officials raised an objection. As Justice Story explained, in admiralty actions in rem,

> "the jurisdiction of the [federal] court is founded upon the possession of the thing; and if the State should interpose a claim for the property, it does not act merely in the character of a defendant, but as an actor. Besides, the language of the [Eleventh] Amendment is, that 'the judicial power of the United States shall not be construed to extend to any suit in law or equity.' But a suit in the admiralty is not, correctly speaking, a suit in law or in equity; but is often spoken of in contradistinction to both." 2 J. Story, Commentaries on the Constitution of the United States § 1689, pp. 491–492 (5th ed. 1891).

Justice Washington, riding Circuit, expressed the same view in United States v. Bright, 24 F. Cas. 1232, 1236 (No. 14,647) (C.C. Pa. 1809), where he reasoned:

> "In cases of admiralty and maritime jurisdiction the property in dispute is generally in the possession of the court, or of persons bound to produce it, or its equivalent, and the proceedings are in rem. The court decides in whom the right is, and distributes the proceeds accordingly. In such a case the court need not depend upon the good will of a state claiming an interest in the thing to enable it to execute its decree. All the world are parties to such a suit, and of course are

bound by the sentence. The state may interpose her claim and have it decided. But she cannot lie by, and, after the decree is passed say that she was a party, and therefore not bound, for want of jurisdiction in the court."

Although those statements might suggest that the Eleventh Amendment has little application in in rem admiralty proceedings, subsequent decisions have altered that understanding of the federal courts' role. In Ex parte Ex parte New York, 256 U.S. 490 (1921) (New York I), the Court explained that admiralty and maritime jurisdiction is not wholly exempt from the operation of the Eleventh Amendment, thereby rejecting the views of Justices Story and Washington.* * *

The Court's most recent case involving an in rem admiralty action, Florida Dept. of State v. Treasure Salvors, Inc., 458 U.S. 670 (1982), addressed whether the Eleventh Amendment "bars an in rem admiralty action seeking to recover property owned by a state." A plurality of the Court suggested that . . . the State's possession of maritime artifacts was unauthorized, and the State therefore could not invoke the Eleventh Amendment to block their arrest. As the plurality explained, "since the state officials do not have a colorable claim to possession of the artifacts, they may not invoke the Eleventh Amendment to block execution of the warrant of arrest."

That reference to a "colorable claim" is at the crux of this case. Both the District Court and the Ninth Circuit interpreted the "colorable claim" requirement as imposing a burden on the State to demonstrate by a preponderance of the evidence that the Brother Jonathan meets the criteria set forth in the ASA. Other Courts of Appeals have concluded that a State need only make a bare assertion to ownership of a res in order to establish its sovereign immunity in an in rem admiralty action.

By our reasoning, however, either approach glosses over an important distinction present here. In this case, unlike in Treasure Salvors, DSR asserts rights to a res that is not in the possession of the State. The Eleventh Amendment's role in that type of dispute was not decided by the plurality opinion in Treasure Salvors, which decided "whether a federal court exercising admiralty in rem jurisdiction may seize property held by state officials under a claim that the property belongs to the State." * * *

Nor did the opinions in New York I or New York II address a situation comparable to this case. The holding in New York I explained that, although the suit at issue was styled as an in rem libel action seeking recovery of damages against tugboats chartered by the State, the proceedings were actually "in the nature of an action in personam against [the Superintendent of Public Works of the State of New York], not individually, but in his [official] capacity." The action in New York II was an in rem suit against a vessel described as being "at all times mentioned in the libel and at present . . . the absolute property of the State of New York, in its possession and control, and employed in the public service of the State for governmental uses and purposes." * * *

It is true that statements in the fractured opinions in Treasure Salvors might be read to suggest that a federal court may not undertake in rem adjudication of the State's interest in property without the State's consent, regardless of the status of the res. Those assertions, however, should not be divorced from the context of Treasure Salvors * * *.

* * * Although the Eleventh Amendment bars federal jurisdiction over general title disputes relating to State property interests, it does not necessarily follow that it applies to in rem admiralty actions, or that in such actions, federal courts may not exercise jurisdiction over property that the State does not actually possess.

* * *[A] requirement that a State possess the disputed res in such cases is "consistent with the principle which exempts the [State] from suit and its possession from disturbance by virtue of judicial process." Based on longstanding precedent respecting the federal courts' assumption of in rem admiralty jurisdiction over vessels that are not in the possession of a sovereign, we conclude that the Eleventh Amendment does not bar federal jurisdiction over the Brother Jonathan and, therefore, that the District Court may adjudicate DSR's and the State's claims to the shipwreck. We have no occasion in this case to consider any other circumstances under which an in rem admiralty action might proceed in federal court despite the Eleventh Amendment.

III.

There remains the issue whether the courts below properly concluded that the Brother Jonathan was not abandoned for purposes of the ASA.* * * In light of our ruling that the Eleventh Amendment does not bar complete adjudication of the competing claims to the Brother Jonathan in federal court, the application of the ASA must be reevaluated. Because the record before this Court is limited to the preliminary issues before the District Court, we decline to resolve whether the Brother Jonathan is abandoned within the meaning of the ASA. We leave that issue for reconsideration on remand, with the clarification that the meaning of "abandoned" under the ASA conforms with its meaning under admiralty law.

Our grant of certiorari also encompassed the question whether the courts below properly concluded that the ASA pre-empts § 6313, which apparently operates to transfer title to abandoned shipwrecks not covered by the ASA to the State. Because the District Court's full consideration of the application of the ASA on remand might negate the need to address the pre-emption issue, we decline to undertake that analysis.

Accordingly, the judgment of the Court of Appeals assuming jurisdiction over this case is affirmed, its judgment in all other respects is vacated, and the case is remanded for further proceedings consistent with this opinion.

It is so ordered.

JUSTICE STEVENS, concurring.

In Florida Dept. of State v. Treasure Salvors, Inc. both the four Members of the plurality and the four dissenters agreed that the District Court "did not have power . . . to adjudicate the State's interest in the property without the State's consent." Our reasons for reaching that common conclusion were different, but I am now persuaded that all of us might well have reached a different conclusion if the position of Justices Story and Washington (that the Eleventh Amendment is no bar to any in rem admiralty action) had been brought to our attention. I believe that both opinions made the mistake of assuming that the Eleventh Amendment has the same application to an in rem admiralty action as to any other action seeking possession of property in the control of state officers.

* * *

Having given further consideration to the special characteristics of in rem admiralty actions, and more particularly to the statements by Justice Story and Justice Washington quoted at pages 9 and 10 of the Court's opinion, I am now convinced that we should have affirmed the Treasure Salvors judgment in its entirety. Accordingly, I agree with the Court's holding that the State of California may be bound by a federal court's in rem adjudication of rights to the Brother Jonathan and its cargo.

JUSTICE KENNEDY, with whom JUSTICE GINSBURG and JUSTICE BREYER join, concurring.

I join the opinion of the Court. In my view, the opinion's discussion of Florida Dept. of State v. Treasure Salvors, Inc., does not embed in our law the distinction between a State's possession or nonpossession for purposes of Eleventh Amendment analysis in admiralty cases. In light of the subsisting doubts surrounding that case and Justice Stevens' concurring opinion today, it ought to be evident that the issue is open to reconsideration.

NOTES AND QUESTIONS

1. Congress found both the law of salvage and the law of finds unsuitable for preservation of historic shipwrecks; the ASA specifically provides that neither shall apply to abandoned shipwrecks that have been transferred into state ownership. ASA § 2106(a). In The Brother Jonathan, the Supreme Court found that "abandoned" under the ASA has the same meaning as under admiralty law; therefore, the question of abandonment cannot be deter-

mined under state law. In admiralty law, a shipwreck is abandoned if the title has been affirmatively renounced or when an inference of abandonment can be made from the circumstances. Consequently, in spite of the statutory language rejecting the application of admiralty law to ships transferred to the states by the ASA, a large body of admiralty law concerning abandonment still remains relevant to determining, as a threshold issue, whether a vessel falls within the ASA. Fairport Int'l Exploration v. The Shipwrecked Vessel known as The Captain Lawrence, 177 F.3d 491 (2000), provides an excellent legal analysis of the term abandonment. Abandonment can be express or by inference. Neither lapse of time alone nor the owner's failure to return to a shipwreck site necessarily establishes abandonment, but these aspects do contribute to circumstantial evidence from which abandonment may be inferred. Id. at 500–501. The case specifically addressed the issue of the burden of proof borne by the party asserting abandonment under the ASA and found: "The uniform rule in admiralty is that a finding of abandonment requires proof by clear and convincing evidence." Id. at 501.

2. The legislative history of the ASA suggests that sovereign vessels must be treated differently than private vessels in regard to abandonment. A State Department letter included in the House Report on the ASA states, "the U.S. only abandons its sovereignty over, and title to, sunken U.S. warships by affirmative act; mere passage of time or lack of positive assertions of right are insufficient to establish such abandonment." The letter goes on to say that the U.S. accords the same presumption of non-abandonment to sovereign vessels of other nations that have sunk in U.S. waters while on the non-commercial service of that state. H.R. Rep. No. 100–514(II), at 13 (1988).

In Sea Hunt v. the Unidentified Shipwrecked Vessel, 221 F.3d 634 (2000), the state of Virginia claimed ownership under the ASA of the La Galga and the Juno, Spanish Navy frigates that sank in 1750 and 1802 respectively. The state issued permits to Sea Hunt, a maritime salvage company, to conduct salvage operations and recover artifacts from the wrecks. After the court rejected the authority of the United States to intervene on behalf of Spain, Spain filed a verified claim asserting ownership over the shipwrecks. The court upheld the title of Spain to the vessels, stating:

> Applying the express abandonment standard to sovereign vessels also respects the legitimate interests of the executive branch. While the ASA confers title to abandoned shipwrecks to the states, it does not vitiate important national interests or undermine the well-established prerogatives of sovereign nations. Department of Interior advisory guidelines on the ASA state that a sovereign vessel that appears to have been abandoned "remains the property of the nation to which it belonged at the time of sinking unless that nation has taken formal action to abandon it or to transfer title to another party." 55 Fed. Reg. 50116, 50121 (1990). The State Department has likewise emphasized that its policy is "to recognize claims by foreign governments—such as in this case by the Government of Spain regarding the warships Juno and La Galga—to ownership of foreign warships sunk in waters of the United States without be-

ing captured, and to recognize that title to such sunken warships is not lost absent express abandonment by the sovereign." Statement of Interest, U.S. Dep't of State. Further, the State Department notes, "U.S. domestic law is consistent with the customary international law rule that title to sunken warships may be abandoned only by an express act of abandonment." Id.

Sea Hunt, 221 F.3rd. See also, Odyssey Marine Exploration, Inc. v. Unidentified Shipwrecked Vessel, 657 F.3d 1159 (11th Cir. 2011) (holding that the vessel and cargo were immune from judicial arrest under the Foreign Sovereign Immunities Act (FSIA), 28 U.S.C.S. §§ 1602–1611, and that the cargo aboard the Mercedes was not severable from the shipwreck of the Mercedes in determining immunity because other statutes, including the Sunken Military Craft Act, Pub. L. No. 108–375, §§ 1401–08 (2004), which would govern the salvage claims against the Mercedes, treated cargo as part of the shipwreck).

3. In The Brother Jonathan, the state of California relied on Florida Department of State v. Treasure Salvors, Inc., 458 U.S. 670 (1982), where four members of the plurality and four dissenters had agreed that Treasure Salvors could not sue Florida in federal admiralty court to recover property owned by the state without the state's consent. In that case, however, the state official was found to have acted beyond his authority and the state did "not have even a colorable claim to the artifacts." Subsequent cases have found federal courts to have no in rem admiralty jurisdiction where the state presents a "colorable claim." How did the Supreme Court distinguish The Brother Jonathan? Why does The Brother Jonathan call the result of Treasure Salvors into question?

In a number of earlier cases, the state's "colorable claim" was based on a state law, like Cal. Pub. Res. Code § 1603, rather than the ASA or the SLA. Are such laws likely to survive a preemption challenge when used to assert jurisdiction over shipwrecks that do not fall within the ASA? Note that even before The Brother Jonathan, it was estimated that only about five percent of the shipwrecks in state waters were affected by the ASA.

4. When is a ship "embedded"? In Zych v. Unidentified, Wrecked and Abandoned Vessel, Believed to be the "Seabird," 941 F.2d 525 (7th Cir.1991), the Seventh Circuit Court of Appeals remanded the case for a determination of whether the ship was "embedded" within the definition of the ASA. The court directed that "embedded" is defined as "firmly affixed in the submerged lands or in coralline formations such that the use of tools of excavation is required in order to move the bottom sediments to gain access to the shipwreck, its cargo, and any part thereof[.]" ASA § 2102(a). The term is to be interpreted consistently with the common law exception from the law of finds.

CHAPTER 3

THE PUBLIC TRUST IN COASTAL LANDS AND WATERS

■ ■ ■

Tide lines play an important role in ocean and coastal law. The zones of ocean jurisdiction recognized by the Law of the Sea Convention are measured from the "baseline," which is normally the mean low water line along the coast. (See Figure 1–1, p. 31.) The U.S. Submerged Lands Act of 1953 defined "lands beneath navigable waters" with reference to the ordinary high water mark. Privately owned lands bordering the oceans are often bounded by the mean high water line, and public rights are defined with reference to the high or low tidelines and held in trust by the state. This chapter explores the challenges of defining property ownership in such a manner and the special principles that govern property rights in dynamic shorelines.

1. INTRODUCTION

Within the coastal zone exists a complex mix of common law private and public rights and interests. Generally, legal title to land located above the mean high-tide line to the line of vegetation (the dry sand area) and beyond (the uplands) will be in private hands. However, legal title to the lands below the mean high-tide line (the wet sand area and submerged lands) will be in the state. (See Figure 3–1, next page.)

Coastal waters themselves, of course, are not subject to private ownership and are under the control of the state. Title to the lands located below the mean high-tide line, sometimes referred to as *sovereignty lands or public trust lands*, is generally in the state, and such lands are said to be held by the state in public trust. The beneficiary of this trust is the public, who has the right, subject to reasonable limitations, to use public trust lands and associated waters for a wide variety of commercial and recreational purposes. In this chapter, the origins and scope of the public trust doctrine are examined first.

Figure 3–1: Legal and Geological Zonation Along a Beach

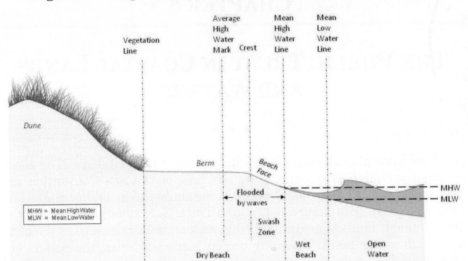

Source: James G. Titus, Rolling Easements Primer 16, Climate Ready Estuaries Web site, U.S. Environmental Protection Agency (June 2011).

Although coastal waters and submerged lands are public trust resources, that does not preclude the existence of private property interests in those same resources. For example, owners of land abutting navigable waters, by reason of their adjacency, may have certain distinctive common law rights or privileges to use adjacent waters and submerged lands. Although the precise nature and extent of these rights or privileges may vary considerably from state to state, to some degree, a common core exists. Historically, these rights were called *littoral rights* if the land abutted the seashore, and *riparian rights* if the land abutted rivers and coastal waters. Today, the distinction is disappearing and being replaced with the generic term *"riparian."*

The extent of, and relationship between, public rights and private property interests in coastal waters and submerged lands implicates fundamental notions of private property that find expression in the "takings" clause of the Fifth Amendment to the United States Constitution. Not infrequently, when the government acts to protect public rights and interests in coastal lands and waters, those adversely affected by the government's actions will claim that there is a "taking" of some private property interest for which compensation is required. However, part of the legal process is the judicial adjustment and redefining of common law property interests. A private property interest *thought* to exist may be defined out of existence. If the asserted private property interest does not exist, the takings claim predicated on it disappears. A significant question is: are there circumstances in which this common law process of shaping and defining the nature and extent of public and private rights can itself be a "taking"?

Whatever restraints the "takings" clause might otherwise place on government conduct, a rather unique exception to the "takings" clause exists when the federal government acts to protect or improve navigation in coastal waters. This exception falls under the heading of the *navigation servitude*. In essence, all state-created property rights and interests in coastal waters and submerged lands are subordinate to this navigation servitude.

As with many rights developed through the common law process, the exact parameters of common law littoral rights and public trust rights are uncertain. The views of private waterfront landowners, public officials, and the general public about access to, and use of, our limited coastal resources frequently diverge. Clashes are inevitable. How the courts resolve these conflicting views, interests, and rights is the heart of this chapter.

2. THE GEOGRAPHIC SCOPE OF THE PUBLIC TRUST

If coastal waters are navigable, normally title to the submerged lands is in the state, with the overlying waters available for use by the public. Such submerged lands are frequently said to be held by the state in a special, distinct capacity and are referred to as either "sovereignty" or "public trust" lands. As such, the state's authority to dispose of such lands may be more limited than its power over other state-owned property.

This concept of "sovereignty" or "public trust" lands is traceable back to Roman law and English common law. The Romans developed the "natural law" principle that the sea belonged to no one, and that use rights in it and on its shores were common to all. This was necessary to protect the empire's dependence upon navigation for trade and communication, as well as fishing. However, during the early Middle Ages, commerce and navigation declined in importance throughout Europe, and in England much of the coast passed into private ownership. Early grants of coastal lands lacked precision, and the English sovereigns seem to have acquiesced as feudal lords assumed that their titles extended out into the sea.

Beginning with the signing of the Magna Carta, and particularly after Sir Matthew Hale's treatise, De Jure Maris (1670), there emerged a new interest in reestablishing public rights (the *jus publicum*) in coastal waters and navigable rivers. Hale's treatise laid the groundwork for the English common law rule that title to lands over which the tide ebbed and flowed was *prima facie* in the Crown and held by it in a sort of trust for the public (the public rights of use being navigation, water commerce, and fishing). This trust did not preclude a Crown grant of tidelands to private individuals, but the burden was on private landowners to prove that such a grant had occurred.

Very early in our nation's history, the principle that submerged lands under navigable waters are public trust lands became part of the law of the United States. The next case—*Phillips Petroleum Company v. Mississippi*—provides some of the history of the public trust doctrine. The specific issue in the case is whether ownership of submerged lands under non-navigable-in-fact tidal waters is in state or private hands. But the broader question in *Phillips Petroleum* is whether the submerged lands are "lands under navigable waters," title to which passed to Mississippi on statehood.

The key concept of "navigable waters" is indeed a slippery one. As you read *Phillips Petroleum*, you will see that the phrase "navigable waters" has different meanings depending on the question being asked. *Phillips Petroleum* is a title determination case, but it is a case involving title to submerged lands in a state other than one of the original thirteen. The definition of navigable waters for purposes of determining title to submerged lands in one of the original thirteen states is not necessarily the same as the one used in *Phillips Petroleum*. To add to the complexity, the definition in *Phillips Petroleum* is not necessarily the definition that would be used to determine whether, as a matter of state law, submerged lands remained in state hands after statehood or passed, in one fashion or another, into private hands. Finally, even when title to submerged lands is in private hands, that does not necessarily mean that the owner of the submerged lands controls the overlying waters. Generally, the public is entitled to use navigable waters for navigation, fishing, and water recreation. But, the definition of "navigable waters" for purposes of public use may be different and broader than "navigable waters" for title determination purposes.

This does not exhaust the different meanings of "navigable waters." Navigable waters may mean one thing if the question is whether a particular federal statute applies; it may mean another if the question is whether the waterway is subject to the federal navigation servitude; and still another if the question is whether federal admiralty jurisdiction exists. With such variations in possible meaning, it is important when reading cases to keep in mind that a definition of navigable waters (or navigability) reached in one context may not be applicable in another context.

PHILLIPS PETROLEUM COMPANY V. MISSISSIPPI

Supreme Court of the United States, 1988
484 U.S. 469

JUSTICE WHITE delivered the opinion of the Court.

The issue here is whether the State of Mississippi, when it entered the Union in 1817, took title to lands lying under waters that were influenced by the tide running in the Gulf of Mexico, but were not navigable in fact.

I

As the Mississippi Supreme Court eloquently put it: "Though great public interests and neither insignificant nor illegitimate private interests are present and in conflict, this in the end is a title suit." Cinque Bambini Partnership v. State, 491 So. 2d 508, 510 (1986). More specifically, in question here is ownership of 42 acres of land underlying the north branch of Bayou LaCroix and 11 small drainage streams in southwestern Mississippi; the disputed tracts range from under one-half acre to almost ten acres in size. Although the waters over these lands lie several miles north of the Mississippi Gulf Coast and are not navigable, they are nonetheless influenced by the tide, because they are adjacent and tributary to the Jourdan River, a navigable stream flowing into the Gulf. The Jourdan, in the area involved here, is affected by the ebb and flow of the tide. Record title to these tracts of land is held by petitioners, who trace their claims back to prestatehood Spanish land grants.

The State of Mississippi, however, claiming that by virtue of the "equal footing doctrine" it acquired at the time of statehood and held in public trust all land lying under any waters influenced by the tide, whether navigable or not, issued oil and gas leases that included the property at issue. This quiet title suit, brought by petitioners, ensued.

The Mississippi Supreme Court, affirming the Chancery Court with respect to the lands at issue here, held that by virtue of becoming a State, Mississippi acquired "fee simple title to all lands naturally subject to tidal influence, inland to today's mean high water mark. * * * " Id. Petitioners' submission that the State acquired title to only lands under navigable [in fact] waters was rejected.[1]

---

[1] The Chancery Court had held that 140 acres of the lands claimed by petitioners were public trust lands. The Mississippi Supreme Court reversed with respect to 98 of these 140 acres, finding that these tracts were artificially created tidelands (caused by road construction), and therefore were not part of the public trust created in 1817. Since these lands were neither tidelands in 1817, nor were they added to the tidelands by virtue of natural forces of accretion, they belonged to their record title holders. 491 So.2d at 520.

Because the State did not cross-petition, this portion of the Mississippi Supreme Court's decision is not before us. The only issue presented here is title to the 42 acres which the Mississippi Supreme Court found to be public trust lands.

We granted certiorari to review the Mississippi Supreme Court's decision, 479 U.S. 1084 (1987), and now affirm the judgment below.

II

As petitioners recognize, the "seminal case in American public trust jurisprudence is Shively v. Bowlby, 152 U.S. 1 (1894)." Reply Brief for Petitioners 11. The issue in Shively v. Bowlby was whether the state of Oregon or a prestatehood grantee from the United States of riparian lands near the mouth of the Columbia River at Astoria, Oregon, owned the soil below the high-water mark. Following an extensive survey of this Court's prior cases, the English common law, and various cases from the state courts, the Court concluded:

> "At common law, the title and dominion in lands flowed by the tide water were in the King for the benefit of the nation. * * * Upon the American Revolution, these rights, charged with a like trust, were vested in the original States within their respective borders, subject to the rights surrendered by the Constitution of the United States. * * *

> The new States admitted into the Union since the adoption of the Constitution have the same rights as the original States in the tide waters, and in the lands under them, within their respective jurisdictions." Id., at 57.

Shively rested on prior decisions of this Court, which had included similar, sweeping statements of States' dominion over lands beneath tidal waters. Knight v. United States Land Association, 142 U.S. 161, 183, (1891), for example, had stated that, "It is the settled rule of law in this court that absolute property in, and dominion and sovereignty over, the soils under the tide waters in the original States were reserved to the States, and that the new States since admitted have the same rights, sovereignty and jurisdiction in that behalf as the original States possess within their respective borders." On many occasions, before and since, this Court has stated or restated these words from *Knight* and *Shively*.

Against this array of cases, it is not surprising that Mississippi claims ownership of all of the tidelands in the State. Other States have done as much. The 13 original States, joined by the Coastal States Organization (representing all coastal States), have filed a brief in support of Mississippi, insisting that ownership of thousands of acres of tidelands under nonnavigable waters would not be disturbed if the judgment below were affirmed, as it would be if petitioners' navigability-in-fact test were adopted. * * *

Petitioners rely on early state cases to indicate that the original States did not claim title to nonnavigable tidal waters. * * * But it has been long established that the individual States have the authority to define the limits of the lands held in public trust and to recognize private rights in such lands as they see fit. Shively v. Bowlby, 152 U.S. at 26. Some of the original States, for example, did recognize more private interests in tidelands than did others of the 13—more private interests than were recognized at common law, or in the dictates of our public trusts cases. * * * Because some of the cases which petitioners cite come from such States (i.e., from States which abandoned the common law with respect to tidelands), they are of only limited value in understanding the public trust doctrine and its scope in those States which have not relinquished their claims to all lands beneath tidal waters.

Finally, we note that several of our prior decisions have recognized that the States have interests in lands beneath tidal waters which have nothing to do with navigation. For example, this Court has previously observed that public trust lands may be used for fishing—for both "shell-fish [and] floating fish." See, e.g., Smith v. Maryland, 18 How. 71, 75 (1855). On several occasions the Court has recognized that lands beneath tidal waters may be reclaimed to create land for urban expansion. E.g., Hardin v. Jordan, 140 U.S. 371, 381–382 (1891); Den v. Jersey Co., 15 U.S. (How.) 426, 432 (1854). Because of the State's ownership of tidelands, restrictions on the planting and harvesting of oysters there have been upheld. McCready v. Virginia, 94 U.S. (4 Otto) 391, 395–397 (1877). It would be odd to acknowledge such diverse uses of public trust tidelands, and then suggest that the sole measure of the expanse of such lands is the navigability of the waters over them.

Consequently, we reaffirm our long standing precedents which hold that the States, upon entry into the Union, received ownership of all lands under waters subject to the ebb and flow of the tide. Under the well-established principles of our cases, the decision of the Mississippi Supreme Court is clearly correct: the lands at issue here are "under tide waters," and therefore passed to the State of Mississippi upon its entrance into the Union.

III

Petitioners do not deny that broad statements of public trust dominion over tidelands have been included in this Court's opinions since the early 19th century. Rather, they advance two reasons why these previous statements of the public trust doctrine should not be given their apparent application in this case.

A

First, petitioners contend that these sweeping statements of state dominion over tidelands arise from an oddity of the common law, or more specifically, of English geography. Petitioners submit that in England practically all navigable rivers are influenced by the tide. Brief for Petitioners 19. See The Propeller Genesee Chief v. Fitzhugh, 12 How. 443, 454 (1852). Thus, "tidewater" and "navigability" were synonyms at common law. See Illinois Central R. Co. v. Illinois, 146 U.S. 387, 436 (1892). Consequently, in petitioners' view, the Crown's ownership of lands beneath tidewaters actually rested on the navigability of those waters rather than the ebb and flow of the tide. * * *

The cases relied on by petitioners, however, did not deal with tidal, nonnavigable waters. And we will not now enter the debate on what the English law was with respect to the land under such waters, for it is perfectly clear how this Court understood the common law of royal ownership, and what the Court considered the rights of the original and the later entering States to be. As we discuss above, this Court has consistently interpreted the common law as providing that the lands beneath waters under tidal influence were given the States upon their admission into the Union. See Shively v. Bowlby, 152, U.S. at 57.* * * It is true that none of these cases actually dealt with lands such as those involved in this case, but it has never been suggested in any of this Court's prior decisions that the many statements included therein—to the effect that the States owned all the soil beneath waters affected by the tide—were anything less than an accurate description of the governing law.

B

Petitioners, in a related argument, contend that even if the common law does not support their position, subsequent cases from this Court developing the American public trust doctrine make it clear that navigability—and not tidal influence—has become the sine qua non of the public trust interest in tidelands in this country.

It is true that *The Genesee Chief*, 12 How. at 456–457, overruled prior cases of this Court which had limited admiralty jurisdiction to waters subject to tidal influence. Cf. The Thomas Jefferson, 10 Wheat. 428, 429 (1825). The Court did sharply criticize the "ebb and flow" measure of admiralty inherited from England in *The Genesee Chief*, and instead insisted quite emphatically that the different topography of America—in particular, our "thousands of miles of public navigable water[s] * * * in which there is no tide"—required that "jurisdiction [be] made to depend upon the navigable character of the water, and not upon the ebb and flow of the tide." 12 How. at 457. Later, it came to be recognized as the "settled law of this country" that the lands under navigable freshwater lakes and rivers were within the public trust given the new States upon their entry into the Union, subject to the federal navigation easement and the power of Congress to control navigation on those streams under the Commerce Clause. Barney v. Keokuk, 94 U.S. (4 Otto) 324, 338 (1877). See also Illinois Central R. Co. v. Illinois, 146 U.S. at 435–436.

That States own freshwater river bottoms as far as the rivers are navigable, however, does not indicate that navigability is or was the prevailing test for state dominion over tidelands. Rather, this rule represents the American decision to depart from what it understood to be the English rule limiting Crown ownership to the soil under tidal waters. In Oregon ex rel. State Land Board v. Corvallis Sand & Gravel Co., 429 U.S. 363, 374 (1977), after recognizing the accepted doctrine that States coming into the Union had title to all lands under the tidewaters, the Court stated that Barney v. Keokuk, had "extended the doctrine to waters which were nontidal but nevertheless navigable, consistent with [the Court's] earlier extension of admiralty jurisdiction."

This Court's decisions in *The Genesee Chief* and Barney v. Keokuk extended admiralty jurisdiction and public trust doctrine to navigable freshwaters and the lands beneath them. But we do not read those cases as simultaneously withdrawing from public trust coverage those lands which had been consistently recognized in this Court's cases as being within that doctrine's scope: all lands beneath waters influenced by the ebb and flow of the tide.* * *

C

Finally, we observe that not the least of the difficulties with petitioners' position is their concession that the States own the tidelands bordering the oceans, bays, and estuaries—even where these areas by no means could be considered navigable, as is always the case near the shore. Tr. of Oral Arg. 6. It is obvious that these waters are part of the sea, and the lands beneath them are State property; ultimately, though, the only proof of this fact can be that the waters are influenced by the ebb and flow of the tide. This is undoubtedly why the ebb-and-flow test has been the measure of public ownership of tidelands for so long.

Admittedly, there is a difference in degree between the waters in this case, and nonnavigable waters on the seashore that are affected by the tide. But there is no difference in kind. For in the end, all tidewaters are connected to the sea: the waters in this case, for example, by a navigable, tidal river. Perhaps the lands at issue here differ in some ways from tidelands directly adjacent to the sea; nonetheless, they still share those "geographical, chemical and environmental" qualities that make lands beneath tidal waters unique. Cf. Kaiser Aetna v. United States, 444 U.S. 164, 183 (1979) (Blackmun, J., dissenting).

Indeed, we find the various alternatives for delineating the boundaries of public trust tidelands offered by petitioners and their supporting amici to be unpersuasive and unsatisfactory. As the State suggested at argument, and as recognized on several previous occasions, the ebb and flow rule has the benefit of "uniformity and certainty, and * * * eas[e] of application." See, e.g., Cobb v. Davenport, 32 N.J.L. 369, 379 (1867). We are unwilling, after its lengthy history at common law, in this Court, and in many state courts, to abandon the ebb and flow rule now, and seek to fashion a new test to govern the limits of public trust tidelands. Consequently, we hold that the lands at issue in this case were within those given to Mississippi when the State was admitted to the Union.

* * *

V

Because we believe that our cases firmly establish that the States, upon entering the Union, were given ownership over all lands beneath waters subject to the tide's influence, we affirm the Mississippi Supreme Court's determination that the lands at issue here became property of the State upon its admission to the Union in 1817. Furthermore, because we find no reason to set aside that court's state-law determination that subsequent developments did not divest the State of its ownership of these public trust lands, the judgment below is Affirmed.

JUSTICE KENNEDY took no part in the consideration or decision of this case.

JUSTICE O'CONNOR, with whom JUSTICE STEVENS and JUSTICE SCALIA join, dissenting.

Breaking a chain of title that reaches back more than 150 years, the Court today announces a rule that will disrupt the settled expectations of landowners not only in Mississippi but in every coastal State. Neither our precedents nor equitable principles require this result, and I respectfully dissent from this undoing of settled history.

* * *

These waterways are not used for commercial navigation. None of the drainage streams is more than a mile long; all are nameless. Mississippi is not pressing its claim for the sake of facilitating commerce, or even to protect the public's interest in fishing or other traditional uses of the public trust. Instead, it is leasing the land to a private party for exploitation of underlying minerals. Mississippi's novel undertaking has caused it to press for a radical expansion of the historical limits of the public trust.

* * *

The Court's decision departs from our precedents, and I fear that it may permit grave injustice to be done to innocent property holders in coastal States. I dissent.

NOTES AND QUESTIONS

1. **The equal footing doctrine.** The subject of the controversy in *Phillips Petroleum* was the ownership of tidelands located in waters that are not navigable-in-fact. What is the basis of the claim of Mississippi, a state carved out of the Southwest Territory? The answer lies in the *equal footing doctrine*. The original thirteen colonies, when they first became independent states, which was prior to the formation of the United States, succeeded to the sovereign rights of the English crown. These rights included the ownership of lands under navigable waters and the authority to convey such *sovereignty* lands, usually subject to public trust rights.

When the United States acquired a new territory, it held any submerged land in trust for future states to be carved out of the territory. When a new state was formed, sovereignty over submerged lands under navigable waters then passed to the new state which continued to hold the lands subject to the public trust. See, e.g., Pollard's Lessee v. Hagan, 44 U.S. 212, 224 (1845).

2. **Federal definitions of navigability.** As the majority opinion in *Phillips Petroleum* points out, no comprehensive federal definition of navigability exists. The earliest federal definitions of navigability appear in admiralty jurisdiction cases. Because torts occurring on navigable waters fall within federal admiralty jurisdiction, the classification of the waters upon which the tort occurred is of some significance.

The history of admiralty jurisdiction in the 1800s is one of expansion beyond what existed in England. In The Steamboat Thomas Jefferson, 23 U.S. 428 (1825), the Court held that admiralty "navigable waters" meant the sea or waters subject to the ebb and flow of the tide, the so-called English rule of navigability. However, as the country grew westward to include the Great Lakes and vast inland river systems, the Court discarded the limitations of the English rule. The reach of admiralty jurisdiction was broadened to include all fresh waters that were used for commercial navigation between the states and between the United States and foreign countries. The Propeller Genesee Chief v. Fitzhugh, 53 U.S. (12 How.) 443 (1851); Jackson v. The Steamboat Magnolia, 61 U.S. (20 How.) 296 (1857); The Eagle, 75 U.S. (8 Wall.) 15 (1868); Ex parte Boyer, 109 U.S. 629 (1884). Although unanswered questions still exist as to the exact definition of navigable waters for purposes of federal admiralty jurisdiction, there has been no significant United States Supreme Court opinion on the topic since the 1880s.

In 1870, the Court's attention shifted to the relationship of navigability to the federal government's power under the Commerce Clause. In The Daniel Ball, 77 U.S. (10 Wall) 557 (1870), the issue was whether a federal safety regulation applied to a ship that operated solely on a river in Michigan, upon which goods moved in interstate commerce. If the river was a "navigable water of the United States" within the meaning of the federal statute, and if Congress had the power under the Commerce Clause to pass such a statute, then The Daniel Ball was subject to the regulation. The Court answered both questions affirmatively. In addressing the first issue, Justice Field, the author of Illinois Central, infra, attempted to provide a comprehensive definition of navigability.

> The doctrine of the common law as to the navigability of waters has no application in this country. Here the ebb and flow of the tide do not constitute the usual test, as in England, or any test at all of the navigability of waters. There no waters are navigable in fact, or at least to any considerable extent, which are not subject to the tide, and from this circumstance tide water and navigable water there signify substantially the same thing. But in this country the case is widely different. Some of our rivers are as navigable for many hundreds of miles above as they are below the limits of tide water, and some of them are navigable for great distances by large vessels, which are not even affected by the tide at any point during their entire length. A different test must, therefore, be applied to determine the navigability of our rivers, and that is found in their navigable capacity. Those rivers must be regarded as public navigable rivers in law which are navigable in fact. And they are navigable in fact when they are used, or are susceptible of being used, in their ordinary condition, as highways for commerce, over which trade and travel are or may be conducted in the customary modes of trade and travel on water. And they constitute navigable waters of the United States within the meaning of the acts of Congress, in contradistinction from the navigable waters of the States, when they form in their ordinary condition by themselves, or by uniting with other waters, a continued highway over which commerce is or may be carried on with other States or foreign countries in the customary modes in which such commerce is conducted by water.

Id. at 563. The "navigability" test of The Daniel Ball was subsequently expanded in other Commerce Clause cases, of which United States v. Appalachian Electric Power Co., 311 U.S. 377 (1940), is perhaps the most significant. In that case, the Court said:

> To appraise the evidence of navigability on the natural condition only of the waterway is erroneous. Its availability for navigation must also be considered. "Natural and ordinary condition" refers to volume of water, the gradients and the regularity of the flow. A waterway, otherwise suitable for navigation, is not barred from that classification merely because artificial aids must make the highway suitable for use before commercial navigation may be undertaken.

> * * * Although navigability to fix ownership of the river bed or riparian rights is determined * * * as of the formation of the Union in the original states or the admission to statehood of those formed later, navigability, for the purpose of the regulation of commerce, may later arise. An analogy is found in admiralty jurisdiction, which may be extended over places formerly nonnavigable. There has never been doubt that the navigability

referred to in the cases was navigability despite the obstruction of falls, rapids, sand bars, carries or shifting currents. The plenary federal power over commerce must be able to develop with the needs of that commerce which is the reason for its existence. * * *In determining the navigable character * * * it is proper to consider the feasibility of interstate use after reasonable improvements might have been made.

Id. at 407–09.

3. **Navigable-in-fact.** For a waterbody to be "navigable-in-fact", by what type of vessels and for what purposes must it be navigable? If it was navigable in the past, but is no longer so, legally is it still navigable-in-fact waters?

4. **Navigable waters of the states.** In *The Daniel Ball*, in dicta, the court provides a definition of "navigable waters of the States." If that is a federal common law definition of state navigable waters, in what situations is it to be applied? *Phillips Petroleum* addresses the "ebb and flow" branch of the test for navigable waters. But what is the test for determining whether non-tidal waters, impressed with the public trust, passed to the state pursuant to the equal footing doctrine? See Utah v. United States, 403 U.S. 9 (1971) (at time of statehood, Utah acquired title to Great Salt Lake, an entirely intrastate body of water).

5. **Navigable waters post–statehood.** After "navigable waters" and associated submerged lands pass to a state, may the state adopt a broader definition of navigable waters? Does the Fifth Amendment permit a state, over time, to modify its definition of navigability? Could a state adopt one definition of navigable waters for title purposes and a broader definition for the purpose of determining what waters are open to public trust uses? Would this avoid any "takings" problem?

The fact of the matter is that state definitions of navigability may evolve over time. For example, the Arkansas Supreme Court expanded its definition of navigable-in-fact to include streams that can be used for recreational purposes. Earlier cases had suggested that a waterway had to be used for commercial navigation to be "navigable." These cases were distinguished on the ground that the issue of whether streams useful for only recreational boating could be "navigable waters" had not been before the court. State v. McIlroy, 268 Ark. 227, 595 S.W.2d 659, cert. denied, 449 U.S. 843 (1980). See also Kelly ex rel. MacMullan v. Hallden, 51 Mich. App. 176, 214 N.W.2d 856 (1974). It is important to note that in these cases, the courts were not deciding whether title to the submerged land lying under the body of water was in the state or in private hands. The issue was only the right of the public to use the water for navigation or other public trust uses. This right of public use is sometimes referred to as a navigation easement. Therefore the public right to use a water body is not dependent upon public ownership of the underlying submerged lands. For a further discussion of these issues, see 1 and 4 Water and Water Rights §§ 6.02(f), 6.03(a), 30.03, 32.01–.03(a) (2011).

3. THE NATURE OF THE PUBLIC TRUST IN TIDELANDS

A. THE PRESUMPTION AGAINST PRIVATE OWNERSHIP

The most important issue for the management of coastal lands and waters is whether the public trust doctrine limits the types of private uses that can be made of tidal lands and waters. The following case, Illinois Central Railroad Co. v. Illinois, 146 U.S 387 (1892), is the cornerstone of the public trust doctrine as it exists today in the United States. The roots of the *Illinois Central* controversy lie in an 1869 Illinois legislative act that purported to grant the railroad title to submerged lands lying in the Chicago harbor. The Act provided, in part, that:

> * * * the fee to said lands shall be held by said company in perpetuity, and * * * said company shall not have power to grant, sell, or convey the fee to the same * * * and provided also, that nothing herein contained shall authorize obstructions to the Chicago harbor, or impair the public right of navigation; nor shall this act be construed to exempt the * * * railroad * * * from any act of the general assembly which may be hereafter passed regulating rates of wharfage and dockage to be charged in said harbor.

Id. at 406, n.3.

If the railroad accepted the grant, it was to pay certain specified sums to the City of Chicago and a percentage of the revenues derived from the use of facilities placed upon the submerged lands to the State of Illinois. The first payment to Chicago was tendered but never accepted by the city. No payment was ever made to the State because the litigation was instituted before any facilities were constructed upon the disputed lands.

The 1869 Act generated substantial adverse publicity and a call for its repeal. A new legislature was elected and, in response to public feeling, it acted quickly in 1873 to repeal the 1869 Act. The State then filed an action to determine title. The action was initially filed in state court, but the railroad subsequently removed the case to the federal circuit court. Although the 1869 Act could be read as conveying only a limited interest in the submerged lands to the railroad, the railroad's position was that the Act conveyed absolute title to the company with the complete power to use and dispose of any of the submerged lands.

When the case reached the United States Supreme Court, two Justices disqualified themselves. One, Chief Justice Fuller, had represented the railroad in the lower courts; the other, Justice Blatchford, was a stockholder in the railroad. The Supreme Court (4–3) affirmed the decision of the circuit court, which had declared the 1869 grant invalid. The majority opinion was written by Justice Field, a Justice known for his railroad sympathies.

ILLINOIS CENTRAL RAILROAD V. ILLINOIS
Supreme Court of the United States, 1892
146 U.S 387

JUSTICE FIELD delivered the opinion of the Court.

The [1869] act, if valid and operative to the extent claimed, placed under the control of the railroad company nearly the whole of the submerged lands of the harbor, subject only to the limitations that it should not authorize obstructions to the harbor or impair the public right of navigation, or exclude the legislature from regulating the rates of wharfage or dockage to be charged. With these limitations the act put it in the power of the company to delay indefinitely the improvement of the harbor, or to construct as many docks, piers and wharves and other works as it might choose, and at such positions in the harbor as might suit its purposes, and permit any kind of business to be conducted thereon, and to lease them out on its own terms, for indefinite periods. * * *

The question, therefore, to be considered is whether the legislature was competent to thus deprive the state of its ownership of the submerged lands in the harbor of Chicago, and of the consequent control of its waters; or, in other words, whether the railroad corporation can hold the lands and control the waters by the grant, against any future exercise of power over them by the State.

That the State holds the title to the lands under the navigable waters of Lake Michigan, within its limits, in the same manner that the State holds title to soils under tide water, by the common law, we have already shown; and that title necessarily carries with it control over the waters above them whenever the lands are subjected to use. But it is a title different in character from that which the State holds in lands intended for sale. It is different from the title which the United States hold in the public lands which are open to pre-emption and sale. It is a title held in trust for the people of the State that they may enjoy the navigation of the waters, carry on commerce over them, and have liberty of fishing therein freed from the obstruction or interference of private parties. The interest of the people in the navigation of the waters and in commerce over them may be improved in many instances by the erection of wharves, docks and piers therein, for which purpose the State may grant parcels of the submerged lands; and, so long as their disposition is made for such purpose, no valid objections can be made to the grants. It is grants of parcels of lands under navigable waters, that may afford foundation for wharves, piers, docks, and other structures in aid of commerce, and grants of parcels which, being occupied, do not substantially impair the public interest in the lands and waters remaining, that are chiefly considered and sustained in the adjudged cases as a valid exercise of legislative power consistently with the trust to the public upon which such lands are held by the State. But that is a very different doctrine from the one which would sanction the abdication of the general control of the State over lands under the navigable waters of an entire harbor or bay, or of a sea or lake. Such abdication is not consistent with the exercise of that trust which requires the government of the State to preserve such waters for the use of the public. The trust devolving upon the State for the public, and which can only be discharged by the management and control of property in which the public has an interest, cannot be relinquished by a transfer of the property. *The control of the State for the purposes of the trust can never be lost, except as to such parcels as are used in promoting the interests of the public therein, or can be disposed of without any substantial impairment of the public interest in the lands and waters remaining.* It is only by observing the distinction between a grant of such parcels for the improvement of the public interest, or which when occupied do not substantially impair the public interest in the lands and waters remaining, and a grant of the whole property in which the public is interested, that the language of the adjudged cases can be reconciled. General language sometimes found in opinions of the courts, expressive of absolute ownership and control by the State of lands under navigable waters, irrespective of any trust as to their use and disposition, must be read and construed with reference to the special facts of the particular cases. A grant of all the lands under the navigable waters of a State has never been adjudged to be within the legislative power; and any attempted grant of the kind would be held, if not absolutely void on its face, as subject to revocation. *The State can no more abdicate its trust over property in which the whole people are interested, like navigable waters and soils under them, so as to leave them entirely under the use and control of private parties, except in the instance of parcels mentioned for the improvement of the navigation and use of the waters, or when parcels can be disposed of without impairment of the public interest in what remains, than it can abdicate its police powers in the administration of government and the preservation of the peace.* In the administration of government the use of such powers may for a limited period be delegated to a municipality or other body, but there always remains with the State the right to revoke those powers and exercise them in a more direct manner, and one more conformable to its wishes. So with trusts connected with public property, or property of a special character, like lands under navigable waters, they cannot be placed entirely beyond the direction and control of the State.

The harbor of Chicago is of immense value to the people of the State of Illinois in the facilities it affords to its vast and constantly increasing commerce; and the idea that its legislature can deprive the State of control over its bed and waters and place the same in the hands of a private corporation created for a different purpose, one limited to transportation of passengers and freight between distant points and the city, is a proposition that cannot be defended.

The area of the submerged lands proposed to be ceded by the act in question to the railroad company embraces something more than 1,000 acres, being, as stated by counsel, more than three times the area of the outer harbor, and not only including all of that harbor but embracing adjoining submerged lands which will, in all probability, be hereafter included in the harbor. It is as large as that embraced by all the merchandise docks along the Thames at London; is much larger than that included in the famous docks and basins at Liverpool; is twice that of the port of Marseilles, and nearly if not quite equal to the pier area along the water front of the city of New York. And the arrivals and clearings of vessels at the port exceed in number those of New York, and are equal to those of New York and Boston combined. Chicago has nearly twenty-five per cent of the lake carrying trade, as compared with the arrivals and clearings of all the leading ports of our great inland seas. * * * It is hardly conceivable that the legislature can divest the State of the control and management of this harbor and vest it absolutely in a private corporation. Surely an act of the legislature transferring the title to its submerged lands and the power claimed by the railroad company to a foreign State or nation would be repudiated, without hesitation, as a gross perversion of the trust over the property under which it is held. * * * It would not be listened to that the control and management of the harbor of that great city—a subject of concern to the whole people of the State—should thus be placed elsewhere than in the State itself. All the objections which can be urged to such attempted transfer may be urged to a transfer to a private corporation like the railroad company in this case.

Any grant of the kind is necessarily revocable, and the exercise of the trust by which the property was held by the State can be resumed at any time. Undoubtedly there may be expenses incurred in improvements made under such a grant, which the State ought to pay; but, be that as it may, the power to resume the trust whenever the State judges best is, we think, incontrovertible. The position advanced by the railroad company in support of its claim to the ownership of the submerged lands and the right to the erection of wharves, piers, and docks at its pleasure, or for its business in the harbor of Chicago, would place every harbor in the country at the mercy of a majority of the legislature of the State in which the harbor is situated.

We cannot, it is true, cite any authority where a grant of this kind has been held invalid, for we believe that no instance exists where the harbor of a great city and its commerce have been allowed to pass into the control of any private corporation. But the decisions are numerous which declare that such property is held by the state, by virtue of its sovereignty, in trust for the public. The ownership of the navigable waters of the harbor and of the lands under them is a subject of public concern to the whole people of the State. The trust with which they are held, therefore, is governmental and cannot be alienated, except in those instances mentioned of parcels used in the improvement of the interest thus held, or when parcels can be disposed of without detriment to the public interest in the lands and waters remaining.

This follows necessarily from the public character of the property, being held by the whole people for purposes in which the whole people are interested. * * *

The soil under navigable waters being held by the people of the State in trust for the common use and as a portion of their inherent sovereignty, any act of legislation concerning their use affects the public welfare. It is therefore appropriately within the exercise of the police power of the State.

* * * The legislature could not give away nor sell the discretion of its successors in respect to matters, the government of which, from the very nature of things, must vary with varying circumstances. The legislation which may be needed one day for the harbor may be different from the legislation that may be required at another day. Every legislature must, at the time of its existence, exercise the power of the State in the execution of the trust devolved upon it. We hold, therefore, that any attempted cession of the ownership and control of the State in and over the submerged lands in Lake Michigan, by the act of April 16, 1869, was inoperative to affect, modify or in any respect to control the sovereignty and dominion of the State over the lands, or its ownership thereof, and that any such attempted operation of the act was annulled by the repealing act of April 15, 1873, which to that extent was valid and effective. There can be no irrepealable contract in a conveyance of property by a grantor in disregard of a public trust, under which he was bound to hold and manage it.

Affirmed.

NOTES AND QUESTIONS

1. **State police powers and the Contract Clause.** The position of the railroad in *Illinois Central* was that the legislation was in effect a contract which could not be repealed by a later legislature without violating the Contract Clause of the United States Constitution. Why wasn't the action of the state of Illinois a violation of the Contract Clause? Consider the following case, Stone v. Mississippi, 101 U.S. 814 (1879).

In 1867, the Mississippi legislature passed legislation incorporating a private corporation and granting that corporation the right to conduct a lottery within the state. Shortly thereafter, in 1869, a new state constitution was adopted. The new constitution declared that "[t]he legislature shall never authorize any lottery; nor shall the sale of lottery-tickets be allowed; nor shall any lottery heretofore authorized be permitted to be drawn, or tickets therein sold." Acting pursuant to this constitutional mandate, the 1870 legislature passed legislation prohibiting all lotteries within the state. The State then sued the corporation on the ground that it was conducting a prohibited lottery. The corporation defended on the basis that the rights granted by the 1867 statute could not be abrogated by a later state constitution or legislation.

The unanimous opinion of the Supreme Court began with the somewhat reluctant acknowledgment that a charter to a private corporation was within the protection of the Contract Clause. However, the Court then noted that, unless a valid contract was entered into, there was nothing to be protected by the Contract Clause. Thus, "[w]hether the alleged contract exists * * * or not, depends on the authority of the legislature to bind the State and the people of the State in that way." Id. at 817. Although nothing in the pre–1869 state constitution prohibited the legislature from granting the right to conduct lotteries, the Court noted "[a]ll agree that the legislature cannot bargain away the police power of a State." Id. Without attempting to define the limits of this police power, the Court stated that it certainly included all matters affecting the public health and public morals and thus a lottery was a proper subject of regulation under state police powers. Consequently, a contract in which the legislature or state purported to give up the right to regulate or prohibit a lottery was invalid and unenforceable.

In explaining its decision the Court stated:

> * * * the power of governing is a trust committed by the people to the government, no part of which can be granted away. The people, in their sovereign capacity, have established their agencies for the preservation of the public health and the public morals, and the protection of public and private rights. These several agencies can govern according to their discretion, if within the scope of their general authority, while in power; but they cannot give away nor sell the discretion of those that are to come after them, in respect to matters the government of which, from the very nature of things, must "vary with varying circumstances." They may create corporations, and give them, so to speak, a limited citizenship; but as citizens, limited in their privileges, or otherwise, these creatures of the government creation are subject to such rules and regulations as may from time to time be ordained and established for the preservation of health and morality.

> The contracts which the Constitution protects are those that relate to property rights, not governmental. It is not always easy to tell on which side of the line which separates governmental from property rights a particular case is to be put; but in respect to lotteries there can be no difficulty. * * * Anyone, therefore, who accepts a lottery charter does so with the implied understanding that the people, in their sovereign capac-

ity, and through their properly constituted agencies, may resume it at any time when the public good shall require, whether it be paid for or not. All that one can get by such a charter is a suspension of certain governmental rights in his favor, subject to withdrawal at will. He has in legal effect nothing more than a license to enjoy the privilege on the terms named for the specified time, unless it be sooner abrogated by the sovereign power of the State. It is a permit, good as against existing laws, but subject to future legislative and constitutional control or withdrawal.

Id. at 820–21.

2. *Illinois Central*: A matter of federal constitutional law or the law of the individual states?

A central issue is the legal foundation of the public trust doctrine. There is no question that the public trust doctrine is widely accepted by the states. And there is no question that state decisions affirming the existence of the public trust doctrine almost always cite *Illinois Central* as authority. See, e.g., CWC Fisheries, Inc. v. Bunker, 755 P.2d 1115, 1117–18 (Alaska 1988); Caminiti v. Boyle, 107 Wash.2d 662, 670, 732 P.2d 989, 997 (1987); Shepard's Point Land Co. v. Atlantic Hotel, 132 N.C. 517, 525–28, 44 S.E. 39, 41–42 (1903); State v. Black River Phosphate Co., 32 Fla. 82, 13 So. 640, 645–47 (1893). However, when faced with determining the validity of an alleged conveyance of submerged lands under navigable waters, the courts frequently avoid the difficult issue of the constitutional basis, if any, for the public trust doctrine.

In most cases, conveyances of public trust lands are treated as valid but as subject to the public's continuing public trust use rights. The courts employ a variety of approaches to find that there is no valid conveyance of the submerged land free of the public trust. In some cases, courts strictly construe against the grantee the language of the authorizing legislation or the deed of conveyance. For example, in Boston Waterfront Dev. Corp. v. Commonwealth, 378 Mass. 629, 637–38, 393 N.E.2d 356, 361 (1979), a statute granting certain submerged land to a corporation in fee simple also contained language that "nothing herein shall be understood as authorizing * * * interfere(nce) with the legal rights of * * * [others]." This language was construed to mean that the submerged lands were conveyed subject to the public trust. See also, e.g., Coastal States Gas Producing Co. v. State Mineral Board, 199 So.2d 554, 557–58 (La. App 1967); CWC Fisheries, Inc. v. Bunker, 755 P.2d 1115 (Alaska 1988) (unless legislative intent to give up the public interest in any tideland statute is clearly expressed or necessarily implied, the court will interpret the grant as preserving the public interest). In other cases, courts conclude that the particular state entity or agency that made the alleged conveyances of submerged lands under navigable water lack the necessary legislative authorization. See, e.g., Martin v. Busch, 93 Fla. 535, 573, 112 So. 274, 286–87 (1927).

But when non-constitutional grounds for invalidating a conveyance of submerged lands do not exist, the issue of what exactly is the constitutional basis of the public trust doctrine cannot be ignored. If the United States Constitution is the source of the doctrine, what federal constitutional provision permits the United States Supreme Court to impose a public trust upon state owned land? Is there both a federal public trust doctrine and the public trust doctrine of individual states? If so, how do the doctrines differ? Finally, if no express provision of the federal or state constitution prohibits legislative disposals of submerged lands, why should a state or federal court be permitted to invalidate state legislation conveying submerged lands to private parties by means of an extra-constitutional doctrine, such as the public trust doctrine? When the people adopt constitutions defining the powers of the various branches of the federal and state governments, and the constitutions do not in any express manner limit the power of the Congress or state legislatures to dispose of federal or state owned submerged land, then haven't the people spoken? Compare C. Wilkinson, The Headwaters of the Public Trust: Some Thoughts on the Source and Scope of the Traditional Doctrine, 19 Envtl. L. 425 (1988), with J. Huffman, A Fish Out Of Water: The Public Trust Doctrine in a Constitutional Democracy, 19 Envtl. L. 527 (1988).

In Gwathmey v. State of North Carolina, 342 N.C. 287, 464 S.E.2d 674 (1995), the North Carolina Supreme Court directly addressed the question of whether a constitutional public trust doctrine limits the authority of a state legislature to dispose of public trust submerged lands. The case involved a state agency's conveyances between 1926 and 1945 of salt marsh located in one of North Carolina's estuarine sounds. The State argued that the marshlands could not be conveyed free of the public trust and the legislature did not have the power to do anything which would impair public trust interests in such lands. The Court responded that

> [i]t is true that lands submerged by waters which are determined to be navigable in law are subject to the public trust doctrine. However, the assumption that such lands may not be conveyed by the General Assembly without reservation of public trust rights is incorrect.

* * *

> No constitutional provision throughout the history of our State has expressly or impliedly precluded the General Assembly from conveying lands beneath navigable waters by special grant in fee simple and free of any rights arising from the public trust doctrine. See [M. Kalo and J. Kalo, The] Battle to Preserve North Carolinas Estuarine Marshes: The 1985 Legislation, Private Claims to Estuarine Marshes, Denial of Permits to Fill, and the Public Trust, 64 N.C. L. Rev. at 576–77. *The public trust doctrine is a common law doctrine.* In the absence of a constitutional basis for the public trust doctrine, it cannot be used to invalidate acts of the legislature which are not proscribed by our Constitution. Thus, in North Carolina, the public trust doctrine operates as a rule of construc-

tion creating a presumption that the General Assembly did not intend to convey lands in a manner that would impair public trust rights. * * * However, this presumption is overcome by a special grant from the General Assembly *expressly* conveying lands underlying navigable waters in fee simple and without reservation of any public trust rights. [citations omitted].

Id. at 301–04; 464 S.E.2d at 682–84, (emphasis added). See also Providence Chamber of Commerce v. State, 657 A.2d 1038, 1041–43 (R.I. 1995) (public trust is a common law doctrine). But see New York v. DeLyster, 759 F. Supp. 982, 990 (W.D.N.Y. 1991) (*Illinois Central* "involved a fundamental issue of federal law concerning the nature of a state's sovereignty, and the powers assumed by the state upon its admission to the Union.").

The North Carolina Supreme Court's view of the essential nature of the public trust doctrine is supported by language in United States Supreme Court cases decided subsequently to *Illinois Central*. Two years after *Illinois Central* was decided, the Court handed down Shively v. Bowlby, 152 U.S. 1 (1894). *Shively* concerned the title to submerged land located below the high water mark in the Columbia River, a navigable river in Oregon. The Court held that the issue was a matter to be determined by state law, stating that:

> * * * The title and rights of riparian or littoral proprietors in the soil below the high water mark * * * are governed by the laws of the several States, subject to the rights granted to the United States by the Constitution.
>
> The United States, while they hold the country as a Territory, * * * may grant * * * titles or rights in the soil below the high water mark of tide waters. But they have never done so by general laws; and * * * have acted upon the policy * * * of *leaving the administration and disposition of the sovereign rights in navigable waters, and in the soil under them, to the control of the States * * * when organized and admitted to the Union.*

Id. at 57–58 (emphasis added). Later, in Appleby v. City of New York, 271 U.S. 364 (1926), the Court seemed to retreat from its holding in *Illinois Central*. In *Appleby*, the Court held that a state could convey fee title to submerged lands if the legislature decided it was in the public interest. In its view, the *Illinois Central*

> * * * case arose in the Circuit Court of the United States, and the conclusion reached was necessarily a statement of Illinois law, but the general principle and the exception have been recognized the country over. * * *

Id. at 395.

More recently, in Idaho v. Coeur d'Alene Tribe of Idaho, 521 U.S. 261, 285–86 (1997), the Court observations were mixed, leaving room for a constitutional norm binding on the states. In that case the Court observed that "[w]hile *Illinois Central* was 'necessary a statement of Illinois law,' Appleby v.

City of New York * * *, it invoked the principle in American law recognizing
the weighty public interests in submerged lands. * * * *these lands are tied in
an unique way to sovereignty.*" (emphasis added). See also E. Pearson, Illinois
Central and the Public Trust Doctrine in State Law, 15 Va. Envir.L.J. 713
(1996).

3. For a detailed discussion of the background of *Illinois Central*, see J.
Kearney and T.Merrill, The Origins of the American Public Trust Doctrine:
What Really Happened in *Illinois Central*, 71 U. of Chicago L. Rev. 799
(2004).

B. ALIENATION OF PUBLIC TRUST LANDS: CRITERIA FOR VALIDITY

What criteria should determine the validity of state created private
rights in public trust lands and waters? Consider the next case.

PEOPLE v. CHICAGO PARK DISTRICT

Supreme Court of Illinois, 1976
66 Ill. 2d 65, 360 N.E.2d 773

WARD, CHIEF JUSTICE.

The General Assembly passed Senate Bill 782 (Laws of 1963, at
1229–31) on June 17, 1963, and it was signed by the Governor on June
26, 1963. The bill, in essence, provided for the conveyance by the State of
Illinois of 194.6 acres of land submerged in waters of Lake Michigan to
the United States Steel Corporation, hereafter referred to as defendant,
upon its paying to the State Treasurer $19,460 and upon the Chicago
Park District reconveying to the State an interest in the land it had received by certain legislation. * * *

The defendant, which proposes to construct a steel plant on the land
to be reclaimed, tendered its draft on August 13, 1973, in the amount of
$19,460 to the State Treasurer, but it was returned three days later. The
Attorney General commenced this action by filing a complaint in the circuit court of Cook County. The complaint sought a declaratory judgment
that "An Act for the sale to United States Steel Corporation of the interest of the State of Illinois in certain lands" (Senate Bill 782) was void.
* * * The trial court allowed the plaintiffs' motion for summary judgment,
holding that Senate Bill 782 was void on the grounds that it violated the
public trust doctrine, the fourteenth amendment of the United States
Constitution, and the following provisions of the Illinois Constitution of
1970: article I, section 2; article IV, section 13; and article VIII, section
1(a). The defendant appealed. * * *

The defendant argues that * * * Senate Bill 782 does not violate the public trust doctrine or any of the constitutional provisions as the Attorney General alleges and that the trial court's judgment was erroneous.

Any discussion of the public trust doctrine in Illinois must begin with Illinois Central Railroad Co. v. Illinois, 146 U.S. 387 [Discussion of *Illinois Central* omitted.]

A short time [after the Illinois Central decision] * * * another question involving submerged lands was presented to this court. In Illinois Central R.R. Co. v. City of Chicago, 173 Ill. 471, 50 N.E. 1104 (Illinois Central II), the plaintiff railroad sought to prevent the city of Chicago from interfering with its plan to fill in 4.48 acres of land submerged in Lake Michigan between 25th and 27th Streets in Chicago. The plaintiff proposed to construct an engine house on the reclaimed land, and it alleged in its complaint the necessity of constructing the engine house on this site. The plaintiff contended that it had the power under the charter granted to it by the State to reclaim this land. This court, citing People ex rel. Moloney v. Kirk, 162 Ill. 138, 45 N.E. 830, declared that the State held title to the submerged lands in trust for the benefit of the people and that it could not sell these lands. 173 Ill. 471, 485, 50 N.E. 1104. It went on to say that in *Illinois Central I* the Supreme Court had held that 'grants of parcels of lands for wharves, piers, docks, and other structures in aid of commerce, and grants of parcels which do not impair the public interests in the lands and waters remaining' could be allowed. 173 Ill. 471, 485, 50 N.E. 1104, 1108. But the court concluded:

> It is not proposed here to take or appropriate the land in question for the erection of wharves, docks or piers, the construction of which may facilitate or aid the navigation of the waters of the lake, but the sole purpose seems to be to appropriate the submerged land for the private use of the railroad company. It is unreasonable to believe that the legislature, in the enactment of section 3 of the charter of the railroad company, ever intended to place in the hands of the company unlimited power to go on, from time to time, and appropriate to its own use parcel after parcel of the lands covered by the waters of Lake Michigan; and, if such unlimited power was contemplated it transcended its authority. It, in effect, undertook to part with governmental powers, which it could not do.

173 Ill. 471, 487, 50 N.E. 1104, 1109.

It can be seen that the State holds title to submerged land, as is involved here, in trust for the people, and that in general the governmental powers over these lands will not be relinquished. (See generally R. Clark, [Waters and Water Rights] § 36.4(A) (1967); R. Powell, The Law of Real Property, par. 160.) It is within this general framework that we are called upon to decide whether the legislative grant here was valid. In two of the discussed decisions (*Illinois Central I* and *II*) direct grants of submerged lands to private interests were held void. In the one case (People ex rel. Moloney v. Kirk) in which a grant of private interests was upheld, it was observed that the main purpose of the statute was to allow public officials to construct a needed extension of Lake Shore Drive for direct public benefit. 162 Ill. 138, 155–56, 45 N.E. 830. In none of these cases, nor in later cases decided by this court (Fairbank v. Stratton, 14 Ill. 2d 307, 152 N.E.2d 569; Bowes v. City of Chicago, 3 Ill. 2d 175, 120 N.E.2d 15), was a grant upheld where its primary purpose was to benefit a private interest.

[I]t may be pointed out that, in considering what is the public interest, courts are not bound by inflexible standards.

> We have no difficulty in finding that, in this latter half of the twentieth century, the public rights in tidal lands are not limited to the ancient prerogatives of navigation and fishing, but extend as well to recreational uses, including bathing, swimming and other shore activities. The public trust doctrine, like all common law principles, should not be considered fixed or static, but should be molded and extended to meet changing conditions and needs of the public it was created to benefit.

Borough of Neptune City v. Borough of Avon–By–The–Sea (1972), 61 N.J. 296, 309, 294 A.2d 47, 54–55, and cases and authorities cited therein; see also Marks v. Whitney (1971), 6 Cal. 3d 251, 98 Cal. Rptr. 790, 491 P.2d 374.

On this question of changing conditions and public needs, it is appropriate to observe that there has developed a strong, though belated, interest in conserving natural resources and in protecting and improving our physical environment. The public has become increasingly concerned with dangers to health and life from environmental sources and more sensitive to the value and, frequently, the irreplaceability of natural resources. This is reflected in the enactment of the Illinois Environmental Protection Act (Ill.Rev.Stat. 1975, ch. 111 1/2, par. 1001 Et seq.) in 1971 and in the ratification by the people of this State of sections 1 and 2 of article XI of the 1970 Constitution, which declare:

> The public policy of the State and the duty of each person is to provide and maintain a healthful environment for the benefit of this and future generations. The General Assembly shall provide by law for the implementation and enforcement of this public policy.

> Each person has the right to a healthful environment. Each person may enforce this right against any party, governmental or private, through appropriate legal proceedings subject to reasonable limitation and regulation as the General Assembly may provide by law.

It is obvious that Lake Michigan is a valuable natural resource belonging to the people of this State in perpetuity and any attempted ceding of a portion of it in favor of a private interest has to withstand a most critical examination.

The defendant steel company plans to construct an additional facility which will extend its South Work's Plant some 194 acres into Lake Michigan. The general area in question is bordered on the north by a public beach, Rainbow Park, at 79th Street; on the south by the United States Government breakwater protecting Calumet Harbor, and on the east by the Illinois–Indiana state line in Lake Michigan. These waters, which are adjacent to waters presently in important public use, would be irretrievably removed from the use of the people of Illinois. It cannot be said there will not be an adverse effect on the public use of these adjacent waters. We would also observe that in Illinois Central II it was said of the grant there: "(T)he sole purpose seems to be to appropriate the submerged land for the private use of the railroad company." 173 Ill. 471, 487, 50 N.E. 1104, 1109. Here, too, we can perceive only a private purpose for the grant.

The defendant contends that the General Assembly has determined that the land in question will be used for a public purpose and that this court should not overturn this determination. The defendant points to section 1 of Senate Bill 782, which states:

> It is hereby declared that the grant of submerged land contained in this Act is made in aid of commerce and will create no impairment of the public interest in the lands and waters remaining, but will instead result in the conversion of otherwise useless and unproductive submerged land into an important commercial development to the benefit of the people of the State of Illinois.

The defendant argues, too, that a public purpose will be served in that the plant facilities which will be erected on the reclaimed land will provide a large number of jobs and will boost the economy of the city of Chicago and of the State. We judge these arguments to be unpersuasive.

While the courts certainly should consider the General Assembly's declaration that given legislation is to serve a described purpose, this court recognized in People ex rel. City of Salem v. McMackin, 53 Ill. 2d 347, 354, 291 N.E.2d 807, 812, that the "self-serving recitation of a public purpose within a legislative enactment is not conclusive of the existence of such purpose."

In order to preserve meaning and vitality in the public trust doctrine, when a grant of submerged land beneath waters of Lake Michigan is proposed under the circumstances here, the public purpose to be served cannot be only incidental and remote. The claimed benefit here to the public through additional employment and economic improvement is too indirect, intangible and elusive to satisfy the requirement of a public purpose. In almost every instance where submerged land would be reclaimed there would be employment provided and some economic benefit to the State. This court has upheld grants where the land was to be used for a water filtration plant (Bowes v. City of Chicago, 3 Ill. 2d 175, 120 N.E.2d 15) and for an exposition hall (Fairbank v. Stratton, 14 Ill. 2d 307, 152 N.E.2d 569), but it has upheld a grant to private individuals in only one instance, People ex rel. Moloney v. Kirk, 162 Ill. 138, 45 N.E. 830. There, however, as has been pointed out, the main purpose of the legislation was to benefit the public by the construction of an extension of Lake Shore Drive. The benefit to private interest was to further a public purpose and was incidental to the public purpose. (See also, City of Milwaukee v. State (1927), 193 Wis. 423, 214 N.W. 820.) Any benefit here to the public would be incidental. We judge that the direct and dominating purpose here would be a private one.

For the reasons given, the judgment of the circuit court is affirmed.

NOTES AND QUESTIONS

1. When a state alienates, in fee simple, submerged lands under navigable waters, must the conveyance be for a "public purpose"? If so, what is an acceptable public purpose? See City of Madison v. State, 1 Wis. 2d 252, 258–59, 83 N.W.2d 674, 678 (1957) (auditorium and civic center); Morse v. Oregon Division of State Lands, 285 Or. 197, 590 P. 2d 709 (1979) (runway for airport). Does it matter whether the conveyance is to a public entity or private party? Must a conveyance to a private party confer a public benefit? Would a conveyance of submerged land, which would be filled, to a group of doctors who were going to construct a hospital be acceptable? Must the contemplated private use be water dependent? Must the use be related to accepted public trust uses? If so, what is the source of the requirement that any conveyance of submerged lands under navigable waters be for a specific purpose or type of use? See generally 4 Water and Water Rights §§ 30.02(d)–(d)(3) (2011).

2. May the state be indirectly divested, free of the public trust, of submerged lands under navigable waters? If the state has a Marketable Title Act or Torrens Act, does either act apply to claims to public trust lands?

Most states have statutes that abrogate the ancient legal maxim "*nullius tempus occurrit regi*," or "time does not run against the king." Nowadays, in most situations, one can acquire title to state-owned land by adverse possession. The courts, however, have been reluctant to apply the doctrine of adverse possession to public trust lands. See, e.g., Romeo v. Sherry, 308 F. Supp. 2d 128 146–48 (E.D. N.Y. 2004) (no adverse possession of foreshore since navigable waterway is inalienable except by grant); State ex rel. Rohrer v. Credle, 322 N.C. 522, 369 S.E. 2d 825 (1988) (exclusive right to take oysters from lands under navigable waters cannot be acquired by prescriptive use); O'Neill v. State Highway Dep't Bd., 50 N.J. 307, 320, 235 A.2d 1, 8 (1967); Coastal States Gas Producing Co. v. State Mineral Bd., 199 So.2d 554, 557 (La. App. 1967). Absent a statute, such as N.C. Gen. Stat. § 1–45.1 (1985), that expressly prohibits the adverse possession of public trust lands, on what grounds can you distinguish allowing adverse possession of some state-owned lands but not public trust lands? Assuming that a state's adverse possession statute applied to public trust lands, what difficulties would a claimant encounter in proving the requisite elements of adverse possession?

In order to increase alienability of land and to simplify title transactions, a number of states have passed Marketable Title Acts. See, e.g., West's Fla. Stat. Ann. §§ 712.01–.10 (1979); N.C. Gen. Stat. §§ 47B–1 to 47B–9 (1984); Conn. Gen. Stat. Ann. § 47–33(b–h) (Supp. 1985). Under the provisions of these acts, the owner of title to land that has been of record for the requisite number of years has a title that is marketable subject only to claims that are exempted from the operation of the acts, encumbrances inherent in or arising after the instrument constituting the root of title, and claims that have been preserved by re-recording. All other conflicting claims are extinguished by the acts. If the particular state act does not expressly exempt the title or interests owned by the state or its political subdivisions, then two questions arise: (1) can the act be invoked to divest the state of title to submerged land under navigable waters, and (2) can the act be invoked to terminate the public's right to engage in public trust activities in such lands and waters?

3. One of our nation's most valuable resources is the millions of acres of saltwater marshlands that serve as vital links in the production of fish and shellfish. Yet, despite the apparent limitations *Illinois Central* placed upon the disposal of submerged lands, many states did sell and purport to convey fee simple title to large portions of these wetlands. Much was sold for pennies an acre. This, of course, was done primarily at a time when such wetlands were viewed as swamps, serving no purpose other than to breed mosquitos and other noxious insects. Today, many of these transactions are being challenged as violations of the public trust doctrine. See M. Kalo and J. Kalo, The Battle to Preserve North Carolina's Estuarine Marshes: The 1985 Legislation, Private Claims to Estuarine Marshes, Denial of Permits To Fill, And The Public Trust, 64 N.C. L. Rev. 565 (1986). Do they violate the public trust? Before you view the challengers as the good guys, charging forth to save the environment from pillagers, think about what the private parties are doing or might do with the land in dispute. If the state or other challengers win the lawsuits and the conveyances are declared invalid, does that prevent the state from entering into a more profitable arrangement that permits other private companies to engage in the same acts as those engaged in or planned by the present private claimant to the land? See, e.g., Phillips Petroleum Co. v. Mississippi, supra at p. 129. In other words, is it just a battle over who gets the money?

4. If a state agency sells submerged lands under navigable waters to private investors and the investors make some improvements, and they invest

significant sums in development plans for a project involving the submerged land, may the state subsequently challenge the validity of the original sale? If the state is successful, must the state reimburse the investors for the original purchase price (with interest?), the real property taxes that were paid, the development planning costs, and other sums invested in the proposed project? Would the answer change if the state was revoking a conveyance that a state agency had the authority to make as opposed to challenging the authority of the agency to make the conveyance in the first instance? See generally 4 Water and Water Rights, § 30.02(d)(1) (2011).

5. In some jurisdictions, even after state-owned submerged lands are filled, they may still retain their public trust status. In such circumstances, transfer of title to such lands may be constrained by the public trust doctrine. See, e.g. West Ann. Cal. Public Resources Code § 6307 (2005) (conditions under which title to such land may be transferred). In other jurisdictions, filled state-owned submerged lands may be subject to appropriation or adverse possession by private parties free of the public trust. See, e.g. Providence & Worcester R.R. v. Pine, 729 A. 2d 202 (R.I. 1999); Greater Providence Chamber of Commerce v. State, 675 A.2d 1038 (R.I. 1995) (filling of submerged lands with express or implicit approval of state and subsequent improvement of filled lands).

6. **The equal footing doctrine and conveyances by the federal government.** The fact that the federal government held territorial submerged lands in trust for future states did not necessarily mean that the federal government could never validly convey those lands to private parties prior to statehood. The Supreme Court, in Shively v. Bowlby, 152 U.S. 1 (1894), declared that the Property Clause permitted Congress to convey territorial public trust lands [and so defeat the title of a new State] "in order to perform international obligations, or to effect the improvement of such lands for the promotion and convenience of commerce with foreign nations and among the several States, or to carry out other public purposes appropriate to the objects for which the United States holds the Territory." Id. at 48. See also Summa Corp. v. California ex rel. State Lands Commission, 466 U.S. 198, 204–09 (carrying out treaty provisions represents an "international duty") reh'g denied, 467 U.S. 1231 (1984) (dicta); United States v. City of Anchorage, 437 F.2d 1081 (1971) (grant of public trust lands to federally owned and operated railroad deemed a "public purpose"); United States v. Alaska, 423 F.2d. 764 ("public purpose" served by grant to game refuge), cert. denied, 400 U.S. 967 (1970).

According to the United States Supreme Court, there is a "strong presumption against conveyance by the United States" of title to the bed of a navigable water. Montana v. United States, 450 U.S. 544, 552, reh'g denied, 452 U.S. 911 (1981). It is unclear whether this "strong presumption against conveyance" is constitutionally mandated or represents merely a congressional policy. See Utah Division of State Lands v. United States, 482 U.S. 193, 207 (1987) (Court inferred a congressional policy, not a constitutional obligation, to retain public trust property for future States); but see State of North Dakota ex rel. Board of University and School Lands v. Andrus, 506 F. Supp. 619, 623 (1981), aff'd, 671 F.2d 271 (1982) (presumption arises from the constitutional doctrine of equal footing). No matter what the source of this presumption, a court will not infer a conveyance of public trust lands unless in the grant itself an "intention was definitely declared or otherwise made very plain, or was rendered in clear and especial words, or unless the claim confirmed in terms embraces the land under the waters of the stream." Utah Division of State Lands, supra, at 198. The United States Supreme Court, however, has never determined that the United States did in fact grant to private parties sovereign lands prior to statehood. But see Choctaw Nation v. Oklahoma, 397 U.S. 620 (United States grant to Indian Nations upheld due to the unusual history behind the particular Indian treaties involved in this case. Arguably the Indian tribes represented a sovereign nation, not individuals), reh'g denied, 398 U.S. 945 (1970).

7. **Eminent domain and public trust rights.** If the federal government acquires title to submerged lands by eminent domain or otherwise, does that extinguish any public trust rights or interests that previously existed under state law? Does it matter whether the purpose for which the federal government acquired the lands is inconsistent with any public use? If the federal government later decides it no longer needs the submerged lands and sells them to a private individual, does the private individual take title subject to public trust rights and interests? If so, were the public trust rights and interests only suspended during federal ownership? Is a conveyance of submerged lands acquired by eminent domain or otherwise subject to the same limitations as conveyances of sovereignty lands in territories prior to statehood?

In Norton v. Town of Long Island, 883 A. 2d 889 (Me. 2005), the issue was whether certain submerged lands in Casco Bay in Maine, to which the United States acquired title by condemnation during World War II to use as part of a Navy fuel station and, subsequently in the 1960s, sold to a private individual, was conveyed to the private individual subject to any public trust interests. In its opinion, the court said:

> Because of the importance of the interest at issue, the United States' taking of the *jus privatum* through a condemnation of land cannot be understood to *implicitly* include a taking of a state's public trust interest in that land. * * * Here, because the description of the property does not include any mention of the public trust easement of the State, we will not imply a reference to that interest, and accordingly, we conclude the United States did not "take" the public trust easement and therefore never extinguished it by transferring it to a private individual.

> The State was appropriately listed as a party to the condemnation proceeding because it held the *jus privatum* title to the submerged lands beyond the low tide mark until the taking. The inclusion of the State as a party did not, however, negate the requirement that the federal gov-

ernment be explicit about the nature of its taking. We will not read into the description an intention to take the easement held by the State for the public. Accordingly, although the United States exercised its powers pursuant to the Property Clause of the United States Constitution, U.S. CONST., art. IV, § 3, cl. 2, in deeding the land to Norton's father, the *jus privatum* interest it deeded remains subject to the State's public trust easement, the *jus publicum,* which allows the public to use the submerged lands for fishing and navigation.

Through the application of the public trust doctrine in the present case, we have determined that Norton's title is subject to the State's public trust easement. This determination does not disrupt the chain of title established by Norton at trial. Norton holds *title* to the small boat pool, but his title is subject to the State's public trust easement permitting the public to use the small boat pool for fishing and navigation. Accordingly, Norton may, as the holder of title to the submerged lands, limit access to his structures, but may not build or arrange them in a manner that unreasonably interferes with the public's right to fish and navigate in the waters. See Opinion of the Justices, 437 A.2d at 605; State v. Wilson, 42 Me. 9, 26–27 (1856). The parties do not dispute that Norton has title to the breakwater structure itself and possesses the right to exclude others from it.

Id. at 900–901.

The *Norton* case does not address the question of whether the federal government *could* permanently extinguish public trust rights. As to that question the cases are in conflict. Compare City of Alameda v. Todd Shipyards Corp., 635 F. Supp. 1447, 1450 (N.D. Cal. 1986) (holding that the federal government may take the *jus publicum* but may not extinguish it and may not transfer it to a private party); United States v. 1.58 Acres of Land, 523 F. Supp. 120 (D. Mass. 1981) (dicta) (federal government is as restricted as the states in the disposition of sovereignty lands); with United States v. 11.037 Acres of Land, 685 F. Supp. 214, 216–17 (N.D. Cal. 1988) (the Supremacy Clause permits the federal government to extinguish the state's public trust easement by exercising the power of eminent domain).

C. STATE PUBLIC TRUST MANAGEMENT OBLIGATIONS

In the management of public trust waters and submerged lands, does the state have any affirmative obligations? Many people and companies use public trust waters and submerged lands for either private recreational purposes or for profit. The uses range from individual recreational piers and duck blinds to fish pound nets, fish farms, large scale marinas, and restaurants built over the water. Each of these uses, and many others, involve some appropriation of public trust lands and waters and, to some extent, the exclusion of the general public from the appropriated area. As the manager of the public trust, can the state charge these users "rent" or "equitable compensation" for their use of public trust waters and submerged lands? Is this good public policy? Is the state under a legal obligation to collect "rent"?

CAMINITI V. BOYLE

Supreme Court of Washington, 1987
107 Wash. 2d 662, 732 P.2d 989

ANDERSEN, JUSTICE.

This action was commenced by a petition filed in this court seeking a writ of mandamus directed to the Commissioner of Public Lands and the State Treasurer. Petitioners ask us to declare unconstitutional the state statute (RCW 79.90.105) which allows owners of residential property abutting state-owned tidelands and shorelands to install and maintain private recreational docks on such lands without payment to the state. * * * Having now considered the parties' briefs and oral argument on the merits, we decline to hold the statute unconstitutional. Issuance of the writ will be denied.

The case was submitted on agreed facts. Those pertinent to our disposition of the case are as follows:

> By the Laws of the State of Washington of 1983 * * * (RCW 79.90.105), the following legislation became effective on June 13, 1983:

> The abutting residential owner to state-owned shorelands, tidelands, or related beds of navigable waters, other than harbor areas, may install and maintain without charge a dock on such areas if used exclusively for private recreational purposes and the area is not subject to prior rights. This permission is subject to applicable local regulation governing construction, size, and length of the dock. This permission may be revoked by the department upon finding of public necessity which is limited to the protection of waterward access or ingress rights of other landowners or public health and safety. The revocation may be appealed as a contested case under chapter 34.04 RCW. Nothing in this section prevents the abutting owner from obtaining a lease if otherwise provided by law.

> Prior to the effective date of RCW 79.90.105, approximately 370 residential owners of private land abutting public aquatic lands were paying the State approximately $35,000 in annual rental for private recreational docks on public aquatic lands, outside of harbor areas, pursuant to the then statutorily authorized leasing program. * * *

There is one principal issue.

ISSUE

Does RCW 79.90.105, which allows owners of residential property abutting state-owned tidelands and shorelands[4] to install and maintain private recreational docks on such lands free of charge, violate article 17, section 1 of the Washington State Constitution or the "public trust doctrine"?

DECISION

The short answer to the question posed by this issue is "no." Upon admission into the Union, the state of Washington was vested with title in, and dominion over, its tidelands and shorelands. Since statehood, the Legislature has had the power to sell and convey title to state tidelands and shorelands. Prior to 1971, when the Legislature by statute changed its policy, the state had sold approximately 60 percent of its tidelands and 30 percent of its shorelands. The Legislature has never had the authority, however, to sell or otherwise abdicate state sovereignty or dominion over such tidelands and shorelands. By enacting the statute at issue in this case (RCW 79.90.105), the Legislature has seen fit to grant only a revocable license allowing owners of land abutting state-owned tidelands and shorelands to build recreational docks thereon subject to state regulation and control. The Legislature did not thereby surrender state sovereignty or dominion over these tidelands and shorelands, but through the Department of Natural Resources and local subdivisions of state government continues to exercise control over them.

By our state constitution, "[t]he state of Washington asserts its ownership to the beds and shores of all navigable waters in the state up to and including the line of ordinary high-tide, in waters where the tide ebbs and flows, and up to and including the line of ordinary high water within the banks of all navigable rivers and lakes. * * * " Const. art. 17, § 1 (part). This was but a formal declaration by the people of rights which our new state possessed by virtue of its sovereignty, and which declaration had the effect of vesting title to such lands in the state.

As this court has repeatedly held, under the foregoing constitutional provision the state of Washington has the power to dispose of, and invest persons with, ownership of tidelands and shorelands subject only to the paramount public right of navigation and the fishery. * * *

---

[4] In addition to referring to state-owned shorelands and tidelands, RCW 79.90.105 also deals with *related beds* of navigable waters, other than harbor areas. * * * "(Italics ours.) Bedlands are those lands lying beyond the line of navigability of rivers and lakes and those lands beyond the low-tide mark of tidal waters. RCW 79.90.050. Bedlands in tidal waters may present unique problems, particularly with respect to federal regulation of navigable waters. However, the parties have chosen to argue this case primarily with respect to tidelands and shorelands which, as a practical matter, are those principally involved. As a consequence, bedlands will not be separately dealt with herein other than to point out by this note that what we hold concerning tidelands and shorelands generally applies to bedlands as well.

The state's ownership of tidelands and shorelands is not limited to the ordinary incidents of legal title, but is comprised of two distinct aspects.

The first aspect of such state ownership is historically referred to as the *jus privatum* or private property interest. As owner, the state holds full proprietary rights in tidelands and shorelands and has fee simple title to such lands. Thus, the state may convey title to tidelands and shorelands in any manner and for any purpose not forbidden by the state or federal constitutions and its grantees take title as absolutely as if the transaction were between private individuals. In the case before us, the state has not by this statute conveyed title to the land, but as will be discussed shortly, has given a revocable license only.

The second aspect of the state's ownership of tidelands and shorelands is historically referred to as the *jus publicum* or public authority interest. The principle that the public has an overriding interest in navigable waterways and lands under them is at least as old as the Code of Justinian, promulgated in Rome in the 5th Century A.D. This *jus publicum* interest as expressed in the English common law and in the common law of this state from earliest statehood, is composed of the right of navigation and the fishery. More recently, this interest was more particularly expressed by this court in Wilbour v. Gallagher, 77 Wash. 2d 306, 316, 462 P.2d 232 (1969), as the right

> of navigation, together with its incidental rights of fishing, boating, swimming, water skiing, and other related recreational purposes generally regarded as corollary to the right of navigation and the use of public waters.

The state can no more convey or give away this *jus publicum* interest than it can "abdicate its police powers in the administration of government and the preservation of the peace." Thus it is that the sovereignty and dominion over this state's tidelands and shorelands, as distinguished from *title*, always remains in the state, and the state holds such dominion in trust for the public. It is this principle which is referred to as the "public trust doctrine." Although not always clearly labeled or articulated as such, our review of Washington law establishes that the doctrine has always existed in the State of Washington.

The test of whether or not an exercise of legislative power with respect to tidelands and shorelands violates the "public trust doctrine" is found in the following language of the United States Supreme Court:

> The control of the State for the purposes of the trust can never be lost, except as to such parcels as are used in promoting the interests of the public therein, or can be disposed of without any substantial impairment of the public interest in the lands and waters remaining.

Accordingly, we must inquire as to: (1) whether the state, by the questioned legislation, has given up its right of control over the *jus publicum* and (2) if so, whether by so doing the state (a) has promoted the interests of the public in the *jus publicum*, or (b) has not substantially impaired it.

* * *

Turning * * * to the above stated test for violations of the "public trust doctrine," and applying that test to the questioned statute (RCW 79.90.105), we observe as follows.

Right of control. Petitioners argue that "[a] common thread in judicially-pronounced public trust doctrine tests is deciding whether the state has retained adequate control over trust resources." We agree.

By enacting RCW 79.90.105, the Legislature has given up relatively little right of control over the *jus publicum*, and has not conveyed title to any state-owned tidelands or shorelands. The statute in question relates only to residential owners whose property abuts public tidelands or shorelands. * * * In Washington, abutting landowners have no riparian rights in state-owned tidelands and shorelands; accordingly, the ultimate state control is that the Legislature having by this statute given abutting landowners the license to use its tidelands and shorelands, can likewise revoke that license by repealing the statute in the event it sees fit to do so. * * *

Promotion of the interests of the public. The statute also promotes the interests of the public in the *jus publicum*, albeit to a limited degree. The Shoreline Management Act of 1971, discussed above, stresses that "coordinated planning is necessary in order to protect the public interest associated with the shorelines of the state while, at the same time, recognizing and protecting private property rights consistent with the public interest." The statute under review expresses a part of that policy; it is a practical recognition that one of the many beneficial uses of public tidelands and shorelands abutting private homes is the placement of private docks on such lands so homeowners and their guests may obtain recreational access to navigable waters. No expression of public policy has been directed to our attention which would encourage water uses originating on public docks, as they do, while at the same time discouraging any private investment in docks to help promote the use of public waters.

Impairment of the jus publicum. In any event, nothing in the statute substantially impairs the *jus publicum*. Private docks cannot, of course, block public access to public tidelands and shorelands, and the public must be able to get around, under or over them. Recreational docks existed on public tidelands and shorelands before enactment of the statute, and still do; the principal difference being that under current statutory policy there is no obligation to pay rental or lease fees.

* * *

The writ petitioned for is denied.

PEARSON, C.J., and DOLLIVER, UTTER, BRACHENBACH, CALLOW and DURHAM, JJ., and SCHUMACHER, J. PRO TEM., concur.

DORE, JUSTICE (dissenting). * * * (omitted)

NOTES AND QUESTIONS

1. In many states, littoral and riparian owners have the right to wharf out to access adjacent waterways with their vessels. In such states, may the state charge littoral and riparian owners a fee or annual rent when the owners exercise their rights and build docks, piers, or similar structures on the public trust lands adjacent to their waterfront property? Does it matter whether the riparian owner's use is commercial or non-commercial? Is the charging of rent simply a tax in disguise?

2. To what extent may the state issue licenses or leases to non-riparian or non-littoral owners that authorize such licensees or lessees to engage in activities on public trust lands? See, e.g. Washington State Geoduck Harvest Association v. Washington State Department of Natural Resources, 124 Wash. App. 441, 101 P.3d. 891 (2004) (auction of geoduck harvesting rights did not violate public trust). Does it matter whether the public will be totally excluded from the area subject to the license or lease? For example, under what circumstances, if any, may the state grant the right to close off public trust lands and associated waters to a fish farm? May the state, by lease, allow a private club to have exclusive use of the wet sand beach and waters that lie adjacent to the club's uplands? Do the terms of the lease matter? Does the length of the lease matter? Must the terms of the lease be the least restrictive of the public's right to use public trust lands and waters that is consistent with the legitimate needs of the licensee or lessee? See, e.g., Cartens v. California Coastal Commission, 182 Cal.App.3d 377, 227 Cal.Rptr. 135 (1986).

3. If the state collects a fee or rent for use of public trust lands or waters, must the funds collected be used for a public trust purpose or may the legislature use them for any public purpose?

4. If the placement of rip-rap or a seawall will inevitably cause the loss of the wet sand beach, may public interest groups challenge the issuance of a permit to construct such beach hardening devices on the grounds that the public trust doctrine requires the preservation of the wet sand beach for public access and use? If an objection based on common law principles to the issuance of the permit is not made before the coastal permit agency, is it waived? If the coastal permit agency nonetheless issues the permit, would a

public interest group have standing to appeal the agency's decision? See, e.g., Save Our Dunes v. Alabama Department of Environmental Management, 834 F.2d 984 (11th Cir. 1987) (under Alabama law, concern, knowledge, and general use of beaches are not sufficient, in and of themselves, to make plaintiffs an "aggrieved" person with standing to appeal adverse agency determination).

4. THE TRADITIONAL TRIAD AND JUDICIAL EXPANSION OF PUBLIC TRUST USES

English common law and the common law of most states recognize the right of any person to use navigable waters for navigation, commerce and fishing—the so-called traditional triad of public trust rights. Many American courts have expanded these public trust rights beyond the traditional triad to include other uses such as hunting, bathing, swimming, general recreation, using the bottom for anchoring, standing or other purposes, and conservation. See, e.g., Matthews v. Bay Head Improvement Ass'n, 95 N.J. 306, 321, 471 A.2d 355, 363, cert. denied, 469 U.S. 821 (1984); Marks v. Whitney, 6 Cal. 3d 251, 259, 491 P.2d 374, 380, 98 Cal.Rptr. 790, 796 (1971); Swan Island Club v. White, 114 F. Supp. 95, 103–05 (1953); White v. Hughes, 139 Fla. 54, 59, 190 So. 446, 449 (1939); Arnold v. Mundy, 6 N.J.L. 1 (1821) (one of the first cases recognizing the existence of the public trust doctrine in the United States); N.C. Gen. Stat. § 1–45.1 (purporting to codify common law public trust rights); see also J. Stevens, The Public Trust: A Sovereign's Ancient Prerogative Becomes The People's Environmental Right, 14 U.C. Davis L. Rev. 195, 221–23 (1980); Comment, The Public Trust Doctrine In Maine's Submerged Lands: Public Rights, State Obligation And The Role of The Courts, 37 Me. L. Rev. 105, 107–13 (1985); Comment, The Public Trust in Tidal Areas: A Sometime Submerged Traditional Doctrine, 79 Yale L.J. 762, 781–86 (1970). In some jurisdictions, public trust rights are apparently open-ended. See, e.g., Marks v. Whitney, supra.

New Jersey is one jurisdiction that has expanded public trust uses to include the incidental right to use privately owned dry sand beaches. In Matthews v. Bay Head Improvement Ass'n, 95 N.J. 306, 471 A. 2d 355, cert. denied, 469 U.S. 821 (1984), the Supreme Court of New Jersey, said

> Exercise of the public's right to swim and bathe below the mean high water mark may depend upon a right to pass across the uplands beach. * * *

> The bather's right in the upland shores is not limited to passage. Reasonable enjoyment of the foreshore and the sea cannot be realized unless some enjoyment of the dry sand area is also allowed. The complete pleasure of swimming must be accompanied by intermittent periods of rest and relaxation beyond the waters edge. * * * [W]here

the use of the dry sand is essential or reasonably necessary for the enjoyment of the ocean, the [public trust] doctrine warrants the public's use of the upland dry sand areas subject to an accommodation of the interests of the owner.

Id. at 324–25, 471 A. 2d at 364–65. The *Matthews* court identified a number of factors relevant to determining whether a particular privately owned dry sand beach was open to such public. Applying the *Matthews* factors in Raleigh Avenue Beach Association v. Atlantis Beach Club, 370 N.J. Super. 171, 851 A. 2d 19 (2005), the court determined that a private beach club's beach must be open to the general public at a reasonable fee for services provided by the owner.

Do these expansions of the traditional public trust doctrine raise a potential issue of a taking through judicial modification of the common law as some private property owners have argued? The "takings" clause of the Fifth Amendment to the United States Constitution provides that:

nor shall private property be taken for public use, without just compensation. * * *

Most "takings" occur through legislative or executive action. For example, the executive branch, through its agents, seizes private property for public use. Or the legislature passes a statute that so restricts the uses to which private property may be put that the court finds that in effect the law is the equivalent of an appropriation of the property for public use. But the "takings" issue may also arise in a different context—the promulgation and modification of property rules through the common law process. If a court expands the definition of "navigable," and thereby gives the public access to waters that everyone formerly thought were closed to the public, or adds to the public uses encompassed by the public trust doctrine, or interprets common law doctrines to assure the public has access to the dry sand beach, is there a "taking" of private property rights for public use in violation of the Fifth Amendment? See Stop The Beach Renourishment, Inc. v. Florida Department of Environmental Protection, 130 S.Ct. 2592, ___ U.S. ___ (2010) (extensive debate among Justices as to whether a "judicial decision determining the rights of property owners can violate the Takings Clause"), discussed further beginning on p. 383. What are relevant factors in determining whether a "taking" has occurred in this context? See id; see also B. Thompson, Judicial Takings, 76 Va. L. Rev. 1449 (1990).

5. PRIVATE PROPERTY INTERESTS IN COASTAL WATERS AND LANDS: LITTORAL AND RIPARIAN RIGHTS

A. INTRODUCTION

Although the state has the power to regulate coastal water uses and generally holds title to coastal submerged lands, property owners whose lands abut coastal waters may also have common law rights in adjacent coastal waters and submerged lands. Although these common law *littoral* and *riparian* rights may vary widely among the individual states, according to an early twentieth century authority, Henry Farnham, the traditional common law rights included:

1. The right to have the water remain in place and to retain, as nearly as possible, its natural character.[1]

2. The right of access, which included:

    i.   The right to maintain contact with the body of water;

    ii. The right to accretions;

    iii. The first right to purchase adjacent submerged land if it is sold by the state;

    iv. If filling of submerged land is permitted by the state, the preferential right to fill adjacent submerged land.

3. Subject to reasonable restrictions, the right to wharf out to the navigable portion of a body of water.

4. The right of free use of the water immediately adjoining the property for the transaction of such business associated with his wharves or other such structures.

I. Farnham, Water and Water Rights § 62 (1904); see also, e.g., Smith Tug & Barge Co. v. Columbia–Pacific Towing Corp. 250 Or. 612, 616, 443 P.2d 205, 208 (1968); 3 American Law of Property § 12.32 (1952); 1 Water and Water Rights § 6.01(a) (2011). For a detailed discussion of the specifics of the general rights listed above, see Game & Fresh Water Fish Commission v. Lakes Islands, Ltd., 407 So.2d 189, 191–92 (Fl. 1982).

One common feature of this list of rights is allowing the waterfront owner to maintain his or her adjacency to the water body. But what is meant by adjacency, and where exactly is the boundary when the level of the body of water may fluctuate with rising and falling tides?

---

[1] The 19th century common law riparian rules were based on the natural flow theory, which required that the riparian owner's use of the waterbody leave it substantially unchanged except for minor effects of the use. As a result of industrialization and increased economic and social needs for water, most American jurisdictions have adopted the reasonable use theory. This theory allows the riparian owner to make reasonable use of the water for any purpose. See generally, e.g., Restatement of Torts, Second, Chapter 41, Introductory Note (1979).

Since the 17th century and the publication of Lord Hale's De Jure Maris, the boundary between privately owned uplands and the publicly owned foreshore or tidelands has generally been the "ordinary high-tide line." In the United States, the federal common law rule is that the "ordinary high-tide line" is the "mean high-tide line,"[2] which is the average of all high-tides over an 18.6 year cycle, as determined by the Department of Commerce's National Oceanic Survey. See Borax Consolidated Ltd. v. Los Angeles, 296 U.S. 10, 26–27 (1935). The "ordinary high-tide line" is not the highest line reached by the tides during any month or period of years, and thus, areas of the foreshore which are flooded on occasion by tidal waters are the subject of private ownership. As the sea level rises, the mean high-tide line will move shoreward. In many areas, the shore has a very gradual slope and small vertical change in water level may cause a significant horizontal movement of a boundary on the ground. See G. Cole, Water Boundaries 1–55 (1997) (a detailed discussion of the techniques used to locate the mean high-tide line); see also F. Maloney and R. Ausness, The Use and Legal Significance of the Mean High Water Line in Coastal Boundary Mapping, 53 N.C. L. Rev. 185 (1974).

In thinking about this division between the public and the private, consider for a moment coastal beaches with which you are familiar and how these beaches are used. In light of these considerations, is using the mean high-tide line a realistic way of separating the public from the private?

In addition to separating publicly owned foreshore from privately owned upland, the *mean high-tide line* marks the outer limits of a body of navigable waters. That which is waterward is part of the navigable body of water; that which is landward is considered part of the uplands.[3] Thus, a navigable body of water is more than its navigable channels. It includes the full breadth of the water body from mean high-tide line to mean high-tide line.[4]

---

[2] The mean high tide line may also be called the "ordinary high water mark."

[3] In some situations, it is physically impossible to use the mean high-water mark as a means of separating uplands from submerged lands. For example, dense mangrove swamps cover parts of Florida's coast. Under those conditions, locating the mean high water mark is not possible. Rather than apply a purely fictional tidal rule, Florida's courts sometimes use *meander lines* to define the boundary between public and private lands. See Florida Bd. of Trustees of the Internal Improvement Trust Fund v. Wakulla Silver Springs Co., 362 So.2d 706 (Fla. Dist. Ct. App. 1978); cf. Utah v. United States, 425 U.S. 948 (1976) (involving title to lands exposed by the evaporation of Utah's Great Salt Lake). But see St. Joseph Land and Dev. Co. v. Florida St. Bd., 365 So.2d 1084 (Fla. Dist. Ct. App. 1979).

The meander line is a straight line or series of straight lines connecting points on the shore. The meander line is primarily for determining the quantity of public land in the subdivision being surveyed and is not intended as an exact measurement. For a discussion of the problems of using meander lines as boundaries, see D. Maloney, The Ordinary High Water Mark: Attempts at Settling an Unsettled Boundary Line, 13 Land & Water L. Rev. 465, 489–92 (1965).

[4] When dealing with non-tidal waters, the outer limits of navigability are determined by the location of the ordinary high water mark.

One further observation is necessary to complete this discussion. The *Borax* rule is a federal common law rule applied to determine the seaward boundary of a federal patent or grant of oceanfront property. This rule may not be applicable in other settings. As a matter of state law, the dividing line between public and private interests may be something other than the mean high-tide line as defined by federal law. In fact, at least five states (Maine, Massachusetts, Virginia, Delaware, and Pennsylvania) recognize the existence of some private interests extending to the low-tide line.

B. ACCRETION, EROSION, AVULSION, AND RELICTION

1. General Principles

In most coastal states, tidal boundaries are considered to be ambulatory; that is, the physical location of the mean high (or low) water line may shift because of natural or artificial changes in the location of the shoreline. Accordingly, littoral owners may gain or lose land by virtue of accretion, reliction, erosion, or avulsion.

* * * Accretions or accreted lands consist of additions to the land resulting from the gradual deposit by water of sand, sediment or other material. The term applies to such lands produced along both navigable and non-navigable water. Alluvion is that increase of earth on a shore or bank of a stream or sea, by the force of the water, as by a current or by waves, which is so gradual that no one can judge how much is added at each moment of time. The term "alluvion" is applied to the deposit itself, while accretion denotes the act, but the terms are frequently used synonymously.

Reliction refers to land which formerly was covered by water, but which has become dry land by the imperceptible recession of the water. Although there is a distinction between accretion and reliction, one being the gradual building of the land, and the other the gradual recession of water, the terms are often used interchangeably. The term "accretion" in particular is often used to cover both processes, and generally the law relating to both is the same.

Erosion is the gradual and imperceptible wearing away of land bordering on a body of water by the natural action of the elements. Avulsion is either the sudden and perceptible alteration of the shoreline by action of the water, or a sudden change of the bed or course of a stream forming a boundary whereby it abandons its old bed for a new one.

As a general rule, where the shoreline is gradually and imperceptibly changed or shifted by accretion, reliction or erosion, the boundary line is extended or restricted in the same manner. The owner of the littoral property thus acquires title to all additions arising by accretion or reliction, and loses soil that is worn or washed away by erosion. However, any change in the shoreline that takes place suddenly and perceptibly does not result in a change of boundary or ownership. Normally a landowner may not intentionally increase his estate through accretion or reliction by artificial means. However, the littoral owner is usually entitled to additions that result from artificial conditions created by third persons without his consent.

* * *

F. Maloney and R. Ausness, The Use and Legal Significance of the Mean High Water Line in Coastal Boundary Mapping, 53 N.C. L. Rev. 185, 224–26 (1974).

2. The Right to Accretions

a. The General Rule

The general common law rule is that all accretions belong to the waterfront owner to whose land they attach. Such a rule has a number of justifications. First, a person is a littoral or riparian owner if a water body constitutes one or more of the described boundaries of his or her property. In such a case, in order for the boundary to remain the same, the accretions must become the property of the waterfront owner. Second, the reason waterfront property commands a premium price is because of its access to the water. Unless the accretions became the property of the waterfront owner, she could gradually be cut off from access to the water and lose one of the most important and valuable features of the property. Third, accretions, in many cases, involve relatively small additions to the upland. To the extent that such additional uplands can be put to productive use, as a practical matter, the waterfront owner is the only one situated to put the accreted land to use. Fourth, if the waterfront owner is to lose land to erosion, then it seems only fair to allow her to benefit from the reverse process of accretion.

b. The General Rule and Equity

FORD V. TURNER

District Court of Appeal of Florida, 1962
142 So. 2d 335

WHITE, JUDGE.

Appellants H. H. Ford and Robert Ford and wives were principal defendants in a quiet title suit which resulted in favor of the plaintiff-appellee Walter S. Turner, Jr. The litigation involves an apparent increment or increase of land in the form of an elongated strip physically attached to the southerly end of Captiva Island near Blind Pass in Lee County on the lower Gulf Coast of Florida. * * *

The record reveals, however, that the general topography of the involved area has altered considerably since the turn of the century. The great geodetic changes between 1900 and 1958 are reflected in the following sketches derived from exhibits in evidence. The approximate relative location of the disputed tract, which purportedly 'accreted' to the plaintiff's land, is indicated on Sketch 2 [which appears following the text of the case].* * *

According to the defendants' exhibits, the Ford property did originally front on the open Gulf of Mexico. A series of aerial photographs dated 1937, 1939, 1944, 1953 and 1958 show that Captiva Island has built up in a southerly direction until that island has almost completely paralleled Ford's original Gulf frontage, leaving only a navigable channel separating Ford's property and the 'accreted' portion of Captiva Island with the Island fronting on the Gulf.* * *

Generally the margin or bed of a stream, or other body of water constituting a boundary, continues to be the boundary notwithstanding any accretion or erosion which changes the location of the body of water. The boundary lines of land so located thus extends or restricts as that margin gradually changes or shifts by reason of accretion or erosion. Feig v. Graves, Fla. App.1958, 100 So.2d 192, 196. The newly formed land belongs to the owner of the land to which it is an accretion, and not to the one originally owning the land in that place. See 8 A.L.R. 640, 41 A.L.R. 395 and numerous cases cited.

One witness testified that the accretion to plaintiff's land extended southeastward approximately 9,000 feet. One of the defendants' contentions, as stated, is that accretion can not thus extend laterally but only frontward.* * *

We have studied the authorities cited by defendants in support of their contention that accretion must be immediately in front of the land to which it has attached and that the owner cannot follow it laterally. See III Farnham, Waters and Water Rights, § 845(a), pgs. 2489–2490. Most of the cited cases, however, applied to rivers and streams or non-tidal waters where the owners' boundaries extended to the center of the stream bed in contradistinction to the instant case where the lands border tidal waters in which the title to the submerged land is held by the State of Florida in trust for the use and benefit of its citizens.* * *

Florida is bordered by water on the east, south and west. The numerous islands or keys are constantly changing by various methods of accretion, alluvion, erosion, reliction and avulsion, giving rise to myriad problems. Public policy demands a definite standard of quieting title to these areas despite the fact that occasionally some hardship may occur. * * *

Affirmed.

NOTES AND QUESTIONS

1. On facts quite similar to *Ford*, the Supreme Court of Washington held that lateral accretions that cut off a littoral owner's direct access to the ocean belonged to that person and not to the littoral owner to whose uplands the accretions actually adhered. Hudson House, Inc. v. Rozman, 82 Wash.2d 178, 509 P.2d 992 (1973). See also Strom v. Sheldon, 12 Wash.App. 66, 527 P.2d 1382 (1974). See generally 3 American Law of Property § 15.27 (1952). For a criticism of *Ford*, see Note, Accretion: A New Slant, 17 U. Miami L. Rev. 417 (1963).

2. Who owns accretions that result from the construction of a groin, jetty, or similar structure? Is the waterfront owner entitled only to accretions created by natural processes? The general common law rule is that the waterfront owner is entitled to all accretions created by natural or artificial sources, unless the accretions are artificially induced by the waterfront owner. See, e.g., Bd. of Trustees of Internal Improvement Trust Fund v. Sand Key Associates, Ltd., 512 So.2d 934 (Fla. 1987) (common law rule); but see, e.g., People v. Hector, 241 Cal. App.2d 484, 50 Cal.Rptr. 654 (1966) (If artificially induced accretions would result in the transfer of state owned tidelands to private ownership, the California rule is that waterfront owners are not entitled to such accretions). Frequently, such questions are resolved by statute. See, e.g., N.C. Gen. Stat. §§ 146–6(a) and (b). If lateral artificial accretions adhering to one littoral owner' land cut off another littoral owner's direct access to the water, should those accretions be equitably apportioned or would they belong only to the littoral owner to whose lands they adhere? See Rayne v. Coulbourne, 65 Md. App. 351, 500 A. 2d 665 (1985) (equitable apportionment).

3. In Norfolk, Virginia, a couple purchased an unbuildable, one acre waterfront lot on Chesapeake Bay in 1981. Then a "miracle" occurred! In 1984 sand rapidly began to accrete. In fact, it accreted as fast as the City of Norfolk could dump it on a withered city beach two miles upshore. Longshore currents carried the City's sand directly to the lot. Today, the lot is fronted by a five acre beach. The City claims the beach is "public land" and plans to scoop up the sand and return it to the beach where it was originally dumped. Can the city do that? See C. Zaneski, "Drifting Sand Shapes into a Property Dispute," The Virginian–Pilot and The Ledger–Star, November 5, 1988, at A1.

4. What happens when erosion causes the mean high-tide line to move shoreward, eventually crossing the fixed boundary line of formerly non-littoral or non-riparian land? Does the land become littoral or riparian and

subject to the rules of erosion and accretion? See generally American Law of Property § 15.27 (1952); C. Dunscombe, Riparian and Littoral Rights 37 (1970). Consider the following situation. In 1965, the plaintiff purchased two inland lots in a development located near the north end of a barrier island. The recorded plat showed the location of the lots and of a planned adjacent public road. Over a period of several years, but before any significant construction occurred in the development, the northern inlet separating this barrier island from the next one migrated southward, completely washing away the northern end of the island, including plaintiff's lots. Neither the plaintiff nor any of the other affected lot owners made any attempt to reclaim submerged lots. However, in 1978, the original developer obtained permits from both the state and the U.S. Army Corps of Engineers allowing him to reconstruct the northern end of the island.

Over the next few years, sand and other fill material was deposited in the inlet until the inlet was completely closed. A new inlet was then opened near the original 1965 location. The filled area was roughly the size of the original washed out area, but not in exactly the same location. Plaintiff's original lots would now be oceanfront lots, but located seaward of the beach setback line and therefore unbuildable.

After the filling was completed, the enterprising developer prepared a new plat, with new lots and a new road, the locations of which did not correspond to the original 1965 plat, and filed the plat with the state. All of these new lots have been sold and summer homes valued at one-half million dollars or more constructed upon them.

The plaintiff has now filed suit seeking a declaration that she is the owner of two lots, located in the positions in which they appear in the 1965 plat, and that she has an easement of ingress and egress over the area identified as a public road on the 1965 plat. At this time, that road would run right through the center of a number of houses constructed upon 76 of the "new" lots. Is the plaintiff still the owner of the two lots? Does she have a right of ingress and egress over the area shown in the original plat? See Ward v. Sunset Beach and Twin Lakes, Inc., 53 N.C. App. 59, 279 S.E.2d 889 (1981); United States v. 2,134.46 Acres of Land, 257 F.Supp. 723 (D.N.D. 1966); N.C. Gen. Stat. § 146–6.

———

3. **Beach Nourishment Projects: Avulsion or Accretion?**

Rising sea levels, ocean storms and the natural wave processes annually cause significant losses of valuable shoreline. Often these property owners will seek to reclaim the lost land. Due to the expense and the likelihood that any private reclamation may be only temporary, property owners will attempt to have the state or federal government finance a beach nourishment project. Following such a project, to whom does the nourished beach belong? In the absence of a statute, where should the line between public and private ownership be drawn? Should the rule of accretion or avulsion apply? Keep in mind that littoral rights attach only to land that abuts the water. See, Slavin v. Town of Oak Island and Walton County v. Stop the Beach Renourishment, which appear below, at p. 202 and p. 193, respectively and accompanying notes.

4. State or Federal Common Law?

Generally state law determines the nature and the extent of a property right. Thus, one would think that the question of whether a waterfront owner was entitled to accretions, or suffered losses as the result of erosion, would be a matter of state common law or statutes. But this is not always true.

In Hughes v. Washington, 389 U.S. 290 (1967), the state of Washington claimed title to accretions to oceanfront property owned by Mrs. Hughes. Mrs. Hughes title was traceable back to a pre-statehood federal patent. The state supreme court held that, under state law, Mrs. Hughes had no right to any accretions that formed between her upland property and the ocean. The United States Supreme Court reversed, holding that the question of Mrs. Hughes' right to accretions was a matter of federal common law. And, the federal common law rule was the traditional common law rule which vested title to accretions in the adjacent upland owner. According to the Court, the question was one that:

> deals with waters that lap both the lands of the State and the boundaries of the international sea. This relationship, at this particular point of the marginal sea, is too close to the vital interest of the Nation in its own boundaries to be governed by any law but the "supreme Law of the Land".

Id. at 293. A few years later, the Court seemed to back away from its conclusion in *Hughes*.

In Oregon ex rel. State Land Board v. Corvallis Sand and Gravel Company, 429 U.S. 363 (1977), the United States Supreme Court held that the *Hughes* rule—that the common law rights of littoral owners whose title is traceable to a federal patent are determined by federal common law—did not apply to riparian owners whose title is also traceable to a federal patent. According to the Court, federal law only determined the initial boundary between submerged lands that passed to the state upon statehood, and the uplands, which were the subject of a federal patent. "[T]hereafter * * * the land is subject the laws of the State." Id. at 376. Thus, the rights of the riparian owner, whose title was traceable to a federal patent, were to be determined by state property law rules and not federal law.

The issue of whether federal common law or state law determines the present-day property rights of persons who trace their title back to a federal patent goes to a fundamental notion inherent in our federal system, that each newly admitted state enters the Union on an "equal footing" regarding political standing and sovereignty. The rights of riparian owners in the original thirteen states, political entities that existed prior to the founding of the Union, were a matter of the states' existing, differing, evolving common law. To hold that "[a]n original State * * * [was] free to choose its own legal principles to resolve property disputes relating to lands under its riverbeds; [but], a subsequently admitted State * * * [must] apply the federal common-law rule, which may result in property law determinations antithetical to the desires of that State * * *" would be a perverse application of the *equal footing doctrine*. Id. at 378. "Under our federal system, property ownership is not governed by a general federal law, but rather by the laws of the several States." Id.

Surprisingly, *Hughes* was not overruled by the *Corvallis* majority. Instead, the majority attempted to distinguish *Hughes* on the dubious basis that the property in *Hughes* was oceanfront property, the boundaries of which are "too close to the vital interest of the Nation in its own boundaries to allow to be governed by any law but the supreme Law of the Land.'" Id. at 377 n.6 (citing Hughes v. Washington, 389 U.S. 290, 293 (1967)).

Later, in California v. United States, 457 U.S. 273, reh'g denied, 458 U.S. 1131 (1982), the Supreme Court reaffirmed the *Hughes* rule. The issue was whether the United States or the State of California had title to oceanfront land created through accretion to land owned by the United States. The accretion followed the construction of two jetties extending seaward from the land owned by the United States. Under California law, a distinction is drawn between accretion resulting from natural forces and that which is the effect of artificial conditions. The former belongs to the littoral owner; the latter belongs to the State. The Court, however, held "that a dispute over accretion to oceanfront property where title rests with or *was derived* from the Federal Government is to be determined by federal law." Id. at 273 (emphasis added). According to the Court, the federal rule is that accretions of whatever cause belong to the littoral owner. Id. at 288. See also Wilson v. Omaha Indian Tribe, 442 U.S. 653 (1979).

The *Hughes* decision and its progeny leave a number of questions unanswered. Does the *Hughes* rule apply to property on all tidal waters if title is traceable to a federal patent? Would it apply to property in Puget Sound? If oceanfront property is located in one of the original thirteen states, and therefore title could not be traced to a federal patent, does federal or state law determine the rights of oceanfront property owners? Does United States v. California, 381 U.S. 139 (1965) or the Submerged

Lands Act of 1953 (see Chapter 4, infra) have any bearing on this question?

5.   Interfering with the Natural Processes of Erosion and Accretion

More often than not the source of interferences with the natural processes of erosion and accretion will be seawalls and other temporary and permanent erosion control structures. Does a littoral owner have a common law right to protect coastal property from erosion? If a proper permit is obtained for such a structure, is the littoral owner nonetheless liable to others for any increased erosion of their property caused by the structure? The following two cases address these issues.

UNITED STATES V. MILNER

United States Court of Appeals, Ninth Circuit, 2009
583 F. 3rd. 1174

FLETCHER, CIRCUIT JUDGE:

[The United States, as trustee for the Lummi Nation, holds title to tidelands in the State of Washington located in the Strait of Georgia. The adjacent uplands are owned by a number of homeowners who have erected shoreline defense structures consisting of rip rap and boulders with bulkheads placed landward of the rip rap and boulders.]

In this appeal we decide whether a group of waterfront homeowners are liable for common law trespass * * * because the ambulatory tideland property boundary has come to intersect shore defense structures the homeowners have erected. * * * [A]fter a bench trial, the district court found against the homeowners and ordered them to remove violating structures * * *We affirm in part and reverse in part.

I.

* * *

After finding liability, [District] Judge Rothstein imposed an injunction under the Rivers and Harbors Act (RHA) ordering the Homeowners to remove any shore defense structures located seaward of the mean high water (MHW) line. * * *

III.

The problem of riparian and littoral property boundaries is a recurring and difficult issue. These disputes can be especially complicated where the land borders tidal waters, because the waters fluctuate dramatically and because private title claims often have to be balanced against federal and state interests in the ownership and use of the submerged lands. At issue in the Homeowners' second challenge to the trespass claim are two competing common law principles. On the one hand, courts have long recognized that an owner of riparian or littoral property must accept that the property boundary is ambulatory, subject to gradual loss or gain depending on the whims of the sea. *See, e.g.,* County of St. Clair v. Lovingston, 23 Wall. 46, 90 U.S. 46, 68–69, 23 L.Ed. 59 (1874). On the other hand, the common law also supports the owner's right to build structures upon the land to protect against erosion. *See, e.g.,* Cass v. Dicks, 14 Wash. 75, 44 P. 113, 114 (1896) ("If a landowner whose lands are exposed to inroads of the sea [ ] . . . erects sea walls or dams for the protection of his land, and by so doing causes the tide, the current, or the waves to flow against the land of his neighbor . . . [he] is not responsible in damages to the latter, as he has done no wrong having acted in self-defense, and having a right to protect his land." (citation omitted)). In this case, the Homeowners' land has eroded away so dramatically that the ambulatory tideland boundary has reached and become fixed at their shore defense structures. While the Homeowners cannot be faulted for wanting to prevent their land from eroding away, we conclude that because both the upland and tideland owners have a vested right to gains from the ambulation of the boundary, the Homeowners cannot permanently fix the property boundary, thereby depriving the Lummi of tidelands that they would otherwise gain.

Under the common law, the boundary between the tidelands and the uplands is ambulatory; that is, it changes when the water body shifts course or changes in volume. *See* Jefferis v. East Omaha Land Co., 134 U.S. 178, 189, 10 S.Ct. 518, 33 L.Ed. 872 (1890); California ex rel. State Lands Comm'n v. United States, 805 F.2d 857, 864 (9th Cir.1986); United States v. Boynton, 53 F.2d 297, 298 (9th Cir.1931). The uplands owner loses title in favor of the tideland owner-often the state-when land is lost to the sea by erosion or submergence. The converse of this proposition is that the littoral property owner gains when land is gradually added through accretion, the accumulation of deposits, or reliction, the exposure of previously submerged land. *See* County of St. Clair, 90 U.S. at 68–69, 23 Wall. 46; Jefferis, 134 U.S. at 189, 10 S.Ct. 518; 65 C.J.S. Navigable Waters § 95 (2009). These rules date back to Roman times, and have been noted in Blackstone's Commentaries and many other common law authorities and cases. * * *

By this logic, both the tideland owner and the upland owner have a right to an ambulatory boundary, and each has a vested right in the potential gains that accrue from the movement of the boundary line. The relationship between the tideland and upland owners is reciprocal: any loss experienced by one is a gain made by the other, and it would be inherently unfair to the tideland owner to privilege the forces of accretion over those of erosion. Indeed, the fairness rationale underlying courts' adoption of the rule of accretion assumes that uplands already are subject to erosion for which the owner otherwise has no remedy.

* * *

The Homeowners concede that the tideland boundary is ambulatory, but only to a point. According to the Homeowners, once the MHW line intersects the face of their defense structures, the boundary becomes fixed and remains so unless the tide line overtops the structures or recedes. The Homeowners rightly note that the common law permits them to erect shore defense structures on their property to prevent erosion. They contend that they lawfully did just that, building landward of the MHW line, and cannot be liable for the movement of the tideland boundary. In particular, the Homeowners draw support for their position from the *1189 common enemy doctrine, which provides that "[a] man may raise an embankment on his own property to prevent the encroachments of the sea, although the fact of his doing so may be to cause the water to beat with violence against the adjoining lands, thereby rendering it necessary for the adjoining landowner to enlarge or strengthen his defenses." Revell v. People, 177 Ill. 468, 52 N.E. 1052, 1059 (1898) (quotation marks and citation omitted).

Typically, the common enemy doctrine applies as a defense to nuisance or trespass actions where a property owner has caused surface waters-the "common enemy" of all landowners-to invade a neighbor's property. *See, e.g.,* Cass v. Dicks, 14 Wash. 75, 44 P. 113, 114 (1896) ("[S]urface water, caused by the falling of rain or the melting of snow, and that escaping from running streams and rivers, is regarded as an outlaw and a common enemy, against which any one may defend himself, even though by doing so injury may result to others."). The doctrine therefore does not apply here. On the one hand, the injury complained of is not the diversion of water onto the tidelands; rather, it is the physical encroachment of the shore defense structures themselves. * * * On the other hand, the rule is inapposite because the water is not acting as a "common enemy" of the parties involved. The tide line is an inherent attribute of the properties at issue, since it dictates where the tidelands end and the uplands begin. That the boundary is ambulatory does not make it a common enemy, since any movement seaward or landward is to the benefit of one party and the detriment of the other. It is unfortunate that the boundary line increasingly has encroached on the Homeowners' property, but they cannot claim that the common enemy doctrine allows them to fix permanently the tideland boundary.

The Homeowners have the right to build on their property and to erect structures to defend against erosion and storm damage, but all property owners are subject to limitations in how they use their property. The Homeowners cannot use their land in a way that would harm the

Lummi's interest in the neighboring tidelands. Given that the Lummi have a vested right to the ambulatory boundary and to the tidelands they would gain if the boundary were allowed to ambulate, the Homeowners do not have the right to permanently fix the property boundary absent consent from the United States or the Lummi Nation. The Lummi similarly could not erect structures on the tidelands that would permanently fix the boundary and prevent accretion benefitting the Homeowners. Although the shore defense structures may have been legal as they were initially erected, this is not a defense against the trespass action nor does it justify denying the Lummi land that would otherwise accrue to them.

We emphasize that this does not mean property owners cannot erect shore defense structures on their property or take other action to prevent erosion. Nor does it mean that the Homeowners must necessarily remove their structures, if they can reach an agreement with the Lummi Nation and the United States that allows the structures to remain. Rather, we hold only that the Homeowners have no defense to a trespass action because they are seeking to protect against erosion. Once the shore has eroded so dramatically that the property owner's shore defense structures fix the ambulatory boundary, the upland owner cannot expect to permanently maintain the boundary there without paying damages to the tideland owner or working out an agreement with the tideland owner. * * *

* * *

LUMMIS V. LILLY

Supreme Judicial Court of Massachusetts, 1982
385 Mass. 41, 429 N.E.2d 1146

NOLAN, JUSTICE.

The defendants filed a motion to dismiss or for summary judgment in answer to a complaint in three counts alleging nuisance, unreasonable use, and unjust enrichment, resulting from the defendants' installation and maintenance of a stone groin on their Cape Cod waterfront property, which almost adjoins the plaintiff's littoral property.* * *

From the record we learn that the defendants have owned their property since at least 1965. * * * The plaintiff purchased his property (Lummis property) in 1975. An engineer's plan of the area reveals that both properties are on that part of the shore of Buzzards Bay in Cape Cod known as Sippewisset Beach and that they are almost contiguous. In 1966, Josiah Lilly applied to the Massachusetts Department of Public Works for a license "to build and maintain a stone groin." The license was granted under the following terms and conditions: " * * * Nothing in this license shall be construed as authorizing encroachment on property not owned or controlled by the licensee except with the consent of the owner or owners thereof. This license is granted subject to all applicable Federal, State, County and Municipal laws, ordinances and regulations." Lilly also received a permit from the United States Army Engineer Division "to construct and maintain a stone groin and place riprap" on his property, under conditions which do not require recital because they are not material to this case. A groin was then built.

A groin was defined in one expert's affidavit as "a solid structure which lies generally perpendicular to the shoreline and extends from the backshore out across the foreshore of the beach. The function of a groin is to interrupt the littoral drifting of sand along the shore, thereby producing deposition of sand on the updrift side of the structure and widening the beach." According to the same expert the "[l]ittoral drifting continues on the downdrift side of the structure and since the sand which is transported away is not replaced by sand from the updrift side, the beach narrows on the downdrift side of the groin." The Lummis property is on the downdrift side and these conditions, as they affect the Lummis property, are precisely the damage alleged by the plaintiff.

The narrow but important issue is whether we should apply the rule of "reasonable use" as most recently enunciated by this court in Tucker v. Badoian, 376 Mass. 907, 384 N.E.2d 1195 (1978), to the rights of owners of oceanfront property.

In *Tucker*, the court rejected, as to the problems of surface water, the standard which came to be known as the "common enemy" rule. * * *

The common enemy rule has never been successfully invoked in decisions adjudicating the rights of riparian landowners. From earliest times, these rights have been enforced under the standard of reasonable use. In Stratton v. Mount Hermon Boys' School, 216 Mass. 83, 85, 103 N.E. 87 (1913), the "reasonable use" rule was articulated as follows: "[E]ach riparian owner must conduct his operations reasonably in view of like rights and obligations in the owners above and below him. The right of no one is absolute but is qualified by the existence of the same right in all others similarly situated. The use of the water flowing in a stream is common to all riparian owners and each must exercise this common right so as not essentially to interfere with an equally beneficial enjoyment of the common right by his fellow riparian owners. Such use may result in some diminution, obstruction or change in the natural flow of the stream, but the interference cannot exceed that which arises from reasonable conduct in the light of all circumstances, having due regard to the exercise of the common right by other riparian owners." Support for this rule * * * can be found in Restatement (Second) of Torts § 850 (1979).

Our jurisprudence on the rule governing littoral rights is not abundant. * * * A more recent case to address the problem directly is Jubilee Yacht Club v. Gulf Ref. Co., 245 Mass. 60, 140 N.E. 280 (1923), in which the plaintiff sought damages and injunctive relief because of the defendant's construction of a breakwater. The defendant in the present action relies heavily on *Jubilee*, in which the court denied the plaintiff relief because the defendant "merely exercised the ordinary rights of an owner in fee." Id. at 64, 140 N.E. 280. There, the court analogized the defendant's construction of the concrete breakwater to "acts * * * committed by the owner of adjoining property away from the seashore. * * * The building of fences, walls or other structures, or making excavations on his own land ordinarily is within the absolute right of the owner of a fee without reference to the incidental injury which may thereby be caused to his neighbor." Id. at 62, 140 N.E. 280.

To the extent that the *Jubilee* decision approved of a rule applicable to littoral owners other than that of reasonable use we choose not to follow it. There is no sound reason for imposing the obligation of reasonable use on riparian owners, while permitting littoral owners to use their property without any limitations. See Mears v. Dole, 135 Mass. 508, 510 (1883).

1. **Reasonable use.** On remand, the trial judge will be faced with weighing the evidence to resolve whether the defendants have made a reasonable use of their property as that use affects the plaintiff's property. There are several factors which the judge may consider in determining whether the maintenance of the stone groin in its present form constitutes a reasonable use. Factors considered relevant to reasonable use by riparian owners can be considered in evaluating the same question when applied to littoral owners.

Among those factors are the license which the defendant secured and whether the conditions of the license have been met. Neither the license from the Department of Public Works nor the permit from the United States Army Engineer Division is conclusive on the issue of reasonable use. It is settled that a license does not immunize the licensee from liability for negligence or nuisance which flows from the licensed activity.

Other factors bearing on the reasonableness of the use are the purpose of the use, the suitability of the use to the water course, the economic value of the use, the social value of the use, the extent and amount of harm it causes, the practicality of avoiding the harm by adjusting the use or method of use of one owner or the other, the practicality of adjusting the quantity of water used by each owner, the protection of existing values of water uses, land, investments, and enterprise, and the justice of requiring the user who is causing harm to bear the loss. Restatement (Second) of Torts § 850A (1979). See Stratton v. Mount Hermon Boys' School, 216 Mass. 83, 85, 103 N.E. 87 (1913).

2. **Nature of relief.** This case was decided by entry of summary judgment for the defendants. As a result, the judge did not consider the

issue of the relief, if any, to which the plaintiff would be entitled. We need not reach this issue. At a minimum, the plaintiff might be entitled to equitable relief from prospective injury, if an unreasonable use of the groin is found. In such case, equitable relief in the form of an injunction or an order to reduce the size of the groin or to modify its shape may be in order.

As to relief for damages sustained prior to the entry of judgment, it appears that the plaintiff's claim is founded more nearly on longstanding principles enunciated in connection with the rights of riparian owners than on principles similar to the rights of landowners concerned with surface water, recently announced prospectively in Tucker v. Badoian, supra. [citations omitted.] On this record, we cannot determine what, if any, damages may be recoverable by the plaintiff.

The judgment dismissing the plaintiff's complaint is reversed and the case is remanded to the Superior Court for action consistent with this opinion.

So ordered.

NOTES AND QUESTIONS

1. **Bans on permanent erosion control structures.** States imposing bans on coastal construction of permanent erosion control structures include Maine, North Carolina, Rhode Island, and South Carolina. In North Carolina, temporary erosion control methods, such as sandbags, are permitted. These sandbag structures, consisting of stacks and rows of sandbags twenty feet long and six feet in diameter, function much the same as a permanent seawall. Although the rules provide that in most circumstances the sandbags may only be in place for five years, the fact of the matter is many have been in place for more than twenty years. When attempts are made to enforce the rules, as one can imagine, the resistance is high. If sea level rise predictions are accurate, the threat of erosion will increase for more and more coastal property and so will the pressure from coastal communities and property owners to allow more and more permanent hardened erosion control structures. See, e.g. N.C. Gen. Stat. 113A–115.1(authorizing the issuance of permits to construct "terminal groins.")

2. If *Milner* was correctly decided, under what circumstances may a state order the removal of seawalls and similar structures that were legally erected in the past? Cf. Scott v. City of Del Mar, 58 Cal. App. 4th 1296, 68 Cal. Rptr. 2d 317 (1997) (upholding removal of seawalls and rip rap obstructing public access as public nuisances).

3. When the *Milner* shoreline defense structures were initially constructed, a permit from the U.S. Army Corps of Engineers was not necessary because they were landward of the mean high water line (MHWL). But, due to shoreline erosion, eventually the MHWL intersected the face of the struc-

tures. Once that happened, according to the *Milner* court, the structures violated Section 10 of the Rivers and Harbors Act of 1899 which prohibits the construction, placement or maintenance of any structures in navigable waters of the United States without first obtaining a permit from the Corps. 33 U.S.C. § 403. In a time of rising sea levels and greater storm activity, increased shoreline erosion is leaving some oceanfront or Gulf-front houses lying in whole or part seaward of the MHWL and therefore in violation of Section 10. Should the federal government force the owners to remove the houses?

C. THE RIGHT OF ACCESS

1. The Water Area of Littoral Access

DORROH V. McCARTHY

Supreme Court of Georgia, 1995
265 Ga. 750, 462 S.E.2d 708

FLETCHER, PRESIDING JUDGE.

Property owners William and Margaret Dorrah sued to stop their neighbor Brian McCarthy from constructing a dock in the navigable tidal waters in coastal Chatham County. The trial court ruled that McCarthy was a riparian owner because his property adjoins the high water mark of the river and that the Department of Natural Resources did not abuse its discretion in allowing equitable access to navigable water in the tidal basin among adjoining waterfront property owners. We agree that the state exercised its discretion reasonably when it adopted an equitable approach in apportioning use of its tidelands among riparian owners on the curving shoreline and affirm.

McCarthy and Dorrahs own adjoining lots that abut the high water mark or marsh line on a curving inlet in a tidal basin of the Wilmington River. In 1987, McCarthy applied for a permit to build a dock in the basin's navigable waters, but DNR rejected the proposal. In 1993, the DNR commissioner requested a legal opinion concerning the proper method for allocating use of state-owned bottoms on the navigable waters between adjoining waterfront property owners. The attorney general concluded that the straight-line extension method, which extends the side boundary lines of property, was generally acceptable, but rigid adherence to it could cause inequitable results by denying access to deep water to a riparian or littoral owner. Based on this official opinion, DNR changed its policy and granted McCarthy a revocable license to construct a dock in the tidal waters. The Dorrahs sued McCarthy and the DNR commissioner, seeking an injunction to stop construction and a declaratory judgment that the license was illegal. The trial court denied both, and the Dorrahs appealed.

* * *

Although the courts in this state have not previously considered how to divide the riparian owner's right of access on a curving shoreline, other states provide persuasive authority for the principle of equitable apportionment. Many jurisdictions have adopted the general rule that allocates access to tidal waters according to the riparian owner's frontage on the high water line. The "fundamental rule" in dividing the tidelands is "to give each parcel a width at its outer or seaward end proportional to that which it has at the high water mark." Other states have eschewed a general rule in favor of case-by-case adjudication based on equitable principles.

We hold that the Georgia Department of Natural Resources exercised its discretion reasonably in adopting a policy granting equitable access to the tidelands and tidal waters among the waterfront property owners. When a shoreline is relatively straight, extending the property lines straight out to the navigable waters is a fair method for allocating access among riparian owners. When the shoreline curves, however, the straight-line method is inadequate. It can result in overlapping claims for use of state-owned water bottoms and in denying access to water altogether to some riparian owners. * * *

Judgment affirmed

All the Justices concur.

NOTE

A number of methods are used by courts and regulatory agencies to allocate, among waterfront property owners, the water area lying between their uplands and the deep water (or line of navigation). In addition to those described in *Dorrah*, there is the method used in the next case—*In Re Protest of Mason*. In *Mason*, the area through and over which the littoral owner is entitled to exercise his or her right of access, including the right to wharf out, is delineated by the following method. First, in front of the littoral property, draw an imaginary line that locates the beginning of navigable or deep water. Next, beginning at the line of deep water, draw two imaginary lines that are (1) perpendicular to the imaginary line of deep water and (2) if extended, will intersect with the shore at the point where the littoral property owner's property lines meet the water's edge.

Another method is to draw the lines perpendicular to the shore and then out to the imaginary line of deep water. See, e.g., C. Dunscombe, Riparian and Littoral Rights 37 (1970). As the *Dorrah* observes, to assure every riparian owner has reasonable access, in many jurisdictions, the delineation of the area of access may be done on a case-by-case basis based on equitable principles. The methodology used is dependent on the contours of the shorelines and angles of the upland properties' side line boundaries relative to the shoreline. See, e.g., Pine Knoll Shores Association v. Cardon, 126 N.C. App 155, 160, 484 S.E.2d 446, 449 (1997) (describing four different methodologies); Water Street Associates Limited Partnership v. Innopak Plastics Corporation, 230 Conn. 764, 774, 646 A.2d 790, 796 (1994) (" 'no rule can be laid down which is applicable to every situation' ").

2.   The Nature of the Right of Access and to Pier Out

IN RE PROTEST OF MASON
North Carolina Court of Appeals, 1985
78 N.C. App. 16, 337 S.E.2d 99

BECTON, JUDGE.

This case began with the application of Joseph A. Huber to the Marine Fisheries Commission (Commission) to lease public bottom land in Core Sound for clam culture. Clyde Mason, Jr., protested the proposed lease. On 14 April 1984, after an administrative hearing and a final agency hearing, the Commission ordered that the lease be issued to Huber with certain conditions. Following is a more detailed recitation of the facts and procedural history of this case.

On 9 July 1982, Huber submitted an application for a lease for shellfish cultivation in a 1.8 acre area of the public bottom of Core Sound, Carteret County, North Carolina.

* * *

Huber's lease application included a map of the proposed area to be used for clam culture. The map showed that the area would begin at the highwater mark of Core Sound and extend outward in such a way as to overlap Mason's area of riparian access across the Sound. The water depth in this area varies from zero at the shore side of the lease area to a depth of one and one-half to four and one-half feet at the waterward side. It is not disputed that Mason owned the riparian rights involved herein, that Core Sound is navigable, or that Mason's riparian area is overlapped by the proposed lease area.

* * *

On 22 September 1983, the Commission approved Huber's proposed lease (which had been amended on 15 September 1983). On 7 October 1983, Mason requested an administrative hearing. An administrative hearing was held, and the hearing officer issued a proposed order on 14 March 1984. The Commission then held a final hearing. It reviewed the entire record, including the findings and conclusions of the administrative hearing officer, and it issued a final order on 14 April 1984 granting to Huber a lease subject to several specific conditions.

Mason petitioned the superior court to review the Commission's decision. * * * In the petition, Mason included a recitation of the facts in the case, some of which varied from the findings of the Commission. The trial court issued its own findings of fact and conclusions of law and held that (1) the Commission violated the United States and North Carolina Constitutions by issuing the lease to Huber because it constituted a taking of the vested riparian rights of Mason for a private purpose without compensation. * * * The trial court reversed the Commission's order and denied the issuance of the lease.

The Commission appeals, asserting that the trial court erred by * * * (3) improperly and erroneously concluding that riparian access areas must extend to the nearest federally maintained channel; and (4) erroneously concluding that Mason's riparian rights were taken and that he was entitled to compensation. We disagree with the Commission on its first two assignments of error, and we hold that the trial court properly reversed the Commission's order. But we agree with the Commission on its last two assignments of error, and we modify the reasoning of the trial court to the extent it relies on the conclusion that Mason's riparian rights were taken.

* * *

Riparian rights are vested property rights that cannot be taken for private purposes or taken for public purposes without compensating the owner, and they arise out of ownership of land bounded or traversed by navigable water. * * * The State may regulate, protect and promote the shellfish industry and protect the public rights in navigable waters. The legislature vested the authority to promote the shellfish industry in the Marine Fisheries Commission, but it also mandated that the Commission may not lease a bottom area if the lease would impinge upon riparian rights. G.S. § 113–202(a)(4).

The trial court in the case at bar concluded that Mason's riparian rights were seriously encumbered in that the lease would interfere with Mason's rights to "navigation, recreation, access to the navigable portions of Core Sound, potential future accretions and all other rights of usage to which petitioner is entitled * * * by virtue of his riparian ownership." We believe the Commission properly and conscientiously considered the potential conflicts between the proposed lease and Mason's riparian rights, and the trial court erroneously concluded that the lease, as issued, would impinge upon Mason's riparian rights. * * *

The * * * area to consider is the area covered by the lease as issued, with the conditions imposed by the Commission. These conditions are explicitly authorized by the legislature:

> In the event the Secretary finds the application inconsistent with the applicable standards, the Secretary shall recommend that the application be denied or *that a conditional lease be issued* which is consistent with the applicable standards.

G.S. § 113–202(d) (emphasis added). And, if a protest is filed, "[t]he Marine Fisheries Commission may impose special conditions on leases so that leases may be issued which would otherwise be denied." Id. § 113–202(h) (quoted language eliminated by 1985 amendments). The Commission used this authority to impose the following conditions: 1. All stakes must be a minimum of nineteen feet apart; 2. All stakes should be at a height clearly visible to boaters; 3. The matting must be maintained so as not to pose a threat to navigation; 4. The lease area must be set back at least 100 feet from the Protestant's shoreline as shown in Protestant's Exhibit 21; and 5. That portion of the lease area within the limits of the Protestant's areas of riparian rights shall be made subject to the lawful exercise of those rights including the right to build a pier for access to navigable waters within the lease. Upon six months notice that the Protestant, or his successor in interest, has obtained the necessary permits for and intends to build a pier within the lease area, the leaseholder shall remove all equipment which interferes with the pier and reasonable access to the pier.

The first three conditions were designed to guard the public's right of navigation and recreation (including Mason's) as required by G.S. § 113–202(a)(3). The Commission recognized the problem:

> On the proposed lease site, the number of stakes, if unregulated as to proximity and height, could pose an impermissible obstruction to navigation in an area commonly plied by boats eighteen to twenty-three feet long, Finding of Fact 4(e). While the Commission requires lease boundary stakes no further than fifty yards apart, 15 NCAC 3C.0305(a)(3), it sets no minimum distance for stakes generally.

And it concluded that the conditions, combined with the protection already afforded the public under G.S. § 76–40(a) (prohibiting deposit of various wastes in navigable water) and (c) (1981) (prohibiting abandonment of structures on floor of navigable waters), would render "such matting and stakes * * * compatible with other public uses of the area." The fourth condition, requiring a one hundred foot set-off, also protects the public's right and Mason's right to navigation and recreation in the riparian area. The set-off, based upon 15 NCAC 3c.0302(a)(3), recognizes Mason's right to make reasonable use of the water as it flows past the shore.

The final condition imposed by the Commission protected Mason's right to access to "deep" or "navigable" water. The Commission concluded that the lease as proposed "could interfere with [Mason's] riparian right to build a pier or other structure out to deep water." The Commission noted, however, that Mason's Exhibit 22 (the map) did not, as a matter of law, show Mason's area of riparian access because it extended the area of access to the federal channel. The Commission nevertheless found that the proposed lease area generally extends substantially waterward of Mason's property. The trial court specially found:

> 7. The riparian area of petitioner's land is that area included within parallel lines drawn from the perpendicular to the water course as established by the NOAA Chart aforesaid to the termini of petitioner's land lines at the highwater mark as shown by protestant's Exhibit 22.

Exhibit 22 shows the riparian area extending all the way to the federally maintained channel.

As the Commission correctly noted, the riparian access zone does not necessarily extend this far. It only extends as far as necessary to provide access to the "navigable parts" of the waterway. See Shepard's Point Land Co., 132 N.C. at 538, 44 S.E. at 46. Thus, the question becomes: What is navigable? In this State, "all water courses are regarded as navigable in law that are navigable in fact." State v. Baum, 128 N.C. 600, 604, 38 S.E. 900, 901 (1901). "The navigability of a watercourse is therefore largely a question of fact for the jury, and its best test is the extent to which it has been so used by the public when unrestrained." Id. Thus, the Commission was correct in concluding that the right of access to "navigable" water in the case at bar depended upon "the context of the actual shoreline, the sound, and local usage." We further point out that the lateral boundaries of the zone of riparian access should be determined in accordance with the Coastal Area Management Act (CAMA) regulation 15 NCAC 7h.0208(b)(6)(F) (1983) (concerning the proper placement of piers that may interfere with adjacent property owner's riparian access area):

> The line of division of areas of riparian access shall be established by drawing a line along the channel or deep water in front of the properties, then draw a line perpendicular to the line of the channel so that it intersects with the shore at the point the upland property line meets the water's edge.

Here we note that these imaginary lines drawn from the channel or deep water represent the lateral boundaries between access zones and do not represent the distance each zone extends away from the shore. Each access zone extends only as far as necessary to ensure access to navigable waters, as described above.

Even though the findings of the Commission indicate that the small craft customarily used in the proposed lease area are able to navigate up to the shore, there was no error in the Commission's conclusion that Mason is entitled to some access to deeper water through the area of the proposed lease. Otherwise, Mason would be boxed in. The Commission was well within its authority to condition the lease on the provision of this zone of access. See G.S. §§ 113–202(d), (h). * * *

For the reasons set forth above, we affirm the result and modify the reasoning of the trial court.

Modified and affirmed.

PROBLEM

A non-profit sailing club requested a permit to build an extension and addition to its pier. The neighboring riparian property owners objected on the ground that there would be too much noise and activity in the waters adjacent to their property and the sailing club's property. The permit was nonetheless granted, and the pier was built. The neighbors subsequently hired a surveyor who determined that part of the extension and addition is located within an adjacent riparian owner's area of access. Does the adjacent riparian owner have a cause of action for removal of the encroachment?

NOTES AND QUESTIONS

1. At common law in England, the placement of a wharf or other structure in navigable waters was unlawful and, if it interfered with public navigation, a public nuisance. But in the United States, to promote the development of navigation and commerce, riparian owners were encouraged to erect wharves and piers. Although the source and nature of the right may differ among the states, in some form the right exists in all states. See generally 1 Water and Water Rights § 6.01(a)(2) (2011). And, in all states the exercise of the right is subject to significant regulation and may require the obtaining of both federal and state permits. Do oceanfront and Gulf front property owners have a common law right to wharf out? See generally C. Dunscombe, Riparian and Littoral Rights 7–15, 21–23 (1970); but see Capune v. Robbins, 273 N.C. 581, 160 S.E.2d 881 (1968). If so, exactly what is the extent of the right?

In some jurisdictions, the right to wharf out is a recognized common law incident of ownership of waterfront property, a vested property right; in others it may be regarded only a priority that riparian owners have. *Compare In Re Mason*, supra, *with* Port Clinton Associates v. Bd. of Selectmen of the Town of Clinton, 217 Conn. 588, 597–98, 587 A.2d 126, 142 (1991) (riparian rights are so limited by superior public rights that they are a mere "franchise."); Watts v. Lawrence, 703 So.2d 236 (Miss. 1997) ("littoral rights * * * are not property rights per se; they are merely licenses or privileges"). Whatever the legal source of the right, it exists in some form in every state. In Pacific Coast states, the recognition of riparian rights was limited. In Washington, the right to wharf out is a revocable, statutory right. Oregon originally granted upland owners no riparian rights of access or wharfage over tidelands as against the state or its grantees. Bowlby v. Shively, 22 Or. 410, 30 P. 154 (1892), aff'd, Shively v. Bowlby, 152 U.S. 1 (1894). Later, the Oregon Supreme Court modified its position in *Bowlby*. The riparian owner on navigable water had, in the absence of any statute regulating or prohibiting such activity, the "right" to construct a log boom or other structure adjacent to his property. Coquille M & M Co. v. Johnson, 52 Or. 547, 98 P. 132 (1908).

2. The traditional common law right of access includes the right to fill in adjacent shallows and dredge channels through adjacent shallows to reach the navigable part of the waters. This right is subject to reasonable regulation. However, if the riparian or littoral owner has reasonable access, the owner has no right to dredge submerged lands to either improve or maintain a particular level of access without the permission of the owner of the submerged lands. See Town of Oyster Bay v. Commander Oil Corporation, 700 N.Y. S. 2d 47 (App. Div. 1999).

3. May non-consumptive riparian rights be conveyed to non-riparian owners? In a number of jurisdiction riparian rights may be severed from the ownership of riparian property. See generally 1 Waters and Water Rights, sec. 7.04(a)(3) (2011). What implications does that have for the purchaser of waterfront property? For the title searcher?

4. Does a riparian owner's right to wharf out mean that she can occupy the whole area of access if she wishes, for example by building a large marina? If the marina will also extend beyond the beginning of deep water, does the riparian owner have a common law right of use measured by the reasonable use doctrine? See, e.g., Walker v. N.C. Department of Environment, Health, and Natural Resources, 111 N.C. App. 851, 433 S.E.2d 767 (N.C. App. 1993) (no independent littoral or riparian right to construct large scale marina without first obtaining easement from the state).

5. Is the right to wharf out limited to water dependent uses? For example, may a riparian owner build a restaurant that extends out over the water? See, e.g. Tewksbury v. City of Deerfield Beach, 763 So. 2d 1071 (Fla. App. 4 Dist. 1999) (operation of outdoor dining area on dock outside scope of riparian and littoral rights); see generally 1 Water and Water Rights § 6.01(a)(2) (2011) (must have navigational function).

6. Along many parts of the coast, the construction and sale of dockominiums is a growing phenomenon. In a dockominium a boat owner purchases a fee interest in a particular boat slip. Prices range from $55,000 for a Lake Huron slip capable for mooring 40 to 80 foot yachts to over $150,000 in the Florida Keys. See e.g. J. Fletcher, No Rooms, Water View, Wall St. J. May 9, 2003 at 12; M. Cheng, Dockominiums: An Expansion of Riparian Rights that Violates the Public Trust Doctrine, 16 B.C. Envtl. Aff. L. Rev. 821 (1989); C. Hall, Dockominiums: In Conflict With the Public Trust Doctrine, 24 Suffolk U. L. Rev. 331, 332–35 (1990). An easy way to create a dockominium is to convert an existing public marina into a dockominium form of ownership.

What exactly is a purchaser of a slip in a dockominium buying? Some dockominium projects purport to give a purchaser a fee title deed to the slip.

Does the slip purchaser actually acquire any title to the water in the slip or the air space above the water?

BECKER V. LITTY

Maryland Court of Appeals, 1989
318 Md. 76, 566 A.2d 1101

ADKINS, JUDGE.

Boone Creek is a tidal estuary located near Oxford, Talbot County, Maryland. A somewhat tortuous channel at its mouth leads to the Choptank River. The Creek is divided into what are known as the North and Southeast Branches. At the confluence of these branches is Sol's Island, containing perhaps as much as five acres of land. A bridge spanning the roughly 240 feet from Sol's Island to the mainland is the focus of controversy in this case, which raises, among other issues, important questions of riparian rights, the preemptive effect of a United States Coast Guard bridge permit, and standing. We shall resolve these issues, but, because the record before us clearly does not reflect a number of matters that bear on the ultimate disposition of the case, we shall remand under Maryland Rule 8–604(d), for further proceedings.

I. Facts

In May 1986, appellee Suzanne Hanks Litty acquired title to Sol's Island, then an essentially uninhabited tract of land accessible only by air or via the waters of Boone Creek. She and her husband, appellee Ernest Litty (the Littys), decided to build a residence on the island. They also decided, it seems, that an aerial or aquatic commute would have its drawbacks. In October 1986, the Littys obtained a United States Coast Guard permit to build a private, one-lane, fixed bridge across the aforesaid 240 feet between Sol's Island and the mainland. The permit specified that the bridge should have three feet of vertical clearance over Boone Creek at mean high water.

Although the Coast Guard had given public notice of the application for the bridge permit, and also had notified certain federal and State agencies, some of the Littys' Boone Creek neighbors did not become aware of the situation until after the permit had issued. When they learned of the permit, those neighbors lost no time in protesting to the Littys, the Coast Guard, and others. Despite these objections, the Littys actively prepared for erection of the bridge.

On 11 January 1988, appellants William B. Becker and his wife Jean, along with 12 others who owned property, or in most cases both owned property and resided on the shores of Boone Creek, filed a complaint against the Littys seeking to enjoin construction of the bridge. Because the individual appellants assert essentially identical interests, we shall refer to them, collectively, as "the Beckers." On 2 February 1988, the Circuit Court for Talbot County (Wise, J.) issued an interlocutory injunction barring construction of the bridge. On 25 August it dissolved that injunction and granted summary judgment in favor of the Littys and against the Beckers. We frame the issues in this appeal by explaining the Beckers' theories below, and the trial court's reasons for rejecting them.

II. Issues and Rulings in the Circuit Court

The Beckers' and their co-parties' properties are located at various spots on the North and Southeast Branches of Boone Creek. In the circuit court they asserted that they owned various vessels by which they navigated between the branches of the Creek and from the Creek to the Choptank River. They alleged that Boone Creek to the south and southeast of Sol's Island was too shallow to permit navigation as a practical matter. Thus, the only way they could move between the branches, and for those whose properties lay on the Southeast Branch, into the Choptank, was through the narrow channel between Sol's Island and the mainland. A bridge with only three feet of vertical clearance would effectively block this navigation. This, averred the Beckers, would deprive them of their riparian rights and cause substantial depreciation in the values of their properties.

Judge Wise did not accept any of these arguments. He held that the Beckers were complaining about interference with a right of navigation, which is a public right, as opposed to one of the bundle of rights possessed by riparian owners. * * *

III. Riparian Rights

Before us the Beckers restate their riparian rights argument. In essence, they assert that there can be no interference with what they claim is their right, as the owners of riparian property, to navigate on the waters of Boone Creek and the Choptank River. We assume, arguendo, that the bridge, if constructed pursuant to the Coast Guard permit, will have that effect. But we hold that Judge Wise did not err in rejecting this argument.

* * *

The riparian owner has * * * a right of access to water. That is, a right of access "to the water in front of his fast land." The owner has the right, under proper circumstances, to reach that water for purposes such as fishing, bathing, and making certain improvements into the water. That is why, for example, the riparian owner is entitled to reliction and accretion. But once the right of access is gratified, this particular right of a riparian owner goes no further. It does not encompass a right of free navigation.

The right to navigate on navigable waters is a public right, not one that attaches only to the owner of riparian property. "The public [has] a right, at common law, to navigate over every part of a common navigable river.* * * "Garitee v. M. & C.C. of Balto., 53 Md. 422, 436 (1880). * * *

Other courts have reached similar results.* * * Webb v. Giddens, 82 So.2d 743, 745 (Fla. 1955), did reach a contrary conclusion. There, a riparian owner who rented boats was totally cut off from the main body of the lake where people used the boats. The Florida court allowed the owner access to the lake. In a later case, the Supreme Court of Florida did state that "a riparian owner's interest in waterway navigation is the same as a member of the public except where there is some special injury to the riparian owner," but the injury was very different from the present case. Game & Fresh Water Fish Comm'n v. Lake Islands, 407 So.2d 189 (Fla. 1982). In *Lake Islands*, the property owners lost all access to their islands, whereas in the present case, the Beckers can still get to their property by land and still have access to Boone Creek.

In short, other jurisdictions, like Maryland, hold that a general right to navigation is not a riparian owner's right, but a right of the general public. The Littys' bridge will not deprive the Beckers of their riparian rights of access to the water in front of their properties. They still have that access. * * *

For the reasons stated, we reject the Beckers' riparian rights claim.

NOTES AND QUESTIONS

1. The right of access to waters fronting littoral and riparian lands is not absolute. As *Lilly* illustrates, it is possible to effectively cut off certain types or levels of access to navigable waters without infringing on the protected common law right of access.

2. Is the right of access to navigable water illusory if once a littoral owner reaches the navigable portion of the water body the littoral owner is unable to actually use the water body for navigation?

D. THE RIGHT OF VIEW

CITY OF OCEAN CITY V. MAFFUCCI

Superior Court of New Jersey, Appellate Division, 1999
326 N.J.Super. 1, 740 A.2d 630

LONG, JUDGE.

Defendants Gerard and Constance Maffucci, individually and as principals of the 2910 Wesley Avenue Condominium, and Louis and Martha Spadaccino, as principals of the 2825 Wesley Avenue Condominium, own beachfront duplexes on Wesley Avenue in Ocean City. In 1993, as a result of a joint project of the State of New Jersey and the Army Corps of Engineers to build new sand dunes along seven miles of Ocean City beach, Ocean City sought to purchase an easement from the beachfront owners. In 1995, when a price could not be negotiated, the city instituted a condemnation action against defendants, the Maffuccis, Wesley Avenue Condominium, and 2825 Wesley Avenue Condominium. Included in the proceeding was a fifty by eighty foot strip of beach in front of 2825 Wesley Avenue in which the Spadaccinos are first floor tenants. As a result of the dune project, the view of the ocean from the Spadaccino's condominium has been completely obstructed and direct access to the beach has been eliminated by nine foot high dune grasses. Beach access must be gained by a pathway 80 feet north of the condominium.

On July 22, 1997, after a hearing, three commissioners appointed to appraise the value of the easement taken by the City and set just compensation, issued a report declaring just compensation to be $1.00. No reasons were stated for this award. Defendants appealed.

A jury trial was held at which the main issue was whether the defendants were entitled to severance damages. Defendants claimed that the easement damaged the remaining part of their property and diminished its market value by $100,000. The City countered that the easement caused no damage to the property as a whole.

Cyril Galvin, a coastal engineering expert, testified for defendants that the dune eliminated any view of or access to the beach from the Spadaccino's condominium. Galvin explained that the dune continually increased in height and width from the date of taking to the time of trial and that it would continue to do so: The dune clearly blocks the line of sight to the water and this obstruction will increase markedly in the coming years because of the vegetation growth and the trapping of the sand from the newly widened beach.* * *

We * * * agree with Judge Callinan's conclusion that loss of ocean view and access are elements for which severance damages may be awarded. While no New Jersey case has had occasion to expressly render such a ruling, the application of the standards governing partial takings leads inevitably to this conclusion.

When the State takes private property for a public purpose under the provisions of the Eminent Domain Act of 1971, N.J.S.A. 20:3–1 to–50, the property owner is entitled to just compensation. State, by Comm'r of Transp. v. Silver, 92 N.J. 507, 513, 457 A.2d 463 (1983) (citing N.J. Const. art. I, & 20). Where the whole of a property is taken, the measure of damages is the fair market value of the property as of the date of the taking, determined by what a willing buyer and a willing seller would agree to, neither being under any compulsion to act. Village of S. Orange v. Alden Corp., 71 N.J. 362, 368, 365 A.2d 469 (1976). However, where only a portion of a property is condemned, the measure of damages includes both the value of the portion of land actually taken and the value by which the remaining land has been diminished as a consequence of the partial taking. Silver, supra, 92 N.J. at 514, 457 A.2d 463. The diminution in value of the remaining property constitutes the "severance damages."

* * *

In valuing the property remaining after a partial taking an examination of all of the characteristics of such remaining property after the time of the taking, as opposed solely to facts in existence at or immediately before condemnation, is inescapable. Therefore, in the case of a partial taking, the market value of property remaining after a taking should be ascertained by a wide factual inquiry into all material facts and circumstances—both past and prospective—that would influence a buyer or seller interested in consummating a sale of the property.

[Id. at 515, 457 A.2d 463 (citations omitted).]

* * *

Here, the City argues that the jury based its award on non-compensable considerations, namely, loss of ocean view, beach access and privacy. We disagree. If a "wide factual inquiry into all material facts and circumstances—both past and prospective—that would influence a buyer or seller interested in consummating a sale of the property" is the standard, ocean view, beach access, use and privacy are fundamental considerations in valuing beachfront property. Indeed every other jurisdiction which has considered this issue has held that loss of view, loss of access, loss of privacy and loss of use are compensable. For example, in Pierpont Inn, Inc. v. State, 70 Cal.2d 282, 74 Cal.Rptr. 521, 449 P.2d 737, 745–46 (1969), overruled on other grounds, Los Angeles County, Metro. Transp. Authority v. Continental Dev. Corp., 16 Cal.4th 694, 66 Cal.Rptr.2d 630, 941 P.2d 809 (1997), the California Supreme Court held that a property owner's loss of view and access to the beach, resulting from a partial taking for freeway construction, were proper elements of severance damages. Like the City here, the appellant in Pierpont contended that the trial judge "erred in permitting the jury to consider the property's loss of view and relatively unrestricted access to the beach in determining severance damages." The California Supreme Court held:

> Where the property taken constitutes only a part of a larger parcel, the owner is entitled to recover, inter alia, the difference in the fair market value of his property in its 'before' condition and the fair market value of the remaining portion thereof after the construction of the improvement on the portion taken. Items such as view, access to beach property, freedom from noise, etc. are unquestionably mat-

ters which a willing buyer in the open market would consider in determining the price he would pay for any given piece of real property. Concededly such advantages are not absolute rights, but to the extent that the reasonable expectation of their continuance is destroyed by the construction placed upon the part taken, the owner suffers damages for which compensation must be paid.

* * *

We note that the City's reliance on "highway access" cases, to support its contention that defendant's loss of direct access to the beach is non-compensable, is misplaced. While those cases make clear that non-compensable, "reasonable access" remains even if it is inconvenient or indirect, they concern an abutting property owner's right of access to and from the public highway. This case presents the claim of a property owner, not to a public highway or byway, but to his own property. Spadaccino established the existence of a riparian grant. Collins testified that the property has riparian rights, namely that "you not only own the portion of your property that your home is on, but you also own the beach all the way out to the water." Judge Callinan confirmed that "in the case of a riparian right . . . you own the property." Accordingly, any loss of the right of access can be compensated. See Board of Trustees of Internal Improvement Trust Fund v. Sand Key Assocs., 512 So.2d 934, 936 (Fla.1987) (riparian and littoral rights include "the right of access to the water" and "the right to an unobstructed view of the water"); Thiesen v. Gulf, F. & A. Ry. Co., 75 Fla. 28, 78 So. 491, 501 (1917) ("The common-law riparian proprietor enjoys [the] right [of ingress and egress], and that of unobstructed view over the waters, and in common with the public the right of navigating, bathing, and fishing* * * "); Tiffany v. Town of Oyster Bay, 234 N.Y. 15, 136 N.E. 224, 225 (1922) ("[R]ights of reasonable, safe, and convenient access to the water * * *commonly belong to riparian ownership.")

In short, we are satisfied that the judgement entered upon the jury verdict could have been reached upon the evidence presented and that the judge properly rejected the City's motion for a new trial.

Affirmed.

NOTE

Several states recognize the right of view. See, e.g., DBL, Inc. v. Carson, 262 Ga. App. 252, 255, 585 S.E. 2d 87, 91 (2003) (docks obstructing view); Lee County, Florida v. Kiesel, 705 So. 2d 1013 (Ct. of Appeals, 1st Dis. 1998) (bridge obstructing view). If a right of view exists, what are the waterward limits of the right? In Hayes v. Bowman, 91 So.2d 795 (Fl. 1957), the Florida Supreme Court stated:

We * * * hold that the common law riparian right to an unobstructed view and access to the Channel over the foreshore across the waters toward the Channel must be recognized over an area as near 'as practicable' in the direction of the Channel so as to distribute equitably the submerged lands between the upland and the Channel. * * * An upland owner must in all cases be permitted a direct, unobstructed view of the Channel and as well a direct, unobstructed means of ingress and egress over the foreshore and tidal waters to the Channel. * * *

91 So.2d at 801–02.

E. LOSS OF LITTORAL RIGHTS

WALTON COUNTY v. STOP THE BEACH RENOURISHMENT, INC.

Supreme Court of Florida, 2008
998 So. 2d 1102

BELL, J.

We have for review the First District Court of Appeal's decision in *Save Our Beaches, Inc. v. Florida Department of Environmental Protection,* * * *

Though it phrased its certified question in terms of an applied challenge, the First District actually addressed a facial challenge. Therefore, we rephrase the certified question as follows:

> On its face, does the Beach and Shore Preservation Act unconstitutionally deprive upland owners of littoral rights without just compensation?

We answer the rephrased certified question in the negative and quash the decision of the First District. * * *

I. The Context

A. Factual and Procedural History

As the First District explained in its opinion,

[t]he Gulf of Mexico beaches of the City of Destin and Walton County were [damaged] by Hurricane Opal in 1995. The . . . problem was identified by the Department [of Environmental Protection (Department)], which placed these beaches on its list of critically-eroded beaches. Destin and Walton County then initiated a lengthy process of beach restoration through renourishment. The process, which included extensive studies and construction design and pre-application conferences with Department staff, culminated in the filing of an Application for a Joint Coastal Permit and Authorization to Use Sovereign Submerged Lands on July 30, 2003.

The application proposed to dredge sand from an ebb shoal borrow area south of East Pass in eastern Okaloosa County, using either a cutter head dredge (which disturbs the sand on the bottom of the borrow area and vacuums it into a pipeline which delivers it to the project area) or a hopper dredge (which fills itself and is moved to the project site). On the project site, heavy equipment moves the dredged sand as specified in the design plans. The project is executed in this manner and progresses along the beach, usually at a pace of about 300 to 500 feet a day.

To determine the mean high water line (MHWL) for the restoration area, a coastline survey was completed in September 2003. The Board of Directors for the Internal Improvement Trust Fund (Board) subsequently established an erosion control line (ECL) at the surveyed MHWL. Pursuant to section 161.191(1) of the Beach and Shore Preservation Act, this ECL became the boundary between publicly owned land and privately owned upland after it was recorded. Then, on July 15, 2004, the Department issued a Notice of Intent to Issue the permit.

* * *

On June 30, 2005, following the administrative hearing, the administrative law judge recommended that the Department enter a final order issuing the permit. The Department entered its final order on July 27, 2005, determining that the permit was properly issued pursuant to existing statutes and rules.

Before the First District, [Plaintiffs, STBR, an association of upland private owners] challenged the Department's final order * * * Specifically, Plaintiffs asserted that section 161.191(1) of the Beach and Shore Preservation Act, which fixes the shoreline boundary after the ECL is recorded, unconstitutionally divests upland owners of all common law littoral rights by severing these rights from the uplands. According to the Plaintiffs, after the recording of the ECL and by operation of section 161.191(1), the State becomes owner of the land to which common law littoral rights attach because it owns all lands seaward of the ECL. Plaintiffs further argued that the littoral rights, which are expressly preserved by section 161.201 of the Act, are an inadequate substitute for the upland owners' common law littoral rights that are eliminated by section 161.191.

The First District agreed the Act divests upland owners of their littoral right to receive accretions and relictions because section 161.191(2) provides that the common law rule of accretion and reliction no longer operates once the ECL is recorded. The First District also agreed that the Act eliminates the right to maintain direct contact with the water since section 161.191(1) establishes the ECL as the shoreline boundary. Furthermore, the First District found that:

Although section 161.201 has language describing a preservation of common law riparian rights, it does not actually operate to preserve the rights at issue . . . [because] Florida's law is clear that riparian rights cannot be severed from riparian uplands absent an agreement with the riparian owner, not even by the power of eminent domain.

* * * Thus, the First District held that the final order issued pursuant to the Act results in an unconstitutional taking of the littoral rights to accretion and to contact with water without an eminent domain proceeding as required by section 161.141, Florida Statutes.

The First District remanded for the Department to provide satisfactory evidence of sufficient upland interest pursuant to Florida Administrative Code Rule 18–21.004(3). *Id.* Then, on July 3, 2006, the First District certified the question of great public importance described earlier.

B. The Beach and Shore Preservation Act

Before addressing the rephrased certified question, it is helpful to provide the relevant portions of the Beach and Shore Preservation Act.

Recognizing the importance and volatility of Florida's beaches, the Legislature in 1961 enacted the Beach and Shore Preservation Act. Ch. 61–246, § 1, Laws of Fla. (codified at §§ 161.011–161.45, Fla. Stat. (2005)). Determining that "beach erosion is a serious menace to the economy and general welfare of the people of [Florida] and has advanced to emergency proportions," the Legislature declared it "a necessary governmental responsibility to properly manage and protect Florida beaches . . . from erosion," and to provide funding for beach nourishment projects. § 161.088. The Legislature then delegated to the Department the authority to determine "those beaches which are critically eroded and in need of restoration and nourishment" and to "authorize appropriations to pay up to 75 percent of the actual costs for restoring and renourishing a critically eroded beach." § 161.101(1).

Pursuant to section 161.141, when a local government applies for funding for beach restoration, a survey of the shoreline is conducted to determine the MHWL for the area. Once established, any additions to the upland property landward of the MHWL that result from the restoration project remain the property of the upland owner subject to all governmental regulations, including a public easement for traditional uses of the beach. § 161.141.

After the MHWL is established, section 161.161(3) provides that the Board must determine the area to be protected by the project and locate an ECL. In locating the ECL, the Board is "guided by the existing line of mean high water, bearing in mind the requirements of proper engineering in the beach restoration project, the extent to which erosion or avulsion has occurred, and the need to protect existing ownership of as much upland as is reasonably possible." § 161.161(5).

Pursuant to section 161.191(1), this ECL becomes the new fixed property boundary between public lands and upland property after the ECL is recorded. And, under section 161.191(2), once the ECL has been established, the common law no longer operates "to increase or decrease the proportions of any upland property lying landward of such line, either by accretion or erosion or by any other natural or artificial process."

However, section 161.201 expressly preserves the upland owners' littoral rights, including, but not limited to, rights of ingress, egress, view, boating, bathing, and fishing, and prevents the State from erecting structures on the beach seaward of the ECL except as required to prevent erosion. Section 161.141 further declares that the State has no intention "to extend its claims to lands not already held by it or to deprive any upland or submerged land owner of the legitimate and constitutional use and enjoyment of his or her property."

Moreover, section 161.141 explains that "[i]f an authorized beach restoration, beach nourishment, and erosion control project cannot reasonably be accomplished without the taking of private property, the taking must be made by the requesting authority by eminent domain proceedings." And, in the event the beach restoration is not commenced within a two-year period, is halted in excess of a six-month period, or the authorities do not maintain the restored beach, section 161.211 dictates that the ECL is cancelled.

II. Discussion

* * *

After reviewing Florida's common law as well as the Beach and Shore Preservation Act's effect upon that common law, we find that the Act, on its face, does not unconstitutionally deprive upland owners of littoral rights without just compensation. In explaining our conclusion, we first describe the relationship at common law between the public and upland owners in regard to Florida's beaches. We then detail the Beach and Shore Preservation Act's impact upon this relationship. In particular, we explore how the Act effectuates the State's constitutional duty to protect Florida's beaches in a way that facially balances public and private interests. Finally, we address the First District's decision.

A. The Relationship at Common Law between the Public and Upland Owners

Since the vast development of Florida's beaches, there has been a relative paucity of opinions from this Court that describe the nature of the relationship at common law between the public and upland owners in regard to Florida's beaches. It is important that we outline this relationship prior to resolving the specific issues in this case.

(1) The Public and Florida's Beaches

[At this point the court discussed the public trust doctrine.]

(2) The Upland Owners and Florida's Beaches

Private upland owners hold the bathing, fishing, and navigation rights described above in common with the public. * * * In fact, upland owners have no rights in navigable waters and sovereignty lands that are superior to other members of the public in regard to bathing, fishing, and navigation. * * * However, upland owners hold several special or exclusive common law littoral rights: (1) the right to have access to the water; (2) the right to reasonably use the water; (3) the right to accretion and reliction; and (4) the right to the unobstructed view of the water. * * * These special littoral rights "are such as are necessary for the use and enjoyment" of the upland property, but "these rights may not be so exercised as to injure others in their lawful rights." * * *

Though subject to regulation, these littoral rights are private property rights that cannot be taken from upland owners without just compensation. * * * Indeed, in Thiesen v. Gulf, Florida & Alabama Railway Co., 75 Fla. 28, 78 So. 491, 506–07 (1918), this Court considered and *rejected* the notion that littoral rights are subordinate to public rights and, as a result, could be eliminated without compensation. * * *

While Florida case law has clearly defined littoral rights as constitutionally protected private property rights, the exact nature of these rights rarely has been described in detail. * * * Early on, this Court described the nature of littoral rights as follows:

> These special rights are *easements* incident to the [littoral] holdings and are property rights that may be regulated by law, but may not be taken without just compensation and due process of law. The common-law [littoral] rights that arise by implication of law *give no title to the land under navigable waters except such as may be lawfully acquired by accretion, reliction,* and other similar rights.

Based upon this early description, the littoral rights to access, use, and view are easements under Florida common law. * * *

Furthermore, based upon this Court's early description of the nature of littoral rights, it is evident that the littoral right to accretion and reliction is distinct from the rights to access, use, and view. The rights to access, use, and view are rights relating to the present use of the foreshore and water. The same is not true of the right to accretion and reliction. The right to accretion and reliction is a contingent, future interest that only becomes a possessory interest if and when land is added to the upland by accretion or reliction * * *

(3) Dealing with a Dynamic Boundary

The boundary between public or sovereignty lands and private uplands is a dynamic boundary, which is located on a shoreline that, by its very nature, frequently changes. Florida's common law attempts to bring order and certainty to this dynamic boundary in a manner that reasonably balances the affected parties' interests.

* * *

Accordingly, under the doctrines of erosion, reliction, and accretion, the boundary between public and private land is altered to reflect gradual and imperceptible losses or additions to the shoreline. * * * In contrast, under the doctrine of avulsion, the boundary between public and private land remains the MHWL as it existed before the avulsive event led to sudden and perceptible losses or additions to the shoreline. * * *

While our common law has developed these specific rules that are intended to balance the interests in our ever-changing shoreline, Florida's common law has never fully addressed how public-sponsored beach restoration affects the interests of the public and the interests of the upland owners. We now turn to the legislative attempt to deal with this subject.

B. The Beach and Shore Preservation Act's Balancing of Public and Private Interests

As explained earlier, the State has a constitutional duty to protect Florida's beaches, part of which it holds in trust for public use. The Beach and Shore Preservation Act effectuates this constitutional duty when the State is faced with critically eroded, storm-damaged beaches.

Like the common law, the Act seeks a careful balance between the interests of the public and the interests of the private upland owners. By authorizing the addition of sand to sovereignty lands, the Act prevents further loss of public beaches, protects existing structures, and repairs prior damage. In doing so, the Act promotes the public's economic, ecological, recreational, and aesthetic interests in the shoreline. On the other hand, the Act benefits private upland owners by restoring beach already lost and by protecting their property from future storm damage and erosion. Moreover, the Act expressly preserves the upland owners' rights to access, use, and view, including the rights of ingress and egress. *See* § 161.201. The Act also protects the upland owners' rights to boating, bathing, and fishing. *See id.* Furthermore, the Act protects the upland owners' view by prohibiting the State from erecting structures on the new beach except those necessary to prevent erosion. *See id.* Thus, although the Act provides that the State may retain title to the newly created dry land directly adjacent to the water, upland owners may continue to access, use, and view the beach and water as they did prior to beach restoration. As a result, at least facially, there is no material or substantial impairment of these littoral rights under the Act. * * *

Finally, the Act provides for the cancellation of the ECL if (1) the beach restoration is not commenced within two years; (2) restoration is halted in excess of a six-month period; or (3) the authorities do not maintain the restored beach. *See* § 161.211. Therefore, in the event the beach restoration is not completed and maintained, the rights of the respective parties revert to the status quo ante.* * *

C. The First District's Decision

* * *In explaining our disagreement with the First District, we first discuss how the First District failed to consider the doctrine of avulsion. The doctrine of avulsion is pivotal because, under that doctrine, the public has the right to reclaim its land lost by an avulsive event. We then address why, in the context of this Act, the littoral right to accretion is not an issue. Thereafter, we explain that there is no independent littoral right of contact with the water under Florida common law. * * *

(1) Doctrine of Avulsion

In its opinion, the First District stated that beach restoration under the Act "will cause the high water mark to move seaward and ordinarily this would result in the upland landowners gaining property by accretion." * * * This statement fails to consider the doctrine of avulsion, most likely because the parties did not raise the issue before the First District. As a result, the First District never considered whether the Act is facially constitutional given the doctrine of avulsion. * * *

Contrary to the First District's statement about accretion, under the doctrine of avulsion, the boundary between public lands and privately owned uplands remains the MHWL as it existed before the avulsive event. * * *

Significantly, when an avulsive event leads to the loss of land, the doctrine of avulsion recognizes the affected property owner's right to reclaim the lost land within a reasonable time. *See generally* 1 Henry Philip Farnham, *The Law of Waters and Water Rights* § 74, at 331 (1904) ("If a portion of the land of the riparian [or littoral] owner is suddenly engulfed, and the former boundary can be determined or the land reclaimed within a reasonable time, he does not lose his title to it."). * * *

To summarize, when the shoreline is impacted by an avulsive event, the boundary between public lands and private uplands remains the pre-avulsive event MHWL. Consequently, if the shoreline is lost due to an avulsive event, the public has the right to restore its shoreline up to that MHWL.

In light of this common law doctrine of avulsion, the provisions of the Beach and Shore Preservation Act at issue are facially constitutional. In the context of restoring storm-ravaged public lands, the State would not be doing anything under the Act that it would not be entitled to accomplish under Florida's common law. Like the common law doctrine of avulsion, the Act authorizes the State to reclaim its storm-damaged shoreline by adding sand to submerged sovereignty lands. *See generally* §§ 161.088, 161.091, 161.101. And similar to the common law, the Act authorizes setting the ECL and the boundary between sovereignty lands and private uplands at "the existing line of mean high water, bearing in mind . . . the extent to which . . . avulsion has occurred." *See* § 161.161(5). In other words, when restoring storm-ravaged shoreline, the boundary under the Act should remain the pre-avulsive event boundary. Thus, because the Act authorizes actions to reclaim public beaches that are also authorized under the common law after an avulsive event, the Act is facially constitutional.

*(2) Common Law Right to Accretion * * ***

(3) Contact is Ancillary to the Littoral Right of Access

The First District concluded that, under section 161.191(1), upland owners "lose the right to have the property's contact with the water remain intact." * * * However, under Florida common law, there is no independent right of contact with the water. Instead, contact is ancillary to the littoral right of access to the water.

The ancillary right to contact with the water exists to preserve the upland owner's core littoral right of access to the water. * * *

In this case, the Act expressly protects the right of access to the water, which is the sole justification for the subsidiary right of contact. The Act preserves the rights of ingress and egress and prevents the State from erecting structures upon the beach seaward of the ECL except as required to prevent erosion. *See* § 161.201. The Act also provides that the State has no intention "to extend its claims to lands not already held by it or to deprive any upland or submerged land owner of the legitimate and constitutional use and enjoyment of his or her property." § 161.141. At least facially, these provisions ensure that the upland owner's access to the water remains intact. Therefore, the rationale for the ancillary right to contact is satisfied.

Furthermore, it is important to understand that contrary to what might be inferred from the First District's conclusion regarding contact, there is no littoral right to a seaward boundary at the water's edge in Florida. Rather, as explained previously, the boundary between sovereignty lands and private uplands is the MHWL, which represents an average over a nineteen-year period. Although the foreshore technically separates upland property from the water's edge at various times during the nineteen-year period, it has never been considered to infringe upon the upland owner's littoral right of access, which the ancillary right to contact is meant to preserve. Admittedly, the renourished beach may be wider than the typical foreshore, but the ultimate result is the same. Direct access to the water is preserved under the Act. In other words, because the Act safeguards access to the water and because there is no right to maintain a constant boundary with the water's edge, the Act, on its face, does not unconstitutionally eliminate the ancillary right to contact. * * *

III. Conclusion

As we have explained, the Beach and Shore Preservation Act effectuates the State's constitutional duty to protect Florida's beaches. And, like Florida common law, the Act facially achieves a reasonable balance between public and private interests in the shore. Specifically, the Act benefits upland owners by restoring lost beach, by protecting their property from future storm damage and erosion, and by preserving their littoral rights to use and view. The Act also benefits upland owners by protecting their littoral right of access to the water, which is the sole justification for the ancillary right of contact. Additionally, the Act authorizes actions to reclaim public beaches that are also authorized under the common law after an avulsive event. Furthermore, the littoral right to accretion is not implicated by the Act because the reasons underlying this common law rule are not present in this context.

In light of the above, we find that the Act, on its face, does not unconstitutionally deprive upland owners of littoral rights without just compensation. Consequently, we answer the rephrased certified question in the negative and quash the decision of the First District. And we again emphasize that our decision in this case is strictly limited to the context of restoring critically eroded beaches under the Beach and Shore Preservation Act.

It is so ordered.

NOTE

Justice Lewis filed a dissent, complaining that the majority had "butchered" Florida law in an attempt to find an equitable solution to the vexing issue of beach renourishment, "erasing well-established Florida law without proper analysis...." Perhaps emboldened by this dissent, the plaintiffs petitioned for certiorari, asking the United States Supreme Court to rule that Florida's Supreme Court effectuated a judicial taking of their littoral rights in violation of the Fifth Amendment. In a decision handed down in December 2010, the Court held it did not. Stop The Beach Renourishment, Inc. v. Florida Department of Environmental Protection, 130 S.Ct. 2592, ___ U.S. ___ (2010). The decision is discussed further in Chapter 4.

SLAVIN V. TOWN OF OAK ISLAND
North Carolina Court of Appeals, 2003
160 N.C.App. 57, 584 S.E.2d 100

ELMORE, JUDGE.

Plaintiffs are owners of oceanfront property located within the municipal boundaries of the Town of Oak Island ("defendant" or "Town"). In May 2001, the United States Army Corps of Engineers ("Corps") completed a beach renourishment project, the Turtle Habitat Restoration Project, within the limits of the Town. The project was conducted with the consent of defendant and was designed to restore a sea turtle nesting habitat that had been damaged by erosion. A second beach renourishment project, the Wilmington Harbor Project, was undertaken in the Town by the Corps but not yet completed by the time this action commenced. Both projects entailed the placement of new sand on the seaward side of the former mean high water mark, which represents the seaward boundary of plaintiffs' properties. The placement of new sand in this manner pushed the mean high water mark seaward, creating a new dry sand beach and dune between plaintiffs' property and the ocean.

In order to protect the new sand dune and the turtle habitat, defendant adopted the Beach Access Plan ("Access Plan") at issue. The Access Plan provides for the construction of fencing on and along the length of the renourished beach. Pursuant to the Access Plan, plaintiffs may only access the ocean via designated public access points. Prior to implementation of the Access Plan and construction of the fencing, each plaintiff enjoyed direct access to the ocean from his or her property.

Plaintiffs filed suit against defendant alleging that plaintiffs had a right of direct access to the ocean and that defendant's Access Plan constituted a taking of that right in violation of the federal and state constitutions. On 13 February 2002, after careful consideration of the pleadings and supporting materials, the trial court ordered that summary judgment be entered in favor of defendant. * * * We * * * affirm the trial court's order.

Plaintiffs * * * contend that summary judgment for defendant was improper because plaintiffs have a vested appurtenant littoral right of direct access to the ocean, which defendant cannot lawfully limit without compensating plaintiffs. Plaintiffs insist that they are entitled to compensation because defendant's Access Plan unlawfully limits plaintiffs' right of access by requiring plaintiffs to access the ocean via designated access points, rather than directly from their respective properties.

While we agree that North Carolina law recognizes a littoral property owner's right of access to adjacent water, plaintiffs misinterpret the nature of that right. A littoral property owner's right of access to the ocean is a qualified one, and is subject to reasonable regulation, Plaintiffs, however, do not argue that the Access Plan is an unreasonable regulation of their littoral property rights. Rather, plaintiffs insist that defendant may not limit their right of access to the ocean at all without compensating plaintiffs.

In Capune the North Carolina Supreme Court stated that a littoral property owner's right of access to adjacent water is " 'subject to such general rules and regulations as the Legislature, in the exercise of its powers, may prescribe for the protection of the public rights in rivers or navigable waters.' " In Week this Court held that appurtenant littoral rights are "subordinate to public trust protections." Weeks, 97 N.C.App. at 226, 388 S.E.2d at 234. Thus, it is well-established that the littoral right of access to adjacent water is a qualified right.

Plaintiffs' contention that the Town may not, without compensation, in any way limit their right of access to the ocean is inconsistent with the qualified nature of that right. Accordingly, we conclude that defendant is entitled to judgment as a matter of law, and the trial court's order granting summary judgment in favor of defendant was proper.

Affirmed.

NOTES AND QUESTIONS

1. Is the continued existence of an oceanfront property owner's littoral rights dependent upon whether the state, as owner of the adjacent submerged lands, decides to fill and raise the submerged lands above the mean high tide line? Does the purpose of the filling matter? Must the filling be related to public trust interests or rights? If so, how closely connected must the filling be to a public trust interest or right? Is it enough that the state wishes to create a wider, public dry sand beach? See, e.g. Michaelson v. Silver Beach Improvement Association, Inc., 342 Mass. 251, 173 N.E. 2d 273 (1961) (beach created by project unrelated to navigation belonged to adjacent littoral owner).

In Tiffany v. Town of Oyster Bay, 234 N.Y. 15, 136 N.E. 224 (1922), a waterfront property owner mistakenly thought he owned the adjacent submerged lands and filled them. Unfortunately for him, the court ruled that the town held title to the submerged lands both before and after that land was raised. Having title to the raised land, the town decided to make full use of the land and build 33 public bath houses on it. The waterfront property owner sued to enjoin the town's plan on the ground that it would interfere with his right of access. Although the town was not precluded from using the filled land as a public beach, it was prohibited from erecting structures which would interfere with the waterfront owner's direct access to the water "along the whole frontage" of his property. Id. at 22, 136 N.E. at 226. The court also stated that the waterfront owner's "rights as a riparian owner continue[d] and he [did not] * * * become an inland owner to the extent of the fill." Id. at 22, 136 N.E. at 226.

On the other hand, in Koyer v. Minor, 172 Cal. 448, 156 P. 1023 (1916), the City of San Pedro erected as a seawall on state-owned submerged land and then filled the area between the shoreline and the seawall. The filled area was then leased to a company for use in connection with an electric railroad franchise. As a result, the plaintiffs' direct access to water was cut off, leaving them with access only by means of the public streets. According to the court

> When the public authorities see fit to make improvements on the land below the high-water mark for purposes of [improving] navigation, the riparian owner must yield. * * *

> If such improvements have the effect of cutting off access * * * it is no ground of complaint * * * because [the upland property owner] had no right to the free and unobstructed access to navigable waters over said tidelands against the right of the state to at any time devote them to the improvement of the harbor * * * in aid of the public easement of navigation and commerce.

Id. at 452–53, 156 P. at 1025. For additional discussion of the issues raised by *Slavin*, see J. Kalo, North Carolina Oceanfront Property And Public Waters: The Rights of Littoral Owners In The Twenty-First Century, 83 N.C. L. Rev. 1427, 1453–83 (2005).

2. In order to create the appropriate beach contour, the typical long-term (50 year) federal beach nourishment project will require the deposit of sand above the mean high tide line. If, in the particular jurisdiction, private title runs to the mean high tide line, will the entity sponsoring the project need the permission of each littoral owner to place fill above the mean high-tide line? Below the mean high-tide line? If so, what if one or more littoral owners refuse to grant the necessary permission? What can be done about such "holdouts"? If the placement of fill below the mean high tide line does not require the consent of the adjacent littoral owner, does that mean that littoral rights may be terminated simply by depositing the sand and other materials seaward of the mean high tide line?

3. If the following statute is in effect, does it mean that, without the consent of affected littoral owners, a beach nourishment project terminates all existing littoral rights?

> The title to land in or immediately along the Atlantic Ocean or Gulf of Mexico raised above the mean high water mark by publicly financed projects that involve hydraulic dredging or other deposition of spoil materials or sand vests in the State. Title to such lands raised through projects

that receive no public funding vests in the adjacent littoral proprietor. All such raised lands shall remain open to the free use and enjoyment of the people of the State, consistent with the public trust rights in ocean beaches, which rights are part of the common heritage of the people of this State.

Remember, in order for land to be littoral, one boundary must be a navigable waterbody.

4. Does it matter that the cases cited by the *Slavin* court, in support of its assertion that the littoral rights of oceanfront property owners are subject to reasonable regulation, are cases involving the right to wharf or pier out? Is that littoral right inherently different from the other traditional littoral rights?

6.   THE NAVIGATION SERVITUDE

A.   FEDERAL NAVIGATION SERVITUDE

Under the Commerce Clause, the federal government has extensive powers over arteries of interstate and foreign commerce. But usually when the federal government acts to aid the movement of goods in interstate commerce by improving the arteries of commerce, such as the interstate highway system and it removes private structures that are impediments to the project, the government is required by the Fifth Amendment of the United States Constitution to pay fair compensation to the owners of such structures. When, however, the federal government acts to aid navigation in the nation's waterways and removes obstructions or private structures or otherwise destroys or diminishes private riparian rights, it is not required to pay compensation to the owners of such structures and property interests! The justification for no-compensation is the *federal navigation servitude*. Although compensation is not required, Congress may elect nonetheless to compensate the property owner for some or all of the loss sustained. See, e.g., 33 U.S.C. § 595a (1982) (compensation for real property above the high water mark taken by the United States shall include the fair market value based upon all uses to which the property may reasonably be put). As you read the following materials, think about these questions:

1.   What kinds of interests are burdened by the navigation servitude?

2.   What is the geographic extent of the navigation servitude?

3.   How does the navigation servitude differ from the public trust doctrine?

4.   What does "in aid of navigation" encompass?

5.   What is the justification for this "taking without paying" power?

LEWIS BLUE POINT OYSTER CO. V. BRIGGS

Supreme Court of the United States, 1913
229 U.S. 82

MR. JUSTICE LURTON delivered the opinion of the court.

This was an action to restrain the defendant in error from dredging upon certain lands under the waters of Great South Bay in the State of New York. The defense was that the lands upon which he was engaged in dredging were under the navigable waters of the bay, which was a navigable area of the sea, over which enrolled and registered vessels passed in interstate commerce; that Congress had provided for the dredging of a channel some 2,000 feet long and 200 feet wide across said Bay, and that defendant was engaged as a contractor with the United States in dredging the channel so authorized. The plaintiff in error, plaintiff below, averred that this channel would pass diagonally across submerged land in said bay which it held as lessee under the owner of the fee in the bed of the bay. The land so held under lease had been planted with oysters and had been long used for the cultivation of that variety of oyster known as the "Blue Point." The claim was that the dredging of such a channel would destroy the oysters of the plaintiff, not only along the line of excavation, but for some distance on either side, and greatly impair the value of his leasehold for oyster cultivation.

The New York Court of Appeals held that the title of every owner of lands beneath navigable waters was a qualified one, and subject to the right of Congress to deepen the channel in the interest of navigation, and such a "taking" was not a "taking" of private property for which compensation could be required. The judgment of the courts below discharging the injunction and dismissing the action was therefore affirmed.

The case comes here upon the claim that the dredging of such a channel, although in the interest of navigation, is a taking of private property without just compensation, forbidden by the Fifth Amendment to the Constitution of the United States.

* * * If the public right of navigation is the dominant right and if, as must be the case, the title of the owner of the bed of navigable waters holds subject absolutely to the public right of navigation, this dominant right must include the right to use the bed of the water for every purpose which is in aid of navigation. This right to control, improve and regulate the navigation of such waters is one of the greatest of the powers delegated to the United States by the power to regulate commerce. Whatever power the several States had before the Union was formed, over the navigable waters within their several jurisdictions, has been delegated to the Congress, in which, therefore, is centered all of the governmental power over the subject, restricted only by such limitations as are found in other clauses of the Constitution.

By necessary implication from the dominant right of navigation, title to such submerged lands is acquired and held subject to the power of Congress to deepen the water over such lands or to use them for any structure which the interest of navigation, in its judgment, may require. The plaintiff in error has, therefore, no such private property right which, when taken, or incidentally destroyed by the dredging of a deep water channel across it, entitles him to demand compensation as a condition.

* * *

The conclusion we reach, is that the court below did not err in dismissing the action of the plaintiff in error, and the judgment is accordingly

Affirmed.

NOTES AND QUESTIONS

1. Before reacting to *Blue Point Oyster*, some more background on the navigation servitude is helpful. Professor Eva Morreale, in Federal Power in Western Waters: The Navigation Power and The Rule of No Compensation, 3 Nat. Resources. J. 1, 2 n.6 (1963), wrote:

> It is important to note * * * that the terms "*navigation power*" and "*navigation servitude*" describe two related but nevertheless distinct phenomena. Navigation power designates the regulatory power which Congress, under the commerce clause and since Gibbons v. Ogden, exercises over navigable waters. Navigation servitude designates the rule that certain private property may be taken in the exercise of the navigation power without the payment of compensation.

What is the justification for this no-compensation rule?

2. The federal navigation servitude, in its traditional form, could be used to avoid payment of compensation to adversely affected private property owners when the only purpose of the particular federal activity was in aid of navigation. Gradually, the navigation servitude was transformed. In 1931, Justice Brandeis wrote: "That purposes other than navigation will also be served could not invalidate the exercise of the authority conferred, even if those other purposes would not alone have justified an exercise of Congressional power." Arizona v. California, 283 U.S. 423, 456 (1931). Justice Brandeis implied, however, that aid of navigation had to be the primary purpose. Ten years later, in Oklahoma v. Atkinson, 313 U.S. 508, 534 (1941), a unanimous Supreme Court noted: "That ends other than flood control will also be served, or that flood control may be relatively of lesser importance, does not invalidate the exercise of the authority conferred on Congress." The requirement that navigation be the primary purpose had vanished. Aid of navigation need only be a purpose.

For example, the owners of 49.3 acre tract of submerged land lying under very shallow (1–3 feet) waters in Lake Worth, Florida, sought compensation following the refusal of the U.S. Army Corps of Engineers to grant a permit to allow filling of the tract. Although the Corps' denial letter made it clear the denial was primarily predicated on environmental grounds, since *one* reason for the denial was that the filling of the shallow waters would eliminate open waters utilized by recreational and commercial fishermen using shallow draft watercraft, the Court of Federal Claims held that the federal navigation servitude was a complete defense to the regulatory taking claim. Palm Beach Isles Associates v. United States, 58 Fed. Cl. 657, 680–682 (2003).

3. In United States v. Certain Parcels of Land Situated in the City of Valdez, 666 F.2d 1236 (1982), the City of Valdez, Alaska, sought compensation for a ferry terminal facility condemned by the federal government and incorporated into a Coast Guard vessel traffic control and safety facility. In part, the City of Valdez asserted that the government could not rely on the navigation servitude to avoid compensation because construction of the facility did not aid "navigation in fact." According to the city, the government only improves navigation when it removes obstructions in navigable waters. Since the ferry terminal was not removed, but instead incorporated into a new dock, the city contended that it did not aid navigation, that the government took the facility for its own use, and that the government had to compensate the city for the value of the terminal. (Interestingly, the ferry terminal facility was constructed entirely with federal funds, by the U.S. Army Corps of Engineers, for the city after a 1964 earthquake destroyed the original facility owned by the State of Alaska).

The Ninth Circuit rejected the petitioners claim. The Court dismissed the City's assertion that the exercise of the navigation servitude requires that the government act to aid navigation in fact. According to the Court, only a purpose to improve and protect navigation is essential. Under such circumstances, "private improvements connected to fastlands but located in navigable waters may be altered or removed by the government without compensating the owner." Id. at 1240.

4. The U.S. Army Corps of Engineers ordered some wharf owners to remove pilings from their wharves and suspended the wharf owners' federal permit right to maintain such structures. When the wharf owners sued, alleging a taking, the district court held that (1) the wharf owners' state-created right to maintain a wharf on state owned submerged lands was subordinate to the federal navigation servitude and (2), under the applicable regulations, the Corps retained the power to modify, revoke, or suspend plaintiffs' rights under their federal permit if such was necessary in the public interest. Donnell v. United States, 834 F.Supp. 19 (D. Me. 1993).

5. What waters are subject to the navigation servitude? Read the discussion in the notes that follows Phillips Petroleum, supra on p. 129. Lake Worth, the waterbody involved in *Palm Beach Isles Associates*, discussed in

note 2, above, was a freshwater lake until in the 1860s an opening was cut in the upland ridge separating it from the Atlantic Ocean. Subsequently, Lake Worth became part of the Atlantic Intracoastal Waterway. In its pre–1860s state, was Lake Worth a "navigable water of the United States" subject to the federal navigation servitude? Under what circumstances will artificial changes in a waterbody make it both a "navigable water of the United States" and subject to the federal navigation servitude? For additional reading on the navigation servitude, See, e.g., W. Stoebuck, Nontrespassory Taking in Eminent Domain 100–20 (1977).

APPLEGATE V. UNITED STATES
United States Court of Federal Claims, 1996
35 Fed Cl. 406

MILLER, JUDGE.

This case is before the court on plaintiffs' motion for summary judgment as to liability; plaintiffs' motion for partial summary judgment based on the Assignment of Claims Act, 31 U.S.C. § 3727 (1994); and defendant's motion for summary judgment. Plaintiffs seek compensation for an alleged taking in violation of the Fifth Amendment through erosion due to construction of a federal harbor project. By their motions plaintiffs contend: 1) that erosion of their properties above the mean high-water mark, beyond the limits of the Federal Government's navigational servitude, amounts to a physical taking; 2) that the Government caused the erosion of their properties through construction of the Canaveral Harbor project * * *. Defendant asserts entitlement to summary judgment on the bases: 1) that plaintiffs have no compensable expectancy in accreting beaches or in the uninterrupted flow of sand. * * *

Facts

The following facts are undisputed, unless otherwise indicated. This constitutional takings case involves over 300 plaintiffs and more than 350 parcels of land. * * *

Plaintiffs are owners of beachfront property south of Port Canaveral in Brevard County, Florida. This coastline fronts on the Atlantic Ocean to the south of the projection of Cape Canaveral. Prior to the events giving rise to this action, the area consisted of a 41-mile long arc of white sandy beaches. All of the plaintiffs, save one, acquired interests in the properties that are the subject of this action at various times after construction began on the federal project in question.

During the 1950s the Corps undertook construction of the Canaveral Harbor Project (the "Project") * * *. The Project was designed to provide a deep-water harbor on the east coast of Florida in Brevard County, immediately south of Cape Canaveral. The Project included the dredging of a channel from the deep water of the Atlantic Ocean through a barrier island into the Banana River Lagoon, as well as turning basins, dikes, locks, and other harbor mechanisms. Construction of the Project began in 1950.

As part of the Project, the Corps constructed two jetties projecting from the shoreline eastward into the Atlantic Ocean. * * * Plaintiffs and defendant contest the purpose of the jetties and their effect on the harbor and adjacent lands.

* * *

Discussion

* * *

2. Permanent Physical Occupation: Taking through Erosion

* * *

Plaintiffs claim a physical invasion of their properties through flooding and erosion caused by the Corps' construction of the Project. They contend that the construction interfered with the natural southerly littoral flow of sand that, before construction of the Project, provided regular, natural replenishment and maintenance of their beachfront properties. Defendant maintains that plaintiffs have no compensable expectancy in the littoral flow of sand because the Government has exceptional power to regulate waters in the public interest, including the flow of sand beneath the MHWM. * * *

It is well settled that flooding and attendant erosion of private property by the Government amount to a taking. United States v. Dickinson, 331 U.S. 745, 750 (1947). * * *

Takings cases involving navigable waters present unique considerations. The United States holds broad powers to regulate along bodies of water and maintains an exclusive navigation servitude, United States v. Rands, 389 U.S. 121, 123 (1967), which reflects the superior interests of the United States in navigation and the nation's navigable waters. United States v. Twin City Power Co., 350 U.S. 222, 224 (1956). * * *

The holdings of the Supreme Court and the Federal Circuit establish that the Government owes no compensation for injury or destruction of a claimant's rights when they lie within the scope of the navigational servitude, which encompasses, at least, properties below the MHWM. * * * However, the Supreme Court "has never held that the navigational servitude creates a blanket exception to the Takings Clause. * * * "Kaiser–Aetna [v. United States,] 444 U.S. [164] at 172.

The Federal Circuit recognizes that compensation may be required "where improvements to navigation made by the government result in erosion to land located above or outside * * * the high-water mark at the time of construction." * * * Whether the Government's action went so far as to amount to a taking then is a separate inquiry from the existence of the navigational servitude itself. Kaiser–Aetna, 444 U.S. at 174; Owen [v. United States,] 851 F.2d [1404,] 1416. * * *

Binding precedent supports a ruling, as a matter of law, that flooding and erosion on plaintiffs' properties caused by governmental action above the MHWM is a compensable taking. Owen, 851 F.2d at 1416. The same line of cases denies compensation to a landowner for damage to property within the broad navigational servitude held by the United States, specifically the littoral flow of sand below the MHWM.

A judgment as a matter of fact and law in a takings case requires proof of causation. Proof of actual and proximate causation of plaintiffs' damages due to construction of the Project by the Corps is a difficult undertaking on summary judgment. * * *

1) Proof of Loss

Fundamental to proving causation in a takings case is marshaling evidence of the actual taking of property. Public Water, 133 Ct. Cl. at 352, 135 F. Supp. at 890. Plaintiffs filed their complaint in 1992. * * * Plaintiffs Don and Gayle Applegate and Noro and Company, d/b/a Pelican Landing Resort, were permitted to represent the claims of similarly situated plaintiffs. Plaintiffs' counsel certified to the court that the test plaintiffs represent the similar claims of all plaintiffs. During the following months, the court ordered plaintiffs to provide defendant with information on the actual and specific physical losses due to dune and bluff erosion caused by construction of the Project. To date plaintiffs have not provided any information on actual loss of property for any plaintiff, including the test plaintiffs. As a result, plaintiffs currently face a June 28, 1996 deadline to provide such information, after which the sanction of dismissal will be imposed. Applegate v. United States, 35 Fed. Cl. 47, 58–59 (1996) (order denying motion to dismiss and compelling discovery); Applegate v. United States, No. 92–832L (Fed. Cl. Mar. 27, 1996) (order denying reconsideration and extending deadline).

* * * Without an appropriate showing of the amount of beachfront allegedly lost, the court cannot rule as a matter of fact and law that any loss occurred and that any plaintiff in this case therefore is entitled to compensation for a taking of property.

2) Proof of Causation

To entitle a claimant to compensation, the Fifth Amendment requires that the Government actually take the property interest at issue. In cases involving indirect action, a necessary and difficult element of proof is causation. Collectively, plaintiffs and defendant have presented hundreds of pages of documents. Review of the evidence submitted on summary judgment leads to the ineluctable conclusion that the burdens attendant to resolution on summary judgment as to causation, in light of the conflicting evidence, are insurmountable. The evidence presents conflicting scenarios regarding the causes, history, and current state of erosion on beaches south of Canaveral Harbor.

Among the disputes that directly relate to causation is the nature of beach creation and renourishment. Plaintiffs assert that Brevard County beaches are the product of the natural southerly littoral flow of sand, which also causes sustaining accretion, relying on letters from Corps engineers, Corps reports, and the holding in Pitman. 457 F.2d at 978. Disputing plaintiffs' theory that the littoral flow of sand created the beaches, defendant rejoins with an alternative explanation of the process by which the beaches of Peninsular Florida were formed, relying on the Affidavit of David V. Schmidt, Chief, Coastal Section, Plan Formulation Branch, Planning Division, Jacksonville District, U.S. Army Corps of Engineers.

* * *

3. Assignment of Claims

Plaintiffs argue that a landowner may recover damages for a taking of property that precedes his ownership of the affected property. Plaintiffs assert that they are entitled to compensation dating back to the initial construction of the Project, regardless of the date of purchase * * *.

"[I]t is undisputed that '[since] compensation is due at the time of taking, the owner at that time, not the owner at an earlier or later date, receives the payment'." [United States v.] Dow [357 U.S.] at 20–21.* * * Furthermore A[i]t is well established * * * that the Assignment of Claims Act prohibits the voluntary assignment of a compensation claim against the Government for the taking of property." * * *

Since plaintiffs are barred by law from claiming damages prior to ownership, and no valid assignment occurred, plaintiffs are precluded from recovering damages for any property taken before the date for each purchase of property. * * *

Plaintiffs' motions for summary judgment are denied.* * *

4. Assuming that plaintiffs comply with the court's order of February 29, 1996, requiring them to respond to outstanding discovery requests by June 29, 1996, a status conference shall be held * * *.

NOTES AND QUESTIONS

1. Did the court hold that the plaintiffs had a property right in the natural littoral flow of sand in the ocean waters lying in front of their beach property? Other than the fact that the federal government is the defendant, isn't this case the same as Lummis v. Lilly, supra on p. 175?

2. Does proof of causation and loss present almost insoluble and extremely expensive problems for plaintiffs attempting to recover in such cases? See Banks v. United States, 62 Fed. Cl. 778 (2004) (Corps jetties in Lake Michigan responsible for some additional erosion but material issue of fact as to how much).

3. Are the critical facts here the construction of the jetty and the cutting of an artificial channel through a barrier island? Should the navigation servitude insulate the federal government from liability if the Corps was dredging a natural coastal river to protect the river channel from siltation and the consequence was increased erosion of down current beaches? Under Section 111 of the Rivers and Harbors Act of 1899 (codified at 33 U.S.C. 426i (2000)), the Corps is authorized to take corrective measures for erosion and damage to adjacent shorelines that result from a federal navigation project.

4. Would a state be liable to oceanfront property owners for the consequences of cutting off the natural movement of littoral sand drift if the state erected a breakwater or other erosion control structure on state-owned submerged lands for the purpose of improving navigation? See, e.g., Miramar Co. v. City of Santa Barbara, 23 Cal. 2d 170, 143 P. 2d 1 (1943) (no liability).

5. In developed areas, it would not be unusual for coastal properties to change hands frequently. If a property owner may only recover for erosion that has taken place during that person's period of ownership, doesn't this, as a practical matter, preclude the successful prosecution of takings claims predicated upon alleged erosion of beach property resulting from governmental activities?

6. The federal government settled the *Applegate* litigation by agreeing to pay for an $8 million beach restoration project and an additional $5 million in damages and attorneys' fees to oceanfront property owners. T. O' Mieilia, Palm Beach Considers Suing U.S. Over Beaches, Palm Beach Post, Wednesday, December 15, 1999.

B. STATE NAVIGATION SERVITUDES

The Commerce Clause grants the federal government power over interstate commerce, including the use of and activities involving navigable waters of the United States. Under the Supremacy Clause, this power of the federal government is superior to any such power of the individual states. But if Congress has not seen fit to exercise its power over a particular navigable waterway, a state may regulate navigation there. In addition to this state navigation power, a state navigation servitude may also exist in a particular state. The existence of such a servitude can be traced back to an early New York case, Lansing v. Smith, 4 Wend. 9 (N.Y. 1829), in which the court held that a riparian owner on navigable water was not entitled to compensation when access to his wharf was impeded by a state-licensed pier. The grant of the riparian property to the owner was viewed as being subject to an implied reservation of power to regulate commerce. By 1897, several other states had recognized such a servitude. E.g., Holyoke Water Power Co. v. Connecticut River Co., 52 Conn. 570 (Conn. 1884); Green Bay & M Canal Co. v. Kaukauna Water Power Co., 90 Wis. 370, 61 N.W. 1121, 63 N.W. 1019 (1895). Most often the existence of a state navigation servitude has been asserted in dicta, recognizing the doctrine, but finding it

> inapplicable because the state's activity has been held not to be carried out under the navigation power. The net result being that the scope of the state navigation power has been most narrowly constricted. * * *

> So reluctant have state courts been to invoke the navigation servitude that one might question the vitality of the state branch of the navigation servitude. * * * W. Stoebuck, Nontrespassory Taking in Eminent Domain 114–15 (1977).

In Wernberg v. State, 516 P.2d 1191 (1973), reh'g denied, 519 P.2d 801 (Alaska 1974), the Alaskan Supreme Court addressed the issue of the existence and extent of the Alaskan state navigation servitude. The case involved highway construction that had the effect of blocking Wernberg's access to the deep waters of Cook Inlet. After the construction of the highway, Wernberg, a commercial fisherman and littoral owner, could no longer navigate his fishing vessels into Cook Inlet. The state opposed the payment of any compensation to the appellant on the ground that any right of access of a littoral owner was subordinate to the state navigation servitude. The court rejected the state's argument. In its opinion, the court observed that, where recognized, state navigation servitudes are governed by one of three rules:

> (1) the general rule; (2) the public purpose rule; * * * [or] (3) the Louisiana exception. The general rule requires the state to compensate the riparian owner for infringement of his property rights unless the project causing the harm is in aid of navigation. The public purpose rule, on the other hand, requires no compensation if the offending project is for any public purpose. Under the Louisiana exception, the scope of the servitude extends to projects "in aid of navigation" that are miles from the actual boundaries of the watercourse, allowing the state to burden all property in between without payment of compensation.

Id. at 1196. The court then said that the state could take riparian or littoral property rights for a purpose other than to aid navigation, but then the Alaskan constitution requires that compensation be paid.

If compensation must be paid, what does the state navigation servitude add to the police powers of the state to take private property rights for a public purpose so long as compensation is paid? Is the state navigation servitude meaningful in Alaska?

In its opinion, the court also stated that state navigation servitudes are subordinate to the federal one,

> but where the federal government has not acted, it allows the state, in aid of navigation, to take private riparian rights without paying the compensation that would otherwise be required by the fourteenth amendment.

Id. Does this mean that if the state had been acting "in aid of navigation," Wernberg would not have been entitled to compensation for loss of his access to the deep waters of Cook Inlet?

> The "public purpose" rule discussed in *Wernberg*, is best exemplified by the California Supreme Court's decision in Colberg, Inc. v. State ex rel. Department of Public Works, 62 Cal.Rptr. 401, 432 P.2d 3 (1967), cert. denied, 390 U.S. 949 (1968), a decision that sharply contrasts to what most other state courts have been doing. In *Colberg*, the plaintiffs owned a shipyard, located on riparian land, at the end of a tidal waterway. The State planned to construct a fixed low level bridge between plaintiff's shipyard and the mouth of the waterway. As a result, the ship access from the mouth of the waterway to the shipyards would be substantially diminished. Relying on the state navigation servitude, the California Supreme Court denied compensation. The court said that "whatever the scope and character of * * * [plaintiffs'] right to have access to those navigable waters,* * * such right is burdened with a servitude in favor of the state which comes into operation when the state properly exercises its power to control, regulate, and utilize such waters." Id. at 12–13. Perhaps more significantly, the court stated:

> The limitation of the servitude to cases involving a strict navigational purpose stems from the time when the sole use of navigable waters for purposes of water commerce was that of surface water transportation* * * That time is no longer with us. The demands of modern commerce, the concentration of population in urban centers fronting on navigable waterways, the achievements of science in devising new methods of commercial intercourse—all of these factors require that the state, in determining the means by which the general welfare is best to be served through the utilization of navigable waters held in

trust for the public, should not be burdened with an outmoded classification favoring one mode of utilization over another.

Id. at 12. Consequently, in California the navigable servitude applies whenever the state exercises its power over navigable waters to improve commercial intercourse, whether navigational or otherwise. See Note, Colberg, Inc. v. State: Riparian Landowner's Right to Eminent Domain Relief for State Impairment of Access to a Navigable Waterway, 72 Dick. L. Rev. 375, 380 (1968).

Would the federal government be required to compensate in a situation in which it engaged in activities with similar consequences to those in *Colberg*? Is the expansion of the state navigation servitude in California in effect a taking by judicial decision in violation of the Fifth Amendment? Does *Colberg* proclaim a state navigational servitude for every form of governmental activity that affects navigable waters?

7. PUBLIC ACCESS AND USE OF BEACHES AND SHORES

A. THE SCOPE OF THE PUBLIC RIGHT OF ACCESS TO COASTAL LANDS AND WATERS

Use by the public of navigable waters and beaches below the mean high tide line boundary is part of the trust in which the states hold these waters. But access by the public to beaches and ocean waters can be problematic. In general, several issues regularly arise concerning the public's access and use of beaches:

- How can members of the public reach the public trust beach and waters (vertical access)? Is there a right to cross private land to access the beach?

- What part of the beach is open to use by the public? Can rights extend to the dry sand portion of the beach?

- What is the scope of the public's right to use the beach? To what extent can the public's use be regulated or limited?

Public use of beaches has become more controversial as the amount of undeveloped beachfront property has dwindled and access to beaches has been cut off by a wall of development. In addition, as the price of beachfront property has soared, owners paying extremely high prices expect peace and privacy. Common law property and public trust principles play an important role in balancing public and private interests, but many states have begun to address the public access issue in legislation.

OPINION OF THE JUSTICES
(PUBLIC USE OF COASTAL BEACHES)

Request of the House of Representatives No. 94–322
139 N.H. 82 (S. Ct. of New Hampshire, 1994)

* * *

To the Honorable House:

The undersigned justices of the supreme court submit the following reply to your questions of May 5, 1994. Following our receipt of your resolution, we invited interested parties to file memoranda with the court on or before September 1, 1994.

SB 636 (the bill), as amended, proposes to amend RSA chapter 483–B (1992) by inserting after section 9 a new section, 483–B:9–a, titled "Public Use of Coastal Beaches." The legislature's purpose is set out in the bill as follows:

It is the purpose of the general court in this section to recognize and confirm the historical practice and common law right of the public to enjoy the existing public easement in the greatest portion of New Hampshire coastal beach land subject to those littoral rights recognized at common law. This easement presently existing over the greater portion of that beachfront property extending from where the 'public trust' ends across the commonly used portion of sand and rocks to the intersection of the beach and the high ground, often but not always delineated by a sea wall, or the line of vegetation, or the seaward face of the foredunes, this being that beach where violent sea action occurs at irregular frequent intervals making its use for the usual private constructions uneco[n]o[m]ical and physically impractical.

The bill defines "coastal beaches" as "that portion of the beach extending from where the public trust shoreland ends, across the commonly used portion of sand and rocks to the intersection of the beach and high ground, often but not always delineated by a seawall, or the line of vegetation, or the seaward face of the foredunes."

The bill states that "New Hampshire holds in 'public trust' rights in all shorelands subject to the ebb and flow of the tide and subject to those littoral rights recognized at common law" and that the " 'public trust' shoreland establishes the extreme seaward boundary extension of all private property rights in New Hampshire except for those 'jus privatum' rights validly conveyed by legislative act without impairment of New Hampshire's 'jus publicum' interests." The bill then provides that

for an historical period extending back well over 20 years the public has made recognized, prevalent and uninterrupted use of the vast majority of New Hampshire's coastal beaches above the 'public trust' shoreland. The legislature recognizes that some public use of the beach area above the public trust lands is necessary to the full enjoyment of the land. The general court recognizes and confirms a public easement flowing from and demonstrated by this historical practice in the coastal beaches contiguous to the public trust shoreland where the public has traditionally had access and which easement has been created by virtue of such uninterrupted public use.

Further, the bill states that "[a]ny person may use the coastal beaches of New Hampshire where such a public easement exists for recreational purposes subject to the provisions of municipal ordinances," but "[t]he provisions of [the bill] shall in no way be construed as affecting the title of property owners of land contiguous to land subject to a public easement." Finally, the new section provides that "[i]n a suit brought or defended under this section, or whose determination is affected by this section, a showing that the area in dispute is within the area defined as 'coastal beach' shall be prima facie evidence that a public easement exists."

Your first question asks "[w]hether New Hampshire law identifies a particular coastal feature or tidal event as outlining the maximum shoreward extension of the public trust area boundary * * * beyond which the probable existence of private property rights may, without a public easement arising from historical practice, restrict any public access under the provisions of Part I, Article 12 of the New Hampshire Constitution and the 5th amendment of the United States Constitution." We answer in the affirmative.

* * *

In 1889, this court rejected a Massachusetts law that adopted the low water mark as the boundary between public and private ownership. Concord Co. v. Robertson, 66 N.H. 1, 26–27, 25 A.m718, 730–31 (1889). * * *

* * *

Your second question asks "[w]hether the effect of [the bill], which recognizes that the public trust extends to those lands 'subject to ebb and flow of the tide' infringes upon existing private property rights as protected by Part I, Article 12 of the New Hampshire Constitution and the 5th amendment of the United States Constitution." We answer in the negative.

As already set out in our answer to your first question, New Hampshire has long recognized that lands subject to the ebb and flow of the tide are held in public trust. "Land covered by public water is capable of many uses." Concord Co. v. Robertson, 66 N.H. at 7, 25 A. at 721. "Rights of navigation and fishery are not the whole estate" but rather the public trust lands are held "for the use and benefit of all the [public], for all useful purposes * * * " Id. at 7–8, 25 A. at 721 (quotation omitted); see St. Regis Co. v. Board, 92 N.H. 164, 170, 26 A.2d 832, 837–38 (1942) (public trust encompasses "all useful and lawful purposes"); State v. Sunapee Dam Co., 70 N.H. 458, 463, 50 A. 108, 110 (1900) ("in this state the law of public waters is what justice and reason require"). These uses include recreational uses. See Hartford v. Gilmanton, 101 N.H. 424, 425–26, 146 A.2d 851, 853 (1958) (public waters may be used to boat, bathe, fish, fowl, skate, and cut ice).

* * *

Therefore, to the extent that the term "lands subject to ebb and flow of the tide" applies to tidelands below the high water mark, the bill simply codifies the common law and does not infringe upon private property rights. Where private title to tidelands is already burdened by preexisting public rights, a regulation designed to protect those same rights will not constitute a taking of property without just compensation.

Your third question asks "[w]hether the provisions of [the bill], which recognize a public easement in the 'dry sand area' of historically accessible coastal beaches is a taking of private property for a public purpose without just compensation in violation of Part I, Article 12 of the New Hampshire Constitution and the 5th amendment of the United States Constitution." Except for those areas where there is an established and acknowledged public easement and subject to the assumptions contained in the discussion below, we answer in the affirmative.

The bill apparently recognizes two property interests in two distinct areas of shoreland. First, the bill establishes that "New Hampshire holds in 'public trust' rights in all shorelands subject to the ebb and flow of the tide." Second, the bill establishes a public easement in land "extending from where the public trust ends across the commonly used portion of sand and rocks to the intersection of the beach and the high ground, often but not always delineated by a sea wall, or the line of vegetation, or the seaward face of the foredunes." This high ground is generally known as the "dry sand" area. * * *

* * * [T]his court has not defined the term "high water mark." Because, however, the bill states that the dry sand area is not within the public trust we will, for purposes of this opinion, base our analysis on that assumption. We construe the bill, therefore, as recognizing public trust rights below the dry sand area and a prescriptive easement in the dry sand. * * * "To establish a prescriptive easement, the plaintiff must prove by a balance of probabilities twenty years' adverse, continuous, uninterrupted use of the land [claimed] in such a manner as to give notice to the record owner that an adverse claim was being made to it." Mastin v. Pres-

cott, 122 N.H. 353, 356, 444 A.2d 556, 558 (1982) (quotation omitted). Although the general public is capable of acquiring an easement by prescription, Elmer v. Rodgers, 106 N.H. 512, 515, 214 A.2d 750, 752 (1965),

[e]vidence of continuous and uninterrupted public use of the premises for the statutory period * * * is insufficient alone to establish prescriptive title as a matter of law. The nature of the use must be such as to show the owner knew or ought to have known that the right was being exercised, not in reliance upon his toleration or permission, but without regard to his consent.

Vigeant v. Donel Realty Trust, 130 N.H. 406, 408, 540 A.2d 1243, 1244 (1988) (ellipses in original) (quotation omitted). While the fact that the owner was also using the premises for the same purposes would not prevent a finding of adverse use by the general public, Elmer v. Rodgers, 106 N.H. at 515, 214 A.2d at 752, "[a] permissive use no matter how long or how often exercised cannot ripen into an easement by prescription." Ucietowski v. Novak, 102 N.H. 140, 145, 152 A.2d 614, 618 (1959). The general public may, therefore, acquire coastal beach land by prescription in New Hampshire.

Problems militate, however, against the use of the prescriptive doctrine. "First, there is the obvious problem of establishing factual evidence of the specialized type of adverse use for the requisite period of time * * * needed to create an easement by prescription." R. Powell, 3 Powell on Real Property § 34.11[6], at 34–171 (1994). "Secondly, prescriptive easements, by their nature, can be utilized only on a tract-by-tract basis, and thus cannot be applied to all beaches within a state." Id. In a suit to quiet title, adequate evidence may well exist to prove that on a given piece of property, the area landward of the public trust across the dry sand is subject to a public easement. Such a determination is, however, a judicial one [and not a legislative one]. * * *

Although the bill does not completely deprive private property owners of use of their property, "[t]he interference with private property here involves a wholesale denial of an owner's right to exclude the public." * * * When the government unilaterally authorizes a permanent, public easement across private lands, this constitutes a taking requiring just compensation.

Because the bill provides no compensation for the landowners whose property may be burdened by the general recreational easement established for public use, it violates the prohibition contained in our State and Federal Constitutions against the taking of private property for public use without just compensation. Although the State has the power to permit a comprehensive beach access and use program by using its eminent domain power and compensating private property owners, it may not take property rights without compensation through legislative decree. * * *

We emphasize that this opinion does not amount to a judicial decision. An opinion of the justices on proposed legislation is not binding upon the court in the event the proposed legislation should become law and a case should arise requiring its construction.

NOTES AND QUESTIONS

1. In 1999, the New Hampshire Supreme Court answered one of the questions left open in The Opinion of the Justices. In Purdie v. Attorney General, 143 N.H. 661, 732 A. 2d 442 (1999), the court defined "high water mark" as the "mean high tide line." Consequently, a legislative act extending public trust rights to the highest high water mark violated the state and federal constitutional prohibitions against the taking of private property for public use without adequate compensation.

2. If the mean high tide line is the measure for determining the boundary between public trust lands and private property, is it an appropriate one or one that can be easily enforced, e.g., through a trespass action? Is it clearly visible on the beach? Can it be judged by the daily reach of the water or the vegetation line? Is it even in the same place every day? The following excerpt explains why the MHWL boundary continues to contribute to the controversy between beach users and upland property owners:

> * * * The mean high water line boundary is found at the point at which the horizontal tidal plane of the mean high water intersects with the shore. The vertical determination of mean high water is basically stable, being based on observations over nineteen years. The horizontal element of the boundary determination on a sandy beach is anything but stable. The intersection of the horizontal plane of mean high water changes with erosion and accretion, seasonal variations in the beach, wind, waves, storms and man-made changes to the beach—anything that changes the profile of the beach. As a result, "[a] water boundary determined by tidal definition is . . . not a fixed visible mark on the ground, but represents a condition at the water's edge during a particular instant of the tidal cycle." It follows that even the most accurate determination of the MHWL for a dynamic sandy beach is no more than a snapshot of the boundary at that particular time and place.

Donna R. Christie, Of Beaches, Boundaries and SOBs, 25 J. L. U. & Envtl. Law 19, 34 (2009)(citations omitted.)

3. Although the New Hampshire Supreme Court rejected the idea that public trust rights include the use of the dry sand beach (the area between the mean high tide line and vegetation line), the New Jersey Supreme Court accepted the concept. In Matthews v. Bay Head Improvement Ass'n, 95 N.J. 306, 326, 471 A.2d 355, cert. denied, 469 U.S. 821 (1984), the court said:

Public Rights in Privately-Owned Dry Sand Beaches

* * * We now address the extent of the public's interest in privately-owned dry sand beaches. This interest may take one of two forms. First, the public may have a right to cross privately owned dry sand beaches in order to gain access to the foreshore. Second, this interest may be of the sort enjoyed by the public in municipal beaches * * * namely, the right to sunbathe and generally enjoy recreational activities. * * *

Exercise of the public's right to swim and bathe below the mean high water mark may depend upon a right to pass across the upland beach. Without some means of access the public right to use the foreshore would be meaningless. To say that the public trust doctrine entitles the public to swim in the ocean and to use the foreshore in connection therewith without assuring the public of a feasible access route would seriously impinge on, if not effectively eliminate, the rights of the public trust doctrine. This does not mean the public has an unrestricted right to cross at will over any and all property bordering on the common property. The public interest is satisfied so long as there is reasonable access to the sea.

* * *

The bather's right in the upland sands is not limited to passage. Reasonable enjoyment of the foreshore and the sea cannot be realized unless some enjoyment of the dry sand area is also allowed. The complete pleasure of swimming must be accompanied by intermittent periods of rest and relaxation beyond the water's edge. The unavailability of the physical situs for such rest and relaxation would seriously curtail and in many situations eliminate the right to the recreational use of the ocean. * * * We see no reason why rights under the public trust doctrine to use of the upland dry sand area should be limited to municipally-owned property. It is true that the private owner's interest in the upland dry sand area is not identical to that of a municipality. Nonetheless, where use of dry sand is essential or reasonably necessary for enjoyment of the ocean, the doctrine warrants the public's use of the upland dry sand area subject to an accommodation of the interests of the owner.

We perceive no need to attempt to apply notions of prescription, dedication, or custom, as an alternative to application of the public trust doctrine. Archaic judicial responses are not an answer to a modern social problem. Rather, we perceive the public trust doctrine not to be "fixed or static," but one to "be molded and extended to meet changing conditions and needs of the public it was created to benefit." Avon, 61 N.J. at 309, 294 A.2d 47 [sic].

Precisely what privately-owned upland sand area will be available and required to satisfy the public's rights under the public trust doctrine will depend on the circumstances. Location of the dry sand area in relation to the foreshore, extent and availability of the publicly-owned upland sand area, nature and extent of the public demand, and usage of the upland sand land by the owner are all factors to be weighed and considered in fixing the contours of the usage of the upper sand.

Today, recognizing the increasing demand for our State's beaches and the dynamic nature of the public trust doctrine, we find that the public must be given both access to and use of privately-owned dry sand areas as reasonably necessary. While the public's rights in private beaches are not co-extensive with the rights enjoyed in municipal beaches, private landowners may not in all instances prevent the public from exercising its rights under the public trust doctrine. The public must be afforded reasonable access to the foreshore as well as a suitable area for recreation on the dry sand.

* * *

Id. at. 322–326. Matthews was reaffirmed in Raleigh Avenue Beach Association v. Atlantis Beach Club, Inc, 185 N.J. 40, 879 A. 2d 112 (2005). (public has right to use a 480 foot privately owned upland sand beach).

4. Contrary to the law in most states, Matthews established a right of access to the beach across private property as well as a right to use the dry sand beach "as reasonably necessary" to exercise rights under the public trust doctrine. In Texas, the Open Beaches Act creates two presumptions for purposes of protecting and facilitating ingress and egress to the sea. The Act originally provided that the title of private owners of dry beach area in Gulf beaches "does not include the right to prevent the public from using the area for ingress and egress to the sea." TEX. NAT. RES. CODE § 61.020(a)(1). In 1991, the OBA was amended to add a second presumption that imposed "on the area a common law right or easement in favor of the public for ingress and egress to the sea." Id. § 61.020(a)(2). Does the fact that these presumptions are rebuttable by the landowner protect the provisions from a constitutional taking challenge? Is it merely a shifting of the burden of proof?

5. In the Northeast, general public access and use of ocean beaches has long been a contentious issue.

> [W]here the beaches were municipally owned, as in parts of Connecticut and New Jersey, the shore municipalities often limited beach use to town residents, or put beach fees or other barriers in the way of non-residents' use of town beaches. Tactics of indirect exclusion included charging more for nonresident beach passes, making cheap seasonal passes difficult or impossible for nonresidents to get, limiting parking near the beach and/or banning on-street parking altogether, making beach access contingent on membership in a beach club which, in turn, would be available only to residents of the community, barring disrobing or wearing a swimsuit on the streets (which effectively meant one had to belong to a beach club), and banning eating on the beach (which discouraged day trippers with picnics).

Marc R. Poirier, Environmental Justice and the Beach Access Movements of
the 1970s in Connecticut and New Jersey, Stories of Property and Civil
Rights, 28 Conn.L. Rev. 719 (1996) (describing the history and important litigation of the period). Some of the disputes over beach access have racial over-
tones. See A. Cowan, Crossing a Line Drawn In Greenwich's Fine Sand,
Thursday, February 9, 2006, New York Times, B1. Public beach access advocates have been less successful in Connecticut than in New Jersey. See Leabo
v. Leninski, 438 A.2d 1153 (Conn. 1981) (refusal to open beach to public); De-
links v. McGowan, 148 Conn. 614, 173 A. 2d 488 (1961) (public trust doctrine
does not give public right to cross beach landward of mean high tide line).
But see, Leydon v. Town of Greenwich, 257 Conn. 318, 777 A. 2d 552 (2001)
(upholding right of non-resident to use town beach park on First Amendment
constitutional grounds).

6. Massachusetts is what is referred to as a "low-tide" state; that is, a littoral owner's boundary extends to the low water, not high water, line. Between the mean high water and extreme low water line, however, the public
has limited rights—the right to "fish and fowl." Historically, these rights did
not include the right of the general public to walk on the wet sand beach.
When the legislature proposed the bill recognizing such a right, the Massachusetts Supreme Judicial Court, in an advisory opinion, held that the proposed law would constitute a taking of private property rights in the foreshore (the right to exclude the general public) and the proposed law failed to
provide fair compensation to those whose property rights would be adversely
affected. Thus, the proposed law would violate both the Massachusetts and
United States Constitutions. In re Opinion of the Justices, 365 Mass. 681,
313 N.E.2d 561 (1974). See also Bell v. Town of Wells, 557 A.2d 168 (Me.
1989) (statute defining public rights to use intertidal land to include general
recreational purposes held to be an unconstitutional taking of private
property).

B. PUBLIC ACCESS AND OTHER COMMON LAW THEORIES

The public trust doctrine is not the only common law theory that has
been advanced in the efforts to assert a public right to use the dry sand
area of the beach or a right to cross uplands to reach the public portion of
the beach. Traditional common law doctrines of prescription, custom, and
dedication are among the other approaches used to address these issues.
While these doctrines vary slightly among jurisdictions, the following case
sets out the general principles:

TREPANIER V. COUNTY OF VOLUSIA

Court of Appeal of Florida, Fifth District, 2007
965 So.2d 276

* * *

SOURCES OF THE PUBLIC'S RIGHT OF USE OF THE BEACH

The common law public trust doctrine is embodied in Article 10, section 11 of the Florida Constitution. Under that provision, title to the portion of the beach below the mean high water line is held by the state in trust for all the people. The "beach," however, includes more land than what is set aside for the people under the public trust doctrine. The area above the mean high water line is subject to private ownership. In Florida, courts have recognized that the public may acquire rights to the dry sand areas of privately owned portions of the beach through the alternative methods of prescription, dedication, and custom.

A. PRESCRIPTIVE EASEMENT

One means by which the public may acquire rights to private lands is by prescription. For the public to gain a prescriptive easement in land, its use of private land must be continuous, for the statutory period of twenty years, actual, adverse under a claim of right, and either known to the owner or so open, notorious, and visible that knowledge of the adverse use by the public can be imputed to the owner. Further, "[i]f the use of an alleged easement is not exclusive and not inconsistent with the rights of the owner of the land to its use and enjoyment, it would be presumed that such use is permissive rather than adverse." The burden is on the claimant to prove that the public's use was adverse. Moreover, in Downing v. Bird, 100 So. 2d 57 [64–65] (Fla. 1958), the court said:

Also, ' * * * the limits, location, and extent of his occupation must be definitely and clearly established by affirmative proof, and cannot be established or extended by presumption * * * ' And the pleadings, as well as the proof, particularly where a prescriptive way is claimed, must show a reasonably certain line, by definite route and termini. Acquisition of rights by one in the lands of another, based on possession or use, is not favored in the law and the acquisition of such rights will be restricted. Any doubts as to the creation of the right must be resolved in favor of the owner.

* * *

B. DEDICATION

* * * The public may acquire a right to use upland property by dedication. The dispositive issue in determining whether or not property has been dedicated appears to be whether the private property owner has expressed "a present intention to appropriate his lands to public use." City of Palmetto v. Katsch, 98 So. 352 (1923). In Katsch, the court said:

The means generally exercised to express one's purpose or intention to dedicate his lands to the public use are by a (1) written instrument executed for that purpose; (2) filing a plat or map of one's property designating thereon streets, alleys, parks, etc., (3) platting one's lands and selling lots and blocks pursuant to said plat indicating there in places for parks, streets, public grounds, etc., (4) recitals in a deed by which the rights of the public are recognized; (5) oral declarations followed by acts consistent therewith; (6) affirmative acts of the owner with reference to his property such as throwing it open in a town, fencing and designating streets thereon; (7) acquiescence of the owner in the use of his property by the public for public purposes. Id. at 511–12.

As explained by the Fourth District Court of Appeal in Hollywood, Inc. v. Zinkil, 403 So. 2d 528, 533 (Fla. 4th DCA 1981):

[M]ere uses by the public although long continued, should be regarded as a license only, revocable at the pleasure of the owner, where it does not appear that any public or private interests have been acquired upon the faith of the supposed dedication, which would be materially impaired if the dedication were revoked. The burden is on the government to prove dedication. This court added * * * that the "proof required of the intention to dedicate is 'clear and unequivocal,' and the burden of proof is on the party asserting the existence of the dedication."

* * *

C. CUSTOM

* * * Florida's Supreme Court first recognized the public's "customary" right to the use of Florida's privately owned dry sand beaches in the Tona–Rama decision. 294 So. 2d at 74. There the court said:

The beaches of Florida are of such a character as to use and potential development as to require separate consideration from other lands with respect to the elements and consequences of title. The sandy portion of the beaches ... [have] served as a thoroughfare and haven for fishermen and bathers, as well as a place of recreation for the public. The interest and rights of the public to the full use of the beaches should be protected.

294 So. 2d at 77. The court recognized that the public may acquire a right to use the sandy area adjacent to the mean high tide line by custom when "the recreational use of the sandy area ... has been ancient, reasonable, without interruption and free from dispute. . . ." Id. at 78. The recognition of a right through "custom" means that the owner cannot use his property in a way that is inconsistent with the public's customary use or "calculated to interfere with the exercise of the right of the public to

enjoy the dry sand area as a recreational adjunct of the wet sand or fore-shore area." Id.

* * *

What evidence is required in order to establish entitlement of the public to use of a particular parcel, based on custom? * * * [A]t common law, establishment of a right through custom required proof of several elements. In addition to the temporal requirement of "ancient" use, three other key elements must be proven: peaceableness, certainty and consistency. Finally, the customary use must be shown to be "reasonable."

* * *

NOTES AND QUESTIONS

1. What advantages and disadvantages do you see as to the use of each of these theories as a means of determining whether the public can use the dry sand or may cross uplands to reach the beach area? Public beach access advocates have successfully used all three common law theories to establish the public right to use privately-owned dry sand beaches in Texas. In Matcha v. Mattox, 711 S.W. 2d 95 (Tex. App. 1986), cert. denied, 481 U.S. 1024 (1987) (custom); Feinman v. State, 717 S.W. 2d 106 (Tex. App. 1986) (prescription); Seaway Co. v. Attorney General, 375 S.W. 2d 923 (Tex. Civ. App. 1964) (dedication). See also, Arrington v. Mattox, 767 S.W. 2d. 2d 957 (Tex. App. 1989) (Texas Open Beaches Act enforces pre-existing easement based on prescription, custom and dedication, and there is not an unconstitutional taking).

2. Establishing public prescriptive use can present insurmountable problems of proof. See, e.g., City of Daytona Beach v. Toma–Rama, Inc., 294 So.2d 73, 77 (Fla. 1974) (use not adverse to owner and treated as permissive); Town of Manchester v. Augusta County Club, 477 A.2d 1124, 1130 (Me. 1984) (presumption that public use of undeveloped land was permissive). See also Comment, Sunbathers Versus Property Owners: Public Access to North Carolina Beaches, 64 N.C.L.Rev. 159, 164–66 (1985). On the other hand, unsuccessful efforts by a landowner to prevent an aggressive public from crossing her land may establish that the use was indeed adverse. Concerned Citizens v. Holden Beach Enterprises, 329 N.C. 37, 404 S.E.2d 677 (1991), describes an on-going battle, spanning 20 years, between sunbathers and fishermen who were using a beach path crossing undeveloped land to reach an inlet, and the owner of the land. Despite the presence of "No Trespassing" signs, which people used for firewood, the placement of fences and gates, which people pulled down and destroyed, and a private security guard and guardhouse, whom people ignored and drove past, the public continued to use the path. According to the court, the repeated, futile attempts by the owner to prevent the public from crossing his land established that the public use was indeed adverse and not permissive. And although some people were deterred, that did not interrupt the public use because most were not. At trial, the frus-

trated agent of the owner asked: " '[W]hat does it take to keep somebody out of a place[?] * * * [H]ave you got to set a tank up, a machine gun, or what [?]' " Id. at 51, S.E.2d at 686.

3. Dedication can be express or implied. But implied dedication still requires clear evidence of intent to dedicate by acts or circumstances that show the landowner intended to donate an easement to the public and such an offer was impliedly accepted. The test applied in the California Supreme Court's decisions in Gion v. Santa Cruz (consolidated with Dietz v. King, 2 Cal.3d 29, 89 Cal. Rpt. 162, 465 P.2d 50 (1970)) left landowners in a precarious situation. The California court found the elements of implied dedication were established by "use by the public for the prescriptive period without asking or receiving permission from the fee owner." Consequently, if a landowner allowed public use of beach property, he or she could be deemed to have "acquiesced" to public dedication of the property; if the owner objected and the public used the property anyway, the public might gain the same rights of use through adverse use.

To protect landowners from unintended dedication of land to public use and encourage landowners to allow the public to use privately-owned land for recreational purposes, some state legislatures have passed statutes that prevent the finding of an implied dedication when the only evidence of an intent to dedicate is the fact that the public used it without objection by the landowner. See West's Ann. Cal. Civ. Code § 1009. However, the statute may not apply to privately-owned property that is used by the public to access the beach. See, e.g., West's Ann. Cal Civ. Code § 1009(d)(key provision is not applicable to coastal property lying within 1000 yards of MHTL of Pacific Ocean). In some jurisdictions, an essential component of an implied dedication are acts of maintenance of the area by public authorities. See, e.g., Seaway Co. v. Attorney General, 375 S.W.2d 923 (Tex.Civ.App. 1964).

4. In State ex rel. Thornton v. Hay, 254 Or. 584, 462 P.2d 671 (1969), the Oregon Supreme Court applied the common law doctrine of customary rights to establish the public's right to use the dry sand ocean beaches of the entire state. The court derived the essential elements of a claim of a right of customary use from Blackstone: (1) long and general usage, which in the case of beach usage the Court traced back to use by Indians prior to the arrival of settlers, (2) without interruption by private landowners, (3) peaceful and free from dispute, (4) reasonable, (5) certain as to its scope and character, (6) without objection by landowners, and (7) is not contrary to other customs or laws. According to the court, these conditions existed with respect to the all the dry sand oceanfront beaches of the state and therefore such beaches are open to public use. Several other jurisdictions also recognize the doctrine of custom although all states do not apply the doctrine as expansively as the Oregon courts, i.e., to the entire beachfront coast of the state. See, e.g., County of Hawaii v. Sotomura, 55 Haw. 176, 182, 517 P.2d 57, 61 (1973); Public Access Shoreline Hawaii v. Hawaii County Planning Commission, 79 Hawaii 425, 903 P.2d 1246 (Haw. 1995), cert. denied, 517 U.S. 1163 (1996) (coastal

zone management act requires protection of customary rights); United States v. St. Thomas Beach Resorts, Inc., 386 F.Supp.73 769, 772–73 (D.V.I. 1974). City of Daytona Beach v. Tona–Rama, Inc., 294 So.2d 73 (Fla.1974). A Washington Attorney General's Opinion, 1970 AGO No. 27, has also concluded that the public is entitled to free use of the wet and dry sand beaches of the state based on the doctrine of custom. Oceanfront property owners in North Carolina challenged that state's claim that the public has a customary right to use all natural dry sand beaches, but the lawsuit was dismissed on procedural grounds. Fabrikant v. Currituck County, 621 S.E. 2d 19 (N.C. App. 2005). See J. Kalo, The Changing Face of the Shoreline: Public and Private Rights to the Natural and Nourished Dry Sand Beaches of North Carolina, 78 N.C. L. Rev. 1869 (2000).

C. ROLLING EASEMENTS FOR PUBLIC ACCESS

Access to the beach over meandering dunes may result in the public using different pathways over time. In Concerned Citizens, discussed in note 2 of the previous section, one of the issues involved whether the evidence established that the public had in fact used a specific, identifiable path for the full statutory prescriptive period. During the relevant time that people were walking or driving across the property to reach the inlet, storms, hurricanes, winds, high water, and erosion altered the configuration of the island and the dune field and other terrain through which people traveled. As a result, the precise course of the pathway they traveled also changed, and the defendant's argument was that no easement existed. The court, however, held that, so long as there was a "substantial identity" to the area traversed, the fact that the dynamic quality of the environment necessitated changes in the precise route would not require a finding that there was no easement. Whether "substantial identity" existed was a question of fact for the jury.

The Supreme Court of Hawaii, however, has rejected the notion that a public access easement can move based on the dynamic nature of the environment of an area. The court maintained that an easement by prescription or dedication must be confined to a "definite and specific line," and that "vague description of the easement literally allows members of the public to redefine its location each time they use the land." In re Banning, 832 P.2d 724 (Ha.1992).

Access along the beach, rather than to the beach, had been subject to a "rolling easement" concept in Texas based on cases starting in the 1980s. When a storm severely eroded a Texas beach, the court in Matcha v. Mattox, 711 S.W. 2d 95 (Tex. App. 1986), cert. denied, 481 U.S. 1024 (1987), recognized the theory of a migratory public easement. The court of appeals explained:

> A public easement on a beach cannot have been established with reference to a set of static lines on the beach, since the beach itself,

and hence the public use of it, surely fluctuated landward and seaward over time. The public easement, if it is to reflect the reality of
the public's actual use of the beach, must migrate as did the customary use from which it arose. The law cannot freeze such an easement
at one place any more than the law can freeze the beach itself.

Id. at 99–100. See also Arrington v. Texas General Land Office, 38 S.W.
3d 764 (Tex. App. 2001) (public beach easement moves with movement of
shoreline after a tropical storm). The rolling easement concept has been
applied to prohibit reconstruction of houses after hurricanes and require
removal of houses sitting on eroded beaches if the structures interfered
with public access. (In Texas, access often means driving on beaches as
well as other traditional public recreational uses.) It was not until recently, however, that the Texas Supreme Court had the necessity to address
the rolling public access easement as a matter of state law. It did so on
certified questions from the U.S. Court of Appeals for the Fifth Circuit,
Severance v. Patterson, 345 S.W.3d 18 (Tex., 2010).

CAROL SEVERANCE V. JERRY PATTERSON

Supreme Court of Texas, 2012
370 S.W.3d 705

ON CERTIFIED QUESTIONS FROM THE UNITED STATES
COURT OF APPEALS FOR THE FIFTH CIRCUIT.

OPINION BY: WAINWRIGHT, J.

* * *

Pursuant to article V, section 3–c of the Texas Constitution and Texas Rule of Appellate Procedure 58.1, we accepted the petition from the
United States Court of Appeals for the Fifth Circuit to answer the following certified question[]:

1. Does Texas recognize a "rolling" public beachfront access easement, i.e., an easement in favor of the public that allows access to and use
of the beaches on the Gulf of Mexico, the boundary of which easement migrates solely according to naturally caused changes in the location of the
vegetation line, without proof of prescription, dedication or customary
rights in the property so occupied?

* * *

II. Background

In April 2005, Carol Severance purchased * * * the Kennedy Drive or
Kennedy Beach property, [which] is at issue in this case. A rental home
occupies the property. The parties do not dispute that no easement has
ever been established on the Kennedy Drive property. A public easement

for use of a privately owned parcel seaward of Severance's Kennedy Drive property pre-existed her purchase. * * * Five months after Severance's purchase, Hurricane Rita devastated the adjacent property burdened by an easement and moved the line of vegetation landward. The entirety of the house on Severance's Kennedy Drive property is now seaward of the vegetation line. The State claimed a portion of her property was located on a public beachfront easement and a portion of her house interfered with the public's use of the dry beach. When the State sought to enforce an easement on her private property pursuant to the OBA [Open Beaches Act], Severance sued several state officials in federal district court. She argued that the State, in attempting to enforce a public easement without proving its existence, on property not previously encumbered by an easement, infringed upon her federal constitutional rights and constituted (1) an unreasonable seizure under the Fourth Amendment, (2) an unconstitutional taking under the Fifth and Fourteenth Amendments, and (3) a violation of her substantive due process rights under the Fourteenth Amendment.

* * * [T]he Fifth Circuit determined her Fifth Amendment takings claim was not ripe, but certified unsettled questions of state law to this Court to guide its determination on her Fourth Amendment unreasonable seizure claim. * * *

A. Texas Property Law in Coastal Areas

* * *

Certainly, there is a history in Texas of public use of public Gulf-front beaches, including on Galveston Island's West Beach. On one hand, the public has an important interest in the enjoyment of the public beaches. But on the other hand, the right to exclude others from privately owned realty is among the most valuable and fundamental of rights possessed by private property owners. The boundary distinguishing private property rights is set forth in the definition of public beaches, prudently set forth in the OBA.

1. Defining Public Beaches in Texas

The Open Beaches Act states the policy of the State of Texas for enjoyment of public beaches along the Gulf of Mexico. The OBA declares the State's public policy to be "free and unrestricted right of ingress and egress" to State-owned beaches and to private beach property to which the public "has acquired" an easement or other right of use to that property. TEX. NAT. RES. CODE § 61.011(a). It defines "[p]ublic beach[es]" as:

> any beach area, whether publicly or privately owned, extending inland from the line of mean low tide to the line of vegetation bordering on the Gulf of Mexico to which the public has acquired the right of use or easement to or over the area by prescription, dedication, pre-

sumption, or has retained a right by virtue of continuous right in the public since time immemorial, as recognized in law and custom. This definition does not include a beach that is not accessible by a public road or public ferry as provided in Section 61.021 of this code.

Id. § 61.001(8). Privately owned beaches may be included in the definition of public beaches. Id.

* * *

The wet beaches are all owned by the State of Texas, which leaves no dispute over the public's right of use. However, the dry beach often is privately owned and the right to use it is not presumed under the OBA. The Legislature recognized that the existence of a public right to an easement in the privately owned dry beach area of West Beach is dependent on the government's establishing an easement in the dry beach or the public's right to use of the beach "by virtue of continuous right in the public since time immemorial. . . ." TEX. NAT RES. CODE § 61.001(8). Accordingly, where the dry beach is privately owned, it is part of the "public beach" if a right to public use has been established on it. See id. Thus, a "public beach" includes but is broader than beaches owned by the State in those instances in which an easement for public use is established in the dry beach area. Id. Public beaches include Gulf-front wet beaches, State-owned dry beaches and private property in the dry beaches on which a public easement has been established.

* * *

2. History of Beach Ownership along the Gulf of Mexico

* * * It is well-established that the "soil covered by the bays, inlets, and arms of the Gulf of Mexico within tidewater limits belongs to the State, and constitutes public property that is held in trust for the use and benefit of all the people." [citations omitted]. * * * Having established that the State of Texas owned the land under Gulf tidal waters, the question remained how far inland from the low tide line did the public trust—the State's title—extend. We answered that question in Luttes v. State. This Court held that the delineation between State-owned submerged tidal lands (held in trust for the public) and coastal property that could be privately owned was the "mean higher high tide" line under Spanish or Mexican grants and the "mean high tide" line under Anglo–American law. 159 Tex. 500, 324 S.W.2d 167, 191–92 (Tex. 1958). * * *

These boundary demarcations, linked to vegetation, high tide, and low tide lines are a direct response to the ever-changing nature of the coastal landscape because it is impractical to apply static real property boundary concepts to property lines that are delineated by the ocean's edge. The sand does not stay in one place, nor does the tide line. While the vegetation line may appear static because it does not move daily like the tide, it is also constantly affected by the tide, wind, and other forces of nature.

A person purchasing beachfront property along the Texas coast does so with the risk that her property may eventually, or suddenly, recede into the ocean. When beachfront property recedes seaward and becomes part of the wet beach or submerged under the ocean, a private property owner loses that property to the public trust. We explained in State v. Balli:

Any distinction that can be drawn between the alluvion of rivers and accretions cast up by the sea must arise out of the law of the seashore rather than that of accession and be based . . . upon the ancient maxim that the seashore is common property and never passes to private hands. . . . [This] remains as a guiding principle in all or nearly all jurisdictions which acknowledge the common law. . . .

144 Tex. 195, 190 S.W.2d 71, 100 (Tex. 1945). Likewise, if the ocean naturally and gradually recedes away from the land moving the high tide line seaward, a private property owner's land may increase at the expense of the public trust. See id. at 100–01. Regardless of these changes, the boundary remains fixed (relatively) at the mean high tide line. See Luttes, 324 S.W.2d at 191–93. Any other approach would leave locating that boundary to pure guesswork. See Coastal Indus. Water Auth. v. York, 532 S.W.2d 949, 952 n.1 (Tex. 1976).

* * *

III. Public Beachfront Easements

* * * We have never held that the State has a right in privately owned beachfront property for public use that exists without proof of the normal means of creating an easement. And there is no support presented for the proposition that, during the time of the Republic of Texas or at the inception of our State, the State reserved the oceanfront for public use. * * * Therefore, considering the absence of any historic custom or inherent title limitations for public use on private West Beach property, principles of property law answer the first certified question.

A. Dynamic Nature of Beachfront Easements

Easements exist for the benefit of the easement holder for a specific purpose. An easement does not divest a property owner of title, but allows another to use the property for that purpose. * * * The existence of an easement "in general terms implies a grant of unlimited reasonable use such as is reasonably necessary and convenient and as little burdensome as possible to the servient owner." Coleman v. Forister, 514 S.W.2d 899, 903 (Tex. 1974). * * *

Easement boundaries are generally static and attached to a specific portion of private property. See Holmstrom v. Lee, 26 S.W.3d 526, 533 (Tex. App.—Austin 2000, no pet.) ("Once established, the location or character of the easement cannot be changed without the consent of the parties.") * * * . Therefore, a new easement must be re-established for it to encumber a part of the parcel not previously encumbered.

Like easements, real property boundaries are generally static as well. But property boundaries established by bodies of water are necessarily dynamic. Because those boundaries are dynamic due to natural forces that affect the shoreline or banks, the legal rules developed for static boundaries are somewhat different.* * *

The nature of littoral property boundaries abutting the ocean not only incorporates the daily ebbs and flows of the tide, but also more permanent changes to the coastal landscape due to weather and other natural forces.

Courts generally adhere to the principle "that a riparian or littoral owner acquires or loses title to the land gradually or imperceptibly" added to or taken away from their banks or shores through erosion, the wearing away of land, and accretion, the enlargement of the land. * * * Avulsion, by contrast, as derived from English common law, is the sudden and perceptible change in land and is said not to divest an owner of title. We have never applied the avulsion doctrine to upset the mean high tide line boundary as established by Luttes.1 324 S.W.2d at 191.

* * *

Property along the Gulf of Mexico is subjected to hurricanes and tropical storms, on top of the everyday natural forces of wind, rain, and tidal ebbs and flows that affect coastal properties and shift sand and the vegetation line. This is an ordinary hazard of owning littoral property. And, while losing property to the public trust as it becomes part of the wet beach or submerged under the ocean is an ordinary hazard of ownership for coastal property owners, it is far less reasonable, and unsupported by ancient common law precepts, to hold that a public easement can suddenly encumber an entirely new portion of a landowner's property or a different landowner's property that was not previously subject to that right of use. * * * Gradual movement of the vegetation line and mean high tide line due to erosion or accretion, as opposed to avulsion, has very different practical implications.

Like littoral property boundaries along the Gulf Coast, the boundaries of corresponding public easements are also dynamic. The easements' boundaries may move according to gradual and imperceptible changes in the mean high tide and vegetation lines. However, if an avulsive event moves the mean high tide line and vegetation line suddenly and perceptibly, causing the former dry beach to become part of State-owned wet beach or completely submerged, the adjacent private property owner is not automatically deprived of her right to exclude the public from the new dry beach. In those situations, when changes occur suddenly and perceptibly to materially alter littoral boundaries, the land encumbered by the easement is lost to the public trust, along with the easement attached to that land. Then, the State may seek to establish another easement as permitted by law on the newly created dry beach and enforce an asserted public right to use the private land.

It would be impractical and an unnecessary waste of public resources to require the State to obtain a new judgment for each gradual and nearly imperceptible movement of coastal boundaries exposing a new portion of dry beach. These easements are established in terms of boundaries such as the mean high tide line and vegetation line; presumably public use moves according to and with those boundaries so the change in public use would likewise be imperceptible. Also, when movement is gradual, landowners and the State have ample time to reach a solution as the easement slowly migrates landward with the vegetation line. Conversely, when drastic changes expose new dry beach and the former dry beach that may have been encumbered by a public easement is now part of the wet beach or completely submerged under water, the State must prove a new easement on the area. Because sudden and perceptible changes by nature occur very quickly, it would be impossible to prove continued public use in the new dry beach, and it would be unfair, and perhaps unlawful, to impose such drastic restrictions through the OBA upon an owner in those circumstances without compensation. * * *

If the public is to have an easement on newly created and privately owned dry beach after an avulsive event, the State must prove it, as with other property. * * * Thus, a public beachfront easement in West Beach, although dynamic, does not roll under Texas law. The public loses that interest in privately owned dry beach when the land to which it is attached becomes submerged underwater. While these boundaries are somewhat dynamic to accommodate the beach's everyday movement and imperceptible erosion and accretion, the State cannot declare a public right so expansive as to always adhere to the dry beach even when the land to which the easement was originally attached is violently washed away. This could divest private owners of significant rights without compensation because the right to exclude is one of the most valuable and fundamental rights possessed by property owners. We have never held the dry beach to be encompassed in the public trust.

We hold that Texas does not recognize a "rolling" easement. Easements for public use of private dry beach property change size and shape along with the gradual and imperceptible erosion or accretion in the coastal landscape. But, avulsive events such as storms and hurricanes that drastically alter pre-existing littoral boundaries do not have the effect of allowing a public use easement to migrate onto previously unencumbered property. This holding shall not be applied to use the avulsion doctrine to upset the long-standing boundary between public and private ownership at the mean high tide line. The division between public and private ownership remains at the mean high tide line in the wake of naturally occurring changes, and even when boundaries seem to change suddenly.

Declining to engraft a "rolling easement" theory onto Texas property law does not render the State powerless to regulate Texas shorelines, within constitutional limits. For example, the State, as always, may validly address nuisances or otherwise exercise its police power to impose reasonable regulations on coastal property, or prove the existence of an easement for public use, consistent with constitutional precepts.

* * *

Justice Medina's dissent also dismisses Severance's grievance as a gamble she took and lost by purchasing oceanfront property in Galveston and argues that she would not be entitled to compensation even though an easement had never been established on her parcel, a portion of which is now in the dry beach. It notes the OBA requirement of disclosure in executory contracts of the risk that property could become located on a public beach and subject to an easement in the future. See TEX. NAT. RES. CODE § 61.025. This is incorrect for three reasons. First, beachfront property owners take the risk that their property could be lost to the sea, not that their property will be encumbered by an easement they never agreed to and that the State never had to prove. Second, putting a property owner on notice that the State may attempt to take her property for public use at some undetermined point in the future does not relieve the State from the legal requirement of proving or purchasing an easement nor from the constitutional requirement of compensation if a taking occurs. We do not hold that circumstances do not exist under which the government can require conveyance of property or valuable property rights, such as the right to exclude, but it must pay to validly obtain such right or have a sufficient basis under its police power to do so. * * * Third, simply advising in a disclosure that the State may attempt to enforce an easement on privately owned beachfront property does not dispose of the owner's rights.

* * *

C. Custom in Texas

A few Texas courts of appeals have reached results contrary to the holding in this opinion. In Feinman v. State, the court held that public easements for use of dry beach can roll with movements of the vegetation line. 717 S.W.2d 106, 110–11 (Tex.App.—Houston [1st Dist.] 1986, writ ref'd n.r.e.). * * * Feinman's specific holding is that a rolling easement is "implicit" in the OBA, a conclusion with which we do not agree. See 717 S.W.2d at 111.

* * *

The first Texas case to address the concept of a rolling easement in Galveston's West Beach is Matcha v. Mattox. In 1983, Hurricane Alicia shifted the vegetation line on the beach such that the Matchas' home had moved into the dry beach. Id. at 96. The court held that legal custom—"a reflection in law of a long-standing public practice"—supported the trial court's determination that a public easement had "migrate[d]" onto private property. Id. at 100. The court reasoned that Texas law gives effect to the long history of recognized public use of Galveston's beaches, citing accounts of public use dating back to time immemorial, 1836 in this case. The Matcha opinion, as with Feinman, fails to cite any Texas authority holding that custom establishes a rolling beachfront easement.

* * *

None of the four Texas courts of appeals cases cited in support of a rolling easement date back to time immemorial nor do they provide a legal basis for recognizing the claimed inherent limitation on West Galveston property titles or continuous legal right since time immemorial. We disapprove of the courts of appeals opinions to the extent they are inconsistent with our holding in this case.

* * *

IV. Conclusion

* * * Although existing public easements in the dry beach of Galveston's West Beach are dynamic, as natural forces cause the vegetation and the mean high tide lines to move gradually and imperceptibly, these easements do not spring or roll landward to encumber other parts of the parcel or new parcels as a result of avulsive events. New public easements on the adjoining private properties may be established if proven pursuant to the Open Beaches Act or the common law.

JUSTICE HECHT, JUSTICE GREEN, JUSTICE JOHNSON and JUSTICE WILLETT joined. JUSTICE WILLETT delivered a concurring opinion. JUSTICE MEDINA delivered a dissenting opinion, in which JUSTICE LEHRMANN joined and JUSTICE GUZMAN joined in part. JUSTICE GUZMAN delivered a dissenting opinion. JUSTICE LEHRMANN delivered a dissenting opinion, in which JUSTICE MEDINA joined. CHIEF JUSTICE JEFFERSON did not participate in the decision. (Opinions omitted.)

NOTES AND QUESTIONS

1. Note that Texas law recognizes the mean high water line (MHWL) as the boundary of public trust lands regardless of whether it has moved because of erosion or avulsion. What is the policy reason given by the court for this position? Does this approach make more sense for ocean beaches than the avulsion rule? Consider a beach that has been subject to erosion, manmade erosion control structures, hurricanes and beach restoration. Can natural acts of erosion or avulsion always be distinguished? Where is the boundary? Can it really be determined by traditional common law rules? See generally Joseph L. Sax, The Accretion/ Avulsion Puzzle: Its Past Revealed, Its Future Proposed, 23 Tul. Envtl. L.J. 305 (2010).

2. The court emphasizes that property owners accept the gamble that their property may eventually or suddenly be lost to the public trust, but not that the property may become subject to a public beach access easement. If beach access had been previously established by custom to the "beach" between the MHWL and vegetation line, wherever that beach and that use moved, why is upland property subject to this easement if the beach movement is caused by erosion or accretion, but not if the movement was avulsive?

3. Why does the court focus on the question of whether the concept of the rolling easement had been part of Texas law since time immemorial? Because of the unique nature of ocean boundaries, could beach access easements be rationally treated differently than other easements? If the rules concerning the "static" nature of easements are primarily to assure that the underlying fee owner has clear notice of the boundaries of the easement, do natural monuments, like the vegetation line, provide that notice—even if it is a moving boundary?

D.   CREATING BEACH ACCESS BY REGULATION

1.   Street Design and Permit Conditions

Another approach available for providing public access is the subdividing of shoreline areas in such a manner as to provide for all streets, other than those running parallel to the beach, to extend to the MHWL or dry sand. This allows development without obstructing the public way of passage to the beach. Where large areas of shoreline are already developed, dedication of a public access easement may be imposed as a condition for remodeling existing homes or putting up seawalls. See, e.g. A. Wagner, "Feud Breaks Out on Beach," Sunday, March 27, 2005, The News and Observer, D–1(describing conflict between oceanfront property owners and California Coastal Commission). Of course, public access really isn't complete unless there are easily visible signs showing the location of a public access point and adequate public parking available within a reasonable walking distance. Both of these are frequently lacking in many coastal areas. See, e.g. J. Costello, "Beach Access: Where Do You

Draw the Line in the Sand?," New York Times, January 21, 2005, F1 (describing lack of access to Florida beaches and lack of signs at many existing public access points).

Developers and individual property owners, who have been required to provide access as a condition of development approval, have often asserted that the government has overstepped its constitutional authority. In the following case, Justice Scalia agreed with the homeowner that in some cases the requirements put on these permits can amount to extortion and be constitutionally untenable.

NOLLAN V. CALIFORNIA COASTAL COMMISSION
U.S. Supreme Court, 1987
483 U.S. 825

[The Nollans owned a beachfront lot near a public beach. A concrete seawall parallel to the shoreline separated the beach portion of their property from the rest of the lot. They decided to demolish an existing, run-down structure and replace it with a three-bedroom house. The Coastal Commission granted them permission to do so only on the condition that they record an easement on behalf of the public to pass along the beach. The Commission reasoned that the new construction would create a "psychological barrier" when combined with other buildings, causing the public to believe that the beach was not open to the public. The Nollans sought judicial review, arguing that the permit condition was an unconstitutional taking. The California court held that the collective burden on public beach access caused by projects like Nollan's justified requiring a dedication in this case. The court also rejected Nollan's "taking" claim.]

JUSTICE SCALIA delivered the opinion of the Court.

* * *

Had California simply required the Nollans to make an easement across their beachfront available to the public on a permanent basis in order to increase public access to the beach, rather than conditioning their permit to rebuild their house on their agreeing to do so, we have no doubt there would have been a taking. To say that the appropriation of a public easement across a landowner's premises does not constitute the taking of a property interest but rather, (as Justice Brennan contends) "a mere restriction on its use," is to use words in a manner that deprives them of all their ordinary meaning. Indeed, one of the principal uses of the eminent domain power is to assure that the government be able to require conveyance of just such interests, so long as it pays for them. * * *

Given, then, that requiring uncompensated conveyance of the easement outright would violate the Fourteenth Amendment, the question becomes whether requiring it to be conveyed as a condition for issuing a land-use permit alters the outcome. We have long recognized that land-use regulation does not effect a taking if it "substantially advance[s] legitimate state interests" and does not "den[y] an owner economically viable use of his land." [citations omitted] Our cases have not elaborated on the standards for determining what constitutes a "legitimate state interest" or what type of connection between the regulation and the state interest satisfies the requirement that the former "substantially advance" the latter. They have made clear, however, that a broad range of governmental purposes and regulations satisfies these requirements. [citation omitted] The Commission argues that among these permissible purposes are protecting the public's ability to see the beach, assisting the public in overcoming the "psychological barrier" to using the beach created by a developed shorefront, and preventing congestion on the public beaches. We assume, without deciding, that this is so ___ in which case the Commission unquestionably would be able to deny the Nollans their permit outright if their new house (alone, or by reason of the cumulative impact produced in conjunction with other construction) would substantially impede these purposes, unless the denial would interfere so drastically with the Nollan's use of their property as to constitute a taking.

The Commission argues that a permit condition that serves the same legitimate police-power purpose as a refusal to issue the permit should not be found to be a taking if the refusal to issue the permit would not constitute a taking. We agree. Thus, if the Commission attached to the permit some condition that would have protected the public's ability to see the beach notwithstanding construction of the new house—for example, a height limitation, a width restriction, or a ban on fences—so long as the Commission could have exercised its police power (as we have assumed it could) to forbid construction of the house altogether, imposition of the condition would also be constitutional. Moreover (and here we come closer to the facts of the present case), the condition would be constitutional even if it consisted of the requirement that the Nollans provide a viewing spot on their property for passersby with whose sighting of the ocean their new house would interfere. Although such a requirement, constituting a permanent grant of continuous access to the property, would have to be considered a taking if it were not attached to a development permit, the Commission's assumed power to forbid construction of the house in order to protect the public's view of the beach must surely include the power to condition construction upon some concession by the owner, even a concession of property right, that serves the same end. If a prohibition designed to accomplish that purpose would be a legitimate exercise of the police power rather than a taking, it would be strange to conclude that providing the owner an alternative to that prohibition which accomplishes the same purpose is not.

The evident constitutional propriety disappears, however, if the condition substituted for the prohibition utterly fails to further the end advanced as the justification for the prohibition. When that essential nexus is eliminated, the situation becomes the same as if California law forbade shouting fire in a crowded theater, but granted dispensations to those willing to contribute $100 to the state treasury. While a ban on shouting fire can be a core exercise of the State's police power to protect the public safety, and can thus meet even our stringent standards for regulation of speech, adding the unrelated condition alters the purpose to one which, while it may be legitimate, is inadequate to sustain the ban. Therefore, even though, in a sense, requiring a $100 tax contribution in order to shout fire is a lesser restriction on speech than an outright ban, it would not pass constitutional muster. Similarly here, the lack of nexus between the condition and the original purpose of the building restriction converts that purpose to something other than what it was. The purpose then becomes, quite simply, the obtaining of an easement to serve some valid governmental purpose, but without payment of compensation. Whatever may be the outer limits of "legitimate state interests" in the takings and land-use context, this is not one of them. In short, unless the permit condition serves the same governmental purpose as the development ban, the building restriction is not a valid regulation of land use but "an out-and-out plan of extortion."

The Commission claims that it concedes as much, and that we may sustain the condition at issue here by finding that it is reasonably related to the public need or burden that the Nollans' new house creates or to which it contributes. We can accept, for purposes of discussion, the Commission's proposed test as to how close a "fit" between the condition and the burden is required, because we find that this case does not meet even the most untailored standards. The Commission's principal contention to the contrary essentially turns on a play on the word "access." The Nollans' new house, the Commission found, will interfere with "visual access" to the beach. That in turn (along with other shorefront development) will interfere with the desire of people who drive past the Nollans' house to use the beach, thus creating a "psychological barrier" to "access." The Nollans' new house will also, by a process not altogether clear from the Commission's opinion but presumably potent enough to more than offset the effects of the psychological barrier, increase the use of the public beaches, thus creating the need for more "access." These burdens on "access" would be alleviated by a requirement that the Nollans provide "lateral access" to the beach.

Rewriting the argument to eliminate the play on words makes clear that there is nothing to it. It is quite impossible to understand how a requirement that people already on the public beaches be able to walk across the Nollans' property reduces any obstacles to viewing the beach created by the new house. It is also impossible to understand how it lowers any "psychological barrier" to using the public beaches, or how it helps to remedy any additional congestion on them caused by construction of the Nollans' new house. We therefore find that the Commission's imposition of the permit condition cannot be treated as an exercise of its land-use power for any of these purposes. Our conclusion on this point is consistent with the approach taken by every other court that has considered the question, with the exception of the California state courts.

Justice Brennan argues that imposition of the access requirement is not irrational. In his version of the Commission's argument, the reason for the requirement is that in its absence, a person looking toward the beach from the road will see a street of residential structures including the Nollans' new home and conclude that there is no public beach nearby. If, however, that person sees people passing and repassing along the dry sand behind the Nollans' home, he will realize that there is a public beach somewhere in the vicinity. The Commission's action, however, was based on the opposite factual finding that the wall of houses completely blocked the view of the beach and that a person looking from the road would not be able to see it at all. * * *

We are left, then, with the Commission's justification for the access requirement unrelated to land-use regulation:

Finally, the Commission notes that there are several existing provisions of pass and repass lateral access benefits already given by past Faria Beach Tract applicants as a result of prior coastal permit decisions. The access required as a condition of this permit is part of a comprehensive program to provide continuous public access along Faria Beach as the lots undergo development or redevelopment.

That is simply an expression of the Commission's belief that the public interest will be served by a continuous strip of publicly accessible beach along the coast. The Commission may well be right that it is a good idea, but that does not establish that the Nollans (and other coastal residents) alone can be compelled to contribute to its realization. Rather, California is free to advance its "comprehensive program," if it wishes, by using its power of eminent domain for this "public purpose," see U.S. Const., Amdt. V; but if it wants an easement across the Nollans' property, it must pay for it.

Reversed.

[Dissenting opinions of Justices Brennan and Blackmun omitted.]

NOTES AND QUESTIONS

1. What is the relationship required by the Nollan majority? Must regulation do no more than require that specific externalities of an activity be internalized? In Dolan v. City of Tigard, 512 U.S. 374 (1994), the Supreme Court reinforced the nexus requirement and further defined the essential nexus as a "rough proportionality" between the dedication of property and the "nature and extent" of the impact of the proposed development.

2. How can Nollan and Dolan be reconciled with the Supreme Court's landmark decision in Village of Euclid v. Amber Realty Co., 272 U.S. 365 (1926), where the Court applied an extremely deferential, "fairly debatable" standard to land use regulation? Aren't trade-offs a necessary part of balancing public and private interests in land use regulation? Consider Justice Brennan's dissent in Nollan:

Nonetheless it is important to point out that the Court's insistence on a precise accounting system in this case is insensitive to the fact that increasing intensity of development in many areas calls for farsighted, comprehensive planning that takes into account both the interdependence of land uses and the cumulative impact of development. As one scholar has noted:

> Property does not exist in isolation. Particular parcels are tied to one another in complex ways, and property is more accurately described as being inextricably part of a network of relationships that is neither limited to, nor usefully defined by, the property boundaries with which the legal system is accustomed to dealing. Frequently, use of any given parcel of property is at the same time effectively a use of, or a demand upon, property beyond the border of the user. Sax, Sax, Takings, Private Property, and Public Rights, 81 Yale L.J. 149, 152 (1971).

> As Congress has declared, "The key to more effective protection and use of the land and water resources of the coastal zone [is for the states to] develo[p] land and water use programs for the coastal zone, including unified policies, criteria, standards, methods, and processes for dealing with land and water use decisions of more than local significance." 16 U.S.C. § 1451(I). This is clearly a call for a focus on the overall impact of development on coastal areas. State agencies therefore require considerable flexibility in responding to private desires for development in a way that guarantees the preservation of public access to the coast. They should be encouraged to regulate development in the context of the overall balance of competing uses of the shoreline. The Court today does precisely the opposite, overruling an eminently reasonable exercise of an expert state agency's judgment, substituting its own narrow view of how this balance should be struck. Its reasoning is hardly suited to the complex reality of natural resource protection in the twentieth century. I can only hope that today's decision is an aberration, and that a broader vision ultimately prevails.

Nollan, 483 U.S. at 3161–3162.

3. To what extent then may the government condition private access to public resources on the private party's grant of some reciprocal right to the public? Assuming that the public has the right to use the wet sand area seaward of the mean high tide line and that a beachfront owner wants to construct seawalls or similar structures that will prevent the natural movement of the mean high tide line landward, ultimately eliminating the wet sand area, could the government condition the grant of a permit to construct a seawall or similar structure on the beachfront owner granting the public an easement landward of the seawall or similar structure? If such a seawall were constructed before any permits for construction were required, could the government require, in the absence of a grant of a public easement landward of the seawall, that the seawall be torn down?

2.   Beach Nourishment Projects and Public Access

PROBLEM

The Town of Gulf Shores is located on a barrier island that is 5 miles long and runs from east to west. There are bridges from the mainland at each end of the island. One major road, which is located approximately 1/4 mile inland, also runs east to west and bisects the island. All of the town's public buildings and private businesses and shopping centers are located along this highway. The area between the highway and the shoreline consists of a number of private developments, four of which are private gated subdivisions. No parking is allowed on any of the streets in these developments. There are no public beach access ways in the private gated subdivisions but there are public beach access points one-quarter mile apart along three miles of the shoreline. None of the public beach access ways has a public parking area adjacent to it. The only parking areas are located along the main road bisecting the island. The beaches located in the Town of Gulf Shores are seriously eroded and a federal beach nourishment project is being proposed to restore the beaches. But under federal law, federal funds may not be used to restore or nourish private beaches. To qualify for federal funding, the restored or nourished beach must be open to public use. Therefore, among the many issues presented by this project, one of considerable importance is the degree of public access to the island's beaches.

The U.S. Army Corps of Engineers Regulations provide that:

14–1. Beach Erosion Control

* * *

    b. Definitions

* * *

  (2) Public Use. The term "public use", particularly of private property, means recreational use by all on equal terms and open to all regardless

of origin or home area. Prohibited is any device for limitation of use to specific segments of the population, such as local residents, or similar restriction on outside visitors, directly or indirectly. This definition allows a reasonable beach entrance fee, uniformly applied to all, for use in payment of local project costs. Normal charges made by concessionaires and municipalities for use of facilities such as bridges, parking areas, bath houses and umbrellas are not construed as a charge for the use of the Federal beach project, as long as they are commensurate with the value of the service they provide and return only a reasonable profit . Fees for such services must be applied uniformly to all concerned and not as a prerequisite to beach use. Lack of sufficient parking facilities for the general public (including non-resident users) located reasonably nearby and accessible to the project beaches or lack of public pedestrian right-of-ways to the beaches at suitable intervals would constitute de facto restriction on public access and use of such beaches, thereby precluding eligibility for Federal assistance.

Digest of Water Resources Policies and Authorities, U.S. Army Corps of Engineers, EP 1165–2–1 (30 July 1999) 14–1 to 14–2. If federal tax dollars are the primary source of funding for a beach project, then what specific steps must be taken to afford adequate public access to the nourished beach? How close together should public access points be? One mile apart? One-half mile? One-quarter mile? An earlier set of regulations stated that "public use is construed to be effectively limited to within one-quarter mile from available points of public access to any particular shore." Federal Participation In Shore Protection, U.S. Army Corps of Engineers, ER 1165–2–130 (15 June 1989) at 13. Does a "one size fits all" requirement make sense?

What will constitute "sufficient parking facilities" and how close to the beach access points should the facilities be located? The earlier Corps regulations stated that in some situations "public transportation facilities may substitute for or complement parking facilities." Under what circumstances should public transportation substitute for parking located reasonably close to the beach itself? If residents in the immediate vicinity of the beach have persuaded the local governmental authority to prohibit parking along the streets near the beach and little or no parking is available at the access points, should a parking lot one-half mile away with a shuttle bus service satisfy the public access requirements? Must there be some parking available at the beach access points? What about parking for people with disabilities?

Can adequate public access really exist in the absence of bath houses and public restrooms located within a reasonable distance of the beach? Should construction of such facilities be a condition of federal participation in a beach project?

3.   Adequate Access for the Disabled

Must the beach access points be constructed to accommodate people with disabilities? Must there be a wooden walkway with benches to allow people with physical disabilities to view the beach? Must the walkway be constructed with ramps to allow easy physical access to the dry sand beach itself? 42 U.S.C. § 12132 of the Americans with Disabilities Act(ADA) states that:

> * * * no qualified individual with a disability shall, by reason of such disability, be excluded from participation in or be denied the benefits of the services, programs, or activities of a public entity, or be subject to discrimination by any such entity.

Although no specific provision of the ADA or ADA regulation directly addresses access to beaches, an ADA regulation does require that new facilities constructed after January 26, 1992, "by or on behalf of, or for the use of a public entity shall be designed and constructed in such a manner that the facility is readily accessible to and usable by individuals with disabilities." 28 C.F.R. § 35.151. The regulation also applies to facilities that are altered. If the facility is altered then, "to the maximum extent feasible, [it shall] be altered in such a manner that the altered portion * * * is readily accessible to and usable by individuals with disabilities." Id.

It is important to remember that adequate access encompasses not only an unobstructed path to the beach but, according to the report of the Regulatory Negotiation Commission established by the U.S. Architectural and Transportation Barrier Compliance Board, also includes access over the surface of the beach to the mean high tide line. See Recommendations for Accessibility Guidelines: Outdoor Developed Areas, Final Report, Regulatory Negotiation Commission (September 1999). The proposal to require adequate access to the mean high tide line has raised concerns relating to maintenance, potential hurricane or tide damage, and emergency vehicle passage along the beach.

E. REGULATORY RESTRICTIONS ON PUBLIC ACCESS

Beach closures have generated a number of lawsuits. In Riveria v. United States, 910 F. Supp. 239 (D.VI. 1996), the plaintiffs challenged the closure of a beach in a federal park that was ordered as part of the partial shutdown of the federal government during the 1995 budget dispute between the President and Congress. The plaintiffs alleged that the closure violated the Virgin Islands Open Shoreline Act which protects the public's right to use and enjoy the beaches of the islands. The district court issued a preliminary injunction ordering the reopening of the beaches. However, the plaintiffs in New England Naturalist Association, Inc. v. Larsen, 692 F. Supp. 75 (D.R.I. 1988), were less successful. In that case, a nudism association unsuccessfully sued to prevent the U.S. Fish and Wildlife Service from erecting fences across a portion of a nude beach to provide additional nesting grounds for threatened species of birds. See also, United

States v. Town of Plymouth, Mass., 6 F. Supp. 2d 81 (D. Mass. 1981) (enjoining the use of off-road vehicles on beach to protect piping plover); People v. Deacon, 151 Cal. Rptr. 277 (1978) (county ordinance prohibiting motorcycle use for tidelands access upheld). If public access to public trust lands is restricted, must the restrictions be the least required to achieve legitimate public interests or needs? See, e.g., Carstens v. California Coastal Comm'n, 182 Cal.App. 3d 277, 277 Cal. Rptr. 135 (1986).

Individuals with disabilities may use motorized modes of transportation, such as motorized wheelchairs, in accessing and using the beach. When does the closure of a beach to all modes of motorized transportation unlawfully discriminate against those with disabilities? Although there are no cases directly on point, a similar issue has arisen in connection with the use in state parks of motorized modes of transportation by individuals with disabilities. In Galusha v. New York State Department of Environmental Conservation, 27 F.Supp. 2d 117 (N.D.N.Y. 1998), three disabled persons challenged a state park prohibition against the use of motorized vehicles in certain areas in Adirondack State Park. The alleged basis for the restriction was to preserve wilderness areas. However, park officials were allowing daily use of roads in the areas by maintenance workers, security patrols, those engaged in data collection and research efforts, independent contractors, and others. The park's policy was characterized by the court as "irrational and unfair." In granting the plaintiffs' request for a preliminary injunction the court also noted that "without the assistance of motorized transport, disabled Plaintiffs effectively have zero access to [the park's] crown jewels." Id. at 124. An earlier, pre-ADA case, Baker v. Department of Conservation of the State of New York, 634 F. Supp. 1460 (N.D.N.Y. 1986), reached a different result. In Baker the challenge was to a regulation prohibiting the use of mechanically propelled vessels and aircraft on certain Adirondack State Park lakes. A group of disabled individuals asserted that the regulation denied them "meaningful access" to the park in violation of then existing federal legislation. The court found that disabled persons had meaningful access to this park as a whole with the only limitation being those areas designated as wilderness. Accommodating the plaintiffs, the court concluded, would "destroy the very benefit sought * * *." Id. at 1466. In Baker there was no finding that park employees or others were allowed to use the prohibited modes of transportation. Based on these two cases, in order to withstand scrutiny any limitations on the use of motorized modes of transportation by the disabled would have to be supported by significant environmental concerns which could not be accommodated by other reasonable means.

To what extent may public access to public waters be restricted in order to accommodate the interests of the owners of submerged lands? If a private hunting club holds title to submerged lands, may the state legislature prohibit public waterfowl hunting without permission of the club? If you represented an association of duck hunters attempting to persuade a court to find such legislation invalid, what objections and arguments would you make?

CHAPTER 4

GOVERNANCE OF THE COASTAL ZONE

■ ■ ■

1. THE COASTAL ZONE MANAGEMENT ACT OF 1972

Starting in the 1960s, public and Congressional awareness of the tremendous stress being placed upon coastal lands and water mounted. Population pressures, increased industrialization, pollution, and growing commercial and recreational uses threatened to overwhelm the capabilities of state and local governments to manage development effectively and to resolve conflicting uses of coastal resources. The unclear division of federal, state and local authority over some coastal lands, waters, and other resources and the lack of co-ordination between federal, state, and local agencies made planning and implementation of efficient, balanced, orderly coastal resources development difficult. Congressional concern led to the passage of the Marine Resources and Engineering Development Act of 1966. One significant feature of this Act was the establishment of the Commission on Marine Science, Engineering and Resources or, as it was called for its chairman, the Stratton Commission. The Stratton Commission's report laid the foundation for the Coastal Zone Management Act of 1972.

The Stratton Commission concluded that the lack of effective management—ultimately a state responsibility—was the primary problem in the coastal zone. However, the federal government's role should not be to compel a state to develop a special organization to deal with its coastal management problems. Instead, the report concluded that the federal government should encourage state action by establishing guidelines, facilitating federal cooperation with state authorities, and providing appropriate financial assistance. The Commission recommended the enactment of a coastal management act to provide policy objectives for the coastal zone and authorize federal grants-in-aid to facilitate the establishment of state authorities empowered to manage the coastal water and adjacent land. Similar concerns were expressed thirty years later by another high-level commission (U.S. COP 2004). Do the legal principles explored in Chapter 2 make the coastal zone an especially difficult space to govern? This chapter explores this question and whether a federal grants and standards program for states is sufficient to safeguard the national interest in the coastal zone.

A. HISTORY OF THE CZMA

The federal Coastal Zone Management Act of 1972 was enacted during the same period as other major federal environmental legislation, but differed substantially from legislation like the Clean Air Act or the Clean Water Act. First, state participation in coastal zone management planning was completely voluntary and federal standards or management would not be imposed if the state did not develop a plan. Second, although there was a recognized national interest in effective coastal management, Congress also recognized that the type of land use planning and management required was primarily within the traditional domain of state and local governments.

The CZMA is a federal-state partnership providing federal funding for states to develop and administer coastal programs according to guidelines set out in the Act. The states are given great flexibility in their approaches to coastal management. Acceptable federal models range from direct state control of land and water use regulation to state review of locally or regionally implemented programs. In addition, the CZMA gives the states substantial discretion in designating the geographic scope of its coastal zone in its management program.

Federal funding for program development is a traditional incentive for state cooperation in reaching coastal management goals. The CZMA provides, however, an additional incentive for state participation—the so-called federal consistency requirement—a limited waiver of federal supremacy that assures a state that, with certain exceptions, federal agency activities or federally-sponsored activities affecting the coastal zone will be consistent with the state-created and federally-approved coastal management plan.

The Washington coastal program was the first to receive federal approval in 1976. With approval of the Illinois program in 2012, all thirty-five eligible states and territories (including the Northern Marianas, Puerto Rico, the Virgin Islands, Guam, and American Samoa) had successfully developed federally-appoved programs. In 2011, however, the legislature of Alaska failed to extend the state program and officially withdrew from the federal progam on July 1st of that year. An initiative added to 2012 ballot to reinstate the program in Alaska failed.

The CZMA is administered by the National Oceanic and Atmospheric Administration (NOAA) in the Department of Commerce. The policies of the CZMA reflect the national interests in the coastal zone and the purposes served by coastal management planning. Initially, the CZMA simply declared the national policy "to preserve, protect, develop, and where possible, to restore or enhance, the resources of the Nation's coastal zone for this and succeeding generations" and to assist the states in this effort. 16 U.S.C. § 1452.

Since the original enactment, the purposes of the Act have been amended to clarify and expand the policies, as follows:

CZMA § 303. Congressional Declaration of Policy

16 U.S.C. § 1452

The Congress finds and declares that it is the national policy—

(1) to preserve, protect, develop, and where possible, to restore or enhance, the resources of the Nation's coastal zone for this and succeeding generations;

(2) to encourage and assist the states to exercise effectively their responsibilities in the coastal zone through the development and implementation of management programs to achieve wise use of the land and water resources of the coastal zone, giving full consideration to ecological, cultural, historic, and esthetic values as well as the needs for compatible economic development, which programs should at least provide for—

(A) the protection of natural resources, including wetlands, floodplains, estuaries, beaches, dunes, barrier islands, coral reefs, and fish and wildlife and their habitat, within the coastal zone,

(B) the management of coastal development to minimize the loss of life and property caused by improper development in flood-prone, storm surge, geological hazard, and erosion-prone areas and in areas likely to be affected by or vulnerable to sea level rise, land subsidence, and saltwater intrusion, and by the destruction of natural protective features such as beaches, dunes, wetlands, and barrier islands,

(C) the management of coastal development to improve, safeguard, and restore the quality of coastal waters, and to protect natural resources and existing uses of those waters,

(D) priority consideration being given to coastal-dependent uses and orderly processes for siting major facilities related to national defense, energy, fisheries development, recreation, ports and transportation, and the location, to the maximum extent practicable, of new commercial and industrial developments in or adjacent to areas where such development already exists,

(E) public access to the coasts for recreation purposes,

(F) assistance in the redevelopment of deteriorating urban waterfronts and ports, and sensitive preservation and restoration of historic, cultural, and esthetic coastal features,

(G) the coordination and simplification of procedures in order to ensure expedited governmental decisionmaking for the management of coastal resources,

(H) continued consultation and coordination with, and the giving of adequate consideration to the views of, affected Federal agencies,

(I) the giving of timely and effective notification of, and opportunities for public and local government participation in, coastal management decisionmaking,

(J) assistance to support comprehensive planning, conservation, and management for living marine resources, including planning for the siting of pollution control and aquaculture facilities within the coastal zone, and improved coordination between State and Federal coastal zone management agencies and State and wildlife agencies, and

(K) the study and development, in any case in which the Secretary considers it to be appropriate, of plans for addressing the adverse effects upon the coastal zone of land subsidence and of sea level rise; and

(3) to encourage the preparation of special area management plans which provide for increased specificity in protecting significant natural resources, reasonable coastal-dependent economic growth, improved protection of life and property in hazardous areas, including those areas likely to be affected by land subsidence, sea level rise, or fluctuating water levels of the Great Lakes, and improved predictability in governmental decisionmaking;

(4) to encourage the participation and cooperation of the public, state and local governments, and interstate and other regional agencies, as well as of the Federal agencies having programs affecting the coastal zone, in carrying out the purposes of this title;

(5) to encourage coordination and cooperation with and among the appropriate Federal, State, and local agencies, and international organizations where appropriate, in collection, analysis, synthesis, and dissemination of coastal management information, research results, and technical assistance, to support State and Federal regulation of land use practices affecting the coastal and ocean resources of the United States; and

(6) to respond to changing circumstances affecting the coastal environment and coastal resource management by encouraging States to consider such issues as ocean uses potentially affecting the coastal zone. 16 U.S.C. § 1452(2)–(6).

With the Arab oil embargo and resulting energy crisis, the 1973–74 political atmosphere made energy independence an objective of national importance. The Federal Energy Administration, the Federal Power Commission, and the Energy Research and Development Administration objected to and criticized the states' failure to identify coastal areas that were particularly suitable for energy development. NOAA acknowledged the problem, but it adopted the view that the CZMA did not obligate states to designate specific energy development sites. The 1976 amendments were a response to this criticism.

The major new initiative contained in these amendments was the Coastal Energy Impact Program (CEIP), a 10-year program to provide financial assistance to coastal states likely to be affected by outer continental shelf energy development. Only coastal states participating in the CZMA program were eligible to receive CEIP funds. The three part program provided planning grants, loans and bond guarantees to assist coastal states in financing public services and facilities necessitated by coastal energy activity, and grant money to ameliorate the negative effects of outer continental shelf development. The 1976 amendments also specifically extended the states' consistency review authority to federal offshore oil and gas exploration and development.

The 1980 amendments again highlighted Congress's concern that coastal states incorporate the national interest in the development and implementation of their CZMPs. States were now required to use an increasing proportion of their federal funds, up to a ceiling of 30%, to address the following new coastal policies: (1) protecting coastal resources; (2) managing improper coastal development; (3) siting facilities related to national defense, energy, fisheries, recreation, ports, and transportation; (4) increasing access to coastal recreation; (5) redeveloping damaged urban forests; (6) simplifying procedures to allow for quicker governmental decisions; (7) continuing to foster cooperation with affected federal agencies, local governments, and public citizens; and (8) assisting the management of living marine resources.

Other important changes contained in the 1980 amendments were a reduction in CZMA funds from $101 million to $86 million annually, the encouragement of special area management planning, and the establishment of a new grant program inducing coastal states to inventory and designate resources of national significance and to establish specific, enforceable standards for this effort. Finally, the amendments continued authorization of the CZMA through fiscal year 1985.

The Coastal Management Reauthorization Act of 1985 (passed in 1986) contained amendments establishing new procedures for review and acceptance of changes in a state's coastal program. In addition, the Act established the National Estuarine Reserve Research System, set specific requirements for the designation of an area as a national estuarine reserve, and authorized the Secretary of Commerce to make grants to coastal states to allow them to acquire land and water rights in such areas as are needed to ensure long-term management.

The Coastal Zone Act Reauthorization Amendments of 1990 (passed in 1991) made major changes in the consistency provisions which went far to clarify the provision and which effectively overruled the Supreme Court's narrow interpretation of consistency in Secretary of Interior v. California, 464 U.S. 312 (1984). In addition, the Coastal Energy Impact Program was repealed and replaced by a more limited Coastal Zone Management Fund. The amendments also created a new Coastal Zone Enhancement Grant Program. This program was designed to encourage states to improve their plans in one or more of eight areas of coastal concern. These areas are: (1) coastal wetlands protection; (2) natural hazards management; (3) public access improvements; (4) coastal growth and development impact; (5) special area management planning; (6) ocean resources planning; (7) siting of coastal energy and government facilities; and (8) reduction of marine debris. To encourage participation of states that did not yet have approved coastal programs, the 1990 amendments authorized grants for program development.

The most controversial provision of the 1990 Amendments has been the section 6217 Coastal Non–Point Pollution Program. This program requires shoreline states to develop and implement plans for protecting coastal water from non-point source pollution from land uses. The EPA has developed national guidelines for five source categories of nonpoint pollution: agricultural runoff, urban runoff, forestry runoff, marinas, and hydromodification. Coastal state programs were to be submitted to NOAA and the EPA by 1995, but implementation of controls over non-point source pollution has not been any less difficult to achieve through the CZMA than it has been under section 319 of the Clean Water Act. Only about half of the state non-point source pollution programs have been approved, while the remaining states have been granted conditional approval.

The 1996 amendments to the CZMA made few major changes, but inserted several provisions concerning the promotion of aquaculture. The latest reauthorization expired in 1999; although several new provisions have been introduced, Congress has repeatedly been unable to pass reauthorization language. A 2010 report outlines why this has been the case and why reauthorization has become controversial:

1. Numerous stakeholders (participants, use and development interests, and environmentalists); and

2. Changing context, including events (like Hurricane Katrina and the BP oil spill), new scientific information (like knowledge concerning marine dead zones), economic trends (like rising energy prices), and climate change.

See generally Harold F. Upton, Coastal Zone Management Background and Reauthorization Issues (Congressional Research Service Report 10–16, Sept. 29, 2010).

For further discussion of the history of CZMA, see, e.g., S. Rep. No. 753, 92nd Cong., 2d Sess. (1972); H.R. Conf. Rep. No. 1544, 92 Cong., 2d Sess. (1972); U.S. Commission on Marine Science, Engineering and Resources, Our Nation and the Sea (Jan. 1969); D. Brower and D. Carol, Coastal Zone Management as Land Planning (1984); W. Allayand, Integrated Planning for Water Quality Management 36 (1979); B. Millemann, And Two If By Sea: Fighting the Attack on America's Coasts (Coastal Alliance 1986).

B. DEVELOPMENT AND IMPLEMENTATION OF STATE COASTAL MANAGEMENT PROGRAMS

The Department of Commerce, primarily through NOAA's Office of Ocean and Coastal Resource Management (OCRM), administers the federal CZMA grant program and approves or disapproves individual state programs. The CZMA provisions on administrative grants set out the basic requirements for approval of a state coastal management program. The Secretary is required to approve programs meeting the statutory requirements.

CZMA § 306. Administrative Grants

16 U.S.C. § 1455(d)

(d)(2) [The Secretary shall find that] The [state] management program includes each of the following required program elements:

(A) An identification of the boundaries of the coastal zone subject to the management program.

(B) A definition of what shall constitute permissible land uses and water uses within the coastal zone which have a direct and significant impact on the coastal waters.

(C) An inventory and designation of areas of particular concern within the coastal zone.

(D) An identification of the means by which the State proposes to exert control over the land uses and water uses referred to in subparagraph (B), including a list of relevant State constitutional provisions, laws, regulations, and judicial decisions.

(E) Broad guidelines on priorities of uses in particular areas, including specifically those uses of lowest priority.

(F) A description of the organizational structure proposed to implement such management program, including the responsibilities and interrelationships of local, areawide, State, regional, and interstate agencies in the management process.

(G) A definition of the term "beach" and a planning process for the protection of, and access to, public beaches and other public coastal areas of environmental, recreational, historical, esthetic, ecological, or cultural value.

(H) A planning process for energy facilities likely to be located in, or which may significantly affect, the coastal zone, including a process for anticipating the management of the impacts resulting from such facilities.

(I) A planning process for assessing the effects of, and studying and evaluating ways to control, or lessen the impact of, shoreline erosion, and to restore areas adversely affected by such erosion.

(3) The State has—

(A) coordinated its program with local, areawide, and interstate plans applicable to areas within the coastal zone * * *.

(B) established an effective mechanism for continuing consultation and coordination between the [state] management agency * * * and with local governments, interstate agencies, regional agencies, and areawide agencies within the coastal zone to assure the full participation of those local governments and agencies in carrying out the purposes of this title; * * *

(8) The management program provides for adequate consideration of the national interest involved in planning for, and managing the coastal zone, including the siting of facilities such as energy facilities which are of greater than local significance. In the case of energy facilities, the Secretary shall find that the State has given consideration to any applicable national or interstate energy plan or program.

(9) The management program includes procedures whereby specific areas may be designated for the purpose of preserving or restoring them for their conservation, recreational, ecological, historical, or esthetic values.

(10) The State, acting through its chosen agency or agencies (including local governments, areawide agencies, regional agencies, or interstate agencies) has authority for the management of the coastal zone in accordance with the management program. Such authority shall include power—

(A) to administer land use and water use regulations to control development to ensure compliance with the management program, and to resolve conflicts among competing uses; and

(B) to acquire fee simple and less than fee simple interests in land, waters, and other property through condemnation or other means when necessary to achieve conformance with the management program. * * *

(12) The management program contains a method of assuring that local land use and water use regulations within the coastal zone do not unreasonably restrict or exclude land uses and water uses of regional benefit.

(13) The management program provides for—

(A) the inventory and designation of areas that contain one or more coastal resources of national significance; and

(B) specific and enforceable standards to protect such resources.

(14) The management program provides for public participation in permitting processes, consistency determinations, and other similar decisions.

(15) The management program provides a mechanism to ensure that all State agencies will adhere to the program.

(16) The management program contains enforceable policies and mechanisms to implement the applicable requirements of the Coastal Nonpoint Pollution Control Program of the State required by section 1455b of this title.

CZMA § 307. Coordination and Cooperation

16 U.S.C. § 1456(b)

(b) Adequate consideration of views of Federal agencies. The Secretary shall not approve the management program submitted by a state pursuant to section 306 [16 U.S.C. § 1455] unless the views of Federal agencies principally affected by such program have been adequately considered.

* * *

American Petroleum Institute v. Knecht, which follows, is an early important judicial consideration of the nature of coastal management programs. The 1977 approval of the California coastal management program was challenged for failure to give adequate consideration to energy facility siting. Reread relevant sections of the CZMA at 16 U.S.C. §§ 1455(d)(2), (3), (8), and (12) which require the Secretary of Commerce to find that a coastal program includes specific provisions relating to such issues as energy facility siting, consideration of the views of federal agencies, and consideration of the national interest.

Increased interest in potential oil and gas deposits off the California coast, especially on the federal outer continental shelf, led to inclusion of a substantial oil and gas element in the California program. But rather than designating certain areas of the coastal zone as suitable for energy facilities, the program provided siting policies and a planning process. Do such general provisions provide "adequate consideration of the national interest" in energy facility siting? Does the CZMA require state programs to accommodate energy facilities? Who determines what is a state's fair share of needed energy facilities?

AMERICAN PETROLEUM INSTITUTE V. KNECHT
United States District Court, C.D. Cal., 1979
456 F. Supp. 889, aff'd, 609 F.2d 1306 (9th Cir. 1979)

KELLEHER, DISTRICT JUDGE.

Plaintiffs American Petroleum Institute, Western Oil and Gas Association, and certain oil company members * * * brought this action * * * seeking declaratory and injunctive relief against defendants' imminent grant of "final approval" of the California Coastal Zone Management Program ("CZMP") pursuant to § 306 of the Coastal Zone Management Act of 1972, as amended ("CZMA") * * *.

In brief, plaintiffs contend that the California Program cannot lawfully be approved by the federal defendants under § 306 of the CZMA, principally for two reasons. First, the CZMP is not a "management program" within the meaning of § 304(11) of the Act in that * * * it fails to satisfy the requirements of §§ 305(b) and 306(c), (d), and (e), and regulations promulgated thereunder, as regards content specificity. * * *

Facts

* * *

The Court has before it for determination both preliminarily and for ultimate disposition questions of the highest importance, greatest complexity, and highest urgency. They arise as the result of high legislative purpose, low bureaucratic bungling, and present inherent difficulty in judicial determination. In other words, for the high purpose of improving and maintaining felicitous conditions in the coastal areas of the United States, the Congress has undertaken a legislative solution, the application of which is so complex as to make it almost wholly unmanageable. In the course of the legislative process, there obviously came into conflict many competing interests which, in typical fashion, the Congress sought to accommodate, only to create thereby a morass of problems between the private sector, the public sector, the federal bureaucracy, the state legislature, the state bureaucracy, and all of the administrative agencies appurtenant thereto. Because the action taken gives rise to claims public and private which must be adjudicated, this matter is now involved in the judicial process.

* * *

Legislative History of the CZMA

A seemingly unbridgeable gulf between the parties concerning the proper construction of the CZMA establishes the cutting edge of this action. First, noted at the outset of this memorandum of decision, plaintiffs complain that the California Program fails to qualify for final approval under § 306 because it lacks the requisite specificity Congress intended management programs to embody, especially with respect to the substantive requirements of §§ 305(b) and 306(c), (d), and (e), so as to enable private users in the coastal zone subject to an approved program to be able to predict with reasonable certainty whether or not their proposed activities will be found to be "consistent" with the program under § 307(c). Second, plaintiffs contend that a proper understanding of § 306(c)(8), particularly in light of the 1976 Amendments, compels the conclusion that in requiring "adequate consideration" Congress intended that an approvable program affirmatively accommodate the national interest in planning for and siting energy facilities and that the CZMP fails so to do. The Court here addresses each of these contentions.

A. The Definition of "Management Program"

Any attempt to resolve this underlying dispute, out of which most of the issues in this lawsuit arise, must begin with Congress' definition of a "management program" in § 304(11) of the Act:

> The term "management program" includes, but is not limited to, a comprehensive statement in words, maps, illustrations, and other media of communication, prepared and adopted by the state in accordance with the provisions of this title, setting forth *objectives, policies and standards to guide* public and private uses of lands and waters in the coastal zone.

[Emphasis supplied.] This definition is exactly as originally contained in the Senate version of the CZMA (S. 3507). In its report on S. 3507, the Committee on Commerce stated:

> "Management program" is the term to refer to the Process by which a coastal State * * * proposes * * * to manage land and water uses in the coastal zone so as to reduce or minimize a direct, significant, and adverse effect upon those waters, including the development of criteria and of the governmental structure capable of implementing such a program. In adopting the term "Management program" the Committee seeks to convey the importance of a *dynamic* quality to the planning undertaken in this Act that permits adjustments as more knowledge is gained, as new technology develops, and as social aspirations are more clearly defined. The Committee does *not* intend to provide for management programs that are *static* but rather to create a *mechanism for continuing review* of coastal zone programs on a regular basis and to provide a framework for the allocation of resources that are available to carry out these programs.

S. Rep. No. 753, 92d Cong., 2d Sess. (1972), U.S. Code Cong. & Admin. News 1972, pp. 4776, 4784 [emphasis supplied]. * * *

The Court agrees with defendants that Congress never intended that to be approvable under § 306 a management program must provide a "zoning map" which would inflexibly commit the state in advance of receiving specific proposals to permitting particular activities in specific areas. Nor did Congress intend by using the language of "objectives, policies, and standards" to require that such programs establish such detailed criteria that private users be able to rely on them as predictive devices for determining the fate of projects without interaction between the relevant state agencies and the user. To satisfy the definition in the Act, a program need only contain standards of sufficient specificity "to guide public and private uses."

The CZMA was enacted primarily with a view to encouraging the coastal states to plan for the management, development, preservation, and restoration of their coastal zones by establishing rational processes by which to regulate uses therein. Although sensitive to balancing competing interests, it was first and foremost a statute directed to and solicitous of environmental concerns. "The key to more effective use of the coastal zone in the future is introduction of management systems permitting conscious and informed choices among the various alternatives. The aim of this legislation is to assist in this very critical goal." S. Rep. No. 753, U.S. Code Cong. & Admin. News 1972, p. 4781 (Legislative History at 198). See H. Rep. No. 1049, 92d Cong., 2d Sess. (1972) (Legislative History at 313 and 315).

The Amendments of 1976 made clear the national interest in the planning for, and siting of, energy facilities. Apparently neither the Act nor the Amendments thereto altered the primary focus of the legislation: the need for a rational planning process to enable the state, not private users of the coastal zone, to be able to make "hard choices." "If those choices are to be rational and devised in such a way as to preserve future options, the program must be established to provide guidelines which will enable the selection of those choices." H. Rep. No. 92–1049 (Legislative History at 315). The 1976 Amendments do not require increased specificity with regard to the standards and objectives contained in a management program. * * *

In conclusion, to the extent plaintiffs' more specific challenges to the Acting Administrator's § 306 approval are premised on an interpretation of congressional intent to require that such programs include detailed criteria establishing a sufficiently high degree of predictability to enable a private user of the coastal zone to say with certainty that a given project must be deemed "consistent" therewith, the Court rejects plaintiffs' contention. * * *

B. Adequate Consideration of the National Interest

Plaintiffs' fundamental grievance with the California Program stems from its assertion that the Program fails to satisfy the mandate of § 306(c)(8) that before the Secretary grant approval to a management program under § 306 she find that it

> provides for adequate consideration of the national interest involved in planning for, and in the siting of, facilities (including energy facilities in, or which significantly affect, such state's coastal zone) which are necessary to meet requirements which are other than local in nature.

Plaintiffs urge that the CZMA, particularly in light of the 1976 Amendments, requires an "affirmative commitment" on the part of the state before § 306 approval is proper. The California Program allegedly fails adequately to make that commitment in that its general lack of specificity, coupled with what plaintiffs characterize as California's overall antipathy to energy development (as embodied in the policies and practices of its Coastal Commission), combine to give the Coastal Commission a "blank check" effectively to veto any or all exploration and development activities subject to § 307(c)(3) simply by finding such activity not to be "consistent" with the CZMP. * * *

The Coastal Zone Management Act Amendments of 1976, Pub.L. 94–370 ("1976 Amendments"), while largely prompted by the 1973 Arab oil embargo and while expressly recognizing the national interest in the planning for and siting of energy facilities, nevertheless did not alter the requirement of "adequate consideration" in § 306(c)(8) or make any changes in the degree of specificity required under the Act. Rather, recognizing that coastal states like California were currently burdened by the onshore impacts of Federal offshore (OCS) activities and likely to be burdened further by the plans for increased leases on the OCS, Congress sought to encourage or induce the affected states to step up their plans vis-a-vis such facilities.

The primary means chosen to accomplish this result was the Coastal Energy Impact Program ("CEIP") contained in new § 308. * * * The Congress was particularly careful to circumscribe the role of the federal government in particular siting decisions. Thus, § 308(I) provides:

> The Secretary shall not intercede in any land use or water use decision of any coastal state with respect to the siting of any energy facility or public facility by making siting in a particular location a prerequisite to, or a condition of, financial assistance under this section.

This provision is consistent with the approach of the CZMA as a whole to leave the development of, and decisions under, a management program to the state, subject to the Act's more specific concern that the development and decision-making process occur in a context of cooperative interaction, coordination, and sharing of information among affected agencies, both local, state, regional, and federal. This last, especially as regards energy facility planning, is the policy behind the Energy Facility Planning Process ("EFPP") of § 305(b)(8) and the Interstate Grants provision of new § 309 (which encourages the coastal states to give high priority to coordinating coastal zone planning utilizing "interstate agreements or compacts"). It should be noted that the only amendment to the national interest requirement of § 306(c) (8) effectuated by the 1976 Amendments is the additional requirement that in fulfilling its obligation to provide "adequate consideration of the national interest" in the case of energy facilities, the state also give such consideration "to any applicable interstate energy plan or program" established under § 309.

* * *

* * * NOAA has promulgated revised program approval regulations * * *. In its response to several reviewers' suggestion that § 306(c)(8) be interpreted to require that facilities be accommodated in a State's coastal zone, the agency reiterated the position it has maintained since the inception of the CZMA that

> the purpose of "adequate consideration" is to achieve the act's "spirit of equitable balance between State and national interests." As such, consideration of facilities in which there may be a national interest must be undertaken within the context of the act's broader finding of a "national interest in the * * * beneficial use, protection, and development of the coastal zone" (Section 302(a)). Subsection 302(g) of the Act gives "high priority" to the protection of natural systems. Accordingly, while the primary focus of subsection 306(c)(8) is on the planning for and siting of facilities, adequate consideration of the national interest in these facilities must be based on a balancing of these interests relative to the wise use, protection and other development of the coastal zone. As the Department of Energy noted in its comments on the proposed regulations:

> > The Act presumes a balancing of the national interest in energy self-sufficiency with State and local concerns involving adverse economic, social, or environmental impacts.

43 Fed. Reg. 8379.

* * *

The Court notes further in this regard that the standards established by the Coastal Act * * * for making energy facilities siting decisions, in the words of the Coastal Commission staff, "establish the general findings that must be made to authorize coastal dependent industrial facilities, liquefied natural gas terminals, oil and gas developments, refineries, petrochemical facilities and electric power plants." FEIS, Part II (Chapter 9) at 66. The key to the California approach, and one which the Acting Administrator and this Court find acceptable under the CZMA, is that the standards require that "findings" be made upon which specific siting decisions ensue. For instance, in dealing with the siting of oil tanker facilities, § 30261(a) requires that

> [t]anker facilities shall be designed to (1) minimize the total volume of oil spilled, (2) minimize the risk of collision from movement of other vessels, (3) have ready access to the most effective feasible containment and recovery equipment for oil spills, and (4) have onshore deballasting facilities to receive any fouled ballast water from tankers where operationally or legally required.

As can readily be seen from these provisions, whether a particular tanker facility siting proposal will be deemed "consistent" with these requirements of the California Program will turn on specific findings of a factual nature. The California Program sensibly does not attempt to map out in advance precisely what type or size tanker facilities will be found to meet these requirements in particular areas of its almost 1,000-mile coastline. Rather, by its very nature, the Coastal Act encourages plaintiffs with a particular facility in mind to address themselves to the standards set forth in the Coastal Act and to plan such a facility in cooperation and communication with the Coastal Commission from the inception. This approach seems consonant with the overall approach of the CZMA itself. * * * To the extent plaintiffs seek not guidance with respect to the way in which coastal resources will be managed but instead a "zoning map" which would implicitly avoid the need to consult with the state regarding planned activities in or affecting its coastal zone, the Court rejects their position. While wholly sympathetic to the legitimate concerns of corporate officers and planners who must conform their activities to the standards of the CZMP, the Court nevertheless concludes that the Acting Administrator's finding that the Program satisfies § 306(c)(8) is supportable and hence not arbitrary or capricious. It proceeds from a correct interpretation of the CZMA. * * *

[U]nder our so-called federal system, the Congress is constitutionally empowered to launch programs the scope, impact, consequences and workability of which are largely unknown, at least to the Congress, at the time of enactment; the federal bureaucracy is legally permitted to execute the congressional mandate with a high degree of befuddlement as long as it acts no more befuddled than the Congress must reasonably have anticipated; if ultimate execution of the congressional mandate requires interaction between federal and state bureaucracy, the resultant maze is one of the prices required under the system. * * *

The administrative action is affirmed; the petition is denied, each side to bear its costs.

NOTES AND QUESTIONS

1. In a section of the opinion not included above, the court considered the standard of review appropriate to the administrative decision in dispute:

> That deference is due an agency's interpretation of its own regulations and the statute is charged with administering is indisputable. * * * The principle of deference itself is premised on the twin notions of agency expertise and congressional acquiescence in that interpretation. 456 F. Supp. at 906.

The court ultimately found both factors important in its decision to give "considerable deference" to the interpretations made by the federal defendants of their regulations:

> * * * Congress placed responsibility for administering the CZMA in the Department of Commerce with the clear expectation that such responsibility ultimately would be delegated to NOAA, an agency favored by Congress expressly because of its technical expertise in matters relating to the Nation's coasts. Moreover, during enactment of the 1976 Amendments Congress applauded NOAA's administration of the Act and directed it to promulgate regulations further clarifying the requirements of the Act. Id. at 908.

What other factors in the case led the reviewing court to defer to NOAA's construction of the statute and implementing regulations?

2. State programs are generally presented in the format of the Environmental Impact Statement (EIS) which is required by the National Environmental Policy Act for all major federal actions that significantly affect the environment. In *API v. Knecht*, API attacked the adequacy of the EIS for not considering relevant information and available alternatives and not discussing potential and unavoidable adverse impacts of approving and implementing the California plan. Upholding the adequacy of the EIS, Judge Kelleher stated:

> [T]he "essence" of the CZMP, in accordance with * * * the CZMA, is sensitivity to environmental concerns in establishing standards for utilization of the coastal zone; consequently, fewer and less detailed environmental studies would be expected because the Program emphasizes environmental preservation. API v. Knecht, 456 F. Supp. 889 (C.D. Cal. 1978).

Was the court correct in its assessment of the "essence" of coastal planning and its conclusion that the CZMA is "first and foremost a statute directed to and solicitous of environmental concerns"? Did the court foreclose the necessity of considering alternatives that might have better accommodated both the environment and development?

3. Implementing these coastal management policies requires states to prioritize coastal uses and make choices among uses where they conflict. To what extent did Congress, in the CZMA, grant or delegate to the states the authority to carry out these policies? Can states effectively make these choices between competing land and water uses in the coastal zone within constitutional limitations?

Due to the inactivity of its port for commercial shipping in the late 1970s, the City of Rochester, New York, developed plans to turn the port into a recreational and marina area. To further this plan, the port was zoned to "create a harbor district, in which the permitted uses will be those water dependent and commercial uses which will enhance the character as an attractive and recreational harbor." The zoning ordinance prohibited all manufacturing, warehouse and distribution centers, and commercial cargo and shipping terminals. Pittston Warehouse Corporation sought to initiate a new "roll-on/roll-off trailer ship" service between Rochester and Canada, but Rochester passed a resolution specifically prohibiting this type of service. Pittston challenged the constitutionality of the ordinances. Among the city's arguments was the claim that the CZMA provides support for cities to exercise their police power for purposes of improving the harbor environment, promoting public access, and enhancing the recreational character of the area. In Pittston Warehouse Corp. v. City of Rochester, 528 F. Supp. 653 (D.C. W.D.N.Y. 1981), the court held that the ordinances violated the Commerce Clause and are "invalid insofar as they impede or obstruct the free flow of interstate and international commerce." See also Norfolk Southern Corp. v. Oberly, 822 F.2d 388, 394–395 (1987) (Noting that Congress can authorize actions by states that would otherwise be forbidden by the dormant Commerce Clause, but congressional consent must be express. "While the CZMA states a national policy in favor of coastal zone management, it does not on its face expand state authority to regulate in ways that would otherwise be invalid under the Commerce Clause").

4. As amended in 1990, the definition of "coastal zone" provides:

The term "coastal zone" means the coastal waters (including the lands therein and thereunder) and the adjacent shorelands (including the waters therein and thereunder), strongly influenced by each other and in proximity to the shorelines of the several coastal states, and includes islands, transitional and intertidal areas, salt marshes, wetlands, and beaches. The zone extends, in Great Lakes waters, to the international boundary between the United States and Canada and, in other areas, seaward to the outer limit * * * of State title and ownership under the Submerged Lands Act. * * * The zone extends inland from the shorelines only to the extent necessary to control shorelands, the uses of which have a direct and significant impact on the coastal waters, and to control those geographical areas which are likely to be affected by or vulnerable to sea level rise. * * * 16 U.S.C. § 1453(1).

How far inland should state coastal zone boundaries extend? See Woodruff, Longley & Reed, Inland Boundary Determinations for Coastal Management Purposes, 4 Coastal Zone Mgmt. J. 189 (1978). The definition leaves considerable room for variation of landward boundaries from one coastal state to another. For example, North Carolina, South Carolina and Georgia define the inland portion of the coastal zone as the area encompassed by coastal counties; Hawaii's, Rhode Island's and Delaware's coastal zones include the entire state; California, on the other hand, generally defines the land portion of its coastal zone as a 1000-yard strip extending inland from its coastal waters; Massachusetts' coastal zone extends landward 100 feet beyond the first major land transportation route encountered (e.g., a road, highway, or rail line), and also includes all of Cape Cod, Martha's Vineyard, Nantucket, and Gosnold. The coastal zone boundary in Alabama is a continuous 10-foot contour in the coastal counties. For an overview of state coastal zone boundaries, see the chart at http://coastalmanagement.noaa.gov/mystate/docs/StateCZ Boundaries.pdf.

5. The CZMA "[e]xclude[s] from the coastal zone * * * lands the use of which is by law subject solely to the discretion of or which is held in trust by the Federal Government, its officers, or agents." See 16 U.S.C. § 1453(1). In California Coastal Commission v. Granite Rock Company, 480 U.S. 572 (1987), a mining company argued that the California Coastal Commission lacked the authority to impose environmental permit conditions upon its mining activities. The mining activities would be conducted in accordance with federal regulations on unpatented mining claims located in a national forest. According to the company, the Commission's permit requirements were per se preempted by Forest Service regulations, the Mining Act of 1872, and by the exclusion of federal lands from the definition of "coastal zone." The United States Supreme Court rejected this broad challenge to the Coastal Commission's authority. The Court concluded "that even if all federal lands are excluded from the CZMA definition of coastal zone the CZMA does not automatically preempt all state regulation of activities on federal lands." Id. at 593. The federal laws applicable to the activity were viewed by the Court as "land use" regulations which would not preempt the state's "environmental" regulation imposing conditions aimed at carrying out the activity in the least environmentally damaging manner. See also Manchester Pacific Gateway v. California Coastal Com., 67 ERC (BNA) 1857 (S.D. Cal. Apr. 25, 2008). ("In California Coastal Com. v. Granite Rock Co., the Supreme Court directly addressed the CZMA in context of the Property Clause. While the Supreme Court noted that the Property Clause invests unlimited power in Congress over use of federal lands, it also concluded that Congress, by enacting the CZMA, contemplated state environmental oversight over coastal zones. Consequently, the CZMA, and not the Property Clause, provides the framework for analyzing environmental review issues in coastal areas.")

6. Some states, such as North Carolina, South Carolina and California, have passed comprehensive coastal management legislation to create their coastal management program; other states, such as Florida, have "networked" existing legislation and regulations under the umbrella of an executive order or policy statement, or enabling legislation. The CZMA gives states a great deal of flexibility in programmatic approaches. CZMA § 306(d)(11), 16 U.S.C. § 1455 (d)(11), recognizes three general approaches a state may adopt:

(A) State establishment of criteria and standards for local implementation, subject to administrative review and enforcement;

(B) Direct State land and water use planning and regulation; or

(C) State administrative review for consistency with the management program of all development plans, projects, or land and water use regulations, including exceptions and variances thereto, proposed by any State or local authority or private developer, with power to approve or disapprove after public notice and an opportunity for hearings.

Two of these approaches leave most coastal land and water use decisions at the local level. What kind of problems are likely to result from leaving the primary management of the coastal zones under local control?

7. Once the state's management plan has been approved, what must the state do to amend it? The federal district court decision in Save Our Dunes v. Pegues, 642 F. Supp. 393 (M.D. Ala. 1985), rev'd on other grounds, 834 F.2d 984 (4th Cir. 1987), posed a threat to continued federal CZMA funding of previously-approved state coastal programs that had been amended or modified without specific federal approval of the amendments or modification. The court strictly interpreted CZMA § 306(g), 16 U.S.C. § 1455(g) [now (e)], as it then read as prohibiting further CZMA program administration grants until such state program changes have been federally approved. According to the court, a supplemental environmental impact statement must be prepared if the changes can significantly affect the environment "in qualitative or quantitative terms," which would have made the amendment approval process potentially a quite elaborate one. With federal funds delayed or cut off, state programs could deteriorate to the point of withdrawal of federal approval, thereby causing the state to lose the benefits of federal consistency as well. Consider whether the following 1990 amendments on program amendment or modification solve the problems caused by the court's analysis.

16 U.S.C. § 1455(e). A coastal state may amend or modify a management program which it has submitted and which has been approved by the Secretary under this section, subject to the following conditions:

(1) The State shall promptly notify the Secretary of any proposed amendment, modification, or other program change and submit it for the Secretary's approval. The Secretary may suspend all or part of any grant

made under this section pending State submission of the proposed amendments, modification, or other program change.

(2) Within 30 days after the date the Secretary receives any proposed amendment, the Secretary shall notify the State whether the Secretary approves or disapproves the amendment, or whether the Secretary finds it is necessary to extend the review of the proposed amendment for a period not to exceed 120 days after the date the Secretary received the proposed amendment. The Secretary may extend this period only as necessary to meet the requirements of the National Environmental Policy Act of 1969. If the Secretary does not notify the coastal state that the Secretary approves or disapproves the amendment within that period, then the amendment shall be conclusively presumed as approved.

(3)(A) Except as provided in subparagraph (B), a coastal state may not implement any amendment, modification, or other change as part of its approved management program unless the amendment, modification, or other change is approved by the Secretary under this subsection.

(B) The Secretary, after determining on a preliminary basis, that an amendment, modification, or other change which has been submitted for approval under this subsection is likely to meet the program approval standards in this section, may permit the State to expend funds awarded under this section to begin implementing the proposed amendment, modification, or change. This preliminary approval shall not extend for more than 6 months and may not be renewed. A proposed amendment, modification, or change which has been given preliminary approval and is not finally approved under this paragraph shall not be considered an enforceable policy for purposes of section 307 [16 U.S.C. § 1456].

8. All changes in state coastal programs are not formal amendments or modifications requiring federal approval. A "change" may be either an "amendment" or a "routine program implementation." See 15 C.F.R. §§ 923.80–.84. An "amendment" involves "substantial changes" in one or more of the following program areas: "(1) Uses subject to management; (2) Special management areas; (3) Boundaries; (4) Authorities and organization; and (5) Coordination, public involvement and the national interest." Id. § 923.80(d). "Substantial" can be related to the degree the change affects national or regional interests. A "routine program implementation" is a "[f]urther detailing of a State's program that is the result of implementing" the approved program, and is not an action covered by § 923.80(d), is not subject to the approval process of an amendment. Id. § 923.84(a). The state must, however, notify OCRM of the changes and provide public notice before the routine program change will require federal consistency. Id. § 923.84(b)(1)–(2), (b)(2)(ii). See also, OCRM, NOAA, Program Change Guidance: The Coastal Zone Management Act and Changes to State and Territory Coastal

Management Programs (July 1996), available at http://coastalmanagement.
noaa.gov/consistency/media/guidanceappendices.pdf.

In AES Sparrows Point LNG, LLC v. Smith, 527 F.3d 120 (4th Cir.
2008), the court found that Baltimore County had attempted to stop development of an LNG terminal by passing a categorical ban on LNG terminals
in the Chesapeake Bay Critical Area that the CMP did not previously contain. The legislation was, however, never presented to NOAA for approval.
The court found that "[t]his, in our view, constitutes a 'substantial change' in
the 'uses subject to management' by the CMP. It also implicates the 'national
interest' in the 'the siting of facilities such as energy facilities which are of
greater than local significance.'" 16 U.S.C. § 1455(d)(8). Without the approval
of the change by NOAA, the ban could not become part of the CMP.

9. Section 312 of the CZMA, 16 U.S.C. § 1458(a), requires periodic review
of state coastal management programs. In 1987, NOAA conducted a periodic
review of the California Coastal Management Program (CCMP). NOAA conditioned continued administrative grants on the Coastal Commission's preparing and submitting "for approval guidelines that would provide greater
predictability for parties seeking consistency determinations for proposed
activities affecting the Outer Continental Shelf. The Commission refused,
contending that it would lose necessary flexibility and that the current case-
by-case, negotiated process was preferable." In California v. Mack, 693 F.
Supp. 821 (N.D. Cal. 1988), California sought to enjoin NOAA's enforcement
of the grant conditions. The court held that:

> * * * NOAA does not have authority to revisit the approvability of a plan.
> In other words, once NOAA determines that a program satisfies the re-
> quirements of the CZMA and grants final approval, it may no longer ex-
> amine the content of the approved program, only the adequacy of its exe-
> cution. Only if NOAA determines that the state is not, in fact, satisfacto-
> rily implementing its plan, and the state refuses to remedy this deficien-
> cy, may NOAA withdraw approval. * * * In short, a careful reading of the
> enforcement provisions of the CZMA leaves the clear impression that
> NOAA may not use its power over funding to accomplish indirectly what
> it may not accomplish directly: enforce alteration of the approved pro-
> gram itself. * * *

Thus, the question here is one of degree. Clearly Congress realized that
NOAA, through its control of federal financial assistance, would wield
considerable influence over state coastal programs. But it is also clear
that Congress did not intend to confer on NOAA the ability to manipu-
late the coastal policy of the states. "There is no attempt to diminish
state authority through federal preemption. The intent of this legislation
is to enhance state authority by encouraging and assisting the states to
assume planning and regulatory powers over their coastal zones." S.
Rep. No. 753, 92d Cong. 2d Sess. 1 * * *. Accordingly, this Court concludes that, whatever authority NOAA may have to impose *implementation* requirements as conditions to grants, it may not revisit the question

of the management program's adequacy by forcing a state to choose between modifying the program and losing federal financial assistance under the CZMA.

Was NOAA attempting to reverse the position it took in *API v. Knecht*, supra?

10. The CZMA established the Estuarine Sanctuaries Program, which has evolved through the 1985 CZMA amendments into the National Estuarine Research Reserve (NERR) System. 16 U.S.C. § 1461. Estuarine Reserves are designated "to enhance public awareness and understanding of estuarine areas, and provide suitable opportunities for public education and interpretation * * *." The NERR system is intended to comprise estuaries that represent all eleven of the country's biological and geographic regions and that will serve as "living laboratories" for long-term research and education. The CZMA provides funds to the states for acquisition, management, education and interpretive programs, and research within the reserves. CZMA § 315, 16 U.S.C. § 1461, authorizes the Secretary of Commerce to grant coastal states up to fifty percent of the costs of acquiring and operating estuarine reserves. What are some alternative mechanisms for comprehensively managing sensitive estuarine areas? See, e.g., 16 U.S.C. § 1425(3) (special area management plans encouraged by the 1980 CZMA amendments). Compare the purposes and management approach of estuarine research reserves to the National Estuary Program, 33 U.S.C. § 1330. Under this program, the EPA chooses estuaries of "national significance" and convenes a management conference to develop a comprehensive conservation and management plan for the estuary that recommends corrective action and a compliance schedule. The management conference includes state, regional and federal agencies, local governments, affected industries, public and private educational institutions, and the public. Estuary plans are to be incorporated into states' coastal management programs.

C. INTERGOVERNMENTAL COOPERATION: THE FEDERAL CONSISTENCY REQUIREMENT

1. History and Development of the Consistency Doctrine

Federal grants to assist states in developing and administering coastal management programs provided an initial impetus for states to participate in coastal zone planning. These funds have continually decreased. The so-called federal consistency requirement provides the major incentive for states to continue and maintain their federally-approved programs. Section 307(c), prior to the 1990 amendments, provided that federal actions and activities "directly affecting" a state's coastal zone be conducted in a manner consistent with the state coastal program to the maximum extent practicable. The section also required that federal permitting, OCS exploration and development, and federal assistance to state and local governments for activities affecting a state's coastal zone must be consistent with the coastal program.

In Secretary of the Interior v. California, 464 U.S. 312 (1984), the state of California and others sued the Secretary of Interior on the grounds that a proposed sale of oil and gas leases on outer continental shelf (OCS) tracts off the California coast could not be conducted without the Department of Interior making a consistency determination as required by CZMA § 307(c)(1). California's position was that the lease sale required a showing by the Secretary of Interior that the sale would be "consistent" to the "maximum extent practicable" with the California coastal zone management plan. The Secretary argued that the proposed lease sale was not an "activity directly affecting" the California coastal zone and therefore, no consistency determination was required by the CZMA.

Development of oil and gas OCS resources is divided by statute into four distinct stages by the provisions of the Outer Continental Shelf Lands Act (OCSLA). The first is the five-year leasing plan prepared by the Department of Interior. 43 U.S.C. § 1344. The second stage is the lease sale itself. 43 U.S.C. § 1337. A successful lease purchaser acquires only the right to conduct limited preliminary activities on the OCS, such as geophysical and other surveys. The issue in this suit was whether the sale and these consequent preliminary activities "directly affected" the coastal zone. The third stage consists of actual exploration. However, exploration cannot take place until exploration plans have been submitted for review and approved by the Secretary of Interior. At this stage the Outer Continental Shelf Lands Act, 43 U.S.C. § 1340(c)(2), itself, as well as § 307(c)(3)(B) of the CZMA, refer to the CZMA consistency requirement, and a consistency determination is specifically required. The final stage is the actual development and production of an OCS oil and gas well. Again, before such activities can be undertaken, the lessee must submit another plan for approval by the Secretary. These activities are also specifically subject to the consistency requirement of the CZMA. At all four stages, it is important to note, the OCSLA requires that affected states are given the opportunity to comment upon the plans. In fact, at both the lease stage and the development and production stage, the Governor of any affected state may submit recommendations regarding the size, timing, or location of any proposed lease sale or development and production activity, and the recommendations must be accepted by the Secretary of Interior unless the Secretary finds the recommendations do not strike a reasonable balance between national interests and state and local interests.

In a 5–4 decision of the Court, Justice O'Connor delivered a majority opinion that left the consistency doctrine in a state of confusion. The Court rejected the state's argument that "leasing sets in motion a chain of events that culminates in oil and gas development, and that leasing therefore 'directly affects' the coastal zone within the meaning of § 307(c)(1)." 464 U.S. at 319. The Court noted that the lease sale authorized only preliminary exploration "that has no significant effect on the coastal zone" and is only one "in a series of decisions that may culminate in activities directly affecting that zone." The Court went on to suggest that only federal activities conducted *in* the coastal zone could have direct effects. "Section 307(c)(1)'s 'directly affecting' language was aimed at activities conducted or supported by federal agencies on federal lands physically situated in the coastal zone but excluded from the zone as formally defined by the Act." 464 U.S. at 330. Ultimately, however, the Court was persuaded by the fact that although consistency of OCS activities during the exploration and development stages is addressed in both the OCSLA and CZMA, neither act requires consistency review at the lease sale stage. The Court stated:

> As we have noted, the logical paragraph to examine in connection with a lease sale is not § 307(c)(1), but § 307(c)(3). Nevertheless, even if OCS lease sales are viewed as involving an OCS activity "conduct[ed]" or "support[ed]" by a federal agency, lease sales can no longer aptly be characterized as "directly affecting" the coastal zone. Since 1978 the sale of a lease grants the lessee the right to conduct only very limited, "preliminary activities" on the OCS. It does not authorize full-scale exploration, development, or production. Those activities may not begin until separate federal approval has been obtained, and approval may be denied on several grounds. If approval is denied, the lease may then be canceled, with or without the payment of compensation to the lessee. In these circumstances, the possible effects on the coastal zone that may eventually result from the sale of a lease cannot be termed "direct."

> It is argued, nonetheless, that a lease sale is a crucial step. Large sums of money change hands, and the sale may therefore generate momentum that makes eventual exploration, development, and production inevitable. On the other side, it is argued that consistency review at the lease sale stage is at best inefficient, and at worst impossible: Leases are sold before it is certain if, where, or how exploration will actually occur.

> The choice between these two policy arguments is not ours to make; it has already been made by Congress. In the 1978 OCSLA amendments Congress decided that the better course is to postpone consistency review until the two later stages of OCS planning, and to rely on less formal input from State Governors and local governments in the two earlier ones. It is not for us to negate the lengthy, detailed, and coordinated provisions of CZMA § 307(c)(3)(B), and OCSLA

§§ 1344–1346 and 1351, by a superficially plausible but ultimately unsupportable construction of two words in CZMA § 307(c)(1).

Id. at 342–43.

Since prospective lease purchasers acquire no rights to explore, produce, or develop any portion of the OCS, no CZMA consistency review is required. The Court held that § 307(c)(1) did not mandate consistency review for OCS lease sales, but some agencies read the case more broadly. The U.S. Army Corps of Engineers, for example, adopted the interpretation that federal activities must be conducted *in* the coastal zone to have direct effects. See, e.g., Corps Ocean Dumping Regulations, 53 Fed. Reg. 14902 (Apr. 26, 1988).

After several years and a number of proposed amendments to CZMA § 307 to reverse Secretary of the Interior v. California, the 1990 Coastal Zone Act Reauthorization Amendments (CZARA) readdressed the federal consistency requirement and provided for a presidential exemption.

CZMA § 307(c)–(d). Coordination and Cooperation

16 U.S.C. § 1456(c)–(d)

(c) Consistency of Federal activities with State management programs; certification.

(1)(A) Each Federal agency activity within or outside the coastal zone that affects any land or water use or natural resource of the coastal zone shall be carried out in a manner which is consistent to the maximum extent practicable with the enforceable policies of approved State management programs. A Federal agency activity shall be subject to this paragraph unless it is subject to paragraph (2) or (3).

(B) After any final judgment, decree, or order of any Federal court that is appealable under section 1291 or 1292 of Title 28, or under any other applicable provision of Federal law, that a specific Federal agency activity is not in compliance with subparagraph (A), and certification by the Secretary that mediation under subsection (h) is not likely to result in such compliance, the President may, upon written request from the Secretary, exempt from compliance those elements of the Federal agency activity that are found by the Federal court to be inconsistent with an approved State program, if the President determines that the activity is in the paramount interest of the United States. No such exemption shall be granted on the basis of a lack of appropriations unless the President has specifically requested such appropriations as part of the budgetary process, and the Congress has failed to make available the requested appropriations.

(C) Each Federal agency carrying out an activity subject to paragraph (1) shall provide a consistency determination to the relevant

State agency designated under section 1455(d)(6) of this title at the earliest practicable time, but in no case later than 90 days before final approval of the Federal activity unless both the Federal agency and the State agency agree to a different schedule.

(2) Any Federal agency which shall undertake any development project in the coastal zone of a state shall insure that the project is, to the maximum extent practicable, consistent with the enforceable policies of approved state management programs.

(3)(A) After final approval by the Secretary of a state's management program, any applicant for a required Federal license or permit to conduct an activity, in or outside of the coastal zone, affecting any land or water use or natural resource of the coastal zone of that state shall provide in the application to the licensing or permitting agency a certification that the proposed activity complies with the enforceable policies of the state's approved program and that such activity will be conducted in a manner consistent with the program. At the same time, the applicant shall furnish to the state or its designated agency a copy of the certification, with all necessary information and data. Each coastal state shall establish procedures for public notice in the case of all such certifications and, to the extent it deems appropriate, procedures for public hearings in connection therewith. At the earliest practicable time, the state or its designated agency shall notify the Federal agency concerned that the state concurs with or objects to the applicant's certification. If the state or its designated agency fails to furnish the required notification within six months after receipt of its copy of the applicant's certification, the state's concurrence with the certification shall be conclusively presumed. No license or permit shall be granted by the Federal agency until the state or its designated agency has concurred with the applicant's certification or until, by the state's failure to act, the concurrence is conclusively presumed, unless the Secretary, on his own initiative or upon appeal by the applicant, finds, after providing a reasonable opportunity for detailed comments from the Federal agency involved and from the state, that the activity is consistent with the objectives of this title or is otherwise necessary in the interest of national security.

(B) After the management program of any coastal state has been approved by the Secretary under section 1455 of this title, any person who submits to the Secretary of the Interior any plan for the exploration or development of, or production from, any area which has been leased under the Outer Continental Shelf Lands Act (43 U.S.C. § 1331 et seq.) and regulations under such Act shall, with respect to any exploration, development, or production described in such plan and affecting any land or water use or natural resource of the coastal zone of such state, attach to such plan a certification that each activity which is described in detail in such plan complies with the enforceable policies of such state's approved management program and will be carried out in a manner consistent with such program. No Federal official or agency shall grant such person any license or permit for any activity described in detail in such plan until such state or its designated agency receives a copy of such certification and plan, together with any other necessary data and information, and until—

(i) such state or its designated agency, in accordance with the procedures required to be established by such state pursuant to subparagraph (A), concurs with such person's certification and notifies the Secretary and the Secretary of the Interior of such concurrence;

(ii) concurrence by such state with such certification is conclusively presumed as provided for in subparagraph (A), except if such state fails to concur with or object to such certification within three months after receipt of its copy of such certification and supporting information, such state shall provide the Secretary, the appropriate federal agency, and such person with a written statement describing the status of review and the basis for further delay in issuing a final decision, and if such statement is not so provided, concurrence by such state with such certification shall be conclusively presumed; or

(iii) the Secretary finds, pursuant to subparagraph (A), that each activity which is described in detail in such plan is consistent with the objectives of this title or is otherwise necessary in the interest of national security.

If a state concurs or is conclusively presumed to concur, or if the Secretary makes such a finding, the provisions of subparagraph (A) are not applicable with respect to such person, such state, and any Federal license or permit which is required to conduct any activity affecting land uses or water uses in the coastal zone of such state which is described in detail in the plan to which such concurrence or finding applies. If such state objects to such certification and if the Secretary fails to make a finding under clause (iii) with respect to such certification, or if such person fails substantially to comply with such plan as submitted, such person shall submit an amendment to such plan, or a new plan, to the Secretary of the Interior. With respect to any amendment or new plan submitted to the Secretary of the Interior pursuant to the preceding sentence, the applicable time period for purposes of concurrence by conclusive presumption under subparagraph (A) is 3 months.

(d) Applications of local governments for Federal assistance; relationship of activities with approved management programs.

State and local governments submitting applications for Federal assistance under other Federal programs, in or outside of the coastal zone, affecting any land or water use of natural resource of the coastal zone shall indicate the views of the appropriate state or local agency as to the relationship of such activities to the approved management program for the coastal zone. Such applications shall be submitted and coordinated in accordance with the provisions of Title IV of the Inter-governmental Coordination Act of 1968 (82 Stat. 1098). Federal agencies shall not approve proposed projects that are inconsistent with the enforceable policies of a coastal state's management program, except upon a finding by the Secretary that such project is consistent with the purposes of this title or necessary in the interest of national security.

NOTES AND QUESTIONS

1. Section 307(c) originally required federal consistency with "approved state management programs." The 1990 Amendments require consistency only with "the enforceable policies of approved State management programs." Is there a difference? The amended CZMA defines "enforceable policy" as "State policies which are legally binding through constitutional provisions, laws, regulations, land use plans, ordinances, or judicial or administrative decisions, by which a State exerts control over private and public land and water uses and natural resources in the coastal zone." 16 U.S.C. § 1453(6a).

Section 307(c)(1)(B) provides a rarely used presidential exemption from the consistency requirement for activities that are found the executive to be in the "paramount interest of the United States." In the case of Navy training and modern sonar operations off California, however, the president provided an exemption from the consistency requirement, finding that continuation of the exercises as limited by the Navy was "essential to national security." He concluded that prohibiting or conditioning the operations would "undermine the Navy's ability to conduct realistic training exercises that are necessary to ensure the combat effectiveness of . . . strike groups." See Winter v. NRDC, 555 U.S. 7 (2008) (discussed in Chapter 8).

2. The consistency requirement was originally intended to provide an inducement to the states to develop coastal management plans. If a state developed a plan that met CZMA guidelines and adequately considered the national interest, the state received some assurance that its coastal policy choices would not be readily overturned by federal officials with a differing philosophy of coastal development. Of course, intergovernmental interactions are never as smooth in reality as they are in theory. The use of the consistency requirement by states to oppose development of oil and gas on the continental shelf has been one of the more controversial issues between state and federal governments. NOAA has avoided some potential conflict by not approving the inclusion of specific policies in state CMPs that would prohibit all oil and gas activities off their coasts on the basis that such policies conflict

with the CZMA requirements to consider the national interest in energy development.

Some critics depict the consistency requirement as a state veto power over federal activities and suggest that it is an unconstitutional violation of the Supremacy Clause. Do you agree? Does your analysis differ if you consider use of the consistency provision by the states as the implementation of a federal statute rather than the imposition of state requirements? For a complete discussion of this debate concerning the consistency requirement, see Whitney, Johnson & Perles, State Implementation of the Coastal Zone Management Consistency Provisions—Ultra Vires or Unconstitutional?, 12 Harv. Envtl. L. Rev. 67 (1988); Archer and Bondareff, Implementation of the Federal Consistency Doctrine—Lawful and Constitutional: A Response To Whitney, Johnson & Perles, 12 Harv. Envtl. L. Rev. 115 (1988); Kuhse, The Federal Consistency Requirement of the Coastal Zone Management Act of 1972: It's Time to Repeal This Fundamentally Flawed Legislation, 6 Ocean & Coastal L. J. 77 (2001); Gibbons, Too Much of a Good Thing? Federal Supremacy & the Devolution of Regulatory Power: The Case of the Coastal Zone Management Act, 48 Naval L. Rev. 84 (2001).

In practice, there has been little evidence that the states have abused any preemptive authority the consistency provisions may have given them. States concur with nearly all consistency certifications, and the few that incur objections are generally resolved through negotiations to develop conditions or mitigating measures. In the case of OCS oil and gas development, NOAA has noted the following:

> Since 1978, MMS has approved over 10,600 EP's [exploration plans] and over 6,000 DPP's [development and production plans]. States have concurred with nearly all of these plans. In the 30-year history of the CZMA, there have been only 18 instances where the offshore oil and gas industry appealed a State's federal consistency objection to the Secretary of Commerce. The Secretary issued a decision in 14 of those cases. The Secretary did not issue a decision for the other 4 OCS appeals because the appeals were withdrawn due to settlement negotiations between the State and applicant or a settlement agreement between the Federal Government and the oil companies involved in the projects. Of the 14 decisions (1 DPP and 13 EP's), there were 7 decisions to override the State's objection and 7 decisions not to override the State.

71 Fed. Reg. 788, 791 (2006). While the consistency provision has provided states with a basis for negotiating changes to thousands of federal actions, "States have concurred with approximately 93%–95% of all federal actions reviewed." Id. at 789.

Regulations adopted in December 2000 encourage further cooperation by allowing a state to issue a "conditional concurrence." The state must include in its concurrence letter the conditions that must be satisfied and explain why the conditions are necessary to ensure consistency with enforceable state policies. If the conditions are not met, then the letter will include notice that it will be treated as an objection. See 15 C.F.R. § 930.4.

3. What is a federal activity that triggers consistency review? NOAA's 2006 regulations provide that:

> The term "Federal agency activity" means any functions performed by or on behalf of a Federal agency in the exercise of its statutory responsibilities. The term "Federal agency activity" includes a range of activities where a Federal agency makes a proposal for action initiating an activity or series of activities when coastal effects are reasonably foreseeable, e.g., a Federal agency's proposal to physically alter coastal resources, a plan that is used to direct future agency actions, a proposed rulemaking that alters uses of the coastal zone. "Federal agency activity" does not include the issuance of a federal license or permit to an applicant or person (see subparts D and E of this part) or the granting of federal assistance to an applicant agency (see subpart F of this part).

15 C.F.R. § 930.31 (a).

In State of California v. Norton, 311 F.3d 1162 (9th Cir. 2002), the 9th Circuit Court of Appeals required the Department of Interior to provide consistency determinations for lease suspensions it issued for 36 OCS leases off the California coast. Does the above definition of federal activity preclude consistency review of other lease suspensions. NOAA's view is that "Federal agency activities do not include interim or preliminary activities incidental or related to a proposed action for which a consistency determination has been or will be submitted and which do not make new commitments for actions with coastal effects. Such interim or preliminary activities are not independent actions subject to federal consistency review." 71 Fed. Reg. 788, 807 (2006). NOAA distinguished the decision in California v. Norton as follows:

> The heart of the Ninth Circuit's decision is that lease suspensions cannot be categorically exempt from CZMA review. Applying the CZMA "effects test," the Ninth Circuit found that the 36 lease suspensions at issue had coastal effects. It is NOAA's view that the Ninth Circuit's coastal effects determination is limited to the 36 leases in that case. NOAA believes that in all other foreseeable instances, lease suspensions would not be subject to federal consistency review since (1) they do not generally authorize activities with coastal effects, and (2) if lease suspensions did result in activities with coastal effects, they should be addressed in a State's consistency review of the lease sale, EP or DPP.

Id. Note that the original lease sales in California v. Norton had not been subject to consistency review. Without the suspension, the leases would have expired.

4. What kind of effects on the coastal zone trigger the consistency requirement? Are environmental effects in the coastal zone necessary? Are economic effects on the coastal zone enough? For example, does an OCS lease

sale that affects an offshore fishery and has only economic effects in the coastal zone require consistency? Does the 1990 amendment deleting the requirement of "direct" effects change your analysis? Current regulations provide the following:

> *Effect on any coastal use or resource (coastal effect).* The term "effect on any coastal use or resource" means any reasonably foreseeable effect on any coastal use or resource resulting from a Federal agency activity or federal license or permit activity (including all types of activities subject to the federal consistency requirement under subparts C, D, E, F and I of this part.) Effects are not just environmental effects, but include effects on coastal uses. Effects include both direct effects which result from the activity and occur at the same time and place as the activity, and indirect (cumulative and secondary) effects which result from the activity and are later in time or farther removed in distance, but are still reasonably foreseeable. Indirect effects are effects resulting from the incremental impact of the federal action when added to other past, present, and reasonably foreseeable actions, regardless of what person(s) undertake(s) such actions. 15 C.F.R. § 930.11(g).

5. Does a state have discretion about whether to exercise its authority under the federal consistency requirement? In Skokomish Indian Tribe v. Fitzsimmons, 982 P.2d 1179 (1999), cert. denied, 143 Wn.2d 1018 (2000), the Washington Court of Appeals held that, as a matter of state law, the state's Department of Ecology (DOE) could not waive its responsibility to object to the City of Tacoma's consistency certification for a dam project that DOE had acknowledged to be inconsistent with the state coastal management program. The court stated that "[b]oth the federal and state regulatory schemes . . . would be rendered meaningless" if the agency could simply "choose" not to follow procedures to object to the federally licensed project. Finding the action arbitrary and capricious, the court ordered the DOE to issue a response consistent with state law.

6. What authority does NOAA have to sanction states for acting inconsistently with its own approved state program? NOAA is required to conduct a "continuing review" of state performance (generally, every three years) assessing the "extent to which the state has implemented and enforced the program approved by the Secretary, addressed coastal management needs * * *, and adhered to the terms of any grant, loan, or cooperative agreement." 16 U.S.C. § 1458(a). The 1990 CZMA amendments clarified the conditions for NOAA's suspension of financial assistance to state coastal programs and the circumstances for withdrawal of approval of state programs:

16 U.S.C. § 1458. * * *

(c) Suspension of financial assistance for noncompliance; notification of Governor; length of suspension.

(1) The Secretary may suspend payment of any portion of financial assistance extended to any coastal state under this title, and may withdraw

any unexpended portion of such assistance, if the Secretary determines that the coastal state is failing to adhere to (A) the management program or a State plan developed to manage a national estuarine reserve * * * or a portion of the program or plan approved by the Secretary, or (B) the terms of any grant or cooperative agreement funded under this title.

(2) Financial assistance may not be suspended under paragraph (1) unless the Secretary provides the Governor of the coastal state with—(A) written specifications and a schedule for the actions that should be taken by the State in order that such suspension of financial assistance may be withdrawn; and (B) written specifications stating how those funds from the suspended financial assistance shall be expended by the coastal state to take the actions referred to in subparagraph (A).

(3) The suspension of financial assistance may not last for less than 6 months or more than 36 months after the date of suspension.

(d) Withdrawal of approval of a program. The Secretary shall withdraw approval of the management program of any coastal state and shall withdraw financial assistance available to that State under this title as well as any unexpended portion of such assistance, if the Secretary determines that the coastal state has failed to take the actions referred to in subsection (c)(2)(A).

(e) Notice and hearing. Management program approval and financial assistance may not be withdrawn under subsection (d), unless the Secretary gives the coastal state notice of the proposed withdrawal and an opportunity for a public hearing on the proposed action. Upon the withdrawal of management program approval under this subsection (d), the Secretary shall provide the coastal state with written specifications of the actions that should be taken, or not engaged in, by the state in order that such withdrawal may be canceled by the Secretary.

2. Application of the Consistency Requirement

In the following problem, the consistency provision is applied in the context of the Department of Interior's authority to lease the outer continental shelf for renewable energy development. The source of this authority is examined in Chapter 5, Section 3, as is the role of state coastal zone management programs. State and federal authorities to manage fisheries, fish habitat and aquaculture is explored in Chapter 6.

PROBLEM

The Department of the Interior has announced it will lease several large tracts on the U.S. continental shelf for the siting of offshore wind turbines. The tracts are 4 to 15 miles offshore of State A. In the same area, there is commercial shrimping and a seasonal recreational mackerel fishery in which both State A's and adjacent State B's fishermen participate. Although State A has not objected to the lease, adjacent State B's coastal zone management agency objects to the proposed leasing as being inconsistent with the state's federally approved coastal zone management program. The State B program restricts any activities that may interfere with established fisheries. The program also contains a policy statement giving priority to exploitation of renewable, over nonrenewable, resources. It further provides that "facilities serving the commercial fishing and recreation boating industries shall be protected and, where feasible, upgraded." The state contends that the proposed wind farm will interfere with commercial shrimping and recreational fishing and that the decline in fisheries will have an adverse impact upon the onshore facilities serving the commercial fishing industry. State B argues further that in addition to destroying the offshore habitat where the wind turbines will be erected, the construction of the turbines and the transmission lines that will go ashore in State A will create turbidity that will impact seagrass beds in state waters which serve as nursery and feeding areas for the shrimp and for numerous species of fish.

Before the Department of the Interior may issue the lease, must it supply the state coastal commission with a certification that the sale is consistent to the maximum extent practicable with the state coastal zone management plan? If not, how would the state raise its objection to the proposed sale? Does the state have a legitimate objection to the proposed sale? If it does, does that mean that the sale must be canceled? Must the Department of Interior seek a Presidential exemption? On what grounds may the President exempt the leasing activity? Do those grounds exist here?

Assume the lease is issued to Energy Solutions, Inc. whose proposal involves not only the installation of the wind turbines, but a second phase of the project which will use the wind turbine structures for anchoring aquaculture pens to raise local, high value fish species that have become depleted in recent years. Energy Solutions argues that the area leased is "hard bottom" with no significant reef or seagrass habitat to support fisheries and that any off-site impacts of the construction will be temporary and mitigated in the nearshore areas where the transmission lines will go ashore by restoration projects replacing impacted seagrasses and wetlands. The company contends that only indigenous fish species will be propagated in the pens (no invasive species from escapes) and that the open ocean environment will assure that there are no water quality issues. The company concedes that the wind farm will interfere with navigation and fishing in the area to some extent, but that the turbines will be placed to avoid the primary navigation routes to State A's and State B's harbors. The company also argues that the benefits more than compensate for any impacts and that both renewable energy production and aquaculture are national priorities. Energy Solutions has applied for federal permits for the wind farm and the aquaculture operation from the relevant federal agencies.

Must Energy Solutions supply a consistency certification for both State A and State B with its federal permit applications? Assuming the federal agencies refuse to issue the permits without the consistency certifications from State B, and Energy Solutions continues to believe that such a certification is not required or is not inconsistent, what legal action should the company take to force the issuance of a permit? Assuming, on the other hand, that Energy Solutions operations are in fact inconsistent with the State B coastal zone management plan, may the company nonetheless appeal the denial of the permit? To whom does Energy Solutions appeal and upon what grounds may the permit be issued notwithstanding the inconsistency of the company's proposed operations with the State B coastal zone management plan? If Energy Solutions successfully appeals after the state's negative determination, what are State B's options?

How would your analysis be affected if State A were issuing the lease in state waters, but Energy Solutions was required to acquire federal permits under the Clean Water Act and the Rivers and Harbors Act before it could proceed?

* * *

Where there is disagreement about whether an activity is consistent with a state coastal management program, the CZMA provides for both mediation and an appeals processes.

CZMA § 307(h). Mediation of Disagreements

16 U.S.C. § 1456(h)

In case of serious disagreement between any Federal agency and a coastal state * * * in the administration of [an approved] management program * * * the Secretary * * * shall seek to mediate the differences in such disagreement. The process of such mediation shall * * * include public hearings which shall be conducted in the local area concerned. * * *

The Secretarial Appeal Process

Findings by a state that a federally permitted activity, an OCS exploration or development plan, or a federal assistance program is inconsistent with a state coastal program may also be appealed to the Secretary of Commerce. See 16 U.S.C. §§ 1456(c)(3)(A)–(B), (d), supra at pp. 274–276. NOAA regulations provide the basis of review for determining when the Secretary can override a state's consistency objection by finding the activity consistent with the objectives of the CZMA or necessary in the interest of national security.

15 C.F.R. § 930.121. Consistent with the Objectives or Purposes of the Act

A federal license or permit activity, or a federal assistance activity, is "consistent with the objectives or purposes of the Act" if it satisfies each of the following three requirements:

(a) The activity furthers the national interest as articulated in § 302 or § 303 of the Act, in a significant or substantial manner.

(b) The national interest furthered by the activity outweighs the activity's adverse coastal effects, when those effects are considered separately or cumulatively.

(c) There is no reasonable alternative available which would permit the activity to be conducted in a manner consistent with the enforceable policies of the management program. The Secretary may consider but is not limited to considering previous appeal decisions, alternatives described in state objection letters and alternatives and other information submitted during the appeal. The Secretary shall not consider an alternative unless the State agency submits a statement, in a brief or other supporting material, to the Secretary that the alternative would permit the activity to be conducted in a manner consistent with the enforceable policies of the management program.

15 C.F.R. § 930.122. Necessary in the Interest of National Security

A federal license or permit activity, or a federal assistance activity, is "necessary in the interest of national security" if a national defense or other national security interest would be significantly impaired were the activity not permitted to go forward as proposed. Secretarial review of national security issues shall be aided by information submitted by the Department of Defense or other interested Federal agencies. The views of such agencies, while not binding, shall be given considerable weight by the Secretary. The Secretary will seek information to determine whether the objected-to activity directly supports national defense or other essential national security objectives.

* * *

The regulations above reflect December 2000 revisions that changed § 930.121(a) to add the requirement that the activity "further the national interest . . . *in a significant or substantial manner.*" This change was intended to exclude from the appeal process projects with only minimal connection to the national goals of the CZMA and focus the process on assuring that national interests are fully considered in the state certification process. NOAA's discussion of the 2000 regulations notes that "a project can be of national import without being quantifiably large in scale or impact on the national economy. . . . To determine whether a project significantly or substantially furthers the national interest, NOAA encourages appellants and States to consider three factors: (1) The degree to which the activity furthers the national interest; (2) the nature or importance of the national interest furthered as articulated in the CZMA; and (3) the extent to which the proposed activity is coastal dependent." 65 Fed. Reg. 77150 (2000).

The siting of energy facilities or OCS oil and gas development significantly further the national interest. "Such activities are coastal dependent industries with economic implications beyond the immediate locality in which they are located." Noncoastal dependent uses, such as a house or a restaurant, are fundamentally local land use decisions having little relation to the national interests furthered by the CZMA. More difficult cases are presented by proposals for marinas or airport runways, which must be considered based on the record presented to the Secretary. Id. Clearly cases like In the Consistency Appeal of Jessie W. Taylor from an Objection by the State of South Carolina, U.S. Department of Commerce, Office of The Secretary (1997), involving a commercial storage facility on .6 acres of coastal wetland, and In the Consistency Appeal of John Bianchi, U.S. Department of Commerce, Office Of The Secretary (1989), involving an individual dock permit will no longer be considered as meeting the most fundamental threshold requirement for overruling a state's negative consistency determination.

The secretarial appeals process often results in rulings important to interpretation of the CZMA and the consistency requirement.

* * *

IN THE CONSISTENCY APPEAL OF THE VIRGINIA ELECTRIC AND POWER COMPANY FROM AN OBJECTION BY THE NORTH CAROLINA DEPARTMENT OF ENVIRONMENT, HEALTH AND NATURAL RESOURCES

U.S. Department of Commerce, Office of the Secretary, 1994

EXECUTIVE SUMMARY

Introduction

The Virginia Electric and Power Company (VEPCO), on behalf of the City of Virginia Beach, Virginia (City), has appealed to the Secretary of Commerce to override the State of North Carolina's objection to the City's proposal to withdraw water from Lake Gaston for the City's water supply needs. This issue has had a long and contentious history, and the decision was reached only after a thorough consideration of all the evidence in the record. As explained in more detail below, the Secretary overrides North Carolina's objection, thereby allowing the City to obtain federal permits to build a pipeline for the withdrawal of up to 60 million gallons a day (mgd) of water from Lake Gaston.

VEPCO's appeal arises under the Coastal Zone Management Act (CZMA), an act administered by the National Oceanic and Atmospheric Administration (NOAA), an agency within the Department of Commerce. Section 307 of the CZMA provides that any applicant for a required federal license to conduct an activity affecting any land or water use or natural resource of the coastal zone, shall provide to the permitting agency a certification that the proposed activity complies with the enforceable policies of a state's coastal zone management program.

VEPCO has requested approval from the Federal Energy Regulatory Commission (FERC) for the City's project. Because North Carolina has objected to the project, FERC may not grant a license or permit, unless the Secretary of Commerce finds that the activity is consistent with the objectives of the CZMA or is otherwise necessary in the interest of national security.

Background

The City, located on the coast of southeastern Virginia, is the largest city in Virginia, with more than 400,000 residents. The City has no water supply of its own and, historically, has purchased all of its water from the adjacent city of Norfolk. A series of droughts plaguing southeastern Virginia over the past 15 years has caused water shortages throughout the area. In response, the City has adopted mandatory year round water restrictions and imposed a moratorium on extensions of its water system. Numerous water studies have shown that southeastern Virginia will need at least an additional 60 mgd of water by the year 2030.

More than a decade ago, after several years of study, the City embarked upon a project to withdraw potable water from Lake Gaston for the consumption of its residents and those of neighboring cities. Lake Gaston, which lies approximately 80 miles west-southwest of the City, is a man-made lake formed by damming a portion of the Roanoke River. Lake Gaston is part of a hydroelectric project constructed in the 1950s by VEPCO, under a license granted by FERC. Lake Gaston lies partly in Virginia and partly in North Carolina. The proposed project involves the permanent, consumptive withdrawal of up to 60 mgd of water from Lake Gaston, which is the equivalent of 22 billion gallons per year.

To gain access to Lake Gaston, the City proposes to construct a pipeline. The proposed pipeline would originate in a branch of Lake Gaston in Brunswick County, Virginia, at a location approximately 400 yards north of the Virginia–North Carolina border, run 76 miles across southeastern Virginia, and end at Lake Prince in Isle of Wight County, Virginia. The proposed pipeline would be located entirely within Virginia. In 1983, in order to construct the pipeline, the City applied to the U.S. Army Corps of Engineers (Corps) for a permit under two federal statutes, the Clean Water Act and the Rivers and Harbors Act. The Norfolk District Corps of Engineers issued the permit after conducting an environmental assessment pursuant to the National Environmental Policy Act (NEPA), and concluded that the project would have no significant environmental effects.

The State of North Carolina (State) challenged the adequacy of the Corps' NEPA review in the federal courts. A decision issued in July 1991, ultimately upheld the issuance of the Corps permit.

To install and operate its water intake facility for Lake Gaston, the City must also obtain permission from VEPCO, and VEPCO, in turn, must obtain approval from FERC. VEPCO applied to FERC on February 20, 1991, to obtain the necessary permit approval for the pipeline project. The State of North Carolina requested that the City and VEPCO submit a certification that the proposed project was consistent with North Carolina's coastal management program, a program which had been approved under the CZMA. The City and VEPCO jointly submitted such a certification.

On September 9, 1991, the State objected to the City's and VEPCO's consistency certification on the ground that the proposed project is inconsistent with several enforceable policies contained in the State's coastal management program. Specifically, the State alleged that the project is not consistent with its guidelines for estuarine waters and public trust areas because the proposed withdrawal of water would significantly increase the number of low flow days experienced by the lower Roanoke River system in coastal North Carolina. This increase, the State asserted, would cause significant adverse effects on its coastal zone, including the Roanoke River striped bass fishery.

Under the CZMA, the State's consistency objection precludes any federal agency from issuing any license or permit necessary for the City's proposed project, unless the Secretary of Commerce (Secretary) finds that the activity is either consistent with the objectives or purposes of the CZMA (Ground I) or is necessary in the interest of national security (Ground II).

On October 3, 1991, VEPCO, on behalf of the City, filed with the Secretary a notice of appeal from the State's objection to the City's proposed project. The City argued that the project satisfies both Ground I and Ground II and raised several threshold issues. On December 3, 1992, then-Secretary of Commerce Barbara Franklin, relying on a Department of Justice opinion, terminated the appeal on the basis that North Carolina lacked the authority under the CZMA to review a proposed project that would occur wholly within Virginia. In February, 1993, the Department of Justice was asked again whether its previous opinion still represented its view, and Justice responded affirmatively. Subsequently, the Department of Justice withdrew its opinion, and on January 7, 1994, the Department of Commerce reopened the appeal.

Upon consideration of the entire record, which included submittals by the City and North Carolina, written information from federal agencies and the public, and views given during a public hearing, the Secretary made the following findings.

DECISION

* * *

IV. THRESHOLD ISSUES

In accordance with prior consistency appeals, I have not considered whether the State was correct in its determination that the proposed activity was inconsistent with its coastal management program. Rather, the scope of my review[1] of the State's objection is limited to determining whether the objection was properly lodged, i.e., whether the State complied with the requirements of the CZMA and implementing regulations in filing its objection.

A. Compliance with the CZMA and its Implementing Regulations

The City has raised certain threshold issues related to whether the State's objection complies with the requirements of the CZMA. The City argues that because certain key provisions of the CZMA do not apply to the proposed pipeline project, the project is not subject to consistency review.

1. The City argues that because VEPCO has not applied for a federal license or permit the right to review is not triggered.

According to the CZMA, the City must first have applied for a federal license or permit in order to trigger the State's right to review an activity for consistency purposes. The City contends that VEPCO has not applied for any such required federal license or permit. The City admits, however, that VEPCO, on the City's behalf, must obtain FERC's approval to transfer easements to the City. NOAA regulations define the term "license or permit" to include approvals.[2] Nonetheless, the City argues that these

---

[1] The term "appeal" is a misnomer. More precisely, I examine the State's objection for compliance with the CZMA and its regulations in order to determine whether the objection was properly lodged. I then determine whether an appellant has filed a perfected appeal. The Then, based on all relevant information in the administrative record, I conduct a de novo inquiry of whether the activity is consistent with the objectives of the CZMA or necessary in the interest of national security.

[2] The term "license or permit" is defined by NOAA regulations as:

[A]ny authorization, certification, approval, or other form of permission which any federal agency is empowered to issue to an applicant * * * [It includes] [r]enewals and major

regulations should not be given effect because they exceed the authority of the CZMA.

I reject the City's argument. NOAA's consistency regulations constitute a reasonable interpretation of the term "license or permit" and thus are entitled to substantial deference. In addition, Congress has endorsed the regulations at issue. NOAA's interpretation is also consistent with other federal statutes, including the Administrative Procedure Act, which define the term "license" to include agency approvals. Therefore, I find NOAA's regulations interpreting the term "license or permit" to include approvals are valid and should be given effect. Because the City admits that FERC approval is required for the project at issue, I find that VEPCO has applied for a required federal license or permit.

B. Interstate Consistency

The second threshold issue raised by the City is that of interstate consistency. * * * "Federal consistency" is the term used to describe the mechanism by which a state can review federal activities, including federally licensed or permitted activities, to determine whether they are consistent with the state's coastal management program. The issue raised by the City is whether, under the CZMA, a state (North Carolina) has a right to review, i.e., comment on and possibly object to, a federally licensed or permitted activity occurring totally within another state (the Lake Gaston pipeline in Virginia) in order to determine if the activity has negative effects on the coastal environment of the reviewing state (North Carolina). This issue is referred to as "interstate consistency."

The two parties have raised three issues regarding interstate consistency. First, Virginia Beach argues that interstate consistency is not authorized by the CZMA. Thus, North Carolina cannot review the Lake Gaston project even if that activity affects its coastal zone, because the project is located in Virginia.

Contrarily, North Carolina believes that interstate consistency is authorized by the CZMA and that it can therefore review the Lake Gaston project if that project affects its coastal zone. Second, in addition to asserting that North Carolina has no right to review activities occurring outside its borders, the City also asserts that I am precluded from considering the interstate consistency issue because that issue was already decided when the Corps considered Virginia Beach's application for a permit related to this project. Finally, the State argues that whether interstate consistency is authorized does not have to be reached in this case because the project occurs within its own borders and thus is not an interstate application of federal consistency. Several non-party commentators submit-

---

amendments of federal license and permit activities not previously reviewed by the State agency * * * 15 C.F.R. § 930.51.

ted comments to me in this appeal supporting the positions of both North Carolina and Virginia Beach on the issue of interstate consistency. * * *

2. Does this project occur in Virginia only, or in both Virginia and North Carolina?

The State argues that the project does not involve interstate consistency because the project will occur in both North Carolina and Virginia. That is to say, the State argues that I need not decide whether it has a right to review an activity occurring in another state, because the activity is also occurring within its own borders. The State asserts that the largest part of the reservoir is in North Carolina, and that the removal of water from Lake Gaston is itself part of the project. In contrast, the City argues that the project will occur totally within the state of Virginia, but concedes that there may be only minimal effects in North Carolina.

This is a question of first impression for a consistency appeal decision. In practice, however, NOAA has considered projects to be occurring at the site where the physical activity required for the project takes place, i.e., the site of construction, the site of a discharge pipe, or the site of dredging and disposal of dredged material. This is true even for projects affecting water bodies shared by two or more states, as evidenced by NOAA's handling of several past consistency appeals (which were withdrawn for other reasons before decisions were reached). The State has, however, confused the effects of the project with the location of the project. If the FERC permit is issued, the City will be granted easements to allow it to build a pipeline and intake pipe in Virginia, from which it will extract water from the Virginia portion of Lake Gaston.

The State's request would, in effect, have me determine as a threshold matter that because the pipeline may cause detrimental effects in North Carolina, the project therefore occurs in North Carolina, and thus it can be reviewed without implicating interstate consistency. Like former Secretary Franklin, I decline to accept this argument. A project does not "occur" in a state merely because its effects might be felt there. I concur with Secretary Franklin's decision that "the proposed activity will occur wholly within the boundaries of the Commonwealth of Virginia."

Having made this threshold determination, I will, however, subsequently consider the effects of the pipeline when I balance the effects against the national interest in the project. The project's effects are thoroughly considered in Element 2 of Ground I of this decision.

3. Does the CZMA authorize one state to review for consistency with its coastal management program an activity occurring totally within another state?

a. Plain Meaning of the Statute

Interpretation of any statute begins with the plain language of that statute. The CZMA, as amended by the 1990 Coastal Zone Act Reauthorization Amendments (hereinafter CZARA), makes it clear that Congress meant to place no geographical boundaries upon the states' use of federal consistency. Two terms are particularly significant for purposes of my examination of the plain meaning of the CZMA: "affect" and "that state." At issue regarding the word "affect" is whether an activity occurring totally within one state, which will affect the coastal zone of another state, can be reviewed for consistency by the state that will be affected. * * *

The fact that Congress [in 16 U.S.C. § 1456(c)] used the term "in or outside of the coastal zone" to describe activities "affecting" the coastal zone indicates that the only test for determining whether a state can review a federal activity for consistency is whether that activity affects the reviewing state's coastal zone. In other words, the focus is not on the activity's location, but rather on its effects. The activity's location is irrelevant to the analysis of the activity's effects on the coastal zone. "Affecting" is the limiting factor in this section of the CZMA, not political and/or geographical lines.

The second significant term for purposes of my analysis is "that state." The section cited above provides that an applicant for a federal permit for an activity affecting the coastal zone of "that state" shall provide a consistency certification. The City argues that the term "that state" refers only to the state in which the activity is being conducted (in this case, Virginia), and therefore, the statute does not authorize interstate consistency review.[3]

I decline to adopt the City's narrow reading of "that state." Rather, I find that the more reasoned approach to interpreting the term is to refer to the beginning of the sentence, where the term "state" is first used. The sentence begins with the phrase, "After final approval of a state's coastal

---

[3] The City makes an often-heard argument that this view of section 307(c)(3)(A) would lead to Louisiana reviewing for consistency with its coastal management program activities occurring considerably north of Louisiana along the Mississippi–Missouri river system. While theoretically possible, this argument is a red herring. There must be a nexus between the activity wherever located and the reviewing state's coastal zone. The activity must cause an effect in the coastal zone of the reviewing state. This limiting factor may be reviewed at two critical junctures in the consistency process. First, OCRM has advised that, if a state has not indicated in its coastal management program the geographic location of activities outside of its coastal zone that it will review for consistency, the preferred method for state review is for a state to request from the Director of OCRM permission to review the activity as an unlisted activity. The standard for allowing such review is that the requesting state must show that the activity can be "reasonably expected to affect" the land and water uses or natural resources of its coastal zone. Clearly, the farther away an activity is from the coastal zone in question, the harder that showing will be. Second, if review is allowed and a state finds the activity inconsistent with its coastal management program, upon appeal, the Secretary will examine the activity within the statutory and regulatory parameters of his review and could find the activity (1) consistent with the objectives of the CZMA or (2) otherwise necessary in the interest of national security.

management program, any applicant * * *." Reading this phrase in conjunction with the use of the term "that state" later in the sentence convinces me that "that state" refers to any state with an approved coastal zone management program. This is consistent with the legislative history and the policies and purposes of the CZMA discussed below.

Therefore, based on the plain language of the statute, I find that the CZMA authorizes interstate consistency review.

b. Additional Statutory Arguments

The City also argues that allowing interstate consistency review would diminish states' "jurisdiction, responsibility, [and] rights" regarding water resources.[4]

It asserts that North Carolina, by its objection to the City's consistency determination, uses a federally delegated authority in an area that should be left to the state of Virginia. This argument erroneously suggests that the CZMA gives a state with a federally approved coastal management program direct authority over activities occurring within another state.

While the CZMA does not give one state direct authority to control activities in another state, the CZMA does grant to states with federally approved coastal management programs the right to seek conditions on or prohibit the issuance of federal permits and licenses that would "affect" their state. Thus, Congress has, in effect, granted to states with a federally approved coastal management program, in exchange for their protecting the nation's coasts, the right to ensure that federal permitees and licensees will not further degrade those coasts. The ability to prevent the granting of federal permits and licenses is a federal authority which has been granted to coastal states, not a state authority which has been usurped from the states. However, as a safeguard to a state's unrestrained use of this authority, an applicant can, as the City has, appeal for an override by the Secretary of Commerce.

The City has also advanced the argument that Congress has by adding the term "enforceable policies" to section 307 of the CZMA limited a state's review to the geographical area where, under state law, the reviewing state's enforceable policies are in effect. Thus, the City argues that the definition of enforceable policies limits a state's objection to activities occurring within the reviewing state because that is the only place the reviewing state's enforceable policies would have effect under state law. The City's interpretation of "enforceable policies" is incongruous with

---

[4] The City cites another portion of the CZMA, section 307(e)(1), as supporting its reading of section 307(c)(3)(A). This section reads, in pertinent part:

Nothing in this title shall be construed * * * to diminish either Federal or state jurisdiction, responsibility, or rights in the field of planning, development, or control of water resources. * * *

the language of section 307. Where possible, one must read various parts of a law consistently; and one must read the term "enforceable policies" in the context of the section in which it appears. As discussed above, in its 1990 amendments to section 307, Congress explicitly clarified that federal consistency under section 307 applies to activities both "in and outside" a state's coastal zone. It is thus illogical that Congress meant to limit this explicit recognition of the broad scope of federal consistency review merely by using the term "enforceable policies."

Furthermore, the City's argument is contrary to the spirit of the CZMA provisions enacted by Congress. By granting states the authority to review federal licenses and permits, Congress has deliberately given states broader authority than they would otherwise have. Similarly, Congress also made clear that enforceable policies included in a state's federally approved coastal management plan should apply, through federal consistency, to activities occurring both "in and outside" of the coastal zone. Congress thereby ensured the broadest possible protection for federally sanctioned activities that might harm a state's coastal zone.

Finally, at the same time that Congress added the term "enforceable policies" to section 307, it made it clear that the amendments to sections 307(c)(3)(A) and (B) were made "solely for the purpose of conforming these existing provisions with the changes to section 307(c)(1) made to overturn the [Secretary of Interior v. California] Supreme Court decision" and "to codif[y] the existing regulatory practice [15 C.F.R. §§ 930.39(c) and 930.58(a) (4).]". Thus, the term "enforceable policies" should not be construed to change NOAA's long-standing position that the CZMA authorizes interstate consistency.

I find, therefore, that contrary to the City's contention, the addition of the term "enforceable policies" in the 1990 CZARA amendments does not preclude interstate consistency review.

c. Legislative History

While I have found that the plain language of the CZMA supports interstate consistency, the parties have extensively quoted the legislative history of the CZMA to support their positions. Before addressing their arguments, a review of some of this history may be instructive.

As mentioned above, on May 2, 1989, * * * General Counsel of NOAA issued a legal opinion concluding that interstate consistency is authorized by the CZMA. That opinion gives a long and thorough legislative and regulatory history of the CZMA on this issue. In 1992, after the CZMA was amended, NOAA General Counsel * * * again reviewed this issue in light of the amendments and concluded, after a thorough review of the legislative history of the amendments, that the amendments "confirm that the 'affects' test of the CZMA consistency provision is not subject to geographic limitation." I thoroughly agree with that conclusion and hereby incorporate that opinion by reference.

d. Comparison to Clean Water Act and Clean Air Act

The City argues that the CZMA does not apply to interstate situations because, unlike the Clean Air Act (CAA) and the Clean Water Act (CWA), the CZMA does not have an explicit mechanism for resolution of interstate disputes. Contrary to the City's claim, the CZMA, although not containing a provision labeled specifically as an interstate dispute mechanism, does have a general method for addressing disputes, including interstate disputes.

The CWA and CAA require that an activity in one state be consistent with the policies of a neighboring state if there will be effects in the neighboring state. If the activity is inconsistent, those statutes prohibit the activity without a finding by the Administrator of EPA that the activity is permissible. Likewise, under the CZMA, a federal agency is prohibited from issuing a license in the face of a state's consistency objection unless the Secretary of Commerce decides that, despite the state's objection, the activity is consistent with the objectives of the CZMA (Ground I) or otherwise necessary in the interest of national security (Ground II). Input from neighboring states is allowed under all three statutes.

Further, the CWA and CAA regulatory schemes are distinguishable from that of the CZMA. Pursuant to the CAA and CWA, the federal government establishes minimum national standards and the states are granted authority to achieve those standards through their laws and policies. Because one state's actions under those laws could prevent a neighboring state from achieving the minimum federal standards, states are given the ability to review the laws and policies of other states.

The CZMA envisions a different type of federal/state partnership. There are no national standards under the CZMA. Instead, because of the unique coastal resources of each state, the CZMA encourages each state to develop its own standards, with enforceable policies, to implement the policies and goals of the [CZMA]. Under the CZMA States do not have the ability to review other State's laws and policies or the object to approvals granted under those state laws. There is no delegation of federal authority for the development of those programs. However, as discussed above, a type of federal authority is granted to the states in that states are able to review federal actions, such as the granting of federal permits and licenses, for consistency with their state programs.

Thus, I find that while there are important differences between the regulatory schemes of the CZMA and the CWA and CAA, Congress provided resolution mechanisms for interstate conflicts under all three acts. For CZMA section 307(c)(3)(A) conflicts, Congress provided Secretarial override of a state's objection as a mechanism for resolution of a state's objection.

Conclusion for Interstate Consistency

For the reasons stated above, including the plain language of the statute and legislative history, I find that the CZMA authorizes North Carolina to review for consistency with its federally approved coastal management program Virginia Beach's proposed Lake Gaston project, although that activity occurs totally within Virginia, if that project affects any land or water use or natural resource in North Carolina's coastal zone.

Further, a proper reading of the policies and goals of the CZMA supports my conclusion. Congress enacted the CZMA in order to more effectively protect the nation's coasts by encouraging states to exercise their full authority over the lands and waters of the coastal zone, both for the state and for the national interest. This congressional objective is expressed in a number of policies in the CZMA.[5] To implement these policies, states were encouraged to develop management plans for their coasts which were to give "full consideration to ecological, cultural, historic, and esthetic values as well as the needs for compatible economic development * * *."

The City's view that interstate consistency is not authorized under the CZMA is a narrow interpretation of the CZMA that would thwart or make incomplete the implementation of CZMA policies. Just as the beauty of the coast knows no boundaries, neither does the ecology of the coast, nor the threats to the coast. An interpretation that restricts consistency review to the state where the activity is taking place undermines the policies of the CZMA by eliminating states' abilities to consider transboundary effects on their coastal zones.

It is difficult to believe that if Virginia thought its coastal zone was being threatened by an activity requiring a federal license or permit occurring in a neighboring state, it would not at that point appreciate the ability, pursuant to the CZMA, to review that activity for consistency with Virginia's coastal management program. One's view of using the CZMA in an interstate situation will often depend on where one stands in the particular matter under consideration. * * *

[The following section is excerpted from the Executive Summary]

---

[5] Those policies included:

to encourage the participation and cooperation of the public, state and local governments, and interstate and other regional agencies, as well as of the Federal agencies having programs affecting the coastal zone, in carrying out the purposes of this title. Section 303(4) of the CZMA.

C. Conclusions Regarding Threshold Issues

The Secretary determined that threshold issues raised by Virginia Beach and the State of North Carolina did not preclude him from considering the merits of this case.

Ground I: Consistent with the Objectives or Purposes of the CZMA

To find that the proposed activity satisfies Ground I, the Secretary must determine that the project satisfies all four of the elements specified in the regulations implementing the CZMA. If the project fails to satisfy any one of the four elements, it is not consistent with the objectives or purposes of the CZMA and federal licenses or permits may not be granted. * * *

The Secretary made the following findings with regard to Ground I:

1. The proposed project will foster development of the coastal zone and coastal zone resources, and thus furthers more than one of the objectives or purposes of the CZMA.

2. The proposed project's individual and cumulative adverse effects on the coastal zone are outweighed by its contribution to the national interest. While the record shows that the project's effects on water flow in the Roanoke River will have individual and cumulative adverse effects on striped bass, those effects will likely be small. The record shows that the project's effects on water quality will be minimal, and will minimally affect striped bass. The record shows that the project's effects on coastal wetlands and on other coastal resources and uses will be minimal.

The proposed project will contribute significantly to the national interest because it will allow the beneficial use of water resources of the coastal zone. Providing potable water for human consumption to a major metropolitan area constitutes a very high priority use among all beneficial uses of water. The record shows that the project will contribute significantly to the national interest because of the extent to which it will further and support economic development in the coastal zone, and the extent to which it will alleviate southeastern Virginia's projected water deficit.

In sum, although the project will affect the Roanoke River striped bass fishery, as well as other coastal resources and uses, the evidence shows that the individual and cumulative adverse effects of the project are outweighed by the national interest contribution of alleviating the City's water supply shortage and encouraging economic development.

3. The proposed project will not violate the Clean Water Act or the Clean Air Act.

4. There are no reasonable alternatives available which would permit the project to be conducted in a manner consistent with the State of North

Carolina's coastal management program. The proposed alternatives failed for one or more reasons. The State failed to describe some alternatives with sufficient specificity. Some alternatives were unreasonable, i.e., environmental advantages of the alternative did not outweigh the increased cost of the alternative over the proposed project. Finally, some alternatives were found to be unavailable either because of technical or legal barriers or because an alternative did not meet the primary purpose of the project, which is to provide up to 60 mgd of additional water to southeastern Virginia.

Ground II: Necessary in the Interest of National Security

Although southeastern Virginia is home to the largest naval complex in the world, the record demonstrates that there would be no significant impairment to a national defense or other national security interest if the City's project is not allowed to go forward as proposed. Therefore, the Secretary found that the requirements of Ground II have not been met.* * *

VI. CONCLUSION AND SECRETARIAL DECISION

I hereby find, for the reasons stated, that the proposed project is consistent with the objectives and purposes of the CZMA, thereby meeting the requirements of Ground I. Accordingly, the proposed project may be permitted by federal agencies.

* * *

NOTES AND QUESTIONS

1. Is the secretarial appeal process mandatory? Does the appeal represent an administrative remedy that must be exhausted before objection to an applicant's consistency determination can be appealed to the courts?

In Acme Fill Corporation v. San Francisco Bay Conservation and Development Commission (BCDC), 187 Cal.App.3d 1056, 232 Cal.Rptr. 348 (1986), the court of appeal found that the petitioner was required to exhaust the administrative remedy provided under the CZMA before a state court challenge to the authority of the BCDC's exercise of consistency review authority. The court based its decision on the fact that although a Secretarial appeal involved different issues, it could have provided petitioner with the relief he sought.

What legal questions does the Secretarial appeal process leave unresolved? In the Consistency Appeal Of Chevron U.S.A., Inc., From An Objection By The State Of Florida, U.S. Department Of Commerce, Office Of The Secretary (1993), the Secretary addressed this issue:

> * * * As in previous decisions, I do not consider in this appeal whether Florida was correct in its determination that the proposed activity is inconsistent with the state's coastal management program, nor do I

consider whether the state's objection is correct as a matter of other state law. Rather, once I have found that the state's objection complies with the CZMA and its implementing regulations, I consider only whether Chevron's proposed project, notwithstanding Florida's objection, is either consistent with the objectives or purposes of the CZMA or otherwise necessary in the interest of national security. The consistency appeals process, therefore, is not the proper forum for an argument on the validity or appropriateness of Florida's consistency determination.

2. What is the standard of review and who bears the burden of proof in Secretarial appeals? See In the Drilling Discharge Consistency Appeal Of Mobil Oil Exploration & Producing Southeast, Inc. From An Objection By The State of North Carolina, U.S. Department of Commerce, Office Of The Secretary (1994) (petitioner bears the burden of proof and is responsible for the adequacy of information to establish by a preponderance of the evidence that the grounds for override have been met).

3. So-called "interstate consistency" is one of the more controversial applications of the CZMA. Was the consistency requirement intended to allow states to exert control over another state's activities? Regulations adopted in December 2000 recognize the requirement of consistency for "interstate coastal effects." 15 C.F.R. § 930.150(a) provides:

A federal activity may affect coastal uses or resources of a State other than the State in which the activity will occur. Effective coastal management is fostered by ensuring that activities having such reasonably foreseeable interstate coastal effects are conducted consistent with the enforceable policies of the management program of each affected State.

15 C.F.R. § 930.154 requires states to list the kind and geographic location of activities for which they intend to conduct interstate consistency review. States must also demonstrate the effects of such activities, as well as "include evidence of consultation with States in which the activity will occur, evidence of consultation with relevant Federal agencies, and any agreements with other States and Federal agencies regarding coordination of activities." The listing must be approved by NOAA as a routine program change in order for a state to subject a federal action to interstate review.

4. The Secretarial appeal of the Lake Gaston project was found proper even though no "permit," only approval, was required to be issued by a federal agency. However, in New Jersey v. Long Island Power Authority, 30 F.3d. 403 (3rd Cir. 1994), the court held that approval by the Coast Guard of an Operations Plan to ship nuclear power plant fuel through New Jersey waters did not trigger the consistency requirement. The submission of the Operational Plan was voluntary, and the failure of the agency to exercise discretionary enforcement power did not constitute an agency action under the CZMA. Id. at 420–421.

New regulations in 2006 define a federal license or permit as follows:

The term "federal license or permit" means any authorization that an applicant is required by law to obtain in order to conduct activities affecting any land or water use or natural resource of the coastal zone and that any Federal agency is empowered to issue to an applicant. The term "federal license or permit" does not include OCS plans, and federal license or permit activities described in detail in OCS plans, which are subject to subpart E of this part, or leases issued pursuant to lease sales conducted by a Federal agency (e.g., outer continental shelf (OCS) oil and gas lease sales conducted by the Minerals Management Service or oil and gas lease sales conducted by the Bureau of Land Management). Lease sales conducted by a Federal agency are Federal agency activities under subpart C of this part.

15 C.F.R. § 930.51(a). NOAA's explained that this new language was intended to "emphasize and clarify NOAA's long-standing view of the elements needed to determine that an authorization from a Federal agency is a 'federal license or permit'. . . . First, Federal law must require that the applicant obtain the federal authorization. Second, the purpose of the federal authorization is to allow a non-federal applicant to conduct a proposed activity. Third, the activity proposed must have reasonably foreseeable effects on a State's coastal uses or resources, and fourth, the proposed activity was not previously reviewed for federal consistency by the State agency * * * " 71 Fed. Reg. 788, 794 (2006).

A consistency determination may also be required for renewals and major amendments to permits which affect a coastal use or resource, particularly if the original activity was not reviewed by the state's agency, if the state program has changed since the original review, or if the effects of the activity will be substantially different than those originally reviewed by the state. See 15 C.F.R. § 930.51(b)–(e). In California Coastal Comm'n v. U.S. Navy, 5 F.Supp. 2d 1106 (S.D.Cal. 1998), after discovering that dredged material from a homeport project that was to be deposited on beaches contained dangerous ordnance, the Navy received a modified permit to dispose the dredged material offshore. The court found that the Navy could not proceed pursuant to a modified permit without determining that the new plan of disposal was consistent with the state plan to the maximum extent practicable.

————

With the expansion of natural gas development facilities, the CZMA has emerged as an important means for resolving interstate disputes. Are the Act's criteria sufficient for such a role?

CONNECTICUT v. U. S. DEPARTMENT OF COMMERCE

United States District Court, Conn. 2007
2007 WL 2349894

UNDERHILL, DISTRICT JUDGE.

Islander East Pipeline Company, LLC ("Islander") wants to build a 45-mile-long natural gas pipeline from Branford, Connecticut to a point in Suffolk County, Long Island (the "project"). The project would involve dredging a trench in the sea floor of Long Island Sound. In order to complete the project, Islander must obtain permits from the Federal Energy Regulatory Commission ("FERC") and the Army Corps of Engineers, which in turn require Islander to get coastal certification from both New York and Connecticut pursuant to the Coastal Zone Management Act ("CZMA"). The State of Connecticut and the Commissioner of the Connecticut Department of Environmental Protection ("Connecticut") objected to the certification. Islander appealed to the Secretary of Commerce ("Secretary"), who overturned Connecticut's objection, finding that the project was consistent with the CZMA. The three interested parties, Connecticut, the Secretary, and Islander have now filed cross-motions for summary judgment, principally asking me to decide whether the Secretary's decision was arbitrary and capricious.

* * *

I. Relevant Background

Islander wants to construct 45 miles of natural gas pipeline, 22 miles of which would be beneath the Long Island Sound * * *. Islander intends to lay the pipeline using horizontal directional drilling (HDD) for 4,000 feet from a point on the Connecticut shore to an exit point on the near shore. From that point, Islander plans to dredge a 1.1 mile trench. The pipeline would then continue under waters greater than 20 feet deep for the remainder of its length. Islander proposes to place "back-fill" of sand and gravel over the pipeline and to use a subsea plow to bury the underwater pipeline.

The project would be sited in a region of the Connecticut coast among the Thimble Islands, which provides a habitat for fish, crabs, urchins, snails, sponges, mussels, oysters, clams, and scallops. The Thimble Island region is "one of the most highly valuable, multiple marine ecological environments" along the coast of Connecticut. The proposed pipeline route would impact up to 3,700 acres of Sound bottom, including commercially leased and potentially leasable shellfish habitats. Shellfish are a species of "considerable ecological, commercial or recreational importance" in the Southern New England and New York regions. * * *

Connecticut objected to Islander's certification that its project complied with Connecticut's coastal management plan. Islander filed an appeal of Connecticut's objection with the Secretary. Islander and Connecticut filed briefs and supporting materials with the Secretary, and the Secretary provided a notice and comment period and held a public hearing in New Haven, Connecticut. * * * In the Decision, the Secretary determined that the project was consistent with the CZMA, thereby overruling Connecticut's objections.

II. Discussion

The State of Connecticut argues that the Secretary's Decision, determining that the project is consistent with the CZMA, was arbitrary and capricious. * * * Defendants argue that the Secretary articulated a reasoned basis for his Decision on each of the three required elements.

A. Arbitrary and Capricious Standard of Review

Jurisdiction is based on the Administrative Procedure Act ("APA"), 5 U.S.C. § 706, which governs judicial review of agency action. The court will set aside agency action when it is "arbitrary, capricious, an abuse of discretion, or otherwise not in accordance with law." 5 U.S.C. § 706(2) The court will also set aside agency action found to be "without observance of procedure required by law." 5 U.S.C. § 706(2)(D). For an agency decision to withstand the arbitrary and capricious standard of review, an agency is required to:

> examine the relevant data and articulate a satisfactory explanation for its action including a rational connection between the facts found and the choice made. In reviewing that explanation, we must consider whether the decision was based on a consideration of the relevant factors and whether there has been a clear error of judgment. Normally, an agency rule would be arbitrary and capricious if the agency has relied on factors which Congress has not intended it to consider, entirely failed to consider an important aspect of the problem, offered an explanation for its decision that runs counter to the evidence before the agency, or is so implausible that it could not be ascribed to a difference in view or the product of agency expertise. The reviewing court should not attempt itself to make up for such deficiencies; we may not supply a reasoned basis for the agency's action that the agency itself has not given. We will, however, uphold a decision of less than ideal clarity if the agency's path may reasonably be discerned.

Islander E. Pipeline Co., LLC v. Conn. Dep't of Envtl. Prot., 467 F.3d 295, 310 (2d Cir. 2006) (quoting Motor Vehicle Mfrs. Ass'n v. State Farm Mut. Auto. Ins. Co., 463 U.S. 29, 42–43 (1983)). * * *

* * *

The Second Circuit has instructed courts applying the arbitrary and capricious standard of review to consider whether the agency: (1) considered the relevant evidence; (2) examined relevant factors; and (3) spelled out a satisfactory rationale for its action, including demonstrating a reasoned connection between the facts and its decision.

B. Statutory Framework and Legislative History of the CZMA

* * *

2. Legislative History of the CZMA

* * * The 1976 amendments to the CZMA clarified the national interest in siting energy facilities. Moreover, it is well-established that, although initially aimed at conservation, the statute is a balancing statute—that is, it balances conservation with commercial development.

C. Whether the Secretary's Decision was Arbitrary and Capricious

Following a careful review of the Secretary's Decision and the voluminous administrative record in this case, I conclude that the Decision was arbitrary and capricious. Although the Secretary (1) considered the three factors relevant to a consistency determination, and (2) considered evidence relevant to each of those factors, he did not (3) demonstrate a reasoned connection between the evidence and his determination. In reaching this conclusion, I have not substituted my judgment for that of the Secretary; rather, I have carefully inquired into the facts and determined whether the Secretary considered relevant factors. Bearing in mind the deferential standard of review, I must set aside the Decision and remand this case for further consideration by the Secretary, because he failed adequately to explain or support the Decision with record evidence and neglected to consider important aspects of the problem raised by Connecticut's objection. Islander East Pipeline Co., LLC, 467 F.3d at 321 (remanding case to agency to "conduct the type of review contemplated by federal law"). Additionally, the Secretary did not follow necessary procedural requirements.

1. Element 1: Whether the Activity Furthers the National Interest in a Significant or Substantial Manner

The Secretary concluded that the project furthers the national interest, as defined in sections 302–03 of the CZMA, in a significant or substantial manner, and he considered relevant evidence in connection with that element. The Secretary's determination of element one demonstrates a reasoned connection between the evidence and his conclusion, because he considered the meaning of "national interest" under the CZMA and applied the evidence in the record to conclude that the project substantially furthered the national interest in three major ways: (1) the project develops the coastal zone; (2) the project is a sited, coastal-dependent energy facility; and (3) the project will preserve and enhance coastal zone resources. Citing to previous administrative decisions, the Secretary accurately noted that it is relatively easy for projects to satisfy the national interest requirement, because Congress broadly construed the CZMA to include both preservation and development objectives.

a. The Project Develops the Coastal Zone

* * *

The Secretary concluded that the project develops the coastal zone, because it would enable the bottom of Long Island Sound to be used in a productive manner, that is, to transport natural gas to be used in energy facilities. The Secretary's reliance on development as a national interest and his application of that national interest to the facts of this case appear to be reasonable.

The consistency regulations require that the proposed activity contribute to the national interest in a "significant or substantial" manner. 15 C.F.R. § 930.121(a). The National Oceanic and Atmospheric Administration's ("NOAA") Rules and Regulations define "significant or substantial" as contributing to the national achievement of the objections described in sections 302 and 303 of the CZMA "in an important way or to a degree that has a value or impact on a national scale." 65 Fed. Reg. 77124, 77150 (2000). A project can be "significant" within the meaning of the CZMA without being "quantifiably large in scale." Id. The siting of an energy facility is "significant."[5]

The Secretary reasoned that the development of Long Island Sound rose to the level of significant national importance, because the pipeline spanned two states, would affect hundreds of thousands of people in major metropolitan areas, and would develop the nation's energy infrastructure. Thus, the Secretary's conclusion that the project would benefit the national interest in a "substantial or significant manner" was not arbitrary and capricious.

b. The Project is a Sited, Coastal-Dependent Energy Facility

The CZMA encourages states to maintain coastal management programs that provide for "priority consideration being given to coastal-dependent uses and orderly processes for siting major facilities related to . . . energy, . . . and the location, to the maximum extent practicable, of

---

[5] NOAA enumerates three factors to consider whether an activity is significant or substantial: (1) the degree to which the activity furthers the national interest; (2) the nature or importance of the national interest furthered as articulated in the CZMA; and (3) the extent to which the proposed activity is coastal dependent." 65 Fed. Reg. 77150.

new commercial and industrial developments in or adjacent to areas where such development already exists." 16 U.S.C. § 1452(2)(D). * * *

Both the CZMA and the NOAA regulations use the term "coastal dependent." The term "coastal dependent" has been construed broadly in the relevant case law. See, e.g., North Carolina v. Brown, 1995 WL 852123 (D.D.C. 1995) (upholding Secretary's finding that, although proposed project was not itself "coastal dependent," it would indirectly promote development of coastal dependent uses) * * *. Connecticut defines "coastal dependent" more narrowly to mean "those uses and facilities which require direct access to, or location in, marine or tidal waters and which therefore cannot be located inland. . . . " Conn. Gen. Stat. § 22a–93(16). The incentive the CZMA provides for state participation is that federally sponsored activities in the coastal zone are supposed to be consistent with the state-created coastal management plan. Because Connecticut's plan includes a definition of coastal-dependent, that definition should guide the determination whether a particular use or facility is coastal dependent.

* * * The Secretary determined that the Islander project falls within the CZMA definition of an energy facility. That conclusion is a reasonable interpretation of the relevant statutory language; thus, the Secretary's conclusion that the project would be a sited energy facility is not arbitrary and capricious.

The Secretary also concluded that the project would be coastal dependent. * * * Arguably, a pipeline is merely a coastal-sited facility, not a "coastal dependent" facility, because it does not inherently depend upon the coast to achieve its desired results. The issue in this case, however, is whether a pipeline transporting gas to Long Island from Connecticut is coastal dependent. Because any such pipeline requires "direct access to, or location in, marine or tidal waters" of Long Island Sound, the project meets the definition of a coastal dependent energy facility.

Finally, the Secretary's Decision addresses why the siting of the pipeline would further the national interest in a significant or substantial manner. * * * According to the NOAA regulations, the siting of coastal dependent energy facilities inherently has economic consequences beyond the immediate locality where the facility is located, that is, involves a significant national interest. See 65 Fed. 77150. In light of the NOAA regulations describing the national importance of the siting of energy facilities, the Secretary's determination of these issues was not arbitrary and capricious.

　　　* * *

2. Element 2: Whether the National Interest Furthered by the Activity Outweighs the Activity's Adverse Coastal Effects, When Those Effects Are Considered Separately or Cumulatively

The Secretary's Decision is arbitrary and capricious because he failed to provide record support for his conclusions regarding the balancing of adverse coastal effects and failed to consider an important aspect of the problem * * *.

The Secretary found, by a preponderance of the evidence, that the national interest furthered by the Project outweighs its adverse coastal effects, considering those effects separately or cumulatively. The Secretary first considered generally what coastal areas would be affected by the project, as well as by the construction techniques that Islander intends to use. He then discussed five types of adverse coastal effects that would result from the project * * *. Despite the existence of those adverse effects, the Secretary concluded that the project's adverse coastal effects would be temporary in duration and limited in scope.

That conclusion is not adequately supported by record evidence and is not sufficiently definite. * * * Applying the deferential standard of review, I conclude that the Secretary's Decision is arbitrary and capricious and remand the case to him for further consideration.

a. The Secretary's Decision

i. Water Quality from Sedimentation

The Secretary examined the possibility that fine particles of sediment from the floor of the Long Island Sound ("Sound") could easily become re-suspended in the water during the construction process. Islander's proposed construction techniques, including the use of dredging, the subsea plow, cables, and anchors, will cause an increase in the turbidity of the waters. Increased turbidity tends to cause re-suspension of sediment into the water column, which affects water quality by reducing dissolved oxygen levels and reducing the depth of light penetration. Increased turbidity could also release contaminants from the Sound bottom.

First, with respect to the possibility of the release of contaminants from the Sound bottom, the Secretary considered evidence that there was a moderate level of contamination in the sediments in the construction area. He also examined record evidence indicating that, even after the increased turbidity due to construction, the level of contamination would remain below state water quality control standards.

Next, concerning the impact to water quality, the Secretary concluded that "the increase in turbidity will result in only limited, temporary adverse impacts on water quality." * * *

ii. Water Quality From Drilling Fluids

The Secretary also considered the effects of the release of drilling fluids * * * [but] concluded, based upon Islander's proposed construction techniques and contingency plan, that the release of drilling fluid would result in limited, temporary adverse effects on the water quality.

iii. Shellfish Habitat

After considering evidence about the adverse effects on the shellfish habitat, the Secretary ultimately concluded that the project will result in temporally and spatially limited adverse effects on shellfish.

The Secretary considered Connecticut's concern that the pipeline will cross shellfish lease areas in Connecticut's waters. He considered that the oyster and clam industry is a multi-million dollar enterprise in Connecticut, with Connecticut ranking first in the nation in terms of the dollar value of oysters harvested.

The Secretary recognized that there is record evidence proving that there will be adverse impacts to the shellfish habitat. The principal damage will occur in the area of the Sound floor where the pipeline is actually installed, as well as to surrounding areas where anchors and cables strike the Sound floor. Connecticut, the National Marine Fisheries Service ("NMFS"), and the Fish and Wildlife Service ("FWS") believe that it may take more than five years for the shellfish habitat to recover, and that the damage may be long-term. [T]here is evidence that the dredging and subsea plowing can cause direct mortality to the shellfish in those areas, and it is possible that the shellfish in the immediate pipeline area will never recover.

iv. Shellfish Harvest

The Secretary * * * concluded that, based upon the measures Islander proposed to mitigate those effects, as well as the lack of support for Connecticut's position, the project's impacts on commercial shellfish harvest would be minimal.

v. Wetlands

Finally, the Secretary considered Connecticut's concern about potential damage to two coastal wetland areas. The Secretary reasoned that, because Islander would monitor the wetlands for three years following construction to make sure they are restored, the damage to the wetlands would be mitigated, and would therefore be minimal.

vi. Cumulative Effects

Citing to prior administrative decisions, the Secretary explained that cumulative effects mean "the effects of an objected-to activity when added to the baseline of other past, present and reasonably foreseeable future activities occurring in the area of, and adjacent to, the coastal zone" of the area in which the objected-to activity has taken place. Here, the Secretary found that there was no evidence in the record that there were other past or reasonably foreseeable future activities within the meaning of the term cumulative effects.

* * *

b. Why the Secretary's Decision is Arbitrary and Capricious

The Secretary concluded that the national interest outweighed the adverse coastal effects just discussed because those effects would be limited in scope and temporary in duration. That conclusion is not supported by evidence or data, and is therefore arbitrary and capricious.

First, with respect to the scope of the adverse effects, * * * the Secretary's conclusion that any adverse coastal effects would be limited in scope * * * is also unsupported by data or evidence, and as a result, I cannot defer to the Secretary's conclusion that the project's adverse impacts would be limited in scope.

Second, the Secretary's conclusion that the adverse effects would be temporary is not supported by the record. * * * A close reading of the Decision reveals that, although he mentions the number three to five years, that number is just a floor, not a ceiling, and more fundamentally, the Secretary does not even point to any evidence that the shellfish will ever recover.

* * *

Third, the Secretary failed to address an important aspect of the problem because he effectively ignored the adverse effects on oysters when concluding that the adverse effects on shellfish would be temporary. * * * The Secretary acknowledged that oysters have not returned to the Sound after construction of the Iroquois pipeline in 1991. * * * [T]he Secretary is not predicting that oysters will return to the Sound bottom, nor is he citing data supporting the conclusion that oysters will likely return.

* * * "There are no findings and no analysis here to justify the choice made, no indication of the basis on which the agency exercised its expert discretion." As a result, the Secretary's Decision is arbitrary and capricious, and I must remand the case to the Secretary for further consideration of the impact of the pipeline on oysters.

* * *

In sum, the level of care given to balancing the adverse effects against the national interest is insufficient. In order for me to uphold the Secretary's Decision, there would need to be "a rational connection between the facts found and the choice made." Here, there is no rational connection between the record evidence and the conclusion that the adverse effects will be temporary or limited in scope. * * * I conclude that the Secretary's Decision is not sufficiently supported by data, and he failed to consider an important aspect of the problem. Therefore, I remand the case to the Secretary for further consideration, so that he can "conduct the type of review contemplated by federal law," meaning that he must provide record support for his conclusions and consider all important aspects of the problem, including the effect of the pipeline construction on oysters.

3. Element 3: No Reasonable Alternative Available

The Secretary also considered the third element required for the consistency analysis and concluded that there was no reasonable alternative to the project. Connecticut did not challenge that aspect of the Decision. Nevertheless, I conclude that the Secretary's Decision on this point is arbitrary and capricious because his analysis does not justify his determination. * * *.

The CZMA gives priority to new energy facilities, but requires, to the extent practicable, that they are to be installed adjacent to existing facilities. 16 U.S.C. § 1452(2)(D) ("[P]riority consideration [should be] given to coastal-dependent uses and orderly processes for siting major facilities related to . . . energy, . . . and the location, to the maximum extent practicable, of new commercial and industrial developments in or adjacent to areas where such development already exists.") (emphasis supplied). * * * Even though the CZMA has also incorporated development goals, it is, nevertheless, a balancing statute that seeks to balance conservation with commercial development.

There is an existing pipeline that spans the Long Island Sound, originating in Milford, Connecticut with the potential to expand to include the Islander project. Combining the Islander project with, or siting the Islander project adjacent to, the existing Iroquois pipeline would further the statutory purpose of concentrating commercial and industrial development in the coastal zone, and presents a potential way to minimize the adverse effects of the Islander project.

* * *

III. Conclusion

Connecticut's motion for summary judgment is GRANTED * * *. The Decision was arbitrary and capricious and is set aside. This matter is remanded to the Secretary for further proceedings consistent with this ruling. The clerk shall close this case.

It is so ordered.

[On March 10, 2009, the Department of Commerce dismissed as moot Islander East's federal consistency appeal, precluding the issuance of certain federal permits necessary for the project as proposed at that point.]

NOTES AND QUESTIONS

1. Review the provisions of CZMA § 307(c)(3)(A)(16 U.S.C. § 1456(c)(3)(A), pp. 273–276. Is the state that found an activity inconsistent a party to the permit applicant's appeal process? If not, what is the basis for the state appealing the Secretary's decision? What is the standard of review? Did the court here simply balance the factors differently? How much discretion does the Secretary have in applying a balancing test that does not include any standards as to priorities or weights of factors?

2. Can the state enjoin a federal permittee's activities that are inconsistent with the state coastal plan? In February 1986, John DeLyser applied to the Corps of Engineers for a permit to build a dock and boathouse on pilings. The permit was issued, but DeLyser instead began construction of a two-story residence with sanitary facilities.

The Corps issued a cease and desist order and required DeLyser to submit an after-the-fact permit application. Because the state of New York found the project inconsistent with its coastal management plan, the Corps denied the permit. DeLyser's appeal to the Secretary of Commerce was also unsuccessful. Despite the adverse rulings, DeLyser completed the building and took up residence. The Corps declined to enforce its order citing consideration of funding allocations and the failure of any party other than the state to object to the structure. Does the state have an implied right of action under the CZMA to require DeLyser to remove the unauthorized structure? See State of New York v. DeLyser, 759 F. Supp 982 (W.D.N.Y. 1991) (holding that the state had no authority under the CZMA to require removal of the structure).

3. States cannot review or object to an activity unless a federal applicant has submitted a consistency determination. See NOAA's Dismissal Letter in the Consistency Appeal of Collier Resources Company (April 17, 2002). What is the state's remedy if a federal applicant refuses to submit a consistency application for an activity the state determines will affect coastal resources or uses?

4. Does the CZMA allow private citizens or local governments to sue to enjoin construction of developments that are inconsistent with a federally approved state coastal management plan? See Town of North Hempstead v. Village of North Hills, 482 F. Supp. 900, 905 (E.D.N.Y. 1979) (finding the CZMA "is neither a jurisdictional grant, nor a basis for stating a claim upon which relief can be granted," the court dismissed CZMA claim against the village by neighboring town); see also Save Our Dunes v. Alabama Department of Environmental Management, 834 F.2d 984 (11th Cir. 1987), rev'g, Save Our Dunes v. Pegues, 661 F. Supp. 18 (M.D. Ala. 1987) (plaintiffs held not to have standing to appeal coastal permit decision); and Serrano–Lopez v. Cooper, 193 F. Supp. 2d 424 (D.P.R. 2002) (private individuals can achieve no prudential standing to sue under the CZMA through the APA). But see, City of Sausalito v. O'Neill, 386 F.3d 1186, 1201 (9th Cir. 2004) where the Ninth Circuit held "that adversely affected local governments are within the zone of

interests of the CZMA, as parties adversely affected or aggrieved by an improper consistency determination." See also Friends of Earth v. U.S. Navy, 841 F.2d 927, 928 (9th Cir. 1988) (recognizing the standing of environmental groups under the CZMA).

5. How much discretion do agencies have in determining whether a federal activity is consistent "to the maximum extent practicable"? NOAA's regulations provide that federal activities must be "fully consistent with the enforceable policies of [state] programs unless full consistency is prohibited by existing law applicable to the Federal agency. * * * The Act was intended to cause substantive changes in Federal agency decision making within the context of the discretionary powers residing in such agencies. Accordingly, whenever legally permissible, Federal agencies shall consider the enforceable policies of management programs as requirements to be adhered to in addition to existing Federal agency statutory mandates." 15 C.F.R. § 930.32(a)(1)–(2).

Assume the U.S. Army Corps of Engineers decides to engage in a project in the coastal zone to which the state objects as being inconsistent with its federally approved coastal zone management program. After the state objects, the Army Corps of Engineers sends the appropriate state agency a letter in which the Corps asserts that the project "is consistent to the maximum extent practicable" with the state program. Does that end the matter? May the Corps proceed with its project? What right does the state have to participate in the determination of whether the activity indeed is consistent to the maximum extent possible? See 15 C.F.R. §§ 930.39 (content of a consistency determination); §§ 930.41(providing guidelines for state response and grounds for disagreement), § 930.39(d) (authorizing the federal agency to apply its more restrictive standards), § 930.36 and § 930.44–.45 (providing for mediation).

6. For federal agency action to be consistent with a state coastal management program, are federal agencies required to get state permits required by legislation included in the state plan? Compare Minnesota v. Hoffman, 543 F.2d 1198 (8th Cir. 1976), cert. denied 430 U.S. 977 (1977) (Clean Water Act section 404 exempts the U.S. Army Corps of Engineers from state requirements relating to the discharge of dredged spoil) with the more recent cases, Friends of the Earth v. United States Navy, 841 F.2d 927 (9th Cir. 1988) (Navy must have a state permit under Washington's Shoreline Management Act before continuing with dredging and filling related to a homeport project) and Sierra Club v. Marsh, 692 F. Supp. 1210 (S.D. Cal. 1988) (The California Coastal Act will not be applied when it is hostile to the federal purpose of discharging its obligation to protect endangered species). See also California Coastal Comm'n v. Granite Rock Co., 480 U.S. 572 (1987).

The NOAA regulations relating to this issue of state permits appear somewhat ambiguous.

(e) State permit requirements. Federal law, other than the CZMA, may require a Federal agency to obtain a State permit. Even when Federal agencies are not required to obtain State permits, Federal agencies shall still be consistent to the maximum extent practicable with the enforceable policies that are contained in such State permit programs that are part of a management program. 15 C.F.R. § 930.39.

In Mountain Rhythm Resources v. FERC, 302 F.3d 958 (9th Cir. Aug. 23, 2002) (cited with approval by NOAA in the publication of 2006 regulations, 71 Fed. Reg. 788, 824), the court found that there are "federal and state law concerns for protecting and managing coastline that Congress has declared to be limitations on FERC's power. Specifically, the [CZMA] provides that if a hydropower project is located in a state's coastal zone, then FERC cannot issue the license unless the state's applicable agency concurs that the proposed project is consistent with the state's Coastal Zone Management Program * * *." Id. at 960. The court also found that requiring a state permit as part of the CZMA federal consistency process, does not "strip" the federal government of its exclusive grant of authority to issue licenses for hydropower projects. But "the [state] permit is not a power permit; it is merely part of the consistency evaluation process invoked by the responsible state agency, [Dept. of Ecology], in exercising its authority to assess consistency with state coastal zone management that Congress has granted to the states in the CZMA." Id. at 967. The court explained that the state "permit does not in any way supplant FERC's authority, but is a confirmation that a proposed project complies with state waterway zoning regulations. FERC remains the only authority that can issue power licenses. And with the deliberate concurrence of the Secretary of Commerce about consistency with the CZMA, FERC may do this even over state objection." Id.

7. How does the consistency requirement apply in the case of general permits issued by federal agencies? 15 C.F.R. § 930.31(d) confirms that proposal of a general permit is a federal agency activity requiring consistency review, but the exercise of a general permit does not involve case-by-case or individual issuance of a license or permit by a federal agency. If a state concurs with the general permit, it "removes the need" for state consistency review of individual uses under the general permit. But what if the state objects to the general permit? Can a state object to activities not subject to individual action by a federal agency?

> * * * [I]f a State agency objects to the general permit, then the Federal agency shall notify potential users of the general permit that the general permit is not available for use in that State unless an applicant * * *, who wants to use the general permit in that State provides the State agency with a consistency certification"

15 C.F.R. § 930.31(d).

For example, in the OCS oil and gas context, if a state has concurred with the EPA's consistency determination for creation of an OCS National Pollutant Discharge Elimination System (NPDES) general permit under the Clean Water Act, then the state may not review the use of the NPDES general permit for consistency at the OCS exploration or development plan stage of review or when a facility files a notice of intent to be covered by a general permit under the NPDES regulations. If, however, a State objects to the OCS NPDES general permit, then each general permit user must file a consistency certification with the state and obtain the state's concurrence before it may undertake the activity authorized by the NPDES general permit.

2. PERVASIVE ISSUES IN COASTAL PLANNING AND MANAGEMENT

State coastal management programs may be approaching major crossroads at which difficult, complex policy choices will have to be made. While escalating coastal property values, ever increasing development pressures, coastal population rise, and the burgeoning flow of day-tripping and vacationing public into coastal regions have made the protection of important coastal land and water resources and resolution of use conflicts perennial issues, this century's overarching issue will be climate change and adaption to sea level rise. Design and criteria for the type, location and extent of development on retreating coastlines will be in the forefront. Gathering the necessary data to support these criteria and continued monitoring of development trends and impacts upon coastal resources may seriously tax available fiscal resources and agency personnel. What beaches will be nourished; what shoreline will be hardened; and, what areas will be left to the unpredictable forces of nature? Complicating such decisions are the necessity to respond to the taxpaying public's demand for continued access to public resources and the limitations on state regulatory power flowing from the Fifth Amendment's Taking Clause. The aim of this Section is to examine some fundamental legal and policy issues inherent in the choices that are being made.

A. CRITERIA FOR COASTAL DEVELOPMENT

1. Water Dependency and Working Waterfronts

National policy reflected in the CZMA is

> to encourage and assist states to exercise effectively their responsibilities in the coastal zone through the development and implementation of management programs * * * which programs should at least provide for—

> * * *

> (D) priority consideration being given to coastal dependent uses * * *

16 U.S.C. § 1452(2)(D). Specifically the CZMA requires states to identify in their coastal management programs:

(B) A definition of what shall constitute permissible land uses and water uses within the coastal zone which have a direct and significant impact on the coastal waters. * * *

(E) Broad guidelines on priorities of uses in particular areas, including specifically those uses of lowest priority.

16 U.S.C. § 1455(d)(2).

Both in defining permissible coastal zone uses and establishing priorities of uses, water dependency has often been identified as a factor. Why? What factors should be taken into account in determining whether to protect or prioritize water dependent uses? Are uses that are dependent upon being on or having access to the water inherently more valuable to a state or community? With waterfront property becoming more scarce and consequently more valuable, can important water dependent uses compete for the space if only market forces control development of the waterfront? Should non-economic factors be taken into account in protecting water dependent uses? How narrowly should this term be construed? How should water dependency be evaluated in the case of multiple use developments? Should multi-use projects be allowed only if the primary purpose is water dependent? Consider these questions in light of the following case and notes.

PAYNE V. CITY OF MIAMI

Court of Appeal of Florida, 2010
53 So. 3d 258,
review denied by Balbino Investments, LLC v. Payne, 2011
69 So.3d 277 (2011)

ROTHENBERG, JUDGE.

Riverside owns a 4.3–acre parcel located on the south side of the Miami River at 2215 N.W. 14th Street, Miami, Florida. Riverside applied for and obtained from the City a small scale amendment to the Future Land Use Map ("FLUM Amendment") of the Miami Comprehensive Neighborhood Plan ("Comprehensive Plan"), changing the land use designation of the property from Industrial to Restricted Commercial. Riverside also applied for and obtained a zoning change from SD–4.2 Waterfront Industrial to C–1 Restricted Commercial, and a Major Use Special Permit ("MUSP"), thereby allowing Riverside to construct a multi-family development project with a maximum density of 150 units per acre on the property. The ordinance approving the FLUM Amendment was adopted by the City Commission on January 26, 2006, and was signed by the Mayor on January 31, 2006. The City approved the rezoning of the property and the MUSP on the same day. The approved development on this 4.3–acre waterfront parcel is for two twelve-story residential condominiums consisting of 633 dwelling units.

* * * After a hearing, the administrative law judge ("ALJ") issued a Recommended Order, which was subsequently adopted by the State of Florida Department of Community Affairs ("the Department"), and to which the appellants now appeal.

* * *

After performing a careful and thorough review of the record, we conclude that because the ALJ: (1) failed to examine the FLUM Amendment's impact upon, and consistency with, fundamental policy decisions contained in both the Comprehensive Plan and the Miami River Master Plan; and (2) made material findings that are unsupported by competent, substantial evidence, we must reverse. We additionally conclude that had the ALJ considered the relevant portions of the Comprehensive Plan and the Miami River Plan and have only relied on the evidence that was supported by competent, substantial evidence, it would have compelled a finding that the Riverside FLUM Amendment is inconsistent with both the Comprehensive Plan and the Miami River Master Plan.

* * *

[The court discussed creation of a special waterfront industrial zoning district in Miami Zoning Code and set out the intent of the designation.]

Sec. 604. SD–4 Waterfront Industrial District.

Sec. 604.1. Intent.

This district designation is intended for application in areas appropriately located for marine activities, including industrial operations and major movements of passengers and commodities. **In view of the importance of such activities to local economy and the limited area suitable and available for such activities, it is intended to limit principal and accessory uses to those reasonably requiring location within such districts, and not to permit residential, general commercial, service, office or manufacturing uses not primarily related to waterfront activities except for office uses in existing office structures. * * ***

* * *

The Miami Comprehensive Neighborhood Plan
("Comprehensive Plan")

A. The Port of Miami River Subelement

* * *

Some of the objectives and policies found in the "Port of Miami River" subelement of the Comprehensive Plan that the ALJ failed to consider when he found that the FLUM Amendment was consistent with the Comprehensive Plan are:

Objective PA–3.1: The City of Miami, through its Land development regulations, shall help protect the Port of Miami River from encroachment by non water-dependent or water-related land uses, and shall regulate its expansion and redevelopment in coordination with the City's applicable coastal management and conservation plans and policies.

Policy PA–3.1.1: The City shall use its land development regulations to encourage the establishment and maintenance of water-dependent and water-related uses along the banks of the Miami River, and to discourage encroachment by incompatible uses.

Policy PA–3.1.2: The City shall, through its land development regulations, encourage the development and expansion of the Port of Miami River consistent with the coastal management and conservation elements of the City's Comprehensive Plan.

* * *

Policy PA–3.3.1: The City of Miami, through its Intergovernmental Coordination Policies, shall support the functions of the Port of Miami River consistent with future goals and objectives of the Comprehensive Plan, particularly with respect to the unique characteristics of the Port of Miami River's location and its economic position and functioning within the local maritime industry, and the necessity for coordination of these characteristics and needs with maritime industry that complements, and often competes with, the Port of Miami River.

Failure to consider these objectives and policies is material, as Riverside's proposed land use is clearly inconsistent with the Port of Miami River subelement of the Comprehensive Plan. Objective PA–3.1 requires the City to **"protect the Port of Miami River from encroachment by non-water-dependent or water-related land uses. . . . "** (emphasis added). This subelement also provides clear policy which requires the

City through its land development regulations to encourage the maintenance of water-dependent and water-related uses along the banks of the Miami River and **to encourage expansion of the Port of Miami River.** Contrary to these objectives and policies, the City approved Riverside's small scale FLUM Amendment to the Comprehensive Plan, changing the land use designation from Industrial to Restricted Commercial, and also permitted this parcel of land, located directly on the Miami River, to be rezoned from SD–4.2 Waterfront Industrial to Restricted Commercial, thereby allowing the construction of a mixed-use project, which is neither water-dependent nor water-related, to be built on the site, thereby limiting future expansion of the Port of Miami River.

* * *

Rather than encouraging the establishment and maintenance of water-dependent, water-related uses along the banks of the Miami River, discouraging encroachment by incompatible uses, encouraging development of compatible land uses, and supporting the functions of the Port of Miami River consistent with the future goals and objectives of the Comprehensive Plan, the City approved the Riverside FLUM Amendment, eliminated the ability of the marine industry to use this Waterfront Industrial site to expand and service the marine industry, and created an incompatible use, and, in fact, created a "spot plan amendment." * * *

We conclude that the ALJ erred in refusing to consider the Port of Miami River subelement, and find that had he done so, the inescapable legal conclusion would have been that the FLUM Amendment is inconsistent with the Comprehensive Plan. * * *

B. Coastal Management

The Comprehensive Plan also contains a section or subelement, titled "Coastal Management," which addresses the coastal areas located within the City. One of the goals specified in this section is to "[p]rovide an adequate supply of land for water dependent uses." Goal CM–3. In order to accomplish this goal, Objective CM–3.1 provides: **"Allow no net loss of acreage devoted to water dependent uses in the coastal area of the City of Miami."** (emphasis added). Moreover, Policy CM–3.1.1 states: "Future land use and development regulations will encourage water dependent uses along the shoreline."

> * * * Instead of providing an adequate supply of land for water dependent uses, allowing no net loss of acreage devoted to water dependent uses in the coastal area of the City of Miami, and using its land use regulations to encourage water dependent uses along the shoreline, the City approved this land use change to enable it to eliminate the special Waterfront Industrial zoning and avoid the restriction against residential development.* * *

The Comprehensive Plan's goals, objectives, and policy considerations regarding coastal areas, and specifically those coastal areas along the Miami River, are in recognition of how important the shipping industry and other water-dependent uses are to the City's economy.

In view of the importance to the local economy, the limited available areas suitable for high intensity water dependent uses, and strong population pressures of the 1960's, the City created in the mid 1960's a zoning classification entitled Waterfront Industrial. **This zoning classification strictly prohibits uses that are not directly related to waterfront activities**.

* * *

Since any new water dependent or related facilities would involve redevelopment of existing waterfront properties, **these zoning ordinances are considered sufficient to insure that adequate land area for water-dependent or related uses is protected**.

* * *

Along the Miami River, an economic study in 1986 reported that the firms located in the study area . . . have a significant impact on the Miami economy. They employ an estimated 7,000 workers on a full time basis and over 600 part time. Total sales are estimated at $613 million, or about $87,000 for a full time worker. An additional indirect impact of $1.2 billion of business activity in the Miami area is created by firms in the study area. Many of the firms located in the study area are marine related businesses in part composed of water dependent and water related activities.

Miami Comprehensive Neighborhood Plan 1989–2000, Volume II, Data and Analysis, Coastal Management Element.

The ALJ, however, failed to consider the importance of the marine industry to the City's economy or to appreciate that the Industrial land use designation and Waterfront Industrial SD–4 zoning classification were created to protect those uses and to ensure that there will be adequate land area for water-dependent and water-related uses. * * *

C. *Future Land Use*

* * *

The Miami River's economic benefit to the City is undisputed. Evidence presented at the hearing clearly establishes that fact. Florida's maritime trade with twenty-nine nations and territories in the Caribbean Basin pass through the Miami River, providing nearly twenty percent of the nation's $22.1 billion in trade with the Caribbean Basin. A study conducted in 2001 by the Miami River Commission, the Beacon Council, and the City, reflects that the Miami River serves approximately one hundred ports of call (up from sixty-two in 1991) generated $216 million in revenues for the marine related businesses on the Miami River, and that jobs along the River have tripled in the last ten years, amounting to a $35 million payroll. In 2005, with forty percent of the Miami River maintenance/dredging project completed, the industry already began to see further growth. Five marine industrial businesses opened on the Miami River in 2005 including two new international terminals and two new recreational boatyards, generating new local jobs and tax revenue. In April 2005, it was determined that waterborne commerce on the Miami River had generated $805 million in output, $406 million in income, 6,700 jobs, and $44 million in tax revenues.

The ALJ also failed to address LU–1(6), which requires the City to "[m]aintain a land use pattern that protects and conserves the city's significant natural and coastal resources." **Since 2000, fifty percent of the properties designated for marine industrial water-related and water-dependent uses along the banks of the Miami River have been lost due to the multiple small scale land use amendments passed to make way for residential high-rises.** These small scale amendments do not require the scrutiny that is normally required to amend the Comprehensive Plan. * * *

Additionally, while diversification and mixed-use classifications may be desirable in certain locations along the Miami River, **the Comprehensive Plan and the River Master Plan make it clear that these goals only apply to appropriately zoned areas, not to land reserved for waterfront industrial purposes[.]** * * *

We therefore find that the ALJ's findings that Riverside's FLUM Amendment is consistent with the Future Land Use section of the Comprehensive Plan is unsupported by the evidence presented. We conclude, that based on the evidence actually presented, it is clearly inconsistent.

MIAMI RIVER MASTER PLAN
("River Master Plan")

The River Master Plan is the result of a planning study undertaken by the City of Miami Department of Planning, Building and Zoning, to provide a long-range and a short-range vision of the Miami River as a "working waterfront." The River Master Plan provides a pattern of land use that encompasses this "vision" and was intended to offer certainty in the marine industry for potential expansion and investment. To accomplish these goals, the River Master Plan specifically provides that:

The function of the Miami River as a "working waterfront" should be preserved. Scarce waterfront land should be reserved, wherever possible, for use by businesses that are dependent on a waterfront location or are essentially related to the maritime economy of the area.

The river should grow as a shallow draft seaport—a lifeline to the Caribbean Basin—providing good-paying jobs for city residents. New shipping terminals should be located where they will not be detrimental to residential neighborhoods.

The river's role in the regional market for repair, sales and service of boats and marine equipment should be maintained and strengthened.

The marine character embodied by the fishing industry on the river should be preserved.

River Master Plan, Executive summary, at 0.2 (emphasis added).

The River Master Plan addresses the limited availability of land suitable to development and expansion of water-dependent marine businesses, stating in pertinent part:

Within Dade County, there is estimated to be only 13.7 acres of undeveloped land with suitable water access and zoning to permit expansion of water-dependent marine businesses. Of that total, 8 acres are located on the Miami River. **Given the economic significance of the marine industry, particularly in terms of the type and number of jobs created, it is important to prevent encroachment upon the limited amount of land available for growth of marine activities in the Miami River area.**

River Master Plan, The Working Waterfront at 1.4—1.5 (emphasis added).

* * *

Lastly, the River Master Plan recognizes that higher land values and the concomitant increase in property taxes would result in the displacement of marine businesses and that the SD–4.2, Waterfront Industrial zoning was created, in part, to protect the maritime industry along the Miami River from being priced out of the location. It, therefore, provides for specific objectives and policies to protect these marine businesses from displacement by higher land values.

* * *

RECOMMENDATIONS

Objective:

1.3 Preserve the marine repair, service, equipment and related industries along the Miami River that are vital to the shipping industry or the recreational boating industry.

Policies:

163.3.1 Protect boatyards and related marine businesses from displacement by higher land values uses by adopting separate "marine industrial" and "marine commercial" zoning district classifications.

River Master Plan, Marinas and Boatyards, at 1.9. Riverside's FLUM Amendment, changing the land use designation from Industrial to Restricted Commercial, is clearly inconsistent with the objectives and policy considerations relating to property values. Riverside's 633-unit residential towers will most likely raise the property values and taxes, not protect them, thereby creating a financial strain on smaller marine businesses critical to the working waterfront. The ALJ erred in failing to consider this issue in finding that the FLUM Amendment was consistent with the River Master Plan.

* * *

CONCLUSION

While we recognize that agency action enjoys great deference, findings of fact must be supported by competent, substantial evidence. Furthermore, when the agency incorrectly interprets the law or fails to apply the law, the decision rendered is subject to reversal. * * * We find that had the ALJ considered these areas of the Comprehensive Plan and the River Master Plan, he could not have concluded that Riverside's FLUM Amendment was consistent with either. We therefore reverse.

We further note that these "small scale" amendments, when viewed together as a whole, are changing the character of the Miami River waterfront without proper long range planning or input from appropriate agencies, departments, and citizen groups. Because the Miami River is such an important asset to the City, County, and State, such piecemeal, haphazard changes are not only ill-advised, they are contrary to the goals and objectives of those who worked together, debated, and determined how the Miami River waterfront should be developed. If the City's vision for the Miami River has changed, then that change should be clearly reflected in its Comprehensive Plan to provide industries and land owners along the Miami River with fair notice.

Reversed.

NOTES AND QUESTIONS

1. The City of Miami had elements of its comprehensive plan addressing the preservation of certain areas for specific water dependent uses. Zoning was required by state law to be consistent with the plan. What are the policies underlying the water-dependency requirement? Are working waterfronts the primary kind of water dependent uses in need of protection? What other kind of uses may require protection?

2. How broadly or narrowly should water dependency be defined? Many states define a use as water dependent only if the use can only be conducted on, in, over or adjacent to the water body or requires direct access to the water body. See, e.g., N.J. Admin. Code 7:7E–1.8; Fla. Admin. Code r. 18–21.003(66). Other states refine this definition by listing certain uses as water dependent, and specifically excluding other uses. See, e.g., Mass. Regs. Code tit. 310 § 9.12. How does the definition relate to how the criteria is used? Would you define the use differently depending on whether water dependency is a requirement for coastal development or merely a factor to be considered in permitting? Should a definition incorporate levels of water dependency, like "water-related" or "water-enhanced;" that is, uses associated with water-dependent uses or uses that benefit economically from locating on or by the water?

How are multi-use projects evaluated? In 1000 Friends of Oregon v. Land Conservation and Development Commission, 302 Ore. 526, 731 P.2d 1015 (1987), a public interest group challenged the permit issued to a project that characterized an "integrated marina project," including a marina, dry boat storage, motel, RV park, restaurant, and shops, as not meeting Oregon's water-dependency requirement. The Oregon Supreme Court found:

> The Botts Marsh project was designed as an integrated marina complex. In adopting its exceptions to Goal 16 [of the State Plan], the county was required to demonstrate a public need for such a complex. 1000 Friends does not challenge in this court [the] finding that such a need exists. Neither does it contend that alternative sites exist for the complex as a whole. Rather, it suggests that the complex be broken up and its component uses placed at various upland locations.

> We agree with respondents that the third criterion under Goal 16 does not require this course of action, which would destroy the integrity of the project and largely defeat the purpose for which it was designed. The county was entitled to reject such an alternative. The manner in which it went about making its finding that Botts Marsh was the only suitable site for the marina complex was sufficient to demonstrate that "no alternative upland locations exist," thereby satisfying the third criterion of the dredge and fill conditions under Goal 16.

Is the permit applicant's definition of the project controlling? How many other uses can be "tacked" to the water-dependent use? Compare to water dependency as a criteria for a CWA § 404 permit.

3. In a study on defining water dependency, the authors identified character of place and public access to the water as important to policy development. Additional considerations include:

1. the rationale and goals of limiting development to water-dependent uses; these may involve the economy and jobs, the culture of the community, the physical environment, access to the waterfront and many other dimensions;

2. the uses or mix of uses the community wants to preserve (the "vision");

3. the area to be regulated;

4. the need to have an inventory of resources in order to make informed, rational policy choices regarding public and private needs;

5. the public trust doctrine and the responsibility of state officials.

* * *

A water-dependency test may emphasize public facilities and commercial land uses which are open to the public, whether free or by payment for services, or it may emphasize maintenance of character of a place by preserving traditional maritime activities. Rather than create a contest between these goals and other competing uses, definitions should first seek to promote both increased public access and preservation of traditional maritime activities by prohibiting uses that do not substantially further either one or both goals.

Thomas T. Ankersen and Thomas Ruppert, Water-Dependent Use Definitions: A Tool to Protect and Preserve Recreational and Commercial Working Waterfronts 19–21 (2010). Evaluate the authors' recommended "Best Policy Practice" set out below:

> Most jurisdictions offer two defined levels of water dependency. Our review of these definitions leads us to maintain two levels of water dependency followed by a clarifying exclusion. These definitions, when combined with special zoning districts for waterfronts or other policy tools, can provide a crucial means for communities to protect recreational and commercial working waterfronts and public access to the waterfront.

> Water-dependent Use: An activity that must physically be located in, on, over, or adjacent to water in order to conduct its primary purpose and which, therefore, cannot be located inland.

Water-related Use: An activity not dependent on direct access to water in order to conduct its primary purpose, but which provides goods or services directly related to water-dependent uses.

Water-enhanced Use: An activity that benefits economically from being located on or near the water but that is neither dependent on direct access to water nor provides goods or services directly related to water-dependent uses. Water-enhanced uses are specifically excluded from definitions of both water-dependent and water-related uses.

Id. at 27.

4. Are state agencies able to monitor and enforce development permit conditions effectively and assure that no significant change of use has occurred after the permit is issued? In Island Venture Ass'n. v. New Jersey DEP, 846 A.2d 1228 (2004), the state supreme court refused to enforce a permit condition restricting an adjacent marina site to water dependent use in perpetuity against a subsequent purchaser. Although the deed restriction was recorded, the court found that the description in the Master Deed of the development did not adequately describe the properties affected and did not provide notice to a subsequent purchaser. In balancing the policies of the state's recording act with the provisions of the Coastal Area Facility Review Act, the court found that protecting a good faith, innocent purchaser "will preserve the significant policy objectives underlying each statute." Id. at 1236.

5. Does the public trust doctrine, examined in detail in Chapter 3, provide a rationale for protecting water dependent uses? Does it require a state to protect such uses? In Samson v. City of Bainbridge Island, 149 Wn. App. 33, 202 P.3d 334 (Wash. App. 2009) (review denied 166 Wn.2d 1036, 218 P.3d 921 (2009)), the court found that a local government ban on private recreational docks by waterfront property owners did not violate the public trust doctrine by restricting access to the water by the owners. Samson further argued that a regulation that "completely eliminates private docks—the most fundamental water-dependent use—from an entire harbor of the City" inappropriately balances shoreline development and protection elements of the Shoreline Management Act. The court found that the Act gave no preferences for private single-family docks—only improvements that facilitate public access to state waters.

———

2.   Ecological and Aesthetic Impacts

Development will inevitably bring change. Some of the impacts may be beneficial and others adverse. The determination of whether to grant or deny coastal development permits requires both the identification of which impacts are relevant to the decision and their measurement. Neither is easy. The controversy over the ever growing number of private docks and piers in estuarine waters and in tidal creeks and rivers illustrates these points.

With little oceanfront and sound front land left undeveloped, development is moving into tidal rivers, streams, and creeks. Most people buying waterfront property along these rivers, streams, and creeks do so with the expectation that they will have access to the water for recreational boating activities and most quickly construct a dock or pier. In many of these areas, there also appears to be a proliferation of private multi-slip structures.

Although it is difficult to separate some of the environmental impacts of docks and piers from the impacts of the accompanying suburban and other upland development, a number of concerns have been raised at dock/pier regulatory workshops. Among the concerns raised are: (1) impacts upon navigation, (2) the effect of shading upon the productivity of salt marsh vegetation, (3) harm to tidal creeks and streams and salt marsh vegetation, (4) chemical contamination from dock-related activities, (5) the impact upon the biological integrity of tidal creeks and streams, (6) the impact of related boating activities on shoreline erosion and stability, and (7) possible reduced public access to shellfish beds and other coastal water resources. See, e.g., Evaluation of the Impacts of Dock Structures on South Carolina Estuarine Environments, Tech. Rep. No. 99, S.C. Dep't of Natural Resources 40 (2002).

With few exceptions, these docks and piers are built on public trust lands over public trust waters but, in many states, one riparian right of a waterfront property owner is the right to pier out. See Chapter 3, Section 5, supra at p. 179. But that right is subject to reasonable regulation. Thus, the question arises as to the circumstances under which, and the extent to which, the state may limit or prohibit the construction of a private dock or pier. The issue is especially difficult when there are already a number of docks and piers in the vicinity and the question is whether the cumulative adverse impacts of another dock or pier is a sufficient basis for denial of the application.

KROEGER V. DEPARTMENT OF ENVIRONMENTAL PROTECTION

Supreme Judicial Court of Maine, 2005
870 A.2d 566

Harold A. Kroeger appeals from a judgment of the Superior Court affirming the Department of Environmental Protection's denial of his application to build a dock. The Department denied the permit because it found that the proposed dock did not meet the requirements of the Natural Resources Protection Act. * * *

I. Background

Kroeger owns property on Mount Desert Island with two hundred feet of shorefront on the eastern shore of Somes Sound in the area known as the Narrows. He applied to the Department for a permit to construct a dock. In the application, Kroeger stated that the dock would be used for recreational boating and that its purpose was to access and store dinghies and to access his large boat that is moored nearby. Kroeger's plan describes a 180-foot long dock, consisting of the following: a permanent pier, 110 feet in length by six feet wide; a seasonal ramp, fifty feet long by four feet wide; and a float, twenty feet long by fifteen feet wide. The plan calls for the pier to be supported by a concrete abutment on shore and two granite cribs. The pier would impact 138 square feet of the coastal wetland substrate.

During the process of reviewing the application for the permit, the Department received letters from citizens who use Somes Sound and who criticized the proposal. These included comments from a neighboring landowner, who opposed the construction of the dock and who was later granted intervener status in the Superior Court. Kroeger was allowed to supplement his application to respond to the various comments. Before the Department rendered its decision, it issued a draft order and gave Kroeger an opportunity to comment on the draft, which he did.

In its final order, the Department made detailed factual findings and concluded that Kroeger's application met seven of the nine [statutory] standards. 38 M.R.S.A. § 480–D (2001 & Supp.2004).[1] However, because a permit cannot be issued unless an applicant has demonstrated that all

---

[1] The relevant Maine statute provides in part:

The department shall grant a permit upon proper application and upon such terms as it considers necessary to fulfill the purposes of this article. The department shall grant a permit when it finds that the applicant has demonstrated that the proposed activity meets the following standards.

1. Existing uses. The activity will not unreasonably interfere with existing scenic, aesthetic, recreational or navigational uses.

2. Soil erosion. The activity will not cause unreasonable erosion of soil or sediment nor unreasonably inhibit the natural transfer of soil from the terrestrial to the marine or freshwater environment.

3. Harm to habitats; fisheries. The activity will not unreasonably harm any significant wildlife habitat, freshwater wetland plant habitat, threatened or endangered plant habitat, aquatic or adjacent upland habitat, travel corridor, freshwater, estuarine or marine fisheries or other aquatic life.

In determining whether there is unreasonable harm to significant wildlife habitat, the department may consider proposed mitigation if that mitigation does not diminish in the vicinity of the proposed activity the overall value of significant wildlife habitat and species utilization of the habitat and if there is no specific biological or physical feature unique to the habitat that would be adversely affected by the proposed activity. For purposes of this subsection, "mitigation" means any action taken or not taken to avoid, minimize, rectify, reduce, eliminate or compensate for any actual or potential adverse impact on the significant wildlife habitat, * * *

38 M.R.S.A. § 480–D.

nine standards are met and because the Department found that Kroeger failed to meet two of the standards, the Department denied the permit. One of the standards he failed to meet requires that an "activity will not unreasonably interfere with existing scenic, aesthetic, recreational or navigational uses." 38 M.R.S.A. 480–D(1) (2001). Regarding this standard, the Department stated that the proposed dock would unreasonably interfere with existing scenic uses because it "would represent a sharp visual contrast to the existing shoreline * * * and the applicant has alternatives that would meet the project purposes making the impacts unnecessary and unreasonable."

The other standard that the Department found that Kroeger failed to meet is the "harm to habitats" standard, which requires that an activity "not unreasonably harm any significant wildlife habitat, freshwater wetland plant habitat, threatened or endangered plant habitat, aquatic habitat, travel corridor, freshwater, estuarine or marine fisheries or other aquatic life." 38 M.R.S.A. § 480–D(3) (Supp. 2001). The Department found that Kroeger's proposed dock "would result in the loss of coastal wetland area, functions and values; would result in a loss of marine aquatic life and habitat; and that the applicant has alternatives that would meet the project purpose making the impacts unnecessary and unreasonable."

Kroeger appealed the denial of the permit to the Superior Court. The Superior Court affirmed the Department's decision, and Kroeger appealed. The neighbor, who was granted intervener status in the Superior Court pursuant to M.R. Civ. P. 24(b) has also participated in this appeal as an appellee.

II. Discussion

* * *

B. Existing Scenic Uses

The construction of a permanent structure in, on, or over a coastal wetland is an activity that requires a permit. An applicant for a permit has the burden to demonstrate that the activity will not unreasonably interfere with existing scenic uses. An applicant also has to meet the standards set forth in the regulations promulgated by the Department. One of those is the "avoidance" standard: "No activity shall be permitted if there is a practicable alternative to the project that would be less damaging to the environment." 2 C.M.R. 06 096 310–4 § 5(A) (2002). The regulation also states that even if there is no practicable alternative, "the application will be denied if the activity will have an unreasonable impact on the wetland." 2 C.M.R. 06 096 310–5 § 5(D)(1) (2002).

In the decision denying Kroeger's application for a permit, the Department described Somes Sound, the location of the proposed dock, as "the only natural fjord on the east coast of the United States." It noted that Acadia National Park is located on the opposite side of Somes Sound from the proposed dock. The Department found that the dock would not blend into the shoreline and that "a light colored, linear structure 17 feet high and extending out into the sound represents a sharp visual contrast to the natural horizontal banding of the shoreline, and would degrade the scenic character of the natural shoreline of the Somes Sound fjord."

The evidence before the Department included reports by experts opining on the visual impact of the proposed dock. Kroeger's expert concluded that the proposed dock would be "prominent only from close range," but that it would blend with the existing shoreline. Kroeger's expert commented that the visual impact of the proposed dock would diminish with distance:

At extremely close range the structures can cross a viewers [sic] entire field of vision. At middle distances the structures cross a small percentage of a viewers [sic] field of vision, while distant viewers see the structures taking a very small percentage of their field of vision.

The intervener submitted an expert's report to the Department that criticized the lack of information in Kroeger's expert's report regarding the existing scenic uses. The intervener's expert stated:

People from all over the world come to view Somes Sound. The people who will see the proposed pier from boats and hiking trails will be largely recreationists who, as a group, and especially in a landscape of such national significance, primarily seek high quality settings. As such, they are very highly sensitive to changes in the landscape.

In addition to the experts' reports on existing scenic uses and the visual impact of the proposed dock, the record contains photographs of the affected area, including photographs submitted by Kroeger containing simulations of the proposed dock. The photographs demonstrate the scenic beauty of the area and the lack of other docks. The photographs with simulations also demonstrate the interference of the proposed dock with the existing scene. The record evidence discloses that there are no other docks within 2000 feet of the location of Kroeger's proposed dock, and the other docks on the Sound are more secluded than the proposed dock and are not on the narrow reach of the Sound.

The administrative record also includes comments by members of the public and neighbors. The comments attest to the unique scenic beauty of the area and the fear that the proposed dock would interfere with the scenery of the Sound. The Department noted that Somes Sound is used by many boaters to enjoy the beauty of the area. Department personnel also visited the site and took notice of the proposed location and its proximity to Acadia National Park. The record adequately supports the Department's finding that the proposed dock will interfere with existing scenic uses of boaters, hikers, and sightseers of Somes Sound.

* * *

C. Practicable Alternatives

The Department determined that the interference that the proposed dock would have on scenic uses would be unreasonable because Kroeger had practicable alternatives to the construction of a dock. The Department regulations require a permit applicant to analyze alternatives to the proposed activity and "demonstrate that a practicable alternative does not exist." 2 C.M.R. 06 096 310–4, 310–7 §§ 5(A), 9(A) (2002). "Practicable" is defined as "[a]vailable and feasible considering cost, existing technology and logistics based on the overall purpose of the project." 2 C.M.R. 06 096 310–3 § 3(R) (2002). The Department found that Kroeger failed to meet his burden of demonstrating that a practicable alternative does not exist.

Kroeger stated in his permit application that the dock would be used for recreational boating and that the purpose was to access dinghies, store them, and access his large boat that is moored nearby. Contrary to the requirement in the regulations to provide information regarding an alternatives analysis with the application, 2 C.M.R. 06 096 310–7 § 9(A), Kroeger failed to provide the information. * * * In response, Kroeger stated the drafts of his fifty-two-foot boat and his twenty-eight-foot powerboat. He noted that the float was designed primarily for skiffs and that there would also be kayaks. He responded that a dinghy and three-point hitch were impractical "because of the physical ability required to use one" and that the rocky shore was not conducive to the use of a three-point hitch. He stated that the public marina was two miles away.

In the letter to the Department commenting on the draft decision, Kroeger stated that the dock would be used primarily by kayaks, canoes, a small rowboat, and an inflatable combination motor/row boat. He stated that he and his wife were ages sixty-two and fifty-eight and that it was not practical for them to load a vessel onto a vehicle and transport it to another location.

The Department found that Kroeger has dock space and a mooring at the Northeast Harbor Town Landing for his large boat and that he is a member of a private marina in the area. The Department found that Kroeger did not demonstrate that he did not have practical alternative access to the water through the public and private marinas nearby and by launching small boats from his shore. The record supports these findings and does not compel a finding that no practicable alternatives existed, particularly in the absence of any information offered by Kroeger as to why shore launching was impracticable.

* * *

The Department also found that Kroeger had not met the [statutory] standard requiring no unreasonable harm to the habitat, and Kroeger challenges that finding on appeal. However, because an applicant must meet all of the NRPA standards in order to obtain a permit, our affirmance of the Department's decision on the existing scenic uses standard renders discussion of the other standard superfluous.

The entry is:

Judgment affirmed.

DANA, J., with whom ALEXANDER, J., joins, dissenting. (dissent opinion omitted).

NOTES AND QUESTIONS

1. What factors may a regulatory agency consider when evaluating an application to build a private dock or pier? In Samson v. City of Bainbridge Island, discussed previously, the restriction on private docks was justified by the impact on scenic vistas ("view shed"), among other factors. The court noted "Blakely Harbor's scenic beauty, unobstructed waters, birds, sea life, and the lack of artificial light at night." Would aesthetic values alone justify the restriction on private docks?

2. The few available studies of the impact upon coastal waters of private docks and piers suggest that the actual adverse environmental impacts of the dock or pier are small in most situations. The significant harmful impacts are primarily associated with the related upland development. The South Carolina study concluded that

> [t]he environmental impacts associated with dock structures are part of the cumulative impact of suburban development on coastal watersheds. As a result, the effects of watershed development and docks cannot be easily separated. The proliferation of docks along the South Carolina coast is therefore a symptom of a much more serious problem— uncontrolled landscape development and associated changes in environmental quality.

See, e.g. Evaluation of the Impacts of Dock Structures on South Carolina Estuarine Environments, Technical Report No. 99, S.C. Department of Natural Resources 45 (2002).

3. The number of boats and other vessels in a waterbody directly impacts its water quality and their wakes may cause shoreline erosion and loss of wetland habitat. In some areas, more boat traffic can also increase the probability of collisions with endangered manatees or other marine animals. How should a state address these problems? See Fla. Marine Contractors v. U.S. FWS, 378 F.Supp.2d 1353 (M.D. Fla. 2005) (because act's prohibition against incidental taking of marine mammals applies to recreational boating on Flor-

ida's inland waters, Army Corps of Engineers was required to consult with FWS before issuing dock permit).

4. Kroeger is unusual. In most cases the applicant is contesting the denial of a permit to build a dock or pier of a certain size or length. See, e.g., Serra v. Maryland Department of the Environment, 133 Md. App. 643, 758 A. 2d 1057 (2000) (denial of permit to add a boathouse to existing pier); Fafard v. Conservation Commission of Barnstable, 432 Mass. 194, 733 N.E. 2d 66 (2000) (denial of permit to build pier of size requested); Stutchin v. Town of Huntington, 71 F. Supp. 2d 96 (E.D. N.Y. 1999); Sea View Estates Beach Club, Inc. v. Department of Natural Resources, 223 Wis. 2d 138, 588 N.W. 2d 667 (1998) (denial of permit for 190 foot pier, but granting permit for 110 foot pier); Weeks v. North Carolina Department of Natural Resources and Community Development, 97 N. C. App. 215, 388 S.E. 2d 228 (1990) (denial of permit to build 900-foot-long pier). Litigation involving the denial of a permit to build any private dock or pier is rare. Why are outright denials rare? Do coastal managers not comprehend the qualified nature of the littoral right to wharf out?

3.   Cumulative and Secondary Impacts

During the past 40 years, increased coastal development has heightened concerns over the degradation of coastal waters and loss of coastal resources. Traditional environmental impact assessments examined only the direct and indirect/secondary impacts of a proposed project and therefore were limited to impacts at the site of the project. Of increasing concern is the cumulative impact of coastal development. Critics note that traditional assessments do not protect coastal waters and resources from the incremental degradation associated with multiple projects spread over time. Instead, they assert, that a full environmental impact assessment must also take into consideration how the immediate effects of a particular project may interact and combine with other projects over time. It is only by taking such cumulative impacts into account that fully-informed permit decisions can be made by regulatory authorities.

During this same 40-year period, the increased availability of computer databases, the creation of sophisticated mapping techniques, the use of new methodologies, and information generated by numerous studies of coastal resources and the effects of development mean that coastal managers and others have more information and better tools for assessing the nature and extent of the adverse environmental impacts of development on coastal waters and resources.

As you read the next case, think about the following questions: What is the difference between a direct and secondary effect? How are cumulative effects distinguishable from secondary effects? Which category is more speculative? What are the legal and practical limits to making cumulative impact assessments? To what extent should other existing projects and future development be taken into account when making an assessment of a particular project for which a permit is being sought? What are the geographic boundaries of a cumulative effects assessment?

CONSERVANCY, INC. V. A. VERNON ALLEN BUILDER

First District Court of Appeals for Florida, 1991
580 So.2d 772

WIGGENTON, JUDGE.

The Conservancy, Inc., and Florida Audubon Society bring this appeal from the final order of the Department of Environmental Regulation granting a dredge and fill permit. Although we affirm a number of the issues raised on appeal, we must on one point reverse and remand for further proceedings.

In April 1988, appellee A. Vernon Allen Builder, Inc. (Builder) submitted its application to the Department of Environmental Regulation (DER or Department) for a dredge and fill permit. The permit application was for the excavation and re-disposition of approximately 1,155 cubic yards of material within Gordon Pass in order to embed a sewage pipeline system along the bottom of Gordon Pass extending from the City of Naples mainland south to Keewaydin (Key) Island. The pipeline will be part of a sewage force-main system which will provide sewer service to present and future development on Key Island.

Gordon Pass is located between the City of Naples and Key Island, a coastal barrier island designated by the United States Congress as a unit to be protected within the coastal barrier resource system pursuant to the provisions of the Coastal Barrier Resources Act (CBRA). The purposes of such congressional designation include prohibiting federal funding of any projects that would enable development on designated coastal barrier islands due to their importance to the estuarine system and public health and safety. Key Island forms the southern shore of Gordon Pass. As a coastal barrier island, Key Island enables the existence and functioning of the estuarine system to the west and serves as a buffer to wave action from the Gulf of Mexico. As numerous witnesses and experts confirmed before the hearing officer, Key Island is a dynamic, evolving and inseparable part of the estuarine system. In turn, the estuarine system is dependent upon and cannot be separated from Key Island for its existence.

The northern tip of Key Island is within the city limits of Naples and contains the Keewaydin Club, a vacation resort long ago developed for an existing small private club. Its existence is so limited that its impact was determined to be minimal by Congress so as to require that Key Island be designated as an undeveloped coastal barrier island entitled to protection pursuant to the CBRA. The proposed subaqueous sewage pipeline is intended to serve the club's existing facilities which presently utilize septic tanks, as well as a proposed new development of 75 exclusive estate homes intended to be built by Builder. * * *

Appellants have raised four issues on appeal challenging DER's decision to grant the dredge and fill permit. We affirm Points I, III and IV. * * * [T]he more troublesome issue involves the hearing officer's exclusion of the proffered evidence regarding the cumulative impacts of the permitted project. It is on this point that we must reverse and remand for further proceedings.

The issue of "cumulative impacts" was initially indirectly addressed in the Department's Notice of Intent, wherein the Builder was advised to make other permit applications before constructing the sewer pipelines if it felt that denial of the other permits would result in unnecessary expenditure of resources. * * *

Thereafter, the hearing officer ruled on the matter in regard to appellees' motion to strike appellants' amended petition. In a pre-hearing order, the hearing officer stated that when the Intent to Issue was filed, the Department was very much aware that the proposed subaqueous sewer main was intended to service a planned 75-unit single-family development. She also ruled that any effect this future planning might have on the design of the system as proposed by the Builder was an appropriate matter for consideration. However, any matters relating to the development beyond the design plans would have to be shown to be probative before they would be considered at the hearing. To that end, the order provided:

> If it can be demonstrated that the sewer main line is currently designed for even more development beyond the proposed 75 units, this aspect of the design and how the design increase affects the review criteria will also be considered at the hearing. However, any extrapolation which predicts future harms from proposed development is irrelevant, and will not be considered as probative evidence during the formal hearing.

* * * In Chapter 403, Florida Statutes, the Legislature specifically set forth the criteria to be considered by DER in its review of an application for a dredge and fill permit. The statutes, the small size of the proposed project, and the representation by the applicant that the pipeline permit is not necessarily related to future development, required that the evidentiary and review limitations be imposed. * * *

Furthermore, in her conclusions of law, the hearing officer made the following additional observations on this point:

> Of particular concern to the Petitioners at hearing was the indirect or secondary impacts from the proposed projects. In the context of this

dredge and fill application, the secondary impacts would be any impact to DER jurisdictional waters not caused by the actual dredging
and filling necessary to embed the sewer pipeline. In this case, DER
considered the project's secondary impacts by requiring the applicant
to have emergency shut-off valves on each side of the pass to limit potential environmental harm from the use of the pipeline within a
sewage transfer system. A total review of the proposed development
in this proceeding is not allowed by the statutory grant of authority
nor is it relevant. The petitioners' concerns regarding construction
activities beyond this permit is not before the agency by way of any
permit application and is therefore not ripe for DER review. DER has
no power to require the applicant to submit all permits for review at
one time.

* * *

In refusing to disturb the hearing officer's ruling on this issue, the
Secretary of DER rejected appellants' exceptions to the hearing officer's
ruling on cumulative impacts. * * *

He went on to conclude that the rule of del Campo [v. Department of
Environmental Regulation, 452 So. 2d 1004 (Fla. 1st DCA 1984)]:

Only requires the impact of future development to be considered
where the likelihood of future development is highly probable given
the economic waste of the permitted activity in the absence of such
future development. Thus, in Caloosa Property Owners' Ass'n. v.
[DEP][citation omitted], the court held that the Department was not
required to consider the impacts of future development where there
was no evidence establishing a reasonable likelihood of prospective
development in the same area. * * *

At the hearing in this case, expert testimony was introduced
showing that the capacity of the pipeline was appropriate for the
loading from the planned 75-unit development, but too small to han-
dle the large additional development which Petitioners claimed
would occur.* * * Therefore, there was competent, substantial evidence to support the Hearing Officer's conclusion that evidence of
impacts of development beyond the planned 75-unit single-family development should be excluded because there was no reasonable likelihood that the pipeline would be economic waste in the absence of
such future development.

* * *

On the other hand, appellee DER urges that appellants' argument is
an attempt to expand the scope of both section 403.919(1)[1] and previous

---

[1] Section 403.919 is as follows:

cases dealing with the Department's examination of impacts that are generally classified as secondary or cumulative. DER explains that "secondary" impacts are those that may result from the permitted activity itself, and "cumulative" impacts are impacts that may result from the additive effects of many similar projects. It, in turn, contends that section 403.919 should be considered to refer to cumulative rather than secondary impacts. However, it does recognize that the distinction is blurred somewhat in cases such as the present one where at least some of the claimed impacts could be considered under either category, in that they include both additional dredge and fill projects (cumulative impacts) and projects or developments that may be facilitated by the installation of the pipe (secondary impacts).* * *

DER's arguments on this point illuminate the difficulties encountered by it and the hearing officer "in attempting to maintain absolute conceptual separations of the permits while simultaneously recognizing that the outcome of each one inextricably influences the outcome of the others." J.T. McCormick v. City of Jacksonville, 12 FALR 960, 981 (Jan. 22, 1990). Thus, it becomes clear that the resolution of the issue involved herein is not limited strictly to analyzing the alleged cumulative impacts, but, rather, depends as well on a consideration of secondary impacts and the subtle tension that exists between the two analyses.

The cumulative impact doctrine was elucidated by the Department in Peebles v. State of Florida, Department of Environmental Regulation, 12 FALR 1961 (1990). Therein, * * * the Secretary of DER ruled that

> in order to [show] entitlement to a dredge and fill permit, an applicant must show that he has provided reasonable assurance that water quality standards will not be violated and that the project is not contrary to the public interest, and both of those tests must take into consideration the cumulative impacts of similar projects which are existing, under construction, or reasonably expected in the future. * * * The applicant's burden of proof includes the burden of giving reasonable assurance that cumulative impacts do not cause a project to be contrary to the public interest or to violate water quality standards.

Id. at 1965–1966. The Secretary went on to explain in Peebles that the role of the cumulative impact analysis is such that the Department is required to take into consideration "the cumulative impacts of similar pro-

---

Equitable distribution.—The department, in deciding whether to grant or deny a permit for an activity which will affect waters, shall consider:

(1) The impact of the project for which the permit is sought. (2) The impact of projects which are existing or under construction or for which permits or jurisdictional determinations have been sought. (3) The impact of projects which are under review, approved, or vested pursuant to s. 380.06, or other projects which may reasonably be expected to be located within the jurisdictional extent of waters, based upon land use restrictions and regulations.

jects which are existing, under construction, or reasonably expected in the future," citing again to the language in section 403.919. The Secretary emphasized that the cumulative impact doctrine "is not a third test, but rather a factor to be considered in determining whether reasonable assurance has been provided that the project will not result in violations of water quality standards and will not be contrary to the public interest." Id. at 1967. He went on to recount that the cumulative impact doctrine was originally developed as department policy and subsequently codified by the legislature in 1984 as section 403.919. * * * In explaining section 403.919, entitled "Equitable Distribution," the Secretary observed that, as the title suggests,

> * * * the purpose of cumulative impact analysis is to distribute equitably that amount of dredging and filling activity which may be done without resulting in violations of water quality standards and without being contrary to the public interest. In order to determine whether the allocation to a particular applicant is equitable, the determination of the cumulative impact is based in part on the assumption that reasonably expected similar future applications will also be granted.

However, in addition to employing a cumulative impact analysis, it has been the Department's policy, for purposes of applying and balancing the statutory public interest criteria in section 403.918, to look "at the actual jurisdictional area to be dredged and filled, and any other relevant activities that are 'very closely linked or causally related to the proposed dredging and filling.' " Thus, in McCormick, the DER Secretary declined to adopt the hearing officer's recommendation not to consider any impacts of the overall landfill project in his review of the dredge and fill permit application to construct an access road to the project. Indeed, the Secretary observed:

> Specifically in the context of permitting access roads and bridges, it has been the policy of the Department to consider what will be at the end of the bridge or road. * * * Of course, if the activities or impacts proposed at the end of the bridge or road are remote in distance or conceptual relationship from the dredge and fill activity, those activities or impacts should be weighed accordingly in applying the statutory balancing test.

Id. at 981. This particular policy, which clearly employs the secondary impact analysis, was specifically countenanced by this court in del Campo.

Based on the foregoing, we do not consider unreasonable DER's position that the cumulative impact doctrine is codified in section 403.919, which requires the Department to take into consideration only those impacts created by the cumulative effects of similar future projects, and not the "secondary" impacts caused or enabled by the project, such as the development in the instant case. However, it is also clear from the Department's decision in McCormick that the Department in certain cases is willing to apply a secondary impact analysis and to consider the impact of the total development as enabled by the proposed dredge and fill permit, which consideration is essential to the Department's evaluating whether the applicant has provided the requisite "reasonable assurances" required by section 403.918. In fact, the statement of Department policy set forth in McCormick is clearly consistent with that set forth in del Campo wherein the Department conceded that it " 'has maintained as a matter of law that in reviewing a permit application for a portion of a project it may consider the impacts of associated development, even where no application has been received for that development.' " 452 So.2d at 1006 (Smith, J., specially concurring and dissenting in part).

In the instant case, we disagree with appellees that the contemplated development of 75 estate homes is speculative and is not closely linked or causally related to the proposed dredging and filling. We perceive there to be little difference between the Department's aforestated need to "consider what will be at the end of the bridge or road," and the necessity here to consider what will be at the end of the pipeline, especially when the evidence, proffered or admitted, suggests that the development enabled by the dredge and fill permit could have devastating environmental impacts. Such evidence would be highly relevant to the Department's consideration of whether the applicant has carried its burden of giving reasonable assurances under section 403.918 that water quality standards will not be violated and the project is not contrary to the public interest. Thus, the Department's consideration of the proposed development solely in relation to the design of the pipeline system itself neglected the necessity in this case to consider potential secondary impacts.

Consequently, it was error for the hearing officer to exclude the evidence proffered by appellants for the reasons set forth in her recommended order. Accordingly, this case must be reversed and remanded for further proceedings and reevaluation of the proffered evidence in a manner consistent with this opinion.

NOTES AND QUESTIONS

1. In Kroeger v. Maine DEP, supra p. 323, the dissenting opinion reminded the majority that in an earlier case the court held

that unsupported speculation about future development of piers that could cause the proposed pier to have an unreasonable impact in the future, even if it would not have an unreasonable impact now, cannot properly support an agency's decision. * * * But we also stated that the

Department could deny an application if a proposed dock would add an incremental effect so as to create a cumulative impact. * * *

Kroeger at 574.

How would you factor in consideration of cumulative impacts into the permitting process? Does it only become a factor when development has proceeded to the point that the environmental systems are severely stressed? Should it be a consideration in evaluating the first application for development in an area? How would this work? See Alison Rieser, Managing the Cumulative Effects of Coastal Land Development: Can Maine Law Meet the Challenge? 139 Maine L. Rev. 321 (1987).

Florida Statute 403.919 (set out in the footnote in the Conservancy case) which incorporates cumulative impact analysis is entitled "Equitable Distribution." Does this name adequately reflect the analysis required by the statute? Does it equitably apportion environmental impacts among present and future users? Compare the Florida approach to the regulations of the Council on Environmental Quality which define cumulative impacts as "the impact on the environment which results from the incremental impact of the action when added to other past, present, and reasonably foreseeable future actions."

2. Although many federal and state agencies are authorized or required to take cumulative effects into consideration, in actual practice, rarely are such effects taken into account. Many agencies still continue to focus on "immediate and direct impacts of a narrow range of activities." NOAA Coastal Ocean Program: Methodologies and Mechanisms of Cumulative Coastal Environmental Impacts 3 (Marine Law Institute, Portland, ME, 1995). Consideration of cumulative effects presents a number of difficulties:

a. the absence of practical, widely accepted methodologies for making such assessments,

b. lack of staff resources to develop the necessary methodologies and databases,

c. limited scientific knowledge about causes and effects,

d. absence of socially-established goals for the resource or a resource-specific comprehensive management plan to provide a normative context for decision-making,

e. jurisdictional constraints which impose inappropriate geographic or subject matter limits on impact assessment and management, and

f. uncertainty about the defensibility or fairness of basing individual permit decisions on potential adverse cumulative impacts.

Id. at 4. Do these difficulties make environmental decisions based on cumulative impact assessments especially vulnerable to legal challenges (i.e., as arbitrary and capricious)?

3. To what extent should remote impacts be considered? How should uncertainty or lack of information be factored into the process? The experience under the National Environmental Policy Act (NEPA) may be helpful. In general, an environmental impact statement need not consider purely speculative impacts or remote "worst case" possibilities. See, e.g., Robertson v. Methow Valley Citizens Council, 490 U.S. 332 (1989). Keep in mind, however, that NEPA merely requires consideration of environmental impacts in the decision making process and does not impose a substantive permitting requirement. How should this affect the analysis?

4. A 1997 CEQ handbook, Considering Cumulative Effects Under the National Environmental Policy Act, sets out general principles and recommendations on approaches and methodologies to use in cumulative impact analysis. Although the handbook applies to the context of environmental impact analysis under NEPA, the principles in the application of the cumulative impact in the chart below have more general application in regulation and permitting.

Table B. Incorporating Principles of Cumulative Effects Analysis (CEA) into the Components of Environmental Impact Assessment (EIA)

EIA Components	CEA Principles
Scoping	• Include past, present, and future actions. • Include all federal, nonfederal, and private actions. • Focus on each affected resource, ecosystem, and human community. • Focus on truly meaningful effects.
Describing the Affected Environment	• Focus on each affected resource, ecosystem, and human community. • Use natural boundaries.
Determining the Environmental Consequences	• Address additive, countervailing, and synergistic effects. • Look beyond the life of the action. • Address the sustainability of resources, ecosystems, and human communities.

Source: Council on Environmental Quality, Considering Cumulative Effects Under the National Environmental Policy Act at vii (1997)
http://ceq.hss.doe.gov/nepa/ccenepa/ccenepa.htm.

5. In the broader context of coastal development, what impacts, in addition to environmental and aesthetic impacts, should be considered in permitting? For example, should hurricane evacuation be a consideration? Should the effects of sea level rise be considered?

B. BEACH EROSION, SEA LEVEL RISE, AND SHORELINE PROTECTION

"Coastal property may present such unique concerns for a fragile land system that the State can go further in regulating its development and use than the common law of nuisance might otherwise permit." Lucas v. South Carolina Coastal Council, 505 U.S. 1003, at 1035 (1992) (Kennedy, J., concurring).

"The beaches are moving." This was the warning by Wallace Kaufman & Orrin H. Pilkey, Jr. in their 1979 book, The Beaches Are Moving: The Drowning of America's Shoreline. Although labeled by some as alarmist at the time, the book's predictions have been largely realized. In 2000, The Heinz Center published Evaluation of Erosion Hazards, a report for FEMA that bolstered Kaufman and Pilkey's conclusions and further factored in the effects of sea level rise.

The average annual erosion rate on the Atlantic coast is roughly 2 to 3 feet/year. States bordering the Gulf of Mexico have the nation's highest average annual erosion rates (6 feet/year). The rates vary greatly from location to location and year to year. A major storm can erode the coast inland 100 feet or more in a day. * * * Id. at xxvii.

The Pacific coastline consists of narrow beaches backed by steep sea cliffs that are composed of crumbly sedimentary bedrock and are therefore unstable. In addition, the cliffs are heavily faulted and cracked, and the resulting breaks and joints are undermined easily by wave action. Cliff erosion is site specific and episodic. In some locations, the cliffs can retreat tens of feet at one time, whereas 50 to 100 feet away, there is no retreat at all. As a result, long-term average annual erosion rates are usually less than 1 foot/year, but these low averages hide the true nature of large, episodic events. Similarly, along the shores of the Great Lakes, rates of bluff and dune erosion vary from near zero to tens of feet per year because of annual variability in wave climate and lake levels. Id. at xxvii.

* * * Approximately 350,000 structures are located within 500 feet of the 10,000-mile open ocean and Great Lakes shorelines of the lower 48 states and Hawaii. This estimate does not include structures in the densest areas of large coastal cities, such as New York, Chicago, Los Angeles, and Miami, which are heavily protected against erosion. Id. at xxv.

Of these, about 87,000 homes [one out of four houses within 500 feet of the U.S. shoreline] are located on low-lying land or bluffs likely to erode into the ocean or Great Lakes over the next 60 years. * * * Assuming no additional beach nourishment or structural protection, roughly 1,500 homes and the land on which they are built will be lost to erosion each year. Id. at xxv.

* * * 80 to 90 percent of the sandy beaches in the United States are eroding. The East Coast erosion rate averages 2–3 ft/yr. However, these rates can vary over short distances (e.g., 1 mile or less) because of geology, inlets, and engineering structures. Two types of losses can be caused by erosional processes. The first is shoreline retreat, characterized by beach and bluff erosion that undermines structures. Id. at 11.

The second is increased flood damage caused by a combination of erosional processes, such as scour, and changes in beach profile that increase flood risk. It is nearly impossible, however, to separate erosion damages from flood damages because both tend to occur together during large storms. Id. * * *

Research has revealed an important relationship between sea level rise and sandy beach erosion. On the U.S. East Coast, historical time-series data show that erosion rates on sandy beaches— uninfluenced by inlets or engineering modifications—are roughly 150 times the rate of sea level rise. For example, a sustained rise of 10 cm in sea level could result in 15 meters of shoreline retreat. This amount of erosion is more than an order of magnitude greater than would be expected from a simple response to sea level rise through inundation of the shore. Id. at 13.

States are attempting to deal with the problems of protecting lives and property, protecting the economic values of the beaches and coasts, and preserving the beach and dunes systems through a number of approaches. These approaches can be grouped in three general categories: 1) restoration; 2) armoring; and 3) retreat.

1. Restoration

From Coney Island to Miami Beach, there are recreational beaches that are such an integral part of a local or state economy that restoration is an economic necessity. The high cost of this management technique is justified by the revenues generated by the beaches. The process is not only expensive, but also perpetual. Restored beaches may last 5–10 years without renourishment or be washed away the next week by a storm. In a comprehensive study by the National Research Council (NRC), Beach Renourishment and Protection (1995), the NRC supports beach renourishment as a viable method for protecting the shoreline from erosion and for restoring lost beaches. The report also contains important warnings:

Although proven engineered shore protection measures exist, there are no quick, simple, or inexpensive ways to protect the shore from natural forces, to mitigate the effects of beach erosion, or to restore beaches, regardless of the technology or approach selected. Available shore protection measures do not treat some of the underlying causes of erosion, such as relative rise in sea level and interruption of sand transport in the littoral systems, because they necessarily address locale-specific erosion problems rather than their underlying systemic causes.

* * *

WALTON COUNTY V. STOP THE BEACH RENOURISHMENT
Supreme Court of Florida, 2008
998 So.2d 1102

[Refer to the case in Chapter 3, Section 5.E., on p. 193.]

PROBLEM AND NOTES

1. Did the Stop the Beach Renourishment decision resolve all the issues related to beach restoration projects in Florida? What issues did the case fail to address? Did the case create any problems for future projects? See generally, Donna R. Christie, Of Beaches Boundaries and SOBs, 25 J. L.U. & Env'tl L.19, 51–62 (2009).

2. Is beach restoration a viable long-term option for shoreline control and protection? From an economic perspective: Some states report that every dollar spent on beach restoration generates more than ten dollars income for the state. From the engineering perspective: The background rate of erosion on many shorelines is so great that it overwhelms projected impacts of sea level rise. As rates of erosion increase in response to sea level rise, beach restorers will require moderately increasing volumes of sand to be placed on beaches, but the practice is expected to continue to be cost effective for perhaps as much as the next 50 years. How do these insights affect your answer to the question?

3. In general, the benefit to upland owners—private or commercial—is so great from beach restoration that challenges to projects were few. In the last decade, however, numerous challenges to these projects have arisen—usually funded by interest groups seeking to establish private property rights principals. Why? If Stop the Beach had won the Florida case, would the landowners have received significant compensation? Would beach restoration have remained a viable coastal management alternative for the state?

2. Armoring

Seawalls and bulkheads are another engineering approach to shore-line erosion that property owners find compelling. Consider the trade-offs to the public interest in the following fact pattern.

PROBLEM

Joe Snowbird bought a coastal lot for his future retirement home in 1977, prior to any state regulation of armoring shores or filling wetlands. Over the subsequent 30 years, storms, government inlet dredging, and other development contributed to the erosion of Joe's property, causing the mean high water mark to move inland more than 60 feet. In 2009, Joe applied to the State Coastal Commission for a permit to bulkhead and backfill his lot to recover enough of the lot to construct a house. The bulkhead was necessary not only to protect the future structure from continuing erosion, but also to meet the state's requirements for coastal setback and the local government's requirements for setback from the highway abutting the rear of the property. However, the tidelands are designated as critical areas by the state coastal protection law and the particular beach area is a nesting area for endangered sea turtles.

Consider the following questions as you read the next few sections of the text:

a. Should Joe be able to recover his eroded lot? Did he assume the risk of erosion when he acquired the property? Did the risk include erosion only from natural forces? If he is able to recover the lot, is he appropriating state property? Is he "taking" endangered species?

b. Does your analysis change if most of the other lots in the area are bulkheaded? Does it matter whether the lots were bulkheaded before or after any regulation was in place?

c. Would your analysis change if Joe had bought a developed lot and the bulkhead is necessary to protect the structure from the retreating shoreline? Is it relevant whether the threatened structure is a 100-unit condominium, rather than a single-family dwelling?

d. If the permit is denied and Joe is unable to build his retirement home, he is likely to bring suit alleging a regulatory taking. Should he be entitled to compensation? The takings issue is considered in detail in Section D, beginning on p. 364.

Armoring or coastline "hardening" is a term that encompasses seawalls, bulkheads, revetments, rip-rap, groins and other fixed structures intended to stabilize the shoreline. Although armoring can provide short-term protection to endangered land and structures, evidence indicates that armoring increases the rate of erosion of adjacent beaches causing damage to adjacent properties, loss of habitat, and loss of beach access. In general, armoring is not a preferred management tool, but is often the only solution when a storm leaves a structure teetering on the brink of destruction. One might argue that all permits for armoring should be denied because shoreline property owners have assumed this risk of erosion and armoring is a potentially dangerous approach for long-term management. Such a policy is difficult to apply in individual cases, however, because of the moral, economic, and political dilemmas that arise. Would such a policy, however, also run into constitutional issues? Do property owners' have a property right to protect their land and structures from encroachment and destruction?

* * *

SHELL ISLAND HOMEOWNERS ASS'N V. TOMLINSON

Court of Appeals of North Carolina, 1999
134 N.C. App. 217, 517 S.E.2d 406

MARTIN, JUDGE.

* * * Shell Island Homeowners Association, Inc., is an association of all unit owners at Shell Island Resort, which is located at the north end of Wrightsville Beach, North Carolina, just south of Mason's Inlet. Plaintiffs filed this action * * * challenging the "hardened structure rule" and variance provision adopted by the Coastal Resources Commission and codified at 15A NCAC 7H.0308 and 7H.0301. The rule provides:

Permanent erosion control structures may cause significant adverse impacts on the value and enjoyment of adjacent properties or public access to and use of the ocean beach, and, therefore, are prohibited. Such structures include, but are not limited to: bulkheads; seawalls; revetments; jetties; groins and breakwaters.

* * * Briefly, plaintiffs have sought permits to construct various hardened erosion control structures to protect Shell Island Resort from the southward migration of Mason's Inlet; defendants, enforcing the "hardened structure rule," have denied those applications and refused plaintiffs' requests for variances. Plaintiffs did not seek administrative review of any of defendants' decisions enforcing the hardened structure rules, and they have not applied for a permit for a permanent erosion control structure since their application for a variance was originally denied on 6 February 1996. Instead, on 7 January 1998, over two years after plaintiffs submitted their original permit request, plaintiffs filed the complaint in this action alleging twelve claims for declaratory and injunctive relief by which they (1) challenge the validity and enforcement of the hardened structure rules; (2) seek a declaration that plaintiffs have the right to build a permanent hardened erosion control structure of unspecified design; and (3) seek damages for a taking of their property without just compensation by reason of defendants' denial of their application for

a [coastal act] permit for construction of a permanent erosion control structure.

* * *

I

[The court dismissed the plaintiff's non-constitutional claims for failure to exhaust administrative remedies.]

II

* * *

B

The remaining issue for decision is whether plaintiffs' * * * claims for relief in which they essentially allege that the hardened structure rules have effected a regulatory taking of plaintiffs' property without just compensation, for which taking they seek damages, state claims upon which relief can be granted. We hold these claims were also properly dismissed.

* * *[P]laintiff's allege that the rules both facially and as applied violate the Fifth and Fourteenth amendments of the Federal Constitution and similar state constitutional provisions in that the rules effect a taking of plaintiffs' property without just compensation. Plaintiffs' Second claim for relief seeks a declaratory judgment that defendants' actions constitute an inverse condemnation of their property, and damages. * * *

However, plaintiffs have failed to identify, on the face of the complaint, any legally cognizable property interest which has been taken by defendants. The invasion of property and reduction in value which plaintiffs allege clearly stems from the natural migration of Mason's Inlet, and plaintiffs have based their takings claim on their need for "a permanent solution to the erosion that threatens its property," and the premise that "the protection of property from erosion is an essential right of property owners. . . . " The allegations in plaintiffs' complaint have no support in the law, and plaintiffs have failed to cite to this Court any persuasive authority for the proposition that a littoral or riparian landowner has a right to erect hardened structures in statutorily designated areas of environmental concern to protect their property from erosion and migration. The courts of this State have considered natural occurrences such as erosion and migration of waters to be, in fact, natural occurrences, a consequence of being a riparian or littoral landowner, which consequence at times operates to divest landowners of their property. Our Supreme Court has stated that when the location of a body of water constituting the boundary of a tract of land,

> is gradually and imperceptibly changed or shifted by accretion, reliction, or erosion, the margin or bed of the stream or body, as so

changed, remains the boundary line of the tract, which is extended or restricted accordingly. The owner of the riparian land thus loses title to such portions as are so worn or washed away or encroached upon by the water. Thus the lots of the plaintiff were gradually worn away by the churning of the ocean on the shore and thereby lost. Its title was divested by "the sledge-hammering seas [and] the inscrutable tides of God."

Carolina Beach Fishing Pier, Inc. v. Town of Carolina Beach, 277 N.C. 297, 304, 177 S.E.2d 513, 517 (1970) (citations omitted).

* * * [I]n the present case, plaintiffs' complaint does not allege that the migration of Mason's Inlet and the resulting erosion of plaintiffs' property have been caused by any regulatory action taken by defendants, and these naturally occurring phenomena are the primary causes of any loss sustained by plaintiffs. Defendants' consistent enforcement of the hardened structure rules, consistent with its statutory powers, is merely incidental to these naturally occurring events. Plaintiffs' complaint fails to allege any right supported by law to construct a hardened erosion control structure in an area designated by statute as one of environmental concern, nor does it allege that plaintiffs have lost all economically beneficial or productive use of their property; rather, plaintiffs have merely asserted that they have "experienced a significant reduction in use/value of the Hotel," which is insufficient to support a takings claim. (Citations omitted). Plaintiffs' takings claim therefore cannot survive a Rule 12(b)(6) motion.

In addition, plaintiffs' complaint specifically alleges that the hardened structure rules which they challenge were adopted in 1982, three years prior to issuance of the original CAMA permit for construction of the Shell Island Resort. The hardened structure rules were contained in the very regulatory scheme under which the original permit was issued, and the land upon which the hotel was constructed was subject to the restrictions at the time the permit was issued.

* * *

* * * [I]in this case, because plaintiff's tract was subject to the challenged restrictions at the time the original permit was issued and the hotel was constructed, there can be no claim of compensable taking by reason of the regulations. (Citations omitted). * * *

Moreover, even assuming arguendo that plaintiffs had the ability to challenge the hardened structure rules on equal protection and due process grounds, the allegations in plaintiffs' complaint nevertheless fail to state a claim upon which relief can be granted. * * *

Here, plaintiffs have not alleged their classification in any suspect class such as race, religion, or alienage, nor have they alleged that the

hardened structure rules discriminate on such a basis. Furthermore, plaintiffs have not alleged that the rules burden any recognized fundamental personal right, and we discern none from the allegations of the complaint. Thus, in reviewing whether plaintiffs have stated an equal protection claim upon which relief may be granted, we must determine whether the hardened structure rules have a "rational relationship to a conceivable, legitimate interest of government," reviewed under a presumption of constitutionality. We hold that they do; the protection of lands of environmental concern is a conceivable and legitimate government interest, as is the preservation of value and enjoyment of adjacent properties and the need for the public to have access and use of the State's ocean beaches. The hardened structure rules, which prevent permanent structures from being erected in environmentally sensitive areas which may adversely impact the value of the land and adjacent properties, as well as the right to public enjoyment of such areas are clearly rationally related to the legitimate government end.

Plaintiffs' allegations that the hardened structure rules "deprive the Plaintiff of property without procedural and substantive due process of law" also fail to state a claim upon which relief can be granted. As earlier noted, plaintiffs have shown no established right to construct hardened structures in areas of environmental concern, thus, they have failed to plead a legally cognizable right to support a claim of due process. In addition, the allegations of the complaint detail the administrative process through which plaintiffs have been provided an ample opportunity to be heard and to seek review of defendants' permit and variance application decisions.

For the foregoing reasons, we affirm the dismissal of the * * * claims for relief alleged in plaintiffs' complaint for their failure to state claims upon which relief can be granted. It follows that plaintiffs' * * * claim for relief, for damages by reason of the matters alleged in the other claims, was also appropriately dismissed.

III

* * * The order dismissing plaintiffs' complaint is affirmed.

JUDGES GREENE and WYNN concur.

NOTES

1. The nine-story Shell Island Resort was built in the late 1980s about one-half mile from Mason's Inlet. The developers signed a permit that provided: "In signing this permit, the permittee acknowledges the risks of erosion associated with developing on the site and recognizes that current state regulations do not allow shoreline erosion control structures such as seawalls to be erected for developments initiated after June 1, 1979." The units were subsequently sold to individuals as condominiums. By 1996, the inlet was

within 200 feet of the structure, and in September 1996 Hurricane Fran exacerbated the erosion and put the Resort in imminent danger. Were the interests of the condominium buyers adequately protected by this notice? A suit by the Shell Island Resort Homeowner's Association against state agencies and Coastal Resources Commission for negligence in granting a permit to the developers of the Shell Island Resort was also dismissed. The Association argued that the state should not have allowed the developers to build the resort because of its location in an inlet hazard area.

Shell Island Resort has recently undergone renovation and touts the resort as the best on Wrightsville Beach. This was possible because of a more than $10 million project to relocate Mason's Inlet to its historic position (3,000 feet north) which the landowners in the area agreed to fund and maintain for 30 years. The Homeowners Association spokesman has stated, "That inlet is staying where it is for the next 30 years. We've gone from having the most threatened piece of property on the island to probably the safest, with the widest beach." A recent study concludes, however: "Future modification (e.g., dredging feeder channels) to the system will be needed in order to mitigate the infilling nature of the inlet that historically has led to increased migration to the southwest. Failure to contain the inlet within the proposed 'inlet corridor' will result in an unsuccessful relocation effort." See John Welsh, Characterization of the Evolution of a Relocated Tidal Inlet: Mason Inlet, North Carolina, available at http://libres.uncg.edu/ir/ listing.aspx?id=1433. In August 2012, New Hanover County announced the need for a $2–3 million project in the coming year to control continued inlet migration. Are property owners likely to be willing or able to control or afford the costs associated with an apparently endless project? Who should pay? What are the alternatives?

NOTE ON FEDERAL GOVERNMENT LIABILITY FOR FLOOD PROTECTION: IN RE KATRINA CANAL BREACHES

Seawalls, levees and other flood protection structures are likely responses to sea level rise in many highly-developed areas. If governments choose to build these structures to protect private and public property, or builds them but fails to maintain them properly, is there liability if these structures fail? In the case of the levees and armoring by the Corps of Engineers, the answer is probably "no." In In re Katrina Canal Breaches Litigation, 696 F.3d 436 (2012), the Fifth Circuit Court of Appeals applied the immunity provisions of the Flood Control Act of 1928 ("FCA"), 33 U.S.C. § 702, to deny claims of, inter alia, the residents of New Orleans' Lower Ninth Ward, and held that "discretionary function" immunity further protected the Corps from liability:

> * * * Congress . . . included Section 702c in the FCA, which affirms the government's sovereign immunity in the flood-control context: "No liability of any kind shall attach to or rest upon the United States for any damage from or by floods or flood waters at any place." The Supreme Court has read Section 702c's legislative history as reflecting Congress's

> "consistent concern for limiting the Federal Government's financial liability to expenditures directly necessary for the construction and operation of the various projects" funded by the FCA. [State v.] *James,* 478 U.S. at 607 (1986). This court had similarly emphasized Congress's reluctance to build flood-control projects without a guarantee of immunity: "[T]he immunity from liability for floodwater damage arising in connection with flood control works was the condition upon which the government decided to enter into the area of nationwide flood control programs." Graci [v. United States, 456 F.2d 20 (5th Cir.1971)] at 26 (internal quotation marks omitted.)

Id. at 444. The court read the immunity broadly, recognizing "immunity for any flood-control activity engaged in by the government, even in the context of a project that was not primarily or substantially related to flood control." Id. The court did, however, recognize an exception to FCA immunity:

> Although the text of Section 702c could not more broadly preserve immunity, in *Graci,* we read the FCA and its legislative history to include a limitation. We determined that it was unreasonable "to suppose that in exchange for its entry into flood control projects[,] the United States demanded complete immunity from liability for the negligent and wrongful acts of its employees *unconnected with flood control projects.*" We therefore held that the *Graci* plaintiffs' claims were not barred by the FCA, because they alleged flood water damage caused by "the negligence of the United States unconnected with any flood control project."

Id. at 444–445. In the case of damages not subject to FCA immunity, the court found the discretionary function exception (DFE) applicable.

> The DFE bars suit on any claim that is "based upon the exercise or performance or the failure to exercise or perform a discretionary function or duty on the part of a federal agency or an employee of the Government, whether or not the discretion involved be abused." 28 U.S.C. § 2680(a). The purpose of the DFE "is to prevent judicial second-guessing of legislative and administrative decisions grounded in social, economic, and political policy through the medium of an action in tort." Spotts v. United States, 613 F.3d 559, 568 (5th Cir. 2010) (internal quotation marks omitted).

> "The Supreme Court has developed a two-part test for determining whether the federal government's conduct qualifies as a discretionary function or duty." Freeman v. United States, 556 F.3d 326, 336–37 (5th Cir.2009). First, the conduct must involve "an element of judgment or choice." Id. at 337 (quoting United States v. Gaubert, 499 U.S. 315, 322, 111 S.Ct. 1267, 113 L.Ed.2d 335 (1991)) (other citation omitted). "If a statute, regulation, or policy leaves it to a federal agency or employee to determine when and how to take action, the agency is not bound to act in a particular manner and the exercise of its authority is discretionary."

Id. (citation omitted). "On the other hand, [t]he requirement of judgment or choice is not satisfied and the discretionary function exception does not apply if a federal statute, regulation, or policy specifically prescribes a course of action for an employee to follow, because the employee has no rightful option but to adhere to the directive." *Id.* (internal quotation marks omitted).

Second, the DFE "protects only governmental actions and decisions based on considerations of public policy." *Id.* (citations omitted). The "proper inquiry" is not whether the decisionmaker "in fact engaged in a policy analysis when reaching his decision but instead whether his decision was susceptible to policy analysis." *Spotts,* 613 F.3d at 572 (emphasis removed) (internal quotation marks omitted). Under Gaubert, 499 U.S. at 324, 111 S.Ct. 1267, "the very existence" of a law or regulation allowing a government employee discretion (satisfying *Berkovitz*'s first prong) "creates a strong presumption that a discretionary act authorized by the regulation involves consideration of the same policies which led to the promulgation of the regulations."

* * * [T]here is ample record evidence indicating the public-policy character of the Corps's various decisions contributing to the delay in armoring Reach 2. Although the Corps appears to have appreciated the benefit of foreshore protection as early as 1967, the record shows that it also had reason to consider alternatives (such as dredging and levee "lifts") and feasibility before committing to an armoring strategy that, in hindsight, may well have been optimal. The Corps's actual reasons for the delay are varied and sometimes unknown, but there can be little dispute that the decisions here were susceptible to policy considerations. Whatever the actual reasons for the delay, the Corps's failure to armor timely Reach 2 is shielded by the DFE.

Id. at 448–449, 451. The court concluded: "Our application of the DFE, however, completely insulates the government from liability." Id. at 454.

3.   Retreat

The third management option is one that is necessary where beach and dune systems are so dynamic that neither restoration nor armoring is feasible, when the economic costs of restoration cannot be justified, and when environmental concerns outweigh justifications for armoring or restoration. It is also a stategy for planning for sea level rise. Retreat may involve strict construction regulations within the sensitive beach/dune system or complete construction prohibitions within particularly sensitive or hazardous areas. Approximately half the coastal states have enacted statutes creating coastal construction zones that regulate or prohibit construction. Some zones are established as lines drawn at a fixed distance from a baseline, usually the mean high water line, the vegetation line, or a line associated with the primary dune. Fluctuating high hazard zones are usually based on local erosion rates. See Houlahan, Comparison of State Construction Setbacks to Manage Development in Coastal Hazard Areas, 17 Coastal Management 219 (1989).

NOTES AND QUESTIONS

1. Early setback lines generally prohibited or limited construction in areas within a prescribed distance from a baseline, usually the mean high water line, the vegetation line, or a line associated with the primary dune. The distances were relatively arbitrary and generally ranged from 40 to 100 feet. As understanding of beach and dune processes increased and as coastal engineering became more sophisticated, delineation of setback lines has also become more sophisticated and highly technical. Many states now have a second type of regulatory setback line based on complicated calculations of seasonal shoreline fluctuations, vulnerability to storms and storm surges, and the rate of shoreline erosion. See, e.g., Island Harbor Beach Club, Ltd. v. Department of Natural Resources, 495 So.2d 209 (Fla.Dist.Ct.App.1986) (finding that because of the complexity of the technical and scientific issues and the high degree of scientific uncertainty involved, agency determinations of coastal construction control lines should be given great deference), review denied, 503 So.2d 327 (Fla. 1987). How does this complexity affect landowners' expectations about how they can use their land? Is it relevant whether control lines are established and recorded on public records or whether they are delimited on a case-by-case basis?

2. Retreat strategies generally apply only to undeveloped beachfront property. Existing development is usually "grandfathered-in" to lessen the impact of the regulation. Two major problems have arisen in relation to grandfathering of existing structures. First, in areas that were almost fully developed prior to the new regulation, new prohibitions on development that apply only to the remaining undeveloped lots may be unreasonable. See, e.g., Lucas v. South Carolina Coastal Council, infra at p. 365; but see, West's Fla. Stat. Ann. § 161.053(5)(b) (creating a variance from some Coastal Construction Control Line (CCCL) permitting requirements where existing adjacent structures form a "reasonably continuous and uniform construction line" seaward of the CCCL and the existing structures have not been "unduly affected by erosion"). Would the conclusion in Lucas have been the same if it concerned the first house to be constructed?

The second problem concerning existing structures relates to the determination of when they may become subject to the new regulatory scheme. South Carolina's Beachfront Management Act places new limitations on rebuilding structures that are "destroyed beyond repair" and originally banned their reconstruction within the dead zone or seaward of the baseline. Destroyed beyond repair means "more than sixty-six and two-thirds percent of the replacement value of the habitable structure * * * has been destroyed." See S.C. Code 1992 § 48–39–270(11). Reacting to the widespread impact of the Act on beachfront homeowners in the wake of Hurricane Hugo, the South

Carolina legislature amended the law in 1990 to give the Coastal Council the authority to issue special permits to allow reconstruction of habitable structures under certain conditions, even if they were located seaward of the baseline. The Florida Coastal Zone Protection Act provides that CCCL and thirty-year erosion zone requirements will apply to all new construction except "modification, maintenance, or repair to any existing structure within the limits of the existing foundation which does not require * * * any additions to, or repair or modification of, the existing foundation." See West's Fla. Stat. Ann. § 161.053(12).

How does the United States Supreme Court's reasoning in Lucas v. South Carolina Coastal Council, infra at p. 365, affect states' treatment of existing nonconforming development? Can states continue to justify differential treatment of developed and undeveloped land? Does *Lucas* suggest that states should be less restrictive on new activity in developed areas or more restrictive on existing development where regulation is justified? Is it realistic to think that nonconforming structures should continue to be allowed because they are really only temporary (until the next big storm) and will be required to conform in the future? Has evidence of sea level rise changed perceptions?

3. A version of the retreat strategy, called the rolling easement, has been advocated by many commentators, but the current version of the concept is attributed to James G. Titus, the project manager for sea level rise in the Climate Change Division of the U.S. EPA. Titus's strategy allows areas that could eventually become submerged to be developed or continue to be used until the use must be abandoned. No efforts would be allowed to protect the shore or hold back the sea. A rolling easement would further require removal of structures as they became seaward of a specifically designated migrating boundary, such as the dune vegetation line, mean high water, or the upper reaches of tidal wetlands. Ecosystems would be allowed to migrate inland, protecting access and habitat in the long term.

The idea is that there must be clear, definitive planning about what lands will be subject to the rolling easement so markets and investors have the certainty necessary to incorporate and manage the risk of sea level rise. "If some lands must give way to the rising sea, the economic, environmental, and human consequences could be much less if the abandonment occurs according to a plan rather than unexpectedly." See James G. Titus, Rolling Easements 4–10 (U.S. Environmental Protection Agency 2011), available at http://water.epa.gov/type/oceb/ cre/upload/rollingeasementsprimer.pdf.

Titus's rolling easement is not an "easement" at all, but a range of strategies, including both regulatory and property rights approaches, to accomplish the goals of the rolling easement described above. His most recent report (cited above), provides a comprehensive "primer on more than a dozen approaches for ensuring that wetlands and beaches can migrate inland, as people remove buildings, roads, and other structures from land as it becomes submerged" as a guide for governments in planning for sea level rise. Titus, Rolling Easements, id.

4. Coastal building codes have come under considerable scrutiny recently because of the damages hurricanes have caused to substandard housing. The National Flood Insurance Program (NFIP), established by the National Flood Insurance Act of 1968, 42 U.S.C. §§ 4001–4128, has led to widespread adoption of minimum federal building standards for flood prone areas, including beaches. The NFIP is intended to reduce federal flood disaster relief by supplying guaranteed flood insurance coverage to communities that adopt building standards and land use controls that minimize flood damages and property losses. State and local regulation may be stricter than federally-imposed safety and building standards, and governments are encouraged to adopt land use regulations that guide development away from flood hazard areas.

In addition to guaranteeing flood insurance for communities participating in the NFIP, the program also imposes penalties for nonparticipation. If a community with areas susceptible to flooding does not join the program, federal agencies, such as the Small Business Administration and the Veterans Administration, are prohibited from providing federal assistance for development in flood-prone areas. See 42 U.S.C. § 4106(a). In challenges to the NFIP, the program has been held neither to be an unconstitutional coercion or imposition of strict federal building standards on the states nor to be a taking of private property as a result of diminished property values in nonparticipating communities. See Adolph v. Federal Emergency Management Agency, 854 F.2d 732 (5th Cir. 1988); Texas Landowners Rights Ass'n v. Harris, 453 F. Supp. 1025 (D.D.C. 1978), aff'd mem., 598 F.2d 311 (D.C. Cir.), cert. denied, 444 U.S. 927 (1979).

C. EFFECTS OF GOVERNMENT FUNDING

Although coastal areas represent both hazardous and fragile environments, government funding and infrastructure development has facilitated, and even encouraged, coastal development. Consider the effects of government actions like building bridges to barrier islands, providing water, sewage and electric utilities, underwriting insurance and mortgages, and providing relief after coastal storms. Do governments regularly or adequately take into account these effects in infrastructure spending? Is government spending sufficiently linked to planning in the coastal zone? This Section considers these questions in the context of the National Flood Insurance Act of 1968, as amended, introduced in the Notes and Questions above, and the Coastal Barrier Resources Act of 1982, two federal laws with practical importance to coastal development.

1. The National Flood Insurance Program

The National Flood Insurance Program (NFIP) is often cited as a program that has led to the boom in growth in sensitive coastal areas after 1970. See, The Heinz Center, Human and Environmental Links to Natural Disasters: Strengthening Coastal Communities 39–40 (2002). The effects of the increase in building have been somewhat offset by a decrease in structural damage attributable to the NFIP's building standards. The fact that the rate of damage to structures may have decreased because of the program does not, however, take into account the program's effects on the environment.

COALITION FOR A SUSTAINABLE DELTA V. FEDERAL EMERGENCY MANAGEMENT AGENCY

United States District Court for the Eastern District of California, 2011
812 F.Supp.2d 1089

WANGER, JUDGE.

I. Introduction

This case is before the Court on the Federal Defendant's Motion for Partial Summary Judgment. This case involves a challenge to the Federal Emergency Management Agency's ("FEMA") administration of the National Flood Insurance Program ("NFIP") in the Sacramento–San Joaquin Delta ("Delta"). Plaintiffs, the Coalition for a Sustainable Delta and Kern County Water Agency, allege in their first claim for relief that FEMA's ongoing implementation of the NFIP, by, among other things, certifying community eligibility for the NFIP, monitoring community compliance and enforcement with FEMA's criteria for eligibility, and revising flood maps, provides incentives for development within the Delta that might otherwise not occur and therefore requires consultation under Section 7 of the [Endangered Species Act](ESA).

Plaintiffs claim that residential, commercial, and agricultural development in the Delta adversely affects four listed species: Sacramento River winter-run Chinook salmon, the Central Valley spring-run Chinook salmon, the Central Valley Steelhead, and the Delta smelt. Plaintiffs assert that FEMA's actions under the NFIP cause "more development in the flood-prone areas of the Delta," which harms listed species. Plaintiffs' challenges to FEMA actions under the NFIP include: (1) issuance, administration, and enforcement of minimum flood plain management criteria; (2) issuance of Letters of Map Changes ("LOMCs"); and (3) providing flood insurance to property owners within participating communities.

* * *

Plaintiffs assert this process encourages third parties to use fill to elevate properties, or build levees to provide flood protection to induce FEMA to remove the property from the SFHA [Special Flood Hazard Area], relieving property owners of the statutory obligation to purchase flood insurance. These floodplain mapping activities are said to "encourage" these harmful actions, requiring section 7(a)(2) consultation. Plaintiffs further complain "FEMA has issued hundreds of new individual flood insurance policies for the new structures within floodplains utilized by and relied upon by the Listed Species without the benefit of consultation in violation of section 7(a)(2)." FEMA * * * move[s] for partial summary judgment * * *.

* * *

III. Background

A. The Endangered Species Act

The ESA provides for the listing of species as threatened or endangered. 16 U.S.C. § 1533. * * *

ESA Section 9 prohibits "any person subject to the jurisdiction of the United States" from "tak[ing] any such species within the United States." 16 U.S.C. § 1538(a)(1)(B). * * * The ESA's citizen suit provision allows a private plaintiff to bring an action to enjoin private activities alleged to be in violation of the ESA. Id. § 1540(g).

Section 7(a)(2) directs each federal agency to insure, in consultation with FWS or NMFS (the "consulting agency"), that "any action authorized, funded, or carried out by such agency . . . is not likely to jeopardize the continued existence of" any listed species or destroy or adversely modify designated critical habitat. Id. § 1536(a)(2). * * * If the agency proposing the action ("action agency") determines that the action "may affect" listed species or critical habitat, it must pursue either informal or formal consultation. 50 C.F.R. §§ 402.13–402.14. Formal consultation is required unless the action agency determines, with the consulting agency's written concurrence, that the proposed action is "not likely to adversely affect" a listed species or its critical habitat. Id. §§ 402.14(b)(1), 402.13(a). If formal consultation is required, the consulting agency must prepare a biological opinion stating whether the proposed action is likely to jeopardize the continued existence of any listed species or destroy or adversely modify critical habitat. 16 U.S.C. § 1536(a)(2); 50 C.F.R. § 402.14.

The ESA's implementing regulations provide that "Section 7 and the requirements of this part apply to all actions in which there is discretionary Federal involvement or control." 50 C.F.R. § 402.03. * * *

B. The National Flood Insurance Act and Program

A 2004 decision in a section 7 challenge to FEMA's implementation of the NFIP in Puget Sound summarizes the NFIP:

> The three basic components of the NFIP are: (1) the identification and mapping of flood-prone communities, (2) the requirement that communities adopt and enforce floodplain management regulations that meet certain minimum eligibility criteria in order to qualify for flood insurance, and (3) the provision of flood insurance. * * *

Nat'l Wildlife Fed'n v. FEMA, 345 F. Supp. 2d 1151, 1155 (W.D. Wash. 2004) ("NWF v. FEMA").

1. FEMA's Floodplain Management Criteria

Congress created the NFIP to, among other things, "provid[e] appropriate protection against the perils of flood losses" and to "minimiz[e] exposure of property to flood losses." 42 U.S.C. § 4001(c). The program seeks to "encourage State and local governments to make appropriate land adjustments to constrict the development of land which is exposed to flood damage and minimize damage caused by flood losses." Id. § 4001(e). To accomplish these objectives, Congress mandated that FEMA "shall make flood insurance available" in communities that have * * * adopted adequate floodplain management regulations consistent with criteria developed by FEMA. See 42 U.S.C. § 4012(c); see id. § 4022(a); 44 C.F.R. § 60.1(a). The criteria must be designed to encourage state and local governments to adopt flood plain regulations that will:

> (1) constrict the development of land which is exposed to flood damage where appropriate,

> (2) guide the development of proposed construction away from locations which are threatened by flood hazards,

> (3) assist in reducing damage caused by floods, and

> (4) otherwise improve the long-range land management and use of flood-prone areas.

42 U.S.C. § 4102(c).

In 1976, after notice and opportunity for public comment, FEMA promulgated regulations setting forth the minimum floodplain management criteria required by the NFIA. * * * In order to qualify for flood insurance under the NFIP, a community must adopt and enforce a floodplain management ordinance that meets or exceeds the regulatory criteria.

The land management criteria for flood-prone areas require participating communities to adopt land use ordinances that restrict development of land susceptible to flooding. See 44 C.F.R. §§ 60.3, 60.1(d). In relevant part, the ordinances must require new or substantially improved structures to be built with the lowest floor at or above the "base flood elevation." Id. § 60.3(c)(2)–(3). The base flood is the flood that has a one percent chance of being equaled or exceeded in any given year (referred to as the "100-year flood"). Id. § 59.1. * * *

2. FEMA's Floodplain Mapping Activities

Under the NFIA, Congress directed FEMA to identify and publish information for floodplain areas nationwide that have special flood hazards (referred to as 'Special Flood Hazard Areas" or "SFHAs") and to establish flood-risk zone data. 42 U.S.C. § 4101. This data is then transferred onto Flood Insurance Rate Maps ("FIRMs"). 44 C.F.R. § 59.1. The SFHA is the "land within a community subject to a 1 percent or greater chance of flooding in any given year," also referred to as the base flood. Id.

The NFIA requires FEMA to assess the need to revise and update FIRMs and flood-risk zones "based on an analysis of all natural hazards affecting flood risks." 42 U.S.C. § 4101(e)–(f). State or local governments may request FIRM revisions, provided they submit sufficient technical data to justify the request. See 42 U.S.C. § 4101(f)(2). Individual landowners may also request that a FIRM be revised by requesting a [Letter of Map Change](LOMC). See 44 C.F.R. §§ 65.4–65.8; 44 C.F.R. pt. 72; 42 U.S.C. § 4104.

3. Letters of Map Change

FEMA periodically revises FIRMs by either publishing a new FIRM or by making minor changes or corrections through Letters of Map Revisions ("LOMRs") or Letters of Map Amendments ("LOMAs"), collectively LOMCs. 44 C.F.R. pts. 70. A LOMR is a modification of the effective FIRM "based on the implementation of physical measures that affect the hydrologic or hydraulic characteristics of a flooding source and thus result in a modification of the existing regulatory floodway[], the effective base flood elevations [BFEs] or the SFHA." 44 C.F.R. § 72.2. A LOMR may also be issued as a result of updated flood hazard data that requires a modification of the FIRM. See 44 C.F.R. §§ 65.4–65.6. * * *

FEMA may issue a LOMR based on fill activities ("LOMR–F"), which is a "modification of the SFHA shown on the FIRM based on the placement of fill outside the existing regulatory floodway." 44 C.F.R. § 72.2. If issued, a LOMR–F revises the SFHA boundary by letter to exclude the elevated property from the coverage under the SFHA.

By the time any LOMR, including an LOMR–F, is requested, the project (in the case of an LOMR–F, the placement of fill) will have already been completed. An individual LOMR itself does not authorize, permit, fund, license, zone or otherwise approve construction of any projects in the floodplain.

* * *

4. Conditional Letters of Map Change

In advance of completing a project (e.g., a fill activity), a community or individual may request FEMA's comments as to whether a proposed project, if built as proposed, would result in a FIRM revision. FEMA's comments in response to such a request are issued in the form of a Conditional Letter of Map Amendment ("CLOMA"), Conditional Letter of Map Revision ("CLOMR"), or Conditional Letter of Map Revision based on Fill ("CLOMR–F"). 44 C.F.R. § 65.8, pt. 70. A CLOMA is FEMA's comment on whether a proposed structure would, upon construction, be located on existing natural ground above the BFE. 44 C.F.R. § 72.2. CLOMA requests do not involve any projects that physically modify the floodplain. Id. A CLOMR is FEMA's comment on whether a project would be compliant with applicable NFIP regulations and would, upon construction, result in modification of the BFE, the SFHA, or other flood hazard data depicted on a FIRM. Id. A CLOMR–F is FEMA's comment on whether a project would, upon construction, be elevated above the BFE and therefore out of the SFHA through the placement of engineered fill. Id.

FEMA mandates that a party requesting a CLOMR or CLOMR–F provide information demonstrating that the proposed project complies with the ESA[.]* * *

5. The Issuance Of Flood Insurance Within Participating Communities

Congress found that "many factors have made it uneconomic for the private insurance industry alone to make flood insurance available to those in need of such protection on reasonable terms and conditions" and, therefore, authorized the creation of the NFIP "with large-scale participation of the Federal Government and carried out to the maximum extent practicable by the private insurance industry." 42 U.S.C. § 4001(b). * * *

C. The Impact of Development on the Delta.

* * * The Sacramento–San Joaquin Delta is the largest estuary on the West Coast. The Delta is crucial to California's economy and provides critical ecosystem services to the State. The Delta also supports more than 750 plant and animal species, including 130 fish species, and provides critical habitat for a number of ESA listed species including the Sacramento River winter-run Chinook salmon, the Central Valley spring-run Chinook salmon, the Central Valley steelhead, (collectively, the "Listed Salmonids"), and the delta smelt, (collectively, the "Listed Species").

Plaintiffs allege that Development in the Delta has eliminated much of the historical habitat of native Delta fishes and harmed the remaining habitat. [M]ore than 95 percent of the historic tidal marshes in the Delta have been leveed and experienced attendant losses in fish and wildlife habitat. Development in the Delta has resulted in the clearing of riparian habitat along the Sacramento River, which reduces the volume of large wood debris needed to form and maintain the stream habitat that salmon depend on in their various life stages. In addition, development leads to increased sedimentation, which can adversely affect salmonids during all freshwater life stages. Other land use activities associated with development, such as road construction, have significantly altered the fish habitat quantity and quality by altering the streambank and channel morphology, altering water temperatures, and eliminating spawning and rearing habitat. Increased development in the Delta also increases wastewater and urban runoff from lawns, sidewalks, and roads. Such runoff contains pesticides and other contaminants harmful to the Listed Species.

According to NMFS, development in floodplains and adjacent riparian habitat is among the activities that can pose a high risk of take of salmonids:

> Shoreline and riparian disturbances (whether in the riverine, estuarine, marine, or floodplain environment) may retard or prevent the development of certain habitat characteristics upon which the fish depend (e.g., removing riparian trees reduces vital shade and cover, floodplain gravel mining, development, and armoring shorelines reduces the input of critical spawning substrates, and bulkhead construction can eliminate shallow water rearing areas).

65 Fed. Reg. 42,422, 42,473 (July 10, 2000); * * *.

Plaintiffs allege that under FEMA's mapping regulations, communities and private landowners may place fill or construct levees to remove land from the regulatory floodplain, thereby enabling them to avoid the requirement to obtain flood insurance.

> * * *

V. Discussioin

A. Elements of an ESA Section 7 Claim

To prevail on a claim against a federal agency under ESA Section 7(a)(2), the plaintiff must establish that the agency has "authorized, funded, or carried out" "any action" without the benefit of consultation. See 16 U.S.C. § 1536(a)(2). NMFS and FWS have interpreted "action" to mean "all activities or programs of any kind authorized, funded, or carried out, in whole or in part, by Federal agencies in the United States or upon the high seas." 50 C.F.R. § 402.02. "Examples [of agency action] include, but are not limited to . . . actions intended to conserve listed species or their habitat; . . . the promulgation of regulations; . . . or . . . actions directly or indirectly causing modifications to the land, water, or air." Id.

Second, the agency action must be one that "may affect" listed species or critical habitat. 50 C.F.R. § 402.14(a). If an agency action may affect the Listed Species or their critical habitat, even in a beneficial way, consultation is required. Cal. ex rel. Lockyer v. U.S. Dep't of Agric., 575 F.3d 999, 1018–19 (2009) (citing 51 Fed. Reg. 19,926, 19,949 (June 3, 1996) ("Any possible effect, whether beneficial, benign, adverse or of an undetermined character, triggers the formal consultation requirement. . . .")).
* * *

B. Does the Statute of Limitations Bar Plaintiffs' Challenge to FEMA's Implementation of the Floodplain Management Criteria?

* * * The crux of this dispute is Plaintiffs' argument that FEMA has the discretion to carry out its floodplain mapping activities in a way that provides alternative mechanisms to protect the species. On this record, FEMA has exercised such discretion in other regions. For example, NMFS issued a jeopardy biological opinion and reasonable and prudent alternative ("RPA") addressing the impacts of the NFIP on listed salmonids in Puget Sound. That RPA required FEMA to process LOMCs created by manmade alterations: "only when the proponent has factored in the effects of the alterations on channel and floodplain habitat function for listed salmon, and has demonstrated that the alteration avoids habitat functional changes, or that the proponent has mitigated for the habitat functional changes resulting from the alteration with appropriate habitat measures that benefit the affected salmonid populations." FEMA is implementing these and other changes to its mapping procedures to reduce impacts on salmonids in Puget Sound.

Given the existence in the regulatory framework of sufficient discretion to accommodate the changes to FEMA's mapping activities described above, * * * FEMA retains authority to modify how and under what circumstances it will consider allowing floodplain modifications in its mapping activities. This "discretionary" action "directly or indirectly causes modifications to the land and water." 50 C.F.R. § 402.02(d).

* * *

The NFIP regulations permit landowners to exempt their property from the flood plain by artificially elevating it. FEMA implements these regulations on a continuing basis by approving map changes to reflect fill activities. FEMA possesses discretion to modify its implementation of the mapping regulations to benefit the species. If it did not, the modifications made to implement the NFIP in Puget Sound would be unlawful. FEMA's floodplain NFIP ongoing mapping activity in the Sacramento–San Joaquin Delta is ongoing agency action and therefore not barred by the six-year statute of limitations. Federal Defendants' partial motion for summary judgment that Plaintiffs' claims regarding FEMA's mapping activities are barred by the statute of limitations is DENIED.

C. FEMA's Argument That LOMCs Do Not Trigger a Duty to Consult Because They Have No Effect on Listed Species

Section 7(a)(2)'s consultation requirement applies only to those actions "authorized, funded, or carried out" by Federal agencies, 50 C.F.R. § 402.02, that "may affect" listed species or critical habitat, id. § 402.14(a) (emphasis added). "ESA section 7 requires that an agency considering action consult with either [FWS or NMFS] if the agency 'has reason to believe that an endangered species or a threatened species may be present in the area' affected by the proposed action, and 'implementation of such action will likely affect such species.' " Ground Zero Ctr. for Non-Violent Action v. U.S. Dep't of Navy, 383 F.3d 1082, 1091 (9th Cir. 2004). * * *

FEMA contends that to the extent Plaintiffs' assert that FEMA's mapping activities violate ESA Section 7(a)(2), these claims fail because the individual mapping actions are "environmentally neutral" * * * activities that could not possibly "affect" listed species. Rather, FEMA maintains that the appropriate targets for ESA compliance action are the private individuals and local and state jurisdictions that actually completed the projects and "are required to comply with the ESA independently of FEMA's process."

FEMA minimizes the programmatic nature of Plaintiffs' challenge, which is not directed against individual mapping actions themselves. Plaintiffs maintain that FEMA's ongoing administration of its floodplain mapping activities encourages communities and developers to use fill or build levees to obtain FEMA-issued LOMRs or LOMR–Fs, removing the covered properties from the SFHA, relieving the property owners of the statutory requirement for flood insurance. This is alleged to encourage land filling and recovery which reduces the species' critical habitat in the Delta.

NWF v. FEMA explains:

FEMA argues that its mapping of a floodplain is "exceedingly ministerial," based solely on a technical evaluation of the base flood elevation. However, FEMA has used its discretion to map the floodplain in a way that allows persons to artificially fill the floodplain to actually remove it from its floodplain status, and thus from regulatory burdens. There is nothing in the NFIA authorizing, let alone requiring, FEMA to authorize filling activities to change the contours of the natural floodplain. Indeed, such regulations may be counterproductive to the enabling statute's purpose of discouraging development in areas threatened by flood hazards. As a result of FEMA's discretion in its mapping activities, FEMA must consult on its mapping regulations and its revisions of flood maps, to determine whether they jeopardize the continued existence of the Puget Sound chinook salmon. Because the NFIA requires FEMA to review flood maps at least once every five years to assess the need to update all floodplain areas and flood risk zones, 42 U.S.C. § 4101(e), (f)(1), the agency activity is clearly an ongoing one that is subject to the ESA's consultation requirements.

345 F. Supp. 2d at 1173.

FEMA argues that this reasoning is "legally untenable, because "FEMA's floodplain mapping regulations do not authorize anyone to place fill, build levees, or construct any type of flood control projects anywhere." NWF v. FEMA makes no such finding. Rather, that case and Plaintiffs here emphasize how FEMA has used its discretion to permit persons to artificially (e.g., through filling activities) remove areas from the floodplain, which causes reduction in habitat.

* * *

[A] 2006 BA [Biological Assessment] concerned a different FEMA program, namely funding to prepare for and/or rebuild after natural disasters. That the direct provision of funds to elevate structures above flood level "causes" such activities to take place is undisputed. Here, the issue is whether FEMA's administration of the NFIP in a manner that permits artificial activities to modify the floodplain so as to exclude structures from its boundaries causes persons to engage in such activities. NMFS's biological opinion on FEMA's implementation of the NFIP in Puget Sound directly addressed this issue:

> The regulatory function of the NFIP recognizes placement of fill in floodplains for two purposes—1) to place habitable structures at or above the elevation of the 100 year flood to reduce risk of loss of life and property, and 2) to remove areas from the floodplain altogether. Where the NFIP is in effect, barring local regulations that preserve floodplain function, the eventual effect of operation of the regulation to place fill, is to allow more development to be "safely" placed in the floodplain. By its very purpose, the NFIP reduces available floodplain storage of water, in particular the slower velocity, more shallow volumes of water of the "flood fringe, which juvenile salmonids rely on for their survival." * * *

This finding about NFIP effects on the same listed species in another area creates a dispute as to whether FEMA's mapping activities indirectly cause development to occur in NFIP participating areas, with resulting effect on the species.

FEMA's motion for summary judgment on the ground that its map revision process has no effect on Listed Species is DENIED.

D. * * *

E. Is FEMA's Issuance of Flood Insurance a Non–Discretionary Act Not Subject to Section 7(a)(2) under Home Builders?

Federal Defendants argue that FEMA's issuance of flood insurance is a non-discretionary act not subject to Section 7 under Home Builders. The Eleventh Circuit explains Home Builders in Florida Key Deer v. Paulison, 522 F.3d 1133 (11th Cir. 2008):

> In National Association of Home Builders, the Supreme Court considered the interplay between the seemingly conflicting mandates of the Clean Water Act ("CWA") and the ESA. The CWA established the National Pollution Discharge Elimination System ("NPDES"), which is "designed to prevent harmful discharges into the Nation's waters." Nat'l Ass'n of Home Builders, 127 S.Ct. at 2525. Although the [EPA] initially administers the NPDES permitting system for each state, it must transfer that permitting authority to a state upon application and satisfaction of nine statutory criteria. Id. Those criteria test the authority under state law of the would-be administering agency to carry out the NPDES program. Id. at 2525 & n. 2. The respondents before the Court argued that the EPA has discretion to consider listed species in making an NPDES transfer decision. Id. at 2537. The Court rejected the argument, stating that "[n]othing in the text of [the CWA's operative provision] authorizes the EPA to consider the protection of threatened or endangered species as an end in itself when evaluating a transfer application." Id. Additionally, the Court noted that "to the extent that some of the [CWA] criteria may result in environmental benefits to marine species, there is no dispute that [the state at issue] has satisfied each of those statutory criteria." Id. In other words, although the CWA "requires the EPA to consider whether [a state] has the legal authority to enforce applicable water quality standards, . . . the permit transfer process does not itself require scrutiny of the underlying standards or of their effect on marine or wildlife." Id. at 2537 n. 10.

Id. at 1142. NWF v. FEMA found that FEMA's issuance of flood insurance was a nondiscretionary act:

> FEMA has no discretion to deny flood insurance to a person in a NFIP-eligible community. See 42 U.S.C. § 4012(c) (requiring FEMA to provide flood insurance to communities which have "evidenced a positive interest in securing flood insurance coverage under the flood insurance program" and have "given satisfactory assurance that . . . adequate land use and control measures will have been adopted

... which are consistent with the comprehensive criteria for land management and use developed" under 42 U.S.C. § 4102). As a result, FEMA has no obligation to consult with NMFS regarding the actual sale of flood insurance.

345 F. Supp. 2d at 1174. * * *

* * * Plaintiffs concede the mandate that FEMA "must make flood insurance available to participating communities" that satisfy the eligibility criteria means what it says, but argue that this does not mean FEMA has no discretion to place additional conditions on the insurance to qualify for coverage. That FEMA hypothetically could amend the conditions for eligibility is irrelevant to resolution of this issue. It is not disputed that "FEMA [] is charged with developing [the eligibility] criteria and enjoys broad discretion in so doing." Fla. Key Deer, 522 F.3d at 1142. However, once the then-governing eligibility criteria have been satisfied, the issuance of flood insurance to qualified applicants is mandatory, and, under Home Builders, is an act not subject to section 7 consultation. * * *

FEMA's motion for partial for summary judgment that its issuance of flood insurance to eligible applicants is non-discretionary under Home Builders is GRANTED.

VI. Conclusion

For the reasons set forth above Federal Defendants' motion for partial summary judgment is GRANTED IN PART AND DENIED IN PART * * *.

NOTES

1. In Fla. Key Deer v. Paulison, 522 F.3d 1133 (2008), quoted by *Coalition*, the Court of Appeals upheld an injunction prohibiting FEMA from issuing flood insurance for new developments in the suitable habitats of the listed Key deer species in Monroe County, the county encompassing the low-lying Florida Keys, on the basis that FEMA failed to fulfill its obligations under section 7(a)(2) of the ESA. The agency obligations under section 7 are discussed in detail in Chapter 7, beginning on p. 864.

2. Has the NFIP accomplished its purposes or has FEMA exercised its discretion in a manner that has increased the vulnerability of U.S. coastal communities to sea level rise? Should the NFIP be modified to broaden the scope of its purposes to specifically take into account habitat and ecosystem impacts and sea level rise? How could this be accomplished?

2.   Coastal Barrier Resources Act

Barrier islands and spits are arguably the most sensitive and unstable lands in the coastal zone. Until the 1950s only ten percent of the barrier islands were developed, but that situation has changed radically. Today, a large proportion of the developable acreage and shoreline is developed, with an additional 5,000 to 6,000 acres being developed each year. Much of this development could not take place without federal and state assistance and subsidies. Federal and state programs, including flood insurance, transportation programs, sewage treatment facility funding, and disaster relief, have tended to subsidize and encourage growth on barriers. Development on barriers also involves tremendous costs with average annual storm damage to coastal property amounting to billions of dollars and disaster relief creating additional public costs.

The Coastal Barrier Resources Act (CBRA), 16 U.S.C. §§ 3501–3510, enacted in 1982, is the first federal environmental law that coordinates environmental protection with federal fiscal policy. CBRA's goal is to preserve the natural resources of coastal barrier islands, minimize danger to human life from poorly located coastal barrier development, and to end federal support for such development. The heart of the Act is the restriction of new federal assistance or expenditures within designated coastal barrier areas. These areas, known as the Coastal Barrier Resources System (CBRS), have been designated through Congressionally-adopted maps of the areas in § 3503 of CBRA. Restricted or prohibited programs include new federal flood insurance coverage, government loans, and other forms of federal assistance and subsidies. Without such federal assistance, the costs of development and the risks of development must be borne by the developer and the purchaser of newly developed coastal barrier island property. See Jones, The Coastal Barrier Resources Act: A Common Cents Approach to Coastal Protection, 21 Envtl. L. 1015 (1991); Creel, Barrier Islands: The Conflict Between Federal Programs that Promote Conservation and Those that Promote Development, 33 S. Car. L. Rev. 373 (1981). With the amount of coastline available for development dwindling, is CBRA likely to be effective as a long term strategy for limiting development? Will the land be so valuable that development will be economically viable even without government support? Note that the property owners on Mason Inlet in Shell Island Homeowners, supra at p. 342, pledged $15 million to rebuild the inlet north of their properties after the seawall permit was denied.

In Bostic v. United States, 753 F.2d 1292 (4th Cir. 1985), developers and landowners of property on Topsail Island, North Carolina, complained that CBRA wrongly designated their land as part of an undeveloped coastal barrier. Their objection centered on the fact that the alleged wrongful designation disqualified them from receiving federal flood insurance. The Bostic court held, however, that since a § 3503 map designated the island as an undeveloped coastal barrier, Congress unquestionably intended to include it in the CBRS. Such a designation, said the court, reduces federal expenditure and discourages development which would otherwise occur. This is accomplished because developers tend not to build in a coastal barrier area if their only recourse, when federal flood insurance is not available, is to purchase insurance in the private market which can be prohibitively expensive.

Some states have followed the lead of the federal government. For example, the coastal infrastructure policy of Florida's Coastal Zone Protection Act of 1985 reinforced the expenditure limitation approach previously ordered by the governor in 1981. Section 380.27, West's Fla. Stat. Ann., mandates that no state funds be used for constructing bridges or causeways to coastal barrier islands that are not currently accessible by bridge or causeway. The coastal infrastructure policy also emphasizes state-local cooperation by prohibiting state allocation of funds to expand infrastructure unless the construction is consistent with the approved coastal management element of local government comprehensive plans. Section 163.3178, West's Fla. Stat. Ann., states the intent of the legislature that local governments also cooperate in developing funding policies. Local governments are instructed to design their comprehensive plans to "limit public expenditures in areas that are subject to destruction in natural disaster."

* * *

D. LIMITATIONS ON STATE AUTHORITY: THE "TAKINGS ISSUE"

Coastal land comprises some of the most valuable property in the country. Poorly conceived or implemented development of private coastal property subjects owners to natural hazards, may damage adjacent properties, endangers or impedes access to important public resources, and may result in enormous public expense for disaster relief. Recent events, like Hurricanes Katrina and Sandy, leave little doubt that there is strong justification, and even an obligation, for conscientious regulation of coastal development.

But attempts to protect the public interest, to promote or preserve public resource values of the coasts or even to protect coastal property and its owners often clash with private property interests. Coastal wetlands may be virtually valueless to a private owner if they cannot be filled. Beachfront land may be wedged between the high water line and a highway, leaving little flexibility for locating a structure. Restrictive building zones may incorporate the entire lot. In addition, new regulations may disproportionately affect unimproved lots in largely developed coastal areas. These factors make regulation of the coast particularly susceptible to claims that regulation "goes too far" in impairing the use and value of coastal land.

Fifth Amendment to the United States Constitution

"nor shall private property be taken for public use, without just compensation."

* * *

LUCAS V. SOUTH CAROLINA COASTAL COUNCIL

Supreme Court of the United States, 1992
505 U.S. 1003

JUSTICE SCALIA delivered the opinion of the Court.

In 1986, petitioner David H. Lucas paid $975,000 for two residential lots on the Isle of Palms in Charleston County, South Carolina, on which he intended to build single family homes. In 1988, however, the South Carolina Legislature enacted the Beachfront Management Act, S.C. Code §§ 48–39–250 et seq. (Supp. 1990) (Act), which had the direct effect of barring petitioner from erecting any permanent habitable structures on his two parcels. See § 48–39–290(A). A state trial court found that this prohibition rendered Lucas's parcels "valueless." This case requires us to decide whether the Act's dramatic effect on the economic value of Lucas's lots accomplished a taking of private property under the Fifth and Fourteenth Amendments requiring the payment of "just compensation."

I

A

South Carolina's expressed interest in intensively managing development activities in the so-called "coastal zone" dates from 1977 when, in the aftermath of Congress's passage of the federal Coastal Zone Management Act of 1972, 86 Stat. 1280, as amended, 16 U.S.C. §§ 1451 et seq., the legislature enacted a Coastal Zone Management Act of its own. See S.C. Code §§ 48–39–10 et seq. (1987). In its original form, the South Carolina Act required owners of coastal zone land that qualified as a "critical area" (defined in the legislation to include beaches and immediately adjacent sand dunes, § 48–39–10(J)) to obtain a permit from the newly created South Carolina Coastal Council prior to committing the land to a "use other than the use the critical area was devoted to on [September 28, 1977]." S.C. Code § 48–39–130(A).

In the late 1970's, Lucas and others began extensive residential development of the Isle of Palms, a barrier island situated eastward of the City of Charleston. Toward the close of the development cycle for one residential subdivision known as "Beachwood East," Lucas in 1986 purchased the two lots at issue in this litigation for his own account. No portion of the lots, which were located approximately 300 feet from the beach, qualified as a "critical area" under the 1977 Act; accordingly, at the time Lucas acquired these parcels, he was not legally obliged to obtain a permit from the Council in advance of any development activity. His intention with respect to the lots was to do what the owners of the immediately adjacent parcels had already done: erect single-family residences. He commissioned architectural drawings for this purpose.

The Beachfront Management Act brought Lucas's plans to an abrupt end. Under that 1988 legislation, the Council was directed to establish a "baseline" connecting the landward-most "point[s] of erosion * * * during the past forty years" in the region of the Isle of Palms that includes Lucas's lots. S.C. Code § 48–39–280(A)(2) (Supp. 1988).[1] In action not challenged here, the Council fixed this baseline landward of Lucas's parcels. That was significant, for under the Act construction of occupiable improvements[2] was flatly prohibited seaward of a line drawn 20 feet landward of, and parallel to, the baseline, S.C. Code § 48–39–290(A) (Supp. 1988). The Act provided no exceptions.

B

Lucas promptly filed suit in the South Carolina Court of Common Pleas, contending that the Beachfront Management Act's construction bar effected a taking of his property without just compensation. Lucas did not take issue with the validity of the Act as a lawful exercise of South Carolina's police power, but contended that the Act's complete extinguishment of his property's value entitled him to compensation regardless of whether the legislature had acted in furtherance of legitimate police power objectives. Following a bench trial, the court agreed. Among its factual determinations was the finding that "at the time Lucas purchased the two lots, both were zoned for single-family residential construction and * * * there were no restrictions imposed upon such use of the property by either the State of South Carolina, the County of Charleston, or the Town of the Isle of Palms." The trial court further found that the Beachfront Management Act decreed a permanent ban on construction insofar as Lucas's lots were concerned, and that this prohibition "deprive[d] Lucas of any reasonable economic use of the lots, * * * eliminated the unrestricted right of use, and render[ed] them valueless." The court thus concluded that Lucas's properties had been "taken" by operation of the Act, and it ordered respondent to pay "just compensation" in the amount of $1,232,387.50.

---

[1] This specialized historical method of determining the baseline applied because the Beachwood East subdivision is located adjacent to a so-called "inlet erosion zone" (defined in the Act to mean "a segment of shoreline along or adjacent to tidal inlets which is influenced directly by the inlet and its associated shoals," S.C. Code § 48–39–270(7) (Supp. 1988)) that is "not stabilized by jetties, terminal groins, or other structures," S.C. Code § 48–39–280(A)(2). For areas other than these unstabilized inlet erosion zones, the statute directs that the baseline be established "along the crest of the primary oceanfront sand dune." § 48–39–280(A)(1).

[2] The Act did allow the construction of certain nonhabitable improvements, e.g., "wooden walkways no larger in width than six feet," and "small wooden decks no larger than one hundred forty-four square feet." S.C. Code § 48–39–290(A)(1) and (2) (Supp. 1988).

The Supreme Court of South Carolina reversed. It found dispositive what it described as Lucas's concession "that the Beachfront Management Act [was] properly and validly designed to preserve * * * South Carolina's beaches." 404 S.E.2d 895, 896 (1991). Failing an attack on the validity of the statute as such, the court believed itself bound to accept the "uncontested * * * findings" of the South Carolina Legislature that new construction in the coastal zone—such as petitioner intended—threatened this public resource. Id., at 898. The court ruled that when a regulation respecting the use of property is designed "to prevent serious public harm," id. at 899 (citing, inter alia, Mugler v. Kansas, 123 U.S. 623 (1887)), no compensation is owing under the Takings Clause regardless of the regulation's effect on the property's value.

* * *

We granted certiorari.

II

[The Court's discussion of the ripeness of Lucas's claim is omitted.]

III

A

Prior to Justice Holmes' exposition in Pennsylvania Coal Co. v. Mahon, 260 U.S. 393 (1922), it was generally thought that the Takings Clause reached only a "direct appropriation" of property, Legal Tender Cases, 12 Wall. 457, 551 (1871), or the functional equivalent of a "practical ouster of [the owner's] possession," Transportation Co. v. Chicago, 99 U.S. 635, 642 (1879). Justice Holmes recognized in Mahon, however, that if the protection against physical appropriations of private property was to be meaningfully enforced, the government's power to redefine the range of interests included in the ownership of property was necessarily constrained by constitutional limits. 260 U.S., at 414–415. If, instead, the uses of private property were subject to unbridled, uncompensated qualification under the police power, "the natural tendency of human nature [would be] to extend the qualification more and more until at last private property disappear[ed]." Id., at 415. These considerations gave birth in that case to the oft-cited maxim that, "while property may be regulated to a certain extent, if regulation goes too far it will be recognized as a taking." Id.

Nevertheless, our decision in Mahon offered little insight into when, and under what circumstances, a given regulation would be seen as going "too far" for purposes of the Fifth Amendment. In 70-odd years of succeeding "regulatory takings" jurisprudence, we have generally eschewed any " 'set formula' " for determining how far is too far, preferring to "engag[e] in * * * essentially ad hoc, factual inquiries." Penn Central Transportation

Co. v. New York City, 438 U.S. 104, 124 (1978) (quoting Goldblatt v. Hempstead, 369 U.S. 590, 594 (1962)). We have, however, described at least two discrete categories of regulatory action as compensable without case-specific inquiry into the public interest advanced in support of the restraint. The first encompasses regulations that compel the property owner to suffer a physical "invasion" of his property. In general (at least with regard to permanent invasions), no matter how minute the intrusion, and no matter how weighty the public purpose behind it, we have required compensation. * * *

The second situation in which we have found categorical treatment appropriate is where regulation denies all economically beneficial or productive use of land. * * * As we have said on numerous occasions, the Fifth Amendment is violated when land-use regulation "does not substantially advance legitimate state interests or denies an owner economically viable use of his land." Agins, supra, at 260 (citations omitted) (emphasis added).[7]

* * *

[T]the functional basis for permitting the government, by regulation, to affect property values without compensation that "Government hardly could go on if to some extent values incident to property could not be diminished without paying for every such change in the general law," [Penn. Coal] at 413, does not apply to the relatively rare situations where the government has deprived a landowner of all economically beneficial uses.

We think, in short, that there are good reasons for our frequently expressed belief that when the owner of real property has been called upon to sacrifice all economically beneficial uses in the name of the common good, that is, to leave his property economically idle, he has suffered a taking.

B

The trial court found Lucas's two beachfront lots to have been rendered valueless by respondent's enforcement of the coastal-zone construction ban. Under Lucas's theory of the case, which rested upon our "no

---

[7] Regrettably, the rhetorical force of our "deprivation of all economically feasible use" rule is greater than its precision, since the rule does not make clear the "property interest" against which the loss of value is to be measured. When, for example, a regulation requires a developer to leave 90% of a rural tract in its natural state, it is unclear whether we would analyze the situation as one in which the owner has been deprived of all economically beneficial use of the burdened portion of the tract, or as one in which the owner has suffered a mere diminution in value of the tract as a whole * * *. The answer to this difficult question may lie in how the owner's reasonable expectations have been shaped by the State's law of property—i.e., whether and to what degree the State's law has accorded legal recognition and protection to the particular interest in land with respect to which the takings claimant alleges a diminution in (or elimination of) value. * * *

economically viable use" statements, that finding entitled him to compensation. Lucas believed it unnecessary to take issue with either the purposes behind the Beachfront Management Act, or the means chosen by the South Carolina Legislature to effectuate those purposes. The South Carolina Supreme Court, however, thought otherwise. In its view, the Beachfront Management Act was no ordinary enactment, but involved an exercise of South Carolina's "police powers" to mitigate the harm to the public interest that petitioner's use of his land might occasion. 404 S.E.2d, at 899. By neglecting to dispute the findings enumerated in the Act or otherwise to challenge the legislature's purposes, petitioner "concede[d] that the beach/dune area of South Carolina's shores is an extremely valuable public resource; that the erection of new construction, inter alia, contributes to the erosion and destruction of this public resource; and that discouraging new construction in close proximity to the beach/dune area is necessary to prevent a great public harm." Id., at 898. In the court's view, these concessions brought petitioner's challenge within a long line of this Court's cases sustaining against Due Process and Takings Clause challenges the State's use of its "police powers" to enjoin a property owner from activities akin to public nuisances. * * *

It is correct that many of our prior opinions have suggested that "harmful or noxious uses" of property may be proscribed by government regulation without the requirement of compensation. * * * "Harmful or noxious use" analysis was, [in early cases], simply the progenitor of our more contemporary statements that "land-use regulation does not effect a taking if it 'substantially advance[s] legitimate state interests' * * *." Nollan, supra, at 834 (quoting Agins v. Tiburon, 447 U.S., at 260); see also Penn Central Transportation Co., supra, at 127; Euclid v. Ambler Realty Co., 272 U.S. 365, 387–388 (1926).

The transition from our early focus on control of "noxious" uses to our contemporary understanding of the broad realm within which government may regulate without compensation was an easy one, since the distinction between "harm-preventing" and "benefit-conferring" regulation is often in the eye of the beholder. It is quite possible, for example, to describe in either fashion the ecological, economic, and aesthetic concerns that inspired the South Carolina legislature in the present case. One could say that imposing a servitude on Lucas's land is necessary in order to prevent his use of it from "harming" South Carolina's ecological resources; or, instead, in order to achieve the "benefits" of an ecological preserve. * * * A given restraint will be seen as mitigating "harm" to the adjacent parcels or securing a "benefit" for them, depending upon the observer's evaluation of the relative importance of the use that the restraint favors. * * * Whether Lucas's construction of single-family residences on his parcels should be described as bringing "harm" to South Carolina's adjacent ecological resources thus depends principally upon whether the describer believes that the State's use interest in nurturing those resources is so important that any competing adjacent use must yield.

When it is understood that "prevention of harmful use" was merely our early formulation of the police power justification necessary to sustain (without compensation) any regulatory diminution in value; and that the distinction between regulation that "prevents harmful use" and that which "confers benefits" is difficult, if not impossible, to discern on an objective, value-free basis; it becomes self-evident that noxious-use logic cannot serve as a touchstone to distinguish regulatory "takings"—which require compensation—from regulatory deprivations that do not require compensation. A fortiori the legislature's recitation of a noxious-use justification cannot be the basis for departing from our categorical rule that total regulatory takings must be compensated.* * *

Where the State seeks to sustain regulation that deprives land of all economically beneficial use, we think it may resist compensation only if the logically antecedent inquiry into the nature of the owner's estate shows that the proscribed use interests were not part of his title to begin with. This accords, we think, with our "takings" jurisprudence, which has traditionally been guided by the understandings of our citizens regarding the content of, and the State's power over, the "bundle of rights" that they acquire when they obtain title to property. It seems to us that the property owner necessarily expects the uses of his property to be restricted, from time to time, by various measures newly enacted by the State in legitimate exercise of its police powers; "[a]s long recognized, some values are enjoyed under an implied limitation and must yield to the police power." Pennsylvania Coal Co. v. Mahon, 260 U.S., at 413. And in the case of personal property, by reason of the State's traditionally high degree of control over commercial dealings, he ought to be aware of the possibility that new regulation might even render his property economically worthless (at least if the property's only economically productive use is sale or manufacture for sale). See Andrus v. Allard, 444 U.S. 51, 66–67 (1979) (prohibition on sale of eagle feathers). In the case of land, however, we think the notion pressed by the Council that title is somehow held subject to the "implied limitation" that the State may subsequently eliminate all economically valuable use is inconsistent with the historical compact recorded in the Takings Clause that has become part of our constitutional culture.

* * * Any limitation [prohibiting all economically beneficial use of land] cannot be newly legislated or decreed (without compensation), but must inhere in the title itself, in the restrictions that background principles of the State's law of property and nuisance already place upon land ownership. A law or decree with such an effect must, in other words, do no more than duplicate the result that could have been achieved in the courts by adjacent landowners (or other uniquely affected persons) under

the State's law of private nuisance, or by the State under its complementary power to abate nuisances that affect the public generally, or otherwise.

On this analysis, the owner of a lakebed, for example, would not be entitled to compensation when he is denied the requisite permit to engage in a landfilling operation that would have the effect of flooding others' land. Nor the corporate owner of a nuclear generating plant, when it is directed to remove all improvements from its land upon discovery that the plant sits astride an earthquake fault. Such regulatory action may well have the effect of eliminating the land's only economically productive use, but it does not proscribe a productive use that was previously permissible under relevant property and nuisance principles. The use of these properties for what are now expressly prohibited purposes was always unlawful, and (subject to other constitutional limitations) it was open to the State at any point to make the implication of those background principles of nuisance and property law explicit. See Michelman, Property, Utility, and Fairness, Comments on the Ethical Foundations of "Just Compensation" Law, 80 Harv. L. Rev. 1165, 1239–1241 (1967). In light of our traditional resort to "existing rules or understandings that stem from an independent source such as state law" to define the range of interests that qualify for protection as "property" under the Fifth and Fourteenth Amendments, Board of Regents of State Colleges v. Roth, 408 U.S. 564, 577 (1972), this recognition that the Takings Clause does not require compensation when an owner is barred from putting land to a use that is proscribed by those "existing rules or understandings" is surely unexceptional. When, however, a regulation that declares "off-limits" all economically productive or beneficial uses of land goes beyond what the relevant background principles would dictate, compensation must be paid to sustain it.

The "total taking" inquiry we require today will ordinarily entail (as the application of state nuisance law ordinarily entails) analysis of, among other things, the degree of harm to public lands and resources, or adjacent private property, posed by the claimant's proposed activities, see, e.g., Restatement (Second) of Torts § 826, 827, the social value of the claimant's activities and their suitability to the locality in question, see, e.g., id., § 828(a) and (b), 831, and the relative ease with which the alleged harm can be avoided through measures taken by the claimant and the government (or adjacent private landowners) alike, see, e.g., id., § 827(e), 828(c), 830. The fact that a particular use has long been engaged in by similarly situated owners ordinarily imports a lack of any common-law prohibition (though changed circumstances or new knowledge may make what was previously permissible no longer so, see Restatement (Second) of Torts, supra, § 827, comment g. So also does the fact that other landowners, similarly situated, are permitted to continue the use denied to the claimant.

It seems unlikely that common-law principles would have prevented the erection of any habitable or productive improvements on petitioner's land; they rarely support prohibition of the "essential use" of land, Curtin v. Benson, 222 U.S. 78, 86 (1911). The question, however, is one of state law to be dealt with on remand. We emphasize that to win its case South Carolina must do more than proffer the legislature's declaration that the uses Lucas desires are inconsistent with the public interest, or the conclusory assertion that they violate a common-law maxim such as sic utere tuo ut alienum non laedas. As we have said, a "State, by ipse dixit, may not transform private property into public property without compensation * * *." Webb's Fabulous Pharmacies, Inc. v. Beckwith, 449 U.S. 155, 164 (1980). Instead, as it would be required to do if it sought to restrain Lucas in a common-law action for public nuisance, South Carolina must identify background principles of nuisance and property law that prohibit the uses he now intends in the circumstances in which the property is presently found. Only on this showing can the State fairly claim that, in proscribing all such beneficial uses, the Beachfront Management Act is taking nothing. * * *

The judgment is reversed and the cause remanded for proceedings not inconsistent with this opinion.

So ordered.

[JUSTICE KENNEDY's concurring opinion, JUSTICE BLACKMUN's and JUSTICE STEVEN's dissenting opinions, and JUSTICE SOUTER's statement are omitted.]

* * *

GOVE V. ZONING BOARD OF APPEALS OF CHATHAM
Supreme Court of Massachusetts, 2005
831 N.E.2d 865

MARSHALL, CHIEF JUSTICE.

* * *

I. Background

Lot 93 is located in the Little Beach section of Chatham, nearly all of which was acquired by Gove's parents (the Horne family) in 1926. In time, members of the Horne family developed a motel, marina, rental "cottage colonies," and a number of single-family houses in Little Beach. The family also sold several lots for development. In 1975, that portion of Little Beach still owned by the Horne family was divided, by the terms of the will of Gove's mother, among Gove and her three brothers. Gove received several lots outright and sixteen other lots in fractional ownership, to be shared with her brothers. Gove also obtained title to at least two cottages. Gove continues to own one cottage in Little Beach; she sold a second in 1996.

Little Beach is part of a narrow, low-lying peninsula, bounded by Chatham Harbor and Stage Harbor, at the extreme southeastern corner of Cape Cod. In recent years, a "breach" has formed in the barrier island that long separated Chatham Harbor from the open ocean. The breach, which is widening, lies directly across the harbor from Little Beach, and a land surveyor familiar with the area testified that Little Beach is now "wide open to the Atlantic Ocean" and prone to northeasterly storm tides. Chatham is known for its vulnerability to storms, and, according to an expert retained by Gove and the Greniers, in recent years Chatham has "as a direct result of the breach" experienced a "significant erosion problem," including "houses falling into the sea." The same expert testified that, since the appearance of the breach, "there had been a significant rise in the mean high water [near lot 93] along Chatham Harbor." The record indicates that virtually no development has occurred in Little Beach since 1980.

Even before the breach developed, Little Beach was prone to inundation by seawater. Gove testified that the area was flooded by hurricanes in 1938, 1944, and 1954, and by a significant off-shore ocean storm in 1991. None of these storms struck Chatham directly, but in the 1944 hurricane, Stage Harbor experienced a storm surge some nine feet above sea level. The 1954 hurricane damaged buildings and flooded roads in Little Beach. The 1991 storm flooded the area around lot 93 to a depth of between seven and nine feet above sea level, placing most, if not all, of the parcel underwater. The 1944, 1954, and 1991 storms, while significant, were less severe than the hypothetical "hundred year storm" used for planning purposes, which is projected to flood the area to a depth of ten feet. According to another expert called by Gove and the Greniers, during storms, roads in Little Beach can become so flooded as to be impassable even to emergency vehicles, and access to the area requires "other emergency response methods," such as "helicopters or boats." The same expert conceded that, in an "extreme" event, the area could be flooded for four days, and that, in "more severe events" than a hundred year storm, storm surge flooding in Little Beach would exceed ten feet.

Lot 93 itself consists of approximately 1.8 acres. The lot is within approximately 500 feet of both Stage Harbor and Chatham Harbor and, according to one expert, is susceptible to coastal flooding "from both the front side and the backside of [the] property." The lot is bisected by a tidal creek, which is prone to flooding as well. The highest point on the property is 8.7 feet above sea level, and much of the property is less than four feet above sea level and technically a "wetland." According to a 1998 map issued by the Federal Emergency Management Agency, lot 93 lies entirely within flood hazard "Zone A," an area defined by its vulnerability to "significant flooding" in "hundred year storms." Lot 93 also lies immediately outside "Zone V" where, during a hundred year storm, significant flooding with wave action can be expected.

Gove inherited lot 93 in 1975, when residential development was permitted on the parcel. In 1985, however, the town placed all of the land within the hundred year coastal flood plain, including lot 93, into the conservancy district. The stated purposes of the conservancy district include maintaining the ground water supply, protecting coastal areas, protecting public health and safety, reducing the risk to people and property from "extreme high tides and the rising sea level," and conserving natural resources. The town zoning officer testified that the conservancy district serves to mitigate the "total public safety problem" of coastal flooding, and was specifically intended to protect both residents and public safety personnel.

The bylaw governing the conservancy district bars without exception the construction of new residential dwellings. The bylaw does allow specified nonresidential uses, either as of right or by special permit. The zoning officer testified that the nonresidential uses are less likely to create a danger in the event of a flood than are residential structures, in part because structures "ancillary" to homes "tend to break off" in storms and "do a lot of collateral damage to other structures and property," whereas such damage is less likely when nonresidential structures, normally more firmly anchored to the ground, are built.

In the years before the zoning regulations were amended to restrict development in the hundred year flood zone, Gove attempted to sell lot 93. She listed the lot and another she owned with a local broker but "had no offers" on the properties, and she withdrew them from the market. Gove further testified that, whatever its value before the breach developed, lot 93's worth had "plummeted" as a result of the breach and the property "had no value . . . whatsoever" in the early 1990's. By the late 1990's, property in the area had gained value, she said, but the land, she clarified, was still most attractive to those who "have lived in the area" and were unswayed by frequent media reports of storm damage in Chatham.

In 1998, the Greniers contracted to purchase lot 93 from Gove for $192,000, contingent on their ability to obtain permits for a home and a septic system on the site. The Greniers proposed to develop a house on lot 93 on land between 5.3 and 7.0 feet in elevation. They proposed to construct the home raised on pilings, so that the level of the first floor would be above the level of a hundred year flood.

A zoning officer denied the Greniers a permit to build a house on the property. The board upheld the decision of the zoning officer. Gove and the Greniers then filed one suit against the selectmen and board and another against the conservation commission of Chatham. A Superior Court judge consolidated the actions, and the parties agreed to a bifurcated trial in which all claims, except for the issue of compensation, would first be tried before a judge, with issues of compensation then tried, if necessary, to a jury.

After a two-day trial during which both parties presented expert testimony, the Superior Court judge found * * * insufficient evidence to support Gove's takings claim, and concluded that she and the Greniers had failed to carry their burden of demonstrating that the board's decision was "legally untenable," "an abuse of discretion, or was arbitrary or capricious."

II. Discussion

At trial, Gove attempted to prove that the board had effected a taking of lot 93 by subjecting the property to land use regulation in a manner that failed substantially to advance legitimate State interests. Gove also contended that the town had deprived her of any beneficial use of lot 93, [see Lucas], and disrupted her reasonable expectation of developing the property. See Penn Cent. Transp. Co. v. New York City, 438 U.S. 104 (1978) (Penn Central). We discuss Gove's theories in turn.

a. Legitimate State interests. * * * Gove argues first that the zoning regulations, as applied to lot 93, failed substantially to advance legitimate State interests. [T]he Supreme Court's holding in Agins v. Tiburon, 447 U.S. 255, 260 (1980) (Agins), [stated] that "the application of a general zoning law to particular property effects a taking if the ordinance does not substantially advance legitimate State interests." This term, however, the United States Supreme Court reconsidered the validity of the Agins "substantially advances State interests" standard "as a freestanding takings test," and concluded that "this formula prescribes an inquiry in the nature of a due process, not a takings test, and that it has no proper place in our takings jurisprudence." Lingle v. Chevron U.S.A. Inc., 161 L Ed. 2d 876, 125 S.Ct. 2074, 2083 (2005) (Lingle).

In practical effect, Lingle renders a zoning ordinance valid under the United States Constitution unless its application bears no "reasonable relation to the State's legitimate purpose." This highly deferential test neither involves "heightened scrutiny," nor allows a court to question the "wisdom" of an ordinance. * * *

In this case, the evidence clearly establishes a reasonable relationship between the prohibition against residential development on lot 93 and legitimate State interests. Gove offered no testimony meaningfully questioning the conservancy district's reasonable relationship to the protection of rescue workers and residents, the effectiveness of the town's resources to respond to natural disasters, and the preservation of neighboring property. Having addressed Gove's due process concerns, we turn now to consider her takings claim.

b. Takings. While the takings clause is directed primarily at "direct government appropriation or physical invasion of private property," the Supreme Court has "recognized that government regulation of private property may, in some instances, be so onerous that its effect is tantamount to a direct appropriation or ouster—and that such 'regulatory takings' may be compensable under the Fifth Amendment." Not every regulation affecting the value of real property constitutes a taking, for "Government hardly could go on if to some extent values incident to property could not be diminished without paying for every such change." Lingle, quoting Pennsylvania Coal Co. v. Mahon, 260 U.S. 393 (1922). A regulation "goes too far" and becomes a "taking" in any case "where government requires an owner to suffer a permanent physical invasion of her property" or where it "completely deprives an owner of 'all economically beneficial use' of her property." "Outside these two relatively narrow categories * * *regulatory takings challenges are governed by the standards set forth in [Penn Central]." Lingle.

Gove does not claim that the conservancy district regulations effected a physical occupation of her property, so we discuss, first, why Gove has not shown a "total" regulatory taking under Lucas. We then address why she has not shown that she is entitled to compensation under Penn Central.

i. "Total" regulatory takings. In Lucas, the Supreme Court concluded that a land use regulation that denies a plaintiff "all economically beneficial use of her property," constitutes a taking "except to the extent that 'background principles of nuisance and property law' independently restrict the owner's intended use of the property. The plaintiff in Lucas had paid $975,000 for two residential lots at a time when he was "not legally obliged to obtain a permit * * * in advance of any development activity." Two years later, the State enacted laws that, a State court found, rendered the two parcels "valueless," leading the Supreme Court to conclude that a total regulatory taking could be established.

In Palazzolo v. Rhode Island, 533 U.S. 606 (2001) (Palazzolo), the Supreme Court further explained that, to prove a total regulatory taking, a plaintiff must demonstrate that the challenged regulation leaves "the property 'economically idle' " and that she retains no more than "a token interest." The plaintiff in Palazzolo was unable to prove a total taking by showing that an eighteen-acre property appraised for $3,150,000 had been limited, by regulation, to use as a single residence with "$200,000 in development value."

Here, the facts are no more indicative of a total taking than those considered by the Supreme Court in Palazzolo. Even if we limit our analysis to lot 93, Gove has failed to prove that the challenged regulation left her property "economically idle." Her own expert testified that the property was worth $23,000, a value that itself suggests more than a "token interest" in the property. Moreover, the expert's $23,000 valuation did not take into account uses allowed in the conservancy district, either as of right or by special permit, which she admitted could make the property "an income producing proposition." The judge's finding that lot 93 retained significant value despite the challenged regulation invalidates Gove's theory: she cannot prove a total taking by proving only that one potential use of her property—i.e., as the site of a house—is prohibited. Lucas requires that the challenged regulation "denies all economically beneficial use" of land. (See Lingle discussing in Lucas context "the complete elimination of a property's value is the determinative factor"). We now turn to the Penn Central inquiry.

ii. The Penn Central inquiry. Recent Supreme Court opinions have emphasized that almost all regulatory takings cases involve the "essentially ad hoc factual inquiries" described in Penn Central * * * The Penn Central framework eschews any "set formula" or "mathematically precise variables" for evaluating whether a regulatory taking has occurred, emphasizing instead "important guideposts" and "careful examination* * *of all the relevant circumstances." The relevant "guideposts" include: the actual "economic impact of the regulation" on the plaintiff; the extent to which the regulation "has interfered with" a landowner's "distinct investment-backed expectations"; and the "character of the governmental action." In the end, "the Penn Central inquiry turns in large part, albeit not exclusively, upon the magnitude of a regulation's economic impact and the degree to which it interferes with legitimate property interests." Lingle, at 2082.

Considering all of the evidence at trial, we agree with the judge that Gove failed to show that the conservancy district regulations had a substantial "economic impact" on her or deprived her of "distinct investment-backed expectations" in lot 93. As an initial matter, Gove's failure to introduce a thorough assessment of lot 93's current value left the judge no basis to conclude that she suffered any economic loss at all. But even if we assume that residential development is the most valuable potential use of lot 93, Gove did not prove that the prohibition against a house on lot 93 caused her a loss outside the range of normal fluctuation in the value of coastal property.

Lot 93 is a highly marginal parcel of land, exposed to the ravages of nature, that for good reason remained undeveloped for several decades even as more habitable properties in the vicinity were put to various productive uses. Lot 93 is now even more vulnerable than ever to coastal flooding. Nevertheless, recent appreciation in coastal property (belatedly, and for the time being) has given the parcel some development value. Absent the coastal conservancy district regulations, lot 93 might well be worth more. But this is a new and insofar as it relates to residential development, wholly speculative value that has arisen after the regulations became effective. Before the enactment of the regulations, Gove had no reasonable expectation of selling the property for residential development, a fact she recognized by removing the property from the market for want of an offer. Nor did Gove have any reasonable expectations of a better outcome as late as the early 1990's, when lot 93 had, by Gove's own estimation, "no value whatsoever." Gove could not have developed reasonable expectations of selling lot 93 for residential development after the early 1990's, by which time the regulations had barred any such development for several years. The takings clause was never intended to compensate property owners for property rights they never had. Gove's argument is not furthered by the Greniers' tentative offer to pay $192,000 for the parcel contingent on receiving approval to build a single-family house, a proposition that all parties reasonably should have known was highly dubious at best, particularly since the regulations did not permit such variances. It is similarly fallacious for Gove to claim that the regulations diminished the value of her property from $346,000 (the appraiser's estimate of the value of lot 93 at the time of the trial if it were suitable for a three-bedroom home) to $23,000 (the appraiser's estimate of the land's "unbuildable" worth).

This is not a case where a bona fide purchaser for value invested reasonably in land fit for development, only to see a novel regulation destroy the value of her investment. Gove did not purchase lot 93; she inherited the property as part of the devise from her mother in which she received other real property of significant value. By this we do not suggest that Gove's takings claim is defeated simply on account of her lack of a personal financial investment. Rather, Gove's failure to show any substantial "personal financial investment" in lot 93 emphasizes her inability to demonstrate that she ever had any reasonable expectation of selling that particular lot for residential development, or that she has suffered any substantial loss as a result of the regulations. In these circumstances "justice and fairness" do not require that Gove be compensated. To the contrary, it seems clear that any compensation would constitute a "windfall" for Gove.

We add that "the character of the governmental action" here is the type of limited protection against harmful private land use that routinely has withstood allegations of regulatory takings. It is not at all clear that Gove has "legitimate property interests" in building a house on lot 93. The judge found that "it is undisputed that [lot 93] lies in the flood plain and that its potential flooding would adversely affect the surrounding areas" if the property were developed with a house. Reasonable government action mitigating such harm, at the very least when it does not involve a "total" regulatory taking or a physical invasion, typically does not require compensation.

Judgment affirmed.

NOTES AND QUESTIONS

1. In the late 1800s and early 1900s, the taking requirement was viewed quite literally. Unless the government appropriated private property for its own use, no compensable taking occurred. Regulation of property uses did not constitute a "taking." This approach is derived from the law of nuisance and starts with the basic proposition that no one can obtain a vested right to injure or endanger the public. Thus, the abatement or prevention of a noxious use is not a taking of property since a use that adversely affects the public interest cannot be a vested private property right. Using this approach the economic consequences of government action are irrelevant. The chief proponent of this view was the elder Justice Harlan.

Justice Holmes, however, viewed the "taking" issue as one of a battle between economic interests and the forces of social change. In his view, the distinction between an unconstitutional taking and a valid regulation was simply one of degree. Thus, his focus was upon the degree of economic harm inflicted as a result of the state regulation. If the economic harm was substantial, a "taking" occurred.

With two such dramatic differences in "takings" theory appearing in earlier United States Supreme Court decisions, the natural question is upon which, if any, has the Court settled? Which theory dominates Lucas?

2. Takings litigation involves a great deal of indeterminacy. Lucas represents an attempt to provide clarity by identifying a second category of per se taking requiring compensation. Did the Court succeed in clarifying takings by identifying regulations that represent categorical takings?

Most recent United States Supreme Court cases are 5–4 decisions, demonstrating that even among our justices, there is considerable disagreement about what kind of regulation constitutes a compensable taking of property. Intelligent, well-informed public officials may in good faith disagree about the validity of specific types of land use regulation. Yet, in First English Evangelical Lutheran Church of Glendale v. County of Los Angeles, 482 U.S. 304 (1987), the United States Supreme Court held that, if a regulation constitutes a taking of property, a private property owner is entitled to compensation for the time during which the property owner was unable to use her property due to a governmental regulation that is ultimately held to be invalid or withdrawn. Local governments and officials must pay the price for the necessarily vague standards in this area of the law.

3. Other than common law nuisance, what are the "background principles" of property law to which Justice Scalia refers? The Court specifically recognizes easements: "[W]e assuredly would permit the government to assert a permanent easement that was a pre-existing limitation on the landowner's title." Lucas, 505 U. S. 1003, at 1028–29. However, Justice Scalia wrote a strong dissent to the Court's denial of certiorari in Stevens v. City of Cannon Beach, 510 U.S. 1207 (1994). Stevens sought review of an Oregon Supreme Court decision finding that he did not suffer a compensable taking when he was denied permits to build a seawall on the dry sand beach that was necessary to further develop his land. The Oregon court found that the doctrine of custom was a background principle of state property law and that Stevens never had the right to obstruct the dry sand beach that was subject to public use based on custom. Justice Scalia found the reliance on Thornton v. Hay, 254 Ore. 584, 462 P.2d 671 (1969), problematic both substantively and procedurally:

> I believe that petitioners have sufficiently preserved their due process claim, and believe further that the claim is a serious one. Petitioners, who owned this property at the time Thornton was decided, were not parties to that litigation. Particularly in light of the utter absence of record support for the crucial factual determinations in that case, whether the Oregon Supreme Court chooses to treat it as having established a "custom" applicable to Cannon Beach alone, or one applicable to all "dry-sand" beach in the State, petitioners must be afforded an opportunity to make out their constitutional claim by demonstrating that the asserted custom is pretextual. If we were to find for petitioners on this point, we would not only set right a procedural injustice, but would hasten the clarification of Oregon substantive law that casts a shifting shadow upon federal constitutional rights the length of the State.

For a discussion of the development of the concept of "background principles" of law, see Michael C. Blumm and Lucus Ritchie, Lucas's Unlikely Legacy: the Rise of Background Principles as Categorical Takings Defenses, 29 Harv. Envt'l. L. Rev. 321 (2005).

4. Is legislation enacted prior to a party's acquisition of land a "background principle"? The majority opinion in Palazzolo v. Rhode Island, 533 U.S. 606 (2001), addressed this question directly (but since the Court found that there was no "total taking," the Court's pronouncement may be no more than dicta). Justice Kennedy wrote:

> * * * In Lucas, the Court observed that a landowner's ability to recover for a government deprivation of all economically beneficial use of property is not absolute but instead is confined by limitations on the use of land which "inhere in the title itself." This is so, the Court reasoned, because the landowner is constrained by those "restrictions that background

principles of the State's law of property and nuisance already place upon land ownership." It is asserted here that Lucas stands for the proposition that any new regulation, once enacted, becomes a background principle of property law which cannot be challenged by those who acquire title after the enactment.

We have no occasion to consider the precise circumstances when a legislative enactment can be deemed a background principle of state law or whether those circumstances are present here. It suffices to say that a regulation that otherwise would be unconstitutional absent compensation is not transformed into a background principle of the State's law by mere virtue of the passage of title.* * * A regulation or common-law rule cannot be a background principle for some owners but not for others. The determination whether an existing, general law can limit all economic use of property must turn on objective factors, such as the nature of the land use proscribed.* * * A law does not become a background principle for subsequent owners by enactment itself.* * *

Id. at 629–30. Can legislation that goes beyond codification of a common law doctrine be a "background principle"?

5. On remand of Lucas, the South Carolina Supreme Court found no common law basis for prohibiting Lucas's proposed use of the land and remanded the case to the trial court for a determination of the actual damages Lucas sustained for the temporary taking of his property. What was the period of the temporary taking? What types of evidence should be presented before the trial court in this kind of a case? See Lucas v. South Carolina Coastal Council, 309 S.C. 424, 424 S.E.2d 484 (1992) (instructing the trial court that the relevant period for determining damages was from the time of the enactment of the statute through the date of the state supreme court's order in 1992).

6. In Lucas, the dissent suggested that the majority had "launched a missile to kill a mouse," and even Justice Scalia admitted that situations where the government has deprived a landowner of all economically beneficial uses are "relatively rare." Are most cases more likely to be like Gove in that the land retains some subsidiary uses and value? How does one determine whether there is more than a "token interest" remaining in the regulated property? See Rith Energy, Inc. v. United States, 270 F.3d 1347, 1349 (Fed. Cir. 2001), cert. denied, 536 U.S. 958 (2002) (discussing "token interest"). How does the Penn Central analysis differ from the Lucas analysis? Who has the burden of proof in each type of case?

7. In Gove, the Penn Central analysis focused on the property owner's investment-backed expectations and the character of the government action. How do recent hurricanes, particularly Katrina and Sandy, affect these factors in the analysis? If we are entering a long period, perhaps a 20 year cycle, of increased hurricane activity, how would this affect the expectations of coastal property owners? Would more extensive government regulation of coastal property be part of these expectations?

8. Is the argument for a "total taking" particularly convincing when a developer can make no use of a coastal wetland? What about the value of the ecosystem services the wetlands provide—pollutant treatment, flood control, storm surge abatement, habitat? How should these values be taken into account? Who "owns" these services? See generally, James Salzman, "The Ecosystem Approach: New Departures for Land and Water, Review Essay: Valuing Ecosystem Services," 24 Ecology L.Q. 887 (1997); James Salzman, Barton H. Thompson, Jr., Gretchen Daily, Protecting Ecosystem Services: Science, Economics and Law, 20 Stanford Envt'l. L.J. 497 (2001).

9. Nollan v. California Coastal Commission, 483 U.S. 825 (1987) [See Chapter 3, Section 7.D., Public Access and Use of Beaches and Shores] is often characterized as a takings case, because the permit imposed an unconstitutional condition that did not have a substantial relation to damage anticipated by the development. In Lingle v. Chevron U.S.A. Inc., 544 U.S. 528 (2005), however, the unanimous Supreme Court rejected the proposition that a regulation effects a takings if it does not "substantially advance" a legitimate state interest. In dicta, the Court went on to explain how this clarification affects the application of Nollan/Dolan analysis:

> We emphasize that our holding today—that the "substantially advances" formula is not a valid takings test—does not require us to disturb any of our prior holdings. * * * [I]n no case have we found a compensable taking based on such an inquiry. * * *

> It might be argued that this formula played a role in our decisions in [Nollan and Dolan]. But while the Court drew upon the language of Agins in these cases, it did not apply the "substantially advances" test that is the subject of today's decision. Both Nollan and Dolan involved Fifth Amendment takings challenges to adjudicative land-use exactions—specifically, government demands that a landowner dedicate an easement allowing public access to her property as a condition of obtaining a development permit. * * *

> In each case, the Court began with the premise that, had the government simply appropriated the easement in question, this would have been a per se physical taking. The question was whether the government could, without paying the compensation that would otherwise be required upon effecting such a taking, demand the easement as a condition for granting a development permit the government was entitled to deny. The Court in Nollan answered in the affirmative, provided that the exaction would substantially advance the same government interest that would furnish a valid ground for denial of the permit. 483 U.S., at 834–837. The Court further refined this requirement in Dolan, holding that an adjudicative exaction requiring dedication of private property must also be " 'rough[ly] proportion[al]' . . . both in nature and extent to the impact of the proposed development." 512 U.S. at 391.

Although Nollan and Dolan quoted Agins' language, the rule those decisions established is entirely distinct from the "substantially advances" test we address today. Whereas the "substantially advances" inquiry before us now is unconcerned with the degree or type of burden a regulation places upon property, Nollan and Dolan both involved dedications of property so onerous that, outside the exactions context, they would be deemed per se physical takings. In neither case did the Court question whether the exaction would substantially advance some legitimate state interest. Rather, the issue was whether the exactions substantially advanced the same interests that land-use authorities asserted would allow them to deny the permit altogether. As the Court explained in Dolan, these cases involve a special application of the "doctrine of 'unconstitutional conditions,'" which provides that "the government may not require a person to give up a constitutional right—here the right to receive just compensation when property is taken for a public use—in exchange for a discretionary benefit conferred by the government where the benefit has little or no relationship to the property." 512 U.S., at 385. That is worlds apart from a rule that says a regulation affecting property constitutes a taking on its face solely because it does not substantially advance a legitimate government interest. In short, Nollan and Dolan cannot be characterized as applying the "substantially advances" test we address today, and our decision should not be read to disturb these precedents.

Lingle, 544 U.S. at 545–548

This dicta seemed to help clarify the circumstances in which the Nollan/Dolan test, the test of rough proportionality between a permit condition and the impact of the permitted activity, would apply. Questions still abound, however, about when this stricter analysis of government action will apply. In the 2012–13 term, the U.S. Supreme Court granted certiorari on Koontz v. St. Johns River Water Management District, Docket No. 11–1447, a Florida case involving the imposition of off-site mitigation as a permit condition for wetlands destruction.

10. For an excellent analysis of the relation of takings analysis to regulation responding to sea level rise, see J. Peter Byrne, The Cathedral Engulfed: Sea-Level Rise, Property Rights, and Time, 73 La. L. Rev. 69–118 (2012).

NOTE ON NOVEL CONSTITUTIONAL TAKINGS REMEDIES: JUDICIAL TAKINGS AND FOURTH AMENDMENT TAKINGS

Although a Fifth Amendment "regulatory taking" has been the primary basis for property owners to make claims for compensation when coastal regulations have affected the value of their land, property rights advocates have continued to be concerned with the indeterminacy of this remedy. Recent cases have advanced new theories that may affect the development of takings analysis and, consequently, coastal management law. In Stop the Beach Renourishment v. Florida Department of Environmental Protection, 130 S. Ct.

2592, 177 L. Ed. 184 (2010), discussed in Chapter 3, the property owners argued that their right to accretion, a vested property interest, had been "taken" by the Florida Supreme Court's changing of the applicable law. Although the Supreme Court unanimously agreed that there had been no Fifth Amendment taking, the plurality, led by Justice Scalia, found that judicial opinions "effect a taking if they recharacterize as public property what was previously private property." Justice Scalia's test for a judicial taking focused on the effect on existing property rights: "If a legislature *or a court* declares that what was once an established right of private property no longer exists, it has taken that property. . . . " Id. at 2602. (emphasis added). Both the nature of Justice Scalia's judicial takings test and how it fits into traditional takings doctrine are left rather unclear. At one level, he speaks in absolute terms about "judicial opinions effect[ing] a taking if they recharacterize as public property what was previously private property," suggesting a per se rule. Id. at 2601. But he also seems to concede that the nature and degree of the infringement on property rights is relevant. "To be sure," he explains, "the manner of state action may matter: Condemnation by eminent domain, for example, is always a taking, while a legislative, executive, *or judicial* restriction of property use may or may not be, depending on its nature and extent." Id. at 2602. Interpreting this language as applying the same test to a judicial impairment of property rights as to a similar impairment of rights by the legislature or an executive agency, i.e., a *Penn Central* balancing test, would be more consistent with Justice Scalia's position that, regarding the Takings Clause, the same standards apply to all branches of government.

Justice Kennedy, joined by Justice Sotomayor, found it unnecessary in the case to adopt a "judicial takings" doctrine and focused on the problems associated with applying the Fifth Amendment to judicial decisions. He did, however, suggest that courts could be constrained appropriately through the Due Process Clause for an arbitrary and irrational decision that eliminates or substantially changes established property rights. Finally, Justice Breyer, joined by Justice Ginsburg, did not discuss the merits of the concept of a judicial taking since reaching a novel constitutional issue was unnecessary to the case's disposition. It is notable, however, that none of the Justices in the case categorically denied the existence of the concept of a judicial taking and that six Justices agreed that state supreme court decisions that eliminated existing property rights might be unconstitutional. The door is definitely open, or at least ajar, for the development of the judicial takings concept.

The other novel theory is assertion of the Fourth Amendment to claim an unreasonable seizure of property (rather than a Fifth Amendment taking). In Severance v. Patterson, 566 F.3d 490 (5th Cir. 2009), the federal case that certified the "rolling easement" question to the Texas Supreme Court, the federal Court of Appeals found that the Fourth Amendment claim was not subsumed in Severance's taking claim. In response to the Texas Supreme Court's ruling that the "rolling easement" is not part of Texas law, the Fifth Circuit has remanded the case for further proceedings on the Fourth Amendment claim. The court stated that it was "unpersuaded" that the case has been rendered moot by the fact that Severance's property has in the interim been taken (and fully compensated for) through eminent domain proceedings. See Severance v. Patterson, 682 F.3d 360 (5th Cir. 2012).

Is there such a thing as a judicial taking? If so, what should the test be for a judicial taking? For a Fourth Amendment seizure of property through regulation? Would there be a difference in the remedy for Fourth Amendment "unreasonable seizure" than for a Fifth Amendment taking?

CHAPTER 5

OCEAN INDUSTRIAL DEVELOPMENT OF THE CONTINENTAL SHELF

■ ■ ■

1. INTRODUCTION

As discussed in Chapter 1, the extension of coastal national jurisdiction and sovereignty over marine areas and resources beyond three miles is a recent development. Most of the law in this area has evolved since the end of World War II and developed primarily in response to coastal nations' perceptions that oil and gas resources and offshore fisheries should be subject to the sovereignty of the adjacent coastal nation. Although these have continued to be the major resources extracted from the seas, their exploitation has come at a high cost to the marine environment, and the use of fossil fuels continues to contribute to climate change.

New uses of the offshore are proliferating, more resources of the seabed and water column are being exploited, and the oceans will be both the site and the source of alternative and renewable energy projects. Renewable ocean energy resource potential includes: "1) kinetic energy unique to the ocean, such as energy provided by surface waves, currents and tides, 2) renewable energy not unique to the ocean, such as wind and solar energy, 3) thermal energy, such as that produced by the temperature differential of surface and deep ocean waters, and 4) marine biofuels, such as those derived from algae." See An Ocean of Energy There For The Taking, Tundi Agardy, Ph.D. (2008) (available at World Ocean Observatory, http://worldoceanobservatory.org/events/oceanenergy/current3.htm.).
While these new energy sources have great potential, they, too, are not without environmental costs. See M. Spaulding & C. de Fontaubert, Conflict Resolution for Addressing Climate Change with Ocean-Altering Projects, 37 Envtl. L. Rep. 10740 (2007).

This chapter will focus on the industrialization of the offshore—the use of the oceans to exploit its nonliving and energy resources—and the impacts of that development.

2. OUTER CONTINENTAL SHELF OIL AND GAS DEVELOPMENT

A. THE GEOGRAPHY OF THE CONTINENTAL SHELF

The original 1945 Truman Proclamation claim to the continental shelf did not make a claim to a specific distance or depth. Its only reference was to the submerged lands that "may be regarded as an extension of the land-mass of the coastal nation and thus naturally appurtenant to it." A press release at the time of the Proclamation indicated that the continental shelf was considered to be the offshore area to a depth of 100 fathoms.

The 1953 codification of the Truman Proclamation, the Outer Continental Shelf Lands Act (OCSLA), 43 U.S.C.A. §§ 1331–1356, provided a definition, but no specifically identified area for the continental shelf.

OCSLA section. 1331. Definitions

(a) The term "outer Continental Shelf" means all submerged lands lying seaward and outside of the area of lands beneath navigable waters as defined in section 1301 of this title, and of which the subsoil and seabed appertain to the United States and are subject to its jurisdiction and control; . . .

Even regulations of the Department of Interior, 30 CFR 552.3, simply mirror the OCSLA definition. Why?

The United States is a party to the 1958 Convention on the Continental Shelf, 15 U.S.T. 473. Article One of Convention provides:

For the purpose of these articles, the term 'continental shelf' is used as referring (a) to the seabed and subsoil of the submarine areas adjacent to the coast but outside the area of the territorial sea, to a depth of 200 metres or, beyond that limit, to where the depth of the superjacent waters admits of the exploitation of the natural resources of the said areas; * * * 15 U.S.T. 473.

In United States v. Ray, 423 F.2d 16 (5th Cir. 1970), the court found that these provisions are not inconsistent. In interpreting both the Submerged Lands Act (SLA) and the OCSLA, U.S. courts have often resorted to international law and treaties to fill in the many problems created and gaps left by the legislation, but no case has addressed the specific geographic extent of the U.S. continental shelf. Most commentators agree, however, that the UN Convention on the Law of the Sea (LOSC) has superceded the 1958 Convention, and that to the extent the LOSC provisions constitute customary international law, the United States may base its claims on its definitions.

The U.S. Department of State maintains a website at http://www.state.gov/e/oes/continentalshelf/ that sets out the current U.S. position:

Defining the Limits of the U.S. Continental Shelf

The continental shelf is an important maritime zone, one that holds many resources and vital habitats for marine life. The majority of the world's continental shelf is unknown and unmapped. Even so, the responsible use and preservation of this unique area depends on the collection of data to better understand where our rights on the continental shelf lie.

Given these important aspects, it is critical for the United States to accurately define the full extent of its continental shelf. Determining the extent of the continental shelf is a bit different than other maritime zones, such as the territorial sea or the exclusive economic zone, because it is not simply a matter of distance from shore. Under customary international law, as reflected in the Convention on the Law of the Sea, every coastal Country automatically has a continental shelf out to 200 nautical miles from its shore (or out to a maritime boundary with another coastal Country). In some cases, a coastal Country can have a continental shelf beyond 200 nautical miles if it meets certain criteria. Typically, the portion of continental shelf beyond 200 nautical miles is called the "extended continental shelf" or simply the ECS.

The State Department estimates "that the U.S. ECS likely totals at least one million square kilometers." The data gathering to define the U.S. ECS is coordinated by the U.S. Extended Continental Shelf Task Force, an interagency body headed by the U.S. Department of State. The United States has also entered into a joint effort with Canada to gather data to define the limits of the continental shelf in the Arctic Ocean.

NOTES AND QUESTIONS

1. It should be noted that the United States and Canada have disputed overlapping lateral boundary claims to OCS and EEZ in the Beaufort Sea and Arctic Ocean. Under these circumstances, why are these countries cooperating on OCS survey and scientific work there?

2. Most of the Gulf of Mexico is surrounded by the land area of the United States and Mexico. The boundaries of the countries' overlapping exclusive economic zones were established in the Treaty on Maritime Boundaries between the United States of America and the United Mexican States, signed at Mexico City May 4, 1978, which entered into force November 13, 1997. Both countries agreed that relatively small gaps in the central Gulf beyond 200 miles (Western Gap) met the international law definition of continental shelf. In the 2000 U.S.–Mexico Treaty on Delimitation of the Continental Shelf in

the Western Gulf of Mexico Beyond 200 Nautical Miles, the two countries divided the areas of continental shelf beyond their EEZs by an equidistant line drawn from the respective U.S. and Mexican coastal baseline, including the baselines of islands. The treaty anticipated that the countries would "seek to reach agreement for the efficient and equitable exploitation of such transboundary reservoirs."

In 2012 the countries concluded the treaty to "establish a legal framework to achieve safe, efficient, equitable and environmentally responsible exploitation of transboundary hydrocarbon reservoirs." Preamble. Both Mexico and the U.S. have had major oil spill disasters while developing the oil resources of the Gulf of Mexico OCS: the 1979 Ixtoc I platform blowout in Mexico's Bay of Campeche, 600 miles south of Texas, when oil spilled for almost 300 days, and the BP–Deepwater Horizon explosion and oil spill in 2010. Does the 2012 agreement provide a basis for harmonizing marine pollution prevention policies as required by the LOSC, article 208(4)? Do the neighboring countries have risk reduction standards consistent with state practice in other areas of OCS development?

AGREEMENT BETWEEN THE UNITED STATES OF AMERICA AND THE UNITED MEXICAN STATES CONCERNING TRANSBOUNDARY HYDROCARBON RESERVOIRS IN THE GULF OF MEXICO

Article 1 Scope

This Agreement shall apply to cooperation between the Parties with regard to the joint Exploration and Exploitation of geological Hydrocarbon structures and Reservoirs that extend across the Delimitation Line, the entirety of which are located beyond 9 nautical miles from the coastline.

Article 6 Unitization Agreement

1. Any joint Exploration and/or Exploitation of a Transboundary Reservoir or Unit Area pursuant to the terms of a unitization agreement must be approved by the Parties. Such joint Exploration and/or Exploitation shall be conducted pursuant to the terms of a unitization agreement negotiated and proposed by the Licensees and approved by the Executive Agencies. The Executive Agencies should develop one or more model unitization agreements for use under this Agreement.

Article 14 Joint Commission

1. A Joint Commission shall be established no later than 90 days after entry into force of this Agreement to assist the Executive Agencies in administering this Agreement.

* * *

5. The Joint Commission shall be the competent body to examine any dispute or other matter referred to it by either Executive Agency relating to the interpretation and implementation of this Agreement, or any unforeseen issues arising under this Agreement.

6. If the Joint Commission is unable within 60 days to resolve all differences concerning the allocation of production pursuant to Article 8, or the reallocation of production pursuant to Article 9, either Party may submit the dispute for Expert Determination. If the Joint Commission is unable within 60 days to resolve all differences related to the determination of a Transboundary Reservoir . . . and relevant data is available from a well in the prospective Transboundary Reservoir on each side of the Delimitation Line, either Party may submit the dispute for Expert Determination.

7. If the Joint Commission is unable within 60 days to resolve all differences concerning any dispute referred to it by the Executive Agencies relating to the interpretation and implementation of this Agreement that is not addressed in paragraph 6 of this Article or referred to it under paragraphs 4 or 5 of Article 6 or paragraph 4 of Article 7, either Party may resort to the dispute settlement provisions. . . . The Joint Commission will have 30 days in which to consider the final recommendation in any arbitration instituted pursuant to Article 17. If the Joint Commission is unable to resolve any remaining differences within that time, the dispute will be returned to the Parties.

8. The Parties will refrain from action with regard to any dispute referred to the Joint Commission or to Expert Determination or dispute resolution under this Agreement where it is reasonably foreseeable that such action would prejudice the implementation of any decision related to the dispute until the dispute resolution procedures are complete.

[The Treaty contains a wide range of dispute settlement mechanisms.]

Article 18 Inspections

1. Subject to applicable national law, each Party shall, under procedures to be developed and agreed under this Agreement, have the right to inspect Facilities in a Unit Area approved pursuant to this Agreement.

2. To enable Inspectors of each Party to safeguard their respective interests with respect to safety, environmental and fiscal matters, the Executive Agencies shall develop specific procedures, subject to national law, for:

(a) consultation among Inspectors of each Party;

(b) timely access to information relevant to inspection activities; and

(c) physical access to Unit Areas for the purpose of inspecting activities therein under a joint inspection regime, including access to metering systems, wherever located. * * *

Article 19 Safety and Environmental Protection

1. The Parties shall adopt, where appropriate, common safety and environmental standards and requirements applicable to activity contemplated under this Agreement. In any event, the Parties shall strive to ensure that their respective standards and requirements are compatible where necessary for the safe, effective, and environmentally responsible implementation of this Agreement.

B. AN INTRODUCTION TO OCS OIL AND GAS DEVELOPMENT

The modern era of offshore oil and gas development began in 1954 with the first lease sale under the OCSLA in the Gulf of Mexico. OCS oil and gas leasing gained momentum quickly, but in 1969 the disastrous oil spill from a platform in the Santa Barbara Channel off the California coast prompted reassessment of the leasing and development program. The Santa Barbara oil is often cited as triggering the environmental movement and plethora of environmental laws that emerged in the next decade. But the decade of the 1970s was also a time of oil embargoes and gas shortages that led to calls for accelerated OCS leasing. The 1978 Amendments to the OCSLA attempted to address both issues by incorporating provisions to protect the marine and coastal environments as well as provisions to expedite OCS oil and gas development.

Under the Reagan Administration, Secretary of the Interior James Watt fundamentally changed the leasing process to allow areawide leasing. Instead of offering only designated tracts or discrete areas, areawide leasing opened up entire OCS planning areas, millions of acres of continental shelf, in lease sales. Consider the effect of this strategy on accelerating leasing, assessment of impacts of the lease sale, competition among bidders, and the amount of bids and revenue to the U.S. This approach to leasing led to increased controversy between the federal government and the states. Starting in 1982, Congress began regularly introducing limitations on leasing in certain areas of the OCS by restricting funding in DOI's appropriations bills. These Congressional moratoria continued for 27 years.

In January 1989, President Bush delayed three controversial lease sales while a presidential task force and the National Academy of Sciences reviewed the leasing and development processes. These reports, which criticized certain leasing as lacking necessary information on the envi-

ronmental effects, led President Bush to announce a moratorium in 1990
on lease sales for a large portion of the continental U.S. from 1990–2000
and to order DOI to revise it process for selecting lease areas. Until recently, however, lease sale areas have continued to incorporate areas
much larger than the pre–1978 lease sales. The presidential moratorium
put in place by President Bush was extended through 2012 by President
Clinton in 1998. See B. Cicin–Sain, R. Gramling, R. Johnson, and C. Wolf,
Appendix C, The Evolution of the Federal OCS Program: National and
Regional Perspectives 107–142, in Commission on Geosciences, Environment and Resources, Assessment of the U.S. Outer Continental Shelf Environmental Studies Program: III. Social and Economic Studies (1992).

   In 2006 Congress passed the Gulf of Mexico Energy Security Act
(GOMESA) which required leasing in 8.3 million acres in the Gulf, including 5.8 million acres that were previously under Congressional moratoria.
GOMESA also established a new moratorium on leasing activities in a
redefined Eastern Gulf planning area within 125 miles of the Florida
coast, as well as a portion of the Central Gulf planning area within 100
miles of coast line of Florida, until June 30, 2022. A moratorium also applies east of the Military Mission Line in the Gulf of Mexico in an area
that has been traditionally used for military testing and training activities. The Act further provided for exchanges, allowing companies to exchange certain leases in moratorium areas for bonus and royalty credits
to be used on other Gulf of Mexico leases.

   In 2008, President George W. Bush issued an executive memorandum that rescinded the presidential moratorium on the OCS created by
the 1990 order of President George H. W. Bush and renewed by President
Clinton. The memorandum left only areas designated as marine sanctuaries subject to the leasing moratorium. On March 31, 2010, President
Obama withdrew Bristol Bay, offshore Alaska, from leasing consideration
through June 30, 2017. The result is that large areas of the U.S. continental shelf are potentially open for leasing. Although the Obama Administration has supported calls for more extensive OCS development, the
new Five-Year Lease Plan includes potential sales only in the Gulf of
Mexico and limited areas of Alaska. The proposed lease sales off the coast
of Alaska, however, include parts of the Cook Inlet and the Chukchi and
Beaufort Seas, areas where native groups and environmentalists have
challenged leases and drilling plans in court. See Section D. in this chapter.

   The future of OCS oil and gas development continues to be unclear.
One key factor will be the status of Middle East oil supplies. As long as
these supplies remain secure, environmentalists and coastal state interests may continue to be able to marshal support for limiting OCS oil and
gas activities. But even among these groups, there are differing views
about the desirability of OCS oil and gas activities. On the one hand, OCS

oil and gas activities do pose risk of oil spills and other damage to sensitive environments; on the other hand, some data suggests that the environmental risks of OCS activities are significantly less than the risks associated with oil tanker traffic. Dependency on Middle East oil supplies means that large numbers of vulnerable oil tankers will be moving through U.S. waters on a daily basis. Historically, all but two major oil spills in U.S. waters, the 1969 Santa Barbara Channel and 2010 Deepwater Horizon Gulf oil spills, have resulted from a tanker mishap. The epic proportions of the Deepwater Horizon spill may, however, change the political calculus.

A second factor is our desire to utilize more environmentally friendly fuels, such as natural gas, and renewable energy sources. Various incentives for increased OCS gas production and imports of liquefied natural gas (LNG) are provided by the Energy Policy Act of 2005 (H.R.6), and the Obama Administration has made a commitment to development of offshore wind energy.

A third factor is the fiscal one. OCS revenues are a large source of revenue for the federal government. Periodic concerns about federal budget deficits could make it more difficult to reduce future OCS production and to implement any federal program to buy back OCS leases.

NOTE ON REVENUE SHARING

When oil and gas are developed on federal lands within the boundaries of a state, the state is entitled to 50% of the rents, bonuses and royalties generated. Alaska receives 90% of the revenues generated. Coastal states have long argued that in view of the human and environmental impacts of OCS development they experience and the great risks to which coastal states are exposed, these states should share in OCS revenues. The following excerpt discusses the limited extent to which Congress has responded.

CURRY L. HAGERTY, OUTER CONTINENTAL SHELF MORATORIA ON OIL AND GAS DEVELOPMENT 13–14, CONGRESSIONAL RESEARCH SERVICE RPT 7–5700
(May 6, 2011)

* * *

Federal Revenues

Fiscal concerns impact moratorium policy alternatives with pressure on policymakers not to diminish OCS receipts, which are a significant source of federal revenue. Moratoria reduce the potential for federal and state revenues from OCS development. Where OCS oil and gas leasing is currently underway, and states participate in specific revenue-sharing policies, revenue management programs seem to have broad support.

Federal funds from offshore production are deposited in the General Treasury, the Land and Water Conservation Fund, and the National Historic Preservation Fund, and go to some states. Revenue sharing between the states and the federal government is established by statute. Congress has enacted three OCS revenue-sharing programs that disburse receipts to coastal states. These programs are discussed in the following sections.

OCSLA Amendments of 1986 Created the § 8(g) Zone

Section 8(g) of the OCSLA amendments of 1986 mandated that the federal government share with affected coastal states 27% of revenues generated from oil and natural gas leases located in the federal zone. The § 8(g) zone is 3 miles wide and is located directly adjacent to a state's seaward boundary. The Energy Policy Act of 2005 (EPAct05; P.L. 109–58) expanded revenue sharing in the § 8(g) zone to include 27% of the revenues generated from renewable energy leases.

Coastal Impact Assistance Program (CIAP)

CIAP grants funds to states pursuant to EPAct05. States with an approved CIAP State Plan are eligible to receive a portion of $250 million for each of FY2007 through FY2010. This revenue is shared among Alabama, Alaska, California, Louisiana, Mississippi, and Texas.

Gulf of Mexico Energy Security Act of 2006 (GOMESA)

GOMESA established a revenue-sharing program for four coastal producing states in the Gulf of Mexico—Alabama, Louisiana, Mississippi, and Texas—and their coastal counties and parishes. There are two phases: (1) starting in FY2007, these four states would receive 37.5% of the oil and gas revenues generated from leases issued in two areas of the Gulf of Mexico where sales were mandated in the Eastern and Central Gulf of Mexico Planning Areas; and (2) beginning in FY2017, the four states will share 37.5% of qualified OCS revenues from Gulf of Mexico leases issued after December 20, 2006. Payments to states are made annually. In March 2009, $25 million of GOMESA qualified revenues were disbursed from bonuses and first year rental payments from leases issued in FY2008.

NOTES AND QUESTIONS

1. Do Section 8(g) funds accurately reflect the circumstances of the grant? Is it likely that oil and gas development adjacent to state boundaries is exploiting transboundary resources? Would that make the circumstances different from other kinds of revenue sharing?

In a 1984 case with important political and fiscal implications, a federal district court in Texas was called upon to decide what was meant by a 'fair and equitable' division of revenues from OCS oil and gas produced from so called '8(g)' lands. Texas v. Secretary of the Interior, 580 F. Supp. 1197 (E.D.

Tex. 1984); see 43 U.S.C. 1337(g). At stake in the litigation was $1 billion. 8(g) lands are the innermost three mile strip of federal offshore lands which lies immediately adjacent to state owned offshore lands. Texas argued that the just and equitable division of monies from these lands should be made after a broad analysis, taking into account things such as the onshore economic impacts of offshore development and the enhancement in value of federal tracts that has occurred because of prior state offshore leasing. The Secretary of Interior claimed that only a single factor should be used in determining a 'fair and equitable' allocation of 8(g) monies, that being the drainage of oil and gas from beneath state lands. The court sided with Texas as to which approach should be used, and based upon the facts and circumstances presented in the immediate case, called for a 50/50 division of the 8(g) monies between Texas and the federal government.

Section 8(g) was amended in 1986 to mandate that future bonuses, rentals and royalties subject to 8(g) would also be split 73%–federal, 27%–states, except that future royalties from existing 8(g) leases would be distributed on the basis of surface acreage actually within three miles of state waters but at a 50% rate. Could amended section 8(g) reduce tensions between the federal and state governments over OCS oil and gas development? See Alabama v. U.S. Dept. of Interior, 84 F.3d 410 (11th Cir. 1996). See generally R. Hildreth, Federal–State Offshore Revenue Sharing Deserves Attention and Expansion, 21 Ocean Devel. and Int'l L. 241 (1990); R. Hildreth, Federal–State Revenue Sharing and Resource Management Under Outer Continental Shelf Lands Act Section 8(g), 17 Coastal Management 171 (1989); R. Hildreth, Outer Continental Shelf Hydrocarbons and Minerals, in Silva, ed., Ocean Resources and Intergovernmental Relations in the 1980s (1986).

Under OCSLA section 8(p), added by the 2005 Energy Policy Act, the Interior Secretary may now grant leases, easements, and rights of way on the OCS for the production, transportation, and transmission of energy sources other than oil and gas, such as wind. In doing so, the Secretary is required to consult with affected state and local governments, collect a 'fair return' from the grantee, and distribute 27% of revenues collected in the 8(g) zone to coastal states within 15 miles of the project. The jurisdiction of other federal and state agencies over such projects under other laws such as the Rivers and Harbors Act and the CZMA is expressly preserved.

2. CIAP and GOMESA funds do not come without "strings attached." Unlike OCS revenues that are paid to the federal treasury, funds from these programs can only spent on specified programs. GOMESA funds, for example, may only be used for:

- Projects and activities for the purposes of coastal protection, including conservation, coastal restoration, hurricane protections, and infrastructure directly affected by coastal wetland losses;

- Mitigation of damage to fish, wildlife, or natural resources;

- Implementation of a federally approved marine, coastal, or comprehensive conservation management plan;

- Mitigation of impacts of OCS activities through funding of onshore infrastructure projects; and

- Planning assistance and the administrative costs not to exceed 3%.

Do these limitations make the revenue sharing less valuable to coastal states?

C. OUTER CONTINENTAL SHELF LANDS ACT

The Outer Continental Shelf Lands Act of 1953, 43 U.S.C.A. §§ 1331–1356, provided basic authority for OCS development and gives primary responsibility for the management of OCS oil and gas resources to the Department of the Interior (DOI). The Bureau of Ocean Energy Management (BOEM) [formerly the Minerals Management Service (MMS)] of the DOI administers the leasing provisions of the OCSLA and oversees the development of a tract once it has been leased as well as the decommissioning process. The current legal framework for oil and gas development was largely created by the Outer Continental Shelf Lands Act Amendments of 1978. The process was divided into four major stages:

1. The Secretary first prepares a nationwide five-year lease program that includes a schedule of potential lease sales.

2. The second stage comprises the individual lease sales scheduled in the 5-year program.

3. After the issuance of a lease, an Exploration Plan (EP) must be approved before an operator may begin exploratory drilling on a site. The EP includes all exploration activities, the timing of these activities, information concerning drilling, the location of each well, and other information.

4. To develop any oil and/or gas that is discovered, the lessee must submit for approval a Development and Production Plan (DPP) which includes the number of wells, where these wells will be located, what type of structure will be used, and how the operator will transport the oil and natural gas.

The process also involves the compliance of DOI with the National Environmental Policy Act (NEPA) and coordination with states and other agencies under provisions of the OCSLA and other acts.

Figure 5–1. OCS Oil and Gas Leasing Process

Pre-Lease   Develop 5-Year Program

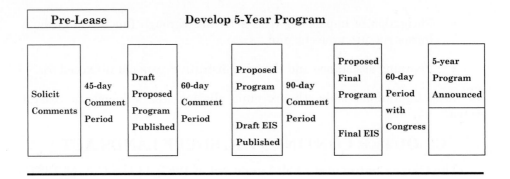

Planning for Specific Sale

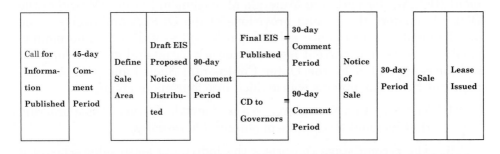

Post-Lease   Exploration Plan Approval

| Exploration Plan Submitted | Environmental Assessment / CZM Review Starts | Exploration Plan Approved | 90-day CZM Review Approved | APD Approved / Permits Granted | Exploration Drilling Starts | First Exploration Well Completed | Delineation Drilling |

Development & Production Plan Approval

Develop-ment and Production Plan	CZM Consistency Review Starts	Draft EIS Pub-lished	90-day Comment Period	Final EIS Pub-lished	CZM Consistency Obtained / Development and Produc-tion Plan Approved	Production Well Application	First Oil/Gas Production

Abbreviations
  APD: Application for Permit to Drill
  CZM: Coastal Zone Management
  EIS: Environmental Impact Statement

* * *

The possible adverse impacts of OCS oil and gas operations upon state beaches, waters, and coastal resources, and the lack of any significant offsetting economic benefits to most coastal states, have resulted in substantial opposition to such operations. At each stage of the process, state objections to OCS oil and gas plans are interposed and, not infrequently, litigation erupts with state, tribal, local, fishing and environmental interests on one side and federal agencies and oil and gas interests on the other. See E. Fitzgerald, The Seaweed Rebellion: Federal–State Conflicts over Offshore Energy Development (2001).

Since OCS operations must comply with a large number of statutory requirements, there are numerous legal avenues available to attempt to thwart OCS development. In most situations, opponents have not been able to prevent OCS oil and gas leasing or drilling. Delay, modification of the most objectionable features of OCS plans, and sometimes Congressional action withdrawing highly sensitive areas from a leasing plan are usually the goals of OCS litigation. The monetary and energy stakes are too high to expect that OCS drilling can be totally precluded.

The National Environmental Policy Act (NEPA), the Endangered Species Act (ESA), and Coastal Zone Management Act (CZMA) are at the core of much of the environmental OCS litigation. The role of the CZMA and its federal consistency requirement was discussed previously in Chapter 4. The following notes and cases discuss the relationship of the requirements of OCSLA, NEPA, and ESA.

NOTE ON OCSLA AND NEPA

There is only one provision in OCSLA mandating the preparation of an EIS and is directed at development and production plans in frontier areas. 43 U.S.C. § 351(e)(1) provides:

> At least once the Secretary shall declare the approval of a development and production plan in any area or region * * * of the outer Continental Shelf, other than the Gulf of Mexico, to be a major Federal action.

When an agency proposes a major Federal action, it must determine if the action has the potential to affect the quality of the human environment. Agencies then apply one of three levels of NEPA analysis:

1. Prepare an Environmental Impact Statement (EIS) when the agency determines that the proposed action has the potential for significant environmental impacts;

2. Prepare an Environmental Assessment (EA) to determine whether the agency can make a Finding of No Significant Impact (FONSI) or proceed to prepare an EIS; or

3. Apply a Categorical Exclusion (CE) when the agency determines that a proposed action falls within the categories of actions described in an established CE and that no extraordinary circumstances apply. Agencies establish CEs through a public comment process, with a finding that the category of actions does not normally, in the absence of extraordinary circumstances, result in individually or cumulatively significant environmental effects.

CEQ, Report Regarding the Minerals Management Service's National Environmental Policy Act Policies, Practices, and Procedures as They Relate to Outer Continental Shelf Oil and Gas Exploration and Development (August 16, 2010) ["CEQ NEPA Report"].

Although nowhere else in OCSLA is there a direct mandate for application of NEPA, the lease sale provisions imply that NEPA requirements must be met and an EIS prepared prior to any lease sale. See, e.g., 43 U.S.C. § 1346. Finally, OCSLA does state:

> (a) Except as otherwise expressly provided in this Act, nothing in this Act shall be construed to amend, modify, or repeal any provision of * * * NEPA * * *

43 U.S.C. § 1866(a). In light of this statutory structure, the courts have little difficulty finding that NEPA applies to the leasing process, see, e.g., Conservation Law Foundation v. Andrus, 623 F.2d 712, 716 (1st Cir. 1979); Natural Resources Defense Council v. Morton, 458 F.2d 827, 836 (D.C. Cir. 1972), to post-sale lease suspensions, California v. Norton, 311 F.3d 1162 (9th Cir. 2002), and to any frontier oil and gas production and development plan ap-

proval, see, e.g., Village of False Pass v. Clark, 733 F.2d 605, 609, 614, 615–16 (9th Cir. 1984).

NEPA also applies to the intermediate stage of the approval of an exploration plan. See 30 C.F.R. § 250.203(g). Potential adverse environmental impacts of exploration activities are an express concern of the OCSLA. 43 U.S.C. § 1340(c)(1) states:

> * * * The Secretary shall approve * * * [an exploration] plan * * * within thirty days of its submission, except that the Secretary shall disapprove such plan if he determines that (A) any proposed activity under such plan would result in any condition described in [section 1334(a)(2)(A)(i)] of this title, and (B) such proposed activity cannot be modified to avoid such condition. * * *

The condition described in 43 U.S.C. § 1334(a)(2)(A)(i) is

> * * * [the proposed] activity * * * would probably cause serious harm or damage to life (including fish and other aquatic life), to property * * * or to the marine, coastal, or human environment.

* * *

NOTE ON OCSLA AND
THE ENDANGERED SPECIES ACT (ESA)

The presence of an endangered species of fish, sea turtle, or birds, and of marine mammals in areas in which operations may take place means that the ESA and Marine Mammal Protection Act (MMPA) can have an effect on the location, timing, and extent of OCS oil and gas activities.

As described in the Coalition for a Sustainable Delta v. FEMA case in Chapter 4, beginning on p. 352, the ESA mandates that:

> Each Federal agency shall, in consultation with * * * the Secretary [of Interior or Commerce] insure that any action authorized, funded or carried out by such agency * * * is not likely to jeopardize the continued existence of any endangered species or threatened species or result in the destruction or adverse modification of habitat of such species which is determined by the Secretary * * * to be critical, unless such agency has been granted an exemption * * *.

Section 7(a)(2) [16 U.S.C. § 1536(a)(2)]. The MMPA's mandate, which is discussed later in Chapter 7, is similar to that of the ESA, and requires federal OCS licensees to obtain incidental take permits.

The ESA phrase "insure that any action" suggests a continuing obligation for all federal agencies to avoid adversely affecting threatened or endangered species. See, e.g., Defenders of Wildlife v. Administrator, EPA, 882 F.2d 1294, 1299 (8th Cir. 1989); Sierra Club v. Lyng, 694 F. Supp. 1260, 1270 (E.D. Tex. 1988). According to the implementing regulations, "action" includes the granting of licenses, * * * leases * * * [or] permits. * * * " 50 C.F.R. § 402.02. Thus the ESA is applicable to all stages of the OCS oil and gas process. See Village of False Pass v. Clark, 733 F.2d 605, 611–12 (9th Cir. 1984).

The act further provides that:

> the Federal agency and the permit or license applicant shall not make any irreversible or irretrievable commitment of resources with respect to the agency action which has the effect of foreclosing the formulation or implementation of any reasonable and prudent alternative measures which would not violate subsection (a)(2) quoted above.

16 U.S.C. § 1536(d). See 50 C.F.R. § 402.09 (prohibition is in force during the consultation process and continues until the requirements of section 7(a)(2) are satisfied). In the OCSLA context, a lease sale is not considered an "irreversible or irretrievable commitment of resources" because the Secretary has the authority to halt any future potentially harmful activities. See, e.g., Conservation Foundation v. Andrus, 623 F.2d. 712, 715 (1st Cir. 1979); North Slope Borough v. Andrus, 642 F.2d 589, 612 (D.C. Cir. 1980). In addition, leasing activities themselves do not pose a direct threat to any endangered species. It is the later stages of the OCS oil and gas process that present the dangers. Exploration and development/production plans thus would result in potentially jeopardizing activities and constitute "irreversible or irretrievable commitment of resources."

The ESA mandates that federal agencies consult with the FWS or the National Marine Fisheries Service whenever their actions may affect a species identified as endangered. 16 U.S.C. § 1536. However, this procedural duty seems only to require a level of compliance similar to that which exists in the NEPA context, with any judicial review applying the "arbitrary and capricious" standard. See, e.g., Cabinet Mountains Wilderness v. Peterson, 685 F.2d 678, 687 (D.C. Cir. 1982).

In the context of some OCS activities, the ESA may lack any real teeth. Although the ESA will halt activities that clearly jeopardize an endangered species, e.g. TVA v. Hill, 437 U.S. 153 (1978), the risks associated with offshore oil and gas activities are usually perceived as minimal due to the low probability of occurrence of an oil spill. Whenever OCS activities do potentially affect endangered species, the ESA provides various mechanisms that allow projects to proceed nonetheless. E.g., 16 U.S.C. §§ 1536(b)(4) and (o) (Secretary may issue biological opinions or incidental take permits setting out certain conditions that will minimize impacts to endangered species).

Have the findings of the Deepwater Horizon investigations concerning risk-taking by OCS operators altered this perception? See Section E of this chapter. Do the impacts of global warming on the Arctic Ocean also alter the risk calculus?

D. IMPLEMENTATION OF THE OCSLA DEVELOPMENT PROCESS

1. The Five-Year Leasing Program

CENTER FOR BIOLOGICAL DIVERSITY v. U.S. DEPARTMENT OF INTERIOR

United States Court of Appeals, District of Columbia Circuit, 2009
563 F.3d 466

SENTELLE, CHIEF JUDGE.

In August 2005, the United States Department of Interior (Interior) began the formal administrative process to expand leasing areas within the Outer Continental Shelf (OCS) for offshore oil and gas development between 2007 and 2012. This new five-year Leasing Program included an expansion of previous lease offerings in the Beaufort, Bering, and Chukchi Seas off the coast of Alaska. Petitioners filed independent petitions for review challenging the approval by the Secretary of the Interior (Secretary) of this Leasing Program on various grounds. Specifically, Petitioners argue that: (1) the Leasing Program violates both the OCSLA, 43 U.S.C. §§ 1331–1356a, and NEPA, 42 U.S.C. §§ 4321–4370f, because Interior failed to take into consideration both the effects of climate change on OCS areas and the Leasing Program's effects on climate change (the climate change claims); (2) the Leasing Program also violates both OCSLA and NEPA because Interior approved the Program without conducting sufficient biological baseline research for the three Alaskan seas, and further failed to provide a research plan detailing how it would obtain this baseline data before the next stage of the Program; (3) Interior violated the ESA, 16 U.S.C. §§ 1531–1544, by failing to consult with either the U.S. Fish and Wildlife Service (Fish and Wildlife) or the National Marine Fisheries Service (NMFS) about potential harm to endangered species in the OCS planning areas before it adopted the Leasing Program; and (4) the Leasing Program violates OCSLA because it irrationally relied on an insufficient study by [NOAA] (the NOAA study) in assessing the environmental sensitivity of the OCS planning areas in the Leasing Program. We hold that Petitioners' NEPA-based climate change claim, Petitioners' NEPA baseline data claim, and Petitioners' ESA claim are not yet ripe for review. We therefore dismiss the petition with respect to these claims.

Nevertheless, we conclude that Petitioners' remaining OCSLA-based challenges are all justiciable. Of these three remaining claims, Petitioners' OCSLA-based climate change claims and their OCSLA-rooted baseline data challenge ultimately lack merit and must fail. However, we find meritorious Petitioners' challenge to the Leasing Program on grounds that the Program's environmental sensitivity rankings are irrational. Accordingly, we vacate the Leasing Program, and remand the Program to the Secretary for reconsideration in accordance with this opinion.

I. Background

A. Introduction

* * * This action concerns a Leasing Program approved by Interior that includes a potential expansion of previous lease offerings in the Beaufort, Bering, and Chukchi Seas off the coast of Alaska. Each of these seas is home to a number of species of wildlife. For instance, the Beaufort and Chukchi Seas are home to two polar bear populations. The North Pacific right whale, an endangered marine mammal, is known to inhabit the Bering Sea. Bowhead whales are also known to feed and migrate through each of these seas. In addition, a number of other species of whale, seals, the Pacific walrus, and various seabirds are indigenous to these seas.

Three petitioners—Center for Biological Diversity, Alaska Wilderness League, and Pacific Environment—are non-profit activist organizations whose members have been working to preserve and protect the waters and living environments off the coast of Alaska. The remaining petitioner—the Native Village of Point Hope, Alaska—is a federally recognized tribal government whose members use the Chukchi Sea coast for subsistence hunting, fishing, whaling, and gathering, as well as cultural and religious activities.

B. Outer Continental Shelf Lands Act

* * *[The OCSLA] leasing program's four-stage process is "pyramidic in structure, proceeding from broad-based planning to an increasingly narrower focus as actual development grows more imminent." California v.Watt I, 668 F.2d 1290, 1297 (D.C. Cir. 1981). This multi-tiered approach was designed "to forestall premature litigation regarding adverse environmental effects that . . . will flow, if at all, only from the latter stages of OCS exploration and production." Sec'y of Interior, 464 U.S. at 341.

First, during the preparation stage, Interior creates a leasing program by preparing a five-year schedule of proposed lease sales. 43 U.S.C. § 1344. At this stage, "prospective lease purchasers acquire no rights to explore, produce, or develop" any of the areas listed in the leasing program. Sec'y of Interior, 464 U.S. at 338. Second, during the lease-sale stage, Interior solicits bids and issues leases for particular offshore leasing areas. 43 U.S.C. § 1337(a). Third, during the exploration stage, Interior reviews and determines whether to approve the lessees' more extensive exploration plans. 43 U.S.C. § 1340. Interior allows this exploration stage to proceed only if it finds that the lessees' exploration plan "will not be unduly harmful to aquatic life in the area, result in pollution, create hazardous or unsafe conditions, unreasonably interfere with other uses of the area, or disturb any site, structure, or object of historical or archeological significance." 43 U.S.C. § 1340(g)(3). Fourth and final is the development and production stage. During this stage, Interior and those affected state and local governments review an additional and more detailed plan from the lessee. 43 U.S.C. § 1351. If Interior finds that the plan would "probably cause serious harm or damage . . . to the marine, coastal or human environments," then the plan, and consequently the leasing program, may be terminated. 43 U.S.C. § 1351(h)(1)(D)(i).

The Leasing Program at issue has only completed its first stage—preparation of the five-year program under Section 18 of OCSLA, 43 U.S.C. § 1344. Under Section 18, the Secretary is required to prepare, periodically revise, and maintain "an oil and gas leasing program" that consists of "a schedule of proposed lease sales indicating, as precisely as possible, the size, timing, and location of leasing activity which he determines will best meet national energy needs for the five-year period following its approval or reapproval." 43 U.S.C. § 1344(a). The Secretary must prepare and maintain a leasing program consistent with several principles. First, the Secretary must ensure that a leasing program is "conducted in a manner which considers economic, social, and environmental values of the renewable and nonrenewable resources contained in the [OCS], and the potential impact of oil and gas exploration on other resource values of the [OCS] and the marine, coastal, and human environments." 43 U.S.C. § 1344(a)(1). Second, the Secretary must consider additional factors with respect to the timing and location of exploration, development, and production of oil and gas in particular OCS areas. These factors include, *inter alia*: a region's "existing information concerning the geographical, geological, and ecological characteristics;" "an equitable sharing of developmental benefits and environmental risks among the various regions;" "the interest of potential oil and gas producers in the development of oil and gas resources;" "the relative environmental sensitivity and marine productivity of different areas of the [OCS];" and "relevant environmental and predictive information for different areas of the [OCS]." 43 U.S.C. §§ 1344(a)(2)(A), (B), (E), (G), (H). Next, Interior must ensure, "to the maximum extent practicable," that the timing and location of leasing occurs so as to "obtain a proper balance between the potential for environmental damage, the potential for the discovery of oil and gas, and the potential for adverse impact on the coastal zone." 43 U.S.C. § 1344(a)(3). Finally Interior's leasing activities must ensure that winning lessees receive "fair market value for the lands leased and the rights conveyed by the Federal Government." 43 U.S.C. § 1344(a)(4). * * *

Section 20 of OCSLA also provides that, subsequent to a first lease in a given area, the Secretary "shall conduct such additional studies to establish environmental information as he deems necessary and shall monitor the human, marine, and coastal environments of such area or region

in a manner designed to provide time-series and data trend information."
43 U.S.C. § 1346(b).

C. National Environmental Policy Act

NEPA's requirements are essentially "procedural in character," and
are designed to "ensure solicitude for the environment through formal
controls and thereby help realize the substantive goal of environmental
protection." North Slope Borough v. Andrus, 206 U.S. App. D.C. 184, 642
F.2d 589, 598 (D.C. Cir. 1980). Ultimately, NEPA ensures that an agency's approval of a project is "a fully informed and well-considered decision." Id. at 599 (quoting Vermont Yankee Nuclear Power Corp. v. Natural Resources Def. Council, Inc., 435 U.S. 519, 558 (1978)). To that end,
the statute requires that each agency "assess the environmental consequences of 'major [f]ederal actions' by following certain procedures during
the decision-making process." Nevada v. Dep't of Energy, 457 F.3d 78, 87
(D.C. Cir. 2006) (quoting 42 U.S.C. § 4332(2)(C)). Before an agency may
approve a particular project, it must prepare a "detailed statement
. . . [on, *inter alia*,] the environmental impact of the proposed action,'
"any adverse environmental effects which cannot be avoided should the
proposal be implemented," and "alternatives to the proposed action." 42
U.S.C. §§ 4332(2)(C)(i)–(iii). When faced with a multi-stage, pyramidic
program such as the Leasing Program at issue here, NEPA's regulations
allow an agency to conduct a tiered approach to preparing an EIS. See 40
C.F.R. § 1508.28; see also Nevada, 457 F.3d at 91 & n.9. Under this approach, an agency may issue a broader EIS at the earlier "need and site
selection" stage of a program, and issue subsequent, more detailed environmental impact statements at the program's later, more site-specific
stage. See 40 C.F.R. § 1508.28.

D. Endangered Species Act

The ESA is designed to ensure that endangered species are protected
from government action. Under the ESA, each federal agency is required
to ensure that any action undertaken by the agency "is not likely to jeopardize the continued existence of any endangered species or threatened
species or result in the destruction or adverse modification" of critical animal habitats. 16 U.S.C. § 1536(a)(2). If an agency concludes that its action "may affect" a listed species or critical habitat, then the agency must
pursue either formal or informal consultation with the NMFS or Fish and
Wildlife. See 50 C.F.R. §§ 402.13, 402.14. If the agency determines that
its action will not affect any listed species or critical habitat, however,
then it is not required to consult with NMFS or Fish and Wildlife. See
Southwest Center for Biological Diversity v. U.S. Forest Serv., 100 F.3d
1443, 1447 (9th Cir. 1996).

E. Leasing Program

* * *

In total, the Leasing Program has scheduled 21 potential lease-sales between July 1, 2007 and June 30, 2012 in eight areas of the OCS. Four of those potential leasing areas are in the Beaufort, Bering, and Chukchi Seas off the Alaska coast. At the time the petitions challenging the approval of the Leasing Program were brought before this court, Interior had not yet conducted any lease-sales in these regions. Since that time, however, Interior has approved one lease-sale in the disputed Alaskan sea areas, Chukchi Sea Lease–Sale 193, which occurred on February 6, 2008. Petitioner Point Hope and others challenged this lease-sale in the federal district court for the District of Alaska.

II. Jurisdiction

We hold that Petitioners' three OCSLA-based claims are justiciable. We also hold that Petitioners' NEPA-based climate change and baseline data challenges, and their ESA claim are not yet ripe for review.

A. Climate Change Claims

Petitioners claim that Interior violated both OCSLA and NEPA because Interior failed to consider both the economic and environmental costs of the greenhouse gas emissions associated with the Program and the effects of climate change on OCS areas. * * * We hold, that Petitioners have standing to bring their climate change claims under their procedural theory of standing.

1. Petitioners' Procedural Theory of Standing

Petitioners argue that they are injured by Interior's failure to comply with both OCSLA and NEPA requirements. Specifically, Petitioners claim that Interior violated both OCSLA and NEPA because Interior failed to consider both the economic costs of the greenhouse gas emissions associated with the Program and the effects of climate change on OCS areas. As the Supreme Court noted in *Defenders of Wildlife*, a plaintiff may have standing if it can show that an agency failed to abide by a procedural requirement that was "designed to protect some threatened concrete interest" of the plaintiff. Lujan v. Defenders of Wildlife, 504 U.S. 555, 573 n.8 (1992). In such cases, the omission of a procedural requirement does not, by itself, give a party standing to sue. Audubon Soc'y, 94 F.3d at 664. Rather, "a procedural-rights plaintiff must show not only that the defendant's acts omitted some procedural requirement, but also that it is substantially probable that the procedural breach will cause the essential injury to the plaintiff's own interest." Id. at 664–65. A plaintiff "must show that he is not simply injured as is everyone else, lest the injury be too general for court action, and suited instead for political redress." Id. at 667 n.4.

Petitioners may bring both their OCSLA- and NEPA-based climate change claims under their procedural standing theory. Petitioners have shown that they possess a threatened particularized interest, namely their enjoyment of the indigenous animals of the Alaskan areas listed in the Leasing Program. The Supreme Court has noted "the desire to use or observe an animal species, even for purely aesthetic purposes, is undeniably a cognizable interest for purpose of standing." Defenders of Wildlife, 504 U.S. at 562–63. This interest, however, will not suffice on its own "without any description of concrete plans, or indeed even any specification of *when*" the plaintiff will be deprived of the opportunity to observe the potentially harmed species. Id. at 564. Petitioners' affidavits demonstrate a sufficiently immediate and definite interest in enjoyment of the animals. Petitioners' members have detailed in their affidavits definitive dates in the near future. Second, Petitioners have shown, solely for the sake of an Article III standing analysis, that Interior's adoption of an irrationally based Leasing Program could cause a substantial increase in the risk to their enjoyment of the animals affected by the offshore drilling, and that our setting aside and remanding of the Leasing Program would redress their harm.

B. NEPA Climate Change and Baseline Data Claims

* * *

Petitioners' NEPA-based claims are not ripe due to the multiple stage nature of the Leasing Program. * * *

At the point that Petitioners filed their petitions, Interior had only approved the Leasing Program at issue. No lease-sales had yet occurred. The Leasing Program here had therefore not yet reached that "critical stage" where an "irreversible and irretrievable commitment of resources" has occurred that will adversely affect the environment.

Additionally, any harm that might befall Petitioners by having to wait until the actual leasing stage to bring their claims is outweighed by the harm to Interior (and other agencies). Allowing a petitioner to bring such NEPA challenges to a leasing program when no rights have yet been implicated, or actions taken, would essentially create an additional procedural requirement for all agencies adopting any segmented program. This would impose too onerous an obligation, and would require an agency to divert too many of its resources at too early a stage in the decision-making process. By contrast, Petitioners suffer little by having to wait until the leasing stage has commenced in order to receive the information it requires. In the meantime, as Interior points out, no drilling will have occurred, and consequently, no harm will yet have occurred to the animals or their environment. * * *

C. ESA Claim

* * *

In order to resolve the ripeness of Petitioners' ESA claim, our inquiry must focus on whether an agency's approval of a leasing program "may affect" a listed species or critical habitat. Petitioners argue that we should consider the Leasing Program's potential effect on endangered species as a whole in resolving this issue. In other words, Petitioners advocate a "but for" approach: if, because of events traceable to the agency's adoption of the multiple-stage leasing plan, it is possible that an endangered species will be affected, then the agency must consult with NMFS or Fish and Wildlife. Interior advocates more of a "proximate cause" approach, viewing each stage of the agency action as a separate intervening act, and linking any effect on endangered species to that particular stage.

* * *

We conclude that Petitioners' ESA claim is not yet ripe. Given the multi-stage nature of leasing programs under OCSLA, we must consider any environmental effects of a leasing program on a stage-by-stage basis, and correspondingly evaluate ESA's obligations with respect to each particular stage of the program. Regardless of whether there has been an agency action under the ESA, the completion of the first stage of a leasing program does not cause any harm to anything because it does not require any action or infringe on the welfare of animals. The welfare of animals is, by design, only implicated at later stages of the program, each of which requires ESA consultation and additional environmental review by Interior. In addition, at this initial stage, leasing programs may list areas that Interior does not intend to lease. It is therefore not certain, at least at this initial stage of the Leasing Program, that any of the endangered species in the areas at issue may be affected by the Program, as the proposed leases in these areas might never come to pass. As a result, both this court and the Secretary of the Interior "would benefit from postponing review until the policy in question has sufficiently 'crystallized' by taking on a more definite form." Venetian Casino Resort, LLC v. EEOC, 409 F.3d 359, 364 (D.C. Cir. 2005) (citing City of Houston v. Dep't of Hous. & Urban Dev., 24 F.3d 1421, 1430–31 (D.C. Cir.1994)). Any hardship to Petitioners from delaying review of their ESA claim until after Interior moves beyond this initial stage of the Leasing Program is insufficient to outweigh the institutional interests of the court and Interior. Petitioners' ESA challenge at this initial stage of the Leasing Program is therefore premature. See Atl. States Legal Found. v. EPA, 325 F.3d 281, 284–85 (D.C. Cir. 2003).

D. OCSLA-based NOAA Study and Baseline Information Claims

Finally, we conclude that we do have jurisdiction over both of Petitioners' remaining OCSLA-based claims. Specifically, Petitioners argue that the Leasing Program violates OCSLA because Interior approved the Program without conducting sufficient biological baseline research. Petitioners also contend that the Leasing Program violates Section 18(a)(2)(G) of OCSLA because it relied on an insufficient NOAA study in assessing the environmental sensitivity of the OCS planning areas in the Leasing Program. See 43 U.S.C. § 1344(a)(2)(G).

First, as we did with Petitioners' OCSLA-based climate change claims, we conclude that Petitioners have standing to bring these remaining two OCSLA-based claims. Petitioners have shown that they possess a threatened particularized interest, namely their enjoyment of the indigenous animals of the Alaskan areas listed in the Leasing Program, and that they have a sufficiently immediate and definite interest in enjoyment of the animals. Second, Petitioners have also shown, solely for the sake of Article III standing analysis, that Interior's adoption of an irrationally based Leasing Program could cause a substantial increase in the risk to their enjoyment of the animals affected by the offshore drilling, and that our setting aside and remand of the Leasing Program would redress their harm. We also conclude that both of these remaining OCSLA-based claims are ripe for review, as both concern OCSLA requirements that are implicated at the initial stage of a leasing program. Accordingly, we may also proceed to the merits of these two claims.

III. Merits of the Remaining Justiciable Claims

A. Standard of Review

This court utilizes a "hybrid" standard of review when reviewing a leasing program for compliance with OCSLA. See Watt I, 668 F.2d at 1300. Findings of ascertainable fact are guided by the substantial evidence test. Id. at 1302. Under this standard, evidence upon which a finding is made must be "more than a scintilla," but may be less than a preponderance of the evidence. FPL Energy Maine Hydro LLC v. FERC, 287 F.3d 1151, 1160 (D.C. Cir. 2002). An agency's policy judgments are reviewed to ensure that "the decision is based on a consideration of the relevant factors and whether there has been a clear error of judgment." Watt I, 668 F.2d at 1302. This court gives substantial deference to the Secretary of Interior's interpretation of ambiguous provisions in OCSLA, so long as that interpretation is a "permissible construction of the statute." See id. at 1302–03. However, a statutory interpretation that does not effectuate Congress' intent must fall. Id. at 1303.

B. OCSLA-based Climate Change Claims

Petitioners raise two distinct but related OCSLA-based climate change claims. First, Petitioners argue that the Secretary violated sections 18(a)(1) and (a)(3) of OCSLA by failing to account for the environmental costs resulting from consumption of the fossil fuels extracted from the OCS. Second, Petitioners contend that Interior violated section 18(a)(2) of OCSLA because Interior failed to adequately consider climate change caused by consumption of these fossil fuels and the present and future impact of climate change on OCS areas as section 18(a)(2)(H) requires. To the extent these claims concern Interior's alleged failure to consider the effects brought about by *consumption* of oil and gas extracted under the Program, we hold that OCSLA does not require Interior to consider the global environmental impact of oil and gas consumption before approving a Leasing Program. Therefore, OCSLA does not require Interior to consider the further derivative environmental impact that oil and gas consumption has on OCS areas. Accordingly, Petitioners' OCSLA climate change claims fail.

Contrary to Petitioners' claims, the text of OCSLA does not require Interior to consider the impact of *consuming* oil and gas extracted under an offshore Leasing Program. Under Section 18(a) of OCSLA, Interior must prepare Leasing Programs so that "the size, timing, and location of leasing activity . . . will best meet national energy needs." 43 U.S.C. § 1344(a). Section 18(a)(1) states further that Interior must consider the values of resources "contained in the outer Continental Shelf," as well as "the potential impact of oil and gas *exploration* on other resource values of the [OCS] and the marine, coastal and human environments." 43 U.S.C. § 1344(a)(1) (emphasis added). Similarly, section 18(a)(3) states that "[t]he Secretary shall select the timing and location of leasing . . . so as to obtain a proper balance between the potential for environmental damage, the potential for the discovery of oil and gas, and the potential for adverse impact on the coastal zone." 43 U.S.C. § 1344(a)(3). We noted in *Watt I* that such a cost-benefit analysis of oil and gas extraction under section 18(a)(3) is satisfactory when an individual area's potential benefits are weighed against its potential costs. See Watt I, 668 F.2d at 1318. The Secretary therefore need only consider the "potential for environmental damage" on a localized area basis. And, under section 18(a)(2), Interior is required to determine the impacts of "exploration, development, and production" of oil and gas. As the statutory language and our precedent show, Interior's obligations under OCSLA extend to assessing the relative impacts of production and extraction of oil and gas on the localized areas in and around where the drilling and extraction occurred. Interior need not consider the impacts of the *consumption* of oil and gas after it has been extracted from the OCS. OCSLA therefore concerns the local environmental impact of leasing activities in the OCS and does not authorize—much less require—Interior to consider the environmental impact of post-exploration activities such as consuming fossil fuels on either the world at large, or the derivative impact of global fossil fuel consumption on OCS areas.

Moreover, Interior's continuing duty to promulgate five-year Leasing Programs under OCSLA renders Interior's consideration of the effects of oil and gas consumption unnecessary. Petitioners argue that Interior's consideration of the environmental impacts of greenhouse emissions associated with the Program might have altered Interior's ultimate decisions concerning the Program's leasing activities, such that the OCS areas at issue here might not have been included in the Program. But Petitioners' argument ignores the fact that Interior's decisions about the size and location of leasing areas or the timing of oil and gas extraction do not affect the impact that *consuming* oil and gas may have on climate change. That environmental impact is the same regardless of where and how the oil and gas are extracted. Therefore, even if, as Petitioners assert, Interior were not to adopt the Program at issue here, Interior's continuing duty to promulgate Leasing Programs would compel it to promulgate a different Leasing Program, potentially approving oil and gas extraction from other areas of the OCS. This extraction would presumably lead to the same overall consumption effects as those under the current Program.

Petitioners' consumption-related claims appear to stem from the flawed premise that, before Interior approves an offshore oil and gas Leasing Program, it must first consider whether it should extract oil and gas from the OCS at all. But Congress has already decided that the OCS should be used to meet the nation's need for energy. Indeed, OCSLA instructs Interior to ensure that oil and gas are extracted *from the OCS* in an expeditious manner that minimizes the *local* environmental damage to the OCS. See 43 U.S.C. § 1344. Interior simply lacks the discretion to consider any global effects that oil and gas consumption may bring about. Interior was therefore correct to point out in its EIS that the more expansive effect of oil and gas consumption is a matter for the Congress to consider "when decisions are made regarding the role of oil and gas generally, including domestic production and imports, in the Nation's overall energy policy." Consequently, it was unnecessary for Interior to consider the climate change effects brought about by the consumption of oil and gas—either as oil and gas consumption affects the global environment generally or the OCS areas specifically.

Interior's decision to limit its inquiry to the effect of the Program's *production* activities on climate change is consistent with its obligations under OCSLA, and was not error. Here, there is no doubt that Interior considered the effects of the Program's production activities on climate change generally, and the present and future impact of climate change on the local OCS areas. In the EIS, which Interior incorporated by reference in its Program approval, Interior estimated the total amount of greenhouse gas emissions that would result from leasing, exploration, and development in the OCS, and examined the cumulative impact of these emissions on the global environment. Interior also noted that potential impacts are "most pronounced in [the] Arctic Subregion," and could affect the areas of Alaska in which Petitioners assert an interest. Accordingly, Petitioners' OCSLA-based climate change claims fail. * * *

As its final EIS demonstrates, Interior considered and chronicled the geological, biological, and environmental information of the Beaufort, Bering, and Chukchi Seas, and many of their inhabitants. To be sure, a review of areas as wide and diversely populated as these Arctic seas will likely miss some of the seas' myriad inhabitants. These gaps in information, however, must be considered in conjunction with the "pyramidic structure" of a five-year leasing program. Watt I, 668 F.2d at 1297. At this early stage of the Leasing Program, the existence of some gaps in the baseline data for these three seas is not fatal to the Leasing Program. This is also tempered by the fact that Interior has recognized that such gaps exist and has indicated its intention to conduct additional research to close them. North Slope Borough v. Andrus, 642 F.2d 589, 613 (D.C. Cir. 1980) (affirming the district court's denial of petitioners' OCSLA claim that research was insufficient because Interior acknowledged that "[m]ore research is necessary; the research is being done"). * * *

D. NOAA Study Claim

Section 18(a)(2)(G) of OCSLA requires agencies to consider "the relative environmental sensitivity of . . . different areas of the outer Continental Shelf." 43 U.S.C. § 1344(a)(2)(G). In its efforts to comply with this requirement, Interior ranked the environmental sensitivity of various program areas in terms of only one factor: the "physical characteristics" of the shoreline of those areas. This ranking was based on Interior's use of the Environmental Sensitivity Index, developed by NOAA, which considered the sensitivity of different shoreline areas to oil spills, and ranked them on that basis. The study ranked each area on a scale of 1 to 10 (with 10 being a rating for an area most likely to be damaged long-term by oil spills). Petitioners contend that Interior's sole reliance on this study to measure the environmental sensitivity of the potential OCS leasing areas in the Leasing Program renders the Program improper. Interior counters that this court has stated that Section 18(a)(2)(G) "provides no method by which environmental sensitivity . . . [is] to be measured." Watt I, 668 F.2d at 1311. Accordingly, Interior argues that its adoption of the NOAA shoreline study to determine environmental sensitivity of OCS areas is a policy judgment that is entitled to substantial deference.

Interior's argument is not consistent with controlling precedent. Our decisions in California v. Watt (Watt II), 712 F.2d 584 (D.C. Cir. 1983), and *Watt I* set forth the standard for Interior's compliance with Section 18(a)(2)(G). In *Watt II*, we affirmed our holding in *Watt I* that all that is required for compliance with Section 18(a)(2)(G) is "that the Secretary make a good faith determination of the relative environmental sensitivity . . . of the various regions based upon the best 'existing information' available to him." Watt II, 712 F.2d at 596 (quoting Watt I, 668 F.2d at 1313)). Accordingly, the Secretary was "free to choose any methodology 'so long as it is not irrational.' " Watt II, 712 F.2d at 596 (quoting Watt I, 668 F.2d at 1320). The Secretary's decision is not irrational so long as it is "based on a consideration of the relevant factors." Watt I, 668 F.2d at 1317.

Interior's interpretation of Section 18(a)(2)(G) is irrational. It was not based on a consideration of the relevant factors set forth therein. Section 18(a)(2)(G) states clearly that an agency must assess the environmental sensitivity of "different areas *of the outer Continental Shelf*" in order to make its determination of when and where to explore and develop additional areas for oil. 43 U.S.C. § 1344(a)(2)(G) (emphasis added). Based on this language alone, Interior's use of the NOAA study runs afoul of this provision because it assesses only the effects of oil spills on shorelines. Interior provides no explanation for how the environmental sensitivity of coastal shoreline areas can serve as a substitute for the environmental sensitivity of OCS areas, when the coastline and proposed leasing areas are so distant from each other. This interpretation runs directly counter to the statutory language.

Moreover, though *Watt II* and *Watt I* afforded Interior a great deal of leeway in determining how to comply with Section 18(a)(2)(G), they did not give Interior carte blanche to wholly disregard a statutory requirement out of convenience. The law plainly requires that Interior examine and compare the environmental sensitivity of different areas of the OCS. Though the law allows Interior to consider the environmental sensitivity of onshore areas to OCS development, it plainly does not allow Interior to consider *only* onshore areas. Interior's sole focus on the environmental sensitivity of shoreline areas to OCS development therefore falls short of what Section 18(a)(2)(G) requires. Accordingly, Interior's Section 18(a)(2)(G) analysis is inadequate.

Our conclusion that Interior failed to properly conduct an environmental sensitivity analysis under Section 18(a)(2)(G) does not end our inquiry. We have consistently linked the adequacy of Interior's analysis under Section 18(a)(2) with its analysis under Section 18(a)(3). Section 18(a)(3) requires that, when preparing a leasing program, Interior select, "to the maximum extent practicable," the "timing and location of leasing . . . so as to obtain a proper balance between the potential for environmental damage, potential for the discovery of oil and gas, and the potential for adverse impact on the coastal zone." 43 U.S.C. § 1344(a)(3). In essence, these three elements are "a condensation of the factors specified in section 18(a)(2)." Though Section 18(a)(3) does not define specifically how Interior shall balance these three elements, Watt I, 668 F.2d at 1315, it stands to reason that a flawed consideration of Section 18(a)(2) factors hinders Interior's ability to obtain a proper balance of the factors under Section 18(a)(3). Interior's failure to properly consider the environmental sensitivity of different areas of the OCS—areas *beyond* the Alaskan coastline—has therefore also hindered Interior's ability to comply with Section 18(a)(3)'s balancing requirement.

Consequently, on remand, the Secretary must first conduct a more complete comparative analysis of the environmental sensitivity of different areas "*of the outer Continental Shelf,*" 43 U.S.C. § 1344(a)(2)(G) (emphasis added), and "must at least attempt to identify those areas whose environment and marine productivity are most and least sensitive to OCS activity." Though Interior may ultimately conclude as a result of this additional analysis that the shorelines of the Beaufort, Bering, and Chukchi Seas are the areas that are most sensitive to OCS development, such a conclusion cannot be reached without considering the effects of development on areas of the OCS in addition to the shoreline. Once Interior has conducted its Section 18(a)(2)(G) analysis, Interior must then determine whether its reconsideration of the environmental sensitivity analysis warrants the exclusion of any proposed area in the Leasing Program. Finally, having reconsidered its Section 18(a)(2) analysis, Interior must reassess the timing and location of the Leasing Program "so as to obtain a proper balance between the potential for environmental damage, the potential for the discovery of oil and gas, and the potential for adverse impact on the coastal zone," as required by Section 18(a)(3). 43 U.S.C. § 1344(a)(3).

* * *

We vacate the Leasing Program and remand the Program to the Secretary for reconsideration in accordance with this opinion.

So ordered.

2. Lease Sale Stage

NATIVE VILLAGE OF POINT HOPE v. SALAZAR

United States District Court, District of Alaska, 2010
730 F.Supp.2d 1009

AMENDED ORDER REMANDING TO AGENCY

I. Motions Presented

Plaintiffs have filed a Complaint for Declaratory and Injunctive Relief challenging Defendants' decision to offer approximately 29.4 million acres of public lands on the outer continental shelf of the Chukchi Sea for oil and gas leasing. Plaintiffs allege that the decision, together with the Chukchi Sea Planning Area Oil and Gas Lease Sale 193 and Seismic Surveying Activities in the Chukchi Sea Final Environmental Impact Statement (FEIS), violates NEPA and the Administrative Procedure Act (APA).

Specifically, Plaintiffs allege that the FEIS:

1. does not adequately analyze and present the impacts of Lease Sale 193 on the environment and human communities;

2. fails to include essential missing information about the Chukchi Sea and the potential impacts of the lease sale, or explain why excluding this information is justified;

3. fails to adequately analyze the impact of the lease sale in the context of a warming climate;

4. understates the potential impacts of oil and gas development pursuant to the leases by analyzing a limited development scenario;

5. understates the risks of an oil spill;

6. fails to fully analyze the cumulative impacts to threatened eiders of the lease sale and other oil and gas development in threatened eiders' Arctic habitat; and

7. provides a misleading analysis of the effects of seismic surveying.

Defendants suggest that the result of their due diligence, review of the best available scientific information, and extensive public process was a three-volume Final EIS comprising over 1,800 pages of analysis, tables, figures, and responses to comments. This EIS was preceded by decades of prior seismic and exploration activity, which included extensive public comment, participation, and analysis of existing scientific data. They say Sale 193 EIS not only incorporates information from the two EIS's prepared in connection with MMS's five-year leasing plans, it also incorporates two Biological Opinions issued by the National Marine Fisheries Service and the Fish and Wildlife Service on the bowhead whale, the spectacled eider, the Steller's eider, and the Ledyard Bay Habitat Unit designated for spectacled eiders, and information from the 2006 Programmatic Environmental Assessment for Seismic Activities in the Beaufort and Chukchi Seas. The Sale 193 EIS contains a nearly 300-page discussion of the impacts of the "Proposed Action" and a 76-page analysis of potential cumulative effects. Defendants argue that the EIS includes a detailed environmental review of each of the areas Plaintiffs allege is deficient—missing baseline information about resources and impacts, the development scenario, climate change, seismic activity, and endangered and threatened species. * * *

II. Background

A. National Environmental Policy Act

NEPA mandates the preparation of an Environmental Impact Statement ("EIS") for any major federal action "significantly affecting the quality of the human environment." The twin objectives of NEPA are to (1) require the federal agency to "consider every significant aspect of the environmental impact of a proposed action," and (2) ensure that the agency "inform[s] the public that it has indeed considered environmental concerns in its decision-making process." NEPA aims to "promote efforts which will prevent or eliminate damage to the environment and biosphere and stimulate the health and welfare of man. . . . " An injunction that prevents harmful activities undoubtedly furthers these purposes and thereby protects the public interest, but the development of the state's natural resources is a competing public interest to consider.

* * *

III. Standard of Review

Judicial review of administrative actions under NEPA is governed by the Administrative Procedure Act ("APA"). Under the APA, the Court must determine whether the agency action was "arbitrary and capricious, an abuse of discretion, or otherwise not in accordance with law," or "without observance of procedure required by law. . . . "When considering whether the action was arbitrary and capricious or an abuse of discretion, "we must ensure that the agency has taken a 'hard look' at the environmental consequences of its proposed action." However, "[t]he standard is narrow and the reviewing court may not substitute its judgment for that of the agency."

An agency decision is arbitrary and capricious if the agency has "relied on factors which Congress has not intended it to consider, entirely failed to consider an important aspect of the problem, offered an explanation for its decision that runs counter to the evidence before the agency, or is so implausible that it could not be ascribed to a difference in view or the product of agency expertise."

As long as the agency "has considered the relevant factors and articulated a rational connection between the facts found and the choice made," a court must uphold the administrative action. Deference is especially appropriate when reviewing the agency's technical analysis and judgments involving the evaluation of complex scientific data within the agency's technical expertise. Deference must be given to the experience and expertise of the agency in light of the Supreme Court's instruction that the Court is not to substitute its own judgment for that of the agency.

Furthermore, the purpose of NEPA is to ensure that environmental considerations are taken into account, but not necessarily elevated over other appropriate considerations. In the context of reviewing an EIS, the Ninth Circuit has explained:

> The adequacy of an EIS depends upon whether it was prepared in observance of the procedure required by law. . . . Under this standard of review, we employ a "rule of reason" that inquires whether an EIS contains a reasonably thorough discussion of the significant aspects of the probable environmental consequences. . . . This standard is not susceptible to refined calibration. It instead requires a reviewing court to make a pragmatic judgment whether the EIS's form, content and preparation foster both informed decision-making and informed public participation. . . . This standard of review, however, does not authorize a reviewing court to substitute its judgment for that of the agency concerning the wisdom or prudence of a proposed action. Once satisfied that a proposing agency has taken a "hard look" at a decision's environmental consequences, the review is at an end.

Finally, where "a court reviews an agency action involv[ing] primarily issues of fact, and where analysis of the relevant documents requires a high level of technical expertise, [the court] must defer to the informed discretion of the responsible federal agencies."

IV. Discussion

NEPA review occurs at each stage of the four-stage process, but MMS issues "more detailed environmental impact statements at the program's later, more site-specific stage." Defendants argue that Plaintiffs' claims under 40 C.F.R. § 1502.22 must be considered exclusively in the context in which this case arises—i.e., in the second stage of the OCS Lands Act's four-stage process for oil and gas leasing. During the second stage, leases are issued by MMS, but "the purchase of a lease entails no right to proceed with full exploration, development, or production." * * *

Defendants argue that Plaintiffs want the same degree of review applicable at a later phase applied at the lease sale phase, which fails to account for the distinct nature of a lease sale. It is the promise of more accurate information and further review at each subsequent stage, Defendants argue, that makes a more limited review at the lease sale stage appropriate. Plaintiffs would have the Department of Interior wait for more information before approving the lease sale, but Defendants argue that the lease sale itself is a catalyst for gathering information.

The Ninth Circuit has previously ruled in the oil and gas leasing context, at the initial leasing stage, NEPA does not require MMS to prepare an EIS that evaluates potential environmental effects on a site-specific level of detail. The Ninth Circuit found that, while plaintiffs had "legitimate concerns about the uncertainty at this stage of gauging the adverse effects that future development may have on this environment," such concerns were "inherent in any program for the development of natural resources." The Court explained that "[t]his is because such projects generally entail separate stages of leasing, exploration and development. At the earliest stage, the leasing stage we have before us, there is no way of knowing what plans for development, if any, may eventually materialize." Intervener–Defendant Conoco Phillips Company notes that as expected in a remote, frontier area, MMS has estimated the probability that Lease Sale 193 will result in a commercial discovery leading to development and production is less than 10%.

Plaintiffs argue that the EIS understates the potential impacts of development from the lease sale. They also argue that MMS's NEPA obligation at the lease sale stage is to analyze the effects of development, "should it occur." The likelihood that commercial discovery leading to development and production is less than 10% is therefore, irrelevant. Plaintiffs further note that once leases are issued, significant rights are transferred to the lessee, and a lessee may immediately conduct preliminary industrial activities without further MMS approval, including certain types of seismic surveying and drilling. The government can suspend or cancel leases, but only after making findings about the potential for harm to the environment, and potentially subjecting itself to substantial liability to the lessees.

A. Seismic Surveying and Threatened Eiders

Plaintiffs allege that MMS failed to take a hard look at the effects of seismic surveying, and failed to fully analyze cumulative effects to threatened eiders. Specifically, Plaintiffs argue that the EIS's discussion of the effects of seismic surveying violated NEPA because, even though it bases its conclusions on successful mitigation measures, it (1) fails to disclose and analyze data from 2006 reports that call into doubt the efficacy of mitigation measures designed to prevent injury to marine mammals from loud noise; and (2) fails to disclose scientific debate about whether broader exclusion zones are needed to protect bowhead cows and calves from disturbance impacts and avoid resulting significant effects to the bowhead population. The government acknowledges that the EIS did not analyze these questions, but justifies the failure by arguing that future permits will impose mitigation measures that will avoid impacts to marine mammals. Plaintiffs suggest this is contrary to what the law requires. In light of these omissions, Plaintiffs argue the EIS does not meet NEPA's requirements.

The Court finds that the record reflects a "hard look" in these areas, acknowledging that necessary mitigation measures can be implemented in stages 3 and 4. To conclude otherwise would require the Court to engage in multiple levels of speculation, which is expressly forbidden under the applicable standard of review, which "is narrow and the reviewing court may not substitute its judgment for that of the agency."

B. Oil and Gas Development

Plaintiffs complain that the EIS omits analysis of natural gas development * * *. Plaintiffs suggest that the government's justification regarding the omission of natural gas development in the EIS (i.e. that there is presently no infrastructure to bring natural gas to market) is unpersuasive. The leases allow the development of natural gas, notwithstanding the current lack of infrastructure. Plaintiffs suggest the guiding assumption underlying the development is that the size of the resources discovered will justify the construction of an infrastructure to bring the resource to market. The Defendants do not dispute that the leases include incentives for natural gas development.

The Court finds that the EIS analysis of "only" the first billion gallons of oil satisfies the "hard look" requirement at this stage. However, the Court agrees with Plaintiffs that the inclusion of incentives for natural gas production, without addressing the impact of natural gas exploration, is arbitrary, because it "entirely failed to consider an important aspect" of the lease sale. The agency cannot have taken a "hard look" at the impact of natural gas exploration if natural gas development is omitted entirely from the EIS.

C. Incomplete or Unavailable Information

NEPA's regulatory requirements impose specific obligations on agencies faced with incomplete or unavailable information. When an agency is evaluating reasonably foreseeable significant adverse effects on the human environment in an environmental impact statement and there is incomplete or unavailable information, *the agency shall always make clear that such information is lacking.*

(a) If the incomplete information *relevant* to foreseeable significant adverse impacts is *essential* to a reasoned choice among alternatives and the overall costs of obtaining it are *not exorbitant*, the agency *shall* include the information in the environmental impact statement.

(b) If the information relevant to reasonably foreseeable significant adverse impacts cannot be obtained because the overall costs of obtaining it are exorbitant or the means to obtain it are not known, the agency shall include within the environmental impact statement:

(1) A statement that such information is incomplete or unavailable;

(2) a statement of the relevance of the incomplete or unavailable information to evaluating reasonably foreseeable significant adverse impacts on the human environment;

(3) a summary of existing credible scientific evidence which is relevant to evaluating the reasonably foreseeable significant adverse impacts on the human environment, and

(4) the agency's evaluation of such impacts based upon theoretical approaches or research methods generally accepted in the scientific community. For the purposes of this section, "reasonably foreseeable" includes impacts which have catastrophic consequences, even if their probability of occurrence is low, provided that the analysis of the impacts is supported by credible scientific evidence, is not based on pure conjecture, and is within the rule of reason. 40 C.F.R. § 1502.22 (emphasis added).

In support of their claim that the EIS suffers from missing information and data gaps, Plaintiffs have provided an exhibit with their Opening Brief ("Exhibit 129"). Exhibit 129 is a compendium of statements made in the EIS for Lease Sale 193. Many of the statements acknowledge missing information about the Chukchi Sea environment and the potential effects of the lease sale on wildlife and subsistence. The exhibit reflects dozens if not hundreds of entries indicating a lack of information about species/habitat, as well as a lack of information about effects of various activities on many species.

Plaintiffs argue that MMS failed to determine whether missing information was relevant or essential under 40 C.F.R. § 1502.22, and failed to determine whether the cost of obtaining the missing information was exorbitant, or the means of doing so unknown. Plaintiffs argue that MMS's failure to do so violates Section 1502.22 and is arbitrary. Having failed to make these determinations under § 1502.22, Plaintiffs argue that Defendants' arguments (on brief) that the missing information was not relevant or essential for the lease sale decision is a post-hoc justification that cannot be credited. Plaintiffs request that the Court dismiss the argument out of hand and remand to the agency to evaluate, as NEPA requires, the importance of the missing information.

Defendants argue that Plaintiffs have the burden to demonstrate that the information they claim is missing meets both the "relevant" and "essential" prongs of § 1502.22, and that Plaintiffs have failed to meet this burden. The Court finds, however, that this conflicts with the plain language of § 1502.22, which requires the agency to make the findings. Furthermore, "It is well established that an agency's action must be upheld, if at all, on the basis articulated by the agency itself," rather than on post-hoc rationalization by its lawyers. The Court finds that MMS's failure to follow § 1502.22 was arbitrary and warrants remand.

V. Conclusion

The Court finds that, although much of the Agency's extensive investigation was appropriate . . . the record reflects that the Agency:

(1) failed to analyze the environmental impact of natural gas development, despite industry interest and specific lease incentives for such development;

(2) failed to determine whether missing information identified by the agency was relevant or essential under 40 C.F.R. § 1502.22; and

(3) failed to determine whether the cost of obtaining the missing information was exorbitant, or the means of doing so unknown. The Court finds the Agency's failure to comply with the clear instructions of § 1502.22 was an abuse of discretion. This does not necessarily require the Agency to completely redo the permitting process, but merely to address the three concerns addressed above. In all other respects the Court finds Defendants have complied with NEPA.

* * * This matter is remanded to the Agency to satisfy its obligations under NEPA in accordance with this opinion. This Order is intended to be narrow and not construed to prevent scientific studies which have already been approved or are pending approval by BOEM (formerly MMS), to include activities under the approved Work Plan that were fully examined in the Agency's EIS and are unrelated to the defects identified by the Court. Furthermore, this Order does not apply to activities outside of Lease Sale 193 or to organizations not a party to this lawsuit, nor does it preclude BOEM from issuing permits under its permitting authorities to Statoil or others or prohibit routine paper transactions relating to Lease Sale 193.

It is so ordered.

NOTES AND QUESTIONS

1. If, under the OCSLA, the Secretary lacks the discretion to consider the global environmental effects of producing oil and gas from the OCS, is the Secretary required to do so under NEPA at the lease sale stage?

2. Where does the president get the authority to impose a moratorium on OCS development?

3. Has President Obama by executive order created a process for the management of the U.S. OCS on a regional, multiple-use basis? See E.O. 13547, Stewardship of the Oceans, Our Coasts, and the Great Lakes, 75 Fed. Reg. 43023 (July 19, 2010).

4. What are the onshore impacts of offshore oil drilling? Are the effects positive or negative? What mechanisms other than the OCSLA and CZMA are available to state and local governments for planning and controlling on-

shore impacts? See Western Oil and Gas Association v. Sonoma County, 905 F.2d 1287 (9th Cir. 1990) (land use ordinances in California that regulate onshore facilities used to support offshore oil and gas development were not subject to challenge by the oil industry association because the plaintiffs had not demonstrated that the ordinances will interfere with their bidding rights for OCS leases); Louisiana v. Lujan, 777 F. Supp. 486 (E.D. La. 1991) (rejecting the state's challenge to a Gulf of Mexico lease sale based on negative impacts on coastal wetlands and inadequately estimated socioeconomic impacts onshore).

---

3. Exploration Stage

ALASKA WILDERNESS LEAGUE V. KEMPTHORNE
United States Court of Appeals, Ninth Circuit, 2008
548 F.3d 815

NELSON, SENIOR CIRCUIT JUDGE.

Petitioners challenge the Minerals Management Service's ("MMS") approval of an exploration plan submitted by Shell Offshore Inc. ("Shell"). Shell seeks to drill multiple offshore exploratory oil wells over a three-year period in the Alaskan Beaufort Sea.

Petitioners challenge the agency's action under NEPA, 42 U.S.C. §§ 4321–4347, and the OCSLA, 43 U.S.C. §§ 1331–56. Petitioners allege that MMS failed to take the requisite "hard look" at the impact of drilling on the people and wildlife of the Beaufort Sea region in violation of the standards set forth by NEPA, OCSLA, and their implementing regulations. Petitioners also argue that MMS erred by failing to prepare an environmental impact statement ("EIS") for the proposed exploration activities, because of the potential for significant harmful effects on the environment.

We vacate the agency's approval of Shell's exploration plan, and remand so that MMS can conduct the "hard look" analysis required by NEPA.

FACTUAL AND PROCEDURAL BACKGROUND

I. Administrative Process

In April 2002, MMS issued a five-year plan establishing a lease sale schedule for the Outer Continental Shelf ("OCS") of the Gulf of Mexico and Alaska. The plan envisions offering three separate lease sales in the Beaufort Sea. In February 2003, MMS prepared a detailed EIS to evaluate the overall impacts of the activities projected to occur pursuant to these lease sales ("multi-sale EIS"). The study analyzes the potential effects of oil exploration and production on the region's wildlife, environment, and subsistence activities. The multi-sale EIS assumes that drilling would begin in 2007, and would require a maximum of two drilling rigs, icebreakers, supply boats, and floating platforms in waters deeper than twenty meters. The multi-sale EIS also evaluates mitigation measures that were developed through the cooperation of federal agencies, the State of Alaska, and Native Alaskans. These measures include an extensive bowhead whale monitoring program and a conflict avoidance process designed to protect subsistence activities. The multi-sale EIS further notes: "Any proposed exploration or development plans that may result for any of the three OCS sales evaluated in this EIS, would require additional NEPA environmental analysis using site specific information."

In 2003, MMS held the first sale, Lease Sale 186, without conducting further NEPA analysis. The agency held two subsequent lease sales in July 2004 (Lease Sale 195), and August 2006 (Lease Sale 202), preparing a supplemental environmental assessment ("EA") for each one. Both of these EAs "tiered" to the multi-sale EIS. In the tiering process, the agency looks to see if the proposed activities are covered by the analysis in previous studies, whether additional mitigation measures are needed, and what level of NEPA evaluation is required. The leases at issue in this case were purchased in July 2004, under Lease Sale 195.

OCSLA requires that a lessee obtain approval of an exploration plan ("EP") before beginning exploratory drilling. 30 C.F.R. § 250.201. The EP must include a project-specific environmental impact analysis assessing the potential effects of the proposed exploration activities. 30 C.F.R. § 250.227. MMS reviews the EP, and the application is deemed "submitted" when it "fulfills requirements and is sufficiently accurate," and the applicant has "provided all needed additional information." 30 C.F.R. § 250.231(a). MMS then conducts its environmental review pursuant to NEPA, 30 C.F.R. § 250.232(c), and within thirty days issues a decision approving, disapproving, or requiring modifications to the EP. 30 C.F.R. § 250.233.

Shell's proposed drilling activities are the first to be considered for the Beaufort Sea in conjunction with these lease sales. In November 2006, Shell submitted the first version of its EP for the Beaufort Sea region. Shell's EP details its plan to drill up to twelve exploratory wells on twelve lease tracts in the Beaufort Sea over the next three years. The lease blocks are grouped into five "prospects" and stretch from the Colville River Delta eastward to the Canadian border. The Cornell Prospect is fifteen to twenty miles offshore of the Colville River Delta, north of the Inupiat Eskimo village of Nuiqsut. The Sivulliq Prospect is ten miles offshore in Camden Bay, between the villages of Nuiqsut and Kaktovik. The Olympia Prospect is located north of Kaktovik. The Fosters and Fireclaw Prospects are located farther east, between Kaktovik and the Canadian border.

In the first year of the plan, Shell aims to drill four wells within the Sivulliq Prospect in Camden Bay. In the following two years "Shell proposes to drill an undetermined number of wells on additional prospects . . . depending on the [initial] drilling results." Throughout this project, Shell plans to use two drilling vessels, two icebreaking ships, various other supply boats, and up to six aircraft. All exploratory activities would occur between June and mid-November as the Beaufort Sea is frozen over for half of the year.

In December 2006, MMS issued its "Completeness Comments" on Shell's EP, indicating what information was still needed before the EP would be considered properly submitted. The agency asked Shell to clarify the specific drilling locations for which it was seeking approval. MMS also sought more information on the "potential impact of underwater noise," conflict avoidance mechanisms, and other mitigation measures that could ameliorate the deleterious effects of the exploratory drilling. The final version of Shell's EP was submitted on January 12, 2007. The application included Shell's Environmental Report and an oil spill contingency plan. No further detail was given identifying specific well locations for the 2008 and 2009 seasons. MMS determined the application was complete and began the approval process on January 17, 2007.

After receiving a completed EP, the agency has thirty days to approve, disapprove, or require modification of a plan. 43 U.S.C. § 1340(c)(1); 30 C.F.R. § 250.233. Throughout this time period, a number of agency experts expressed concern about the potentially significant impacts the drilling would have on bowhead whales, polar bears, and the Inupiat subsistence harvest.

Despite these concerns, MMS issued an eighty-seven page EA and a Finding of No Significant Impact ("FONSI") on February 15, 2007. The EA "tiers" to the prior environmental studies, pursuant to 40 C.F.R. § 1502.20. The EA states: "The level and types of activities proposed in the Shell EP are within the range of the activities described and evaluated in the Beaufort Sea multiple-sale EIS . . . and updated in EA's [sic] for Sales 195 and 202." The agency concluded that the proposed activities "would not significantly affect the quality of the human environment" or "cause 'undue or serious harm or damage to the human, marine, or coastal environment,' " in accordance with 40 C.F.R. § 1508.27. As a result of this finding, the agency did not prepare an EIS specific to this project.

MMS's approval of the EP was subject to many conditions. Shell had to: (1) obtain a determination from the State of Alaska that its operations were consistent with the Alaska Coastal Management Plan; (2) take measures to avoid conflicts with subsistence harvests; and (3) get approval of its project from both the National Marine Fisheries Service and the

Fish and Wildlife Service. The State of Alaska approved Shell's plan on June 19, 2007. Shell reached a conflict avoidance agreement with local whaling captains on July 24, 2007. On July 31, 2007, the Fish and Wildlife Service issued its Letter of Authorization. The National Marine Fisheries Service approved the project on October 25, 2007. * * *

On August 14, 2007, this court granted Petitioners' motion to stay, ordering the agency's decision inoperative until this matter could be considered on the merits.

II. BEAUFORT SEA RESOURCES AND WILDLIFE

The Alaskan Beaufort Sea is part of the Arctic Ocean, bordering Alaska's north shore. It stretches from Point Barrow and the Chukchi Sea in the west, to the Canadian border in the east. The Beaufort Sea is home to a wide range of fish, mammal, and bird species. The Western Arctic stock of bowhead whales lives within the Beaufort region. Bowhead whales are designated as an endangered species under 50 C.F.R. § 17.11(h). * * *

Bowhead whales are sensitive to noise in the marine environment. The noise generated by icebreakers and drill ships has the potential to cause serious consequences for bowhead whales. The impacts of a specific project would vary depending on the placement, quantity, and quality of vessels operating at each site. High levels of underwater noise can cause temporary or permanent hearing damage. Even low levels of noise can affect the biological functions and behavioral patterns of marine mammals. In particular, increased noise can cause avoidance behaviors that displace migratory routes. Females traveling with young calves may be especially susceptible to harm, as disturbances could separate a dependent from its caregiver.

The Inupiat Eskimos reside on the north coast of Alaska and have long relied upon the resources of the Beaufort Sea and its environs for subsistence. Eight different villages are scattered along the coast. As noted by the multi-sale EIS:

> [T]his close relationship between the spirit of a people, their social organization, and the cultural value of subsistence hunting may be unparalleled when compared with other areas in America where energy development is taking place. The Inupiat's continuing strong dependence on subsistence foods, particularly marine mammals and caribou, creates a unique set of potential effects from onshore and offshore oil exploration and development on the social and cultural system.

Subsistence activities are an important component of the Inupiat's long-term health, as this diet and lifestyle protects against degenerative health risks. Further, as the multi-sale EIS states "[s]ubsistence activities are assigned the highest cultural values by the Inupiat and provide a sense of identity in addition to being an important economic pursuit."

Bowhead whales are an important subsistence resource for the Inupiat. The harvest of bowhead whales is regulated by the International Whaling Commission, which sets guidelines on the number of whales that can be taken for subsistence purposes. The whale hunt is a dangerous and arduous process for Inupiat whalers, but it produces large amounts of meat consumed by Inupiat communities. Shell's proposed activities take place in and adjacent to the subsistence bowhead whale hunting grounds for the villagers of both Nuiqsut and Kaktovik. As a result, there is the potential that Shell's activities may disrupt the Inupiat whaling activities.

STANDARDS OF REVIEW

* * *

We review a decision to forego preparation of an environmental impact statement under the arbitrary and capricious standard. Nat'l Parks & Conservation Ass'n v. Babbitt, 241 F.3d 722, 730 (9th Cir.2001). We look to whether the agency has: (1) taken a "hard look" at the potential impact of its actions; (2) considered all of the relevant factors in its decision; and (3) provided an adequate statement of reasons to explain why a project's impacts are insignificant. *Id.* * * *

OCSLA's jurisdictional provision provides that a petition for review must be filed with the court within sixty days of any contested action. 43 U.S.C. § 1349(c)(3).

I. Compliance with NEPA "Hard Look" Review

A. Statutory Background

OCSLA provides for a four-stage process for oil and gas development, with NEPA review at each stage. * * * The continuing review process allows an agency to adjust its analysis to make sure energy production activities are conducted in an environmentally sound manner. The case before us involves exploration, the third stage of the process. At this phase, a lessee submits an EP for review and approval. 43 U.S.C. § 1340(c). The agency has thirty days to review the EP. Id. § 1340(c)(1). The agency must disapprove the plan if it would result in "serious harm or damage" to the marine, coastal, or human environment. See 43 U.S.C. § 1334(a)(2)(A)(i).

* * *

NEPA requires that, "to the fullest extent possible," all federal agencies shall prepare an EIS when considering proposed activities "significantly affecting the quality of the human environment." 42 U.S.C. § 4332; Robertson v. Methow Valley Citizens Council, 490 U.S. 332, 348 (1989). ... * * * Federal regulations encourage agencies to tier their environmental analyses in order to streamline and focus the review process. 40 C.F.R. § 1502.20 ("Whenever a broad [EIS] has been prepared . . . the subsequent statement or environmental assessment need only summarize the issues discussed in the broader statement and incorporate discussions from the broader statement by reference and shall concentrate on the issues specific to the subsequent action.").

"[A]n EIS *must* be prepared if 'substantial questions are raised as to whether a project . . . *may* cause significant degradation of some human environmental factor.' " Idaho Sporting Congress v. Thomas, 137 F.3d 1146, 1149 (9th Cir.1998). If an agency finds an EIS is not required and issues a FONSI, it must provide a "convincing statement of reasons" to explain its decision. Blue Mountains, 161 F.3d at 1212; see also 40 C.F.R. §§ 1501.4(e), 1508.13. An agency cannot rely on mere "conclusory assertions that an activity will have only an insignificant impact on the environment." Ocean Advocates v. U.S. Army Corps of Eng'rs, 402 F.3d 846, 864 (9th Cir.2005). Rather, the agency must demonstrate that it took the requisite "hard look" at the potential environmental impacts of a project, thereby justifying its action. Blue Mountains, 161 F.3d at 1212; Ocean Advocates, 402 F.3d at 864; Kern v. U.S. Bureau of Land Mgmt., 284 F.3d 1062, 1066–67 (9th Cir.2002).

To provide guidance on how NEPA should be applied, the Council on Environmental Quality promulgated regulations explaining what factors an agency must consider in determining if a project's potential effects are "significant." See 40 C.F.R. § 1508.27. This requires "considerations of both context and intensity." Id. Context refers to the location and interests that would be affected by the proposed action. Id. § 1508.27(a). Intensity refers to "the severity of the impact." Id. § 1508.27(b). In considering intensity, an agency should consider up to ten factors that shed light on the "significance" of a project. Id. Those factors include: the effect on public health and safety; the unique characteristics of the geographic area; the degree to which the effects on the quality of the human environment are likely to be highly controversial; the degree to which the possible effects are highly uncertain or involve unknown risks; and the possible impacts on an endangered or threatened species. Id. §§ 1508.27(b)(2), (3), (4), (5), (7).

B. Sufficiency of MMS's Environmental Analysis

MMS has not provided a convincing statement of reasons explaining why Shell's exploratory drilling plans at these *specific* sites would have an insignificant impact on bowhead whales and Inupiat subsistence activities. As a result, we are unpersuaded that MMS took the requisite "hard look" at the environmental impact of this project. There remain substantial questions as to whether Shell's plan may cause significant harm to the people and wildlife of the Beaufort Sea region.

Respondents' primary response is that, through the tiering process, the agency sufficiently analyzed all possible environmental impacts of this project. The EA is "tiered" to the multi-sale EIS and the EAs for Lease Sales 195 and 202 pursuant to 40 C.F.R. § 1502.20. According to Respondents, any analysis that is allegedly missing from the EA is adequately covered in those previous documents. Respondents point out that OCSLA only allows thirty days to approve an EP, see 43 U.S.C. § 1340(c)(1), and argue that this short statutory deadline encourages a streamlined review process. The agency may not, however, hide behind the cloak of its generalized multi-sale EIS. NEPA applies to all stages of the OCSLA cycle. Vill. of False Pass v. Clark, 733 F.2d 605, 614 (9th Cir.1984). When the agency is tasked with assessing the environmental impacts of a particular exploration plan, it has a duty to take a hard look at the consequences of drilling in specific sites. As the agency itself noted in the multi-sale EIS, "[a]ny proposed exploration or development plans that may result for [the area] evaluated in this EIS, would require additional NEPA environmental analysis using site specific information." MMS's environmental analysis is inadequate because it fails to consider the impacts this specific project will have on bowhead whales and Inupiat subsistence activities.

1. Impacts on Bowhead Whales

MMS's EA fails to take a hard look at whether Shell's exploratory drilling program would have a "significant" effect on bowhead whales, an endangered species.* * *

The major shortcoming of the agency's environmental analysis is that it does not assess the impacts that would be felt by the bowhead whale population from a project in the migratory route that involves two drill ships and two icebreakers. The multi-sale EIS envisions "[a] maximum of two drilling rigs" would be used during this time, and the EA "assumed that two drilling rigs with icebreaker support might operate during any year." However, aside from nominally mentioning the possible extent of this project, the studies relied upon by the agency do not actually assess the potential significance of underwater noise from a drilling operation of this scope.

The multi-sale EIS discusses, in a general sense, the impact of noise on bowhead whales, citing a number of studies that have been conducted on the topic. However, that document contains no studies that analyze the effects of noise from a project with two drill ships and two icebreakers. * * *

MMS realizes the distinguishing characteristics between Shell's specific proposal and the scope of prior studies, but does not then engage in any additional analysis.* * *

Notably, the EA also states that the "effect on bowheads is likely to be greater than for [the 1993 activities] because of Shell's proposal to use two drill ships, two large icebreakers, and several associated vessels." Although the agency mentions the possibility for increased impacts on bowhead whales and the human populations who depend on them, it fails to take a hard look at whether a proposal of this magnitude will have significant impacts on this endangered species.

The agency's attempt to rely upon a monitoring program as a mitigation measure is similarly ill-founded. This section of the EA ends with a discussion of "Stipulation No. 4" which requires that Shell conduct a site-specific whale monitoring program during its drilling operations. Instead of insisting on alternative mitigation measures or conducting a full EIS at this time, MMS states it "has the authority to modify approved operations to ensure that significant biological populations or habitats deserving protection are not subject to a threat of serious, irreparable, or immediate harm."

Federal regulations define "mitigation" as a way to avoid, minimize, rectify, or compensate for the impact of a potentially harmful action. 40 C.F.R. §§ 1508.20(a)–(e). An agency can rely upon mitigation measures in determining whether an environmental impact is significant. See Nat'l Parks & Conservation Ass'n, 241 F.3d at 734. In order to be effective, a mitigation measure must be supported by analytical data demonstrating why it will "constitute an adequate buffer against the negative impacts that may result from the authorized activity." Id. A mitigation measure must render potential impacts "so minor as to not warrant an EIS." Id. The proposed monitoring program fails this test, as it could detect impacts only after they have occurred. MMS's statement that it would reserve the authority to modify approved operations does not provide enough protection under this standard. A court must be able to review, in advance, how specific measures will bring projects into compliance with environmental standards. See id. at 733 ("The Parks Service proposes to increase the risk of harm to the environment and then perform its studies. . . . This approach has the process exactly backwards."). Monitoring may serve to confirm the appropriateness of a mitigation measure, but that does not make it an adequate mitigation measure in itself. See EPIC, 451 F.3d at 1015–16.

After considering the gaps in the multi-sale EIS and the EA, we conclude that the agency failed to take a "hard look" under NEPA because it did not provide a well-reasoned analysis of site-specific impacts to the endangered bowhead whale population. The tiered OCSLA process allows general analysis at the lease-sale stage, but the agency must then consider site-specific impacts before approving an individual exploration plan.* * *

As the agency itself notes in the multi-sale EIS, the tiered approach "builds on the premise that as both the agencies and companies involved move from general planning, to leasing, to exploration . . . the specificity of the information improves. The accompanying environmental analysis that flows from each stage also is more specific with respect to location, timing, and magnitude." * * * The agency may not rely on past studies on the general impact of noise on bowhead whales to justify its failure to conduct a particularized assessment here. This is especially true when past studies acknowledged that noise levels may, in certain circumstances, cause significant disturbances to whales. Additionally, MMS's analysis should take a closer look at the locations of Shell's individual wells in relationship to the migratory patterns of the bowhead whales.

In sum, MMS abrogated its NEPA duties because neither the EA nor the documents it tiers to considers the specific parameters and potential dangers of Shell's project.* * * Furthermore, the proposed mitigation measure does not save the plan because it is not clear that a monitoring program will ameliorate potentially serious negative impacts. See Nat'l Parks & Conservation Ass'n, 241 F.3d at 734.

2. Impacts on Inupiat Subsistence Activities

i. *Bowhead Whale Harvest*

MMS also failed to take a "hard look" at the effects Shell's project would have on the Inupiat's subsistence uses of bowhead whales. The agency's review should consider how the proposal affects public health or safety, and the degree to which its impact on the human environment is unknown or highly controversial. 40 C.F.R. §§ 1508.27(b)(2), (4), (5). MMS defines a "significant" effect on a sociocultural system as: "A chronic disruption of sociocultural systems that occurs for a period of 2–5 years, with a tendency toward the displacement of existing social patterns."

* * *

* * * The EA itself notes that even if underwater noise does not cause a significant biological effect for the whales themselves, "there could be a significant sociocultural effect if the bowheads do not migrate back" into the "migration corridor." MMS acknowledges this possibility, but then comes to the inexplicable conclusion that this project can proceed without other modifications.* * *

Without examining the possible level of disruption to the Inupiat harvest of bowhead whales, MMS offers only "conclusory assertions" that impacts will not be significant.* * *

MMS asserts that any threat to the Inupiat's subsistence whaling would be minimized through a conflict avoidance agreement. Again, the deficiencies in the agency's analysis are not cured through its proposed mitigation measure. In order to rely on mitigation to obviate further analysis, the measure must be identified and its effectiveness analyzed. * * * The agency must provide analytic data on the efficacy of a proposed measure, and the court must decide whether it "will render such impacts so minor as to not warrant an EIS." Nat'l Parks & Conservation Ass'n, 241 F.3d at 734.

The conflict avoidance agreement process is too vague and uncertain as a mitigation measure to justify the agency's decision not to engage in further analysis. Conflict avoidance agreements come about through a voluntary process and are renegotiated every year. The agency is not party to the process, and any agreement made is not legally binding. The EA itself notes that without an agreement, there are serious questions about whether the project would have significant impacts on Inupiat communities. The agency states: "Without such conflict avoidance measures in place, significant impacts to the subsistence resources and hunts for bowhead whales, seals, and polar bears could occur." It goes on to say: "Only a carefully constructed and monitored [conflict avoidance agreement] could produce some remedy to disturbances to bowhead whales and the subsistence hunt." The language used by MMS reveals the real risks this project poses to the bowhead population and Inupiat communities. An annual voluntary re-negotiation process does not sufficiently mitigate the concerns raised by Petitioners and acknowledged by the agency.

Simply because conflict avoidance agreements have been used effectively in the past does not mean that an agency can rely on them to cure inadequacies in the environmental assessment. * * By relying on the uncertain outcome of the conflict avoidance agreement process, the agency deprives this court of its ability to review whether the measure is sufficiently protective. In sum, the agency is not relieved of its responsibility to conduct more specific analysis on how this project will affect the Inupiat harvest of bowhead whales.

Before this court stayed drilling operations in August 2007, Shell and the local whaling captains negotiated a year-long agreement that would have deferred drilling operations until after completion of the Nuiqsut whale hunt.

ii. *Other Subsistence Activities*

Shell's activities will also affect other Inupiat subsistence resources, such as beluga whales, caribou, and fish. Petitioners urge the agency to take a closer look at the impacts of exploration because of the proximity of the proposed activities to the Inupiat hunting and fishing grounds. The EA's comments focus almost entirely on the subsistence use of bowhead whales. It notes only in one sentence that "helicopter and aircraft supply flights have the potential to disturb caribou movements and alter the subsistence hunt." The multi-sale EIS takes a cursory glance at these other animal populations, stating that drilling activities "could affect the availability of" beluga whales to subsistence hunters. The study further acknowledges that flight activity may disturb caribou populations.

The biggest gap in the agency's multi-sale EIS and EA is the lack of both information and analysis examining the impacts this project will have on fish populations. In analyzing fish populations, the EA acknowledges: "Given scientific uncertainty surrounding how several important fish species would react to varying levels of drilling program noise, we believe it possible there will be more than a minimal level of effect on some species." MMS acknowledges that it "cannot concur" with Shell's assurances that its activities "may have minimal to no impact on fish." The agency goes on to state:

> The MMS also cannot concur that the effects on all fish species would be 'short term' or that these potential effects are insignificant, nor would they be limited to the '. . . localized displacement of fish . . .', because they could persist for up to five months each year for three consecutive years and they could occur during critical times in the life cycle of important fish species.

> The MMS remains concerned that the potential adverse effects described for several fish species will occur to an unknown degree, however none are expected to exceed the level that would require three generations to recover (the threshold for a significant effect).

After this lengthy discussion on concerns and gaps in the data, the EA's abrupt conclusion that any potential effects will be insignificant is unsubstantiated. This is the type of "conclusory assertion" that is disfavored by this court because the agency has not provided any scientific data that justifies this position. See Ocean Advocates, 402 F.3d at 864.

* * *

The EA ultimately concludes that Inupiat communities may suffer cultural consequences from drilling activities, but does not state whether these effects will be "significant." Instead, the EA relies on mitigation measures in the hopes that they would ameliorate any harm done: "Required mitigation, monitoring, and conflict avoidance measures . . . would serve collectively to mitigate disturbance effects on Native lifestyles and subsistence practices and likely would mitigate any consequent impacts on sociocultural systems." As discussed above, these mitigation measures do not go far enough to rectify the potential that Shell's project will cause substantial harm to Inupiat communities on Alaska's northern shore.

In sum, MMS failed to take a "hard look" at the impacts this plan will have on Inupiat subsistence activities. * * *

3. Impacts of Potential Crude Oil Spills

Despite any other insufficiencies, MMS's environmental analysis does adequately examine the impacts of a potential crude oil spill. The EA states, "[f]or purposes of this EA analysis, no crude oil spills are assumed from exploration activities. This assumption is based on the low rate of exploratory drilling blowouts per well drilled and the history of exploration spills on the Arctic OCS. . . . " * * * The agency's assessment makes the proper inquiry into the risk of an oil spill, and no further analysis is required in relationship to this exploration plan.

* * *

Although the language in the EA may not have been ideal, MMS's "assumption" that there would not be an oil spill was supplemented with comprehensive studies on the likelihood and impact of such an event. Accordingly, the agency did not act arbitrarily and capriciously in its assessment of the potential effects of an oil spill from this project.

C. Necessity of a Revised EA or an EIS

MMS has violated NEPA by failing to take a "hard look" at the impacts of Shell's proposal on bowhead whales and Inupiat subsistence activities. MMS has not provided a convincing statement of reasons to justify its decision not to complete an EIS. See Blue Mountains, 161 F.3d at 1211.

* * *

Accordingly we remand to the agency to either prepare a revised EA or, as necessary, an EIS.

* * *

II. MMS's Compliance with OCSLA

The agency's approval of this project also violated OCSLA. OCSLA's implementing regulations require that, when evaluating exploration plans, an agency should consider information about "proposed well location and spacing." 30 C.F.R. § 250.203. Exploration plans must be "project specific" and describe the "resources, conditions, and activities" that could be affected. 30 C.F.R. § 250.227. In particular, an EP must include "[a] map showing the surface location and water depth of each proposed well and the locations of all associated drilling unit anchors." 30 C.F.R. § 250.211(b). Shell submitted the locations of the 2007 drilling sites, but did not specify where it wished to drill in 2008 and 2009. Shell noted that future drilling locations will depend on what is found in the first Sivulliq exploration. Without specific information about future well locations, the agency cannot meet its obligation to "review and approve proposed well location and spacing" in accord with 30 C.F.R. § 250.203. As a result, the agency erred by approving an EP for 2007–2009 without knowing where Shell would be drilling for the last two years.

* * *

CONCLUSION

For the foregoing reasons, we vacate the agency's approval of Shell's exploration plan and remand for the agency to prepare a revised EA or, as necessary, an EIS. Shell's motion to lift the stay is denied.

* * *

NOTE ON NEPA AND THE DEEPWATER HORIZON SPILL

Although the Alaska Wilderness League case predates the Deepwater Horizon spill, the court finds many of the same problems with the NEPA process that were reported by the Council on Environmental Quality (CEQ) in its Report Regarding the Minerals Management Service's National Environmental Policy Act Policies, Practices, and Procedures as They Relate to Outer Continental Shelf Oil and Gas Exploration and Development (August 16, 2010) ["CEQ NEPA Report"].

The CEQ NEPA Report analyzes the failures of the NEPA in the context of leasing and exploration process leading to the Deepwater Horizon oil spill. The Report identified several steps of the review process that contributed to inadequate NEPA review, including:

1. The tiering process, a strategy used to avoid repetitive discussions of the same issues, and to prevent unnecessary duplication of work by reviewers, lacked transparency and failed to assure that that information from one level of review was effectively carried forward to—and reflected in—subsequent reviews.

2. Tiering foreclosed site specific environmental assessment of the lease sale.

3. The agency did not deem a catastrophic spill, comparable to the BP Oil spill, to be a reasonably foreseeable impact. The analysis associated such a spill, therefore, was not taken into account in the agency's Environmental Assessment of the lease and issuance of a Finding of No New Significant Impact (FONNSI).

4. The process for applying categorical exclusions was not designed to incorporate oil spill details or analyses from previous EIS or EA reviews.

5. The Deepwater EA included a proposal to evaluate certain mitigation measures to prevent and contain oil spills. These measures did not appear in the Programmatic EIS, the Multi-Sale EIS, the Lease Sale 206 EA, or the Lease Stipulations applicable to Lease Sale 206, the CERs, and the CEs.

The CEQ Report also addressed the 30-day period for approval of exploration plans. Does this statutorily imposed limit, which was intended to expedite progress on the exploration stage, provide adequate time to assess environmental impacts? Did Congress assume that impacts as the exploration stage would be insignificant? The CEQ has recommended amendment of the OCSLA to eliminate the 30-day decisional timeframe for approval of submitted Exploration Plans. See CEQ NEPA Report, at 8–9.

The Report also contains comprehensive recommendations, most of which have been implemented for the current Five-Year Lease Program. Since 2010 CEQ has also issued a number of guidance documents intended to "modernize and reinvigorate" NEPA. See CEQ, Steps to Modernize and Reinvigorate NEPA, available at http://www.whitehouse.gov/administration/eop/ceq/initatives/nepa.

NOTE ON THE FUTURE OF OFFSHORE DRILLING IN ALASKA

Several months after the above decision, and after President Barack Obama took office, Shell withdrew its EP. The analysis used in the decision, however, remains valid and sheds light on how the Ninth Circuit will analyze similar cases in the future. In accordance with OCSLA, any decision of the Secretary regarding an exploration plan or development and production plan is subject to judicial review only in a United States Court of Appeals for a circuit in which an affected state is located. Therefore, decisions regarding drilling in the Beaufort Sea or on any part of the OCS in Alaska will be reviewed by the Ninth Circuit and by the tests laid out in this decision. This precedent may prove to be an insurmountable obstacle to offshore exploration, development, and production. See J. Larson, Challenges Under OCSLA and the Future of Offshore Drilling Under the Obama Administration, 13 SMU Sci. & Tech. L. Rev. 55 (2009). But see Gulf Restoration Network, Inc. v. Salazar, 2012 U.S. App. LEXIS 10892 (5th Cir. May 30, 2012) (rejecting challenge to renewed deepwater exploration in the Gulf of Mexico); Native Village of Point Hope v. Salazar, 2012 U.S. App. LEXIS 10760 (9th Cir. May 25, 2012) (BOEM's approval of a Beaufort Sea exploration plan upheld). See also Shell Offshore Inc. v. Greenpeace, Inc., 2012 U.S. Dist. LEXIS 74387 (NGOs ordered to stay away from Arctic exploratory drilling vessels).

Of what significance to OCS oil and gas development off Alaska is the 2011 removal (Federal Register, July 7, 2011) of Alaska's coastal zone management program from federal funding and the federal consistency process under the federal Coastal Zone Management Act discussed in Chapter 4? See *California v. Norton* and *Amber Resources Co. v. United States* discussed below.

―――――

4. Development and Production Stage

UNION OIL CO. OF CALIFORNIA V. MORTON

United States Court of Appeals, Ninth Circuit, 1975
512 F.2d 743

CHOY, CIRCUIT JUDGE.

* * *

FACTUAL BACKGROUND

In February 1968, Union paid over $61 million for oil and gas rights on tract OCS–P 0241. The leased tract lies on the continental shelf in the Santa Barbara Channel, beyond the jurisdiction of the State of California. The Interior Department granted the lease under the authority of the Outer Continental Shelf Lands Act, 43 U.S.C. § 1331 et seq.

The lease gives Union the right to erect floating drilling platforms, subject to the provisions of the Act and to "reasonable regulations" not inconsistent with the lease issued by the Secretary. Two platforms, A and B, were installed, each supporting many productive wells. In September 1968, Union sought permission to install a third platform, C. The Secretary approved the application, and the Army Corps of Engineers issued the necessary permit. In January 1969, before platform C was installed, a blow-out occurred on one of the wells on platform A. The blowout caused the disastrous Santa Barbara oil spill, which killed birds and marine organisms, damaged beaches and seafront properties, and restricted fishing and recreational activities in the area.

On February 7, 1969, the Secretary ordered all activities on this and certain other leases suspended pending further environmental studies. After these studies were completed, the Secretary announced on September 20, 1971, that Union would not be allowed to install platform C, because operation of that platform would be "incompatible with the concept of the Federal Sanctuary [which the Secretary had proposed to Congress]." He stated that all operations would remain suspended on certain other Channel leases, pending action by Congress canceling the leases. See Gulf Oil Corp. v. Morton, 493 F.2d 141 (9th Cir. 1973).

The Department formally notified Union the following month that the Secretary "has determined that the installation of Platform 'C' would be inconsistent with protection of the environment of the Santa Barbara Channel and has directed [the Regional Supervisor] to withdraw the approval of September 16, 1968." This suit resulted. On November 3, 1972, just prior to trial, the Secretary issued a statement further clarifying the environmental concerns contributing to his decision.

* * *

We upheld the Secretary's suspension of the leases pending congressional action in Gulf Oil, supra. Because Congress had not acted within a reasonable time to cancel the leases in question, however, we declared the suspension invalid after October 18, 1972. Id. at 149. This appeal is limited to the validity of the order withdrawing permission for Union to install platform C.

THE ACT

The Outer Continental Shelf Act authorizes the Secretary to issue oil and gas leases on the outer continental shelf to the highest bidder. 43 U.S.C. § 1337(a). A lease issued under this Act, like a mineral lease granted under the Mineral Leasing Act of 1920, 30 U.S.C. § 181 et seq., does not convey title in the land, nor does it convey an unencumbered estate in the oil and gas. The lease does convey a property interest enforceable against the Government, of course, but it is an interest lacking many of the attributes of private property. Oil and gas deposits beneath the continental shelf are precious resources belonging to the entire nation. Congress, although encouraging the extraction of these resources by private companies, provided safeguards to insure that their exploitation should inure to the benefit of all. These safeguards are not limited to those provided by covenants in the lease; Congress also authorized the Secretary to maintain extensive, continuing regulation of the oil companies' day to day drilling operations.

Careful study of the Act confirms that Congress intended to exercise both proprietary powers of a landowner and the police powers of a legislature in regulating leases of publicly owned resources. Cf. Forbes v. United States, 125 F.2d 404, 408 (9th Cir. 1942). The Secretary, to whom Congress has delegated these powers, may prescribe at any time those rules which he finds necessary for the conservation of natural resources. 43 U.S.C. § 1334(a)(1). Exercising its legislative power, Congress has provided criminal penalties for knowing violation of these rules. 43 U.S.C. § 1334(a)(2). In addition, those rules in effect at the time a lease is executed are incorporated statutorily into the terms of the lease. 43 U.S.C. § 1334(a)(2). The Secretary, like a private property owner, may obtain cancellation of the lease if the lessee breaches such a rule. 43 U.S.C. § 1334(b)(1). Violation of rules issued after the lease has been executed does not enable the Secretary to cancel the lease, however. The property rights of the lessee are determined only by those rules in effect when the lease is executed. See generally W. Christopher, The Outer Continental Shelf Lands Act: Key to a New Frontier, 6 Stan. L. Rev. 23, 43–47 (1953).

* * *

SUSPENSION: REGULATION OR TAKING?

Pursuant to 43 U.S.C. § 1334(a)(1), the Secretary issued a regulation on August 22, 1969, authorizing emergency suspension of any operation which threatens immediate, serious, or irreparable harm or damage to life, including aquatic life, to property, to the leased deposits, to other valuable mineral deposits or to the environment. Such emergency suspension shall continue until in his judgment the threat or danger has terminated." 30 C.F.R. § 250.12. Refusal to allow installation of a previously approved platform could be justified only as a suspension of operations under this regulation.

The regulation properly provides for "conservation of the natural resources of the outer Continental Shelf," as we have construed that phrase. Nevertheless, Union points to the distinction between a suspension and a revocation, asserting that the Secretary did not in fact merely suspend operations, because a suspension by definition possesses a "temporary nature." The structure of the Act demonstrates that Congress intended vested rights under the lease to be invulnerable to defeasance by subsequently issued regulations. Although 30 C.F.R. § 250.12 provides expressly that a "suspension" shall be limited in time only by the Secretary's judgment that the environmental threat has ended, and although 43 U.S.C. § 1334(a)(1) authorizes regulations providing not only for suspensions but for any other action affecting operations which the Secretary determines "necessary and proper" for "conservation of natural resources," Congress clearly did not intend to grant leases so tenuous in nature that the Secretary could terminate them, in whole or in part, at will.

Congress itself can order the leases forfeited even now, subject to payment of compensation. But without congressional authorization, the Secretary or the executive branch in general has no intrinsic powers of condemnation. Congress' clear concern to distinguish police power regulation from invasion of property rights in these leases convinces us that Congress did not confer powers of condemnation upon the Secretary by implication.

The degree to which the Government may interfere with the enjoyment of private property by exercise of its police power without having to pay compensation is not a simple question. The courts, under a variety of tests, have recognized that regulation of private property can become so onerous that it amounts to a taking of that property. If, as Union contends, platform C is a necessary means for the extraction of oil from a portion of the leased area, refusal to permit installation of that platform now or at any time in the future deprives Union of all benefit from the lease in that particular area. We therefore conclude that an open-ended suspension of the right granted Union to install a drilling platform would be a pro tanto cancellation of its lease.

Such a taking by interference with private property rights is within the constitutional power of Congress, subject to payment of compensation. See Dugan v. Rank, 372 U.S. 609 (1963). But Congress no more impliedly authorized the Secretary to take the leasehold by prohibiting its beneficial use than by condemnation proceeding. A suspension for which the fifth amendment would require compensation is therefore unauthorized and beyond the Secretary's power.

Whether the Secretary has taken Union's property depends on the conditions of the suspension. If operations are suspended indefinitely, property rights have been taken. To determine whether the suspension is indefinite, or, on the other hand, is a temporary suspension whose termination is conditioned by the occurrence of certain future events, we must examine the justifications which the Secretary has offered for the suspension. The Secretary explained the suspension most recently in his statement of November 3, 1972:

> The following were the primary factors that led to my decision denying the platform applications:
>
> (1) construction of the proposed platform and drilling wells would increase the risk of oil pollution in the Santa Barbara Channel by reason of:
>
> (a) the risks inherent in offshore oil drilling;
>
> (b) location of the Channel in an active seismic belt, and
>
> (c) with regard to Platform "C," the fact that the platform would be located on the damaged Dos Quadros [sic] structure;
>
> (2) oil pollution in the Santa Barbara Channel would have adverse consequences both short and longer term, because of the characteristics of the Channel environment; the following attributes of the Channel that would be affected by oil pollution were given particular consideration:
>
> (a) animal and plant marine life;
>
> (b) commercial and sport fisheries;
>
> (c) recreational use;
>
> (d) beaches and shore line of the Channel;
>
> (e) birds;
>
> (3) the lack of systems and equipment which are completely effective in controlling and removing oil pollution under all weather and sea conditions;

(4) the suitability of the Dos Quadros [sic] structure (leases OCS–P 0241 and 0240) for unitization and the suitability of leases OCS–P 0240 and 0166 for unitization;

(5) additional platforms would increase interference with other uses of the Channel for recreational and commercial fishing;

(6) additional platforms would be aesthetically undesirable.

Factors 2, 4, 5, and 6 amount simply to a weighing of conflicting interests which the Secretary should have undertaken before the lease was granted. For the Secretary to offer these factors now to justify suspending Union's drilling activities asserts in effect that he can cancel the lease because he has changed his mind. These enumerated interests are not temporary concerns which the passage of time may eliminate.

Factors 1 and 3, however, suggest conditions which the development of new technology or further study may lessen as threats to the environment. Further study of seismic risks in the Channel, or of the geology of the Dos Quadros structure, for example, may produce evidence of environmental risks unanticipated at the time the lease was executed. Knowledge of these newly discovered risks might induce Congress to cancel the lease. A suspension also might provide time for an improved pollution control technology to be developed. A suspension whose termination was conditioned on the occurrence of events or the discovery of new knowledge which can be anticipated within a reasonable period of time would be a valid exercise of the Secretary's regulatory power, and not a fifth amendment taking.

The vague assertion of potential risks advanced in the Secretary's 1972 statement is totally inadequate to enable this court to decide whether such justifications for a suspension do exist, however, and whether they sufficiently restrict the duration of the suspension to avoid the need for compensation. The trial court decided without explanation that the suspension deprived Union of no property rights. We are uncertain as to the basis for this conclusion.

In view of the insufficient nature both of the Secretary's explanation for the suspension and the district court's justification of its judgment, we vacate the decision of the district court and remand the case to the district court for a determination whether the Secretary is taking property rights from Union. The court should allow the Secretary to prepare and present an amended statement of the grounds on which he bases the suspension. The court may, at its discretion, receive additional evidence and testimony in support of and in opposition to the Secretary's amended justification. The court should then determine whether each justification advanced by the Secretary is appropriate under 30 C.F.R. § 250.12, whether the Secretary has offered sufficient evidence to demonstrate that his decision was not arbitrary and capricious or an abuse of discretion, and whether the duration of a suspension based on the grounds offered is sufficiently conditioned on the occurrence of future events to avoid fifth amendment requirements of compensation.

If the trial court finds that the suspension, as limited by the Secretary's amended statement, complies with these requirements, Union's complaint should be dismissed. Otherwise, the order of suspension should be set aside as beyond the Secretary's statutory powers. 5 U.S.C. § 706(2)(C).

Because of the Secretary's continuing supervisory obligations, injunctive relief against further interference with Union's operations would be inappropriate.

Vacated and remanded.

NOTES AND QUESTIONS

1. Congress attempted to clarify the rights of lessor and lessee in the OCS Lands Act Amendments of 1978. The section dealing with suspension and termination of leases provides in part (43 U.S.C. § 1334(a)):

* * *

The regulations prescribed by the Secretary under this subsection shall include, but not be limited to, provisions—

(1) for the suspension or temporary prohibition of any operation or activity, including production, pursuant to any lease or permit (A) at the request of a lessee, in the national interest, to facilitate proper development of a lease or to allow for the construction or negotiation for use of transportation facilities, or (B) if there is a threat of serious, irreparable, or immediate harm or damage to life (including fish and other aquatic life), to property, to any mineral deposits (in areas leased or not leased), or to the marine, coastal, or human environment, and for the extension of any permit or lease affected by suspension or prohibition under clause (A) or (B) by a period equivalent to the period of such suspension or prohibition, except that no permit or lease shall be so extended when such suspension or prohibition is the result of gross negligence or willful violation of such lease or permit, or of regulations issued with respect to such lease or permit;

(2) with respect to cancellation of any lease or permit

(A) that such cancellation may occur at any time, if the Secretary determines, after a hearing, that—

(i) continued activity pursuant to such lease or permit would probably cause serious harm or damage to life (including fish and other aquatic life), to property, to any mineral (in areas leased or not leased), to the national security or defense, or to the marine, coastal, or human environment;

(ii) the threat of harm or damage will not disappear or decrease to an acceptable extent within a reasonable period of time; and

(iii) the advantages of cancellation outweigh the advantages of continuing such lease or permit in force;

(B) that such cancellation shall not occur unless and until operations under such lease or permit shall have been under suspension, or temporary prohibition, by the Secretary, with due extension of any lease or permit term continuously for a period of five years, or for a lesser period upon request of the lessee;

(C) that such cancellation shall entitle the lessee to receive such compensation as he shows to the Secretary as being equal to the lesser of (i) the fair value of the canceled rights as of the date of cancellation, taking account of both anticipated revenues from the lease and anticipated costs, including costs of compliance with all applicable regulations and operating orders, liability for cleanup costs or damages, or both, in the case of an oilspill, and all other costs reasonably anticipated on the lease, or (ii) the excess, if any, over the lessee's revenues, from the lease (plus interest thereon from the date of receipt to date of reimbursement) of all consideration paid for the lease and all direct expenditures made by the lessee after the date of issuance of such lease and in connection with exploration or development, or both, pursuant to the lease (plus interest on such consideration and such expenditures from date of payment to date of reimbursement). * * *

2. Has the leasehold become so tenuous as to discourage new ventures by industry? Alternative bidding systems could lessen the impact of cancellation. For example, the Secretary of Interior could be required to lease some of the area offered for lease each year by a bidding system other than the bonus bid/fixed royalty method, which has been the usual system. Lessees under an alternative bidding system such as variable royalty bidding would not be required to make such a high initial capital outlay as under the bonus bid system, and so would not have as much at stake in a suspension or termination.

3. What proprietary rights, if any, does a lessee retain under the above statutory provisions? In the following case, what rights does Mobil have when the lease is cancelled? Does it matter whether the cancellation was based on the OCSLA, other legislation, or a negative consistency determination by the state under the CZMA that is not overruled by the Secretary?

MOBIL OIL EXPLORATION & PRODUCING SOUTHEAST, INC. v. UNITED STATES

Supreme Court of the United States, 2000
530 U.S. 604

JUSTICE BREYER delivered the opinion of the Court.

Two oil companies, petitioners here, seek restitution of $156 million they paid the Government in return for lease contracts giving them rights to explore for and develop oil off the North Carolina coast. The rights were not absolute, but were conditioned on the companies' obtaining a set of further governmental permissions. The companies claim that the Government repudiated the contracts when it denied them certain elements of the permission-seeking opportunities that the contracts had promised. We agree that the Government broke its promise; it repudiated the contracts; and it must give the companies their money back.

I

A

A description at the outset of the few basic contract law principles applicable to this case will help the reader understand the significance of the complex factual circumstances that follow. "When the United States enters into contract relations, its rights and duties therein are governed generally by the law applicable to contracts between private individuals." United States v. Winstar Corp., 518 U.S. 839, 895, 116 S.Ct. 2432, 135 L.Ed.2d 964 (1996) (plurality opinion) (internal quotation marks omitted). The Restatement of Contracts reflects many of the principles of contract law that are applicable to this case. As set forth in the Restatement of Contracts, the relevant principles specify that, when one party to a contract repudiates that contract, the other party "is entitled to restitution for any benefit that he has conferred on" the repudiating party "by way of part performance or reliance." Restatement (Second) of Contracts § 373 (1979) (hereinafter Restatement). The Restatement explains that "repudiation" is a "statement by the obligor to the obligee indicating that the obligor will commit a breach that would of itself give the obligee a claim for damages for total breach." Id., § 250. And "total breach" is a breach that "so substantially impairs the value of the contract to the injured party at the time of the breach that it is just in the circumstances to allow him to recover damages based on all his remaining rights to performance." Id., § 243.

As applied to this case, these principles amount to the following: If the Government said it would break, or did break, an important contractual promise, thereby "substantially impair[ing] the value of the contract[s]" to the companies, ibid., then (unless the companies waived their rights to restitution) the Government must give the companies their money back. And it must do so whether the contracts would, or would not, ultimately have proved financially beneficial to the companies. The Restatement illustrates this point as follows:

"A contracts to sell a tract of land to B for $100,000. After B has made a part payment of $20,000, A wrongfully refuses to transfer title. B can recover the $20,000 in restitution. The result is the same even if the market price of the land is only $70,000, so that performance would have been disadvantageous to B." *Id.*, § 373, Comment *a*, Illustration 1.

B

In 1981, in return for up-front "bonus" payments to the United States of about $158 million (plus annual rental payments), the companies received 10-year renewable lease contracts with the United States. In these contracts, the United States promised the companies, among other things, that they could explore for oil off the North Carolina coast and develop any oil that they found (subject to further royalty payments) provided that the companies received exploration and development permissions in accordance with various statutes and regulations to which the lease contracts were made "subject." * * * The statutes and regulations, the terms of which in effect were incorporated into the contracts, made clear that obtaining the necessary permissions might not be an easy matter. In particular, the Outer Continental Shelf Lands Act (OCSLA), 67 Stat. 462, as amended, 43 U.S.C. § 1331 *et seq.* (1994 ed. and Supp. III), and the Coastal Zone Management Act of 1972 (CZMA), 16 U.S.C. § 1451 *et seq.*, specify that leaseholding companies wishing to explore and drill must successfully complete the following four procedures.

First, a company must prepare and obtain Department of the Interior approval for a Plan of Exploration. 43 U.S.C. § 1340(c). Interior must approve a submitted Exploration Plan unless it finds, after "consider[ing] available relevant environmental information," § 1346(d), that the proposed exploration

"would probably cause serious harm or damage to life (including fish and other aquatic life), to property, to any mineral * * *, to the national security or defense, or to the marine, coastal, or human environment." § 1334(a)(2)(A)(i).

Where approval is warranted, Interior must act quickly—within "thirty days" of the company's submission of a proposed Plan. § 1340(c)(1).

Second, the company must obtain an exploratory well drilling permit. To do so, it must certify (under CZMA) that its Exploration Plan is consistent with the coastal zone management program of each affected State. 16 U.S.C. § 1456(c)(3). If a State objects, the certification fails, unless the Secretary of Commerce overrides the State's objection. If Commerce rules against the State, then Interior may grant the permit. § 1456(c)(3)(A).

Third, where waste discharge into ocean waters is at issue, the company must obtain a National Pollutant Discharge Elimination System permit from the Environmental Protection Agency. 33 U.S.C. §§ 1311(a), 1342(a). It can obtain this permit only if affected States agree that its Exploration Plan is consistent with the state coastal zone management programs or (as just explained) the Secretary of Commerce overrides the state objections. 16 U.S.C. § 1456.

Fourth, if exploration is successful, the company must prepare, and obtain Interior approval for, a Development and Production Plan—a Plan that describes the proposed drilling and related environmental safeguards. 43 U.S.C. § 1351. Again, Interior's approval is conditioned upon certification that the Plan is consistent with state coastal zone management plans—a certification to which States can object, subject to Commerce Department override. § 1351(a)(3).

C

The events at issue here concern the first two steps of the process just described—Interior's consideration of a submitted Exploration Plan and the companies' submission of the CZMA "consistency certification" necessary to obtain an exploratory well drilling permit. The relevant circumstances are the following:

1. In 1981, the companies and the Government entered into the lease contracts. The companies paid the Government $158 million in up-front cash "bonus" payments.

2. In 1989, the companies, Interior, and North Carolina entered into a memorandum of understanding. In that memorandum, the companies promised that they would submit an initial draft Exploration Plan to North Carolina before they submitted their final Exploration Plan to Interior. Interior promised that it would prepare an environmental report on the initial draft. It also agreed to suspend the companies' annual lease payments (about $250,000 per year) while the companies prepared the initial draft and while any state objections to the companies' CZMA consistency certifications were being worked out, with the life of each lease being extended accordingly.

3. In September 1989, the companies submitted their initial draft Exploration Plan to North Carolina. Ten months later, Interior issued the promised ("informal" pre-submission) environmental report, after a review which all parties concede was "extensive and intensive." App. 179 (deposition of David Courtland O'Neal, former Assistant Secretary of the Interior) (agreeing that the review was "the most extensive and intensive" ever "afforded an exploration well in the outer continental shelf (OCS) program"). Interior concluded that the proposed exploration would not "significantly affec[t]" the marine environment or "the quality of the hu-

man environment." *Id.,* at 138–140 (U.S. Dept. of Interior Minerals Management Service, Environmental Assessment of Exploration Plan for Manteo Area Block 467 (Sept.1990)).

4. On August 20, 1990, the companies submitted both their final Exploration Plan and their CZMA "consistency certification" to Interior.

5. Just two days earlier, on August 18, 1990, a new law, the Outer Banks Protection Act (OBPA), § 6003, 104 Stat. 555, had come into effect. That law prohibited the Secretary of the Interior from approving any Exploration Plan or Development and Production Plan or to award any drilling permit until (a) a new OBPA-created Environmental Sciences Review Panel had reported to the Secretary, (b) the Secretary had certified to Congress that he had sufficient information to make these OCSLA-required approval decisions, and (c) Congress had been in session an additional 45 days, but (d) in no event could he issue an approval or permit for the next 13 months (until October 1991). § 6003(c)(3). OBPA also required the Secretary, in his certification, to explain and justify in detail any differences between his own certified conclusions and the new Panel's recommendations. § 6003(c)(3)(A)(ii)(II).

6. About five weeks later, and in light of the new statute, Interior wrote a letter to the Governor of North Carolina with a copy to petitioner Mobil. It said that the final submitted Exploration Plan "is deemed to be approvable in all respects." It added:

"[W]e are required to approve an Exploration Plan unless it is inconsistent with applicable law or because it would result in serious harm to the environment. Because we have found that Mobil's Plan fully complies with the law and will have only negligible effect on the environment, we are not authorized to disapprove the Plan or require its modification." App. to Pet. for Cert. in No. 99–253, at 194a (letter from Regional Director Bruce Weetman to the Honorable James G. Martin, Governor of North Carolina, dated Sept. 28, 1996).

But, it noted, the new law, the "Outer Banks Protection Act (OBPA) of 1990 . . . prohibits the approval of any Exploration Plan at this time." It concluded, "because we are currently prohibited from approving it, the Plan will remain on file until the requirements of the OBPA are met." In the meantime a "suspension has been granted to all leases offshore the State of North Carolina." *Ibid.* See also App. 129–131 (letter from Lawrence H. Ake, Minerals Management Service, to William C. Whittemore, Mobil Exploration & Producing U.S. Inc., dated Sept. 21, 1990 (notice of suspension of leases, citing 30 CFR § 250.10(b)(7) (1990) as the basis for the suspensions)).

About 18 months later, the Secretary of the Interior, after receiving the new Panel's report, certified to Congress that he had enough information to consider the companies' Exploration Plan. He added, however, that he would not consider the Plan until he received certain further studies that the new Panel had recommended.

7. In November 1990, North Carolina objected to the companies' CZMA consistency certification on the ground that Mobil had not provided sufficient information about possible environmental impact. A month later, the companies asked the Secretary of Commerce to override North Carolina's objection.

8. In 1994, the Secretary of Commerce rejected the companies' override request, relying in large part on the fact that the new Panel had found a lack of adequate information in respect to certain environmental issues.

9. In 1996, Congress repealed OBPA. § 109, 110 Stat. 1321–177.

D

In October 1992, after all but the two last-mentioned events had taken place, petitioners joined a breach-of-contract lawsuit brought in the Court of Federal Claims. On motions for summary judgment, the court found that the United States had broken its contractual promise to follow OCSLA's provisions, in particular the provision requiring Interior to approve an Exploration Plan that satisfied OCSLA's requirements within 30 days of its submission to Interior. The United States thereby repudiated the contracts. And that repudiation entitled the companies to restitution of the up-front cash "bonus" payments it had made. Conoco Inc. v. United States, 35 Fed.Cl. 309 (1996).

A panel of the Court of Appeals for the Federal Circuit reversed, one judge dissenting. The panel held that the Government's refusal to consider the companies' final Exploration Plan was not the "operative cause" of any failure to carry out the contracts' terms because the State's objection to the companies' CZMA "consistency statement" would have prevented the companies from exploring regardless. 177 F.3d 1331 (C.A.Fed.1999).

We granted certiorari to review the Federal Circuit's decision.

II

The record makes clear (1) that OCSLA required Interior to approve "within thirty days" a submitted Exploration Plan that satisfies OCSLA's requirements, (2) that Interior told Mobil the companies' submitted Plan met those requirements, (3) that Interior told Mobil it would not approve the companies' submitted Plan for at least 13 months, and likely longer, and (4) that Interior did not approve (or disapprove) the Plan, ever. The Government does not deny that the contracts, made "pursuant to" and "subject to" OCSLA, incorporated OCSLA provisions as promises. The Government further concedes, as it must, that relevant contract law entitles a contracting party to restitution if the other party "substantially" breached a contract or communicated its intent to do so. See Restatement § 373(1); 11 W. Jaeger, Williston on Contracts § 1312, p. 109 (3d ed.1968) (hereinafter Williston); 5 A. Corbin, Contracts § 1104, p. 560 (1964); see also Ankeny v. Clark, 148 U.S. 345, 353 (1893). Yet the Government denies that it must refund the companies' money.

This is because, in the Government's view, it did not breach the contracts or communicate its intent to do so; any breach was not "substantial"; and the companies waived their rights to restitution regardless. We shall consider each of these arguments in turn.

A

The Government's "no breach" arguments depend upon the contract provisions that "subject" the contracts to various statutes and regulations. Those provisions state that the contracts are "subject to" (1) OCSLA, (2) "Sections 302 and 303 of the Department of Energy Organization Act," (3) "all regulations issued pursuant to such statutes and in existence upon the effective date of" the contracts, (4) "all regulations issued pursuant to such statutes in the future which provide for the prevention of waste and the conservation" of Outer Continental Shelf resources, and (5) "all other applicable statutes and regulations." * * * The Government says that these provisions incorporate into the contracts, not only the OCSLA provisions we have mentioned, but also certain other statutory provisions and regulations that, in the Government's view, granted Interior the legal authority to refuse to approve the submitted Exploration Plan, while suspending the leases instead.

First, the Government refers to 43 U.S.C. § 1334(a)(1)(A), an OCSLA provision that authorizes the Secretary to promulgate regulations providing for "the suspension * * * of any operation or activity * * * *at the request of a lessee,* in the national interest, to facilitate proper development of a lease." (Emphasis added.) This provision, as the emphasized terms show, requires "the request of a lessee," *i.e.,* the companies. The Government does not explain how this requirement was satisfied here. Hence, the Government cannot rely upon the provision.

Second, the Government refers to 30 CFR § 250.110(b)(4) (1999), formerly codified at 30 CFR § 250.10(b)(4) (1997), a regulation stating that "[t]he Regional Supervisor may * * * direct * * * a suspension of any operation or activity * * * [when the] suspension is necessary for the implementation of the requirements of the National Environmental Policy Act or to conduct an environmental analysis." The Government says that this regulation permitted the Secretary of the Interior to suspend the companies' leases because that suspension was "necessary * * * to conduct an environmental analysis," namely, the analysis demanded by the new statute, OBPA.

The "environmental analysis" referred to, however, is an analysis the need for which was created by OBPA, a later enacted statute. The lease contracts say that they are subject to then-existing regulations and to certain future regulations, those issued pursuant to OCSLA and §§ 302 and 303 of the Department of Energy Organization Act. This explicit reference to future regulations makes it clear that the catchall provision that references "all other applicable * * * regulations," *supra,* at 2433, must include only statutes and regulations already existing at the time of the contract, see 35 Fed.Cl., at 322–323, a conclusion not questioned here by the Government. Hence, these provisions mean that the contracts are not subject to future regulations promulgated under other statutes, such as new statutes like OBPA. Without some such contractual provision limiting the Government's power to impose new and different requirements, the companies would have spent $158 million to buy next to nothing. In any event, the Court of Claims so interpreted the lease; the Federal Circuit did not disagree with that interpretation; nor does the Government here dispute it.

Instead, the Government points out that the regulation in question— the regulation authorizing a governmental suspension in order to conduct "an environmental analysis"—was not itself a *future* regulation. Rather, a similar regulation existed at the time the parties signed the contracts, 30 CFR § 250.12(a)(iv) (1981), and, in any event, it was promulgated under OCSLA, a statute exempted from the contracts' temporal restriction. But that fact, while true, is not sufficient to produce the incorporation of future statutory requirements, which is what the Government needs to prevail. If the pre-existing regulation's words, "an environmental analysis," were to apply to analyses mandated by *future* statutes, then they would make the companies subject to the same unknown future requirements that the contracts' specific temporal restrictions were intended to avoid. Consequently, whatever the regulation's words might mean in other contexts, we believe the contracts before us must be interpreted as excluding the words "environmental analysis" *insofar as* those words would incorporate the requirements of future statutes and future regulations excluded by the contracts' provisions. Hence, they would not incorporate into the contracts requirements imposed by a new statute such as OBPA.

Third, the Government refers to OCSLA, 43 U.S.C. § 1334(a)(1), which, after granting Interior rulemaking authority, says that Interior's "regulations * * * shall include * * * provisions * * * for the suspension * * * of any operation * * * pursuant to any lease * * * *if there is a threat of serious,* irreparable, or immediate *harm* or damage to life * * *, to property, to any mineral deposits * * *, or to the marine, coastal, or *human environment.*" (Emphasis added.)

The Government points to the OBPA Conference Report, which says that any OBPA-caused delay is "related to * * * environmental protection" and to the need "for the collection and analysis of crucial oceanographic, ecological, and socioeconomic data," to "prevent a public harm." H.R. Conf. Rep. No. 101–653, p. 163 (1990), U.S. Code Cong. & Admin.News 1990, pp. 722, 842; see also Brief for United States 32. At oral argument, the Government noted that the OBPA mentions "tourism" in North Carolina as a "major industry * * * which is subject to potentially significant disruption by offshore oil or gas development." § 6003(b)(3). From this, the Government infers that the pre-existing OCSLA provision authorized the suspension in light of a "threat of * * * serious harm" to a "human environment."

The fatal flaw in this argument, however, arises out of the Interior Department's own statement—a statement made when citing OBPA to explain its approval delay. Interior then said that the Exploration Plan "fully complies" with current legal requirements. And the OCSLA statutory provision quoted above was the most pertinent of those current requirements. * * * The Government did not deny the accuracy of Interior's statement, either in its brief filed here or its brief filed in the Court of Appeals. Insofar as the Government means to suggest that the new statute, OBPA, *changed* the relevant OCSLA standard (or that OBPA language and history somehow constitute findings Interior must incorporate by reference), it must mean that OBPA in effect created a *new* requirement. For the reasons set out * * * however, any such new requirement would not be incorporated into the contracts.

Finally, we note that Interior itself, when imposing the lengthy approval delay, did not rely upon any of the regulations to which the Government now refers. Rather, it relied upon, and cited, a different regulation, 30 CFR § 250.110(b)(7) (1999), which gives Interior the power to suspend leases when "necessary to comply with judicial decrees prohibiting production or any other operation or activity." The Government concedes that no judicial decree was involved in this case and does not rely upon this regulation here.

We conclude, for these reasons, that the Government violated the contracts. Indeed, as Interior pointed out in its letter to North Carolina, the new statute, OBPA, *required* Interior to impose the contract-violating delay. See App. 129 ("The [OBPA] contains provisions that specifically prohibit the Minerals Management Service from approving any Exploration Plan, approving any Application for Permit to Drill, or permitting any drilling offshore the State of North Carolina until at least October 1, 1991"). It therefore made clear to Interior and to the companies that the United States had to violate the contracts' terms and would continue to do so.

Moreover, OBPA changed pre-existing contract-incorporated requirements in several ways. It delayed approval, not only of an Exploration Plan but also of Development and Production Plans; and it delayed the issuance of drilling permits as well. It created a new type of Interior Department environmental review that had not previously existed, conducted by the newly created Environmental Sciences Review Panel; and, by insisting that the Secretary explain in detail any differences between the Secretary's findings and those of the Panel, it created a kind of presumption in favor of the new Panel's findings.

The dissent argues that only the statements contained in the letter from Interior to the companies may constitute a repudiation because "the enactment of legislation is not typically conceived of as a 'statement' of anything to any one party in particular," and a repudiation requires a "statement by the obligor to the obligee indicating that the obligor will commit a breach." *Post,* * * * n. 4 (quoting Restatement § 250). But if legislation passed by Congress and signed by the President is not a "statement by the obligor," it is difficult to imagine what would constitute such a statement. In this case, it was the United States who was the "obligor" to the contract. See App. to Pet. for Cert. in No. 99–253, at 174a (lease, identifying "the United States of America" as the "Lessor"). Although the dissent points out that legislation is "addressed to the public at large," *post,* * * * n. 4, that "public" includes those to whom the United States had contractual obligations. If the dissent means to invoke a special exception such as the "sovereign acts" doctrine, which treats certain laws as if they simply created conditions of impossibility, see Winstar, 518 U.S., at 891–899, 116 S.Ct. 2432 (principal opinion of SOUTER, J.), 923–924, 116 S.Ct. 2432 (SCALIA, J., concurring in judgment), it cannot do so here. The Court of Federal Claims rejected the application of that doctrine to this case, * * * and the Government has not contested that determination here. Hence, under these circumstances, the fact that Interior's repudiation rested upon the enactment of a new statute makes no significant difference.

We do not say that the changes made by the statute were unjustified. We say only that they were changes of a kind that the contracts did not foresee. They were changes in those approval procedures and standards that the contracts had incorporated through cross-reference. The Government has not convinced us that Interior's actions were authorized by any other contractually cross-referenced provision. Hence, in communicating to the companies its intent to follow OBPA, the United States was communicating its intent to violate the contracts.

B

The Government next argues that any violation of the contracts' terms was not significant; hence there was no "substantial" or "material" breach that could have amounted to a "repudiation." In particular, it says that OCSLA's 30-day approval period "does not function as the 'essence' of these agreements." Brief for United States 37. The Court of Claims concluded, however, that timely and fair consideration of a submitted Exploration Plan was a "necessary reciprocal obligation," indeed, that any "contrary interpretation would render the bargain illusory." 35 Fed.Cl., at 327. We agree.

We recognize that the lease contracts gave the companies more than rights to obtain approvals. They also gave the companies rights to explore for, and to develop, oil. But the need to obtain Government approvals so qualified the likely future enjoyment of the exploration and development rights that the contract, in practice, amounted primarily to an *opportunity* to try to obtain exploration and development rights in accordance with the procedures and under the standards specified in the cross-referenced statutes and regulations. Under these circumstances, if the companies did not at least buy a promise that the Government would not deviate significantly from those procedures and standards, then what did they buy? Cf. *id.,* at 324 (the companies bought exclusive rights to explore and develop oil *"if they met"* OCSLA requirements (emphasis added)).

The Government's modification of the contract-incorporated processes was not technical or insubstantial. It did not announce an (OBPA-required) approval delay of a few days or weeks, but of 13 months minimum, and likely much longer. The delay turned out to be at least four years. And lengthy delays matter, particularly where several successive agency approvals are at stake. Whether an applicant approaches Commerce with an Interior Department approval already in hand can make a difference (as can failure to have obtained that earlier approval). Moreover, as we have pointed out, OBPA changed the contract-referenced procedures in several other ways as well. * * *

The upshot is that, under the contracts, the incorporated procedures and standards amounted to a gateway to the companies' enjoyment of all other rights. To significantly narrow that gateway violated material conditions in the contracts. The breach was "substantia[l]," depriving the companies of the benefit of their bargain. Restatement § 243. And the Government's communication of its intent to commit that breach amounted to a repudiation of the contracts.

C

The Government argues that the companies waived their rights to restitution. It does not deny that the United States repudiated the contracts *if* (as we have found) OBPA's changes amounted to a substantial breach. The Government does not claim that the United States retracted its repudiation. Cf. *id.,* § 256 (retraction will nullify the effects of repudiation if done before the other party either changes position in reliance on the retraction or communicates that it considers the repudiation to be final). It cannot claim that the companies waived their rights simply by urging performance. *Id.,* § 257 (the injured party "does not change the effect of a repudiation by urging the repudiator to perform in spite of his repudiation"); see also 11 Williston § 1334, at 177–178. Nor has the Government convinced us that the companies' continued actions under the contracts amount to anything more than this urging of performance. See 2 E. Farnsworth, Contracts § 8.22, p. 544 (2d ed.1998) (citing United Cal. Bank v. Prudential Ins. Co., 140 Ariz. 238, 282–283, 681 P.2d 390, 433–434 (App.1983) (urging performance and making "efforts of its own to fulfill the conditions" of the contract come to the same thing)); cf. 11 Williston § 1337, at 186–187. Consequently the Government's waiver claim must come down to a claim that the companies *received* at least partial performance. Indeed, acceptance of performance under a once-repudiated contract can constitute a waiver of the right to restitution that repudiation would otherwise create. Restatement § 373, Comment *a;* cf. Restatement of Restitution § 68, Comment *b* (1936).

The United States points to three events that, in its view, amount to continued performance of the contracts. But it does not persuade us. First, the oil companies submitted their Exploration Plan to Interior two days *after* OBPA became law. * * * The performance question, however, is not just about what the oil companies did or requested, but also about what they actually received from the Government. And, in respect to the Exploration Plan, the companies received nothing.

Second, the companies subsequently asked the Secretary of Commerce to overturn North Carolina's objection to the companies' CZMA consistency certification. And, although the Secretary's eventual response was negative, the companies did at least receive that reply. * * * The Secretary did not base his reply, however, upon application of the contracts' standards, but instead relied in large part on the findings of the new, OBPA-created, Environmental Sciences Review Panel. See App. 224, 227, n. 35, 232–233, 239, 244 (citing the Panel's report). Consequently, we cannot say that the companies received from Commerce the kind of consideration for which their contracts called.

Third, the oil companies received suspensions of their leases (suspending annual rents and extending lease terms) pending the OBPA-mandated approval delays. * * * However, a separate contract—the 1989 memorandum of understanding—entitled the companies to receive these suspensions. See App. to Brief for United States 2a (letter from Toni D. Hennike, Counsel, Mobil Exploration & Producing U.S. Inc., to Ralph Melancon, Regional Supervisor, U.S. Dept. of Interior Minerals Management Service, dated Feb. 21, 1995 (quoting the memorandum as a basis for the requested suspensions)). And the Government has provided no convincing reason why we should consider the suspensions to amount to significant performance of the lease contracts in question.

We conclude that the companies did not receive significant postrepudiation performance. We consequently find that they did not waive their right to restitution.

D

Finally, the Government argues that repudiation could not have hurt the companies. Since the companies could not have met the CZMA consistency requirements, they could not have explored (or ultimately drilled) for oil in any event. Hence, OBPA caused them no damage. As the Government puts it, the companies have already received "such damages as were actually caused by the [Exploration Plan approval] delay," namely, none. Brief for United States 43–44; see also 177 F.3d, at 1340. This argument, however, misses the basic legal point. The oil companies do not seek damages for breach of contract. They seek restitution of their initial payments. Because the Government repudiated the lease contracts, the law entitles the companies to that restitution whether the contracts would, or would not, ultimately have produced a financial gain or led them to obtain a definite right to explore. * * * If a lottery operator fails to deliver a purchased ticket, the purchaser can get his money back— whether or not he eventually would have won the lottery. And if one party to a contract, whether oil company or ordinary citizen, advances the other party money, principles of restitution normally require the latter, upon repudiation, to refund that money. Restatement § 373.

III

Contract law expresses no view about the wisdom of OBPA. We have examined only that statute's consistency with the promises that the earlier contracts contained. We find that the oil companies gave the United States $158 million in return for a contractual promise to follow the terms of pre-existing statutes and regulations. The new statute prevented the Government from keeping that promise. The breach "substantially impair[ed] the value of the contract[s]." *Id.,* § 243. And therefore the Government must give the companies their money back.

For these reasons, the judgment of the Federal Circuit is reversed. We remand the cases for further proceedings consistent with this opinion.

It is so ordered.

JUSTICE STEVENS, dissenting.

Since the 1953 passage of the Outer Continental Shelf Lands Act (OCSLA), 43 U.S.C. § 1331 *et seq.,* the United States Government has conducted more than a hundred lease sales of the type at stake today, and bidders have paid the United States more than $55 billion for the opportunity to develop the mineral resources made available under those leases. The United States, as lessor, and petitioners, as lessees, clearly had a mutual interest in the successful exploration, development, and production of oil in the Manteo Unit pursuant to the leases executed in 1981. If production were achieved, the United States would benefit both from the substantial royalties it would receive and from the significant addition to the Nation's energy supply. Self-interest, as well as its duties under the leases, thus led the Government to expend substantial resources over the course of 19 years in the hope of seeing this project realized. Conoco, Inc. v. United States, 35 Fed.Cl. 309, 315, n. 2 (1996); see also U.S. Dept. of Interior, Minerals Management Service, Mineral Revenues 1999, Report on Receipts From Federal and American Indian Leases 35 (reporting more than $64 billion in royalties from federal offshore mineral leases from 1953–1999).

From the outset, however, it was apparent that the Outer Banks project might not succeed for a variety of reasons. Among those was the risk that the State of North Carolina would exercise its right to object to the completion of the project. That was a risk that the parties knowingly assumed. They did not, however, assume the risk that Congress would enact additional legislation that would delay the completion of what would obviously be a lengthy project in any event. I therefore agree with the Court that the Government did breach its contract with petitioners in failing to approve, within 30 days of its receipt, the plan of exploration petitioners submitted. As the Court describes, * * * the leases incorporate the provisions of the OCSLA into their terms, and the OCSLA, correspondingly, sets down this 30-day requirement in plain language. 43 U.S.C. § 1340(c).

I do not, however, believe that the appropriate remedy for the Government's breach is for petitioners to recover their full initial investment. When the entire relationship between the parties is considered, with particular reference to the impact of North Carolina's foreseeable exercise of its right to object to the project, it is clear that the remedy ordered by the Court is excessive. I would hold that petitioners are entitled at best to damages resulting from the delay caused by the Government's failure to approve the plan within the requisite time.

* * *

The Federal Water Pollution Control Act, 86 Stat. 816, 33 U.S.C. § 1251 *et seq.,* requires lessees to obtain a National Pollutant Discharge Elimination System (NPDES) permit from the Environmental Protection Agency (EPA) before lessees may move forward with any exploration plan that includes discharging pollutants into the ocean, §§ 1311(a), 1342(a). The EPA cannot issue an NPDES permit, however, before the lessee has certified to the State's satisfaction that the discharge would comply with the State's CZMA requirements. Unless the Secretary of Commerce overrides any state objection arising during this process, 16 U.S.C. § 1456(c)(3), lessees will not receive the necessary permit.

After the State of North Carolina filed its formal CZMA objections on November 19, 1990 (indicating that the State believed a contract still existed), petitioners promptly sought in December 1990—again under statutory terms incorporated into the contracts—to have the Secretary of Commerce override the objections, 43 U.S.C. § 1340(c)(1), to make it possible for the exploration permits to issue. In a response explainable solely on the basis that the Government still believed itself to be performing contractually obligatory terms, the Secretary of Commerce undertook to evaluate petitioners' request that the Secretary override the State's CZMA objections. This administrative review process has, I do not doubt, required a substantial expenditure of the time and resources of the Departments of Commerce and Interior, along with the 12 other administrative agencies whose comments the Secretary of Commerce solicited in evaluating the request to override and in issuing, on September 2, 1994, a lengthy "Decision and Findings" in which he declined to do so.

* * *

Indeed, petitioners have pending in the United States District Court for the District of Columbia at this very moment their appeal from the Secretary of Commerce's denial of petitioners' override request of North Carolina's CZMA objections. *Mobil Oil Exploration & Producing Southeast, Inc. v. Daley,* No. 95–93 SSH (filed Mar. 8, 2000).

Absent, then, any repudiation, we are left with the possibility that the nature of the Government's breach was so "essential" or "total" in the scope of the parties' contractual relationship as to justify the remedy of restitution. As above, I would reject the suggestion that the OBPA somehow acted *ex proprio vigore* to render a total breach of the parties' contracts. * * * The OBPA was not passed as an amendment to statutes that the leases by their terms incorporated, nor did the OBPA state that its terms were to be considered incorporated into then existing leases; it was, rather, an action external to the contract, capable of affecting the parties' actions but not of itself changing the contract terms. The OBPA did, of course, impose a legal duty upon the Secretary of the Interior to take actions (and to refrain from taking actions) inconsistent with the Government's existing legal obligations to the lessees. Had the Secretary chosen, despite the OBPA, to issue the required approval, he presumably could have been haled into court and compelled to rescind the approval in compliance with the OBPA requirement. But that this possibility remained after the passage of the OBPA reinforces the conclusion that it was not until the Secretary actually took action inconsistent with his contractual obligations that the Government came into breach.

The result of such a proceeding may well have been the issuance of a judicial decree enjoining the Secretary's actions. Ironically, the Secretary would then have been authorized under the regulatory provisions expressly incorporated into the parties' contracts to suspend the leases. 30 CFR § 250.10(b)(7) (1990) ("The Regional Supervisor may also direct * * * suspension of any operation or activity, including production, because * * * (7)[t]he suspension is necessary to comply with judicial decrees prohibiting production or any other operation or activity, or the permitting of those activities * * * "). Indeed, this was the very provision the DOI relied on in explaining why it was suspending petitioners' leases. App. 129–130.

* * *

Whether the breach was sufficiently "substantial" or material to justify restitution depends on what impact, if any, the breach had at the time the breach occurred on the successful completion of the project. See E. Farnsworth, Contracts § 8.16 (3d ed. 1999) ("The time for determining materiality is the time of the breach and not the time that the contract was made * * * Most significant is the extent to which the breach will deprive the injured party of the benefit that it justifiably expected"). In this action the answer must be close to none. Sixty days after the Government entered into breach—from September 19, 1990, to November 19, 1990—the State of North Carolina filed its formal objection to CZMA certification with the United States. App. 141–148. As the OCSLA makes clear, "The Secretary *shall not grant any license or permit for any activity described* in detail in an exploration plan and affecting any land use or water use in the coastal zone of a State with a coastal zone management program * * * unless the State concurs or is conclusively presumed to concur with the consistency certification accompanying such plan * * *, or the Secretary of Commerce makes the finding [overriding the State's objection]." 43 U.S.C. § 1340(c)(2) (emphasis added); see also § 1351(d). While this objection remained in effect, the project could not go forward unless the objection was set aside by the Secretary of Commerce. Thus, the Government's breach effectively delayed matters during the period between September 19, 1990, and November 19, 1990. Thereafter, implementation was contractually precluded by North Carolina.

This fact does not, of course, relieve the Government of liability for breach. It does, however, make it inappropriate to conclude that the Government's pre-November 19 actions in breach were sufficiently "material" to the successful completion of the parties' project to justify giving petitioners all of their money back. * * *

IV

The risk that North Carolina would frustrate performance of the leases executed in 1981 was foreseeable from the date the leases were signed. It seems clear to me that the State's objections, rather than the enactment of OBPA, is the primary explanation for petitioners' decision to take steps to avoid suffering the consequences of the bargain they made. As a result of the Court's action today, petitioners will enjoy a windfall reprieve that Congress foolishly provided them in its decision to pass legislation that, while validly responding to a political constituency that opposed the development of the Outer Banks, caused the Government to breach its own contract. Viewed in the context of the entire transaction, petitioners may well be entitled to a modest damages recovery for the *two months* of delay attributable to the Government's breach. But restitution is not a default remedy; it is available only when a court deems it, in all of the circumstances, just. A breach that itself caused at most a delay of two months in a protracted enterprise of this magnitude does not justify the $156 million draconian remedy that the Court delivers.

Accordingly, I respectfully dissent.

5.   The Decommissioning Stage

The OCSLA regulations define decommissioning as: "(1) Ending oil, gas, or sulphur operations; and (2) Returning the lease or pipeline right-of-way to a condition that meets the requirements of regulations of MMS and other agencies that have jurisdiction over decommissioning activities." 30 C.F.R. § 250.1700. This broad definition encompasses all forms of decommissioning covered by the regulations: permanently plugging wells, temporarily abandoned wells, removing platforms and other facilities, site clearance, and pipeline decommissioning. Id. at § 250.1703.

The regulations also address who is subject to the regulations and decommissioning duties (lessees and owners of operating rights, right-of-way holders), when decommissioning obligations accrue (e.g. when you drill a well, install a platform, pipeline or facility, create an obstruction to other OCS users, or re-enter a previously plugged well), and when the major deadlines, which vary from region to region, arise for the decommissioning of an offshore facility. See Noble Energy v. Salazar, 42 ELR 20056 (D.C. Cir. March 2, 2012).

DOI regulations require that all structures on a lease be removed within one year after the lease is terminated. 30 C.F.R. §§ 250, 256. Generally a lease is terminated when the last structure on the lease ceases production. A post-removal report is due within 30 days after removing a platform or other facility. After the decommissioning is complete, the agency must assess whether it has been undertaken properly.

* * *

E. OIL SPILL CLEAN-UP AND LIABILITY FOR DAMAGES TO PROPERTY AND THE ENVIRONMENT

1. The Oil Spill Clean-Up Process

OIL POLLUTION ACT OF 1990

Section 1001.

(32) "responsible party" means the following:

(A) VESSELS.—In the case of a vessel, any person owning, operating, or demise chartering the vessel.

* * *

(C) OFFSHORE FACILITIES.—In the case of an offshore facility * * * the lessee or permittee of the area in which the facility is located or the holder of a right of use and easement granted under applicable State law or the Outer Continental Shelf Lands Act (43 U.S.C. 1301–1356) for the area in which the facility is located (if the holder is a different person than the lessee or permittee) * * *.

Section 1002.

(a) IN GENERAL.–* * [E]ach responsible party for a vessel or a facility from which oil is discharged, or which poses the substantial threat of a discharge of oil, into or upon the navigable waters or adjoining shorelines or the exclusive economic zone is liable for the removal costs and damages specified in subsection (b) that result from such incident

(b) COVERED REMOVAL COSTS AND DAMAGES.—

(1) REMOVAL COSTS.—The removal costs referred to in subsection (a) are—

(A) all removal costs incurred by the United States, a State, or an Indian tribe under subsection (c), (d), (e), or (l) of section 311 of the Federal Water Pollution Control Act (33 U.S.C. 1321), as amended by this Act, under the Intervention on the High Seas Act (33 U.S.C. 1471 et seq.), or under State law; and

(B) any removal costs incurred by any person for acts taken by the person which are consistent with the National Contingency Plan.

* * *

IN RE OIL SPILL BY THE OIL RIG "DEEPWATER HORIZON"

United States District Court, E.D. Louisiana, 2012
2012 WL 5960192

BARBIER, DISTRICT JUDGE.

Before the Court is Defendant Nalco's Motion for Summary Judgment, Rec. Doc. 6541, and related briefing. Nalco's motion seeks to dismiss all claims asserted against it * * *.

I. FACTUAL AND PROCEDURAL HISTORY

On April 20, 2010, a blowout, explosion, and fire occurred aboard the semi-submersible drilling rig DEEPWATER HORIZON as it was preparing to temporarily abandon the "Macondo Well," located on the Outer Continental Shelf approximately fifty miles south of the Louisiana coast. * * *

The oil spill instigated a massive response involving government entities and officials, BP and its contractors and subcontractors, and thousands of individuals. Responders attempted a number of countermeasures, including skimming, absorbing, burning, and—most relevant here—chemically dispersing oil. Dispersants "are chemical agents that emulsify, disperse, or solubilize oil into the water column or promote the surface spreading of oil slicks to facilitate dispersal of the oil into the water column." 40 C.F.R. § 300.5. The intended result is to reduce the risk of direct contact by wildlife and reduce the amount of oil impacting sensitive near-shore and shoreline areas. Furthermore, "microbial biodegradation of oil appears to be enhanced by dispersal because of the larger surface area available as compared to a surface slick." Approximately 1.8 million gallons of the dispersants Corexit EC9500A and Corexit EC9527A (collectively, "Corexit") were applied either to the water's surface or beneath the water's surface, near the source of the discharge. Nalco is the manufacturer of Corexit.

[This part of the In re Oil Spill litigation addressed claims under general maritime law and state law on behalf of individuals allegedly injured by exposure to oil, chemical dispersant, or a mixture of oil and dispersant.]

III. DISCUSSION

* * *

B. Statutory and Regulatory Background

Since it was enacted in 1972, Section 311 of the Clean Water Act ("CWA") has declared, "it is the policy of the United States that there should be no discharges of oil . . . into or upon the navigable waters of the

United States. . . . " Pub.L. No. 92–500, 86 Stat. 816, 863 (1972) (codified at 33 U.S.C. § 1321(b)(1)). Consistent with this policy statement, the CWA established certain federal obligations and powers with respect to an oil spill. As detailed below, the Oil Pollution Act of 1990 ("OPA") made significant changes to these provisions. However, even before OPA's amendments the CWA authorized the President "to act to remove or arrange for the removal" of discharged oil, "unless he determines such removal will be done properly by the owner or operator of the vessel, onshore facility, or offshore facility from which the discharge occurs." 33 U.S.C. § 1321(c)(1) (1988), *amended by* OPA, Tit. II, Sec.2001, Pub.L. No. 101–380, 104 Stat 484, 523–27 (1990). In the case of a large discharge of oil that "created a substantial threat of a pollution hazard to the public health or welfare of the United States" (hereinafter, "Substantial Spill") the CWA permitted, but did not require, the federal government to "coordinate and direct" all public and private response efforts and "summarily remove, and, if necessary, destroy such vessel by whatever means are available without regard to any provisions of law governing the employment of personnel or the expenditure of appropriated funds." *Id.* § 1321(d) (1988).

OPA amended the CWA to, among other things, expand federal authority over, and responsibility for, oil spill responses. For all spills, regardless of size or character, the CWA now requires that "[t]he President shall, in accordance with the National Contingency Plan and any appropriate Area Contingency Plan, *ensure effective and immediate removal* of a discharge . . . of oil. . . . " 33 U.S.C. § 1321(c)(1)(A) (emphasis added). In the case of smaller spills, the President may choose from a variety of options when determining how to ensure effective and immediate removal: the President may remove or arrange for the removal of the discharge; direct removal actions; remove or destroy a vessel discharging oil "by whatever means are available"; or simply monitor removal efforts. *Id.* § 1321(c)(1)(B). However, when there is a Substantial Spill, the CWA deletes the option of monitoring removal efforts. Instead, "[t]he President *shall direct all Federal, State, and private actions* to remove" a Substantial Spill. *Id.* § 1321(c)(2)(A) (emphasis added). Legislative history states that this provision was "designed to eliminate the confusion evident in recent spills where the lack of clear delineation of command and management responsibility impeded prompt and effective response." H.R.Rep. No. 101–653, at 45 (1990) (Conf.Rep.), *reprinted in* 1990 U.S.C.C.A.N. 779, 825. When addressing a Substantial Spill, the President may remove the discharge, arrange for the removal of the discharge, or destroy a discharging vessel, as he could for smaller spills; however, to "facilitate emergency response," the President may perform these actions "without regard to any other provision of law governing contracting procedures or employment of personnel by the Federal Government." 33 U.S.C. § 1321(c)(2)(B); H.R.Rep. No. 101–653, at 45.

The CWA also required the President to prepare a National Contingency Plan ("NCP"), which "shall provide for efficient, coordinated, and effective action to minimize damage from oil . . . , including containment, dispersal, and removal . . . ," as well as a National Response System that is consistent with the NCP. *Id.* § 1321(d), (j). The National Response System establishes three levels of federal contingency plans: the NCP, Regional Contingency Plans, and Area Contingency Plans. 40 C.F.R. § 300.210.

The NCP mirrors the CWA's provision regarding federal authority and responsibility. Under the NCP, the Federal On-Scene Coordinator ("FOSC")[6] "directs response efforts and coordinates all other efforts at the scene of the discharge or release." *Id.* § 300.120(a).[7] When there is a Substantial Spill, "the [F]OSC must direct all response efforts" and "should declare as expeditiously as practicable to spill response participants that the federal government will control the response." *Id.* § 300.305(d)(2); *see also id.* § 300.322(b). The FOSC also may take additional response actions not explicitly provided in the NCP. *Id.* § 300.322(c)(3); *see also id.* § 300.324(a)(4) (permitting similar actions when there is a "worst case discharge"). If a spill "is so complex that it requires extraordinary coordination of federal, state, local, and responsible party resources to contain and clean up the discharge," the Coast Guard may declare a "spill of national significance" and name a National Incident Commander who will "assume the role of the [F]OSC in communicating with affected parties and the public, and coordinating federal, state, local, and international resources at the national level." *Id.* §§ 300.5, 300.323.

The CWA similarly states that each federal agency, State, or private party participating in an oil spill response under the CWA shall act in accordance with the NCP (or other response plan required by the CWA), unless directed otherwise by the President or the FOSC. 33 U.S.C. § 1321(c)(3); *see also id.* § 1321(d)(4) ("After publication of the [NCP], "the removal of oil . . . and actions to minimize damage from oil . . . shall, to the greatest extent possible, be in accordance with the [NCP].""). Furthermore, parties rendering care, assistance, or advice consistent with the NCP or as directed by the President are explicitly immunized from removal costs or damages that result from their actions or omissions. *Id.*

---

[6] The President may delegate his responsibilities under the CWA to other federal entities. 33 U.S.C. § 1321(l). When a discharge occurs within or threatens the "coastal zone," the United States Coast Guard provides the FOSC. 40 C.F.R. § 300.120(a)(1).

[7] See also 40 C.F.R. § 300.135(d) ("The basic framework for the response management structure is a system (e.g., a unified command system), that brings together the functions of the federal government, the state government, and the responsible party to achieve an effective and efficient response, where the [F]OSC maintains authority." (emphasis added)).

§ 1321(c)(4)(A).[8] Legislative history states that this immunity is intended to encourage "immediate and effective responses" and that "[w]ithout such a provision the substantial financial risks and liability exposures associated with spill response could deter vessel operators, cleanup contractors, and cleanup cooperatives from prompt, aggressive response." H.R.Rep. No. 101–653, at 45. The CWA also immunizes the federal government "for any damages arising from its actions or omissions relating to any response plan required by [Section 311 of the CWA]. 33 U.S.C. § 1321(j)(8).

The CWA and the NCP contemplate that chemical dispersants may be used in response to an oil discharge. The CWA requires the NCP to contain, *inter alia,* "[p]rocedures and techniques to be employed in identifying, containing, *dispersing,* and removing oil . . . ," *id.* § 1321(d)(2)(F) (emphasis added), as well as:

A schedule, prepared in cooperation with the States, identifying—

(i) *dispersants,* other chemicals, and other spill mitigating devices and substances, if any, that may be used in carrying out the Plan,

(ii) the waters in which such *dispersants,* other chemicals, and other spill mitigating devices and substances may be used, and

(iii) the quantities of such *dispersant,* other chemicals, or other spill mitigating device or substance which can be used safely in such waters. . . .

Id. § 1321(d)(2)(G) (emphasis added); *see also id.* § 1321(j)(4) (requiring Area Contingency Plans to list available "dispersants or other mitigating substances and devices"). Furthermore, "in the case of any dispersant . . . not specifically identified in such schedule[,] . . . the President, or his delegate, may, on a case-by-case basis, identify the dispersants . . . which may be used, the waters in which they may be used, and the quantities which can be used safely in such waters." *Id.* § 1321(d)(2)(G).

Accordingly, the EPA prepared and maintains the NCP Product Schedule. 40 C.F.R. §§ 300.900(a), 300.905. If a dispersant is listed on the NCP Product Schedule, then the FOSC may authorize its use if the EPA (and sometimes other state representatives) concurs in such use and, when practicable, after consulting with certain natural resource trustees. *Id.* § 300.910(b). However, if a dispersant listed on the NCP Product Schedule is also "preauthorized" for use in specified circumstances under a Regional Contingency Plan or Area Contingency Plan, then the FOSC

---

[8] This immunity does not extend to "responsible parties" under OPA, claims for personal injury or wrongful death, acts of gross negligence or willful misconduct, or responses under the Comprehensive Environmental Response, Compensation, and Liability Act of 1980, 42 U.S.C. § 9601 et seq. 33 U.S.C. § 1321(c)(4)(B). The "responsible party" is liable for removal costs and damages immunized by this provision. Id. § 1321(c)(4)(C).

may authorize the use of that dispersant without the concurrence of, or consulting with, any other agency or officer. *Id.* § 300.910(a). The NCP also permits the FOSC to authorize the use of dispersants not listed on the NCP Product Schedule when it is necessary to prevent or substantially reduce a hazard to human life. *Id.* § 300.910(d).

To be included on the NCP Product Schedule, the manufacturer must submit certain data to the EPA. *See id.* §§ 300.905(2), 300.920(a). This includes special handling and worker precautions; shelf life; recommended application procedures, concentrations, and conditions for use depending on water salinity, water temperature, and types and ages of pollutants; results of certain effectiveness tests; results of certain toxicity tests; and component information. *Id.* § 300.915(a) & app. C. After reviewing the submission, the EPA determines whether to add the dispersant on the NCP Product Schedule. *Id.* § 300.920(a)(2). The EPA may also request further documentation or conduct its own testing on the product. *Id.* The regulation notes, however, that "[t]he listing of a product on the NCP Product Schedule does not constitute approval of the product." *Id.* § 300.920(e).

C. The Use of Corexit during the DEEPWATER HORIZON/Macondo Well Oil Spill

Corexit EC9527A and Corexit EC9500A have been listed on the NCP Product Schedule since 1978 and 1994, respectively, and continue to be listed to this day. Both versions of Corexit also were preauthorized for use under the circumstances described in the Regional Response Plans for Region IV (covering Gulf waters adjacent to Mississippi, Alabama, Florida, and other areas) and Region VI (covering Gulf waters adjacent to Texas and Louisiana). Preauthorization under these plans generally permitted the FOSC to quickly authorize surface application of any dispersant on the NCP Product Schedule to waters either ten meters deep or three nautical miles from shore, whichever is farther from the shore.

The Commander of the Coast Guard's Marine Safety Unit at Morgan City, Louisiana became the first FOSC to direct the response to the DEEPWATER HORIZON/Macondo Well incident. On April 23, Rear Admiral Mary Landry succeeded as FOSC and established the Unified Area Command (discussed below). On April 29, the United States Coast Guard classified the spill as a "spill of national significance" * * *.

The Unified Area Command included representatives from the Coast Guard, EPA, BP, and Transocean (owner of the DEEPWATER HORIZON). Each day, the FOSC and other members of the Unified Area Command would evaluate the risks posed by the oil spill, the tools available to minimize the damage, and otherwise manage the response. However, the FOSC exercised ultimate decision-making authority over response activities, including the use of dispersants.

On April 21, 2010, the FOSC determined that the use of dispersants would likely provide a net environmental benefit and authorized the first aerial application of Corexit under the preauthorization guidelines of the Regional Contingency Plan for Region VI. Between April 22 and July 19, the FOSC, with the appropriate concurrence of and/or consultation with other officials (when required), approved surface and subsea applications of Corexit on a daily basis. * * * At times the FOSC authorized the use of dispersants outside the preauthorization zones (e. g., within three nautical miles of the shore) when it was deemed necessary to prevent or substantially reduce a hazard to human life. Nalco did not decide whether, when, where, how, or in what quantities Corexit was applied in response to the DEEPWATER HORIZON/Macondo Well oil spill.

D. Arguments and Law Regarding Preemption

[The Court held that state law is preempted by general maritime law and by OPA].

E. Analysis

A fundamental objective of the CWA is to "ensure effective and immediate removal of a discharge . . . of oil. . . . " 33 U.S.C. § 1321(c)(1)(A). Likewise, a goal of the NCP is to "provide for efficient, coordinated, and effective action to minimize damage from oil. . . . " *Id.* § 1321(d)(2). In the case of an oil spill as massive and dangerous as the one from the DEEPWATER HORIZON/Macondo Well (i.e., a Substantial Spill and a "spill of national significance"), Congress determined that these objectives are best achieved if the President directs all levels of the response—federal, state, and private. *See id.* § 1321(c)(2)(A). The purpose was to eliminate confusion that impeded past oil spill responses by establishing a clear chain of command and responsibility. *See* H.R.Rep. No. 101–653, at 45 (1990) (Conf.Rep.), *reprinted in* 1990 U.S.C.C.A.N. 779, 825. Notably, the EPA's comments accompanying its post-OPA revisions to the NCP similarly reflect that when the FOSC directs a response, States and private parties cannot deviate from this direction:

> Two commenters suggested that, contrary to proposed language in [40 C.F.R.] § 300.305(c), the [F]OSC lacks authority to direct state and local agency actions, but rather should/must coordinate with these parties through the unified command system. However, the language to which the commenters objected, that the [F]OSC "may direct or monitor all Federal, State, and private actions to remove a discharge" is taken directly from CWA section 311(c) [33 U.S.C. § 1321(c)], as amended by the OPA. *Thus, EPA disagrees that the OSC does not have the authority to direct state, local, or private actions.*

* * *

Another commenter suggested that inclusion of the unified command concept would clarify that a state is not at liberty to impose more stringent measures when a federal OSC is directing the response. EPA disagrees with the commenter's view that a state could initiate more stringent measures than the [F]OSC when the latter is directing the response. *When directing a response, the [F]OSC is more than managing the response.* He or she has specific legal authority to guide the activities of all parties responding to a discharge, and *all actions would have to be authorized or approved by the [F]OSC.*

59 Fed. Reg. 47,384, 47,399–400 (Sept 15, 1994) (emphasis added).

The CWA/NCP also expressly contemplated that dispersants may be used in response to an oil spill. *See* 33 C.F.R. § 1321(d)(2), (d)(2)(F), (d)(2)(G); 40 C.F.R. § 300.910. The NCP established procedures for submitting and listing a dispersant on the NCP Product Schedule, and empowered the FOSC (sometimes with the concurrence of the EPA, etc.) to determine when to use a dispersant. 40 C.F.R. § 300.910.

Although chemical dispersants have been used as an oil spill countermeasure for decades, it is clear that they are not without controversy. *See, e.g.,* [Abby J. Queale, Responding to the Response: Reforming the Legal Framework for Dispersant Use in Oil Spill Response Efforts in the Wake of Deepwater Horizon, 18 Hastings W.–Nw. J. Envtl. L. & Pol'y 63, 65 (2012)] at 66–67 (noting that dispersants have been used over 213 times since 1967 and explaining that "[i]t is the trade-off between effectiveness and toxicity that is at the heart of the dispersant controversy"). Likewise, the fact that the NCP Product Schedule requires the manufacturer to provide toxicity data and handling precautions suggests that the federal government has long been aware that there may be dangers or drawbacks associated with dispersants. *See* 40 C.F.R. § 300.920(a)(8). However, this also reflects that these dangers do not preclude the use of a dispersant—they are one of several factors to be considered by the FOSC. According to the EPA:

EPA believes that the best approach to regulating dispersants is to . . . provide [F]OSCs, RRTs [Regional Response Teams], and Area Committees the toxicity data and *allow them to make decisions on dispersant use by weighing the toxicity data against other variables and the effectiveness data* for those dispersants that meet or exceed the effectiveness threshold.

59 Fed. Reg. 47,384, 47,410 (Sept. 15, 1994) (emphasis added). The documents provided to the Court similarly evince that the FOSC knew there were potential dangers associated with Corexit, but also that there may be significant negative consequences if Corexit was not used.

Thus, the design of the CWA/NCP is that the FOSC (and sometimes with the concurrence of the EPA, etc.), after weighing the pros and cons, will determine whether it is appropriate to use a particular dispersant. When this is considered with the fact that the CWA and NCP required the FOSC to direct all levels of this response, it follows that it would be improper for the Court to second guess the FOSC's decision to use (or not use) a particular dispersant—just as it would be improper for a State or private person to disobey the FOSC's direction during a response. This conclusion is clear even if the CWA did not expressly immunize the government from suit. *See* 33 U.S.C. § 1321(j)(8). The PSC essentially admits this point, but urges that the B3 claims are not preempted because they target the allegedly defective nature of Corexit, not the government's decision to use it. *See* Hr'g Tr., July 13, 2012, pp. 100, 105, 107, Rec. Doc. 6932. This distinction lacks significance, however, because—as further discussed below—the B3 claims would still create an obstacle to federal law. *Cf.* Ouellette, 479 U.S. at 497 ("This delineation of authority represents Congress' considered judgment as to the best method of serving the public interest and reconciling the often competing concerns of those affected by the pollution. *It would be extraordinary for Congress, after devising an elaborate permit system that sets clear standards, to tolerate common-law suits that have the potential to undermine this regulatory structure.*" (emphasis added)).

* * * If the Court were to permit the B3 claims (and irrespective of whether Corexit is found to be defective or unreasonably dangerous), then, during the next Substantial Spill or "spill of national significance," the threat of liability might cause the manufacturer of dispersant X to refuse to provide its product, even though the FOSC determined that dispersant X should be used. Such a refusal, or perhaps even a hesitation by the manufacturer, would conflict with the statutory and regulatory design of placing the FOSC in charge of all levels of the response and empowering him or her to determine if, when, where, and how dispersants should be used. More importantly, this refusal would deprive the response of a tool expressly contemplated by federal law and, consequently, impede the FOSC's ability to "ensure effective and immediate removal" of oil and the "efficient, coordinated, and effective" response intended by the NCP. Thus, despite the fact that the B3 claims avoid a direct attack on the FOSC's decisions to use Corexit, they still stand as an obstacle to the accomplishment and execution of the full purposes and objectives of Congress.* * *

* * *Although the Court finds that the instant personal injury claims are preempted, other personal injury or gross negligence claims that do not create an obstacle to the CWA or NCP might be viable. * * *

* * *The issue before the Court is whether the claims against Nalco are, as a matter of law, preempted by the CWA and NCP. For clarity, the

Court does not decide whether Corexit was toxic, defective, unreasonably dangerous, etc. While the Court is sympathetic to these complaints, they are irrelevant to the issue of preemption.

The Court also makes clear that today's decision is limited to Nalco. The Court does not address the pending motions by the Clean-Up Defendants, nor does this decision affect the liability of BP or any other defendants.* * *

IV. CONCLUSION

For the reasons explained above, the Court finds that the claims in the B3 Master Complaint asserted against Nalco, whether brought under state law or general maritime law, are preempted by the Clean Water Act and the National Contingency Plan. Accordingly,

IT IS ORDERED that Nalco's Motion for Summary Judgment is GRANTED and the claims against Nalco in the B3 Master Complaint are DISMISSED WITH PREJUDICE.

NOTES AND QUESTIONS

1. Why did OPA make the President responsible for directing the clean-up of substantial oil spills? Why did Congress shift the primary responsibility for directing clean-up from the discharger to the government and then provide immunity for any "damages arising from its actions or omissions relating to any response plan"? Who else can claim immunity when participating in oil spill clean-up? Why?

2. How clean is "clean"? As of December 18, 2012, an oil sheen was still being reported at the Deepwater Horizon spill site. See Michael Kunzelman, Gulf Oil Sheen At BP's Deepwater Horizon Rig Disaster Site Remains A Mystery, Huffington Post (12/19/2012). A 2008 report prepared for the U.S. Coast Guard on a San Francisco Bay spill described the process of determining a clean-up endpoint:

Overview

The treatment termination endpoints or so-called "how clean is clean," determination represents the end of visible activity on the shorelines and, for all practical purposes, the end of the response phase of the spill (the NRDA and restoration process will proceed for months and years, but the activity is far less visible to the public and stakeholders). These endpoints, while informed by previous cleanups around the country, are determined on a case-by-case basis by consensus of key decision-makers and stakeholders, including the [Responsible Party](RP). There is no official federal guidance as to the determination of "clean" and even when state law identifies maximum contamination standards, these are rarely helpful for the treatment of gross oil contamination and speak more to post-natural attenuation conditions. While it might seem prudent to establish these termination endpoints well in advance of a release, here the process is as important as the product.

The development of endpoints necessarily involves both responders (the UC) and key stakeholders. As it represents the end of the response for many, it can involve emotionally charged meetings between those wishing to "go home" and those concerned about lingering oil on their resources. Often hidden agendas are suspected from both sides. Stakeholders fear the RP is trying to reduce their costs and the RP fears the stakeholders are being punitive. Usually neither is the case completely. Nevertheless, the activity of having both parties work through the process with open dialogue, in the best of circumstances, building an uneasy trust along the way, seems to work the best. As in all human endeavors, however, once trust is perceived to have been broken, regaining it is very difficult.

In general, there are several guiding principles in the development of a treatment termination endpoint agreement. First, unless extraordinary circumstances exist (e.g., the presence or imminent arrival of an endangered species), treatment activity will be terminated where and when the activity itself poses a greater threat to the resource than the remaining contaminant. The best example is that of oiled vegetation where activity can drive the oil into the root system and threaten the seasonal regrowth of the perennial. Second, sheen emanating from the shoreline must be controlled until it stops. Third, human exposure must be minimized in areas of human use. Finally, and perhaps most critically, shoreline treatment will not occur if doing so jeopardizes worker safety. Again, there is typically no formal guidance for these criteria; rather, they are in the record of many, if not most, previous spills. The remainder of the agreement is usually based on the potential user of the habitat and minimizing the impact of the remaining oil. (In all spills, some oil remains in the environment after active treatment is terminated. This remaining oil will be naturally degraded over time, aided by the physical processes affecting that piece of the environment: natural weathering, storm activities and the senescence and re-growth of vegetation. Eventually, most of this oil is consumed at a microbial level, which is a natural process. Of course the time involved in this natural attenuation process differs dramatically from location to location. In Prince William Sound, Alaska, many areas still contain oil from the Exxon Valdez spill in 1989. Debate continues to rage as to whether this oil represents a threat to local organisms and if so, how it can be alleviated without causing greater injury.)

Incident Specific Preparedness Review (ISPR), M/V Cosco Busan Oil Spill in San Francisco Bay at 24, PART II AND FINAL REPORT (7 May 2008).

3. If parties in the above case have no claim under state or general maritime law, do they possibly have a claim under OPA? Consider this question as you read the next section.

———

2. Liability for Damages to Property and the Environment

OIL POLLUTION ACT OF 1990

SEC. 1002. ELEMENTS OF LIABILITY.

(a) (2) DAMAGES.—The damages referred to in subsection (a) are the following:

(A) NATURAL RESOURCES.—Damages for injury to, destruction of, loss of, or loss of use of, natural resources, including the reasonable costs of assessing the damage, which shall be recoverable by a United States trustee, a State trustee, an Indian tribe trustee, or a foreign trustee.

(B) REAL OR PERSONAL PROPERTY.—Damages for injury to, or economic losses resulting from destruction of, real or personal property, which shall be recoverable by a claimant who owns or leases that property.

(C) SUBSISTENCE USE.—Damages for loss of subsistence use of natural resources, which shall be recoverable by any claimant who so uses natural resources which have been injured, destroyed, or lost, without regard to the ownership or management of the resources.

(D) REVENUES.—Damages equal to the net loss of taxes, royalties, rents, fees, or net profit shares due to the injury, destruction, or loss of real property, personal property, or natural resources, which shall be recoverable by the Government of the United States, a State, or a political subdivision thereof.

(E) PROFITS AND EARNING CAPACITY.—Damages equal to the loss of profits or impairment of earning capacity due to the injury, destruction, or loss of real property, personal property, or natural resources, which shall be recoverable by any claimant.

(F) PUBLIC SERVICES.—Damages for net costs of providing increased or additional public services during or after removal activities, including protection from fire, safety, or health hazards, caused by a discharge of oil, which shall be recoverable by a State, or a political subdivision of a State.

* * *

SEC. 1004. LIMITS ON LIABILITY.

(a) GENERAL RULE.—Except as otherwise provided in this section, the total of the liability of a responsible party under section 1002 and any removal costs incurred by, or on behalf of, the responsible party, with respect to each incident shall not exceed—

  (1) for a tank vessel, the greater of—

    (A) $1,200 per gross ton; or

    (B) (i) in the case of a vessel greater than 3,000 gross tons, $10,000,000; or

    (ii) in the case of a vessel of 3,000 gross tons or less,$2,000,000;

  (2) for any other vessel, $600 per gross ton or $500,000, whichever is greater;

  (3) for an offshore facility except a deepwater port, the total of all removal costs plus $75,000,000; and

  (4) for any onshore facility and a deepwater port, $350,000,000.

(b) DIVISION OF LIABILITY FOR MOBILE OFFSHORE DRILLING UNITS.—

  (1) TREATED FIRST AS TANK VESSEL.—For purposes of determining the responsible party and applying this Act and except as provided in paragraph (2), a mobile offshore drilling unit which is being used as an offshore facility is deemed to be a tank vessel with respect to the discharge, or the substantial threat of a discharge, of oil on or above the surface of the water.

  (2) TREATED AS FACILITY FOR EXCESS LIABILITY.—To the extent that removal costs and damages from any incident described in paragraph (1) exceed the amount for which a responsible party is liable (as that amount may be limited under subsection (a)(1)), the mobile offshore drilling unit is deemed to be an offshore facility. For purposes of applying subsection (a)(3), the amount specified in that subsection shall be reduced by the amount for which the responsible party is liable under paragraph (1).

(c) EXCEPTIONS.—

  (1) ACTS OF RESPONSIBLE PARTY.—Subsection (a) does not apply if the incident was proximately caused by—

    (A) gross negligence or willful misconduct of, or

    (B) the violation of an applicable Federal safety, construction, or operating regulation by, the responsible party, an agent or employee of the responsible party, or a person acting pursuant to a contractual relationship with the responsible party (except where the sole contractual arrangement arises in connection with carriage by a common carrier by rail).

* * *

What is the policy or rationale for setting limitations on damages for oil spills?

Liability for damages from spills of oil or hazardous substances has proved to be an unending source of confusion. Rather than provide a single, comprehensive statute for liability, Congress has specifically retained certain available remedies and has often left it to the courts to determine whether other remedies have been preempted or displaced. The choice of law determination is often critical to who can recover damages and what the limits of the polluter's liability may be.

SEC. 1018. RELATIONSHIP TO OTHER LAW.

(a) PRESERVATION OF STATE AUTHORITIES; SOLID WASTE DISPOSAL ACT.—Nothing in this Act or the Act of March 3, 1851 [Limitation of Liability Act] shall—

(1) affect, or be construed or interpreted as preempting, the authority of any State or political subdivision thereof from imposing any additional liability or requirements with respect to—

(A) the discharge of oil or other pollution by oil within such State; or

(B) any removal activities in connection with such a discharge; or

(2) affect, or be construed or interpreted to affect or modify in any way the obligations or liabilities of any person under the Solid Waste Disposal Act (42 U.S.C. 6901 et seq.) or State law, including common law.

* * *

(c) ADDITIONAL REQUIREMENTS AND LIABILITIES; PENALTIES.-Nothing in this Act, the Act of March 3, 1851 (46 U.S.C. 183 et seq.), or section 9509 of the Internal Revenue Code of 1986 (26 U.S.C. 9509), shall in any way affect, or be construed to affect, the authority of the United States or any State or political subdivision thereof—

(1) to impose additional liability or additional requirements; or

(2) to impose, or to determine the amount of, any fine or penalty (whether criminal or civil in nature) for any violation of law; relating to the discharge, or substantial threat of a discharge, of oil.

It has fallen to the United States District Court for the Eastern District of Louisiana to sort out the law, the claims, and the plaintiffs for damages for the BP oil spill.

IN RE OIL SPILL BY THE OIL RIG "DEEPWATER HORIZON"

United States District Court, E.D. Louisiana, 2011
808 F.Supp.2d 943

BARBIER, DISTRICT JUDGE.

This multi-district litigation ("MDL") consists of hundreds of consolidated cases, with thousands of claimants, pending before this Court. These cases arise from the April 20, 2010 explosion, fire, and sinking of the DEEPWATER HORIZON mobile offshore drilling unit ("MODU"), which resulted in the release of millions of gallons of oil into the Gulf of Mexico before it was finally capped approximately three months later. The consolidated cases include claims for the death of eleven individuals, numerous claims for personal injury, and various claims for environmental and economic damages.

In order to efficiently manage this complex MDL, the Court consolidated and organized the various types of claims into several "pleading bundles." The "B1" pleading bundle includes all claims for private or "non-governmental economic loss and property damages." There are in excess of 100,000 individual claims encompassed within the B1 bundle.

I. PROCEDURAL HISTORY

In the B1 Master Complaint, the PSC identifies a number of categories of claimants seeking various types of economic damages, including Commercial Fishermen * * *, Processing and Distributing Plaintiffs, Recreational [and] Commercial Business[es], Recreation Plaintiffs, Plant and Dock Worker[s], Vessel of Opportunity Plaintiffs, Real Property Plaintiffs, Real Property/Tourism Plaintiffs, Banking/Retail Business[es], Subsistence Plaintiffs, Moratorium Plaintiffs, and Dealer Claimants.

* * *

Plaintiffs allege claims under general maritime law, the Oil Pollution Act of 1990 ("OPA"), 33 U.S.C. § 2701 et seq., and various state laws. Under general maritime law, Plaintiffs allege claims for negligence, gross negligence, and strict liability for manufacturing and/or design defect. Under various state laws, Plaintiffs allege claims for nuisance, trespass, and fraudulent concealment. . . . Additionally, Plaintiffs seek punitive damages under all claims and request declaratory relief regarding any settlement provisions that purport to affect the calculation of punitive damages.

* * *

III. PARTIES' ARGUMENTS AND DISCUSSION

The subject Motions to Dismiss go to the heart of Plaintiffs' claims in this case. * * * At bottom, however, all Defendants seek dismissal of all non-OPA claims for purely economic damages resulting from the oil spill. Essentially, Defendants move to dismiss all claims brought pursuant to either general maritime law or state law.* * * The Defendants' Motions raise a number of issues involving choice of law, and especially the interplay among admiralty, the Outer Continental Shelf Lands Act ("OCSLA"), 43 U.S.C. § 1301 et seq., OPA, and various state laws.

A. Vessel Status

* * * [Except for Cameron], Plaintiffs and all other Defendants agree that the DEEPWATER HORIZON MODU was at all material times a "vessel" as that term is defined and understood in general maritime law. Cameron argues that although the DEEPWATER HORIZON may have been a vessel during the times it was moved from one drilling location to another, at the time of the casualty it was stationary and physically attached to the seabed by means of 5,000 feet of drill pipe. Cameron relies on a line of cases beginning with Rodrigue v. Aetna Casualty Co., 395 U.S. 352, 89 S.Ct. 1835, 23 L.Ed.2d 360 (1969), for the proposition that a drilling platform permanently or temporarily attached to the seabed of the Outer Continental Shelf is considered an "fixed structure" and not a vessel. Accordingly, argues Cameron, admiralty jurisdiction is absent and general maritime law does not apply. * * * Under clearly established law, the DEEPWATER HORIZON was a vessel, not a fixed platform. * * *

In the seminal case of Offshore Co. v. Robison, the Fifth Circuit held that a "special purpose vessel, a floating drilling platform" could be considered a vessel. 266 F.2d 769, 779 (5th Cir.1959). Specifically, the defendants in that case, who claimed that the floating platform should not be considered a vessel, argued that "[t]he evidence shows that Offshore 55 was a platform designed and used solely for the purpose of drilling oil wells in offshore waters—in this instance, the Gulf of Mexico. That the platform was not self-propelled and when moved from one well to another, two large tugs were used. Further, when an oil well was being drilled the platform was secured to the bed of the Gulf in an immobilized position with the platform itself raised forty to fifty feet above the water level. . . . " Id. at 773 n. 3. Nonetheless, the Fifth Circuit held that such a "floating drilling platform" can be a vessel, though secured to the seabed while drilling a well.

* * *More recently, the Supreme Court held "a 'vessel' is any watercraft practically capable of maritime transportation." Stewart v. Dutra Constr. Co., 543 U.S. 481, 497 (2005). * * *

B. OCSLA Jurisdiction

All parties agree that at the time of the spill, the DEEPWATER HORIZON was operating in the Gulf of Mexico approximately fifty miles offshore, above the Outer Continental Shelf, triggering OCSLA jurisdiction. Indeed, this Court has already held in this MDL that it has OCSLA jurisdiction pursuant to 43 U.S.C. § 1349 because "(1) the activities causing the injuries in question could be classified as an operation on the OCS involving exploration or production of minerals, and (2) because the case arises in connection with the operation." In re Oil Spill by the Oil Rig Deepwater Horizon in the Gulf of Mexico, on April 20, 2010, 747 F.Supp.2d 704 (E.D.La.2010).* * *

C. Admiralty Jurisdiction

The test for whether admiralty jurisdiction exists in tort cases was outlined by the Supreme Court in Grubart, Inc v. Great Lakes Dredge & Dock Co.:

> [A] party seeking to invoke federal admiralty jurisdiction pursuant to 28 U.S.C. § 1333(1) over a tort claim must satisfy conditions both of location and of connection with maritime activity. A court applying the location test must determine whether the tort occurred on navigable water. The connection test raises two issues. A court, first, must assess the general features of the type of incident involved to determine whether the incident has a potentially disruptive impact on maritime commerce. Second, a court must determine whether the general character of the activity giving rise of the incident shows a substantial relationship to traditional maritime activity.

513 U.S. 527, 534 (1995) (citations and internal quotations omitted).

The location test, which is satisfied when the tort occurs on navigable water, is readily satisfied here. The B1 Master Complaint alleges that the blowout, explosions, fire, and subsequent discharge of oil, occurred on or from the DEEPWATER HORIZON and its appurtenances, which was operating on waters overlying the Outer Continental Shelf; i.e., navigable waters. The connection test is also met. First, there is no question that the explosion and resulting spill caused a disruption of maritime commerce, which exceeds the "potentially disruptive" threshold established in Grubart. Second, the operations of the DEEPWATER HORIZON bore a substantial relationship to traditional maritime activity. See Theriot v. Bay Drilling Corp., 783 F.2d 527, 538–39 (5th Cir.1986) ("oil and gas drilling on navigable waters aboard a vessel is recognized to be maritime commerce"). Further, injuries incurred on land (or in the seabed) are cognizable in admiralty under the Admiralty Extension Act, 46 U.S.C. § 30101.

This case falls within the Court's admiralty jurisdiction. With admiralty jurisdiction comes the "application of substantive admiralty law." Grubart, 513 U.S. at 545, 115 S.Ct. 1043. "[W]here OCSLA and general maritime law both could apply, the case is to be governed by maritime law." Tenn. Gas Pipeline v. Houston Cas. Ins. Co., 87 F.3d 150, 154 (5th Cir.1996).

D. Plaintiffs' State Law Claims

[The state law claims section of this case is reproduced at Chapter 2, Section 2. A. The court held that Plaintiffs' state common-law claims for nuisance, trespass, and fraudulent concealment and state statutory claims were dismissed. State law does not apply because admiralty jurisdiction and admiralty law apply and OPA preemption.]

E. General Maritime Law Claims

Defendants seek to dismiss all general maritime claims, contending that when Congress enacted OPA, it displaced pre-existing federal common law, including general maritime law, for claims covered by OPA. Defendants argue that OPA provides the sole remedy for private, non-governmental entities asserting economic loss and property damage claims. They urge that when Congress enacts a comprehensive statute on a subject previously controlled by federal common law, the federal statute controls and displaces the federal common law. Defendants further argue that under OPA, Plaintiffs are allowed to pursue their claims for economic damages solely against the designated "Responsible Party" and that OPA does not allow claims directly against non-Responsible Parties.

Prior to the enactment of OPA in 1990, a general maritime negligence cause of action was available to persons who suffered physical damage and resulting economic loss resulting from an oil spill. General maritime law also provided for recovery of punitive damages in the case of gross negligence, Exxon Shipping Co. v. Baker, 554 U.S. 471, 128 S.Ct. 2605, 171 L.Ed.2d 570 (2008), and strict product liability for defective products, E. River S.S. Corp., 476 U.S. 858 (1986). However, claims for purely economic losses unaccompanied by physical damage to a proprietary interest were precluded under Robins Dry Dock & Repair Co. v. Flint, 275 U.S. 303 (1927). The Fifth Circuit has continuously reaffirmed the straightforward application of the Robins Dry Dock rule, explaining that "although eloquently criticized for its rigidity, the rule has persisted because it offers a bright-line application in an otherwise murky area." Mathiesen v. M/V Obelix, 817 F.2d 345, 346–47 (5th Cir.1987) [additional citations omitted].

One relevant exception to the Robins Dry Dock rule applies in the case of commercial fishermen. See Louisiana v. M/V Testbank, 524 F.Supp. 1170, 1173 (E.D.La.1981) ("claims for [purely] economic loss [resulting from an oil spill and subsequent river closure] asserted by the commercial oystermen, shrimpers, crabbers, and fishermen raise unique considerations requiring separate attention . . . seamen have been recognized as favored in admiralty and their economic interests require the fullest possible legal protection."). A number of other courts have recognized that claims of commercial fishermen are sui generis because of their unique relationship to the seas and fisheries, treating these fishermen as akin to seamen under general maritime law. See Yarmouth Sea Prods. Ltd. v. Scully, 131 F.3d 389 (4th Cir.1997); Union Oil Co. v. Oppen, 501 F.2d 558 (9th Cir.1974).

Accordingly, long before the enactment of OPA, this was the state of general maritime law. Persons who suffered physical damage to their property as well as commercial fisherman had a cause of action under general maritime law to recover losses resulting from unintentional maritime torts. In the case of gross negligence or malicious, intentional conduct, general maritime law provided a claim for punitive or exemplary damages. Baker, 554 U.S. 471, 128 S.Ct. 2605. And, in the case of a defective product involved in a maritime casualty, maritime law imposed strict liability. E. River S.S. Corp., 476 U.S. 858, 106 S.Ct. 2295 (1986).

In the wake of the EXXON VALDEZ spill in 1989, there were large numbers of persons who suffered actual economic losses but were precluded from any recovery by virtue of the Robins Dry Dock rule. At that time, an oil spill caused by a vessel on navigable water was governed by a web of different laws, including general maritime law, the CWA, and the laws of states affected by the spill in question. Various efforts had been made in the past to enact comprehensive federal legislation dealing with pollution from oil spills. With impetus from the EXXON VALDEZ incident, Congress finally enacted OPA in 1990.

OPA is a comprehensive statute addressing responsibility for oil spills, including the cost of clean up, liability for civil penalties, as well as economic damages incurred by private parties and public entities. Indeed, the Senate Report provides that the Act "builds upon section 311 of the Clean Water Act to create a single Federal law providing cleanup authority, penalties, and liability for oil pollution." S. Rep. 101–94 (1989), 1990 U.S.C.C.A.N. 722, 730. One significant part of OPA broadened the scope of private persons who are allowed to recover for economic losses resulting from an oil spill. OPA allows recovery for economic losses "resulting from" or "due to" the oil spill, regardless of whether the claimant sustained physical damage to a proprietary interest. OPA allows recovery for "[d]amages equal to the loss of profits or impairment of earning capacity due to the injury, destruction, or loss of real property, or natural resources, which shall be recoverable by any claimant." 33 U.S.C. § 2702(b)(2)(E) (emphasis added). Furthermore, the House Report noted that "[t]he claimant need not be the owner of the damaged property or resources to recover for lost profits or income." H.R. Conf. Rep. 101–653 (1990), 1990 U.S.C.C.A.N. 779, 781.

Clearly, one major remedial purpose of OPA was to allow a broader class of claimants to recover for economic losses than allowed under general maritime law. Congress was apparently moved by the experience of the Alaskan claimants whose actual losses were not recoverable under existing law. Another obvious purpose of OPA was to set up a scheme by which a "Responsible Party" (typically the vessel or facility owner) was designated and made strictly liable (in most instances) for clean up costs and resulting economic damages. The intent is to encourage settlement and reduce the need for litigation. Claimants present their claims to the Responsible Party, who pays the claims and is then allowed to seek contribution from other allegedly liable parties. 33 U.S.C. §§ 2709, 2710, 2713. If the Responsible Party refuses or fails to pay a claim after ninety days, the claimant may either pursue its claim against the government-created Oil Spill Liability Trust Fund or file suit in court. Id. § 2713. There was much debate in Congress about whether or not this new federal statute should completely preempt or displace other federal or state laws. Ultimately, the statute included two "saving" provisions, one relating to general maritime law1 and the other to state laws (discussed above). The question arises in this case as to whether, or to what extent, OPA has displaced any claims previously existing under general maritime law, including claims for punitive damages.

Only a handful of courts have had the opportunity to address whether OPA displaces general maritime law. For example, the First Circuit in South Port Marine, LLC v. Gulf Oil Limited Partnership, 234 F.3d 58 (1st Cir.2000), held that punitive damages were not available under OPA. The First Circuit began by noting that in enacting OPA "Congress established a comprehensive federal scheme for oil pollution liability" and "set[ ] forth a comprehensive list of recoverable damages." Id. at 64. "Absent from that list of recoverable damages is any mention of punitive damages." Id.

* * *

In Gabarick v. Laurin Maritime (America) Inc., 623 F.Supp.2d 741, 747 (E.D.La.2009), the district court determined that OPA preempted maritime law claims for economic loss, using the four factors articulated in United States v. Oswego Barge Corp., 664 F.2d 327 (2d Cir.1981), to analyze whether OPA displaced general maritime law: "(1) legislative history; (2) the scope of legislation; (3) whether judge-made law would fill a gap left by Congress's silence or rewrite rules that Congress enacted; and (4) likeliness of Congress's intent to preempt 'long established and familiar principles of the common law or the general maritime law.' "

However, more recent Supreme Court precedents cause this Court to question the notion that long-standing federal common law can be displaced by a statute that is silent on the issue. See Exxon Shipping Co. v. Baker, 554 U.S. 471 (2008) (holding that the CWA did not displace a general maritime remedy for punitive damages) * * *

* * *The question presented in Baker was whether the CWA preempted or displaced general maritime punitive damages for economic loss. The Court first stated that it saw no clear indication of congressional intent to occupy the entire field of pollution remedies. Next, the Court noted that the CWA made no mention of punitive damages, and that "[i]n order to abrogate a common-law principle, the statute must speak directly to the question addressed by the common law." Finally, the Court did not perceive that punitive damages for private harms would have any frustrating effect on the CWA remedial scheme. Accordingly, the Court concluded that the CWA did not preempt punitive damages under general maritime law.

* * *

The B1 Master Complaint alleges economic loss claims on behalf of various categories of claimants, many of whom have not alleged physical injury to their property or other proprietary interest. Pre–OPA, these claimants, with the exception of commercial fishermen, would not have had a viable cause of action and would be precluded from any recovery by virtue of Robins Dry Dock. Accordingly, claims under general maritime law asserted by such claimants are not plausible and must be dismissed.

However, the Court finds that the B1 Master Complaint states a viable cause of action against the non-Responsible Parties under general maritime law on behalf of claimants who either allege physical damage to a proprietary interest and/or qualify for the commercial fishermen exception to Robins Dry Dock. In brief, these claims are saved and not displaced by OPA for the following reasons.

First, when reading OPA and its legislative history, it does not appear that Congress intended to occupy the entire field governing liability for oil spills, as it included two savings provisions—one that preserved the application of general maritime law and another that preserved a State's authority with respect to discharges of oil or pollution within the state. 33 U.S.C. §§ 2718, 2751.

Second, OPA does not directly address or speak to the liability of non-Responsible Parties to persons who suffer covered losses. Although OPA contains provisions regarding the Responsible Party's ability to seek contribution and indemnification, Id. §§ 2709, 2710, it is silent as to whether a claimant can seek redress directly from non-Responsible Parties. Prior to OPA's enactment, commercial fisherman and those who suffered physical damage had a general maritime law cause of action against these individuals.

Third, there is nothing to indicate that allowing a general maritime remedy against the non-Responsible Parties will somehow frustrate Congress' intent when it enacted OPA. Under OPA, a claimant is required to first present a claim to the Responsible Party. If the claim is not paid within ninety days, the claimant may file suit or file a claim against the Oil Spill Liability Trust Fund. A Responsible Party is strictly liable and damages are capped unless there is gross negligence or violation of a safety statute or regulation that proximately caused the discharge. To allow a general maritime claim against the Responsible Party would serve to frustrate and circumvent the remedial scheme in OPA.

Thus, claimants' maritime causes of action against a Responsible Party are displaced by OPA, such that all claims against a Responsible Party for damages covered by OPA must comply with OPA's presentment procedure. However, as to the non-Responsible Parties, there is nothing in OPA to indicate that Congress intended such parties to be immune from direct liability to persons who either suffered physical damage to a proprietary interest and/or qualify for the commercial fishermen exception. Therefore, general maritime law claims that existed before OPA may be brought directly against non-Responsible parties.

F. Claims for Punitive Damages

OPA is also silent as to the availability of punitive damages. Plaintiffs who could assert general maritime claims pre-OPA enactment may plausibly allege punitive damages under general maritime for several reasons. First, "[p]unitive damages have long been available at common law" and "the common-law tradition of punitive damages extends to maritime claims." Townsend, 129 S.Ct. at 2569. Congress has not occupied the entire field of oil spill liability in light of the OPA provision preserving admiralty and maritime law, "[e]xcept as otherwise provided." OPA does not mention punitive damages; thus, while punitive damages are not available under OPA, the Court does not read OPA's silence as meaning that punitive damages are precluded under general maritime law. Congress knows how to proscribe punitive damages when it intends to, as it did in the commercial aviation exception under the Death on the High Seas Act, 46 U.S.C. § 30307(b) ("punitive damages are not recoverable").

There is also nothing to indicate that allowing a claim for punitive damages in this context would frustrate the OPA liability scheme. As stated above, claims against the Responsible Party must comply with OPA's procedure, regardless of whether there is also cause of action against the Responsible Party under general maritime law. However, the behavior that would give rise to punitive damages under general maritime law—gross negligence—would also break OPA's limit of liability. See 33 U.S.C. § 2704(a). Thus, the imposition of punitive damages under general maritime law would not circumvent OPA's limitation of liability.

* * *

Thus, OPA does not displace general maritime law claims for those Plaintiffs who would have been able to bring such claims prior to OPA's enactment. These Plaintiffs assert plausible claims for punitive damages against Responsible and non-Responsible parties.

* * *

H. Presentment under OPA

Defendants also seek to dismiss all OPA claims because the B1 Master Complaint does not properly allege that the B1 Claimants have complied with the "presentment" requirements of OPA. Defendants argue that presentment to the Responsible Party is either a jurisdictional requirement or, alternatively, a mandatory condition precedent before filing suit.

The Court finds that the text of OPA clearly requires that OPA claimants must first "present" their OPA claim to the Responsible Party before filing suit. * * * [The statute provides that all claims for removal costs or damages shall be presented first to the responsible party, who is given 90 days to settle the claims. 33 U.S.C. § 2713 (emphasis added).]

The text of the statute is clear. Congress intended presentment to be a mandatory condition precedent to filing suit. See Boca Ciega Hotel, Inc. v. Bouchard Transp. Co., Inc., 51 F.3d 235 (11th Cir.1995) (presentment is a mandatory condition precedent to filing suit under OPA); Gabarick v. Laurin Maritime (America), Inc., 2009 WL 102549 (E.D.La.2009) (noting that the purpose of the claim presentation procedure is to promote settlement and avoid litigation).

* * *Claimants who have not complied with the presentment requirement are subject to dismissal without prejudice, allowing them to exhaust the presentment of their claims before returning to court. In the ordinary case, the Court would simply dismiss those claims without prejudice. However, as the Court has previously noted, this is no ordinary case. * * * It would be impractical, time-consuming, and disruptive to the orderly conduct of this MDL and the current scheduling orders if the Court or the parties were required to sort through in excess of 100,000 individual B1 claims to determine which ones should be dismissed at the current time.* * *

In summary on this issue, the Court finds that presentment is a mandatory condition-precedent with respect to Plaintiffs' OPA claims. The Court finds that Plaintiffs have sufficiently alleged presentment in their B1 Master Complaint, at least with respect to some of the Claimants. For the reasons stated above, the Court does not intend to engage in the process of sorting through thousands of individual claims at the present time to determine which claims have or have not been properly presented.

I. Vessel of Opportunity and Moratorium Claims

The parties disagree as to whether the Vessel of Opportunity ("VoO") and Moratorium Plaintiffs have stated plausible B 1 claims. Plaintiffs argue that OPA may apply to some of the claims presented by VoO claimants because OPA provides for liability on the part of Responsible Parties for damages that "result from "discharges of oil. At least some of the VoO claimants allege property damage to their vessels. Moratorium Plaintiffs argue that they have stated a viable OPA claim because there are some losses that would have been incurred regardless of the Moratorium and further because the Moratorium was a foreseeable response to the spill.* * *

Few courts have had occasion to address the question of OPA causation. See, e.g., Gatlin Oil Co. v. United States, 169 F.3d 207 (4th Cir.1999) (holding that a plaintiff could not recover for fire damage because the evidence did not show that the fire caused the discharge of oil into navigable waters); In re Settoon Towing LLC, 2009 WL 4730969 (E.D.La. Dec. 4, 2009) (explaining that it was potentially possible for an injured party to recover for damages incurred as the result of a shutdown of the Gulf Intracoastal Waterway in the wake of a spill).* * *

The Court notes that OPA does not expressly require "proximate cause," but rather only that the loss is "due to" or "resulting from" the oil spill. While the Court need not define the precise contours of OPA causation at this time, it is worth noting that during oral argument both counsel for BP and the PSC conceded that OPA causation may lie somewhere between traditional "proximate cause" and simple "but for" causation. See CSX Transp., Inc. v. McBride, ___ U.S. ___, 131 S.Ct. 2630, 2642–43 (2011) ("Congress, it is true, has written the words 'proximate cause' into a number of statutes. But when the legislative text uses less legalistic language, e.g., 'caused by,' 'occasioned by,' 'in consequence of,' . . . and the legislative purpose is to loosen constraints on recovery, there is little reason for courts to hark back to stock, judge-made proximate-cause formulations.").

The Court need not define causation under OPA—necessarily a highly factual analysis—at this stage of the pleadings. The Court is satisfied that the VoO and Moratorium Plaintiffs have alleged sufficient facts to state plausible claims in the B1 bundle.

* * *

IV. SUMMARY

In summary, the Court finds as follows:

1. The DEEPWATER HORIZON was at all material times a vessel in navigation.

2. Admiralty jurisdiction is present because the alleged tort occurred upon navigable waters of the Gulf of Mexico, disrupted maritime commerce, and the operations of the vessel bore a substantial relationship to traditional maritime activity. With admiralty jurisdiction comes the application of substantive maritime law.

3. OCSLA jurisdiction is also present because the casualty occurred in the context of exploration or production of mineral on the Outer Continental Shelf.

4. The law of the adjacent state is not adopted as surrogate federal law under OCSLA, 43 U.S.C. § 1333(a)(2)(A).

5. State law, both statutory and common, is preempted by maritime law, notwithstanding OPA's savings provisions. All claims brought under state law are dismissed.

6. General maritime law claims that do not allege physical damage to a proprietary interest are dismissed under the Robins Dry Dock rule, unless the claim falls into the commercial fishermen exception. OPA claims for economic loss need not allege physical damage to a proprietary interest.

7. OPA does not displace general maritime law claims against non-Responsible parties. As to Responsible Parties, OPA does displace general maritime law claims against Responsible Parties, but only with regard to procedure (i.e., OPA's presentment requirement).

8. Presentment under OPA is a mandatory condition precedent to filing suit against a Responsible Party.

9. There is no presentment requirement for claims against non-Responsible Parties.

10. Claims for punitive damages are available for general maritime law claimants against Responsible Parties (provided OPA's presentment procedure is satisfied) and non-Responsible Parties.

* * *

12. Plaintiffs have plausibly alleged OPA claims for VoO claimants and Moratorium claimants.

* * *

Accordingly,

IT IS ORDERED that Defendants' Motions to Dismiss the B1 Master Complaint are hereby GRANTED IN PART and DENIED IN PART, as set forth above.

NOTES AND QUESTIONS

1. The court finds that OPA, unlike general maritime, does not limit the recovery of economic damages to plaintiffs who have also suffered some physical damage. The Robins Dry Dock rule provided a "brightline." Some courts have found the results somewhat arbitrary, but there is no doubt that it is clear and easy to apply. What standard applies for OPA causation? How removed from the physical event can a claimant be?

What are the conditions for purely economic claims under OPA? In In re Oil Spill by the Oil Rig "DEEPWATER HORIZON," 902 F.Supp.2d (E.D.La. 2012), the court dismissed a number of claims dubbed as "pure stigma" claims. These claims were not cognizable under maritime law because they alleged only economic losses with no actual property damage; the court also found that they did not state an OPA claim. The dismissed claims included:

1. allegations that the values of real properties were reduced as result of oil spill, even though the properties were not sold;

2. allegations that BP dealers suffered damages as result of "consumer animosity and resulting loss of value to the 'BP' brand or name; and

3. allegations that plaintiffs suffered a loss of enjoyment as result of the oil spill. There were two types of Recreational Claims: (a) "Loss of Enjoyment" claims, which alleged loss of enjoyment from the plaintiffs' inability to engage in preferred recreational activities (e.g., fishing, diving, boating, or beachgoing), and (b) "Loss of Deposit" claims, which allege that plaintiffs wasted money spent in preparation for such recreational activities.

Why should these kinds of claims be disallowed?

2. The court notes that OPA does not provide for punitive damages, but that OPA does not preempt punitive damages under maritime law. In Exxon Shipping Co. v. Baker, 554 U.S. 471 (2008), the Supreme Court held that punitive damages, traditionally available in maritime law, were not preempted by the CWA. The Court limited punitive damages in maritime cases, however, stating that it "consider[s] that [a] 1:1 ratio [between compensatory damages and punitive damages], is a fair upper limit in such maritime cases." Id. at 513. The Court was equally divided on whether maritime law allows corporate liability for punitive damages based on the acts of managerial agents. What relevance is this case for the Deepwater Horizon litigation?

3. Who is likely to fit into the category of "non-responsible" parties? In the Deepwater Horizon litigation, major non-responsible parties include:

- **QBE Underwriting LTD., Lloyd's Syndicate 1036** (insured the *Deepwater Horizon)*;

- **Halliburton Co.** (formulated the cement intended to seal the well against leaks);

- **Cameron International Corp.**(designed the blowout preventer used on the well);

- **Weatherford U.S., L.P.** (produced the float collar used at the well) . . .

- **Several subsidiary and parent companies of responsible parties.**

See Environmental Law Insitute, *Deepwater Horizon* Litigation, available at http://eli-ocean.org/gulf/understanding-litigation/.

4. Maritime law is primarily a kind of federal common law, but also includes some notable statutes. The Limitation of Liability Act of 1851, 46 U.S.C. §§ 30501–30512, which is referred to in OPA as the Act of March 3, 1851, is an early enactment that was intended to promote commerce and shipping by limiting a shipowner's potential liability In summary, if a shipowner establishes that a loss caused by its vessel was not due to negligence within the owner's privity or knowledge, the owner's liability for the loss is limited to the value of the owner's interest in the vessel and her pending freight. In the case of a catastrophic accident without fault, the liability of the owner of a sunken vessel, for example, may be virtually nothing. However, OPA effectively repeals the 1851 Act's liability limits with respect to oil spill clean up costs and damages recoverable under OPA. Can non-responsible parties still potentially rely on the Act?

5. Although the federal government established an Oil Spill Liability Trust Fund in 1986 to assist with the cleanup costs after an oil spill, it was not actually funded until OPA 1990. OPA consolidated the liability and compensation requirements of several prior federal oil pollution laws and their related funds, including: the CWA § 311k revolving fund; the Deepwater Port Liability Fund, the Trans–Alaska Pipeline Liability Fund, and the Offshore Oil Pollution Compensation Fund. The Energy Policy Act of 2005 increased the amount of money in the Fund to a maximum of $2.7 billion. Expenditures from the Fund are limited to $1 billion for any one oil spill event. OPA § 1012 (33 U.S.C. 2712) provides uses of the Fund to include:

- Immediate funds for removal costs incurred by USCG and EPA Federal On-Scene Coordinators;

- Payments to Federal, state, and Indian tribe trustees to conduct Natural Resource Damage Assessments (NRDAs) and restorations;

- Payment of claims for uncompensated removal costs and damages; and

- Administrative, operational, and personnel costs and expenses for implementation, administration, and enforcement of OPA.

The Fund also provides a mechanism for individuals to be compensated for removal costs and other damages if the claim is submitted to the responsible party, and the responsible party does not pay or settle the dispute within 90 days. If a responsible party denies a claim that is subsequently awarded monies from the Fund, the federal government may seek to recover these costs from the responsible party.

6. Beyond recovery costs and liability for damages, a polluter may be liable for civil penalties and criminal liability. Criminal liability may arise under a number of laws including the Clean Water Act, the Refuse Act and the Migratory Bird Treaty Act. In the case of the Deepwater Horizon spill, on November 15, 2012, BP agreed to pay $4 billion in criminal fines and penalties and plead guilty to eleven counts of felony manslaughter, one count of felony obstruction of Congress, and violations of the Clean Water and Migratory Bird Treaty Acts. In addition, a former BP executive is charged with obstruction of Congress and making false statements to law enforcement officials, and a Louisiana grand jury has returned indictments against the two highest-ranking BP supervisors on the well site for eleven felony counts of seaman's manslaughter, eleven felony counts of involuntary manslaughter and one violation of the Clean Water Act. See Department of Justice Press Release, BP Exploration and Production Inc. Agrees to Plead Guilty to Felony Manslaughter, Environmental Crimes and Obstruction of Congress Surrounding Deepwater Horizon Incident, available at http://www.justice.gov/opa/pr/2012/November/12-ag-1369.html (includes links to guilty plea and indictments).

NOTE ON NATURAL RESOURCES DAMAGES

One of the most important goals of OPA is to restore natural resources and natural resources services that are injured or lost as a result of oil spills. Natural resources services are defined broadly by NOAA regulations and guidance to include both ecological (physical, chemical, or biological functions that one natural resource provides for another) and human services (human uses of natural resources or functions of natural resources that provide value to the public). Federal, state, tribal, and foreign natural resource trustees are designated to act on behalf of the public. OPA directs the trustees to (1) return injured natural resources and services to the condition they would have been in if the incident had not occurred, and (2) recover compensation for interim losses of natural resources and services through the restoration, rehabilitation, replacement, or acquisition of equivalent natural resources or services.

The Natural Resources Damage Assessment Process proceeds in three phases. In the Preassessment Phase, the Trustees must determine jurisdiction and assess the need for restoration. The Restoration Planning Phase includes injury assessment and quantification, development of restoration alternatives, selection of restoration alternatives and development of a restoration plan. Injury assessment determines the nature, degree, and spacial and temporal extent of injuries to natural resources and services. NOAA's Guidance provides the following instructions concerning restoration plans:

(a) Developing Restoration Alternatives

Once injury assessment is complete or nearly complete, trustees develop a plan for restoring the injured natural resources and services. Under the OPA regulations, trustees must identify a reasonable range of restoration alternatives, evaluate and select the preferred alternative(s), and develop a Draft and Final Restoration Plan. Acceptable restoration actions include any of the actions authorized under OPA (restoration, rehabilitation, replacement, or acquisition of the equivalent) or some combination of those actions.

Restoration actions under the OPA regulations are either primary or compensatory. Primary restoration is action taken to return injured natural resources and services to baseline, including natural recovery. Compensatory restoration is action taken to compensate for the interim losses of natural resources and/or services pending recovery. Each restoration alternative considered will contain primary and/or compensatory restoration actions that address one or more specific injuries associated with the incident. The type and scale of compensatory restoration may depend on the nature of the primary restoration action, and the level and rate of recovery of the injured natural resources and/or services given the primary restoration action.

When identifying the compensatory restoration components of the restoration alternatives, trustees must first consider compensatory restoration actions that provide services of the same type and quality, and of comparable value as those lost. If compensatory actions of the same type and quality and comparable value cannot provide a reasonable range of alternatives, trustees then consider other compensatory restoration actions that will provide services of at least comparable type and quality as those lost.

(b) Scaling Restoration Actions

To ensure that a restoration action appropriately addresses the injuries resulting from an incident, trustees must determine what scale of restoration is required to return injured natural resources to baseline levels and compensate for interim losses. The approaches that may be used to determine the appropriate scale of a restoration action are the resource-to-resource (or service-to-service approach) and the valuation approach.

Under the resource-to-resource or service-to-service approach to scaling, trustees determine the appropriate quantity of replacement natural resources and/or services to compensate for the amount of injured natural resources or services.

Where trustees must consider actions that provide natural resources and/or services that are of a different type, quality, or value than the injured natural resources and/or services, or where resource-to-resource (or service-to-service) scaling is inappropriate, trustees may use the valuation approach to scaling, in which the value of services to be returned is compared to the value of services lost. Responsible parties (RPs) are liable for the cost of implementing the restoration action that would generate the equivalent value, not for the calculated interim loss in value. An exception to this principle occurs when valuation of the lost services is practicable, but valuation of the replacement natural resources and/or services cannot be performed within a reasonable time frame or at a reasonable cost. In this case, trustees may estimate the dollar value of the lost services and select the scale of the restoration action that has the cost equivalent to the lost value.

(c) Selecting a Preferred Restoration Alternative

The identified restoration alternatives are evaluated based on a number of factors that include:

- Cost to carry out the alternative;

- Extent to which each alternative is expected to meet the trustees' goals and objectives in returning the injured natural resources and services to baseline and/or compensating for interim losses;

- Likelihood of success of each alternative;

- Extent to which each alternative will prevent future injury as a result of the incident, and avoid collateral injury as a result of implementing the alternative;

- Extent to which each alternative benefits more than one natural resource and/or service; and

- Effect of each alternative on public health and safety.

Trustees must select the most cost-effective of two or more equally preferable alternatives.

Preassessment Phase: Guidance Document for Natural Resource Damage Assessment Under the Oil Pollution Act of 1990, the Damage Assessment Remediation and Restoration Program, NOAA, August 1996 at pp.1–4 to 1–6.

The final Restoration Implementation Phase involves funding or fully implementing the plan. The responsible party works with the trustees and is often involved in implementing the restoration plan. The responsible party pays the costs of assessment and restoration, and if the party does not agree to damages, the trustees may file a lawsuit or submit a claim for damages to the Oil Spill Liability Trust Fund. The federal government may seek recovery from the responsible party for any damages paid by the Fund.

Damages to natural resources and services are inherently difficult to assess. What methods are available for assessment? What methods does the Guidance use? Is the methodology outlined above likely to meet OPA's goals?

3. OCEAN RENEWABLE ENERGY

The jurisdictional issues surrounding the fast-developing technology of ocean renewable energy were the subject of *Ten Taxpayer Citizens Group v. Cape Wind Associates*, in Chapter 2. This category of ocean industrial uses includes wind turbines embedded into the seafloor in single numbers or in vast arrays called windfarms. They generate electricity carried to shore and to the land-based electrical grid by cables buried in the seafloor. Other forms include wave energy and tidal power, called "marine hydrokinetic" energy. The Cape Wind project, if built, would be the first large-scale offshore wind project in the U.S. Its proposed location in waters off the coast of Massachusetts, on a portion of the OCS that is almost entirely surrounded by state waters, raised some unusual jurisdictional issues. But all offshore renewable energy facilities necessarily involve both state and federal authorities because transmission cables must cross state submerged lands. Approval by the applicable state and federal agencies therefore represents a commitment by the U.S. to decrease our dependence on fossil fuels by developing renewable sources of energy including those from the oceans.

Cape Wind triggered a firestorm of local opposition, from private property owners and towns on Cape Cod and on the islands of Martha's Vineyard and Nantucket. Opponents feared the proposed 25-square-mile wind farm would degrade their views and enjoyment of Nantucket Sound and desecrate this historically and culturally significant body of water. See Kenneth Kimmel and Dawn S. Stalenhoef, The Cape Wind Offshore Wind Energy Project: A Case Study of the Difficult Transition to Renewable Energy, 5 Golden Gate U. Envtl. L.J. 197 (2011). The opposition led to contentious proceedings before Massachusetts state agencies and to a challenge that these agencies' approval violated the Commonwealth's well-developed public trust doctrine. Id. at 219–26. It also motivated Congress to amend the Outer Continental Shelf Lands Act to clarify federal authority and responsibility in leasing the shelf for renewable energy. As other states grappled with proposals for generating renewable energy from the oceans and in the coastal zone, legal challenges brought into question the role of private parties under provisions of the federal Coastal Zone Management Act that encourage states to provide for the siting of regionally-significant energy facilities.

A. OCEAN RENEWABLE ENERGY AND THE PUBLIC TRUST DOCTRINE

ALLIANCE TO PROTECT NANTUCKET SOUND, INC. V. ENERGY FACILITIES SITING BOARD

Supreme Judicial Court of Massachusetts, 2010
457 Mass. 663

BOTSFORD, JUDGE.

Cape Wind plans to construct a wind farm consisting of 130 wind turbine generators, each 440 feet tall, on Horseshoe Shoal in Nantucket Sound, a location that is more than three miles from any Commonwealth coast and entirely in Federal waters. As a result, the wind farm itself requires only Federal permits. However, the transmission lines at issue in this case, which Cape Wind proposes to build to connect the wind farm to the regional power grid, will pass under Massachusetts territorial waters in Lewis Bay and Nantucket Sound for approximately six miles and therefore require State and local permits, licenses, and approvals for their construction and operation. The transmission lines—two cables, each comprised of three copper conductors and one fiber optic cable bundled together—will carry electricity across an approximately 18.4 mile route, running under the seabed through Nantucket Sound and Lewis Bay for 12.5 miles, coming ashore in the town of Yarmouth, and continuing underground for 5.9 miles through Yarmouth and Barnstable to an existing switching station in Barnstable.

Cape Wind's efforts to secure the necessary Federal and, of greater significance here, State and local regulatory approvals for its wind farm and transmission project have a lengthy history. In November, 2001, Cape Wind began to seek the permits required for the transmission project by filing an expanded environmental notification form (ENF) with the Executive Office of Energy and Environmental Affairs (EOEEA). The filing set in motion a joint review by the EOEEA under the Massachusetts Environmental Protection Act (MEPA),[6] and by the commission under

---

[6] Review of the petition to build and operate two 115 kilovolt underground and undersea electric transmission cables or lines (transmission project, or transmission lines) under the Massachusetts Environmental Protection Act (MEPA) occurred jointly with Federal review by the Minerals Management Service (MMS) under the National Environmental Policy Act (NEPA). NEPA review covered the offshore wind-powered energy generating facility (wind farm) itself, in addition to the transmission project. MEPA review did not. The Secretary of the Executive Office of Energy and Environmental Affairs (EOEEA) gave this explanation in the final environmental impact report:

§ 12(i) of St.1989, c. 716, "An Act establishing the Cape Cod commission" (Cape Cod Act). Cape Wind stated in the ENF that it sought a [Development of Regional Impact (DRI)] approval from the commission. After holding a public hearing, the Secretary of the EOEEA determined that the transmission project would require Cape Wind to file an environmental impact report (EIR) in order to comply with MEPA, and outlined the scope of the joint DRI–EIR review. Pursuant to a memorandum of understanding with the EOEEA, the commission held public hearings and submitted comment letters to provide input for the MEPA review.

In 2002, Cape Wind sought permission from the siting board pursuant to § 69J, to construct the transmission lines.[7, 8] "The approval of the [siting] board is required prior to the commencement of construction of any 'facility'[9] . . . in the Commonwealth, and no State agency may issue a construction permit for any such facility unless the petition to construct the facility has already received approval from the [siting] board." *Alliance I*, 448 Mass. at 46–47, citing § 69J. Following a three-year review, the siting board approved construction of the transmission line facility under § 69J in 2005,[10] a decision this court affirmed in 2006. See *id.* at 56.

"Because MEPA (like the Cape Cod Commission Act) is the product of state law, not federal law, MEPA review (and by extension Cape Cod Commission review) applies only to those portions of the project that are located within Massachusetts, including its territorial waters (generally within three nautical miles of the low water mark of the shore). The proposed [wind farm] is located outside of Massachusetts and, therefore, is not subject to state regulatory requirements. There is one notable exception . . . federal law (pursuant to the Coastal Zone Management Act) specifically delegates review authority over projects in federal waters to the Coastal Zone Management Office of the adjacent coastal state. . . . "

[7] The siting board is "an independent review board established within the department of telecommunications and energy and charged by the Legislature with administering the provisions contained in G.L. c. 164, §§ 69H through 69Q" in order to fulfil its "governing mandate, set forth in § 69H . . . to 'provide a reliable energy supply for the commonwealth with a minimum impact on the environment at the lowest possible cost.' " *Alliance to Protect Nantucket Sound, Inc. v. Energy Facilities Siting Bd.,* 448 Mass. 45, 46–47 (2006) (*Alliance I*).

[8] General Laws c. 164, § 69J (§ 69J), states in relevant part: "No applicant shall commence construction of [an electric] facility . . . unless a petition for approval of construction of that facility has been approved by the [siting] board. . . . In addition, no state agency shall issue a construction permit for any such facility unless the petition to construct such facility has been approved by the [siting] board. . . . "

[9] The definition of "[f]acility" in G.L. c. 164, § 69G, includes "a new electric transmission line having a design rating of [sixty-nine] kilovolts or more and which is one mile or more in length on a new transmission corridor."

[10] At the same time that Cape Wind sought § 69J approval in 2002, it also petitioned the Department of Public Utilities (DPU) under G.L. c. 164, § 72 (§ 72), for a determination that the transmission lines were necessary, would serve the public convenience, and were consistent with the public interest. The DPU chairman referred the § 72 petition to the siting board for review, to be consolidated with Cape Wind's § 69J petition. The siting board's presiding officer ultimately bifurcated the petitions because a § 72 decision could not be made until the completion of MEPA review. In May, 2008, the siting board issued its § 72 decision, finding the transmission project necessary and in the public interest and convenience pursuant to § 72, approving minor changes to the transmission project as it had been originally approved in the siting board's § 69J decision in 2005, and granting a three-year extension to begin construction.

In March, 2007, the Secretary of the EOEEA issued a final environmental impact report, finding the transmission project in compliance with MEPA. Cape Wind then renewed its efforts to obtain DRI approval from the commission. In deciding whether to grant such approval under the Cape Cod Act, the commission assesses whether a project complies with minimum performance standards (MPS) set forth in its regional policy plan (RPP), a county ordinance enacted under the Barnstable County Home Rule Charter.

In its review of Cape Wind's DRI application, the commission first deemed it incomplete for failure to include certain engineering plans and proof of control of the property along the transmission line route. Nevertheless, the commission held three days of public hearings in May, 2007, and after receiving additional information from Cape Wind, found the application complete as of August 3, 2007. The commission closed public hearings on August 8, 2007, triggering, under § 13(a) of the Cape Cod Act, a sixty-day period for the commission to make a decision, in the absence of which Cape Wind's DRI application would receive constructive approval. The commission held additional public hearings in September, 2007, and sought still more information. At the commission's request, on September 11, 2007, Cape Wind agreed to extend the decision deadline to October 21, 2007, and provided responses to the specific information requests. On October 18, 2007, the commission denied the DRI application "without prejudice" on grounds that Cape Wind had not submitted the full body of information that it had sought and that Cape Wind would not agree to another extension of the decision deadline.

Cape Wind did not appeal from the DRI decision, but in November, 2007, filed an initial petition with the siting board to obtain a § 69K certificate.[13] See 980 Code Mass. Regs. § 6.00 (1993). As previously indicated, such a certificate, if issued, serves as "a composite of all individual permits, approvals or authorizations which would otherwise be necessary for the construction and operation of the facility." G.L. c. 164, § 69K. Cape Wind requested that the certificate include the equivalent of the necessary DRI approval by the commission, and eight additional State and local permits. Among the eight was a tidelands license under G.L. c. 91 (c. 91); tidelands licenses are generally within the regulatory jurisdiction of DEP. See c. 91, § 14.[14]

---

[13] General Laws c. 164, § 69K, states in relevant part: "Any electric, gas or oil company which proposes to construct or operate facilities in the commonwealth may petition the [siting] board for a certificate of environmental impact and public interest with respect to such facility. The [siting] board shall consider such petition providing: . . . the facility cannot be constructed due to any disapprovals, conditions or denials by a state or local agency or body, except with respect to any lands or interests therein, excluding public ways, owned or managed by any state agency or local government."

[14] In October, 2008, Cape Wind filed with DEP an application for a tidelands license pursuant to G.L. c. 91, § 14, and 310 Code Mass. Regs. §§ 9.00 (2008). This replaced and superseded

In December, 2007, Cape Wind filed a formal certificate application, which the siting board consolidated with Cape Wind's initial petition. The siting board granted intervener status to the five government entities with permits at issue—Barnstable, Yarmouth, DEP, the Executive Office of Transportation and Public Works, and the commission; and to three nonprofit organizations—Conservation Law Foundation, Clean Power Now, Inc., and the Alliance. From August through October, 2008, the parties conducted written discovery. Cape Wind, the commission, and DEP each submitted prefiled testimony of witnesses. Also before the siting board were 330 exhibits, consisting mainly of responses to information requests. The siting board's presiding officer held two days of hearings, during which witnesses whose direct testimony had been prefiled were subject to cross-examination. The siting board issued a tentative decision on May 11, 2009, and then a final decision granting the certificate on May 21, 2009.

Each of the petitioners challenges the siting board's decision on several grounds, and the Alliance and Barnstable separately challenge the validity of a DEP regulation relevant to that decision, 310 Code Mass. Regs. § 9.12(2)(b)(10) (2008). We discuss first the challenges that may be described loosely as claims concerning aspects of the siting board's jurisdictional authority in this case; we then review the challenges that go to the validity of the siting board's decision. Finally, we consider the challenge to the DEP regulation.

A. Jurisdictional Authority Claims

* * * 2. *Authority to include the equivalent of a c. 91 tidelands license in a § 69K certificate.* The Alliance, joined by Barnstable, claims that § 69K does not authorize the siting board to include in a certificate granted under that section any type of license relating to the Commonwealth's tidelands.[25] The argument is that these tidelands are both owned and

the application Cape Wind had filed with DEP on December 13, 2004. DEP did not act on Cape Wind's 2004 application because the MEPA process had not yet been completed. On December 22, 2008, after public hearing, DEP issued a draft license and written determination that the proposed transmission project satisfied the requirements of G.L. c. 91 (c. 91). DEP found that the project, as infrastructure to be used to deliver electricity from an offshore facility outside the Commonwealth, qualified as a water-dependent industrial use of tidelands under 310 Code Mass. Regs. § 9.12(2)(b)(10). DEP further found that the "project serves a proper public purpose which provides greater public benefit than detriment to the public's rights in said tidelands" and "preserves public rights of access to [the] tidelands for fishing, fowling, navigation and the natural derivatives thereof." DEP conditioned the draft license on receipt of all Federal, State, and local approvals, including State and local permits obtained in the form of a § 69K certificate. On January 9, 2009, the Alliance to Protect Nantucket Sound, Inc. (Alliance), filed a claim for an administrative adjudicatory hearing on the DEP draft license under c. 91, § 18, and 310 Code Mass. Regs. § 9.17. On July 10, 2009, DEP stayed further proceedings pending decision in this case.

[25] Tidelands are a "broad but single category of the estuarine complex comprising the shore and submerged lands lying between mean high water and the seaward boundary of the Commonwealth." Final Report: A Study of the Law Pertaining to the Tidelands of Massachusetts, 1971 House Doc. No. 4932, at 15. Chapter 91, § 1, defines "[t]idelands" as "present and former

held in trust by the Commonwealth to protect the public's rights in them, and that no one—including a State agency such as the siting board—may claim authority to act in connection with the tidelands unless granted express legislative authority to do so. The Alliance contends that § 69K contains no language of delegation or even mention of the tidelands or the public trust with which they are imbued, and therefore, the siting board cannot grant a certificate that incorporates, in effect, a c. 91 tidelands license.

The public trust doctrine expresses the government's long-standing and firmly established obligation to protect the public's interest in the tidelands and, in particular, to protect the public's right to use the tidelands "for, traditionally, fishing, fowling, and navigation." Moot v. Department of Envtl. Protection, 448 Mass. 340, 342 (Moot I). See Trio Algarvio, Inc. v. Commissioner of the Dep't of Envtl. Protection, 440 Mass. 94, 97 (2003); Fafard v. Conservation Comm'n of Barnstable, 432 Mass. 194, 198 (2000) (*Fafard*); Boston Waterfront Dev. Corp. v. Commonwealth, 378 Mass. 629, 632 (1979). There is no question that the Commonwealth tidelands through which Cape Wind's transmission lines will pass are held in the public trust to which the Alliance refers. We also agree with the Alliance that under the public trust doctrine, "only the Commonwealth, or an entity to which the Legislature properly has delegated authority, may administer public trust rights." Fafard, supra at 199. See id. at 196. See also Commonwealth v. Charlestown, 18 Mass. (1 Pick.) 180, 184–185 (1822). The question, then, is whether the Legislature in § 69K "properly has delegated authority," Fafard, supra at 199, to the siting board to exercise public trust rights. The answer requires examination of c. 91, the waterways statute administered by DEP, § 69K, and the statutory scheme of which § 69K is a part.

The Legislature has delegated to DEP the authority to license "structures" in the Commonwealth's tidelands, provided that they "serve a proper public purpose and that said purpose shall provide a greater public benefit than public detriment to the rights of the public in said lands." G.L. c. 91, § 14. See *id.* at § 18. In doing so, DEP is to "protect the interests of the Commonwealth" in the tidelands. *Id.* at § 2. Section 69K, in turn, grants authority to the siting board to issue a certificate in accordance with §§ 69K–69O, which

> "shall be in the form of a composite of *all* individual permits, approvals or authorizations which would otherwise be necessary for the con-

---

submerged lands and tidal flats lying below the mean high water mark." The section further separates "[t]idelands" into "Commonwealth tidelands" and "[p]rivate tidelands." "Commonwealth tidelands" are defined as "tidelands held by the commonwealth in trust for the benefit of the public or held by another party by license or grant of the commonwealth subject to an express or implied condition subsequent that it be used for a public purpose." G.L. c. 91, § 1. The portions of Lewis Bay and Nantucket Sound within the Commonwealth's territorial jurisdiction are Commonwealth tidelands.

struction and operation of the facility[26] and that portion of the certificate which relates to subject matters within the jurisdiction of a state or local agency shall be enforced by said agency under the applicable laws of the commonwealth as if it had been directly granted by the said agency" (emphasis added).

We read the quoted provision in § 69K as an express legislative directive to the siting board to stand in the shoes of any and all State and local agencies with permitting authority over a proposed "facility"—that is, a directive to assume all the powers and obligations of such an agency with respect to the decision whether to grant the authorization that is within the agency's jurisdiction, with regulatory enforcement thereafter returned to that agency. DEP, as a State agency, is by definition included within the broad coverage of § 69K. There is no mention of public trust rights or obligations in § 69K, but there does not need to be. The Legislature has designated DEP as the agency charged with responsibility for protecting public trust rights in tidelands through the c. 91 licensing program, and where a tidelands license is necessary for a proposed facility, the Legislature has, in § 69K, expressly vested authority in the siting board to act in DEP's stead with respect to the initial permitting decision. Accordingly, an evaluation of § 69K's relationship to the public trust doctrine must take into account the fact that in a case such as this, § 69K operates as an overlay of c. 91.

Other sections of the siting board statute support our reading of § 69K, most significantly, G.L. c. 164, § 69O (§ 69O). That section specifies the issues on which the siting board must make findings in its decision whether or not to grant a § 69K certificate, and provides that the siting board must take into account whether the facility seeking the certificate will conform to the various laws, ordinances, and regulations that would otherwise govern it in the absence of a § 69K certificate. G.L. c. 164, § 69O (3).[26a] See note 36, *infra,* where § 69O is quoted in full. One set of

---

[26] There is overlap between the definition of the term "facility" as it is used in § 69K (see G.L. c. 164, § 69G, which sets out the definition, quoted in note 9, *supra*); and "structure" as used in c. 91, § 14 (see c. 91, § 1, which defines the term). The transmission lines that Cape Wind seeks to construct qualify both as a "facility" for purposes of § 69K and as a "structure" under c. 91, §§ 14 and 18.

[26a] General Laws c. 164, § 69O, states, in relevant part:

"The [siting] board shall make its decision [on a petition for a certificate] in writing and shall include therein its findings and opinions with respect to the following:

"(1) the need for the facility to meet the energy requirements of the applicant's market area taking into account wholesale bulk power or gas sales or purchases or other co-operative arrangements with other utilities and energy policies as adopted by the commonwealth;

"(2) the compatibility of the facility with considerations of environmental protection, public health and public safety;

"(3) [t]he extent to which construction and operation of the facility will fail to conform with existing state and local laws, ordinances, by-laws, rules and regulations and reasonableness of exemption thereunder, if any, consistent with the implementation of the energy policies

such laws is c. 91, §§ 2, 14 and 18, with their requirement that DEP protect the public's interest in tidelands in issuing any license or permit pursuant to c. 91. Because § 69K delegates to the siting board both the power *and the obligation* to stand in the shoes of DEP, if DEP had not made the findings that the siting board adopted here,[27] the siting board would have had to undertake the same reviewing process that DEP did in evaluating Cape Wind's c. 91 tidelands license application.[28]

In sum, we find in § 69K a sufficiently articulated legislative delegation of authority to the siting board to act in the place of DEP, and to administer the public trust rights within DEP's jurisdiction in the limited context of deciding whether to approve the equivalent of a c. 91 tidelands license.[29] Contrast *Fafard,* 432 Mass. at 198–199, 207 (where there was *no* grant of authority by Legislature, local conservation commission could not exercise public trust rights, and bylaw purporting to do so was inva-

---

contained in this chapter to provide a necessary energy supply for the commonwealth with a minimum impact on the environment at the lowest possible cost; and

"(4) the public interest, convenience and necessity requiring construction and operation of the facility."

[27] As previously discussed, Cape Wind initially sought a c. 91 license directly from DEP, and in December, 2008, DEP issued a draft license and written determination that the transmission project met the requirements of c. 91. The siting board incorporated DEP's findings into its certificate decision and included the equivalent of a tidelands license in the certificate it granted. DEP expressly stated that it had no objection.

[28] General Laws c. 164, § 69O (3), authorizes the siting board in certain instances to issue a § 69K certificate that would not require the certificate holder to conform fully "with existing state and local laws, ordinances, by-laws, rules and regulations." The Commonwealth's public trust obligations exist independently of such State and local laws and other regulatory measures. See *Moot v. Department of Envtl. Protection,* 448 Mass. 340, 347 (2007) (*Moot I*), citing *Fafard v. Conservation Comm'n of Barnstable,* 432 Mass. 194, 200 n. 11 (2000) (*Fafard*) ("the Commonwealth's authority and obligations under [G.L. c. 91] are not precisely coextensive with its authority and obligations under the public trust doctrine"). We do not read § 69O (3) as a delegation of authority to the siting board effectively to exempt a facility from otherwise applicable requirements of the public trust doctrine. Rather, in any case where public trust obligations are in play because a c. 91 tidelands license at issue, those obligations must be fully met by the applicant seeking a certificate in the absence of further legislative action. Cf. *Moot I, supra* at 350, 352–353 (under public trust doctrine, DEP could not, without specific legislative authorization, adopt regulation exempting filled landlocked tidelands from c. 91's licensing requirements). Cf. also *Arno v. Commonwealth,* 457 Mass. 434, 453 n. 21 (2010) (land registration proceedings concerning plaintiff's parcel of filled tidelands could not have effect of relinquishing public trust rights in that parcel absent specific legislative authorization).

[29] While not directly bearing on the delegation question discussed in the text, additional sections of the siting board statute reflect the Legislature's interest in having DEP, the agency to which the Legislature generally has granted authority to issue such licenses, play a role in the siting board's decision where a c. 91 tidelands license is in issue. Thus, G.L. c. 164, §§ 69L and 69N, read together, define the "parties in interest" in any certificate proceeding to include, among others, any person or entity that the siting board permits to intervene. In the present case, DEP was an intervener in the § 69K proceeding concerning Cape Wind, and fully participated in that proceeding. Moreover, in G.L. c. 164, § 69H, as amended through St.2007, c. 19, § 37, the Legislature has designated the Secretary of EOEEA, the Executive Office in which DEP resides, as the chair of the siting board itself, and the commissioner of DEP as one of the siting board's nine members. We view these provisions as steps taken by the Legislature to facilitate the siting board's obligation to address DEP's statutory and regulatory mandate—including the protection of public trust rights—when, as in this case, they are implicated by a § 69K certificate application.

lid). Contrast also *Moot I,* 448 Mass. at 347–353.[30] Accordingly, the siting board in this case did not exceed its authority by including the equivalent of a c. 91 tidelands license in the certificate it granted Cape Wind.

We agree with the Chief Justice, [separate opinion concurring and dissenting in part], that an express statement from the Legislature is necessary both to relinquish public rights in tidelands and to delegate authority to administer public trust rights and duties. See, e.g., *Arno v. Commonwealth, supra* at 438 n. 7, 453 n. 21. The decisions of this court, however, have recognized a difference between a legislative delegation of authority to administer public trust rights and duties through regulation or use of tidelands subject to conditions, and a permanent relinquishment of the public's rights in tidelands. The latter can only happen where the Legislature has undertaken specific steps and made explicit findings to signal its intent to relinquish. Compare *Fafard,* 432 Mass. at 199 n. 10 ("The Commonwealth may delegate, and has delegated, its authority to preserve and regulate Commonwealth tidelands to State agencies or municipalities"), and Boston Waterfront Dev. Corp. v. Commonwealth, 378 Mass. 629, 649 (1979) (wharfing statutes granting landowners fee simple title to certain Commonwealth tidelands "subject to the condition subsequent that it be used for the public purpose for which it was granted"), with Opinions of the Justices, 383 Mass. 895, 901–905 (1981) (setting forth steps Legislature must take to "abandon, release, or extinguish the public interest in submerged land" and noting that *"Boston Waterfront* . . . concerned the consequences of the Lewis Wharf statutes, . . . which did not undertake by their express terms to transfer all the Commonwealth's or the public's interests in the disputed land"). Cf. *Moot II,* supra at 313–315 (legislation enacted after *Moot I* did not relinquish public rights in landlocked tidelands but permissibly exempted them from c. 91 licensing scheme; court therefore rejected plaintiffs' claim that legislation exceeded Legislature's authority by effectively extinguishing public trust rights without explicit findings required by Opinions of the Justices, supra). While it is clear from our case law what steps the Legislature must take to relinquish the public's rights in tidelands, see Opinions of the Justices, supra, our cases addressing delegation of authority to regulate tidelands, and in doing so to administer public trust rights and duties, have said only that such delegation must be express. See Commonwealth v. Charlestown, 18 Mass. (1 Pick.) 180, 184–185 (1822). And the statutory provisions effecting this type of delegation have generally been broadly

---

[30] In *Moot I,* 448 Mass. at 347, 352–353, we held that DEP exceeded its authority under G.L. c. 91, § 18, by promulgating a regulation exempting filled landlocked tidelands from c. 91's licensing requirements. "By exempting filled 'landlocked' tidelands from the statute's licensing requirements, [DEP was] relinquishing all control over the use of the filled land . . . without legislative authorization, effectively relinquishing all public rights that the Legislature has mandated be preserved through the licensing requirements." *Id.* at 350. See *Moot v. Department of Envtl. Protection,* 456 Mass. 309, 310 (2010) (*Moot II*). Here, there has been no relinquishment or extinguishment of the public's rights in the tidelands at issue.

phrased, offering few specific directives to the designated agency or official on how to exercise the authority given them. See Fafard, supra, and statutes cited. As we have discussed, our view is that in § 69K, the Legislature has expressly delegated to the siting board the authority to grant a revocable c. 91 license to use the tidelands at issue, and encompassed in that delegation is the authority, and obligation, to administer public trust rights and duties.* * *

3. *Jurisdiction to consider "in-State impacts" of the wind farm.* In its decision, the siting board adopted the presiding officer's determination that it lacked jurisdiction to consider the "in-State impacts" of the wind farm itself due to the location of the wind farm in Federal waters, and therefore that the scope of the certificate proceeding would be limited to the transmission lines only and evidence concerning the wind farms's impacts would be excluded. See note 14, *supra.* The petitioners assert that no such jurisdictional limitation exists, and the siting board was obliged to assess the in-State impacts of the entire wind farm project in making its § 69K certificate decision.[31]

There is no dispute that the wind farm, located entirely in Federal waters, will lie outside the jurisdiction of the siting board as well as the State and local permitting agencies with permits at issue in the siting board's § 69K proceeding. See Alliance I, 448 Mass. at 48, 858 N.E.2d 294 ("The area in which the wind farm itself is proposed to be built is located in Federal waters and, thus, falls beyond the scope of the [siting] board's jurisdiction"). The petitioners assert, however, that whether as a matter of making the findings required by § 69O or of complying with public trust doctrine obligations, the siting board had the power and the duty to consider the potential effects of the wind farm on the Commonwealth. The thrust of their claim appears to be that as a general tenet of environmental and perhaps all regulation of private development projects, regulatory agencies consider—and must consider—all direct and indirect impacts of the entire project; and because Cape Wind's transmission lines will connect directly to and service the wind farm, evaluation of the impacts of the wind farm itself was a mandatory part of the siting board's review of the transmission project. The claim fails for two reasons.

First, the siting board statute generally, and §§ 69J, 69K, and 69O in particular, state with unmistakable clarity that the siting board's regulatory point of focus at all times is to be on the proposed "facility." The petitioners do not, and could not, dispute that Cape Wind's two new 115 kilovolt electric transmission lines constitute the only "facility" subject to the

---

[31] The petitioners mention, in particular, impacts of the wind farm's turbine generators on "state waters, air space, lands, and public safety," alleging that the wind farm will cause harm to navigation, aviation, fisheries, birds, and water quality, as well as create an increased set of risks relating to public safety and environmental damage that a town such as Barnstable will be forced to confront.

siting board's review in this case. Accordingly, insofar as § 69O (2) directs the siting board to make findings relating to "considerations of environmental protection, public health and public safety," those findings are solely to concern "the compatibility of *the facility* "with such considerations (emphasis added).[32] Cf. Villages Dev. Co. v. Secretary of the Executive Office of Envtl. Affairs, 410 Mass. 100, 112–115 & n. 13 (1991) (where Secretary of [then] EOEA had jurisdiction under MEPA to review private development project based on one necessary State "permit" [grant of easement over bicycle path to construct bridge], MEPA review statutorily restricted to direct and indirect environmental impacts related to easement itself, not impacts of entire development project, even if bridge necessary for entire project to go forward).

The second reason the petitioners' bid for review of the wind farm's impacts fails is the one the siting board cites: the wind farm itself will be within Federal jurisdiction, and Federal jurisdiction in this area is paramount. See United States v. Maine, 420 U.S. 515, 522, 524 (1975) ("control and disposition [of all lands underlying sea] in the first instance are the business of the Federal Government rather than the States"; "paramount rights to the offshore seabed inhere in the Federal Government as an incident of national sovereignty"); *Ten Taxpayer Citizens Group v. Cape Wind Assocs., LLC,* 373 F.3d 183, 196–197 (1st Cir.2004), cert. denied, 543 U.S. 1121 (2005) *(Ten Taxpayer Citizens)* (by enacting Outer Continental Shelf Lands Act of 1953 [OCSLA], 43 U.S.C. §§ 1331 et seq., "Congress retained for the federal government the exclusive power to authorize or prohibit specific uses of the seabed beyond three miles from shore"); *Alliance to Protect Nantucket Sound, Inc. v. Department of the Army,* 398 F.3d 105, 107–108 (1st Cir.2005).[33] Contrary to the Alliance's claim, the express assertion of exclusive Federal power and control over the outer continental shelf (defined in OCSLA as all submerged lands lying in navigable waters beyond three miles from shore, see 43 U.S.C. § 1331 [a]), serves to preempt any attempt by the Commonwealth or its

---

[32] This point is reinforced by the fact that since the passage of the 1997 Restructuring Act, St.1997, c. 164, which amended the siting board statute in several respects, the Legislature has mandated that a proposed "generating facility" (a term that describes the wind farm) be reviewed by the siting board separately from a "facility" (the term that describes the transmission lines). See, e.g., G.L. c. 164, §§ 69J1/4, 69K1/2, 69L1/2, 69O1/2, inserted by St.1997, c. 164, §§ 210, 214, 216, and 223, respectively.

[33] Despite the fact that our public trust doctrine relating to, inter alia, Commonwealth tidelands is "an age-old concept with ancient roots," *Trio Algarvio, Inc. v. Commissioner of the Dep't of Envtl. Protection,* 440 Mass. 94, 97 (2003), the United States Supreme Court has made it clear "that the United States enjoys exclusive title in the lands underlying the sea [below the low water mark], regardless of a state's historical claims to the waters off its coast." *Ten Taxpayer Citizens Group v. Cape Wind Assoc., LLC,* 373 F.3d 183, 188 (1st Cir.2004), cert. denied, 543 U.S. 1121 (2005), citing *United States v. California,* 332 U.S. 19, 29–39 (1947); *United States v. Louisiana,* 339 U.S. 699, 705–706 (1950); *United States v. Texas,* 339 U.S. 707, 719–720 (1950); and *United States v. Maine,* 420 U.S. 515, 522 (1975). Massachusetts, like all other coastal States, has title to the three-mile margin of seabed off its coast only because, in 1953, Congress passed the Submerged Lands Act of 1953, 43 U.S.C. §§ 1301 et seq. (2006), which granted this right.

agencies to regulate structures or facilities placed in that area. See Ten Taxpayer Citizens, supra at 197 ("If adopted and enforced on the outer Continental Shelf, statutes like [c.] 91 . . . which require[s] the approval of state agencies prior to construction, would effectively grant state governments a veto power over the disposition of the national seabed," a result "fundamentally inconsistent with the OSCLA").

If the siting board were to assert authority to consider the impacts of the wind farm itself, as the petitioners argue that it should, presumably that authority would encompass the power to deny or condition Cape Wind's requested certificate on account of such impacts. But a denial of the certificate on that ground, or even conditioning, would be tantamount to a denial of the wind farm project itself, because, as the siting board found in its § 69J decision approving construction of the transmission project in 2005, the transmission lines are necessary for the wind farm's operation. See Alliance I, 448 Mass. at 49–50, 55–56. The siting board does not have authority to do indirectly what it cannot do directly. See Ten Taxpayer Citizens, supra. Cf. New England Legal Found. v. Massachusetts Port Auth., 883 F.2d 157, 174 1st Cir.1989) (holding defendant authority's landing fee regulations invalid under Federal law; fee regulations "appear to be an attempt to modify conduct [e.g., control air traffic] rather than to recover operational cost, and are thus an incursion into an area of regulation preempted by [Federal law]. [The authority] cannot do indirectly what it is forbidden to do directly"). Contrast Leisure Time Cruise Corp. v. Barnstable, 62 F.Supp.2d 202, 208–209 (D.Mass.1999) (where local and regional authorities sought to regulate aspects of actual docking of plaintiff's boat in Hyannis Harbor, this regulation was "ancillary to Leisure Time's operation of its gambling cruise" in Federal waters, and not preempted under applicable Federal law).[34]

We emphasize that the siting board properly could, and did, consider the in-State impacts of the entire length of Cape Wind's transmission lines even though the lines will lie in part in Federal waters because those impacts relate *directly* to the "facility" over which the siting board has jurisdiction. See Leisure Time Cruise Corp. v. Barnstable, supra. In doing so, the siting board met its public trust obligations arising from the fact that the facility under review is located in Commonwealth tidelands. Here, the siting board, through the presiding officer, allowed the testimony of the petitioners' witnesses so far as it pertained to the transmission project; the testimony deemed inadmissible related solely to the claimed

---

[34] The legislative history of the siting board statute indicates an early recognition of the limits Federal law places on the scope of the siting board's authority. The Legislature enacted the siting board statute in 1973. St.1973, c. 1232. The following year, it amended a savings clause in the 1973 statute, see *id.* at § 6, to include the following language: "This act shall not apply to any matter over which any agency, department, or instrumentality of the federal government has exclusive jurisdiction." St.1974, c. 852, § 21. The Legislature reiterated this limitation in St.1992, c. 141, § 54.

impacts of the wind farm's turbines. See note 16, *supra*. The siting board's presiding officer did not abuse her discretion or commit other error of law by ruling that evidence related to general in-State impacts of the wind turbines, unconnected to the transmission project, was inadmissible.

The wind farm, including its in-State impacts, has undergone extensive scrutiny by Federal and State agencies. In addition to the National Environmental Policy Act review by the Minerals Management Service, the Coastal Zone Management Office (CZM) has certified to Federal permitting authorities that Cape Wind's entire project, including the wind farm, will be consistent with CZM policies. Moreover, the siting board has conditioned the certificate it granted Cape Wind for the transmission project on Cape Wind's receipt of all necessary Federal and State permits for the wind farm. In reviewing the siting board's decision under § 69J to authorize Cape Wind's construction of the transmission lines, this court approved of the siting board's determination that it was required to defer to Federal review. See *Alliance I,* 448 Mass. at 53–54. We do so again here.* * *

MARSHALL, C.J. (concurring in part and dissenting in part, with whom SPINA, J., joins).

The development of clean energy resources is an important national and State policy. The offshore wind-powered energy generating facility (wind farm) that Cape Wind, LLC (Cape Wind), proposes to construct in Nantucket Sound may further that policy by providing clean energy for the Commonwealth. It is not our role, however, to evaluate whether as a matter of sound policy the project should be constructed. Rather, we must determine whether the approval process of the Cape Wind project comports with the laws of the Commonwealth. It does not. Today's decision that the "certificate of environmental impact and public interest" (certificate), G.L. c. 164, § 69K (§ 69K), issued by the Energy Facilities Siting Board (siting board) was proper is contrary to existing law and seriously undermines the public trust doctrine, which for centuries has protected the rights of the people of Massachusetts in Commonwealth tidelands.

The court concludes that the *Commonwealth* has fulfilled its fiduciary obligation to the people of Massachusetts because the *siting board* has issued a certificate to Cape Wind under § 69K authorizing transmission cables to traverse Commonwealth tidelands. See ante at 679–681, 932 N.E.2d at 800–02. The siting board, however, does not have, and was not intended by the Legislature to have, the right to act as fiduciary on behalf of the people with regard to Commonwealth tidelands or to approve energy projects up and down the coastline of Massachusetts in Commonwealth tidelands. It may be that the Legislature or the Legislature's expressly authorized designee, exercising its responsibility as fiduciary, would conclude that transmission cables stretching across Commonwealth tidelands from the shore to the Commonwealth's seaward boundary should be approved. But that authorization has not occurred. The court's ruling to the contrary establishes a dangerous and unwise precedent, which has far-reaching consequences. A wind farm today may be a drilling rig or nuclear power plant tomorrow.

The court also concludes that the siting board acted appropriately by granting the certificate without considering *any* of the in-State impacts of the wind farm. See ante at 686–687, 932 N.E.2d at 805–06. Centuries of legislation and jurisprudence concerning the paramount rights of the people of the Commonwealth to the use of the sea and shore lead me to disagree. The stakes are high. As we have recently seen in the Gulf of Mexico, the failure to take into account in-State consequences of federally authorized energy projects in Federal waters can have catastrophic effects on State tidelands and coastal areas, and on all who depend on them.

The public trust doctrine stands as a covenant between the people of the Commonwealth and their government, a covenant to safeguard our tidelands for all generations for the use of the people, traditionally for fishing, fowling, and navigation. See Moot v. Department of Envtl. Protection, 448 Mass. 340, 342 (2007) (Moot I); Fafard v. Conservation Comm'n of Barnstable, 432 Mass. 194, 198 (2000) (Fafard), and cases cited. The doctrine, and with it the public's trust in government, once undermined is not easily restored. The court's judgment, I fear, is a step in the wrong direction. I respectfully dissent.

A

The court acknowledges, as it must, that only the Commonwealth, or an entity to which the Legislature "properly has delegated authority," may administer public trust rights. Ante at 677, 932 N.E.2d at 799, quoting Fafard, supra at 199, 733 N.E.2d 66. I cannot agree with the court's conclusion that the Legislature has delegated such authority to the siting board. In Fafard, supra at 197, 733 N.E.2d 66, we once again made clear that only the Commonwealth or an "entity to which the Commonwealth has delegated authority *expressly* "may administer public trust rights (emphasis added). Accord Moot I, supra at 347, 861 N.E.2d 410 (same). See Commonwealth v. Charlestown, 18 Mass. 180, 1 Pick. 180, 185 (1822) (Legislature may "delegate" power under public trust doctrine to authorize construction of bridge over navigable waterway, "but, until they have made such delegation in *express* terms, it is a branch of sovereign power to be exercised by the [L]egislature alone" [emphasis added]). The siting board's enabling legislation provides for no such express delegation.

The requirement that any delegation by the Legislature of authority to administer public trust rights be "express" is rooted in the "history of the origins of the Commonwealth's public trust obligations and authority, as well as jurisprudence and legislation spanning two centuries." Fafard, supra at 199, 733 N.E.2d 66. That history, jurisprudence, and legislation has been recounted frequently and at length elsewhere. See, e.g., Arno v. Commonwealth, 457 Mass. 434, 449–453, 931 N.E.2d 1 (2010) (Arno); Boston Waterfront Dev. Corp. v. Commonwealth, 378 Mass. 629, 631–649, 393 N.E.2d 356 (1979). Briefly, as protector of the public trust, the Commonwealth sits "in a fiduciary relation" to the people. Commonwealth v. Roxbury, 75 Mass. 451, 9 Gray 451, 492 (1857). Commonwealth tidelands are "impressed with a public trust, which gives the public's representatives an interest and responsibility" in their development. Boston Waterfront Dev. Corp. v. Commonwealth, supra at 649, 393 N.E.2d 356. See Trio Algarvio, Inc. v. Commissioner of the Dep't of Envtl. Protection, 440 Mass. 94, 97, 795 N.E.2d 1148 (2003) (Legislature has "obligation to protect the public's interest").

The Commonwealth may delegate, and of course has delegated, the responsibility, or some of it, to administer its tidelands to a State agency. See Moot I, supra, and cases cited. As noted, that delegation, when it occurs, must be explicit. Thus, pursuant to G.L. c. 91, the Department of Environmental Protection (DEP) may issue licenses for the construction of structures "in or over tide water" or cables "under tide water." *Id.* at § 14. See *id.* at § 18 (such licenses are "revocable"). The Legislature has been unmistakably clear that in granting such licenses DEP "shall protect the interests of the commonwealth" and its inhabitants in "lands, rights in lands, flats, shores," "rights in tide waters," and "tidelands" within the Commonwealth. *Id.* at § 2. See Moot I, supra at 342–343, 861 N.E.2d 410 ("obligation to preserve the public trust" has been expressly delegated by Legislature to DEP).* * *

. . . . I cannot agree. The siting board cannot "stand in the shoes" of DEP with respect to the administration of public trust rights unless the Legislature has expressly authorized it to do so. Such an express authorization is the only "articulation" that is "sufficient" to delegate fiduciary responsibilities. See Fafard, supra at 198–199, 733 N.E.2d 66 (town may not administer public trust rights in DEP's place without express delegation of authority).

The court supports its conclusion by pointing to language in § 69K authorizing the siting board, in certain circumstances, to issue a certificate with respect to a proposed energy facility that "shall be in the form of a composite of all individual permits, approvals or authorizations which would otherwise be necessary for the construction or operation of the facility." That language, as does the rest of § 69K, makes no reference to tidelands and lacks any recognition of public trust rights, and, contrary to the court's conclusion, the Legislature has *not* "expressly vested authority" in the siting board to act with respect to public trust rights. The court cites no precedent supporting its "reading" of the statute, and there is none. See ante at 678–681, 932 N.E.2d at 799–802. Rather, the court's "reading" of the statute is at odds with our prior public trust jurisprudence, both ancient and contemporary.* * *

    . . . The court correctly notes that the decisions of this court have "recognized a difference" between a legislative delegation of authority to *administer* public trust rights and duties and a permanent *relinquishment* of the public's rights in tidelands. *Ante* at n. 30. But that difference is inconsequential in the context of this case. In either circumstance (delegation of authority to administer the rights or relinquishment of the rights) our jurisprudence has made abundantly clear that the Legislature *must* act *expressly*. It has not done so here.

    Were the siting board statute itself and the case law not sufficiently clear to require a different outcome of this case, and they are, the legislative history of the creation of the siting board confirms that the Legislature did *not* in fact delegate authority to the siting board to administer public trust rights. * * *

    . . . The extensive legislative history, including three commission reports, multiple drafts of the legislation, amendments in both houses, and memoranda to the Governor from various executive agencies, contains *no* reference to tidelands, tidewaters, tidal flats, land under coastal waters, the public trust, or the traditional rights of navigation, fishing, and fowling. The silence is deafening.

    * * * The Legislature's decision expressly to exempt issues concerning "offshore energy resources activities and offshore facilities" from its expansion of the commission's scope of study reflects an understanding within the Legislature that concerns relating to offshore facilities were *not* part of the commission's scope of inquiry. This singular indication of the Legislature's consideration of issues potentially relevant to public trust rights in relation to the creation of the siting board suggests that the Legislature understood that the creation of the siting board would not implicate those rights.

    The siting board's authority to grant a composite certificate is broad, but nothing in the statutory language, or its legislative history, indicates that such authority encompasses the power to act with respect to public trust rights. I would reverse on this ground alone.

B

    The siting board's lack of any authority to act with respect to public trust rights is sufficient to overrule its decision to grant the certificate to proceed with the transmission cables in the absence of final approval from DEP. I also dissent for a second, and independent, reason. Even if the siting board had the authority to act with respect to public trust rights, which I do not accept, the siting board's position that it was under no obligation to consider—and indeed could not consider—any in-State impacts of the operation of the wind farm is untenable. What is the role of a State agency if not to safeguard in-State interests?

The court acknowledges the petitioners' argument that if the siting board had the authority to administer public trust rights, as a matter of "complying with public trust doctrine obligations," the siting board had the "duty" to consider the potential effects of the wind farm on the Commonwealth. It then rejects that claim by recharacterizing it as one based on a "general tenet of environmental and perhaps all regulation of private development projects." The court makes but a passing reference to the obligations imposed by the public trust doctrine and its rationales for approving the siting board's refusal to consider the impact of the wind farm on Commonwealth tidelands are unpersuasive.[11]

First, the court reasons that the siting board's enabling statute states "with unmistakable clarity" that the siting board's "regulatory point of focus at all times is to be on the proposed 'facility,' " and the proposed transmission lines constitute the only "facility" subject to the siting board's review in this case. That may be so, but it says nothing about the responsibilities the siting board must exercise if it is (as the court concludes) wearing DEP's fiduciary hat. Rather, the court's reasoning on this point undermines its own rationale for concluding that the siting board has the authority to act with respect to public trust rights in the first place. The court concludes that the siting board may administer public trust rights because it is authorized to "stand in the shoes" of DEP. The Legislature, of course, has charged DEP with the fiduciary responsibility to "protect the interests of the commonwealth" and its inhabitants, in the "tidelands." G.L. c. 91, § 2. If, as the court would have it, the siting board may act to affect public trust rights because it may stand in DEP's shoes, then, as the court explicitly acknowledges, the siting board has the obligation to act as fiduciary on behalf of the people of the Commonwealth when reviewing the proposal to construct and operate the transmission cables. No fiduciary—whether DEP or the siting board—can (or would) fulfill that fiduciary responsibility while turning a blind eye to the in-State impacts of the wind farm. To the contrary, consideration of in-State impacts is integral to a determination whether the public trust has been violated.

Second, moving beyond the siting board's enabling statute, the court concludes that neither the siting board, nor DEP, nor any other State en-

---

[11] The Attorney General asserts that the "only question" here is whether the siting board "reasonably construed its enabling act" when it did not review the in-State impacts of the wind farm. To the contrary, the question is whether any State entity, be it the siting board or DEP, could fulfil its fiduciary obligations under the public trust doctrine by approving the construction and operation of the transmission cables *without* considering the in-State impact of the wind farm.

tity,[14] may consider the in-State impacts of the federally located wind farm because to do so would involve the assertion of authority that "presumably" would encompass the "power to deny or condition" a certificate or license "on account of such impacts." Ante at 685, 932 N.E.2d at 804. Such a denial or conditioning, the court reasons, would be "tantamount to the denial of the wind farm project itself," which the court says no State entity may do. Ante at 685, 932 N.E.2d at 804. The reasoning is flawed.

Procedure does not determine outcome. As noted, no fiduciary acting on behalf of the people could or would *ignore* the potential impact on the public's rights that might flow from the construction and operation of the wind farm. The court condones the disregard of those fiduciary obligations by concluding that consideration of the in-State impacts would *necessarily* result in a denial or contingent approval for the transmission cables (and thereby the wind farm). I cannot accept that reasoning. Our role is not to assume the outcome but to ensure that the proper process has been followed. The cases on which the court relies for its statement that the siting board "does not have authority to do indirectly what it cannot do directly" are inapposite. Ante at 685, 932 N.E.2d at 805, citing Ten Taxpayer Citizens Group v. Cape Wind Assoc., LLC, 373 F.3d 183, 197 (1st Cir.2004), cert. denied, 543 U.S. 1121 (2005) (*Ten Taxpayer Citizens*), and New England Legal Found. v. Massachusetts Port Auth., 883 F.2d 157, 174 (1st Cir.1989) (*New England Legal Found.*). Each involved Federal and State efforts to regulate the same activity (construction of a data tower in Federal water in the *Ten Taxpayer Citizens* case; control of air traffic in the *New England Legal Found.* case). Such an overlap is not at issue here: the Federal government has exclusive jurisdiction to provide approvals necessary for the wind farm to be constructed in Federal waters,[15] while the State has exclusive jurisdiction to approve the construction of transmission cables through Commonwealth tidelands. See 43 U.S.C. § 1311(a) (2006) (States have "the right and power to manage, ad-

---

[14] As a single narrow exception, the court recognizes the authority of the Massachusetts Office of Coastal Zone Management to "review and comment on Federal permitting decisions" concerning the wind farm itself.

[15] To the extent that the court relies on our decision in *Alliance to Protect Nantucket Sound, Inc. v. Energy Facilities Siting Bd.*, 448 Mass. 45 (*Alliance I*), this reliance is misplaced. There, the plaintiff was seeking review of the siting board's conditional approval for the building and operation of the transmission lines. See *Alliance I, supra* at 46. The approval was conditioned on the submission by Cape Wind of all of the necessary Federal, State, and local permits for the construction of the wind farm. *Id.* We were in that case concerned primarily with the siting board's determination of "need," as well as the contingent nature of the siting board's decision. *Id.* at 50. We noted that "[t]he area in which the wind farm itself is proposed to be built is located in Federal waters and, thus, falls beyond the scope of the [siting] board's jurisdiction and this case." *Id.* at 48. As the petitioners suggest, that statement, while true, does not address whether the siting board must consider the in-State impacts of the wind farm when considering whether to approve the construction and operation of the transmission cables. It merely indicates that the siting board's jurisdiction does not extend to the permitting and approval of the wind farm itself. See *id.* at 53 ("Federal agencies will be making critical decisions about . . . permitting" of wind farm).

minister, lease, develop, and use" "lands beneath navigable waters within the boundaries of the respective States . . . in accordance with applicable State law"). No one would suggest—or reasonably could suggest—that a private landowner would be "preempted" from denying permission to run transmission cables across its land to serve a facility built by a second private party on adjacent Federal land merely because the second party's project had won Federal approval.

The question here is whether the Commonwealth is required to *consider* the potential impacts on the Commonwealth and its people were it to allow use of its tidelands for the transmission cables. How the siting board or DEP ultimately would respond after considering such impacts is not before us. I am not willing to assume, as the court does, that *any* action that could possibly result from such consideration would necessarily be preempted by Federal law. Nor am I willing to assume that the results of any evaluation of the in-State impact of the wind farm would never be taken into consideration by Federal authorities. Comity within our Federal system has more meaning than the court's crabbed approach.[17]

C

The public trust doctrine and government energy policy are not at odds. Indeed, they are complementary. Both express the people's paramount interest in the wise and fruitful use of natural resources. Today's opinion, however, casts these two allies in opposition, and exalts regulatory expediency at the cost of fiduciary obligation. By issuing a certificate pursuant to G.L. c. 164, § 69K, which purports to include the "equivalent" of a G.L. c. 91 tidelands license, the siting board has purported to act as the protector of the public's long-standing rights under the public trust doctrine without the necessary express legislative authority to do so. Its usurpation of the Commonwealth's fiduciary responsibility to the people, and DEP's complicit agreement with that usurpation, should not be condoned. Moreover, even if the siting board had the authority to act, it has failed to exercise its role of fiduciary on behalf of the public because it failed to consider the in-State impacts of the wind farm. For these reasons, I respectfully dissent.

---

[17] The court references the holding of the United States Supreme Court that "control and disposition" of lands beneath the sea "in the first instance are the business of the Federal Government rather than the States," *United States v. Maine,* 420 U.S. 515, 522 (1975), and cases cited, and notes that under Federal law the Commonwealth's claim to title to the three mile margin of seabed off its seacoast derives from the Submerged Lands Act, 43 U.S.C. §§ 1301 et seq. (2006). The source of the Commonwealth's current authority over Commonwealth tidelands is immaterial to the scope of responsibility that has long been impressed on the Commonwealth under the public trust doctrine to protect the public's rights in those tidelands. See 43 U.S.C. § 1311(a) (States have "title to and ownership of the lands beneath navigable waters within the boundaries of the respective States" and "the right and power to manage, administer, lease, develop, and use" such lands *"in accordance with applicable State law"* [emphasis added]). Cf. *Stop the Beach Renourishment, Inc. v. Florida Dep't of Envtl. Protection,* ___ U.S. ___, 130 S.Ct. 2592, 2597–2598, 177 L.Ed.2d 184 (2010) (recognizing Florida's ownership of permanently submerged lands off its coast "in trust for the public").

NOTES AND QUESTIONS

1. Which of the two opinions in *Alliance II* makes the better argument under the public trust doctrine? (*Alliance I* cited above is at 448 Mass. 45 (2006)). Recall the doctrine's discussion in Chapter 3. See also Alexandra B. Klass, Renewable Energy Development and the Public Trust Doctrine, 45 U.C. Davis L. Rev. 1021 (2012); Raphael D. Sagarin and Mary Turnipseed, The Public Trust Doctrine: Where Ecology Meets Natural Resource Management, 37 Ann. Rev. Environ. Resour. 473 (2012).

2. In colonial era Massachusetts, the legislature modified the common law public trust doctrine to allow landowners to claim title to the low tide line but reserved an easement for the public uses of "fishing, fowling, and navigation." The legislature sought to encourage landowners to build commercial wharves and piers without fear that the Crown, as the sovereign owner of title to tidelands, would claim these structures and control commercial development. See Boston Waterfront Devt Corp. v. Commonwealth, cited above in *Alliance II*. Is the Massachusetts Supreme Judicial Court making a modern-day modification to the public trust in order to put Massachusetts at the forefront of the new "blue" economy?

3. Does Chief Justice Marshall suggest in her separate opinion that the majority may have been influenced by the urgency of a national energy policy that emphasizes renewable sources? What if the Department of Environmental Protection had previously denied the ch. 91 license? Could the energy board have approved the certificate nevertheless? In warning the court it was establishing "a dangerous and unwise precedent" with far-reaching consequences, Chief Justice Marshall's separate opinion states that "[a] wind farm may be a drilling rig or nuclear power plant tomorrow." Alliance II, 457 Mass. 663, 702. Does the chief justice imply that while ocean renewables appear to be an environmentally positive development, industries are just as likely to propose energy facilities that present much higher risks to the coastal environment? The justice may have recalled the General Electric proposal in the 1970s to construct "floating" nuclear power plants off the coast of New Jersey. See John McPhee, A Reporter at Large: The Atlantic Generating Station, The New Yorker (May 12, 1975); John W. Kindt, Ocean Resources Development: The Environmental Considerations Involved in the Offshore Siting of Nuclear Power Plants, 3 Suffolk Transnat'l L.J. 35 (1979).

4. In another wind farm case from New England, In re Review of Proposed Town of New Shoreham Project, 25 A.2d 482 (RI, 2011), the Rhode Island Supreme Court held that the state public utilities commission's approval of a power purchase agreement between a wind farm developer and an electric utility that did not include costs for a transmission cable from state waters near Block Island did not violate Rhode Island's renewable energy legislation. Despite this result, the court was plainly concerned by the state legislature's ambitious "blue economy" goals. Jacqueline S. Rolleri, Comment, Offshore Wind Energy in the United States: Regulations, Recommendations, and Rhode Island, 15 Roger Williams U. L. Rev. 217 (2010).

B. FEDERAL AUTHORITY OVER OCEAN RENEWABLE ENERGY ON THE OCS

As we saw in Chapter 2, in *Ten Taxpayer Citizens Group v. Cape Wind Associates*, the First Circuit Court of Appeals ruled that Massachusetts state laws did not govern placement of the initial, data-collecting structure for a wind turbine farm on the OCS and that the Army Corps of Engineers could license the structure under section 10 of the Rivers and Harbors Act of 1899. Alarmed that this might prove to be the only regulatory lever on such a massive project, opponents of Cape Wind then sought relief in Congress. A turf battle also ensued to determine which federal agencies had authority over ocean renewable energy. See Kimmel and Stalenhoef, cited supra at p. 490. Congress eventually responded with Section 388 of the Energy Policy Act of 2005, amending the OCSLA in language authored by the Department of the Interior. Section 388 gave Interior lead responsibility for leasing federal OCS lands for renewable energy. After the Federal Energy Regulatory Commission asserted jurisdiction over non-wind, renewable energy in marine waters, the federal agencies resolved their battle over regulatory primacy.

The text of 43 U.S.C. § 1337(p) is as follows:

OUTER CONTINENTAL SHELF LANDS ACT, SECTION 1337 (AS AMENDED BY THE ENERGY POLICY ACT OF 2005)

(p) Leases, easements, or rights-of-way for energy and related purposes

(1) In general

The Secretary, in consultation with the Secretary of the Department in which the Coast Guard is operating and other relevant departments and agencies of the Federal Government, may grant a lease, easement, or right-of-way on the outer Continental Shelf for activities not otherwise authorized in this subchapter, the Deepwater Port Act of 1974 (33 U.S.C. 1501 et seq.), the Ocean Thermal Energy Conversion Act of 1980 (42 U.S.C. 9101 et seq.), or other applicable law, if those activities—* * *

(C) produce or support production, transportation, or transmission of energy from sources other than oil and gas; or

(D) use, for energy-related purposes or for other authorized marine-related purposes, facilities currently or previously used for activities authorized under this subchapter . . .

(2) Payments and revenues

(A) The Secretary shall establish royalties, fees, rentals, bonuses, or other payments to ensure a fair return to the United States for any lease, easement, or right-of-way granted under this subsection.

(B) The Secretary shall provide for the payment of 27 percent of the revenues received by the Federal Government as a result of payments under this section from projects that are located wholly or partially within the area extending three nautical miles seaward of State submerged lands. Payments shall be made based on a formula established by the Secretary by rulemaking no later than 180 days after August 8, 2005, that provides for equitable distribution, based on proximity to the project, among coastal states that have a coastline that is located within 15 miles of the geographic center of the project.

(3) Competitive or noncompetitive basis

Except with respect to projects that meet the criteria established under section 388(d) of the Energy Policy Act of 2005, the Secretary shall issue a lease, easement, or right-of-way under paragraph (1) on a competitive basis unless the Secretary determines after public notice of a proposed lease, easement, or right-of-way that there is no competitive interest.

(4) Requirements

The Secretary shall ensure that any activity under this subsection is carried out in a manner that provides for—

(A) safety;

(B) protection of the environment;

(C) prevention of waste;

(D) conservation of the natural resources of the outer Continental Shelf;

(E) coordination with relevant Federal agencies;

(F) protection of national security interests of the United States;

(G) protection of correlative rights in the outer Continental Shelf;

(H) a fair return to the United States for any lease, easement, or right-of-way under this subsection;

(I) prevention of interference with reasonable uses (as determined by the Secretary) of the exclusive economic zone, the high seas, and the territorial seas;

(J) consideration of—

(i) the location of, and any schedule relating to, a lease, easement, or right-of-way for an area of the outer Continental Shelf; and

(ii) any other use of the sea or seabed, including use for a fishery, a sealane, a potential site of a deepwater port, or navigation;

(K) public notice and comment on any proposal submitted for a lease, easement, or right-of-way under this subsection; and

(L) oversight, inspection, research, monitoring, and enforcement relating to a lease, easement, or right-of-way under this subsection.

(5) Lease duration, suspension, and cancellation

The Secretary shall provide for the duration, issuance, transfer, renewal, suspension, and cancellation of a lease, easement, or right-of-way under this subsection.

(6) Security

The Secretary shall require the holder of a lease, easement, or right-of-way granted under this subsection to—

(A) furnish a surety bond or other form of security, as prescribed by the Secretary;

(B) comply with such other requirements as the Secretary considers necessary to protect the interests of the public and the United States; and

(C) provide for the restoration of the lease, easement, or right-of-way.

(7) Coordination and consultation with affected State and local Governments

The Secretary shall provide for coordination and consultation with the Governor of any State or the executive of any local government that may be affected by a lease, easement, or right-of-way under this subsection.

(8) Regulations

Not later than 270 days after August 8, 2005, the Secretary, in consultation with the Secretary of Defense, the Secretary of the Department in which the Coast Guard is operating, the Secretary of Commerce, heads of other relevant departments and agencies of the Federal Government, and the Governor of any affected State, shall issue any necessary regulations to carry out this subsection.

(9) Effect of subsection

Nothing in this subsection displaces, supersedes, limits, or modifies the jurisdiction, responsibility, or authority of any Federal or State agency under any other Federal law.

(10) Applicability

This subsection does not apply to any area on the outer Continental Shelf within the exterior boundaries of any unit of the National Park System, National Wildlife Refuge System, or National Marine Sanctuary System, or any National Monument.

NOTES AND QUESTIONS

1. The inadequacies of the regulatory regime for offshore renewable energy prior to the Energy Policy Act of 2005 were assessed by marine policy scholars from the University of Delaware:

> The inadequacy of this piecemeal regulatory regime perhaps is most apparent when one considers that, at present, it is the Army Corps of Engineers that is the lead agency, through a Rivers and Harbors Act (RHA)/Outer Continental Shelf Lands Act (OCSLA) permit, . . . (perhaps in conjunction with an Army Corps' dredge and fill permit, . . . rather than an agency charged with managing and conserving the ocean's biodiversity. While it is true that the Army Corps of Engineers makes its determinations based on what it perceives to be the "public interest," its public interest standard is so infused with competing considerations and value judgments as to give the Corps almost unbridled discretion. Indeed, the Corps states in its regulations that it will consider "conservation, economics, aesthetics, general environmental concerns, wetlands, historic properties, fish, and wildlife values, flood hazards, floodplain values, land use, navigation, shore erosion and accretion, recreation, water supply and conservation, water quality, energy needs, safety, food and fiber production, mineral needs, considerations of property ownership, and, in general, the needs and welfare of the people," not to mention the areas that the Army Corps of Engineers holds most dear— navigation and national security—and that "how important a factor is and how much consideration it deserves will vary with each proposal." Moreover, given that concerns expressed regarding the development of offshore wind power and marine aquaculture are likely to involve environmental and aesthetic impacts that will be aired as part of the environmental evaluation process, having an agency whose focal point and expertise are grounded in navigation results in a regulatory mismatch (footnotes omitted).

Jeremy Firestone, Willett Kempton, Andrew Kreuger, and Christen E. Loper, Regulating Offshore Wind Power and Aquaculture: Messages from Land and

Sea, 14 Cornell J. L. & Pub. Pol'y 71, 82 (2004). Do the criteria of § 1337(p)(4) improve the criteria for the Secretary of Interior's discretion?

2. After six years of administration by the Interior Department's reorganized Minerals Management Service, now named the Bureau of Ocean Energy Management (BOEM), concerns remain:

> The federal government's process, in contrast, is still driven by the project proponent's individual choice of sites. While there is now a leasing process administered by [BOEM], the primary function of [BOEM] is to select a lessee that offers the best financial bid. There is no statutory ocean planning authority under federal law with an agency empowered to make zoning/planning designations of appropriate sites for offshore wind projects. Nor is there any process to assure developers that if they select certain sites and abide by known performance standards, they will receive a permit. Thus, the Cape Wind experience both highlights the need for reform and provides models for the types of reform that are needed (footnotes omitted).

Kenneth Kimmel and Dawn S. Stalenhoef, The Cape Wind Offshore Wind Energy Project: A Case Study of the Difficult Transition to Renewable Energy, 5 Golden Gate U. Envtl. L.J. 197 (2011). Issues that have arisen in implementation of § 1337(p) are analyzed in Jack K. Stern et al., The Seven Principles of Ocean Renewable Energy: A Shared Vision and Call for Action, 14 Roger Williams U. L. Rev. 600 (2009). How would the Marine and Hydrokinetic Renewable Energy Promotion Act, proposed (as Senate Bill 630) in the 112th Congress, address these challenges?

3. Note that § 1337(p)(9) is a savings clause, meaning that the Army Corps' regulatory jurisdiction still applies to offshore wind power. Why did Congress give the Department of Interior responsibility for overseeing development of ocean renewable energy on the outer continental shelf while retaining other agencies' regulatory jurisdiction?

4. Before the Energy Policy Act was enacted, the Army Corps of Engineers and the Commonwealth of Massachusetts had prepared a joint environmental impact statement (EIS) for the Cape Wind development. When Cape Wind's applications were transferred from the Army to Interior, the Mineral Management Service decided not to accept the joint Massachusetts–Army Corps' draft EIS. An explanation of this decision is in the press release of April 28, 2010, online at http://www.doi.gov/news/doinews/upload/FactSheet-Cape-Wind-with-SOL-edits-04-28-10.pdf.

If the Minerals Management Service had adopted the draft EIS, would opponents of Cape Wind have had a good claim for a violation of NEPA? See the Council on Environmental Quality's regulations on NEPA, 40 C.F.R. Parts 1500–1506. In 2007, the Service published a Programmatic PEIS for Alternative Energy Development and Production and Alternative Use of Facilities on the OCS. This assessment establishes a baseline for site-specific environmental assessments. Adam Vann, CRS Report to Congress, Wind Energy: Offshore Permitting, 8 (7–5700, R 40175, Oct. 17, 2012).

5. Does OCSLA § 1337(p) strike the right balance between federal and state interests? Does the revenue sharing provision in subsection (2)(B) give states an incentive to cooperate on regional development of ocean renewable energy? For a discussion of federalism considerations of renewable energy development see Benjamin J. Sovacol, The Best of Both Worlds: Environmental Federalism and the Need for Federal Action on Renewable Energy and Climate Change, 27 Stan. Envtl. L.J. 397 (2008).

6. The Minerals Management Service (now BOEM) issued final regulations under § 1337(p) in April 2009; these rules were codified at 30 C.F.R. Parts 250, 285, and 290. Renewable Energy and Alternate Uses of Existing Facilities on the Outer Continental Shelf, 74 Fed. Reg. 19638, 19659 (April 29, 2009). For an analysis of these rules, see Peter J. Schaumberg and Angela F. Colamaria, Siting Renewable Energy Projects on the Outer Continental Shelf: Spin, Baby, Spin!, 14 Roger Williams U. L. Rev. 624 (2009). Under these rules, BOEM issued a commercial lease to Cape Wind Associates in December 2010. For information on current proposals for leases and licenses, see http://www.boem.gov/Renewable-Energy-Program/Current-Projects/Index.aspx. In 2009, using the administrative flexibility afforded by 43 U.S.C. § 1337(p), Secretary of Interior Ken Salazar directed the BOEM to implement a comprehensive expedited leasing framework for developing the wind resources of the Atlantic OCS region. The goal is to "accelerate responsible renewable wind energy development" through advanced designation of areas, coordinated environmental studies, large-scale planning, and expedited approval processes. The program is called (ironically, in view of the Cape Wind saga) the "Smart from the Start" Atlantic OCS Offshore Wind Initiative. See, e.g., BOEM, Intent to Prepare EISs: Potential Commercial Wind Lease Issuance and Decision Regarding Approval of Construction and Operations Plan on the Atlantic OCS Offshore Maine, 77 Fed. Reg. 47876 (Aug. 10, 2012).

7. When BOEM's predecessor, the Minerals Management Service, proposed its OCS wind development regulations in 2005, the Federal Energy Regulatory Commission (FERC) asserted exclusive jurisdiction to license wave and tidal energy production in U.S. waters. The Federal Power Act grants FERC authority to license hydroelectric projects in "navigable waters" and in "streams and other bodies of water over which Congress has jurisdiction." See Policy Statement on Conditioned Licenses for Hydrokinetic Projects, 121 FERC 61, 221 (2007). See also M. Walsh, A Rising Tide in Renewable Energy: The Future of Tidal In-Stream Energy Conversion, 19 Vill. Envtl. L.J. 193 (2008). The Department of Interior argued that the Energy Policy Act of 2005 (implicitly) withdrew FERC jurisdiction over projects in the OCS. After a protracted debate, the two agencies signed a memorandum of understanding on shared jurisdiction in April 2009, and joint Guidelines on the Regulation of Marine and Hydrokinetic Energy Projects on the OCS on July

19, 2012 (including hybrid wind-MHK projects and projects straddling the state-federal boundary). See www.ferc.gov/industries/hydropower/gen-info/licensing/hydrokinetics/pdf/mms080309.pdf.

8. Note that the Submerged Lands Act withheld "water power" from the list of natural resources over which the states have sovereign rights and the "production of power" from its grant of authority. 43 U.S.C. §§ 1301(e), 1311(d). This means the MHK energy projects within state seaward boundaries are subject to licensing by FERC under the Federal Power Act. FERC coordinates its licensing with states under memoranda of understanding. See Rachel Salcido, Siting Offshore Hydrokinetic Energy Projects: A Comparative Look at Wave Energy Regulation in the Pacific Northwest, 5 Golden Gate University Envtl L.J. 109 (2011).

9. Note that BOEM and FERC cannot issue leases or licenses for either wind or marine hydrokinetic (MHK) energy project in a national park or national monument located on the OCS. BOEM–FERC Joint Guidelines, at 7. BOEM is also prohibited from leasing within a national marine sanctuary or a national wildlife refuge (under the terms of OCSLA § 1337(p)(10)). FERC, on the other hand, may be authorized to issue MHK licenses without a BOEM lease in such areas. Id. Given the purposes and policies of the National Marine Sanctuaries Act, 16 U.S.C. 1431 et seq., would it be inconsistent with the Act to authorize an ocean renewable energy project in a national marine sanctuary, e.g., in the one of the national marine sanctuaries adjacent to the coast of California, the state with the greatest energy demand in the U.S.? The National Marine Sanctuaries Act is discussed further in Chapter 8.

10. What coastal management issues arise in connection with wave and tidal energy? Is FERC the appropriate federal agency to take the lead? Might states be in a better position to oversee and regulate hydrokinetic energy given its impact on state energy and coastal policies? See Laura Koch, Comment, The Promise of Wave Energy, 2 Golden Gate U. Envtl. L. J. 162 (2008–09). See also Timothy H. Powell, Note: Revisiting Federalism Concerns in the Offshore Wind Energy Industry in Light of Continued Local Opposition to the Cape Wind Project, 92 B.U. L. Rev. 2023 (2012).

C. OCEAN RENEWABLE ENERGY AND STATE COASTAL ZONE MANAGEMENT PROGRAMS

In Chapter 3, we learned that under the federal consistency provisions of the Coastal Zone Management Act (CZMA), states with federally approved coastal zone management plans can influence in significant ways ocean industrial activities that require federal licenses and permits. But under section 306(d) of the CZMA, Congress also established as a matter of national policy that states give priority consideration to the siting of energy facilities in the coastal zone as long as it is consistent with the other national goals of protecting coastal resources. In order to obtain federal approval, Section 306(d) of the CZMA requires the Secretary of

Commerce to find that the state coastal management plan "provides for adequate consideration of the national interest involved in planning for, and managing the coastal zone, including the siting of facilities such as energy facilities which are of greater than local significance. In the case of energy facilities, the Secretary shall find that the State has given consideration to any applicable national or interstate energy plan or program.

COASTAL ZONE MANAGEMENT ACT, 16 U.S.C.
§ 1452(2)(D); § 1453(5),(6)

§ 1452 The Congress finds and declares that it is the national policy—

. . . (2) to encourage and assist the states to exercise effectively their responsibilities in the coastal zone through the development and implementation of management programs to achieve wise use of the land and water resources of the coastal zone, giving full consideration to ecological, cultural, historic, and esthetic values as well as the needs for compatible economic development, which programs should at least provide for—

* * *

(D) priority consideration being given to coastal-dependent uses and orderly processes for siting major facilities related to national defense, energy, fisheries development, recreation, ports and transportation, and the location, to the maximum extent practicable, of new commercial and industrial developments in or adjacent to areas where such development already exists. . .

§ 1453 For purposes of this chapter [CZMA]—

* * *

(5) The term "coastal energy activity" means any of the following activities if, and to the extent that (A) the conduct, support, or facilitation of such activity requires and involves the siting, construction, expansion, or operation of any equipment or facility; and (B) any technical requirement exists which, in the determination of the Secretary, necessitates that the siting, construction, expansion, or operation of such equipment or facility be carried out in, or in close proximity to, the coastal zone of any coastal state;

(i) Any outer Continental Shelf energy activity.

(ii) Any transportation, conversion, treatment, transfer, or storage of liquefied natural gas.

(iii) Any transportation, transfer, or storage of oil, natural gas, or coal (including, but not limited to, by means of any deepwater port, as defined in section 1502(10) of Title 33).

For purposes of this paragraph, the siting, construction, expansion, or operation of any equipment or facility shall be "in close proximity to" the coastal zone of any coastal state if such siting, construction, expansion, or operation has, or is likely to have, a significant effect on such coastal zone.

(6) The term "energy facilities" means any equipment or facility which is or will be used primarily—

(A) in the exploration for, or the development, production, conversion, storage, transfer, processing, or transportation of, any energy resource; or

(B) for the manufacture, production, or assembly of equipment, machinery, products, or devices which are involved in any activity described in subparagraph (A).

The term includes, but is not limited to (i) electric generating plants; (ii) petroleum refineries and associated facilities; (iii) gasification plants; (iv) facilities used for the transportation, conversion, treatment, transfer, or storage of liquefied natural gas; (v) uranium enrichment or nuclear fuel processing facilities; (vi) oil and gas facilities, including platforms, assembly plants, storage depots, tank farms, crew and supply bases, and refining complexes; (vii) facilities including deepwater ports, for the transfer of petroleum; (viii) pipelines and transmission facilities; and (ix) terminals which are associated with any of the foregoing.

* * *

In Alliance II, we saw the application of state laws influencing the siting of coastal energy facilities, specifically the Massachusetts Ocean Sanctuaries Act and the Energy Facility Siting Act. The following case involves the consistency review that is at the heart of state coastal management plans, where state administrative agencies review their actions and decisions for consistency with the state's federally-approved and enforceable coastal management policies.

COASTAL HABITAT ALLIANCE V. PATTERSON

U.S. District Court for the Western District of Texas, 2009
601 F.Supp.2d 868, aff'd without opinion (5th Cir. 2010)

YEAKEL, DISTRICT JUDGE.

I. Background and Statutory Scheme

Defendants Texas Gulf Wind, LLC and Iberdrola Renewables, Inc. (collectively, the "Private Defendants") are building wind-energy-generation facilities ("wind farms") in Kenedy County, Texas, on land adjoining the Laguna Madre.[3] The area encompasses biologically diverse expanses of undeveloped land through which three major migratory-bird pathways converge. Plaintiff Coastal Habitat Alliance states it is an alliance of area ranchers and [conservation] organizations dedicated to protecting the Laguna Madre and its associated environmental resources. Coastal Habitat Alliance filed suit against the Private Defendants; Jerry Patterson, in his capacity as Commissioner of the Texas General Land Office; and Chairman Barry Smitherman, Julie Carruthers Parsley, and Paul Hudson in their capacities as Commissioners of the Texas Public Utility Commission ("Commission") (collectively, "State Defendants"). The Alliance alleges it has been deprived of its rights under the Coastal Zone Management Act ("Act") and the Texas Coastal Management Program ("Texas Program" or "Program"), in violation of the United States Constitution's Supremacy Clause and the Due Process Clauses of the Fifth and Fourteenth Amendments. The Alliance seeks declaratory and injunctive relief and attorney's fees.

Texas proposed a coastal-management program to the Secretary [of Commerce] in 1995. The Office of Ocean and Coastal Resource Management, within the National Oceanic and Atmospheric Administration of the Department of Commerce, reviewed Texas's proposed program and prepared the Texas Program documents. *See* Office of Ocean and Coastal Resource Management, National Oceanic and Atmospheric Administration, Department of Commerce & Coastal Coordination Council, State of Texas, Final Environmental Impact Statement, at iii (August 1996) ("Texas CMP FEIS") ("It is the general policy of the Federal Office of Ocean and Coastal Resource Management (OCRM) to issue combined environmental impact statements and program documents.").

The Texas Program designates the General Land Office as its lead agency. Texas CMP FEIS, Part II, at 3–5; *see* 16 U.S.C. § 1455(d)(6); 15 C.F.R. § 923.47. The Program is networked to combine the expertise and resources of eight state agencies, eighteen local governments, and the Coastal Coordination Council. Texas CMP FEIS, Part I, at 4; *see generally* 16 U.S.C. § 1455(d)(11)(C). The Coastal Coordination Council consists of the heads of Texas's resource agencies and four gubernatorial appointees and is responsible for, *inter alia,* "program oversight and dispute resolution through the state consistency review procedures . . . ," and monitoring Program agencies to assure their compliance with the Program. Texas CMP FEIS, Part I, at 6; Part II, at 3–7. The General Land Office's Coastal

---

[3] Kenedy County is located on the Gulf of Mexico coast, in far south Texas. The Laguna Madre is a long, shallow bay, which in Texas extends from Corpus Christi on the north to Port Isabel on the south, and continues southward along the Mexican coast. It is bounded on the east by Padre Island and on the west by the Texas mainland.* * *

Division staffs the Coastal Coordination Council and coordinates implementation of the energy-facility siting plan.

The Texas Program provides a framework for ensuring that new electric-generating facilities do not harm the [coastal] environment. First, the Texas Program establishes policies for managing the siting, construction, and maintenance of electric-generating facilities and electric-transmission lines. *Id.* at 1–7. The Program includes an "enforceable policy" of siting new electric-generating facilities at previously developed sites. *Id.,* Part II, at 4–6; 31 Tex. Admin. Code Ann. § 501.16(1). Enforceable policies are "[s]tate policies which are legally binding through constitutional provisions, laws, regulations, land use plans, ordinances, or judicial or administrative decisions. . . . " 16 U.S.C. § 1453(6a). In siting facilities at undeveloped sites, the Texas Program policy is to avoid construction in critical areas and to locate facilities at sites selected to have the least adverse effects practicable on areas used for "spawning, nesting, and seasonal migrations of terrestrial and aquatic fish and wildlife species." Texas CMP FEIS, Part II, at 4–6; 31 Tex. Admin. Code Ann. § 501.16. "Critical areas" include coastal wetlands. 31 Tex. Admin. Code Ann. § 501.3(a)(8). "Adverse effects" occur when an effect results in the physical destruction or detrimental alteration of a coastal zone. 31 Tex. Admin. Code Ann. § 501.3(a)(1). Adverse effects include alterations that harm the coastal zone as a habitat for terrestrial and aquatic life, that disrupt wildlife corridors or fish or migratory bird routes, and that alter water in ways that are harmful to terrestrial or aquatic life. *Id.* § 501.3(a)(1)(D)–(E), (H).

The Texas Program requires that the Public Utility Commission comply with the Program's energy-siting policies when issuing Certificates of Convenience and Necessity ("Certificates") to new electric-generating facilities. Texas CMP FEIS, Part II, at 4–6 (citing Public Utility Regulatory Act (PURA)(requiring public utility to obtain certificate of convenience and necessity)); *see* 16 U.S.C. § 1455(d)(10). A public utility may not render services without "having obtained from the [C]ommission a [C]ertificate that the present or future public convenience and necessity requires or will require" such service. The Commission performs consistency review when issuing a Certificate. Act of May, 19, 1995, 74th Leg., R.S., ch. 416, § 4, sec. 33.2053(b), 1995 Tex. Gen. Laws 3017, 3025 (codified at Tex. Nat. Res.Code Ann. § 33.2053(b)). The Commission must affirm in writing that the Certificate is consistent with Program goals and policies (current version at Tex. Nat. Res.Code Ann. § 33.205). Any person interested in a public utility's application for a Certificate may intervene at a hearing on such Certificate.

The Coastal Coordination Council ensures that interested and affected parties are involved in the planning process for siting energy facilities through *inter alia,* "publish[ing] notice in the *Texas Register . . .* " of "consistency determinations and other program decisions." This in addition to "the public participation prescribed by the permitting procedures of individual agencies." Texas CMP FEIS, Part II, at 8–5; *see* 15 C.F.R. § 923.13(d). Citizens may challenge the result of the Commission's consistency review in a contested-case hearing before an agency, and may seek judicial review of the Commission's decision as provided by law.

In summary, the Texas Program prioritizes siting electric-generating facilities at developed sites and in areas where the facilities will cause the least environmental damage. Citizens who desire to participate in assuring the General Land Office, Public Utility Commission, and other state agencies implement the Program's environmental-protection policies will receive notice of a decision as to a project's consistency with such policies through the *Texas Register,* and may raise issues at a Certificate hearing. Citizens may challenge such determination in a contested case, and seek judicial review of the decision.

The parties agree that this case arises because when the Texas Legislature deregulated the utility industry, it eliminated the statutory requirement that many electric-generating facilities obtain a Certificate. In doing so, the legislature eliminated the process through which the Public Utility Commission conducted consistency review. In 1995, the legislature narrowed the definition of "public utility" to exclude "exempt wholesale generators," among other types of entities. Current law requires electric utilities to obtain a Certificate, but the narrow definition of "electric utility" effectively means few electric-generating facilities must obtain one. *See* Tex. Util.Code Ann. § 37.051(a). Defendants argue the Private Defendants' wind farms are exempt wholesale generators and have been excluded from the definition of electric utilities and the Certificate requirement since September 1, 1995. Defendants argue these wind farms were therefore never subject to Texas Program because even before Program approval they would not have been required to obtain a Certificate.

The Court finds that because the Texas [Coastal] Program cites Article 1446c [of the Public Utility Regulatory Act] as the authority under which the Public Utility Commission shall issue Certificates and conduct consistency review, Article 1446c's definition of "public utility" applies in this case. A public utility is "any . . . corporation . . . now or hereafter owning or operating for compensation in this state equipment or facilities for: (1) producing, generating, transmitting, distributing, selling, or furnishing electricity . . . ," and includes the wind farms. The wind farms are therefore subject to the Texas Program's requirements. Such requirements include obtaining a Certificate, because "no public utility may in any way render service directly or indirectly to the public under any franchise or permit without first having obtained from the [C]ommission a[Ce]rtificate that the present or future public convenience and necessity require or will require such installation, operation, or extension." PURA, 64th Leg., R.S., ch. 721, sec. 50(1), 1975 Tex. Gen. Laws 2327, 2345.

Coastal Habitat Alliance argues that Texas lacked the unilateral authority to eliminate consistency review. To obtain approval for such an elimination, Texas should have engaged in a statutorily prescribed process for making the change, which would have involved public participation. 16 U.S.C. § 1455(e)(1), (3). Amendments that affect authorities and public involvement are considered substantial changes. 15 C.F.R. § 923.80(d). The state must conduct at least one public hearing on proposed amendments to a management plan and the amendment request must document the opportunities of the public and private parties to participate in development and approval of the proposed amendment. *Id.* § 923.81(a), (b)(5).

The National Oceanic and Atmospheric Administration's Office of Ocean and Coastal Resource Management reviews a state's amendment request to determine whether the program, including the proposed amendment, still constitutes an approvable program. *Id.* § 923.81(a). If the Office determines that the amended program is approvable, it then determines whether the amended program requires an environmental impact statement pursuant to the National Environmental Policy Act. *Id.* § 923.81(c). Routine program changes that do not result in substantial changes are not subject to the described amendment procedures, but the public must still be notified of the proposed routine changes. *Id.* § 923.84(a), (b)(2), (b)(4).

Coastal Habitat Alliance alleges Texas never attempted to amend its Program after deleting the statutory requirement that many electric-generating facilities obtain a Certificate. The Alliance states Texas submitted proposed Program changes to the federal government on July 11, 2006, which it called routine program changes, which did not disclose the elimination of Certificate review. *See id.* §§ 923.84(a), .80(d). The Alliance alleges the federal government never received notice that consistency review for projects like the wind farms had been omitted from Texas law.

Coastal Habitat Alliance alleges no environmental review has been conducted for the wind farms. The Alliance further alleges the wind farms have been under development for many years and that it has asked the State Defendants to assure consistency review, but they have refused, citing the statutory repeal of the Public Utility Commission's Certificate requirements as the reason they cannot conduct consistency review of these wind farms. The Alliance alleges that groups opposed to these wind farms and other members of the Coastal Coordination Council have repeatedly alerted General Land Office Commissioner Patterson that repeal of Public Utility Commission Certificate review for electricity-generating facilities in the coastal zone would eliminate meaningful review of the environmental consequences of siting such wind farms in the coastal zone. The Alliance alleges it has been denied a meaningful opportunity to raise concerns about the environmental implications of the wind farms.

By this action, Coastal Habitat Alliance seeks declarations that the Private Defendants may not build the wind farms before consistency review is conducted pursuant to the Coastal Zone Management Act and Texas Program, and that during such consistency review the State Defendants must allow the Alliance an opportunity to be heard and an opportunity for judicial review. The Alliance also seeks an injunction prohibiting Private Defendants from building the wind farms in the coastal zone until and unless consistency review occurs with participation by the Alliance.* * *

II. Analysis

Coastal Habitat Alliance alleges two causes of action against Defendants. First, the Alliance alleges Defendants' course of action in not conducting consistency review and in not properly amending the Texas Program is preempted by the Coastal Zone Management Act and the Texas Program ("preemption claim"). The Alliance relies on *Planned Parenthood of Houston v. Sanchez* for the proposition that a party may bring an action for declaratory and injunctive relief based on preemption. 403 F.3d 324, 331 (5th Cir.2005). The Alliance argues Texas is "bound by the strings" accompanying the federal funds it has accepted. *Id.* at 337. The Alliance argues Congress clearly intended environmental review and public participation to occur in implementation of the Act, and Texas's failure to follow through with those elements of its Program render its actions in conflict with federal law. The Alliance further argues that its right to participate in any proceeding regarding a Certificate, or any other proceeding in which it could obtain environmental and consistency review under the Act, is a constitutionally protected property interest that Defendants have taken without due process of law ("Due Process claim").

Defendants argue Coastal Habitat Alliance lacks standing to pursue its claims against them. Specifically, they argue the Alliance has not alleged a cognizable injury because the [Coastal Zone Management] Act does not create a private right of action, and Defendants' actions therefore invade no legally protected interest of the Alliance. *See* Day v. Bond, 500 F.3d 1127, 1139 (10th Cir.2007). Defendants additionally argue that the Alliance cannot demonstrate causation sufficient for standing because no act of Defendants caused the Alliance's injury; instead, any injury suffered by the Alliance was caused by the legislature's deregulation of the utility industry. Finally, Defendants argue the Alliance cannot demonstrate redressability on its preemption claim because the Alliance is unable to show how nullification of a state statute would redress its alleged injuries. . . .

The Defendants argue the Court must dismiss this action for failure to state a claim because the Coastal Zone Management Act does not create a private right of action. *See e.g.* George v. NYC Dept. of City Planning, 436 F.3d 102 (2d Cir.2006); New Jersey Dept. of Envtl. Protection v. Long Island Power Auth., 30 F.3d 403 (3d Cir.1994) (*Long Island Power Auth.*). Coastal Habitat Alliance responds it is not relying on an Act-created right of action; instead it asserts the Act and the Texas Program preempt Texas's action contrary to such law.

In response to the Alliance's preemption contention, the Private Defendants argue that the Alliance's preemption claim against them must be dismissed because a preemption claim cannot lie against private actors. The State Defendants argue the preemption claim must be dismissed because no state law exists to be preempted, to which the Alliance responds that the preempted state statute is the statute which eliminated consistency review for energy-generating facilities in the coastal zone. . . . Finally, Defendants argue the Court must dismiss the Alliance's procedural Due Process claim because the Coastal Zone Management Act does not confer protected rights on the Alliance.

The Court begins its analysis, as it must, by inquiring whether Coastal Habitat Alliance has standing to bring its claims against Defendants. Steel Co. v. Citizens for a Better Env't, 523 U.S. 83, 93–102, 118 S.Ct. 1003, 140 L.Ed.2d 210 (1998). Because the Court holds the Alliance does not have standing, it does not address Defendants' substantive arguments.

B. Standing Generally

Standing is "built on a single basic idea—the idea of separation of powers." Allen v. Wright, 468 U.S. 737, 752 (1984). Standing is an essential part of the case-or-controversy requirement of Article III of the Constitution. *See* U.S. Const. art. III, sec. 2; Lujan v. Defenders of Wildlife, 504 U.S. 555, 560 (1992). As such, the standing inquiry addresses whether a plaintiff's claims are appropriately resolved by the court. Warth v. Seldin, 422 U.S. 490, 498. Standing implicates the court's jurisdiction and must be addressed before determining whether the plaintiff has adequately stated claims against defendants. *See* Steel Co., 523 U.S. at 93–102; Ramming v. United States, 281 F.3d 158, 161 (5th Cir.2001)("When a Rule 12(b)(1) motion is filed in conjunction with other Rule 12 motions, the court should consider the Rule 12(b)(1) jurisdictional attack before addressing any attack on the merits. This requirement prevents a court without jurisdiction from prematurely dismissing a case with prejudice."). At the pleading stage of proceedings, the plaintiff need only make general factual allegations of injury caused by defendants. Lujan, 504 U.S. at 561. The court must assess the plaintiff's standing to bring each of its claims against each defendant. *See* James v. City of Dallas, 254 F.3d 551, 563 (5th Cir.2001).

The familiar "irreducible constitutional minimum of standing" requires first that the plaintiff have suffered an injury in fact, that is, an actual or imminent invasion of a concrete and particularized legally protected interest. Lujan v. Defenders of Wildlife, 504 U.S. at 560 (1992). Second, there must be a causal connection between the plaintiff's complained-of injury and the defendants' actions. *Id.* Third, it must be likely that the plaintiff's injury will be redressed by a favorable decision from the court. Id. at 561. To seek injunctive relief, a plaintiff must also allege defendants will cause it future injury and that the relief sought will redress such injury. James, 254 F.3d at 563. Further, an organization must demonstrate associational standing. An organization has standing to bring suit on its members' behalf when its members would otherwise have standing, it seeks to protect interests germane to the organization's purpose, and neither the claims asserted nor relief sought requires participation in the lawsuit by individual members of the organization (citations omitted).

Coastal Habitat Alliance alleges two injuries in its First Amended Complaint to support its standing to bring this lawsuit against Defendants. The Alliance's first alleged injury is the environmental harm the wind farms will allegedly cause to the fragile wetlands and dependent wildlife in the Laguna Madre area ("environmental harm"). "Construction, operation, and maintenance of these wind farms will harm Alliance members' economic, environmental, and recreational interests uniquely entwined with the endangered and threatened species, Laguna Madre and surrounding wetlands, as well as migratory birds and animals living in, traveling through, and otherwise using 'the last great habitat.' "The Alliance's second alleged injury is deprivation of the consistency review through which it alleges it should have been able to educate state officials and the public of the dangers of locating the wind farms in such a vulnerable area ("deprivation of consistency review"). The "Alliance and its members have been denied any opportunity to participate in any proceeding regarding a [Certificate], or any other proceeding in which to obtain environmental review and to assure consistency with [the] Texas [Program] regarding the challenged wind farms."

Although the Alliance alleges both the injury of environmental harm and the injury of deprivation of consistency review, the Alliance does not expressly assign each type of injury to a type of Defendant. The Alliance alleges the Private Defendants' wind farms are causing environmental harm and the State Defendants' decisions are causing deprivation of consistency review, but it does not allege the State Defendants are causing environmental harm, nor does it allege the Private Defendants are causing the State Defendants' failure to conduct consistency review, besides approving of the lack of regulation. Thus, for purpose of standing, the Court evaluates whether the Alliance has standing to pursue its claims against the Private Defendants for the injury of environmental harm, and whether the Alliance has standing to pursue its claims against the State Defendants for the injury of deprivation of consistency review. The Court analyzes the Alliance's standing to bring both its preemption and Due Process claims. The Court concludes the Alliance lacks standing to bring its preemption claim against the State Defendants because the injury of deprivation of consistency review is not sufficiently concrete or particularized. Further, the Alliance lacks standing to pursue its Due Process claim against the State Defendants and preemption and Due Process claims against the Private Defendants, because the relief it seeks will not redress its alleged injuries.

C. Injury: Coastal Habitat Alliance does not have standing to bring its preemption claim against the State Defendants for the injury of deprivation of consistency review

To convey standing, an injury must be "particularized," meaning it must affect a plaintiff's members in a direct and individual way. Lujan, 504 U.S. at 561; Hunt, 432 U.S. at 343. Defendants argue that because the Act does not create a private right of action, Coastal Habitat Alliance has only alleged invasion of a procedural right, and its alleged injury is not concrete and particularized as required by the standing test. The Public Utility Commission Commissioners direct the Court to Day v. Bond. In *Day,* plaintiffs sued to prevent implementation of a Kansas state statute that deemed certain Kansas nonresidents residents for university-tuition purposes. 500 F.3d at 1130. The plaintiffs alleged the state statute was preempted by federal immigration law, and their only alleged injury was violation of the relevant federal statute. Id. at 1130, 1136. The court determined the federal statute did not confer a private right of action, and plaintiffs therefore had not alleged an invasion of a legally protected interest sufficient to confer standing to bring the preemption claim. Id. at 1139. The Commissioners argue the result in *Day* requires dismissal of the Alliance's preemption claim because the Coastal Zone Management Act does not create a private right of action (citations omitted).

Coastal Habitat Alliance responds that *Day* is distinguishable because the Alliance faces the injury of environmental harm in additions to violation of the Act. For purposes of its preemption claim against the State Defendants, however, the only relevant injury is deprivation of consistency review, a violation of the Act. Under *Day's* reasoning, if the Act does not confer a private right of action on the Alliance, the Alliance has not alleged a concrete injury sufficient for standing purposes.

When a statute does not expressly create a private right of action, a court may only find an implied right of action in the statute if it is clear

Congress intended such a result. Alexander v. Sandoval, 532 U.S. 275, 286 (2001); *Long Island Power Auth.*, 30 F.3d at 421; *see generally* Cort v. Ash, 422 U.S. 66, 78 (1975). To determine whether Congress intended a statute to create a private right of action, the court analyzes the text and structure of the statute. *See* Alexander, 532 U.S. at 288; *George,* 436 F.3d at 103. If the text "explicitly contemplates public enforcement only, courts will assume Congress intended to preclude private enforcement." *George,* 436 F.3d at 103. Additionally, when a statute does not provide an explicit or clearly articulated right of action in a party, a court may only imply such a right when the statute creates a pervasive legislative scheme governing rights between the plaintiff and defendant classes. *Long Island Power Auth.,* 30 F.3d at 422.

No text of the Coastal Zone Management Act indicates Congress intended to confer a private right of action on private parties. *George,* 436 F.3d at 103; *see also* 16 U.S.C. § 1456; *Long Island Power Auth.,* 30 F.3d at 422. Similarly, the Act does not create a pervasive legislative scheme governing the relationship between plaintiffs like the Alliance and defendants like the State and Private Defendants in this case. *Long Island Power Auth.,* 30 F.3d at 422. The Court also notes the Alliance disclaims a private right of action under the Act. The Court holds that the Coastal Zone Management Act does not create a private right of action under which the Alliance may sue the Private and State Defendants.

The Alliance's preemption claim is therefore anchored by nothing more than its desire that the State Defendants follow the law, which, alone, is not an injury sufficient to confer standing. Lujan, 504 U.S. at 573–74; Allen, 468 U.S. at 753; *Day,* 500 F.3d at 1136; Delta Commercial v. Gulf of Mexico Fishery Mgmt. Council, 364 F.3d 269, 272–73 (5th Cir.2004) (holding plaintiff failed to show injury where alleged injury was deviation from statutory requirement).

D. Redressability

To demonstrate redressability sufficient for standing purposes, a plaintiff must "allege facts from which it could be reasonably inferred that . . . if the court affords the relief requested, the asserted [injury] will be removed." Warth, 422 U.S. at 504. The Court finds the Alliance lacks standing to bring its preemption and Due Process claims against the Private Defendants and its Due Process claim against the State Defendants because its requested relief would not redress its alleged injuries. The Alliance requests that the Court issue:

A. Declaratory judgments:

1. Defendants Texas Gulf Wind, Babcock & Brown, and PPM Energy may not build any part of the challenged wind farms in the Texas Coastal Zone before completing environmental review required

pursuant to the [Coastal Zone Management Act] and Texas [Program]; and

2. In any proceeding to consider the environmental consequences of the challenged wind farms under the [Act] and Texas [Program], Defendants must allow Plaintiff an opportunity to be heard as an interested and affected party and, as specifically promised by the Texas [Program], the opportunity of judicial review as appropriate;

The Alliance further requests:

B. Permanent and, as may be appropriate, preliminary injunctive relief that, until and unless they undergo proper environmental review under the [Act], with the required public participation including Plaintiff, the proposed wind farms in the Texas Coastal Zone may not be built, in whole or part, by Defendants Texas Gulf Wind/Babcock & Brown or PPM Energy.

The Alliances's requested relief does not redress its alleged injuries. Most significantly, the Alliance does not ask the Court to command the State Defendants to conduct consistency review. The Alliance's requested relief therefore does not lead to a reasonable inference that the injury of deprivation of consistency review will be removed, because granting such relief would not direct the State Defendants to do anything to remedy such injury. The relief sought, by prohibiting the Private Defendants from building the wind farms until and unless they undergo consistency review, would temporarily halt environmental harm because construction would halt pending consistency review. But such relief merely penalizes the Private Defendants for State Defendant-caused injury, without requiring the State Defendants to remedy such injury, where there is no allegation that the Private Defendants caused deprivation of consistency review.

Because the Alliance's requested relief would not redress its injuries, the Alliance lacks standing.

NOTES AND QUESTIONS

1. Do you agree that the plaintiffs' requested relief and alleged injuries were not redressable? Was this a matter of insufficient pleadings, a problem that could have been remedied had the court been more sympathetic to the claims of the plaintiffs?

2. When the Texas legislature deregulated the utility industry and eliminated the requirement that new electric-generating facilities obtain a certificate of need and convenience, including the Kenedy County wind farms near the critical area of Laguna Madre, could the Coastal Alliance have sued the Secretary of Commerce for not disapproving the revision to the approved pro-

gram? The Coastal Zone Management Act was enacted in 1972, and most state programs were submitted for approval by the Secretary of Commerce in the 1980s. Why was Texas's program not submitted until 1995?

3. Does the federal Coastal Zone Management Act require states that deregulate their coastal energy industries to submit a program amendment to the Secretary of Commerce? Does NEPA require the Secretary in turn to prepare an environmental assessment before approving that amendment? See NOAA Office of Ocean and Coastal Resource Management regulations, 15 C.F.R. Part 923, discussed in Chapter 4. Given the goal of the CZMA is to strengthen the comprehensive management of coastal lands and waters and to ensure public participation in land and water use decisions, should the Commerce secretary intervene when states take actions that undermine their approved programs? What are the political risks of pro-active implementation of the Act?

4. The Coastal Habitat Alliance tried other legal theories to stop the wind farm as the following article explains (footnotes omitted).

ERNEST E. SMITH & BECKY H. DIFFEN, WINDS OF CHANGE: THE CREATION OF WIND LAW

5 Texas Oil, Gas, and Energy J. 65, 190, 195–200 (2009–10)

* * *

The primary argument against the location of the wind farms [near Laguna Madre] is that they are in the migratory pathway of hundreds of species of birds that migrate north to south in the fall and back north in the spring. Typically these migratory flyways are above even the tallest of the wind turbines; however, during fogs or bad weather, the birds commonly fly much lower, where, it is feared, thousands will collide with the wind turbines. From the plaintiff's standpoint, the legal problem was finding some way to get involved in the process, which was particularly difficult in Texas since there is no regulation or required permitting for wind farms.* * *

The Texas [coastal] program under the [federal Coastal Zone Management] Act designates the General Land Office as the lead agency and requires the Public Utilities Commission of Texas ("PUCT" or "Commission") to comply with specified energy-siting policies that minimize environmental damage. A review or consideration of the environmental and other impacts is to be made when the PUCT issued Certificates of Convenience and Necessity ("CCNs") to new electric-generating facilities within the coastal zone. However, when the Texas Legislature deregulated the utility industry, it also eliminated the requirement for a CCN for many electric-generating facilities, including the wind farms in question. Plaintiffs argued that Texas lacked the unilateral authority to eliminate the consistency review process, and that, instead, it was required to adhere to an amendment process set out in the Act. This process required at least one public hearing with public participation as well as approval by the appropriate federal agencies. By failing to follow this procedure, plaintiffs argued the state had deprived them of their due process right to a hearing (citations omitted). The court ruled for the defendants, primarily on the ground that plaintiffs lacked standing. . . . * * *

The second method utilized by the Coastal Habitat Alliance in its attempt to stop the wind farms in Kenedy County involved the one aspect of wind farms where there is regulation: the construction of electric transmission lines. The Alliance sought to intervene in American Electric Power Texas Central Company's application for a CCN for a Double Circuit Transmission Line in Kenedy County that would transmit the electricity generated by the wind farms. The PUCT denied the Alliance's motion to intervene, and the denial was upheld in district court and by the Austin Court of Appeals. The appellate court ruled that the Texas Administrative Procedure Act does not authorize a non-party such as the Alliance to seek judicial review of a final order by the PUCT and that in any event denial of intervention was within the discretion of the PUCT. * * *

A permitting requirement of general concern for wind farms is that required by the Federal Aviation Administration ("FAA"). Modern wind turbines typically stand on 80-meter (262-foot) high towers, and their blades often reach over 400 feet into space. Many wind farms fall under FAA jurisdiction because they exceed the height threshold it has established. In such situations the developer of the wind farm must file a notice with the FAA, which determines if the wind farm will be an airspace hazard.

The third tactic that the Coastal Habitat Alliance has used in its attempts to halt further construction and operation of wind farms along the Texas coast has been a petition to the FAA to force it to conduct an environmental review under NEPA. The Alliance's argument is that the FAA's administrative determination constitutes a "major federal action" and is thus subject to NEPA requirements.

Although it is not clear that a private litigant or an individual landowner has standing to oppose an FAA determination favoring a wind farm, a governmental entity, such as a county that is opposed to a wind farm, may find that fighting an FAA permit is a way to stop or at least slow a project. Although no cases on this topic have arisen yet in Texas, a case involving a project in Nevada that was decided by the D.C. Circuit Court held that the FAA improperly approved a proposed wind farm located near the site of Las Vegas' future airport. Clark County, where the airport was to be located, was concerned because the turbines would be in the path of airplanes that were taking off or landing. The court held that the FAA did not properly support its findings that the turbines would not interfere with the airport's radar system and that the turbines would be a safe distance below the take-off and landing paths. Thus, fighting the FAA permits required for wind farms is one more way opponents may try to fight or stall the installation of wind farms.

* * *

TOWN OF BARNSTABLE, MASS. V. FEDERAL AVIATION ADMINISTRATION

First Circuit U.S. Court of Appeals, 2011
659 F.3d 28

WILLIAMS, SENIOR CIRCUIT JUDGE.

Cape Wind Associates has proposed building 130 wind turbines, each 440 feet tall, in a 25-square-mile area of Nantucket Sound—an area roughly the size of Manhattan island. If constructed, the project would be the nation's first offshore wind farm. See Impact Study of 130 Offshore Wind Turbines in Nantucket Sound at 1 fig. 1, Joint Appendix ("J.A.") 59, shown below:

As required by federal regulations, Cape Wind notified the Federal Aviation Administration of its proposed construction. See 14 C.F.R. § 77.13. After a preliminary investigation, the FAA issued a Notice of Presumed Hazard, J.A. 43, and initiated more extensive aeronautical studies to decide whether the project would "result in an obstruction of the navigable airspace or an interference with air navigation facilities and equipment or the navigable airspace." 49 U.S.C. § 44718(b). The FAA also circulated a public notice of these studies and invited interested persons to submit comments.

The FAA ultimately issued 130 identical Determinations of No Hazard, one for each of the proposed wind turbines. In the determinations, the FAA concluded that the turbines "would have no substantial adverse effect on the safe and efficient utilization of the navigable airspace by aircraft or on the operation of air navigation facilities." See, e.g., Determination of No Hazard to Air Navigation, No. 2009–WTE–332–OE (May 17, 2010) ("Determination") at 1, J.A. 1. Although it ultimately decided that the project was not a hazard, its decision was contingent on Cape Wind's implementing a number of measures to mitigate the turbines' adverse impact on nearby radar facilities. See Determination at 5–6, J.A. 5–6.

Petitioners—the town of Barnstable, Massachusetts and the Alliance to Protect Nantucket Sound, a non-profit organization of private citizens and other organizations—challenge these No Hazard determinations. They argue that the FAA violated its governing statute, misread its own regulations, and arbitrarily and capriciously failed to calculate the dangers posed to local aviation.

In response, the FAA claims that petitioners lack standing to challenge the FAA's determinations and that their merits claims are faulty. We find that petitioners do have standing and that the FAA did misread its regulations, leaving the challenged determinations inadequately justified.

* * *

Petitioners bear the burden of providing, "by affidavit or other evidence," "specific facts" sufficient to demonstrate standing; once provided, however, those facts "will be taken as true" by this Court. Sierra Club v. EPA, 292 F.3d 895, 899 (D.C.Cir.2002) (quoting Lujan v. Defenders of Wildlife, 504 U.S. 555, 560, 112 S.Ct. 2130, 119 L.Ed.2d 351 (1992)). At this stage, however, we must assume the petitioners will prevail on the merits, see City of Waukesha v. EPA, 320 F.3d 228, 235 (D.C.Cir.2003), which means we must assume the FAA would determine the wind farm poses a hazard of the degree and kind the petitioners allege.

Of the three familiar prerequisites to Article III standing—injury, causation, and redressability—the FAA acknowledges the adequacy only of petitioners' injury claims. These include the risk of collisions, as well as delay and inconvenience for pilots and other members of the Alliance involved in aviation over and about the proposed wind farm area, with collateral damage for Barnstable as owner and operator of the town's municipal airport (HYA) and for members of the Alliance affected by the adverse impact on aviation. Accordingly, petitioners seek a determination from the FAA that the wind farm poses an unmitigable hazard.

But the FAA sharply asserts inadequacy as to causation and redressability. Here petitioners' burden is to show that their injuries are fairly traceable to the challenged conduct and that any ultimate success on the merits would yield a "significant increase in the likelihood that [they] would obtain relief that directly redresses the injur[ies] suffered." Utah v. Evans, 536 U.S. 452, 464, 122 S.Ct. 2191, 153 L.Ed.2d 453 (2002); see also Nat'l Parks Conservation Ass'n v. Manson, 414 F.3d 1, 7 (D.C.Cir.2005) (quoting the same). Put another way, there must be a "substantial probability" that a favorable outcome would redress petitioners' injuries. St. John's United Church of Christ v. FAA, 550 F.3d 1168, 1170 (D.C.Cir.2009).

Potentially undermining petitioners' showing of causation and redressability is the fact that the FAA's hazard determinations, by themselves, have "no enforceable legal effect." BFI Waste Sys. v. FAA, 293 F.3d 527, 530 (D.C.Cir.2002) (quoting Aircraft Owners & Pilots Ass'n v. FAA, 600 F.2d 965, 966 (D.C.Cir.1979)). The Interior Department, as lessor of the project area to Cape Wind, is the ultimate arbiter of whether the wind farm receives government permission. See 43 U.S.C. § 1337(p) (delineating Interior's authority to grant leases on the outer continental shelf).

Thus, answering the causation and redressability questions requires us, first, to assume that the FAA will determine that the wind farm poses a hazard of the degree and kind petitioners allege, and second, to appraise the likely effects of such a finding on Interior—specifically whether it would generate a significant increase in the likelihood that Interior would exercise its authority to revoke the lease or to modify it in a way that would in whole or in part redress petitioners' threatened injuries. See Commercial Lease of Submerged Lands for Renewal Energy Development on the Outer Continental Shelf (Oct. 6, 2010) ("Lease").

We conclude that petitioners have shown the requisite likelihood. Interior repeatedly assigned the FAA a significant role in its decision-making process, mandating that Cape Wind "could not begin construction until [its] receipt of the FAA's final determination on whether a hazard exists and [Cape Wind's] compliance with any resulting mitigation measures." Record of Decision, Cape Wind Energy Project, Horseshoe Shoal, Nantucket Sound (Apr. 28, 2010) ("Record of Decision"), *available at* http:// boemre. gov/ offshore/ renewable energy/ PDFs/ Cape Wind ROD. pdf, at 24. And despite recognizing that "FAA [hazard] determinations are advisory in nature," Interior incorporated in the lease a requirement that Cape Wind abide by *any* mitigation measures FAA might propose in its ultimate determination. Id. at 59. Thus the final lease with Cape Wind states that if the FAA "imposes requirements on the Lessee which supersede those in the [prior] FAA Determination [ ], the Lessee shall comply instead with such superseding post-lease requirements." Lease at C–28. Interior thereby gave its blessing to the FAA to impose any future mitigation measures that the FAA might deem necessary to reduce or eliminate a hazard on Cape Wind, and to do so without any further consultation.

In a curious display of agency modesty, the FAA dismisses its influence with Interior. It emphasizes that Interior reached its decision only after years of deliberation that involved consultation with over a dozen agencies, and that Interior decided to move forward with the project only "[a]fter careful review of the project need, the various alternatives considered, the concerns expressed through years of public comment, as well as the many agency consultations that were conducted and the potential impact to Nantucket Sound and environs therein." Record of Decision at 5.

But in fact the evidence seems to us to show that Interior would take an FAA finding of hazard very, very seriously. First, the statutory mandate under which Interior issued the lease explicitly requires it to take into account the "safety" of the activities enabled by the lease. 43 U.S.C. § 1337(p)(4). Interior acknowledges this obligation in the lease itself. Lease at 3.

And the record contains numerous contentions indicating that the wind farm might pose just such a safety risk. For example, petitioners cite evidence that the many pilots who regularly operate under visual flight rules ("VFR") near the proposed wind farm would have a difficult time staying beneath the foggy and otherwise inclement weather that often plagues Nantucket Sound, while at the same time maintaining a safe distance from the wind turbines. During such times, there would be a "clear risk of collision with the wind turbine generators." Submission of managers of the Barnstable, Nantucket and Martha's Vineyard airports (May 14, 2010) at 4, J.A. 586. The "finely balanced airspace over Nantucket Sound is already one of the most congested, foggy, and dangerous airspaces on the eastern seaboard." Submission of chairman of Barnstable airport (Mar. 17, 2009) at 3, J.A. 109. A group of air traffic controllers summed it up by saying that adding the turbines to the area would be a "disaster waiting to happen." Submission of National Air Traffic Controllers Association (Oct. 19, 2004) at 3, J.A. 343.

Petitioners also submitted evidence that attempts to circumvent the turbines would not solve the problem. Such attempts, said the CEO and president of Island Airways after reviewing the volume of traffic and its multiple layers, would be "problematic because even horizontal diversions of only one or two miles can further compress air traffic into concentrated corridors." Aff. of W. Scott LaForge (June 15, 2010) at 5, J.A. 857. A "horizontal diversion around a 25 square mile project would certainly lead to concentrated corridors of travel" and thereby "increase the possibility of a collision." *Id.* Moreover, such "encroachment of established VFR routes [would] severely compromise [pilots'] ability to execute collision avoidance maneuvers in the dead center of the three airports of Nantucket Sound." Letter from W. Scott LaForge (Apr. 14, 2009) at 2, J.A. 138.

While of course the wind farm may be one of those projects with such overwhelming policy benefits (and political support) as to trump all other considerations, even as they relate to safety, the record expresses no such proposition.

Moreover, of the many agencies that Interior consulted, it adopted prospective, automatic incorporation of mitigation measures proposed by only two—the Coast Guard and the FAA. See Lease at C–28, C–30. Interior's deference to these two agencies, one tasked with protecting safety on the sea and the other in the air, appears to reflect a serious effort to meet its statutory obligation to ensure safety. We note, moreover, that the Coast Guard determined only that navigation at sea would be "moderately impaired." Record of Decision at 25. The required assumption of the merits in favor of petitioners precludes our supposing that the FAA's ultimate label will speak only of a "moderate" aviation hazard.

The FAA also argues that Interior did not wait for a final determination before approving the project. But it is hardly surprising that Interior's decision came shortly before the FAA's final determination. In 2001, when Cape Wind first proposed the project, the turbines had been designed to be 417 feet tall; only later did it raise them to 440 feet. The FAA had studied the impact of the original configuration and had issued a no-hazard determination. See Record of Decision at 24. Interior cited this previous study in its Record of Decision, *id.*, and likely did not expect that the 23-foot height increase would alter the FAA's viewpoint. Despite this expectation, Interior still conditioned any start of construction on receipt of a final FAA determination. *Id.*

The facts here are rather similar to those underlying our decision in National Parks Conservation Ass'n v. Manson, 414 F.3d 1 (D.C.Cir.2005), where we found that petitioners had standing to challenge a non-binding Department of Interior opinion on the visibility impact of a project over which the State of Montana had sole and final authority. Id. at 6–7. The state agency there retained "discretionary authority" over whether the challenged project ultimately went forward, id. at 6; the only legal effect of a federal finding on visibility would have been to require the state agency to consider the federal report, and, if it disagreed, to justify its decision in writing, *id.* In fact, in an opinion we cited, the Montana Supreme Court had reversed the state agency's earlier determination in part because it found that Montana law compelled the state agency to make its decision independently of Interior's opinion. See Mont. Envtl. Info. Ctr. v. Mont. Dep't of Envtl. Quality, 326 Mont. 502, 112 P.3d 964, 972 (2005). Although we noted in *National Parks* that Interior's opinion had been "virtually dispositive" of the state's earlier decision, 414 F.3d at 6, this fact was not necessary to our standing determination as the intervening Montana Supreme Court decision had relegated Interior's opinion to an important, but nevertheless advisory role. Yet we still found standing because a changed ruling "doubtless would significantly affect" the state decision. Id. at 7.

Indeed, courts have often found standing where there was no binding legal mechanism by which the challenged action might be redressed. See, e.g., Bennett v. Spear, 520 U.S. 154, 170, 117 S.Ct. 1154, 137 L.Ed.2d 281 (1997) (finding standing despite noting that the ultimate decision-maker was "technically free to disregard" the challenged opinion). Given Interior's incorporation in the lease of all past and prospective mitigation measures proposed by the FAA, its conditioning of initial construction on the final FAA decision, and its persistent attention to the safety mandate in its authorizing statute, we think it improbable that Interior would then turn around and blithely disregard a determination that the project posed a substantial danger to aviation safety that defied cure through mitigation measures. We find it "likely, as opposed to merely speculative," that the Interior Department would rethink the project if faced with an FAA determination that the project posed an unmitigable hazard. Lujan, 504 U.S. at 561, 112 S.Ct. 2130.

* * *

Petitioners make two arguments on the merits. They contend that the FAA's No Hazard determinations are arbitrary and capricious because they depart from the agency's own internal guidelines. They also argue that the FAA failed to fulfill its obligations under 49 U.S.C. § 44718(b). We need reach only the first of these arguments because we agree with petitioners that, in light of the FAA's improper application of its own handbook, the FAA did not "adequately explain its result." Public Citizen v. FAA, 988 F.2d 186, 197 (D.C.Cir.1993).

According to the handbook, see Procedures for Handling Airspace Matters, FAA Order 7400.2G (Apr. 10, 2008) (hereafter "handbook"), the FAA can find a hazard if the proposed structure would have a "substantial adverse effect." Id. § 7–1–3(e). A "substantial adverse effect" is defined to include one that would have an "[a]dverse effect" on a "significant volume of aeronautical operations." Id. § 6–3–5 (defining "Substantial Adverse Effect"); see also id. § 6–3–4 (noting that the volume of flights is significant "if one or more aeronautical operation per day would be affected"). We will return shortly to the concept of "adverse effect."

After discussing the adverse effects the turbines would have on nearby radar facilities, the FAA's Determination addressed the impact on VFR operations, purporting to find no adverse effect on such operations. In so doing, the FAA relied solely on § 6–3–8(c)1 of the handbook, which says:

> A structure would have an adverse [aeronautical] effect upon VFR air navigation if its height is greater than 500 feet above the surface at its site, and within 2 statute miles of any regularly used VFR route.

Handbook, § 6–3–8(c)1 (accurately paraphrased in Determination at 7, J.A. 7). After acknowledging that a regularly used VFR route would be affected, and correctly reciting § 6–3–8(c)1, the FAA leapt to the conclusion that the turbines would not have an adverse effect because they would not exceed the 500-foot threshold. Id. ("Therefore, . . . , the wind turbines . . . do not meet the criteria to have an adverse effect.").

But under any reasonable reading of the handbook, § 6–3–8(c)1 simply identifies one circumstance in which a structure could have an adverse effect, potentially one among many. A different part of the handbook, § 6–3–3 (including subsections (a) through (f)), introduces the concept of "adverse effect":

6–3–3. Determining adverse effect.

A structure is considered to have an adverse aeronautical effect if it first exceeds the obstruction standards of part 77, *and/or* is found to have physical or electromagnetic radiation effect on the operation of air navigation facilities. A proposed or existing structure, if not amended, altered, or removed, has an adverse effect if it would:

* * *

b. Require a VFR operation, to change its regular flight course or altitude.

§ 6–3–3 (emphasis added). It is undisputed that the project turbines would (i) have the threshold "physical or electromagnetic radiation effect on the operation of air navigation facilities" (per the first sentence), and would (ii) "[r]equire a VFR operation, to change its regular flight course or altitude" (per the second sentence, together with § 6–3–3(b)). See Determination at 5, 7. The FAA's complete reliance on § 6–3–8(c)1 is therefore inconsistent not only with the language of that provision (reading into it a non-existent "only"), but with the organization of the handbook, which anticipates that structures qualifying under either segment of § 6–3–3's first sentence are to be assessed for the harms identified in the second sentence's subsections (a) through (f).

Improperly relying solely on § 6–3–8(c)1, the FAA failed to supply any apparent analysis of the record evidence concerning the wind farm's potentially adverse effects on VFR operations. A study by a consulting firm, MITRE, commissioned by the FAA, charted how many flights flew through a three-dimensional zone around the project, the boundaries of which were 500 feet to the side and 1000 feet above the turbines. The study found that over the course of a 90-day period 425 VFR flights flew through the immediate vicinity of the project site and that 94.1% of these 425 were flying at an altitude of 1000 feet or less. J.A. 381, 391–92. The 425 flights would be, of course, more than four and a half times the one flight per day that § 6–3–4 sets as the threshold of significance.

Once the turbines are built, many of these flights may be forced to be rerouted or to proceed in violation of the FAA's own regulation, 14 C.F.R. § 91.119, which requires a 500-foot distance between an aircraft and any structure. Further, the FAA's own weather compressibility study concluded that, during instances of inclement weather, "VFR aircraft could potentially be compressed to a lower altitude" to avoid cloud cover, such that they also would come within 500 feet of the turbines in violation of § 91.119. J.A. 469. Indeed, § 6–3–8(b)2 of the handbook says that any structure "that would interfere with a significant volume of low altitude flights by actually excluding or restricting VFR operations in a specific area would have a substantial adverse effect and may be considered a hazard to air navigation." The FAA may ultimately find the risk of these dangers to be modest, but we cannot meaningfully review any such prediction because the FAA cut the process short in reliance on a misreading of its handbook and thus, as far as we can tell, never calculated the risks in the first place.

The FAA repeatedly notes in its brief that the handbook "largely consists of criteria rather than rules to follow." Respondent's Br. at 40. We agree. Any sensible reading of the handbook, and of § 6–3–8(c)1 in particular, would indicate there is more than one way in which the wind farm can pose a hazard to VFR operations. Indeed, other sections of the handbook, especially when read in light of some of the evidence noted above, suggest that the project may very well be such a hazard. Here, by abandoning its own established procedure, see D & F Afonso Realty Trust v. Garvey, 216 F.3d 1191, 1197 (D.C.Cir.2000), the FAA catapulted over the real issues and the analytical work required by its handbook.

Whether in fact an application of the handbook's guidelines to the studies discussed above will cause the FAA to find the project a hazard, and if so, of what degree, we obviously cannot tell at this stage. But it surely is enough to trigger the standard requirement of reasoned decision-making, i.e., to require the FAA to address the issues and explain its conclusion. *Public Citizen,* 988 F.2d at 197. The FAA's misplaced reliance on § 6–3–8(c)1 is no substitute.

* * *

The petitions for review are accordingly granted, and the FAA's determinations are

Vacated and Remanded.

NOTES AND QUESTIONS

1. Under the Secretarial consistency appeal process discussed in Chapter 4, if a state objected to an ocean renewable energy developer's federal consistency certification, and the developer appealed the objection, would the Secretary of Commerce sustain or overturn the objection? Could the developer argue that national security requires an override of the state's objection?

2. For the Reedport wave energy array off the coast of Oregon, Oregon's coastal management agencies concurred with the developer's federal consistency statement in July 2012 after the developer entered into a settlement agreement with all intervenors (including state and federal agencies) in August 2010. The agreement contained specific mitigation, enhancement, and adaptive management measures, including crabbing and fishing mitigation plans. See FERC's order on issuance of license, 140 FERC P. 62,120 (Aug. 13, 2012). Does the ability of renewable energy developers to negotiate an agreement with all federal, state, and private intervenors make it more likely

an ocean renewable project will receive federal consistency concurrence? If this process is an administrative innovation of FERC's like the preliminary permit, should other regulatory agencies emulate it? Are there procedural and substantive requirements in the OCLSA that would preclude BOEM's adoption of a similar process?

3. Should the FAA's determinations be subject to federal consistency? Are there likely to be enforceable state coastal laws and policies that would impinge upon the judgment of the FAA, e.g., designated transportation modes and corridors for seasonal tourism?

4. What is the role of Section 106 of the National Historic Preservation Act, 16 U.S.C. § 470f, in the siting offshore wind farms? In 2010, two Native American tribes petitioned the Secretary of the Interior to have Nantucket Sound listed on the National Register of Historic Places. After the National Park Service determined that the Sound was eligible for listing, a consultation process was initiated (but later terminated) under Section 106, which provides as follows:

> The head of any Federal agency having direct or indirect jurisdiction over a proposed Federal or federally assisted undertaking in any State and the head of any Federal department or independent agency having authority to license any undertaking shall, prior to the approval of the expenditure of any Federal funds on the undertaking or prior to the issuance of any license, as the case may be, take into account the effect of the undertaking on any district, site, building, structure, or object that is included in or eligible for inclusion in the National Register. The head of any such Federal agency shall afford the Advisory Council on Historic Preservation established under Title II of this Act a reasonable opportunity to comment with regard to such undertaking.

The tribes claimed that the Cape Wind project would adversely affect their cultural rights and practices by altering the seascape and by disturbing burial grounds in the seafloor. The Advisory Council recommended that the secretary not approve the wind farm's license, but the Interior secretary issued Cape Wind a lease to operate effective Nov. 1, 2010. Is the legal framework for leasing and siting renewable energy facilities in the oceans adequate for addressing this kind of claim? The tribes filed suit against BOEM in July, 2011. Wampanoag Tribe of Gay Head (Aquinnah) v. Bronwich (complaint, D.D.C. July 6, 2011). Powell, Note, cited supra on p. 516, 92 B.U. L. Rev. 2023, 2039-43 (2012). See also Danielle E. Horgan, Note, Reconciling the Past with the Future: The Cape Wind Project and the National Historic Preservation Act, 36 Vt. L.Rev. 409 (2011–12); M. W. Marinakos, Comment, A Mighty Wind: The Turbulent Times of America's First Offshore Wind Farm and the Inverse of Environmental Justice, 2 Earth Juris. & Envtl. Justice J. 82 (2012).

4. LIQUEFIED NATURAL GAS AND DEEPWATER PORTS

Natural gas is generally considered a cleaner and less expensive energy alternative to oil or coal. But in its gas form, natural gas is difficult to transport or store. Liquefied natural gas (LNG)—natural gas that has been converted into a liquid by cooling to approximately–259ĖF—is about 1/600th the volume of natural gas making storage and transport more efficient.The process of creating LNG also removes most impurities, making it a "clear, colorless, odorless liquid that is neither corrosive nor toxic."

The infrastructure for LNG transportation includes a liquefaction facility, "a load-out terminal for loading the LNG onto ships, LNG ships for long-distance transportation, and a regasification terminal at the destination, where the LNG is reheated and reverted to a gas. Regasification terminals usually are connected to a pipeline distribution network." See David MacDuffee and Patricia Delgado, Liquified Natural Gas: A Primer on Needs, Regulations, Environmental Implications and Trends, The Coastal Society Bulletin Vol. 27.3 (2005) (available at http://www.thecoastalsociety.org/pdf/bulletin/Issue_2005n3.pdf); Federal Energy Regulatory Commission, LNG, available at http://ferc.gov/industries/gas/indus-act/lng.asp.

Despite the benefits of natural gas over oil or coal, controversy continues over siting facilities. Critics fear that onshore LNG facilities and LNG tankers in ports and nearshore waterways pose serious safety risks, particularly in high population areas. Offshore LNG facilities and terminals have important advantages in reaching markets where onshore siting is unlikely to occur. In 2002, Congress passed the Maritime Transportation Security Act amending the Deepwater Port Act (DWPA) to expedite the licensing of offshore LNG facilities. Among other measures, the DWPA establishes that only one national federal license is required to be issued by the Department of Transportation (DOT); only a single EA or EIS is required for NEPA compliance. It also creates a specific time frame of 330 days from the date of publication in the Federal Register (for notice of a complete application) for approval or denial of the deepwater port license. How well has the expedited decisionmaking process worked? Did the 2002 amendments weaken the marine environmental review?

GULF RESTORATION NETWORK V. UNITED STATES DEPARTMENT OF TRANSPORTATION

United States Court of Appeals, Fifth Circuit, 2006
452 F.3d 362

Petition for Review of an Order of the United States Department of Transportation

DAVIS, CIRCUIT JUDGE.

Petitioners seek review of a decision by the Secretary of the Department of Transportation granting a license for a liquified natural gas ("LNG") facility in the Gulf of Mexico under the Deepwater Port Act, 33 U.S.C. § 1501 et seq. Petitioners submit two issues for review. First, they contend that the Environmental Impact Statement ("EIS") prepared by the Secretary as required by the National Environmental Policy Act ("NEPA"), 42 U.S.C. § 4321 et seq., was deficient in that it did not adequately consider the "environmental impacts of the proposed action." More particularly, Petitioners contend the Secretary acted arbitrarily and capriciously in concluding that the effects of three potential future projects in the Gulf of Mexico were too speculative to consider in evaluating the cumulative impact of the licensing decision under NEPA. Second, Petitioners argue that the Secretary violated the Deepwater Port Act by failing to require that the proposed facility use a closed loop system, which they assert is the "best available technology to prevent or minimize adverse impact on the marine environment." * * *

I. Background

On November 3, 2003, Gulf Landing LLC filed a complete application with the Secretary of Transportation, pursuant to the Deepwater Port Act, for a license to operate a deepwater port off the coast of Louisiana, 38 miles south of Cameron, described in more detail below. The facility will receive ultra-cooled liquid natural gas, store it, regasify it by heating, and transfer it to existing pipelines for delivery to the Gulf Coast. It will be located in 55 feet of water and will consist of two units fixed to the seabed, including two LNG storage tanks. The LNG will be vaporized using "open rack" vaporizers. This system, known as an "open loop" system, will heat the LNG by pumping warm seawater to the top of each open rack vaporizer and allowing it to flow down panels, in which LNG is flowing through tubes, warming and regasifying the LNG. A "closed loop" system, by contrast, burns natural gas to heat water which is used repeatedly to heat the LNG.

Because open loop systems require the uptake and release of a large volume of seawater, they affect the marine environment, primarily by entrapping fish, fish eggs, and larvae in the intake screens, decreasing water temperature, and emitting anti-biofouling agents necessary for production into the water. A closed loop system, while more expensive to run, is friendlier to the environment in most respects.

The facility will be located in what the NOAA Fisheries Service has considered the " 'fertile fisheries crescent,' the most biologically productive area in the Gulf of Mexico marine ecosystem." Accordingly, the facility will affect many types of animals, including fish, turtles, mammals, and birds. Of primary concern is the red drum, a popular sport-fish not commonly fished commercially. According to the Final Environmental Impact Statement ("FEIS") for the project, the Gulf Landing facility alone could destroy annually a number of red drum equal to 3.8% of Louisiana's annual red drum fish harvest.

Under the Deepwater Port Act, the Secretary has approximately one year after receiving a complete application to issue a decision. 33 U.S.C. § 1504(c)(1), (g), (i)(1),(4). During this time, he must take various steps, including conducting an environmental review and issuing an Environmental Impact Statement ("EIS") under NEPA and holding a public hearing. Id.

* * *In following NEPA's mandate that an EIS take into account cumulative effects from "reasonably foreseeable future actions," the Secretary took into account only two of the five pending applications. The Secretary considered the other three applications too speculative, and two of the other three as too geographically distant from the Gulf Landing project as well.

On January 3, 2005, the NOAA Fisheries Service wrote to the Secretary that a license decision without analysis of the cumulative impacts from the other three facilities would not be "adequately evaluated" and that the draft EIS and FEIS should have analyzed the cumulative impact from those facilities. It also stated in a letter that the open loop system was not the "more environmentally responsible action:" "[a]s we have consistently stated in our previous comments on this project, we are convinced that the use of a [closed loop system] would greatly reduce ecological impacts and yield a stronger, more environmentally responsible action." Louisiana Governor Kathleen Blanco, the Louisiana Department of Wildlife and Fisheries, the Gulf States Marine Fisheries Commission, and the Gulf of Mexico Fishery Management Council expressed the same two concerns in a letter to the Secretary.

Despite these concerns, the Secretary approved the Gulf Landing license on February 16, 2005, subject to certain conditions and environmental monitoring requirements. On April 15, the Petitioners filed a petition in this court, pursuant to the Deepwater Port Act, arguing: (1) that the Secretary should have analyzed the cumulative impact from the other three proposed LNG facilities; and (2) that a closed loop system should have been required for the license to issue.

* * *

III. Cumulative Impacts Analysis under NEPA

We first address Petitioners' contention that the Secretary failed to adequately consider the cumulative impact of the Gulf Landing deepwater port with three other ports for which applications were filed. Under the Deepwater Port Act, organizations wishing to construct the type of facility contemplated here must apply to the Secretary of Transportation for a license. 33 U.S.C. § 1503(a). As part of the approval process, the Act requires the Secretary to prepare an EIS pursuant to NEPA. 33 U.S.C. § 1504(f). In accord with NEPA, the Secretary must include a detailed statement of "the environmental impacts of the proposed actions." 42 U.S.C. § 4332(2)(C)(i). Impacts include "ecological . . . aesthetic, historic, cultural, economic, social, or health, whether direct, indirect, or cumulative." 40 C.F.R. § 1508.8. Cumulative impact "is the impact on the environment which results from the incremental impact of the action when added to other past, present, and reasonably foreseeable future actions" and "can result from individually minor but collectively significant actions taking place over a period of time." 40 C.F.R. § 1508.7 (emphasis added).

* * * [T]his court has held that "[a]n impact is 'reasonably foreseeable' if it is 'sufficiently likely to occur that a person of ordinary prudence would take it into account in reaching a decision.' " City of Shoreacres v. Waterworth, 420 F.3d 440, 453 (5th Cir.2005) (citing Sierra Club v. Marsh, 976 F.2d 763, 767 (1st Cir.1992)).

In issuing the FEIS for the Gulf Landing project, the Secretary limited his analysis of "cumulative impacts" to the two ports for which "an approved public Draft NEPA document [was] available for review at the time of the Draft EIS for Gulf Landing". The Secretary therefore did not consider the impact of the three facilities for which applications had been filed but the consideration of the application had not progressed to the draft EIS stage.* * *

The Petitioners argue that the Secretary's decision to exclude consideration of the three ports for which applications had been filed was arbitrary and capricious. They contend that the effects of the proposed projects are not speculative because the details required in an application give the Secretary ample information to evaluate the effects of the projects.

Appellants also argue that the dire need for natural gas, the sums expended by the applicants, the expense entailed in preparing such applications, and the financial stability of the applicants make the projects "sufficiently likely to occur that a person of ordinary prudence would take

[them] into account in reaching a decision." City of Shoreacres, 420 F.3d at 453.

* * *

We agree that the Secretary did not act arbitrarily or capriciously when he included only two of the five ports for which applications were filed. We recognize the high demand for natural gas and these LNG ports, thereby increasing the possibility that the ports will be built. We also recognize that the companies which have filed the applications certainly have the resources to build the ports.

However, the Secretary was entitled to conclude that the occurrence of any one of a number of contingencies could cause the plans to build the ports to be cancelled or drastically altered. For example, one or more of the applicants may decide for a number of reasons to withdraw its application before the Secretary's approval, such as ExxonMobil did with its application for the Pearl Crossing GBS platform. The Secretary, after receiving input from other agencies, may deny an application or make changes to the application's construction specifications such as demanding that the port be closed loop rather than open loop. The technology in this area is also advancing rapidly and may change the effects of the planned ports. Finally, based on public statements and correspondence from Louisiana Governor Kathleen Blanco, the Secretary was aware that she might well decide to veto any open loop port approved by the Secretary.

Under the facts presented to us and under the deferential standard which we review the agency's determination, we find that the Secretary did not abuse his discretion or act arbitrarily or capriciously in concluding that the three ports were not "reasonably foreseeable future actions," or, as this court has put it, actions that "a person of ordinary prudence would take [ ] into account in reaching a decision." City of Shoreacres, 420 F.3d at 453.

IV

We next address Petitioners' argument that the Secretary violated the Deepwater Port Act by issuing a license for a facility that does not require the "best available technology, so as to prevent or minimize adverse impact on the marine environment," as required by the Act.

Under § 1503(c) of the Act, the Secretary "may" issue a license if:

> (2) he determines that the applicant can and will comply with applicable laws, regulations, and license conditions;

> (3) he determines that the construction and operation of the deepwater port will be in the national interest and consistent

with national security and other national policy goals and objectives, including energy sufficiency and environmental quality;

* * *

(5) he determines, in accordance with the environmental review criteria established pursuant to section 1505 of this title, that the applicant has demonstrated that the deepwater port will be constructed and operated using best available technology, so as to prevent or minimize adverse impact on the marine environment . . .

33 U.S.C. § 1503(c)(emphasis added).

The implementing regulations also provide that the application must use "the best available technology to prevent or minimize adverse impact on the environment." 33 C.F.R. § 148.710(a)(2). The regulation further instructs the Secretary to evaluate "a deepwater port proposal and reasonable alternatives . . . on the basis of how well they: (a) Reflect the use of best available technology in design, construction procedures, operations, and decommissioning; . . . (g) avoid interference with biotic populations, especially breeding habitats or migration routes." 33 C.F.R. § 148.725.

The Petitioners argue that the Secretary violated the plain language of subsection (5) by failing to require a closed loop system, a system which would "prevent or minimize adverse impact on the marine environment." They point out that the Secretary admitted in the FEIS that the open loop system will have a "higher effect" on the "water quality and marine life" than a closed loop system, a conclusion other agencies agree with. They argue that the FEIS reflects that the Secretary approved open loop technology because of lower operating costs:

The Applicant selected [open loop] technology because it is widely used and highly proven technology, is a simple process (highly reliable), and has low fuel-usage requirements and resultant reduced operating costs. The Applicant has also made sound arguments on the basis of safety and availability of means to ensure protection of environment.

Thus, appellants argue that because the open loop system is more harmful to the environment than the closed loop system, the Secretary's approval of a port with an open loop system was "contrary to law" under § 706(2)(A) of the APA [Administrative Procedure Act].

The Secretary argues that the Congressional directive to require the applicant to demonstrate it will construct the port, using the best technology "so as to prevent or minimize adverse impact on the marine environment" is best read to require construction that reasonably minimizes adverse impact to a reasonable degree given all relevant circumstances. He also contends that the Petitioners' reading ignores the prior clause in subsection (5)-"in accordance with the environmental review criteria established pursuant to 33 U.S.C. § 1505". The Secretary points out that § 1505 requires the Secretary to consider broad criteria other than marine environment; he argues that the Petitioners would have him ignore these criteria entirely whenever a technology marginally better for the marine environment is worse for the rest of the environment.

The Petitioners' reading of the subsection at issue in isolation cannot be correct. First, under the Petitioners' reading, the Secretary could not apply the overall environmental criteria of § 1505, which is mandated by subsection (5) itself. Second, under petitioner's reading, the Secretary could not properly follow NEPA, as mandated by subsection (5) and § 1505, because he would have to ignore NEPA-mandated variables not related to the marine environment. See, e.g., 42 U.S.C.A. § 4331(b)(5) (requiring the federal government to "achieve a balance between population and resource use which will permit high standards of living and a wide sharing of life's amenities."). Third, the Petitioners' reading would prevent the Secretary from considering the factors in subsection (3): whether the license was in the "national interest" and good for "energy sufficiency and [overall] environmental quality." 33 U.S.C. § 1503(c)(3). The Secretary's cost-analysis of the technology also complies with Congress' intent to "promote the construction and operation of deepwater ports as a safe and effective means of importing oil or natural gas into the United States." 33 U.S.C. § 1501(a)(5). As the Secretary points out, this goal would be compromised if the "best available technology" requirement demanded the use of the technology that is best for the marine environment, even if the costs were so prohibitive that no applicant could ever construct a port using that technology.

For these reasons, we conclude that the Secretary's issuance of the Gulf Landing license was not contrary to law.

Petition for review DENIED.

NOTES AND QUESTIONS

1. The Deepwater Ports Act of 1974 (DWPA), 33 U.S.C. § 1501 et seq., established licensing requirements for deepwater ports located beyond the traditional three mile limit of state waters. By use of such facilities connected to land by pipelines, large oil tankers could discharge their cargo miles at sea. Although a number of Gulf States considered such superport development, the Louisiana Offshore Oil Port (LOOP), located 16 miles southeast of Port Fourchon in the Gulf of Mexico, is the only Deepwater Port petroleum terminal in existence today.

2. The case refers to the power of governors of adjacent states to "veto" the offshore facility. Originally applicable to offshore ports, this power was extended to LNG facilities by amendments to the DWPA. The provisions of the DWPA are:

(a) Designation; direct pipeline connections; mileage; risk of damage to coastal environment, time for designation

(1) The Secretary, in issuing notice of application pursuant to section 1504 (c) of this title, shall designate as an "adjacent coastal State" any coastal State which

(A) would be directly connected by pipeline to a deepwater port as proposed in an application, or

(B) would be located within 15 miles of any such proposed deepwater port.

(2) The Secretary shall, upon request of a State, and after having received the recommendations of the Administrator of the National Oceanic and Atmospheric Administration, designate such State as an "adjacent coastal State" if he determines that there is a risk of damage to the coastal environment of such State equal to or greater than the risk posed to a State directly connected by pipeline to the proposed deepwater port. This paragraph shall apply only with respect to requests made by a State not later than the 14th day after the date of publication of notice of an application for a proposed deepwater port in the Federal Register in accordance with section 1504 (c) of this title. The Secretary shall make the designation required by this paragraph not later than the 45th day after the date he receives such a request from a State.

(b) Applications; submittal to Governors for approval or disapproval; consistency of Federal licenses and State programs; views of other interested States

(1) Not later than 10 days after the designation of adjacent coastal States pursuant to this chapter, the Secretary shall transmit a complete copy of the application to the Governor of each adjacent coastal State. The Secretary shall not issue a license without the approval of the Governor of each adjacent coastal State. If the Governor fails to transmit his approval or disapproval to the Secretary not later than 45 days after the last public hearing on applications for a particular application area, such approval shall be conclusively presumed. If the Governor notifies the Secretary that an application, which would otherwise be approved pursuant to this paragraph, is inconsistent with State programs relating to environmental protection, land and water use, and coastal zone management, the Secre-

tary shall condition the license granted so as to make it consistent with such State programs.

(2) Any other interested State shall have the opportunity to make its views known to, and shall be given full consideration by, the Secretary regarding the location, construction, and operation of a deepwater port.

DWPA, 33 U.S.C. § 1508. What is the nature of the "veto"? Two governors, Blanco of Louisiana and Christie of New Jersey, have vetoed offshore facilities.

3. The DWPA also severely limits legal challenges to a license issued for offshore LNG terminals. 33 U.S.C. § 1516 provides:

Any person suffering legal wrong, or who is adversely affected or aggrieved by the Secretary's decision to issue, transfer, modify, renew, suspend, or revoke a license may, not later than 60 days after any such decision is made, seek judicial review of such decision in the United States Court of Appeals for the circuit within which the nearest adjacent coastal State is located. A person shall be deemed to be aggrieved by the Secretary's decision within the meaning of this chapter if he—

(A) has participated in the administrative proceedings before the Secretary (or if he did not so participate, he can show that his failure to do so was caused by the Secretary's failure to provide the required notice); and

(B) is adversely affected by the Secretary's action.

4. The success of hydraulic fracturing in increasing natural gas supplies in the United States is changing the nature of LNG facilities. While only a few years earlier these facilities were being proposed and developed only for importing LNG, facilities are now being designed or converted to export LNG as well. How is this development likely to affect the further development of LNG facilities? The environmental effects of hydraulic fracturing are still largely unknown. New LNG export facilities can create new markets and lead to increased production of natural gas by fracturing. Should the environmental effects of the process used to produce the natural gas be a factor in approving new LNG terminals?

5. OCEAN MINERALS MINING

A. OCS AND EEZ MINERALS MINING

Historically, U.S. offshore mining had concentrated on sand, gravel and phosphorites, with some recovery of strategic minerals and heavy metal placers. In 1980, however, Congress passed the national Materials and Minerals Policy, Research and Development Act, 30 U.S.C. §§ 1601 et seq., directing the president to "encourage federal agencies to facilitate availability of domestic resources to meet critical needs," and declaring a policy to encourage private development of the nation's mineral resources. President Reagan directed this policy toward marine minerals development in his 1982 National Minerals and Materials Program.

Shortly after President Reagan issued his 1983 EEZ proclamation, officials at the Minerals Management Service of the Interior Department announced plans to lease a Pacific Ocean seabed site potentially rich in polymetallic sulfides for exploration and eventual mineral extraction. This proposed lease sale would have been one of the first offerings of hardrock minerals from the seabed under U.S. jurisdiction, and it would have opened up some 12,000 square miles (7.68 million acres) of the Gorda Ridge off Northern California and Southern Oregon for competitive bidding. The 250-mile-long Gorda Ridge stretches from 35 to 250 miles off the coastlines of those states and is unique among potential deposit sites thus far discovered in that it lies mostly within the U.S. EEZ. In contrast, a preliminary Interior Department assertion of jurisdiction over the Juan de Fuca Ridge off the Washington State coast was withdrawn after the Canadian government protested that the site lay beyond U.S. jurisdiction.

To date, however, no lease sale of Gorda Ridge minerals has been held. The Interior Department, acknowledging that current regulations focusing on extraction of oil, gas and sulphur were inadequate, did proceed to develop an OCS minerals regulatory regime predicated on the Department's authority under OCSLA § 8(k)(1) (43 U.S.C. § 1337(k)(1)). Section 8(k)(1) states:

> The Secretary is authorized to grant to the qualified persons offering the highest cash bonuses on a basis of competitive bidding leases of any mineral other than oil, gas, and sulphur in any area of the outer Continental Shelf not then under lease for such mineral upon such royalty, rental, and other terms and conditions as the Secretary may prescribe at the time of offering the area for lease.

In response to the question of whether the Presidential Proclamation on the EEZ was intended to affect the Department of Interior's jurisdiction under the OCSLA, the Department responded that the OCSLA definition of "Outer Continental Shelf includes all lands seaward of those granted to the States in the Submerged Lands Act * * * to which the United States claims jurisdiction and control under international law. The Presidential Proclamation on the EEZ formally claimed U.S. jurisdiction to a minimum of 200 nautical miles from its coasts." 53 Fed. Reg. 25246 (July 5, 1988). Such an assertion of authority, the Department further asserted, is consistent with existing international law, "which now accepts that the continental shelf extends to a minimum of 200 nautical

miles for all nations, essentially concurrent with the 200-mile EEZ." * * *
Id.

The first set of regulations addresses geological and geophysical prospecting and scientific research activities relating to minerals other than
oil, gas and sulphur. 30 C.F.R. part 280. The regulations require a permit
for all prospecting-related research and some types of scientific research
activities.

The second set of regulations addresses leasing and post-lease operations. 30 C.F.R. parts 281, 282. The regulations authorize the issuance of
leases with a 20-year initial term. Notices of proposed leasing will be sent
to the governors of affected states in addition to being published in the
Federal Register. If a lease will be near the federal-state boundary offshore, joint management agreements are suggested. In 2011, these regulations were substantially revised and published at 30 C.F.R. 580, 581,
and 582.

It is anticipated that an EIS will be prepared when the initial lease
sale in a given area is offered. In addition, the 1990 amendments to
CZMA require that all OCS mineral activities that affect any land or water use or natural resource of the coastal zone be conducted in a manner
that is consistent with the state's federally approved coastal zone management plan, unless either a Presidential exemption is obtained or the
Secretary of Commerce overrides any state consistency objection.

Through a judicial proceeding, MMS may cancel a lease or suspend
operations for noncompliance with the lease regulations or the OCSLA.
Leases may also be cancelled in some circumstances to protect from harm
aquatic life, property, minerals, national security, or the environment. If
a lease is cancelled for violation of lease regulations or the OCSLA, no
compensation is paid to the lessee, but if it is cancelled for environmental
or other reasons, then compensation is paid in accordance with a formula
contained in the regulations.

OCSLA section 8(k) was amended in 1994 by P.L. 103–426, 108 Stat.
4371, to authorize negotiated contracts rather than competitive lease
sales when OCS sand and gravel resources are needed for public works
projects such as beach and coastal wetlands restoration.

NOTES AND QUESTIONS

1. When the OCSLA was amended in 1978 to add substantial requirements for protection of the environment and state participation in the OCS
development, the provisions applied almost exclusively to oil and gas development. Even the original OCSLA made little reference to minerals other
than oil, gas and sulphur. Did OCSLA § 8(k)(1) provide sufficient authority
and guidance for leasing of hard minerals? Should provisions of the 1978
amendments apply to such leases?

2. The role of the states concerning the prospecting and research stage of the mining operations are addressed in the current regulations as follows:

33 C.F.R. § 580.31 Whom will BOEM notify about environmental issues?

(a) In cases where Coastal Zone Management Act consistency review is required, the Director will notify the Governor of each adjacent State with a copy of the application for a permit immediately upon the submission for approval.

(b) In cases where an environmental assessment is to be prepared, the Director will invite the Governor of each adjacent State to review and provide comments regarding the proposed activities. The Director's invitation to provide comments will allow the Governor a specified period of time to comment.

(c) When a permit is issued, the Director will notify affected parties including each affected coastal State, Federal agency, local government, and special interest organization that has expressed an interest.

3. The current regulations involving the role of states in the minerals leasing process are found at 33 C.F.R. 581.13.

33 C.F.R. § 581.13 Joint State/Federal Coordination.

(a) The Secretary may invite the adjacent State Governor(s) to join in, or the adjacent State Governor(s) may request that the Secretary join in, the establishment of a State/Federal task force or some other joint planning or coordination arrangement when industry interest exists for OCS mineral leasing or geological information appears to support the leasing of OCS minerals in specific areas. Participation in joint State/Federal task forces or other arrangements will afford the adjacent State Governor(s) opportunity for access to available data and information about the area; knowledge of progress made in the leasing process and of the results of subsequent exploration and development activities; facilitate the resolution of issues of mutual interest; and provide a mechanism for planning, coordination, consultation, and other activities which the Secretary and the Governor(s) may identify as contributing to the leasing process.

(b) State/Federal task forces or other such arrangements are to be constituted pursuant to such terms and conditions (consistent with Federal law and these regulations) as the Secretary and the adjacent State Governor(s) may agree.

(c) State/Federal task forces or other such arrangements will provide a forum which the Secretary and adjacent State Governor(s) may use for planning, consultation, and coordination on concerns associated with the offering of OCS minerals other than oil, gas, or sulphur for lease.

(d) With respect to the activities authorized under these regulations each State/Federal task force may make recommendations to the Secretary and adjacent State Governor(s) concerning:

(1) The identification of areas in which OCS minerals might be offered for lease;

(2) The potential for conflicts between the exploration and development of OCS mineral resources, other users and uses of the area, and means for resolution or mitigation of these conflicts;

(3) The economic feasibility of developing OCS mineral resources in the area proposed for leasing;

(4) Potential environmental problems and measures that might be taken to mitigate these problems;

(5) Development of guidelines and procedures for safe, environmentally responsible exploration and development practices; and

(6) Other issues of concern to the Secretary and adjacent State Governor(s).

(e) State/Federal task forces or other such arrangements might also be used to conduct or oversee research, studies, or reports (e.g., Environmental Impact Statements).

Do these regulations give the states and their governors protections and input into the OCS mining process comparable to their role in oil and development?

B. DEEP SEABED MINERALS MINING

Prior to the LOS Convention, it was widely presumed that customary international law applied to the exploration for and recovery of seabed mineral resources beyond the limits of national jurisdiction. The principle of freedom of the seas seemed to incorporate the notion that ownership of mineral resources (like ownership of fish) would vest upon capture. No sovereign claim to the seabed itself would be necessary to support a claim to harvest the resources thereon, any more than a sovereign claim to the seabed would be necessary to sustain a claim to mid-oceanic fishing rights. The resolutions of the UN General Assembly and declaration in the LOS Convention that the resources of the deep seabed are the common heritage of mankind have changed customary international law in regard to the mineral resources of the deep seabed, referred to as the "Area." See discussion in Chapter 1, on pp. 53–55.

In the waning years of the LOS negotiations, Congress in June 1980 passed the Deep Seabed Hard Mineral Resources Act (DSHMRA) (30 U.S.C. § 1401 et seq.). The act was intended to improve the investment climate for private ocean mining interests during the interim period prior to the adoption of an acceptable comprehensive law of the sea treaty regime for the seabed. It was Congress' view that substantial investment and a relatively long lead time are needed to develop fully the technology and capability necessary for commercial exploitation of the nodule resource. Congress feared that this private investment would not take place because of the uncertainty as to the nature of an UNCLOS treaty regime and the degree of seabed access the treaty rules would provide to investing U.S. companies. The legislation was intended to create a domestic legal regime to encourage private investment and technology development through an interim regulatory program that also ensures that ocean mining is conducted in a manner which conserves the resources, protects the environment, and promotes safety at sea.

The act requires U.S. citizens and vessels to obtain a license from the Administrator of the National Oceanic and Atmospheric Administration (NOAA) to explore for nodules and a permit before the miner may engage in commercial recovery. Each license or permit gives the holder the exclusive right to explore or mine a specific area, but only as against other U.S. citizens.

NOAA regulations recognize seabed mining as a freedom of the high seas, and issuance of licenses should "not unreasonably interfere with the exercise of the freedoms of the high seas by other nations, as recognized under general principles of international law." 15 C.F.R. § 970.503.

Exploration licenses are issued to qualified applicants on a first come, first served basis. The holder of a ten year license to explore a specific area then has a preference to secure a permit to commercially recover nodules from the explored area. Currently, licenses for deep seabed exploration are in effect for two areas of the Clarion–Clipperton zone of the south Pacific Ocean, known as USA–1 and USA–4. See 67 Fed. Reg. 50,631 (Aug. 5, 2002).

A "reciprocating states" provision of the DSHMRA allows the Administrator of NOAA to designate other nations as reciprocating states, if they meet certain criteria. The U.S. and the designated nations can coordinate their respective license and permit programs to avoid conflicts over mining areas. To become a reciprocating state, another nation must create a domestic regulatory system for its miners that is compatible with the U.S. act and that respects licenses and permits issued by the U.S. By 1983, France, Italy, Japan, the United Kingdom, and West Germany had enacted domestic seabed mining legislation and were designated by NO-AA as reciprocating states The U.S. has negotiated agreements with Belgium, China, France, Germany, Japan, Russia, and the United Kingdom. The problem is that all of the agreements and cooperative arrangements entered into by the U.S. and these nations were concluded before the LOS Convention came into force and were, generally, intended to be interim arrangements. It is not clear whether these arrangements are all now considered viable.

Because of potential environmental impacts of seabed mining, several provisions of the act address environmental concerns. The Act extends Clean Water Act jurisdiction to any discharge of a pollutant from vessels and other floating craft engaged in commercial recovery or exploration under the Act. Vessels are subject to Clean Water Act regulation even when on the high seas. Programmatic environmental impact statements must be prepared by NOAA in certain circumstances. A site-specific EIS must be prepared for each license or permit NOAA issues. NOAA was also directed to expand its Deep Ocean Mining Environmental Study to collect basic scientific information on the ocean environment.

The Administrator of NOAA is directed to consult with regional fishery management councils prior to issuance of any license or permit if it appears that a fishery resource could be adversely affected. The Act makes no provision for the approval by or consultation with coastal states prior to license issuance. However, since the Act requires any shore-based processing of minerals to take place in the U.S., deep seabed mining may have some effects on U.S. coastal areas.

The act has been reauthorized several times without significant change. NOAA regulations governing permits for commercial recovery of deep seabed mineral resources define the "deep seabed" as the area beyond any nation's continental shelf. As written, the commercial recovery regulations lack specific regulatory standards. NOAA addressed the information deficit by requiring licensees and permittees to conduct monitoring programs to ensure early and accurate detection of significant adverse impacts on the environment. The regulations do not define significant adverse impact, leaving it to case-by-case determination. Moreover, NOAA concluded that the occurrence of such impacts due to commercial scale mining is unlikely. The commercial recovery regulations also contain extensive state consultation provisions even though the act itself does not require them. However, commercial recovery remains a distant prospect at best.

Historically, scientific and mining industry attention has focused on manganese nodule mining. However, polymetallic sulfides have recently dominated discussions of deep seabed mining issues, because they contain high concentrations of strategically important minerals, such as cobalt, zinc, copper, and silver. First discovered at seafloor spreading centers in the Eastern Pacific, polymetallic sulfides precipitate out of hot aqueous solutions emitted at "smokers" (hydrothermal vents in the ocean floor), accumulating in vast deposits. Active vent sites are inhabited by unique, previously unknown life forms not dependent on photosynthesis for their existence. See generally J. Edmond and K. Von Damm, Hot Springs on the Ocean Floor, Sci. Am., Apr. 1983, at 78.

NOTES AND QUESTIONS

1. Is the United States bound by the development of customary international law concerning the deep seabed? Recall that in his proclamations and statements on the law of the sea, President Reagan accepted most of the provisions of the LOS Convention as reflecting customary international law, but rejected the seabed mining provisions. Could the U.S. claim the status of a persistent objector? The United States signed the 1994 U.N. Agreement Relating to Implementation of Part XI of UNCLOS on July 29, 1994, and President Bill Clinton transmitted both the agreement and the convention to the Senate for advice and consent to ratification and accession. U.S. Dept. of State, Dispatch Suppl vol.6, Supp. No.1 (Feb. 1995). How does this differ from becoming a party? Does it affect any potential claims to persistent objector status? Does the signing entail any obligations on the part of the United States?

2. NEPA requires an environmental impact statement for all "major Federal actions significantly affecting the quality of the human environment." 42 U.S.C. § 4332(2)(C). Does the coverage of NEPA include only those areas clearly under U.S. jurisdiction? Compare Natural Resources Defense Council v. U.S. Navy, 2002 WL 32095131 (C.D. Cal. Sept. 19, 2002) (NEPA applies to Navy sonar tests in the U.S. EEZ) with Basel Action Network v. Maritime Administration, 2005 U.S. Dist. LEXIS 3278 (D.D.C. March 2, 2005) (NEPA not applicable to vessel towing on the high seas). Can the deep seabed be considered a "human environment"?

3. Deep sea hydrothermal vents provide an oasis-like environment for highly specialized and bizarre life forms, unique in that they are dependent on geothermal rather than solar energy for sustenance. Scientists believe that some of these creatures may be remnants of the earth's earliest life forms, and thus an irreplaceable scientific treasure. Could the Endangered Species Act be extended to cover primitive deep sea creatures whose only habitat lies far from U.S. shores? If so, is it likely that mining will proceed without first learning much more about these animals?

* * *

Although the United States is still outside the U.N. seabed mining regime, the program is going forward. Since 2001, the International Seabed Authority has been entering into 15-year contracts to explore in specified parts of the deep oceans outside national jurisdiction. Each contractor has the exclusive right to explore an initial area of up to 150,000 square kilometers. The Authority has also set aside reserve areas for future exploitation by the Enterprise, the seabed development arm of the Authority, or by joint ventures in association with developing countries.

The Authority has also been developing a comprehensive Mining Code. To date, the Authority has issued Regulations on Prospecting and Exploration for Polymetallic Nodules in the Area (2000) and the Regulations on Prospecting and Exploration for Polymetallic Sulphides in the Area (2010). In addition to technical and legal requirements, the Mining Code provisions provide guidance on the assessment of the environmental impacts.

In 2010, the Republic of Nauru submitted a request to the Authority to provide an interpretation of states' responsibilities under the LOSC "so that developing States can assess whether it is within their capabilities to effectively mitigate such risks and in turn make an informed decision on whether or not to participate in activities in the Area." Nauru's concern was that if exposed to potentially significant liability, developing countries could be effectively precluded from participating in seabed mining activities. The Council—the executive and policy making arm of the Authority—requested an advisory opinion from the specialized Seabed Disputes Chamber of the International Tribunal for the Law of the Sea, the judicial body created by the LOS Convention. This opinion provides the first judicial interpretation of the obligations and potential liability of states in regard to seabed mining operations.

RESPONSIBILITIES AND OBLIGATIONS OF STATES SPONSORING PERSONS AND ENTITIES WITH RESPECT TO ACTIVITIES IN THE AREA

Seabed Disputes Chamber of the International Tribunal for the Law of the Sea
Case No. 17 (2011)

ADVISORY OPINION

[The Council of the International Seabed Authority requested an Advisory Opinion from the Seabed Disputes Chamber of the International Tribunal for the Law of the Sea (hereinafter "the Chamber") on issues of sponsoring state responsibility in regard to mining activities in the Deep Seabed.]

72. The first question submitted to the Chamber is as follows:

What are the legal responsibilities and obligations of States Parties to the Convention with respect to the sponsorship of activities in the Area in accordance with the Convention, in particular Part XI, and the 1994 Agreement relating to the Implementation of Part XI of the United Nations Convention on the Law of the Sea of 10 December 1982?

* * *

I. Sponsorship

74. The notion of "sponsorship" is a key element in the system for the exploration and exploitation of the resources of the Area * * *.

76. The role of the sponsoring State, as set out in the Convention, contributes to the realization of the common interest of all States in the proper application of the principle of the common heritage of mankind which requires faithful compliance with the obligations set out in Part XI. The common-interest role of the sponsoring State is further confirmed by its obligation, set out in article 153, paragraph 4, of the Convention, to "assist" the Authority, which, as stated in article 137, paragraph 2, of the Convention, acts on behalf of mankind. * * *

77. The connection between States Parties and domestic law entities required by the Convention is twofold, namely, that of nationality and that of effective control. All contractors and applicants for contracts must secure and maintain the sponsorship of the State or States of which they are nationals. If another State or its nationals exercises effective control, the sponsorship of that State is also necessary. * * *

78. No provision of the Convention imposes an obligation on a State Party to sponsor an entity that holds its nationality or is controlled by it or by its nationals.* * *

    * * *

IV. Responsibilities and Obligations

    * * *

100. [The key provisions concerning the obligations of the sponsoring States are:]

Article 139, paragraph 1

States Parties shall have the responsibility to ensure that activities in the Area, whether carried out by States Parties, or state enterprises or natural or juridical persons which possess the nationality of States Parties or are effectively controlled by them or their nationals, shall be carried out in conformity with this Part. The same responsibility applies to international organizations for activities in the Area carried out by such organizations.

Article 153, paragraph 4

The Authority shall exercise such control over activities in the Area as is necessary for the purpose of securing compliance with the relevant provisions of this Part and the Annexes relating thereto, and the rules, regulations and procedures of the Authority, and the plans of work approved in accordance with paragraph 3. States Parties shall assist the Authority by taking all measures necessary to ensure such compliance in accordance with article 139.

Annex III, article 4, paragraph 4

The sponsoring State or States shall, pursuant to article 139, have the responsibility to ensure, within their legal systems, that a contractor so sponsored shall carry out activities in the Area in conformity with the terms of its contract and its obligations under this Convention. A sponsoring State shall not, however, be liable for damage caused by any failure of a contractor sponsored by it to comply with its obligations if that State Party has adopted laws and regulations and taken administrative measures which are, within the framework of its legal system, reasonably appropriate for securing compliance by persons under its jurisdiction.

* * *

Obligations of the contractor whose compliance the sponsoring State must ensure

103. The three provisions mentioned in paragraph 100 specify that the obligation (responsibility) of the sponsoring State is "to ensure" that the "activities in the Area" conducted by the sponsored contractor are "in conformity" or in "compliance" with the rules to which they refer.

"Responsibility to ensure"

* * *

110. The sponsoring State's obligation "to ensure" is not an obligation to achieve, in each and every case, the result that the sponsored contractor complies with the aforementioned obligations. Rather, it is an obligation to deploy adequate means, to exercise best possible efforts, to do the utmost, to obtain this result. To utilize the terminology current in international law, this obligation may be characterized as an obligation "of conduct" and not "of result", and as an obligation of "due diligence".

* * *

112. The expression "to ensure" is often used in international legal instruments to refer to obligations in respect of which, while it is not considered reasonable to make a State liable for each and every violation committed by persons under its jurisdiction, it is equally not considered satisfactory to rely on mere application of the principle that the conduct of private persons or entities is not attributable to the State under international law (see ILC Articles on State Responsibility, Commentary to article 8, paragraph 1).

113. An example may be found in article 194, paragraph 2, of the Convention which reads: "States shall take all measures necessary to ensure that activities under their jurisdiction or control are so conducted as not to cause damage by pollution to other States and their environment . . .". * * *

The content of the "due diligence" obligation to ensure

117. The content of "due diligence" obligations may not easily be described in precise terms. Among the factors that make such a description difficult is the fact that "due diligence" is a variable concept. It may change over time as measures considered sufficiently diligent at a certain moment may become not diligent enough in light, for instance, of new scientific or technological knowledge. It may also change in relation to the risks involved in the activity. * * * The standard of due diligence has to be more severe for the riskier activities.

* * *

V. Direct Obligations of Sponsoring States

121. * * * [S]ponsoring States also have obligations with which they have to comply independently of their obligation to ensure a certain behaviour by the sponsored contractor. These obligations may be characterized as "direct obligations".

122. Among the most important of these direct obligations incumbent on sponsoring States are: the obligation to assist the Authority in the exercise of control over activities in the Area; the obligation to apply a precautionary approach; the obligation to apply best environmental practices; the obligation to take measures to ensure the provision of guarantees in the event of an emergency order by the Authority for protection of the marine environment; the obligation to ensure the availability of recourse for compensation in respect of damage caused by pollution; and the obligation to conduct environmental impact assessments. * * *

123. It must nevertheless be stated, at the outset, that compliance with these obligations can also be seen as a relevant factor in meeting the due diligence "obligation to ensure" and that the said obligations are in most cases couched as obligations to ensure compliance with a specific rule.

* * *

Precautionary approach

125. The Nodules Regulations and the Sulphides Regulations contain provisions that establish a direct obligation for sponsoring States. * * * These are regulation 31, paragraph 2, of the Nodules Regulations and regulation 33, paragraph 2, of the Sulphides Regulations, both of which state that sponsoring States (as well as the Authority) "shall apply a pre-

cautionary approach, as reflected in Principle 15 of the Rio Declaration" in order "to ensure effective protection for the marine environment from harmful effects which may arise from activities in the Area".

126. Principle 15 of the 1992 Rio Declaration on Environment and Development (hereinafter "the Rio Declaration") reads:

> In order to protect the environment, the precautionary approach shall be widely applied by States according to their capabilities. Where there are threats of serious or irreversible damage, lack of full scientific certainty shall not be used as a reason for postponing cost-effective measures to prevent environmental degradation.

127. The provisions of the aforementioned Regulations transform this non-binding statement of the precautionary approach in the Rio Declaration into a binding obligation. The implementation of the precautionary approach as defined in these Regulations is one of the obligations of sponsoring States.

* * *

131. * * *[I]t is appropriate to point out that the precautionary approach is also an integral part of the general obligation of due diligence of sponsoring States, which is applicable even outside the scope of the Regulations. The due diligence obligation of the sponsoring States requires them to take all appropriate measures to prevent damage that might result from the activities of contractors that they sponsor. This obligation applies in situations where scientific evidence concerning the scope and potential negative impact of the activity in question is insufficient but where there are plausible indications of potential risks. A sponsoring State would not meet its obligation of due diligence if it disregarded those risks. Such disregard would amount to a failure to comply with the precautionary approach.

* * *

135. The Chamber observes that the precautionary approach has been incorporated into a growing number of international treaties and other instruments, many of which reflect the formulation of Principle 15 of the Rio Declaration. In the view of the Chamber, this has initiated a trend towards making this approach part of customary international law. This trend is clearly reinforced by the inclusion of the precautionary approach in the Regulations . . . contained in Annex 4, section 5.1, of the Sulphides Regulations. So does the following statement in paragraph 164 of the ICJ Judgment in *Pulp Mills on the River Uruguay* that "a precautionary approach may be relevant in the interpretation and application of the provisions of the Statute" (i.e., the environmental bilateral treaty whose interpretation was the main bone of contention between the parties). This

statement may be read in light of article 31, paragraph 3(c), of the Vienna Convention, according to which the interpretation of a treaty should take into account not only the context but "any relevant rules of international law applicable in the relations between the parties".

* * *

VI. Environmental Impact Assessment

141. The obligation of the contractor to conduct an environmental impact assessment is explicitly set out in section 1, paragraph 7, of the Annex to the 1994 Agreement as follows: "An application for approval of a plan of work shall be accompanied by an assessment of the potential environmental impacts of the proposed activities . . .". The sponsoring State is under a due diligence obligation to ensure compliance by the sponsored contractor with this obligation.

* * *

145. It should be stressed that the obligation to conduct an environmental impact assessment is a direct obligation under the Convention and a general obligation under customary international law.

146. As regards the Convention, article 206 states the following:

> When States have reasonable grounds for believing that planned activities under their jurisdiction or control may cause substantial pollution of or significant and harmful changes to the marine environment, they shall, as far as practicable, assess the potential effects of such activities on the marine environment and shall communicate reports of the results of such assessments in the manner provided in article 205. [Article 205 refers to an obligation to publish reports.]

147. With respect to customary international law, the ICJ, in its Judgment in *Pulp Mills on the River Uruguay*, speaks of:

> a practice, which in recent years has gained so much acceptance among States that it may now be considered a requirement under general international law to undertake an environmental impact assessment where there is a risk that the proposed industrial activity may have a significant adverse impact in a transboundary context, in particular, on a shared resource. Moreover, due diligence, and the duty of vigilance and prevention which it implies, would not be considered to have been exercised, if a party planning works liable to affect the régime of the river or the quality of its waters did not undertake an environmental impact assessment on the potential effects of such works. (Paragraph 204)

148. Although aimed at the specific situation under discussion by the Court, the language used seems broad enough to cover activities in the

Area even beyond the scope of the Regulations. The Court's reasoning in a transboundary context may also apply to activities with an impact on the environment in an area beyond the limits of national jurisdiction; and the Court's references to "shared resources" may also apply to resources that are the common heritage of mankind. Thus, in light of the customary rule mentioned by the ICJ, it may be considered that environmental impact assessments should be included in the system of consultations and prior notifications set out in article 142 of the Convention with respect to "resource deposits in the Area which lie across limits of national jurisdiction".

149. It must, however, be observed that, in the view of the ICJ, general international law does not "specify the scope and content of an environmental impact assessment" (paragraph 205 of the Judgment in *Pulp Mills on the River Uruguay*). While article 206 of the Convention gives only few indications of this scope and content, the indications in the Regulations . . . add precision and specificity to the obligation as it applies in the context of activities in the Area.

150. In light of the above, the Chamber is of the view that the obligations of the contractors and of the sponsoring States concerning environmental impact assessments extend beyond the scope of application of specific provisions of the Regulations.

VII. Interests and Needs of Developing States

* * *

159. Equality of treatment between developing and developed sponsoring States is consistent with the need to prevent commercial enterprises based in developed States from setting up companies in developing States, acquiring their nationality and obtaining their sponsorship in the hope of being subjected to less burdensome regulations and controls. The spread of sponsoring States "of convenience" would jeopardize uniform application of the highest standards of protection of the marine environment, the safe development of activities in the Area and protection of the common heritage of mankind.

160. These observations do not exclude that rules setting out direct obligations of the sponsoring State could provide for different treatment for developed and developing sponsoring States.

* * *

Question 2

164. The second question submitted to the Chamber is as follows:

What is the extent of liability of a State Party for any failure to comply with the provisions of the Convention in particular Part XI, and the

1994 Agreement, by an entity whom it has sponsored under Article 153, paragraph 2(b), of the Convention?

* * *

171. * * * The Chamber considers that . . . rules [of international law] supplement the rules concerning the liability of the sponsoring State set out in the Convention.

172. * * * [I]t is evident that liability arises from the failure of the sponsoring State to carry out its own responsibilities. The sponsoring State is not, however, liable for the failure of the sponsored contractor to meet its obligations * * *.

III. Failure to Carry Out Responsibilities

* * *

176. [T]he Convention clearly establishes two conditions for liability to arise: the failure of the sponsoring State to carry out its responsibilities . . . ; and the occurrence of damage.

* * *

IV. Damage

178. * * * [T]he failure of a sponsoring State to carry out its responsibilities entails liability only if there is damage. * * * This constitutes an exception to the customary international law rule on liability since, . . . a State may be held liable under customary international law even if no material damage results from its failure to meet its international obligations.

* * *

182. Article 139, paragraph 2, of the Convention establishes that sponsoring States are responsible for ensuring that activities in the Area are carried out in conformity with Part XI of the Convention. This means that the sponsoring State's liability arises not from a failure of a private entity but rather from its own failure to carry out its own responsibilities. In order for the sponsoring State's liability to arise, it is necessary to establish that there is damage and that the damage was a result of the sponsoring State's failure to carry out its responsibilities. Such a causal link cannot be presumed and must be proven. The rules on the liability of sponsoring States set out in article 139, paragraph 2, of the Convention and in the related instruments are in line with the rules of customary international law on this issue. Under international law, the acts of private entities are not directly attributable to States except where the entity in question is empowered to act as a State organ (article 5 of the ILC Articles on State Responsibility) or where its conduct is acknowledged and

adopted by a State as its own (article 11 of the ILC Articles on State Responsibility). As explained in the present paragraph, the liability regime established in Annex III to the Convention and related instruments does not provide for the attribution of activities of sponsored contractors to sponsoring States.

* * *

Question 3

212. The third question submitted to the Chamber is as follows:

> *What are the necessary and appropriate measures that a sponsoring State must take in order to fulfill its responsibility under the Convention, in particular Article 139 and Annex III, and the 1994 Agreement?*

I. General Aspects

* * *

214. Article 139, paragraph 2, of the Convention provides that the sponsoring State shall not be liable for damage caused by any failure to comply with Part XI of the Convention by an entity sponsored by it under article 153, paragraph 2(b), of the Convention, "if the State Party has taken all necessary and appropriate measures to secure effective compliance under article 153, paragraph 4, and Annex III, article 4, paragraph 4".

215. Article 139, paragraph 2, of the Convention does not specify the measures that are "necessary and appropriate". It simply draws attention to article 153, paragraph 4, and Annex III, article 4, paragraph 4, of the Convention. The relevant part of Annex III, article 4, paragraph 4, reads as follows:

> A sponsoring State shall not, however, be liable for damage caused by any failure of a contractor sponsored by it to comply with its obligations if that State Party has adopted laws and regulations and taken administrative measures which are, within the framework of its legal system, reasonably appropriate for securing compliance by persons under its jurisdiction.

* * *

II. Laws and Regulations and Administrative Measures

218. * * * [T]he adoption of laws and regulations and the taking of administrative measures are necessary. The scope and extent of the laws and regulations and administrative measures required depend upon the legal system of the sponsoring State. The adoption of laws and regulations is prescribed because not all the obligations of a contractor may be enforced through administrative measures or contractual arrangements alone

* * *. Administrative measures aimed at securing compliance with them may also be needed. Laws, regulations and administrative measures may include the establishment of enforcement mechanisms for active supervision of the activities of the sponsored contractor. They may also provide for the co-ordination between the various activities of the sponsoring State and those of the Authority with a view to eliminating avoidable duplication of work.

* * *

IV. Content of the Measures

227. The Convention leaves it to the sponsoring State to determine what measures will enable it to discharge its responsibilities. Policy choices on such matters must be made by the sponsoring State. In view of this, the Chamber considers that it is not called upon to render specific advice as to the necessary and appropriate measures that the sponsoring State must take in order to fulfill its responsibilities under the Convention. * * *

229. The measures to be taken by the sponsoring State must be determined by that State itself within the framework of its legal system. This determination is, therefore, left to the discretion of the sponsoring State. Annex III, article 4, paragraph 4, of the Convention requires the sponsoring State to put in place laws and regulations and to take administrative measures that are "reasonably appropriate" so that it may be absolved from liability for damage caused by any failure of a contractor sponsored by it to comply with its obligations. The obligation is to act within its own legal system, taking into account, among other things, the particular characteristics of that system.

* * *

230. * * * The sponsoring State does not have an absolute discretion with respect to the action it is required to take * * *. In the sphere of the obligation to assist the Authority acting on behalf of mankind as a whole, while deciding what measures are reasonably appropriate, the sponsoring State must take into account, objectively, the relevant options in a manner that is reasonable, relevant and conducive to the benefit of mankind as a whole. It must act in good faith, especially when its action is likely to affect prejudicially the interests of mankind as a whole. The need to act in good faith is also underlined in articles 157, paragraph 4, and 300 of the Convention. Reasonableness and non-arbitrariness must remain the hallmarks of any action taken by the sponsoring State. * * *

* * *

242. For these reasons, THE CHAMBER,

* * *

3. Unanimously,

Replies to Question 1 submitted by the Council as follows:

Sponsoring States have two kinds of obligations under the Convention and related instruments:

A. _The obligation to ensure compliance by sponsored contractors with the terms of the contract and the obligations set out in the Convention and related instruments._

This is an obligation of "due diligence". The sponsoring State is bound to make best possible efforts to secure compliance by the sponsored contractors. The standard of due diligence may vary over time and depends on the level of risk and on the activities involved.

This "due diligence" obligation requires the sponsoring State to take measures within its legal system. These measures must consist of laws and regulations and administrative measures. The applicable standard is that the measures must be "reasonably appropriate".

B. _Direct obligations with which sponsoring States must comply independently of their obligation to ensure a certain conduct on the part of the sponsored contractors._

Compliance with these obligations may also be seen as a relevant factor in meeting the "due diligence" obligation of the sponsoring State. The most important direct obligations of the sponsoring State are:

(a) the obligation to assist the Authority * * *;

(b) the obligation to apply a precautionary approach as reflected in Principle 15 of the Rio Declaration and set out in the Nodules Regulations and the Sulphides Regulations; this obligation is also to be considered an integral part of the "due diligence" obligation of the sponsoring State and applicable beyond the scope of the two Regulations;

(c) the obligation to apply the "best environmental practices" set out in the Sulphides Regulations but equally applicable in the context of the Nodules Regulations;

(d) the obligation to adopt measures to ensure the provision of guarantees in the event of an emergency order by the Authority for protection of the marine environment; and

(e) the obligation to provide recourse for compensation.

The sponsoring State is under a due diligence obligation to ensure compliance by the sponsored contractor with its obligation to conduct an environmental impact assessment set out in section 1, paragraph 7, of the Annex to the 1994 Agreement. The obligation to conduct an environmental impact assessment is also a general obligation under customary law and is set out as a direct obligation for all States in article 206 of the Convention and as an aspect of the sponsoring State's obligation to assist the Authority under article 153, paragraph 4, of the Convention.

Obligations of both kinds apply equally to developed and developing States, unless specifically provided otherwise in the applicable provisions, such as Principle 15 of the Rio Declaration, referred to in the Nodules Regulations and the Sulphides Regulations, according to which States shall apply the precautionary approach "according to their capabilities".

The provisions of the Convention which take into consideration the special interests and needs of developing States should be effectively implemented with a view to enabling the developing States to participate in deep seabed mining on an equal footing with developed States.

4. Unanimously,

***Replies* to Question 2 submitted by the Council as follows:**

The liability of the sponsoring State arises from its failure to fulfill its obligations under the Convention and related instruments. Failure of the sponsored contractor to comply with its obligations does not in itself give rise to liability on the part of the sponsoring State.

The conditions for the liability of the sponsoring State to arise are:

(a) failure to carry out its responsibilities under the Convention; and

(b) occurrence of damage.

The liability of the sponsoring State for failure to comply with its due diligence obligations requires that a causal link be established between such failure and damage. Such liability is triggered by a damage caused by failure of the sponsored contractor to comply with its obligations.

The existence of a causal link between the sponsoring State's failure and the damage is required and cannot be presumed. The sponsoring State is absolved from liability if it has taken "all necessary and appropriate measures to secure effective compliance" by the sponsored contractor with its obligations. This exemption from liability does not apply to the failure of the sponsoring State to carry out its direct obligations.

* * *

The rules on liability set out in the Convention and related instruments are without prejudice to the rules of international law. Where the sponsoring State has met its obligations, damage caused by the sponsored contractor does not give rise to the sponsoring State's liability. If the sponsoring State has failed to fulfill its obligation but no damage has occurred, the consequences of such wrongful act are determined by customary international law.

* * *

5. Unanimously,

Replies to Question 3 submitted by the Council as follows:

The Convention requires the sponsoring State to adopt, within its legal system, laws and regulations and to take administrative measures that have two distinct functions, namely, to ensure compliance by the contractor with its obligations and to exempt the sponsoring State from liability.

The scope and extent of these laws and regulations and administrative measures depends on the legal system of the sponsoring State.

Such laws and regulations and administrative measures may include the establishment of enforcement mechanisms for active supervision of the activities of the sponsored contractor and for co-ordination between the activities of the sponsoring State and those of the Authority.

* * *

The sponsoring State does not have absolute discretion with respect to the adoption of laws and regulations and the taking of administrative measures. It must act in good faith, taking the various options into account in a manner that is reasonable, relevant and conducive to the benefit of mankind as a whole.

As regards the protection of the marine environment, the laws and regulations and administrative measures of the sponsoring State cannot be less stringent than those adopted by the Authority, or less effective than international rules, regulations and procedures.

* * *

It is inherent in the "due diligence" obligation of the sponsoring State to ensure that the obligations of a sponsored contractor are made enforceable.

Specific indications as to the contents of the domestic measures to be taken by the sponsoring State are given in various provisions of the Convention and related instruments. This applies, in particular, to the provision in article 39 of the Statute prescribing that decisions of the Chamber shall be enforceable in the territories of the States Parties, in the same manner as judgments and orders of the highest court of the State Party in whose territory the enforcement is sought.

* * *

NOTES AND QUESTIONS

1. What is the role of the requirement of state sponsorship? Under what circumstances may a state sponsor a mining corporation? As in the case of "flags of convenience," is there a likelihood of "sponsors of convenience" emerging on the international scene?

2. What are the "activities in the Area" that are the subject of state responsibility? Article 145 of the Convention requires the taking of "[n]ecessary measures . . . with respect to activities in the Area to ensure effective protection for the marine environment from harmful effects which may arise from such activities" and indicates that regulations should extend to "drilling, dredging, excavation, disposal of waste, construction and operation or maintenance of installations, pipelines and other devices related to such activities". In the view of the Chamber, these activities are included in the notion of "activities in the Area". Annex III, article 17, paragraph 2(f), of the Convention also refers to "shipboard processing immediately above a mine site of minerals derived from that mine site." While the Chamber excluded transportation of materials to land from the high seas, "transportation within that part of the high seas, when directly connected with extraction and lifting, should be included in activities in the Area," including transshipment between vessels and installations involved in the lifting from seabed and other ships or installations involved in preliminary processing and disposal of materials.

3. The LOS Convention specifies neither what constitutes compensable damage nor who may be entitled to claim compensation. The Chamber posits that: "It may be envisaged that the damage in question would include damage to the Area and its resources constituting the common heritage of mankind, and damage to the marine environment. Subjects entitled to claim compensation may include the Authority, entities engaged in deep seabed mining, other users of the sea, and coastal States." Para. 179. The Chamber goes on to support its view as follows:

> 180. No provision of the Convention can be read as explicitly entitling the Authority to make such a claim. It may, however, be argued that such entitlement is implicit in article 137, paragraph 2, of the Convention, which states that the Authority shall act "on behalf" of mankind. Each State Party may also be entitled to claim compensation in light of the *erga omnes* character of the obligations relating to preservation of the environment of the high seas and in the Area. In support of this view, reference may be made to article 48 of the ILC Articles on State Responsibility, which provides:

> Any State other than an injured State is entitled to invoke the responsibility of another State . . . if: (a) the obligation breached is owed to a group of States including that State, and is established for the protection

of a collective interest of the group; or (b) the obligation breached is owed to the international community as a whole.

4. Is the United States bound by the Chamber's interpretation of the treaty obligations?

CHAPTER 6

PRODUCING FOOD FROM THE OCEANS

∎ ∎ ∎

1. FROM STATE TO FEDERAL REGULATION OF FISHERIES

In 1976, Congress enacted the Fishery Conservation and Management Act (FCMA), extending U.S. fisheries jurisdiction seaward 200 miles from the coastline. The Act also created a framework for the governance of U.S. fisheries. Pressure on coastal fish stocks from foreign, distant-water fishing fleets had grown enormously in the previous decade. Members of Congress and representatives of the U.S. fishing industry were frustrated by the presence of foreign vessels like the F/V Taiyo Maru 28, arrested off of Maine in September 1974, for violating the contiguous fishing zone (see first case in Chapter 1). They believed the U.S. could not afford to wait for the conclusion of the Third U.N. Conference on the Law of the Sea (UNCLOS III), where nations were negotiating a comprehensive new treaty that would validate the emerging juridical concept of a 200-mile Exclusive Economic Zone (EEZ). The U.S. FCMA asserted exclusive management authority for all fish stocks other than "highly migratory species" of tuna. It thereby subjected any foreign fishing in the zone to U.S. licensing and regulations. As numerous other countries followed suit and declared similar exclusive fishery zones, the era of freedom of fishing on the high seas came rapidly to a close.

The FCMA's regulatory system for the domestic marine fishing industry covers all commercial and recreational fishing that occurs beyond state waters. Before 1976, management of commercial and sport fishing was almost exclusively the concern of the individual states, which adopted regulations to conserve fish stocks and to prevent conflicts among different sectors of the fishing industry. Occasionally, these regulations triggered retaliatory measures by neighboring states and constitutional challenges by stakeholders disadvantaged by these state laws.

A. THE LIMITS OF STATE FISHERIES AUTHORITY

Traditionally, the management of coastal and internal waters fisheries was the province of the individual coastal states. While state regulation was certainly common, the legal nature of the states' interests in fishery resources was always somewhat unclear. That they had an important interest was uncontested, at least from the time of the Supreme

Court's decision in Manchester v. Massachusetts, 139 U.S. 240 (1891), where the Court upheld Massachusetts' restrictions on the menhaden seine net fishery in Buzzards Bay. The Court held that if Congress "does not by affirmative legislation assert its right or will to assume control of menhaden fisheries in such bays, the right to control such fisheries must remain with the State which contains such bays." Id. at 266.

Confusion stemmed, at least in part, from the Court's earlier opinions in cases like McCready v. Virginia, 94 U.S. 391 (1876), upholding a Virginia law that prohibited citizens of other states from planting oysters in a Virginia tidewater river. There the Court held that the citizens of a state collectively own "the tide-waters * * * and the fish in them, so far as they are capable of ownership while running." Id. at 394. This ownership rationale has been used over the years in defense of state regulations that discriminated against out-of-state or nonresident interests. See Haavik v. Alaska Packers Assn., 263 U.S. 510 (1924) (upholding fishing licenses discriminating between residents and nonresidents); Foster Packing Co. v. Haydel, 278 U.S. 1 (1942) (Louisiana shrimp local processing requirement before out-of-state shipment violates Commerce Clause); Toomer v. Witsell, 334 U.S. 410 (1948) (shrimp landing and packing requirement violated Commerce Clause as did a nonresident licensing fee one hundred times greater than resident fee). As Justice Reed stated in his dissent in the equal protection case Takahashi v. Fish and Game Commission, 334 U.S. 410 (1948), "Whether the philosophical basis of * * * the power over fish and game is a theory of ownership or trusteeship for its citizens or residents or conservation of natural resources or protection of its * * * coasts is not material. The right to control [fishing] rests in sovereign governments and, in the United States, it rests with the individual states in the absence of federal action by treaty or otherwise." Id. at 428, n. 3.

In Douglas v. Seacoast Products, Inc., 431 U.S. 265 (1977), the Court considered the validity of two Virginia statutes that limited the right of nonresidents and aliens to catch menhaden in state coastal and inland waters. The statutes were challenged by a New Jersey-based company, owned almost exclusively by foreign stockholders, whose vessels obtained licenses from the federal government. Under the applicable statutes the vessels were enrolled and licensed to be employed in the mackerel fishery, a license that entitled the holder to catch fish of any description, 46 U.S.C. § 325 (1976). The company asserted that the Virginia statutes purporting to limit its fishing operations in Virginia coastal and inland waters were preempted by the federal enrollment and licensing statutes. The state argued that the federal statutes only granted the company the right to navigate in state waters and no more. The Court held, however, that the federal statute granted the company the right to fish in Virginia waters on the same terms as Virginia residents and thus the conflicting Virginia statute was preempted.

Although the case turned on the Supremacy Clause analysis of the state laws under the federal enrollment and licensing statutes, one very interesting aspect of the decision is the Court's treatment of the state's argument that the Submerged Lands Act of 1953, as well as a number of prior U. S. Supreme Court decisions, recognize that "the States have title or ownership interest in the fish swimming in their territorial waters." Id. at 283. And, "that because the States 'own' the fish, they may exclude federal licensees." Id. The Court made two responses to this argument. First, the Submerged Lands Act expressly retained for the federal government all constitutional powers of regulation and control for purposes of commerce, navigation, national defense, and international affairs. Since the grant of the federal fisheries license was pursuant to the federal government's commerce power, the Submerged Lands Act did not affect the validity of the license. Second, the Court said:

> * * * it is pure fantasy to talk of "owning" wild fish, birds, or animals. Neither the States nor the Federal Government, any more than a hopeful fisherman or hunter, has title to these creatures until they are reduced to possession by skillful capture. The "ownership" language of [earlier United States Supreme Court] cases such as those cited by appellant must be understood as no more than 19th-century legal fiction expressing "the importance to its people that a State have the power to preserve and regulate the exploitation of an important resource." [Citations omitted.] Under modern analysis, the question is simply whether the State has exercised its police power in conformity with the federal laws and Constitution * * * Virginia has failed to do so here.

While the Court may have laid to rest the ownership theory for constitutional analysis of state non-residency discriminations, the constitutional limits on state fisheries regulation continue to be tested. The first case presented here is from the early years of modern fisheries management, where ecological effects of fishing were just being recognized. The second is from a decade and a half after the enactment of the FCMA.

CORSA V. TAWES

United States District Court, District of Maryland, 1957
149 F.Supp. 771

SOBELOFF, CIRCUIT JUDGE.

By this suit an individual Delaware plaintiff and corporate plaintiffs of New Jersey and Delaware challenge the constitutionality of certain provisions of Maryland's fishing laws. Two sections of the law are under attack: one, Section 259 of Article 66C of the Annotated Code of Maryland 1951, prohibits the use of purse nets in any of the tidal waters of the State; the other, Section 258, excludes non-residents from fishing privileges in Maryland's tidal waters. Pursuant to Title 28 U.S.C.A. §§ 2281, 2284, this three-judge Court was convened.

The plaintiffs are engaged in various aspects of the menhaden fishing industry—some are menhaden fishing boat owners, others are lessees of such boats and operate processing plants out of the State. The individual plaintiff, Corsa, is a menhaden boat captain. The menhaden is a migratory fin fish which travels in large schools and is found during the summer months off the coast of Maryland and neighboring states, both within and beyond the three-mile belt, and to some extent in the Chesapeake Bay. They are commercially valuable as a source of fish oil and meal and other useful by-products, and plaintiffs' plants, after processing the fish, ship substantial quantities of these products in interstate commerce.

The established practice of the industry is to catch the fish by means of a purse net, for they cannot be caught economically in commercial quantities in any other way. When a school is sighted, the mother boat sends out two smaller seine boats with the purse net. This device, which is often a quarter of a mile in length and eighty feet deep, is designed to capture entire schools of menhaden in one quick operation. Rings on the lower edge of the net rest upon the ocean floor, and the net reaches to within one or two feet above sea bottom. When the school is encircled, the seine boats draw the ends of the net together, closing the purse and entrapping the fish within. Plaintiffs' operations, so far as Maryland territorial waters are concerned, are limited to the ocean strip; they do not fish in the Maryland portion of the Chesapeake Bay or its tributaries.

On June 26, 1956 Corsa's vessel, by use of a purse net, caught a load of menhaden in the Atlantic Ocean within three miles of the Maryland coast. He was thereupon served with a summons by an agent of the defendant Commission of Tidewater Fisheries of Maryland, charging him with violating Article 66C, Section 259, Annotated Code of Maryland 1951, the pertinent provisions of which are not limited to menhaden but prohibit the catching of any fin fish in Maryland tidal waters by use of a purse net. Criminal proceedings thereafter were instituted against Corsa in the Circuit Court for Worcester County.

This suit was brought by the plaintiffs to enjoin the enforcement of Section 259 on the grounds that it violates the due process clause of the 14th Amendment and unduly burdens interstate commerce in contravention of Article I, Section 8 of the United States Constitution. Others similarly engaged in the menhaden industry and faced with prosecution under Section 259 have joined as intervening plaintiffs. The criminal prosecution against Corsa has been continued by the Circuit Court of Worcester County awaiting the outcome of this case. Pending the proceeding in this Court further enforcement of the statute against the plaintiffs has, with the consent of the State, been temporarily restrained by us.

Since the decision in Manchester v. Commonwealth of Massachusetts, [1891], 139 U.S. 240, it has been beyond dispute that in the absence of conflicting Congressional legislation under the commerce clause, regulation of the coastal fisheries is within the police power of the individual states under the doctrine of Cooley v. Board of Wardens of Port of Philadelphia, 12 How. 299, 53 U.S. 299; Manchester v. Commonwealth of Massachusetts, supra; Skiriotes v. State of Florida, 313 U.S. 69, 75; Toomer v. Witsell, 334 U.S. 385, 393. Congress has not sought to impose uniformity, but has been content to leave the matter to local authority and has recently made this intention explicit in the Submerged Lands Act of 1953, Title 43 U.S.C.A. §§ 1301(e) and 1311(a).

While in the exercise of this power the State is not immune from recognized constitutional limitations, it is to be remembered that in the field of conservation, as in others, courts will not strike down legislative enactments as violative of due process unless the means chosen bear no reasonable relation to the objective sought to be accomplished. Lacoste v. Department of Conservation, 263 U.S. 545, 552; Bayside Fish Flour Co. v. Gentry, 297 U.S. 422, 427–428. Upon such concepts, prohibitions against the use and possession of purse nets and other particular kinds of fishing devices have been upheld. See Miller v. McLaughlin, 281 U.S. 261.

The objection to purse nets is said to be their excessive efficiency. In seeking to prove that the legislation in question bears no reasonable relation to conservation, it has been argued before us that restrictions upon the catching of some species of fish, including menhaden, have no effect upon conserving the supply. It is said that natural factors, beyond the control of man, such as weather, currents, and salinity, predominantly determine the abundance of fish, and it is the plaintiffs' insistence that the amount of menhaden withdrawn by fishing, regardless of the means employed, is infinitesimal in relation to the present menhaden population. Though there doubtless are differences of opinion among experts as to this and as to the need for and effectiveness of specific conservation measures, we cannot close our eyes to the manifold illustrations of experience, where man's over-exploitation has sharply diminished or even extinguished the supply of natural resources, wild game, and fish. As was said by the Supreme Court in Bayside Fish Flour Co. v. Gentry, supra, regarding such legislative enactments, ' * * * we cannot invalidate them because we might think, as appellant in effect urges, that they will fail or have failed of their purpose.' Moreover, plaintiffs' witnesses who expressed the opinion that such conservation measures in the case of menhaden are unavailing to achieve protection of the supply, admitted that man's activities are the only factor which may be controlled. While insisting that depletion of the supply of menhaden was a possibility too remote to merit serious consideration, they conceded that no resource is inexhaustible and that a point may be reached, due to man's fishing pressure or to natural causes, where further exploitation could bring serious results.

We think, however, that the protective hand of the State may be extended before the danger is unmistakably imminent. Conditions may go unnoticed so long that when the threat is demonstrated it is too late to avert the harm. One witness for the plaintiffs testified that no matter how much a supply may be reduced by over-fishing, provided that the stock is not completely annihilated, it may in time replenish itself. We need not quarrel with this statement of scientific opinion, but in the practical management of its resources, the State may conclude that the time for action is long before the destruction has gone that far. The State is interested not merely in the preservation of specimens for museums but in conserving and perpetuating a constant supply.

That a natural resource is subject to injury by causes beyond man's control is not a sufficient reason for us to require the State to refrain from such measures as may reasonably be taken to prevent unnecessary depredations by man. A similar aspect of human experience is in the field of medicine. While it is realized that human health and the life span are largely governed by factors beyond man's control, this realization is not deemed sufficient reason for excluding such efforts as the medical profession can make to protect man against disease and death.

If there is any fact so firmly fixed in the public consciousness as to justify judicial notice of it by judges residing in Maryland it is that the formulation and reformulation of policy, and the administration and enforcement of the State's fishing laws have been matters of perennial and spirited discussion and not infrequent legislation in the General Assembly.[1] Again and again elaborate studies have been made by public officers and commissions. Their recommendations have been debated by the commercial interests concerned, by sports fishermen, in the press and in the legislative chambers. The need for and the effectiveness of various measures regulating the practices, places, and instrumentalities of fishing, have been argued at length at almost every legislative session.

Opinion as to many of these matters is sharply divided, both as to whether particular regulatory provisions have the desired result upon fish population, and also as to the social policy that the State should follow in the management of its resources. It is a difficult problem or complex of problems, and the issues cannot be resolved for all time by any single enactment. Questions as to the adequacy of existing laws bring serious conflict, and no one is in a position to demonstrate absolutely at what point certain protective measures are no longer required. Wide fluctuation in the abundance of various species is not unknown and is a fact

---

[1] Where should these conflicts be resolved? Certainly the courts are not the appropriate forum. These matters are peculiarly legislative in character, and not within the judicial sphere.

acknowledged by the plaintiffs' witnesses. Men disagree as to what is a reasonable and benign utilization of natural resources, and what is destructive exploitation.

It was suggested that menhaden are not fit for human consumption and are not a chief source of food for edible species. Upon this foundation it is argued that menhaden are not a fit subject for conservation, and that to avoid violation of due process, we should carve out of the statutory prohibition against purse netting an exception for this particular fish. In addition to what we have already said there are further considerations which require us to deny this contention.

Considering that fishing has been a principal occupation of man for countless centuries it is astonishing how little precise information we have as to the habits, migrations, propagation, and proper methods of conserving the supply of fish generally. In this nebulous field the menhaden is no exception; indeed it may take rank among those about which least is known. In recent years, marine biologists have been conducting experiments to enlarge the sphere of knowledge. Some of these experiments were testified to by plaintiffs' witnesses, particularly with regard to the extent to which menhaden constitute a food supply for other fish. While these studies indicate that menhaden are not the principal food supply for food fish in Maryland waters, they are a source of some consequence.

A witness for plaintiff supported his testimony by reliance upon an examination of the contents of the stomachs of 750 blue fish caught in Maryland waters. Menhaden were found in 11 per cent of them, and many of the other 89 per cent contained no food. Reasoning from this slender basis he inferred that menhaden constitute but 11 per cent of the food supply of blue fish. Eleven per cent strikes us as non-inconsiderable, but the inference itself seems dubious. It is about as logical to draw from this meager data the broad conclusion that 11 per cent is the limit of the menhaden role in the blue fish diet, as it would be to interpret the experiment as establishing that considerable numbers of blue fish live without food.

Moreover, were the supply of menhaden diminished it might mean that the fish which feed in part upon menhaden would look to other sources, perhaps other food fish, as the witness Hollis supposed. Nor has it been ruled out that other non-edible fish which live in whole or in part on menhaden are themselves eaten by food fish. These assuredly are factors that may be considered. Neither the duration nor the scope of the scientific studies to which we have been directed is such that this court could find in them demonstration beyond further debate that, as applied to menhaden, the regulation here challenged has no reasonable relation to the ends sought to be achieved. The matter was at the time of its enactment and still is one fairly within the province of legislative judgment. We cannot say that the observation made in Manchester v. Commonwealth of Massachusetts, supra, that menhaden are food for other fish has been clearly proved to be erroneous. If there is new light that is claimed to cast doubt on these legislative assumptions, it should be called to the attention of the legislature. If the legislature deems it appropriate to carve out exceptions it may do so. It is not a judicial function to write amendments into the law to accord with the court's ideas of wisdom and appropriateness.

The difficulty of enforcement is also a salient feature entitled to weight. It was given point by the plaintiff Corsa while on the stand. Testifying that he was aware of the Maryland prohibition against purse nets within the three-mile belt, he stated with astonishing candor that he habitually fished for menhaden within this area whenever he thought he would not be apprehended. The difficulty of enforcement would be compounded if purse netting for menhaden were permitted within the three-mile coastal area. It is obvious that it would be more burdensome to police against purse netting for food fish if purse netters were permitted to enter the area in pursuit of menhaden; an enforcement official so testified.

Decision as to whether the State's interest requires a prohibition of all purse netting in this area in order to protect sports fishing, which itself supports a considerable industry in this State, is also a legislative prerogative. It is a legitimate objective for the State to sponsor sports fishing and the economic interests dependent upon it. Ocean City, the principal seacoast vacation resort of Maryland, is along this coast and numerous sport fishing boats sail from it. While there was testimony of isolated instances where menhaden fishermen operated side by side with game fishermen, the testimony also showed, and it is a matter of common knowledge, that sports fishermen seriously object to purse netting as interfering with their pursuits. The Chairman of the defendant Tidewater Fisheries Commission, Mr. John P. Tawes, testified that his office receives many such complaints from the sports fishermen.

Other witnesses testified that New York and New Jersey regulate purse netting within particular areas for the protection of the sports fishery. New York, they said, restricts purse netting in the vicinity of Coney Island, and New Jersey does not allow the practice within two miles of shore in certain areas. If Maryland deems it necessary or desirable to apply the restriction for the entire three-mile width of its short coastal jurisdiction, it may do so.

For these reasons we do not think that the Maryland statute, Section 259, as applied to fishing for menhaden, deprives the plaintiffs of their liberty or property without due process of law.

We now turn to the second objection raised by the plaintiffs, namely, that the purse-netting prohibition effects an undue burden upon interstate commerce. This, likewise, we find without merit.

Doubtless catching menhaden and processing them into useful products is a legitimate occupation and is commerce the interstate aspects of which cannot be interfered with arbitrarily. But the same Constitution which puts interstate commerce under the protection of Congress, recognizes the sovereignty of the states in local regulation for the protection of their natural resources. If the adverse effect on interstate commerce is only incidental and indirect and is outweighed by the local benefits which the statute is designed to achieve, the commerce clause will not render the enactment invalid. Southern Pacific Co. v. State of Arizona, 325 U.S. 761, 770–771. The local benefits to which we have previously referred clearly indicate a rational basis for the legislation here questioned, and that the interference with interstate commerce is merely incidental. There is nothing to prevent menhaden fishermen from seeking their catch beyond the three-mile belt, for the evidence shows that during the menhaden season the fish are present in plentiful numbers as far as seventy-five miles off coast, and it is the practice to fish up to at least eight miles out.

The plaintiff Corsa testified on direct examination that excluding him from the Maryland three-mile coastal belt would affect his catch 20 per cent. On cross-examination, however, he clarified his statement, saying that he merely meant that he caught 20 per cent of his catch opposite the Maryland shore both within and beyond the three-mile belt. Regardless of the actual per cent of loss caused, we may, in any event, assume that it would be more convenient, and financially advantageous for him and others engaged in the same business to fish close to shore. But we cannot say that the commerce clause requires the State to yield to mere convenience and advantage to particular industries, when it may reasonably consider conservation of paramount importance. Such questions are primarily of a local nature. In Toomer v. Witsell, supra, 334 U.S. at pages 394–395, which dealt with a poundage tax upon fish levied by South Carolina, the Court held that the tax was not a burden on interstate commerce because the taking of the fish occurred before interstate commerce began.

The legislative policy of Congress manifested in the Black Bass Act recently expanded to include other fish[4] is pertinent to the inquiry here, if

---

[4] C. 348, 61 Stat. 517, amended c. 911, 66 Stat. 736, 16 U.S.C.A. § 852. 'Transportation forbidden where law has been violated. It shall be unlawful for any person to deliver or knowingly receive for transportation, or knowingly to transport, by any means whatsoever, from any State, Territory, or the District of Columbia, to or through any other State, Territory, or the District of Columbia, or to or through any foreign country, any black bass or other fish, if (1) such transportation is contrary to the law of the State, Territory, or the District of Columbia from which such black bass or other fish is or is to be transported, or is contrary to other applicable law, or (2)

not controlling. That statute makes it unlawful for anyone to transport fish out of a state where such transportation is prohibited by state law or where the taking of fish is, in the first instance, prohibited by state law. It can be inferred that this statute broadly recognizes the right of the states to burden interstate commerce in fish by forbidding their transportation or by interposing restrictions earlier in the chain of events by prohibiting fishing altogether. It may at least be said that whatever burden Section 259 imposes upon interstate commerce by prohibiting purse netting has been condoned by the Congress.

We conclude, therefore, that Section 259 is not repugnant either to the due process clause of the 14th Amendment or to the commerce clause of the Constitution. The relief prayed, must therefore be denied.

The plaintiffs' challenge is aimed also at Section 258 of Article 66C, on the ground that it discriminates against non-residents in violation of the privileges and immunities clause of the 14th Amendment or, perhaps more accurately, Article IV, Section 2 of the Constitution of the United States. Inasmuch as the State has not attempted to enforce Section 258 against the plaintiffs and has indicated its intention not to do so, and the plaintiffs did not further press for an adjudication of their rights under Section 258, we do not decide the constitutional question raised as to this section in the bill of complaint. Even though serious constitutional doubts may be raised, see Toomer v. Witsell, supra, a court will not adjudicate constitutional issues unless necessary to dispose of the instant case.

Accordingly, the bill of complaint will be dismissed with costs.

* * *

NOTES AND QUESTIONS

1. Consider Judge Sobeloff's question in footnote 1. Do you agree that fisheries matters are particularly legislative in character? By "legislative" the judge presumably means they are matters of public policy, for which scientific studies are relevant but not dispositive. Do you think the Magnuson-Stevens Act creates a legislative-type process for resolving the kinds of "perennial and spirited" debates the judge was referring to?

2. Note how the judge considered the evidence plaintiff Corsa presented on whether menhaden are an important part of the diet of bluefish. Given the wisdom displayed in this paragraph, does the judge undermine his conclusion in footnote 1 that courts are not the appropriate forum for resolving conflicts over fishery regulations?

---

such black bass or other fish has been either caught, killed, taken, sold, purchased, possessed, or transported, at any time contrary to the law of the State, Territory, or the District of Columbia in which it was caught, killed, taken, sold, purchased, or possessed, or from which it was transport-ed or contrary to other applicable law; * * *.'

3. Two Supreme Court cases decided just prior to *Corsa*, discussed constitutional limitations on state regulation—Toomer v. Witsell, 334 U.S. 385 (1948) and Takahashi v. Fish and Game Commission, 334 U.S. 410 (1948)— were both decided in 1948. *Toomer* concerned a challenge to two South Carolina statutes, the first of which imposed a state license fee upon fishermen who were nonresidents of South Carolina that was one hundred times greater than the fee for South Carolina residents. The alleged justification for the difference was the need to conserve the supply of shrimp in South Carolina waters, a justification not supported by the record. The United States Supreme Court held that there was no reasonable relationship between any potential harm to the South Carolina shrimp fishery associated with the fishing efforts of nonresidents in South Carolina waters and the large difference in the fees charged residents and nonresidents. The nonresident licensing fee statute violated the Privileges and Immunities Clause, Art. IV, sec. 2, U.S. Constitution. A second issue in *Toomer* involved a South Carolina statute that required all boats licensed to trawl for shrimp in state waters to dock in a state port, unload the shrimp, and pack and stamp the catch before shipping or transporting the catch to another state. The Court found that the costs of nonresident shrimpers would be materially increased by requiring them to follow this procedure in South Carolina rather than unloading their catch in their out-of-state home ports. In addition, the effect of the statute was to divert to South Carolina ports work that might otherwise be done in the out-of-state ports. Such legislation, the Court held, imposes an improper burden on interstate commerce and thus violates the commerce clause of Art. I, § 8, U.S. Constitution.

In *Takahashi*, fishermen challenged a California statute barring the issuance of fishing licenses to resident aliens who were Japanese. The Court held that this statute violated the Equal Protection Clause of the Fourteenth Amendment. According to the Court, the Equal Protection Clause guaranteed resident aliens the same right to livelihoods as state citizens.

4. Prior to the Supreme Court's decision in *Douglas v. Seacoast Products*, states used the ownership theory to shield their treatment of out-of-state fishing vessels and companies from constitutional scrutiny. Since *Douglas*, states have had to craft their restrictions more carefully in order to enable their regulations to qualify as "evenhanded regulations" necessary for the conservation of natural resources. After a relatively quiet period in terms of constitutional claims against fishing regulations, new constitutional questions have begun to surface as states deal with dwindling fish stocks by, among other means, banning the use of particular fishing gears or fishing vessel type and/or size.

* * *

Once the Magnuson–Stevens Act was enacted, the Supremacy Clause became another constitutional basis for challenging state laws as the following case illustrates, featuring the now-familiar and highly contested waters of Nantucket Sound.

DAVROD CORPORATION V. COATES

United States Court of Appeals, First Circuit, 1992
971 F.2d 778

POLLAK, SENIOR DISTRICT JUDGE.

This case challenges the enforcement by an agency of the Commonwealth of Massachusetts—the Division of Marine Fisheries of the Department of Fisheries, Wildlife and Environmental Law—of certain rules governing fishing and the processing of fish in the coastal waters of Massachusetts. The rule that was the catalyst of this controversy is a regulation, adopted by the Division of Marine Fisheries in 1985, that bars vessels longer than ninety feet from fishing in Massachusetts waters. By a margin of six inches, Huntress I, a so-called "freezer-trawler" home-berthed at Point Judith, Rhode Island, ran afoul of the regulation and hence was barred by the Division from fishing for loligo squid in 1990 in the squid-rich waters of Nantucket Sound and Vineyard Sound. In the following year, the Division did give Huntress I a permit for at-sea processing (i.e., cleaning, freezing and packaging) of loligo squid caught by other vessels. But the 1991 permit set a cap of two hundred and fifty metric tons on the quantity of loligo squid Huntress I could process. In an action filed in the District Court for the District of Massachusetts, both the vessel-length limitation on fishing and the quantity limitation on at-sea processing were challenged on dual grounds. First, it was contended that the limitations constitute an undue burden on commerce. Second, it was contended that the Massachusetts limitations are incompatible with supervening, and hence preemptive, provisions of a federal statute, namely, the Fishery Conservation and Management Act (16 U.S.C. § 1851, *et seq.*), more generally known either as the Magnuson Act or as the FCMA.

* * *

Davrod's appeal and the Division's cross-appeal will be addressed in sequence. With respect to each, we will examine first the question whether the Fishery Conservation and Management Act (FCMA)—i.e., the Magnuson Act—is preemptive of state authority and hence wholly forecloses fisheries regulation by the Division in the waters adjacent to Nantucket and Martha's Vineyard. We consider the preemption issue first because, if Davrod is correct on what is essentially a question of statutory interpretation, it becomes unnecessary to consider Davrod's constitutional claims.

A. *The ninety-foot length limitation*

(1) Preemption

It is Davrod's submission that "the state regulation is preempted by federal law, namely, the Magnuson Fishery Conservation and Management Act." Brief of Appellant, p. 25.

The statute in question, enacted in 1976, was an elaborate and path-breaking legislative enterprise intended to protect the American fishing industry, and to preserve endangered stocks of fish, from what were perceived to be predatory incursions by foreign fishing fleets into American waters. The general design of the legislation was compendiously summarized by Congressman Forsythe of New Jersey in 1982 when explaining to his colleagues in the House of Representatives the need for certain strengthening amendments (128 *Cong. Rec.* 31695 (97th Cong.2d Sess., Dec. 16, 1982)):

The purpose of this historic act was to provide for the conservation and management of important fishery resources found off the coasts of the United States. The significance of this legislation can be appreciated by considering the state of the fishing industry and of the fisheries themselves in the 20 years which preceded enactment of this legislation. During that period world fish production multiplied more than threefold, from 20 million metric tons to approximately 72.4 million metric tons, yet the U.S. share of the catch hovered between 2 and 2.2 million metric tons. While the U.S. harvest of fish remained relatively stable, other nations with large and efficient fleets—many of which were subsidized—substantially increased the amount of fish harvested off our coasts. This situation led to the over-fishing of at least 10 major commercial stocks and caused serious economic consequences for the U.S. industry.

As a means of mitigating this over-fishing and of achieving the objective of effectively conserving fishery resources, the FCMA established a 197-mile fishery conservation zone adjacent to the 3-mile territorial sea. Approximately 20 percent of the world's fishery resources are contained within this 200-mile zone. The act also provided for the creation of eight regional fishery management councils which have the responsibility of developing fishery management plans. These plans identify, for each fishery, the optimum yield which could be harvested annually, the U.S. harvest, the total allowable level of foreign fishing, and the management rules governing foreign and domestic harvests. The Secretary of Commerce is responsible for the review and approval of each plan and the Secretary of State, in consultation with the Secretary of Commerce, is charged with the responsibility of allocating, among foreign nations, the surplus fish not harvested by U.S. fishermen.

As originally enacted, section 306(a) of the Magnuson Act–16 U.S.C. § 1856(a)—provided as follows with respect to "state jurisdiction:"

> Except as provided in subsection (b), nothing in this Act shall be construed as extending or diminishing the jurisdiction or authority of any State within its boundaries. No State may directly or indirectly regulate any fishing which is engaged in by any fishing vessel outside its boundaries, unless such vessel is registered under the laws of such State.[5]

The statutory reservation of "state jurisdiction" was explained in the House Report in the following terms (H. Rep. No. 94–445, p. 29) (Merchant Marine and Fisheries Committee, August 20, 1975), 2 U.S.C.C.A.N. 94th Cong.2d Sess.1976, pp. 593, 602:

> Under United States law, the biological resources within the territorial sea of the United States (i.e., out to 3 miles) are the management responsibility of the adjacent several States of the Union. Whatever regulation of both fishermen and fish harvest, that occurs in this area is as deemed necessary and appropriate by each concerned State.

Thus, the Magnuson Act as originally framed confirmed state jurisdiction over fisheries within a State's internal waters and, for coastal states, out to the three-mile limit. By an amendment adopted in 1983, Congress expanded the jurisdiction of coastal states by adding to section 306(a), 16 U.S.C. § 1856(a), the following language:

> (2) For the purposes of this chapter, except as provided in subsection (b) of this section, the jurisdiction and authority of a State shall extend—

>> (A) to any pocket of waters that is adjacent to the State and totally enclosed by lines delimiting the territorial sea of the United States pursuant to the Geneva Convention on the Territorial Sea and Contiguous Zone or any successor convention to which the United States is a party;

>> (B) with respect to the body of water commonly known as Nantucket Sound, to the pocket of water west of the seventieth meridian west of Greenwich . . .

This enlargement of State jurisdiction was explained by Congressman Studds of Massachusetts as follows:

---

[5] The exception contained in subsection (b) is one which, as described in the Senate Conference Report, was designed to permit the United States "to regulate a fishery . . . within a state's boundaries" when the Secretary of Commerce makes a finding that state regulatory action or omission "will substantially and adversely affect the carrying out of a fishery management plan covering such fishery." Senate Conference Report No. 94–711, March 24, 1976, page 55, 2 U.S.C.C.A.N., 94th Cong.2d Sess.1976, 679. No suggestion has been made in this case that the exception bears in any way on the issues presented.

Section 9 of the amendment addresses those limited situations where Federal waters are surrounded by State waters. The presence of these pockets creates incongruous fishery management schemes and presents significant problems in the area of fisheries law enforcement. Nantucket Sound is identical to these areas and creates the same fishery management problems, although not totally enclosed by the territorial sea. At the eastern edge of the sound the lines delimiting the territorial sea come within 1 mile of intersecting each other.

I am pleased that the amendment now before us includes language which I requested to resolve this problem. Quite simply, it treats Nantucket Sound as the other affected areas. Historically, the Massachusetts Division of Marine Fisheries provided the management of the fisheries in the sound, fisheries law enforcement, conducted stock assessments and other fishery related research, and continues to do so today. By insuring a unified fisheries management regime, this amendment will enhance fishery conservation and fisheries law enforcement in the sound.[6]

Thus, the Magnuson Act, as amended in 1983, does not preempt the Commonwealth's regulatory authority with respect to Massachusetts' offshore waters; to the contrary, section 1856(a), as amended, expressly confirms that regulatory authority. The district court correctly concluded that "Nantucket and Vineyard Sounds are subject to the jurisdiction of Massachusetts . . . "

Three years after § 1856(a) was amended, the Court had occasion, in United States v. Maine, 475 U.S. 89, 91 (1986), to consider the legal status of Vineyard Sound and the legal status of Nantucket Sound:

> . . . [T]he United States and Massachusetts in 1977 filed a joint motion for supplemental proceedings to determine the location of the Massachusetts coastline. After our appointment of a Special Master, the parties agreed on a partial settlement, which we approved in 1981. Left unresolved was the status of Vineyard Sound and Nantucket Sound, a dispute which gave rise to extensive hearings before the Special Master. The Master concluded that Vineyard Sound is a "historic bay" and therefore a part of the inland waters of Massachusetts. However, he reached a contrary conclusion concerning Nantucket Sound. Explaining that the decision concerning Vineyard Sound has only minimal practical significance,[2] the United States has taken no exception to the Master's report. Massachusetts, how-

---

[6] 128 *Cong. Rec.* 31685 (97th Cong.2d Sess., Dec. 16, 1982). A year later, section 1856(a) was again amended to extend state jurisdiction to cover portions of "the waters of Southeastern Alaska (for the purpose of regulating fishing for other than any species of crab)."

[2] According to the Solicitor General, all but 1,000 acres of the submerged lands of Vineyard Sound belong to the Commonwealth of Massachusetts as underlying territorial waters, even under its view that those waters are not inland.

ever, has excepted to that part of the report concerning Nantucket Sound. Specifically, although Massachusetts acquiesces in the determination that the doctrine of "historic title" does not support its claim, it continues to maintain that it has "ancient title" to Nantucket Sound.

The Court overruled Massachusetts' exception to the Special Master's report.

(2) Burden on Commerce

In Hyde Park Partners, L.P. v. Connolly, 839 F.2d 837, 843 (1st Cir.1988), we said:

> Article I, section 8 of the Constitution gives Congress "Power . . . [t]o regulate Commerce with foreign Nations, and among the several States, and with the Indian Tribes." If a state regulates interstate commerce in a manner inconsistent with that prescribed by Congress, the state regulation is preempted by the federal law, and is therefore constitutionally impermissible. Where Congress has not acted directly, nothing in the Commerce Clause explicitly prohibits the states from regulating interstate commerce. Nevertheless, the Supreme Court has established a doctrine, sometimes denominated the "dormant Commerce Clause," under which the states are barred from regulating interstate commerce in a manner which significantly interferes with the national economy.

In Maine v. Taylor, 477 U.S. 131, 138 (1986), the Supreme Court observed that:

> In determining whether a State has overstepped its role in regulating interstate commerce, this Court has distinguished between state statutes that burden interstate transactions only incidentally, and those that affirmatively discriminate against such transactions. While statutes in the first group violate the Commerce Clause only if the burdens they impose on interstate trade are "clearly excessive in relation to the putative local benefits," Pike v. Bruce Church, Inc., 397 U.S. 137, 142 (1970), statutes in the second group are subject to more demanding scrutiny. The Court explained in *Hughes v. Oklahoma,* 441 U.S. [322], at 336 (1979), that once a state law is shown to discriminate against interstate commerce "either on its face or in practical effect," the burden falls on the State to demonstrate both that the statute "serves a legitimate local purpose," and that this purpose could not be served as well by available nondiscriminatory means.

In challenging the district court's determination that "the 90-foot length restriction is a proper regulation of the means of catching fish, and is reasonably related to conservation of the fishery," Davrod contends that the length restriction must be judged under the strict *Hughes v. Oklahoma* standard. Davrod contends that, although the length limitation "may appear neutral on its face, it is discriminatory in practical effect because there are no Massachusetts freezer/trawler squid fishing vessels which are greater than 90-feet in length." Brief of Appellant, p. 18.

Davrod's attempt to characterize the length limitation as one aimed at "freezer-trawler squid fishing vessels" is not persuasive. The limitation—"vessels greater than ninety (90) feet registered length may not conduct fishing activities in any waters under the jurisdiction of this Commonwealth"—is comprehensive in its terms. And the district court found the limitation to be comprehensive in its actual application. "The 90-foot limitation applies to all types of fishing in Massachusetts waters and to the numerous Massachusetts fishing vessels over 90 feet in length." Both aspects of this finding are grounded in the record. The district court's recital that "[t]he 90-foot limitation applies to all types of fishing" is confirmed by the testimony of David E. Pierce, an aquatic biologist on the staff of the Division of Marine Fisheries: "The 90-foot limit was not applied to freezer-trawlers. It was applied to all vessels." The district court's reference to "the numerous Massachusetts fishing vessels over 90 feet in length" finds support in a 1990 Division of Marine Fisheries list of ninety vessels, with offshore lobster permits, exceeding ninety feet in length: seventy-one of the ninety vessels were berthed in Massachusetts, nineteen in other states. In short, the limitation "is nondiscriminatory, because it applies equally to both intrastate and interstate [enterprises]." Hyde Park Partners, supra, 839 F.2d at 844.

Davrod does make the further argument that the Massachusetts length limitation should be struck down because Judge Glasser, in the District Court for the Eastern District of New York, "found the identical New York 90-Foot Rule . . . violative of the Commerce Clause," Brief of Appellant, p. 16, in Atlantic Prince, Ltd. v. Jorling, 710 F.Supp. 893 (E.D.N.Y.1989). "Strange as it appears," says Davrod, "our Court below never mentioned or cited *Atlantic Prince* even though the facts and applicable law of that case are mirror images to the instant case." Brief of Appellant, p. 16.

Davrod's statement is doubly flawed: *First,* the district court, in its memorandum/order denying Davrod's motion for preliminary injunction, did discuss *Atlantic Prince. Second*—and more important—the record in *Atlantic Prince* was far from the "mirror image" of the record in this case. In *Atlantic Prince,* the challenged 1986 statute was adopted at a time when "there was, at most, only one New York commercial fishing vessel exceeding 90 feet in length." Atlantic Prince, 710 F.Supp. at 897. Moreover, Judge Glasser found, on the record before him, "that economic protectionism, and not environmental protection, motivated the State [of New

York] to enact this law." *Id.* at 902.[11] In the instant case, the district court, in denying a preliminary injunction against enforcement of the length limitation, noted that:

> In *Atlantic Prince,* the court found a clear paper trail showing the discriminatory intent of the New York authorities to protect local fishermen and processors from out-of-state competition. Among other circumstances it appeared that the New York 90-foot rule would not affect the local fleet, which contained no vessels over 90 feet in length.

No such heavy discriminatory footprints appear in this case. There are a number of Massachusetts fishing vessels over 90 feet in length which could be converted to squid fishing.

Given that the Massachusetts length limitation applies to all fishing vessels, wherever berthed, and given the further fact that Massachusetts fishing vessels longer than ninety feet greatly outnumber out-of-state vessels, it is apparent that the challenged regulation is not open to any general challenge that it burdens interstate commerce. If the limitation is considered more narrowly—i.e., as a regulation affecting squid fishing, rather than fishing generally—Huntress I is barred from participating, but it is also the case that Massachusetts fishing vessels exceeding ninety feet in length that are not now equipped for squid fishing but "which could be converted to squid fishing" are likewise barred. From this perspective, the strongest claim to be made against the length limitation is that it "burdens interstate transactions only incidentally," not that it "affirmatively discriminates against such transactions." Maine v. Taylor, supra, 477 U.S. at 138. This means that the operative test of the length limitation is not the strict *Hughes v. Oklahoma* standard, under which "the burden falls on the State to demonstrate both that the statute 'serves a legitimate local purpose,' and that this purpose could not be served as well by available non-discriminatory means." Maine v. Taylor, supra, 477 U.S. at 138. Rather, the test is whether "the burdens ... on interstate trade are 'clearly excessive in relation to the putative local benefits.' " *Ibid.*

The "putative local benefits" of the ninety-foot length limitation ... relate to conservation of the fish stock-a dominant regulatory concern at the state level as well as at the national level. With respect to loligo squid, Davrod contends that the Division of Marine Fisheries' conservation concern is over-blown. Dr. Steven Murawski, Chief of the Population Dynamics Branch of the National Marine Fisheries Service, at Woods Hole, testi-

---

[11] "Indeed," wrote Judge Glasser, "this case may present one of those 'rare instance[s] where a state artlessly discloses an avowed purpose to discriminate against interstate goods.' " *Id.* at 901 (quoting *Dean Milk Co. v. Madison,* 340 U.S. 349, 354 (1951)). It is also to be noted that it was NY which, in 1986, replicated Massachusetts' earlier (1985) rule, not vice-versa.

fied that he did not regard loligo squid, in Nantucket and Vineyard Sounds, as "threatened" or "endangered," words which he recognized as having "a legal connotation." App. 521. And when the district court inquired whether loligo squid are "at risk," Dr. Murawski responded: "I guess I will reserve judgment. I haven't looked at the information. We haven't developed sufficient information to come to a consensus on the status in that area." *Id.* at 521–22. When the district court rephrased the question, the following colloquy ensued:

> THE COURT: Let me change the question a little bit.
>
> If this regulation was ruled to be unconstitutional and these large freezer trawlers were permitted without restriction to fish in the Sound, would they put the stock of squid at risk?
>
> THE WITNESS: I guess I'd have to see it in the context of other regulations. If it was certainly an unrestricted access to all comers.
>
> One thing about squid, that stock is relatively healthy compared to the other fish in fishery sources like cod and haddock in this region. And so that's one of the reasons we have seen a greater interest in squid, just because all the alternatives have been over fished.
>
> So if, in fact, this is the only viable resource that is available to a lot of large trawlers, then, the potential certainly is there to collapse this stock quite quickly.
>
> THE COURT: Quite quickly?
>
> THE WITNESS: Yes. That's, in fact, what we saw when we had unrestricted fishing by the distant—the foreign fleets.

Id. at 522–23.

On the basis of this and other testimony, the district court made findings "Concerning Squid":

> Loligo squid are migratory, but their migrations are east and west, in contrast to the north-south migrations of other fish. They spend the winter on the continental shelf and return to shallow coastal estuaries in the spring to spawn. Nantucket Sound is one of the principal spawning grounds for loligo squid, which congregate there in greater concentration than anywhere else on the east coast of North America. (It is not clear whether spawning squid return to the place where they were themselves spawned.) Although the loligo squid in Nantucket sound represent only 14% of the squid population of the northeast Atlantic coast, 72% of the worldwide catch of this particular variety of squid is taken from Nantucket Sound. While the National Marine Fisheries Service has concluded that loligo squid in general is not endangered and is in fact underexploited, this conclusion relates to the deep water population off the northeastern coast of

the United States. The Chief of the Population Dynamics Branch, Dr. Murawski, testified, however, that these findings have no bearing on the risk to the population of squid in shallow enclosed waters, such as Nantucket Sound. He testified that permitting fishing in spawning grounds creates a risk of depletion of the stock of fish, which can happen rapidly. Squid have an average life expectancy of about eighteen months, and the population is subject to considerable seasonal variation. It is therefore difficult to tell whether or not the stock of squid is in imminent danger of depletion from overfishing.

The number of immature squid that appears in the nets greatly increases after the second week in June. Such squid would otherwise be likely to survive to maturity and spawn the following season.

The district court further found:

Squid are harvested by dragging large nets through the water. The capacity of a fishing vessel to catch squid is directly related to the size of the net it can drag, which in turn is a function of the horsepower of the vessel's engine. In general, larger vessels have greater horsepower than smaller ones, although this is not necessarily so.

In light of the testimony of record, these factual findings cannot be deemed clearly erroneous, see Maine v. Taylor, supra, 477 U.S. at 145, and they adequately support the district court's conclusions of law that "the 90-foot length restriction is a proper regulation of the means of catching fish, and is reasonably related to conservation of the fishery." The ninety-foot rule is not "clearly excessive in relation to the putative local benefits." Accordingly, the district court's rejection of Davrod's commerce clause challenge to the rule was warranted.

(3) Equal Protection

Given what we have determined with respect to the commerce clause challenge to the ninety-foot rule, the equal protection challenge need not detain us long. Suffice it to note that (1) the rule applies to all fishing vessels, including those engaged in fishing for loligo squid; (2) of the fishing vessels longer than ninety feet in length, far more of them are Massachusetts vessels than out-of-state vessels; (3) the district court found that "[t]here are a number of Massachusetts fishing vessels over 90 feet in length which could be converted to squid fishing;" and (4) the district court further found that "[t]he exception created by the defendants for purse seiners has in fact benefitted out-of-state fishermen." We conclude that the equal protection challenge is unavailing.

(4) Privileges and Immunities

Article IV, section 2, clause 1 of the Constitution provides that: "The citizens of each State shall be entitled to all privileges and immunities of citizens in the several States." The district court findings canvassed with respect to Davrod's commerce clause and equal protection clause claims make it plain that the Massachusetts length limitation does not differentiate among fishing vessels on the basis of the states in which they are berthed or the states of citizenship, residence or incorporation of the vessels' owners. The regulation "was evidently passed for the preservation of the fish, and makes no discrimination in favor of citizens of Massachusetts and against citizens of other States." Manchester v. Massachusetts, 139 U.S. 240, 265 (1891). Any privileges and immunities challenge would be without merit.

(5) Summary

In the foregoing portion of this opinion we have addressed the validity of the rule adopted by the Division of Marine Fisheries in 1985 barring fishing vessels longer than ninety feet from fishing in Massachusetts waters. As applied in 1990 to prevent Davrod's Huntress I, a ninety-foot-six-inch freezer/trawler, from fishing for loligo squid in Nantucket and Vineyard Sounds, the rule was challenged in the district court as preempted by the Magnuson Act and as violative of the commerce clause and the equal protection clause. The district court rejected those challenges. On Davrod's appeal, we have sustained the district court's ruling; and we have also foreclosed any possible challenge predicated on the privileges and immunities clause. In sum, we conclude that the Division's ninety-foot length limitation is free of legal infirmity: it is not preempted by federal legislation and it is not unconstitutional.

* * *

FRANK M. COFFIN, SENIOR CIRCUIT JUDGE (concurring in part and dissenting in part).

While agreeing with the results reached by my brethren on the equal protection, privileges and immunities and preemption questions, I respectfully disagree with their Commerce Clause analysis. I am unable to conclude that the 90-foot rule burdens interstate commerce only "incidentally." An array of evidence presented in the district court suggests the rule affirmatively discriminates in practical effect against out-of-state concerns.

As the majority points out, the vessel length limitation, as written, applies to Massachusetts and non-Massachusetts vessels, alike. However, there is persuasive evidence of its having a discriminatory effect on a particular class of out-of-state interests-squid freezer-trawlers such as plaintiffs' *Huntress I.* It is undisputed that the rule effectively bars all freezer-trawlers from squid fishing in Massachusetts waters. David Pierce, a senior fisheries manager for the state, offered uncontradicted testimony that there are no squid freezer-trawlers less than ninety feet long in the region. Moreover, it appears that there are no Massachusetts freezer-trawlers of any size. To the extent the rule bars squid freezer-trawlers from Massachusetts waters, it manifestly discriminates against out-of-state interests.

Focusing on the beneficiaries of the 90-foot rule, rather than those burdened by it, likewise suggests discriminatory effect. Plaintiffs contend that the length limitation was enacted, in part, to protect Massachusetts's shore-based squid processors from out-of-state competition. Since freezer-trawlers process their own catch, permitting such vessels to fish for squid will divert revenues from Massachusetts shore-based processors to out-of-state interests. Granted, not all shore-based squid processors are Massachusetts operations. It appears that at least one Rhode Island processor currently benefits from the vessel length limitation. Uncontradicted testimony in the district court, however, suggests that three of the four largest shore-based processors are, indeed, Massachusetts outfits. Thus, while the 90-foot rule does not benefit Massachusetts interests exclusively, it appears to do so disproportionately.

The district court's conclusion of no discriminatory effect (and, to some extent, the majority's as well) rests in part upon a determination that the rule would burden Massachusetts freezer-trawlers longer than ninety feet if there were any. When analyzing the practical effect of a regulation our focus ought to be on its actual as opposed to its theoretical impact. That there are no Massachusetts squid freezer-trawlers longer than ninety feet, nor, apparently, were there any at the time the regulation was promulgated, tends to highlight, rather than undercut, the discriminatory nature of the statute.

To be sure, the length limitation is neutral on its face; it does not single out non-Massachusetts freezer-trawlers for exclusion. Defendant produced a computer print-out suggesting that of the one hundred or so fishing boats longer than ninety feet licensed by the Massachusetts Division of Marine Fisheries, the majority are berthed in Massachusetts. On close analysis, though, this evidence proves exceedingly slight. Testimony offered in conjunction with the print-out suggests that the Massachusetts boats supposedly affected by the rule generally fish off shore in federal rather than Massachusetts waters. Defendant's star witness, David Pierce, explained that the printout (entitled "offshore lobster permits") identifies vessels licensed by the state to catch lobsters "in offshore grounds"—in "federal," as opposed to "inland," waters.

I suspect the 90-foot limitation affects Massachusetts boats in name only. There was no testimony at trial concerning any Massachusetts vessel adversely affected by the rule. Nor has any Massachusetts concern joined plaintiffs in challenging it. *See* Minnesota v. Clover Leaf Creamery

Co., 449 U.S. 456, 473 (1981).[24] This silence is all the more deafening in light of the ruckus raised by Massachusetts fishermen in response to a proposed *65*-foot vessel limitation. That this proposal was rejected in favor of the 90-foot one, with apparently no such hue and cry, casts further doubt as to the evenhandedness of the regulation.

In sum the record suggests: (1) the 90-foot rule adversely affects out-of-state interests; (2) it has no such impact on in-state ones; and (3) it disproportionately benefits local interests. On such a record, to label the effect on interstate commerce "incidental" seems to me to create too wide an escape hatch from the Commerce Clause. I would find affirmative discriminatory effect.[26]

This determination, of course, does not settle matters. "[O]nce a state law is shown to discriminate against interstate commerce 'either on its face or in practical effect,' the burden falls on the State to demonstrate both that the statute 'serves a legitimate local purpose,' and that this purpose could not be served as well by available nondiscriminatory means." Maine v. Taylor, 477 U.S. 131, 138 (1986) (quoting Hughes v. Oklahoma, 441 U.S. 322, 336 (1979)). The district court concluded that the 90-foot rule furthers a legitimate local purpose (squid conservation) and that "other conservation means would not impose a substantially lighter burden on interstate commerce."

I take no issue with the first of the district court's findings. Indeed, I agree wholeheartedly with it. The second, however, I find neither supported nor refuted by the record. (I therefore disagree with the majority's affirmance of it *supra,* at 791.) There was a good deal of testimony in the district court concerning the ineffectiveness of certain alternatives to the 90-foot rule. Defendant explained the drawbacks of regulations limiting the horsepower, door-size, gear-type, net/mesh-size, and total catch of squid fishing vessels. There was also some discussion of the difficulty of enforcing night and regional closures of overfished grounds. Doubtless the district court was well within its discretion to credit this testimony. I, however, am aware of no evidence that Massachusetts's conservationist

---

[24] There the Court upheld against a Commerce Clause attack a state regulation barring the sale of milk in Minnesota in non-reusable, non-returnable (i.e., plastic) containers. The Court found no evidence that Minnesota pulp and paper firms would gain and non-Minnesota firms lose, on balance, under the statute. In so concluding, it relied, in part, upon the fact that two of the dairies challenging the statute were in-state firms. "The existence of major in-state interests adversely affected by the Act is a powerful safeguard against legislative abuse," it reasoned. 449 U.S. at 473 n. 17. No such safeguard is present in this case.

[26] I also wish to express my disagreement with the majority's view of *Atlantic Prince v. Jorling,* 710 F.Supp. 893 (E.D.N.Y.1989). I find that case indistinguishable in any meaningful way from the one before us. In *Atlantic Prince,* the court found New York's 90-foot vessel length limitation to discriminate in practical effect against out-of-state interests. There, as here, the regulation was neutral on its face, but adversely affected out-of-state boats ("almost exclusively"). That there was also evidence of discriminatory intent in *Atlantic Prince* does not blunt the force of these similarities.

goals could not be served as well by shortening the squid fishing season for all vessels. . . .

In light of my conclusion of affirmative discriminatory effect, I would vacate and remand this branch of the case for further factfinding under *Taylor*. Specifically, I would ask the court to address the feasibility of replacing the 90-foot rule with a shortened squid fishing season.

* * *

NOTES AND QUESTIONS

1. Should Commerce Clause analysis turn on whether any in-state commercial vessels are affected by the fishing restriction? Which opinion in *Davrod* reflects a more searching review of the state regulation? Do you agree that the decision in Atlantic Prince, Ltd. v. Jorling was distinguishable? Can a state law be said to "regulate evenhandedly" when no state residents are constrained by it because none are engaged in the restricted fishery? Was the purpose of the Massachusetts statute to conserve the squid stock of Nantucket Sound? What if the goal was to conserve the squid as prey for recreational fishing in Massachusetts waters for the voraciously piscivorous bluefish?

2. Senior Circuit Judge Frank Coffin hailed from Maine, a state with a significant lobster industry, sensitive to economic competition from neighboring states and provinces and to the political power of processors and dealers. See Ron Formisano, The Great Lobster War (U. Mass. Press 1997)(out of state dealers and U.S. Justice Dept bring successful price-fixing suit against Maine lobster fishermen on strike to protest low ex vessel prices). Do you think Judge Coffin believed the 90-foot rule would never affect the 71 offshore lobster fishing vessels from Massachusetts because they were unlikely to convert to freezer-trawling? See also James M. Acheson, The Lobster Gangs of Maine (U. Press New Eng. 1988)(Maine lobster fishermen have traditionally used de facto territorial use rights to govern their extractive activities).

3. In Ampro Fisheries, Inc. v. Yaskin, 606 A.2d 1099 (NJ 1992), the court upheld regulations prohibiting purse-seine fishing for menhaden for other than bait purposes closer than 1.2 nautical miles from the Atlantic coastline. The rule also prohibited menhaden fishing for industrial production purposes in the Delaware, Raritan, and Sandy Hook Bays, fishing which had previously been permitted. The rule was enacted after the one New Jersey-based menhaden processing plant owned by Seacoast Products closed. The plaintiff, a Virginia commercial fishing company with plants in Virginia, North Carolina, and on the Gulf of Mexico, operated more than a dozen fishing vessels, nine of which were licensed by New Jersey for taking menhaden. The court found that Ampro's fishing rights were protected by the Commerce Clause but that the regulation did not discriminate against interstate commerce and was reasonable: "New Jersey should not be prevented from correcting inshore problems simply because New Jersey fleets have withdrawn from the state." The court noted also that other states in the region had already re-

stricted purse-seining close to shore. "Absent evidence of economic protectionism directed at out-of-state fishing fleets or clear abuse of authority, courts do well to recognize that the complex regulation of fisheries resources is within the primary jurisdiction of the councils established under state and federal law." Does New Jersey's closure of state waters to all commercial menhaden fishing once the only in-state commercial menhaden company has closed or left the state suggest a discriminatory intent or effect?

5. If the Mid–Atlantic Fishery Management Council were to adopt the Atlantic States Marine Fisheries Commission's recommended interstate menhaden plan, and that plan affirmatively allowed purse seining for menhaden and allocated a portion of the total annual quota to vessels of that gear type, would the New Jersey law discussed in *Ampro* be preempted by the FMP? See *Davrod,* supra, for discussion of plaintiff's claim of preemption by federal squid regulations.

6. Several states have adopted state-wide bans on the use of certain types of fishing nets, often of the so-called "gillnet" variety. In many instances, these acts have been adopted by citizen initiatives, after campaigns by sport fishing groups. The state courts have had little trouble upholding the constitutionality of these laws under current constitutional doctrine.

In Lane v. Chiles, 698 So.2d 260 (Fla. 1997), the Supreme Court of Florida upheld the constitutionality of Article X, § 16, of the Florida Constitution, the "net ban" amendment adopted through the citizen initiative process. The court found that fishing was not a fundamental right and commercial fishermen were not a suspect class, thus the rational basis test rather than the strict scrutiny standard applied. The court found that the net ban bore a reasonable relationship to a permissible governmental objective and was not discriminatory or oppressive. Lane also claimed that the ban deprived him of his right to due process by denying a right to engage in a lawful occupation and his right to possess and enjoy private property, his nets, which had been taken without just compensation. The court rejected these claims as well, finding:

> [A] state regulation violates a protected liberty interest if it completely interferes with the right to engage in a lawful occupation. However, that is not the case with respect to Article X Section 16. The amendment satisfies the rational basis test in that it serves to accomplish a legitimate governmental objective. The amendment is designed to conserve marine resources and it attempts to meet that objective by a reasonable regulation on commercial fishing. While citizens of differing views could argue the wisdom of the amendment, it would be hard to say that the amendment is without any rational basis.
>
> Moreover, the amendment does not completely prevent the plaintiffs from engaging in their chosen occupation. Commercial fishermen can still fish with nets beyond the territorial limits set by the amendment and they can still fish with nets of a smaller size within the territorial

limits. Article X, Section 16 is widely known as the "net ban amendment" but despite this reference the amendment does not actually ban all net fishing. It is more accurate to say the amendment restricts certain methods of net fishing.

* * * Article X, Section 16 is a valid exercise of the police power and it operates uniformly to prohibit all persons from using certain kinds of fishing equipment in certain areas of the State waters. It does not set arbitrary restrictions that apply only to some persons or classes of persons and not others.

Furthermore, the amendment does not prohibit all possible uses for the property and equipment in question. State statutes that limit fishing seasons, restrict permitted gear, and define certain zones for particular activities have been upheld. The State clearly has an interest in preserving and protecting the resources of the State, which are commonly owned by the people, and restrictions on the harvest of marine fish does not constitute a taking of property from particular individuals.

* * *

See A. Renard, Will Florida's New Net Ban Sink or Swim?: Exploring the Constitutional Challenges to State Marine Fishery Restrictions, 10 J. Land Use & Envtl. L. 273, 290 (1995).

7. Can a state charge non-resident commercial fishermen a higher license fee? See Oliver F.C. Murray, Note, Carlson v. State: Fair Fees for Fishing Far From Home, 4 Ocean & Coastal L.J. 157 (1998)(discussing Carlson v. Alaska Comm'l Fisheries Entry Comm'n, 919 P.2d1337 (Alask. 1996)).

8. In Crotty v. State of Connecticut, Connecticut succeeded in its *parens patriae* suit against New York on behalf of its commercial lobstermen. New York's nonresident lobster law allowed nonresident lobstermen to obtain a commercial lobster permit but excluded them from fishing in a restricted area of Long Island Sound. The court found that the statute violated the Privileges and Immunities Clause because New York failed to show the conservation necessity of the nonresident restriction. Connecticut's Commerce Clause claim was therefore moot. 346 F.3d 84 (2d Cir. 2003).

B. STATE JURISDICTION UNDER THE MAGNUSON–STEVENS ACT

As noted above, the authority of a state to regulate fishing vessels and activities within state waters is confirmed by section 306(a) of the Magnuson–Stevens Act, 16 U.S.C. § 1856(a). The one exception is the Secretary's power to preempt state authority and impose federal FMP regulations if the Secretary finds the state is undermining the effectiveness of an approved FMP and the fishery is largely a federal waters fishery. 16 U.S.C. § 1856(b). State authority to enforce regulations on fishing in the EEZ is provided for in section 306(a)(3), 16 U.S.C. § 1856(a)(3).

Prior to the 1976 enactment of the Act, many states regulated fisheries through laws that applied to fishing vessels licensed by state law, often without regard to where they fished, or through landing laws, which applied to all fish landed in the state regardless of where they were caught. In the FCMA of 1976, section 306(a) contained only a one sentence statement that a state *may not* regulate a fishing vessel outside the state's boundaries either directly or indirectly unless the vessel is registered under the laws of the state. Although short, the language was subject to different interpretations.

Congress' intent in the 1976 act apparently was to allow states to continue to regulate fishing beyond state waters through direct regulation and enforcement at sea and by dockside enforcement of possession and landing laws. The wording of the 1976 Act needed revision to more accurately reflect Congress' intent. Federal courts in Florida, a state with extensive fisheries regulation that often applies beyond state waters, concluded that section 306(a) reflected a Congressional intent to occupy the field of fisheries regulation in the EEZ, leaving no room for concurrent state jurisdiction, even for vessels registered under state laws. See Southeastern Fisheries Assoc. v. Chiles, 979 F.2d 1504 (11th Cir. 1992).

In an effort to clarify its intent, in the 1996 amendments Congress replaced this sentence with an affirmative statement: "A State *may* regulate a fishing vessel outside the boundaries of the State in the following circumstances * * * " This statement is then followed by three paragraphs that define three alternative scenarios under which a state could regulate fishing outside it waters.

The intent of this change was to make it clear to federal and state courts that Congress did not intend to displace all state regulation of fisheries in the EEZ, either by the enactment of the Magnuson–Stevens Act or by the Secretary of Commerce's approval of an FMP and implementing regulations. Such displacement would occur only if the state and federal regulations conflicted with one another.

16 U.S.C. § 1856. State Jurisdiction

(a) In general.

(1) Except as provided in subsection (b), nothing in this Act shall be construed as extending or diminishing the jurisdiction or authority of any State within its boundaries.

* * *

(3) A State may regulate a fishing vessel outside the boundaries of the State in the following circumstances:

(A) The fishing vessel is registered under the laws of that State, and (i) there is no fishery management plan or other applicable Federal fishing regulations for the fishery in which the vessel is operating; or (ii) the State's laws and regulations are consistent with the fishery management plan and applicable Federal fishing regulations for the fishery in which the vessel is operating.

(B) The fishery management plan for the fishery in which the fishing vessel is operating delegates management of the fishery to a State and the State's laws and regulations are consistent with such fishery management plan. If at any time the Secretary determines that a State law or regulation applicable to a fishing vessel under this circumstance is not consistent with the fishery management plan, the Secretary shall promptly notify the State and the appropriate Council of such determination and provide an opportunity for the State to correct any inconsistencies identified in the notification. If, after notice and opportunity for corrective action, the State does not correct the inconsistencies identified by the Secretary, the authority granted to the State under this subparagraph shall not apply until the Secretary and the appopriate Council find that the State has corrected the inconsistencies. For a fishery for which there was a fishery management plan in place on August 1, 1996 that did not delegate management of the fishery to a State as of that date, the authority provided by this subparagraph applies only if the Council approves the delegation of management of the fishery to the State by a three-quarters majority vote of the voting members of the Council.

(C) The fishing vessel is not registered under the laws of the State of Alaska and is operating in a fishery in the exclusive economic zone off Alaska for which there was no fishery management plan in place on August 1, 1996, and the Secretary and the North Pacific Council find that there is a legitimate interest of the State of Alaska in the conservation and management of such fishery. The authority provided under this subparagraph shall terminate when a fishery management plan under this Act is approved and implemented for such fishery.

(b) Exception.

(1) If the Secretary finds, after notice and an opportunity for a hearing in accordance with section 554 of title 5, United States Code, that—

(A) the fishing in a fishery, which is covered by a fishery management plan implemented under this Act, is engaged in predominately within the exclusive economic zone and beyond such zone; and

(B) any State has taken any action, or omitted to take any action, the results of which will substantially and adversely affect the carrying out of such fishery management plan; the Secretary shall promptly notify such State and the appropriate Council of such finding and of his intention to regulate the applicable fishery within the boundaries of such State (other than its internal waters), pursuant to such fishery management plan and the regulations promulgated to implement such plan.

(2) If the Secretary, pursuant to this subsection, assumes responsibility for the regulation of any fishery, the State involved may at any time thereafter apply to the Secretary for reinstatement of its authority over such fishery. If the Secretary finds that the reasons for which he assumed such regulation no longer prevail, he shall promptly terminate such regulation.

* * *

NOTES AND QUESTIONS

1. A court will resolve any legal challenge to a state's fisheries enforcement actions beyond state waters by determining how much authority Congress intended the states to have in the EEZ. As the principal statement of this intent, is section 306 clear? Does it dispel all uncertainty over the scope of state regulation in the EEZ?

2. Would defendants in state fisheries law enforcement actions still be able to argue that "registered under the laws of the state" refers to federal enrollment and licensing laws and not state fishing licensing laws? Such challenge is unlikely to succeed, as several courts have now concluded that the term covers a wide variety of state laws that require licenses, permits, and other acknowledgments from the state before a fishing vessel can operate in its waters. In People v. Weeren, 163 Cal. Rptr. 255, 607 P.2d 1279 (1990), cert. denied, 449 U.S. 839 (1980), the California Supreme Court reasoned that the Congress meant to incorporate the variety of state fishing registration schemes such as California's, "premis[ing] continued state jurisdiction on the undefined and generic concept of local 'registration'." Id. at 1286. This broad reading of the term was appropriate because to do otherwise, at least when no FMP was in place, would leave important food resources without effective controls.

3. As "registered under the laws of the state" is not defined in the Act, how broadly may states define vessel registration under their own laws? May they cover fishing vessels registered and home-ported in other states and owned by citizens of another state? For contrasting views on the Congressional intent behind the state registration requirement, compare Comment, The Fishery Conservation and Management Act of 1976: State Regulation of Fishing Beyond the Territorial Sea, 31 Me. L. Rev. 303 (1980) and Comment, Alaska's Regulation of King Crab on the Outer Continental Shelf, 6 U.C.L.A. Alaska L. Rev. 375, 405 (1977).

4. The 1996 amendments to section 306(a) allow a state to regulate fishing vessels in the EEZ that are not licensed or registered under state law. This may happen if the applicable Council adopts an FMP delegating management of the fishery to the state. The Council must approve the delegation by a three-quarters majority and the state's regulations must be consistent with the FMP. Section 306(a)(3)(B), 16 U.S.C. § 1856(a)(3)(B). This provision was modeled on a federal-state cooperative arrangement contained in the North Pacific Council's FMP for Alaska king and Tanner crabs. It extends the option of delegating EEZ management to all the Councils and their constituent states, not just the North Pacific Council and Alaska.

For a discussion of the policy implications of allowing state fishery regulation in the EEZ, see E.V.C. Greenberg and M. Shapiro, Federalism in the Fishery Conservation Zone: A New Role for the States in an Era of Regulatory Reform, 55 Cal. L. Rev. 641 (1982).

5. Although the Secretary's state waters preemption power under section 306(b), 16 U.S.C. § 1856(b), has been used infrequently, it remains an important lever to ensure that state law loopholes do not undermine enforcement of an FMP. The procedures and criteria for preemption are detailed in Subpart G of NOAA's regulations for the Magnuson-Stevens Act, 50 C.F.R. §§ 600.605-600.630 (2013). Should the Secretary's power to preempt state fisheries laws be limited to fisheries "predominately" within the EEZ or beyond?

C. THE TRANSITION FROM INTERNATIONAL FISHERIES MANAGEMENT

The 1976 FCMA adopted a de-centralized structure for regulating fisheries that directly involves fishermen, fish processors, and other members of the seafood and sports fishing industries. The law was thus an experiment in both foreign and domestic fisheries governance.

Although initial controversy over the Act focused on its impact on foreign fishing, implementation of the domestic regulatory program proved to be the most challenging. Congress has amended the Fishery Act many times since 1976 to adjust policies and requirements for allocating increasingly scarce fishery resources as the domestic industry expanded to fill the apparent void left by the departed foreign fleets. Meanwhile, the scientific underpinnings of fisheries management changed from a paradigm based on "maximum sustainable yield" as a production goal to a much more precautionary approach based on considerations of marine ecosystem health.

STATE OF MAINE V. KREPS

United States Court of Appeals, First Circuit, 1977
563 F.2d 1043

CAMPBELL, CIRCUIT JUDGE.

This is an action brought by the State of Maine[1] seeking a declaration that the quotas set by the United States Secretary of Commerce for foreign fishing of herring stock in certain offshore waters of Maine is in violation of the Fishery Conservation and Management Act, 16 U.S.C. § 1801 et seq., (the "Act"). The area, so called 5Z–SA6, includes the Georges Bank fishing grounds. The Secretary published regulations under the Act governing herring fishing on February 11, 1977, and the plaintiffs brought this challenge on February 28. At the plaintiffs' request, the Department of Commerce reexamined its quotas, and the district court postponed taking action until the review could be completed. The administrative record was reopened and hearings were held on April 19 and 20. On May 13, the Department announced it would not change the limits set on the herring catch, although it did make one minor modification in the rules for tabulating the catch. On July 18, the district court held a hearing and then granted defendant's motion for summary judgment and dismissed the complaint. Plaintiffs appealed, seeking expedited review of the dismissal in this court.

The Fishery Conservation and Management Act, enacted on April 13, 1976, established a two hundred mile fishery conservation zone around the United States within which fishing by foreign vessels is prohibited, except to the extent authorized by the Act. To coordinate the various economic, ecological, and other interests in fish stock, § 1852 of the Act established eight Regional Fishery Management Councils, each with authority to prepare and submit to the Secretary of Commerce a fishery management plan for the species within its geographical area. Section 1821(g) provides that in the event the Secretary is notified that eligible foreign vessels have applied for permission to fish in protected waters and she determines that a management plan for the species sought to be fished will not be prepared by the appropriate regional council before March 1, 1977, she shall prepare a preliminary fishery management plan for those species. To the extent practicable, the Secretary is required to

---

[1] The plaintiffs here are the State of Maine, its Governor, Commissioner of Marine Resources, and a representative to the New England Regional Fishery Management Council, who also is president of a canning business that will depend heavily on the herring catch.

adhere to the same procedures of notice and hearing and same substantive standards that the regional council would have used had it promulgated a plan. 16 U.S.C. §§ 1821(g); 1851–61.

Before enactment of the Fishery Conservation and Management Act, the Georges Bank fishery had been managed by the International Commission for the Northwest Atlantic Fisheries (ICNAF), an international organization from which the United States withdrew at the end of 1976. ICNAF had a spotty record as a conservator of fishing resources, and in particular had permitted the Georges Bank herring stock to sink below acceptable levels.[2] In recent years, however, the member nations had begun to recognize the long term dangers of a depleted fishing stock and gradually reduced their catches. At a meeting of ICNAF delegates in June, 1976, the scientific advisory committee reported that 50,000 metric tons (m.t.) could be taken from the Georges Bank herring stock in 1977 without further decreasing the school population. The Commission agreed to reduce this quota to 33,000 m.t. to permit some replenishment. The allocation of the agreed maximum catch among the member nations took place at a meeting in December, 1976, shortly before the American with-

---

[2] According to Dr. Vaughn Anthony, the Deputy Chief of the Northeast Fisheries Center of the National Marine Fisheries Service and a member of the herring working group of ICNAF, the Commission had achieved the following management record:

Year	Scientists' Recommended Catch	ICNAF Quota	Catch	Potential New Stock	Stock Size at End of Season
1972	50–90	150	174	96	146
1973	83–135	150	199	496	359
1974	150	150	146	85	285
1975	90–150	150	146	85	204
1976	60	60	42	85	234
1977	50	33	28 *	85 *	260 *

all figures in metric tons   * predictions

Scientists advising ICNAF had determined that a stock size below 225,000 m.t. might lead to "recruitment failure", or irreversible depletion. Dr. Anthony testified that the catches in excess of quota for 1972 and 1973 were caused by ICNAF's inability to control the fishing of the German Democratic Republic, not then a member of ICNAF. The estimated catch for 1977, which is lower than the quota, is based on an expectation that the United States fishermen will not consume their entire allocation. The variations in stock size that occurred in spite of fairly similar catches was caused by fluctuations in the number of fish joining the school each year. Dr. Anthony indicated that scientists were unable to anticipate the size of annual recruitment to the stock with great exactitude.

The overall failure of ICNAF to manage the fishing resources under its control, particularly the haddock stock, was a factor in Congressional enactment of the Fishery Conservation and Management Act. See, e. g., 16 U.S.C. s 1801(a)(4); H.R.Rep.No.445, 94th Cong., 1st Sess. 48 (1975); Senate Commerce Comm., Memorandum on S. 961 to the Senate Foreign Relations Comm., 94th Cong., 1st Sess. 3–4 (Comm.Print 1975).

drawal. The United States originally had sought a quota of 18,000 m.t. for its own fishermen but agreed to a reduction to 12,000 m.t. in return for economic concessions from the Federal Republic of Germany and acceptance by all the members of a limited fishing season for foreign fishermen.

Because the New England Regional Council would not be able to prepare a management plan for Georges Bank by the March 1 deadline, and in anticipation of applications to fish the area by foreign vessels, the Secretary prepared a draft preliminary management plan in September, 1976. Hearings were held, comments were received and responded to, and the final plan was published in February, 1977. The Secretary then determined the "optimum yield" of herring for the duration of the plan, a key factor which the Act requires to be ascertained.[4] She also estimated

---

[4] Maximum sustainable yield (MSY), a term not defined by the Act, refers to a scientific appraisal of "the safe upper limit of harvest which can be taken consistently year after year without diminishing the stock so that the stock is truly inexhaustible and perpetually renewable." H.R.Rep.No.445, 94th Cong., 1st Sess. 48 (1975). Counsel for both sides informed this court at oral argument that, by its reference to a constant amount to be taken each year, maximum sustainable yield referred to a healthy, not a depleted stock. In the case of Georges Bank herring, Dr. Anthony testified during the April administrative hearing that MSY would be 100,000 to 150,000 m.t., if the presently depleted stock were to grow to its proper size, estimated to be 350,000 to 500,000 m.t.

The legislative history of the Fishery Conservation and Management Act indicates both Congressional recognition of the precise scientific meaning of maximum sustainable yield and dissatisfaction with the manner ICNAF had employed the concept:

> The concept of maximum sustainable yield is well understood, not only by expert fisheries biologists, but by fishermen also. For this reason, there was considerable support before the Committee for adopting MSY as the basis for management. On the other hand, a responsible body of opinion supported the proposition that the Committee should not give statutory recognition to MSY since it was felt that the concept had been discredited as an effective management tool, largely as a result of the notable failures of the International Commission for the Northwest Atlantic Fisheries under the ICNAF Convention. The Committee believes that the failure of ICNAF has not discredited MSY as a management tool, but rather points up clearly the fact that MSY is only a tool and cannot be expected to accomplish anything in the absence of a sound, comprehensive management system. The Committee believes that MSY must be established for each managed species before intelligent decisions regarding optimization can be achieved.

H.R.Rep.No. 445, 94th Cong., 1st Sess. 48 (1975).

The legislative history then describes in detail the manner in which the optimum yield standard is to apply:

> Once the MSY of the fisheries or stock has been determined with reasonable scientific accuracy, and the same determination made with respect to the total biomass of an ocean area where many different, but inter-related fisheries occur, the developer of a management plan can begin to think in terms of the optimum sustainable yield (OSY). Thus while biologists in the past have tended to regard any unused surplus of a fishery as waste, the resource manager may well determine that a surplus harvest below MSY will ultimately enhance not only the specific stock under management, but also the entire biomass. Conversely, the fisheries manager may determine that the surplus harvest of the entire biomass must be reduced substantially below MSY, in order to restore a valuable depleted stock which is taken incidentally to the harvesting of other species in this biomass. An example of such a situation has occurred in the Northwest Atlantic where mindless overfishing for haddock has virtually wiped out the species. A zero quota for haddock will not permit that species to restore itself since other fisheries in the Northwest Atlantic cannot be conducted without taking haddock. . . .

that a portion of this quota would be harvested by United States fishermen and remitted the balance to be apportioned among foreign fishermen.[5] Following the ICNAF guidelines, the Secretary determined that the optimum yield for Georges Bank herring in 1977 would be 33,000 m.t. and the United States share would be 12,000 m.t. The remainder was allocated according to the ICNAF quotas negotiated in December.

The evidence before the Secretary indicated that present stocks in Georges Bank approximate 218,000 m.t., 7,000 m.t. below the level at which recruitment failure of herring is feared (225,000 m.t.). It was projected that an allowed yield of 33,000 m.t. in 1977 will permit the herring stocks to increase by some ten to thirteen percent by 1978, bringing the stock to a level of 247,000 m.t. Even so, that level will be substantially below the 350,000–500,000 m.t. level which experts regard as an appropriate, healthy stock for the area. Until the stock can be rebuilt to that level, it would obviously be imprudent to allow fishermen to catch herring at the rate of 100,000 to 150,000 m.t. per annum, the figures said by the Government's expert to be the area's "maximum sustainable yield".

Maine argues that since the stock has declined to well below the norm for a healthy stock, and is indeed below the 225,000 m.t. "danger" level, the Act must be construed to ban foreign fishing altogether. The allowable level of foreign fishing under the statute "shall be that portion of the optimum yield . . . which will not be harvested by vessels of the United States". § 1821(d). Maine attacks the Secretary's 33,000 m.t. optimum yield figure as too high, and the Secretary's allocation of 12,000 m.t. to U.S. vessels as too low.

Maine's second point is readily disposed of. The Secretary's assessment of domestic fishing potential was supported by substantial evidence in the record. American fishermen have taken an average of 2,000 m.t. annually from Georges Bank since 1960 and have never exceeded an annual catch of 4,600 m.t. during that period. In 1976 domestic fishermen took 735 m.t. from the stock. Although evidence was presented to the agency indicating a growing desire on the part of American fishermen to increase their herring take from Georges Bank, the Secretary heard and credited evidence as to the economic infeasibility of greatly expanded fish-

---

The concept of optimum sustainable yield is, however, broader than the consideration of the fish stock and takes into account the economic well-being of the commercial fisherman, the interests of recreational fishermen, and the welfare of the nation and its consumers. The optimum sustainable yield of any given fishery or region will be a carefully defined deviation from MSY in order to respond to the unique problems of that fishery or region.

Id. at 48–49.

[5] 16 U.S.C. s 1821(d) provides:

The total allowable level of foreign fishing, if any, with respect to any fishery subject to the exclusive fishery management authority of the United States, shall be that portion of the optimum yield of such fishery which will not be harvested by vessels of the United States, as determined in accordance with the provisions of this chapter.

ing operations at this time. Contrary to Maine's contention, the plaintiffs had sufficient notice that economic considerations would be a factor in weighing the potential domestic catch. The district court properly sustained the portion of the preliminary management plan that estimated the potential American catch for 1977. This figure, of course, is subject to further consideration for future years.

Turning to Maine's attack on the optimum yield estimate, it is to be noted that Maine does not quarrel with the basic data testified to by Dr. Anthony, the Government's expert. Maine accepts his thesis that a yield of 33,000 m.t. will allow for at least a ten percent recoupment of the stock in 1977, although it points out that the stock is now dangerously depressed.

The state's chief contention is that where an area's stock is so depressed as to be unable to maintain fishing at the level of the maximum sustainable yield, priority has to be given to cultivating a surplus so as to rebuild the stock as rapidly as possible, with only U.S. fishing to be allowed.

So stated, we have to agree with the district court that the argument is without support in the Act. We find nothing in the Act which declares that all foreign fishing is to be disallowed whenever stocks are incapable of sustaining the MSY. The statute does, it is true, give first crack at the "optimum yield" to U.S. fishermen. Only such portion thereof "as will not be harvested by vessels of the United States" is available to foreign vessels. But we find nothing in the Act which prescribes a particular annual rate at which a below-par stock need be rebuilt. To be sure, the strong conservation and management aims of the Act clearly preclude the setting of an optimum yield which permits overfishing, see 16 U.S.C. § 1801; but the Secretary's present allotment is based on credible evidence that 33,000 m.t. will allow a ten percent increase in the stock. We cannot say this rate of increase is too slight to promote the purposes of the Act.

Maine is on firmer ground, however, insofar as it questions the adequacy of the present record to show that the Secretary considered fully the Act's definition of optimum yield in promulgating the 33,000 m.t. figure. The "optimum" yield, as defined in the Act, must be selected "on the basis of" the maximum sustainable yield as modified by "any relevant economic, social or ecological factor". In addition, the optimum yield must be such as "will provide the greatest overall benefit to the Nation, with particular reference to food production and recreational opportunities". Arguably the Nation would be better benefitted by leaving in the sea the 21,000 m.t. allotted to foreign vessels, thus allowing a faster buildup of stock. Or, put another way, the optimum yield figure should perhaps be no higher than what is likely to be taken by United States vessels, thus leaving nothing for the foreigners. There is virtually nothing in the record to reflect a rational weighing of these considerations by the Secretary. To the contrary, there is some suggestion that the Secretary may have uncritically taken ICNAF's total allowable catch figure on the assumption that optimum yield and total allowable catch were the same thing. However, optimum yield requires a finding, among others, that the figure selected reflects the greatest overall benefit to this nation.

This is not to question that the "greatest overall benefit to the Nation" criterion, and the companion reference to "relevant economic, social or ecological" factors, both found in the 16 U.S.C. § 1802(18) definition of "optimum" yield, are broad enough to include such national benefits as are to be derived from permitting foreign fishing. While the Act, in its preamble, makes clear that it was enacted in reaction to the ineffectiveness of international fishery agreements to prevent overfishing, § 1801(a), it speaks of a purpose, among others, to encourage such international agreements in the future, and to encourage continued active United States efforts to obtain an internationally acceptable treaty at the upcoming Third United Nations Conference on the Law of the Sea. § 1801(c)(5). Congress plainly did not intend the cardinal aim of the Act the development of a United States' controlled fishing conservation and management program designed to prevent overfishing and to rebuild depleted stocks to be subordinated to the interests of foreign nations. But within a framework of progress towards this goal, the Secretary is directed and empowered within specified limits to accommodate foreign fishing, §§ 1801(c)(4); 1821. We find no congressional purpose that she disregard the benefits to be derived from cooperating with other nations. American consumers depend not only on United States producers; they benefit from our trade with the rest of the world. United States fishermen as well as consumers benefit from international cooperation. Indeed, the continued existence of fish stocks throughout the oceans of the world may well be dependent on actions by foreign nations as well as ourselves. Management of the oceans' fish resources cannot be accomplished solely within our own coastal areas. We think Congress did not require the Secretary to set optimum yield figures entirely without regard to the effects upon this country of allowing or denying foreign fishing.

On the other hand, Congress has expressly directed the Secretary to consider the overall welfare of the United States in setting the optimum yield figure. Our nation's welfare may be considered in terms of its foreign relations as well as its purely domestic needs, but the touchstone is the benefit of this nation, not that of some other. Moreover, by "particular reference to the food supply", Congress underscored that priority was to be given to food requirements: the nation's fisheries were not, for example, to be swapped for a world banking agreement. The international considerations that are given weight must ordinarily relate to fishing, fish and other activities and products pertaining to the food supply (apart from any recreational benefits).

While we, therefore, conclude that the Secretary could consider the effect of international factors on this nation's welfare in setting an optimum yield figure, we are troubled by the lack of information in the record indicating what factors the Secretary considered in the instant case. The figure of 33,000 m.t. adopted by the Secretary was taken unaltered from the quota determined by ICNAF. The final plan stated:

> Since the US withdrew from ICNAF, the decisions made in that forum are no longer binding. However, the scientific assessments made in ICNAF are the bases of the PMP.

The record would indicate that more than the scientific assessments of ICNAF went into the plan. For example, the Secretary accepted the compromise figure for the United States catch set by the December ICNAF meeting, even though the bargaining over the figure had little to do with scientific judgment.

Before the draft plan had become final, several persons criticized the allotment to foreign fishermen as not justified by corresponding benefits to the United States. The point was made most directly in a comment letter from the National Coalition for Maine Conservation, Inc.:

> It is inaccurate and misleading to characterize ICNAF's determination of total allowable catch as a "determination of optimum yield", because optimum yield is a defined term in the Act and the considerations taken into account by ICNAF bear no relation to the considerations required by the Act to be taken into account in determining optimum yield as defined therein.

The Department of Commerce responded:

> The (ICNAF total allowable catch) figures are determined by USA scientists working in cooperation with qualified scientists from other nations as part of a long-range program to maximize productivity from the resource given a set of management goals or options agreed upon. As such, the TAC should provide the greatest "overall benefit to the nation" as long as USA requirements (which are based on socio-economic considerations) are first satisfied.

After the plan was published in final form, representatives of Maine renewed the criticism. At the hearing held on April 19, Mr. William Gordon, the Regional Director for the National Marine Fisheries Service and a member of the American delegation to the December, 1976, ICNAF meeting, explained that the allocation to the Federal Republic of Germany was based on reciprocal economic benefits but that the balance of the foreign quota was intended only to accommodate those countries with historical fisheries in the area.

None of this evidence indicates by itself that the Secretary ignored her statutory duty to weigh benefits to the United States in allocating a portion of the 1977 herring catch to foreign fishermen. In adopting the ICNAF quotas, the Secretary may very well have observed international considerations not immediately apparent to the United States delegation. The Secretary certainly is in a much better position to observe interrelationships among particular international economic concessions that would lead to significant advantages for the nation. At the same time, these considerations are not apparent from the record, with the exception of the advantages obtainable from the Federal Republic of Germany allocation.

Where Congress has vested the authority to resolve technical questions of fact in a specialized administrative body with experience and expertise in that field, considerable deference is due its conclusions. At the same time, the record must provide some basis for a reviewing court to determine that the agency has exercised its discretion consistently with standards set by Congress. Judicial review cannot take place in a vacuum (citations omitted).

The foregoing leads us to this conclusion: while Maine has not at this time persuaded us that the Secretary's optimum yield figure is necessarily "arbitrary, capricious, an abuse of discretion, or otherwise not in accordance with law", 5 U.S.C. § 706(2)(A), it has persuaded us that, in order to obtain the judicial review to which Maine is entitled, the Secretary must provide some "additional explanation of the reasons for the agency decision." There is sufficient indication of possible misunderstanding on the Secretary's part of the criteria applicable to the "optimum" yield figure to render it improper for a court merely to rely upon the presumptive correctness of the Secretary's bottom line result. We think the Secretary should be asked to supplement the record to provide an explanation of the basis of her optimum yield determination insofar as it exceeds amounts needed by United States fishermen and provides for less than the optimum rebuilding of the stock.

On the other hand, although the present record is inadequate, leading us to require the Secretary to address the deficiencies, it does not follow that Maine has as yet made a showing which will entitle it to receive equitable relief, in the form of an injunction against implementation of the preliminary management plan pending production of the Secretary's supplemental explanation. Because the foreign fishing season is hard upon us and of limited duration, interference with implementation would come close to reversing the Secretary's decision. Having in mind both plaintiff's burden of proof and the broad implementation authority vested in the Secretary by Congress, we cannot at present say that it is unlikely that the Secretary can demonstrate a reasonable basis for the decision, or that it is likely that domestic fishermen will suffer irreversible harm from the plan. While the Act requires a determination reflecting substantive consideration, something not satisfied by resort to a conclusory verbal formula, the likelihood of the Secretary specifying relevant factors which would support a conclusion that setting the yield at this figure, which will allocate a portion of the Georges Bank herring catch to foreign fishermen, will serve "the greatest overall benefit to the Nation," would seem substantial. And both parties conceded that the present quota would probably permit some rebuilding of the stock, thereby increasing the resource available to domestic fishermen in the future. In light of these considerations, we are constrained to let the present plan go forward at least until such time as the Secretary supplements the record and it can be ascertained whether or not the 33,000 m.t. figure is rationally supported. However, Maine is entitled to speedy supplementation of the present record, and to further review thereof in the district court, with all reasonable dispatch. Accordingly, in remanding we direct the district court to order forthwith that the Secretary specify and file in court within ten days from the date of the present judgment the reasons which led her to conclude that an optimum yield figure of 33,000 m.t., which allows foreign fishermen to take herring from a depleted stock, provides the greatest overall benefit to the Nation, with particular reference to food supplies and recreation, and including relevant economic, social or ecological factors.

NOTES AND QUESTIONS

1. Why did the United States withdraw from ICNAF? As a signatory to the treaty since 1949, the United States was actively involved in managing the foreign fishing fleets off the U.S. coast and assessing the fish stocks through the Northeast Fisheries Science Center in Woods Hole, Massachusetts, where Dr. Anthony was the chief stock assessment scientist for herring. What does the chart comparing the recommendations, quotas, and actual catches suggest?

2. In the years after 1977, could the Secretary of Commerce have continued to set the OY for Georges Bank herring high enough to allow a "total allowable level of foreign fishing" (TALFF)?

3. In Associated Vessel Services, Inc. v. Verity, the court held that the FCMA did not create a cause of action for foreign fishing companies to challenge TALFFs set by the Secretary of State in consultation with the Secretary of Commerce. 688 F.Supp. 13 (D.D.C. 1980). At the time, the secretaries were following a "fish and chips" policy, allocating surplus to foreign fishing fleets in proportion to the amount of U.S.-caught fish products their countries were importing.

* * *

In 1983, when President Ronald Reagan by proclamation established a 200-mile Exclusive Economic Zone, Proclamation No. 5030, 48 Fed. Reg. 10601 (1983), the Act was amended to reflect this change in nomenclature.

In 1990, further amendments brought tunas and other highly migratory fish species under U.S. management authority. By the late 1990s, the policy emphasis had shifted from 'Americanization' of all U.S. fisheries to the conservation and rebuilding of overfished fish stocks.

2. EVOLUTION OF THE FCMA

The 1996 Sustainable Fisheries Act, Pub. L. No. 104–294, made major substantive changes to the FCMA, to refocus implementation toward the goals of conservation and ecosystem protection. The Act was renamed in 1980 in honor of the late Senator Warren G. Magnuson, its original sponsor in the Senate, and again in 1996, to honor Alaska's Senator Ted Stevens, who was responsible for major amendments restructuring the fisheries of the North Pacific. The law is now officially known as the Magnuson–Stevens Fishery Conservation and Management Act (hereafter the "Magnuson–Stevens Act" or "MSA"). Significant amendments in 2006 tightened the rebuilding requirements by requiring greater adherence to scientific recommendations and making fisheries accountable for exceeding annual catch limits. New permit systems were authorized that held promise of reducing or "rationalizing" commercial fishing fleets where necessary to restore fishery ecosystems damaged by overfishing.

The Secretary of Commerce is legally responsible for implementing the MSA, acting through the National Oceanic and Atmospheric Administration (NOAA) and its National Marine Fisheries Service (NMFS). The Service in turn works with eight advisory bodies called "regional fishery management councils" to develop plans and regulations for fisheries within their respective regions of the EEZ. The councils are composed largely of members of the fishing industry and state fishery officials. The private sector members are appointed by the Secretary of Commerce from lists supplied by the governors within the region. The councils have significant authority to determine the nature of regulations for commercial and recreational fisheries within their areas. Because the councils were created by Congress and the appointed members are constituents of individual senators and representatives, council members often seek relief from Congress when they find the Act's requirements too onerous or they disagree with the scientific advice. NOAA has had difficulty at times asserting the national interest in sustainable fisheries over industrial interests in the fishery resources. Environmental and marine conservation groups have gone to court frequently to enforce the conservation and ecosystem provisions of the Act.

After the 1996 amendments, for instance, a flood of litigation engulfed the National Marine Fisheries Service, triggering congressional inquiries into the scientific basis of fisheries management and the utility of tools such as individual fishing quotas to manage fisheries. During this period of legal challenges, litigants also sought to use the National Environmental Policy Act as a legal lever for requiring an ecosystem-based approach to managing the fisheries of the U.S. EEZ. That the oceans should be managed on an ecosystem basis was the central recommendation of the U.S. Commission on Ocean Policy created by the Oceans Act of 2000, Pub. L. 106–256. See U.S. Commission on Ocean Policy, An Ocean Blueprint for the 21st Century, 288–290 (2004), http://jointoceancommission.org/documents/USCOP_report.pdf.

A. NATIONAL STANDARDS FOR FISHERY MANAGEMENT

The basic standards for conservation and management are laid out in the National Standards, 16 U.S.C. § 1851, which embody the twin goals of preventing overfishing while achieving "optimum yield" from each fishery and require that management measures be based on the "best scientific information available." At the time the Act was written, it was unknown whether it was possible to achieve these goals, especially through the novel system of regional management councils. See, e.g., W. Rogalski, The Unique Federalism of the Regional Councils Under the Fishery Conservation and Management Act of 1976, 9 B.C. Envt'l Aff. L. Rev. 163 (1980).

16 U.S.C. § 1851. National Standards for Fishery Conservation and Management

(a) In general

Any fishery management plan prepared, and any regulation promulgated to implement any such plan, pursuant to this subchapter shall be consistent with the following national standards for fishery conservation and management:

(1) Conservation and management measures shall prevent overfishing while achieving, on a continuing basis, the optimum yield from each fishery for the United States fishing industry.

(2) Conservation and management measures shall be based upon the best scientific information available.

(3) To the extent practicable, an individual stock of fish shall be managed as a unit throughout its range, and interrelated stocks of fish shall be managed as a unit or in close coordination.

(4) Conservation and management measures shall not discriminate between residents of different States. If it becomes necessary to allocate or assign fishing privileges among various United States fishermen, such allocation shall be (A) fair and equitable to all such fishermen; (B) reasonably calculated to promote conservation; and (C)

carried out in such manner that no particular individual, corporation, or other entity acquires an excessive share of such privileges.

(5) Conservation and management measures shall, where practicable, consider efficiency in the utilization of fishery resources; except that no such measure shall have economic allocation as its sole purpose.

(6) Conservation and management measures shall take into account and allow for variations among, and contingencies in, fisheries, fishery resources, and catches.

(7) Conservation and management measures shall, where practicable, minimize costs and avoid unnecessary duplication.

(8) Conservation and management measures shall, consistent with the conservation requirements of this Chapter (including the prevention of overfishing and rebuilding of overfished stocks), take into account the importance of fishery resources to fishing communities in order to (A) provide for the sustained participation of such communities, and (B) to the extent practicable, minimize adverse economic impacts on such communities.

(9) Conservation and management measures shall, to the extent practicable, (A) minimize bycatch and (B) to the extent bycatch cannot be avoided, minimize the mortality of such bycatch.

(10) Conservation and management measures shall, to the extent practicable, promote the safety of human life at sea.

(b) Guidelines—The Secretary shall establish advisory guidelines (which shall not have the force and effect of law), based on the national standards, to assist in the development of fishery management plans.

———

Under the Magnuson–Stevens Act, the Secretary of Commerce approves and implements fishery management plans, devised by the regional councils. Each plan must identify those fish stocks that are below the population levels that are necessary to produce the "optimum yield" from that fishery, the level of fishing that will allow fish stocks to rebuild to the population levels at which they can be exploited on a sustainable basis, and the management measures that will constrain fishing to that level.

B. THE REGIONAL FISHERY MANAGEMENT COUNCILS

The Magnuson–Stevens Act gives the eight regional councils leading roles in designing management policies for the fisheries within their geographic area. 16 U.S.C. § 1852. The Act requires the voting members of each council to include each constituent state's chief marine fisheries official, the NMFS regional administrator, and individuals nominated by the governors and appointed by the Secretary who are "by reason of their occupational or other experience, scientific expertise or training, are knowledgeable regarding the conservation and management, or the commercial or recreational harvest, of the fishery resources of the geographical area concerned." Id. § 1852(b).

In making appointments, the Secretary must, "to the extent practicable, ensure a fair and balanced apportionment, on a rotating or other basis, of the active participants (or their representatives) in the commercial and recreational fisheries under the jurisdiction of the Council," reporting annually to Congress on how the required balance among active industry members has been achieved. Id. § 1852(b)(2)(B). Appointed members may serve a maximum of three consecutive 3-year terms. Voting members are compensated at the daily rate for GS–15, step 7 of the General Schedule. Non-voting members of the council include representatives of the Coast Guard, the State Department, and the interstate fishery commission.

Each council determines its organization, practices and procedures and is required to establish a scientific and statistical committee, a fishing industry advisory committee, and other advisory panels as needed to carry out its functions. Id. § 1852(g). The councils hire their own scientific and administrative staffs who receive and analyze information from the NMFS science centers, the fishing industry, and academic and consulting institutions. Councils must hold public hearings in their geographical areas to allow interested persons an opportunity to participate in the development of FMPs and amendments and in meeting other requirements of the Act. Id. § 1852(h). The councils and their committees and panels are exempt from the Federal Advisory Committee Act, 5 U.S.C. App. 2. Id. § 1852(I), but must follow procedures outlined in the Act regarding notice and conduct of their meetings.

Some critics of the decision-making structure of the Magnuson–Stevens Act argue that it gives too much authority to those with a financial interest in any resulting fishery regulation. Prior to the 1996 amendments, some commentators concluded that the financial interests of some council members made them less willing to accept conservation restrictions on fisheries in which they had a stake. See R.J. McManus, America's Saltwater Fisheries: So Few Fish, So Many Fishermen, 9 Nat. Resources & Envt. 13 (Spring 1995); World Wildlife Fund, Managing U.S.

Marine Fisheries: Public Interest or Conflict of Interest? (Aug. 1995). The conflict of interest issue is analyzed in T. Cloutier, Comment, Conflicts of Interest on Regional Fishery Management Councils: Corruption or Cooperative Management?, 2 Ocean & Coastal L.J. 101 (1996).

A study of the composition of the regional councils found that between 1990 and 2001, 49% of the appointed voting members of the eight councils represented commercial fishing interests, recreational interests made up 33%, and only 17% represented all other interests combined. T.A. Okey, Membership of the Eight Regional Fishery Management Councils in the United States: Are Special Interests Over-Represented? 27 Marine Policy 193 (2003).

The Act requires council voting members to disclose their financial interests in fisheries after their nomination for an appointment and to keep current financial disclosure forms, which are kept on file at the council offices. 16 U.S.C. § 1852(j). This requirement covers financial interests "in any harvesting, processing, or marketing activity that is being, or will be, undertaken within a fishery over which the council concerned has jurisdiction." Id. § 1852(j)(2). Failure to make disclosures in accordance with the Secretary's regulations, however, will not serve as grounds for invalidation of the council's action. Id. § 1852 (j)(6).

The Sustainable Fisheries Act amended the council process to require recusal prior to voting of a member with a financial interest in a Council decision if that decision would have "a significant and predictable effect on such financial interest." Id. § 1852(j)(7)(A). A council decision is to be considered to have a such an effect "if there is a close causal link between the council decision and an expected and substantially disproportionate benefit to the financial interest of the affected individual relative to the financial interests of other participants in the same gear type or sector of the fishery." Id. The recusing member can still participate in the council's deliberations, however, and may indicate for the record how he or she would have voted. Id. Voting members in compliance with NOAA regulations on disclosure are exempt from federal conflict of interest laws of 18 U.S.C. § 208. Id. § 1852(j)(8). Intentional failures to disclose, false disclosures, or failures to recuse are punishable by civil penalties. 16 U.S.C. § 1857(1)(O). The Secretary may remove for cause, after notice and opportunity for a hearing, any member who violates this prohibition. 16 U..S.C. § 1852(b)(6). In 2006, Congress responded to criticism of the council system by adding a provision, 16 U.S.C. § 1852(k), requiring new council members to take a training course on the scientific, economic, environmental, legal, and conflict of interest requirements of the Magnuson-Stevens Act, and a provision to strengthen the recusal requirement. Id. at § 1852(j).

NOTES AND QUESTIONS

1. When President Bill Clinton signed the 1996 amendments to the Magnuson–Stevens Act into law, he offered the following statement:

> Section 107 does not provide adequate protections against conflicts of interest on the part of members of the fishery management councils. A council member will be able to vote in many situations where the member could derive a significant financial gain from the matter. Further, the conflict provisions will not be consistent with other Government-wide conflict laws.

President's Statement on Signing the Sustainable Fisheries Act, Public Papers of the President, Oct. 11, 1996, 32 Weekly Comp. Pres. Doc. 2040.

NOAA regulations on the financial disclosure requirements are found in 50 C.F.R. § 600.235.

2. What is lacking in these safeguards? Is any kind of financial disclosure requirement likely to reduce the tendency of the regional councils to make risk-prone decisions in the face of clear scientific information about the effect of fishing rates on fish stock recovery? Is the problem a result of "the foxes guarding the chicken coop", or are there more subtle factors involved? For a fascinating discussion of the cognitive psychology of resource users who are trapped in a commons dilemma, see B.H. Thompson, Jr., Tragically Difficult: The Obstacles to Governing the Commons, 30 Envtl L. 241 (2000).

3. Should Congress amend the Act to require council members to reflect a balanced representation among not only commercial and recreational fisheries, but the broader public interest? Or should Congress focus on strengthening the authority and accountability of the Secretary of Commerce who has reined in councils' excessively risk-prone decisions in only a few cases? See J. Eagle, S. Newkirk, B.H. Thompson Jr., Taking Stock of the Regional Fisheries Management Councils, Pew Science Series in Conservation and the Environment (2003).

4. Does the Secretary of Commerce have enough authority to ensure that the regional councils do not favor short-term economic considerations over long-term sustainability in their votes on fishery management plans and amendments?

Section 304, 16 U.S.C. § 1854, provides:

> (a)(3) The Secretary shall approve, disapprove, or partially approve a plan or amendment within 30 days of the end of the [public] comment period * * * by written notice to the Council. A notice of disapproval shall specify—
>
> > (A) the applicable law with which the plan or amendment is inconsistent;
> >
> > (B) the nature of such inconsistencies; and

(C) recommendations concerning the actions that could be taken by the Council to conform such plan or amendment to the requirements of applicable law.

* * *

(c)(1) The Secretary may prepare a fishery management plan [FMP] * * * or amendment * * * in accordance with the national standards, the other provisions of this Act, and any other applicable law, if—

(A) the appropriate Council fails to develop and submit to the Secretary, after a reasonable period of time, a FMP * * * or necessary amendment * * * if such fishery requires conservation and management;

(B) the Secretary disapproves or partially approves any such plan or amendment, or disapproves a revised plan or amendment, and the Council involved fails to submit a revised or further revised plan or amendment * * *

* * *

(e)(5) If, within the one-year period beginning on the date of identification or notification that a fishery is overfished, the Council does not submit to the Secretary a FMP, plan amendment, or proposed regulations [to end overfishing * * * and to rebuild affected stocks of fish], the Secretary shall prepare a FMP or plan amendment and any accompanying regulations to stop overfishing and rebuild affected stocks of fish within 9 months under subsection (c).

Are the Secretary's powers to approve, disapprove, or partially approve a fishery management plan or amendment too narrow to allow NMFS to prevent overfishing if a council is determined to allow it?

5. For a concise explanation of the fish stock assessment process, See R. Wallace and K. Fletcher, Understanding Fisheries Management (2nd ed.), available online at http://nsglc.olemiss.edu/Fisheries/fishman.pdf. Since the 2006 amendments, council members are now required to receive training in the scientific aspects of stock assessments.

6. As you read the following cases and materials, consider whether the decentralized and industry-centered council model has worked as intended. In light of the difficulties experienced, why has it survived largely unchanged since 1976?

C. PREVENTING OVERFISHING AND REBUILDING FISH STOCKS

As noted above, the 1996 Sustainable Fisheries Act added provisions to the Magnuson–Stevens Act requiring the regional councils and the Secretary of Commerce to stop overfishing, to rebuild overfished stocks, and to address the ecological impacts of fisheries. These amendments reflect recognition that fisheries management can no longer afford to be concerned only with achieving the maximum sustainable harvests from exploited fish stocks and allocating that harvest among competing user groups.

Under section 304(e)(1), 16 U.S.C. § 1854(e)(1), the Secretary of Commerce is now required to report annually to Congress and councils on the status of fisheries and identify those within each council's geographical area of authority that are either overfished or are approaching a condition of being overfished, using the criteria specified in the applicable FMP or international agreement. "A fishery shall be classified as approaching a condition of being overfished if, based on trends in fishing effort, fishery resource size, and other appropriate factors, the Secretary estimates that the fishery will become overfished within two years." Id. § 1854(e)(1). The annual report to Congress on the condition of U.S. fish stocks is also posted on the Fisheries Service's web site for public review.

The major elements of the Act that add ecological concerns to the management process are the bycatch reduction provisions and the essential fish habitat requirements. In addition, the new provisions on fishing gear registration provides at least some check on the introduction of new fishing technology that may have unacceptably high levels of impact on the surrounding habitat and associated species. Finally, Congress required the Fisheries Service to convene an expert panel to prepare a report on the degree to which ecosystem goals, principles, and policies are applied and can be applied under the Magnuson–Stevens Act. See Ecosystem Principles Advisory Panel, Ecosystem-Based Fishery Management, A Report to Congress (Nov. 15, 1998); M. Macpherson, Integrating Ecosystem Management Approaches into Federal Fishery Management Through the Magnuson–Stevens Fishery Conservation and Management Act, 6 Ocean & Coastal L.J. 1 (2001).

At the same time that these ecosystem-related provisions were added, Congress sought to insure that the economic impact of conservation and management measures were adequately considered. Most notable in this regard is the addition of National Standard 8, the requirement that conservation and management measures—

> shall, consistent with the conservation requirements of this Chapter (including the prevention of overfishing and rebuilding of overfished stocks), take into account the importance of fishery resources to fishing communities in order to (A) provide for the sustained participation of such communities, and (B) to the extent practicable, minimize adverse economic impacts on such communities.

16 U.S.C. § 1851(a)(8).

Do you see any potential for conflict among the conservation and economics provisions? If the capacities of the commercial and recreational fishery sectors are larger than that which can be supported by the biologically acceptable catch level, how are the councils likely to interpret the mandate of National Standards 1 and 8, that is, to prevent overfishing while taking into account the needs of fishing communities?

1. Ending "Overfishing"

The most important requirement for each FMP is that it prevent overfishing while achieving optimum yield "for the United States fishing industry." For the first twenty years of the Act's implementation, the goal of achieving optimum yield for the benefit of commercial fishing, as it was variously defined in the many FMPs, took center stage. The Act contained a definition of OY but not of overfishing. This focus led in many key fisheries to the institutionalization of a condition of overfishing.

The Act's ability to constrain the growth of the commercial fishing industry turned out to be limited, necessitating a series of emergency actions followed by a substantial overhaul in the 1996 Sustainable Fisheries Act. The Act now contains an express definition of "overfished" and "overfishing." Also, the definition of optimum yield has been changed to preclude setting OY at a level that exceeds the maximum sustainable catch level.

16 U.S.C. § 1802. Definitions

(28) The term "optimum", with respect to the yield from a fishery, means the amount of fish which—

> (A) will provide the greatest overall benefit to the Nation, particularly with respect to food production and recreational opportunities, and taking into account the protection of marine ecosystems;
>
> (B) is prescribed on the basis of the maximum sustainable yield from the fishery, as reduced by any relevant economic, social, or ecological factors; and
>
> (C) in the case of an overfished fishery, provides for rebuilding to a level consistent with producing the maximum sustainable yield in such fishery.

(29) The terms "overfishing" and "overfished" mean a rate or level of fishing mortality that jeopardizes the capacity of a fishery to produce the maximum sustainable yield on a continuing basis.

———

Within one year of receiving notice that a fishery is overfished, the responsible council must submit a plan amendment or proposed regulations to end or prevent overfishing and to rebuild the affected stocks. Id.

§ 1854(e)(4). The council's submission must specify a rebuilding period that is as short as possible, taking into account the nature of the stocks and their ecosystem and the needs of fishing communities. The period must not exceed 10 years, unless the biology of the stock, environmental conditions, or international management measures dictate otherwise. If the council does not submit a plan or regulations to stop overfishing or to rebuild the affected stocks within one year, the Secretary is required to prepare such amendment and to publish regulations that stop overfishing and begin to rebuild the stocks within 9 months. Id. § 1854(e)(5).

At the council's request the Secretary can implement interim measures to reduce overfishing until a full rebuilding or overfishing plan can be put into place. The Secretary must also regularly review the rebuilding and overfishing plans to ensure their effectiveness, and notify the council if insufficient progress toward these goals is being made, recommending further measures the council should consider to achieve adequate progress, triggering again the one-year time period for action. Id. § 1854(e)(7).

Do these changes give the Secretary sufficient authority to insure rebuilding plans are put in place in a timely manner? Do they increase the accountability of federal fishery managers for the condition of fishery resources in the U.S. EEZ?

After the 1996 amendments, the pace and intensity of judicial review of fishery management decisions increased dramatically, reflecting in part the resistance of the fishery councils to the tough new controls on overfishing, but also the entry of environmental non-governmental organizations (NGOs) into debates over the management and protection of marine fisheries. These groups have used litigation to push NMFS and the councils to adopt a more ecosystem-based approach. The 1996 amendments' reinvigoration of the conservation goal of the Act provided a basis for this intervention. In A.M.L. International, Inc. v. Daley, 107 F. Supp.2d 90 (D. Mass. 2000), the court described the genesis and impact of the amendments:

> In 1996, Congress ushered in a new era in fisheries management by making significant revisions to the Magnuson–Stevens Act through the Sustainable Fisheries Act. See Pub.L. No. 104–297, 110 Stat. 3559 (1996). The Magnuson–Stevens act was revised because, "it was very clear that major changes were needed. Despite numerous efforts to improve the law over the past two decades, the sad reality [was] that the act did not prevent the current crisis in * * * groundfish stocks, a crisis for the conservation of both fish stocks and fishing families." See 142 Cong.Rec. H11418, 11439 (September 27, 1996) (statement of Rep. Studds). Indeed, Congress recognized that revisions to the Magnuson–Stevens act were critical in order to "put our

fisheries back onto a sustainable path and literally avert an environmental catastrophe on a national level * * * We are precariously close to fisheries failures in many of our most commercially important fish stocks, and it is imperative that we take immediate action if we are to avert disasters." See 142 Cong.Rec. S10794, 10811–12 (September 18, 1996) (statement of Sen. Kerry).

Perhaps the most significant revision to the Magnuson–Stevens Act was the removal of some discretion regarding "overfished" fisheries. If the Secretary determines at any time that a fishery is overfished, the Secretary must immediately notify the appropriate fishery council, and request that action be taken to end overfishing in the fishery and to implement conservation and management measures to rebuild affected stocks of fish. Once a council has been notified that a particular stock is overfished, it has only one year to prepare a fishery management plan to end overfishing and rebuild the stocks.[1] The primary purpose of a plan is to establish conservation and management measures which are "necessary and appropriate for the conservation and management of the fishery, to prevent overfishing and rebuild overfished stocks, and to protect, restore, and promote the long-term health and stability of the fishery." The ultimate goal, therefore, of any fishery management plan is to establish measures which achieve a rate or level of fishing mortality that allows the fishery to produce the maximum sustainable yield on a continuing basis.[2]

A.M.L. Int'l v. Daley, 1007 F. Supp.2d at 94.

———————

Congress clearly intended to change the way in which fisheries were managed, to require the councils and NMFS to set limits on fishing that would allow stocks to rebuild to levels that could produce a long-term sustainable catch level. But several questions remained, including: how

[1] Significantly, Congress imposed the one-year time limit on fishery councils because of the perceived inability of fishery councils to quickly enact needed conservation measures. Indeed, Congress recognized that "it actually took a lawsuit by two Massachusetts environmental groups to force the notoriously slow New England Fishery Management council to draft and implement a fishery management plan that contained the teeth needed to stem continued overfishing and stock decimation." See 142 Cong.Rec. S10906, 10910 (September 19, 1996) (statement of Sen. Chafee).

[2] The Magnuson–Stevens Act requires that fishery management plans must ultimately "prevent overfishing." As discussed above, "overfishing" means a rate of mortality that jeopardizes the capacity of a fishery to produce MSY on a continuing basis. The Magnuson–Stevens Act also calls for fishery management plans to specify the "optimum yield." The statute defines "optimum yield" as the amount of fish which will provide the greatest overall benefit to the nation, with respect to food production and recreational opportunities, and taking into account the protection of marine ecosystems. Optimum yield is prescribed on the basis of the MSY from the fishery, as reduced by any relevant social, economic, or ecological factor. More importantly, the optimum yield for an overfished fishery *must rebuild to a level consistent with producing the maximum sustainable yield.*

much discretion do the councils and NMFS have to set the pace of the rebuilding, in order to reduce economic hardship on the industry? How much certainty must there be that the chosen conservation measures will achieve the goal of preventing overfishing? Must the councils end overfishing immediately or can they wait until the end of the rebuilding period? Recall that National Standard One provides that "[c]onservation and management measures shall prevent overfishing while achieving, on a continuing basis, the optimum yield from each fishery for the United States fishing industry." 16 U.S.C. § 1851(a)(1).

On the issue of the degree of certainty, the following case set an important standard for the Secretary to enforce through the plan amendment approval/disapproval process under 16 U.S.C. § 1854(a).

NATURAL RESOURCES DEFENSE COUNCIL, INC. V. DALEY
United States Court of Appeals, D.C. Circuit, 2000
209 F.3d 747

EDWARDS, CHIEF JUSTICE.

* * *

From a commercial standpoint, the summer flounder is one of the most important species of flounder in the United States. All parties agree that the summer flounder fishery is "overfished" and has been for some time. The Mid–Atlantic Fishery Management Council (MAFMC), covering New York, New Jersey, Delaware, Pennsylvania, Maryland, Virginia, and North Carolina, developed the original summer flounder management plan with the assistance of two other regional Management Councils and the Atlantic States Marine Fisheries Commission ("the Commission"), a consortium of 15 coastal states and the District of Columbia. The Service approved the original management plan in 1988; however, the Service has amended the plan several times. At the time relevant to the instant case, the plan was designed to achieve a fishing mortality rate equal to F submax by 1998.

Pursuant to the management plan, the Service must set a quota each year fixing the total weight of summer flounder that may be harvested by commercial and recreational fishers. This quota is referred to as the "total allowable landings" for the year, or "TAL." The Service allocates 60% of the TAL to commercial fisheries and 40% of the quota to recreational fisheries, and states receive allocations based upon their share of the summer flounder fishery. States may subdivide their allocated commercial quota between "incidental" and "directed" catch. Directed fisheries intentionally harvest summer flounder. Fishers who catch juvenile flounder, or who are part of the directed fishery for another species and catch summer flounder unintentionally, have harvested incidental catch.

* * *

There is a relatively direct relationship between the TAL and the likelihood of achieving the target F. In general, the higher the TAL, the less likely a plan is to achieve the target F. In other words, the lower the target F, the lower the TAL must be to attain the target F. The basic dispute between the parties concerns whether the 1999 TAL provides a sufficient guarantee that the target F for summer flounder will be achieved.

For 1999, the summer flounder fishery management plan mandated a target F equivalent to F submax, which was 0.24. The Summer Flounder Monitoring Committee, a MAFMC committee, had recommended a TAL of 14.645 million pounds, while MAFMC had recommended a TAL of 20.20 million pounds. The Service rejected MAFMC's recommendation as "unacceptably risk-prone" for several reasons: (1) it had an "unacceptably low probability" of 3% of achieving the target F; (2) it had a 50% probability of achieving an F of 0.36, which was "significantly higher" than the target F; (3) the proposal relied on unpredictable data; and (4) MAFMC had "yet to specify a harvest level that has achieved the annual target F." The Service also rejected the Summer Flounder Monitoring Committee's recommendation of a 14.645 million pound TAL. Although the Committee's recommendation had a 50% chance of achieving the target F, the Service rejected the proposal without any meaningful explanation.

On October 21, 1998, the Service proposed a TAL of 18.52 million pounds. All parties agree that, at most, the Service's proposal afforded only an 18% likelihood of achieving the target F. * * *

Between the time of proposal of the 1999 TAL and its adoption, the Service concluded that it did not have the authority to impose any incidental catch restrictions on the states. Therefore, the Service merely *recommended* that the states adopt the incidental catch proposal [of allocating 32.7% of the TAL to incidental catch], making the proposal entirely voluntary. The Commission, the body representing 15 coastal states and the District of Columbia, also declined to command the states to adopt the proposal. According to an advisor to the Service's Assistant Administrator for Fisheries, this development "result[ed] in an unknown but probably substantial reduction in the likelihood that [MAFMC's] rebuilding schedule will be achieved," and he therefore recommended that the Service adopt the Summer Flounder Monitoring Committee's recommended 14.645 million pound TAL.

The Service rejected this recommendation and, on December 31, 1998, issued the final TAL, adopting its initial proposal. The Service acknowledged that the Summer Flounder Monitoring Committee's recommended quota had a 50% chance of achieving the target F, while the Service's TAL had only an 18% chance of achieving the target F.

* * *

Appellants filed suit in District Court on January 29, 1999, seeking, *inter alia,* (1) a declaratory judgment that defendants violated the Fishery Act, the Administrative Procedure Act ("APA"), and NEPA, and (2) remand to the agency to impose a new summer flounder TAL. The District Court upheld the Service's adoption of the 18.52 million pound TAL, deferring to the agency under Chevron, U.S.A., Inc. v. Natural Resources Defense Council, Inc., 467 U.S. 837 (1984). The District Court first determined that [National Standards #1 and #8] in the Fishery Act evinced competing interests between advancing conservation and minimizing adverse economic effects and that Congress offered no insight as to how to balance these concerns. See Natural Resources Defense Council, Inc. v. Daley, 62 F. Supp.2d 102 (D.D.C.1999), at 106–07. In addition, the trial court found that the Fishery Act expressed no clear intent as to the particular level of certainty a TAL must guarantee to be consistent with [National Standard #1]. Given these perceived ambiguities, the District Court deferred to the Service pursuant to *Chevron* Step Two. This appeal followed.

* * *

As for the Service's disputed interpretations of the Fishery Act, we are guided by the Supreme Court's seminal decision in *Chevron U.S.A., Inc.,* [which] governs review of agency interpretation of a statute which the agency administers. Under the first step of *Chevron,* the reviewing court "must first exhaust the 'traditional tools of statutory construction' to determine whether Congress has spoken to the precise question at issue." The traditional tools include examination of the statute's text, legislative history, and structure; as well as its purpose. This inquiry using the traditional tools of construction may be characterized as a search for the plain meaning of the statute. If this search yields a clear result, then Congress has expressed its intention as to the question, and deference is not appropriate. If, however, "the statute is silent or ambiguous with respect to the specific issue," Congress has not spoken clearly, and a permissible agency interpretation of the statute merits judicial deference.

Although agencies are entitled to deferential review under *Chevron* Step Two, our judicial function is neither rote nor meaningless:

> [W]e will defer to [an agency's] interpretation[ ] if [it is] reasonable and consistent with the statutory purpose and legislative history. However, a court will not uphold [an agency's] interpretation "that diverges from any realistic meaning of the statute."

* * * This case presents a situation in which the Service's quota for the 1999 summer flounder harvest so completely diverges from any realistic meaning of the Fishery Act that it cannot survive scrutiny under *Chevron* Step Two.

As an initial matter, we reject the District Court's suggestion that there is a conflict between the Fishery Act's expressed commitments to conservation and to mitigating adverse economic impacts. *Compare* [National Standard #1] (directing agency to "prevent overfishing" and ensure "the optimum yield from each fishery"); *with* [National Standard #8] (directing agency to "minimize adverse economic impacts" on fishing communities). The Government concedes, and we agree, that, under the Fishery Act, the Service must give priority to conservation measures. It is only when two different plans achieve similar conservation measures that the Service takes into consideration adverse economic consequences. This is confirmed both by the statute's plain language and the regulations issued pursuant to the statute. See id. § 1851(a)(8) (requiring fishery management plans, "consistent with the conservation requirements of this chapter," to take into account the effect of management plans on fishing communities) (emphasis added); 50 C.F.R. § 600.345(b)(1) (1999) ("[W]here two alternatives achieve similar conservation goals, the alternative that * * * minimizes the adverse impacts on [fishing] communities would be the preferred alternative.") (emphasis added).

The real issue in this case is whether the 1999 TAL satisfied the conservation goals of the Fishery Act, the management plan, and the Service's regulations. In considering this question, it is important to recall that the Service operates under constraints from three different sources. First, the statute requires the Service to act both to "prevent overfishing" and to attain "optimum yield." 16 U.S.C. § 1851(a)(1). Overfishing is commonly understood as fishing that results in an F in excess of F submax. Since F submax for 1999 was equivalent to 0.24, this constraint required the Service to issue regulations to prevent F from exceeding 0.24. Second, any quota must be "consistent with" the fishery management plan adopted by the Service. In this case the fishery management plan called for an F of 0.24. Therefore, the quota had be to "consistent with" achieving that F. Third, the Service is required to adopt a quota "necessary to assure that the applicable specified F will not be exceeded." The "applicable specified F" for 1999 was F submax, or 0.24.

All of these constraints, then, collapse into an inquiry as to whether the Service's quota was "consistent with" and at the level "necessary to assure" the achievement of an F of 0.24, and whether it reasonably could be expected to "prevent" an F greater than 0.24. In other words, the question is whether the quota, as approved, sufficiently ensured that it would achieve an F of 0.24. Appellants argue that the quota violates applicable standards under both *Chevron* Step One and *Chevron* Step Two * * *

Appellants' *Chevron* Step One "plain meaning" argument is virtually indistinguishable from their *Chevron* Step Two reasonableness argument. Appellants acknowledge that the statutory terms "assure," "prevent," and "consistent with" do not mandate a precise quota figure. However, appellants contend that a TAL with only an 18% likelihood of achieving the target F is so inherently unreasonable that it defies the plain meaning of the statute. This is an appealing argument on the facts of this case, because, as we explain below, the Service's action is largely incomprehensible when one considers the principal purposes of the Fishery Act. Nonetheless, we still view this case as governed by *Chevron* Step Two. The statute does not prescribe a precise quota figure, so there is no plain meaning on this point. Rather, we must look to see whether the agency's disputed action reflects a reasonable and permissible construction of the statute. In light of what the statute *does* require, short of a specific quota figure, it is clear here that the Service's position fails the test of *Chevron* Step Two.

The 1999 quota is unreasonable, plain and simple. Government counsel conceded at oral argument that, to meet its statutory and regulatory mandate, the Service must have a "fairly high level of confidence that the quota it recommends will not result in an F greater than [the target F]." We agree. We also hold that, at the very least, this means that "to assure" the achievement of the target F, to "prevent overfishing," and to "be consistent with" the fishery management plan, the TAL must have had at least a 50% chance of attaining an F of 0.24. This is not a surprising result, because in related contexts, the Service has articulated precisely this standard.

The disputed 1999 TAL had at most an 18% likelihood of achieving the target F. Viewed differently, it had at least an 82% chance of resulting in an F greater than the target F. Only in Superman Comics' Bizarro world, where reality is turned upside down, could the Service reasonably conclude that a measure that is at least four times as likely to fail as to succeed offers a "fairly high level of confidence."

Rather than argue that the quota alone provided enough assurance, the Service contends instead that two additional measures were adopted to increase the likelihood of achieving the target F. These measures were: (1) the provision relating to minimum mesh size; and (2) the recommendation that states voluntarily allocate a certain portion of the directed commercial fishery toward incidental catch. There is nothing in this record, however, to indicate that the proposals on mesh size and voluntary state action would improve the level of confidence so as to assure a reasonable likelihood of achieving the target F.

* * *

As we noted at the outset of this opinion, the Service's quota for the 1999 summer flounder harvest so completely "diverges from any realistic meaning" of the Fishery Act that it cannot survive scrutiny under *Chevron* Step Two. The Service resists this result by suggesting that we owe deference to the agency's "scientific" judgments. While this may be so, we do not hear cases merely to rubber stamp agency actions. To play that role would be "tantamount to abdicating the judiciary's responsibility under the Administrative Procedure Act." The Service cannot rely on "reminders that its scientific determinations are entitled to deference" in the absence of reasoned analysis "to 'cogently explain' " why its additional recommended measures satisfied the Fishery Act's requirements. Indeed, we can divine no scientific judgment upon which the Service concluded that its measures would satisfy its statutory mandate.

Here, the adopted quota guaranteed only an 18% probability of achieving the principal conservation goal of the summer flounder fishery management plan. The Service offered neither analysis nor data to support its claim that the two additional measures aside from the quota would increase that assurance beyond the at-least-50% likelihood required by statute and regulation.

* * *

NOTES AND QUESTIONS

1. Why did the NMFS approve a summer flounder quota that had only an 18% chance of meeting the overfishing target? Chief Justice Edwards said the court could "divine no scientific judgment upon which the Service concluded that its measures would satisfy" the Magnuson–Stevens Act. What judgment was the agency relying upon if not a scientific one?

2. Is "at least 50% likelihood" of preventing overfishing a demanding enough standard? Note that this term refers to the statistical probability that the fishery will be limited to the target fishing mortality rate. Recall that the fishing mortality rate is the rate of exploitation associated with removing a given percentage of the stock's current population in a year. Setting a target rate and staying at or below it is critical to rebuilding the stock to the population size (biomass) that can produce the maximum sustainable yield over the long term.

2. Considering Fishing Communities

What happens when the definition of "overfishing" and the associated rebuilding requirements of an FMP point to a fishing mortality rate or target spawning stock biomass size that require setting a quota that is too low to allow an existing commercial fishery to operate?

As mentioned above, in the 1996 amendments Congress added a national standard requiring conservation and management measures to "consistent with the conservation requirements of this Act (including the prevention of overfishing and rebuilding of overfished stocks), take into account the importance of fishery resources to fishing communities in order to (A) provide for the sustained participation of such communities, and (B) to the extent practicable, minimize adverse economic impacts on such communities." 16 U.S.C. § 1853(a)(8).

In the A.M.L. International, Inc. v. Daley case cited above, the fishing industry challenged the quota restrictions adopted to implement the rebuilding plan for spiny dogfish. The Atlantic dogfish fishery developed after other, more-desirable groundfish populations (cod, haddock, and flounder) crashed due to overfishing. Dogfish landings increased ten-fold to 40 million pounds per year before regulations were put in place. To rebuild the dogfish population, the two northeastern councils adopted catch limits of 300 pounds per trip, an amount equivalent only to an incidental catch, effectively shutting down the directed fishery for five years. The industry argued that this effective closure violated the Act's provisions requiring councils to consider the adverse economic impacts of implementing the rebuilding mandates. The following decision was the result.

A.M.L. INTERNATIONAL, INC. V. DALEY
United States District Court for Massachusetts, 2000
107 F. Supp.2d 90

The plaintiffs argue that the Spiny Dogfish FMP (SDFMP) does not comply with National Standard 8 because (1) there was no attempt to minimize economic consequences, (2) the descriptions of economic impacts, fishery demographics and the fishing communities are inadequate, (3) the consideration of alternative measures was inadequate, and most importantly, (4) the plan shuts down an entire industry. For example, the plaintiffs assert that they will suffer revenue losses of thirty (30) to one hundred (100) percent, and the elimination of at least two hundred (200) jobs in the processing sector.

The record, however, establishes that the Secretary and the councils considered the importance of the fishery to numerous communities. Indeed, the Secretary concluded that without the measures contained in the SDFMP, data indicates that the fishery will collapse completely within two or three years. *A collapsed fishery will not be economically viable for decades, creating drastically worse economic consequences than the temporary measures contained in the SDFMP.*

* * *

Much of the plaintiffs' argument is based on the fact that the implementation of the SDFMP will likely result in the closure of the spiny dogfish directed fishery for at least the next five years. Indeed, the record indicates that some members of the NEFMC and state agencies are confused about the requirements and priorities of the Magnuson–Stevens Act. The National Standards * * * *must be consistent with the ultimate conservation requirements of the Magnuson–Stevens Act.* Any fishery management plan must, first and foremost, contain measures which prevent overfishing and rebuild overfished stocks. Where the Secretary has designated a fishery as overfished, measures *must* provide for rebuilding to a level consistent with producing the maximum sustainable yield, or suitable proxy, within a time period as short as possible but not exceeding ten (10) years.

The requirements of the [Regulatory Flexibility Act] as well as the National Standards pertaining to adverse economic impacts, efficiency, and bycatch, are to be applied *to the extent practicable* given this primary conservation objective. Measures contained in a fishery management plan may well result in the closure of a fishing industry. This terrible and unfortunate consequence, however, was readily anticipated by Congress when it amended the Magnuson–Stevens Act in 1996 * * *

As a sick person must undergo painful surgery and then convalesce for a short time in order to regain his health, a sick fishery must suffer this drastic procedure and then conserve itself for a short time in order to recover its full vitality.

* * *

NOTES AND QUESTIONS

1. Does this decision settle the issue? Are fishing industry groups likely to stop challenging FMP regulations on economic grounds?

2. Among the numerous questions left unanswered by the Sustainable Fisheries Act, as the 1996 amendments are called, was how long the rebuilding period can be. Given the economic impacts of depleted fish stocks on fishing businesses and communities, are the councils likely to want to rebuild as quickly as possible, or are the short-term costs of restricting fishing of more concern? What guidance does the Act and the NMFS give the councils on these difficult choices?

3.   Rebuilding Overfished Stocks

NATURAL RESOURCES DEFENSE COUNCIL, INC. v. NMFS

United States Court of Appeals, Ninth Circuit, 2005
421 F.3d 872

FISHER, CIRCUIT JUDGE.

I. Background

A. The National Marine Fisheries Service, the Magnuson Act, Section 1854 and the National Standards Guidelines

Congress enacted the Magnuson Act to "conserve and manage the fishery resources found off the coasts of the United States." 16 U.S.C. § 1801(b)(1). The Agency is charged with developing and implementing rebuilding plans for overfished fish species. § 1854. In 1996, Congress amended the Act by passing the Sustainable Fisheries Act ("SFA"). Pub.L. No. 104–297, 110 Stat. 3559 (1996). The SFA added new requirements to the Act to accelerate the rebuilding of overfished species.

The Act, as amended by the SFA, contains a provision the proper interpretation of which is the main subject of this appeal. Section 1854 of the Act provides in part that when any species is found to be overfished, the Agency must approve a rebuilding plan that:

> (A) specif[ies] a time period for ending overfishing and rebuilding the fishery that shall—
>
>> (i) be as short as possible, taking into account the status and biology of any overfished stock of fish, the needs of fishing communities, * * * and the interaction of the overfished stock of fish within the marine ecosystem; and
>>
>> (ii) not exceed 10 years, except in cases where the biology of the stock of fish, [or] other environmental conditions * * * dictate otherwise.

§ 1854(e)(4).

The Act also sets forth a series of "national standards" with which any rebuilding plans must be "consistent," and provides for the establishment of National Standards Guidelines ("NSGs") that must be "based on the national standards" for use in "assist[ing] in the development of fishery management plans." §§ 1851(a), (b). The Act provides that NSGs "shall not have the force and effect of law." Id.

There is some ambiguity to § 1854(e)(4). Section 1854(e)(4)(i) specifies that the rebuilding time period be as "short as possible," but also directs that the Agency "tak[e] into account the status and biology of [the] * * * overfished stock" and "the needs of fishing communities." Section

1854(e)(4)(ii) in turn plainly mandates that the rebuilding plan be no longer than 10 years, so long as biologically or environmentally possible. However, if it is not possible to rebuild within 10 years, the Act is not clear as to the exact limits on the length of the rebuilding period. [A separate provision allowing for a longer period if necessary to comply with the terms of an international agreement is not relevant here. See § 1854(e)(4)(A)(ii).]

Seeking to clarify the proper interpretation of § 1854(e)(4), the Agency in 1997 sought "comment on whether or not it is correct in its interpretation that the duration of rebuilding programs should not be unspecified and, if so, what factors should be considered in determining that duration." See 62 Fed. Reg. 67,610 (Dec. 29, 1997). The Agency propounded two alternate interpretations for public comment: that whenever it would take longer than 10 years to rebuild an overfished species, either (1) all fishing of that species would be banned until the rebuilding was complete or (2) the Agency would set a ceiling on the rebuilding duration that would be reached by adding the shortest possible time to rebuild plus "one mean generation time * * * based on the species' life-history characteristics." Id. at 67,609–10. A "mean generation time" is a scientific term, not mentioned in the Act itself, measuring how long it will take for an average mature fish to be replaced by its offspring. After notice and comment, the Agency adopted the second interpretation in a NSG ("the 1998 NSG"). See 50 C.F.R. § 600.310(e)(4)(ii)(B). The Agency reasoned that:

> [f]or stocks that will take more than 10 years to rebuild, the guidelines [adopted] impose an outside limit that is objective, measurable, and linked to the biology of the particular species * * * The guidelines strike a balance between the Congressional directive to rebuild stocks as quickly as possible, and the desire * * * to minimize adverse economic effects on fishing communities. For stocks that cannot be rebuilt within 10 years, the guideline allows flexibility in setting the rebuilding schedule beyond the no-fishing mortality period, but places a reasonable, species-specific cap on that flexibility by limiting the extension to one mean generation time.

63 Fed. Reg. 24, 217 (May 1, 1998).

B. The 2001 and 2002 Limits for Darkblotched Rockfish

The Pacific Coast Groundfish Fishery is one of the fisheries the Agency oversees, covering the bottom-feeding fish species dwelling in the waters off the coasts of California, Oregon and Washington. In 2000, the Agency assessed the status of one species of Pacific groundfish within the fishery—darkblotched rockfish. It found that the species was at 22% of its unfished population level (its predicted level absent any fishing), and therefore concluded that the species was "overfished" within the meaning of the Act. 66 Fed. Reg. 2,347, 2349–50 (Jan. 11, 2001). The Agency further concluded that the species could be rebuilt in 10 years or less, triggering § 1854(e)(4)(ii)'s mandatory requirement that the rebuilding take place within 10 years. The Agency then set a 130 metric ton "fishing harvest level," or quota, i.e., a set limit of darkblotched rockfish that could be fished in 2001.

In 2001, the Agency updated its assessment of darkblotched rockfish and concluded that it had significantly overestimated the health of the species. The Agency now estimated that the species was almost twice as depleted as previously thought—it was at only 12% of its unfished population level. In the Agency's calculations, rebuilding therefore could not be accomplished within 10 years; the minimum period for rebuilding was now 14 years.

This increased rebuilding time meant, by necessity, that the rebuilding plan was no longer limited by § 1854(e)(4)(ii)'s mandatory 10-year cap; instead, the only applicable statutory time limit was § 1854(e)(4)(i)'s command that the rebuilding period be "as short as possible." Further, according to the interpretation of the Act set forth in the 1998 NSG, the revised minimum rebuilding period triggered a new ceiling that was the 14-year period *plus* "one mean generation time," which in the case of the long-lived darkblotched rockfish was 33 years. The Agency, in short, switched from operating under the statutory constraint of *10 years* rebuilding time to a new constraint, dictated by the 1998 NSG, of *47 years*. The Agency then set a "target" rebuilding time of 34 years, and in accordance with this target, *raised* the fishing level harvest for 2002 from the previous year's 130 metric tons to 168 metric tons.[4]

NRDC brought suit alleging that the new quota violated the Act, the Administrative Procedure Act and the National Environmental Policy Act. The district court concluded that the quota violated none of these statutes and granted summary judgment for the Agency. Natural Res. Def. Council, Inc. v. Nat'l Marine Fisheries Serv., 280 F. Supp.2d 1007, 1014–15 (N.D.Cal.2003).

* * *

II. Standard of Review

* * *

We should not defer to an agency's interpretation of a statute if Congress' intent can be clearly ascertained through analysis of the language, purpose and structure of the statute. Chevron, U.S.A., Inc. v. Natural Res. Def. Council, Inc., 467 U.S. 837 (1984). If, however, Congress' intent

---

[4] The new quota meant only that the "target rebuilding time" had even odds of being reached; it had a 70% chance of being reached within the outer limit of 47 years. 67 Fed. Reg. 10,491 (Mar. 7, 2002).

is not clear, and if "Congress delegated authority to the agency generally to make rules carrying the force of law, and [ ] the agency interpretation claiming deference was promulgated in the exercise of that authority," United States v. Mead Corp., 533 U.S. 218, 226–27 (2001), then we must defer to the agency's construction of the statute so long as "the agency's answer is based on a permissible construction of the statute." Chevron, 467 U.S. at 843. If the *Mead* requirements for *Chevron* deference are not met, we review the agency's interpretation under the *Skidmore* standard, whereby the interpretation is "entitled not to deference but to a lesser 'respect' based on the persuasiveness of the agency decision." Wilderness Soc'y v. U.S. Fish & Wildlife Serv., 353 F.3d 1051, 1067(9th Cir.2003); Skidmore v. Swift & Co., 323 U.S. 134 (1944).

III. Discussion

A. *The 2002 Darkblotched Rockfish Quota*

1. *Chevron* Deference

The Agency arrived at its increased 2002 darkblotched rockfish quota by applying its interpretation of § 1854(e)(4) of the Magnuson Act as set forth in the 1998 NSG. NRDC argues that this interpretation of the Act is not entitled to *Chevron* deference for two separate reasons.

First, NRDC argues that Congress' intent in this section of the Act is clear, thereby precluding the need for any deference to the Agency's interpretation of the statute. We disagree. As we noted above, § 1854(e)(4)(ii) is explicit that *if* a species can be rebuilt within 10 years, it must be. But § 1854(e)(4)(i), which states that the rebuilding period must be as "short as possible, taking into account the status and biology of any overfished stock of fish [and] the needs of fishing communities," introduces an ambiguity into the calculus. When it is not biologically possible to rebuild within 10 years, may the Agency extend the rebuilding period beyond the shortest possible rebuilding time to account for the needs of fishing communities? It would be possible to resolve the ambiguity by concluding that the Act as a whole makes it clear that the needs of fishing communities are perfectly aligned with the environmental goal of rebuilding fish stocks in as short a time as possible. But if this were the case, the language "the needs of fishing communities" would be redundant (as these needs would be no different than the need to rebuild stocks in as short a time as possible). But see Natural Res. Def. Council, Inc. v. Daley, 209 F.3d 747, 753 (D.C.Cir.2000) ("[W]e reject the District Court's suggestion that there is a conflict between the [Act's] expressed commitments to conservation and to mitigating adverse economic impacts.").[5] There is therefore an ambiguity in this part of the statute, requiring in-

---

[5] *Daley* may be correct as to the long-term needs of fishing communities, but undoubtedly the short-term economic interests of fishing communities diverge in some respects from the needs of fish species.

terpretation. See Chevron, 467 U.S. at 843 (holding that "[if] Congress has not directly addressed the precise question at issue," it is necessary to move to the second step of the *Chevron* analysis).

NRDC next argues that because the Act explicitly provides that NSGs do not have the force of law, *Chevron* deference is not appropriate. See Mead, 533 U.S. at 226–27 (holding *Chevron* deference to be appropriate only if "Congress delegated authority to the agency generally to make rules carrying the force of law, and [ ] the agency interpretation claiming deference was promulgated in the exercise of that authority"). The Agency responds that although the 1998 NSG does not have the force of law, the 2002 darkblotched rockfish quota itself—which is what is actually being challenged here—is a binding regulation that does have the force of law, requiring *Chevron* deference, and that to hold otherwise would mean punishing the Agency for taking the additional step of setting out the interpretation in an NSG.

We need not resolve this question here, because even under the *Chevron* standard of review, the 2002 quota was based on an impermissible construction of the Act. We therefore will assume that *Chevron* review is appropriate even as to the 1998 NSG's statutory interpretation that was applied to reach the quota, without deciding the issue.

2. The 2002 Quota Is Based on an Impermissible Construction of the Act

Under *Chevron,* we must determine whether "the agency's [quota] is based on a permissible construction of the statute." Chevron, 467 U.S. at 843. *Chevron* review is also described as determining whether the quota reflects "a reasonable interpretation" of the statute. Id. at 844.

The interpretation of § 1854(e)(4) stated in the 1998 NSG, as applied in the 2002 quota, is not a permissible (or reasonable) construction of the statute; it is directly at odds with the text and purpose of the Act. Section 1801 of the Act contains its "Findings, purposes and policy." The "Findings" section states that the nation's fishery resources "constitute valuable and renewable natural resources," that many of these species' "survival is threatened" and that others' survival will soon be threatened by "increased fishing pressure, * * * the inadequacy of fishery resource conservation and management practices and controls." §§ 1801(a)(1),(2). The next subsection recognizes "commercial and recreational fishing" as a "major source of employment" that "contributes significantly to the economy of the Nation." § 1801(a)(3). But even here, the Act urges that the economies of many coastal areas "have been badly damaged by the overfishing of fishery resources at an ever-increasing rate over the past decade." Id. The Act goes on to explain that "[i]f placed under sound management before overfishing has caused irreversible effects, the fisheries can be conserved and maintained so as to provide optimum yields on a continuing basis." § 1801(a)(5). These observations lead to the conclusion that "[a] national program for the conservation and management of the fishery resources of the United States is necessary to prevent overfishing, to rebuild overfished stocks, to insure conservation, to facilitate long-term protection of essential fish habitats, and to realize the full potential of the Nation's fishery resources." § 1801(a)(6). The "purposes" section adds that "[i]t is therefore declared to be the purposes of the Congress in this chapter * * * to take immediate action to conserve and manage the fishery resources * * *" § 1801(b)(1).

The purpose of the Act is clearly to give conservation of fisheries priority over short-term economic interests. See Daley, 209 F.3d at 753 ("[U]nder the [Act], the [Agency] must give priority to conservation measures."). The Act sets this priority in part because the longer-term economic interests of fishing communities are aligned with the conservation goals set forth in the Act. Without immediate efforts at rebuilding depleted fisheries, the very long-term survival of those fishing communities is in doubt. See id. This background provides helpful context for interpreting § 1854. However, even if we turn to the plain language of § 1854(e)(4) and, without such context, ask how its two subsections interact, we still must reject the interpretation of the Act contained in the 1998 NSG as it was applied to this species.

Section 1854 contains two significant mandates that constrain the Agency's options in adopting a rebuilding plan for an overfished species. First, the time period must be *as short as possible,* although the Agency may take into account the status and biology of the overfished species and the needs of fishing communities. See § 1854(e)(4)(i). Subsection (i)'s commands apply to all rebuilding periods, whatever their length. Second, Congress specified a presumptive *cap of 10 years* on any rebuilding period, subject to exceptional circumstances beyond the Agency's control— such as an international treaty or, relevant here, "the biology of the stock of fish." See § 1854(e)(4)(ii).

We have noted some ambiguity in subsection (i)'s mandate to rebuild a species in "as short [a time period] as possible" while giving consideration to "the needs of fishing communities." The natural reading of this language, however, is that Congress intended to ensure that overfished species were rebuilt as quickly as possible, but wanted to leave some leeway to avoid disastrous short-term consequences for fishing communities. To use an example relevant here, even if a fishing community is actively seeking not to fish for a certain species, it will inevitably catch some of the overfished species in the process of fishing for other, more plentiful fish—what is known as "bycatch." Because almost no groundfish that are caught as bycatch survive even if they are thrown back into the ocean, an absolute ban on catching any of a species of groundfish could mean a total moratorium on all fishing in the parts of the fishery containing groundfish, with obvious adverse consequences for fishing communities. Section

1854(e)(4)(i), then, allows the Agency to set limited quotas that would account for the short-term needs of fishing communities (for example, to allow for some fishing of plentiful species despite the inevitability of bycatch), even though this would mean that the rebuilding period would take longer than it would under a total fishing ban.[7]

Reading subsection (i) in this light, it is apparent that Congress intended subsection (ii) as a limit on the Agency's discretion. The Agency may consider the short-term economic needs of fishing communities in establishing rebuilding periods, but may not use those needs to go beyond the 10-year cap set by subsection (ii). To breach this cap, the Agency may only consider circumstances that "dictate" doing so. One such circumstance, albeit not relevant here, would be an international agreement. Another that *is* relevant is "the biology of the stock of fish"—that is, when the current number of fish in the fishery and the amount of time required for the species to regenerate make it impossible to rebuild the stock within 10 years, even with a total moratorium on fishing. In such cases, subsection (ii) recognizes that the presumptive 10-year cap cannot apply. That said, it is manifestly unreasonable to conclude, as the Agency apparently has, that Congress intended in such circumstances to relieve the Agency of its continuing obligation to rebuild the species in a time frame that is "as short as possible."

The 2002 quota was not based on a permissible construction of the Act, because the Agency altered dramatically the balance between the needs of a species and of fishing communities with no statutorily grounded justification.[8] NRDC argues that if the rebuilding period must exceed 10 years, the Act mandates a total moratorium on all fishing—the alternative interpretation of § 1854 that the Agency rejected when it adopted the 1998 NSG. Although NRDC's interpretation of the statute is reasonable, it is not the only reasonable one. It is also reasonable to conclude that the needs of fishing communities may still be taken into account even when the biology of the fish dictates exceeding the 10-year cap—so long as the weight given is proportionate to the weight the Agency might give to such needs in rebuilding periods under 10 years. This interpretation would allow the Agency's rebuilding periods to account for short-term concerns such as bycatch in the same manner whether the rebuilding period exceeds 10 years or not.

---

[7] This appears to explain the 2001 quota. The Agency determined that the darkblotched rockfish stock could be rebuilt within 10 years, but it still had the flexibility under the statute to set a fishing quota of 130 metric tons for 2001 rather than ban fishing entirely.

[8] In cases of species with much shorter mean generation times, the 1998 NSG might dictate a quota that limits the Agency's discretion in a way that appropriately reflects congressional intent. It is no answer to the irrationality of the interpretation as applied to this species, however, that it may be rational as applied to some other species. As the Agency itself has noted, it is the 2002 darkblotched rockfish quota that is being challenged here.

The 2002 darkblotched rockfish quota is patently unreasonable, however, and reflects no such measured proportionality. Freed from the 10-year cap because of the biology of the rockfish (its long regeneration time and its dire condition), the Agency simply applied the 1998 NSG's formulaic approach and *increased* the annual take. In 2001, the Agency set a quota of 130 million tons of darkblotched rockfish because it believed the species had been reduced to only 22% of its unfished population. When its revised estimate revealed that the species was doing much worse, the Agency expanded the fishing of the species from 130 million tons to 168 million tons, a 29% increase. Whatever the outer limits of the range of permissible constructions of the Act, we are certain that what lies beyond them is an interpretation allowing the Agency, upon discovering that a species is in significantly worse shape than previously thought, to increase dramatically the fishing pressure on that species. Increasing the annual take in these circumstances is simply incompatible with making the rebuilding period as short as possible.

We are not prepared to accept NRDC's argument that once the 10-year cap is lifted because the biology of the fish dictates it, the Act in turn dictates that the Agency can no longer consider the short-term economic needs of fishing communities at all. Such an argument, although plausible, does not appear to give due consideration to the continuing operation of subsection (i)'s command to take the needs of fishing communities into account. But neither are we prepared to accept the Agency's interpretation, which would ignore the primary mandate of subsection (i)—that the rebuilding period be "as short as possible." At least as applied here, the Agency's interpretation not only increased the fishing take by almost 30% but extended the maximum rebuilding period from less than 10 years to 47 years. Plainly, the Act does not contemplate that the Agency grant the least protection to the fish species in the worst shape.

The arguments of the Agency and Intervenors regarding potentially dire consequences for fishing communities seem persuasive at all only because they assume that the sole alternative is NRDC's strict moratorium. The district court made this same flawed assumption:

> Faced with a choice between an interpretation of the [Act] that requires a moratorium on harvesting of fish species that take more than ten years to regenerate naturally, and an interpretation that permits limited harvesting over the course of a longer rebuilding period, [the Agency] selected * * * the latter interpretation. In light of [the Act's] dual conservationist and commercial objectives, an interpretation that accommodates both objectives, rather than selecting one to the exclusion of the other, is permissible.

280 F. Supp.2d at 1014. The Agency was "faced with [this] choice" only because it proposed these two extreme interpretations, and no others.[9]

Our rejection of the Agency's interpretation is compelled by the language of § 1854, which requires that rebuilding take place in "as short [a time] as possible" and, if biologically possible, in less than 10 years. § 1854(e)(4). That simple command cannot be reconciled with a rebuilding period that is from 20 to 33 years longer than the biologically shortest possible rebuilding period (and that increases the annual take in the meanwhile). We hold that even granting the Agency some leeway in extending rebuilding periods when the 10-year cap is not applicable, the 2002 darkblotched rockfish quota was based on an impermissible construction of the Act.

NOTES AND QUESTIONS

1. Which alternative interpretations of the rebuilding time requirement did the agency consider before adopting the one at issue in the case? Was this interpretation consistent with the other amendments to the Act? Did the agency propose too narrow a set of alternative interpretations to define the rebuilding time requirement?

2. Final rules setting the 2006 optimum yield specifications for darkblotched rockfish were published in 71 Fed. Reg. 8489 (Feb. 17, 2006). As a result of the above decision, in March, 2006, NMFS published a notice of intent to prepare an environmental impact statement reevaluating and revising the rebuilding plans for all seven of the overfished species managed under the Pacific groundfish FMP. 71 Fed. Reg. 13097 (March 14, 2006). Does NEPA require the council to consider a wider range of alternative rebuilding strategies and timeframes than the Sustainable Fisheries Act?

3. On the East coast, efforts to rebuild the New England groundfish stocks have also brought to light ambiguities in the Sustainable Fisheries Act. In 2000, a federal district court ordered the New England Council and NMFS to prepare a new rebuilding plan for the dozen or more species in the Northeast multi-species groundfish complex, Conservation Law Foundation v. Evans, 209 F.Supp.2d 1 (D.D.C. 2001), and imposed a remedial order of interim conservation measures while the new plan was being prepared, CLF v. Evans, 211 F. Supp.2d 55 (D.D.C. 2002). The Secretary then approved Amendment 13, a plan that allowed fishing to continue at rates above the overfishing rate in the first several years of the rebuilding period. In Oceana, Inc. v. Evans, 2005 WL 555416 (D.D.C. 2005) (slip opinion), environmental-group plaintiffs challenged the approval of Amendment 13 on grounds that it failed to halt overfishing on those fish stocks that were the most severely de-

---

[9] The closest any party came to explaining the Agency's justification for its decision to increase the quota was Intervenors' counsel's assertion that the Act was "not written by biologists," apparently a criticism of the stringency of its rebuilding commands, and in particular of the presumptive 10-year cap.

pleted. The New England Council had selected among several alternative rebuilding plans one that would phase in stricter fishing limits over time, postponing lowering the fishing mortality rate to Fmsy until later in the rebuilding period instead of sharply cutting it in the first year. Relying in part on the lower court decision in the darkblotched rockfish case above, the court upheld the council's choice, finding that the MSA applies only to the MSY amount not to the Fmsy. By not ending overfishing immediately the council was enabling "more fishermen to remain in business while stocks rebuild * * * The Secretary may * * * allow overfishing for a time in order to take account of fishing communities' needs, so long as, * * * the MSA's conservation goals are achieved * * *" Slip copy at 15. Do the provisions on overfishing and rebuilding and the National Standards, as interpreted by the 9th Circuit in NRDC v. NMFS (the darkblotched rockfish case, above) support this holding?

For background on the failures of the federal fishery management system to provide an effective control on New England fisheries, see R. Fleming, P. Shelley, and P.M. Brooks, Twenty-Eight Years and Counting: Can the Magnuson–Stevens Act Deliver on Its Conservation Promise? 28 Vt. L. Rev. 579 (2004).

D. THE ECOSYSTEM APPROACH

The 1996 Sustainable Fisheries Act kept the basic elements of the U.S. fishery management plans and process intact, with its focus on individual fish species or groups of species that comprise a management unit. The Act grafted onto these provisions requirements that the councils consider the other biological and physical features of marine ecosystems that allow fish stocks to persist: ecologically related species and habitat.

1. Bycatch Reduction

The Magnuson–Stevens Act defines "bycatch" as "fish which are harvested in a fishery, but which are not sold or kept for personal use, and include economic discards and regulatory discards. Such term does not include fish released alive under a recreational catch and release fishery management program." 16 U.S.C. § 1802(2). "Economic discards" are those fish that are "the target of a fishery, but which are not retained because they are of an undesirable size, sex, or quality, or for other economic reasons." Id. at § 1802(9). "Regulatory discards" are defined as "fish harvested in a fishery which fishermen are required by regulation to discard whenever caught, or are required by regulation to retain but not sell." Id. at § 1802(32).

The Act defines "fish" as "finfish, mollusks, crustaceans, and all other forms of marine animal and plant life *other than* marine mammals and birds. Id. at § 1802(12)(emphasis added). Therefore, the bycatch requirements of the Act do not apply to marine mammals and other wildlife. The incidental mortality of these species in commercial fisheries can be the subject of FMP regulations, as the Secretary of Commerce has frequently used the Regional Councils or their FMPs to implement the Marine Mammal Protection Act and Endangered Species Act provisions affecting marine wildlife. These laws are covered in the next chapter.

National Standard 9 provides the basic requirements regarding bycatch. "Conservation and management measures shall, *to the extent practicable*, (A) minimize bycatch and (B) to the extent bycatch cannot be avoided, minimize the mortality of such bycatch." 16 U.S.C. § 1851(a)(9)(emphasis added). Also, all FMPs are required to include "a standardized reporting methodology to assess the amount and type of bycatch occurring in the fishery, and include conservation and management measures that, *to the extent practicable* and in the following priority—(A) minimize bycatch; and (B) minimize the mortality of bycatch which cannot be avoided[.]" 16 U.S.C. § 1853(a)(11)(emphasis added).

What does it mean to minimize bycatch "to the extent practicable"? Is "practicable" a technological feasibility standard or one that takes costs into account? In a statement on the House floor during debates on the reauthorization, Congressman Don Young of Alaska said Councils should make "reasonable efforts," but that:

> "it is not the intent of Congress that the councils ban a type of fishing gear or a type of fishing in order to comply with this standard. 'Practicable' requires an analysis of the costs of imposing a management action; the Congress does not intent that this provision will be used to allocate among fishing gear groups, nor to impose costs on fishermen and processors that cannot be reasonably met.

14 Cong. Rec. H11437 (daily ed. September 27, 1996).

The guidelines on the bycatch National Standard is found at 50 CFR § 600.350—National Standard Guideline on Bycatch. It provides further insight into the nature of the fish bycatch problem.

> * * * Bycatch can, in two ways, impede efforts to protect marine ecosystems and achieve sustainable fisheries and the full benefits they can provide to the Nation. First, bycatch can increase substantially the uncertainty concerning total fishing-related mortality, which makes it more difficult to assess the status of stocks, to set the appropriate [optimum yield (OY)] and define overfishing levels, and to ensure that OYs are attained and overfishing levels are not exceeded. Second, bycatch may also preclude other more productive uses of fishery resources.

50 C.F.R. § 600.350(d).

To help the regional councils determine how far it is practicable to minimize bycatch, NOAA offers the following guidance:

(i) A determination of whether a conservation and management measure minimizes bycatch or bycatch mortality to the extent practicable, consistent with other national standards and maximization of net benefits to the Nation, should consider the following factors:

(A) Population effects for the bycatch species.

(B) Ecological effects due to changes in the bycatch of that species (effects on other species in the ecosystem).

(C) Changes in the bycatch of other species of fish and the resulting population and ecosystem effects.

(D) Effects on marine mammals and birds.

(E) Changes in fishing, processing, disposal, and marketing costs.

(F) Changes in fishing practices and behavior of fishermen.

(G) Changes in research, administration, and enforcement costs and management effectiveness.

(H) Changes in the economic, social, or cultural value of fishing activities and nonconsumptive uses of fishery resources.

(I) Changes in the distribution of benefits and costs.

(J) Social effects.

(ii) The Councils should adhere to the precautionary approach * * * when faced with uncertainty concerning any of the factors listed in this paragraph.

Id. at § 600.350(d).

PACIFIC MARINE CONSERVATION COUNCIL V. EVANS

United States District Court, N.D. California, 2002
200 F. Supp.2d 1194

LARSON, MAGISTRATE JUDGE.

In October 1998 the Pacific Council submitted to NMFS proposed Amendment 11 to the Pacific Coast Groundfish FMP. This was an effort to bring the FMP into compliance with the new requirements of SFA. In 1999, NMFS approved most of Amendment 11 but disapproved the amendment's bycatch provisions. NMFS concluded that Amendment 11 was not responsive to the bycatch requirements of the Magnuson–Stevens Act because it contained no specific measures to collect bycatch information. NMFS concluded that a bycatch amendment would also have to include "an analysis of all practicable alternatives to the current year-round trip limit management system that could be expected to result in a reduction of bycatch rates."

In an effort to respond to NMFS' disapproval of the bycatch provisions of Amendment 11, the Pacific Council subsequently prepared Amendment 13 to the Pacific Groundfish FMP and submitted the proposed amendment to the NMFS in 2000. The purpose of Amendment 13 is to bring the FMP into compliance with the bycatch-related requirements of the MSA. Unfortunately, as discussed below, Amendment 13 falls short of what is required by the MSA.

To comply with MSA's requirement that each plan establish a standardized reporting methodology to assess the amount and type of bycatch, Amendment 13 *permits* but does not *require* an observer program.[2] Amendment 13 provides: "The Regional Administrator *may* implement an observer program through a Council-approved federal regulatory framework." Amendment 13 does not make the observer program mandatory despite the NMFS' own conclusion that an at-sea observer program is essential for adequately assessing bycatch in the Pacific groundfish fishery (NMFS concluded that "critical information on the portion of the catch that is discarded at sea is available only through the placement of onboard observers.")

Similarly, to attempt to comply with MSA's requirement to minimize both bycatch and bycatch mortality, Amendment 13 *lists* but does not *require* certain types of bycatch reduction techniques for the non-whiting groundfish fishery. The sentence in Amendment 13 that introduces this list of potential bycatch reduction techniques reads:

> These [bycatch reduction measures] may include but are not limited to: Full retention or increased utilization programs; setting shorter-than-year-round fishing season in combination with higher cumulative landing limits; allowing permit stacking in the limited entry fleet; gear modification requirements; catch allocation to, or gear flexibility for, gear types with lower bycatch rates; re-examining/improving species-to-species landings limit ratios; and time/area closures.

3 AR B.14, Appendix A, at A–5. Amendment 13 did not make these techniques mandatory ("may include"), despite MSA's unambiguous intent to minimize bycatch and bycatch mortality to the extent practicable.

* * *

Plaintiffs challenge Amendment 13 * * * [T]hey allege that the NMFS failed to adopt an adequate bycatch methodology. [T]hey [also] al-

---

[2] An observer program documents bycatch by placing trained individuals in fishing boats for the duration of a fishing trip. While at sea, the observer records the numbers and species of fish that are discarded overboard, giving fishery managers hard and reliable data on the amount and type of bycatch that is occurring in the fishery.

lege that the NMFS failed to adequately consider the adoption of bycatch measures * * *

Adequate Bycatch Assessment Methodology

First, Plaintiffs challenge Amendment 13 for failing to adopt an adequate bycatch assessment methodology in violation of MSA's requirement that each FMP "establish a standardized reporting methodology to assess the amount and type of bycatch occurring in the fishery." 16 U.S.C. § 1853(a)(11). Plaintiff directs this court's attention to NMFS's admission that it lacks adequate data on the amount and type of bycatch in the Pacific ground fishery; that this absence of bycatch data seriously harms its ability to manage the Pacific groundfish fishery and to protect overfished groundfish species; and that an at-sea observer program is essential for adequately assessing bycatch in the Pacific groundfish fishery. While the administrative record makes it clear that an adequate groundfish observer program is essential to account for bycatch in the Pacific, NMFS has yet to implement such an observer program.

Amendment 13 discusses the possible use of observers to assess bycatch at some point in the future. However, it contains no requirement to adopt either an observer program or any other bycatch assessment methodology. As NMFS admits in its Federal Register notice announcing its approval of Amendment 13, the rule "itself does not require implementation of an observer program." 66 Fed. Reg. at 29,729, 29,730 (June 1, 2001).

Defendants argue that Amendment 13 provides for an at-sea observer program and that implementation of this program is underway. NMFS contends that its observer program provides adequate bycatch assessment as required by MSA. This court finds the program legally insufficient to meet NMFS's bycatch assessment duties under 16 U.S.C. section 1853(a)(11), because it is not mandated by Amendment 13. That section of MSA requires that bycatch assessment methods be established in the fishery management plan itself. Because the observer program is optional under Amendment 13, NMFS in theory could decide not to implement an observer program for the ground fishery, and nothing in Amendment 13 would prohibit the agency from making that decision.

Furthermore, NMFS admits that its observer program cannot provide the data necessary to assess the amount and type of bycatch occurring in the fishery. NMFS calls the current observer program "a limited observer program," and the agency admits that at the current level of funding, the observer program will not be able to provide sufficiently accurate new discard estimates for each area/time/gear strata. See 66 Fed. Reg. at 29,731 (only "a limited program is practicable at current funding levels").

MSA requires that a fishery management plan establish a bycatch assessment methodology sufficient to assess the amount and type of bycatch occurring in the fishery. 16 U.S.C. § 1853(a)(11). Because Amendment 13 fails to establish a mandatory and adequate observer program—a program that the NMFS itself concedes is critical—this court finds that Amendment 13 is "not in accordance with" the MSA. Accordingly, this court grants Plaintiffs motion for summary judgment on this claim and remands Amendment 13 to NMFS for further consideration and action. 5 U.S.C. § 706(2)(A).

Amendment 13 Does Not Minimize Bycatch and Bycatch Mortality

The MSA requires that fishery management plans include conservation and management measures to (a) minimize bycatch and (b) to the extent bycatch cannot be avoided, minimize the mortality of such bycatch, to the extent practicable. 16 U.S.C. § 1851(a)(9), 1853(a)(11); see also 63 Fed. Reg. at 24,244 ("bycatch must be avoided as much as practicable, and bycatch mortality must be reduced until further reductions are not practicable."). By Congressional mandate, fishery managers must bring each existing FMP into compliance by October 11, 1998. Sustainable Fisheries Act § 108(b), Pub.L. No 104–297, 110 Stat. 3359, 3575.

Plaintiffs allege that Amendment 13 fails to minimize bycatch and mortality arising from bycatch, and that, in consequence, NMFS is in violation of the MSA. Amendment 13 fails to adopt any bycatch reduction measures with one limited exception. See 66 Fed. Reg. at 29,733. Amendment 13 contains only a voluntary increased-utilization program for at-sea whiting processors. NMFS did not adopt any bycatch reduction requirement for the non-whiting groundfish fishery. Rather, Amendment 13 lists a series of potential bycatch reduction measures that NMFS and the Council might consider for adoption at some undetermined point in the future.... This court finds that by using this discretionary language, ("may include"), Amendment 13 fails to implement the mandate of MSA to reduce bycatch and bycatch mortality.

This court finds that Defendants' adoption of Amendment 13 does not comply with the MSA. MSA requires timely action on bycatch reduction and further requires that all practicable measures be included in the fishery management plan. 16 U.S.C. § 1853(a)(11). Amendment 13 also ignores the fact that overfished Pacific groundfish species need protection from excessive bycatch now, not at some undetermined time in the future. By establishing a two-year deadline for amending FMP to meet the bycatch reduction requirements of 16 U.S.C. section 1853(a)(11), Congress demanded timely action to reduce bycatch. See Sustainable Fisheries Act § 108(b), Pub.L. No 104–297, 110 Stat. 3359, 3575 (establishing two-year deadline). For the foregoing reasons, Amendment 13 falls short of MSA's requirement that FMP's be amended to include conservation and management measures that minimize bycatch to the extent practicable.

Plaintiffs next allege that Amendment 13 violates the legal requirements for reasoned agency decision-making in its dismissal of four viable bycatch reduction measures. Specifically, Plaintiffs allege that Defendants dismiss without justification: 1) reduction of the size of the fishing fleet; and 2) establishment of marine reserves as potential bycatch reduction measures. Plaintiffs claim that the dismissal of these potential measures were based not on their merits, but on Defendants' belief that these are "currently impracticable because implementation would require Council discussion and exploration beyond the scope of this draft amendment."

In response, Defendants argue that Amendment 13 did not dismiss the aforementioned measures that might reduce bycatch. Rather, these measures "were discussed, considered, and reasonably determined to be impracticable for immediate implementation through Amendment 13." Defendants also argue that NMFS has "rationally concluded that implementing a major new regulatory program such as fleet reduction or marine protected areas-both of which are highly complex and controversial-was impractical in the context of Amendment 13." To the contrary, it is evident in the administrative record that NMFS specifically rejected both measures because their implementation would require Council discussion and exploration beyond the scope of Amendment 13.

NMFS rejected both fishing capacity reduction and marine reserves as bycatch reduction measures because it arbitrarily deemed them beyond the scope of Amendment 13. By failing to evaluate these measures on their substantive merits, NMFS violated the requirement that agency decisions be "founded on reasoned evaluation of the relevant factors." Marsh v. Oregon Natural Resources Council, 490 U.S. 360, 378 (1989). Because the record demonstrates that NMFS' decision making was unreasoned here, Amendment 13 should be rejected and remanded to NMFS. See Hall v. U.S. E.P.A., 263 F.3d 926, 940 (9th Cir.2001). ("If the decision of the agency is not sustainable on the administrative record made, then the decision must be vacated and the matter remanded * * * for further consideration.)" (Citations omitted).

Plaintiffs also challenge NMFS's dismissal of two additional bycatch reduction methods as "impracticable without an observer program." The first of these potential measures is the use of incentives for vessels with lower bycatch rates, such as allowing higher landing limits (and thus greater fishing profits) for fishing vessels that fish selectively and thus have relatively low discard rates. The second potential measure is the use of discard caps to manage the fishery.

In response, NMFS argues that these bycatch reduction measures were "reasonably found impracticable without 100 percent observer coverage." As Plaintiffs correctly point out, this argument begs the question of whether full observer coverage is itself practicable in the groundfish fishery in light of the criteria for practicability set forth at 50 C.F.R. 600.350(d)(3)(i). These criteria are:

> Population effects for the bycatch species. Ecological effects due to changes in the bycatch of that species. Changes in the bycatch of other species of fish and the resulting population and ecosystem effects. Effects on marine mammals and birds. Changes in fishing, processing, disposal, and marketing costs. Changes in fishing practices and behavior of fishermen. Changes in research, administration, and enforcement costs and management effectiveness. Changes in the economic, social, or cultural value of fishing activities and nonconsumptive uses of fishery resources. Changes in the distribution of benefits and costs. Social effects.

50 C.F.R. § 600.350.

Defendants argue that "both alternatives are deemed impracticable without a full observer program, since both would require individual vessel monitoring." According to the Defendants, both alternatives are also discussed in the preamble to the final rule implementing Amendment 13. 66 Fed. Reg. 29729, 29731 (June 1, 2001). With respect to the vessel incentives, NMFS states in the preamble that:

> While a limited observer program is practicable at current funding levels, the type of observer program that would be needed to implement a vessel incentive program is not practicable.

Id. With respect to the discard caps, NMFS opines that:

> [A] discard cap program with only limited observer coverage tends to exaggerate the "observer effect" in information about vessels sampled, meaning that the vessels carrying observers have a significant incentive to change their fishing behavior to lower their bycatch rates and keep the entire fishery open. Unobserved vessels do not have this same incentive to reduce discards; thus, there is a strong chance that the whole fleet would reach the discard cap before the observed fleet's expanded data indicated that the cap has been reached. Stronger observer effect under incentives like discard cap management leads to less scientific accuracy from the observer program.

Id.

NMFS did not fully consider the practicability of the more comprehensive observer program necessary to administer vessel incentives or discard caps in light of the factors set forth in 50 C.F.R. 600.350(d)(3)(i). Consequently, NMFS has engaged in unreasoned decision-making in dismissing these two potential bycatch reduction measures. Defendants' failure to minimize bycatch and bycatch mortality is arbitrary, capricious, and contrary to law, and in violation of the MSA, SFA and APA. Accordingly, this court finds that Amendment 13 violates MSA's requirements at 16 U.S.C. §§ 1851(a)(9), 1853(a)(11), and the APA's reasoned agency decision-making. This court also remands Amendment 13 to NMFS for further consideration in light of these requirements. See Hall v. EPA, 263 F.3d 926, 940 (9th Cir.2001) ("If the decision of the agency is not sustainable on the administrative record made, then the * * * decision must be vacated and the matter remanded * * * for further consideration.")

NOTES AND QUESTIONS

1. Note that the court ordered that the bycatch plan amendment be remanded to the Fisheries Service. Should the Service send the amendment back to the council, and if so, how long should it give it to remedy the deficiencies? What happens to the non-target species being caught in the fishery during the time it takes the council to develop new, proposed bycatch measures? If the Fisheries Service doesn't have a default bycatch mitigation plan that takes effect if the council fails to decide, what are the council's incentive to prepare a plan that meets the bycatch minimization mandate? Do councils "care" about the population levels of bycatch species?

In the New England groundfish litigation, federal district court Judge Gladys Kessler did not remand the deficient plan to prevent overfishing and to minimize bycatch to the Fisheries Service but instead ordered the parties to develop a negotiated remedial plan to take effect while the council prepared Amendment 13. Conservation Law Foundation v. Evans, 211 F. Supp.2d 55 (D.D.C. 2002). After Amendment 13 was approved and then challenged, the court found the bycatch provisions to be inadequate and remanded the plan to the Fisheries Service to develop a bycatch monitoring provision. Oceana, Inc. v. Evans, 2005 WL 555416 (D.D.C. 2005) (slip opinion).

2. Are the councils required to adopt bycatch mitigation measures or merely to consider and evaluate if they are needed, adopting measures only to the extent practicable, with discretion in determining what is "practicable"?

3. To ensure that bycatch is accurately counted, onboard observers are often required. Can the government require vessel owners to take an official observer on their boat and remain onboard throughout the lengthy fishing trip? When owners of U. S. purse seine tuna fishing vessels were required to take observers onboard to insure accurate reporting of dolphin mortality, they challenged the regulation as an "unreasonable" search in violation of the 4th Amendment. The Ninth Circuit held that there was no violation as the tuna fishery was highly regulated industry with no reasonable expectation of privacy. Balelo v. Baldrige, 724 F.2d 753 (9th Cir. 1984).

4. In addition to the above general requirements for all FMPs, Congress enacted separate provisions addressing bycatch and regulatory discards in fisheries of the North Pacific and in the shrimp trawl fishery in the Gulf of Mexico and South Atlantic. 16 U.S.C. §§ 1862(f),(g); 1881d(d). In the North Pacific, the council is authorized to develop a program of individual vessel discard quotas and other incentive-based programs to reduce bycatch and discards in all North Pacific fisheries. For the shrimp fishery, Congress required the Secretary to undertake a bycatch reduction program. Without specific congressional authorization are these measures precluded in other fisheries? Why does Congress "micro-manage" certain fisheries?

5. Bycatch of marine wildlife in fisheries is also addressed under the "incidental take" provisions of the Marine Mammal Protection Act and the Endangered Species Act (ESA), which are considered in the next Chapter. When incidental take measures are adopted as Magnuson–Stevens Act bycatch regulations, for example, in the case of sea turtles protected under the ESA, plaintiffs wishing to challenge them must be aware of the 30-day requirement to seek judicial review. In Turtle Island Restoration Network v. Dept. of Commerce, even though NMFS adopted a regulation requiring the use of circle hooks and fish bait after a biological consultation under section 7 of the ESA, because it was implemented as a fishery management measure, plaintiffs were held to the 30-day filing requirement under the MSA. Turtle Island Restoration Network v. Dept. of Commerce, 438 F.3d 937 (9th Cir. 2006). Compare this ruling with Blue Water Fishermen's Assoc. v. NMFS, 158 F. Supp.2d 118 (D. Mass. 2001) (upholding NMFS's closure of Grand Banks offshore fishing grounds to U.S. pelagic longlining for swordfish due to high incidental takes of endangered sea turtles, rejecting claim that 30-day limit under MSA applies). Why did Congress require that any lawsuits challenging the validity of fishery regulations be filed within 30 days of final promulgation or plaintiffs would lose their day in court?

6. Under the Magnuson-Stevens Act, "fish" is defined as meaning "finfish, mollusks, crustaceans, and all other forms of marine animal and plant life other than marine mammals and birds." 16 U.S.C. § 1802(12). Does this mean that a regional fishery management council could develop a management plan for a species or "stock" of sea turtles if one is no longer listed as endangered or threatened under the ESA? Does the MSA give councils the authority to petition the secretary to remove a species from ESA protection including consultation under section 7?

2. Essential Fish Habitat

To address the need for conservation of the habitat on which fish and other marine species depend, the 1996 amendments to the Magnuson–Stevens Act added the following findings on the significance of habitat to fisheries:

Certain stocks of fish have declined to the point where there survival is threatened, and other stocks of fish have been so substantially reduced in number that they could become similarly threatened as a consequence of (A) increased fishing pressure, (B) the inadequacy of * * * conservation and management practices and controls, or (C) direct and indirect habitat losses which have resulted in a diminished capacity to support existing fishing levels.

16 U.S.C. § 1801(a)(2).

One of the greatest long-term threats to the viability of commercial and recreational fisheries is the continued loss of marine, estuarine, and other aquatic habitats. Habitat considerations should receive increased attention for the conservation and management of fishery resources of the United States.

16 U.S.C. § 1801(a)(9).

The Act establishes the concept of "essential fish habitat," defined as "those waters and substrate necessary to fish for spawning, breeding, feeding or growth to maturity." 16 U.S.C. § 1802(10). The Councils are now required in their FMPs to:

describe and identify essential fish habitat for the fishery based on the guidelines established by the Secretary * * *, minimize to the extent practicable adverse effects on such habitat caused by fishing, and identify other actions to encourage the conservation and enhancement of such habitat[.] * * *

16 U.S.C. § 1853(a)(7).

Under the terms of the EFH provisions, the Councils had to submit amendments to the thirty-six existing FMPs by October 11, 1998. These amendments had to identify EFH, the adverse impacts to EFH from both fishing and non-fishing sources, and measures to conserve and enhance EFH. The three Secretarial FMPs prepared directly by NOAA's Fisheries Service for Atlantic highly migratory species were to be amended in a similar fashion.

After the Secretary approved the councils' EFH amendments, environmental groups challenged the adequacy of five of them (New England, Caribbean, Gulf of Mexico, Pacific, and North Pacific). The district court found that all councils had identified EFHs within each of their jurisdictions, yet none adopted further measures that would restrict fishing gear in order to minimize adverse effects of fishing related activities on EFH. The court held that the amendments were sufficient for meeting the requirements of Section 303(a)(7) of the MSA, 16 U.S.C. § 1853(a)(7), but the environmental impact and alternatives analyses required by NEPA were inadequate. American Oceans Campaign v. Daley, 183 F. Supp.2d 1 (D.D.C. 2000). The plaintiffs settled with NOAA on a timetable for the completion of the required analyses and the consideration of additional measures to protect habitat from adverse fishing gear effects.

The regional councils prepared the first round of EFH amendments pursuant to guidance published by NOAA's Fisheries Service as interim final rules on how to identify EFH and assess the effects of fishing gear on EFH. 62 Fed. Reg. 66531 (Dec. 17, 1997). After the American Oceans Campaign challenged the EFH plans in 1999, the Fisheries Service reopened the comment period on the interim rules, seeking input specifically on whether additional regulatory guidance was needed on how to minimize the effects of fishing on habitat. The final rules were published in early 2002 with no major substantive changes, but with several clarifications. 67 Fed. Reg. 2343 (Jan. 17, 2002).

The second round of FMP amendments and environmental impact statements identifying and conserving EFH were completed in 2005, with implementation in 2006. During this period, the Fisheries Service evaluated council-proposed fishery management actions for the extent to which they minimized bycatch and adverse fishing effects on EFH. The Service's decisions to approve these measures continued to generate controversy and, to some degree, inconsistent interpretations of the Act's impact-minimization requirements and of the available scientific information on the adverse effects of fishing gear. After several challenges, it was clear that the councils did not agree on what the best available science was on the habitat impacts of fishing gear such as bottom trawling and dredging. How did the Fisheries Service interpret the available science and whether habitat-protective measures were "practicable"? Consider the following cases.

CONSERVATION LAW FOUNDATION V. EVANS

United States Court of Appeals, First Circuit, 2004
360 F.3d 21

HOWARD, CIRCUIT JUDGE.

On May 31, 2001, the plaintiffs initiated an action challenging Framework 14, a rule that adjusted certain restrictions on sea scallop fishing in the Atlantic coastal waters. * * *

Conservation Law Foundation and Oceana contend that Framework 14 [a regulatory revision] is arbitrary and capricious in failing to mandate the closure of scallop-harvesting in four areas [of fish habitat]. To succeed on this claim, they must demonstrate that NMFS lacked a rational basis for adopting the framework. See Associated Fisheries of Maine, Inc. v. Daley, 127 F.3d 104, 109 (1st Cir.1997). That showing may be made where "the agency relied on improper factors, failed to consider pertinent aspects of the problem, offered a rationale contradicting the evidence before it, or reached a conclusion so implausible that it cannot be attributed to a difference of opinion or the application of agency expertise." Id.

Under the Magnuson–Stevens Act, NMFS has a duty to minimize to the extent practicable (1) adverse effects on essential fish habitat ("EFH"), 16 U.S.C. § 1853(a)(7); and (2) bycatch (fish that are caught but not sold or kept for personal use) and bycatch mortality, 16 U.S.C. §§ 1851(a)(9), 1853(a)(11). [EFH refers to "those waters and substrate necessary to fish for spawning, breeding, feeding or growth to maturity." 16 U.S.C. 1802(10).] The plaintiffs argue that NMFS violated these statutory obligations in rejecting the closure of the four fishing areas. As they see it, NMFS's decision was irreconcilable with record evidence that the closures would be beneficial with respect to EFH and bycatch. The plaintiffs also fault NMFS's analysis, claiming that the agency ignored relevant factors they should have considered and failed to articulate a rational basis for declining to implement the closures.

These arguments are flawed to the extent that they consider the closure alternative in isolation, discounting numerous other restrictions on scallop fishing imposed by Framework 14. See CLF, 229 F. Supp.2d at 34 (noting that Framework 14 maintained closures of three large scallop fishing areas, as well as "restrictions on days at sea, catch and mesh sizes, and seasonal access to sensitive areas"). Moreover, the plaintiffs essentially call for an interpretation of the statute that equates "practicability" with "possibility," requiring NMFS to implement virtually any measure that addresses EFH and bycatch concerns so long as it is feasible. Although the distinction between the two may sometimes be fine, there is indeed a distinction. The closer one gets to the plaintiffs' interpretation, the less weighing and balancing is permitted. We think by using the term "practicable" Congress intended rather to allow for the application of agency expertise and discretion in determining how best to manage fishery resources.

We also note that CLF's and Oceana's characterization of the record is somewhat faulty. NMFS in fact considered the closure alternative and other potential management measures in a Final Supplemental Environmental Impact Statement ("FSEIS") that analyzed the probable effects of Framework 14. The FSEIS concluded, *inter alia,* that the closures would provide only limited, short-term benefits to habitat. These benefits would be "mitigated to some degree" because other (non-scallop) fishing would continue in the closed areas. The FSEIS also found that (1) implementing no new closures would have a greater economic benefit for the fishing seasons Framework 14 was intended to address than would the closure alternative, and (2) any long-term benefits that might accrue as a result of closures were uncertain and might not outweigh the benefits of forgoing new closures. It is not our role to second guess these determinations. See Associated Fisheries, 127 F.3d at 109 ("Even if a reviewing court disagrees with the agency's conclusions, it cannot substitute its judgment for that of the agency."). On this record, the plaintiffs have not shown that NMFS acted irrationally in implementing Framework 14 without imposing additional closures.

* * *

NATURAL RESOURCES DEFENSE COUNCIL V. EVANS

United States District Court, S.D. New York, 2003
254 F. Supp.2d 434

BERMAN, DISTRICT JUDGE.

I. Introduction

* * * Plaintiffs claim that Defendants wrongly refused to limit the use of "bottom-tending mobile gear" to protect tilefish habitat * * *[1] Defendants respond that there is no evidence that bottom-tending mobile gear causes an "identifiable adverse effect" upon tilefish habitat * * *

* * *

In 1998, the Nat'l Marine Fisheries Service declared tilefish (*Lopholatilus chamaeleonticeps*) to be overfished, thus triggering the need for an FMP. The Mid–Atlantic Fishery Management Council issued a draft tilefish FMP and Environmental Impact Statement in May 1999 for comment. The draft considered, among other things, the impact of bottom-tending mobile gear on tilefish habitat and, despite the paucity of evidence in respect of adverse effects on tilefish habitat, stated:

> Based on the best available scientific information, it can be *inferred* that trawling is causing long-term physical adverse impacts to tilefish EFH [i.e., "essential fish habitat"]. It is further *implied* that in some cases those adverse impacts may be severe, at least locally.

The draft FMP cited studies of the impact of bottom-tending mobile gear on other (i.e., non-tilefish) habitats. The draft recommended changes to the use of bottom-tending mobile gear.

The draft FMP gave rise to a great deal of comment. For example, the Northeast Fisheries Science Center challenged the draft FMP's inference, stating that "[t]he use of shallow water examples of possible gear effects to biogenic habitat is misleading." Public hearings in Rhode Island, New York and New Jersey gave rise to the following reactions: "Emerson Hasbrouck (Cornell), * * * a port agent from 1975 through 1988 * * * disagree[d] with conclusion [sic] specifically for tilefish. Assumed impacts to tilefish are not relatable." [citations to record omitted]Bonnie Aripotch commented that "[t]here is no science for 'tilefish.' " Fisherman Dan

---

[1] Bottom-tending mobile gear is a category of fishing device, such as the otter trawl, which uses metal boards to hold open a net towed behind a fishing boat. AR1929–31. (AR ___ refers to pages in the Administrative Record.)

Farnham argued that "gear impacts are not specifically identified for tilefish" and that "[t]he best tilefish landings occur where bottom gear is fished heavily." Maggie Raymond, a representative of Garden State Seafood and other organizations, commented that the Council should research the gear impacts on tilefish habitats before implementing the draft FMP or "[t]here will be lost revenues with this alternative." Fisherman Joe Nolan believed the conclusions in the draft "would destroy historic fishermen." Likewise, Kevin Maguire asked the Council "not [to] put people out of business," and Diana Weir commented that the " 'flawed' plan * * * will decimate our Montauk fisherman." In contrast, Sonja Fordham from the Center for Marine Conservation stated "that a precautionary approach is warranted for such a long-lived, slow-growing, habitat-dependent species, that's in such an overfished state. We recognize that data on specific—the specific association are [sic] not strong."

Commenters who opposed the "inference" that bottom-tending mobile gear negatively impacts tilefish habitat generally based their arguments on the lack of available evidence. Commenters who supported the inference generally sought a precautionary approach, that is, limiting or banning the use of bottom-tending mobile gear despite the lack of evidence of its effects on tilefish habitat.

Interested parties, including Dr. Ken Able, a recognized expert on tilefish, representatives from the National Marine Fisheries Service and Mid–Atlantic Fishery Management Council, and others met in September 1999 as a working group to discuss, among other things, bottom-tending mobile gear's impact on tilefish habitat. Dr. Able was "unaware of any work on the east coast that would address gear impact questions for tilefish * * * Theoretically, trawls could pass over the burrows without destroying them or could potentially cause sediments to fill the burrows. Able ha[d] not seen evidence of burrows filled in by trawls in his submersible work." In short, no scientific data existed which proved a negative impact on tilefish habitat, according to Dr. Able. The Mid–Atl. Fish Mgmt. Council acknowledged that they lacked evidence for their opinion that bottom-tending mobile gear had an adverse impact on tilefish habitat.

At an October 14, 1999 meeting of the MAFMC, the chairman of the Council stated that "what [Dr. Able] said and what the rest of the researchers concluded was that there really is nothing definitively known on tilefish gear or on bottom tending gear impacting tilefish habitat * * * We can make all the associations we want, but we don't have any direct evidence. There's nothing in the literature. He knows of nothing."

At a November 1999 meeting of the council, one staff member noted that "the conclusion of the working group was that nothing definitively was known directly about tilefish being directly impacted by bottom tending mobile gear. There is nothing direct in the literature. Unquestionably, trawl gear-patterns are found in tilefish burrows * * * What the working group and the tilefish technical team now is recommending is that there not be gear impact measures in this FMP at this time, that there be a research approach." A Council member noted: "The fact is there is no evidence as to what mobile gear does. It's not that there isn't much. *There isn't any* * * * We simply have no information to justify . . . the proposals we went out to public hearing with. *We just had nothing.*" (emphasis added). Consequently, the Council voted to "eliminate the recommendation [from the draft FMP] to close ocean areas to protect tilefish habitat from supposed impact from mobile gear at this time." Rather, the Council approved a plan to implement a research program to study the impact of bottom-tending mobile gear on tilefish habitat within two years.

The Council submitted the revised tilefish FMP * * * to the National Marine Fisheries Service in March 2000. The final FMP states:

> It was concluded that there is nothing definitively known about tilefish-mobile fishing gear interactions. There is nothing specifically described about the sensitivity of tilefish burrows in the scientific literature. Unquestionably, from submersible vessel research, there are trawl door patterns observed in areas with tilefish burrows, but how much of an impact the doors have and how quickly tilefish can reopen their burrows, if sediment closed, is completely unknown at this time * * * *[I]mpacts of bottom tending mobile gear specifically to tilefish habitat are unquantifiable at this time.* (emphasis added).

The Secretary approved the FMP on May 10, 2001.

> Based on the adverse economic effects that a prohibition on the use of bottom-tending mobile gear in tilefish HAPC would have upon several other fisheries and on the lack of scientific evidence showing identifiable adverse effects caused by such gear on tilefish EFH, the Council did not propose gear prohibitions in the HAPC on other than limited access tilefish vessels.

> NMFS and the Council support a cooperative research program to further investigate this issue.

* * *

(i) Effects of Bottom-Tending Mobile Gear

Plaintiffs advance a number of arguments to support their claim that Defendants acted arbitrarily in concluding that bottom-tending mobile gear does not have an identifiable adverse effect on tilefish habitat. Plaintiffs argue that Defendants ignored evidence of physical disruption to tilefish habitat, which is an adverse effect; that Defendants failed to explain their change in position from the draft FMP to the final one; and that Defendants wrongly declined to act without definitive proof, among other things.

Defendants respond that Plaintiffs have not established physical disruption to tilefish habitat, and even if they had, physical disruption does not necessarily reduce "quality or quantity of essential fish habitat," as required by the regulations under the Magnuson Act and that Defendants changed their position based on the best scientific information available, i.e., the "absence of any evidence that trawl gear is actually causing any adverse effects to the [essential fish habitat], as defined by the regulations."

The implementing regulations for the Magnuson Act provide that "Councils must act to prevent, mitigate, or minimize any adverse effects from fishing, to the extent practicable, if there is evidence that a fishing practice is having an identifiable adverse effect on [essential fish habitat]." 50 C.F.R. § 600.815(a)(3)(iii). Section 600.810(a) defines "adverse effect" as "any impact which reduces quality and/or quantity of [essential fish habitat]. Adverse effects may include direct (e.g., contamination or physical disruption), indirect (e.g., loss of prey, or reduction in species' fecundity), site-specific or habitat-wide impacts." Id. at § 600.810(a). "Identifiable" means "both more than minimal and not temporary in nature." 62 Fed. Reg. 66, 531, 66,538 (Dec. 19, 1997). To make the adverse effect determination, "[c]ouncils should use the best scientific information available." 50 C.F.R. § 600.815(a)(3)(ii).

Ample record evidence—including, among other things, the comments and reports of academics and fishing industry representatives—establishes clearly that the Defendants arrived at the conclusion that no identifiable adverse effects on tilefish essential fish habitat from bottom-tending mobile gear exists upon a rational analysis of the best scientific information available. The preparers of the FMP concluded that studies of mobile gear's effects on other habitats were not sufficiently analogous and there was a complete lack of evidence to prove an identifiable adverse effect on tilefish habitat (FMP stating that "none of the existing literature discusses or documents specific impacts to subterranean burrow communities such as those used by tilefish."); (Memo from Patricia Kurkul, Regional Administrator for the Nat'l Marine Fish. Serv. stating that "[t]he Council found that there is a paucity of information on the specific impact of trawling on tilefish burrows, with no evidence that tilefish burrows are being adversely impacted by trawling."); see American Oceans Campaign v. Daley, 183 F. Supp.2d 1, 11–17 (D.D.C.2000) ("Since neither the statute nor the regulations requires the Councils to affirmatively conduct research to better identify [essential fish habitat] and the adverse effects of fishing on them, reliance on the best available scientific information is sufficient.").

Plaintiffs note that the final FMP states: "Unquestionably, from submersible vessel research, there are trawl door patterns observed in areas with tilefish burrows." Plaintiffs claim that this observation constitutes per se evidence of physical disruption, and that adverse effect may include a "physical disruption." 50 C.F.R. § 600.810(a). Thus, Plaintiffs contend, the Defendants missed an identifiable adverse effect. Defendants argue that door patterns do not prove physical disruption and, even if they did, Defendants' conclusion was correct because there is no evidence of an impact that reduces "quality or quantity of essential fish habitat." Id. at § 600.18(a).

Record evidence indicates unequivocally that in hundreds of submersible dives, Dr. Able, a renowned expert on tilefish, observed bottom-tending mobile gear patterns in active twenty-to thirty-year old tilefish burrows. ("These fish survived multiple annual trawling during the most intense time of fishing * * * *We can safely postulate that trawling does not impact the local environment or food chain to the detriment of the Tilefish lifecycle.* This is a more reasonable hypothesis than the assumption that trawling does significantly impact the habitat or food chain to the detriment of Tilefish. Our hypothesis of low impact is based upon what we know from trawl surveys and from what has been observed during submersible dives, while the draft plan's assumptions of significant impact on the [essential fish habitat] has no direct evidence or basis other than pure conjecture." (emphasis added)). Based on these observations, Defendants reasonably found no evidence of a reduction in quality or quantity of essential fish habitat and did not deem "door marks" an identifiable adverse effect. The Court defers to the Defendants' expertise, which is supported by the record. See American Oceans, 183 F. Supp.2d at 11–12 (stating that a court must " 'look at the decision not as the chemist, biologist, or statistician that we are qualified neither by training nor experience to be, but as a reviewing court exercising our narrowly defined duty of holding agencies to certain minimal standards of rationality.' "); see also Baltimore Gas & Elec. Co. v. Natural Res. Def. Council, Inc., 462 U.S. 87, 103 (1983).

Plaintiffs' argument that Defendants' changed position from the draft FMP to the final FMP reflects Defendants' arbitrary decision-making process is unpersuasive. The record demonstrates that Defendants based the original inferred hypothesis on studies of other habitats, and that this hypothesis was, subsequently, called into question by Dr. Able, the fishing industry and the Council. (Dr. Tom Hoff, staff member of the Council testified: "[W]hat the technical team believed was that this was a reasonable inference * * * However, there really is nothing known and what [Dr. Able] said and what the rest of us concluded was that there really is nothing definitively known on tilefish gear or on bottom tending gear impacting tilefish habitat, specifically that. We can make all the associations we want, but we don't have any direct evidence. There is nothing in the literature. He knows of nothing."). Defendants based their final conclusion upon the lack of any evidence of effects on tilefish habitat. ("[N]one of the existing literature discusses or documents specific impacts to subterranean burrow communities such as those used by tilefish."); see Muszynski, 268 F.3d at 98 (" '[C]onsiderable weight should be accorded to an executive department's construction of a statutory scheme it is entrusted to administer.' " (quoting United States v. Mead Corp., 533 U.S. 218 (2001))). Moreover, "an agency does not have a burden to explain a change in position from a proposed rule to the final rule, and * * * a lack of an explanation for the change is not in itself evidence of arbitrariness." Fed'n of Fly Fishers v. Daley, 131 F. Supp.2d 1158, 1163 (N.D.Cal.2000).

Plaintiffs' arguments that Defendants declined to act without definitive proof; that Defendants yielded to fishing industry pressure; and that Defendants used the impracticability of implementing precautionary measures as an excuse to reverse their original hypothesis, are equally unpersuasive. The record clearly supports Defendants' conclusion that no evidence existed that bottom-tending mobile gear caused an identifiable adverse impact upon tilefish. (Council member Bill Wells testified that "The fact is there is no evidence as to what mobile gear does. It's not that there isn't much. There isn't any * * * We simply have no information to justify * * * the proposals we went to public hearing with. We just had nothing."). At oral argument, in response to the Court's question whether there is evidence of an impact on tilefish habitat, Plaintiffs' counsel acknowledged that "there is no information[ ], besides inferences, based on the kind of evidence that the Council considered and that is in the record." The Court finds that it was reasonable for Defendants not to impose new restrictions on bottom-tending mobile gear given the lack of evidence that the gear had an identifiable adverse effect. See Evans, 162 F. Supp.2d at 167 ("For a court to set aside the Secretary's decision as arbitrary and capricious, it must conclude that the administrative record is devoid of any justification for the action.").

NOTES AND QUESTIONS

1. Was the First Circuit correct in affording the Secretary so much discretion in determining whether closures are "practicable" to protect essential fish habitat?

2. In another case from New England, plaintiffs challenged the failure of the New England Fishery Management Council and the Fisheries Service to close to bottom trawling certain gravel habitat known to be important refuge for juvenile Atlantic cod, a severely overfished fish stock on Georges Bank that was subject to Amendment 13, the controversial rebuilding plan discussed previously. The court upheld the decision not to close these areas, relying in part on the First Circuit's reading of the "to the extent practicable"

standard of the EFH provision, finding that the qualifier gives the Secretary "substantial discretion in determining what EFH protective measures are realistic, and thereby defining the alternatives to be evaluated in conformity with that practicability assessment." Oceana v. Evans, 2005 WL 555416 (D.D.C. 2005) (slip opinion at 35–37); order dismissing appeal not reported (May 2006) (for Oceana's appellate brief see 2006 WL 789101).

In approving the habitat provisions of Amendment 13, the Fisheries Service cited a National Research Council finding that both closures and fishing effort reductions are necessary to prevent adverse fishing effects on habitat to support its determination that the effort reductions in Amendment 13, intended to rebuild the biomass of overfished stocks, would protect EFH. See National Research Council, Effects of Trawling and Dredging on Seafloor Habitat (2002).

3. Does National Standard Two and the EFH provision require a council to have site-specific evidence that trawling adversely affects the habitat of a specific fish species or may it rely on evidence of such effects in other fisheries? Does the Magnuson–Stevens Act's EFH provision require councils to take a precautionary approach in minimizing adverse fishing effects? Six weeks after the court ruled in NRDC v. Evans, the federal district court in Rhode Island overturned NMFS's approval of the Mid–Atlantic Council's decision to exclude vessels that use bottom trawls to catch tilefish from the limited access permit program and allocate all available quota to longline vessels. The council's decision was justified in part by the evidence that trawling had adverse effects on the habitat of tilefish. The court found, based on the record, that the trawler exclusion was not in fact based on the best available scientific information, noting that the tilefish subcommittee had requested further research on the question.

4. After completed the new EFH amendment and environmental impact analysis required by the district court in American Oceans Campaign, the North Pacific Council adopted a new identification of EFH for all the FMPs for the EEZ off Alaska, including a process for further identifying "habitat areas of particular concern," and measures to minimize adverse fishing effects on EFH. Although the council's EIS determined that the effects of fishing for groundfish, crab, scallops, and salmon on the EFH are minimal, the council adopted protective measures pursuant to its stated policy of taking precautionary action. The minimization measures include closing 38,000 square nautical miles of ocean floor to trawling. The measures also include conservation areas for deep sea coral but keep open all areas that have produced the largest groundfish landings. Final rules implementing the North Pacific council's EFH provisions are published at 71 Fed. Reg. 36694 (June 28, 2006). For a spatial analysis of the conservation value of these closures, see A. Rieser, L. Watling, and J. Guinotte, Trawl Fisheries, Catch Shares and the Protection of Benthic Marine Ecosystems: Has Ownership Generated Incentives for Habitat Stewardship? 40 Marine Policy 75 (2013). The Pacific Fishery Management Council's EFH amendment to its groundfish FMP also

closed certain areas of the EEZ off California to bottom trawling. The amendment included a coastwise ban on the use of bottom trawling. The Fisheries Service, however, disapproved the portion of the amendment that would have closed waters deeper than 3,500 meters, as these areas had not been identified as EFH in the amendment. The amendment also designated specific oil production platforms in southern California as habitat areas of particular concern. 71 Fed. Reg. 27408 (May 11, 2006).

3. Management for Forage and Prey Species

In the following case, we return to the management of Atlantic herring (*Clupea harengus*), one of the most abundant species of fish on the planet, and the focus of the State of Maine's suit against the Secretary of Commerce in 1977. How far has herring management progressed since enactment of the Fishery Conservation and Management Act? Which factors account most for this progress: changes in marine science, public participation in fisheries governance, or changes in agency mandates through amendments to the Magnuson-Stevens Act?

FLAHERTY V. BRYSON

United States District Court for the District of Columbia, 2012
850 F.Supp.2d 38

GLADYS KESSLER, DISTRICT JUDGE.

Atlantic herring inhabit the Atlantic Ocean off of the East coast of the United States and Canada, ranging from North Carolina to the Canadian Maritime Provinces. Atlantic herring can grow to about 15.6 inches in length and live 15–18 years. Atlantic herring play a vital role in the Northwest Atlantic ecosystem, serving as a "forage species," i.e. food, for a number of other fish, marine mammals, and seabirds.

Human beings also hunt Atlantic herring. Fishermen and women predominantly catch Atlantic herring using midwater trawl gear, paired midwater trawls, and purse seines. To do this, boats working alone or in tandem drag nets through the water scooping up fish as they go. Not surprisingly, these nets snare large numbers of other fish and marine wildlife at the same time. [citations omitted]

Of particular concern to Plaintiffs are four species, often caught incidentally with Atlantic herring, collectively referred to as "river herring": (1) blueback herring *(Alosa aestivalis)*, (2) alewive *(Alosa pseudoharengus)*, (3) American shad *(Alosa sapidissima)*, and (4) hickory shad *(Alosa mediocris)*. River herring are apparently so-called because they are anadromous—that is, they spawn in rivers but otherwise spend most of their lives at sea, whereas Atlantic herring spend their entire lives at sea. It is undisputed that river herring play a similar role to Atlantic herring, providing forage for large fish and mammals, including cod, striped bass, bluefin tuna, sharks, marine mammals, and seabirds. The Atlantic Herring Fishery Management Plan, as updated by Amendment 4, provides Annual Catch Limits (ACLs) and Accountability Measures (AMs) for Atlantic herring but not for river herring.

* * *

Plaintiffs challenge Defendants' decision to approve Amendment 4 because the Amendment includes only Atlantic herring, and excludes river herring, as a stock in the fishery. Once a fish is designated as a "stock in the fishery," the Council must develop conservation and management measures, including ACLs and AMs, for that stock. 16 U.S.C. § 1853(a). Hence, the Atlantic Herring FMP includes no protective measures for river herring.

As described above, the MSA requires the Council to prepare an FMP "for each fishery under its authority that requires conservation and management." 16 U.S.C. § 1852(h)(1). The Act defines a "fishery" as "one or more stocks of fish which can be treated as a unit for purposes of conservation and management and which are identified on the basis of geographical, scientific, technical, recreational, and economic characteristics." *Id.* § 1802(13). A "stock of fish" is "a species, subspecies, geographical grouping, or other category of fish capable of management as a unit." *Id.* § 1802(42). The Council determines which "target stocks" (fish that are deliberately caught), and/or "non-target stocks" (fish that are incidentally caught), to include in the fishery. 50 C.F.R. § 600.310(d)(1).

In other words, in developing an FMP, the Council must decide which species or other categories of fish are capable of management as a unit, and therefore should be included in the fishery and managed together in the plan. This decision entails two basic determinations. The Council must decide (1) which stocks "can be treated as a unit for purposes of conservation and management" and therefore should be considered a "fishery" and (2) which fisheries "require conservation and management." 16 U.S.C. §§ 1802(13), 1852(h)(1). The Council must then set ACLs and AMs for all stocks in the fishery. *Id.* § 1853(a)(15). After the Council completes its proposed plan or amendment, NMFS must review it for compliance with applicable law and standards. *Id.* § 1854(a)(1)(A).

Plaintiffs contend that Amendment 4 contravenes the Act's requirements by failing to include river herring as a stock in the Atlantic herring fishery. Consequently, Plaintiffs argue, Defendants have violated the MSA and APA by erroneously concluding that Amendment 4 comports with the provisions of the MSA. 16 U.S.C. § 1854(a)(1)(A) (NMFS must determine whether FMPs are consistent with provisions of MSA); *N.C. Fisheries Ass'n*, 518 F.Supp.2d at 71–72 ("Secretarial review of a FMP or plan amendment submitted by a regional council focuses on the proposed action's consistency with the substantive criteria set forth in, and the overall objectives of, the MSA.").

The Court must now consider whether NMFS acted arbitrarily and/or capriciously in approving Amendment 4. 16 U.S.C. § 1855(f)(1); 5 U.S.C. § 706(2). The Court's "task is not to review *de novo* whether the amendment complies with [the MSA's] standards but to determine whether [NMFS's] conclusion that the standards have been satisfied is rational and supported by the record." *C & W Fish,* 931 F.2d at 1562; *see also* Blue Ocean Inst. v. Gutierrez, 585 F.Supp.2d 36, 43 (D.D.C.2008).

Defendants argue that the Administrative Record fully supports their decision and rely on two basic rationales. First, Defendants argue that, because of the imminence of the 2011 statutory deadline for completion of Amendment 4, the decision to postpone consideration of inclusion of river herring in the fishery until development of Amendment 5 was reasonable. Second, Defendants argue that NMFS properly deferred to the Council's determination as to the makeup of the fishery.

1. Delay Due to Statutory Deadline

Defendants first point to the pressure imposed by the MSRA's deadline. Defendants state that, in June 2009, they determined that consideration of measures specifically designed to protect river herring should be delayed so that they could meet the 2011 statutory deadline for providing measures to protect Atlantic herring. Defendants' logic was that because time was limited and the MSA required ACL and AM rules for all stocks in the fisheries and Atlantic herring had already been identified as a stock in the fishery, they could best comply with the MSA by formulating only the Atlantic herring regulations and postponing consideration of regulations for the management of river herring. *See* Pub.L. No. 109–479, § 104(b), 120 Stat. 3575, 3584 (requiring that FMPs including processes for setting ACLs and AMs take effect "in fishing year 2011 for all . . . fisheries" not determined to be overfished, including the Atlantic herring fishery).

While it is correct that the MSRA did impose the 2011 deadline, Defendants fail to provide any explanation or analysis from which the Court can conclude that the delay in considering the composition of the fishery, which entailed exclusion of river herring, was reasonable. *McDonnell Douglas Corp.,* 375 F.3d at 1186–87 ("we do not defer to the agency's conclusory or unsupported suppositions."). The MSRA was signed at the beginning of 2007. Defendants identify nothing in the Administrative Record that explains why, when the Council had more than four years to meet the statutory deadline for fishing year 2011, it could not address whether river herring, in addition to Atlantic herring, were in need of ACLs and AMs and still meet its deadline.

The Administrative Record discloses only vague and conclusory statements that "there was not sufficient time to develop and implement all the measures originally contemplated in Amendment 4 by 2011." The closest Defendants come to providing a substantive explanation is to quote a slide from a January 26, 2011, meeting regarding proposed Amendment 5, which reads, "the Herring [Plan Development Team] cannot generate a precise enough estimate of river herring catch on which to base a cap." That document does not explain why an estimate could not have been generated prior to issuance of Amendment 4, nor why the Council could not at the very least have devised an interim Acceptable Biologic Catch control rule based on the best available science, as it did in Amendment 4 for Atlantic herring. Defendants point to no other evidence in the Administrative Record to explain why the Council was unable to address management of river herring in the four years of lead time that elapsed between the signing of the MSRA and the final promulgation of Amendment 4.

The reason that Defendants' failure matters is that the MSRA requires ACLs and AMs for *all* stocks in need of conservation and management, not just for those stocks which were part of the fishery prior to passage of the MSRA. Although the MSRA does not explicitly require the Council to reassess the makeup of the fishery, it does require the Council and NMFS to set ACLs and AMs by 2011 "such that overfishing does not occur in the fishery." 16 U.S.C. § 1853(a)(15). The setting of ACLs and AMs necessarily entails a decision as to which stocks require conservation and management. *Id.* §§ 1802(13), 1853(a)(15). Hence, Defendants must provide some meaningful explanation as to why it was not possible to consider which stocks, other than Atlantic herring, should be subject to the ACLs and AMs which are so central to effective fishery management and avoidance of overfishing. NetCoalition v. SEC, 615 F.3d 525, 539 (D.C.Cir.2010) ("an agency may not shirk a statutory responsibility simply because it may be difficult.").

Moreover, Defendants have not explained why the information in the Administrative Record cited by Plaintiffs was deemed insufficient to justify including river herring as a stock, as urged in many comments submitted on the Proposed Regulation, or to permit setting at least an interim Acceptable Biological Catch limit for the species, just as was done for Atlantic herring.

In short, Defendants themselves cite to no evidence or facts supporting the Council's excuse that "there was not sufficient time" to consider the fishery's composition. ... While a looming statutory deadline may in some instances provide justification for an agency's delay in decision-making, it does not relieve Defendants of the duty to "articulate a satisfactory explanation for its action including a rational connection between the facts found and the choice made"—especially when the agency was given a four-year lead time to meet that deadline and failure to meet it could have serious consequences for the species to be protected. *Motor Vehicle Mfrs. Ass'n*, 463 U.S. at 43, 103 S.Ct. 2856 (internal quotation omitted). Defendants' conclusory statement that river herring would simply have to wait until a future amendment does not suffice.

2. Deference to the Council

Defendants also argue that river herring were not designated as a stock in the fishery because the Council decided to include only target stocks in the fishery, and river herring is a non-target stock. According to Defendants, NMFS deferred to the Council's decision not to include any non-target stocks in the fishery, and needed to do no more. The crux of Defendants' argument is that under both the structure of the MSA and the agency's own regulations, unless a species is determined by NMFS to be "overfished" or the Council's decision is in clear violation of the MSA, NMFS should simply defer to the Council's determination of what stocks are in the fishery rather than conduct an independent review of whether that determination complies with the MSA's provisions and standards.

a. Statutory Provisions

Defendants argue that the "Magnuson–Stevens Act entrusts the Councils with the responsibility to prepare FMPs for those fisheries requiring conservation and management" and that the "inclusion of a species . . . in a fishery management unit is based on a variety of judgment calls left to the Council." Defendants rely on 16 U.S.C. § 1852(h), giving the Council the responsibility to prepare and submit FMPs and amendments, and on 16 U.S.C. § 1854(e), requiring an FMP only where NMFS has determined that a fishery is "overfished." Therefore, Defendants contend, in the absence of a finding of overfishing, council decisions about the make-up of a fishery are unreviewable by NMFS and are entitled to deference.

Plaintiffs view Defendants' argument as "threaten[ing] to unravel the entire fabric of the Act." They caution that, under the Defendants' interpretation of the MSA, "councils would be left with the sole discretion to include any, or no, stocks in their FMPs, regardless of whether there is scientific information demonstrating the need for their conservation and management."

Defendants are correct that "it is the *Council* that has the responsibility to prepare the FMP in the first instance for those fisheries requiring conservation and management," which includes describing the species to be managed. As explained above, except in special circumstances, the council prepares and submits proposed FMPs and amendments to NMFS. 16 U.S.C. § 1852(h)(1).

What Defendants fail to fully appreciate, however, is that once the council completes its work, the MSA requires NMFS to review its plan to determine whether it comports "with the ten national standards, the other provisions of [the Act], and any other applicable law." *Id.* § 1854(a)(1)(A). Thus, it is Defendants' responsibility to decide whether an FMP, including the composition of its fishery, satisfies the goals and language of the MSA. *N.C. Fisheries Ass'n,* 518 F.Supp.2d at 71–72 ("Secretarial review of a FMP or plan amendment submitted by a regional council focuses on the proposed action's consistency with the substantive criteria set forth in, and the overall objectives of, the MSA."). While Defendants are correct that it is the Council's role to name the species to be managed "in the first instance," it is NMFS's role, in the second instance, to ensure that the Council has done its job properly under the MSA and any other applicable law.

It is true that the MSA requires management measures when NMFS finds overfishing. But it certainly does not follow that in the absence of overfishing NMFS may simply rubber stamp the Council's decisions. Section 1854(a) is clear: NMFS must examine whether the FMP "is consistent with the national standards, the other provisions of [the MSA], and any other applicable law." 16 U.S.C. § 1854(a)(1)(A). While NMFS may defer to the Council on policy choices, the Act plainly gives NMFS the final responsibility for ensuring that any FMP is consistent with the MSA's National Standards, and "the overall objectives" of the Act. *N.C. Fisheries Ass'n,* 518 F.Supp.2d at 71–72.

Defendants' responsibilities therefore include ensuring compliance with Section 1852(h)'s requirement that the Council prepare an FMP or amendment for any stock of fish that "requires conservation and management." 16 U.S.C. § 1852(h)(1). That Section requires FMPs and necessary amendments for all "stocks of fish which can be treated as a unit for purposes of conservation and management" and which are in need of conservation and management. *Id.* §§ 1802(13)(a), 1852(h)(1). Thus, NMFS must make its own assessment of whether the Council's determination as to which stocks can be managed as a unit and require conservation and management is reasonable. Motor Vehicle Mfrs. Ass'n, 463 U.S. at 52 ("agency's explanation . . . [must] enable us to conclude that [its decision] was the product of reasoned decisionmaking.").

There is no basis for concluding, as Defendants do, that the structure of the MSA weakens Section 1854's command that NMFS review proposed plans and amendments for compliance with the statute. The standards to be applied in reviewing NMFS's conclusion that Amendment 4 complies with Section 1852(h) are therefore no different than review of NMFS's conclusion that an amendment complies with the National Standards. *See N.C. Fisheries Ass'n,* 518 F.Supp.2d at 71–72 ("Secretarial review of a FMP or plan amendment submitted by a regional council focuses on the proposed action's consistency with the substantive criteria set forth in, and the overall objectives of, the MSA."). Merely deferring to the Council's exclusion of non-target species like river herring without any explanation for why that exclusion complies with the MSA fails to meet APA standards.

b. Defendants' Regulation

National Standard 1 of the MSA states, "Conservation and management measures shall prevent overfishing while achieving, on a continuing basis, the optimum yield from each fishery for the U.S. fishing industry." 16 U.S.C. § 1851(a)(1). Defendants cite to 50 C.F.R. § 600.310(d)(1), which interprets that Standard, and states: "[t]he relevant Council determines which specific target stocks and/or non-target stocks to include in a fishery." According to Defendants, this provision justifies NMFS's failure to explain why the Council's decision comports with the MSA.

However, Section 1854 states in no uncertain language that NMFS must "determine whether [the plan or amendment] is consistent with the national standards, the other provisions of this chapter, and any other applicable law." 16 U.S.C. § 1854(a)(1)(A). A mere regulation can never override a clear Congressional statutory command—i.e., that NMFS shall review FMP amendments for compliance with all provisions of the MSA. Nor, it should be noted, need 50 C.F.R. § 600.310(d)(1) be interpreted as Defendants do. It is absolutely correct that under the MSA, the councils do have the responsibility to determine what stocks to include in the fishery. But that is not the end of the process. After the councils make their determination, NMFS must still make its final compliance review.

Simply put, 50 C.F.R. § 600.310(d)(1) cannot be understood to permit NMFS to ignore its duty to ensure compliance with the MSA. The councils do not have unlimited and unreviewable discretion to determine the make-up of their fisheries.

Therefore, Defendants were required to review Amendment 4 for compliance with the MSA. Defendants need not prove that the decision to designate only target stocks as stocks in the fishery was the best decision, but they must demonstrate that they reasonably and rationally considered whether Amendment 4's definition of the fishery complied with the National Standards and with the MSA's directive that FMPs be generated for any fisheries requiring conservation and management. Mere deference to the Council, with nothing more, does not demonstrate reasoned decision-making.

* * *

NOTES AND QUESTIONS

1. Does the Secretary, acting through the National Marine Fisheries Service, have authority to notify a council that an FMP amendment under preparation is likely to be disapproved if the council submits it without including measures to conserve non-target forage species? Do the guidelines for the National Standards, required by MSA section 301(b), make it clear to the councils that forage species must be conserved for the benefit of other marine species that "harvest" them? In 2012, NMFS published an Advanced Notice of Proposed Rulemaking on the guidelines for implementing National Standard Number 1, 77 Fed. Reg. 26238 (May 3, 2012). The intent is to provide guidance on issues that have arisen since the 2007 Magnuson Act reauthorization amendments.

2. The New England Fishery Management Council submitted Amendment 5 to the Atlantic Herring FMP and a draft environmental impact statement to NMFS in 2012. The 2013 fishing year for Atlantic herring opened, however, on January 1, with no measures in place to conserve river herring. The Mid–Atlantic Fishery Management Council proposed measures to conserve alewife and blueback herring in its Atlantic Mackerel, Squid and Butterfish FMP, including catch monitoring, observer, and bycatch reduction measures. How much of the river herring resource should be "allocated" to other species in the ecosystem? Are the councils the appropriate entities to determine this amount?

3. Judge Kessler's opinion reflects a better understanding of the MSA's structure than most decisions. Why would NMFS, on behalf of the Secretary of Commerce, allow the Justice Department to defend its approval of the FMP by arguing that the MSA's structure limits its authority to carry out the act's mandates? Has the Commerce Department (or NMFS) developed a codependent relationship with the regional councils?

E. ALLOCATING CONSERVATION BENEFITS AND BURDENS

1. National Standard #4: Allocating Privileges Fairly

The Magnuson–Stevens Act's National Standard Four states that * * * "if it becomes necessary to allocate or assign fishing privileges among various United States fishermen, such allocation shall be (A) fair and equitable to all such fishermen; (B) reasonably calculated to promote conservation; and (C) carried out in such a manner that no particular individual, corporation, or other entity acquires an excessive share of such privileges." 16 U.S.C. § 1851(a)(4).

Does this provision give the councils and the Secretary adequate guidance on how allocate fishery resources among competing sectors? The following cases highlight the issues that have arisen with respect to allocation.

HADAJA, INC. V. EVANS

United States District Court, D. Rhode Island, 2003
263 F. Supp.2d 346

SMITH, DISTRICT JUDGE.

Factual Background

The tilefish, *Lopholatilus chameleonticeps,* and commonly known as the "Clown of the Sea," is one of the most colorful fishes in North American waters with a body that is blue-green, yellow, rose, silver with golden spots and a yellow mask around the eyes. It inhabits the outer continental shelf from Nova Scotia to South America, and is relatively abundant in the Southern New England to Mid–Atlantic area at depths of 80 to 440 meters. It is generally found in and around submarine canyons where it occupies burrows along the ocean floor.

While tilefish have been fished since the late 1800s, the frequency of tilefish landings has decreased over the past fifty years. On June 15, 1993, the National Marine Fisheries Service ("NMFS") established a control date for entry into the tilefish fishery, which meant that commercial vessels after that date "would not be assured of future access to or an allocation of the tilefish resource if a management regime [was] developed and implemented." [record citations omitted] In 1998, the NMFS determined that the tilefish fishery was overfished.

* * *

B. The Tilefish FMP

1. Limited Access

After determining that the tilefish fishery was overfished, the Council assessed the stock of tilefish in the Middle Atlantic–Southern New England region and created a Tilefish Committee (the "Committee") to make recommendations. The Committee determined that a limited access scheme was appropriate for dealing with the tilefish fishery. A limited access scheme restricts the number of vessels allowed to fish in a particular fishery with the goal of ending overfishing and rebuilding the fish population. Public hearings were held in Rhode Island, New York, and New Jersey during August of 1999. Hadaja did not attend any of these hearings.

The Council has the authority to enact permitting restrictions pursuant to 50 C.F.R. § 648.293. At the direction of the Council, the Committee contemplated five limited access schemes, with the preferred scheme providing for various full-time and part-time access permits. Under the preferred scheme, the majority of the full-time permit holders were located in Montauk, New York. The majority of part-time vessels were located in Rhode Island and New Jersey. However, the Historic Tilefish Coalition and the Montauk Tilefish Association, industry groups from New Jersey and New York, did not agree with this proposal because they felt the preferred scheme did not adequately represent their memberships. In response to the objections, the Committee urged the industry groups to reach a compromise regarding the limited entry option for later inclusion in the FMP.

As a compromise, the industry groups split the full-time permit category into two tiers of four vessels each. The four vessels that qualified for the first tier are from Montauk, New York. The second tier is composed of boats from New York and New Jersey. The compromise also provided for a part-time category, which would consist of forty-two vessels, eleven of which would be able to pre-qualify for a part-time permit based upon their historical participation [i.e., the vessels' history of fishing for a particular fish in light of the vessels' economic dependence on fishing for that species] in the tilefish fishery.

The compromise also provided that incidental permits would be available to all other vessels that do not qualify for full-time or part-time permits. An incidental permit would allow a vessel to obtain up to 300 pounds of tilefish per trip regardless of a vessel's historical participation in the tilefish fishery. Importantly, however, vessels that would not qualify for full-time or part-time permits under the compromise would not receive priority to fish in the tilefish fishery once the fishery had been sufficiently rebuilt. It is this provision with which Hadaja is most concerned. Because Hadaja only is eligible for an incidental permit under the compromise plan, it would be unable to fully participate in the tilefish fishery in the event it is rebuilt.

In other words, Hadaja has been relegated to perennial secondary status once the fishery is rebuilt, because he does not qualify for part-time status now. Other vessels, blessed by this plan with "part-time" permits will stand to ramp-up to full-time status when the fishing is rebuilt, leaving Hadaja and others in their wake.

2. Trawling

In addition to creating the permit-based limited access scheme, the Committee evaluated the use of different types of fishing gear on the tilefish population. Based on available studies, the Committee determined that trawling was having a long-term, negative impact on the tilefish population. While trawling represented a low percentage of the total tilefish landings, the Committee concluded that trawling contributed to a high rate of tilefish mortality. Additionally, the Committee inferred that trawling had a negative impact on tilefish burrows due to the trawl gear's contact with sediment that tilefish use as burrows. As a result, the Committee determined that limiting the use of trawl gear was an effective means of halting the decline of tilefish, and therefore provided that any vessel issued a limited access tilefish permit could not fish for tilefish with gear other than longline gear, or possess gear other than longline gear.

The Council adopted the recommendations of the Committee with respect to the limited access scheme and trawl gear restrictions. These recommendations were then published in the Federal Register pursuant to 16 U.S.C. § 1854(b)(1)(A).

* * *

The limited access scheme set forth in the TFMP, in pertinent part, is as follows:

Vessel permits.

(a) * * *

(12) Tilefish vessels. Any vessel of the United States must have been issued and carry on board a valid tilefish vessel permit to fish for, possess, or land tilefish in or from the tilefish management unit.

(i) Limited access tilefish permits—(A) Eligibility. A vessel may be issued a limited access tilefish permit if it meets any of the following limited access tilefish permit criteria, provided that the vessel landed the specified amounts of tilefish to meet such criteria within the tilefish management unit:

(1) Full-time tier 1 category. The vessel landed at least 250,000 lb (113,430 kg) of tilefish per year for any 3 years between 1993 and 1998, at least 1 lb (2.20 kg) of which was landed prior to June 15, 1993.

(2) Full-time tier 2 category. The vessel landed at least 30,000 lb (13,612 kg) per year for any of 3 years between 1993 and 1998, at least 1 lb (2.20 kg) of which was landed prior to June 15, 1993.

(3) Part-time category. The vessel landed 10,000 lb (4,537 kg) of tilefish in any 1 year between 1988 and 1993 and 10,000 lb (4,537 kg) in any 1 year between 1994 and 1998, or landed 28,000 lb (12,904 kg) of tilefish in any 1 year between 1984 and 1993, at least 1 lb (2.20 kg) of which was landed prior to June 15, 1993.

50 C.F.R. § 648.4(a)(12)(i). Hadaja argues that parts of this limited access scheme violate a number of the Act's National Standards.

* * *

2. National Standard Two

National Standard Two provides that "[c]onservation and management measures shall be based upon the best scientific information available." 16 U.S.C. § 1851(a)(2). Under the agency's national standard guidelines, the Secretary must base his determinations upon information available at the time of the preparation of the FMP or implementing regulations. See 50 C.F.R. § 600.315(b)(2).

Hadaja argues that the Defendant violated National Standard Two with respect to the part-time permits because it failed to base the limitations on any available scientific information. Rather, it accepted the limits based on an industry group "hallway compromise" submitted by the New York and New Jersey vessel owners. Specifically, the Plaintiff takes issue with the qualifying time periods and weight thresholds needed to obtain a part-time permit. The TFMP allows for landings of over 28,000 lbs. made between 1984–1993 to be sufficient to qualify a vessel for a part-time permit. Prior to consideration of the industry compromise, the Committee was prepared to use 1988 as the cutoff date, as opposed to 1984. Hadaja asserts that the only reason that these limitations were selected by the Committee is because they represented a compromise acceptable to the New York and New Jersey contingents. Therefore, the limitations were not based on the best scientific information available (or any scientific basis, for that matter).

> While National Standard Two does not compel the use of specific analytic methods or require that an agency gather all possible scientific data before acting, the Standard does prohibit an agency from simply creating a rule based on mere political compromise. See *Hall,* 165 F. Supp.2d at 133; The Fishing Company of Alaska v. United States, 195 F. Supp.2d 1239, 1248 (W.D.Wash.2002); Parravano v. Babbitt, 837 F. Supp. 1034, 1047 (N.D.Cal.1993). See also Midwater Trawlers Co-operative v. Dept. of Commerce, 282 F.3d 710, 720–21 (9th Cir.2002) ("A plain reading of the proposed NMFS rule * * * demonstrate[s] that the rule was a product of pure political compromise, not reasoned scientific endeavor. Although the NMFS allocation may well be eminently fair, the Act requires that it be founded on science and law, not pure diplomacy."). "[A] regulation must be based on concrete analysis that permits the Secretary to 'rationally conclude that his approach would accomplish his legitimate objectives.'" The Fishing Company of Alaska, 195 F. Supp.2d at 1248 (quoting Parravano, 837 F. Supp. at 1047).

In response, the Defendant contends that the limited access scheme was based on the best scientific evidence available because after receiving the compromise in 1999, the Committee compiled and analyzed fifteen years worth of tilefish data. This data, the Defendant contends, is contained in Table 79 of the Record. The Secretary also argues that the he did not approve the compromise at that time, but instead waited to make a final decision on the rules until 2001 after he had the entire record in front of him and could analyze the relevant data.

The TFMP candidly acknowledges that the limited access scheme was adopted directly from the compromise reached between the New York and New Jersey industry groups.[5] However, despite the Defendant's argument that the compromise was only adopted after considering additional scientific evidence, that conclusion is not evident in the record. While Table 79 indicates the historical participation in the tilefish fishery from 1984 through 1998, merely stating in conclusory fashion that the compromise was considered in light of scientific evidence does not bring the TFMP within the requirements of National Standard Two. Conclusory statements regarding the consideration of scientific data are not sufficient—the FMP must inform its audience of the actual scientific basis supporting it.

Therefore, this Court holds that the TFMP's limited access scheme is not based on scientific evidence, but born of a political compromise between two powerful industry groups. It is clearly arbitrary and should be set aside. The Secretary must adopt a plan that is based upon the best available scientific evidence. That may well be the same plan that was adopted—but only if the record evidence clearly supports it.

3. National Standard Four

National Standard Four provides as follows:

Conservation and management measures shall not discriminate between residents of different States. If it becomes necessary to allocate or assign fishing privileges among various United States fishermen, such allocation shall be (A) fair and equitable to all such fishermen; (B) reasonably calculated to promote conservation; and (C) carried out in such manner that no particular individual, corporation, or other entity acquires an excessive share of such privileges.

---

[5] The TFMP states as follows:

Representatives of the two major factions of tilefish fishermen, the Historic Tilefish Coalition * * * and the Montauk Tilefish Association * * * met, discussed often, and worked very hard to develop a compromise that best represented their memberships. They presented the compromise position to the Council at the 23 November Council meeting and the Council adopted their position.

16 U.S.C. § 1851(a)(4). In interpreting National Standard Four, courts have held that regulations that result in minor discriminatory impact do not automatically violate National Standard Four.

Hadaja argues that the TFMP violates National Standard Four because the tilefish fishermen who were granted full-time and part-time status under the limited access scheme are from New York and New Jersey, while New England fishermen did not qualify for these permits. However, the Record indicates in detail the fishermen who were excluded from receiving a part-time tilefish permit. Fishermen from Rhode Island were among the largest group excluded, but they were not the only group. The Record makes clear that numerous fishermen from Hampton Bay, New York and Montauk, New York were also denied permits under the scheme. The scheme provided permits based on the fishermen's current reliance on the tilefish fishery. It is only logical that if most of the fishermen who currently rely on the tilefish fishery are from New York and New Jersey, they will be the ones who receive the full-time permits. If Rhode Island fishermen do not rely on the fishery they cannot expect to receive full-time permits. While there may be some adverse impact on Rhode Island fishermen as a result, the Record reveals no evidence that the Committee specifically sought to exclude Rhode Island fishermen to the advantage of New York or New Jersey fishermen. This result merely stems from the Committee's belief that such a scheme would benefit the overall fishery to the (unfortunate) detriment of certain fishermen, including those from Rhode Island. With respect to National Standard Four, such an interest-weighing approach is neither arbitrary, nor capricious, nor contrary to law. See Alliance Against IFQs v. Brown, 84 F.3d 343, 349 (9th Cir.1996) (holding that the Secretary is allowed to sacrifice the interests of some fishermen to benefit the interests of the fishery as a whole); *Hall,* 165 F. Supp.2d at 142 ("The Secretary is permitted to sacrifice the interests of a group of fishermen under * * * National Standard Four, if in so doing he ameliorates the depleted state of monkfish."). Therefore, this Court concludes that the TFMP's limited access scheme does not violate National Standard Four.

C. The TFMP's Prohibition Against Trawling

The TFMP's restriction on the use of trawl gear provides that "[a] vessel issued a limited access tilefish permit issued under § 648.4(a)(12)(i) cannot fish for tilefish with any gear other than longline, or possess gear other than longline gear unless properly stowed in accordance with § 648.23." 50 C.F.R. § 648.294. Hadaja argues that the TFMP's restriction on the use of trawl gear also violates National Standards Two and Four.

1. National Standard Two

The Defendant contends that the TFMP's restriction on the use of trawl gear in the tilefish fishery is proper for two reasons: (1) trawling in the tilefish fishery should be prohibited because it has a negative effect on the tilefish habitat, and (2) trawling results in an increased level of fish mortality due to excessive "bycatch." Hadaja claims that these conclusions violate National Standard Two because they are not supported by scientific evidence contained in the Record.

Despite the Defendant's arguments to the contrary, a review of the Record indicates that the Committee lacked the necessary scientific data to determine that trawl gear has a negative impact on the tilefish habitat. The following excerpt from the TFMP is instructive in this regard.

> During the public hearing process, the Council received significant input from both the directed tilefish fishing industry and other fishing industry representatives that bottom-tending mobile gear was not significantly having an identifiable adverse effect on tilefish EFH. The environmental community strongly supported the association that bottom tending mobile gear can destroy bottom structures and that since tilefish are significantly dependent on bottom structure for their burrows, bottom tending mobile gear should be banned in tilefish [Habitat Area of Particular Concern] HAPC.

> On 30 September 1999, the Tilefish Technical Team consisting of Council staff, a Council member, NMFS (both NERO and NEFSC) personnel, academics and industry representatives were hosted in a workshop * * * to discuss the impacts of fishing gear to tilefish habitat. It was concluded that there is nothing definitively known about tilefish-mobile fishing gear interactions * * * *Any short-term or long-term impacts of bottom tending mobile gear specifically to tilefish habitat are unquantifiable at this time. The scientists * * * concluded that a research program to answer these questions was the appropriate approach to take * * * The scientific research program will be developed within the near term.*

As illustrated by the above passage, the TFMP itself indicates that the Committee needed further scientific information before it could determine whether trawling has a negative impact on the tilefish fishery. Despite this conclusion, the Committee determined that the use of trawl gear should be prohibited in the tilefish fishery. This conclusion, however, while appealing from a common-sense point of view, is not based on scientific evidence.

The Defendant argues that habitat protection was not the only basis for the Defendant's implementation of the restriction on trawl gear. The Defendant asserts that the TFMP's gear restriction was also implemented as part of a broader effort to decrease tilefish mortality. In support of this argument, the Defendant refers the Court to testimony from the Tilefish Industry Advisory Subcommittee regarding reasons for the gear restriction.

There are tremendous advantages in having a longline fishery. I wish we had our otter trawl individual here today, * * * I wish we had representation at this Committee of the Rhode Island otter trawl fishermen. They take very small fish * * * 1 lb to 2 lbs * * * they take them in January, February and March, often in association with summer flounder fisheries, but often it is targeted. The price per lb of those fish is 1/3 the price per pound of what the longline fishermen get. They could be contributing as much mortality potentially as the longline fishery, because there are significant discards from what we understand, but we don't have any sea sampling data to quantify it. There is a concept that I am thinking that maybe the otter trawl fishery that is directed for summer flounder should be an experimental fishery, and we should be mandating that an at-sea observer be onboard that, to get discard information, to get the length frequency of the catch, because they can be contributing a tremendous amount to fishing mortality.

The Defendant's reference to this testimony in support of its argument that the gear restriction is supported by the best scientific evidence available is perplexing. This language implies the exact opposite conclusion of that asserted by the Defendant. The Committee had no data to quantify trawling's impact on the tilefish fishery, and the Committee recommended that observers should be placed on board fishing vessels to make determinations regarding tilefish mortality. See id. Such a lack of information demonstrates even more clearly that the Committee had no scientific evidence on which to base its conclusions. It is true that an FMP only needs to rely on the *best* information *available* when implementing its rules. See 50 C.F.R. § 600.315(b) ("fact that scientific information concerning a fishery is incomplete does not prevent the preparation and implementation of an FMP"); Nat'l Coalition for Marine Conservation v. Evans, 231 F. Supp.2d 119, 130 (D.D.C.2002); Massachusetts v. Daley, 170 F.3d at 30 (regulations can be enacted despite lack of complete information). However, there is a difference between relying on conflicting evidence or incomplete evidence and relying on no evidence. This is not a case of conflicting or incomplete evidence where the Committee has determined what is the best available evidence from among conflicting sources. Here, the evidence that the Defendant put forth in support of the gear restriction actually establishes that the Committee did not have *any* evidence to support a restriction on trawl gear.

Therefore, the TFMP's restriction on the use of trawl gear violates National Standard Two and shall be set aside.

2. National Standard Four

Hadaja also appears to allege in the Complaint that the TFMP's restriction on the use of trawl gear discriminates between residents of different states in violation of National Standard Four. However, Hadaja has not addressed this allegation since it was raised in the Complaint. Upon reviewing the TFMP's restriction on the use of trawl gear in light of the requirements of National Standard Four, it is clear to this Court that the restriction is applied even-handedly and does not discriminate against fishing vessels based on their locality or homeport. Therefore, this Court finds that the TFMP's restriction on the use of trawl gear does not violate National Standard Four.

This Court * * * orders that the regulations 50 C.F.R. § 648.4(a)(12) and 50 C.F.R. § 648.294 shall be set aside pending further proceedings, based on the regulations' failure to comport with National Standard Two of the Magnuson–Stevens Fishery Conservation and Management Act.

NOTES AND QUESTIONS

1. National Standard Two applies to economic data as well as biological and ecological information. In order to meet this standard, in assessing economic impacts of proposed management measures should councils be required to obtain earnings data from companies, ports and fishing communities? Does this require access to confidential information?

2. If the total allowable catch in a commercial fishery is allocated to different gear-sectors of the commercial fishery, should the sector with higher bycatch and habitat impacts receive a smaller quota so as to minimize these ecological impacts? In Churchman v. Evans, 2004 WL 2271596 (N.D. Cal. 2004) (slip opinion) plaintiffs claimed the Pacific Council's annual groundfish specifications, which allocated higher catch limits to the trawling sector even though trawlers were responsible for higher bycatch and discard mortality than fixed gear, violated the Act. The court, however, found that the plaintiffs had failed to prosecute their claim in a timely manner and refused to allow the plaintiffs to amend their complaint. If their claim had been timely, would they have prevailed on the merits?

3. Which fishermen are entitled to receive an allocation of a annual catch limit? In Midwater Trawlers Coop. v. Dept. of Commerce, fishing companies and processors challenged the Secretary of Commerce's decision to allocate a portion of the Pacific whiting annual catch to the Makah Indian Tribe. The court held that the Fisheries Service, after remand, had adequately justified its use of a sliding scale to allocate the catch to meet National Standard Two's best available science requirement and treaty fishing rights under the 1855 Treaty of Neah Bay, as required by the MSA. 393 F.3d 994 (9th Cir. 2004). This case is excerpted beginning on p. 694.

2.   Restricting Access and Reducing Capacity

The task of allocating limited fishery resources is much more difficult when the commercial and recreational fishing sectors have more participants than the biological resources can support. When a fish stock is abundant and the fishery is profitable, new vessels often enter the fishery before restrictions can be put in place to prevent overfishing. Also, the reduced abundance of fish leads fishermen who are already in the fishery to borrow money to increase the capacity of their vessels in terms of size, ability to travel longer distances, and fishing power. Restricting catches to allow stocks to rebuild is nearly impossible when the fleet has excess capacity because fishermen have to continue to fish in order to pay for these investments. What are the mechanisms for restricting access and reducing "capacity" under the Magnuson–Stevens Act?

a. Limited Entry under the Magnuson–Stevens Act

In Section 303 (b)(6), 16 U.S.C. § 1853 (b)(6), the Act specifically allows the regional councils and the Secretary of Commerce to adopt and implement systems for limiting the number of fishing vessels or other units of fishing effort that may be used in a fishery. In developing such systems, the council and the Secretary must take into account—

(A) present participation in the fishery,

(B) historical fishing practices in and dependence on, the fishery,

(C) the economics of the fishery,

(D) the capability of fishing vessels used in the fishery to engage in other fisheries,

(E) the cultural and social framework relevant to the fishery and any affected fishing communities, and

(F) any other relevant considerations.

16 U.S.C. § 1853(b)(6).

Most fisheries managed under the Act are now under a limited license program. Fishing vessels are permitted to catch and land managed species only if they obtain a limited access permit for that fishery. Limited access permits are generally available only to vessels with a record of landings before the "control date." That is the date established by NMFS regulations after which landings will not qualify a vessel for a permit unless circumstances beyond the control of the permit applicant prevented the vessel from making or documenting the necessary landings. What happens when state fishery law prevents a vessel from harvesting certain species and thus establishing a catch record? See F/V Robert Michael, Inc. v. Kantor, 961 F. Supp. 11 (D. Me. 1997).

States have adopted various programs to limit access to state fisheries through license limitations and other schemes. For a discussion of legal methods for limiting entry into fisheries and the federal constitutional law claims raised against them in state courts, see M. Lansford and L.S. Howarth, Legal Impediments to Limited Entry Fishing Regulation in the

Gulf States, 34 Nat. Resources J. 411, 415–24 (1994). Alaska's extensive limited entry licensing system was upheld against claims of violations of federal and state equal protection clauses. See Commercial Fisheries Entry Comm'n v. Apokedak, 606 P.2d 1255 (Alaska 1980). For more on the design and early challenges to Alaska's limited entry system, see R. Groseclose and G. Boone, An Examination of Limited Entry as a Method of Allocating Commercial Fishing Rights, 6 U.C.L.A.–Alaska L. Rev. 201 (1977); Owers, Court Tests of Alaska's Limited Entry Law, 11 UCLA–Alaska L. Rev. 87 (1981).

b. *Individual Fishing Quotas*

Individual fishing quotas (IFQs) are perhaps the most controversial form of limited access or capacity reduction regulation. When the quotas are made transferable and fisherman can sell them on the open market, they are called individual transferable quotas (ITQs). The Mid–Atlantic Fishery Management Council was the first regional council to recommend adoption of ITQ program for a federally managed fishery. The Secretary of Commerce approved for implementation the council's surf clam and ocean quahog ITQ program in 1990. The Magnuson Act at the time had no specific criteria or guidelines for ITQ program design. In Sea Watch International v. Mosbacher, 762 F. Supp. 370 (D.D.C. 1991), the court addressed a number of issues of first impression and for which the Magnuson Act gave little guidance at the time. (Congress subsequently revisited these issues in the 1996 reauthorization of the Magnuson Act and added new language regarding IFQs.) The plaintiffs in Sea Watch claimed, inter alia, that the ITQ system amounted to a privatization of the surf clam and quahog resource, thereby transferring private ownership interests in a fishery, a result prohibited by Magnuson Act. The court found:

> * * * The present ITQ system differs only in degree from the system of aggregate quotas and transferable permits previously in use and unchallenged by plaintiffs, and the interests created by it fall short of actual full-scale ownership * * * The new quotas do not become permanent possessions of those who hold them, any more than landing rights at slot-constrained airports become the property of airlines, or radio frequencies become the property of broadcasters. These interests remain subject to the control of the federal government which, in the exercise of its regulatory authority, can alter and revise such schemes, just as the Council and the Secretary have done in this instance. An arrangement of this kind is not such a drastic departure from ordinary regulation, nor is it so akin to the sale of government property, that the Court must require a more precise expression of congressional intent to uphold it.

762 F. Supp. at 376.

The plaintiffs had cited a number of instances in which NMFS had referred to the ITQs as property rights. To this argument the court noted that those references had used the term "property" only as an analogy and always qualified with references to the possibility that the management program could change and not rely on ITQs. Id. at n. 10.

The plaintiffs also claimed that the ITQ program violated National Standard 4 by discriminating against owners of smaller fishing fleets. The court concluded:

> Plaintiffs next contend that the ITQ system violates National Standard 4 because it is intended to drive a particular group of individuals, the single vessel and small fleet owners, out of the fisheries. Since Amendment 8 permits owners to catch their entire ITQ with a few vessels, the argument runs, it will result in lower average costs to the owners of large fleets, and provide them with an unfair competitive advantage. Moreover, it is alleged, small fishermen lack the capital to purchase sufficient ITQs to operate their vessels at full capacity, and ultimately will be driven out of business. It is quite possible that scale economies and transferability of ITQs will produce some consolidation. It is also possible that small fishermen enjoy advantages of their own, and nothing prevents coalitions of small owners from pooling their allocations to obtain efficiencies. Moreover, single vessel or small fleet owners may happen to have substantial allocations depending upon their history. Even where a fisherman with a small allocation decides to exit, transferability of the ITQ provides at least some compensation. There is nothing intentionally invidious or inherently unfair in the plan adopted by the Council and the Secretary. "Inherent in an allocation is the advantaging of one group to the detriment of another." 50 C.F.R. § 602.14(c)(3)(i).

Id. at 377.

To the plaintiffs' contention that the IFQ program would lead to consolidation of quota in the hands of a few fishermen in violation of the National Standard 4 prohibition against "excessive shares," the court responded:

> Plaintiffs * * * allege that two fishermen now hold ITQs totaling forty percent of the annual catch quota for ocean quahogs, and that fragmentation of the remaining shares will necessarily result in further consolidation, as holders of smaller shares sell their interest. This figure does give pause, although the raw number may not be economically significant. The defendants have acknowledged that increased efficiency due to consolidation was one of the explicit objectives of Amendment 8. However, the Act contains no definition of "excessive shares," and the Secretary's judgment of what is excessive in this context deserves weight, especially where the regulations can be

changed without permission of the ITQ holders. The record reflects that the Council and the Secretary considered the problem, and addressed it by providing for an annual review of industry concentration, with the possibility of referral to the Department of Justice.

NOTES AND QUESTIONS

1. Do you agree that the ITQ is more akin to "ordinary regulation" than a property right? What does the economic theory underlying the ITQ approach say regarding the nature of the allocated interest? For a discussion of the ITQ system in the surf clam and ocean quahog fisheries, see generally Note, Protecting Common Property Resources Through the Marketplace: Individual Transferable Quotas for Surf Clams and Ocean Quahogs, 16 Vt. L. Rev. 1127 (1991). For a discussion of the nature of the right created, see Note, Harnessing Market Forces in Natural Resources Management: Lessons From the Surf Clam Fishery, 21 B.C. Envl. L. Rev. 335, 354–58 (1994). For an earlier discussion of the nature of the right created by limited access programs, see Note, Legal Dimensions of Entry Fishery Management, 17 William & Mary L. Rev. 757, 767 (1976).

2. The 1996 Sustainable Fisheries Act defines an IFQ as "a federal permit under a limited access system to harvest a quantity of fish, expressed by a unit or units representing a percentage of the total allowable catch of a fishery that may be received or held for exclusive use by a person * * * " 16 U.S.C. § 1802(21). The Act provides that an IFQ shall not confer any right of compensation to the holder of the IFQ if it is revoked or limited at any time. Id. at § 1853(d)(3).

3. Are IFQs "property"? In October, 1994, the Internal Revenue Service prevented the issuance of halibut and sablefish IFQs to approximately 300 Alaska fishermen who owed back taxes or who had failed to file returns. The IRS issued a Notice of Levy to NMFS asserting a lien for nearly nine million dollars in unpaid taxes, interest, and penalties. The Justice Department concluded that the halibut IFQs, although not yet delivered to the qualifying fishermen, "constitute a right to intangible property—i.e., a valuable and transferable legal right to catch and land certain quantities" and as such were property or rights to property which are subject to the tax lien or levy. Office of Legal Counsel, Dep't of Justice, Internal Revenue Service Notices of Levy on Undelivered Commerce Dep't Fishing Quota Permits, 1995 WL 944019 (Jan. 26, 1995). See J. Weiss, Comment, A Taxing Issue: Are Limited Entry Fishing Permits Property? 9 Alaska L. Rev. 93 (1992).

4. How are IFQs treated in divorce proceedings? The Supreme Court of Alaska ruled that a federal IFQ is property subject to division as marital property, but that the husband's interest is separate property to the extent the size of his quota share was calculated on the basis of landings he made prior to the marriage. Ferguson v. Ferguson, 928 P.2d 597 (Alaska 1996). In Johns v. Johns, 945 P.2d 1222 (Alaska 1997), the court retained jurisdiction over the husband's state permits for herring roe for which he qualified during

marriage that were currently valueless but could become marketable and transferable.

5. As we saw in *Hadaja*, the tilefish case, National Standard 4 requires any fishery allocation to be fair, conservation-oriented, and calculated to prevent any one individual or company from obtaining an excessive share. 16 U.S.C. § 1851(a)(4). Recall that in Sea Watch International, two fishermen held 40% of the ocean quahog quota. Is it sufficient for the Secretary and the Mid–Atlantic Council to rely on an annual review of concentrations and possible referral to the Department of Justice's Antitrust Division to meet the no "excessive share" standard? What standards would apply under the Sherman Antitrust Act? See William Milliken, Comment, Individual Transferable Fishing Quotas and Antitrust Law, 1 Ocean & Coastal L. J. 35 (1994).

6. The Secretary of Commerce may not implement a limited access system unless the program receives approval by a majority of the appropriate regional council members present and voting. 16 U.S.C. § 1854 (c)(3). Also, the Secretary may by regulation set the level of fees that may be charged for fishing permits required in a FMP. However, the level of fees charged for the permits may not exceed the administrative costs incurred in issuing the permits. 16 U.S.C. § 1854 (d)(1). For IFQ programs, the Secretary is allowed to collect a fee to cover the actual costs "directly related to the management and enforcement" of the program, but the fee may not exceed 3 percent of the ex vessel value of the fish harvested under it. Id. at § 1854(d)(2).

7. The North Pacific Fishery Management Council developed an ITQ plan for the Gulf of Alaska halibut and sablefish fixed gear fisheries which received the Secretary's approval in January, 1993, for implementation in 1994 and 1995. 58 Fed. Reg. 59375 (Nov. 9, 1993). When it went into effect, this program was the world's largest individual quota program in number of participants. David Fluharty, Magnuson Fishery Management and Conservation [sic] Act Reauthorization and Fishery Management Needs in the North Pacific Region, 9 Tulane Env'l L. J. 301, 310 (1996). By setting restrictions on transfers of ITQ ownership to owners of vessels in the same vessel category and fishing area, the plan addressed one of the chief concerns of ITQ opponents—that the individual allocations will become concentrated in the hands of a small number of large-scale operators, to the detriment of the family-scale operators. 50 C.F.R. § 676.21.

The North Pacific Council also created a Western Alaska Community Development Quota (CDQ) Program, allocating a fixed portion of the annual total allowable catch (TAC) to the native Alaskan villages of western Alaska. 50 C.F.R. § 676.24. One objective of the CDQ was to allocate at least a portion of the fish resources of the Bering Sea to the communities closest to them, but which were unlikely on their own to develop the fishing fleet to take advantage of that proximity, or to have the money to purchase quota shares. Fluharty supra at 310–11. The communities use their quotas to generate economic development, primarily in partnership with the trawlers owned by companies based in the Seattle, Washington area. Does the idea of reserving a portion of the TAC for allocation as an IFQ to a coastal community rather than an individual vessel owner have other potential applications? Could such a mechanism help reduce the economic and social impacts of IFQs on those fishermen who do not benefit from the initial allocation of quota shares? See Alison Rieser, Property Rights and Ecosystem Management in U.S. Fisheries: Contracting for the Commons?, 24 Ecology L.Q. 813 (1997).

ALLIANCE AGAINST IFQS V. BROWN
United States Court of Appeals, Ninth Circuit, 1996
84 F. 3d 343, cert. denied, 520 U.S. 1185, 1997

KLEINFELD, CIRCUIT JUDGE.

* * *

Commercial ocean fishing combines difficult and risky labor with large capital investments to make money from a resource owned by no one, the fish. Unlimited access tends to cause declining fisheries. The reason is that to get title to a fish, a fisherman has to catch it before someone else does. Pierson v. Post, 3 Caines 175, 2 Am. Dec. 264 (N.Y.1805). This gives each fishermen an incentive to invest in a fast, large boat and to fish as fast as possible. As boats and crews get more efficient, fewer fish escape the fishermen and live to reproduce. "The result is lower profits for the too many fishermen investing too much capital to catch too few fish." Terry L. Anderson and Donald R. Leal, Free Market Environmentalism, 123 (1991).

* * * The Secretary of Commerce, pursuant to the Magnuson Act and the Northern Pacific Halibut Act of 1982 ("Halibut Act"), 16 U.S.C. § 773 et seq., promulgated regulations to limit access to sablefish and halibut fisheries in the Gulf of Alaska and the Bering Sea and Aleutian Islands area.

The Secretary of Commerce implemented by regulation a management plan for sablefish and Pacific halibut fishing. The basic scheme is that any boat that fishes commercially for the regulated fish in the regulated area must have an individual quota share (IFQ) permit on board, specifying the individual fishing quota allowed for the vessel, and anyone who receives the regulated fish must possess a "registered buyer permit."

The regional director of the National Marine Fisheries Service (NMFS) in the Department of Commerce assigns to each owner or lessee of a vessel which made legal landings of halibut or sablefish during 1988, 1989, or 1990, a quota share (QS) based on the person's highest total legal landings of halibut and sablefish during 1984 to 1990. Each year, the regional director allocates individual fishing quotas (IFQs) by multiplying the person's quota share by the annual allowable catch. Subject to some restrictions, the quota shares and individual fishing quotas can be sold, leased and otherwise transferred. If someone who did not fish in the regulated waters during 1988 to 1990 wants a quota share, he has to buy it from someone who did.

Like any governmental regulatory scheme, this one substitutes a governmental decision for myriad individual decisions to determine who shall be permitted to make money in the regulated industry. The plaintiffs are people who suffer from the economic impact of the regulation. Some have invested in fishing vessels and fished in the regulated waters for halibut or sablefish, but not during the critical three years which would give them a quota share. Some have consistently fished for the regulated fish in the regulated waters, but did not own or lease the boats. Of those who acquired quota shares under the scheme, some probably never fished, and just invested in fishing boats to get investment tax credits and depreciation. The regulatory scheme has the practical effect of transferring economic power over the fishery from those who fished to those who owned or leased fishing boats. For these reasons, among others, the case is troubling and difficult.

* * *

Where we review regulations promulgated by the Secretary of Commerce under the Magnuson Act, our only function is to determine whether the Secretary "has considered the relevant factors and articulated a rational connection between the facts found and the choice made." We determine only if the Secretary acted in an arbitrary and capricious manner in promulgating such regulations. We cannot substitute our judgment of what might be a better regulatory scheme, or overturn a regulation because we disagree with it, if the Secretary's reasons for adopting it were not arbitrary and capricious.

Plaintiffs urge us to adopt a more onerous standard of review and cite Atwood v. Newmont Gold Co., Inc., 45 F.3d 1317 (9th Cir.1995), as support. *Atwood* is distinguishable, because we were reviewing an ERISA plan fiduciary's duty, not those of the Secretary of Commerce, and were doing so in light of facts indicating a conflict of interest.

* * *

Plaintiffs argue that the allocation of quota shares to vessel owners and lessees violates the statutory requirement that allocation be "fair and equitable to all such fishermen." 16 U.S.C. § 1851(a)(4). The statute requires that a fishery management plan comply with a number of national standards. * * *

Plaintiffs make the sensible argument that a crew member is just as much of a fisherman as a vessel owner. If all the quota shares go to vessel owners and lessees during that period, and none to the crew, as the Secretary's approved plan provides, then this violates the statutory command of fairness and equity to "all" the fishermen.

As the quoted section of this statute shows, the Secretary's duty was not solely limited to allocating quota shares fairly and equitably among the fishermen. The plan also had to "prevent overfishing while achieving, on a continuing basis, the optimum yield," be "reasonably calculated to promote conservation," "promote efficiency," "minimize costs and avoid unnecessary duplication," and achieve several other criteria. There is a necessary tension, perhaps inconsistency, among these objectives. The tension, for example, between fairness among all fishermen, preventing overfishing, promoting efficiency, and avoiding unnecessary duplication, necessarily requires that each goal be sacrificed to some extent to meeting the others.

The Council and Secretary directed their attention to the fairness problem plaintiffs raise, but decided that the other standards imposed by the statute required allocation of quota shares to boat owners and lessees as opposed to all the fishermen. The Council thought that equity to people who had invested in boats, and the greater ease of ascertaining how much fish boats, as opposed to individual fishermen, had taken, favored allocating quota shares according to owner and lessees of boats:

> There is no question that the IFQ program will restructure the current fixed gear fishery for halibut and sablefish. Some fishermen will be better off and some will be worse off under the IFQ program * * * In brief, those persons benefited by receiving an initial allocation are vessel owners or lease holders * * * The Council's rationale for this particular allocation is that vessel owners and lease holders are the participants who supply the means to harvest fish, suffer the financial and liability risks to do so, and direct the fishing operations.

* * *

> The advantaging of one group to the detriment of another is inherent in allocation * * * The Council considered allocating [quota share] to crew members but decided against it because of the practical difficulties of documenting crew shares. Instead, the Council decided to give eligibility for initial allocations only to vessel owners and lease holders because they have a capital investment in the vessel and gear that continues as a cost after crew and vessel shares are paid from a fishing trip.

[NOAA, Preamble to the Final Rules]

The Secretary thought that the problem of overfishing resulted more from investment in boats than occupational choices of fishermen, so the administrative remedy should be measured by ownership and leasing of boats:

The Council's consideration of "present participation" also included the form of involvement in the fishery (e.g., as a vessel owner, crew member, or processor). As explained under national standard 4, above, the Council perceived vessel owners and lease holders as the most directly involved persons in terms of capital investment. The conservation and management problems resolved by this program stem largely from excess capital in the fisheries. Therefore, it is reasonable to define the group of persons who make the capital investment decision to either enter or exit a fishery as "present participants" for initial allocation purposes.

[Id.]

The Secretary promulgated a regulation [the National Standards Guidelines] requiring that allocations be "rationally connected with the achievement of [optimum yield] or with the furtherance of a legitimate [fishery management plan] objective." In consideration of the fact that "[i]nherent in an allocation is the advantaging of one group to the detriment of another," the regulation provided:

The motive for making a particular allocation should be justified in terms of the [fishery management plan]; otherwise, the disadvantaged user groups or individuals would suffer without cause. * * *

(B) An allocation of fishing privileges may impose a hardship on one group if it is outweighed by the total benefits received by another group or groups. An allocation need not preserve the status quo in the fishery to qualify as fair and equitable, if a restructuring of fishing privileges would maximize overall benefits.

[Id.]

Congress required the Secretary to exercise discretion and judgment in balancing among the conflicting national standards in section 1851. "[U]nless the Secretary acts in an arbitrary and capricious manner promulgating such regulations, they may not be declared invalid." Alaska Factory Trawler Ass'n v. Baldrige, 831 F.2d 1456, 1460 (9th Cir. 1987). Although the Secretary's approval of the plan sacrificed the interest of non-owning crew members to boat owners and lessees, the Secretary had a reason for doing that which was consistent with the statutory standards. Controlling precedent requires that a plan not be deemed arbitrary and capricious, "[e]ven though there may be some discriminatory impact," if the regulations "are tailored to solve a gear conflict problem and to promote the conservation of sablefish." Id. The Secretary is allowed, under this authority, to sacrifice the interests of some groups of fishermen, for the benefit as the Secretary sees it of the fishery as a whole. Id.

The plan adopted will undoubtedly have an adverse impact on the lives of many fishermen who have done nothing wrong. Their entirely legitimate interest in making a living from the fishery has been sacrificed to an administrative judgment about conservation of fish and efficiency of the industry. That is, however, an unavoidable consequence of the statutory scheme. Despite the harshness to the fishermen who were left out, there is no way we can conclude on this record that the Secretary lacked a rational basis for leaving them out. The Secretary considered their interests, "considered the relevant factors and articulated a rational connection between the facts found and the choice made." Washington Crab, 924 F.2d at 1441. Because this standard was met, we do not have the authority to substitute our judgment for the Secretary's with regard to allocation of all the quota shares to boat owners and lessees.

* * *

This is a troubling case. Perfectly innocent people going about their legitimate business in a productive industry have suffered great economic harm because the federal regulatory scheme changed. Alternative schemes can easily be imagined. The old way could have been left in place, where whoever caught the fish first, kept them, and seasons were shortened to allow enough fish to escape and reproduce. Allocation of quota shares could have been on a more current basis, so that fishermen in 1996 would not have their income based upon the fish they had caught before 1991. Quota shares could have been allocated to all fishermen, instead of to vessel owners and lessees, so that the non-owning fishermen would have something valuable to sell to vessel owners. But we are not the regulators of the North Pacific halibut and sablefish industry. The Secretary of Commerce is. We cannot overturn the Secretary's decision on the ground that some parties' interests are injured. Government regulation of an industry necessarily transfers economic rewards from some who are more efficient and hardworking to others who are favored by the regulatory scheme. We have authority to overturn the Secretary's decisions only if they are arbitrary and capricious, or contrary to law. In this case, they are not.

NOTES AND QUESTIONS

1. Note the degree of deference afforded the Secretary of Commerce in fashioning the ITQ allocation scheme. The Court refused the plaintiffs' request for the more searching standard of review it had recently applied in reviewing the ERISA plan fiduciary's duty when the facts indicated a conflict of interest. Does the Secretary have a fiduciary's duty under the Magnuson–Stevens Act as trustee of the public's marine resources? Had the Secretary made sure that crew members were represented on the North Pacific Council during the years it was creating the halibut-sablefish limited access plan? Is a high degree of deference appropriate when the regulations are creating quasi-private property rights in the harvesting of public fish resources?

2. Applicants for individual quota share permits under the Alaska program had to prove they were either owners or lessees of vessels that had made legal landings of halibut or sablefish during 1988–1990. Applicants whose applications NMFS denied had the right to an administrative appeal. 60 C.F.R. § 676.20. What kind of procedure is NMFS required to give a disappointed applicant, given the importance of the IFQ permit to his or her livelihood? Does the due process clause of the U.S. Constitution require NMFS to provide compulsory process (i.e., the appeals officer has subpoena power) as part of the administrative adjudication of the application?

In Dell v. Dep't of Commerce, 191 F.3d 460 (Table), 1999 WL 604217 (9th Cir. 1999) (unpublished opinion), Dell was granted a quota share initially as the lessee of a fishing vessel. The owner of the vessel (and Dell's former father-in-law), however, appealed the decision to NMFS, claiming that Dell was his employee, not lessee. The appeals officer concluded that the relationship between the two claimants was that of owner and captain, not lessor and lessee. She held that the vessel owner was entitled to the IFQ, and NMFS denied Dell's application. When Dell challenged the agency's decision, the district court granted summary judgment for NMFS, and the Ninth Circuit affirmed, finding that while Dell had a "protectable [private] property interest in obtaining IFQ permits," citing Foss v. NMFS, 161 F.3d 584, 589 (9th Cir. 1998), the regulations' appeals procedures without compulsory process were more than adequate to protect them, the risk of erroneous deprivation of the permit was very low, and the government had an interest in a timely and efficient resolution of IFQ applications, thus meeting the test of Matthews v. Eldridge, 424 U.S. 319, 334–35 (1976). In dissent, Judge Reinhardt argued that without the ability to compel production of documents in the possession of his former wife, Dell was denied a fair resolution of his appeal, and that society's interest in speedy resolution of fishing license claims did not outweigh Dell's interest in a fair hearing. Do you agree? Should Congress amend the Magnuson–Stevens Act to require a compulsory process for IFQ appeals?

3. The *Alliance Against IFQs* decision leaves no doubt that IFQ programs have significant redistributive effects on power and wealth among different sectors of the fishing industry.

> Under an ITQ program, the redistribution of economic resources in a fishery occurs because overfishing and overcapitalization is controlled using free market forces to create a smaller, more efficient fishery. The market in ITQs encourages less efficient fishers to sell off their quota shares and leave the fishery. Generally, the sector of the fishing industry made up of smaller, community-based operations is less efficient. The redistributive effects of ITQs can be mitigated by Congress and NMFS, but such measures come at a cost to efficiency. Therefore, the question for any government interested in implementing an ITQ program is how many local fishers can be sacrificed in order to remove overfishing and overcapitalization* * * Whether ITQs become the management tool of choice and the manner in which the tool is utilized ultimately depend on

the degree to which we value the environmental and economic benefits afforded by ITQs over certain [smaller, community-based] fishers' livelihood.

N. Black, Note, Balancing the Advantages of Individual Transferable Quotas Against Their Redistributive Effects: The Case of Alliance Against IFQs v. Brown, 9 Geo. Int'l Envt'l L. Rev. 727, 745–46 (1998).

4. The halibut-sablefish IFQ program attempts to maintain the existing structure of the fishery by restricting the sale of quota shares to vessels within the same size and gear category and by setting a cap on the total percentage of the TAC any one quota share holder could hold. 50 C.F.R. §§ 679.41(e),(g). Also, amendments to the program set aside some quotas for purchase by crew members.

5. In the 1996 Sustainable Fisheries Act, Congress placed a moratorium on the submission, approval or implementation of any new federal ITQ programs until October 1, 2000. 16 U.S.C. § 1853(d)(1). Even before the moratorium was enacted, Congress had attached a rider to the appropriations bill for fiscal year 1997, prohibiting the use of funds to develop new IFQ programs. Section 208 of the Omnibus Consolidated Appropriations Act of 1997, Pub.L. No. 104–208, 110 Stat. 3009 (1996).

During the moratorium, Congress called upon the National Academy of Sciences (NAS) to conduct a comprehensive review of the experience to date with IFQs, and to evaluate a number of issues, including the desirability of limiting or prohibiting the transferability of IFQs, mechanisms to minimize their adverse effects on fishing communities, and methods for ensuring fair and equitable treatment of vessel owners, crew, and processors in the initial allocation of fishing quotas. P.L. 104–297, § 108(f), 16 U.S.C. § 1853 note.

The moratorium and NAS study was a compromise between the proponents of IFQs and those who favored either their complete prohibition under the Act or their non-transferability and 'sunset' after no more than seven years. The debate became a forum for the intense intra-regional competition over the fishery resources of the North Pacific Ocean off Alaska. Senators from Washington State, who favored the ability of the North Pacific council to develop IFQ programs, clashed with members of the Senate from Alaska, who feared Alaska-based fishing interests would not fare as well as the large (and largely overcapitalized and foreign-owned) Seattle-based catcher-processor fleet in any initial allocation of IFQs for the lucrative North Pacific pollock fishery. The catcher-processor sector was promoting IFQs as a way to reduce the number of vessels in their fishery and to lengthen their season. See S. Hsu and J. Wilen, Ecosystem Management and the 1996 Sustainable Fisheries Act, 24 Ecology L. Q. 799 (1997). See also David Dana, Overcoming the Political Tragedy of the Commons: Lessons Learned from the Reauthorization of the Magnuson Act, 24 Ecology L.Q. 833 (1997).

6. The National Academy of Sciences study was released in 1999. National Research Council, Sharing the Fish: Toward a National Policy on Indi-

vidual Fishing Quotas (1999). The Committee recommended that the moratorium be lifted and that IFQs be made an option in fisheries management, if regional councils find them to be warranted by a particular fishery's condition, and if appropriate measures are imposed to avoid potential adverse effects. The report urged that the councils and the Secretary of Commerce gives careful consideration to issues of initial allocation, transferability, and accumulation of shares when IFQ programs are developed. The report gave detailed recommendations on how these issues could be addressed in the design and implementation of a program.

7. During the moratorium, some of the companies that owned catcher-processors in the North Pacific pollock fishery, but who also had vessels engaged in the smaller Pacific whiting fishery off the coasts of Washington, Oregon, and California under the jurisdiction of the Pacific Fishery Management Council, looked for a solution to a similar problem of overcapitalization of that fishery. The council had set a total allowable level of fishing (TAC) for whiting, adopted a limited entry licensing program, and an allocation of part of the TAC to each sector, but there were still more vessels and fishing power than was needed to catch the TAC. In 1997, the companies in the catcher-processor sector developed a private agreement among themselves to end their wasteful practice of racing against each other for the fish. They created a non-profit cooperative and a contractual agreement not to harvest any more than a specific percentage of their sector allocation, which was 34% of the TAC. Their agreement was reviewed and approved by the Anti-trust Division of the U.S. Justice Department. By all accounts, this arrangement eliminated the race to fish. It allowed the companies to reduce the number of vessels in the fishery and to fish at a rate that allowed greater efficiency and product quality in their processing and reduced levels of bycatch because they could move vessels away from areas where bycatches were high. See J. LeBlanc, U.S. Fishery Cooperatives: Rationalizing Fisheries Through Privately Negotiated Contracts, a presentation to the National Fishery Law Symposium, University of Washington Foundation, Seattle, Wash., Nov. 2001.

In 2000, Congress extended the moratorium on IFQs until October 1, 2002, but authorized the Gulf of Mexico and North Pacific regional fishery management councils to study the possibility of quota management programs for fisheries under their jurisdiction. Pub. L. 106–554, § 1(a)(4) [Div.B, Title I, § 144(a)(1),(2)], Dec. 21, 2000; 114 Stat. 2763, 2763A–238, amending 16 U.S.C. § 1853(d). This extension was adopted in lieu of bills introduced by Senators Kerry (D–Mass.) and Snowe (R–Maine) that would have lifted the moratorium and enacted specific criteria for individual quota programs. See, e.g., S. 2973, S. 2832, and S. 637 introduced in the 107th Congress. The Snowe bill, S. 637, for example, would had authorized the adoption and approval of individual quota programs only if they expired after 5 years, created non-transferable quotas, could be held only by citizens and active participants in the fishery, and were twice approved by a two-thirds majority of votes cast by eligible permit holders.

8. Section 407(c) of the Magnuson–Stevens Act requires that before an IFQ program is adopted for the Gulf of Mexico commercial red snapper fishery, NMFS must hold a two referenda, one authorizing the council to prepare a proposed plan and the second to approve the completed plan. 16 U.S.C. § 1883(c). Only licensed red snapper fishermen who actually landed red snapper in the past decade can vote, and the vote is weighted by the landings each license-holder made in the fishery from 1993 to 1996. NMFS held the referenda in 2005 and 2006 which passed the program by a large margin. In 1995, an ITQ program was approved by NMFS, 60 Fed. Reg. 61200, but it could not be implemented due to the Congressional moratorium. After the moratorium expired, NMFS approved the council's new IFQ program, which went into effect in 2007. See Final Rules to Implement Reef Fish FMP Amendment 26, 71 Fed. Reg. 67447 (Nov. 22, 2006) (effective Jan. 1, 2007).

9. The U.S. Commission on Ocean Policy endorsed the broader use of quota programs, which it called "dedicated access privileges" (DAPs), to end the race to fish. U.S. Commission on Ocean Policy, An Ocean Blueprint for the 21st Century, 288–290 (2004), available online at http://jointoceancommission.org/documents/USCOP_report.pdf. The Commission recommended that national guidelines for DAPs should "mandate fees for exclusive access based on a percentage of quota shares held. These user fees should be used to support ecosystem-based management * * * " Id. at 290. Do you see a way in which fishing quotas and fees could be fashioned to assist in the transition to ecosystem-based management of the oceans? How would you answer the concerns raised in the following materials? In 2010, NOAA adopted a national policy on catch shares. See http://www.nmfs.noaa.gov/sfa/domes_fish/catchshare/docs/noaa_cs_policy.pdf.

c. *The 2007 Reauthorization Amendments and Catch Share Programs*

In Lovgren v. Locke, the court reviewed the New England multispecies groundfish sector allocation program. The court determined that the groundfish sectoral program was not an IFQ and thus did not trigger the special voting provisions of the Act. 701 F.3d 5 (1st Cir. 2012). The program was also upheld under the Magnuson-Stevens Act's national standards.

The 2007 MSA amendments profoundly affected the New England fishery council's willingness to consider IFQs, sectoral allocations and other output-based management measures, but made special accommodation to New England fishermen's deep resistance to limited access policies. The court described the impact as follows:

On January 12, 2007, the Reauthorization Act took effect. *See* 2007 U.S.C.C.A.N. S83 (Jan. 12, 2007). The Reauthorization Act established new conservation mandates for all FMPs. FMPs were now required to include "annual catch limits" ("ACLs") that were set at a level "such that overfishing does not occur in the fishery," as well as "measures to ensure accountability" ("AMs") to these limits. 16 U.S.C. § 1853(a)(15). Reflecting Congress's intent to increase the role of science in fishery management, proposed ACLs could "not exceed the fishing level recommendations of [a council's] scientific and statistical committee or the peer review process."

Id., § 1852(h)(6).

Congress also added a section to the MSA governing the implementation of new "limited access privilege programs," or LAPPs. 16 U.S.C. § 1853a. Unlike with the Reauthorization Act's mandatory ACLs and AMs, councils were not required to adopt LAPPs in managing fisheries within their jurisdiction. *Id.,* § 1853a(a). However, councils that chose to develop a LAPP through an FMP had to incorporate certain protections elaborated in section 1853a. Most of section 1853a's requirements applied to all councils, *e.g., id.* § 1853a(b)(1), (5), but Congress both imposed a unique requirement on the N.E. Council and created a unique exception to that requirement. The N.E. Council could not adopt an "individual fishing quota" ("IFQ"), a type of LAPP, unless such a measure was first approved in a referendum by more than two-thirds of the Fishery's "eligible permit holders" and other "fishery participants," as determined by the Secretary. *Id.,* § 1853a (c)(6)(D)(i). But Congress also exempted "sector allocation[s]" from the referendum requirement. *Id.,* § 1853a (c)(6)(D)(vi).

Councils and the NMFS were required to implement new FMPs by the 2010 fishing year for all fisheries subject to overfishing, and by the 2011 fishing year for all others. *See* Pub. L. No. 109–479, Tit. I, § 104(b), 120 Stat. at 3584 (providing effective dates for 16 U.S.C. § 1853(a)(15)).

Id., slip opinion at 17.

* * *

d. IFQs and Ecosystem-Based Management

How are IFQ systems likely to affect the ability of managers to take account of the ecosystems of which the target fish stocks are components? With increasing awareness of the importance of predator-prey relationships among species, the dangers of bycatch, the potential competition between a commercial fishery and marine wildlife, and the significance of habitat for fisheries and for marine biodiversity, many commentators call for greater application of a precautionary approach to fisheries. See, e.g., National Research Council, Sustaining Marine Fisheries 7 (1999). Does the creation of IFQs make it more or less likely that managers can exercise caution and protect marine ecosystems especially where scientific uncertainty surrounds our understanding of the dynamics of such systems? See Alison Rieser, Prescriptions for the Commons: Environmental

Scholarship and the Fishing Quotas Debate, 23 Harv. Envtl. L. Rev. 393 (1999).

e. *Reducing Capacity by Direct Congressional Action*

While the IFQ moratorium was in place, Congress enacted the American Fisheries Act of 1998, Pub. L. No. 105–277, section 208(e), 112 Stat. 2681, 2681–625 (1998)(provisions at 16 U.S.C. 1851 notes). The bill, S.1221, was introduced in the final days of the 105th Congress as part of the Omnibus Consolidated and Emergency Supplemental Appropriations for Fiscal Year 1999.

A complex piece of legislation, the American Fisheries Act (AFA) achieved a major restructuring of the largest North Pacific fishery, the Alaska pollock fishery, although because of the bill's timing, was subject to very little review and debate. The AFA requires owners of all U.S.-flag fishing vessels to meet a 75% U.S.-controlling interest standard and eliminated certain exceptions to restrictions on foreign-rebuilt vessels that had purportedly allowed a huge buildup in the at-sea processing sector of the fishery. The AFA identified a specific list of fishing vessels by name and federal number that are eligible to participate in the Bering Sea and Aleutian Islands pollock fishery. For some of those vessels not eligible to participate, the Act includes a vessel buy-back program for nine catcher/processor vessels financed by a combination of up to $90 million dollars in taxpayer funds and private industry funds borrowed from the government but repaid through a landings fee.

The AFA redefined the pollock allocations for the major (competing) sectors of the fishery: for the offshore component—40% for catcher/processors and 10% for catcher vessels delivering to motherships; for the inshore processing component—50% for catcher vessels delivering to onshore processing plants (located in Alaska). Ten percent of the total pollock quota is to be allocated as a directed fishery allowance to the western Alaska community development quota program created under section 305(i), 16 U.S.C. § 1855(i). The Act also authorized and defined terms for cooperatives for both fishing vessel owners and fish processors participating in the Alaska pollock fishery. (See discussion at note #7 above on p. 687.) The AFA prohibited entry into any fishery managed under the Magnuson–Stevens Act of new vessels over 165 feet in length or 750 tons, or with engines of greater than 3,000 horsepower, unless the vessel's entry is specifically approved by the Secretary of Commerce and the regional fishery management council. Vessels fishing in the U.S. EEZ under the jurisdiction of the Western Pacific Fishery Management Council or tuna purse seine vessels fishing outside the U.S. EEZ are excluded from these size limits.

The FY 2002 Commerce appropriations bill included language amending a provision of the AFA to delete a sunset provision on the allocation and entitlement provisions of the Act. The change make permanent the prohibition on direct pollock fishing by non-AFA catcher/processors, even though these vessels had some history of pollock catches prior to 1998. H.R. Conf. Rep. 107–278, 2001 WL 1402218.

In Arctic King Fisheries, Inc. v. United States, 59 Fed. Cl, 360 (Ct.Cl. 2004), the Court of Claims rejected a regulatory takings challenge to the American Fisheries Act. The court found that the passage of the AFA "did not effect a taking of plaintiffs' property. Rather, * * * this comprehensive reform of the rules governing the [Bering Sea–Aleutian Islands] pollock fishery resulted, at best, only in a noncompensable diminution in the value of plaintiff's' property. The AFA, moreover, neither prevented plaintiff from realizing any reasonable investment-backed expectations nor targeted plaintiff in a fashion inconsistent with the offered reasons for the passage of the legislation." Id. at 385–86.

The American Fisheries Act is an example of the Congress using the budget appropriations process rather than the regional council process under the MSA to determine which vessels should be permitted to participate in U.S. fisheries in the EEZ and at what level. In American Pelagic Fishing Co., L.P. v. United States, 49 Fed. Cl. 36 (Ct. Cl. 2001), the U.S. Court of Federal Claims held that a series of legislative riders introduced by Senator Snowe of Maine, which effectively precluded the owner of a fishing trawler from fishing for Atlantic mackerel and herring in the U.S. EEZ, effected a taking of the owner's property interest in the use of its vessel. Applying the *Penn. Central* analysis for a regulatory taking, discussed in Chapter 4, the court found the owner had a reasonable investment-backed expectation that he would be able to use the vessel for such purpose (he had obtained a permit from NMFS), an economic impact of $40 million, and the legislation was retroactive and aimed specifically at the plaintiff's vessel, the Atlantic Star. (The riders had prohibited NMFS from using appropriations to issue or renew fishing permits or other authorizations for any vessel greater than 165 feet in length or of more than 750 tons, with an engine capacity of 3000 horsepower or more. Id. at 42.) On appeal, the Federal Circuit reversed the judgment, finding that the fishing company did not suffer the taking of a property interest that is legally cognizable under the Fifth Amendment. The fishing company did not possess a property interest in its fishing permits and authorization letter because these did not confer exclusive fishing privileges and the government retained the right to suspend, modify, or revoke them. American Pelagic Fishing Company v. United States, 379 F.3d 1363 (Fed. Cir. 2004).

f.   Vessel and Permit Buyback Programs

In its 1999 report, Sustaining Marine Fisheries, the National Research Council's Committee on Ecosystem Management for Sustainable
Marine Fisheries made the following findings:

> Excess fishing capacity and overcapitalization reduce the economic
> efficiency of the fisheries and usually are associated with overfishing.
> Substantial global reductions in fleet capacity are the highest priori-
> ty for dealing with uncertainty and unexpected events in fisheries
> and to help reduce overfishing. However, overcapacity is a symptom
> of socioeconomic incentive systems and management regimes, not a
> fundamental property of fisheries. Overcapacity has been created un-
> intentionally by many national and international institutions
> through lack of property rights, subsidies, and other activities that
> circumvent market forces.
>
> Fishers adapt ingeniously to regulations designed to reduce fishing
> capacity, by improving technology, fishing "smarter" or harder, and
> modifying their techniques. So fishing capacity is difficult to manage
> directly without also changing other socioeconomic and management
> incentives * * * [M]anagers' primary focus [should] not be on direct
> management of fishing capacity alone. Instead, managers and policy
> makers should focus on developing or encouraging socioeconomic and
> other management incentives that reward conservative use of marine
> resources and their ecosystem and should learn to understand and
> address the problems of subsidies. Direct management of fishing ca-
> pacity is more appropriate in extreme or urgent circumstances or as a
> first step in establishing a more sustainable system of using marine
> resources. Then the degree of overcapacity can be used as one indica-
> tor of the sustainability of a fishery.
>
> * * * Simple buy-back programs have often been ineffective and even
> counterproductive in the past when large amounts of money have
> been spent to buy out the least efficient vessels. If there are no incen-
> tives to reduce fishing power further, the remaining individuals may
> invest additional capital and increase overall fleet capacity.

Id. at 121–122.

The 1996 Sustainable Fisheries Act added Section 312, "Transition to
Sustainable Fisheries," authorizing the Secretary, at the request of a
council or the governor of a state, to conduct a voluntary fishing capacity
reduction program if the Secretary determines the program (1) is necessary to prevent or end overfishing, rebuild stocks, or achieve measurable
and significant improvements in the conservation and management of the
fishery, (2) is consistent with the FMP in effect for the fishery and (3) that
the FMP will prevent the replacement of fishing capacity removed

through the program through a moratorium on new entrants, restrictions on vessel upgrades, and other effort control measures. The FMP must also establish a specified or target TAC to trigger closure of the fishery. 16 U.S.C. § 1861a(b). The objective of the program is to obtain the "maximum sustained reduction in fishing capacity at the least cost and in a minimum period of time." Id. 1861a(b)(2).

Vessel buy-back programs are one way to reduce capacity in fisheries. See Congressional Research Service, Commercial Fishing: Economic Aid and Capacity Reduction, ENR Report 97–441 (1997). Section 312 authorizes the Secretary to "buy out" either or both fishing vessels and fishing permits, and may fund such programs either with appropriations or funds provided under an industry fee system, provided a two-thirds majority of those participating in a referendum among all permit holders or vessel owners vote in favor of the industry fee system. Id. at § 1861a(e). Under an industry fee program, the fishers who remain in the fishery pay for the buyouts, as they are the chief beneficiaries of the capacity reduction plan.

NMFS published interim final framework rules in 2000 setting out the procedures for requesting and conducting a fishing capacity reduction program, including procedures for reverse auction bidding by permit holders and vessel owners and referenda to determine the industry's willingness to participate. 65 Fed. Reg. 31430 (May 18, 2000). The maximum term for buyout loans to is twenty years. A final notice announcing the procedures for a voluntary capacity reduction program for the Pacific groundfish fishery is published at 68 Fed. Reg. 42613 (July 18, 2003). A proposed program for the Northeast multispecies groundfish fishery is described in 66 Fed. Reg. 17668 (April 3, 2001). In 2006, the Nature Conservancy and Environmental Defense announced a privately-funded buyout of permits and vessels in the Pacific groundfish fishery, in exchange for a binding commitment from the Pacific Regional Fishery Management Council to protect certain areas of the seafloor off central California from bottom trawling as part of its Essential Fish Habitat amendment to the FMP. See J. Christensen, Unlikely Partners Create Plan to Save Ocean Habitat Along with Fishing, The New York Times, Aug. 8, 2006. The final rules designating the EFH and creating the no-trawl zones are published at 71 Fed. Reg. 27408 (May 11, 2006).

3. Acknowledging Tribal Fishing Rights

MIDWATER TRAWLERS COOPERATIVE V. DEPARTMENT OF COMMERCE

United States Court of Appeals for the Ninth Circuit, 2002
282 F.3d 710

THOMAS, CIRCUIT JUDGE.

We consider in this appeal a challenge by fishing industry groups and the States of Oregon and Washington to a federal regulation that increased the amount of Pacific whiting fish allocated to four Indian tribes. We affirm in part and reverse in part, with instructions to the district court to remand to the agency for more specific findings.

I

Isaac I. Stevens, Washington's first Territorial Governor and the first Superintendent of Indian Affairs of the Washington Territory, negotiated a series of treaties in the mid-1850s involving a number of Indian tribes located in the Northwest.[1] These treaties, commonly referred to as the "Stevens Treaties," reserved to the signing Tribes certain fishing rights. The treaties at issue in this action are the Treaty of Neah Bay, a treaty with the Makah Tribe; and the Treaty of Olympia, a treaty with the Quinault, Quileute and Hoh Tribes.

As to the right of the Makah Tribe, the Treaty of Neah Bay provided that:

> [t]he right of taking fish and of whaling or sealing at usual and accustomed grounds and stations is further secured to said Indians in common with all citizens of the United States, and of erecting temporary houses for the purpose of curing, together with the privilege of hunting and gathering roots and berries on open and unclaimed lands: Provided, however, That they shall not take shellfish from any beds staked or cultivated by citizens. (Treaty of Neah Bay, 12 Stat. 939, art. 4 (1855)).

[1] See, e.g., Treaty of Medicine Creek, 10 Stat. 1132 (Dec. 26, 1854); Treaty of Point Elliot, 12 Stat. 927 (Jan. 22, 1855); Treaty of Point No Point, 12 Stat. 933 (Jan. 26, 1855); Treaty of Neah Bay, 12 Stat. 939 (Jan. 31, 1855); Treaty with the Yakamas, 12 Stat. 951 (June 9, 1855); Treaty of Olympia, 12 Stat. 971 (July 1, 1855). See generally Wash. V. Wash. State Commercial Passenger Fishing Vessel Ass'n, 443 U.S. 658, 661–69, 99 S.Ct. 3055, 61 L.Ed.2d 823 (1979). Affected Indian tribes include the following: Hoh; Lower Elwha Band of Clallam Indians; Lummi; Makah; Muckleshoot; Nisqually; Nooksack; Port Gamble Band of Clallam Indians; Puyallup; Quileute; Quinault; Sauk Suiattle; Skokomish; Squaxin Island; Stillaguamish; Suquamish; Swinomish; Tulalip; Upper Skagit; and Yakama.

We have construed similar treaty language[2] as entitling "the Tribes to take fifty percent of the salmon and other free-swimming fish in the waters controlled by Washington State." U.S. v. Wash., 135 F.3d 618 (9th Cir.1998), opinion amended and superceded by 157 F.3d 630, 638–39 (9th Cir.1998) ("Shellfish II").[3]

More than a century after the execution of the Stevens Treaties, Congress responded to concerns about preservation of the nation's fishery resources and enacted the Magnuson–Stevens Fishery Conservation and Management Act, 16 U.S.C. §§ 1801–1883 ("the Magnuson–Stevens Act" or "the Act"). "The purpose of the Magnuson[–Stevens] Act was to protect United States fisheries by extending the exclusive fisheries zone of the United States from 12 to 200 miles and to provide for management of fishing within the 200-mile zone."

The Magnuson–Stevens Act vested the National Marine Fisheries Service ("NMFS") of the Department of Commerce with the authority to issue fishery management regulations. 16 U.S.C. §§ 1853, 1855; see generally Washington v. Daley, 173 F.3d 1158, 1162 (9th Cir.1999). However, under the Act, fishery management regulations must be consistent with "applicable law" defining Native American treaty fishing rights. See, e.g., Parravano v. Babbitt, 70 F.3d 539, 544 (9th Cir.1995). In 1996, the NMFS promulgated a regulation (the "Framework Regulation") that established a limit on the total number of Pacific whiting fish to be taken in any year and a framework for allocating these fish to the Hoh, Makah, Quileute, and Quinault Tribes. 50 C.F.R. § 660.324. The regulation stipulated coordinates that identified "usual and accustomed" fishing areas ("U & As") for the tribes, extending about forty miles into the ocean off the coast of Washington. Daley, 173 F.3d at 1163. In so doing, the NMFS recognized that the "Stevens Treaties" reserved rights to harvest Pacific whiting in the tribes' U & As. The Framework Regulation also made a specific allocation of 15,000 m. tons of P. whiting to the Makah Tribe for 1996.

Shortly after the 1996 regulation was enacted, Midwater Trawlers Co-operative, West Coast Seafood Processors, and the Fishermen's Marketing Association (collectively, "Mid-water"), the State of Oregon, and the State of Washington challenged the regulation and its annual allocations of Pacific whiting to the Makah. The action originally was brought in the Oregon federal district court, but was transferred to the federal district court in Washington. In 1997, the district court dismissed the plaintiffs' claims for failure to join the tribes as necessary and indispen-

---

[2] The precise language at issue in Shellfish II was the "right of taking fish, at all usual and accustomed grounds and stations . . . in common with all citizens of the Territory. . . ." Shellfish II, 157 F.3d at 638.

[3] The district court's opinion in the same case, U.S. v. Wash., 873 F.Supp. 1422 (W.D.Wash.1994), has generally been referred to as "Shellfish I."

sable parties. In 1999, this Court reversed the dismissal of the claims and remanded for further proceedings.

In 1999, Midwater and Oregon challenged in Oregon federal district court another NMFS regulation, which increased the 1999 amount of Pacific whiting allocated to the Makah Tribe to 32,500 metric tons. 64 Fed. Reg. 27928 (May 24, 1999). This case was transferred to Washington federal district court and consolidated with the 1996 suit pending on remand. The federal government moved for summary judgment, which the district court granted in 2000 for all the cases. The Washington district court held that (1) the federal defendants did not act arbitrarily and capriciously in recognizing the tribes' right to harvest Pacific whiting, because the Stevens Treaties are "other applicable law" under the Magnuson–Stevens Act; (2) the Secretary of Commerce did not act arbitrarily and capriciously in recognizing the U & A fishing areas beyond the three-mile territorial limit off Washington's coast; and (3) the NMFS's allocation of whiting in 1999 was not arbitrary and capricious. Midwater and Oregon appealed.

We review the district court's grant of summary judgment de novo. . . . Our only task is to determine whether the Secretary has considered the relevant factors and articulated a rational connection between the facts found and the choices made. Wash. Crab Producers, Inc. v. Mosbacher, 924 F.2d 1438, 1441 (9th Cir.1990).

* * *

III

Midwater argues that tribal treaty rights to Pacific whiting could not be recognized as "applicable law" at the time the 1996 Framework Regulation was adopted, because no express judicial adjudication of tribal treaty rights to Pacific whiting had been made. Contrary to Midwater's contention, we need not determine tribal fishing rights under the Stevens Treaties on a case by case, "fish by fish," basis. Indeed, to do so would contravene settled law of this circuit and prior Supreme Court determinations. Indeed, we previously rejected this notion in Shellfish II. There, the State of Washington had argued to the district court that the tribes should be required to prove their historic fishing for Pacific whiting. We rebuffed the argument as inconsistent with the language of the Stevens Treaties, the law of the case, and the intent and understanding of the signatory parties. As explained by the district court in Shellfish I and adopted by us in Shellfish II:

At [Treaty] time, . . . the Tribes had the absolute right to harvest any species they desired, consistent with their aboriginal title. . . . The fact that some species were not taken before treaty time—either because they were inaccessible or the Indians chose not to take them—does not mean that their right to take such fish was limited. Because the "right of taking fish" must be read as a reservation of the Indians' pre-existing rights, and because the right to take any species, without limit, pre-existed the Stevens Treaties, the Court must read the "right of taking fish" without any species limitation.

Shellfish II, 157 F.3d at 644 (quoting Shellfish I, 873 F.Supp. at 1430).

Our reasoning in Shellfish II was a natural outgrowth of the Supreme Court's detailed analysis of tribal fishing rights under the Stevens Treaties in Wash. v. Wash. State Commercial Passenger Fishing Vessel Ass'n, 443 U.S. 658 (1979). In that case, the Court concluded:

In our view, the purpose and language of the treaties are unambiguous; they secure the Indians' right to take a share of each run of fish that passes through tribal fishing areas. Id. at 679.

The fact that we considered tribal rights concerning shellfish specifically in Shellfish II was not incongruous with this treaty interpretation: the Stevens Treaties contained a separate proviso for shellfish, requiring an analysis distinct from that governing free-swimming fish. Shellfish II, 157 F.3d at 639–40.

Pacific whiting are not shellfish. They are free-swimming fish, managed by the NMFS as a unitary stock,that range from the Gulf of California to the Gulf of Alaska. Adult whiting migrate annually from spawning grounds off southern California and northern Mexico to feeding grounds, which range from northern California to British Columbia. They migrate through the Makah Tribe's usual and accustomed fishing grounds. The fact that whiting pass through the U & A in a manner different from anadromous fish, such as salmon, is not relevant. The analysis of the Stevens Treaties conducted in Passenger Fishing Vessel and in Shellfish II applies with equal force to Pacific whiting. The term "fish" as used in the Stevens Treaties encompassed all species of fish, without exclusion and without requiring specific proof. Shellfish II, 157 F.3d at 643 (quoting Shellfish I, 873 F.Supp. at 1430). The district court did not err in so holding.

IV

The Framework Regulation described the U & A fishing grounds for the four tribes as extending to 125 degrees 44' W. longitude, or approximately forty miles off the Washington coast. See 50 C.F.R. § 660.324(c). Although no U & A had been adjudicated beyond three miles for the Hoh, Quileute, and Quinault Tribes, the NMFS extended the Makah Tribe's U & A coordinates south to provide U & As for these other three tribes. 61 Fed. Reg. 28789. The district court did not err in upholding the Secretary of Commerce's recognition of U & A fishing areas beyond the three-mile territorial limit.

The Treaty of Neah Bay, which is the applicable treaty with respect to the Makah tribal interests, provides that the fishing rights are "secured to said Indians in common with all citizens of the United States." 12 Stat. 939, art. 4. Nothing in the plain language of the treaty provides a geographic limitation, and longstanding case law establishes that U & A fishing grounds properly extend into waters under United States jurisdiction. See, e.g., Passenger Fishing Vessel, 443 U.S. at 685–87, 99 S.Ct. 3055 (salmon); U.S. v. Wash., 459 F.Supp. 1020, 1065 (W.D.Wash.1978) (herring); Makah v. Brown, No. C85–1606R, and U.S. v. Wash., Civil No. 9213—Phase I, Subproceeding No. 92–1 (W.D.Wash.), Order on Five Motions Relating to Treaty Halibut Fishing, at 6, Dec. 29, 1993 (halibut); U.S. v. Wash., 873 F.Supp. 1422, 1445 & n. 30 (W.D.Wash.1994), aff'd in part and rev'd in part, 157 F.3d 630, 651–52 (9th Cir.1998) (shellfish); U.S. v. Wash., Subproceeding 96–2 (Order Granting Makah's Motion for Summary Judgment, etc. at 4, Nov. 5, 1996) (Pacific whiting); see also Seufert Bros. Co. v. U.S., 249 U.S. 194, 199, 39 S.Ct. 203, 63 L.Ed. 555 (1919) (rejecting an argument that tribal fishing rights are limited to historic territorial boundaries).

Indeed, we have held specifically that the Makah's "historic fishing grounds extend forty miles out to sea. The Makah are guaranteed the right to fish in these grounds by treaty." Makah Indian Tribe v. Verity, 910 F.2d 555, 556 (9th Cir.1990). Thus, the Secretary of Commerce's recognition of U & A fishing areas beyond the three-mile territorial limit was entirely appropriate.

V

After a careful examination of the administrative record, we conclude that the specific allocation in 1999 to the Makah Tribe was inconsistent with the scientific principles set forth in the Magnuson–Stevens Act. Thus, a remand to the NMFS is required.

The starting point for any examination of the rightful allocation of Pacific whiting to the Makah Tribe must be the tribe's right under the Treaty of Neah Bay. The Supreme Court provided the analytical framework in Passenger Fishing Vessel:

[A]n equitable measure of the common right should initially divide the harvestable portion of each run that passes through a "usual and accustomed" place into approximately equal treaty and nontreaty shares, and should then reduce the treaty share if tribal needs may be satisfied by a lesser amount.

443 U.S. at 685, 99 S.Ct. 3055.

The concept of "harvestable portion" embraces the "conservation necessity principle," meaning that government regulation must not cause "demonstrable harm to the actual conservation of fish." U.S. v. Wash., 384

F.Supp. 312, 415 (W.D.Wash.1974). Conversely, the conservation necessity principle also permits regulation of marine fisheries as necessary to conserve the fish resource, including regulation of Native American fishers harvesting under treaty rights. Passenger Fishing Vessel Ass'n, 443 U.S. at 682, 99 S.Ct. 3055 ("Although non-treaty fishermen might be subjected to any reasonable state fishing regulation serving any legitimate purpose, treaty fishermen are immune from all regulation save that required for conservation."). In the NMFS allocation context, the conservation necessity principle became incorporated in the description of the available stock for harvesting, namely the "harvestable surplus."

Applying these general principles to the case at hand, the Makah Tribe is entitled, pursuant to the Treaty of Neah Bay, to one-half the harvestable surplus of Pacific whiting that passes through its usual and accustomed fishing grounds, or that much of the harvestable surplus as is necessary for tribal subsistence, whichever is less. See Passenger Fishing Vessel Ass'n, 443 U.S. at 685–86, 99 S.Ct. 3055.

In making regulatory allocations of fish based on these legal principles, the NMFS is also bound by the requirements of the Magnuson–Stevens Act, which dictates that the NMFS base fishery conservation and management measures on the "best scientific information available." 16 U.S.C. § 1851(a)(2).

The immediate origins of the present controversy date to 1996, when the NMFS sought public comment on its initial proposal to determine the Makah allocation based on a "biomass" theory, that is, an estimate of the percentage of Pacific whiting in the Makah's usual and accustomed area. The initial proposal included a multiplier, based on deviations from average harvest rates in prior years. Under the proposal, the Makah allocation was estimated to be 6.5% of the harvest available to all United States fishermen, or approximately 13,000 to 18,000 metric tons.

The Makah Tribe argued that the NMFS should employ a harvest-based approach, under which it would be entitled to half the whiting harvested in the North Columbia/Vancouver area, or 25% of the total United States harvest. This contention was based on the Makah Tribe's assertion that the majority of the unitary stock of whiting pass through the Makah Tribe's usual and accustomed area. Therefore, it reasoned, it was entitled to up to 50% of all whiting on the Pacific coast.

The NMFS never implemented the biomass-based methodology it had proposed, in part because that methodology had been rejected in United States v. Washington, which involved allocation of halibut, as contrary to the conservation necessity principle. The NMFS was apparently also concerned about legal proceedings that the tribe had instituted. Instead, the NMFS and the Makah Tribe entered into a compromise agreement, under which the Tribe was to be allocated 15,000 metric tons in 1996. 61 Fed. Reg. 28787.

Subsequently, the tribe proposed a two-year interim allocation of 10.8% of the United States Harvest Guidelines for 1997 and 1998. After determining that the proposal would have a negligible biological impact, the NMFS approved the proposal.

In 1998, the Makah Tribe made a five-year compromise proposal to the NMFS, under which the tribe would receive a treaty share not to exceed 17.5% of the United States harvest guideline in any one year. In 1999, the NMFS proposed an allocation to the Makah Tribe, in accordance with the compromise agreement, of 32,500 metric tons, or 14% of the estimated total United States harvest. Subsequently, the NMFSpublished a proposed rule requesting comments on (1) the Makah Tribe's sliding-scale proposal, which under the 1999 United States Harvest Guidelines would result in an allocation of 32,500 metric tons or 14% of the total United States harvest; (2) a "status quo" allocation of 25,000 metric tons. 64 Fed. Reg. 1341, 1341–42. In an environmental assessment prepared for the 1999 tribal allocation, the NMFS concluded that the Makah proposal would have no significant impact on the environment. 64 Fed. Reg. 27928, 27933. In the end, the NMFS approved the Makah proposal. Id. at 27930. In doing so, the agency stated:

The Makah have made a proposal for 32,500 mt of whiting in 1999 that NMFS accepts as a reasonable accommodation of the treaty right for 1999 in view of the remaining uncertainty surrounding the appropriate quantification. This 1999 amount of 32,500 mt (14 percent of the 232,000–mt OY) is not intended to set a precedent regarding either quantification of the Makah treaty right or future allocations. NMFS will continue to attempt to negotiate a settlement in U.S. v. Washington regarding the appropriate quantification of the treaty right to whiting. If an appropriate methodology or allocation cannot be developed through negotiations, the allocation will ultimately be resolved in the pending subproceeding in U.S. v. Washington. Id.

The difficulty with the published justification for the rule is, of course, that it is devoid of any stated scientific rationale. The Magnuson–Stevens Act requires the Secretary to describe the "nature and extent" of the tribal fishing right, 16 U.S.C. § 1853(a)(2), based on the "best scientific information available." 16 U.S.C. § 1851(a)(2). In sum, the best available politics does not equate to the best available science as required by the Act.

An agency's action is "normally" considered arbitrary and capricious when it:

has relied on factors which Congress has not intended it to consider, entirely failed to consider an important aspect of the problem, offered an explanation for its decision that runs counter to the evidence before the agency, or is so implausible that it could not be ascribed to a difference in view or the product of agency expertise.

In examining the Magnuson–Stevens Act, there is little doubt of congressional intent: the agency was directed to employ the "best available scientific information" as its methodology in making its decisions.

A plain reading of the proposed NMFS rule, and the undisputed history leading up to the allocation decision, demonstrate that the rule was a product of pure political compromise, not reasoned scientific endeavor. Although the NMFS allocation may well be eminently fair, the Act requires that it be founded on science and law, not pure diplomacy. For these reasons, a remand to the NMFS is required to either promulgate a new allocation consistent with the law and based on the best available science, or to provide further justification for the current allocation that conforms to the requirements of the Magnuson–Stevens Act and the Treaty of Neah Bay.

* * *

NOTE

1. What does the court mean that "… the best available politics does not equate to the best available science as required by the Act"? In 2004, the Ninth Circuit upheld the Pacific whiting allocation to the Makah Tribe. Midwater Trawlers Cooperative v. Dept of Commerce, 393 F.3d 994 (9th Cir. 2004). In 2013, a federal district court further vindicated tribal treaty rights by ordering the State of Washington to repair over 600 fish-passage blocking culverts under state-owned roads. U.S. v. Washington, __, 2013 WL 1334391 (W.D. Wash. 2013).

2. How do these outcomes differ from the decision in Native Village of Eyak v. Blank, 688 F.3d 619 (9th Cir. 2012), excerpted in Chapter 2, beginning on p. 92? Note that Native Alaskan villages have cooperative management responsibilities for bowhead whales, seals and walrus herds in the Arctic Ocean. Should the treaty tribes of the Pacific Northwest have a seat on the regional fishery management councils under the Magnuson-Stevens Act?

3. U.S. MANAGEMENT OF HIGHLY MIGRATORY SPECIES

The original FCMA did not assert U.S. management authority over highly migratory species—defined as tuna in the 1976 act—in an attempt to deny other nations the authority to govern tuna fisheries in their 200-mile zones. The U.S. concern was that distant-water tuna fishing vessels of the U.S. would be excluded from the rich fish grounds off other nations. *See, e.g.,* Jon Van Dyke & Susan Heftel, *Tuna Management in the Pacific: An Analysis of the South Pacific Forum Fisheries Agency,* 3 Univ. Hawaii L. Rev.1, 12–17 (1981). However, in 1990 amendments to the FCMA, Congress acknowledged the validity of coastal state jurisdiction over high migratory fish species (HMS) by extending the act to highly migratory species. 16 U.S.C. §§ 1811–12, as amended. The Secretary of Commerce was given responsibility for HMS management plans in the Atlantic. For Pacific tunas in U.S. waters, the Western Pacific Fishery Management Council has lead responsibility.

The U.S. continues to participate in several international tuna management bodies and negotiated a new one for the Pacific. In 2000, the U.S. signed the Convention on the Conservation and Management of Highly Migratory Fish Stocks in the Western and Central Pacific Ocean (sometimes referred to as the Honolulu Convention). The convention created a new management body composed of all the nations that fish for tuna in the Pacific and the Pacific island nations in whose EEZs most of the tuna fishing occurs. The treaty is based on new, precautionary standards for management articulated in the United Nations Agreement on Straddling Fish Stocks and Highly Migratory Fish Stocks of 1995. Since the late 1980s, over three dozen U.S. purse-seine tuna vessels have been licensed to fish for tuna in the Pacific states' EEZs, under the Treaty on Fisheries Between the Governments of Certain Pacific Island States and the Government of the United States of America, for which the U.S. government pays over $18 million in economic development aid. The U.S. is a longstanding member of several other international tuna management bodies, most notably the International Commission for the Conservation of Atlantic Tunas (ICCAT) and the Inter–American Tropical Tunas Commission (IATTC), which governs tuna fisheries in the eastern Tropical Pacific. This membership necessarily affects the governance of the domestic tuna fisheries in U.S. waters and beyond under the Magnuson-Stevens Act.

A. ATLANTIC TUNAS, SWORDFISH, AND SHARKS

Given the pervasive scheme of federal regulation of Atlantic highly migratory species under the Magnuson–Stevens Act, do state or municipal governments have any authority to exclude from their port facilities vessels from fisheries they deem to be unsustainable?

CITY OF CHARLESTON, SOUTH CAROLINA V.
A FISHERMAN'S BEST, INC.

United States Court of Appeals, Fourth Circuit, 2002
310 F.3d 155

GODBOLD, SENIOR CIRCUIT JUDGE.

I. Background

This appeal concerns whether federal law preempts a resolution of the City Council of the City of Charleston, South Carolina enacted July 21, 1998, relating to its Maritime Center docks. The resolution included these prohibitions, which we have numbered for convenience:

[Par. 1]: "the use of the Charleston Maritime Center and its appurtenant facilities is hereby prohibited to fishing vessels utilizing pelagic longline tackle, which shall be prohibited from docking or tying up at the Charleston Maritime Center and its appurtenant facilities for any purpose other than to purchase fuel or ice or in the case of a storm or other emergency."

[Par. 2]: "any Lessee or user of any part of the Charleston Maritime Center and its appurtenant facilities shall be prohibited from selling, purchasing, processing or unloading any fish from or caught by pelagic longline fishing vessels."

[Par. 3]: "no billfish or swordfish from any source of any kind shall be sold, purchased, processed or unloaded at the Charleston Maritime Center and its appurtenant facilities."

* * *

Pelagic refers to fish that live in ocean waters. Swordfish are a highly mobile species (HMS) of pelagic fish that move freely in ocean waters of the world, including waters off United States coasts. HMS are subject to many statutory provisions and regulations that do not apply to other species. . . .

Shrimping and longline fishing for swordfish are the two major components of the fishing industry in waters off the South Carolina coast. Over ninety-eight percent of the swordfish catch made by swordfish vessels in waters off South Carolina is made with longline tackle. Longline fishing tackle employs long lines, two to thirty or forty miles in length, with shorter lines attached at intervals carrying baited hooks. It is a relatively new method of fishing in this country, developed over the past twenty to twenty-five years. Substantially all commercial swordfishing occurs in the EEZ.

Waters off the South Carolina coast are a highly desirable locale for swordfish fishing. Swordfish migrate there for reproduction and nurturing. This produces an abundance of swordfish, especially small fish. Most of the commercial fishermen landing fish off South Carolina fish from the Florida Straits (south tip of Florida) to Cape Hatteras (in North Carolina). *Briefing Paper, Concerning the Pelagic Longline Fishery Off South Carolina A Special Report to the Marine Advisory Committee, South Carolina Department of Natural Resources, Marine Resources Division, Office of Fisheries Management.* App. at 195. Some of these vessels are transients that follow fish up and down the Atlantic coast, some as far north as New England.

In the late 1980s the commercial fishing industry in the Charleston area was in distress. Hurricane Hugo damaged vessels, docks and other facilities. The Mayor of Charleston was approached by a representative of shrimpers who requested that the City help the fishing industry. The City responded. It retained an expert in seaport planning to evaluate market support by commercial fishermen for dock space at the Maritime Center, an existing dock site owned by the City. The expert's report described the fishing industry as contributing strongly to the state's cultural diversity and identity, particularly in coastal counties, and to South Carolina's international commerce since much of its seafood harvest is sent out of state. The report also described a decline in economic health of the Charleston community. It identified Shem Creek, a privately owned dock not far from the Maritime Center, as Charleston's closest link to the commercial fishing industry. The expert reported that within approximately 100 miles of Charleston, except for the Maritime Center, there was no major landing dock for fin fish (i.e., not shrimp) that serviced transient offshore vessels.

* * *

The City concluded that the commercial fishing industry was on a slow and constant decline. The number of transient out-of-state vessels coming to Charleston was declining. John Deehan, Director of Revitalization for the City of Charleston, described the situation this way: without help, families that engaged in fishing and shrimping in South Carolina were going to be "out of business and gone." The City completed a plan to extend and improve the Maritime Center. It requested an Economic Development Agency (EDA) grant of $2,150,000 and agreed to designate for the project an acre of water-front land valued at $1,600,000.

* * *

A bitter public controversy arose in Charleston involving newspapers, television, radio, public meetings, and organized protests against public figures including the Mayor. During the spring and summer of 1997 a sunburst of events occurred. The precise sequence is not always clear from the record, but the tide of events, the roles of players, and their relative positions are clear.

Recreational and sport fishing interests in Charleston opposed the project for improving the Maritime Center. Generally they oppose commercial longline fishing and longline fishing for swordfish. They regard swordfish as a top trophy for saltwater sports fishermen and they compete with commercial fishermen for available swordfish. In Charleston they asserted that the swordfish stock was decreasing and they feared that additional demands on the stock might destroy the species. They felt that the improved facility would attract more transient vessels to fish for swordfish in the EEZ, which would increase pressure on swordfish resources off South Carolina. They submitted that swordfishing contributes excessively to by-catch (fish caught and discarded because not desired or too small), especially small swordfish that must be thrown away. They viewed swordfishing and swordfish vessels as disastrous to the environment. They considered government regulation of fish and fisheries as slow and inefficient and felt that management of swordfish by the United States and by international entities is not satisfactory.

On the other hand commercial swordfish fishermen and their proponents felt that they had been "ganged up on" by politicians, the South Carolina Department of Natural Resources Board, and the National Marine Fisheries Service (an agency of the Commerce Department to which the Secretary has delegated some of his fish and fish management responsibilities). They pointed out that they make their living in a highly-regulated and legally-defined industry and must compete for swordfish with persons who fish only for sport. They considered that they lack political and public support comparable to that enjoyed by more affluent sportsfishermen. They felt that they are branded as dishonest and as having no concern for the health of fishing resources. They pointed to the significance of swordfish as a food resource and to the emphasis placed by Congress on this function. They felt that they are the chief supporters of government regulations.

* * *

II. Structure of the Federal Management System

* * * Statutes of the United States have brought actions of international bodies into our country's regulatory system for fish. The United States is authorized to participate in international agreements, § 1821, and the Secretary of State is authorized to negotiate and renegotiate them. § 1822. Agreements concerning HMS are specifically authorized. *See* § 1822(e).

The United States is a member of the International Convention for the Conservation of Atlantic Tunas (ICCAT), a multinational cooperative management body consisting of more than twenty nations. The convention meets annually to review and revise scientific and catch information for various species of fish including swordfish. An important task is recommending quotas for fish allocated to each member nation.

Congress has implemented ICCAT by the Atlantic Tunas Convention Act, § 971 (ACTA). The United States receives reports and recommendations of ICCAT and accepts or rejects them. If recommendations are accepted, regulations are promulgated to carry them out. This source of regulations is important because swordfish are an international fish, an HMS, in which many nations have interests and assert rights. Many provisions of the United States regulatory system for swordfish have originated in ICCAT and through United States statutory procedures have been adopted as part of the federal regulatory system. These include such matters as size, mortality, quotas, allowable catch, and sanctions to enforce quotas.

III. Preemption: An Overview

* * *

The issue before us is not whether this court favors the commercial fishing industry, particularly longline swordfish fishing, or favors recreational fishermen and environmentalists and the policies they favor. Rather we must determine whether state action, in the form of the City's resolution, interferes with or is contrary to the laws of Congress, made in pursuance of the Constitution. The ultimate touchstone of preemption analysis is the intent of Congress. One of the most familiar recitals is that federal and state law conflict when "the state law stands as an obstacle to the accomplishments of the full purposes and objectives" of federal law.

* * *

The present case is a paradigm of multiple statutes and regulations, and varying governmental institutions, pervasive in depth, breadth and detail, in a regulatory system that Congress intends to be national in character. The system has been described as being as tightly regulated as atomic energy. The Eleventh Circuit has said that the legislative history of the Magnuson Act preempts the entire field of fishery management of the EEZ. Southeastern Fisheries Ass'n., Inc. v. Chiles, 979 F.2d 1504, 1509 (11th Cir.1992). Whether holding or dictum is not clear.

* * *

V. The 1996 Act: A New FMP and New Regulations

Before 1996 management of HMS had been implemented by FMPs covering them and other species jointly.

The 1996 Congress added significant provisions to the system of managing fish and fisheries. It readopted the Magnuson–Stevens Act. It adopted a new system governing identification, testing and approval of fishing gear, now appearing in § 1855 *et seq.,* P.L. 104–297, 539 (1996). The Secretary of Commerce was directed to complete a comprehensive study on the feasibility of implementing a comprehensive management program for HMS participating in fisheries for Atlantic HMS, which included swordfish. § 109(H), Pub. Law, 104–297, *as amended,* Pub. Law 104–108. Waters off South Carolina are within this specially directed fishery to be studied by the Secretary.

A panel was appointed under the authority of the Magnuson–Stevens Act and ATCA. It included representatives of academic organizations, regional councils involved in HMS management, Atlantic and Gulf Coastal States, and ICCAT. The panel met seven times. National Marine and Fisheries Service (NMFS), an agency of the Commerce Department, distributed a scoping document to serve as a starting point for consideration of issues. It described major issues, including legal requirements for management and potential management measures. This document was the subject of public hearings and provided a mechanism for public input.

A draft FMP was circulated in October 1998 with a comment period to end on March 12, 1999. A copy of this draft is in the record of this case, but the district court did not refer to it at the summary judgment hearing or in its order.

A proposed rule that accompanied the draft FMP was published in the Federal Register on January 20, 1999. After the comment period expired on March 12, 1999 NMFS held more than twenty public hearings in communities from Texas to Maine and the Caribbean. An Executive Summary of the proposed FMP was issued in early April which listed fishing proposed for approval for North Atlantic swordfish. It said:

> *The U.S. directed fishery for north Atlantic swordfish is confined by regulation to two gear types: longline and handgear. Pelagic longlining accounts for approximately 98 per cent of U.S. directed swordfish landings.*

Executive Summary, Final Fishery Management Plan for Atlantic Tuna, Swordfish and Sharks, April 1999, p. 45 (Emphasis added.)

A formal rule approving the FMP and regulations implementing it was issued May 28, 1999, less than thirty days before the district court decision was entered in this case on June 22, 1999. It is styled "Fishing Management Plan for Atlantic Tuna, Swordfish and Sharks." It is not in the record and the district court did not refer to it. We take judicial notice of it, however, even if it was not called to the attention of the trial court. The new FMP became effective July 1, 1999, except for a few regulations that do not relate to this case. Formal adoption on May 28 was sufficient to subject the FMP and accompanying regulations to judicial consideration.

The new FMP described the provisions of the 1996 Act:

In 1996, the United States Congress reauthorized the Magnuson–Stevens Act. This reauthorization included a new emphasis on the precautionary approach in U.S. fishery management policy. New provisions of the Magnuson–Stevens Act require managers to halt overfishing; to rebuild overfished fisheries; to minimize bycatch and bycatch mortality, to the extent practicable; and to identify and protect essential fish habitat (EFH). These provisions are coupled with the recognition that management of HMS requires international cooperation and that rebuilding programs must reflect traditional participation in the fisheries by U.S. fishermen, relative to foreign fleets. Besides the Magnuson–Stevens Act, U.S. fisheries management must be consistent with the requirements of other regulations including the Marine Mammal Protection Act, the Endangered Species Act, the Migratory Bird Treaty Act, and several other Federal laws. These laws are described in Chapter 1 of this document. This FMP addresses these new requirements, as well as the requirements of other applicable legislation, and incorporates the best available scientific information into Atlantic HMS management.

Final Fishery Management Plan for Atlantic Tuna, Swordfish, and Sharks, April 1999, p. viii.

The FMP described the area from the Florida east coast north to Cape Hatteras (off North Carolina) as a sector in which pelagic longline vessels primarily target swordfish year round. And, it said, smaller swordfish vessels make trips from the Florida Straits (the south tip of Florida) to the Charleston Hump (an area in the waters off South Carolina), while larger vessels migrate seasonally from the Yucatan Peninsula to the West Indies in the Caribbean and as far north as the mid-Atlantic coast of the United States.

The objectives of the new FMP reflect the complex balancing of interests and concerns that culminated in the 1999 final rule. Among the aims of the new FMP were establishing a foundation for the development of international rebuilding programs, analyzing and implementing management measurements to control bycatch, minimizing social and economic impact to meet the goals of the FMP and the Act, rebuilding overfished fisheries, and bringing about changes that meet the same objectives but with lesser impact on affected communities.

As a consequence of the 1996 Act the federal government began working on a system of closed areas to reduce pelagic longline catch of undersized swordfish, with substantial focus on fishing grounds off the coast of South Carolina.

VI. Preemption Applied

The resolution conflicts in numerous ways with federal laws and, therefore, is preempted.

* * *

Part 635 of the Code of Federal Regulation covers Atlantic Highly Migratory Species. Section 635.21 covers gear operation and deployment restrictions. Subsection (b) provides:

> *General.* No person shall use any gear to fish for Atlantic HMS other than those gears specifically authorized in this part. A vessel using or having on board in the Atlantic Ocean any unauthorized gear may not have on board an Atlantic HMS.

The gear specifically authorized for swordfish appears in (d)(4):

> *Swordfish.* (i) No person may possess north Atlantic swordfish taken from its management unit by any gear other than handgear or long-line, except that such swordfish taken incidentally while fishing with a squid trawl may be retained, subject to restrictions specified in § 635.24(b)(2). No person may possess south Atlantic swordfish taken from its management unit by any gear other than longline.

The resolution also conflicts with Prohibitions under 50 C.F.R. § 635.71. Subsection (e), headed "Swordfish," makes it unlawful to fish for North Atlantic swordfish from, or possess or land North Atlantic swordfish, on board a vessel using or having on board gear other than pelagic longline, harpoon, rod and reel, or handline. *Id.* at 223.

The forces that were directed by Congress to prepare an FMP for HMS in the Atlantic had responded. They had gathered thousands of views through hearings and responses and submissions by experts and state and government agents. They had distributed their views as required by administrative procedures. They had concluded with a choice of tackle for swordfish. The City, pursuing its own interests and goals, had made its own choice, diametrically opposed, for fishing tackle and, indirectly for fishing vessels condemned by their use of gear of which the City disapproved. Compliance with its requirements would violate the law.

* * *

VII. Alleged Barriers to Preemption

The City presents several barriers to preemption. First, it says that it is not engaged in regulating anything but if it is regulating anything it is not regulating fish, therefore there is no issue of whether federal fishing law preempts state action. Along with this it describes its resolution as a mere announcement of a policy that longline vessels are not welcome at its dock, that, like a private landowner, it has the right to announce what persons are welcome, to ask those not welcome to leave, and to pursue a remedy of trespass if they refuse. The City asks for the status of a private landowner. The government grant it secured was to meet needs of a state or local area from economic adjustment problems, and the only entities that could secure such grants were a "redevelopment area or economic development district established under subchapter IV of this chapter, an Indian tribe, a State, a city or other political subdivision of a State, or a consortium of such political subdivisions." 42 U.S.C. § 3242 (repealed 1998).

* * *

When an FMP is in effect and a fisherman has harvested fish in federal waters and is headed for shore to land his cargo, the state cannot exercise its authority over state waters for the purpose or effect of preventing him from landing at an available facility. Federal and state authority is in conflict and the Supremacy Clause requires that the federal law prevails. The Congressional policy of commitment to a national regulatory system is honored. Congress does not intend Balkanization of our coastlines. Were this not so a state or municipal sovereign owning a dock can effectively bring to its knees an industry engaged in bringing ashore fish caught in federal waters—Boston could shut down codfishing and a California seaport can idle the tuna fleet.

* * *

LUTTIG, CIRCUIT JUDGE, dissenting.

I respectfully dissent from my colleagues' disposition of this case. There are two flaws with the majority's opinion. First, it assumes wrongly (with little analysis) that the municipal resolution under review constitutes government regulation, which is subject to preemption, rather than proprietary action of the municipality, which is not, when it is clear that the City acted in the latter capacity when it passed the resolution in question. Second, even were the majority correct in its unexamined assumption that the resolution constitutes regulation as opposed to the exercise of proprietary power, the Magnuson Act does not preempt the resolution because this single jurisdiction's limitation of docking privileges at this single dock does not *actually* interfere with the activities protected by the Act.

As to the first flaw, "preemption doctrines apply only to state *regulation.* [The Supreme Court's] decisions in this area support the distinction between government as regulator and government as proprietor," Building and Constr. Trades Council v. Associated Builders and Contractors, 507 U.S. 218, 227 (1993) (emphasis added). And, as the district court noted, "[w]hether or not a governmental entity is acting as a market participant is a very fact specific determination." Here, the facts unequivocally demonstrate that the City was "a lessor of its property, [ ] participating in the economic marketplace for the provision of physical marketplaces."

That the City's only remedy when longline fishing boats dock at the Maritime Center lies in trespass as the majority itself acknowledges, *see ante* at 176–77, confirms that the City acted in its proprietary capacity when it enacted the instant resolution: The resolution has no enforcement mechanism and gains force *only in so far as the City acts like a private landowner* and exercises private property rights that exist independently of the resolution.

Simply, the resolution is a decision by the City, as a participant in the market, as to how it will manage its own property. The citizens weighed in, a legislative decision was made, and now, the City's land is to be managed in conformity with the democratically-derived directive. The only federal restraint imposed on the conduct of a governmental entity acting in such a capacity is the *direct* command of federal law.

Even were the majority correct in its characterization of the resolution as regulatory in nature, the resolution would yet be valid because it does not interfere with activities protected by the Magnuson Act. As the district court held, this single resolution, of a single local jurisdiction, governing a single dock, does not interfere at all, much less significantly, with longline fishing. It does not even prevent longline fishermen from landing within this one City's jurisdiction.

Allowing individual municipalities to prevent longline fishermen from landing in their respective jurisdictions would allow municipalities to produce, piecemeal, conflict such as that held to be preempted in Southeastern Fisheries Assoc. Inc. v. Chiles, 979 F.2d 1504 (11th Cir.1992). But when, as here, a municipality does not close its shores, no such piecemeal conflict is even possible. Not only may longline fishermen continue to dock elsewhere along the South Carolina coast, they may continue to dock in the City of Charleston itself—just not at the one dock reached by the resolution.

Appellants failed to contest the City's claims that there are other docks in Charleston Harbor (*i.e.,* also advantageously positioned with respect to being in a deep-water port), at which longline fishermen may dock, unaffected by the resolution. Alone, this failure is fatal to appellants' claim.

Appellants did offer testimony that in Charleston Harbor there is currently no other dock site presently complete with all of the services necessary for landing swordfish. But none of that testimony creates a genuine issue of fact as to whether dock space that could be configured to land such fish is in fact rendered unavailable in Charleston Harbor by the resolution. In the absence of any evidence contradicting that offered by the City on this issue, the district court was certainly correct to grant summary judgment.

The "motive" of the City's officials in enacting the resolution is irrelevant to the actual conflict analysis. . . . Here, the only relevant inquiry is whether the resolution renders unavailable all, or substantially all, dock space within the City's jurisdiction that could be configured to allow longline fishermen to land their fish. Were this a case in which the municipality had, in some manner, actually prevented such landings, then the argument for pre-emption would indeed be strong. But this is academic at the moment, because nothing approaching the actual prevention of docking by these fishermen has occurred.

This resolution does not even regulate longline fishing, nor does it prohibit or effectively prohibit such fishing. It merely limits access to one, single municipal dock; other docks remain unaffected by the resolution. As such, there is neither need nor authorization for the heavy hand of federal preemption today sanctioned by the majority.

* * *

NOTES AND QUESTIONS

1. Which opinion contains the better analysis? Does it undermine the dissent's "proprietary action" analysis that the dock was financed by a federal grant? If the recreational fishing lobby was powerful enough to convince the local government to ban longliners at the municipal facility, why does the HMS FMP for U.S. waters favor this fishing sector? Why does the Magnuson-Stevens Act require the NMFS to develop the Atlantic HMS FMP and not the regional fishery management councils for the Atlantic?

2. The Atlantic sharks FMP was challenged by commercial fishermen and upheld in Southern Offshore Fishing Ass'n v. Verity, 995 F.Supp. 1411 (M.D. Fla. 1998). See also Southern Offshore Fishing Ass'n v. Guiterrez, 2008 WL 2669344 (M.D. 2008). Given the life histories and ecological role of sharks as apex predators, is any directed fishery for sharks sustainable? Does the Magnuson–Stevens Act and the science upon which it relies make adequate provision for these ecological considerations?

3. In the 1970s, Massachusetts created a limited entry fishery for Atlantic bluefin tuna by purse-seine fishing vessels owned by one company. This fishing method is controversial as it has the capacity to catch entire schools of small tunas. In Sea Rover Fishing, Inc. v. Diomati, 24 Mass. L. Rptr. 387 (Mass. Super. Ct. 2008), the court upheld seasonal restrictions on purse seining to protect recreational fishers' access to bluefin tuna when they are in

Cape Cod Bay, an important summer feeding ground for this highly migratory species.

4. The Atlantic Tunas Convention Act requires that any regulation of U.S. fishing vessels must ensure that U.S. fishermen have comparable opportunity to catch Atlantic tunas (e.g., Atlantic bluefin tuna) to those of foreign fishermen. 16 U.S.C. § 971. Does this provision prevent NMFS from setting more restrictive provisions to conserve and rebuild W. Atlantic tuna stocks than the parties to ICCAT will agree to?

B. WESTERN AND CENTRAL PACIFIC FISHERIES FOR HIGHLY MIGRATORY SPECIES

1. U.S. Longline Fishing in the Pacific

In the Pacific, the U.S. longline fishing fleet is much smaller than most foreign fleets. Based in Honolulu, HI, it targets tuna and swordfish in the EEZs around Hawaii and the U.S. Pacific territories of Guam and American Samoa. Since NMFS adopted a limited-entry license scheme to control entry, and gear conflicts are minimized by fishing zones, the principal management concern is the tendency of pelagic longline gear, deployed over hundreds of miles of ocean, to "take" migrating sea turtles and catch the juveniles of target fish species. The Western Pacific Fishery Management Council, therefore, has had to adopt and modify fishing management measures to accommodate protections under the Endangered Species Act. In Chapter 7, application of the Endangered Species Act to U.S. fisheries managed under the Magnuson–Stevens Act is explored, beginning on p. 864.

2. U.S. Tuna Fisheries in the Western and Central Pacific Ocean

The Western and Central Pacific Fisheries Convention Implementation Act, 16 U.S.C. §§ 6901 et seq., authorizes the Secretary of Commerce to promulgate regulations to meet U.S. obligations under the Convention on the Conservation and Management of Highly Migratory Fish Stocks in the Western and Central Pacific Ocean, and to implement the decisions of the treaty's Commission. Initial regulations for U.S. vessels were promulgated in 2010, 75 Fed. Reg. 3335 (Jan. 21, 2010).These include requirements for permits, vessel monitoring systems, observers, reporting and recordkeeping, at-sea transshipment, and boarding and inspection on the high seas. Further regulations to cover discards of purse seines were implemented in 2012. 75 Fed. Reg. 71501 (Dec. 3, 2012).

The U.S. tuna treaty with certain Pacific island states is implemented by the South Pacific Tuna Act of 1988, 16 U.S.C. §§ 973–973r. NOAA promulgated regulations in 2010 to govern the allocation of licenses to U.S. purse seine vessels in the event that fewer licenses are authorized by the treaty. The purse seine fishery is largely for the highly-competitive canned tuna market. The regulations established a control date for entry into the fishery. 75 Fed. Reg. 74640 (Dec. 1, 2010). The number of U.S.-flagged vessels grew in the 2000s as U.S. companies entered joint ventures with Pacific island states and as the skipjack and yellowfin tuna stocks they target become scarcer and more valuable.

4. FOREIGN AND INTERNATIONAL FISHERIES

Since 1977, when the U.S. withdrew from ICNAF following enactment of the Fishery Conservation and Management Act, as described in State of Maine v. Kreps, supra, its challenge has been to create institutions and norms that will prompt other fishing nations to conserve fish stocks. A number of new treaties have been negotiated to create regional fisheries management bodies similar to the tuna conventions. Their function is to agree to measures necessary to conserve fish stocks caught in high seas fisheries. Composed solely of nations with high seas fishing fleets, the member states are often more concerned with preserving their own access to the dwindling stocks than with the long-term sustainability of the fisheries. After the enactment of 200-mile EEZs, many distant-water fishing fleets moved to high seas fisheries, where industrial fishing vessels must use thousands of miles of longlines, millions of hooks, and massive nets to catch commercially viable quantities of fish. In addition, illegal and foreign-subsidized fishing put the U.S. high seas fishing industry at a severe economic disadvantage, making U.S. fishermen ambivalent at best about complying with international conservation and management rules. The U.S. seafood industry is a large market for illegal and under-managed high seas fisheries. Can the U.S. use access to its seafood markets to "export conservation" to foreign-flag fisheries?

A. U.S. ROLE IN INTERNATIONAL FISHERIES GOVERNANCE

1. Certification for High Seas Large-Scale Driftnet Fishing

THE HUMANE SOCIETY OF THE UNITED STATES V. CLINTON
United States Court of Appeals for the Federal Circuit, 2001
236 F.3d 1320

PLAGER, SENIOR CIRCUIT JUDGE.

Large-scale driftnet fishing is defined in 16 U.S.C. § 1826c(2)(A) as "a method of fishing in which a gillnet composed of a panel or panels of webbing, or a series of such gillnets, with a total length of two and one-half kilometers or more is placed in the water and allowed to drift with the currents and winds for the purpose of entangling fish in the webbing." A fishing boat deploys the driftnets by suspending them vertically beneath the surface of the water, between buoys at the ocean surface and a weighted lead line at the bottom of the nets. The driftnets are deployed at night when they are less visible to marine life. Though intended to catch fish, the nets indiscriminately catch virtually all aquatic life including fish, whales, dolphins, sea turtles, and sea birds. The fish are captured when the mesh catches behind their gills, and the whales, dolphins, and other air-breathing sea life are caught when they become entangled in the net. At dawn, fishermen collect the driftnets, remove the target fish, and discard any non-target species, often drowned, that were caught in the nets.

In 1991, the United Nations General Assembly passed numerous resolutions calling for a worldwide moratorium on large-scale high seas driftnets. The resolutions were aimed primarily at driftnet fishing in the area of the seas beyond what is known in international law as the Exclusive Economic Zone ("the EEZ"). The EEZ is the area of the seas that lies within 200 nautical miles from the shore of a coastal nation; the area beyond the EEZ is known as the high seas.

In implementing the resolutions, the United States passed the High Seas Driftnet Fisheries Enforcement Act, Pub.L. No. 102–582, 106 Stat. 4900 (1992) (codified as amended at 16 U.S.C. §§ 1826–1826g) (the "Driftnet Act"). The Driftnet Act establishes a process under which the United States may take various actions against a foreign nation whose fishing vessels on the high seas engage in large-scale driftnet fishing, as the Act defines it. (Large-scale driftnet fishing by United States nationals and vessels, both within the United States EEZ and on the high seas, is prohibited by 16 U.S.C. § 1857(1)(M), the Magnuson Fishery Conservation and Management Act.) We will examine the provisions of the Act in detail below. For now, it will be enough to outline the way the Act works.

Whenever the Secretary of Commerce has reason to believe that the nationals or vessels of any nation are conducting large-scale driftnet fishing beyond the EEZ of any nation, the Secretary is to identify that nation, and notify the President and the nation of the identification. 16 U.S.C. § 1826a(b)(1)(B).

Thereafter, the President is to enter into consultations with the government of the identified nation "for the purpose of obtaining an agreement that will effect the immediate termination of large-scale driftnet fishing by the nationals or vessels of that nation. . . . " 16 U.S.C. § 1826a(b)(2). If those consultations are not "satisfactorily concluded," the President is to order the Secretary of the Treasury to prohibit the importation into the United States of fish and fish products from that nation. 16 U.S.C. § 1826a(b)(3)(A)(ii).

In addition, the Act provides that the Secretary of Commerce, after giving notice to the nations involved, is to publish periodically a list of nations whose nationals or vessels conduct large-scale driftnet fishing beyond the EEZ of any nation, and the Secretary of the Treasury shall thereafter deny entry of any such vessel to any place in the United States. 16 U.S.C. § 1826a(a)(1)–(3). Denial of port privileges, as well as import sanctions if imposed, remain in effect until the Secretary of Commerce certifies to the President and the Congress that such nation has terminated large-scale driftnet fishing by its nationals and vessels beyond the EEZ. 16 U.S.C. § 1826b.

In 1995, the Humane Society and other plaintiffs filed suit in the Court of International Trade. They alleged that, in the face of evidence to the contrary, the Secretary of Commerce had failed to identify Italy as a nation whose nationals or vessels conduct large-scale driftnet fishing in violation of the Driftnet Act. Humane Society of the United States v. Brown, 901 F.Supp. 338, 345 (CIT 1995). Ultimately, the Court of International Trade agreed, and held that the Secretary of Commerce had reason to believe that Italian nationals were conducting large-scale driftnet fishing on the high seas and that, therefore, the decision not to identify was an abuse of discretion. Humane Society of the United States v. Brown, 920 F.Supp. 178, 192–196 (CIT 1996). The Government did not appeal the decision. Pursuant to the trial court's decision, the Secretary of Commerce on March 28, 1996 identified Italy as a nation for which there was reason to believe its nationals or vessels were conducting large-scale driftnet fishing beyond the exclusive economic zone of any nation, and notified the President of Italy's identification.

Acting through the Department of State, the President entered into consultations with Italy. In July 1996, the Italian government sent documents formalizing its agreement with the United States to end proscribed driftnet fishing by its nationals and vessels. The United States informed Italy that its proposals were sufficient to avoid the imposition of sanctions under the Driftnet Act. Thereafter, on January 7, 1997, the Secretary of Commerce certified to the President and Congress that Italy had terminated illegal driftnet fishing.

This case arose when, in 1998, pursuant to the authority of 28 U.S.C. § 1581(i) (1994), the Humane Society plaintiffs brought another suit in the Court of International Trade against the President and the Secretary of Commerce. The suit asked for injunctive and declaratory relief. The Humane Society alleged that, despite the earlier agreement, illegal driftnet fishing by Italian nationals and vessels continued in the Mediterranean Sea in the 1997 and 1998 fishing seasons. . . . the United States Navy had sighted several vessels, suspected of being Italian, which were presumed to be engaging in illegal driftnet fishing. Also, Greenpeace reported twenty driftnet vessels in March of 1997; in 1998, nine violations were confirmed.

* * *

The two decisions that are challenged on appeal by the Humane Society plaintiffs are (1) the refusal by the trial court to order the President, after Italy was identified by the Secretary of Commerce pursuant to the court's 1996 Order, to direct imposition of import restrictions; and (2) the conclusion by the trial court that the Secretary's later certification, that Italy had terminated large-scale driftnet fishing, was not arbitrary and capricious.

The Humane Society argues that as a matter of law the President has a non-discretionary duty under the Driftnet Act to direct the imposition of import sanctions against nations whose nationals or vessels engage in large-scale driftnet fishing on the high seas, and this duty can be the basis for a writ of mandamus. The Humane Society also argues that the Secretary of Commerce, in certifying that Italy had terminated large-scale driftnet fishing based solely on an agreement that had not yet been fully implemented and without any evidence that the driftnet fishing had, in fact, ceased, had acted arbitrarily and capriciously.

* * *

We turn ... to the first issue raised by the appellant Humane Society: whether the issuance of sanctions by the President pursuant to § 1826a(b)(3)(A)(ii) is nondiscretionary, and thus the issuance of mandamus would be appropriate. As a general proposition, two requirements must be satisfied in order for a writ of mandamus to issue: 1) the plaintiff must have exhausted all avenues for relief; and 2) the defendant must owe the plaintiff a clear non-discretionary duty. Here, it is uncontested that the Humane Society plaintiffs have satisfied the first requirement. Humane Society of United States v. Clinton, 44 F.Supp.2d 260, 268 (CIT 1999). Thus, the issue is whether the second requirement has been satisfied.

The Driftnet Act is not a model of clarity in statutory drafting. Not surprisingly, the parties find in the statute very different understandings. Part of the problem lies in the order in which the several sections of the Act are presented. The Act in section 101 (16 U.S.C. § 1826a) begins by requiring that the Secretary of Commerce, not later than 30 days after enactment, "and periodically thereafter," publish a list of nations whose nationals or vessels conduct large-scale driftnet fishing beyond the EEZ. The Secretary of the Treasury "shall" then deny port privileges to any such nation's large-scale driftnet fishing vessels.

Subsection (b) of section 101 (16 U.S.C. § 1826a(b), entitled "Sanctions" but actually containing extensive procedural requirements), requires the Secretary of Commerce, not later than January 10, 1993, and "[a]t any time after ... whenever the Secretary ... has reason to believe" that the nationals or vessels of any nation are conducting large-scale driftnet fishing beyond the EEZ, to (i) identify that nation, and (ii) notify the President of the identification. The President is then required to enter into consultations with the government of that nation "for the purpose of obtaining an agreement that will effect the immediate termination of large-scale driftnet fishing by the nationals or vessels of that nation beyond the exclusive economic zone of any nation." 16 U.S.C. § 1826a(b)(2).

"The President[,] ... if the consultations with the government of a nation under paragraph (2) are not satisfactorily concluded within ninety days, shall direct the Secretary of the Treasury to prohibit the importation into the United States of fish and fish products and sport fishing equipment [from such nation]. . . . " 16 U.S.C. § 1826a(b)(3)(A) (emphasis added).

The Humane Society contends that the only logical way to assess whether the negotiations have been "satisfactorily concluded" is by reference to the purpose of the negotiations-specifically, to determine objectively whether they "produce an agreement that will effectuate an immediate end to the illegal driftnet fishing." The Humane Society notes the evidence of continuing violations by Italian vessels as clear evidence that the President failed to act in accordance with the statutory standard. In the view of the Humane Society plaintiffs, if the agreement fell short, then the President was obligated to direct the Secretary of the Treasury to impose import sanctions. The Humane Society asks this court to remand the case to the trial court for its determination of the question of whether the agreement met that standard, and if the agreement did not, then to order the President to take the required action.

The Government responds that the phrase "satisfactorily concluded" refers to a highly subjective state of mind, such as "to make happy," or "to please," phrases taken from dictionary definitions of "satisfy." The Government further notes that, in cases in which international relations are concerned, the President plays a dominant role. In these matters, it is generally assumed that Congress does not set out to tie the President's hands; if it wishes to, it must say so in clear language. *See* United States v. Curtiss–Wright Export Corp., 299 U.S. 304, 320 (1936) ("It is quite apparent that if, in the maintenance of our international relations, embarrassment ... is to be avoided and success ... to be achieved, congressional legislation which is to be made effective through negotiation and inquiry within the international field must often accord to the President a degree of discretion and freedom from statutory restriction which would not be admissible were domestic affairs alone involved.")...

In this setting, when Congress has chosen a broad and ill-defined phrase such as "satisfactorily concluded," this court cannot say with certainty that there is a fixed, measurable standard that limits the President's discretion. The agreement with Italy, negotiated on the President's behalf pursuant to the Act, consisted of six documents, covering a variety of enforcement practices and policies to which the Italian Government committed itself. Whether these commitments should have satisfied the President that they would effect the immediate termination of large-scale driftnet fishing by Italian vessels is a question of judgment about the good faith of the Italian government, and what is possible for the United States to demand and what will work. The fact that there is evidence of later, continuing violations is troubling, but the Act seems to allow for that possibility by providing for subsequent listing of a nation whose vessels or nationals again are in violation.

Furthermore, because of the broad discretion that is delegated to the President by Congress in § 1826a(b)(3)(A), even without the added complication of the mandamus remedy, there would be serious doubt whether a court could review the President's determination of whether the consultations were "satisfactorily concluded." *See* Dalton v. Specter, 511 U.S. 462, 474–76 (1994) ("Where a statute . . . commits decisionmaking to the discretion of the President, judicial review of the President's decision is not available.") . . . We conclude that the trial court was correct when it held that the question of whether consultations were "satisfactorily concluded," and thus whether the requirement for import sanctions was triggered, is a matter that lies within the broad discretion of the President. Therefore, the trial court was also correct in finding that it cannot issue a writ of mandamus. Nothing in the facts of this case suggests that the President acted in other than good faith, or otherwise was in violation of his duties under the Act.

The second issue raised is whether the Secretary of Commerce acted in violation of the Act when he certified in 1997 that Italy had terminated large-scale driftnet fishing. Here again the statute leaves something to be desired. Section 102 (16 U.S.C. § 1826b) of the Act states in its entirety:

> Any denial of port privileges or sanction under section 101 [16 U.S.C. § 1826a, which includes the import sanctions] with respect to a nation shall remain in effect until such time as the Secretary of Commerce certifies to the President and the Congress that such nation has terminated large-scale driftnet fishing by its nationals and vessels beyond the exclusive economic zone of any nation.

The Act does not explain what evidence or circumstances should guide the Secretary in making this certification, or guide our determination of whether the Secretary's action is arbitrary or capricious.

* * *

[T]he Humane Society argues that the Secretary's certification was based solely on the July 1996 agreement, and that the Secretary conducted no investigation of Italian driftnet practices. They argue further that the Secretary relied on the Secretary of State's announcement that an agreement had been reached, without independently scrutinizing that agreement to determine whether it would in fact effectuate an end to the illegal driftnet fishing. From this, the Humane Society concludes that any certification that fails to consider actual fishing practices must be struck down as arbitrary and capricious.

The Government acknowledges that the Secretary's sole stated reason for certifying that Italy has terminated large-scale driftnet fishing by its nationals and vessels was the agreement reached with the United States in 1996. The Government argues that this was reason enough to conclude that Italy had terminated such fishing. The fact that certain elements of the agreement remained to be implemented was immaterial, according to the Government, as was the fact that the State Department was urging Italy to pursue its enforcement program more vigorously. With regard to the Humane Society's allegations that illegal driftnet fishing had not ended, the Government argues that the record indicates that, between the conclusion of the July 1996 Agreement and January 1997, reports of illegal driftnet fishing were limited, sporadic, and unsubstantiated.

The trial court drew a distinction between the Secretary's decision to initially identify a nation under section 101 (16 U.S.C. § 1826a) whose nationals or vessels are engaged in illegal driftnet fishing, and the Secretary's decision to certify under section 102 (16 U.S.C. § 1826b) that a nation has terminated large-scale driftnet fishing. Humane Society of the United States v. Clinton, 44 F.Supp.2d 260, 271 (CIT 1999). The trial court viewed the focus in the first decision to be on the conduct of individuals and vessels, whereas the focus in the latter was on the conduct and intentions of the nation's government. We concur; this is a sensible way to parse the language of the Act and to understand the differences between the two decisions, and it illuminates the kind of inquiry appropriate to testing the Secretary's decision.

Accordingly, the trial court looked to the circumstances that prevailed in January 1997, when the certification was issued. The court concluded that the evidence supported the Secretary's determination that the agreement, though not fully implemented, was substantially so, and that adequate assurances had been given that it would be completed before the commencement of the 1997 fishing season. Given the court's focus, the fact that there may have been some individual violations by Italian vessels would not be determinative. The trial court concluded that in light of this analysis, it cannot be said that the Secretary's decision was so unreasonable as to be legally arbitrary and capricious. We concur in the trial court's analysis and conclusions; the trial court's ruling in that regard is upheld.

NOTES AND QUESTIONS

1. The U.S. uses the threat of trade sanctions to urge foreign governments to ensure their fishing vessels follow international fishery conservation and management regulations. Enacted in 1971 to bolster international conservation of Atlantic salmon, the Pelly Amendment to the Fishermen's Protective Act, 22 U.S.C. 1971–79, authorizes the president to prohibit the importation of products from countries that allow fishing operations that diminish the effectiveness of an international fishery conservation program or that engage in trade or taking that diminishes the effectiveness of an international program for endangered or threatened species. See Japan Whaling Ass'n v. American Cetacean Society, 478 U.S. 221 (1986). Also, the Magnuson-Stevens Act has been amended several times to give the President and the Secretary of Commerce authority to identify and certify nations whose fishing fleets are violating international norms and standards.

2. While Congress appears to have little trouble authorizing market-access sanctions, the Executive Branch has been less than enthusiastic in using them. Why? What incentive does the U.S. have to use its customs laws to enforce international conservation? Are these sufficient to overcome the political and economic disincentives?

2.   Lacey Act and U.S. Seafood Dealers

Illegal fishing has become a major challenge to sustainable management of fisheries for food production. As overfished species of fish and shellfish become depleted and regulations increase, the prices also increase, and seafood mislabeling and smuggling are now global problems. As a major importer of seafood, the United States is now prosecuting smugglers under the Lacey Act of 1900. Originally aimed at the smuggling of wildlife taken in violation of state fish and game laws, the Act provides in pertinent part: "It is unlawful for any person . . . (2) to import, export, transport, sell, receive, acquire, or purchase in interstate or foreign commerce—(A) any fish or wildlife taken, possessed, transported, or sold in violation of any law or regulation of any State or in violation of any foreign law." 16 U.S.C. § 3372(a)(2)(A). The definition of the term "fish or wildlife" to include crustaceans, such as lobsters, 16 U.S.C. § 3371(a), proved vital in the following landmark enforcement case.

UNITED STATES V. BENGIS

United States Court of Appeals for the Second Circuit, 2001
631 F.3d 33, *cert. denied*, 131 S.Ct. 2911

HALL, CIRCUIT JUDGE.

I. Background

From 1987 to 2001, Arnold Bengis, Jeffrey Noll and David Bengis (jointly, "defendants") engaged in an elaborate scheme to illegally harvest large quantities of South Coast and West Coast rock lobsters in South African waters for export to the United States in violation of both South African and U.S. law. Arnold Bengis was the Managing Director and Chairman of Hout Bay Fishing Industries, Ltd. ("Hout Bay"), a fishing and fish-processing operation in Capetown, South Africa, through which defendants principally organized their conspiracy to capture, process and export lobster to the United States. Jeffrey Noll and David Bengis were presidents of two U.S. corporations that imported, processed, packed, and distributed the fish within the United States on behalf of Hout Bay. At all relevant times, the harvesting, processing and exporting of South Coast and West Coast rock lobsters from South Africa was governed under South African law principally by the Marine Living Resources Act 18 of 1998 ("MLRA"), the regulations promulgated under the MLRA, and the Convention on the Conservation of Marine Living Resources. The South African Department of Marine and Coastal Management regulated the harvesting, processing and exporting of fish from South Africa's waters by, *inter alia,* establishing fishing season quotas and issuing harvesting and exporting permits. Defendants caused Hout Bay to harvest South Coast and West Coast rock lobsters in amounts exceeding authorized quotas and to export those lobsters to the United States.

In May 2001, South African authorities seized and opened a container of unlawfully harvested fish and alerted U.S. authorities that another container was scheduled to arrive in the United States soon thereafter. Following the May 2001 seizure, the defendants continued to attempt to avoid detection and to perpetuate their scheme.

Although South African authorities obtained arrest warrants for defendants, after concluding that defendants' financial resources and presence outside of South Africa rendered them "beyond the reach of South African authorities," South Africa declined to charge, much less prosecute, them. Instead, South Africa focused its prosecution on the "South African-based entities involved in the scheme," including Hout Bay, its operational manager, Collin van Schalkwyk, several West Coast lobster fisherman with whom Hout Bay had contracted, and fourteen fisheries inspectors who had taken bribes during the course of the scheme. In April 2002, Arnold Bengis returned to South Africa to enter a plea of guilty on behalf of Hout Bay for, *inter alia,* over-fishing of South and West Coast rock lobster in violation of the MLRA. According to its plea agreement with the South African government, Hout Bay paid a fine of 12 million Rand (approximately $1.2 million in April 2002) and forfeited two fishing boats and the contents of the container seized by the government. The South African government also cooperated with the United States in its investigation and prosecution of the Bengises and Noll for their violation of U.S. law.

Following their indictments in the United States, Arnold Bengis and Jeffrey Noll pleaded guilty to: (i) conspiracy to violate the Lacey Act and to commit smuggling in violation of 18 U.S.C. § 371; and (ii) violations of the Lacey Act, 16 U.S.C. § 3372(a)(2)(A). David Bengis pleaded guilty to the conspiracy charge only. In 2004, the defendants were sentenced to various terms of imprisonment and supervised release and together forfeited a total of $13,300,000 to the United States. Although the defendants' plea agreements acknowledged that restitution might be ordered, with the parties' consent, the district court deferred the restitution hearing to a later date.

Following the court's decision to hold a restitution hearing, the United States submitted a report prepared by the Ocean and Land Resource Assessment Consultants ("OLRAC"), a group of experts commissioned by the South African Department of Marine and Coastal Management, setting out two different methods for calculating restitution. OLRAC Method I focused on the cost of remediation, i.e., what it would cost South Africa to restore the rock lobster fishery to the level it would have been had the defendants not engaged in overharvesting (the "catch forfeit" amount).[2] OLRAC estimated restitution using the catch forfeit amount to be $46,775,150. OLRAC Method II focused on the market value of the overharvested fish and was calculated by multiplying the quantity of overharvested fish by the prevailing market price. OLRAC estimated restitution using OLRAC Method II to be $61,932,630.

The government recommended that the district court adopt OLRAC Method I restitution amount—the lower of the two calculations—which totaled $39,700,000 after deducting the value of the fine and vessels previously forfeited by Hout's Bay to South Africa. Alternatively, the government recommended adopting the OLRAC Method II calculation totaling $54,900,000 after those same deductions. The district court held its decision on a restitution award in abeyance pending the outcome of settlement discussions, which ended unsuccessfully. Consequently, on June

---

[2] OLRAC Method I also included an additional cost measure, "overharvesting costs," which measured the costs incurred by Hout Bay's competitors as a result of Hout Bay's overharvesting. The government elected not to seek the amount of "overharvesting costs" in its application for restitution because those costs were not borne directly by South Africa, but rather by Hout Bay's competitors.

2, 2006, the district court referred the restitution issues to a magistrate judge for a report and recommendations.

II. The Decisions Below

In separate orders, the district court denied the government's request for restitution for South Africa under the MVRA, United States v. Bengis, 2007 WL 241370, at * 1 (S.D.N.Y. Jan. 29, 2007), and the VWPA, United States v. Bengis, 2007 WL 2669315, at *2 (S.D.N.Y. Sept.12, 2007). In each order, the district court adopted by reference the reasoning in the report and recommendation ("R & R") of the magistrate judge.

A. The MVRA

With respect to the MVRA, the R & R concluded that pursuant to the limited categories of crimes for which restitution is mandatory, South Africa is entitled to restitution in this case only if the conduct to which defendants plead guilty constitutes "an offense against property" under Title 18 of the United States Code, 18 U.S.C. § 3663A(c)(1)(A)(ii). United States v. Bengis, 2006 WL 3735654, at *2 (S.D.N.Y. Dec.19, 2006). Under our precedents, the R & R continued, the definition of "property" is limited to "tangible property," see United States v. Cummings, 189 F.Supp.2d 67, 74 (S.D.N.Y.2002), and not "purely regulatory" interests in which "the nature of [the] property cannot not be economic," Cleveland v. United States, 531 U.S. 12, 13, 121 S.Ct. 365, 148 L.Ed.2d 221 (2000).

Here, the magistrate judge concluded, South Africa confronts two obstacles. First, under South African law, the state does not "own" the fish in its territorial waters. "Defendants' acts of taking fish from South African waters that the South African government did not own," therefore "does not provide the basis for any offenses against South African property that would trigger restitution under the MVRA." Id. at *7. Moreover, because "the South African laws that provide the basis for defendants' underlying violations here involve no type of taxes or significant revenue for South Africa," the government cannot claim a property interest in a "tax or other form of revenue" connected to defendant's activity. Id. at *8 (distinguishing Pasquantino v. United States, 544 U.S. 349, 355–57 (2005), which concluded that the Canadian government holds a property interest in the substantial liquor tax revenue that defendants avoided paying as a result of their smuggling scheme).

Finally, the district court rejected the argument that defendant's violation of the Lacey Act, itself, constituted an offense against property pursuant to Title 18. Like the MLRA, the Lacey Act, 16 U.S.C. § 3372(a)(2)(A) (criminalizing trade in "any fish or wildlife taken, possessed, transported, or sold . . . in violation of any foreign law."), was enacted for regulatory, and not economic, purposes, as a result of which a violation thereof is not an offense against property.

B. The VWPA

Having denied mandatory restitution under the MVRA, the district court considered and rejected discretionary restitution under the VWPA, adopting the magistrate judge's conclusion that South Africa was not a "victim" of defendants' crime. In order to be a victim for the purposes of the VWPA, the loss sustained must be " 'caused by the offense of conviction.' " United States v. Bengis, 2007 WL 1450381, at *3 (S.D.N.Y. May 17, 2007) (quoting United States v. Silkowski, 32 F.3d 682, 689 (2d Cir.1994)). The underlying violation of the Lacey Act—the crime to which defendants pleaded guilty—related to the *trade* in illegally obtained lobsters and not the overfishing of lobster in South African waters. That is, the district court concluded, "[i]t was not necessary for the government to have proved that the defendants . . . were the ones who took the fish in violation of South African law." Because the government's loss theories were predicated on the injury associated with the consequences of defendants' *overfishing*—as opposed to its *trading*—and the overfishing of lobster is not directly related to any of the required criminal conduct under the statutes to which defendants plead guilty, the district court concluded that South Africa is not a victim under the VWPA.

Finally, the district court observed that, if discretionary restitution were available, calculating South Africa's injury would involve "complex issues of foreign law as well as intricate questions of fact," as a result of which "extensive further proceedings would be required." United States v. Bengis, 2007 WL 2669315, at *2. Accordingly, the district court held that, even if a restitution order pursuant to the VWPA were permissible, "the complication and prolongation of the sentencing process resulting from the fashioning of an order of restitution under this section would outweigh the need to provide restitution" in this case.

III. Discussion

On appeal, the government challenges the district court's conclusions that South Africa had no property interest in the overharvested lobsters and that it was not directly harmed as a result of the defendants' illegal scheme.

We review a district court's decision to deny an order of restitution for abuse of discretion. "To identify such abuse, we must conclude that a challenged ruling rests on an error of law, a clearly erroneous finding of fact, or otherwise cannot be located within the range of permissible decisions."

A. South Africa's Property Interest in the Illegally Harvested Rock Lobsters

The MVRA provides for mandatory restitution in all sentencing proceedings for convictions of any offense that is, *inter alia,* "an offense against property under [Title 18] . . . in which an identifiable victim or victims has suffered a . . . pecuniary loss." 18 U.S.C. § 3663A(c)(1)(A)(ii)–(c)(1)(B). Accordingly, the threshold question is whether South Africa has a property interest in the illegally harvested rock lobsters. We conclude that South Africa has a property right in illegally harvested rock lobsters.

Under South African law the rock lobsters may be harvested lawfully pursuant to a regulatory scheme administered by the Department of Marine and Coastal Management. Furthermore, under South African law, lobsters caught illegally are not the property of those who caught them, MLRA § 44(2), and the South African government is authorized to seize illegally harvested lobsters, sell them, and retain the proceeds, §§ 51(3)(c)(iii), 63(1)(b), 68(1). Put differently, lobsters possessed in violation of the regulatory scheme do not become property of the possessors, rather they are subject to seizure and sale by the government of South Africa. Under this logic, the moment a fisherman pulls an illegally harvested lobster out of the sea, a property right to seize that lobster is vested in the government of South Africa. Evading seizure of overharvested lobsters thus deprives South Africa of an opportunity to sell those illegally captured lobsters at market price and retain the proceeds, representing an economic loss to South Africa each time an illegally harvested lobster goes unseized. South Africa's interest in those illegally harvested lobsters, therefore, goes beyond a mere regulatory interest in administering the fishing activities in its waters.

Contrary to the District Court's conclusion, the Supreme Court's holding in *Pasquantino*—and not *Cleveland*—provides the closest analogy to South Africa's interest in the lobsters seized by the defendants and guides our analysis here. In *Cleveland,* the Supreme Court concluded that, because its interest was "purely regulatory," the State of Louisiana *did not* have a "property" right in an unissued license to a video poker operator, despite the pre-issuance processing fees collected by the state. 531 U.S. at 20–21. As Justice Ginsburg explained, "The State receives the lion's share of its expected revenue not while the licenses remain in its own hands, but only after they have been issued to licensees. Licenses pre-issuance do not generate an ongoing stream of revenue." *Id.* Importantly, the Supreme Court noted that "as to the character of Louisiana's stake in its video poker licenses," the licensee in *Cleveland* did not "defraud the state of any money to which the State was entitled by law." *Id.* at 22.

By contrast, in *Pasquantino,* the Supreme Court held that Canada *did* possess a "property" right to uncollected excise taxes on liquor that was illegally imported into the country. The uncollected tax, Justice Thomas reasoned, was a right to "collect money" which is a "valuable entitlement" considered to be " 'property' as that term ordinarily is employed." Pasquantino, 544 U.S. at 355–56 (*citing* Black's Law Dictionary

1382 (4th ed. 1951) (defining "property" as "extend[ing] to every species of valuable right and interest") (citations omitted); *see also* Pasquantino, 544 U.S. at 356 ("The right to be paid money has long been thought to be a species of property.") (citing 3 W. Blackstone, Commentaries on the Laws of England 153–155 (1768)). The Court had no doubt that the right to collect that revenue was " 'something of value' to the Government of Canada." *Id.* at 355 (quoting McNally v. United States, 483 U.S. 350, 358 (1987)).

As a result, the *Pasquantino* Court clearly distinguished its earlier holding in *Cleveland*. In *Cleveland,* the "State's interest in an unissued video poker license was not 'property,' because the interest in choosing particular licensees was 'purely regulatory' and '[could not] be economic,' " *id.* at 357 (quoting Cleveland, 531 U.S. at 22–23). Indeed, "the Government nowhere allege[d] that [the defendant] defrauded the State of any money to which the State was entitled by law." In *Pasquantino,* on the other hand, "Canada's entitlement to tax revenue is a straightforward 'economic' interest . . . the Government alleged and proved that petitioners' scheme aimed at depriving Canada of money to which it was entitled by law."

Like the defendants in *Pasquantino,* Arnold Bengis, Jeffrey Noll, and David Bengis' conspiracy to conceal their illegal trade in lobster deprived South Africa of money it was due. Had the defendants not undertaken efforts to conceal their overharvesting, including off-loading overharvested lobsters at night and under-reporting the amounts of their catch to South African authorities, those lobsters caught in excess of the legal limits would have been seized and sold by the government. As a consequence, the defendants' conduct deprived South Africa of proceeds from the sale of the illegally harvested lobsters, i.e., "money to which it was entitled by law." *Id.* Just as in *Pasquantino,* "had [defendants] complied with [their] legal obligation, they would have paid money to [South Africa]." Like Canada's entitlement to its uncollected excise tax revenue in *Pasquantino,* South Africa's entitlement to the revenue from the lobsters that were taken illegally does constitute "property." The defendants' conduct in depriving South Africa of that revenue is, therefore, an offense against property.

B. South Africa as a "Victim" under the MVRA and VWPA

Both the MVRA and VWPA contemplate that a court must or may order the defendant to pay restitution to a "victim." 18 U.S.C. § 3663A(a)(1); § 3663(a)(1)(A). Both statutes define a "victim" as:

a person directly and proximately harmed as a result of the commission of an offense for which restitution may be ordered including, in the case of an offense that involves as an element a scheme, conspiracy, or pattern of criminal activity, any person directly harmed by the defendant's criminal conduct in the course of the scheme, conspiracy, or pattern.

Id. § 3663A(a)(2); § 3663(a)(2). In its second order adopting the magistrate judge's report, the district court denied restitution under the VWPA on the ground that South Africa was not a "victim" entitled to restitution because it had failed to show that it had suffered any losses directly caused by the defendants' illegal scheme. We disagree.

Relying on the magistrate judge's report and district court's order, the defendants contend that, even if South Africa had a property right in the lobsters, it is not a victim of the conspiracy because the conspiracy to which the defendants pleaded guilty did not involve the illegal harvesting of the lobsters, only their importation to the United States with the knowledge that the lobsters had been obtained in violation of South African law. We are not persuaded. The defendants need not have personally harvested the lobsters in order to have deprived the South African government of its property right in the lobsters. By smuggling the lobsters out of South Africa knowing that they had been harvested unlawfully, defendants deprived the South African government of its right to seize and sell the poached lobsters. The defendants' conduct facilitated the illegal harvesting of the lobsters by providing access to the United States market and enabled the poaching to go undetected by the South African government by, for example, off-loading the overharvested lobster at night, under-reporting catch amounts to South African authorities, bribing officials, and submitting false export documents. In doing so, the defendants' criminal conduct "directly harmed" the South African government, which in turn makes South Africa eligible for restitution under the VWPA and MVRA. *See* 18 U.S.C. § 3663A(a)(2); § 3663(a)(2).

Because South Africa had a property interest in the illegally harvested lobsters and is a victim for purposes of restitution, we hold that the MVRA governs the restitution award at issue here.

C. Calculating a Restitution Award

We further conclude that the facts on the record do not support the district court's finding that the complexity of fashioning an award of restitution would further complicate and prolong the sentence so that the burden on the sentencing process outweighs any need to provide restitution to which South Africa is entitled. *See* 18 U.S.C. § 3663A(c)(3). Given our analysis of the nature of South Africa's property interest and our review of the record, OLRAC Method II seems to us a sufficient loss calculation methodology under the circumstances presented by this case. This method most directly traces the nature of the loss inflicted on South Africa because, had the poaching been detected, South Africa would have been entitled to seize the illegally harvested lobsters at that time and sell them at market price for its own benefit. Restitution would thus be calculated by multiplying the number of poached lobsters by the corresponding market price (based on the prevailing market rates at the time the lobsters were poached). Every overharvested lobster that South Africa did not seize and sell represents a loss that has not been recovered.

We note, furthermore, that there is no problem in imposing both a restitution award and a forfeiture award in this case. *See* United States v. Kalish, 626 F.3d 165, 169–70 (2d Cir.2010) (noting that "simultaneous imposition" of both a forfeiture remedy and a restitution remedy, authorized by separate statutes, "offends no constitutional provision"). We leave to the district court's determination in the first instance all relevant issues relating to the amount of restitution, whether any off-set should apply, and if so, whether there should be one based on the forfeiture. We note in passing, however, that to the extent that a restitution award for South Africa that is derived from the market value of the illegally harvested lobsters might be duplicative of the sums that defendants have already forfeited to the United States, the government may exercise its discretion to transfer the forfeited funds to South Africa, in order to reduce the restitution award by the amount defendants have already forfeited. *See* Gov't Br. 56 n.* ("Under the Department of Justice's Restoration Policy, once the District Court orders restitution, the Government would have the discretion to forward those monies to South Africa in partial satisfaction of the defendants' restitution obligations."). We express no view as to how such issues should be resolved.

IV. Conclusion

For the foregoing reasons, the judgments of the district court are VACATED, and the case is REMANDED to the district court with instructions to calculate restitution and enter an order of restitution in favor of the Republic of South Africa.

* * *

NOTES AND QUESTIONS

1. On remand, the district court accepted the magistrate judge's recommendation South Africa's restitution should total $54,883,550. The judge found that the OLRAC Method II, using the market value of the overfished fish, was a reasonable loss calculation.

2. If the court had used the OLRAC Method I, which estimated restitution based on the cost to South Africa of rebuilding the overfished fishery, what property interest would that reflect?

3. The defendants were convicted also of smuggling Patagonian toothfish from the Southern Ocean around Antarctica, which are "high seas" managed by CCAMLR. To calculate victim's restitution, who is the victim of this smuggling and how would the restitution amount be calculated?

4. On May 28, 2004, the Justice Department released a press release announcing that U.S. District Judge Kaplan sentenced the conspirators to prison sentences ranging from 46 months for Arnold Bengis to 12 months for his son, David Bengis. In illegal operations of this scale, are prison sentences likely to have a greater deterrent effect than $55 million in restitution? See Dept. of Justice Press Release, Three Seafood Industry Executives Sentenced to Federal Prison in Massive Seafood Poaching and Smuggling Scheme (May 28, 2004). The release states in part:

> At today's sentencing, Judge Kaplan rejected the defendants' motion for a downward departure on the ground that the South African government previously had investigated the matters at issue in the case. (The Government had filed a brief opposing the defendants' departure motion noting, among other things that, while Arnold Bengis's company, Hout Bay, had been prosecuted in South Africa, these defendants had never been arrested in South Africa; never were charged there; and never spent a day in jail there.) In rejecting the defendants' motion, Judge Kaplan acknowledged (among other things) the important United States interests involved in the prosecution, and noted that the defendants were living in the United States while the South African investigation was pending.

Judge Kaplan determined that he had no authority to depart under United States law, and that, even if he had the authority to depart, he would decline to do so. In ruling, Judge Kaplan remarked on Arnold Bengis's "astonishing display of arrogance" tied to his wealth and power. Among other things, Judge Kaplan pointed to the facts, undisputed by the defendants, that Arnold Bengis, during the course of the United States investigation, had: (i) withheld documents responsive to grand jury subpoenas; (ii) shredded important documents to keep from the hands of U.S. law enforcement; and (iii) even hired a private investigator to follow the United States agents during their investigation. Judge Kaplan also noted the evidence proffered by the Government that Arnold Bengis had previously expressed his skepticism about ever being prosecuted because he had "f___ y___ money."

5. Successful prosecution of illegal toothfish fishing is rare. See G. Bruce Knecht, HOOKED: Pirates, Poaching and the Perfect Fish (2007). The Australian fisheries patrol vessel, the Southern Supporter, chased the Viarsa I pirate longline fishing vessel from the EEZ around Australia's sub-Antarctic territories for thousands of miles through the Southern Indian Ocean and sub-Antarctic waters. Aided in the end by South African mercenaries who boarded the fleeing vessel at-sea, the prosecution under Australian law resulted in a mistrial and a hung jury.

6. The U.S. Antarctic Marine Living Resources Conservation Act of 1984, 16 U.S.C. § 2431 et seq., authorizes the United States to implement international fishery rules adopted by the Commission for the Conservation of Antarctic Marine Living Resources (CCAMLR). Final rules implementing CCAMLR's vessel monitoring and catch documentation scheme for toothfish

(*Dissostichus spp.*) were promulgated in 2010, 75 Fed. Reg. 18110 (April 9, 2010).

B. INDIRECT REGULATION THROUGH SEAFOOD MARKETS

Industrial, pelagic longline fshing has given rise to an additional, unsustainable practice: shark finning. In 2000 and 2002, Congress added provisions regarding the cruel and wasteful practice of shark finning to the Magnuson-Stevens Act. See Notes and Questions below. Given the high demand and prices paid for shark fins, are sharks a target or by-catch species of pelagic longlining? Can state law "supplement" international and U.S. management of pelagic longline fisheries by prohibiting the sale and possession of shark fins by seafood dealers and restaurants? Given the popularity of shark fin soup in Asian communities, are such restrictions constitutional?

CHINATOWN NEIGHBORHOOD ASSOCIATION V. BROWN

United States District Court, Northern District of California, 2013
2013 WL 60919

P. J. HAMILTON, DISTRICT JUDGE.

BACKGROUND

The California Legislature has determined that the practice of shark finning, where a shark is caught, its fins cut off, and the carcass is dumped back into the water, causes tens of millions of sharks to die each year. Stats.2011, ch. 524 (A.B.376), § 1(d). Sharks occupy the top of the marine food chain and their decline constitutes a serious threat to the ocean ecosystem and biodiversity. *Id.,* § 1(c). The Legislature also found that shark fin often contains high amounts of mercury, which has been proven dangerous to people's health. *Id.,* § 1(g). In order to address these problems and promote the conservation of sharks by, among other things, eliminating the California market for fins, the California Legislature enacted Assembly Bills 376 and 853, codified as Fish and Game Code §§ 2021 and 2021.5 ("the Shark Fin Law"), which became effective on January 1, 2012.

Plaintiffs Chinatown Neighborhood Association and Asian Americans for Political Advancement filed this action on July 18, 2012, challenging the implementation of the Shark Fin Law. Named as defendants are Edmund G. Brown, Governor of California; Kamala D. Harris, Attorney General of California; and Charlton H. Bonhan, Director of the California Department of Fish and Game.

According to the complaint, plaintiff Chinatown Neighborhood Association is a "nonprofit corporation/voluntary association having its headquarters in San Francisco." Its members are "people of Chinese origin who are engaged in cultural practices involving the use of shark fins and in business practices involving the buying and selling of shark fins in interstate commerce."

Plaintiff Asian Americans for Political Advancement ("AAPA") is "a political action committee registered in the State of California and headquartered in Burlingame, California." Its members are "people of Chinese national origin who are engaged in cultural practices involving the use of shark fins and in business practices involving the buying and selling of shark fins in interstate commerce." AAPA's website describes the organization as a PAC and Lobbying Coalition "formed to create a political voice for Asian Americans regarding political issues and candidates."

Plaintiffs contend that the history of the Shark Fin Law indicates that it was directed at suppressing the practices and traditions of Californians of Chinese national origin. They assert that shark fin soup is a key traditional dish at many Chinese banquets and special events, such as weddings, birthdays of elders, and festivals, and that the use of shark fin soup dates back to the 14th century Ming Dynasty.

Plaintiffs argue that Assemblyman Paul Fong, one of the bill's sponsors, made it clear that the Law was directed at changing a Chinese practice. They contend that when asked about the implications of the Shark Fin Law on Chinese culture, Assemblyman Fong replied that "Chinese culture used to promote foot binding on women." Plaintiffs assert that this comparison between binding feet and eating shark fin soup shows that the intent of the Legislature was to compel the Chinese to change their cultural practices. They also note that Assemblyman Jared Huffman, another sponsor of the bill, stated that the intent of the Shark Fin Law was to "target the demand for these shark fins," which plaintiffs contend is simply another way of saying that the Chinese people are being targeted, since they are "the only people seeking fins."

Plaintiffs also note that at a press conference organized by proponents of the Shark Fin Law, the Executive Director of WildAid (an organization that worked to promote the passage of the Law) stated that while it is difficult to regulate shark finning on a boat in Indonesia, it's "very easy to regulate if something is happening in Chinatown here" and "very easy to go around to restaurants and find out who's having what." Plaintiffs claim that this comment is clear evidence of the pervasive discrimination against Chinese Californians that underlies the Shark Fin Law. Plaintiffs also point to a comment by an unnamed "San Francisco chef" to the effect that while shark fin soup may be "deeply rooted in Chinese culture, ... some people are going to take a while to crack-that nut," which plaintiffs assert reflects an opinion that the Chinese preference for shark fin soup is a hardheaded tradition that needs to be broken.

Plaintiffs argue that while the Shark Fin Law was ostensibly passed to prevent the practice of shark finning and to further the practice of shark conservation, in actuality it does not and cannot accomplish those goals, because it includes no restrictions on the practice of shark finning—only on the possession and selling of fins. Moreover, plaintiffs assert, because the practice of shark finning in U.S. waters is already illegal under state and federal law, it is clear that the Shark Fin Law was "promoted under fear-mongering-type false pretenses" and has no practical effect on the already outlawed practice of shark finning.

With regard to any argument defendants might make that the Shark Fin Law protects sharks by halting the import of shark fins from foreign countries that do not have laws against shark-finning, plaintiffs respond that if that were the goal, the law could have banned the importation of shark fins from countries without protective laws, instead of enacting a blanket prohibition on all shark fin trade and possession.

Plaintiffs contend that the real effect of the law is to ban the possession and sale of fins taken from legally caught sharks, and that since the trade and possession of those legally-caught sharks is still legal in California, the result of the Shark Fin Law will be that the fins of those legally caught sharks will have to be discarded, which will harm the environment by unnecessary creation of significant amounts of "shark fishing waste." Plaintiffs assert that despite defendants' claims that the Shark Fin Law will save sharks from extinction, the fact is that the populations of many of the approximately 400–500 species of sharks are healthy and not in danger of extinction—and that no country considers sharks to be "globally endangered."

Finally, plaintiffs argue that due to the ban, the supply of lawfully possessed shark fins (those obtained prior to January 1, 2012) is dwindling rapidly and will imminently be exhausted, which in turn will greatly impact Chinese cultural practices involving shark fin soup. They assert that Californians of Chinese national origin will experience difficulty in obtaining shark fins to use to make this traditional dish, which will take away their rights to practice their cultural traditions. Restaurants will also be impacted, as they will not be able to satisfy their customers' requests for shark fin soup at banquets and other events. Moreover, they assert, merchants will be affected, as the ban has already cost merchants "millions of dollars and numerous jobs," and importers—particularly those who deal almost exclusively in shark fins—will lose their livelihoods.

Plaintiffs have attached numerous declarations from restaurant owners, merchants, and importers detailing sums of money lost in the past year due to lost sales of shark fin soup and shark fins, and what they expect to lose in the years to come. Plaintiffs claim that Enterprise 1180, a Milbrae restaurant, has lost $40,000 this year, and stands to lose $100,000 a year; that Far East Café has lost $50,000, and stands to lose $200,000 a year; that Tai Wu Inc. in Daly City has lost $30,000, and stands to lose $100,000 a year; that Koi Palace, a Daly City restaurant, expects to lose $850,000 per year. As for merchants, plaintiffs claim that Chung Chou City sells $341,390.24 worth of fins per year; and that Ho Kee Market sells $30,000 per year. As for importers, plaintiffs assert that A & B Seafood has already lost $373,373.30, and will totally lose its business; that Tony Siu Nam Mak has lost $500,000 since January 2012; and that Pacific Seafood Company sells $900,000 a year.

In the complaint, plaintiffs allege violations of their rights under the Equal Protection Clause of the Fourteenth Amendment; the Commerce Clause; the Supremacy Clause; and 42 U.S.C. § 1983. Plaintiffs assert that the Shark Fin Law targets only the Chinese—some of whom use the shark fins as an ingredient in shark fin soup, and others of whom make a living from buying and selling shark fins—and constitutes cultural discrimination, thereby violating the Equal Protection Clause and its guarantee of equal treatment. Plaintiffs argue that the Shark Fin Law also violates the Commerce Clause because it interferes with the power of the United State to regulate commerce, and violates the Supremacy Clause because it unlawfully preempts federal law, including the Magnuson Stevens Act, 16 U.S.C. §§ 1801–1884, which implemented the Shark Finning Prohibition Act of 2000, and was amended by the Shark Conservation Act of 2010—all of which already prohibit shark finning.

Plaintiffs seek judicial declarations that the Shark Fin Law violates the Equal Protection Clause by discriminating against people of Chinese national origin; that it unlawfully interferes with Congressional authority to regulate interstate commerce; that it unlawfully preempts federal law that already regulates the sale of shark fins and the permitted legal trade of fins obtained in compliance with federal standards; and that enforcement of the Law will violate § 1983 because it will deprive plaintiffs and their members of their rights, privileges, and immunities secured under the Equal Protection Clause, the Commerce Clause, and the Supremacy Clause.

The court previously granted the motion of The Humane Society of the United States, the Asian Pacific American Ocean Harmony Alliance, and the Monterey Bay Aquarium Foundation to intervene in the case as defendant-intervenors, and also granted the request of the National Resources Defense Counsel for leave to file an amicus brief in connection with the motion. Plaintiffs now seek an order preliminarily enjoining the enforcement of the Shark Fin Law.

DISCUSSION

An injunction is a matter of equitable discretion and is "an extraordinary remedy that may only be awarded upon a clear showing that the plaintiff is entitled to such relief." *Winter v. Natural Resources Defense Council, Inc.*, 555 U.S. 7, 22, 129 S.Ct. 365, 172 L.Ed.2d 249 (2008)...

* * *

Plaintiffs argue that they can establish a likelihood of success on the merits of each of the constitutional claims (or a combination of likelihood of success on the merits and that serious questions are raised), and can also establish that they will suffer irreparable injury if the enforcement of the Law is not enjoined. Thus, they assert, a preliminary injunction is warranted.

Plaintiffs contend that the Shark Fin Law discriminates against people of Chinese national origin in California, because it "almost solely" affects people of Chinese national origin—assertedly the only group that utilizes shark fins in "cultural practices." Plaintiffs contend that the comments of the supporters of the Shark Fin Law (Assemblymen Fong and Huffman, the Executive Director of WildAid, and the unnamed "San Francisco chef") demonstrate that the law was passed with the discriminatory purpose of targeting the Chinese. Plaintiffs also note that it is still legal to use sharks for food, or to make sharkskin products, and argue that the fact that the possession of fins is no longer legal means that the Law targets a uniquely Chinese practice. Thus, plaintiffs argue, the statute must be subjected to a strict scrutiny level of review by the court.

Further, plaintiffs contend that the ban on possession of shark fins is not necessary to the accomplishment of a legitimate state interest or a compelling societal interest, and that to the extent that defendants argue that the Shark Fin Law will protect sharks, plaintiffs argue that the Law does nothing to secure the ethical treatment of sharks, as it is still legal to kill them. And, they assert, since shark finning in U.S. waters is already illegal, the Shark Fin Law is not necessary to achieve the stated objectives of protecting sharks.

Second, plaintiffs argue that the Shark Fin Law places an excessive burden on interstate commerce in relation to any local benefits, which they claim is sufficient to show a Commerce Clause violation. They note that the Law places no further restrictions on shark fishing, and that existing law already prohibits shark finning in U.S. waters, and argue that while federal law permits the trade of humanely obtained fins, the Shark Fin Law unnecessarily restricts the shark fin trade entirely—while still permitting the trade of other products from the very same sharks—and therefore constitutes an excessive restriction on interstate commerce.

Third, plaintiffs assert that because the Shark Fin Law render federal regulations pertaining to shark fins moot, it "usurps and preempts" federal law. Plaintiffs contend that this is a violation of the Supremacy Clause, which provides that federal law takes precedence over state law when there is a conflict between the two laws. Here, plaintiffs argue, there is a conflict between federal law permitting trade of legally obtained shark fins and the Shark Fin Law which unwarrantedly prohibits such trade.

Finally, plaintiffs contend that they are likely to prevail on their § 1983 cause of action because they have established the existence of serious questions on the merits as to their three constitutional claims.

As for irreparable injury, plaintiffs contend that the mere fact of a constitutional injury—particularly the denial of plaintiffs' equal protection rights and the "suppression of their cultural practices"—is a harm that cannot be remedied by an award of monetary damages, and is therefore sufficient to establish irreparable injury. They assert that Chinese people have already been compelled to forego participating in the ancient tradition of serving shark fin soup at banquets, and that they will be totally prevented from engaging in this cultural practice in the future, and that the court should enjoin enforcement of the Law to prevent current and future discrimination against the Chinese people.

Moreover, plaintiffs argue that while pure economic harm may not be sufficient to constitute "irreparable harm," the fact that many merchants and importers will be driven out of business if they can no longer buy and sell shark fins is sufficient to show irreparable harm.

Finally, plaintiffs contend that a balancing of the equities tips in their favor, and that an injunction is in the public interest, because it would serve to eliminate discrimination.

In opposition, defendants argue that plaintiffs' facial challenge fails because the Shark Fin Law is race-neutral on its face; and that the Shark Fin Law does not violate the Equal Protection Clause, does not violate the Commerce Clause, and is not preempted by federal law. The defendants also contend that plaintiffs have failed to demonstrate irreparable injury, and that the balance of hardships and the public interest tip in favor of denying the motion.

The court finds that plaintiffs' motion must be DENIED. With regard to likelihood of success, the court agrees with defendants that plaintiffs have not met their burden, ...

First, the court finds that plaintiffs have not established a likelihood of success as to the equal protection claim. The Equal Protection Clause of the Fourteenth Amendment provides that no state shall "deny to any person within its jurisdiction the equal protection of the laws." U.S. Const.

amend XIV, § 1. This is "essentially a direction that all persons similarly situated should be treated alike." (citations omitted).

Laws that facially discriminate on the basis of race are subject to strict scrutiny. *Shaw v. Reno,* 509 U.S. 630, 642 (1993). In order to succeed on a facial challenge, a plaintiff "must establish that no set of circumstances exists under which the [statute] would be valid." *United States v. Salerno,* 481 U.S. 739, 745 (1987). Where, as here, a law is facially neutral, the plaintiff must prove that the intent and purpose of the law was to discriminate against an identifiable class of persons on the basis of a protected classification (*e.g.,* race). *See Washington v. Davis,* 426 U.S. 229, 239 (1976).

Here, plaintiffs have provided no evidence that the Law was *enacted* for the purpose of discriminating against Chinese–Americans. They cite to some anecdotal evidence that is unconnected to the reasons the Legislature passed the law, but have made no showing that any member of the Legislature intended to "target" Chinese–Americans. Plaintiffs' own evidence shows that only a small percentage of Chinese–Americans eat shark fin soup regularly, and that approximately half of Chinese–Americans actually support the Shark Fin Law; and further, one of the Law's sponsors in the Legislature (Assemblyman Paul Fong) is Chinese–American, and enactment of the Law was supported by at least one Asian American organization.

The fact that the Law may end up having a disparate impact on a group of ChineseAmericans—those who want to consume shark fin soup, or those who make a living from selling shark fins to others who want to make or consume shark fin soup—is not sufficient to show that the Law was enacted because of its disparate impact on Chinese–Americans. Where a law is neutral on its face, and is also within the power of government to pursue, it is not invalid under the Equal Protection Clause *simply because* it affects people of one race more than people of another. *See id.* at 239–41; *Village of Arlington Heights v. Metropolitan Housing Dev. Corp.,* 429 U.S. 252, 264–66 (1977).

In light of the fact that the Shark Fin Law is not facially discriminatory and the fact that plaintiffs have failed to show discriminatory intent, a challenge to the Law is subject only to rational basis review, which requires a showing that the Law is "rationally related to legitimate legislative goals." *See Lee v. City of Los Angeles,* 250 F.3d 668, 686–87 (9th Cir.2001) (quotation and citations omitted). The Shark Fin Law easily passes rational basis review.

At the time the Law was enacted, the Legislature was acting in pursuit of a legitimate government interest that bears a rational relationship to the means chosen to achieve that interest (citation omitted). The Law is based on legislative findings that sharks occupy the top of the marine food chain and their decline constitutes a serious threat to the ocean eco-system and biodiversity; that the practice of shark finning causes the death of tens of millions of sharks every year; and that by eliminating an important end market (sales in California), and thereby impacting the demand for shark fins, California can help ensure that sharks do not become extinct. *See* Stats.2011, ch. 524 (A.B.376) § 1.

The stated conservation and public health purposes are legitimate state interests, and prohibiting the possession, sale, and trade of shark fins is rationally related to that purpose. Because the California Legislature has articulated a plainly legitimate purpose for enacting the law, and because it is undisputed that the Shark Fin Law is facially neutral, any facial challenge fails, because it essentially rests on the speculation that at some future time the application of the statute will result in constitutional violations (citation omitted).

Nevertheless, regardless of the level of scrutiny, a plaintiff alleging denial of equal protection under 42 U.S.C. § 1983 based on race or other suspect classification must plead intentional unlawful discrimination or allege facts that are at least susceptible of an inference of discriminatory intent. Here, plaintiffs have provided no evidence showing that the California Legislature enacted the Shark Fin Law for the purpose of discriminating against ChineseAmericans.

As for plaintiffs' claim that the Law does nothing to protect sharks, the evidence provided by the defendant-intervenors and by amici provides strong support for defendants' contention that the Law is intended to protect and conserve sharks and the marine ecosystems dependent on them by means of regulating local *market* conditions, which laws targeting the actual practice of shark finning in domestic waters alone do not address.

In sum, because the Shark Fin Law neither discriminates on the basis of race, nor is based on a discriminatory purpose, and because it is rationally related to a legitimate government purpose, plaintiffs cannot meet their burden of showing a likelihood of success on the merits of the equal protection claim.

The court finds further that plaintiffs have failed to establish a likelihood of success as to the claim under the Commerce Clause. The Commerce Clause authorizes Congress to "regulate Commerce with foreign Nations, and among the several States." U.S. Const., art. I § 8. It includes an implied limitation on the states' authority to adopt legislation that affects commerce, which is referred to as the "negative" or "dormant" Commerce Clause.

The purpose of the dormant Commerce Clause is to "prohibit state or municipal laws whose object is local economic protectionism, laws that would excite those jealousies and retaliatory measures the Constitution was designed to prevent." That is, its purpose is to prevent local economic protectionism at the expense of out-of-state interests, not to protect the economic interests of local businesses engaged in interstate commerce. *See id.*

A statute is considered per se invalid under the dormant Commerce Clause if it directly regulates or discriminates against interstate commerce, or if its effect is to favor instate economic interests over out-of-state interests. *Brown–Forman Distillers Corp. v. New York State Liquor Auth.,* 476 U.S. 573, 578–79 (1986). If a statute does not regulate or discriminate against interstate commerce, and has only indirect effects on interstate commerce and regulates evenhandedly, the court need only consider whether the state's interest is legitimate and whether the burden on interstate commerce, if any, clearly exceeds the local benefits. *Id.* at 579 (citing *Pike v. Bruce Church, Inc.,* 397 U.S. 137, 142 (1970)).

Here, given that the Shark Fin Law is facially neutral, and treats all shark fins the same, regardless of their origin, plaintiffs have not shown (and cannot show) that the Shark Fin Law either regulates extraterritorial ly, or discriminates in favor of in-state interests. Thus, in order to prevail on this claim, plaintiffs will have to establish that any incidental burdens on interstate commerce caused by the Shark Fin Law are clearly excessive in relation to the putative local benefits.

For the reasons stated above, the court finds that the Shark Fin Law serves a legitimate local purpose, which includes protection of public health, wildlife, and the ecosystem. Plaintiffs have identified no cognizable burden on interstate commerce, notwithstanding that they have asserted that the Law places an excess burden in relation to any putative benefits because it is overbroad and duplicative of existing legislation.

Finally, the Shark Fin Law is not preempted by federal law, and therefore does not violate the Supremacy Clause. Federal law may preempt state law where Congress expressly states its intent to preempt state law; or where Congressional intent to preempt state law can be inferred from the fact that Congress indicated an intent to occupy the field by passing a comprehensive scheme that leaves no room for supplemental legislation; or where state law directly conflicts with federal law. *Gonzales v. Arrow Fin. Servs., LLC,* 660 F.3d 1055, 1066 (9th Cir.2011) (citing *English v. Gen. Elec. Co.,* 496 U.S. 72, 79–80 (1990)).

Here, there is no showing of any Congressional intent to preempt state regulation of or relating to shark finning. Moreover, the implementing federal regulations to the Federal Shark Fin Law expressly provide that "[n]othing in this regulation supercedes more restrictive state laws or regulations regarding shark finning in state waters." 50 C.F.R. § 600.1201(c). And as for federal management authority over fishing, the Magnuson Stevens Act provides that states retain concurrent jurisdiction over their own waters and limited concurrent authority over fishing in federal waters. *See, e.g.,* 16 U.S.C. § 1856(a). Nor have plaintiffs established that it will be impossible to comply with both existing federal law and California's Shark Fin Law. Federal law primarily regulates shark finning and the taking and landing of sharks within U.S. waters, while the Shark Fin Law prohibits the sale, trade, or possession of shark fins in California.

Finally, plaintiffs have not established a likelihood of success on the § 1983 claim, because they have not shown any discriminatory conduct by any government official—*e.g.,* enforcing the Law against Chinese–Americans and not against other individuals whose activities are regulated by the Law. Indeed, plaintiffs have provided declarations from fishermen who claim that the Shark Fin Law has caused them harm based on the fact that they have engaged in shark fishing and the subsequent sale of fins—not because they are Chinese.

As for irreparable harm, in general, loss of business revenue or monetary harm in the form of damages is not sufficient to establish irreparable injury. *See Oakland Tribune, Inc. v. Chronicle Pub. Co. ., Inc.,* 762 F.2d 1374, 1376 (9th Cir.1985). Plaintiffs have cited no other type of economic harm, apart from unsupported claims by two declarants that if the Shark Fin Law is not overturned, they will "lose [their] livelihood entirely."

While it is well-established that the deprivation of constitutional rights "unquestionably constitutes irreparable injury," *see Elrod v. Burns,* 427 U.S. 347, 373 (1976); *Melendres v. Arpaio,* 695 F.3d 990, 1002 (9th Cir.2012), in this case, because plaintiffs have not established a likelihood of success on their constitutional claims, the presumption of irreparable harm does not arise. Thus, the court need not consider whether the harm plaintiffs claim (loss of profits and business) is in fact "irreparable." Moreover, the evidence presented by defendant-intervenor Asian Pacific American Ocean Harmony Alliance shows that not all Chinese–Americans believe that a ban on buying and selling shark fins violates the Chinese cultural tradition, as many adhere to a cultural belief that preservation of the environment is of primary importance.

Similarly, with regard to public interest, while it is generally in the public interest to prevent the violation of a party's constitutional rights, *Sammartano v. First Judicial District Court,* 303 F.3d 959, 974 (9th Cir.2002), this factor need not be addressed in the absence of a showing of likelihood of success on the merits of the constitutional claims. Plaintiffs have not shown that the future inability to obtain shark fins by the relatively small percentage of the population that actually wants to do so, or the loss of profits by a small group of merchants, importers, or restauranteurs, outweighs the interests of the Legislature in protecting the marine ecosystem by eliminating a product that drives the pernicious practice of finning.

Finally, it is clear from the papers filed in opposition to plaintiffs' motion that there is support for the Shark Fin Law within the Chinese community. In addition, the evidence shows strong public interest bases for the Law, including conservation (protection of declining shark populations, including populations of shark species vulnerable to shark finning), animal welfare (reducing the economic motivation for shark finning, which leaves sharks unable to swim and causes death by starvation), and public health (bioaccumulation of contaminants such as methyl mercury in shark fins) interests.

NOTES AND QUESTIONS

1. Shortly after the *Chinatown* case was decided, NOAA published proposed rules to implement the Shark Conservation Act of 2010. See 78 Fed. Reg. 25685 (May 2, 2013). NOAA noted that state laws banning possession of shark fins "have the potential to undermine *significantly* conservation and management of federal shark fisheries." Id., 25686 (emphasis added). It concluded that such laws may interfere with achieving the optimum yield from the shark fisheries authorized under fishery management plans for Atlantic spiny dogfish, Atlantic highly migratory species, and Hawaii and American Samoa-based pelagic longline fisheries. Such state laws, the proposal concludes, "are preempted if they are inconsistent with the Magnuson-Stevens Act as amended by the SCA, ... [unless] interpreted not to apply to sharks legally harvested in federal waters." Does the Magnuson Act provision on state law preemption, 16 U.S.C. 1856(b), require the Secretary of Commerce to hold a hearing before making this determination?

2. Is cultural consumption of certain marine species or their use for traditional medicines a practice entitled to some consideration in fisheries management? If shark populations were at no risk of extinction or depletion and sharks were landed whole with no evidence of cruelty in their handling, would the California law have been more constitutionally suspect? For more on the limitations of international governance of shark fishing, see Student Note, Save Our Sharks: Using International Fisheries Law Within Regional Fishery Management Organizations to Improve Shark Conservation, 33 Mich. J. Int'l L. 383 (2012).

3. Which argument was more persuasive on the issue of legitimate state interest: that sharks are essential to healthy marine ecosystems or that the majority of Californian Chinese-Americans supported the ban? For more on the animal cruelty and other social considerations, see Walker, Oceans in the Balance: As the Sharks Go, So Do We, 17 Animal L. 97 (2010).

4. The court points out that the Magnuson-Stevens Act (MSA) was amended in 2000 and again in 2010 to address shark finning. Why was the

2000 anti-finning amendment insufficient? The language of the two provisions is below:

The Shark Finning Prohibition Act of 2000, P.L. No. 105-557, codified at 16 U.S.C. 1857(1)(P).

SEC. 3. PROHIBITION ON REMOVING SHARK FIN AND DISCARDING SHARK CARCASS AT SEA.

Section 307(1) of the Magnuson–Stevens Fishery Conservation and Management Act (16 U.S.C. 1857(1)) is amended—

* * *

(3) by adding at the end [of a list of acts prohibited by any person] the following:

"(P)(i) to remove any of the fins of a shark (including the tail) and discard the carcass of the shark at sea;

"(ii) to have custody, control, or possession of any such fin aboard a fishing vessel without the corresponding carcass; or

"(iii) to land any such fin without the corresponding carcass.

For purposes of subparagraph (P) there is a rebuttable presumption that any shark fins landed from a fishing vessel or found on board a fishing vessel were taken, held, or landed in violation of subparagraph (P) if the total weight of shark fins landed or found on board exceeds 5 percent of the total weight of shark carcasses landed or found on board.".

* * *

The Shark Conservation Act of 2010, P.L. No. 111-348, codified at 16 U.S.C. 1857(1)(P).

§ 1857. Prohibited acts

It is unlawful—

(1) for any person—

(P)(i) to remove any of the fins of a shark (including the tail) at sea;

(ii) to have custody, control, or possession of any such fin aboard a fishing vessel unless it is naturally attached to the corresponding carcass;

(iii) to transfer any such fin from one vessel to another vessel at sea, or to receive any such fin in such transfer, without the fin naturally attached to the corresponding carcass; or

(iv) to land any such fin that is not naturally attached to the corresponding carcass, or to land any shark carcass without such fins naturally attached ...

* * *

5. The federal regulation requiring the use of nylon leaders in pelagic longline fishing gear is designed to minimize bycatch of non-target species. As discussed previously, National Standard #9 of the Magnuson-Stevens Act requires the Secretary to ensure fisheries management plans minimize bycatch to the extent practicable. Can MSA regulations be based on animal cruelty considerations? For example, could the Secretary of Commerce ban a type of fishing method or gear that research shows causes the target fish to suffer before it is landed? Or could the Secretary adopt a regulation to prevent suffering in marine wildlife species that are caught unintentionally in fishing gear, e.g., large whales or dolphins caught by lobster pot gear? See Michael J. Moore et al., Right Whale Mortality: A Message from the Dead to the Living, 358-79, in Scott Krass and Rosalind M. Rolland, eds., The Urban Whale: North Atlantic Right Whales at the Crossroads (2007).

6. The California shark fin ban law, which was also challenged in state court, includes a provision regarding the independent certification of shark fisheries as meeting "accepted standards for sustainable seafood." Does this language create a potential loophole in the ban on shark fins possession in the State of California? The language is as follows:

Notwithstanding section 2021 ... (b)(1) The Ocean Protection Council shall submit an annual report to the Legislature that lists any shark species that have been independently certified to meet internationally accepted standards for sustainable seafood, as defined in Section 35550 of the Public Resources Code, and adopted by the Ocean Protection Council pursuant to Section 35617 of the Public Resources Code, including chain of custody standards; (2) A report to be submitted pursuant to paragraph (1) shall be submitted in compliance with Section 9795 of the Government Code.

7. Conservationists have sought to reduce demand for high-trophic level, pelagic species by publicizing the risks to human health of consuming fish products with high levels of toxic substances. Currently, federal law relies on publishing fish consumption advisories under the Food, Drug and Cosmetic Act, 21 U.S.C. § 301 et seq et seq. In People ex rel. Brown v. Tri-Union Seafoods, LLC, 90 Cal.Rptr. 3d 644 (Cal.App 1st Dist, 2009), application of California's "right to know" law to seafood required the court to resolve scientific questions regarding mercury in fish, including whether it is naturally occurring or anthropogenic in origin. Are courts equipped to deal with these questions?

8. Non-governmental organizations have begun to address the deficiencies in international governance of fisheries through direct appeals to con-

sumers. On the assumption that seafood consumers prefer to buy products from sustainable fisheries, third-party certification of fisheries is now a business enterprise in its own right. Large fishing companies and seafood trade associations pay for certification and the right to have their products labeled eco-friendly. Does this create a conflict of interest for third-party certifiers? What criteria do certifiers apply to determine whether a fishery is sustainable? How does the emergence of private criteria affect the standards applied under international fisheries treaties? Are consumers willing to forego favorite fish dishes in order to save ocean ecosystems for future generations? For more on the criteria used by the Marine Stewardship Council, see Marine Stewardship Council, MSC Principles and Criteria for Sustainable Fishing, available at http://www.msc.org.

CHAPTER 7

MARINE WILDLIFE CONSERVATION: LAW AND SCIENCE

. . .

This chapter explores the major U.S. laws aimed at preserving marine wildlife: the Marine Mammal Protection Act of 1972 (MMPA) and the Endangered Species Act of 1973 (ESA). Since their enactment in the early 1970s, both laws have been amended several times to deal with the challenge of implementing such far-reaching commitments to conservation. Each now contains policies and regulatory processes for protecting marine wildlife from a constantly widening array of human activities and technologies. The evolution of these laws reflects both the development of more pragmatic approaches to marine wildlife conservation and a sober recognition of the irreversibility of the losses associated with any extinction within the marine realm.

The agencies responsible for protecting marine wildlife under these laws face complex legal, scientific, and political challenges. Assessing the size and health of populations of species who spend their entire lives in the sea and whose ocean habitat faces a growing range of threats is difficult under the best of circumstances. Both statutes require that decisions be made on the basis of the best scientific information available, a mandate often referred to as the "best available science" standard. This mandate has become particularly challenging as agencies struggle to implement conservation statutes in a rapidly changing global climate and a political atmosphere often hostile to science and expertise.

1. THE STATUTORY BASIS FOR MARINE WILDLIFE CONSERVATION

Following World War II, the major whaling nations realized that their quarry, the great whales of the world's oceans, were scarce and vulnerable to over-exploitation. They adopted a treaty, the International Convention for the Regulation of Whaling (Whaling Convention or ICRW), done Dec. 2, 1946, 62 Stat. 1716, 161 U.N.T.S. 72, with the dual purposes of "safeguarding for future generations the great natural resources represented by the whale stocks" and the "orderly development of the whaling industry." Preamble, ICRW. In the post-War era, marine conservation meant to manage the exploitation of living marine resources for their continuing utilization by humankind. However, the whaling nations were not able to control the wasteful excesses of their pelagic whaling industries through the management body created by the Convention, the International Whaling Commission (IWC). By the 1960s, international conservationists classified most great whale species as endangered with extinction. The IWC had attempted to manage whaling under the fisheries science concept of "maximum sustainable yield," a data-intensive and risk-prone standard inappropriate for long-lived and slow-reproducing marine mammals. By the late 1960s, the new environmental consciousness brought a reaction against the commercial exploitation of all marine mammals and efforts to prevent the extinction of wild species.

In 1970, the U.S. Secretary of the Interior, Walter J. Hickel, signed an order adding eight commercially-exploited whale species to the list of wildlife species that were at risk of extinction. Congress had recently enacted the Endangered Species Conservation Act of 1969, Pub. L. No. 91–135, 83 Stat. 275 (1969), authorizing the Secretary to list any species or subspecies of fish or wildlife that was at such risk and to prohibit its importation. The Secretary was directed to determine which species warranted listing "based on the best scientific and commercial data available" and to convene a meeting for the purpose of concluding an international treaty to protect endangered species. The Marine Mammal Protection Act of 1972, Pub. L. No. 92–522, 86 Stat. 1027, codified at 16 U.S.C. §§ 1361–1421h, was drafted largely by cetacean scientists who were eager to replace the IWC's unworkable MSY management standard with the notion of an ecologically optimum population level. Animal conservationists pushed for a permanent moratorium on the taking of all marine mammals. They were reacting to the controversial killing methods of the fur seal industry, the tuna fishing fleet that set their nets around pods of oceanic dolphins, polar bear trophy hunters, the captive display industry, and numerous other practices they perceived as inhumane. The 93rd Congress enacted the Endangered Species Act to extend protection to those species or subspecies not yet in danger of extinction but threatened. It authorized the secretary to designate the critical habitat of listed species, spelled out the duties of all federal agencies to avoid jeopardizing listed species and their habitats, and created mechanisms allowing the U.S. to carry out CITES, the Convention on International Trade in Endangered Species of Wild Fauna and Flora, March 3, 1973, 27 U.S.T. 1087, T.I.A.S. No. 8249. Thus, by the end of 1973, the cornerstones of federal marine wildlife conservation law and policy were laid. See Etienne Benson, Endangered Science: The Regulation of Research by the U.S. Marine Mammal Protection and Endangered Species Acts, 42 Historical Studies in the Natural Sciences 30 (2012).

Both the ESA and MMPA prohibit the "taking" of protected species, mandate the use of the "best available science" and create permit programs and consultation processes to ensure that industries and federal agencies do not harm marine wildlife and their habitats. Key differences include the ESA's listing process and citizen suit provisions, the enforceable federal agency duties to prevent jeopardy to species and adverse modification of habitat, and the recovery planning requirement. The MMPA emphasizes the role of marine mammals in their ecosystems and preempts state authority, while the ESA focuses on the risk of extinction and encourages states to enact stronger protections. As climate change alters conditions for species that inhabit the coasts and oceans, the interplay of these two statutes is increasingly important.

A. THE MARINE MAMMAL PROTECTION ACT

In 1972, Congress heard urgent calls for action from members of the scientific and conservation communities who believed the mammals inhabiting the world's oceans were in jeopardy. By enacting the Marine Mammal Protection Act, it established one of the first comprehensive federal programs to address an entire class of wildlife. The law Congress passed reflected a diverse array of viewpoints on the significance of marine mammals and their role in the environment. During the legislative debates, there were those who considered marine mammals a natural resource that through careful management can be utilized in a sustained manner for food and other commercial uses. Others believed these animals should be put off-limits to exploitation because of their intelligence, their complex social interactions, or their beauty. Congress responded to these conflicting views with a statute that was so replete with ambiguities that it would take at least twenty years, extensive litigation, and several amendments to resolve them.

The full text of Section 101, 16 U.S.C. § 1361, Congressional findings and declarations of policy is:

16 U.S.C. § 1361. Congressional Findings and Declaration of Policy

The Congress finds that—

(1) certain species and population stocks of marine mammals are, or may be, in danger of extinction or depletion as a result of man's activities;

(2) such species and population stocks should not be permitted to diminish beyond the point at which they cease to be a significant functioning element in the ecosystem of which they are a part, and, consistent with this major objective, they should not be permitted to diminish below their optimum sustainable population. Further measures should be immediately taken to replenish any species or population stock which has already diminished below that popula-

tion. In particular, efforts should be made to protect essential habitats, including the rookeries, mating grounds, and areas of similar significance for each species of marine mammal from the adverse effect of man's actions;

(3) there is inadequate knowledge of the ecology and population dynamics of such marine mammals and of the factors which bear upon their ability to reproduce themselves successfully;

(4) negotiations should be undertaken immediately to encourage the development of international arrangements for research on, and conservation of, all marine mammals;

(5) marine mammals and marine mammal products either—

(A) move in interstate commerce, or

(B) affect the balance of marine ecosystems in a manner which is important to other animals and animal products which move in interstate commerce, and that the protection and conservation of marine mammals and their habitats is therefore necessary to insure the continuing availability of those products which move in interstate commerce; and

(6) marine mammals have proven themselves to be resources of great international significance, esthetic and recreational as well as economic, and it is the sense of the Congress that they should be protected and encouraged to develop to the greatest extent feasible commensurate with sound policies of resource management and that the primary objective of their management should be to maintain the health and stability of the marine ecosystem. Whenever consistent with this primary objective, it should be the goal to obtain an optimum sustainable population keeping in mind the carrying capacity of the habitat.

* * *

Aimed initially at protecting marine mammals from U.S. and foreign tuna fisheries, by 1994 the Act contained a complex regime for regulating the "incidental take" of marine mammals in many marine fisheries, a regime requiring increasingly detailed information about the populations and habitat requirements of virtually every population of marine mammals in U.S. waters. Similarly, the drafters of the Act in 1972 no doubt could not foresee that in thirty years the Act would become a battle ground over the impact of military activities on ocean life, an issue that would challenge the nation's commitment to affording marine mammals the highest level of protection.

The Act achieves its policy goals by making it illegal for an person to "take" a marine mammal in United States waters. 16 U.S.C.

§ 1372(a)(2)(A). To "take" is defined to mean to harass, hunt, capture, or kill, or attempt to do any of these things to a marine mammal. 16 U.S.C. § 1362(13).

While the statutory definition of "take" is broad, there is also a broad range of exceptions to the ban and one very large exemption, for Alaskan Native subsistence hunting. Id. at § 1371(a). Native Alaskan subsistence hunting may be regulated by the Secretary only if the species in question is "depleted," i.e., is below its optimum sustainable population level.

The Secretaries can issue regulations and permits allowing takes for scientific research or public display, or to allow the taking of marine mammals incidental to commercial fishing operations and other maritime activities. The taking of dolphins in certain tuna fisheries was the most notorious example of the latter but, after 1994, all commercial fisheries that take marine mammals may get authorization to take subject to regulation.

B. THE ENDANGERED SPECIES ACT OF 1973

The Endangered Species Act of 1973 (ESA), as amended, is the legal basis for most of the protection afforded imperiled marine wildlife species and the ecosystems upon which they depend. Although most of Act's principles and programs have been worked out in the context of terrestrial species and ecosystems, the increasing intensity of marine uses and the decline of many marine wildlife species and ecosystems have given its mandates increasing prominence in marine conservation efforts.

Because many marine wildlife species are also marine mammals, implementation of the ESA and the MMPA may in some instances appear indistinguishable, especially under their similar incidental take provisions. Like the MMPA, the ESA recognizes the intrinsic value of wildlife, stating that endangered species "are of esthetic, ecological, educational, historical, recreational, and scientific value to the Nation and its people" and declaring as its purpose, to provide "a means whereby the ecosystems upon which [they] depend may be conserved." 16 U.S.C. § 1531(a)(3), (c). The ESA is a stronger mandate in this regard, however, as it requires that all federal agencies insure their actions neither jeopardize the survival and recovery of an endangered or threatened species nor adversely modify its critical habitat. The ESA's petition and citizen suit provisions have been used increasingly to extend this mandate to a number of marine species, including several whose habitat is threatened directly by ocean warming and acidification associated with greenhouse gas emissions.

How does a fish or a species of marine wildlife qualify for such protection? The process for listing a species under the ESA is described in Section 4, 16 U.S.C. § 1533. A species is "endangered" when it is in "danger of extinction throughout all or a significant part of its range," and is "threatened" when it is "likely to become an endangered species within the foreseeable future." 16 U.S.C. §§ 1532(6),(20), 1533(c).

The Secretary is required to determine whether any species or subspecies is either endangered or threatened because of any of the following factors, and one of which is sufficient to support a listing determination: (a) the present or threatened destruction, modification, or curtailment of its habitat or range; (b) overutilization for commercial, recreational, scientific, or educational purposes; (c) disease or predation; (d) the inadequacy of existing regulatory mechanisms; or (e) other natural or manmade factors affecting its continued existence. 16 U.S.C. § 1533(a)(1). The application of these criteria is explored further in Section 3 of this Chapter.

The ESA divides responsibility for endangered and threatened species between the Secretaries of the Interior and of Commerce. 16 U.S.C. § 1533(a)(2). The Secretaries have delegated their authority under the Act to the Fish and Wildlife Service (FWS) and the National Marine Fisheries Service (NMFS). See 50 C.F.R. § 402.01(b).

For species for which programmatic responsibilities have been vested in the Secretary of Commerce, the Secretary of Interior is to accept the recommendations of the Commerce Secretary with respect to listings. 16 U.S.C. § 1533(a)(2). Listing decisions are to be made "solely on the basis of the best scientific and commercial data available * * * after conducting a review of the status of the species and after taking into account those efforts, if any, being made by any State or foreign nation." 16 U.S.C. § 1533(b).

Once a species or a population segment (of vertebrates) is listed under the ESA, three major provisions of the Act are then triggered:

(a) Section 9's prohibition against taking the listed species and the civil penalties for doing so are invoked. 16 U.S.C. §§ 1538(a), 1540(a). If the species is listed as "threatened", however, the take prohibitions only become applicable once the Secretary adopts a special rule under Section 4(d), 16 U.S.C. § 1533(d).

(b) The Secretary assumes the responsibility to develop protective regulations and recovery plans for the conservation and survival of the listed species "us[ing] all methods and procedures which are necessary to bring any [listed] species to the point" where the species would no longer require listing. 16 U.S.C. §§ 1533(d),(f); 1532(3).

(c) It becomes incumbent upon any federal agency to insure that its actions are not likely "to jeopardize the continued existence of" the listed species or result in the adverse modification of its critical habitat, and to consult with the Secretary and seek her biological opinion to insure no jeopardy. 16 U.S.C. § 1536(a),(b). Citizens can challenge the adequacy of agency performance of these duties under the citizen suit provision. 16 U.S.C. § 1540(g).

The Act requires the Secretary also to designate the critical habitat of a species concurrently with its listing "to the maximum extent prudent and determinable." 16 U.S.C. § 1533(a)(3)(A). Critical habitat designations are also required to be based on the best scientific data available, but the Secretary must also consider the economic impact of the designation, unlike the listing determination, which is to be made without regard to economic or commercial considerations. 16 U.S.C. § 1533(b)(2). The Secretary is allowed to exclude any area from critical habitat upon determining that the benefits of such exclusion outweigh the benefits of specifying the area as critical, unless the area's exclusion will result in the species extinction. Id.

Section 4 allows persons to petition the Secretary under the Administrative Procedure Act, 5 U.S.C. § 553(e), to determine whether the status of a species warrants its listing or to revise a critical habitat designation. 16 U.S.C. § 1533(b)(3)(C), (D).

If the petitioner for listing or designation is dissatisfied with the decision, the petitioner may challenge it under the Administrative Procedure Act. Cases challenging the listing or decisions not to list are presented in Section 3 of this Chapter. The following section explores the prohibitions of the ESA and the MMPA against intentional and unintended takes of marine wildlife.

2. TAKING MARINE WILDLIFE

The Endangered Species Act makes it illegal for any person subject to the jurisdiction of the United States to "take" any endangered species within the U.S. or its territorial sea, or upon the high seas. 16 U.S.C. §§ 1538(a)(1)(B), (C). The term "take" is defined to mean to harass, harm, pursue, hunt, shoot, wound, kill, trap, capture, or collect, or to attempt to do so. Id., § 1532(18). The MMPA prohibits the taking of marine mammals and defines "take" to mean "to harass, hunt, capture, or kill," or to attempt to do so. 16 U.S.C. § 1371(a), § 1362(13). Both acts prohibit both intentional and unintended takes, and authorize regulations to implement these prohibitions. The MMPA, however, has the most explicit set of exceptions for intentional takes. Some of these are explored below.

A. INTENTIONAL TAKES

When the MMPA was enacted in 1972, the captive display industry of zoos, aquaria, and sea life parks insisted on an exception to the moratorium to allow for takes of marine mammals to populate their displays. 16 U.S.C. § 1371(a)(1). This exception also covers scientific research and recovery efforts. The Act also makes an exception for the subsistence takes by Alaskan Natives, as long as the hunted populations are not below their optimum sustainable populations, 16 U.S.C. § 1371(b), and for the take of dolphins in the purse seine fisheries for Pacific tunas. 16 U.S.C. § 1371(a)(2). The geographic reach of the take prohibitions of the Endangered Species Act and the Marine Mammal Protection Act is broad but not without limits, constrained to a degree by international law principles and regimes we were introduced to in Chapter One.

1. Captive Display Takes and Permits

UNITED STATES V. MITCHELL
United States Court of Appeals for the Fifth Circuit, 1977
553 F.2d 996

WISDOM, CIRCUIT JUDGE.

This appeal turns on whether the Marine Mammal Protection Act of 1972 (MMPA), 16 U.S.C. s 1361 et seq., and related regulations, 50 C.F.R. § 216.11 (1974), apply to an American citizen taking dolphins within the territorial waters of a foreign sovereign state. The defendant-appellant, Jerry Mitchell, is an American citizen convicted of violating the Act by capturing 21 dolphins within the three-mile limit of the Commonwealth of the Bahamas. We hold that the criminal prohibitions of the Act do not reach conduct in the territorial waters of a foreign sovereignty. We reverse the conviction.

* * *

II

Congress passed the Marine Mammal Protection Act in 1972 after finding that "certain species and population stocks of marine mammals are, or may be, in danger of extinction or depletion as a result of man's activities". 16 U.S.C. § 1361(1). Section 1361(2) states, in part:

such species and population stocks should not be permitted to diminish beyond the point at which they cease to be a significant functioning element in the ecosystem of which they are a part, and, consistent with this major objective, they should not be permitted to diminish below their optimum sustainable population.

To attain this goal, section 1371[7] establishes what the Conference Report terms a "permanent moratorium." This is defined as a "complete cessation of the taking of marine mammals and a complete ban on the importation into the United States of marine mammals and marine mammal products, except as provided in this chapter". Id. at § 1362(7). During the moratorium, however, the Secretary of Commerce may issue permits for the taking of marine mammals for various purposes, including public display, provided that the taking is reviewed by the Marine Mammal Commission and the Committee of Scientific Advisors on Marine Mammals established by the Act. The Commission and Committee must recommend approval of any proposed taking that is consistent with the purposes stated in section 1361. Id. at § 1371(a). After consultation with the Commission, the Secretary must promulgate regulations governing takings, importation, permits, applications for permits, and general waivers of the moratorium. Id. at §§ 1373(a), 1374(b), 1371(a)(3)(A). The statute does not attempt to define the geographic extent of the moratorium.

The Act also announces a series of specific prohibitions with clear geographic scope. Id. at § 1372. Except as permitted by regulation, permit, or treaty, "it is unlawful for any person subject to the jurisdiction of the United States . . . to take any marine mammal on the high seas", id. at § 1372(a) (1), or from the "waters or on lands under the jurisdiction of the United States", id. at § 1372(a)(2)(A). It is also unlawful for any person to "possess any such mammal; or to transport, sell or offer for sale any such mammal", id. at § 1372(a)(3), or "to import into the United States . . . any marine mammal taken in violation" of the Act or "taken in another country in violation of the law of that country", id. at § 1372(c)(1). In Section 1375(b) Congress imposed criminal liability on those who knowingly commit violations of the Act, regulations, or permit conditions.

This legislative scheme is a hybrid of the bill reported by the House Merchant Marine and Fisheries Committee, which did not include a separate moratorium section, and the bill reported by the Senate Commerce Committee, which did. According to the House Report, the principal element of the House bill was the prohibitions section, now section 1372 of

---

[7] 16 U.S.C. § 1371 states in part:

    (a) There shall be a moratorium on the taking and importation of marine mammals and marine mammal products, commencing on the effective date of this chapter, during which time no permit may be issued for the taking of any marine mammal and no marine mammal or marine mammal product may be imported into the United States except in the following cases:

    (1) Permits may be issued by the Secretary for taking and importation for purposes of scientific research and for public display if (A) the taking proposed in the application for any such permit. . . . is first received by the Marine Mammal Commission and the Committee of Scientific Advisors on Marine Mammals. . . . The Commission and Committee shall recommend any proposed taking or importation which is consistent with the purposes and policies of section 1361 of this title.

the Act. The Committee reasoned that a de facto moratorium would develop from the prohibitions because any taking without a permit would be deemed unlawful. H.R.Rep.No.707, 92d Cong., 1st Sess., reprinted in (1972) U.S.Code Cong. & Ad.News p. 4144. Nevertheless, a five-year moratorium was added to the measure on the floor of the House. 118 Cong.Rec. 7704 (1972). The sponsors of the amendment did not discuss its geographic scope. They apparently intended to expand the protection of the bill by limiting the purposes for which permits could be issued. See id. at 7698, 7701. The Senate version originally proposed a 15-year moratorium in addition to the prohibitions. S.Rep. No. 863, 92 Cong., 2d Sess. 13 (1972). The Committee report does not explain the need for both the moratorium and the prohibitions. In fact, the report demonstrates the interrelated nature of the sections. After explaining the establishment of the moratorium, the report adds:

There are certain important exceptions to this moratorium:

(1) The prohibitions of the Act do not apply to the taking or importation of mammals or marine mammal products pursuant to international agreements. Thus, no permit is necessary (and therefore the moratorium does not apply) to the taking of Alaska fur seals pursuant to the North Pacific Fur Seal Convention. . . .

Consequently, it is not clear from the Senate Report or from the legislative history as a whole whether the moratorium was intended to have broader territorial effect than the prohibitions, which do not reach conduct in the territory of other sovereigns.

III

Mitchell argues that Congress did not intend to exercise its legislative authority to establish subject matter jurisdiction over takings, possessions, and sales of marine mammals in foreign countries. He concedes, as he must, that Congress has the power to control the conduct of American citizens overseas. The Supreme Court has held repeatedly that the legislative authority of the United States over its citizens extends to conduct by Americans on the high seas and even within the territory of other sovereigns. In Blackmer v. United States, 284 U.S. 421 (1932), for example, the Court held that a district court had subject matter jurisdiction to hold an American citizen residing in Paris in criminal contempt for failure to return to the United States in reply to a subpoena. More recently, this Court relied on Blackmer to uphold the power of a district court to try for criminal contempt a prospective witness who refused to return from Israel to testify. As the Restatement explains, international law principles do not constrain this legislative authority, because citizenship alone is generally recognized as a relationship sufficient to justify the exercise of jurisdiction by a state. Restatement (Second) of the Foreign Relations Law of the United States s 30 (1965). Consequently, Mitchell poses a question not about the authority of Congress but instead about the congressional purposes embodied in the statute.

Two principles of statutory construction must be considered in determining whether Congress intended to apply the criminal prohibitions of the MMPA extraterritorially. First, United States v. Bowman, 260 U.S. 94, 98 (1922), requires us to examine the nature of the law:

(Some laws) are such that to limit their locus to the strictly territorial jurisdiction would be greatly to curtail the scope and usefulness of the statute and leave open a large immunity for frauds as easily committed by citizens on the high seas and in foreign countries as at home. In such cases, Congress has not thought it necessary to make specific provision in the law that the locus shall include the high seas and foreign countries, but allows it to be inferred from the nature of the offense.

Second, if the nature of the law does not mandate its extraterritorial application, then a presumption arises against such application. To overcome the presumption and to apply the statute beyond the territory of the United States, the Government must show a clear expression of congressional intent.

With regard to the first proposition, the nature of the MMPA does not compel its application in foreign territories. The MMPA is a conservation statute, designed to preserve marine mammals. The nature of such a bill is based on the control that a sovereign such as the United States has over the natural resources within its territory. It can exploit them or preserve them or establish a balance between exploitation and preservation. See, e. g., 16 U.S.C. §§ 1131, 1361, 1371(a)(2), 1531, 1539. The nature of such control is not limited to the sovereignty of the United States. Other sovereign states enjoy similar authority. For example, the United Nations resolution on "Permanent Sovereignty over National Resources", G.A.Res. 1803, 17 U.N. GAOR 1193–94 (1962), recognizes the control of sovereigns over the natural resources within their territories, including the ability to nationalize or expropriate such resources from private ownership. Restatement (Second) of the Foreign Relations Law of the United States s 185 (1965) (Reporters' Note 4). In addition, Article 14 of the Convention on the Territorial Sea and the Contiguous Zone, April 29, 1958, states that the passage of foreign fishing vessels shall not be considered innocent if the crews do not observe the laws promulgated by coastal states to prevent such vessels from fishing in territorial seas. Thus each sovereign may regulate the exploitation of natural resources within its territory. Id. at s 45 (Reporters' Note 1).

When Congress considers environmental legislation, it presumably recognizes the authority of other sovereigns to protect and exploit their own resources. Other states may strike balances of interests that differ substantially from those struck by Congress. The traditional method of

resolving such differences in the international community is through negotiation and agreement rather than through the imposition of one particular choice by a state imposing its law extraterritorially. With regard
to the MMPA, Congress stated in section 1383 that the Act is not intended to contravene "the provisions of any existing international treaty, convention, or agreement, or any statute implementing the same, which may
otherwise apply to the taking of marine mammals". Furthermore, section
1378 establishes the United States approach to international protection of
marine mammals by directing the Secretary of State to initiate negotiations for both bilateral and multilateral agreements on the subject. The
basic purpose of the moratorium, prohibitions, and permit system therefore appears to be the protection of marine mammals only within the territory of the United States and on the high seas. Conservation in other
states is left to diplomatic negotiations. Restricting the territorial scope of
the Act would not "greatly curtail the scope and usefulness of the statute"
nor frustrate its purpose. We cannot then infer from the nature of the
MMPA that Congress intended to apply its restrictions to the territories
of foreign sovereigns.

With regard to the second proposition of statutory construction, neither the statute nor its legislative history provide a clear expression of
congressional intent for application of the Act in foreign territories.[14]

First, section 1371, which announces the moratorium, and section
1362(7), which defines it, do not deal with the geographic scope of the ban
on takings and importation. The Government argues that the definition of
the moratorium is absolute: " 'moratorium' means a complete cessation of

---

[14] The appellant argues that the legislative history of the Act indicates that Congress expressly rejected the extraterritorial application of the Act. In support of that position, counsel
quotes the language from the House Report:

In its deliberations, the Committee gave careful thought to the possibility of imposing
restrictions upon U.S. citizens and companies engaging in activities in foreign countries
which would not be permitted to them in the United States. . . . Ultimately, the decision
was made not to include the authority. . . .

H.R.Rep.No.707, 92d Cong., 1st Sess.—, reprinted in (1972) U.S.Code Cong. & Ad.News pp. 4144,
4154. We are not impressed. As quoted, the language does support the appellant's argument. But
the language is quoted out of context. The full paragraph from which the language is taken
shows that Congress was referring to funds invested in foreign corporations. The full paragraph
reads:

In its deliberations, the Committee gave careful thought to the possibility of imposing
restrictions upon U.S. citizens and companies engaging in activities in foreign countries
which would not be permitted to them in the United States. This was done as the result of
suggestions made during the course of the hearings which indicated that there might be significant U.S. investments in companies taking animals from depleted or endangered species
or stocks. Ultimately, the decision was made not to include the authority to require the re-
patriation of funds used for this purpose, largely on the basis that there was no solid information available on which a judgment might be made. The matter does continue to be of
considerable interest, however, and it is the expectation of the Committee that the affected
Departments of the government and the Marine Mammal Commission will look into this
question and will report back on the need for legislation to plug what may or may not be a
loophole in H.R.10420. Id.

the taking of marine mammals and a complete ban on the importation into the United States of marine mammals. . . . " The Government therefore concludes that the geographic scope of the moratorium should extend world-wide. In Foley Bros. v. Filardo, 336 U.S. 281 (1949), however, the statute in question used all-inclusive language:

> Every contract hereafter made to which the United States . . . is a party, and every such contract made for or on behalf of the United States . . . which may require or involve the employment of laborers or mechanics shall contain a provision that no laborer or mechanic doing any part of the work contemplated by the contract . . . shall be required or permitted to work more than eight hours in any one calendar day upon such work. . . .

40 U.S.C. § 324 (1946). Nevertheless, the Supreme Court concluded that the statute and its legislative history did not evidence intent specifically for extraterritorial application. The Court held that the Eight Hour Law did not cover American employees working for American contractors in Iraq and Iran. Similarly, with regard to the MMPA all inclusive language that does not expressly address territoriality cannot be held to indicate clear intent for extraterritorial application.

Second, when Congress did define the geographic scope of the prohibitions in section 1372, it did not make conduct in foreign territory unlawful. Takings without permits were prohibited only in United States territory and on the high seas. The omission of the territory of other sovereigns permits the reasonable inference that Congress concluded the prohibitions should not extend extraterritorially.

Third, the permit system established in sections 1373 and 1374 does not seem to contemplate extraterritorial jurisdiction. No mammal may be taken without a permit under sections 1371 and 1372. Any permit issued must be consistent with regulations established under section 1373. And the regulations must be promulgated "on the basis of the best scientific evidence available and in consultation with the Marine Mammal Commission". How the Secretary of Commerce or the Commission would gather scientific evidence to promulgate regulations regarding takings in other sovereign countries is unclear. Because of the reliance on scientific data, the permit system seems designed for application in the United States and on the high seas where such data may be collected without restriction from other jurisdictions. The inference again arises that extraterritorial application beyond the high seas was not intended.

Fourth, the legislative history expressly discussed one conservation problem in the territorial waters of another sovereign, namely the annual hunt of baby harp seals off the Canadian coast. H.R.Rep.No.707, 92d Cong., 1st Sess. reprinted in (1972) U.S.Code Cong. & Ad.News pp. 4144, 4149. The committee noted the "great public concern and indignation" over the hunt. Id. In response, however, it proposed only a ban on importing the skins from the animals. It could have forbade Americans from participating in the hunt. But the legislative history indicates no such intent and does not suggest that any provision of the statute would do so.

Fifth, the addition of the moratorium to the House bill provides no insight into whether the five-year moratorium was to extend the territorial reach of the Act beyond the scope indicated by the prohibitions. The debate on the amendment does not include any discussion of territoriality. See 118 Cong.Rec. 7698–7704 (1972). Although the sponsors of the amendment viewed the moratorium as providing additional protection for the animals, the primary effect discussed on the floor, and the only effect indicated by the words of the amendment, was to deny the Secretary the authority to issue permits except in certain limited circumstances. 118 Cong.Rec. 7700 et seq. It is no small matter when, in effect, this nation countermands a permit of another nation allowing the permittee to work in the territorial waters of the foreign country. We cannot say that the interests of the United States in preserving dolphins outweighs the interest of the Commonwealth of the Bahamas in preserving its character as a tourist attraction by the issuance of a limited number of permits for the capture of dolphins within its narrow band of territorial waters. If the moratorium was meant to extend the reach of the statute to the territorial waters of every country in the world, the sponsors of the amendment would certainly have recognized a duty to explain the need for such an extension on the floors of Congress and in the committee reports.

In summary, then, the Act and its legislative history do not demonstrate the clear intent required by Bowman and its progeny to overcome the presumption against extraterritorial extension of American statutes. Congress did extend the force of the MMPA to the high seas, but any further extension to regulate the taking of marine mammals in the territory of other sovereign states is not justified by the Act. The legislative scheme requires the State Department to pursue international controls by the usual methods of negotiation, treaty, and convention. Without a clearer expression from Congress to the contrary, we must presume that United States jurisdiction under the Act ceases at the territorial waters and boundaries of other states.

* * *

NOTES AND QUESTIONS

1. For a discussion of the legislative history of the 1972 MMPA, see S. Gaines and D. Schmidt, Wildlife Population Management Under the Marine Mammal Protection Act of 1972, 6 ELR 50096, 50103–08 (1976). A detailed and comprehensive examination of the MMPA is presented in M. J. Bean and

M. J. Rowland, The Evolution of National Wildlife Law 109–149 (3rd ed. 1997).

2. How did the design and terms of the MMPA complicate the question of its geographical scope? How did the court use that design to resolve the statutory interpretation question?

3. In Florida Marine Contractors v. US Fish & Wildlife Service, 378 F.Supp. 2d 1353 (M.D. Fla. 2005), the court held that the Act applied geographically to recreational docks which extend over Florida's inland waterways inhabited by Florida manatees, and it applied substantively to takings caused by recreational boating.

4. Note that Mitchell was hired to capture bottlenose dolphins for an aquarium in the Bahamas. If that aquarium were located in the United States, it would need to obtain a permit from the Secretary of Commerce under section 1374(d)(2) of the MMPA. Before it could issue the permit, would NMFS need to prepare an environmental impact statement?

* * *

JONES v. GORDON

United States Court of Appeals for the Ninth Circuit, 1986.
792 F.2d 821

WALLACE, CIRCUIT JUDGE.

The National Marine Fisheries Service (the Service) and Sea World, Inc. (Sea World) appeal from a district court order granting summary judgment in favor of Jones, other tour boat operators, environmental organizations, and the State of Alaska (hereafter referred to collectively as Jones). The district court declared that a Service permit authorizing Sea World to capture killer whales was invalid and void because the Service had failed to prepare an environmental impact statement. The district court further enjoined Sea World from capturing killer whales pursuant to the permit. Jones v. Gordon, 621 F.Supp. 7 (D. Alaska 1985). We have jurisdiction under 28 U.S.C. § 1291. We affirm in part and reverse in part.

I

In March 1983, Sea World, an operator of aquatic zoological parks, applied to the Service for a permit to capture killer whales (*Orcinus orca*) for purposes of scientific research and public display. The Marine Mammal Protection Act of 1972 (the MMPA), 16 U.S.C. §§ 1361–1407mposes a general moratorium on the taking of marine mammals, including killer whales. MMPA § 101(a), 16 U.S.C. § 1371(a). One exception to this moratorium authorizes permits "for taking . . . for purposes of scientific research and for public display." MMPA § 101(a)(1), 16 U.S.C. § 1371(a)(1). Section 104 of the MMPA, 16 U.S.C. § 1374, governs the issuance of such permits. The Secretary of Commerce has delegated responsibility for issuing permits authorizing the taking of killer whales, *see* MMPA §§ 3(11)(A), 104(a), 16 U.S.C. §§ 1362(11)(A), 1374(a), to the National Oceanic and Atmospheric Administration (the Administration) and its subagency, the Service.

In its permit application, Sea World requested permission to collect up to 100 killer whales over a five-year period from Alaska and California coastal waters. Up to ten killer whales would be maintained permanently in captivity for research and display, and up to 90 would be held temporarily (no more than three weeks) for research. The numerous scientific tests proposed included liver biopsies, gastric lavages, hearing and respiratory tests, tooth extractions, and blood tests. Sea World also proposed to tag, mark, and attach radio transmitters to killer whales held temporarily.

Pursuant to MMPA § 104(d)(2), 16 U.S.C. § 1374(d)(2), the Service in March 1983 published notice in the Federal Register of Sea World's application and invited public comment. The Service extended the public comment period four times until it closed in August 1983. During this time, the Service received approximately 1,200 comments supporting the application and 1,000 comments opposing part or all of it. In response to requests for a public hearing, the Service also held a two-day hearing on the permit application in August 1983.

On November 1, 1983, the Service issued a permit to Sea World authorizing the permanent removal of up to 10 killer whales and the temporary capture of up to 90. The permit imposed several conditions not present in Sea World's original application. For example, Sea World was required to conduct a study of local killer whale population in Alaska areas and to submit a report to the Service. No captures could be conducted without further authorization by the Service, and the length of temporary captures was restricted. No more than 2% of a local population could be permanently removed over a two-year period, and no more than two animals could be removed from a distinct social group (pod). Killer whales temporarily captured could be recaptured no more than twice. Many of the planned tests also required further authorization by the Service.

On May 1, 1984, Jones sought declaratory and injunctive relief against the Service in federal district court, alleging that the Service's issuance of the permit without preparation of an environmental impact statement violated the National Environmental Policy Act of 1969 (NEPA), 42 U.S.C. § 4332(2)(C). Sea World intervened as a defendant, and the State of Alaska intervened as a plaintiff. On cross-motions for summary judgment, the district court granted summary judgment in favor of Jones, declared the Service permit void and invalid, and enjoined Sea World from capturing killer whales pursuant to the permit.

* * *

IV

The Service and Sea World . . . argue that issuance of the Sea World permit by the Service did not require preparation of an environmental impact statement. The district court ruled that an environmental impact statement was required. Federal courts must uphold an agency decision not to prepare an environmental impact statement unless that decision is unreasonable.

To address the argument made by the Service and Sea World, we must first sketch the statutory and regulatory framework that governed the Service's action. NEPA requires that federal agencies prepare an environmental impact statement for "major Federal actions significantly affecting the quality of the human environment." 42 U.S.C. § 4332(2)(C). Regulations promulgated by the Council on Environmental Quality (CEQ), *see* 40 C.F.R. §§ 1500–1517 (1985), bind federal agencies in implementing this requirement. *Id.* § 1500.3. Under these regulations, if the proposal would not normally require an environmental impact statement, an agency generally must prepare an environmental assessment in order to decide whether an environmental impact statement must be prepared. *Id.* § 1501.4(a), (b), (c). At the same time, an agency must identify categories of actions that do not have a significant effect on the human environment; neither an environmental assessment nor an environmental impact statement is normally required for such "categorical exclusions." *Id.* §§ 1501.4(a)(2), 1507.3(b)(2)(ii), 1508.4. A categorical exclusion, however, must "provide for extraordinary circumstances in which a normally excluded action may have a significant environmental effect." *Id.* § 1508.4. CEQ regulations further outline factors "of both context and intensity" that an agency must consider in determining whether an action "significantly" affects the environment within the meaning of NEPA. *Id.* § 1508.27. These factors include the "degree to which the effects on the quality of the human environment are likely to be highly controversial," *id.* § 1508.27(b)(4), and the "degree to which the possible effects on the human environment are highly uncertain or involve unique or unknown risks," *id.* § 1508.27(b)(5).

Pursuant to these CEQ regulations, [NOAA]—the parent agency of the Service—issued Revised Administration Directive 02–10, 45 Fed. Reg. 49312 (1980). This directive included among actions falling within a categorical exclusion "[p]ermits for scientific research and public display under the MMPA." *Id.* § 6.c.(5), 45 Fed. Reg. 49316. Consistent with CEQ regulations, this directive further provided for exceptions to its categorical exclusions. An environmental assessment *or* an environmental impact statement must be prepared for actions falling within a categorical exclusion if the actions (a) Are likely to result in significant environmental impacts as defined in [40 C.F.R.] Sec. 1508.27, or (b) Involve a geographic area with unique characteristics, are the subject of public controversy based on potential environmental consequences, have uncertain environmental impacts or unique or unknown risks, establish a precedent or a decision in principle about future proposals, may result in cumulatively significant impacts, or may have any adverse effects upon endangered or threatened species or their habitats. *Id.* § 6.c.(7), 45 Fed. Reg. 49316.

The Service and Sea World argue that the issuance of the Sea World permit by the Service fell within the categorical exclusion of Revised Administration Directive 02–10 for permits for scientific research and public display under the MMPA. The district court ruled, however, that the Service action fell within an *exception* to the categorical exclusion under section 6.c. (7)(b) of the Administration directive, since it both was the subject of public controversy based on potential environmental consequences and had uncertain environmental impacts or unique or unknown risks. The court ruled that the Service was required to prepare an environmental impact statement. The Service and Sea World argue that the conditions imposed in the Sea World permit sufficiently mitigated any significant effects that might have resulted from unconditional approval of Sea World's permit application and thus precluded operation of the exceptions to the categorical exclusion. The Service further argues that even if an exception to the categorical exclusion applies, the Service would not be obligated to prepare an environmental impact statement; rather, as the Administration directive provides, the Service would have the discretion to prepare either an environmental assessment or an environmental impact statement.

While mindful that we may not substitute our judgment for an agency judgment that is fully informed and well-considered, . . . , we hold that the district court did not err in concluding that the decision of the Service not to prepare an environmental impact statement was unreasonable. The Service failed to explain adequately its decision not to prepare an environmental impact statement. In its final report on Sea World's permit application, the Service merely stated:

> Issuance of the permit is not a major Federal action significantly affecting the quality of the human environment; therefore, it has been determined that an Environmental Impact Statement is not necessary in this case. The permit authorizes the removal of ten animals from the wild and the conduct of field research on up to 90 additional animals. Regulations establishing public display and scientific research permit procedures under the MMPA have been in effect since 1974, and over 400 permits involving a take of 586,000 marine mammals have been issued. None have required an EIS and none have been prepared.

The Service did not address the applicability of the Administration directive. In particular, it did not discuss whether an exception to the categorical exclusion for issuance of MMPA permits for scientific research and public display applied.

"An 'agency cannot ... avoid its statutory responsibilities under NEPA merely by asserting that an activity it wishes to pursue will have an insignificant effect on the environment.' " (citations omitted). Instead, an agency must provide a reasoned explanation of its decision.

The Service's explanation is deficient in that it fails to explain why issuance of the permit does not fall within an exception to the categorical exclusions under section 6.c.(7) of the Administration directive. The elements of section 6.c.(7)(b) are stated in the disjunctive: if any of the elements is present, the Service must prepare an environmental assessment or an environmental impact statement. The Service's final report on the Sea World permit application reveals the arguable existence of "public controversy based on potential environmental consequences." Major points presented by public comments included the following: killer whales in captivity cannot perform their ecological role; permitting Sea World to capture killer whales would severely undercut the United States position against whaling; killer whales do not survive long in captivity; issuing a permit would encourage further exploitation; any exploitation would have long-term impacts on population size and structure; removing a killer whale from a group (pod) may disrupt or destroy the group's social structure. While the Service report disputes or rebuts several of these points, it nowhere explains why these points do not suffice to create a public controversy based on potential environmental consequences.

Similarly, the Service's final report reveals the arguable existence of "uncertain environmental impacts or unique or unknown risks." The Service report acknowledged the uncertain life expectancy of captive killer whales. It further recognized that the impact of removing killer whales was uncertain since so little is known concerning the size, composition, structure, and productivity of the killer whale populations at issue. It also stated that even temporary removals might affect the reproductive potential of killer whale groups.

The Service argues that the conditions contained in the permit issued to Sea World substantially mitigated any uncertain environmental effects. We agree that conditions mitigating the environmental consequences of an action may justify an agency's decision not to prepare an environmental impact statement. The conditions contained in this permit, however, rather than mitigating environmental consequences, generally operate simply to defer important agency decisions until more information has been obtained. At most, they "provide only general guidelines. Their effectiveness depends on how they are applied and enforced." Moreover, the Service, in issuing the permit, provided no reasoned explanation—indeed, no explanation at all—of how these conditions would prevent application of an exception to the categorical exclusions.

We conclude, therefore, that the district court did not err in deciding that the Service has unreasonably decided not to prepare an environmental impact statement. We emphasize, however, that we disagree with the district court's conclusion that the Service must prepare such a statement for the Sea World permit. Rather, the Service must consider the requirements of NEPA and regulations thereunder, and must provide a reasoned explanation of whatever course it elects to pursue.

* * *

NOTES AND QUESTIONS

1. What criteria must the Secretary apply to captive display permits under the MMPA, 16 U.S.C. § 1371(a)(1)? See Animal Protection Inst. of America v. Mosbacher, 799 F.Supp. 173 (D.D.C. 1992) (Secretary did not abuse his discretion in issuing import permits for public display of whales without determining the optimum sustainable population when available information suggests stocks were abundant). How have these changed since the MMPA's 1994 amendments, when primary authority to manage the care of captive marine mammals was delegated to the U.S. Dept. of Agriculture under the Animal Welfare Act, 7 U.S.C. §§ 2131–2159? See 50 C.F.R. §§ 216.34-216.35.

2. If U.S. marine mammal populations recover from past practices and become more abundant, should NMFS issue permits for their captive display? Should U.S. aquaria be allowed to import marine mammals taken from foreign waters? In 2012, the Aquarium of Georgia submitted an application to import 18 beluga whales that had been taken from the Sea of Okhotsk off Russia. The first application in over 20 years to import wild cetaceans captured in foreign waters, NMFS released an environmental assessment for public comment. The application argued that the proposed importation will allow the industry to increase "the population base of captive beluga whales to a self-sustaining level" and thereby "reduce the demand for wild-caught beluga whales for public display." E. Underwood, Oh, Baby: Fight Brews Over U.S. Import of Beluga Whales, 338 Science 180 (12 Oct 2012; 77 Fed. Reg. 52694 (Aug. 30, 2012); http://www.nmfs.noaa.gov/pr/permits/public_display.htm. A similar argument was made in an application for a permit to import maricultured green sea turtles listed as "threatened" under the ESA. See Alison Rieser, The Case of the Green Turtle: An Uncensored History of a Conservation Icon (2012) (discussing, inter alia, Cayman Turtle Farm, Ltd. v. Andrus, 478 F.Supp.125 (D.D.C. 1979), aff'd per curiam, unpublished opinion (D.C. Cir. 1980)).

3. What role can the states play in authorizing or disapproving proposed takes for captive display? Does the State of Georgia have authority under the MMPA or other law to block the display of captive marine mammals? See

MMPA section 109, 16 U.S.C. § 1379(a). A bill introduced in the House of Representatives in 1993, the "Marine Mammal Public Display Reform Act" (H.R. 585, 103rd Cong., 1st Sess.), would have given a state 30 days in which to disapprove a proposed public display permit if animals were to be taken from state waters designated as "protected," i.e., as having special value or requiring protection from certain activities under state law. Without this provision, could a state use the federal consistency provision of the Coastal Zone Management Act, 16 U.S.C. § 1456(c), discussed in Chapter 4, to object to a NMFS permit allowing a commercial resort facility to display dolphins? Must the state have a law prohibiting such displays listed as one of the enforceable policies of the state's approved coastal management program? Does such a state law "relate to a taking" and is therefore preempted by the MMPA's Section 1379(a)?

4. The MMPA provides that "[n]o State may enforce, or attempt to enforce, any State law or regulation relating to the taking of any species * * * of marine mammal within the State unless the Secretary has transferred authority for the conservation and management of that species * * * to the State * * * " 16 U.S.C. § 1379(a). Does this language of Section 1379(a) preclude state regulation of commercial and recreational maritime activities to prevent the disturbance or injury of marine mammals in state waters? See UFO Chuting of Hawaii v. Smith, 508 F.3d 1189 (9th Cir. 2007) (Coast Guard license did not preempt state statute banning thrillcraft and parasailing seasonally in Maui Humpback Whale Protected Waters). For the complete history of the protracted litigation, see K.L. Kaulukukui, The Brief and Unexpected Preemption of Hawaii's Humpback Whale Laws: The Authority of the States to Protect Endangered Marine Mammals Under the ESA and the MMPA, 36 ELR 10712 (2006).

5. Why has the Federal Government not transferred authority to any state under section 109 of the MMPA? See 16 U.S.C. § 1379(g). Only two states have attempted to use the transfer provision of the MMPA. California applied for a transfer of management authority over sea otters shortly after the MMPA was enacted. California eventually withdrew its application when the sea otter was listed as "threatened" under the Endangered Species Act. For an account of this effort, see J. Armstrong, The California Sea Otter: Emerging Conflicts in Resources Management, 16 San Diego L. Rev. 249 (1979). Alaska's efforts to return management authority for walrus to the State met with significant problems after the court in People of Togiak v. United States, 470 F. Supp. 423 (D.D.C. 1979), ruled that the Federal Government could not transfer authority to the State if Native Alaskans were not afforded the same opportunities to hunt marine mammals under Alaska law as under the native take exception to the MMPA.

The preemptive effect of § 1379(a) applies to state laws on importations as well as takings. This prevents a state from prohibiting the importation of a marine mammal product if the Secretary has waived the moratorium and granted a permit to the importing company. In Fouke Co. v. Mandel, 386 F.

Supp. 1341 (D. Md. 1974), a Maryland law prohibiting importation into the State of seal skins was found to be implicitly preempted by § 1379(a), even though the provision referred only to "taking." For a criticism of this ruling, see Note, Federal Preemption: A New Method for Invalidating State Laws Designed to Protect Endangered Species, 47 U. Colo. L. Rev. 261 (1976).

6. Although dolphin and killer whale displays are popular, marine life parks are controversial. Are local ordinances prohibiting captive display preempted by the MMPA? Recall City of Charleston, SC v. A Fisherman's Best, supra in Chapter 5 at p. 703. If a park closes, does the release of the captive animals back into the wild constitute a "taking"? If the animals are fitted with satellite trackers is it scientific research and thus subject to a permit under 16 U.S.C. 1371(a)(1)? Issues surrounding marine mammal captivity in commercial facilities are examined in the documentary, Blackfish, directed by Gabriela Cowperthwaite, premiered at the Sundance Film Festival in 2013.

2. Subsistence Whaling and Cultural Takes

In the MMPA, Congress directed the secretaries of state and commerce to initiate negotiations to amend the international whaling convention and other treaties to make them "consistent with the purposes and policies" of the MMPA. 16 U.S.C. § 1378(a)(4). In the case of subsistence and cultural whaling by Native Americans and other indigenous people, this has proven to be a difficult mandate, especially in light of provisions of the ESA providing for the de-listing of recovered species and NEPA, which requires an environmental impact statement and discussion of alternatives for proposed actions that are controversial. What can be more controversial than the resumption of whaling in the coastal waters of the U.S.?

In 1994, the Eastern North Pacific stock of the North Pacific gray whale became one of the first marine species to be removed from the endangered species list, after the Northwest Indian Fisheries Commission and others petitioned for its removal. NMFS determined the stock had recovered to between 60 and 90% of its carrying capacity. 59 Fed. Reg. 31094 (June 16, 1994). A petition to relist the gray whale was filed in March 2001 on behalf of Australians for Animals, The Fund for Animals, and several other groups, who claimed the gray whale was inadequately protected under the MMPA and the subsistence takes policies of the International Whaling Commission (which had granted a gray whale quota in 1997 on a joint request from the U.S. and Russia on behalf of the Makah Tribe and native peoples in Russia). NMFS found that the petition did not present substantial scientific or commercial information to warrant listing as either threatened or endangered. The best available information shows that the gray whales are within their MMPA-required population levels. 66 Fed. Reg. 32305 (June 14, 2001). On the Makah Tribe's subsistence take of gray whales, see R. Fowles, Note, Metcalf v. Daley: Consideration of the Significant Impact on the Gray Whale Population in an Environmental Assessment, 6 Ocean & Coastal L. J. 397 (2001); Anderson v. Evans, 314 F.3d 1006 (9th Cir. 2002) (tribal hunt violates MMPA unless Secretary makes findings to support waiver of the moratorium and prepares EIS due to precedential questions and uncertain recruitment of the resident gray whale population).

ANDERSON V. EVANS

United States Court of Appeals for the Ninth Circuit, 2004
371 F.3d 475 (2nd amended opinion)

BERZON, CIRCUIT JUDGE.

"[W]hile in life the great whale's body may have been a real terror to his foes, in his death his ghost [became] a powerless panic to [the] world." Herman Melville, Moby Dick 262 (W.W. Norton & Co.1967) (1851). This modern day struggle over whale hunting began when the United States granted support and approval to the Makah Tribe's ("the Tribe's") plan to resume whaling.

The Tribe, a traditional Northwest Indian whale hunting tribe, had given up the hunt in the 1920s. In recent years, the Tribe's leaders came to regret the cultural impact on the Tribe of the lapse of its whale hunting tradition. As part of a general effort at cultural revival, the Tribe developed plans to resume pursuing gray whales off the coast of Washington State and in the Strait of Juan de Fuca. The worldwide hunt for whales in the years the real-life Captain Ahabs roamed the high seas, however, seriously depleted the worldwide stock of the cetaceans. As a result of the near extinction of some species of whales, what had been a free realm for ancient and not-so-ancient mariners became an activity closely regulated under both federal and international law. This case is the second in which we have considered whether the federal government's approval of the Tribe's plans to pursue once again the Leviathan of the deep runs afoul of that regulation. *See* Metcalf v. Daley, 214 F.3d 1135 (9th Cir.2000).

The plaintiffs, citizens and animal conservation groups, challenge, as did the plaintiffs in *Metcalf,* the government's failure to prepare an environmental impact statement ("EIS") pursuant to the National Environmental Policy Act of 1969 ("NEPA"), 42 U.S.C. § 4321 et seq. They also contend that the Tribe's whaling plan cannot be implemented because the Tribe has not complied with the Marine Mammal Protection Act of 1972 ("MMPA"), 16 U.S.C. § 1361 et seq. Having reviewed the environmental assessment ("EA") prepared by the government agencies and the administrative record, we conclude that there are substantial questions remaining as to whether the Tribe's whaling plans will have a significant effect on the environment. The government therefore violated NEPA by failing to prepare an EIS before approving a whaling quota for the Tribe. We also conclude that the MMPA applies to the Tribe's proposed whale hunt.

I. Background

A. The Whales

The record discloses that there are two genetically distinct North Pacific gray whale populations—an eastern stock, also known as the California gray whale, and a western stock, confined to East Asian waters. The California gray whales migrate annually between the North Pacific and the West Coast of Mexico. These whales were at one time nearing extinction and were therefore listed on the Endangered Species Act list. *See* Endangered Species Act of 1973, 16 U.S.C. § 1531 et seq.; *Metcalf*, 214 F.3d at 1138. Protected by the endangered species designation and by other conservation measures, the California gray whale stock revived, so that by 1994 the whale was removed from the endangered species list. *See* 59 Fed. Reg. 31,094 (Jun. 16, 1994). The NMFS has determined that the eastern North Pacific gray whale stock has now recovered to between 17,000 and 26,000 whales, a number near its carrying capacity. *See* 63 Fed. Reg. 16,701, 16,704 (Apr. 6, 1998); 58 Fed. Reg. 3121, 3122 (Jan. 7, 1993). Most of the migrating whales pass through the Olympic Coast National Marine Sanctuary ["Marine Sanctuary"], adjacent to the Makah Tribe's home territory on the coast of Washington State, on their way to the Bering and Chukchi Seas, and again when heading south for the winter.

Not all of the gray whales, however, make the entire journey to the Far North each summer. On this much the parties agree, although they disagree about the habits of the nonmigrating whales as they pertain to this case.

The plaintiffs contend that a separate group of gray whales remains in and around the Marine Sanctuary waters and within the Strait of Juan de Fuca (south of Vancouver Island and east of the Pacific Ocean) during the summer and early fall, rather than migrating to the Bering and Chukchi Seas with the other eastern stock North Pacific gray whales. *See* Appendix (map depicting area). This resident group, plaintiffs maintain, arrives in the late spring with the northward migration and remains in the area for the summer, leaving only when the larger contingent of behemoths migrate south for the winter.

The government, in contrast, posits that the whales in the Marine Sanctuary area and the Strait of Juan de Fuca are not a distinct group but rather a rotating one changing from year to year, albeit with some repeat visitors. *See* Environmental Assessment on Issuing a Quota to the Makah Indian Tribe for a Subsistence Hunt on Gray Whales for the Years 2001 and 2002, at 22–29 (July 12, 2001) ["Final EA"]. The government points to several studies that suggest that if there is any identifiable whale subgroup, it is a much larger one than the plaintiffs suppose. This larger subgroup is denominated by the government the Pacific Coast Feeding Aggregation ("PCFA"). The PCFA, the government maintains, does not migrate all the way north for the summer but ranges over a long stretch of the Pacific Coast from California to Southern Alaska. According to this analysis, although some whales in the PCFA show a tendency to return to the same area along the Pacific Coast, most of them move around among different areas along the West Coast rather than staying in a particular area. Some frequent different locations throughout the summer, and others visit different places each year.

Despite this disagreement among the parties about the habits of the nonmigrating whales, there are some concepts that are not disputed. Scientists, including those relied upon by the government agencies, generally support the assessment that there is a fairly small number of whales who spend some or all of the summer in the general area of the planned Tribe hunt, and that some of these whales return to the area for more than one summer, albeit not necessarily in successive years. See, e.g., . . . J.L. Quan, U. Wash. Masters' thesis, Summer Resident Gray Whales of Washington State: Policy, Biological and Mgt Implications of Makah Whaling, at 1, 7–11 (2000).

Further, while the parties disagree in their assessment of the scientific literature as it pertains to many details regarding the behavior of these returning whales, they agree—and our review of the administrative record confirms—that overall, the best current scientific evidence indicates that each summer about sixty percent of the whales in the area around Neah Bay and the Strait of Juan de Fuca are returning whales.

The total number of whales frequenting the area of the planned Makah Tribe hunt each summer is not known. It is common ground, however, that the whales in the Tribe's proposed whaling area are a relatively small subgroup of the larger number of nonmigrating whales that forego the complete trip to the North.

B. The Makah Tribe and Its Efforts to Resume Whaling

The Tribe is composed of Native Americans whose traditional territory is in Washington State, on the northwestern Olympic Peninsula. In 1855, the United States entered into a treaty with the Tribe, the Treaty of Neah Bay, providing that the Tribe would give up most of its land on the Olympic Peninsula. *See* 12 Stat. 939, 940 (1855). In exchange, the Tribe was given, *inter alia,* the "right of taking fish and of whaling or sealing at usual and accustomed grounds and stations. . . . " *Id.* That the Treaty of Neah Bay is the only treaty between the United States and a Native American tribe that specifically protects the right to hunt whales suggests the historic importance of whaling to the Makah Tribe.

Despite the central place of whaling in their lives, the Tribe ended their whaling expeditions in the late 1920s. Explanations regarding the reasons for the abandonment of this custom include: the federal government's discouragement and lack of assistance; a decline in demand for whale oil; social and economic dislocation within the Tribe; and the drastic decline of the gray whale population.

Then came, in the early 1990s, both a renewed interest within the Tribe in reviving its traditional whaling customs and the removal of the California gray whale from the Endangered Species Act list. The Tribe therefore determined to resume its traditional whale hunting. In the seventy years since the last hunt, however, whaling had become an activity tightly regulated internationally, through the International Whaling Commission, and domestically, through the Whaling Convention Act,[6] and the MMPA, as well as through more general federal environmental legislation. Pursuant to the ICRW, aboriginal subsistence whaling is permitted,[7] but such whaling must conform to quotas issued by the IWC for various whale stocks.

In 1996 the NOAA entered into a written agreement with the Tribe committing the NOAA to seek an aboriginal subsistence quota from the IWC. The United States presented a proposal for such a quota at the annual IWC meeting in June 1996. The proposal proved controversial, however, and some members of the IWC blocked its passage. The House of Representatives Committee on Resources also passed a unanimous bipartisan resolution opposing the Tribe's hunting proposal. In the face of this opposition the United States withdrew its request.

Before the United States began its next attempt to gain IWC approval, some animal conservation organizations, whale watching groups, and individual citizens wrote a letter to the NOAA expressing concern about the prospect of a renewed whale hunt in the waters off the continental United States. The letter charged that the government had violated

---

[6] The International Convention for the Regulation of Whaling ("ICRW") was established in 1946 to restrict and regulate whaling. 62 Stat. 1716, 161 U.N.T.S. 72 (Dec. 2, 1946). The ICRW created the International Whaling Commission ("IWC"), comprised of one member from each of the ratifying countries. The IWC is empowered to set international whaling regulations and annual whaling quotas. *Id.* at arts. III, V § 1. The United States signed the Convention, 62 Stat. 1716 (1946), and implemented it domestically in the Whaling Convention Act of 1949 ("WCA"), 16 U.S.C. § 916 et seq. *See also* 50 C.F.R. § 230.1 (WCA implementing regulations).

[7] This exception originated in the first quota (termed a "Schedule") approved under the ICRW, which stated that "[it] is forbidden to take or kill gray whales . . . *except when the meat and products of such whales are to be used exclusively for local consumption by the aborigines.*" 62 Stat. at 1723 (emphasis added). The articulation of the aboriginal subsistence exception has varied in ICRW Schedules over time. The precise reach of the exception has remained unclear. *See, e.g.,* Brian Trevor Hodges, *The Cracking Facade of the International Whaling Commission as an Institution of International Law: Norwegian Small-Type Whaling and the Aboriginal Subsistence Exemption,* 15 J. Envtl. L. & Litig. 295, 304–05 (2000); Nancy C. Doubleday, *Aboriginal Subsistence Whaling: The Right of Inuit to Hunt Whales and Implications for International Environmental Law,* 17 Denv. J. Int'l L. & Pol'y 373, 384–94 (1989).

NEPA by agreeing to help the Tribe obtain hunting rights without conducting an EA. The NOAA quickly produced for public comment a Draft EA, concluding that the Tribe's hunt would have no significant environmental impact.

A few months later, the NOAA and the Tribe entered into a new agreement similar to the prior one except that the new version required that the Tribe's management plan provide time and area restrictions "including . . . confining hunting activities to the open waters of the Pacific Ocean outside the Tatoosh–Bonilla Line." Agreement Between the NOAA and the Makah Tribal Council, at 5 (1997). This provision sought to reduce the likelihood that the Tribe would take nonmigrating whales. Four days after this agreement was reached, the NMFS issued a final EA and a finding of no significant impact ("FONSI") concerning the proposed hunt.

The United States thereupon presented a joint proposal with the Russian Federation to the IWC's 1997 annual meeting. The joint proposal combined the desired Makah Tribe quota with the Russian request for a whaling quota for its Siberian aboriginal people, the Chukotka, into a single request for permission to take 620 whales over a five-year period. *See* IWC Chairman's Report of the 49th Annual Meeting, at 19 (Oct.1997).

Delegates at the IWC meeting again disagreed about whether the Tribe qualified under the aboriginal subsistence exception. Rather than resolving the disagreement, the delegates papered it over with ambiguous language: The new Schedule approved by a majority of IWC members limited use of the California gray whale quota to aboriginal groups "whose traditional aboriginal subsistence needs have been recognised," but did not say who was to recognize those needs, or how. *See* id. at 20. So it remained unclear whether a majority of the members considered the Tribe entitled to the aboriginal subsistence exception, or whether instead such recognition was to be conferred by the country issuing the quota. In March 1998, the NMFS announced a quota permitting the Tribe to take five gray whales in a one-year period and allowing no more than thirty-three strikes over a five year period. See 63 Fed. Reg. 16,701 (Apr. 6, 1998).

Meanwhile, on the day the 1997 FONSI was released and before the IWC and NMFS quotas were issued, a group of concerned citizens and animal conservation organizations filed a complaint in federal court against the federal defendants for violations of NEPA, the WCA, and the Administrative Procedure Act. The primary allegation was that the EA was a deficient effort, put together simply to justify the prior agreement allowing the Tribe to hunt whales. After the district court granted summary judgment for the defendants, the Tribe began whaling and in 1999 killed one whale.

The whale's demise did not bring this prolonged dispute to an end, for this court reversed the district court in *Metcalf.* We held that the EA was invalid because it was not produced until after the agreement with the Tribe had been consummated. A new EA must be drafted, we ordered," under circumstances that ensure an objective evaluation free of the previous taint." Because we viewed the government defendants' actions as having been undertaken improperly, we stated that when the new EA was completed and returned to the courts for evaluation, it should be subject to "additional scrutiny [and] the burden shall be on the Federal Defendants to demonstrate . . . that they have complied with [the] requirement" to evaluate the environmental impact of the proposal objectively and in good faith.

After the decision in *Metcalf,* the federal defendants dissolved the agreement with the Makah Tribe (over the Tribe's protest) and began the EA process anew. The NMFS and the NOAA published a new Draft EA in January 2001. The Draft EA, like the 1997 EA, presented as the most desirable option a whale quota targeted at migrating whales. The restriction was to be accomplished by limiting the hunt to the area west of the Tatoosh–Bonilla line and to months when northward or southward migration was underway. Draft EA at 7. Similarly, the proposed Makah Management Plan only allowed whaling in the "open waters of the Pacific Ocean which are outside the Tatoosh–Bonilla Line." Management Plan for Makah Treaty Gray Whale Hunting for the Years 1998–2002 (pre-amendment), at 6.

Before the Final EA issued but after the comments period on the Draft EA had closed, the Tribe amended the Management Plan. The amended plan, in contrast to the earlier ones, does not contain any general geographic limitations on the whale hunt. Instead, the new plan allows for the taking of five whales in any one calendar year, with the aggregate number taken from 1998 to 2002 not to exceed twenty whales. See Makah Management Plan at 3. No more than thirty-three whales can be struck between 1998 and 2002, and the number of gray whales struck between 2001 and 2002 cannot exceed fourteen. *Id.* The amended plan does limit the number of strikes—but not the number of takes—likely to affect non-migrating whales: For 2001 and 2002, the plan limits to five the number of strikes (1) during the months of the migration, between June 1 and November 30; and (2) at all times in the Strait of Juan de Fuca. *Id.*

On July 12, 2001, the NOAA and NMFS published a Final EA, based on the amended Management Plan and once again found no significant environmental impact. The Draft EA did not evaluate the amended Management Plan, so there has been no opportunity for public comment on the important amendments. Nor did any of the scientific studies relied on in the EA specifically evaluate the impact of the revised Management

Plan. Rather, to the extent those studies and comments discuss the proposed hunt at all, they assume a hunt limited to areas west of the Tatoosh–Bonilla line.

The final step in the administrative saga took place when the NOAA and the NMFS issued a Federal Register notice on December 13, 2001 announcing a quota for the "land[ing]" of five gray whales in 2001 and 2002 and approving the latest Makah Management Plan. 66 Fed. Reg. 64,378 (Dec. 13, 2001).

C. The Current Litigation

The plaintiffs filed this action in January 2002, alleging violations of both NEPA and the MMPA. The Tribe intervened. In April, the plaintiffs moved for a preliminary injunction to prevent an anticipated whale hunt, but the district court denied the motion. Concluding that the federal agencies had taken the requisite "hard look" at the risks associated with the whale hunt and that the court was required to defer to their decision, the district court determined that the plaintiffs did not have a probability of success on the merits. The district court also held that the Treaty of Neah Bay's preservation of the Tribe's whaling rights takes precedence over the MMPA's requirements; the plaintiffs therefore were unlikely to prevail on their MMPA claim as well. The plaintiffs appealed these rulings.

II. NEPA Analysis

* * *

D. Controversy and Uncertainty

Under the CEQ regulations, we must consider whether the effects of the Tribe's whaling on the human environment are "likely to be highly controversial," 40 C.F.R. § 1508.27(b)(4), and also whether the "possible effects . . . are highly uncertain or involve unique or unknown risks." 40 C.F.R. § 1508.27(b)(5). A proposal is highly controversial when there is "a substantial dispute [about] the size, nature, or effect of the major Federal action rather than the existence of opposition to a use." Put another way, a proposal can be considered controversial if "substantial questions are raised as to whether a project . . . may cause significant degradation of some human environmental factor."

There is no disagreement in this case concerning the EA's conclusion that the impact of the Makah Tribe's hunt on the overall California gray whale population will not be significant. What is in hot dispute is the possible impact on the whale population in the local area where the Tribe wants to hunt. In our view, the answer to this question—of greatly increased importance with the revision of the Makah Management Plan so as expressly to allow hunting of local nonmigrating animals—is sufficiently uncertain and controversial to require the full EIS protocol.

Our reasoning in this regard is as follows: The government agrees that a relatively small group of whales comes into the area of the Tribe's hunt each summer, and that about sixty percent of them are returning whales (although, again, not necessarily whales returning annually). Even if the eastern Pacific gray whales overall or the smaller PCFA group of whales are not significantly impacted by the Makah Tribe's whaling, the summer whale population in the *local* Washington area may be significantly affected. Such local effects are a basis for a finding that there will be a significant impact from the Tribe's hunts. *See* 40 C.F.R. § 1508.27(a). Thus, if there are substantial questions about the impact on the number of whales who frequent the Strait of Juan de Fuca and the northern Washington Coast, an EIS must be prepared.

The crucial question, therefore, is whether the hunting, striking, and taking of whales from this smaller group could significantly affect the environment in the local area. The answer to this question is, we are convinced, both uncertain and controversial within the meaning of NEPA. No one, including the government's retained scientists, has a firm idea what will happen to the local whale population if the Tribe is allowed to hunt and kill whales pursuant to the approved quota and Makah Management Plan. There is at least a substantial question whether killing five whales from this group either annually or every two years, which the quota would allow, could have a significant impact on the environment.

The government estimates that a conservative allowable take from a group of 222 to 269 whales is 2.5 whales per year,[12] while a less conservative approach would allow killing up to six whales per year from the PCFA. Final EA at 57. Thus, with a smaller group, it would appear that a take of less than 2.5 whales per year could exceed the allowable Potential Biological Removal level or "PBR" established under the MMPA's standards.

Some of the scientists relied upon by the government worry that takes from the local resident whale population may deplete the number of local whales in the area off the coast of Washington State and in and around the Strait of Juan de Fuca. *See Review of Studies* at 15 ("[The whales'] fidelity to specific locations could subject them to differential harvests and potential depletions if there are unregulated *local takes*.")

[12] The government's calculation of the acceptable Potential Biological Removal level ("PBR") number for the PCFA is not without controversy. The PBR is calculated based on an MMPA formula which strives to prevent any marine mammal from being reduced below its optimum sustainable population level. The EA relies on an estimate that there are 222 to 269 whales in the PCFA. Studies, however, suggest that these figures are not representative and overestimate the actual number of whales in the group. *See* Calambokidis et al., *Range and Movements, supra,* at 9. . . . Based on the higher range of 222 to 269, the EA finds that a conservative estimate allows for the taking of 2.5 whales per year without jeopardizing the PCFA population. The Makah Management Plan, however, is set at five per year—the higher end of the range of acceptable removal levels (2.5 to 6) for this possibly exaggerated number of whales.

(emphasis added); Quan, *supra,* at 13 (finding that there could be an adverse impact on the local whale population in the area of the Tribe's hunt if the whales' site fidelity is based on social or familial recruitment); *see also* Darling Decl. ¶ 7 ("[I]t remains a reasonable possibility that removals of resident whales would deplete their presence in specific areas from which they would require an extended time period to recover."). These concerns, it should be noted, were expressed at a time when it was expected that the Tribe's hunt would be structured so as to avoid targeting the nonmigrating whales in the area, a restriction that has in large part been lifted.

The government tries in two ways to minimize the importance of the possible local impact. First, the government maintains that the PCFA—or summer resident whale group, if one exists—is not genetically distinct from the other California gray whales. For purposes of applying the CEQ regulations, this consideration is irrelevant. If California gray whales disappear from the area of the Strait of Juan de Fuca, the Marine Sanctuary, or both, that would be a significant environmental impact even if the PCFA whales populating the rest of the Pacific Coast in the summer are genetically identical to the local whales, and even if the PCFA whales are genetically identical to the migrating whales.

Second, the government implies that any whales taken from the local resident group will be replaced in the local area by other whales from the PCFA, so the number of whales locally will not decline. The EA describes the PCFA as composed of whales that move from one feeding area to another rather than staying in one locale for all the summer months. That some of the whales who return, whether annually or intermittently, to the area of the proposed hunt also visit other areas of the coast cannot, however, eliminate concern about the local impact. The fact remains that a majority of the fairly small number of whales identified in the Makah Tribe's hunting area have been there in previous years, wherever else they have also journeyed. Whether there will be fewer or no whales in the pertinent local area if the hunt is permitted depends not on whether the whales who frequent that area also travel elsewhere, but upon the opposite inquiry: whether whales who heretofore have *not* visited the area will do so, thereby replenishing the summer whale population in the area, if some of the returning whales are killed.

It is on this latter question that the scientific uncertainty is at its apogee. Almost all of the scientific experts relied upon in the EA state that the effect of taking whales who demonstrate some site fidelity within the Tribe's hunting area is uncertain. Quan, for example, suggests that much depends on how whales are recruited to the area, an open question requiring further study. *See* Quan, *supra,* at 11–13. If the local whales are recruited randomly, removing four whales annually from the Tribe's hunt area should not have any long-term impact. If the whales are recruited familially, however, "the annual removal of four gray whales could direct-ly[affect the number of whales] observed and utilizing the area." Quan, *supra,* at 13.

Similarly, Darling states that "the recruitment mechanism that in-fluences or maintains the resident group of gray whales found in Wash-ington is not known. As a result, it is difficult to predict at this time how the harvesting of resident whales could affect the resident population." Darling Decl. ¶ 10. *See also* Calambokidis et al., *Range and Movements, supra,* at 4 ("It is unclear how loyal these [seasonal resident] animals are to the feeding grounds, how they adopt this alternate feeding strategy, and their range of movements."); *Review of Studies,* at 20 ("Relatively lit-tle is known about how individuals choose feeding grounds throughout their lives. . . . It is plausible that females may learn their migration route and preferred feeding areas from their mothers. . . . A summer hunt that is localized and very coastal has the potential to adversely af-fect such localized feeding groups and could lead to distributional changes and local extirpation.").

The EA's *only* substantive attempt to address the impact of the Tribe's whaling on the number of whales in the area of the Marine Sanc-tuary and the Strait of Juan de Fuca is as follows: "With the extreme movements of whales in the [PCFA] both within and between seasons . . . a limit of five strikes over two years should also alleviate any poten-tial local depletion issues." Final EA at 58.[15] The EA's conclusion simply does not follow from its premise: That PCFA whales do not spend all summer or every summer in the area of the Tribe's hunt does not elimi-nate the possibility that the killing of returning whales present in any given year may lead to a depletion of whales in the local area. Obviously, with the demise of some returning whales, fewer whales with the habit of returning to that area in the summer will survive. As the underlying studies establish, the local impact of the Tribe's whaling therefore turns on whether different PCFA whales will fill in for the killed, struck, or frightened whales no longer in the area. This critical question is never analyzed, numerically or otherwise, in the EA.

In short, the record establishes that there are "substantial questions" as to the significance of the effect on the *local* area. Despite the com-mendable care with which the EA addresses other questions, the EA simply does not adequately address the highly uncertain impact of the Tribe's whaling on the *local* whale population and the local ecosystem. This major analytical lapse is, we conclude, a sufficient basis for holding

---

[15] The EA also quotes from the IWC's Scientific Committee: "[T]he Committee agreed that there is a need for better understanding of site fidelity and potential stock substructure in east-ern gray whales to improve advice on management." Far from negating scientific uncertainty, this conclusion by an international group of experts supports the conclusion that there are unre-solved issues critical to assessing the possible local environmental impact of the Tribe's hunt.

that the agencies' finding of no significant impact cannot survive the level of scrutiny applicable in this case. And because the EA simply does not adequately address the local impact of the Tribe's hunt, an EIS is required.

E. Precedential Effect

There is a second consideration that buttresses the conclusion that an EIS must be prepared. If approval of a single action will establish a precedent for other actions which may cumulatively have a negative impact on the environment, an EIS may be required. *See* 40 C.F.R. § 1508.27(b)(6). The plaintiffs argue that the approval of the Tribe's hunting quota could have such a significant precedential impact on future IWC quotas. Approval of a whaling quota for one group for a limited time period is not binding, however, on future IWC or WCA decisions regarding other groups, or even regarding the same group in the future. This factor is therefore insufficient on its own to demonstrate a significant environmental impact.

There is nonetheless sufficient merit to plaintiffs' concerns to lend support to the conclusion that there are substantial questions concerning whether the Makah Tribe's hunt will adversely affect the environment. As noted, it appears that the IWC quota language concerning the aboriginal subsistence exception was left purposely vague. The quota issued jointly to Russia and the United States was limited to whaling by aboriginal groups "whose traditional aboriginal subsistence needs have been recognised." Conspicuously absent from this phrase is any delineation of who must do the recognizing or how.

Prior to adoption of this language, the understanding among IWC members was that only the IWC could decide which groups met the subsistence exception. The 1997 IWC gray whale quota, as implemented domestically by the United States, could be used as a precedent for other countries to declare the subsistence need of their own aboriginal groups, thereby making it easier for such groups to gain approval for whaling.[17] If such an increase in whaling occurs, there will obviously be a significant impact on the environment.

The EA does not specifically address the impact of the quota on any IWC country besides the United States. Instead, the EA only analyzes the

---

[17] There have been disputes in the IWC in recent years over efforts by other countries to gain approval for quotas for whaling communities viewed domestically, but not internationally, as meeting the aboriginal exception. *See, e.g.,* Leesteffy Jenkins & Cara Romanzo, *Makah Whaling: Aboriginal Subsistence or a Stepping Stone to Undermining the Commercial Whaling Moratorium,* 9 Colo. J. Int'l Envtl. L. & Pol'y 71, 88–99 (1998); *see also* James Brooke, *Japan Cuts Whaling Rights for Native Peoples of Arctic,* N.Y. Times, May 25, 2002, at A4 (describing Japan's efforts to block whaling quotas for Alaskan and Siberian aboriginal people until quota was approved for its own whaling communities).

possible precedent with regard to other Native American tribes in this country and Canada.

We agree that because Canada is not a member of the IWC, it will not be heavily swayed one way or the other by approval of the Makah Tribe's whaling quota. But we cannot agree with the agencies' assessment that because the Makah Tribe is the only tribe that has an explicit treaty-based whaling right, the approval of their whaling is unlikely to lead to an increase in whaling by other domestic groups. And the agencies' failure to consider the precedential impact of our government's support for the Makah Tribe's whaling in future IWC deliberations remains a troubling vacuum. We conclude that the possible impact on the heretofore narrow aboriginal subsistence exception supports our conclusion that an EIS is necessary.

In sum, given the substantial uncertainty and controversy over the local impact of the Makah Tribe's whaling and its possible precedential effect, an EIS should have been prepared. Of course scientific inquiry rarely yields certainty. But here the agencies' inquiry itself was deficient. Thus, an EIS is required.

There is no doubt that the government put much effort into preparing the lengthy environmental assessment now before us. While a notable attribute of the creatures we discuss in this opinion, girth is not a measure of the analytical soundness of an environmental assessment. No matter how thorough, an EA can never substitute for preparation of an EIS, if the proposed action could significantly affect the environment.

We stress in this regard that an EIS serves different purposes from an EA. An EA simply assesses whether there will be a significant impact on the environment. An EIS weighs any significant negative impacts of the proposed action against the positive objectives of the project. Preparation of an EIS thus ensures that decision-makers know that there is a risk of significant environmental impact and take that impact into consideration. As such, an EIS is more likely to attract the time and attention of both policymakers and the public.

In addition, there is generally a longer time period for the public to comment on an EIS as opposed to an EA, and public hearings are often held. Furthermore, preparation of an EIS could allow additional study of a key scientific issue, the local recruitment scheme of the whales in the Makah Tribe's hunting area. See, e.g., Review of Studies at 21 ("A better understanding of site fidelity and potential stock structure will be gained through continuation and expansion of photographic identification and satellite tagging research on the feeding grounds. . . . ").

Because the agencies have not complied with NEPA, we set aside the FONSI, suspend implementation of the Agreement with the Makah Tribe, and vacate the approved whaling quota for the Tribe.

GOULD, CIRCUIT JUDGE, with whom HILL and BERZON, CIRCUIT JUDGES, concur:

III. MMPA Analysis

In addition to arguing their NEPA claim, plaintiffs maintain that the federal defendants issued a gray whale quota to the Tribe in violation of the Marine Mammal Protection Act (MMPA), 16 U.S.C. § 1361 et. seq., which prohibits the taking of marine mammals absent a permit or waiver. The Tribe has not applied for a permit or waiver under the MMPA. Defendants maintain that the MMPA does not apply because the Tribe's whaling quota has been expressly provided for by an international treaty, or, in the alternative, because the Tribe has an Indian treaty whaling right that is not affected by the MMPA.

A. Exemption

The federal defendants, including NOAA, and the Makah Tribe as defendant-intervenor first assert that § 1372(a)(2) of the MMPA exempts the Tribe's whaling from the MMPA moratorium. Section 1372(a)(2) provides an exception to the MMPA's blanket moratorium on the taking of marine mammals when takes have been "expressly provided for by an international treaty, convention, or agreement to which the United States is a party and which was entered into before [1972] or by any statute implementing any such treaty, convention, or agreement." 16 U.S.C. § 1372(a)(2). Defendants argue that § 1372(a)(2) applies here because the International Whaling Commission (IWC) approved a gray whale quota for the Tribe in 1997. We reject this argument for several reasons.

First, there is the problem of timing. Defendants recognize that a 1997 approval does not pre-date the MMPA as required by § 1372(a)(2), but argue that the 1997 approval relates back to the International Convention for the Regulation of Whaling (ICRW), which the United States signed in 1946. The ICRW enacted a schedule of whaling regulations (Schedule) and granted the IWC the power to amend the Schedule by adopting subsequent regulations, including quotas. International Convention for the Regulation of Whaling, 62 Stat. 1716, 1717–19 (1946). Defendants argue that, because the IWC was given the power to adopt quotas in 1946, the Tribe's quota approved in 1997 should be considered a right under the 1946 Convention that pre-dates the MMPA.

We disagree. The 1997 Schedule was adopted more than twenty-four years after the MMPA became effective. Section 1372(a)(2) exempts only international treaties that pre-date the MMPA, without also exempting amendments to those treaties. If Congress wanted to exempt subsequent amendments, then Congress could have done so explicitly. But Congress did not do so. That Congress did not intend to exempt subsequent amendments is clear when § 1372(a)(2) is considered alongside the mandates of § 1378(a)(4). Section 1378(a)(4) requires "the amendment of any existing international treaty for the protection and conservation of any species of marine mammal to which the United States is a party in order to make such treaty consistent with the purposes and policies of this [Act]." 16 U.S.C. § 1378(a)(4). Far from intending amendments of international treaties to escape the restrictions of the MMPA moratorium by relating back to the treaties' pre-MMPA inception, Congress mandated that existing treaties be amended to incorporate the conservation principles of MMPA. It would be incongruous to interpret § 1372(a)(2) to exempt the amendments that were mandated by § 1378(a)(4). And, if we accepted the defendants' view, then we would read the MMPA to disregard its conservation principles whenever in the future the IWC made unknown decisions for unknown reasons about the killing of unknown numbers of whales. We do not believe that Congress subordinated its goal of conservation in United States waters to the decisions of unknown future foreign delegates to an international commission.

Second, there is a problem of specificity. Even if we were to read the 1997 Schedule to relate back to the 1946 Convention and thus to pre-date the MMPA, § 1372(a)(2) still would not apply here because the Schedule fails expressly to provide any whaling quota for the Tribe.[18] Defendants do not dispute that the Schedule fails to mention the Tribe on its face. But defendants argue that IWC Schedules in practice never mention particular aboriginal tribes, but rather provide general quotas based on specific needs of particular tribes. Whatever may be the IWC's practice, the MMPA unambiguously requires express approval for § 1372(a)(2) to apply and to excuse the takings of marine mammals without a permit.

Third, there is a problem of uncertainty. We cannot tell whether the IWC intended a quota specifically to benefit the Tribe. Even if timing and specificity were no problem, the surrounding circumstances of the adoption of the Schedule cast doubt on the intent of the IWC to approve a quota for the Tribe. The Schedule extends the quota only to those aborigines whose "subsistence and cultural needs have been recognised." This language was inserted into the Schedule after some IWC delegates ques-

---

[18] The Schedule provides for:

The taking of gray whales from the Eastern stock in the North Pacific is permitted, but only by aborigines or a Contracting Government on behalf of aborigines, and then only when the meat and products of such whales are to be used exclusively for local consumption by the aborigines whose traditional aboriginal subsistence and cultural needs have been recognised. . . . For the years 1998, 1999, 2000, 2001, and 2002, the number of gray whales taken in accordance with this subparagraph shall not exceed 620, provided that the number of gray whales taken in any one of the years 1998, 1999, 2000, 2001, or 2002 shall not exceed 140.

tioned whether the Tribe qualified for the aboriginal subsistence quota. *See* Metcalf v. Daley, 214 F.3d 1135, 1140 (9th Cir.2000). Whether recognition must formally come from the IWC or from the United States is not clear.

In light of the circumstances giving rise to this language, the IWC presumably intended that such recognition, whether it came from the IWC or the United States, would depend on the Tribe's ability to satisfy the definition of aboriginal subsistence whaling. When the United States presented its request for a quota for the Makah Tribe to the IWC, the United States, in response to issues raised by the IWC during subcommittee, represented that the IWC had adopted the following definition of aboriginal subsistence whaling:

> whaling, for purposes of local aboriginal consumption carried out by or on behalf of aboriginal, indigenous, or native peoples who share strong community, familial, social, and cultural ties related to a *continuing traditional dependence* on whaling and on the use of whales.(emphasis added).

While NOAA issued a Federal Register Notice in April 1998 recognizing the Tribe's subsistence and cultural needs, Notice of Aboriginal Subsistence Whaling Quotas, 63 Fed. Reg. 16,701 (1998), it is not clear that the IWC anticipated such recognition, given that the United States relied on a definition of subsistence whaling that requires a "continuing traditional dependence" on whaling and given that the Tribe had not engaged in whaling since 1927.

Because the IWC adopted the "has been recognised" language in response to opposition to the Tribe's whaling, and because it was not a foregone conclusion that the Tribe would satisfy the definition of aboriginal subsistence whaling, the IWC's intent to approve a whaling quota for the Tribe has not been demonstrated. The "expressly provided for" requirement of § 1372(a)(2) is not satisfied.

Fourth, § 1372(a)(2) does not apply in this case by way of a statute implementing an international treaty because there is no domestic statute implementing the ICRW that expressly permits the Tribe's whaling. The Whaling Convention Act (WCA), 16 U.S.C. § 916, implements the ICRW domestically, making it unlawful to take whales without first obtaining a quota from the IWC. 16 U.S.C. § 916c. The WCA does not mention quotas or aboriginal subsistence whaling, much less the Tribe's whaling, and therefore is of no assistance to defendants.

In sum, the defendants' reliance on § 1372(a)(2) to exempt the Tribe's whaling from the MMPA's general moratorium is misplaced. The federal defendants' view so clearly offends the express, unambiguous language of the statute that the statutory interpretation offered by NOAA and the federal defendants cannot properly be afforded deference under Chevron, U.S.A., Inc. v. NRDC, 467 U.S. 837 (1984).

B. Conservation Necessity

We consider whether the MMPA must apply to the Tribe to effectuate the conservation purpose of the statute. In *Fryberg,* we set out a three-part test for determining when reasonable conservation statutes affect Indian treaty rights: (1) the sovereign has jurisdiction in the area where the activity occurs; (2) the statute is non-discriminatory; and (3) the application of the statute to treaty rights is necessary to achieve its conservation purpose. 622 F.2d at 1015. Applying this rule, the MMPA may regulate any pre-existing Makah Tribe whaling rights under treaty if (1) the United States has jurisdiction where the whaling occurs; (2) the MMPA applies in a non-discriminatory manner to treaty and non-treaty persons alike; and (3) the application of the statute to regulate treaty rights is necessary to achieve its conservation purpose. *See id.*

As to the first prong of the test, the MMPA extends to "any person subject to the jurisdiction of the United States," 16 U.S.C. § 1372(a)(1), and reaches 200 nautical miles outward from the seaward boundary of each coastal state, 16 U.S.C. § 1362(15). Thus, the MMPA would clearly apply to the Tribe's whaling off the coast of Washington State in the Strait of Juan de Fuca. As to the second prong, the MMPA places a general moratorium on all persons except certain Native Alaskans with subsistence needs. The MMPA cannot be said to discriminate between treaty and non-treaty persons because members of the Tribe are not being singled out any more than non-treaty people in the lower forty-eight states.

The third prong of the *Fryberg* test requires that the application of the MMPA to the Tribe be necessary to achieve its conservation purpose. This prong frames for us the critical issue under this test: whether restraint on the Tribe's whaling pursuant to treaty rights is necessary to effectuate the conservation purpose of the MMPA. In assessing this issue, we are mindful that the major objective of the MMPA is to ensure that marine mammals continue to be "significant functioning element[s] in the ecosystem." 16 U.S.C. § 1361(2). In fact, "[marine mammals] should not be permitted to diminish below their optimum sustainable population." *Id.* To carry out these conservation objectives, the MMPA implements a sweeping moratorium in combination with a permitting process to ensure that the taking of marine mammals is specifically authorized and systematically reviewed. For example, the MMPA requires that the administering agency consider "distribution, abundance, breeding habits, and times and lines of migratory movements of such marine mammals" when deciding the appropriateness of waiving requirements under the MMPA, 16 U.S.C. § 1371(a)(3)(A). And, when certain permits are issued, the permit may be suspended if the taking results in "more than a negligible impact on the species or stock concerned." 16 U.S.C. § 1371(a)(5)(B)(ii). One need only review Congress's carefully selected language to realize that Congress's concern was not merely with survival of marine mammals, though that is of inestimable importance, but more broadly with ensuring that these mammals maintain an "optimum sustainable population" and remain "significant functioning elements in the ecosystem." The MMPA's requirements for taking are specifically designed to promote such objectives. Without subjecting the Tribe's whaling to review under the MMPA, there is no assurance that the takes by the Tribe of gray whales, including both those killed and those harassed without success, will not threaten the role of the gray whales as functioning elements of the marine ecosystem, and thus no assurance that the purpose of the MMPA will be effectuated.

If the Tribe's plans for whaling could proceed without regulation, we cannot be certain that future whaling by the Tribe will not jeopardize the gray whale population either through its current plan or through future expanded quotas. While the Tribe's current Gray Whale Management Plan allows the Tribe to hunt whales with rifles and motorized boats, the Tribe is not limited to a particular method of hunting by the terms of the Treaty of Neah Bay. *See* United States v. Washington, 384 F.Supp. 312, 407 (W.D.Wash.1974) (commonly referred to as the "Boldt" decision), aff'd, 520 F.2d 676 (9th Cir.1975), cert. denied, 423 U.S. 1086 (1976) ("Just as non-Indians may continue to take advantage of improvements in fishing techniques, the Treaty Tribes may, in exercising their rights to take anadromous fish, utilize improvements in traditional fishing methods, such for example as nylon nets and steel hooks."). The Tribe, therefore, could use evolving technology to facilitate more efficient hunting of the gray whales. The tribal council of the Makah Tribe has shown admirable restraint in limiting its aim to a small number of whales, and seeking the umbrella approval of the United States for a share of a quota approved by the IWC. But it is not clear the extent to which the Tribe's treaty right is limited to the approvals of the IWC or the Tribe's Gray Whale Management Plan. The intent of Congress cannot be hostage to the goodwill or good judgment or good sense of the particular leaders empowered by the Tribe at present; it must be assumed that Congress intended to effectuate policies for the United States and its residents, including the Makah Tribe, that transcend the decisions of any subordinate group.

If the MMPA's conservation purpose were forced to yield to the Makah Tribe's treaty rights, other tribes could also claim the right to hunt marine mammals without complying with the MMPA. While defendants argue that the Makah Tribe is the only tribe in the United States with a treaty right expressly guaranteeing the right to whale, that argument ignores the fact that whale hunting could be protected under less specific treaty language. The EA prepared by the federal defendants notes that

other Pacific Coast tribes that once hunted whales have reserved traditional "hunting and fishing" rights in their treaties. These less specific
"hunting and fishing" rights might be urged to cover a hunt for marine
mammals. Although such mammals might not be the subject of "fishing,"
there is little doubt they are "hunted."

Defendants argue that the conservation necessity test under *Fryberg*
is not triggered until species preservation emerges as an issue. We have
rejected the idea that species preservation must be an issue for the conservation necessity principle to apply. *Eberhardt,* 789 F.2d at 1362, *citing*
United States v. Oregon, 718 F.2d 299, 305 (9th Cir.1983). Satisfaction of
the *Fryberg* test depends on the conservation purpose of the statute. Here
the purpose of the MMPA is not limited to species preservation. Whether
the Tribe's whaling will damage the delicate balance of the gray whales in
the marine ecosystem is a question that must be asked long before we
reach the desperate point where we face a reactive scramble for species
preservation. To effectuate the purpose of the MMPA, which is to make
informed, proactive decisions regarding the effect of marine mammal
takes, we conclude that the MMPA must apply to the Tribe, even if its
treaty rights must be considered and given weight by NMFS in implementing the MMPA, an issue we do not decide.[24]

The application of the MMPA to the Tribe to uphold the conservation
purpose of the MMPA goes hand in hand with the principles embedded in
the Treaty of Neah Bay itself. The treaty language, when considered on
its face, supports our conclusion that the conservation purpose of the
MMPA requires it be applied to the Tribe. The Treaty of Neah Bay provides the Tribe with a right to fish and hunt whales "in common with all
citizens of the United States." 12 Stat. 939, 940 (1855). We have recognized that the "in common with" language creates a relationship between
Indians and non-Indians similar to a cotenancy, in which neither party
may "permit the subject matter of [the treaty] to be destroyed." United
States v. Washington, 520 F.2d 676, 685 (9th Cir.1975). *See also* United
States v. Washington, 761 F.2d 1404, 1408 (9th Cir.1985) (recognizing
that "in common with" has been interpreted to give rise to cotenancy type
relationship). While this "in common with" clause does not strip Indians
of the substance of their treaty rights, *see* Washington v. Washington
Commercial Passenger Fishing Vessel Ass'n, 443 U.S. 658, 677 n. 22
(1979), it does prevent Indians from relying on treaty rights to deprive
other citizens of a fair apportionment of a resource. In *Washington Commercial Passenger Fishing Vessel Ass'n,* the Supreme Court concluded
that: "Nontreaty fishermen may not rely on property law concepts, devic-

---

[24] This conclusion is reinforced by our holding in *Midwater Trawlers Co-operative v. Dep't of
Commerce,* 282 F.3d 710 (9th Cir.2002), wherein we held that the Magnuson–Stevens Act, which
has as its purpose the protection of U.S. fisheries, applies to the Makah's fishing rights despite
the Treaty of Neah Bay.

es such as the fish wheel, license fees, or general regulations to deprive the Indians of a fair share of the relevant runs of anadromous fish in the case area. Nor may the treaty fishermen rely on their exclusive right of access to the reservations to destroy the rights of other 'citizens of the Territory.' Both sides have a right, secured by the treaty, to take a fair share of the available fish. That, we think, is what the parties to the treaty intended when they secured to the Indians a right of taking fish in common with other citizens." Id. at 684–85. This holding might be read to suggest that the Tribe's treaty right gives the Tribe a right to a "fair share" of whales that are to be taken. The "fair share" formula, however, does not provide a ready answer in this case, which involves now-protected marine mammals rather than salmon and other fish available, within limits, for fishing. The question presented to us is not how whaling rights can be fairly apportioned between Indians and non-Indians. Rather, the Tribe asserts a treaty right that would give the Tribe the exclusive ability to hunt whales free from the regulatory scheme of the MMPA. Just as treaty fisherman are not permitted to "totally frustrate . . . the rights of the non-Indian citizens of Washington" to fish, the Makah cannot, consistent with the plain terms of the treaty, hunt whales without regard to processes in place and designed to advance conservation values by preserving marine mammals or to engage in whalewatching, scientific study, and other non-consumptive uses. The Supreme Court has recognized that regulation for the purpose of conservation is permissible despite the existence of treaty rights. Washington Commercial Passenger Fishing Vessel Ass'n, 443 U.S. at 682 ("Although nontreaty fishermen might be subjected to any reasonable state fishing regulation serving any legitimate purpose, treaty fishermen are immune from all regulation *save that required for conservation.*") (emphasis added). Mindful of that recognition, we conclude that to the extent there is a "fair share" of marine mammal takes by the Tribe, the proper scope of such a share must be considered in light of the MMPA through its permit or waiver process. The MMPA will properly allow the taking of marine mammals only when it will not diminish the sustainability and optimum level of the resource for all citizens. The procedural safeguards and conservation principles of the MMPA ensure that marine mammals like the gray whale can be sustained as a resource for the benefit of the Tribe and others.

Having concluded that the MMPA is applicable to regulate any whaling proposed by the Tribe because the MMPA's application is necessary to effectuate the conservation purpose of the statute, and because such application is consistent with the language of the Neah Bay Treaty, we conclude that the issuance by NOAA of a gray whale quota to the Tribe, absent compliance with the MMPA, violates federal law. Whether or not the Tribe may have sufficient justification to gain a permit or waiver allowing whaling under the MMPA, we must now set aside NOAA's approval of the

Tribe's whaling quota absent MMPA compliance as "arbitrary, capricious, an abuse of discretion, or otherwise not in accordance with law."

Of course, in holding that the MMPA applies to the Tribe, we need not and do not decide whether the Tribe's whaling rights have been abrogated by the MMPA. We simply hold that the Tribe, to pursue any treaty rights for whaling, must comply with the process prescribed in the MMPA for authorizing a "take" because it is the procedure that ensures the Tribe's whaling will not frustrate the conservation goals of the MMPA.

IV. Conclusion

We hold that the federal defendants did not satisfy NEPA when they issued a finding of no significant impact as a result of an environmental assessment: For the reasons set forth above in section II, it is necessary that the federal actions be reviewed in an environmental impact statement. Also, we hold that both the federal defendants and the Tribe did not satisfy the permit or waiver requirements of the MMPA, and, for the reasons set forth above in section III, they must do so before any taking of a marine mammal.

NOTES AND QUESTIONS

1. When the science is uncertain, does the MMPA require the agency to give the whales the benefit of the doubt?

2. Are tribal whaling rights provided for in the MMPA and ESA? See Emily Brand, The Struggle to Exercise a Treaty Right: An Analysis of the Makah Tribe's Path to Whale, 32 U.C. Davis Environs 287 (2009).

3. Setting on Dolphins to Catch Tunas

The most significant exception to the MMPA's moratorium on the taking of marine mammals is that provided for their incidental taking in the course of commercial fishing operations. 16 U.S.C. § 1371(a)(2). The Secretary may either issue permits under Section 1374 according to regulations promulgated under Section 1373, or may grant "authorizations" under Section 1387 and its implementing regulations. Takes allowed under either route are subject to the following overriding policy standard:

> In any event it shall be the immediate goal that the incidental kill or incidental serious injury of marine mammals permitted in the course of commercial fishing operations be reduced to insignificant levels approaching a zero mortality and serious injury rate; provided that this goal shall be satisfied in the case of the incidental taking of marine mammals in the course of purse seine fishing for yellowfin tuna by a continuation of the application of the best marine mammal safety techniques and equipment that are economically and technologically practicable.

16 U.S.C. § 1371(a)(2)(emphasis added). This language set out what has come to be known as the "Zero Mortality Rate Goal" standard. The proviso to this standard for the purse seine tuna fishery was added in 1981, in the aftermath of the following case.

a.　The U.S. Tuna Fishery in the E. Tropical Pacific

COMMITTEE FOR HUMANE LEGISLATION V. RICHARDSON
United States Court of Appeals, District of Columbia Circuit, 1976
540 F.2d 1141

PER CURIAM.

* * *

A. Purse-Seine Fishing "On Porpoise"

Prior to 1960 the most common method of fishing for yellowfin tuna was use of pole, line, and live bait. In the eastern tropical Pacific yellowfin tuna fishery, fishermen observed in the late 1950's that yellowfin habitually associate with certain species of dolphin (commonly called porpoise), and began setting their nets "on porpoise." When porpoise are spotted at the ocean surface, speedboats are deployed to herd them to where the net will be set. The tuna follow below the porpoise. The porpoise then are encircled with a cup-like purse-seine net, the open bottom of which is then drawn closed in the manner of a drawstring purse, trapping both the porpoise and the tuna beneath.

Although efforts are made to free the trapped porpoise,[4] purse-seine fishing has resulted in substantial incidental deaths of porpoise. Porpoise are air-breathing mammals, and may be suffocated if they become entangled in the net, or drowned as a result of shock or physical injury. The number of incidental porpoise deaths in recent years has been as follows:

---

[4] Speedboats are used to stretch the net in an open position to permit the porpoise to swim out of the net without becoming entangled. 40 C.F.R. § 216.24(d)(2)(vi). As the net is brought aboard the seining vessel, the porpoise tend to congregate at the extreme end of the net, while tuna swim back and forth between the porpoise and the seiner. The seiner then follows a "backdown" procedure whereby it is backed rapidly to cause the corkline of the net to submerge at the end where the porpoise are located. When tuna swim toward this escape route, the vessel slows and the corkline bobs to the surface. The "backdown" procedure allows a substantial number of porpoise to escape unharmed. The net itself is provided with a safety panel, known as a Medina panel, of very fine mesh net along the outer edge of the net. 40 C.F.R. § 216.24(d)(2)(iv). The fine mesh panel is intended to help prevent entanglement of porpoise in the net. Other devices are being studied, such as a "porpoise apron" to prevent entrapment of porpoise during the backdown procedure, improved net gear to prevent delays in a seining operation, and methods of removing porpoise from the net manually. It is estimated that 98% of the netted porpoise are released, primarily through the backdown procedure, and that 2% die.

1971   312,400

1972   304,600

1973   175,000

1974   97,800

1975   130,000 (est.)

The average number of porpoise killed each time purse-seine nets are "set" was 70 in 1971, 43 in 1972, 19 in 1973, 12 in 1974, and 17 in 1975.

The effectiveness of purse-seine fishing has led to dramatic increases in its use by the United States tuna fishing fleet. The catch of yellowfin tuna caught by United States purse-seiners on porpoise was 99,000 tons in 1974, or 60 percent of the total United States yellowfin catch (of 165,000 tons) and about 43 percent of the total United States tuna catch. For the period 1971–1974 purse-seiners fishing on porpoise accounted for 72 percent of the total catch of yellowfin.

B. The Marine Mammal Protection Act of 1972

The Marine Mammal Protection Act of 1972 was addressed in part to the growing problem of porpoise deaths incidental to commercial fishing. The Act was founded on a concern that certain species of marine mammals were in danger of extinction or depletion as a result of man's activities, and a concomitant belief that those species "should not be permitted to diminish below their optimum sustainable population." A moratorium was imposed on taking and importation of all marine mammals, with a two-year exemption from the moratorium for taking of marine mammals incidental to the course of commercial fishing operations. Although the Secretary of Commerce was permitted to license incidental taking of marine mammals subsequent to the two-year exemption, the statute directs that "(i)n any event it shall be the immediate goal that the incidental kill or incidental serious injury of marine mammals permitted in the course of commercial fishing operations be reduced to insignificant levels approaching a zero mortality and serious injury rate."

The permits to be issued after the exemption period expired on October 21, 1974 were authorized under 16 U.S.C. § 1374, which in turn required compliance with regulations issued under Section 1373. Section 1374 requires that the permit specify, inter alia, "the number and kind of animals which are authorized to be taken or imported," and the location, period, and method of the authorized taking. Section 1374(b)(2), (c). The applicant for a permit "must demonstrate to the Secretary that the taking or importation of any marine mammal under such permit will be consistent with the purposes of this chapter and the applicable regulations established under section 1373 of this title." Section 1374(d)(3) (emphasis added).

Section 1373, in turn, authorizes the Secretary to promulgate regulations "on the basis of the best scientific evidence available" for permits for taking marine mammals, "as he deems necessary and appropriate to insure that such taking will not be to the disadvantage of those species and population stocks and will be consistent with the purposes and policies set forth in section 1361 of this title." The Act requires that prior to promulgating any such regulations:

> the Secretary shall publish and make available to the public either before or concurrent with the publication of notice in the Federal Register of his intention to prescribe regulations under this section—
>
> (1) a statement of the estimated existing levels of the species and population stocks of the marine mammal concerned;
>
> (2) a statement of the expected impact of the proposed regulations on the optimum sustainable population of such species or population stock;
>
> (3) a statement describing the evidence before the Secretary upon which he proposes to base such regulations; and
>
> (4) any studies made by or for the Secretary or any recommendations made by or for the Secretary or the Marine Mammal Commission which relate to the establishment of such regulations.

16 U.S.C. § 1373(d).

C. The Regulations

On March 13, 1974 NMFS published notice of its intent to prescribe regulations for taking porpoise incidental to commercial fishing. 39 Fed. Reg. 9685. It took this action despite its professed lack of knowledge as to the actual populations of porpoise, the optimum sustainable populations, or the effect of the takings on the optimum sustainable populations of porpoise.[13] Final regulations were promulgated on September 5, 1974, 39 Fed. Reg. 32117, and the American Tunaboat Association was granted a general permit for the period October 21, 1974 to December 31, 1975 under which fishermen holding certificates of inclusion in the general permit were permitted to take an unlimited number of porpoise.

---

[13] "Estimates of porpoise kills by U.S. fishermen were 214,000 in 1970, 167,000 in 1971, and 228,000 in 1972. The importance of these kills in relation to optimum sustainable population is not known due to lack of knowledge of the sizes of porpoise populations and other population dynamics factors. Population modeling studies underway are scheduled to provide information on population sizes by October, 1974." 39 Fed. Reg. at 9685.

Despite subsequent warnings by the Marine Mammal Commission[17] that the levels of incidental porpoise deaths would remain unacceptably high, NMFS did not impose a quota, although it later amended its regulations to require improved gear and techniques. The number of porpoise killed by commercial fishermen increased from 97,800 in 1974 to about 130,000 in 1975.

The American Tunaboat Association's application for renewal of its permit was granted on December 19, 1975. Although NMFS published population estimates for two species of porpoise, it again stated that it could not make any statement as to the optimum sustainable populations or the effect of the proposed taking, and determined to set no quota as to incidental deaths unless it appeared that the total number of deaths would exceed 70 percent of the final 1975 estimate. Although the Marine Mammal Commission again warned that there was no basis for assurance that porpoise stocks would not be harmed by the taking, NMFS expressed its belief in proposing regulations that existing porpoise populations would neither increase nor decrease as a result of the taking.

* * *

The * * * major issue presented by this appeal is whether NMFS has discretion under the Marine Mammal Protection Act of 1972 to issue permits for incidental taking of marine mammals in the course of commercial fishing when estimates of the optimum sustainable populations of the species involved and of the effect of that taking upon the optimum sustainable populations are not available.

As a preliminary matter, we may state our agreement with the District Court's conclusion that the Act was to be administered for the benefit of the protected species rather than for the benefit of commercial exploitation.[27] That general legislative intent, however, is not dispositive of the instant question. Congress was confronted directly with the conflict between protection of the porpoise and protection of the American tuna fishing industry; one result of that conflict was the express two-year exemption granted commercial fishermen from the moratorium on taking

---

[17] The Marine Mammal Commission, created by 16 U.S.C. § 1401 et seq. (Supp. IV 1974), is an independent three-member commission of individuals knowledgeable in the fields of marine ecology and resource management. Among its duties it is to study and make recommendations to federal officials for protection and conservation of marine mammals. 16 U.S.C. § 1402(a)(4).

[27] Appellants have sought to infer a different interpretation from 16 U.S.C. § 1361(6), which states the belief of Congress that marine mammals should be protected and encouraged "to the greatest extent feasible commensurate with sound policies of resource management * * * To the extent that that phrase may imply a qualification of the legislative purpose, we believe it is sufficient to note that the section goes on to provide that "the primary objective of this management should be to maintain the health and stability of the marine ecosystem. We also note that the explanation of this provision in H.R.Rep.No.92–707, U.S.Code Cong. & Admin.News 1972, p. 4154, stated that it "indicates that the animals must be managed for their benefit and not for the benefit of commercial exploitation.

marine mammals. More significantly for this case, the committee reports contain strong language indicating that the Act was not intended to force tuna fishermen to cease operations * * *

The specific requirements of the Act are indeed so clear as to require little discussion. 16 U.S.C. § 1373(d) requires that the Secretary publish, inter alia, a statement of "the estimated existing levels of the species and population stocks" of the marine mammals to be taken, and a statement of the expected impact of the takings on the optimum sustainable populations of the species. As the House committee report explained, the Act was deliberately designed to permit takings of marine mammals only when it was known that taking would not be to the disadvantage of the species:

> In the teeth of this lack of knowledge of specific causes, and of the certain knowledge that these animals are almost all threatened in some way, it seems elementary common sense to the Committee that legislation should be adopted to require that we act conservatively that no steps should be taken regarding these animals that might prove to be adverse or even irreversible in their effects until more is known. As far as could be done, we have endeavored to build such a conservative bias into the legislation here presented.

H.R.Rep.No.92–707 [Dec. 4, 1971], supra, at 15, U.S.Code Cong. & Admin.News 1972, p. 4148. In promulgating the instant regulations in both 1974 and 1975, NMFS did not fulfill the requirement that it determine the impact of the takings on the optimum sustainable populations of the species of porpoise involved. The statement that "(t)here is no evidence that the porpoise populations would substantially increase or decrease as a result of the regulations and reissuance of the general permit" is not at all responsive; the fact that actual stocks may be stable may supply little or nothing to the determination of effect on optimum sustainable populations. We therefore affirm the judgment of the District Court on this issue.* * *

NOTES

In *Committee for Humane Legislation*, the general permit issued by NMFS to the American Tunaboat Association had allowed the killing of an unlimited number of dolphins in the purse-seine yellowfin tuna fishery because the agency was unable to determine either the stocks' OSPs or the impact of the proposed takes upon these levels. After that decision, NMFS significantly increased the restrictions on the U.S. yellowfin tuna purse-seine fishery to meet the requirements of the Act.

The U.S. yellowfin tuna purse-seine fishery is now regulated by a general permit dating from 1980, extended indefinitely by the Act subject to compliance with a number of operational conditions, including the duty to use the "best marine mammal safety techniques and equipment that are economically and technologically practicable" and to carry official observers. 16 U.S.C. § 1374(h)(2).

The tuna-dolphin conflict continued to generate controversy and litigation as it became the focus of MMPA provisions requiring bans on the importation of tuna products to the U.S. market from foreign-flag purse-seine fisheries that are not as heavily regulated to prevent injury and death of dolphins as the U.S. tuna purse-seine fleet.

b. Embargoes on Foreign Tuna and the Dolphin-Safe Label

The MMPA was not the first federal statute to use trade sanctions as leverage for conservation. The U. S. Congress has a long history of authorizing trade sanctions to enforce international fisheries and wildlife conservation agreements and resolutions, beginning with the Pelly Amendment to the Fishermen's Protection Act of 1967, 22 U.S.C. § 1978(a), and extending to the High Seas Driftnet Fisheries Enforcement Act of 1992, 16 U.S.C. §§ 1826a–1826c. As we saw in Chapter 6, the latter enactment amended the Magnuson–Stevens Act to require sanctions against nations whose vessels or nationals engage in large-scale driftnet fishing in waters beyond the Exclusive Economic Zone of any nation.

Officials in the Executive Branch, however, are often reluctant to impose the sanctions called for in these laws, and environmental groups have sought judicial orders requiring action. In Japan Whaling Association v. American Cetacean Society, 478 U.S. 221 (1978), the U.S. Supreme Court, in a 5–to–4 decision, held that the Pelly Amendment gave the Secretary of Commerce discretion not to impose sanctions against Japan for refusing to comply with whaling quotas set by the International Whaling Commission.

After *Japan Whaling Association*, Congress enacted provisions mandating trade embargoes and other sanctions to support marine mammal and endangered species protection efforts. By far the most controversial trade sanction provisions have been those aimed at "leveling the playing field" for U.S. fisheries subject to incidental take restrictions and other regulations under the MMPA and ESA. Often these fisheries compete in the U.S. market with foreign fisheries not subject to as stringent domestic conservation measures. See R. McLaughlin, Settling Trade-Related Disputes Over the Protection of Marine Living Resources: UNCLOS or the WTO?, 10 Geo. Int'l Envtl L.Rev. 29 (1997). Also, to avoid the increasingly stringent MMPA regulations, many U.S. fishing vessels changed to foreign flags of registry. See Marine Mammal Commission, 1990 Annual Report to Congress 99 (1991). Protection of marine mammals vulnerable to tuna fisheries in the Eastern Tropical Pacific Ocean (ETP) required Congress to tighten the MMPA's application to foreign-caught tuna.

The tuna-dolphin controversy has played a major role in the development of U.S. and international marine resources law and policy, and in its intersection with international trade law. A series of MMPA amendments sought to access the U.S. market as leverage for international dolphin conservation efforts. After an unsettling though non-binding disapproval of these measures by the World Trade Organization's predecessor, Congress shifted away from the embargo approach in favor of a promising new international regime created by the tuna-fishing nations, the International Dolphin Conservation Program. The new regime, however, created regulatory standards that may be at odds with the standards Congress expected to be implemented.

While the MMPA required embargoes of tuna products caught by encircling dolphins, the Executive Branch was never enthusiastic about implementing these provisions. Animal welfare groups, led by the Earth Island Institute, got the U.S. Court of International Trade to order the Secretary of Commerce to implement the embargoes. In a recent appellate brief, Earth Island Institute gives the following concise account of the tuna embargo legislation and its implementation:

> Largely due to enforcement of the MMPA, the number of dolphins killed by the American fleet declined dramatically, from 360,000 in 1972 to about 20,000 per year in 1980. S. Rpt. 104–383. The success of the American fleet in reducing dolphin deaths, however, was offset by increased killing by foreign tuna fleets. Id. The foreign vessels, comprising more than 70% of all the tuna vessels in the ETP, killed nearly four times the number of dolphins than the U.S. fleet, resulting in estimates of more than 100,000 dolphin deaths annually in the 1980s. Id.

> Since dolphins do not heed sovereign borders or territorial waters, Congress passed two additional measures of protection to attempt to ensure the continued survival of dolphin species. These two measures, while both important, should not be confused with one another, as the Applicants intentionally attempt to do in their papers. The first measure involved efforts directly to affect foreign fishing practices by conditioning imports of tuna from foreign countries on their particular fishing practices. This measure provides for embargoes of tuna imports from countries failing to comply with certain fishing standards, and has been the subject of much litigation, both domestically in the Court of International Trade ("CIT") and at the General Agreement of Trade and Tariffs ("GATT"), and its successor the World Trade Organization ("WTO"). E.g., Defenders of Wildlife v. Hogarth, 350 F.3d 1358 (Fed. Cir. 2003).

* * *

In 1984, Congress amended the MMPA to establish specific restrictions on foreign nations seeking to import tuna into the United States. H. Rpt. 105–74 (I)(1997). These amendments allowed importation of tuna harvested with purse seine nets in the ETP only upon a demonstration by the government of the foreign nation that it (1) has in place a "comparable" regulatory program to that of the United States fleet for protecting dolphins from commercial fishing operations; and (2) has an average incidental marine mammal taking rate "comparable" to that of the United States fleet. H. Rpt. 105–74 (I)(1997). Without such documentation, the nation was subject to an automatic embargo on the importation of yellowfin tuna. Id. These amendments also prevented the export of tuna from those nations not meeting the comparability standard through third party to intermediary nations. Id.

The 1984 amendments were not implemented until March of 1988. Id. In August of 1990, the United States imposed an embargo on Mexico and Venezuela for failure to achieve comparability with U.S. tuna harvesting standards. H.R. Rep. No. 105–74(I), at 13; S. Rpt. 104–373; Defenders of Wildlife v. Hogarth, 177 F. Supp.2d at 1339.

On January 25, 1991, Mexico filed a formal complaint challenging the MMPA as a non-tariff trade barrier under the General Agreement on Tariffs and Trade (GATT). S. Rpt. No. 104–373; H.R. Rep. No. 105–74(I). The GATT panel hearing the Mexican complaint found that the U.S. ban on tuna imports was in violation of GATT and concluded that the MMPA embargo provisions were not permissible. S. Rpt. No. 104–373. The panel's decision, however, was ultimately not adopted by the GATT Council, and Mexico did not pursue the decision further in the WTO. Id.

In 1997, Congress enacted another set of amendments to the MMPA, called the International Dolphin Conservation Program Act (the "1997 Amendments"). Brower v. Evans, 257 F.3d at 1061; Defenders of Wildlife, 177 F. Supp.2d at 1340. In part to address the GATT panel decision, the 1997 Amendments set forth "new import criteria for tuna products," which are codified under 16 U.S.C. § 1371 (the "Embargo Statute"). Defenders of Wildlife v. Hogarth, 330 F.3d at 1362.

Under the Embargo Statute, Congress permitted lifting of the tuna embargo if a nation provides documentary evidence that (1) it participates in on "International Dolphin Conservation Program" and is a member of the Inter–American Tropical Tuna Commission

(IATTC); (2) it meets its obligations under the International Dolphin Conservation Program and is a member of the IATTC; and (3) it does not exceed specified dolphin mortality limits (DMLs). 16 U.S.C. § 1371(a)(2)(B); Defenders of Wildlife, 177 F. Supp.2d at 1340, 1367; Defenders of Wildlife v. Hogarth, 330 F.3d at 1362.

Pursuant to Section 1371, the Secretary of Commerce on April 12, 2000 found that the Government of Mexico met the requirements to import yellowfin tuna harvested in the ETP by purse seine vessels into the United States. Notice of this finding was published in the Federal Register on May 8, 2000. Taking and Importing of Marine Mammals, 65 Fed. Reg. 26585 (May 8, 2000). The United States Customs Service was instructed to lift the embargo against Mexican yellowfin tuna and tuna products on April 14, 2000. Defenders of Wildlife, 177 F. Supp.2d at 1367.

In 2000, Defenders of Wildlife filed a suit challenging the affirmative finding by the U.S. Department of Commerce pursuant to the Embargo Statute to lift the U.S. tuna embargo against Mexico. Defenders of Wildlife, 177 F. Supp.2d at 1336, aff'd, 330 F.3d 1358 (Fed. Cir. 2003) * * *

Earth Island Institute, Appellees' Answering Brief (opposing intervention by Mexican and Venezuelan tuna fishing associations in Earth Island Institute v. Evans, 2003 WL 22767923 (Oct. 2003)).

* * *

The Federal Circuit upheld the affirmative finding allowing the U.S. tuna embargo against Mexico to be lifted. See Defenders of Wildlife v. Hogarth, 330 F. 3d 1358; pet. for rehearing en banc denied, 344 F.3d 1335 (Fed. Cir. 2003); cert. denied, 124 S.Ct. 2093 (2004). Has this decision brought closure to the question of whether Mexican tuna fishing activities under the IATTC's International Dolphin Conservation Program are "dolphin-safe"?

In addition to the embargo statute, Congress directed the Secretary of Commerce to determine what tuna products could be labeled as "dolphin-safe." Under the Dolphin Protection Consumer Information Act of 1990, 16 U.S.C. § 1385, tuna was "dolphin safe" only if it was caught without encirclement and capture of dolphins. 16 U.S.C. § 1385(d)(1)(1990). By the mid-1980s, almost all U.S. vessels that fished in the ETP for yellowfin tuna had either transferred their vessel registration and flag to foreign countries or moved their operations to the Western Pacific where tuna can be caught without setting on dolphins. By 2002, the U.S. ETP tuna fleet was down to only three vessels and these did not set on dolphins, leaving the largest purse seine fleets still setting on dolphins to be those of Mexico, Venezuela, and Ecuador.

After the 1995 Panama Declaration, the Commerce and State Departments sought amendments that would allow them to lift the embargoes and to change the dolphin-safe definition, allowing foreign-caught tuna products to enter the U.S. market if they were caught in compliance with the Panama Declaration and new IATTC program. In the International Dolphin Conservation Program Act of 1997 (IDCPA), Congress amended the "dolphin safe" definition to allow the importation of tuna caught with dolphin-encircling purse seines in compliance with the IATTC's protocol on one condition: if, after conducting research on the effects of repeated chasing and encirclement by fishing vessels on dolphin populations, the Secretary, using the best available science, found that such activities did not have significant adverse effects. 16 U.S.C. § 1385(d).

NOAA's Assistant Administrator for Fisheries made an initial finding in 1999 that there was "insufficient evidence that chase and encirclement by the tuna purse seine fishery is having a significant adverse impact" on the depleted dolphin stocks in the ETP. Judge Henderson of the federal district court for the N.D. California set this finding aside as an abuse of discretion and not in accordance with the law, largely due to the failure of the National Marine Fisheries Service to complete the required studies before allowing the dolphin-safe label definition to be changed. Brower v. Evans, 93 F. Supp.2d 1071 (Brower I) (N.D. Cal. 2000). The Ninth Circuit Court of Appeals affirmed, Brower v. Evans (Brower II), 257 F.3d 1058 (9th Cir. 2001), ruling that the Secretary's finding was not based on the best available scientific information as required by the statute and had been influenced by factors not intended by Congress.

EARTH ISLAND INSTITUTE V. EVANS

United States District Court, N.D. California, 2004
2004 WL 1774221, not reported in F. Supp.2d

HENDERSON, DISTRICT JUDGE.

* * *

B. The Best Available Scientific Evidence

All parties agree that the Secretary was required to make the final finding based on the "best available scientific evidence." As *Brower II* emphasized, and Defendants acknowledge, this standard does not require that the scientific data be complete or conclusive. 257 F.3d at 1070–71. Rather, "[s]cientific findings in [the] marine mammal conservation area are often necessarily made from incomplete or imperfect information." Id. at 1070; Defs.' Mot. at 16 (Brower provides that "decisions under the IDCPA must be made using the best available evidence standard, even if that evidence is not entirely conclusive or complete"). Further, this standard is "intended to give 'the benefit of the doubt to the species.' " *Brower II*, 257 F.3d at 1070.

The parties also agree that the "best available scientific evidence" in this case consists of the Final Science Report (including the underlying research), along with the reports of members of the Ecosystems and Indirect Effects expert panels. See *EII*, 256 F. Supp.2d at 1071 (and citations therein); see also Defs.' Mot. at 5.

As noted above, the Secretary adopted an Organized Decision Process or "ODP" which directed the Secretary to focus on four general issues in making his final finding: (1) whether there have been changes to the ETP ecosystem that have affected the ability of depleted dolphin stocks to recover (the Ecosystem Question), (2) current direct mortality levels (the Direct Mortality Question), (3) whether stress or other indirect effects of the fishery are affecting the ability of dolphin stocks to recover (the Indirect Effects Question), and (4) the grow rates of depleted dolphins stocks (the Growth Rate Question). 67 Fed. Reg. 54633, 54641–42 (Aug. 23, 2002).

Defendants characterize the best available scientific evidence relating to these four issues as being mostly inconclusive, with the remaining evidence divided equally between evidence that supports the Secretary's finding and evidence that does not support the finding. See Defs.' Opp'n at 12 (The "scientific record * * * contains evidence supporting a 'significant adverse' impact, evidence supporting a 'no significant adverse impact' finding and mostly equivocal evidence"). This Court concludes, however, that Defendants' effort to portray the record as providing even-handed support for either finding does not withstand scrutiny. Rather, while the record is hampered by the limited data obtained from the [Congressionally-specified stress] studies, a fair reading of the science that is available—and one that does not improperly ignore evidence simply because it is not conclusive—indicates that virtually all of the best available scientific evidence points toward the fishery having a significant adverse impact. In reaching this conclusion, the Court examined the record with respect to each of the four issues identified in the ODP, as set forth below.

* * *

* * * [T]he best available scientific evidence clearly shows that the Northeastern offshore spotted dolphins and the Eastern Spinner dolphins remain severely depleted, and that while reported direct mortality is very low—and not a threat to the dolphins' recovery—the dolphins are still not recovering at expected rates and may never fully recover. Rather, the very low growth rates indicate that the dolphin populations are being significantly adversely impacted by something—i.e. that "some process is acting to suppress population growth."

As to the cause of the suppression, scientists examined two potential explanations: (1) changes to the ecosystem and (2) indirect effects from the fishery. With the respect to the former, the available scientific evidence indicates that while the ecosystem may have changed to some degree it is not the likely explanation for the dolphins' failure to recover. With respect to the latter, scientists identified potential indirect effects of the fishery, including cow-calf separation, delayed stress effects, and under-reporting of mortality. While inconclusive, the best available scientific evidence all suggests that these combined effects can explain the dolphins' failure to recover, particularly given the intensity of the fishery. As such, the Final Science Report concludes that "[t]he final determination of whether or not the purse seine fishery is having a significant adverse impact * * * should be made in consideration of the evidence for adverse fishery effects *beyond reported mortality and the lack of evidence for substantial ecosystem change*." Id. at 5537 (emphasis added). Indeed, it appears clear that, as with the case of the initial finding, virtually all of the best scientific evidence that is available points in favor of finding that the fishery is having a significant adverse impact on the depleted dolphin stocks.

* * *

As noted above, the Secretary, in explaining his final finding, repeatedly focuses on the fact that the evidence concerning indirect effects is inconclusive and that additional data is needed. Thus, while he concedes that "[i]n the aggregate, available data suggest the possibility that purse seining activities result in indirect effects that negatively impact dolphins," he concludes that because the available data is insufficient to draw population-level inferences, and "[a]dditional research is necessary," that the indirect effects are "not impacting dolphins to a degree that would risk or appreciably delay recovery." As discussed above, however, findings in the area of marine science must often be based on incomplete information, and doubts should be resolved in favor of the depleted species. *Brower II,* 257 F.3d at 1070. As such, the Secretary can not rely on "insufficient evidence" to default to a finding of no significant adverse impact-particularly where, as here, the Secretary continued to drag his feet on critical research. Id. at 1066–67, 1070–71. Indeed, the Secretary's heavy reliance on the fact that the indirect effects evidence is not definitive is completely unavailing. Finally, as discussed above, Defendants' efforts to demonstrate that the record contains significant affirmative evidence supporting a finding that the fishery is not having a significant adverse impact is based either on a misreading of the record or improper post-hoc justifications, which in any event do not hold up under scrutiny.

C. Integrity of the Decision-Making Process

In seeking to uphold his initial finding, the Secretary expressly argued that "international concerns and competing policies for protecting dolphins" should be taken into account. *Brower II*, 257 F.3d at 1065–66. As both this Court and the Ninth Circuit have plainly held, however, Defendants were required to make the final finding based solely on the best available scientific data, and without deference to trade politics or competing policy viewpoints. *Brower I*, 93 F. Supp.2d at 1087, 1089–90, aff'd, 257 F.3d at 370; *EII*, 256 F. Supp.2d at 1066, 1069–71. Indeed, the prior decisions in this matter made it patently clear that "international concerns" and "competing policies" regarding the best approach to dolphin conservation had no place in the Secretary's decision-making because such factors had already been weighed by Congress—and resulted in the specific and mandatory requirements of the IDCPA. "Such [policy] decisions are within Congress' bailiwick, and both the Secretary and this court must defer to congressional intent as reflected in the IDCPA." *Brower II*, 257 F.3d at 1066 (emphasis added). Indeed, Defendants agreed at oral argument that the Congressional compromise was to leave the decision to NOAA's scientific expertise.

Despite these explicit warnings and admissions, the record is replete with evidence that the Secretary was influenced by policy concerns unrelated to the best available scientific evidence. In fact, while Defendants maintain that Plaintiffs' claim of political influence is only "mere * * * conjecture," Defs.' Opp'n at 20, this Court has never, in its 24 years, reviewed a record of agency action that contained such a compelling portrait of political meddling. This portrait is chronicled in documents which show that both Mexico and the United States Department of State ("DOS") engaged in a persistent effort to influence both the process and the ultimate finding, and that high ranking-officials in the Department of Commerce were willing to heed these influences notwithstanding the scientific evidence to the contrary. Aiding this process was the fact that the Department of Commerce's own trade policy objectives in this area were consistent with the interests of Mexico and the DOS * * *

Mexico also threatened to withdraw from the IDCP if the dolphin label was not changed, and both the DOS and the Department of Commerce strongly favored keeping this agreement intact.

* * *

During the month of December 2002, on the eve of the final finding, the political pressures intensified * * * On December 3, 2002, Secretary of State Colin L. Powell also personally wrote Secretary Evans that "[t]he Department of State has an ongoing interest in this matter because this finding will profoundly affect our role as the lead USG [United States

Government] representative to the IDCP [International Dolphin Conservation Program].” The Secretary further argued the importance of the IDCP, emphasizing that the DOS, “[w]orking in close cooperation with your staff at NOAA * * * [has] successfully developed the IDCP from its origins in 1992 as an informal arrangement to a binding international agreement * * * ” Finally, Secretary Powell argued that the evidence was not sufficient to find a significant adverse impact and requested that Secretary Evans “carefully consider the sufficiency of the evidence in reaching [his] decision.” * * *

During this same period, the record shows that, within the Department of Commerce, the decision-making process was shifting away from the science and toward the larger policy issues * * * By December 16, 2002, a revised set of Talking Points prepared in anticipation of the final finding had a considerably different approach. Instead of focusing on the science, it emphasized the larger policy considerations:

- We’ve all seen the science. We know that dolphin stocks aren’t recovering.

- Now, let’s take a step back and look at the bigger picture * * *

- We also know that, given the information in-hand, we can’t prove that either the fishery is or is not having a significant adverse impact on the dolphins * * *

- So, we’ve identified what our overarching goals are and would like to take the road that best gets us to these goals.

- Our basic goals are: dolphin recovery, continued international cooperation, getting better compliance with the [IDCP] Agreement, and maintaining a sustainable fishery * * *

- We think we can package either decision to demonstrate that we are conservation minded, pro-active, and are dedicated to recovering dolphins as well as cooperating with our international partners.

On December 31, 2002, the Secretary issued his final finding that the fishery is not having a significant adverse impact on depleted dolphin stocks in the ETP, thus triggering a weakening of the dolphin-safe standard.

To be sure, there is no “smoking gun” document that explicitly admits that the final finding was motivated by larger policy considerations that Congress did not intend the Secretary to consider. The Court would not, however, expect such a document to exist. The plentiful circumstantial evidence, however, readily leads the Court to this conclusion. Indeed, it appears that while the scientists at NMFS undertook their research mission extremely seriously, at the end of the day, the intense pressures to secure larger policy objectives led to a decision driven more by politics than science. Indeed, the record reflects an agency that gave short shrift to the conclusions of its own scientists, dragged its feet on crucial research, and essentially ignored the explicit warning of the appellate court not to invoke "insufficient evidence" as a justification for its finding.

* * *

As this Court has previously held, the Secretary must be held to the Congressional compromise that resulted in the IDCPA. *Brower I,* 93 F. Supp.2d at 1089. Under this compromise, the dolphin-safe standard would not be changed in order to support the IDCP or otherwise promote the international trade policies and objectives sought by the Executive Branch either in 1997 or today. Rather, the compromise required that the fate of the dolphin-safe standard would turn solely on the *scientific* evidence of the impact of the fishery on depleted dolphin stocks * * * Given all of the above, this Court is convinced that the Secretary's decision-making process was infected by the very policy considerations that Congress had directed should not be considered. Accordingly, the Court has no choice but to conclude that the final finding was based on "factors which Congress has not intended [the agency] to consider." *Brower II,* 257 F.3d at 1065; Midwater Trawlers Coop. v. Dep't. of Commerce, 282 F.3d 710, 720 (9th Cir.2002); New York v. Gorsuch, 554 F. Supp. 1060, 1065–66 (S.D.N.Y.1983) (agency can not fail to comply with statutory mandate based on competing concerns).

NOTES AND QUESTIONS

1. Why did Judge Henderson not defer to the Fisheries Service's scientific expertise as is often the case under the arbitrary and capricious standard of review for agency actions?

2. Does the dramatic reduction in the direct kill of dolphins under the international dolphin conservation progam vindicate the Commerce Department's reluctance to impose trade embargoes as a lever for conservation? Or does it support the use of embargoes for conservation?

3. In 2012, Denmark sought a subsistence quota on behalf of Greenland whale hunters at the annual meeting of the International Whaling Commission. When the proposal failed to pass, Denmark issued a subsistence whaling quota to Greenland under its own authority. Does this action "diminish the effectiveness of an international fishery conservation program" under the U.S. Pelly Amendment, 22 U.S.C. § 1978? Can the president negotiate an agreement with Denmark to avoid certifying Denmark and imposing sanctions under the Pelly Amendment? See Japan Whaling Ass'n v. American Cetacean Society, 478 U.S. 221 (1986). Do Canada's quotas for polar bear hunting by Native Canadians violate the Agreement on the Conservation of Polar Bears and trigger certification under the Pelly Amendment?

B. INCIDENTAL TAKES

1.   Sea Turtles and Shrimp Trawling

While still grappling with the incidental take of oceanic dolphins in tuna purse-seine fisheries, the National Marine Fisheries Service had to confront the high levels of mortality in the domestic shrimp trawling fisheries in the Gulf of Mexico and South Atlantic. Several species of sea turtles are listed under the ESA, and NMFS implemented regulations in 1987, requiring special equipment in shrimp nets called turtle excluder devices (TEDs) and limiting towing times, in order to reduce the incidental drowning of sea turtles in the trawls. On behalf of its shrimp fishermen, the State of Louisiana challenged the regulations on grounds they did not reflect the best available scientific information and failed to regulate other major causes of sea turtle mortality, such as development on sea turtle nesting beaches. The regulations were upheld in State of Louisiana, ex rel. Guste v. Verity, 853 F.2d 322 (5th Cir. 1988). Land-based activities that take sea turtles incidentally, including beachfront development, construction of seawalls, and driving on the beach, must obtain incidental take permits under Section 10(a)(1)(B), 15 U.S.C. § 1539(a)(1)(B), of the ESA from the U.S. Fish & Wildlife Service. Permits must be accompanied by a habitat conservation plan. See Loggerhead Turtle v. County Council of Volusia County, 896 F. Supp. 1170 (M.D. Fla. 1995); Loggerhead Turtle v. County Council of Volusia County, 148 F.3d 1231 (11th Cir. 1998); and Loggerhead Turtle v. County Council of Volusia County, 92 F. Supp.2d 1296 (M.D. Fla. 2000) (protracted litigation challenging incidental take permits issued to a Florida county).

In a 1988 bill, Congress delayed implementation of the TEDs rule until the National Academy of Sciences could study all the sources of sea turtle mortality and the contribution that reducing mortality in shrimp fisheries would make to the species' survival. The resulting report endorsed the TEDs rule, concluding that the incidental take of adult and juvenile sea turtles in shrimp fisheries was the leading cause of sea turtle population declines and not habitat destruction of nesting beaches. See Bean and Rowland, supra at 224, note 148, citing National Research Council, Decline of the Sea Turtles: Causes and Prevention (1990).

In 1989, Congress enacted Public Law 101–162, Title VI, Section 609, 103 Stat. 1037 (1989)(codified at 16 U.S.C. § 1537 note), requiring the United States to embargo imported shrimp harvested with commercial fishing technology that may incidentally catch sea turtles. Under the law, a foreign country that has adopted a sea turtle protection program is not subject to the import ban if that program is comparable to the U.S. in its requirement and enforcement of the use of TEDs, or if sea turtles do not occur in the area of that country's shrimp fishery. The U.S. State Department implements the 609 program. To comply with the law, nations that seek to import shrimp into the U.S. must be certified annually. Certification of an exporting nation requires U.S. inspection of that nation's shrimp trawl fleet, although the certification guidelines allow the importation of individual shipments of TED-harvested shrimp from uncertified countries. The latter provision has been upheld by a divided U.S. Court of Appeals for the Federal Circuit. Turtle Island Restoration Network v. Evans, 284 F.3d 1282 (Fed. Cir. 2002), cert. denied, 538 U.S. 960 (2003).

Note that the TEDs rule was issued under the authority of Sections 4(d) (for threatened species of sea turtles) and 11(f) (for endangered species) of the ESA, 16 U.S.C. §§ 1533(d) and 1540(f). The plaintiffs in *Verity* did not challenge the agency's authority to promulgate the rules, only whether there was sufficient evidence to justify them. Should the NMFS make greater use of this regulatory authority to implement the recovery plans for endangered species? Does the agency have a duty to carry out the recommendations of the recovery plans? See generally, F. Cheever, The Road to Recovery: A New Way of Thinking About the Endangered Species Act, 23 Ecol. L.Q. 1 (1996).

NMFS has since expanded the application of the TEDs rule to the summer flounder trawl fishery and required larger openings in the TEDs to reduce the risk to larger sea turtles such as leatherbacks. See 50 C.F.R. § 223.206(d)(2)–(8). In the days following the BP-Deepwater Horizon disaster, before the oil came ashore, shrimp fishermen began fishing intensively, some with the TEDs either not deployed or sewn shut. A large number of dead sea turtles washed up on the shores. Should these turtle deaths be included in the natural resources damages assessed under the Oil Pollution Act of 1990 against the BP-Deepwater Horizon responsible parties? The oil spill provisions of OPA are discussed in Chapter 5.

2.   Marine Mammal Takes in Non–Purse Seine Fisheries

The overall goal of the MMPA from its inception was to reduce marine mammal deaths and injury in all fisheries operations to insignificant levels. The 1972 Act's mechanism for individually permitting incidental takes in commercial fisheries under Section 1374, however, proved unworkable, and not just in the U.S. tuna purse-seine fishery. In 1989, a federal court ruled that the MMPA did not allow the Secretary to issue permits for incidental mortality for fisheries that encountered either depleted stocks or those whose population sizes were unknown. Kokechik Fishermen's Ass'n v. Secretary of Commerce, 839 F.2d 795 (D.C. Cir. 1988), cert. denied, Verity v. Center for Env'l Educ., 488 U.S. 1004 (1989). Because so little information had been collected about the extent of commercial fisheries takes and their impact on mammal populations, this ruling threatened to tie up many economically significant U.S. fisheries.

Congress quickly amended the Act in 1988 to provide a five-year interim exemption to the incidental take provision while the NMFS collected more information on the extent of mortality and injuries in commercial fisheries. During the interim period, a new regulatory regime was developed in consultation with the industry, conservation groups, and the Marine Mammal Commission, which oversees implementation of the Act under 16 U.S.C. § 1402. This regime was added to the Act by the 1994 amendments. See G. Chmael II, K.W. Ainsworth, R. Kramer, The 1994 Amendments to the Marine Mammal Protection Act, 9–SPG Nat. Resources & Env't 18 (1995) and N. Young and S. Iudicello, Blueprint for Whale Conservation: Implementing the 1994 Amendments to the Marine Mammal Protection Act, 3 Ocean & Coastal L.J. 149 (1997).

The new regime requires the Secretary to prepare and revise annually a list of commercial fishing operations that have frequent, occasional, or remote likelihood of incidentally taking marine mammals.

The 1994 amendments also require the Secretary of Commerce to prepare stock assessments on all marine mammal stocks that occur in U.S. waters. 16 U.S.C. § 1386. These assessments must describe the stock's geographic range; estimate its population size, reproduction or "productivity" rates, and rates of mortality due to human activities; and determine its "potential biological removal level" (PBR). The Secretary must also categorize the status of the stock as either "strategic" or as being at a level of human-caused mortality and serious injury that is not likely to cause the stock to be reduced below its optimum sustainable population. Id. at § 1386(a)(5). The assessments and PBR determinations are made through a public process, and the Secretary is assisted by scientific review groups convened from each of the three major marine regions of the U.S.: Alaska, the Pacific, and the Atlantic. Id. at § 1386(b),(d) . Assessments for strategic stocks must be reviewed at least annually; all other stocks, unless significant new information is available, must be reviewed at least once every three years. Id. at § 1386(c).

a.   The *Classification of Fisheries*

As mentioned above, under the MMPA, NMFS must publish at least annually a List of Fisheries that classifies U.S. fisheries based on the level of serious injury and mortality of marine mammals that occurs incidental to each fishery. NMFS has chosen to classify fisheries using a two-tiered, stock specific approach. The first tier addresses the total impact of all fisheries on each marine mammal stock and the second-tier addresses the impact of individual fisheries on each stock. The impact is judged with respect to the rate of incidental takes in number of animals per year relative to a mammal stock's "Potential Biological Removal" (PBR) level, This level is defined in the MMPA and in regulations as the maximum number of animals that may be removed while allowing that mammal stock to reach or maintain its optimum sustainable population. 16 U.S.C. § 1362(20); 50 C.F.R. 229.2.

Does this approach make sense, given the likely paucity of information about incidental take rates and the population dynamics of marine mammal stocks? Does this sound like the Service is setting quotas for the number of animals that can be killed or injured in U.S. commercial fisheries?

In Hui Malama I Kohala v. NMFS, 314 F. Supp.2d 1029 (D. Haw. 2004), environmental groups charged NMFS with violating the MMPA by classifying the Hawaii longline fishery for swordfish and tuna as "category III" in the 2003 List of Fisheries. The Pacific Scientific Review Group had for several years recommended changing the classification to I or II, based on data indicating that between four and nine false killer whales (*Pseudorca crassidens*) per year are caught in the longlines, an annual mortality rate exceeding 50% of the species' potential biological removal level. The court held that the agency had not abused its discretion in taking into account the reliability of the available data that likely led led to an underestimation of the minimum population size. The Ninth Circuit later vacated the court's decision and remanded it for dismissal after the Secretary published the 2004 List of Fisheries which classified the Hawaii longline fishery as Category 1. 156 Fed. Appx. 16 (9th Cir. 2005). In a 2004 Report to Congress, NMFS reported that it did not plan to convene a take reduction team for the Hawaiian longline fishery's take of false killer whales.

Fisheries in either the "frequent" or "occasional" categories must register for incidental take authorizations and must comply with any regulations required to reduce the incidence of such takes to insignificant levels. These regulations also may require that fishing vessels subject to the authorization carry observers. In Balelo v. Baldrige, 724 F.2d 753 (9th Cir. 1984), the tuna purse seiners unsuccessfully challenged the observer requirement of MMPA regulations for U.S. tuna fishing as a violation of their Fourth Amendment protection from unreasonable searches and seizures. Can you make an argument for why an observer on board is not an unreasonable search?

Should the fisheries classification process apply to recreational fisheries? In testimony to the House Resources Committee, an Alaska commercial fisherman argued that the law was unfair in its application solely to commercial fisheries. In 2003, Rep. Young (R–Ak) introduced a bill to reauthorize the MMPA that would amend Section 118 to require the classification of marine recreational fisheries.

b. Take Reduction Planning

The Act requires the Secretary to develop and implement take reduction plans to assist in the recovery or prevent the depletion of each strategic stock which interacts with a commercial fishery on either a frequent or occasional basis, as determined by the Secretary's classification process. 16 U.S.C. § 1387(f)(1). NMFS convenes take reduction teams to develop these plans. The plans are the vehicle by which the Act's goal are to be achieved. Strategic stocks are those that are below their optimum sustainable population (i.e., listed as "depleted"), are listed as endangered or threatened under the Endangered Species Act, or have a direct, human-caused mortality which exceeds the stock's potential biological removal level.

If the affected stock is strategic, the plan's immediate goal must be to reduce, within six months of implementation, the incidental mortality or serious injury rate to levels less than the PBR level established for that stock under the stock assessment process of § 1386. The long-term goal must be to reduce incidental takes to incidental levels approaching a zero mortality and serious injury rate, "taking into account the economics of the fishery, the availability of existing technology, and existing state or regional fishery management plans." This goal must be achieved within five years of implementation of the plan. Id. at § 1387(f)(3). The plans must include recommended regulatory or voluntary measures for reducing death and injury and recommended dates for achieving the plan's objectives. The plans are to be prepared by take reduction teams composed of representatives of the commercial fisheries and conservation communities, scientists, and others, consisting of "to the maximum extent practicable, * * * an equitable balance among representatives of resource user interests and nonuser interests." Id. at § 1387(f)(6)(C). The teams are not subject to the Federal Advisory Committee Act, but their meetings must be publicized and open to the public.

For strategic stocks for which the incidental take rate is estimated to be equal to or greater than the PBR level, the team has six months to develop a draft plan. These plans are to be developed by consensus, but in the event a consensus cannot be reached, the team is to advise the Secretary in writing on the possibilities the team considered and the views of the majority and minority of its members. Id. at § 1387(f)(7). The Secretary is required to take the plan into consideration and publish the plan in the Federal Register for public comment with an indication of changes proposed to it. If the team fails to submit a draft plan within six months, the Secretary must publish a proposed plan and implementing regulations for public comment. If the incidental rates are less than the estimated PBR level, the team has eleven months to prepare the plan. Id. at § 1387(f)(8).

A review of the take reduction planning process is presented in N. Young and S. Iudicello, Blueprint for Whale Conservation: Implementing the 1994 Amendments to the Marine Mammal Protection Act, 3 Ocean & Coastal L.J. 149, 203–216 (1997). Rules governing the implementation of § 1387 are published in 50 C.F.R. Part 229. How successful do you think this approach has been in addressing the problem?

The most controversial take reduction plan is the one developed for the large whales of the Northwest Atlantic that are entangled by fixed fishing gear such as lobster traps and gillnets. Litigation and actions related to the implementation of this plan is described infra in Section 2.C.(2).

c. The Zero Mortality Rate Goal Rule

How far must incidental takes in commercial fisheries be reduced? What did Congress mean when it set the long-term goal as "insignificant levels approaching a zero serious injury and mortality rate"?

A number of conservation and animal welfare groups sued NMFS in 2002 for its failure to promulgate rules to define the zero mortality rate (ZMR) goal, for not convening take reduction teams for certain strategic stocks interacting with category I and II fisheries, and for not reporting to Congress on its progress in meeting the ZMR goal. A settlement in 2003 resulted in the promulgation of a rule defining the insignificance threshold for the long term ZMR goal as equal to or less than 10% of the mammal stocks's PBR level. 69 Fed. Reg. 43338 (July 20, 2004). NMFS also agreed to convene a take reduction team for the pelagic longline fishery in the Atlantic Ocean.

The ZMR goal has been sharply criticized by some commercial fisheries. A bill introduced by Rep. Young of Alaska in 2005 to reauthorize the MMPA would allow the ZMR goal to be met "if fishermen use the best technology that is economically and technologically feasible." H.R. 3839, introduced Sept. 20, 2005. The bill also states that "the fundamental principles of ecosystem management are defeated by giving one species a preeminent position in the ecosystem through imposition of a zero mortality rate goal." Is Congress likely to adopt this provision in the final reauthorization of the MMPA? If it did, how would this language change the overall policy and approach of the Act?

3. Taking Marine Mammals by Harassment

The MMPA authorizes the Fish & Wildlife Service and the NMFS to allow U.S. citizens to take small numbers of marine mammals incidentally in connection with a "specified activity" within a specified geographical region of the ocean if such takes will have no more than a "negligible impact" on the species or stock. 16 U.S.C. § 1371(a)(5)(A). The authorization can be for a five-year period. If the incidental take is by "harassment" authorization can be requested for a one-year period and issued under an expedited process for these relatively short-term activities. 16 U.S.C. § 1371(a)(5)(D). An interim final rule governing the issuance of "incidental harassment authorizations" in Arctic waters is published at 50 C.F.R. Part 216.101–108.

Most letters of authorization and incidental harassment authorizations are issued for acoustic harassment of marine mammals, by such sources as seismic airguns (for scientific research or for exploring for subsea oil and gas deposits), ship and aircraft noise, high energy sonar systems, and explosives. In 1994 amendments, the definition of "harassment" was changed to distinguish between two types of harassment. Level A harassment is an act of pursuit or torment that has the potential for physical injury to a marine mammal. Level B is such an act that has the potential to disrupt behavioral patterns, such as migrating, feeding, and mating. 16 U.S.C. § 1362(18)(A).

By far the most controversial authorizations have been those issued to the U.S. Navy for the testing and deployment of high-intensity active sonar systems designed to detect the new class of "stealth" submarines. First, the Navy funded and undertook an at-sea research program to supply information for its environmental impact statement. Once this was done, NMFS issued rules authorizing the Navy's one-year use of the active sonar program for "training, testing, and routine military operations" in roughly 75% of the world's oceans. The authorization was subject to certain mitigation measures and exclusion zones and was based on a finding that such operations would have a negligible impact on marine mammals. See NMFS, Final Rule, Taking of Marine Mammals Incidental to Navy Operation of SURTASS Low-Frequency Active Sonar, 67 Fed. Reg. 46712 (July 16, 2002).

When environmental groups challenged the authorization, a federal district court issued a preliminary injunction on grounds that it violated the MMPA's small numbers and negligible impact criteria. *Natural Resources Defense Council, Inc. v. Evans (Evans I)*, 232 F. Supp.2d 1003 (N.D. Cal. 2002). The court approved an agreement by the parties to limit the sonar's use to a one million-square mile area of the Western Pacific Ocean where marine mammals were thought to be relatively rare. In 2003, the court ruled on the plaintiffs' motion for a permanent injunction on grounds that the authorization decision violated the National Environmental Policy Act, the Endangered Species Act, and the Marine Mammal Protection Act. The decision in *Evans II* on the several elements of the MMPA claim is presented below. The aftermath of the decision is described in notes following the case.

NATURAL RESOURCES DEFENSE COUNCIL, INC. V. EVANS

United States District Court, N.D. California, 2003
364 F. Supp.2d 1083

LAPORTE, MAGISTRATE JUDGE.

Plaintiffs, various environmental organizations and a concerned individual, seek a permanent injunction against federal officials to prevent the United States Navy's peacetime use of a low frequency sonar system for training, testing and routine operations. This new technology, Surveillance Towed Array Sensor System ("SURTASS") Low Frequency Active Sonar ("LFA"), sends out intense sonar pulses at low frequencies that travel hundreds of miles in order to timely detect increasingly quiet enemy submarines. Plaintiffs charge that the National Marine Fisheries Service ("NMFS") improperly approved use of LFA in as much as 75% of the world's oceans in violation of the Marine Mammal Protection Act ("MMPA"), the Endangered Species Act ("ESA"), and the Administrative Procedure Act ("APA"). Plaintiffs also claim that the Navy participated in the ESA violation and issued an inadequate Environmental Impact Statement ("EIS") in violation of the National Environmental Policy Act ("NEPA") and the APA. Plaintiffs claim that these violations will cause irreparable injury by harassing, injuring and killing marine mammals and other sea creatures with sensitive hearing, many of them rare and endangered, including whales, dolphins, seals, sea turtles and salmon. Defendants counter that they have fully complied with the applicable laws. Defendants argue further that enjoining the peacetime use of LFA sonar would harm national security because training and testing is necessary for military readiness.

* * *

Citizens of the United States who engage in a specified activity other than commercial fishing within a specified geographical region may petition the Secretary to authorize the incidental, but not intentional, taking of small numbers of marine mammals within that region. 16 U.S.C. § 1371(a)(5)(A). Such authorization is limited to a period of not more than five consecutive years. Id. The Secretary "shall allow" the incidental taking if the Secretary finds that "the total of such taking during each five-year (or less) period concerned will have a negligible impact on such species or stock and will not have an unmitigable adverse impact on the availability of such species of stock for taking for subsistence uses * * * " Id. If the Secretary allows the incidental taking, the Secretary also must prescribe regulations setting forth: (i) permissible methods of taking pursuant to such activity, and other means of effecting the least practicable adverse impact on such species or stock and its habitat, paying particular attention to rookeries, mating grounds, and areas of similar significance, and on the availability of such species or stock for subsistence uses; and

(ii) requirements pertaining to the monitoring and reporting of such taking. Id.

Thus, to receive a "small take" authorization, an activity must: (i) be limited to a "specified geographical region," (ii) result in the incidental take of only "small numbers of marine mammals of a species or population stock," and (iii) have no more than a "negligible impact" on species and stocks. In addition, in issuing an authorization, the Secretary must: (iv) provide for the monitoring and reporting of such takings, and (v) prescribe methods and means of effecting the "least practicable adverse impact" on species and stock and their habitat. 16 U.S.C. § 1371(a)(5)(A) * * *

Plaintiffs argue that the Final Rule issued by NMFS violates the MMPA in five ways. First, they contend that the Final Rule is not limited to a specified geographical region. Second, they argue that the Final Rule uses an improper definition of "small numbers." Third, they claim that the Final Rule uses an improper definition of "harassment." Finally, plaintiffs argue that the Final Rule will have more than a negligible impact on marine mammals, and fails to set forth sufficient requirements for monitoring and reporting impacts on marine mammals.

1. Specified Geographical Region

The Final Rule authorizes incidental taking by Level A and Level B harassment of mysticete whales (whales without teeth), odontocete whales (whales with teeth), and pinnipeds (seals, sea lions, fur seals, and walruses) in fifteen different biomes, divided into numerous provinces and subprovinces. 67 Fed. Reg. 46785–76 (50 C.F.R. § 216.180). Plaintiffs argue that the "provinces" identified by NMFS are gargantuan in scale and far too large to meet the MMPA's requirement of a "specific geographical region." 16 U.S.C. § 1371(a)(5)(A). Defendants argue, on the other hand, that there is no requirement in either the statute or the regulations that the specified geographic regions must be small, as long as they are no larger than necessary to accomplish the specified activity.

* * *

The Code of Federal Regulations defines "specified geographical region" as "an area within which a specified activity is conducted and which has similar biogeographic characteristics." 50 C.F.R. § 216.103.

Initially, NMFS' proposed rule divided the world's oceans into sixteen regions. 66 Fed. Reg. 15390 (2001) (proposed 50 C.F.R. § 216.180) * * * NMFS then adopted its current approach of dividing the oceans into fifteen biomes, and fifty-four provinces within those biomes, as designed by Longhurst (1998). 67 Fed. Reg. 46768. NMFS stated that it believed that this approach met the statutory definition because "a biome is the most likely geographic region to contain the majority of a specific marine mammal stock, especially those that are migratory." Id.

* * * "These provinces and biomes effectively delineate the area wherein discrete population units reside thereby allowing NMFS to analyze impacts from SURTASS LFA sonar on a species and/or stock basis." Id. at 46769.

Plaintiffs object that the biomes and provinces identified by NMFS are still far too large * * * Plaintiffs are on stronger ground when they assert that because the Final Rule contains no limitation on how many provinces may be involved in any given deployment of the LFA system, the Final Rule in fact imposes no specific geographical limitation on LFA's deployment at all. NMFS has conceded that "no world-wide authorizations have previously been granted." 66 Fed. Reg. 15378. NMFS acknowledges in the Final Rule that "[t]he total area that would be available for SURTASS LFA sonar to operate includes about 70–75% of the world's oceans." 67 Fed. Reg. 46761. NMFS noted, however, that:

> this in no way equates to affecting 70–75 percent of the world's ocean area. The current authorization is for only two SURTASS LFA sonar vessels—normally one in the Atlantic Ocean/Mediterranean Sea and the other in the Pacific/Indian ocean.

Id. The Navy is "required to notify NMFS annually as to which provinces or subprovinces it intends to operate SURTASS LFA sonar system in the upcoming year, and the extent of the take (by harassment) it expects to encounter during the mission." 67 Fed. Reg. 46769; see also id. at 46788 (50 C.F.R. § 216.187). Thus, according to defendants, in practice the Navy will be limited to operating in certain specified geographical regions each year.

* * *

Given the enormous scope of the SURFASS LFA system, the geographic areas need to be quite large. It is troublesome that NMFS has chosen large areas that undisputedly do not have homogeneous ecological or biogeographical characteristics. Plaintiffs have not established, however, that NMFS failed to consider any alternative biogeographical scheme that existed at the time the Final Rule was adopted * * * Thus, the Court finds that NMFS did not act in an arbitrary and capricious manner in choosing the specified geographical regions identified in the Final Rule, *provided* that NMFS takes the additional step of carving out locations within those regions, during particular seasons, where known high concentrations of marine mammal activities in those areas would otherwise render the effects on marine mammals throughout the region very disparate.

* * *

Plaintiffs have shown, however, that the Final Rule does not preclude the Navy from applying to proceed in all fifty-four provinces in a given year, nor does it preclude the NMFS from authorizing worldwide deployment of LFA. The Navy has not indicated that it intends to operate in all fifty-four provinces simultaneously, and with only two ships, it is not currently capable of doing so. As written, however, the Final Rule does not limit the Navy's operations to a specified geographic region. Thus, plaintiffs have shown that the Final Rule violates the MMPA by failing to limit the take of marine mammals to a "specified geographic region." In order to comply with the MMPA, the Final Rule must authorize the Navy to operate in only a limited number of geographical regions at any given time * * *

* * *

5. Mitigation and Monitoring

When NMFS issues a small take permit, the MMPA requires the Secretary to provide for the monitoring and reporting of the takes, and to prescribe methods and means of effecting the "least practicable adverse impact" on species and stock in their habitat. 16 U.S.C. § 1371(a)(5)(A). The purpose is to assure that the take allowed under the permit is, in fact, small, and also has only a negligible impact on affected species. H. Rpt. No. 228, 97th Cong., 1st Sess. 18–20 (1981).

In requiring the agency to adopt measures to ensure the "least practicable adverse impact" on marine mammals, Congress imposed a stringent standard. Although the agency has some discretion to choose among possible mitigation measures, it cannot exercise that discretion to vitiate this stringent standard.

In the Final Rule, NMFS adopted certain measures to limit harm to marine mammals. First, it adopted a two kilometer (1.2 nautical miles) exclusion zone around the LFA source, within which operations would be shutdown if marine mammals or sea turtles are detected. To detect the animals within this area, NMFS required use of a high frequency active sonar system ("HF/M3"), visual observation from the deck of the source ship, and passive acoustic monitoring. 67 Fed. Reg. 46787. In addition, NMFS excluded as "off limits" coastal areas within twelve nautical miles of the shoreline, as well as a few "Offshore Biologically Important Areas" ("OBIAs") outside the coastal areas, and limited received levels of LFA sonar to 145 dB at known human dive sites. LFA will also not be deployed in the Arctic or the Antarctic, although defendants explained at oral argument that this exclusion was for LFA operational reasons. Plaintiffs argue that these measures are insufficient to achieve the least practicable adverse impact, and that NMFS arbitrarily failed to adopt additional, more stringent measures. NMFS responds that the measures chosen are within its discretion and additional measures are unnecessary or impractical.

* * *

b. Exclusion Zones

Defendants established geographic exclusion zones that prevent LFA sonar from exposing marine mammals to signals at 180 dB or above in: coastal waters within a twelve nautical mile zone from shore (as well as 145 dB within known human dive sites); the Arctic and Antarctic; and three "Offshore Biologically Important Areas (OBIAs)." These OBIAs are the 200 meter isobath of the North American Eastern Coast, year round; the Costa Rico Dome, year round; and the Atlantic Convergence Zone, October through March.

* * *

NMFS has the ability to identify which areas and which seasons to avoid based on its own data. However, NMFS chose not to do so. In response to a proposal by environmental groups, NMFS official Hollingshead commented in an e-mail to the Navy's consultant, Clay Spikes:

> Clay, [f]irst it's Marine-Protected Areas and now they are proposing to establish Special Ocean Sites. If the Navy does not formally raise objections the enviros may succeed in locking up a lot of offshore territory. We will need to ensure that [Special Ocean Sites] and [Marine Protected Areas] do not ipso facto become OBIAs.

(NMFS Vol. 17 at 362.) Another e-mail from the Navy consultant to the NMFS official recapped their prior discussion about the need to divert public attention from the fact that the agencies knew of gray whale migratory paths outside the Olympic national marine sanctuary, but had nonetheless chosen not to mitigate for those paths. (AR 24633) ("It is true that the dates related to gray whale migration, but at some point we discussed the fact that we did not want to emphasis [sic] this fact because we were not 'mitigating' for gray migratory paths outside of the Olympic NMS"). Thus, despite NMFS' and the Navy's awareness of specific areas and seasons that are potentially sensitive, NMFS arbitrarily and capriciously refused to designate more OBIAs. Instead, NMFS delayed doing so and shifted the burden to members of the public to prove that additional exclusion zones are warranted.

* * *

The Court concludes that defendants acted arbitrarily and capriciously in failing to (1) extend the coastal exclusion zone in all areas except for those few coastal areas where close to shore training is necessary,

(2) use aerial surveys or observational vessels for LFA sonar missions operated close to shore, and (3) designate additional off-limit areas or seasons and OBIAs. Thus, plaintiffs' motion for summary judgment is granted and defendants' motion for summary judgment is denied with respect to the adequacy of defendants' mitigation and monitoring under the MMPA.

* * *

[The Court finds NMFS violated NEPA and ESA as well as MMPA.]

VI. Permanent Injunction

The traditional test for a permanent injunction is actual success on the merits, irreparable injury, and in adequacy of legal remedies * * * Here, the certain harassment and possible injury of marine mammals and other sea creatures, many of them endangered, plainly cannot be remedied by money, and is likely to be long lasting. It is undisputed that marine mammals, many of whom depend on sensitive hearing for essential activities like finding food and mates and avoiding predators, and some of whom are endangered species, will at a minimum be harassed by the extremely loud and far traveling LFA sonar. For example, the important reproductive behavior of singing by the endangered humpback whale is affected at levels well below 180 dB, although how significantly it is affected is debated. While defendants argue that harassment cannot be presumed to constitute irreparable injury because it is permissible under the MMPA subject to appropriate conditions, these conditions have not been met, as the Court found above. In enacting the MMPA, Congress clearly expressed its concern about the harm caused by harassment of marine mammals.

* * *

In determining whether to issue an injunction, courts also consider the public interest * * * The Court has balanced the hardships and considered the public interest. On one hand, the interest of the plaintiffs and the public in the survival and flourishing of marine mammals and endangered species, as well as a healthy marine environment, is extremely strong. Indeed, Congress enacted the MMPA and the ESA in recognition of this compelling public interest, not only to the American public but to the international community, and not only to present generations but to future generations to come. For example, Congress found that "marine mammals have proven themselves to be resources of great international significance, esthetic and recreational as well as economic * * * " 16 U.S.C. § 1361. Stewardship of the world's precious oceans and the marine life within them is undoubtedly of utmost importance.

On the other hand, the total ban on use of LFA sonar for training and testing sought by plaintiffs would pose a hardship to the Navy. More broadly, the public has a compelling interest in protecting national security by ensuring military preparedness and the safety of those serving in the military from attacks by hostile submarines * * * Defendants have provided classified information to the Court in camera regarding the reality of the threat. But even if they had not done so, the Court will not second guess the Navy's determination within its expertise that it needs to test and train with LFA sonar in a variety of oceanic conditions.

* * *

Balancing the harms and weighing the public interest, the Court concludes that it should issue a permanent injunction, but that it should not impose the complete ban on peacetime use of LFA sonar that is requested by plaintiffs. Rather, the permanent injunction should be carefully tailored to reduce the risk to marine mammals and endangered species by restricting the sonar's use in areas that are particularly rich in marine life, while still allowing the Navy to use this technology for testing and training in a variety of oceanic conditions * * *

A tailored injunction reconciles the very compelling interests on both sides of this case, by enabling the Navy to continue to train with and test LFA sonar as it needs to do, while taking some additional measures to better protect against harm to marine life. In particular, the permanent injunction will extend the coastal buffer zone beyond twelve nautical miles in the vast majority of the coastal areas where LFA sonar can effectively operate at a greater distance and where training closer to shore is not necessary. Where the Navy does need to train close to shore, it will conduct pre-operation surveys by air or small craft where weather conditions permit. These protections should reduce the likelihood of irreparable injury to the abundant marine life that flourishes in coastal areas, and help protect marine mammals like beaked whales from the risk of stranding. In addition, the injunction should provide that the Navy will not operate LFA sonar in other areas of the deep ocean which have special features that support concentrations of marine mammals and endangered species, such as reasonable candidates for designation as additional Offshore Biologically Important Areas.

NOTES AND QUESTIONS

1. The court ordered the parties to negotiate the terms of the "carefully tailored injunction" but directed the Navy to refrain from operating in those coastal and open ocean areas that have features known to support concentrations of marine mammals, taking into consideration their migratory requirements. See Stephen Dycus, Osama's Submarine: National Security and Envi-

ronmental Protection After 9/11, 30 Wm. & Mary Envtl. L. & Pol'y. Rev. 1, 35 (2005).

2. Despite the Navy's agreement to the settlement, Congress gave the Pentagon a broad exemption from the MMPA late in 2003. As part of the Department of Defense Authorization Act of 2004, Congress added language to the MMPA creating separate "harassment" provisions for the military and for federally-supported scientific research. Pub. L. No. 108–136, 319, 117 Stat. 1392 (2003). The amendments narrowed significantly the definition of harassment for "military readiness activities" to cover only (1) acts that actually injure or have a significant potential to injure, and (2) acts that actually disturb or are likely to disturb by disrupting natural behavioral patterns to the point where they are abandoned or significantly altered. Id., § 319(a) (amending 16 U.S.C. § 1362(18)). The amendments also removed the "small numbers" and specific geographic region limitations from § 1371(a)(5)(D) and require the Secretary to impose restrictions to insure the least practicable adverse impact on the marine mammals only after taking into account personnel safety, practicality, the impact on military readiness, and the views of the Department of Defense. Id., § 319(c). The Secretary of Defense was authorized to exempt any action or category of actions from the MMPA for up to two years if "necessary for the national defense." Id., § 319(b), 117 Stat. at 1434 (adding 16 U.S.C. § 1371(f)).

3. After receiving MMPA authorization to take marine mammals by harassment during its 2006 Rim of the Pacific (RIMPAC) anti-submarine warfare exercises in the waters around Hawaii using mid-frequency active sonar, 71 Fed. Reg. 20986, the Navy received a National Defense Exemption under the new MMPA provision. The plaintiffs in *Evans II* led by NRDC got a temporary restraining order on grounds that the actions would likely cause irreparable harm and the plaintiffs were likely to succeed in proving the Navy violated NEPA in its finding of no significant impact. NRDC v. Winter, CV No. 06–4131 FMC (JCx) (C.D. Cal., July 3, 2006) (temporary restraining order). After negotiations on conditions, the court allowed the exercises to go forward with a 25-mile buffer zone around the new Northwestern Hawaiian Islands National Monument created by President George W. Bush in June, 2006. J. McKinley, Navy Settles Sonar Dispute Over Whales, The New York Times, July 8, 2006.

4. The National Academy of Sciences latest report on acoustic harassment is National Research Council, Marine Mammal Populations and Ocean Noise: Determining When Noise Causes Biologically Significant Effects (2005). A federal advisory committee convened by the Marine Mammal Commission to advise the Federal Government on how to study the effects of sonar on marine mammals failed to reach consensus in its report to Congress in late 2005. R. Dalton, Panel Quits in Row over Sonar Damage, 439 Nature 376 (Jan. 26, 2006).

5. The court in *Evans II* noted that the MMPA does not have a citizens suit provision. Given the limited resources the Fisheries Service has to issue

authorizations for all the potential sources of ocean acoustic harassment and to enforce the harassment prohibition against sources that do not apply for authorization, would a citizen suit provision improve compliance? Should reauthorization of the MMPA add such a provision?

6. Should the Fisheries Service rely on noise sources to apply for authorization for specific activities before developing mitigation regulations or should it adopt programmatic regulations for categories of noise sources? Should it set acoustic habitat quality criteria for waters known to be important to marine mammals? See the recommendations in Sounding the Depths II: The Rising Toll of Sonar, Shipping and Industrial Ocean Noise on Marine Life, a report of the Natural Resources Defense Council (2005), 51–53.

3. CLASSIFYING SPECIES AND HABITAT

The Endangered Species Act of 1973 (ESA), as amended, is the legal basis for most of the protection afforded imperiled marine wildlife species and the ecosystems upon which they depend. Although most of Act's principles and programs have been worked out in the context of terrestrial species and ecosystems, the increasing intensity of marine uses and the decline of many marine wildlife species and ecosystems have given its mandates increasing prominence in marine conservation efforts.

Because many marine wildlife species are also marine mammals, implementation of the ESA and the MMPA may in some instances appear indistinguishable, especially under their similar incidental take provisions. The ESA is a stronger mandate, however, due to its requirement that all federal agencies insure their actions neither jeopardize the survival and recovery of an endangered or threatened species nor adversely modify its critical habitat. The ESA's petition and citizen suit provisions have been used in recent years to extend this mandate to a number of marine species.

A. LISTING MARINE SPECIES AS THREATENED OR ENDANGERED

How does a fish or a species of marine wildlife qualify for such protection? The process for listing a species under the ESA is described in Section 4, 16 U.S.C. § 1533. A species is "endangered" when it is in "danger of extinction throughout all or a significant part of its range," and is "threatened" when it is "likely to become an endangered species within the foreseeable future." 16 U.S.C. §§ 1532(6),(20), 1533(c).

The Secretary is required to determine whether any species is either endangered or threatened because of any of the following factors, and one of which is sufficient to support a listing determination: (a) the present or threatened destruction, modification, or curtailment of its habitat or range; (b) overutilization for commercial, recreational, scientific, or educational purposes; (c) disease or predation; (d) the inadequacy of existing regulatory mechanisms; or (e) other natural or manmade factors affecting its continued existence. 16 U.S.C. § 1533(a)(1).

The ESA divides responsibility for endangered and threatened species between the Secretaries of the Interior and of Commerce. 16 U.S.C. § 1533(a)(2). The Secretaries have delegated their authority under the Act to the Fish and Wildlife Service (FWS) and the National Marine Fisheries Service (NMFS). See 50 C.F.R. § 402.01(b).

For species for which programmatic responsibilities have been vested in the Secretary of Commerce, the Secretary of Interior is to accept the recommendations of the Commerce Secretary with respect to listings. 16 U.S.C. § 1533(a)(2). Listing decisions are to be made "solely on the basis of the best scientific and commercial data available * * * after conducting a review of the status of the species and after taking into account those efforts, if any, being made by any State or foreign nation." 16 U.S.C. § 1533(b).

Once a species or a population segment (of vertebrates) is listed under the ESA, three major provisions of the Act are then triggered:

- Section 9's prohibition against taking the listed species and the civil penalties for doing so are invoked. 16 U.S.C. §§ 1538(a), 1540(a). If the species is listed as "threatened", however, the take prohibitions only become applicable once the Secretary adopts a special rule under Section 4(d), 16 U.S.C. § 1533(d).

- The Secretary assumes the responsibility to develop protective regulations and recovery plans for the conservation and survival of the listed species "us[ing] all methods and procedures which are necessary to bring any [listed] species to the point" where the species would no longer require listing. 16 U.S.C. §§ 1533(d),(f); 1532(3).

- It becomes incumbent upon any federal agency to insure that its actions are not likely "to jeopardize the continued existence of" the listed species or result in the adverse modification of its critical habitat, and to consult with the Secretary and seek her biological opinion to insure no jeopardy. 16 U.S.C. § 1536(a),(b). Citizens can challenge the adequacy of agency performance of these duties under the citizen suit provision. 16 U.S.C. § 1540(g).

The Act requires the Secretary also to designate the critical habitat of a species concurrently with its listing "to the maximum extent prudent and determinable." 16 U.S.C. § 1533(a)(3)(A). Critical habitat designations are also required to be based on the best scientific data available, but the Secretary must also consider the economic impact of the designation, unlike the listing determination, which is to be made without regard to economic or commercial considerations. 16 U.S.C. § 1533(b)(2). The Secretary is allowed to exclude any area from critical habitat upon determining that the benefits of such exclusion outweigh the benefits of specifying the area as critical, unless the area's exclusion will result in the species extinction. Id.

Section 4 allows persons to petition the Secretary under the Administrative Procedure Act, 5 U.S.C. § 553(e), to determine whether the status of a species warrants its listing or to revise a critical habitat designation. 16 U.S.C. § 1533(b)(3)(C), (D).

If the petitioner for listing or designation is dissatisfied with the decision, the petitioner may challenge it under the Administrative Procedure Act, but the petitioner must show that the agency's finding that adequate protection is afforded by the other statutes is "arbitrary, capricious, an abuse of discretion, or otherwise not in accordance with law."

* * *

STATE OF ALASKA V. LUBCHENCO

United States District Court for the District of Columbia, 2011
825 F.Supp.2d 209

R.C. LAMBERTH, CHIEF JUDGE.

The absence of an expected change is sometimes indistinguishable from the presence of an observed one. So when the best available science predicts that a recently enacted ban on subsistence hunting will reverse the abrupt depletion of a species, a decade without any noticeable recovery in the species' population should raise a concern that the true cause of its decline has not been fully addressed. The species in this case—beluga whales in Alaska's Cook Inlet—was nearly wiped out by a catastrophic spree of subsistence whaling between 1994 and 1998. More than a decade later, and despite the passage of a legislative moratorium on subsistence hunting in 1999, the population of Cook Inlet beluga whales has failed to show any appreciable signs of recovery. For this and other reasons, the National Marine Fisheries Service ("Service") granted a petition to list the species as endangered under the Endangered Species Act ("ESA"), 16 U.S.C. § 1531 *et seq.* The Service's decision is rational and is supported by the administrative record, and the defendants are therefore entitled to summary judgment.

I. Background

Thirty years ago, the number of beluga whales in Cook Inlet—a glacial fjord reaching 180 miles from Anchorage to the Gulf of Alaska—likely exceeded 1,300, but now hovers around 350. Although the population dwindled steadily through the 1980s and early 1990s, its decline was accelerated between 1994 and 1998 by Alaska Natives, who depend to some extent on beluga whales for subsistence. Aided by modern technology, Alaska Natives decimated the beluga population in Cook Inlet, harvesting nearly half of the remaining 650 whales in only four years. This unregulated harvest led to what could fairly be described in conservation terms as an emergency.

The Service initially responded by designating the stock of Cook Inlet beluga whales as "depleted" under the Marine Mammal Protection Act ("MMPA"), 16 U.S.C. § 1371 *et seq.,* allowing the agency to regulate subsistence hunting. 65 Fed. Reg. 34590 (May 31, 2000). The Service also considered a petition to list the Cook Inlet beluga under the ESA, which defines an "endangered species" as one that is in "danger of extinction throughout all or a significant portion of its range." 16 U.S.C. § 1532(6). Relying on the assumption that the legislative and regulatory action already taken to control subsistence hunting would allow the population to recover, the Service determined that ESA listing was not warranted at that time. 65 Fed. Reg. 38778 (June 22, 2000). That decision was previously upheld by this Court. Cook Inlet Beluga Whale v. Daley, 156 F.Supp.2d 16, 22 (D.D.C.2001) (Robertson, J.). However, the Service determined that the stock of beluga whales in Cook Inlet is a distinct population segment ("DPS"), making it eligible for future listing under the ESA despite the existence of healthy populations in other parts of the world.[1]

The fundamental assumption on which the Service based its 2000 decision proved too optimistic. Aerial surveys performed annually over Cook Inlet—the state-of-the-art method for estimating abundance of marine mammals—indicated that the population had not shown any appreciable signs of recovery since 1999, when hunting restrictions began. Instead of the 2 to 6 percent annual population growth the Service expected, the abundance estimates for the next several years indicated that the population was still declining at a rate of 4.1 percent. Concerned that the cause of the species' decline was more complicated than the residual effects of subsistence whaling, the Service initiated a status review of the Cook Inlet beluga whale in March 2006.

To determine the probability of extinction, the Service developed a time-series model that extrapolated the negative population trend observed in Cook Inlet over 50, 100, and 300 years. The parameters for this

---

[1] The ESA defines "species" to include "any distinct population segment of any species." 16 U.S.C. § 1532(16); *see* Policy Regarding the Recognition of Distinct Vertebrate Population Segments Under the Endangered Species Act, 61 Fed. Reg. 4722 (Feb. 7, 1996) (describing a DPS as isolated from and an important component of the species to which it belongs). Plaintiffs do not challenge the Service's determination that the Cook Inlet beluga whale is a DPS.

model—which include a "constant mortality effect" for killer whale predation and an "unusual mortality effect" for irregular (but devastating)
events such as mass strandings and oil spills—were subject to extensive
peer review by independent researchers, including representatives from
Alaska's own Department of Fish and Game. The Service also tested the
model's sensitivity to these parameters by varying assumptions about
growth rates, mortality effects, and the optimum sustainable population
size for Cook Inlet (known as the "carrying capacity"). After performing
over ten thousand trial runs, the Service selected a model that best fit the
observed trend in the abundance estimates. The most realistic model resulted in a 1 percent risk of extinction in 50 years, a 26 percent risk of
extinction in 100 years, and a 70 percent risk of extinction in 300 years.
The Service concluded that "[t]aken as a whole, these modeling results
indicate clearly that it is likely that the Cook Inlet beluga population will
continue to decline or go extinct over the next 300 years unless factors
determining its growth and survival are altered in its favor."

Following another petition to designate the stock as endangered, the
Service published a Proposed Rule to list Cook Inlet belugas under the
ESA. 72 Fed. Reg. 19854 (April. 20, 2007). The effect of this publication
was to initiate the public notice and comment process required by the
Administrative Procedure Act ("APA"), 5 U.S.C. § 553(c). The majority of
comments supported listing the Cook Inlet beluga whale as endangered.
However, and of particular importance to this case, the State of Alaska
opposed the listing determination, arguing that nothing had changed
with respect to potential threats to the population since the Service's 2000
determination that listing was not warranted. Alaska also disputed
whether the population was actually trending downward, arguing that
the ban on subsistence hunting had effectively stopped the population
slide, and that growth could not reasonably be expected until the breeding
age component of the population had stabilized.

In April 2008, the Service extended the one-year deadline for a final
listing determination to October 2008, noting "substantial disagreement"
regarding the population trend. 73 Fed. Reg. 21578 (April 22, 2008); see
16 U.S.C. § 1533(b)(6)(B)(i). This six-month extension allowed the Service
to incorporate into its population viability analysis the results of the June
2008 aerial survey of Cook Inlet. When the 2008 abundance estimate was
included in the model, however, the rate of population decline was still
1.45 percent annually—not significantly less than zero, but significantly
less than the expected growth rate of 2 to 6 percent for a healthy population.

Satisfied that listing the species as endangered was now appropriate,
the Service published its Final Rule on October 22, 2008. 73 Fed. Reg.
62919. Alaska then sued for declaratory and injunctive relief under the
APA, 5 U.S.C. § 702 et seq., and the ESA's citizen-suit provision, 16

U.S.C. § 1540(g), seeking to have the Service's listing determination vacated by this Court. The State's six-count complaint alleges that the Service failed to consider the relevant statutory factors and did not conform to the required procedures for making a listing determination. On September 7, 2010, the Court allowed Escopeta Oil Company, LLC to file an intervenor complaint raising substantially identical claims. The Court also allowed Alaska Center for the Environment and several other non-profit corporations to intervene as plaintiffs. The parties then moved for judgment on the administrative record, and the case is now ripe for summary judgment.

* * *

A listing determination is inherently fact-specific and science-dependent, and federal courts are particularly deferential toward agency findings—like those here—that involve "scientific determination[s]," *Baltimore Gas,* 462 U.S. at 103, since those findings are presumed to be the product of agency expertise. In such cases, the court "must look at the decision not as the chemist, biologist or statistician that [it is] qualified neither by training nor experience to be, but as a reviewing court exercising [its] narrowly defined duty of holding agencies to certain minimum standards of rationality." Ethyl Corp. v. EPA, 541 F.2d 1, 36 (D.C.Cir.1976) (en banc).

* * *

A. The Service Rationally Considered the ESA's Listing Factors

The Service's decision to list the Cook Inlet beluga whale as endangered is rational because the small, isolated population has not shown any appreciable signs of recovery since 1999, when hunting restrictions began. Everyone agrees that the already-declining population suffered unsustainable losses from the mid- to late-1990s. *Daley,* 156 F.Supp.2d at 20. Although the Service reasonably expected that the regulation of subsistence whaling would result in immediate population growth, the most recent estimates show unmistakably that the population is not recovering and that there is a meaningful risk that the number of beluga whales in Cook Inlet is actually continuing to decline. As the Service explained, this unexpected development "strongly suggests other factors may now be involved in the lack of recovery," and that "cessation of excessive harvests is not enough to bring about recovery." 73 Fed. Reg. 62922. Because the regulation of subsistence whaling failed to reverse the downward trend in population numbers, the Service acted rationally in looking beyond this factor as the sole cause of the species' decline.

Recall that in identifying species that qualify for protection under the ESA, the Service must consider five statutorily prescribed factors, any

one of which is sufficient to support a listing determination. 16 U.S.C.
§ 1533(a)(1). These factors include:

> (A) the present or threatened destruction, modification, or curtail-
> ment of its habitat or range; (B) overutilization for commercial, rec-
> reational, scientific, or educational purposes; (C) disease or preda-
> tion; (D) the inadequacy of existing regulatory mechanisms; or (E)
> other natural or manmade factors affecting its continued existence.

Id. The Service must list a species as endangered or threatened if "any of
§ 1533(a)(1)'s five factors are sufficiently implicated." *Babbitt,* 215 F.3d at
60. Here, the administrative record demonstrates that the Service
thoughtfully considered each of the § 1533(a)(1) factors and found that all
five factors support a listing determination.

First, the Service found that the "habitat for this species has been
modified by municipal, industrial, and recreational activities in upper
Cook Inlet, where belugas concentrate." 72 Fed. Reg. 19857. The Service
cited examples of significant projects—including port expansions and coal
mining—that threaten to destroy or modify beluga habitat. *Id.* at 19858.
The Service also identified a number of ongoing activities that may impact this habitat, including:

> (1) continued oil and gas exploration, development, and production;
> and (2) industrial activities that discharge or accidentally spill pollu-
> tants (e.g., petroleum, seafood processing waste, ship ballast dis-
> charge, effluent from municipal wastewater treatment systems, and
> runoff from urban, mining, and agricultural areas).

Id. In addition, the Service noted that with the contraction of the species'
range into the upper Cook Inlet, the population was more vulnerable to
losses due to stranding, predation, or disease. Thus, the Service reasonably concluded that the cumulative effects of this development along Cook
Inlet weigh in favor of listing the beluga as endangered because these activities could result in the "present or threatened destruction, modification, or curtailment of its habitat or range." 16 U.S.C. § 1533(a)(1)(A).

Second, the Service found that "[s]ubsistence removals reported during the 1990s are sufficient to account for the declines observed in this
population and must be considered as a factor in the proposed classification of the Cook Inlet beluga whale DPS as endangered." 73 Fed. Reg.
62927. Indeed, the agency found that residual effects from past subsistence hunting were "significant" and were sufficient—by themselves—to
account for much of the decline observed in the Cook Inlet beluga population. 72 Fed. Reg. 19858. As the Service explained:

> While subsistence harvest occurred at unknown levels for dec-
> ades, the observed decline from 1994 through 1998 and the reported
> harvest (including estimates of whales that were struck but lost, and

assumed to have perished) indicated these harvest levels were unsustainable. Annual subsistence take by Alaska Natives during 1995–1998 averaged 77 whales. The harvest was as high as 20 percent of the population in 1996.

73 Fed. Reg. 62927 (citations omitted). The Service also noted that there may be other residual effects on the stock from commercial and sport whaling operations that existed prior to the enactment of the MMPA in 1972. 72 Fed. Reg. 19858. Thus, the Service reasonably concluded that the "overutilization for commercial, recreational, scientific, or educational purposes" also contributed to the Cook Inlet beluga's status as endangered. 16 U.S.C. § 1533(a)(1)(B).

Third, the Service considered whether "disease or predation" might be contributing to the population decline. *Id.* § 1533(a)(1)(C). The Service noted that "killer whales are thought to take at least one Cook Inlet beluga per year." 72 Fed. Reg. 19858. Compared to the enormous impact on the species from subsistence whaling, the mortality effects of killer whale predation are obviously slight. But the Service was particularly concerned that mortality due to killer whales may be underestimated, and that the loss of more than one beluga whale annually could impede recovery. 73 Fed. Reg. 62921. And in any event, the precariously low level of beluga whales predisposed the population to significant consequences from any increase in killer whale predation. Thus, the Service reasonably concluded that this factor too weighed in favor of an endangered designation.

Fourth, the Service found that the "absence of legal authority to control subsistence harvest prior to 1999 is considered a contributing factor" to the Cook Inlet beluga whale's decline. 73 Fed. Reg. 62928. The Service noted that subsequent regulations promulgated pursuant to the MMPA "constitute an effective conservation plan regarding Alaska Native subsistence harvest, but they are not comprehensive in addressing the many other issues now confronting Cook Inlet beluga whales." Thus, the Service acted rationally in finding that the "inadequacy of existing regulatory mechanisms" contributed to the Cook Inlet beluga's status as endangered. 16 U.S.C. § 1533(a)(1)(D).

Fifth, the Service found that the small population of beluga whales in Cook Inlet was vulnerable to "other natural or manmade factors"— including strandings, oil spills, noise from oil and gas exploration, ship strikes, and the effects of pollutants and urban runoff—that could affect its continued existence. *See* 16 U.S.C. § 1533(a)(1)(E). Specifically, the Service found:

> Cook Inlet beluga whales are known to strand along mudflats in upper Cook Inlet, both individually and in number. The cause for this is uncertain, but may have to do with the extreme tidal fluctuations, predator avoidance, or pursuit of prey, among other possible causes.

We have recorded stranding events of more than 200 Cook Inlet beluga whales. Mortality during stranding is not uncommon. We consider stranding to be a major factor establishing this DPS as endangered.

73 Fed. Reg. 62928. Of particular concern was a fundamental ecological
shift: "[t]he contraction of the range of this population northward into the
upper inlet," which "makes it far more vulnerable to catastrophic events
with the potential to kill a significant fraction of the population." In sum,
the Service concluded that each of the five statutory factors supports—to
some extent—a determination that the Cook Inlet beluga whale is currently "in danger of extinction throughout all or a significant portion of its
range," 16 U.S.C. § 1532(6); considered together, these factors present a
strong case for listing under the ESA.

Plaintiffs' principal argument in opposition is that nothing has
changed with respect to potential threats to the population since the Service's 2000 determination that listing was not warranted. Plaintiffs characterize the Service's 2008 decision as an "about face" that was not justified by any change in circumstances. There is some appeal to this argument. After all, if it was rational to conclude that listing was "not warranted" in 2000, *see Daley,* 156 F.Supp.2d at 22, why is the opposite conclusion—that listing is now required—not "arbitrary and capricious"
when nothing has changed in the intervening eight years? But it is precisely the lack of changed circumstances that led the Service to conclude
in 2008 that listing was now appropriate. The key assumption underlying
the agency's 2000 decision—that subsistence whaling was the only factor
responsible for the decline in beluga abundance—has proven false. Instead of the expected 2 to 6 percent annual increase in abundance, the
population has shown no appreciable signs of recovery, and the best
available scientific data indicate a very high probability that the population is continuing to decline (albeit at a statistically insignificant rate).
Under these circumstances, and after nearly a decade during which the
expected recovery failed to materialize, the Service could rationally conclude that the species warranted protection under the ESA.

This Court all but held that listing would be necessary if the Service
ultimately determined that the population was not recovering. As the
Court explained in 2001, "[i]f a moratorium fails to control Native American harvesting in the future, ESA listing will be warranted. That much is
agreed." *Daley,* 156 F.Supp.2d at 20. Indeed, when the Service determined that listing was not warranted in 2000, it recognized that the logic
of its decision was heavily dependent on the assumption that cessation of
the excessive harvest would reverse the decline in the beluga whale's
population. As the agency explained in 2000, "a failure to restrict the subsistence harvest would likely cause CI beluga whales to become in danger
of extinction in the foreseeable future." 65 Fed. Reg. 38783.

To be sure, the record reflects that excessive whaling by Alaska Natives remains the most significant factor in the declining whale population over the past thirty years. But that does not undermine the Service's choice to look beyond this factor after the regulation of subsistence harvest failed to reverse the negative population trend. Although subsistence hunting occurred at unknown levels prior to 1994, there is very little reliable information for the period between 1979 and 1994 to identify a mechanism for the apparent decline of this population from approximately 1,300 to 650 whales. And although listing is not required "simply because the agency is unable to rule out factors that could contribute to a population decline," *Daley,* 156 F.Supp.2d at 22, there is a world of difference between an inability to eliminate certain factors, on one hand, and a determination that a *single* factor no longer explains the observed population trend, on the other. Indeed, the agency affirmatively found that all five statutory factors were implicated to some extent. Under the circumstances, what the agency did here makes sense and therefore passes muster under the "highly deferential" standard of review that applies to this case. *See Costle,* 657 F.2d at 283.

Plaintiffs raise two other objections to the Service's reasoning, both unavailing. First, plaintiffs claim that the Service failed to consider Alaska's own conservation efforts in determining that the Cook Inlet beluga is endangered. Section 4(b)(1)(A) of the ESA provides that the Service shall make such a determination only "after taking into account those efforts, if any, being made by any State or foreign nation . . . to protect the species." 16 U.S.C. § 1533(b)(1)(A). This obligation is separate from—but similar to—the agency's obligation to consider the "inadequacy of existing regulatory measures" under Section 4(a)(1)(D). *See id.* § 1533(a)(1)(D). The Service considers a State's conservation efforts in accordance with its Policy for Evaluating Conservation Efforts When Making Listing Decisions ("PECE"), which requires that current conservation efforts demonstrate some degree of certainty as to their "implementation" and "effectiveness." *See* 68 Fed. Reg. 15100 (Mar. 28, 2003). In other words, it is not enough for the State to identify conservation efforts that *may* be beneficial to a species' preservation; those efforts must actually be in place and have achieved some measure of success in order to count under the Service's policy. *See id.*

Plaintiffs argue that the Service failed to consider Alaska's formal conservation programs designed to improve the habitat and food supply of beluga whales in Cook Inlet. But most of these conservation efforts are not specifically directed toward the protection of beluga whales, and instead address much broader conservation goals having only an incidental impact on the beluga's chances for survival. For example, Alaska argues that its conservation measures directed at maintaining fisheries in Cook Inlet protect a source of food for beluga whales and therefore contribute to the preservation of their habitat. The State also points to its "extensive permitting program to address discharges into the waters of Cook Inlet." But the Service could reasonably conclude that these conservation efforts "lack the certainty of implementation and effectiveness so as to have removed or reduced threats to Cook Inlet belugas." 72 Fed. Reg. 19860.

Likewise, the Service identified a Draft Conservation Plan for the Cook Inlet Stock of Beluga Whales, 70 Fed. Reg. 12853), but noted that many of the Plan's recommendations were unfunded, and it was therefore uncertain whether they would ever be implemented. 72 Fed. Reg. 19860. Ultimately, whatever conservation efforts were already being made by the State or pursuant to the MMPA clearly had not demonstrated a degree of effectiveness sufficient to alleviate concern over the small population size in Cook Inlet, since the population had shown no signs of recovery and was indeed continuing to decline.[4]

Second, plaintiffs claim that the Service could have taken a less drastic step in response to the beluga population's failure to immediately recover. Plaintiffs argue that the Service should have listed the Cook Inlet beluga as a "threatened species," which is defined as one that "is likely to become endangered in the foreseeable future." 16 U.S.C. § 1532(20). But this argument confuses a species that is "likely to become endangered in the foreseeable future" with one that is already "in danger of extinction." *See* 16 U.S.C. § 1532(6). There is no requirement that the Service separately consider a "threatened" designation for a species that *already* qualifies as "endangered" under the ESA. It is enough that the species is presently "in danger of extinction throughout all or a significant portion of its range."

Under the Service's definition of an unacceptably high risk of extinction for large whales, the Cook Inlet beluga easily qualifies as endangered. The Service has previously concluded that a "reasonable, conservative definition" for endangered status for large whales is a probability of extinction greater than or equal to 1 percent in 100 years. 72 Fed. Reg. 19860. The results of the status review for the Cook Inlet beluga whale indicate a 26 percent risk of extinction in 100 years. Thus, the Service acted rationally in designating this species as endangered rather than threatened. Indeed, it would not be appropriate to designate as merely "threatened" a species that is already teetering on the edge of extinction.

---

[4] In its summary judgment briefing, Alaska also cited its Coastal Management Program ("ACMP") as a conservation measure that the Service should have considered in making its listing determination. Alaska Mem. at 10, 35–36. However, on July 1, 2011, the sunset provision of the ACMP was triggered, effectively repealing the program. *See* AK ST §§ 46.39.010–46.40.210; 2005 Alaska Sess. Laws Ch. 31 §§ 18 and 22. Though perhaps not relevant to the Service's obligation to consider conservation efforts in effect at the time it made the challenged listing determination, the subsequent expiration of Alaska's Coastal Management Program certainly does not help plaintiffs' argument that the Service somehow overlooked an important state-sponsored conservation effort.

B. The Service Based Its Decision on the Best Available Scientific Data

Unable to overcome the rationale behind this decision, plaintiffs attack the underlying science on which it rests. The ESA requires the Service to make its listing determinations "solely on the basis of the best scientific and commercial data available." 16 U.S.C. § 1533(b)(1)(A). Here, the administrative record demonstrates that the Service's listing decision is supported by the overwhelming weight of scientific evidence. To appreciate the strength of this evidence requires a crash course in population viability analysis—an exercise involving a "great deal of predictive judgment" that is "entitled to particularly deferential review." Trout Unlimited v. Lohn, 559 F.3d 946, 959 (9th Cir.2009).

The science underlying the Service's listing determination is essentially a two-step process. In the first step, the Service gathered information about the estimated population of beluga whales in Cook Inlet over a period of fourteen years. These population estimates come from aerial surveys conducted each June from 1994 to 2008 using a consistent methodology: when a group of whales was sighted, researchers would circle the group several times to allow multiple counts and the collection of video data. The surveys documented a decline in abundance of nearly 50 percent between 1994 and 1998, from an estimated 653 whales to an estimated 347 whales.[5] When the aerial surveys between 1999 and 2008 are included in the analysis, the results of these abundance estimates indicate that "the trend for the period 1999 to 2008 is a negative 1.45% annually." 73 Fed. Reg. 62919.

In the second step, the Service extrapolated this trend using a time-series model to determine the probability of extinction. This model focuses on the behavior of a declining population at sizes of less than 500 whales and incorporates several parameters specific to the Cook Inlet stock. For example, the model includes a "constant mortality effect" for killer whale predation and an "unusual mortality effect" for events—such as mass strandings and oil spills—that do not occur annually but that have a significant impact on the population's chances for survival, particularly where the population is already small. The model was also "age-structured" to account for the time lag from birth to sexual maturity and the preference of hunters for adult animals. A value of 1,300 belugas was used as the carrying capacity for Cook Inlet, and a control model—known as the "healthy population" model—included a "density-dependent component" which adjusted for an expected population growth rate of be-

[5] Differences in survey methods prior to 1994 rule out a precise statistical assessment of trends using the available population estimate of 1,293 whales from 1979. However, a comparison of the 1,293 estimate in 1979 with 375 belugas in 2008 indicates a 71 percent decline in 29 years.

tween 2 and 6 percent annually while the population remains below its carrying capacity.

The Service performed extensive testing on the model's sensitivity to these variables by running more than ten thousand individual trials for further analysis. Using statistical methods, the Service then compared models with these different effects to the observed population trend from 1994 to 2008 in order to determine which model best matched the existing data. The model was also peer-reviewed by independent scientists, including researchers from Alaska's own Department of Fish and Game. On the basis of this sensitivity analysis, the Service selected a model that most closely fit the observed population trends. The "most realistic" model predicted a 1 percent risk of extinction in 50 years, a 26 percent risk of extinction in 100 years, and a 70 percent risk of extinction in 300 years. But even under the "base case scenario" or "healthy population" model, there was 29 percent risk of extinction in 300 years. As a measure of confidence in this negative trend, the model estimated that there is only a 5 percent probability that the population growth rate is above 2 percent, while there is at least a 62 percent probability that the population will decline further.

There is no "better" way to assess a species' likelihood of extinction. Plaintiffs do not suggest a more accurate method for estimating the abundance of marine mammals, nor do they point to a superior method of projecting the observed population trend into the future. "If no one propose [s] anything better, then what is available is the best." Massachusetts ex rel. Div. of Marine Fisheries v. Daley, 170 F.3d 23, 30 (1st Cir.1999).

Nevertheless, Alaska criticizes several of the assumptions underlying these models, arguing that the models are very sensitive to the inputs the Service used. Renewing an objection raised during the public notice and comment period, Alaska first claims that the population has in fact stabilized since 1999, when hunting restrictions began, pointing to the Service's conclusion that the trend of negative 1.45% "is not significantly different from zero." 73 Fed. Reg. 62919. But regardless of whether the trend is static or ever-so-slightly negative, the Service emphasized that it is "significantly less than the expected growth for an un-harvested population (2–4 percent)." *Id.* This matters because the population is already less than one-third of the Cook Inlet carrying capacity for beluga whales, and a healthy population so far below carrying capacity would be expected to immediately begin growing. Stated differently, plaintiffs confuse the expected behavior of a population that is already functioning at carrying capacity, on one hand, with that of a smaller population that is no longer being actively depleted but is still below carrying capacity, on the other. The former would not be expected to show consistent annual growth, while a failure of the latter to immediately begin growing would raise a concern about the population's health.

Alaska protests that the Service should not have expected population growth until five to seven years after the cessation of subsistence harvest because the population's breeding age component—those adults capable of reproduction—would require several years to stabilize after the cessation of subsistence harvest. Yet the record indicates that this "lag time" was already baked into the Service's model via its assumption of an "age-structured" population. As the Service explained in responding to comments on the Proposed Rule:

> [E]ven if the age structure was significantly reduced through selective harvests ending in 1998, the recruitment into the adult population would have been expected to occur continuously, beginning the following year and continuing to the present. This would have resulted in a gradual increase in abundance figures and, by now, the "signal" from such selective removals would have grown through the population. The population model used to estimate the risk of extinction accounted for the reduction in the adult population during unrestricted harvest and the lag time of 9 or more years between birth and age of first reproduction.

73 Fed. Reg. 62926. Indeed, Alaska's own peer reviewer, who examined the Service's proposed rule, agreed that the expected 2 to 6 percent growth rate was reasonable:

> Even with a disruption of the age structure of the population due to over harvest of adults, there were still at least 150 adults that would be capable of breeding in 1999. If 75 are female and one third give birth each year, a minimum of 25 calves per year could be produced since 1999 (200 calves in 8 years).

Overall, the peer reviewers agreed that the assessment represented the best available science and that the conclusions were supported by the scientific findings presented in the status review. Thus, the Service's expectation that the population would immediately begin growing following the regulation of subsistence whaling is grounded in the best available scientific data.

Alaska also argues that Service did not justify its reliance on extinction risk at the 100- and 300-year ranges. But a shorter time horizon would be nonsensical given the longevity of the average beluga whale. Belugas typically live to be older than 60 years, with some living to be older than 70 years. Statistically, it is very unlikely that even a small population of animals that live 60–70 years in age will decline to zero within 50 years. Such a scenario would require the unrealistic assumption that the reproduction rate would be zero for 50 years. Thus, the long-lived nature of this species makes it appropriate to consider projections with longer time horizons.

Alaska also argues that the "most reasonable" population model was arbitrarily chosen from among the thousands of trial runs produced by the Service's population viability analysis. But this argument misapprehends the purpose of testing the model through sensitivity analysis. The Service relied on a comparison of all of these trial runs—not merely the results of a single model—in determining that the population is declining. As the Service explained, "[w]hile several of the sensitivity trials showed some improvement in extinction risk, only the assumption of a growth rate greater than 2%, the least likely model, removed the risk of decline and extinction." Alaska presses the point that the Service gave no explanation for relying on one model—the "most realistic" one—out of the thirty-one possible models that could result from mixing and matching the independent variables. But twenty-three of those model runs were based on unrealistic parameters and were run only for sensitivity analysis or to test the model's assumptions.

Finally, plaintiffs claim that the Service never justified its use of 1,300 as the value for carrying capacity in Cook Inlet. But the Service stated a rational basis for using this value: it represents the best estimate of the population in 1979. The Service explaining that "the 1979 estimate was based on a valid survey protocol that is documented and repeatable," and is "the best available estimate" for the population prior to the commencement of comprehensive aerial surveys in 1994. 73 Fed. Reg. 62924. If anything, the 1979 estimate may understate the carrying capacity for Cook Inlet, since subsistence whaling occurred at unknown levels prior to 1994 and there is very limited empirical data regarding the rate of harvest before this date. It is entirely possible that the number of beluga whales in Cook Inlet once numbered in the thousands. Under the circumstances, the Service's use of 1,300 for carrying capacity is totally reasonable and is probably a very conservative estimate of this value.

The most important thing to remember is that even if plaintiffs can poke some holes in the agency's models, that does not necessarily preclude a conclusion that these models are the best available science. Some degree of predictive error is inherent in the nature of mathematical modeling. The standard under the ESA is that "the Service must utilize the 'best scientific . . . data *available*,' not the best scientific data *possible*." Building Indus. Ass'n of Superior Cal. v. Norton, 247 F.3d 1241, 1246 (D.C.Cir.2001) (emphasis in original). In this case, plaintiffs do not point to any *superior* data that the Service should have considered. *See* id. at 1246–47. And the State's own peer reviewer concluded that although the model assumptions "could have been more detailed" or "better discussed," "the assumptions made considering what is known about beluga biology and life history were reasonable." Thus, it ultimately makes no difference that plaintiffs can point to a few shortcomings here and there in the Service's modeling. The agency's population viability analysis represents the best available science and is therefore entitled to deference.

NOTES AND QUESTIONS

1. In 2001, the same court upheld the agency's determination that listing was not warranted. Cook Inlet Beluga Whale v. Daley, 156 F.Supp.2d 16 (D.D.C. 2001). For a discussion of the case, see Sara Edmonds, Comment: A Whale's Tale: Efforts to Save the Cook Inlet Alaska Beluga Whale, 7 Ocean & Coastal L.J. 131 (1994). Why was the second petition attempt successful? Was the agency's analysis of Section 4's five factors more persuasive because of new scientific evidence? Was the law interpreted differently the second time around?

2. Are the Native Alaskans being unfairly blamed for endangering the survival of the Cook Inlet beluga whale? Who was responsible for the "catastrophic spree of subsistence whaling"? What was the status before the 1999 restrictions on subsistence hunting? Why wasn't the population classified as "depleted" before that time, i.e., as below the OSP? What other factors may have contributed to the population's decline? Was the population in 1980 (1,300) the optimum sustainable population?

3. Oil and gas drilling has been conducted in Cook Inlet for decades. In 1975, the U.S. and Alaska litigated the ownership of Cook Inlet under the Submerged Lands Act of 1953. The State of Alaska unsuccessfully claimed it was an historic bay with a baseline across the mouth of the inlet. U.S. v. Alaska, 422 U.S. 184 (1975).

4. In 2005, the Fish & Wildlife Service listed the southwest Alaska distinct population segment (DPS) of the northern sea otter (*Enhydra lutris kenyoni*) as threatened, in light of its overall population decline of 55–67% and of more than 90% in some areas of SW Alaska. 70 Fed. Reg. 46366 (Aug. 9, 2005). At the same time, the Service proposed a special Section 4(d) rule regarding Native Alaskan takes for native handicrafts to align the conditions with those established under the MMPA. 16 U.S.C. 1371(b)(2). See Didrickson v. Dept. of Interior, 982 F.2d 1332 (9th Cir. 1992) (invalidating federal regulations restricting definition of "authentic native articles of handicrafts and clothing" to the type of articles commonly produced prior to Dec. 21, 1972). Under the FWS's regulations, the take prohibition of Section 9 is extended to all threatened species but authorizes the Service to adopt a special take rule tailored for a particular threatened species. 50 C.F.R. § 17.31(a). As noted elsewhere, NMFS determines on a case-by-case basis whether to extend the take prohibition of Section 9 to protect a threatened species.

5. In 2006, the National Marine Fisheries Service published the final listing of two species of reef-building corals as "threatened," the elkhorn (*Acropora palmata*) and staghorn (*A. cervicornis*) corals. 71 Fed. Reg. 26852 (May 9, 2006). At the same time, the Service declined to list a third species,

the fused-staghorn coral (*A. prolifera*), finding that it was a hybrid of the other two Acroporids and therefore did not meet the definition of a species. After receiving a petition to list an additional 82 species of coral as endangered, due to ocean warming and other factors, on Dec. 7, 2012, the Service published a determination that 12 of the petitioned coral species warrant listing as endangered (five Caribbean and seven Indo-Pacific), 54 coral species warrant listing as threatened (two Caribbean and 52 Indo-Pacific), and 16 coral species (all Indo-Pacific) do not warrant listing as threatened or endangered under the ESA. In addition, the Service determined, based on the best scientific and commercial information available and efforts undertaken to protect the species, that the two Caribbean coral species listed as threatened in 2006 warrant reclassification from threatened to endangered. 77 Fed. Reg. 73220 (Dec. 7, 2012).

6. Another species affected by rising sea temperatures due to global warming is the polar bear (*Ursus maritimus*). The Center for Biological Diversity petitioned the Fish & Wildlife Service (FWS) to list this marine mammal as threatened in 2005 largely due to threats to the bear's Arctic habitat from global warming and the loss of sea ice. The Service published a 90-day finding that the petition presented substantial scientific information indicating that the listing may be warranted, 71 Fed. Reg. 6745 (Feb. 9, 2006), and then reopened the public comment period on the status review, 71 Fed. Reg. 28653 (May 17, 2006). During the reopened public comment period, the Service received more than 200,000 letters from scientists, members of the public, and members of Congress, urging the agency to list the bear as threatened. After the FWS listed the polar bear as "threatened, the following litigation ensued.

IN RE POLAR BEAR ENDANGERED SPECIES ACT LISTING AND SECTION 4(d) RULE

United States Court of Appeals, District of Columbia
709 F.3d 1 (2013)

EDWARDS, Senior Circuit Judge:

***

B. The Listing Rule

On February 16, 2005, the Center for Biological Diversity petitioned the Secretary of the Interior to list the polar bear as threatened under the ESA because of the effects of global climate change on polar bear habitat. In re Polar Bear, 794 F.Supp.2d at 72. On December 21, 2006, following peer review and multiple opportunities for public comment, FWS completed a 262–page Status Review. See generally SCOTT SCHLIEBE ET AL., RANGE–WIDE STATUS REVIEW OF THE POLAR BEAR (URSUS MARITIMIS) (Dec. 21, 2006). (The Status Review is posted on FWS's website at http://www.fws.gov/.) Shortly thereafter, on January 9, 2007, FWS published a proposed rule to list the species as threatened; this ac-

tion triggered a 90–day public comment period. See generally 12–Month
Petition Finding and Proposed Rule to List the Polar Bear (Ursus maritimus) as Threatened Throughout Its Range, 72 Fed. Reg. 1064 (Jan. 9,
2007).

During the course of the rulemaking process, FWS sought the assistance of the U.S. Geological Survey ("USGS") in "collecting and analyzing
scientific data and developing models and interpretations that would enhance the base of scientific data for [FWS's] use in developing the final
decision." Listing Rule, 73 Fed. Reg. at 28,235. USGS produced "nine scientific reports that analyze and integrate a series of studies on polar bear
population dynamics, range-wide habitat use, and changing sea ice conditions in the Arctic." Id. These reports were also subject to public comment.

FWS published the final Listing Rule on May 15, 2008. The Listing
Rule concludes that "the polar bear is likely to become an endangered
species within the foreseeable future throughout all of its range" and
should therefore be listed as threatened. Id. at 28,212.

The Listing Rule explains in detail the taxonomy, evolution, and
population of the species. Some of the principal findings are as follows:

> Polar bears evolved in sea ice habitats and as a result are evolution-
> arily adapted to this habitat.
>
> * * * *
>
> Over most of their range, polar bears remain on the sea ice year-
> round or spend only short periods on land. However, some polar bear
> populations occur in seasonally ice-free environs and use land habi-
> tats for varying portions of the year.
>
> * * * *
>
> Although polar bears are generally limited to areas where the sea is
> ice-covered for much of the year, they are not evenly distributed
> throughout their range on sea ice. They show a preference for certain
> sea ice characteristics, concentrations, and specific sea ice features.
> Sea-ice habitat quality varies temporally as well as geographically.
> Polar bears show a preference for sea ice located over and near the
> continental shelf, likely due to higher biological productivity in these
> areas and greater accessibility to prey in near-shore shear zones and
> polynyas (areas of open sea surrounded by ice) compared to deep-
> water regions in the central polar basin. Bears are most abundant
> near the shore in shallow-water areas, and also in other areas where
> currents and ocean upwelling increase marine productivity and serve
> to keep the ice cover from becoming too consolidated in winter.
>
> * * * *

Polar bears are distributed throughout the ice-covered waters of the circumpolar Arctic, and rely on sea ice as their primary habitat. Polar bears depend on sea ice for a number of purposes, including as a platform from which to hunt and feed upon seals; as habitat on which to seek mates and breed; as a platform to move to terrestrial maternity denning areas, and sometimes for maternity denning; and as a substrate on which to make long-distance movements.

* * * *

The total number of polar bears worldwide is estimated to be 20,000–25,000. Polar bears are not evenly distributed throughout the Arctic, nor do they comprise a single nomadic cosmopolitan population, but rather occur in 19 relatively discrete populations. The use of the term "relatively discrete population" in this context is not intended to equate to the Act's term "distinct population segments." Boundaries of the 19 polar bear populations have evolved over time and are based on intensive study of movement patterns, tag returns from harvested animals, and, to a lesser degree, genetic analysis. The scientific studies regarding population bounds began in the early 1970s and continue today. [The Listing Rule adopts] the use of the term "population" to describe polar bear management units consistent with their designation by the World Conservation Union–International Union for Conservation of Nature and Natural Resources (IUCN), Species Survival Commission (SSC) Polar Bear Specialist Group (PBSG) with information available as of October 2006, and to describe a combination of two or more of these populations into "ecoregions." ... Although movements of individual polar bears overlap extensively, telemetry studies demonstrate spatial segregation among groups or stocks of polar bears in different regions of their circumpolar range. These patterns, along with information obtained from survey and reconnaissance, marking and tagging studies, and traditional knowledge, have resulted in recognition of 19 relatively discrete polar bear populations. Genetic analysis reinforces the boundaries between some designated populations while confirming the existence of overlap and mixing among others.

Id. at 28,212–15 (citations omitted).

The Listing Rule also explains that studies of the nineteen polar bear populations have divided the species into four "physiographically different functional groups or 'ecoregions' in order to forecast future polar bear population status on the basis of current knowledge of polar bear populations, their relationships to sea ice habitat, and predicted changes in sea ice and other environmental variables." Id. at 28,217. The Listing Rule then discusses the Archipelago, Seasonal Ice, Divergent, and Convergent ecoregions in some depth. Id. at 28,217–19.

FWS cited three principal considerations in determining that polar bears should be listed as a threatened species. First, the polar bear depends on sea ice for its survival. Id. at 28,214. Second, sea ice is declining. On this point, the Listing Rule states:

 Polar bears evolved to utilize the Arctic sea ice niche and are distributed throughout most ice-covered seas of the Northern Hemisphere. We find, based upon the best available scientific and commercial information, that polar bear habitat—principally sea ice—is declining throughout the species' range, that this decline is expected to continue for the foreseeable future, and that this loss threatens the species throughout all of its range. Therefore, we find that the polar bear is likely to become an endangered species within the foreseeable future throughout all of its range.

Id. at 28,212. Third, climatic changes have and will continue to reduce the extent and quality of Arctic sea ice. See id. at 28,244.

FWS concluded that these findings satisfied two of the statutory listing factors: (A) the threatened destruction of the species' habitat or range, id. at 28,275–77, and (D) the inadequacy of existing regulatory mechanisms to preserve the species, id. at 28,288.

In aggregating data on climate change and sea ice, FWS relied on a variety of published studies and reports, including those of the Intergovernmental Panel on Climate Change ("IPCC"). See id. at 28,212. FWS explained that

[t]he rapid retreat of sea ice in the summer and overall diminishing sea ice throughout the year in the Arctic is unequivocal and extensively documented in scientific literature. Further extensive recession of sea ice is projected by the majority of state-of-the-art climate models, with a seasonally ice-free Arctic projected by the middle of the 21 st century by many of those models.

Id. at 28,292. Noting that sea ice had reached a record low in the summer of 2007, FWS also explained that "[t]he observational record indicates that current summer sea ice losses appear to be about 30 years ahead of the ensemble of modeled values, which suggests that a transition towards a seasonally ice-free Arctic might occur sooner than the models indicate." Id. at 28,234.

The agency's assessment of the species' dependence on sea ice derives from peer reviewed studies on polar bear biology and behavior, observed polar bear demographics, and population modeling. As noted above, FWS explained that the bears are highly dependent on sea ice, "including as a platform from which to hunt and feed upon seals; as habitat on which to seek mates and breed; as a platform to move to terrestrial maternity denning areas, and sometimes for maternity denning; and as a substrate on which to make long-distance movements." Id. at 28,214. The Listing Rule anticipates that changes to the polar bear's habitat will soon pose an existential threat to the species:

> Productivity, abundance, and availability of ice seals, the polar bear's primary prey base, would be diminished by the projected loss of sea ice, and energetic requirements of polar bears for movement and obtaining food would increase. Access to traditional denning areas would be affected. In turn, these factors would cause declines in the condition of polar bears from nutritional stress and reduced productivity. As already evidenced in the Western Hudson Bay and Southern Beaufort Sea populations, polar bears would experience reductions in survival and recruitment rates. The eventual effect is that polar bear populations would decline. The rate and magnitude of decline would vary among populations, based on differences in the rate, timing, and magnitude of impacts. However, within the foreseeable future, all populations would be affected, and the species is likely to become in danger of extinction throughout all of its range due to declining sea ice habitat.

Id. at 28,292–93.

C. The District Court's Decision

Soon after publication of the Listing Rule, nearly a dozen challenges were filed to contest FWS's action. See In re Polar Bear, 794 F.Supp.2d at 77–78. Several plaintiffs argued that the listing was unwarranted because the agency failed to establish a foreseeable risk of extinction. Others argued the opposite—that the species should have been listed as endangered because it faced an imminent risk of extinction. These actions were consolidated before the District Court as a Multidistrict Litigation case.

The litigants filed cross-motions for summary judgment. On October 20, 2010, the District Court held an initial hearing on the parties' cross-motions for summary judgment.

At that hearing, the [District] Court focused only on a threshold question: whether it must review the agency's interpretation of the ESA listing classifications under step one or step two of the familiar framework set forth in Chevron, U.S.A., Inc. v. Natural Resources Defense Council, Inc., 467 U.S. 837 (1984). In a Memorandum Opinion issued on November 4, 2010, the [District] Court held that FWS had improperly relied on an erroneous plain-meaning reading of the definition of an endangered species that could not be upheld under step one of Chevron. In re Polar Bear Endangered Species Act Listing and § 4(d) Rule Litigation, 748 F.Supp.2d 19, 29 (D.D.C.2010). Finding that the term "endangered species" under the ESA is instead ambiguous, the Court remanded the

Listing Rule to the agency "to treat the statutory language as ambiguous." Id.

In response to the [District] Court's remand order, on December 22, 2010, the federal defendants submitted the agency's memorandum of supplemental explanation. In their Supplemental Explanation, FWS concluded that, even treating the phrase "in danger of extinction" in the definition of an endangered species as ambiguous, the administrative record does not support a finding that the polar bear qualified for endangered status at the time of listing. Because the agency determined that the species is likely to become endangered within the foreseeable future, however, FWS reiterated that the polar bear met ESA's ... definition of a threatened species at the time of listing.

In re Polar Bear, 794 F.Supp.2d at 79 (citations omitted)

The District Court held another hearing on February 23, 2011, after which it granted summary judgment in favor of FWS. The District Court rejected all of the challenges to the Listing Rule. See generally id. After a lengthy review of Appellants' arguments, the District Court concluded that it was "simply not persuaded that [FWS's] decision to list the polar bear as a threatened species under the ESA was arbitrary and capricious." Id. at 81. Appellants challenge this decision and several conservation groups have intervened on behalf of FWS.

II. Analysis

Appellants' principal claim on appeal is that FWS misapplied the statutory criteria for a listing decision by ignoring or misinterpreting the record before it and failing to articulate the grounds for its decision. In particular, Appellants contend that: (1) FWS failed to adequately explain each step in its decisionmaking process, particularly in linking habitat loss to a risk of future extinction; (2) FWS erred by issuing a single, range-wide determination; (3) FWS relied on defective population models; (4) FWS misapplied the term "likely" when it determined that the species was likely to become endangered; (5) FWS erred in selecting a period of 45 years as the "foreseeable future"; (6) FWS failed to "take into account" Canada's polar bear conservation efforts; and (7) FWS violated Section 4(i) of the ESA by failing to give an adequate response to the comments submitted by the State of Alaska regarding the listing decision. For the reasons discussed below, we find these arguments meritless.

***

B. The Agency's Decision

The Listing Rule rests on a three-part thesis: the polar bear is dependent upon sea ice for its survival; sea ice is declining; and climatic changes have and will continue to dramatically reduce the extent and quality of Arctic sea ice to a degree sufficiently grave to jeopardize polar bear populations. See Listing Rule, 73 Fed. Reg. at 28,212. No part of this thesis is disputed and we find that FWS's conclusion—that the polar bear is threatened within the meaning of the ESA—is reasonable and adequately supported by the record.

The Listing Rule is the product of FWS's careful and comprehensive study and analysis. Its scientific conclusions are amply supported by data and well within the mainstream on climate science and polar bear biology. Thirteen of the fourteen peer reviewers to whom FWS submitted the proposed rule found that it generally "represented a thorough, clear, and balanced review of the best scientific information available from both published and unpublished sources of the current status of polar bears" and that it "justified the conclusion that polar bears face threats throughout their range." Listing Rule, 73 Fed. Reg. at 28,235. Only one peer reviewer dissented, "express[ing] concern that the proposed rule was flawed, biased, and incomplete, that it would do nothing to address the underlying issues associated with global warming, and that a listing would be detrimental to the Inuit of the Arctic." Id.

As we discuss below, several of Appellants' challenges rely on portions of the record taken out of context and blatantly ignore FWS's published explanations. Others, as the District Court correctly explained, "amount to nothing more than competing views about policy and science," on which we defer to the agency.   In re Polar Bear, 794 F.Supp.2d at 69; see also Am. Wildlands, 530 F.3d at 1000 (reviewing courts must "avoid[ ] all temptation to direct the agency in a choice between rational alternatives").

Significantly, Appellants point to no scientific findings or studies that FWS failed to consider in promulgating the Listing Rule. At oral argument, Appellants' counsel acknowledged that Appellants do not claim that FWS failed to use the "best scientific and commercial data available" as required by 16 U.S.C. § 1533(b)(1)(A). See Oral Argument at 25:22. Rather, "Appellants merely disagree with the implications of the data for the species' continued viability." Br. of Appellees at 14.

Where, as here, the foundational premises on which the agency relies are adequately explained and uncontested, scientific experts (by a wide majority) support the agency's conclusion, and Appellants do not point to any scientific evidence that the agency failed to consider, we are bound to uphold the agency's determination. Therefore we affirm the District Court's decision to uphold the Listing Rule.

———

B. DESIGNATION OF CRITICAL MARINE HABITAT

Once a species is listed, what obligation are the Secretaries under to designate critical habitat? What additional protection from extinction does the designation of critical habitat provide a listed species? In the sea otter listing, the FWS announced that critical habitat was not determinable at that time. It was unable to identify the physical and biological features essential to the conservation of the DPS, a requirement for critical habitat, because the reasons for the population decline is unclear. 70 Fed. Reg. 46366, 46384. When the Fish & Wildlife Service or NMFS find that critical habitat is not determinable at the time of the final listing decision, they are required within one year to propose a critical habitat designation unless they find the designation not to be prudent. 16 U.S.C. § 1533(a)(3); 50 C.F.R. 424.12 (implementing regulations for Section 4, 16 U.S.C. § 1533(a)(3)). When would it be not prudent to designate critical habitat for a marine species listed as threatened or endangered?

How is critical habitat defined for a marine species with an extensive migratory range or whose whereabouts for long periods or most seasons are largely unknown to science? If the species population is so reduced that it is rarely sighted, what information can the agency use to define critical habitat?

CENTER FOR BIOLOGICAL DIVERSITY V. EVANS

U.S. District Court, N.D. California, 2005
2005 WL 1514102, not reported in F. Supp.2d

ALSUP, DISTRICT JUDGE.

One of the most endangered mammals is the right whale. It was among the first group of species to be listed as endangered in 1971. After 34 years, the agency responsible has yet failed to designate any critical habitat in the Pacific Ocean. This order directs the agency to make the required statutory decision by October 28, 2005.

In this action, the Center for Biological Diversity and certain individuals seek declaratory and injunctive relief against the National Marine Fisheries Service for unreasonable delay in the determination and designation of critical habitat for the right whale in the Pacific Ocean. Plaintiffs assert defendants' violations of the Endangered Species Act, 16 U.S.C. 1532 et seq., and the Administrative Procedure Act, 5 U.S.C. 706(1) and (2). Relief is granted for the following reasons.[1]

---

[1] The scientific name of the right whale is the Northern Right Whale, *Eubalaena glacialis*. In 2003, NMFS published a Federal Register Notice that listed the Right Whale in the Pacific Ocean as a distinct species, *Eubalaena japonica*, *i.e.* as distinct from the Atlantic version (68 Fed. Reg. 17560–62 (2003)). In 2005, after plaintiffs filed this action, defendants announced that they were rescinding the 2003 action because NMFS had allegedly failed to meet procedural requirements. The notice further stated that the agency would conduct a status review to determine

STATEMENT

1. Right Whale

The right whale is the most endangered of all large whale species. A baleen whale, it has a thick body and a huge head that accounts for about one-third of its length. Adults range between 45 and 55 feet in length and weigh up to 70 tons. It has distinctive callosities on the head.

Right whales were once abundant throughout the Pacific and Atlantic. Prized for their oil and easy to catch, commercial whaling during the nineteenth century decimated the species. By 1935, they were so near extinction that the League of Nations convinced the whaling nations to stop hunting them; in 1949, with the passage of international whaling regulations, the Pacific population gained international protection. In the 1960's, however, right whales were still being poached in the Pacific. Today, right whales are injured by collisions with large vessels and net entanglement and by habitat degradation through pollution, sea-bed mining and oil-and-gas exploration. The Pacific population may now be as few as "tens of animals," as even NMFS now acknowledges (67 Fed. Reg. 7660, 7660 (2002)).

habitat harm [handwritten marginalia]

2. Procedural History

The right whale was listed as an endangered species in 1971 (id. at 7661). In 1991, the NMFS issued the "Final Recovery Plan for the Northern Right Whale." The recovery plan called for the identification and protection by 1996 of "critical habitat(s)"—habitats essential to the survival and recovery of right whales in the Pacific Ocean. The plan stated that the recovery plan team could not yet determine what habitat areas were critical to the survival of the right whales in the Pacific. Nevertheless, the recovery team recommended that once areas essential to the survival and recovery were identified in the Pacific, those areas should be protected under the Act. The plan gave a time-frame of five years (i.e., until 1996) to identify critical habitat for right whales in the Pacific.

In 1994, the NMFS designated three "critical habitats" for right whales in the Atlantic (59 Fed. Reg. 28793, 28805 (1994)). No Pacific habitat was designated. Nor was any designated in 1996, as called for in the plan-or ever, which provoked this suit. In 2000, the CBD submitted a formal petition to NMFS to revise the critical habitat designation to include a zone off of the Alaskan coast. The petition identified areas concentrated in the middle shelf and inner front of the southeast Bering Sea to be designated as a critical habitat for the right whale in the Pacific Ocean. NMFS agreed that "the petition present [ed] substantial scientific

---

whether more than one species exists. At the hearing of this case, government counsel acknowledged that the separate listing would have triggered, at least arguably, an independent statutory duty to designate critical habitat in the Pacific Ocean. This order does not reach any such further issues. Rather, this order treats, as does the government, the right whale as a single species.

information that the designation of a critical habitat may be warranted" and took the petition under consideration (66 Fed. Reg. 29773 (2001)).

In 2002, however, even after receiving many comments supporting designation, NMFS declined to designate any Pacific habitat. Despite "agree [ing] that designation of critical habitat may be a necessary component of any effort to conserve and recover" the right whale, NMFS concluded that the extent of the critical habitat could not be determined at that time because of alleged inadequate information (67 Fed. Reg. at 7662). Significantly, NMFS stated that "the most reasonable conclusion is that a smaller area than that petitioned may contain physical and biological features that are essential to the conservation of the species" (*id.* at 7664). Nonetheless, NMFS did not designate even the "smaller area" as critical habitat but said that it would continue to analyze the issues (id. at 7665). That was in 2002. Now in 2005, NMFS has yet to designate any critical habitat for the right whale in the entire Pacific Ocean. The 2002 notice further stated that a draft plan was expected to be available for comment later the same year for the Pacific right whale (id. at 7662). Although there have been multiple internal draft recovery plans for the right whales in the Pacific since 2002, no plan has been released.

ANALYSIS

Under the Endangered Species Act, when the Secretary lists a species as endangered, the Secretary is required to publish "concurrently" a final regulation designating critical habitat "to the maximum extent prudent" unless the Secretary determines that the critical habitat is not then "determinable" (§ 1533(a)(3)). ("The Secretary" refers to the Secretary of the Interior or the Secretary of Commerce, depending on the species; here it means the latter, who, in turn, has delegated the responsibility to NMFS.) If a habitat determination is not then possible, then the Secretary must publish a final critical habitat designation "to the maximum extent prudent" within one year following the listing (ibid.). The regulations give "not prudent" a very narrow meaning: "Not prudent" is defined as "not * * * beneficial to the species" or "increasing the degree of [takings] threat to a species" (50 C.F.R. 424.12(a)(1)(i)–(ii)).

Thereafter, any "interested person" may petition for a revision in the critical habitat (§ 1533(b)(3)(D)(i)). Within ninety days, the Secretary must "make a finding as to whether the petition presents substantial information indicating that the revision may be warranted" (ibid.). Upon a so-called "positive finding," the Secretary must then determine and publish "how he intends to proceed with the requested revision" within one year following the petition (§ 1533(b)(3)(D)(ii)). Specifically:

> Within 12 months after receiving a petition that is found under clause (i) to present substantial information indicating that the requested revision may be warranted, the Secretary shall determine

how he intends to proceed with the requested revision, and shall promptly publish notice of such intention in the Federal Register.

The standards governing critical habitat revisions are the same as for original designations (§ 1533(B)(2)):

> The Secretary shall designate critical habitat, and make revisions thereto, under subsection (a)(3) of this section on the basis of the best scientific data available and after taking into consideration the economic impact, the impact on national security, and any other relevant impact, of specifying any particular area as critical habitat. The Secretary may exclude any area from critical habitat if he determines that the benefits of such exclusion outweigh the benefits of specifying such area as part of the critical habitat, unless he determines, based on the best scientific and commercial data available, that the failure to designate such area as critical habitat will result in the extinction of the species concerned.

Not prudent

To the "maximum extent prudent and determinable," the Secretary has an ongoing duty to revise such designations "as appropriate" (§ 1533(a)(3)(A)).

In combined effect, these provisions inform the statutory phrase "how he intends to proceed" in the habitat-revision paragraph. With respect to a petition for habitat revision, the Secretary has these options: (i) publish a proposed rule revising the critical habitat or finding that a statutory factor (e.g., economic impact or national security) overrides the need for species protection or (ii) find that revision of critical habitat is either not "prudent" or not "determinable." The Secretary must chose one of the above and publish his intent within one year of the petition.

options

The Act permits any person to commence a civil action against the Secretary "where there is alleged a failure of the Secretary to perform any act or duty under section 1533 * * * which is not discretionary with the Secretary" (§ 1540(g)(1)(C)). Under the APA, an aggrieved person may sue to set aside final agency action that is arbitrary and capricious and to compel an agency to act when it reasonably delays action.

APA

In the present action, NMFS, acting as the Secretary's delegate, did, in fact, respond to the petition by publishing "how [it] intends to proceed." The notice stated (in 2002) that NMFS would study the problem (67 Fed. Reg. 7660). This was, in effect, a finding that a revision was not "determinable" and a ruling that no Pacific habitat at all would be made at that time. No suggestion was made that a designation would be imprudent.[2]

---

[2] Since the filing of this complaint, the agency has noticed that it will conduct a status review of the listing of the right whale in the Pacific and issue a final rule and any necessary critical habitat designation by 2006 (70 Fed. Reg. 1830, 1831 (2005)). The agency relies on this representation to attempt to side-step the entire "unreasonable delay" issue by arguing that because it is in the process of listing the Pacific population of right whales as a separate species and in do-

The circumstances presented are very similar to those in Biodiversity Legal Foundation v. Norton, 285 F. Supp.2d 1 (D.D.C.2003) ("*BLF*"). There, Judge Rosemary M. Collyer held that the Secretary of Interior (through the Fish and Wildlife Service) had unreasonably withheld agency action in violation of the Administrative Procedure Act, 5 U.S.C. 555(b), 706(1) * * *

The present record presents an even stronger case for relief. The right whale was listed as endangered 34 years ago, yet no Pacific habitat has ever been designated—despite the statutory duty to determine to revise (or not) critical habitat in a timely manner and the duty to act based on the best scientific data available. See BLF, 285 F. Supp. at 16; Fund for Animals, Inc. v. Rice, 85 F.3d 535, 547 (11th Cir. 1996). The surviving Pacific right whales are numbered "in the tens." The 1991 recovery plan here committed the agency to "identifying and protecting as necessary habitat(s) essential to the survival and recovery of the North Pacific Right Whale" by 1996. The plan stated that "North Pacific right whale habitats * * * and certain geographic areas are probably essential for meeting the biological requirements of the North Pacific right whales". Although critical habitat was designed for the Atlantic in 1994, no critical habitat has ever been designated for the Pacific—then or now. By the reasoning in *BLF,* NMFS has been overdue on the designation since at least 1996. The delay here has thus been at least nine years, if not 34 years.

Another consideration under *BLF* is the extent to which the delay has undermined the statutory scheme. It is true that the Act places more priority on original designations than over later revisions. Yet, again, it must be remembered that no Pacific habitat has yet been determined for 34 years. The Pacific fleet of right whales is verging on extinction now, numbering "in the tens" by the agency's own admission (67 Fed. Reg. at 7660). Without question, the delay has been severe in light of the statutory goal. Indeed, the Act does not contemplate critical habitat as an afterthought in the preservation of a species; Congress considered the critical habitat designation an essential component of preservation of a species: "classifying a species as endangered or threatened is only the first step in insuring its survival. Of equal or more importance is the determination of the habitat necessary for the species' continued existence." H.R.Rep. No. 94–887, at 3 (1976).

Another *BLF* consideration is the consequence of further delay. Put differently, it is theoretically conceivable that right whales would be able to protect themselves in the face of more delay and/or that there are no imminent threats to them in the Pacific, such that more delay could be

---

ing so will designate critical habitat, the issues plaintiffs present are moot. This argument is not valid. For the last fourteen years the agency has said that it plans to designate critical habitat for the right whale in the Pacific and it has not—there is no reason to believe that the agency will now follow-through with promulgating the rule without judicial intervention.

tolerated. For example, in the 1991 recovery plan, the agency surmised that natural conditions—such as extremely low abundance and scattered distribution rather than direct human interaction—posed the greatest threat to recovery of the right whales in the Pacific. The administrative record, however, illustrates that over the last decade, increasing amounts of contaminants in the sea and the larger, faster, ocean-going fishing vessels that are being built are increasing the danger of collision and death for right whales in the Pacific. Given that there are a few precious right whales left in the Pacific and even fewer females, delay—of any length of time—brings the species closer to extinction.

Another *BLF* consideration is whether there are any difficulties faced by the agency in carrying out the congressional mandate. While the defendants do not raise this issue in their briefs, the administrative record illustrates that one of the difficulties faced by the agency in determining critical habitat is the impact a designation would have on commercial fishing and transportation businesses. As an example, in a memorandum regarding critical habitat, an Alaskan administrator writes "[f]urther actions to establish additional critical habitat for any species will likely be met with concern by the Alaskan Congressional delegation, the State of Alaska, and various private interests in particular the commercial fishing and transportation industries." While the Act directs the agency to analyze all impacts of critical habitat, including economic impact, the agency may not exclude an area from critical habitat if it is determined that failure to designate that area as a critical habitat will result in extinction of the species, as quoted above (See also 50 C.F.R. 424.19 (2004)).

A final factor makes this case an even stronger case for relief than in *BLF*. Here, the agency has all but admitted that the record presented a case for at least designating a smaller geographic region in the Pacific than that proposed by plaintiff—yet the agency designated no critical habitat at all in the Pacific Ocean. In its final decision, the agency denied CBD's petition yet stated that "[t]he most reasonable conclusion is that a much smaller area than that petitioned may contain physical and biological features that are essential to the conservation of the species, but information is insufficient to extrapolate that conclusion to the entire area petitioned" (67 Fed. Reg. 7660, 7664). Furthermore, numerous correspondences in the administrative record indicate the agency's willingness to designate critical habitat. For example, a July 2003 agency memo reads "[we] are now prepared to go forward with a Proposed Rule sometime this winter to designate some portion of the Bering Sea as a critical habitat". The agency even drafted a proposed rule—although it was never published for public comment.

Congress instructed the agency to act on the basis of the "best scientific data available" (§ 1533(b)(1)(A)). As the Ninth Circuit has said:

The Endangered Species Act requires agencies to make determinations on the basis of the best scientific data available. Thus, a review of ESA case law provides insightful and analogous provisions and analysis. In Conner v. Burford, 848 F.2d 1441, 1454 (9th Cir.1988), this court held that an agency's claim of insufficient information to prepare comprehensive biological opinions violated the ESA requirement that opinions use best data available, and ordered the agency to comply with the ESA requirement. See also Greenpeace v. Nat'l Marine Fisheries Serv., 55 F. Supp.2d 1248, 1261–62 (W.D. Wash. 1999) (best scientific data available standard requires less than conclusive proof; Secretary must issue biological opinion); Defenders of Wildlife v. Babbit, 958 F. Supp. 670, 679–81 (D.D.C. 1997) (Secretary must determine whether any species is threatened or endangered using the best available evidence).

Brower v. Evans, 257 F.3d 1058, 1070–71 (9th Cir.2001) (emphasis added).

Here, the best available evidence supports critical habitat designation. Beginning in 1996, small groups of right whales—including calves—were seen congregating, feeding and engaging in courtship behavior in the southeast Bering Sea. According to the Marine Mammal Commission, (a federal body of marine mammal experts charged with making recommendations to NMFS) concluded that the repeated occurrence of right whales in summer and fall months, coupled with the fact that the petitioned area lies within a broader area in which whaling records document that right whales were once abundant, provides a reasonable basis for concluding that the petitioned area contains physical or biological features essential for the species' survival.

Under the best available standard, Congress required the agency to consider the scientific information available *at the time* of consideration, giving the species the benefit of the doubt. See e.g. Conner v. Buford, 848 F.2d 1441, 1454 (9th Cir.1998).

Congress did not contemplate paralysis while critical habitat issues were studied to death. Congress wanted, "to the maximum extent prudent," prompt protection based on the "best scientific data available" so long as the data is adequate to make a "determination." No critical habitat will ever be knowable with geographic exactitude. The interwoven character of our ecology here on Earth bars that. Our best approximations must do, at least so Congress concluded. As stated by the Ninth Circuit in Brower v. Evans, 257 F.3d 1058, 1070 (2001), "scientific findings in marine mammal conservation are often necessarily made from incomplete or imperfect information." The record presented to the agency seems clearly to have presented a strong case for designating at least the smaller zone referenced by the agency itself—yet the agency punted by calling for more study (67 Fed .Reg. 7664).

To be sure, the Act is controversial. Economic interests, often with political influence, can be expected to resist efforts to designate critical habitat. Congress took this into account. It charged the Secretary, in making critical habitat designations, to consider "the economic impact, the impact on national security, and any other relevant impact." The Secretary "may exclude any area from critical habitat if he determines that the benefits of exclusion outweigh the benefit of [inclusion] unless he determines, based on the best scientific and commercial data available, that the failure to [include] will result in the extinction of the species concerned." Hard decisions are called for. Commercial interests will legitimately prevail in some. The species will legitimately prevail in others. But Congress expected the hard decisions to be made. Except where designations are simply not determinable, the agency must act based on the best evidence available to the maximum extent prudent.

NMFS had a statutory duty to make the hard decision, i.e., to designate or not, unless it reasonably found the habitat was not determinable. The agency's conclusion that the issue was not "determinable" was not supported by administrative record and was arbitrary and capricious. The agency was legally obligated to make the hard decision based on the evidence available. The agency's failure to do so not only amounted to an unreasonable delay but was "arbitrary, capricious, an abuse of discretion or otherwise not in accordance with law" (5 U.S.C. 706).

Summary

NOTES AND QUESTIONS

1. The court ordered NMFS to use the best available scientific evidence, either to designate an area of the Pacific Ocean as critical habitat for the right whale, or to publish a notice explaining why no Pacific critical habitat should be designated due to a more paramount statutory consideration (e.g., commercial or national security interests), by June 30, 2006. On July 9, 2006, NMFS issued final rules revising the current critical habitat for the northern right whale by designating additional areas within the North Pacific: one in the Gulf of Alaska and another in the Bering Sea. 71 Fed. Reg. 38277 (July 7, 2006).

2. Why would the FWS or NMFS be reluctant to designate critical habitat for a listed species?

3. How much information must the Secretary have about the biology and ecology of a species before its critical habitat is "determinable" within the meaning of section 4(a)(3) of the ESA, 16 U.S.C. § 1533(a)(3)? See 50 C.F.R. § 424.12(a).

4. As the court noted, NMFS designated three areas in the North Atlantic as critical habitat for northern whales in 1994. These include the Great South Channel, Cape Cod Bay, and waters of the southeastern U.S. off the coasts of Florida and Georgia. The Service rejected a petition to revise this critical habitat designation after finding that it was not supported by sufficient new information and analysis. 68 Fed. Reg. 51758 (Aug. 28, 2003). The North Atlantic right whale numbers in the 300s and is one of the most closely studied great whales in U.S. waters. Entanglement in fixed-gear fisheries (by trap and gillnet) in North Atlantic waters frequented by the right whale are a major source of injury and mortality.

5. In designating critical habitat, unlike the listing of the species itself, the Services are authorized to take economic impacts into account and to exclude some habitat if the costs outweigh the benefits. What methods do the agencies use to make such determinations? Does the listed species get the benefit of the doubt?

6. A federal district court judge in Alaska vacated and remanded the FWS's final rules designating critical habitat for the polar bear, following its listing as threatened. Alaska Oil and Gas Assoc. v. Salazar,__F.Supp.2d__, 2013 WL 222259 (D.Ak. 2013). Judge Beistline found much of the rule was based on the best available scientific information, but remanded to the agency to better explain why such extensive areas should be designated and to remedy certain procedural defects.

BUILDING INDUSTRY ASS'N OF THE BAY AREA V. COMMERCE

U. S. District Court, Northern District of California, 2012
__ F.Supp. 3d __, 2012 WL 6002511

HAMILTON, District Judge.

BACKGROUND

This is a case about environmental regulations and the designation of the "critical habitat" for a threatened species, namely, the green sturgeon. The facts of the case are largely undisputed. The Endangered Species Act ("ESA") provides for the protection of species that are either "endangered" (in danger of becoming extinct) or "threatened" (likely to become endangered in the foreseeable future). If a species meets either of those criteria, it is "listed" as either threatened or endangered. Once a species is listed, the government has the authority to designate certain areas as "critical habitat" that are necessary to the conservation of the species, and which may require special protection. The Departments of Commerce and the Interior are responsible for these decisions, and have delegated those responsibilities (in the context of certain species, including the green sturgeon) to the National Marine Fisheries Service ("NMFS").

The green sturgeon was listed as a threatened species, which enabled NMFS to determine which areas, if any, were to be designated as "critical habitat," and thus deserving of special protection. Section 4(b)(2) of the ESA sets forth the procedure by which "critical habitat" areas are designated:

> The Secretary shall designate critical habitat, and make revisions thereto, under subsection (a)(3) on the basis of the best scientific data available and after taking into consideration the economic impact, the impact on national security, and any other relevant impact, of specifying any particular area as critical habitat. The Secretary may exclude any area from critical habitat if he determines that the benefits of such exclusion outweigh the benefits of specifying such area as part of the critical habitat, unless he determines, based on the best scientific and commercial data available, that the failure to designate such area as critical habitat will result in the extinction of the species concerned. 16 U.S.C. § 1533(b)(2).

As the text of section 4(b)(2) shows, the ESA is designed not only to protect the habitats of certain species, but also to achieve that protection without creating unnecessary economic impact. Congress delegated to the Secretary of Commerce (who then delegated to the NMFS) both the power to "designate" critical habitats for the green sturgeon, and to "exclude" those areas from designation based on economic impact, national security impact, or any other relevant impact.

NMFS endeavored to perform this "critical habitat" designation for the green sturgeon, and performed various analyses of the species, the physical and biological areas necessary to conservation of the species, the economic interests that would be impacted by conservation, and ultimately, the conservation value of each specific area. NMFS looked at each area that it was considering designating as a "critical habitat," and assigned each area a conservation value rating of "high," "medium," or "low." NMFS also was aware of section 4(b)(2)'s language regarding exclusion of those areas where designation would have a large economic impact, and thus analyzed the economic impact of designating each area. NMFS ultimately decided that all areas found to have a "high" conservation value rating would not be eligible for exclusion; in other words, they would all be designated as critical habitat. NMFS issued a "final rule" codifying this decision, and this final rule gave rise to this litigation.

Plaintiffs Building Industry Association of the Bay Area ("BIABA") and Bay Planning Coalition ("BPC") both represent property owners impacted by NMFS' decision to designate certain lands as "critical habitat." Specifically, BIABA is a "nonprofit association of builders, contractors, and related trades and professions involved in the residential construction industry," and BPC is a nonprofit organization representing the interests of "business and property owners in the San Francisco Bay Area" whose "mission is to ensure a healthy and thriving San Francisco Bay Area for commerce, recreation, and the natural environment." Plaintiffs filed suit against defendants Department of Commerce (and John Bryson in his official capacity as Secretary of the Department of Commerce), NMFS (and Eric C. Schwaab in his official capacity as assistant administrator for NMFS), and the National Oceanic and Atmospheric Administration, asserting three causes of action: (1) failure to take into consideration economic impacts in high conservation value ("HCV") areas under ESA section 4(b)(2); (2) failure to balance the benefits in HCV areas under ESA section (4)(b)(2); and (3) violations of the National Environmental Policy Act ("NEPA") and the Administrative Procedure Act ("APA"). NEPA requires federal agencies to examine the environmental effects of proposed federal actions and to inform the public of the environmental concerns that went into the agency's decision making, and requires the government to prepare environmental impact statements to that effect. The APA provides a right of judicial review to a person "suffering legal wrong because of agency action, or adversely affected or aggrieved by agency action within the meaning of a relevant statute," if agency action is "arbitrary, capricious, an abuse of discretion, or otherwise not in accordance with law."

DISCUSSION

* * *

Plaintiffs' first and second causes of action both arise under section 4(b)(2) of the ESA, and both are premised on the argument that defendants' blanket designation of all high conservation value areas, without any balancing of economic interests, constituted a violation of defendants' duties under the ESA. Even though plaintiffs' first and second causes of action are based on the same legal theory, each uses a different statutory hook from the text of the ESA. The first cause of action is based on defendants' alleged "failure to take into consideration economic impacts in high conservation value areas." The second cause of action is based on defendants' alleged "failure to balance the benefits in HCV areas." For reference, section 4(b)(2) of the ESA is as follows, with relevant portions underlined:

> The Secretary shall designate critical habitat, and make revisions thereto, under subsection (a)(3) on the basis of the best scientific data available and *after taking into consideration the economic impact,* the impact on national security, and any other relevant impact, *of specifying any particular area as critical habitat.* The Secretary *may exclude* any area from critical habitat if he determines that *the benefits of such exclusion outweigh the benefits of specifying such area as part of the critical habitat,* unless he determines, based on the best scien-

tific and commercial data available, that the failure to designate such area as critical habitat will result in the extinction of the species concerned.

Plaintiffs argue that the first sentence of section 4(b)(2) -specifically, the words "shall designate ... after taking into consideration the economic impact"-creates a nondiscretionary duty to account for economic impact in all areas, even HCV areas, when making a decision to designate critical habitat. In plaintiffs' words, "[n]o area, now matter how it may be classified by NMFS, is excepted from the requirement to consider economic impacts."

Plaintiffs then point to the second sentence as setting forth the methodology for such a "consideration." Plaintiffs argue that the word "outweigh" serves to "direct the government to conduct the assessment of economic impacts specifically by a balancing-of-the-benefits methodology." In plaintiffs' view, the "second sentence of Section 4(b)(2) prescribes the manner in which the duty to consider economic impacts mandated in the first sentence must be performed." Plaintiffs do concede that "the ultimate decision whether to exclude any area from critical habitat is discretionary," but they emphasize that "the requirement to consider economic impacts by means of balancing the benefits is mandatory."

For their part, defendants do concede that they had a mandatory duty to "consider" the economic impacts of designating an area as critical habitat. However, they take issue with plaintiffs' interpretation of section 4(b)(2)'s second sentence as imposing a "mandatory" balancing test. They argue that "[t]here is no statutory requirement that NMFS balance the benefits of designation of critical habitat against the benefits of exclusion," and that NMFS "was not required to use any particular methodology" to "consider" the economic impact of designation. Instead, defendants characterize section 4(b)(2) as having two components: (1) an initial, mandatory requirement to consider economic (and other) impacts, and (2) a "wholly discretionary process" by which the agency can exclude certain areas from designation. And as defendant-intervenor adds, the ESA "does not dictate the manner in which NMFS performs the analysis," and "[h]ad Congress intended NMFS [ ] to conduct critical habitat designations using a balancing-of-the-benefits methodology, it would have explicitly so required."

As evidence of NMFS' consideration, the federal defendants point to an economic analysis report prepared by an outside consultant, Industrial Economics, Inc. According to defendants, the Indecon report "considered 14 potentially affected economic activities, calculated a total economic impact score for each critical habitat unit, and characterized the associated economic costs for each unit as high, medium, or low." After reviewing the Indecon report, NMFS prepared a report of its own, titled the "Final

ESA Section 4(b)(2) Report." Defendant-intervenor argues that the section 4(b)(2) report shows that NMFS actually did balance the benefits of conservation with the economic impact, even though it was not obligated to do so. Specifically, defendant-intervenor points to the report's use of specific dollar thresholds to represent the economic impact of designating each particular area as critical habitat. Even though NMFS ultimately concluded that no HCV areas would be excluded from designation, defendant-intervenor argues that this "does not mean NMFS did not weigh the benefits of exclusion against those of designation," but instead shows only that NMFS "determined that because HCV areas were critical to the recovery of the green sturgeon, those areas would not be eligible for exclusion even when economic costs were high."

The parties thus present two issues for the court to decide:

(1) What is the scope of NMFS' duty under section 4(b)(2) of the ESA? Was it obligated only to "consider" the economic impact of designation, or both to "consider" the economic impact and to balance that impact with the environmental effects of designation?

(2) Whatever the scope of the duty, did NMFS comply with it?

Regarding the first issue, the court finds that the text of section 4(b)(2) is clear in requiring NMFS to "consider" the economic impact of designation. *See* Bennett v. Spear, 520 U.S. 154, 172 (1997) ("the fact that the Secretary's ultimate decision is reviewable only for abuse of discretion does not alter the categorical *requirement* that, in arriving at his decision, he 'tak[e] into consideration the economic impact, and any other relevant impact.'") (emphasis in original). However, the statutory text does not specify any particular methodology that must be used to accomplish this "consideration." Thus, the court rejects plaintiffs' argument that defendants were obligated to perform a balancing test. In fact, the second sentence of section 4(b)(2) shows that the entire "exclusion" process itself is discretionary. A simple reordering of the sentence (without changing the meaning) makes this clearer: "If the Secretary determines that the benefits of such exclusion outweigh the benefits of specifying such area as part of the critical habitat, he may exclude any area from critical habitat." Based on the plain text of the statute, even if the secretary does determine that the benefits of exclusion outweigh the benefits of designation, he is still not obligated to exclude that area from designation. Instead, he "may exclude" the area from designation. Accordingly, even if NMFS was somehow obligated to perform a balancing test, it was not obligated to exclude any area from designation regardless of the results of that balancing test.

Thus, the key question is whether NMFS did indeed "tak[e] into consideration the economic impact" of designation before issuing its final rule. The court finds that the administrative record, especially NMFS'

"Final ESA Section 4(b)(2) Report," shows that NMFS did satisfy its duty to consider economic impacts. The section 4(b)(2) report makes clear each step of the NMFS' analysis. After identifying the specific areas to be analyzed, the report "determine[s] the benefits of designation," and then "determine[s] the benefits of exclusion." In the section describing the economic benefits of exclusion, NMFS notes that it was "able to monetize estimates of the economic impacts resulting from a critical habitat designation," and that "[s]everal factors were considered in developing the economic impacts, including the level of economic activity within each area, the level of baseline protection afforded to green sturgeon by existing regulations for each economic activity within each area, and the estimated economic impact (in dollars) associated with each activity type." After describing the benefits of both designation and exclusion, the report then sets forth NMFS' "exclusions based on economic impacts." This section specifically states that "to weigh the benefits of designation against the benefits of exclusion, we compared the conservation value ratings with the range of high to low annualized economic cost estimates," and includes a chart showing this comparison. NMFS "selected dollar thresholds representing the levels at which the potential economic impact associated with a specific area appeared to outweigh the potential conservation benefits of designating that area." To determine those thresholds, NMFS "examined the range in economic impacts across all areas within a conservation value rating category, determined where the breakpoint occurred between relatively low economic impacts and relatively high economic impacts, and selected a value within the range of that breakpoint where economic impacts may outweigh the conservation benefits for that area." After determining this dollar "threshold" for all areas, including HCV areas, "four decision rules were established based on these dollar thresholds." While plaintiffs obviously disagree with NMFS' rule that "all areas with a conservation value rating of 'High' were not eligible for exclusion regardless of the level of economic impact because of the threatened status of the green sturgeon," the record shows that NMFS did properly consider the economic impacts before deciding that HCV areas would be ineligible for exclusion, and thus satisfied its duty under section 4(b)(2) of the ESA. In fact, the mere presence of these economic analyses in the record would be enough to establish that NMFS satisfied its duty, because in this circuit, an agency is entitled to a presumption that it considered all relevant information "unless rebutted by evidence in the record." Rock Creek Alliance v. U.S. Fish & Wildlife Service, 663 F.3d 439, 443 (9th Cir.2011); *see also* Kern County Farm Bureau v. Allen, 450 F.3d 1072, 1081 (9th Cir.2006). Even if the court accepted plaintiffs' reading of the statute and required NMFS to perform the "balancing" test urged by plaintiffs, it appears that defendants cleared that higher bar. Regardless, the court holds only that defendants were required to, and did, "consider" economic impacts, and makes no determination as to the exact methodology required for such consideration.

As to the ultimate designation decision reached by NMFS, the court notes that the Administrative Procedure Act does not allow for court review of an agency's action if "agency action is committed to agency discretion by law." 5 U.S.C. § 701(a)(2). An agency action is committed to agency discretion by law if the underlying "statute is drawn so that a court would have no meaningful standard against which to judge the agency's exercise of discretion." Heckler v. Chaney, 470 U.S. 821, 830 (1985). In this case, section 4(b)(2) of the ESA does not provide any standard by which to judge an agency's decision *not* to exclude an area from critical habitat designation. As explained above, the second sentence of section 4(b)(2) establishes a discretionary process by which the secretary *may* exclude areas from designation, but does not set forth any standard governing when a certain area *must* be excluded from designation. Put another way, section 4(b)(2) provides a standard of review to judge decisions to exclude, but provides no such standard to review decisions not to exclude. Thus, the agency action in this case is committed to agency discretion by law, and the APA precludes court review of NMFS' ultimate decision. *See also* Cape Hatteras Access Preservation Alliance v. U.S. Dept. of the Interior, 731 F.Supp.2d 15, 29 (D.D.C.2010) ("The plain reading of the statute fails to provide a standard by which to judge the Service's decision not to exclude an area from critical habitat."); Home Builders Ass'n of Northern California v. U.S. Fish & Wildlife Service, 2006 WL 3190518 (E.D.Cal.2006) ("[T]he court has no substantive standards by which to review the [agency's] decisions not to exclude certain tracts based on economic or other considerations, and those decisions are therefore committed to agency discretion.").

———

C. REGULATION TO PREVENT TAKES OF ENDANGERED SPECIES

1. Scope of the Take Prohibition

Like the Marine Mammal Protection Act (MMPA), the Endangered Species Act protects wildlife by prohibiting a broad range of public and private activities that could constitute a "take" of the protected species. 16 U.S.C. § 1538(a)(1). The Act defines the term "take" as meaning "to harass, harm, pursue, hunt, shoot, wound, kill, trap, capture or collect, or to attempt to engage in any such activity." Id. at § 1532(19). Federal regulations interpreting the term "harm" under the ESA, however, also encompass "significant habitat modification or degradation." This interpretation was upheld by the Supreme Court in Sweet Home Chapter of Communities for a Great Oregon v. Babbitt, 515 U.S. 687 (1995). Regulations proposed in 1998 by the National Marine Fisheries Service adopt this interpretation of the Section 9 takings prohibition for marine listed species. 63 Fed. Reg. 24148 (1998). Under these regulations, an action that changes or degrades the habitat of a listed marine species where it actually kills or injures the species by significantly impairing essential behavior patterns, including breeding, spawning, rearing, migrating, feeding, and sheltering, will be a violation of the Act. Given the range of activities that occur in coastal waters and the shared jurisdiction between state and federal governments, Section 9 has the potential to alter state as well as private actions in significant ways.

STRAHAN V. COXE

United States Court of Appeals, First Circuit, 1997
127 F.3d 155

TORRUELLA, CHIEF JUDGE.

* * *

I. Status of the Northern Right Whale

Strahan is an officer of GreenWorld, Inc., an organization dedicated to the preservation and recovery of endangered species. Strahan, 939 F. Supp. at 966 & n. 6. Strahan brought suit on behalf of the Northern Right whale, listed as an endangered species by the federal government. See 50 C.F.R. § 222.23(a). Northern Right whales are the most endangered of the large whales, Strahan, 939 F. Supp. at 968, presently numbering around 300, 62 Fed. Reg. 39157, 39158 (1997). Entanglement with commercial fishing gear has been recognized as a major source of human-caused injury or death to the Northern Right whale. Final Recovery Plan for the Northern Right Whale (Eubalaena Glacialis), NMFS (December 1991)("Right Whale Recovery Plan") at 24; see also Strahan, 939 F.Supp. at 972. Collision with ships is also a significant cause of Northern Right whale death. See Right Whale Recovery Plan at 10; Strahan, 939 F. Supp. at 972.

The majority of Northern Right whales are present in Massachusetts waters only during spring feeding. Strahan, 939 F. Supp. at 968. The district court found, based on statements made by defendants as well as on affidavits from three scientists, that Northern Right whales have been entangled in fixed fishing gear in Massachusetts coastal waters at least nine times. See Strahan, 939 F. Supp. at 984 ("On May 15, 1983, a Right whale was observed 'thrashing around' a location three miles east of Manomet Point in Plymouth, MA because of its entanglement in ropes attached to lobster buoys. * * * Right whales were also found entangled in lobster and other fishing gear in Massachusetts waters on June 16, 1978,

May 13, 1982, October 14, 1985, May 15, 1983, August 29, 1986, August 7, 1993, November 17, 1994, and August 17, 1995. At least one of these whales was not expected to survive its injuries from the gear."). Moreover, a Northern Right whale mortality was reported off Cape Cod, Massachusetts in May 1996. 61 Fed. Reg. 41116, 41117 (Aug. 7, 1996).

The NMFS issued a final interim rule proposing to close off entirely the critical habitat of the Northern Right whale and to modify fishing practices to enhance the viability of the Northern Right whale. Taking of Marine Mammals Incidental to Commercial Fishing Operations; Atlantic Large Whale Take Reduction Plan Regulations, 62 Fed. Reg. 39157, 39158–39159 (July 22, 1997). The report accompanying the proposed rule recognized that entanglement with fishing gear is one of the leading causes of the depletion of the Northern Right whale population and indicated that more than half of the Northern Right whale population bear scars indicating unobserved and unrecorded earlier entanglement. Id. The report calls for a ban on gillnet fishing and lobster pot fishing, the two manners of fishing at issue in this case, during the Northern Right whales' high season in the Cape Cod Bay Critical Habitat from January 1 to May 15 of each year, and in the Great South Channel from April 1 to June 30, until modified fishing equipment is developed that will diminish the risk of injury and death to the Northern Right whale. Id. at 39159–39160.

II. Massachusetts' Regulatory Authority Scheme

The Massachusetts Division of Marine Fisheries ("DMF") is vested with broad authority to regulate fishing in Massachusetts's coastal waters, Mass. Gen. L. c. 130, which extend three nautical miles from the shoreline, see Strahan, 939 F. Supp. at 974. Nearly all commercial fishing vessels must receive a permit from DMF in order to take fish, including shellfish, from Massachusetts coastal waters. 322 C.M.R. §§ 7.01–7.05, 8.08. DMF is a division of the Department of Fisheries, Wildlife and Environmental Law Enforcement, which is part of the Executive Office of Environmental Affairs. The Division of Fisheries and Wildlife, a subcomponent of the Department of Fisheries, Wildlife and Environmental Law Enforcement, "has authority over all endangered species of Massachusetts including marine mammals."

The DMF has limited the use of gillnets and lobster pot fishing gear in certain areas * * * "In 1994, in response to the alarming depletion of the Harbor porpoise, DMF ordered that all sink gillnets be removed from coastal waters north of Cape Ann every November and from Massachusetts Bay and Cape Cod Bay every March." 939 F. Supp. at 975 (citing DMF Rules Update (Nov. 2, 1994)).

In addition, the DMF has established a 500-yard "buffer zone" around Northern Right whales in Massachusetts coastal waters. 322

C.M.R. § 12.00–12.05 (1993). Defendant Coates admitted that he had "issued a limited number of scientific research permits to some whale watch vessels exempting them from the 500 yard buffer zone surrounding right whales for scientific research purposes upon application."

* * *

II. Endangered Species Act

A. Statutory and Regulatory Background

The Endangered Species Act was enacted with the purpose of conserving endangered and threatened species and the ecosystems on which they depend. See 16 U.S.C. § 1531. The ESA is "the most comprehensive legislation for the preservation of endangered species ever enacted by any nation." TVA v. Hill, 437 U.S. 153, 180 (1978) * * * The Northern Right whale has been listed as endangered pursuant to the ESA. See 50 C.F.R. § 222.23(a).

As it relates to this litigation, the ESA prohibits any person from "tak [ing] any [endangered] species within the United States or the territorial sea of the United States." § 1538(a)(1)(B). In addition, the ESA makes it unlawful for any person "to attempt to commit, solicit another to commit, or cause to be committed, any offense defined" in the ESA. See § 1538(g). The term " 'take' means to harass, harm, pursue, hunt, shoot, wound, kill, trap, capture, or collect, or to attempt to engage in any such conduct." § 1532(19). " 'Take' is defined * * *. in the broadest possible manner to include every conceivable way in which a person can 'take' or attempt to 'take' any fish or wildlife." S.Rep. No. 93–307, at 7 (1973); see also Babbitt v. Sweet Home Chapter of Communities for a Great Oregon, 515 U.S. 687, 703–04 (1995) (citing Senate and House Reports indicating that "take" is to be defined broadly). The Secretary of the Interior has defined "harm" as "an act which actually kills or injures wildlife. Such act may include significant habitat modification or degradation where it actually kills or injures wildlife by significantly impairing essential behavioral patterns, including breeding, feeding, or sheltering." See 50 C.F.R. § 17.3 (1994); Sweet Home, at 695–701 (upholding the regulation as a reasonable interpretation of the statutory language). The term "person" includes "any officer, employee, agent, department, or instrumentality * * * of any State, municipality, or political subdivision of a State * * * [or] any State, municipality, or political subdivision of a State * * * " 16 U.S.C. § 1532(13).

Under the ESA regulatory scheme, the National Marine Fisheries Service ("NMFS"), part of the National Oceanic and Atmospheric Administration ("NOAA") within the Department of Commerce, is responsible for species of the order Cetacea (whales and dolphins) under the ESA and the MMPA. See ESA, 16 U.S.C. §§ 1532(15), 1540; MMPA, 16 U.S.C. §§ 1362(12), 1377; Incidental Take of Endangered, Threatened and Other

Depleted Marine Mammals, 54 Fed. Reg. 40,338 (1989). Under the ESA, the Secretary of Commerce, acting through the NMFS, may permit the taking of an endangered species if that taking is "incidental to, and not the purpose of, the carrying out of an otherwise lawful activity." § 1539(a)(1)(B). Pursuant to an application for an incidental take permit, an applicant must submit a conservation plan discussing the impact of the incidental takings, the steps the applicant will take to minimize the impact, and the alternatives considered with reasons why the alternatives would not be implemented. See § 1539(2)(A).

On August 31, 1995, the NMFS implemented a prohibition on any taking of a Northern Right whale incidental to commercial fishing operations. See Taking of Threatened or Endangered Marine Mammals Incidental to Commercial Fishing Operations; Interim Permit, 60 Fed. Reg. 45,399 (NMFS) (Aug. 31, 1995). In addition, the NMFS recently implemented a ban on approaches within 500 yards of a Northern Right whale. See North Atlantic Northern Right Whale Protection; Interim Final Rule, 62 Fed. Reg. 21562 (Apr. 25, 1997). This restriction brings the federal approach distance in line with the Massachusetts 500 yard approach prohibition. See 322 Code Mass. Reg. § 12.05.

Furthermore, the NMFS has proposed an interim final rule, modifying 50 C.F.R. pt. 229 and set to become effective November 15, 1997, 62 Fed. Reg. 39157 (July 22, 1997), that restricts the use of gillnet and lobster pot fishing gear during specific times of the year unless the gear conforms to marking and design requirements set forth within the provision. See 62 Fed. Reg. at 39184 * * * These proposed restrictions, however, do not impact on the district court's and this court's consideration of whether Massachusetts, through its fishing licensure scheme, has violated the provisions of the ESA.

B. Legal Challenges

The district court's reasoning, in finding that Massachusetts' commercial fishing regulatory scheme likely exacted a taking in violation of the ESA, was founded on two provisions of the ESA read in conjunction. The first relates to the definition of the prohibited activity of a "taking," see § 1538(a)(1)(B), and the second relates to the solicitation or causation by a third party of a prohibited activity, such as a taking, see § 1538(g). The district court viewed these provisions, when read together, to apply to acts by third parties that allow or authorize acts that exact a taking and that, but for the permitting process, could not take place. Indeed, the district court cited several opinions that have also so held. See, e.g., * * * Palila v. Hawaii Dep't of Land and Nat. Resources, 639 F.2d 495, 497–98 (9th Cir.1981) (holding state's practice of maintaining feral goats and sheep in palila's habitat constituted a taking and ordering state to remove goats and sheep); Loggerhead Turtle v. County Council of Volusia County,

896 F. Supp. 1170, 1180–81 (M.D.Fla.1995) (holding that county's author-ization of vehicular beach access during turtle mating season exacted a taking of the turtles in violation of the ESA). The statute not only prohib-its the acts of those parties that directly exact the taking, but also bans those acts of a third party that bring about the acts exacting a taking. We believe that, contrary to the defendants' argument on appeal, the district court properly found that a governmental third party pursuant to whose authority an actor directly exacts a taking of an endangered species may be deemed to have violated the provisions of the ESA.

The defendants argue that the statute was not intended to prohibit state licensure activity because such activity cannot be a "proximate cause" of the taking. The defendants direct our attention to long-standing principles of common law tort in arguing that the district court improper-ly found that its regulatory scheme "indirectly causes" these takings. Spe-cifically, the defendants contend that to construe the proper meaning of "cause" under the ESA, this court should look to common law principles of causation and further contend that proximate cause is lacking here. The defendants are correct that when interpreting a term in a statute which is, like "cause" here, well-known to the common law, the court is to pre-sume that Congress intended the meaning to be interpreted as in the common law. We do not believe, however, that an interpretation of "cause" that includes the "indirect causation" of a taking by the Com-monwealth through its licensing scheme falls without the normal bounda-ries.

The defendants protest this interpretation. Their first argument is that the Commonwealth's licensure of a generally permitted activity does not cause the taking any more than its licensure of automobiles and driv-ers solicits or causes federal crimes, even though automobiles it licenses are surely used to violate federal drug laws, rob federally insured banks, or cross state lines for the purpose of violating state and federal laws. The answer to this argument is that, whereas it is possible for a person li-censed by Massachusetts to use a car in a manner that does not risk the violations of federal law suggested by the defendants, it is not possible for a licensed commercial fishing operation to use its gillnets or lobster pots in the manner permitted by the Commonwealth without risk of violating the ESA by exacting a taking. Thus, the state's licensure of gillnet and lobster pot fishing does not involve the intervening independent actor that is a necessary component of the other licensure schemes which it ar-gues are comparable. Where the state has licensed an automobile driver to use that automobile and her license in a manner consistent with both state and federal law, the violation of federal law is caused only by the actor's conscious and independent decision to disregard or go beyond the licensed purposes of her automobile use and instead to violate federal, and possibly state, law. The situation is simply not the same here. In this instance, the state has licensed commercial fishing operations to use gill-nets and lobster pots in specifically the manner that is likely to result in a violation of federal law. The causation here, while indirect, is not so re-moved that it extends outside the realm of causation as it is understood in the common law.

The defendants' next argument need only detain us momentarily. They contend that the statutory structure of the ESA does not envision utilizing the regulatory structures of the states in order to implement its provisions, but that it instead leaves that implementing authority to NMFS. The point that the defendants miss is that the district court's rul-ing does not impose positive obligations on the Commonwealth by con-verting its regulation of commercial fishing operations into a tool of the federal ESA regulatory scheme. The Commonwealth is not being com-pelled to enforce the provisions of the ESA. Instead, the district court's ruling seeks to end the Commonwealth's continuing violation of the Act.

Defendants also contend that the district court's ruling is erroneous because it fails to give deference to the position of NMFS, the federal agency charged with enforcing the ESA. The defendants' position is flawed for two reasons. First, the ESA gives NMFS, through the Secre-tary, discretion in authorizing takings incidental to certain commercial activity; the Act does not give a federal court, having determined that a taking has occurred, the same discretion in determining whether to grant injunctive relief. Second, the fact that NMFS has expressly declined to ban gillnet or lobster pot fishing in Cape Cod Bay does not reflect a policy determination by NMFS that such a ban is unnecessary. For these two reasons, we find the defendants' deference arguments without merit.

* * *

The defendants * * * contend that the district court ignored evidence of the significant efforts made by the Commonwealth to "minimize North-ern Right Whale entanglements in fishing gear," and evidence of other causes of takings of Northern Right whales. With respect to the determi-nation of whether a taking has occurred, the district court quite rightly disregarded such evidence. Given that there was evidence that any en-tanglement with fishing gear injures a Northern Right whale and given that a single injury to one whale is a taking under the ESA, efforts to minimize such entanglements are irrelevant. For the same reasons, the existence of other means by which takings of Northern Right whales oc-cur is irrelevant to the determination of whether the Commonwealth has engaged in a taking.

Finding neither any error of law nor any clear error with respect to the factual findings, we believe that the district court properly applied the ESA to the facts presented and was correct in enjoining the Commonwealth so as to prevent the taking of Northern Right whales in violation of the ESA.

* * *

NOTES AND QUESTIONS

1. Why did Massachusetts's enactment of right whale protection regulations fail to be a mitigating factor in determining whether the State's licensing of fixed fishing gear in the right whale's critical habitat violated Section 9's takings prohibition?

2. The First Circuit also rejected Massachusetts's claim that the preliminary injunction violated the 10th Amendment. Massachusetts then petitioned for certiorari on grounds that the Section 9 take prohibition violates the 10th Amendment to the U.S. Constitution. Massachusetts relied on the Supreme Court's rulings in New York v. U.S., 505 US 144 (1992) and Printz v. U.S., 117 S.Ct. 2365 (1997). 1998 WL 34103383. The United States filed a brief arguing that Supreme Court review of the injunction was not needed in light of the regulatory action NMFS had subsequently taken under the take reduction planning program of the MMPA. 1998 WL 34103625. Can you explain why this action would render Massachusetts no longer liable for takes under Section 9?

———

2. Regulations to Prevent Takes

The Atlantic Large Whale Take Reduction Plan (ALWTRP) The court in *Coxe* referred to measures NMFS had adopted to restrict seasonally the use of fixed fishing gear in Massachusetts waters that had been designated critical habitat for North Atlantic right whales. These regulations were the first rules to implement the take reduction plan that had been created under the MMPA's Section 118 program. The plan aims to protect three whale species (fin, humpback, and North Atlantic right) from entanglement in fishing gear. The plan covers a large number of fixed gear fisheries, the largest of which is the New England and Mid–Atlantic lobster trap fisheries. The plan relies on a combination of regulatory and non-regulatory measures, including broad gear modifications, time-area closures, disentanglement efforts, outreach and education, and right whale surveillance. As entanglements continue to occur, the plan has been amended several times, including the addition of a dynamic area management program to protect "unexpected aggregations" of right whales by restricting temporarily the type of gear that can be used in a designated area. 67 Fed. Reg. 1133 (Jan. 9, 2002); 67 Fed. Reg. 65722 (Oct. 28, 2002).

In 2002, eight right whales were seen entangled in fishing gear despite the adoption of these measures and some of these whales were later found dead. NMFS reconvened the take reduction team and additional measures were developed. NMFS then released a draft environmental impact statement assessing the alternatives and proposed regulations to amend the ALWTRP on June 21, 2005. 70 Fed. Reg. 35894. Scientists estimate from analysis of photographs of all known right whales that almost 62% of the overall population shows physical evidence of entanglements and that between 10 and 28% experience entanglements each year.

The proposed changes to the Plan include expanding the geographic and temporal requirements of the Plan, include more fisheries within its scope, and further gear modifications to reduce the profile in the water column of lines connecting the traps to the surface and to other traps along the sea floor. 70 Fed. Reg. 35898. These latter changes are very controversial, especially in Maine where lobster gear is placed among rocks and boulders and fishermen rely on floating groundline to avoid chafing and snagging on rocks. For an excellent account of the reaction of fishermen to the right whale take reduction planning process and resulting regulations, see Tora Johnson, Entanglements: The Intertwined Fates of Whales and Fishermen (2005).

The final ALWTRP included area closures, gear modification requirements in areas open to fixed gear fishing, a right whale sighting advisory system, a disentanglement program, and gear research. 50 C.F.R. 229.32. Reducing the risk of entanglement in groundlines by requiring fisheries of the U.S. east coast to use sinking material in their groundlines was the first priority. 72 Fed. Reg. 57104, Oct. 5, 2007. (The groundline connects strings of lobster traps that sit on the seafloor. Between 80 and 85% of all adult right whales have scars indicating prior gear entanglement). These rules exempted inshore areas of the Gulf of Maine, inter alia, from the sinking groundline rule.

In an article in the journal *Science*, leading right whale biologists, several of whom have participated on take reduction teams, wrote of the ALWTRP regulations:

> These closures do not adequately encompass the seasonal movement of right whales, and gear modifications implemented thus far have not reduced entanglement rates. Eight dead right whales in the past 16 months [including 6 adult females, from both ship strikes and gear entanglement injuries] provide clear evidence that management efforts have been woefully inadequate, and much stronger measures are needed to reverse the right whale's decline. [T]he amount of fixed fishing gear in the water column should be eliminated or minimized. There are many steps that could be taken to do this, including (1) mandating changes in the pot-fishing industry (lobster, crab, hagfish,

etc.); (ii) requiring use of alternative rope types (e.g., sinking ground lines) to minimize entanglement deaths; (iii) developing and implementing fishing methods that do not use vertical lines attached to surface buoys; and (iv) developing a fast-track process for permitting and experimenting with conservation-focused fishing gear modifications and implementation. This means streamlining the current rulemaking and NEPA process for right whale research and gear modifications, which now takes years.

Kraus et al., "North Atlantic Right Whales in Crisis," 309 *Science* 561 (July 22, 2005).

In 2011, on the advice of the Atlantic Large Whale Take Reduction Plan team, NMFS held public scoping meetings to aid in the development of a vertical line rule to reduce further the risk of gear entanglement. 76 Fed. Reg. 34654 (June 14, 2011). In the notice of intent to prepare an EIS, the agency discussed its plan to apply the resulting rule selectively and not throughout the Northeast. A "co-occurrence model" is under development to identify areas of greatest overlap between fixed gear fisheries and the three species of large whales covered by the plan. Final rules are projected for publication in 2014.

Ship strikes and right whales Back in 1994, the same plaintiff who brought the *Coxe* case sued both the U.S. Coast Guard and the NMFS for their alleged failure to address the impact of Coast Guard activities on right whales and other endangered marine mammals, including ship strikes during search and rescue missions, and to prepare adequate recovery plans. In Strahan v. Linnon, 967 F. Supp. 581 (D. Mass. 1997), the federal district court ordered the Coast Guard to comply with the ESA, NEPA, and the MMPA in 1995. 967 F. Supp. at 609.

The Coast Guard prepared an EIS, revised its procedures to reduce the likelihood of ship strikes, and conducted ESA consultations with NMFS to determine if these actions were likely to jeopardize the continued existence of northern right whales. The Coast Guard's conservation program and NMFS's actions to implement the recovery plan were later deemed adequate by the district court, and the federal defendants were granted summary judgment. NMFS's consultations with the U.S. Coast Guard resulted in the requirement of the following measures: posting lookouts, reducing speed, providing training, and improving vessel operations to avoid interactions with the listed species. Endangered Species Act Implementation: Hearing Before the House Comm. on Resources, 105th Cong., 2d Sess., March 5, 1998 (statement of Rolland D. Schmitten, Ass't Administrator for Fisheries, National Oceanic and Atmospheric Administration).

The Coast Guard's actions, however, did not reduce the incidence of ship strikes of endangered right whales by merchant vessels. At the urging of the North Atlantic Right Whale Recovery Team's Ship Strike Sub-committee and after a lengthy process of interagency review and numerous stakeholder meetings, the National Marine Fisheries Service announced that it was adopting a Ship Strike Reduction Strategy. 69 Fed. Reg. 30857 (June 1, 2004). The Strategy identified a number of regulatory and non-regulatory actions to reduce the incidence of ship strikes along the right whale's migratory route. Implementation of the Strategy is examined in Chapter 8, Sec. 2, A.

NOTES AND QUESTIONS

1. Are selective area closures, gear modifications, and a dynamic area management system likely to be sufficient to reduce the risk of entanglement in fixed fishing gear? Is it possible that there is just too much fixed fishing gear in the waters that make up the right whale's habitat and migration routes? Should the MMPA's Take Reduction Planning Process process require the stakeholders to consider whether there is more gear in the water than is needed to catch the fishery's sustainable yield? What coordination occurs between implementation of the Sustainable Fisheries Act and Section 118 of the MMPA (16 U.S.C. § 1387)?

2. Given the length of time it takes to review proposed take reduction alternatives under NEPA, is it appropriate to apply NEPA to regulatory actions to protect endangered whales? Is it helpful for identifying and applying the best scientific information available? Note that listing decisions are not subject to NEPA. Should NMFS use its regulatory authority under the ESA to prevent takes instead of the MMPA's take reduction planning process for such a highly endangered marine mammal as the North Atlantic right whale?

3. In 2009, observations of right whale aggregations on previously undocumented wintering grounds in the Gulf of Maine, and the birth of at least 38 calves, suggests measures enacted under the MMPA and the ESA to reduce ship strikes and gear entanglement may be working. See C. Dean, The Fall and Rise of the Right Whale, New York Times (Mar. 16, 2009). In July 2008, shipping lanes across Stellwagen Bank en route to the port of Boston were shifted slightly. Similar action was taken at the entrance to the Bay of Fundy in cooperation with the International Maritime Organization.

3.   Federal Agency Duties under Section 7

Consultation and preparation of a biological opinion on fishery management plans has become the major vehicle used by the National Marine Fisheries Service to address fisheries impacts on endangereded marine species through incidental takes or indirect effects such as competition for or disturbance or prey.

Section 7 of the ESA directs the Secretaries of Interior and Commerce and all other federal agencies to carry out programs to conserve endangered and threatened species. 16 U.S.C. § 1536(a)(1). Section 7 also requires all federal agencies to insure that their actions do not jeopardize the continued existence of listed species. This directive "has been the single most significant provision" of the ESA. Bean and Rowland, The Evolution of National Wildlife Law 240 (3rd ed. 1997). It was the basis for the Supreme Court's decision prohibiting the Tennessee Valley Authority from completing the Tellico Dam because it would jeopardize the snail darter's continued existence. TVA v. Hill, 437 U.S. 153 (1978). Section 7 has also played a major role in U.S. fisheries management, forcing the regional fishery management councils to take account of the role fish and shellfish play in the diets of marine wildlife and in the ecosystems that support them.

In the following case, the court considered whether the commercial fisheries allowed by the Western Pacific Regional Fishery Management Council in the waters around the coral reefs and atolls of the Northwestern Hawaiian Islands were liable for taking the endangered monk seal under Section 9 and whether the NMFS had meet its obligations to prevent jeopardy and adverse habitat modification under Section 7.

GREENPEACE FOUNDATION V. MINETA

U.S. District Court, D. Hawaii, 2000
122 F. Supp.2d 1123

KING, DISTRICT JUDGE.

The Hawaiian monk seal (*Monachus schauinslandi*) ("monk seal") is an endangered species. Statistics on the status of the monk seal paint a grim picture. Recent population estimates indicate that the current monk seal population numbers at approximately 1,300 to 1,400. A 1997 National Marine Fisheries Service ("NMFS") report noted that the seal population at French Frigate Shoals ("FFS") atoll, which is home to one of the largest monk seal colonies, has declined nearly 55% since 1989. The survival rate of monk seal pups is another portent of the bleak outlook for the monk seal. In the mid-1980's, approximately 90% of seal pups at FFS survived to age two. The survival rate declined to about 10% in the mid-1990's. Indeed, NMFS scientists agree that "[t]he overall status of the Hawaiian monk seal is extremely grave."

The monk seal is endemic to Hawaii. It inhabits eight areas in the Northwestern Hawaiian Islands ("NWHI"): FFS, Laysan Island, Lisianski Island, Pearl and Hermes Reef, Midway Atoll, Kure Atoll, Necker Island, and Nihoa Island. Defendant NMFS has designated the NWHI as the monk seal's "critical habitat."

An active lobster fishery and bottomfish fishery operate in the NWHI. NMFS and the Western Pacific Regional Fishery Management

Council ("Council") manage each fishery via separate Fishery Management Plans ("FMP") prepared pursuant to the Magnuson–Stevens Fishery Conservation and Management Act. NMFS adopted the FMP for the Crustacean Fisheries of the Western Pacific Region ("Crustacean FMP") in 1983, and the FMP for the Bottomfish and Seamount Groundfish Fisheries of the Western Pacific Region ("Bottomfish FMP") in 1986. The lobster fishery harvests spiny lobster (*Panulirus marginatus*) and slipper lobster (*Scyllarides squammosus*). The bottomfish fishery targets snappers, groupers, and jacks. Monk seals are known to prey on the species harvested by the fisheries.

Plaintiffs Greenpeace Foundation, Center for Biological Diversity, and Turtle Island Restoration Network ("Plaintiffs") brought this suit against Defendants Norman Mineta, Secretary of Commerce; and Penelope D. Dalton, Assistant Administrator of the NMFS (collectively, "Defendants"). The target of the suit is the embattled NMFS, whom Plaintiffs allege is violating the Administrative Procedure Act ("APA"), by managing the fisheries in a manner that does not comply with Sections 7 and 9 of the Endangered Species Act ("ESA") * * *

The crux of the ESA claims is that the fisheries are depleting the monk seal's food supply and interacting with monk seals in an injurious manner. Cast in the language of the ESA, the claims allege that (1) NMFS has been remiss in performing its Section 7 duty to consult with the Secretary of Commerce regarding the impact of the FMPs on protected species, and (2) the operation of the fisheries has resulted in "takes" of monk seals in violation of Section 9.

* * *

II. Endangered Species Act

A. Section 7

Section 7 of the ESA requires every federal agency to "insure that any action authorized, funded, or carried out by such agency * * * is not likely to jeopardize the continued existence" or "result in the destruction or adverse modification of habitat" of listed species. To fulfill its obligation under Section 7, an agency must consult with the Secretary of Commerce. See id. An agency must use "the best scientific and commercial data available" in conducting the consultation. Id.

Consultation can be informal or formal. Informal consultation is an optional process designed to assist an agency in determining whether formal consultation is required. If an agency determines during informal consultation that the proposed action is not likely to adversely affect listed species or critical habitat, and the Director concurs, the consultation process is terminated, and no further action is required. See id. If, however, the agency determines that the proposed action may affect listed species or critical habitat, formal consultation is required.

After consultation is complete, the Secretary must prepare a biological opinion. The biological opinion must include a "detailed discussion of the effects of the action on listed species or critical habitat" and the Secretary's "opinion on whether the action is likely to jeopardize the continued existence of a listed species or result in the destruction or adverse modification of critical habitat," (a "jeopardy opinion"), or whether the proposed action poses no threat of jeopardy or adverse modification (a "no jeopardy opinion"). If new information reveals effects of the action that may affect listed species or critical habitat in a manner or to an extent not previously considered, the agency must reinitiate consultation. Consultation must also be reinitiated if the action is modified in a manner that causes an effect to a listed species or its habitat that was not previously considered.

Plaintiffs contend that NMFS ignored the best scientific and commercial data available in preparing the biological opinions on the Crustacean FMP. In reviewing whether NMFS's past consultation efforts satisfied Section 7 requirements, the Court applies the standard set forth in the APA, which requires that an agency action be set aside if it is "arbitrary, capricious, an abuse of discretion or otherwise not in accordance with law."

NMFS issued the first biological opinion on the Crustacean FMP in 1981. The theme pervading the opinion is that insufficient information prevented detailed assessment of the impact of the FMP on the monk seal. The opinion identified spiny lobster as a prey species for monk seals, but it could not ascertain its relationship to the monk seal diet. The opinion stated that monk seals are "opportunistic feeders supported by a diverse prey base." NMFS believed that monk seals could adapt to other prey species if lobster were to become unavailable. However, the available information did not permit NMFS to assess the amount of shift in the monk seal's diet from lobster to other prey caused by lobster fishing or the impact of that stress. NMFS opined that the lobster fishery did have the "potential of reducing the lobster populations to levels at which lobsters are no longer available to monk seals." NMFS further admitted that the maximum sustainable yield ("MSY") and optimum yield ("OY") estimates of the lobster population calculated by the Council were too high and rested on the erroneous assumption that the lobster stocks in the NWHI were unexploited. The opinion warned: "[I]f OY is overestimated the fishery could result in depletion of the lobster resources. Therefore the FMP does not insure the availability of lobster to monk seals." The opinion concluded that "[t]here is insufficient information available for the Council to be able to insure that the proposed activity will not jeopardize the continued existence of the monk seal * * * " NMFS stressed that the opinion was not to be construed as a "no jeopardy opinion" and that it "in no way alleviate[d] the Council of its obligation under Section 7(a)(2) of the ESA to insure that the activities conducted under the spiny lobster FMP are not likely to jeopardize the continued existence of the threatened and endangered species which occur in the NWHI * * * " Despite this conclusion, the opinion paradoxically recommended implementation of the FMP.[11]

The conclusions of the 1981 biological opinion are difficult to reconcile with the recommendation of NMFS that the FMP be implemented. NMFS has an affirmative obligation under Section 7(a)(2) to insure that agency action will not jeopardize the continued existence of listed species or adversely modify their habitat. Certainly, an agency's assessment of proposed action is limited by the best scientific and commercial information available. Data on the role of lobster in the monk seal's diet was admittedly sparse at the time the 1981 biological opinion was prepared. Nonetheless, when an agency concludes after consultation that it cannot insure that the proposed action will not result in jeopardy, and yet proceeds to implement such action, the agency has flouted the plain requirements of Section 7.

The next biological opinion prepared in connection with the lobster fishery, issued in 1996, assessed the impact of Amendment 9 to the Crustacean FMP. Amendment 9 established a new harvest guideline system that allowed fishermen to retain berried and undersized lobsters in a catch. The rationale was that the retention limits then in effect resulted in waste from mortality of lobsters that are captured and released without contributing to the protection of the reproductive potential of lobster stocks. The new proposed harvest management program was based on the existing model for calculating the exploitable lobster population. The models indicated that stocks of spiny lobster would remain healthy over the long term. At the same time, the opinion noted a "continuing decline in pup production, and total seal counts over the past six years, [which] is cause for significant concern. NMFS attributed the decline to several factors, one of which was the reduction of the availability of prey such as lobster due to lobster fishing. The availability of lobster had been particularly low at FFS for a number of years. NMFS maintained, as it did before and does today, that "monk seals appear to be very opportunistic and catholic feeders." However, NMFS still had not elucidated the importance of lobsters to the monk seal's diet. Regarding the effect of Amendment 9 on the monk seal, the opinion stated: "[G]iven the relatively healthy status of the stocks of lobsters and the small contribution of French Frigate Shoals to the fishery, it is expected that catch competition with monk

---

[11] The biological opinion reasoned that implementing the Crustacean FMP was preferable to taking no action because the FMP would regulate the fishing industry, whereas the fishery would operate and expand without restriction in the absence of an FMP. NMFS constructs a false dichotomy. If conservation of the monk seal is a high priority objective for NMFS, an unconsidered alternative would have been to regulate lobster fishing by banning it until more information regarding the impacts of lobster fishing on listed species was available.

seals at French Frigate Shoals would not likely occur." The opinion concluded that the annual harvest guidelines formulated under the proposed harvest rate strategy would protect the reproductive capacity and existing stock of lobster in the NWHI.

The 1996 opinion in many ways perpetuated the errors of the 1981 opinion. As a memorandum from one NMFS scientist to another regarding the 1996 opinion reveals, NMFS takes the position in the opinion that its knowledge of monk seal behavior had not advanced much in the past fifteen years. And so management of the lobster fishery remained relatively unchanged. The harvest management system under Amendment 9 was predicated on the existing model of calculating the exploitable population of lobster, with the addition of a guideline permitting retention of berried and undersized lobsters. NMFS ignored the flaws of that model, as evidenced by its observation in the 1996 opinion that the status of the lobster stocks was relatively healthy. In fact, the lobster stocks showed signs of stress. From 1983 to 1991, the catch per unit effort ("CPUE") declined from 2.71 to 0.56 legal spiny and slipper lobsters per trap haul. NMFS closed the lobster fishery in 1991 and 1993. It reopened the fishery briefly in 1994, but aborted the season shortly after it began when it realized that its harvest quota was too high. In the year before the 1996 biological opinion issued, the CPUE was an anemic 0.60. Such data should have alerted NMFS that the existing model of calculating the exploitable lobster population was in need of revision. NMFS ignored the data.

Moreover, the 1996 opinion overemphasized the importance of the status of the lobster stocks at FFS. A 1992 NMFS report on the status of the monk seal found that monk seals at FFS may depend on the availability of food at Gardner Pinnacles and Necker Island, where most of the lobster harvest has occurred for many years. The 1996 opinion did not examine the availability of lobster in those areas of the NWHI.

A review of the 1996 opinion convinces the Court that NMFS did not adequately discharge its duties under Section 7(a)(2). If, in the 1981 opinion NMFS was uncertain of the impact of the FMP because it knew too little about the monk seal diet, by 1996 it was emboldened by its ignorance to draw definitive conclusions about the impact. NMFS reiterated in the 1996 opinion that the available information still had not clarified the importance of lobster in the monk seal diet, yet, in a departure from its conclusion in 1981, NMFS this time concluded that no jeopardy to the monk seal would result. NMFS arrived at this conclusion despite the fact that the fishery operated up to the 10- and 20-fathom isobath areas of Maro Reef, FFS, and Necker Island—all within the critical habitat of the monk seal, which by then had been designated. The explanation for the reversal in judgment is that the 1996 opinion focused on Amendment 9 alone. But ESA regulations require NMFS to consider "the effects of [agency action] as a whole." While Amendment 9 might be an innocuous measure as far as monk seal survival is concerned, it is appended to an FMP that NMFS could not insure would be consistent with the continued existence of the monk seal. In making a "no jeopardy" determination in the 1996 opinion, NMFS essentially affirmed that the existing model of calculating lobster stocks was workable. The available data indicated it was not. By neglecting such data, and by failing to evaluate the Crustacean FMP's impact on prey availability for the monk seal in all areas of the NWHI (not just FFS), NMFS was arbitrary and capricious in reaching the conclusions contained in the 1996 biological opinion.

* * *

NMFS has failed to fulfill its "rigorous" affirmative duty under Section 7 to "insure" that implementation of the Crustacean FMP does not result in jeopardy or adverse modification. NMFS cannot speculate that no jeopardy to monk seals or adverse modification of their critical habitat will occur because it lacks enough information regarding the impact of the fishery on seals. Such a conclusion is arbitrary and capricious. Accordingly, the Court GRANTS summary judgment to Plaintiffs and DENIES summary judgment to Defendants on the claim that past consultation on the Crustacean FMP violates Section 7(a)(2) and the APA.

B. Section 9

Section 9(a)(1)(B) of the ESA makes it unlawful for any person to take any endangered species of wildlife within the United States or the territorial seas of the United States. "Take" is defined as "harass, harm, pursue, hunt, shoot, wound, kill, trap, capture, or collect, or to attempt to engage in any such conduct." The term "harm" includes "significant habitat modification or degradation which actually kills or injures fish or wildlife by significantly impairing essential behavioral patterns, including breeding, spawning, rearing, migrating, feeding or sheltering." 50 C.F.R. § 222.102; see also Babbitt v. Sweet Home Chapter of Communities for a Great Oregon, 515 U.S. 687, 115 S.Ct. 2407, 132 L.Ed.2d 597 (1995) (upholding ESA regulation that included "significant habitat modification" in the definition of "harm").

1. The Lobster Fishery

Plaintiffs claim that the lobster fishery adversely modifies the habitat of the monk seal by depleting the lobster population in the NWHI. It is undisputed that the fishery removes prey from the critical habitat of the monk seal. The question is whether the removal of prey results in adverse habitat modification. Plaintiffs offer circumstantial evidence that it does. One study revealed that monk seals at FFS dive deeper and travel farther to forage than seals at Pearl and Hermes Reef because there is less food available at FFS. Another study found that monk seals at FFS consume more cephalopods than seals elsewhere because other prey is less available to them. Decreased prey availability has been hypothesized to be a cause of the decline in the reproduction, survival, and condition of surviving immature seals. Plaintiffs also rely on studies of the monk seal's diet. One study found that lobster contains amino acids and macrominerals important to bodily functions of the monk seal. Fatty acid signature analysis of monk seal blubber suggests that lobster comprises a significant part of the monk seal's diet.

The information in the record is insufficient to establish as a matter of law that lobster is absolutely critical to the diet of the monk seal. Plaintiffs may of course rely on circumstantial evidence to show a causal link between lobster fishing and the monk seal population. Circumstantial evidence was the basis for the findings of adverse habitat modification in Palila v. Hawaii Department of Land & Natural Resources, 471 F. Supp. 985 (D. Haw.1979), aff'd, 639 F.2d 495 (9th Cir.1981), and Sierra Club v. Lyng, 694 F. Supp. 1260 (E.D. Tex.1988), aff'd in relevant part, Sierra Club v. Yeutter, 926 F.2d 429 (5th Cir.1991). The difference is that the agency action in those cases destroyed or modified a feature of the species' habitat that was decidedly critical to the continued existence of the species. In *Palila,* this Court found that mamane trees were clearly essential to the endangered Palila's survival. See Palila, 471 F. Supp. at 989; see also Palila v. Hawaii Dep't of Land & Natural Resources, 73 F. Supp.2d 1181, 1182 (D. Haw.1999). In *Lyng,* the court found that the very shelter upon which the red-cockaded woodpecker depended for survival was threatened by the Forest Service's management of the Texas national forests.

Here, it is not certain that lobster plays such an essential role in the monk seal diet that a reduction of lobster prey dooms the monk seal to extinction. The studies Plaintiffs rely upon do not prove otherwise. Studies of monk seal foraging behavior may indicate a decrease in prey availability in general, but they do not show that it is a reduction in the availability of *lobster that causes* monk seals to consume other prey. Indeed, one study hypothesized that monk seals were consuming more octopi because fewer teleosts (ray-finned fish) were available. Nor do the data based on fatty acid signature analysis prove that the monk seal relies heavily on lobster as part of its diet. Dr. Sara Iverson, the researcher conducting the studies, submits a declaration to the Court in which she states that her findings "cannot be conclusive and should not be used as a basis for decisions concerning possible interactions between fisheries and monk seals." Dr. Iverson emphasizes that her research is "preliminary" and that it has not been peer reviewed. She anticipates an additional three years of research before she can make "firm and defensible conclusions" about the importance of various prey in the monk seal diet.[14]

The Court agrees that preliminary findings are not a basis for a conclusive determination that lobster comprises a significant and essential portion of the monk seal diet. On the basis of the currently available scientific information, this Court cannot find as a matter of law that the removal of lobster from the monk seal's critical habitat results in "harm" to the monk seal within the meaning of Section 9. The role of lobster in the monk seal diet is a question of fact that precludes summary judgment on the Section 9 claim.

The ruling does not assure victory for NMFS. NMFS's position is essentially that it is innocent of Section 9 violations because it is not aware of any data that confirms that it is in violation of Section 9; such is a head-in-the-sand attitude we do not condone.[15] It is also a position in conflict with the underlying philosophy of the ESA. But to this problem we assign the requirements of NEPA and Section 7 of the ESA, not section 9.[16]

Because a material question of fact exists, the Court DENIES summary judgment to Plaintiffs and DENIES summary judgment to Defendants on the Section 9 claim with respect to the lobster fishery.

NOTES AND QUESTIONS

1. NMFS designated the waters around the Northwestern Hawaiian Islands as critical habitat for monk seal out to a depth of 10 fathoms in 1986. 51 Fed. Reg. 16047 (April 30, 1986). The Marine Mammal Commission had recommended in 1976, when the monk seal was listed as endangered, that waters out to three miles be designated critical habitat. Why did it take the Service ten years to designate critical habitat? Was scientific uncertainty responsible? For an account of the contentious designation and the roles of poli-

---

[14] Dr. Iverson has presented her preliminary findings to NMFS's Monk Seal Recovery Team, but chiefly for the purpose of demostrating fatty acid signature analysis as an ainnovative technique of examining diets in free-ranging animals, and to report on the progress of her research.

[15] With all this talk of seals, fish, and lobsters, we break the monotony by tendering a fact about a terrestrial member of the animal kingdom. The legend that ostriches bury their heads when faced with danger is just that: a legend. The real story is that ostriches lie on the ground with their necks outstretched to avoid detection. See Flightless Birds, *in Compton's Interactive Encyclopedia* (1996).

[16] Under NEPA, federal agencies are under a duty "to gather information and do independent research when missing information that is 'important,' 'significant,' or 'essential' to a reasoned choice among alternatives. Section 7 of the ESA requires agencies to use the "best scientific and commercial data available" in conducting consultation on agency action. Moreover, an agency has a correlative duty to conduct independent research and to make projections of impact to protected species based on existing information.

tics and scientific information, see R. Tobin, The Expendable Future: U.S. Politics and the Protection of Biological Diversity (1990), 220–223.

2. In *Mineta*, Judge King noted that with respect to federal fisheries management, the NMFS consults with itself. Because it has responsibility for approving and implementing FMPs and amendments that authorize the fisheries that potentially affect the listed species, NMFS is both the action agency and the consulting agency under Section 7 (a)(2). Can the agency simultaneously meet its mandates under the Magnuson–Stevens Act and the ESA? Note that the Magnuson–Stevens Act requires the Secretary of Commerce, upon receipt of an FMP or amendment, to "immediately commence a review of the plan or amendment to determine whether it is consistent with the national standards, the other provisions of this Act, and any other applicable law; * * * " 16 U.S.C. § 1854(a).

3. When in the FMP process is the agency required to prepare a biological opinion? Is the regional fishery management council the action agency under the ESA, responsible for determining if a listed species is likely to be affected by its management of a fishery? Are the commercial fishermen who will be subject to the FMP's regulations "applicants" and therefore entitled under FWS and NMFS regulations to review the draft biological opinion? See 50 C.F.R. Part 402 (interagency consultation guidelines).

In, Hawaii Longline Assoc. v. NMFS 2002 WL 732363 (DDC 2002) (not reported in F. Supp.2d), the magistrate judge recommended that the federal court invalidate the 2001 biological opinion on the FMP for the W. Pacific pelagic longline fishery for tuna and swordfish. The biological opinion had found that the fishery as operated under the FMP jeopardized the continued existence of the green, leatherback, and loggerhead sea turtles, and set out mandatory alternative regulations for the fishery to avoid jeopardy. Invalidation was recommended on the procedural grounds that association was entitled to comment on a draft of the biological opinion because it was an "applicant" under the terms of 50 C.F.R. Part 402.

4. **The Steller Sea Lion and Alaskan Groundfish Fisheries.** One of the possible indirect effects of a fishery on endangered wildlife is the impact it may have on the availability of fish that are the species' prey. Will a regional fishery management council be required to lower a commercial fishing quota to meet the prey requirements of an endangered marine mammal? Section 7 of the ESA requires such action if the operation of the fishery would jeopardize the existence of the species or alter its critical habitat. But the scientific evidence needed to support a jeopardy determination is not readily available, nor is it clear how a fishery can be modified to fashion a reasonable and prudent alternative that will not lead to jeopardy. The impact of the Alaskan pollock fishery's removal of vast amounts of fish from the Bering Sea and Aleutian Islands marine ecosystem on the endangered Steller sea lion has been hotly contested, resulting in some very important case law, but no consensus. See J. McBeath, Management of the Commons for Biodiversity: Lessons from the North Pacific, 28 Marine Policy 523 (2004) for a review of

the cases, especially the Greenpeace v. NMFS quartet, decided by Judge Zilly of the Western District of Washington federal district court, beginning with Greenpeace v. NMFS, 55 F. Supp.2d 1248 (W.D. Wash. 1999) and Greenpeace v. NMFS, 80 F. Supp.2d 1137 (W.D. Wash. 2000).

Senator Stevens of Alaska attached an amendment to an FY 2001 appropriations bill requiring phased implementation of the new measures required under Section 7 and a National Academy of Sciences review of the scientific underpinning of the biological opinion. He also added language authorizing $30 million in disaster relief for Alaska fishing communities and $30 million for additional research. These studies were directed to test the validity of competing theories of what is causing the sea lion's decline, including the theory of nutritional stress and localized prey depletion NMFS relied on, climate regime shifts, and the 'trophic cascade' effect of killer whale predation on the Bering Sea ecosystem.

The National Academy of Sciences report on the role of Alaskan fisheries in the decline of the Steller sea lion is National Research Council, Decline of the Steller Sea Lion in Alaskan Waters: Untangling Food Webs and Fishing Nets (2003).

For a discussion of U.S. management of the Bering Sea in light of evolving principles of international environmental law regarding ecosystem management, see T. Smith, Comment, United States Practice and the Bering Sea: Is It Consistent with a Norm of Ecosystem Management?, 1 Ocean & Coastal L.J. 141 (1995).

4.   Recovery Plans and Species Reintroductions

Sometimes, takes of individuals for the purpose of reintroduction of an endangered species can fail to meet the "no jeopardy or adverse modification" standard of Section 7. Species reintroductions to marine ecosystems are less common than in terrestrial ecosystems, but they are no less controversial. When Congress strikes a political compromise and specifies the conditions for the reintroduction program, as it did for the threatened California sea otter, under what circumstances can the Fish & Wildlife Service or NMFS terminate the program?

The Fish & Wildlife Service was directed by Congress to undertake a reintroduction and translocation program for the California sea otter after it was listed as threatened in 1977 (42 Fed. Reg. 2968, Jan. 14, 1977). Public Law 99–625 (1986). The special authorization was necessary because the southern sea otter is a threatened species under the ESA and depleted under the MMPA, but the MMPA does not have a provision similar to Section 10(j) of the ESA authorizing translocations for the purpose of establishing experimental populations. The Marine Mammal Commission and the FWS believed it was appropriate to reintroduce southern sea otters to areas in their historic range to reduce the risk that a catastrophic oil spill would wipe out the remaining population. When Congress enacted the provision, however, it directed the agency to establish a management zone around the translocation zone from which sea otters would be recaptured and removed, in order to prevent conflicts with shellfish fisheries and military activities. 50 C.F.R. § 17.84(d). See W. Booth, Reintroducing a Political Animal, 241 Science 156 (1988), cited by Holly Doremus, Restoring Endangered Species: The Importance of Being Wild, 23 Harv. Envtl. L.R. 1 (1999). Under the special act, Congress exempted the military from Section 7 consultation requirements regarding the experimental, translocated population.

After several years and several deaths of recaptured otters and the disappearance of others, the Service decided to terminate the program. It reached this decision after a Section 7 biological opinion determining that continuation of the program jeopardized the survival and recovery of the California sea otter. Dept. of Interior, Fish & Wildlife Service, Notice of Policy Regarding Capture and Removal of Southern Sea Otters in a Designated Management Zone, 66 Fed. Reg. 6649 (Jan. 22, 2001). Commercial sea urchin fishermen sued to keep the program operating, while conservation groups sued FWS to make a final decision to end the program and let otters expand their range naturally into southern California waters. The Otter Project v. Salazar, 712 F.Supp.2d 999 (N.D. Cal. 2010)(FWS regulations required the agency to make a failure determination which was unreasonably delayed in violation of the Adminstrative Procedure Act). See FWS, Final Rule and NEPA Record of Decision on Southern Sea Otter Translocation, 77 Fed. Reg. 75266 (Dec. 19, 2012).

NOTES AND QUESTIONS

1. If it is not working, why is it necessary for the FWS, the agency responsible for the recovery of the sea otter, to undertake a Section 7 consultation on the continuation of the sea otter translocation project? In April 2000, after the FWS circulated a draft biological opinion recommending termination of the program, California shellfish fishermen filed suit challenging the FWS's decision not to continue capturing and removing sea otters from the management zone. Public Law 99–625 exempts translocation and management activities from the Section 9 take prohibition and from the MMPA take provision, but the FWS argues that this exemption does not extend to the program if it has been found under Section 7 to jeopardize the continued survival and recovery of the species. The Defenders of Wildlife intervened in the suit in support of the FWS after the Service published the Jan. 2001 policy statement. The plaintiffs voluntarily dismissed their suit in July 2001.

2. For background on the reintroduction under the ESA, see Federico Cheever, From Population Segregation to Species Zoning: The Evolution of Reintroduction Law Under Section 10(j) of the Endangered Species Act, 1 Wyo. L. Rev. 287 (2001).

3. In Limon v. California Dept. of Fish & Game, 2004 WL 2092223, un-published in Cal. Rptr. 3d (Cal. App. 2d Dist. 2004), the court upheld a state regulation restricting the use of gillnets and trammel nets to waters deeper than 60 fathoms off California's central coast to prevent entanglement of sea otters. California's Endangered Species Act declares sea otters a "fully pro-tected" species and permits no takes. The State had extended the ban to deeper waters and to the central coast region after it became clear the otter had extended its range and frequently dove to such depths (and wildlife groups had threatened an ESA citizen suit for California's alleged violation of Section 9). Fishermen challenged the statistical evidence on which the Fish & Game Dept. had based its estimated mortality rate due to entanglement. The State of California argued that if its regulations banning gillnets in central California waters were invalidated, the State would be liable for a take of the threatened species under the holding in Strahan v. Coxe, supra. To the fish-ermen's substantive due process claim, the court reiterated a previous hold-ing that there is no constitutional right to use gillnets and trammel nets in state waters where it endangers sea otters. California Gillnetters Assoc. v. Dept. of Fish & Game, 39 Ca. App. 4th 1145 (1995) (upholding Proposition 132 (Cal. Const., art. 10B, § 3) prohibiting gill and trammel nets in Marine Resources Protection Zones).

CHAPTER 8

SHIPPING, MARINE PROTECTED AREAS, AND MILITARY USES OF THE SEA

■ ■ ■

Historically, navigation and shipping have been the primary uses of the oceans. As such these uses have benefited the most from the traditional "freedom of the seas" principle of international law. Provisions of the Law of Sea Convention require coastal nations to allow "innocent passage" of foreign-flag surface vessels within their territorial seas and to abide by international standards on the construction, design, manning and equipment of vessels in regulating shipping. Federal regulation of shipping in the U.S. is a complex scheme of licensing and navigational standards, with an overlay of environmental regulation that is often a secondary concern. Negotiated under the auspices of the U.N. International Maritime Organization, these standards often lag behind the needs of coastal states for protections from the risks of oil spills. Even when these standards reflect the best available technology, compliance can be difficult to ensure with the increasing prominence of open registry states, often called "flags of convenience," and the competition of ports for global trade.

When U.S. coastal states perceive the risks to their coastlines to be especially high, they may enact laws that supplement federal regulation of shipping and face legal challenge under the Supremacy Clause. But coastal shipping also produces air pollution, introduces non-native species into ports and harbors, and can increase the risk of extinction of imperiled species. The federal statutes that address these threats, such as the Clean Water Act, the Endangered Species Act, and NEPA, encourage states to set their own standards. And the National Marine Sanctuaries Act authorizes federal-state cooperation in the management of marine areas of special value. In the past decade, spatial planning has emerged as a process that may be able to work through the federalism challenges of protecting marine and coastal ecosystems. Can federal agencies, with their numerous and often competing mandates and authorities, effectively participate in spatial planning? In the face of ocean warming and the need to protect the resilience of rare or vulnerable marine ecosystems, can the U.S. president decree large-scale marine reserves by executive order or proclamation in the U.S. EEZ?

1. ENVIRONMENTAL REGULATION OF SHIPPING

A. PREVENTING OIL POLLUTION

UNITED STATES V. MASSACHUSETTS

U.S. Court of Appeals, First Circuit, 2007
493 F.3d 1

LYNCH, CIRCUIT JUDGE.

The states and the federal government have ongoing conflicts about the adequacy of federal laws protecting against maritime oil spills. Several states, including Massachusetts, have passed laws to protect particularly sensitive waterways. The framework for analyzing such conflicts derives from the several preemption analyses set forth in United States v. Locke, 529 U.S. 89 (2000), and Ray v. Atlantic Richfield Co., 435 U.S. 151 (1978). In short, depending on the nature of state and federal regulations, either field preemption, conflict preemption, or overlap analysis is used to determine whether state law impermissibly infringes on federal authority.

After a catastrophic oil spill in Buzzards Bay in 2003, the Commonwealth of Massachusetts enacted the Massachusetts Oil Spill Prevention Act (MOSPA). *See* 2004 Mass. Acts 920 (codified as amended primarily at Mass. Gen. Laws ch. 21, §§ 42, 50B–50E, and ch. 21M). MOSPA imposes requirements designed to reduce the risk of oil spills, and to ensure that adequate resources are available to remedy such spills.

The United States sued Massachusetts on January 18, 2005, seeking to enjoin the enforcement of several MOSPA provisions. The United States alleged that these provisions were preempted by the Ports and Waterways Safety Act of 1972, as amended by the Port and Tanker Safety Act of 1978 (collectively, the "PWSA"), and by regulations promulgated thereunder by the Coast Guard. This allegation included a claim that MOSPA's financial assurance requirement, which requires certain vessels to post a bond to ensure their ability to respond financially to an oil spill, *see* Mass. Gen. Laws ch. 21, § 50C, was preempted by Title II of the PWSA, notwithstanding relevant savings clauses in the Oil Pollution Act of 1990 ("OPA") (codified at 33 U.S.C. § 2718). The United States did not assert violations of any treaties or claim that federal foreign affairs powers were at issue.

The Commonwealth disputed each claim of preemption. It argued that Congress had given the states leeway to regulate particularly sensitive local waterways, at least in the absence of an actual conflict with a federal statute or regulation. In the state's view, there was no such conflict.

The district court, acting on the United States' motion for judgment on the pleadings, and thus without taking evidence, entered judgment for plaintiffs and permanently enjoined all of the challenged provisions. United States v. Massachusetts, 440 F.Supp.2d 24, 48 (D. Mass. 2006).

On appeal, three sets of amici have filed briefs in support of Massachusetts: the "state amici" (which include the states of Washington, Alaska, California, Maine, Oregon, and Rhode Island, and the Commonwealth of Puerto Rico), the "local government amici" (which include the towns of Bourne, Fairhaven, Falmouth, Gosnold, Marion, and Westport, and the city of New Bedford), and the Conservation Law Foundation.

The Commonwealth's appeal challenges the injunction only insofar as it blocked three of MOSPA's provisions: an enhanced manning requirement for tank barges and tow vessels in Buzzards Bay, *see* Mass. Gen. Laws ch. 21M, § 4; a tug escort requirement for special interest waters, *see id.* § 6; and a requirement that certain vessels obtain a certificate of financial assurance, the amount of which can vary, *see id.* ch. 21, § 50C.

We vacate the entry of judgment and the permanent injunction for the United States, and we remand for further proceedings consistent with this opinion. As we explain, the district court did not adhere to the analytical structure the Supreme Court has required to resolve federal-state conflicts in this area. The district court acted prematurely.

I. Factual Background

Buzzards Bay is one of five recognized Estuaries of National Significance. *See* 69 Fed. Reg. 62,427, 62,428 (Oct. 26, 2004); *see also* 33 U.S.C. § 1330 (establishing a national estuary program). Massachusetts has designated the Bay as part of an "Ocean Sanctuary." Mass. Gen. Laws ch. 132A, § 13(c). The bay is characterized by unusually dangerous ledges, reefs, and currents. Most of the Bay is less than 50 feet deep, and the Bay is less than 8 miles wide. *See* B. Howes et al., *Ecology of Buzzards Bay: An Estuarine Profile* 7, 23–24 (U.S. Dep't of the Interior, Biological Report No. 33, 1996), *available at* http://cuadra.cr.usgs.gov/Techrpt/96–33.pdf. The Bay's Cape Cod Canal has unusually strong tidal currents, and it "represents a significant navigational challenge." *Id.* at 98.

Significant volumes of oil are transported through the Bay and Canal each year. In 2002, about 80% of the trips were made in single-hull barges. 71 Fed. Reg. 15,649, 15,650 (Mar. 29, 2006). In the state's view, the waters of Buzzards Bay are subject to a disproportionate and unnecessary risk of an oil spill. A Coast Guard-sponsored report has concluded that "the risk for oil or hazardous material discharge in Buzzards Bay is relatively high." There have already been several damaging spills in the Bay. In 1969, roughly 175,000 gallons of No. 2 fuel oil spilled into the Bay after the barge *Florida* ran aground. *Id.* In 1974, a sizable amount of oil spilled from the *Bouchard No. 65,* inflicting significant damage on local marine life. Howes et al., *supra,* at 102–03. In 1977, there was yet another *Bouchard* spill, this one releasing 81,000 gallons of fuel oil into the water. 71 Fed. Reg. at 15,650. In 1986, the tank barge *ST–85* was grounded in the Bay, spilling 119,000 gallons of gasoline. In 1999, there was another grounding, this one involving a vessel carrying 4.7 million gallons of No. 6 fuel oil. Most recently, in April 2003 the barge *Bouchard–120* released an estimated 98,000 gallons of heavy fuel oil into the Bay, killing hundreds of birds, closing thousands of acres of shellfish beds, affecting over 90 miles of coastline, and generating significant clean-up costs. Massachusetts responded by enacting MOSPA on August 4, 2004. 2004 Mass. Acts at 933.

II. Description of Federal Law

A. Background

Federal regulation of maritime commerce has existed since the founding of the country. *See* Act of Sept. 1, 1789, ch. 11, § 1, 1 Stat. 55. Federal regulation specifically geared toward the transport of dangerous cargoes started with the Tank Vessel Act of 1936, Pub.L. No. 74–765, 49 Stat. 1889. *See* K. Brooks, California Oil Spill Laws in the Wake of United States v. Locke, 12 U.S.F. Mar. L.J. 227, 230 (1999–2000). Regulatory involvement increased after 1967, the year of a massive oil spill involving a supertanker [Torrey Canyon] off the coast of England. Indeed, Congress has since enacted more stringent legislation for oil tankers and more comprehensive remedies for oil spills.

The Ports and Waterways Safety Act (PWSA) is a key component of this congressional response. It has two titles, both of which are at issue here, which we describe in greater detail later. Title I authorizes the Coast Guard to issue regulations on subjects within that title, although it does not so mandate. 33 U.S.C. § 1223(a). Title II works differently; it *requires* the Coast Guard to issue federal regulations governing subjects covered by that title. 46 U.S.C. § 3703(a).

Several states have enacted statutes and regulations designed to give still greater protection against oil spills. The Supreme Court's 1978 decision in *Ray* concerned such state laws. *Ray* held that certain provisions of a Washington statute (concerning tanker design, tanker size, and pilotage requirements for enrolled vessels) were preempted by federal law. 435 U.S. at 159–60, 168, 178. *Ray* did uphold Washington's limited tug escort requirement for Puget Sound against a preemption challenge. Id. at 173.

Despite the protections of the PWSA, in 1989 the supertanker *Exxon Valdez* ran aground in Alaska, causing the largest oil spill in United States history. The key congressional response was the 1990 enactment of the Oil Pollution Act (OPA). OPA has nine titles, including provisions imposing liability on parties responsible for damages and other costs stemming from oil spills. *See* 33 U.S.C. § 2702. Two "savings clauses" in OPA's Title I expressly preserve and recognize state authority to impose additional liability requirements and penalties. *Id.* § 2718(a)(1), (c).

The scope of these savings clauses was at issue in *Locke*. On certiorari to the Supreme Court, the United States argued that several provisions of the Washington Administrative Code were preempted; the federal government stressed the foreign relations and international commerce aspects of the case. Locke, 529 U.S. at 102–03.

Locke thus presented issues regarding the need for national uniformity for this country in the international community. Id. at 102–03; *cf.* Crosby v. Nat'l Foreign Trade Council, 530 U.S. 363, 373–74 (2000). The United States argued that various treaties preempted Washington's regulations, including the International Convention for the Safety of Life at Sea, 1974, 32 U.S.T. 47; the International Convention for Prevention of Pollution from Ships, 1973, S. Exec. Doc. C, 93–1, 12 I.L.M. 1319, as amended by 1978 Protocol, S. Exec. Doc. C, 96–1, 17 I.L.M. 546; and the International Convention of Standards of Training, Certification and Watchkeeping for Seafarers, with Annex, 1978 (STCW), S. Exec. Doc. EE 96–1, C.T.I.A. No. 7624. Locke, 529 U.S. at 102–03. The Court did not reach the United States' arguments based on these treaties and international agreements. Id. at 103.

Locke governs this case. The distinctions that *Locke* drew are the subject of dispute among the parties here. *Locke* held that several provisions of Washington's regulations were preempted by federal law. *Id.* at 112–17. The *Locke* Court held that PWSA's Title II preempted three state regulations (requiring training for tanker crews, mandating English language proficiency, and imposing a general statewide navigation-watch requirement). *Id.* at 112–14. The Court also held that a fourth regulation (governing the reporting of marine casualties) was preempted by a different federal statute, 46 U.S.C. § 6101. *Id.* at 114–16.

Locke did not definitively rule on all of the regulations before it. Instead, the Court remanded the issue of whether certain regulations, such as the state's watch requirement in times of restricted visibility, were of limited extraterritorial effect and were necessary to address the peculiarities of Puget Sound-factors that would weigh in favor of a Title I conflict preemption analysis rather than a Title II field preemption analysis. *Id.* at 116–17. The Court stated that the resolution of these matters would benefit from a full development of the record, noting that the United States did not enter the case until appeal. *Id.*

For our purposes, *Locke* established a number of significant rules. *Locke* held that OPA's savings clauses preserved only "state laws of a scope similar to the matters contained in Title I of OPA," id. at 105, and

did not constitute a reversal of *Ray*'s preemption rules as to Title I and
Title II of the PWSA, *id.* at 105–07. Rather, OPA only preserved state authority in the limited area of establishing liability rules and imposing financial requirements regarding oil spills. Id. at 105.

Locke also rejected the use of general presumptions, either for or
against preemption, and instead called for close analysis of the federal
statutory structure. *Locke* expressly repudiated any notion, which might
have survived *Ray,* that there is any presumption of non-preemption of
state rules. *Id.* at 107–08. *Locke* pointed out that the federal interest in
national and international maritime commerce was one of the reasons
cited in the Federalist Papers for adopting the Constitution, and the
Court detailed the numerous federal statutes and treaties in the area. *Id.*
at 99–103, 108. At the same time, however, *Locke* did not put in place the
opposite presumption, a presumption favoring preemption. Rather, the
validity of state regulation must be judged against the "federal statutory
structure." Id. at 108. Indeed, "[n]o artificial presumption aids us in determining the scope of appropriate local regulation under the PWSA." *Id.*;
see also P. Gudridge, Comment, United States v. Locke, 120 S.Ct. 1135,
94 Am. J. Int'l L. 745, 748 (2000).

Locke reinforced *Ray*'s two-category approach to preemption: either
field preemption or conflict preemption is to be used. Locke, 529 U.S. at
109–11. *Locke* also went further, recognizing that it would not always be
clear which of the two models would apply. It added a new overlap analysis to resolve that question. *See* id. at 112.

Field preemption applies to state law on subjects which are within
the province of Title II of the PWSA. Id. at 110–11. Other sources of federal maritime regulation may also preempt state law, even if the state
law is consistent with federal law. Id. at 114–16.

By contrast, *Locke* held that conflict preemption applies to state regulations within the scope of Title I. Title I of the PWSA does not expressly
preserve state power (unlike OPA). But Title I also does not preempt with
the same force as Title II. Rather, state law in areas within the province
of Title I are subject to standard conflict preemption analysis, primarily
the model which the Court has utilized in Commerce Clause cases. Id. at
109–10; *see also* Bethlehem Steel Co. v. N.Y. State Labor Relations Bd.,
330 U.S. 767, 773–74 (1947) (discussing federal preemption of state regulation in the Commerce Clause context).

Locke's conflict preemption analysis involves an initial inquiry into
whether federal authority has been exercised through a regulation intended to displace state law, or by a federal decision of the Coast Guard
that there should be no regulation of the subject in question. A conflict
arises "when compliance with both state and federal law is impossible, or
when the state law stands as an obstacle to the accomplishment and exe-

cution of the full purposes and objective of Congress." *Id.* at 109, 120 S.Ct. 1135 (quoting California v. ARC Am. Corp., 490 U.S. 93, 100–101(1989)) (internal quotation marks omitted). "In this context, Coast Guard regulations are to be given pre-emptive effect over conflicting state laws."

Overlap analysis applies when a state law falls within the overlapping coverage of Title I and Title II. We describe that overlap analysis below.

B. Title I, Title II, and Overlap Analysis

The respective scopes of Title I and Title II play a crucial role in any preemption analysis under the PWSA. This necessitates a more detailed discussion of these provisions. Congress has, by statute, occupied the field with respect to subject matters addressed in Title II of the PWSA. The subject matter of Title II, "Vessels Carrying Certain Cargoes in Bulk," is generally defined at 46 U.S.C. § 3703(a):

> The Secretary shall prescribe regulations for the design, construction, alteration, repair, maintenance, operation, equipping, personnel qualification, and manning of vessels to which this chapter applies, that may be necessary for increased protection against hazards to life and property, for navigation and vessel safety, and for enhanced protection of the marine environment.

Congress has required the Coast Guard to issue regulations under Title II, which "shall include requirements about . . . (3) equipment and appliances for . . . prevention and mitigation of damage to the marine environment; [and] (4) the manning of vessels and the duties, qualifications, and training of the officers and crew." 46 U.S.C. § 3703(a).

By contrast, conflict preemption is applied to state statutes and regulations concerning subject matters within Title I of the PWSA. *See* Locke, 529 U.S. at 109. The subject matter of Title I is defined by statute:

> Subject to the requirements of section 1224 of this title, the Secretary—

> > (1) in any port or place under the jurisdiction of the United States, in the navigable waters of the United States, or in any area covered by an international agreement negotiated pursuant to section 1230 of this title, may construct, operate, maintain, improve, or expand vessel traffic services, consisting of measures for controlling or supervising vessel traffic or for protecting navigation and the marine environment and may include, but need not be limited to one or more of the following: reporting and operating requirements, surveillance and communications systems, routing systems, and fairways. . . .

33 U.S.C. § 1223(a). As the United States has stated, the subject matter of Title I is characterized generally by matters of local concern, and, absent issuance of federal regulations or a decision not to allow state regulation under Title I, state regulation is not preempted in areas subject to that title.

Title I and Title II overlap in some instances. For example, both titles cover, in different contexts, "operating" requirements. *See id.* § 1223(a)(1) (Secretary may impose measures including, inter alia, "operating requirements"); *id.* § 1223(a)(4)(D) (Secretary may "restrict[ ] operation, in any hazardous area or under hazardous conditions, to vessels which have particular operating characteristics or capabilities which he considers necessary for safe operation under the circumstances"); 46 U.S.C. § 3703(a) (requiring Secretary to "prescribe regulations for the . . . operation . . . and manning of vessels to which this chapter applies"); *see also* Locke, 529 U.S. at 116 (remanding for consideration of whether a state navigation-watch requirement should be analyzed under Title I conflict preemption or Title II field preemption). Further, each title purports to have as one of its purposes the protection of the environment. *See* 33 U.S.C. § 1223(a)(1) (authorizing regulations on covered subjects "for protecting navigation and the marine environment"); 46 U.S.C. § 3703(a) (requiring regulations on covered subjects "that may be necessary . . . for enhanced protection of the marine environment").

As a result, *Locke* recognized that "[t]he existence of some overlapping coverage between the two titles of the PWSA may make it difficult to determine whether a pre-emption question is controlled by conflict pre-emption principles, applicable generally to Title I, or by field pre-emption rules, applicable generally to Title II." 529 U.S. at 111. In such instances of overlap, not every question will be resolved "by the greater pre-emptive force of Title II." *Id.* Rather, "conflict pre-emption under Title I will be applicable in some, although not all, cases." Id. at 111–12.

In resolving preemption questions in cases of overlapping coverage, *Locke* instructs courts to consider these factors: (1) "the type of regulations the Secretary has actually promulgated under [Title II]"; (2) whether the regulation falls within the specific type listed in § 3703(a) as required to be promulgated; (3) whether the federal rule is "justified by conditions unique to a particular port or waterway" (e.g., a Title I regulation based on water depth in Puget Sound or other local peculiarities); (4) whether the state regulation is "of limited extraterritorial effect, not requiring the tanker to modify its primary conduct outside the specific body of water purported to justify the local rule"; and (5) whether the state regulation is one that "pose[s] a minimal risk of innocent noncompliance, do[es] not affect vessel operations outside the jurisdiction, do[es] not require adjustment of systemic aspects of the vessel, and do[es] not impose a substantial burden on the vessel's operation within the local jurisdiction itself." Id. at 112.

In the same vein, *Ray* instructed federal courts addressing such maritime environmental cases to look to the respective purposes of the federal and state laws. 435 U.S. at 164–65. This "purpose" rule emerged from earlier Supreme Court Commerce Clause cases such as Huron Portland Cement Co. v. City of Detroit, 362 U.S. 440 (1960), and Kelly v. Washington, 302 U.S. 1 (1937). Overlap analysis thus involves some identification of the relative purposes and domains of Title I and Title II. *See* Medtronic, Inc. v. Lohr, 518 U.S. 470, 484 (1996) (stressing the need to identify the "domain" of the statutory clause said to preempt state law). *Ray* appeared to consider Title II to be concerned with matters that are properly subject to national rules, *see* 435 U.S. at 165–66 & n. 15, while Title I is more concerned with rules "arising from the peculiarities of local waters that call for special precautionary measures," id. at 171.

"[T]he principles developed [under Commerce Clause preemption] are not limited to [that] context; essentially the same techniques are used to determine the consequences for state action of *any* exercise of a plenary federal authority." Tribe, *supra,* § 6–29, at 508. Nonetheless, there are some distinctions between Commerce Clause preemption rules and maritime preemption rules. *See* Am. Dredging Co. v. Miller, 510 U.S. 443, 452 n. 3 (1994) (distinguishing "negative Commerce Clause" jurisprudence, and commenting that "[w]hatever might be the unifying theme of this aspect of our admiralty jurisprudence, it assuredly is *not* . . . the principle that the States may not impair maritime commerce").

Against this background, we turn to the preemption analysis of the specific MOSPA sections.

* * *

[The court remanded the vessel manning requirements for a proper overlap analysis and the tug escort requirements to determine if the USCG intended to preempt them by its recently promulgated regulations under Title I of the PWSA.]

V. The State's Financial Assurance Requirement

The parties again disagree on the proper frame of analysis of the state's financial assurance statute and its exception. Nonetheless, the parties do agree that the analysis here is different from that of the other regulations at issue because Congress (through its enactment of OPA) has expressly saved the states' power to establish liability rules and related requirements. *See* 33 U.S.C. § 2718. Indeed, the Supreme Court has clarified that OPA did not preempt state power to "establish liability rules and financial requirements relating to oil spills." Locke, 529 U.S. at 105.

MOSPA's financial assurance requirement has two relevant parts, one of which is under attack, and the other of which is conceded not to be preempted (assuming it is severable). In pertinent part, the state statute provides:

(a) Any vessel, whether or not self-propelled, in or entering upon the waters of the commonwealth for the purpose of transporting, discharging or receiving a cargo of oil, hazardous material, or hazardous waste, shall be subject to the financial assurance requirements and penalty authority as provided in subsections (b) to (d), inclusive.

(b) A certificate of financial assurance obtained individually or jointly by the vessel, its owner or agent, its charterer, or by the owner or operator of the terminal at which the vessel discharges or receives its cargo, shall be provided to the department in the amount of at least $1,000,000,000. Vessels with a capacity of less than 6,000 barrels shall present a certificate of financial assurance to the department of environmental protection in the amount of $5,000,000. A copy of the financial assurance shall be posted on the vessel.

(c) . . . .

(d) The department may allow financial assurance in a lower amount based upon criteria that includes, but is not limited to, the type and amount of the above cargo transported by the vessel; the size and construction of the vessel, including whether the vessel is double hulled; the safety record of the vessel or the vessel owner, the loss or accident history of the vessel or vessel owner involving maritime spills and the safety equipment used by the vessel. The financial assurance shall be in a form approved by the department.

Mass. Gen. Laws ch. 21, § 50C.

The United States concedes that, standing alone, the provisions for the $1 billion and $5 million financial assurance certificates (subsections (a) and (b)) are within the state's power under OPA's savings clauses, 33 U.S.C. § 2718(a)(1), (c). The dispute is over section 50C(d), which provides that the state Department of Environmental Protection may lower the amount of the bond according to certain criteria, some of which are defined by statute. The specified criteria include: "the type and amount of cargo transported . . . ; the size and construction of the vessel, including whether the vessel is double hulled; the safety record of the vessel or the vessel owner"; and the vessel's safety equipment. Mass. Gen. Laws ch. 21, § 50C(d). The department is also given discretion to use other criteria. *Id.*

There are two relevant OPA savings clauses. The first, 33 U.S.C. § 2718(a)(1)(A), provides:

Nothing in this Act . . . shall—

(1) affect, or be construed or interpreted as preempting, the authority of any State or political subdivision thereof from imposing any additional liability or requirements with respect to—

(A) the discharge of oil or other pollution by oil within such State. . . .

The second clause, 33 U.S.C. § 2718(c)(1), provides:

Nothing in this Act . . . shall in any way affect, or be construed to affect, the authority of the United States or any State or political subdivision thereof—

(1) to impose additional liability or additional requirements [relating to the discharge, or substantial threat of a discharge, of oil]. . . .

These clauses in OPA do not define "requirements." The clauses save state laws from preemption by OPA's Title I, but not from OPA's other titles, or from other federal statutes. Locke, 529 U.S. at 106, 120 S.Ct. 1135. EXPLAIN THAT OPA TITLE I sets liability amounts for oil spills. . .

The United States asserts that MOSPA is problematic because the exceptions in section 50C(d) encompass criteria at the core of PWSA's Title II. Moreover, the state statute merely provides that the criteria are to be administered by the state agency, and it offers no further guidance.

The United States asserts that the state may not regulate indirectly what it cannot regulate directly under Title II. The state and the Coalition acknowledge that an indirect regulation argument *might* survive *Ray*. *Ray* did consider such an indirect regulation theory, although there the theory did not concern a state financial assurance certification under OPA's savings clauses. *See* 435 U.S. at 173 & n. 25 (inquiring whether a state's tug escort rule indirectly regulated primary conduct, and rejecting that possibility on the facts presented). Nonetheless, even assuming arguendo that some theory of impermissible indirect regulation is viable even in a savings clause case, the United States has not to date met its burden on its argument that the statute is not within the powers reserved to the states.

In this case, the two sides take fundamentally different views of what constitutes impermissible indirect regulation. There is a lack of clarity regarding the exact nature of both the United States' claim and the state's defense. The issue can be viewed as a spectrum problem. On the one hand, there is the state's statutory choice to establish a financial assurance program, the cost of which may be reduced by criteria which are attuned to degree of risk. Such gradations are common to most insurance schemes. On the other hand, there is a federal fear that implementation of this scheme will lead to state regulation of primary conduct-conduct that is exclusively under federal control pursuant to Title II.

In the United States' view, MOSPA's impermissible indirect effect is inherent in the structure of its financial assurance provision. Because here, according to the United States, "the potential to influence primary conduct cannot be eliminated or even discounted," the statute is preempted as a matter of law. Under this theory, there is no need to present facts demonstrating that the provision would impose an actual burden or impediment to federal Title II authority.

One might ask why, if the state may impose a $1 billion financial assurance requirement, a state may not also reduce the amount based on the objective criteria set forth in the statute-criteria which appear, on their face, to be rationally related to the degree of the risk posed. After all, there would appear to be less risk of spillage from a double-hulled vessel. Similarly, a vessel's capacity would presumably be related to the amount of expected liability if a spill did occur. Tellingly, OPA itself has a federal financial assurance requirement; as recently amended by Congress, the statute requires differing amounts of financial assurance based on whether or not a vessel is single-hulled, based on whether or not the vessel is a "tank vessel," and based on the gross tonnage of the vessel. 33 U.S.C. §§ 2704, 2716.

The United States responds that MOSPA's $1 billion requirement is effectively no more than a ceiling, and that in practice the amounts charged will vary depending on criteria that are exclusively under federal control under PWSA's Title II. The United States argues that a state may never use criteria within Title II to ground its decisions. That is because the state's mechanism amounts to a financial incentive "for any design, cargo or equipment changes that [state regulators] think appropriate." We are doubtful that when Congress authorized the states to set financial assurance requirements it at the same time meant *per se* to preempt states from using graduated levels rationally related to risk. It is again worth observing that OPA itself imposes federal financial assurance requirements that are not uniform for all vessels. Under the OPA regime, vessels over 300 gross tons with oil on board, and certain other vessels of any size, are required to provide evidence of financial responsibility sufficient to meet OPA's liability maximums. 33 U.S.C. § 2716; *see also id.* § 2704 (setting forth liability maximums). At the time OPA was enacted, these maximums differed based on the vessel's gross tonnage, and based on whether or not the vessel was a tank vessel. Pub.L. No. 101–380, § 1004(a), 104 Stat. at 491–92. In light of this, it is difficult to believe that Congress intended to preclude the states from similarly calibrating their financial assurance requirements to account for different vessel characteristics.

The Coast Guard has yet to revise its financial assurance regulations to respond to this statutory amendment. While it "anticipate[s] initiating a rulemaking" to institute the changes, 71 Fed. Reg. 47,737, 47,738 (Aug. 18, 2006), it has told vessel operators that the prior requirements for submitting evidence of financial responsibility remain in effect until such rulemaking takes place, *id.*

Moreover, we should not be quick to assume that Congress intended preemption here. One commentator has read *Ray* to mean that when a state provides for alternative courses of behavior, one preempted and one not, the overall state scheme is not preempted unless the state's requirements act to exert pressure on operators in preempted areas. *See* Tribe, *supra,* § 6–26, at 486–87. *Ray* considered and rejected such a claim on its facts, and in light of the Court's treatment of the issue, Professor Tribe has concluded that "the basic teaching of the [*Ray*] decision is that state pressure to act in derogation of a federal statutory scheme is not to be inferred lightly." Id. at 487.

That principle has even more force in our case. In OPA, Congress expressly preserved state power to require financial assurance. *Ray's* discussion of indirect regulation did not involve any such explicit congressional preservation. Moreover, *Ray* decided the indirect regulation issue on a detailed record replete with factual stipulations. 435 U.S. at 156, 173 & n. 25. In this context, we reject the United States' arguments that the existence of pressure to conform conduct can be decided here as a matter of law, and that the actual effects of the state statute are irrelevant.

As a fallback argument, the United States contends that it *has* established the existence of burdensome pressure, as MOSPA gives a state agency the authority to calibrate the assurance requirement on a case-by-case basis with only general guidance. It is not clear whether the United States means to argue that the state could constitutionally enact a financial assurance provision which, for example, allowed reductions according to a legislatively set schedule based on various design and other defined criteria. Nor is it clear if the United States' position would permit a state to use regulations (rather than a statute) to enact such a provision, if these regulations reduced and cabined administrative discretion.

The district court took a different approach. It correctly held that the effect of the statute was relevant. It asked whether the practical effect of the $1 billion rule was to force vessels to seek reductions pursuant to the exemption scheme. The court then decided, without hearing any evidence and on a motion for judgment on the pleadings, "that the Commonwealth's one billion dollar financial assurance requirement imposes such an onerous financial obligation on a tank vessel owner that it in effect forces compliance with the statutory exception criteria." *Id.*

As an initial matter, the $1 billion amount does not appear to be plainly unreasonable when measured against risk. The remedial costs of the *Exxon Valdez* spill in 1989 surpassed $2 billion (as measured in 1990 dollars). A. Rodriguez & P. Jaffe, The Oil Pollution Act of 1990, 15 Tul. Mar. L.J. 1, 16 (1990). In Buzzards Bay, while the clean-up costs from the 2003 spill were significantly lower, they were still sizable.

Moreover, the record does not yet contain evidence about the requirements other states have set, industry usage and practice, or the costs of obtaining financial assurance. Nor have the parties even discussed or presented evidence about the requirements set by the federal government. While our own research on this last point has uncovered the federal rules, *see* 33 U.S.C. §§ 2704, 2716, those rules simply highlight the need for further facts. Indeed, the federal requirements set a complicated formula based in part on a vessel's gross tonnage, and there is nothing in the record informing us about the gross tonnages of vessels that traverse Buzzards Bay.

Of course, even if the $1 billion amount were not in itself unreasonable, it is possible that such an amount would still place strong pressure on the industry to change its primary conduct. Yet there is simply no evidence on this point.

The district court also found it significant that there was a lack of notice to vessel owners about the specific criteria that the state would use in lowering the bond amount; this was the crux of its concern about the vagueness of the criteria and the untrammeled delegation to the state agency. *See Massachusetts,* 440 F.Supp.2d at 46. Given its finding that the state system necessarily forced vessels into compliance with the exemptions, the court held that the exemption scheme necessarily undercut the certainty that federal regulation under Title II afforded the industry. *Id.*

The state characterizes the indirect regulation issue differently. It agrees with the district court that the analysis might turn on the practical effect of the $1 billion amount and the implemented exceptions. But it argues that there was no evidence of record to support the district court's conclusion. It also points out that an offer of proof was made to the court of evidence that no real burden is posed by the exemptions to the statute.

The analysis presented thus far is insufficient to permit resolution of the matter on its merits. As the state has not yet exercised its administrative authority, it is unclear how it would choose to grant exceptions to the financial assurance requirement. We simply cannot yet say that MOSPA's section 50C(d) is incapable of any constitutional application. It may well be that the state will structure its decision making as to the exemption in a way that would frame the preemption question differently. It may even be that discussions between state and federal authorities would produce an agreed-upon scheme that adequately protects both state and federal interests. Given the absence of evidence at this stage, it is too early to know whether the state exception scheme would intrude impermissibly on the Coast Guard's exclusive authority under Title II. On this record, the district court was not warranted in permanently enjoining any aspects of the financial assurance provision.

Nonetheless, we do share the concerns of the United States that the state has yet to make a showing, by regulation or otherwise, explaining how it will utilize its discretion under section 50C(d). Since the state has not structured its exemption scheme, there is no operational scheme to enjoin. The state should make such a showing on remand; we leave it to the district court to consider the appropriateness of a preliminary injunction thereafter.

NOTES AND QUESTIONS

1. Given how developed is the doctrine of federal preemption, why aren't federal statutes like the Oil Pollution Act and the Ports and Waterways Safety Act, which are enacted in the wake of actual, non-hypothetical disasters, more clear on the scope of permissible, concurrent state regulation?

2. Why is the U.S. Coast Guard so reluctant to exercise its authority under Title I and II of the Ports and Waterways Safety Act? Is it concerned about imposing costs on the shipping industry and disadvantaging U.S. ports? Note that several shipping nations sent a diplomatic note urging the U.S. to challenge the Massachusetts law. After the Coast Guard promulgated rules regarding navigation in Buzzards Bay without analyzing the impacts of alternatives through a NEPA process, it sought and obtained an injunction against Massachusetts' special rules for Buzzards Bay. The following case ensued. Do federal agency obligations under NEPA alter the federalism equation of the Ports and Waterways Safety Act?

UNITED STATES V. COALITION FOR BUZZARDS BAY

U.S. Court of Appeals, First Circuit, 2011
644 F.3d 26

SELYA, CIRCUIT JUDGE.

Buzzards Bay is a brilliant jewel in the diadem of Massachusetts waters. It comprises an inlet flowing landward from the Atlantic Ocean, thirty miles long and up to ten miles wide. Many people regard it as the gateway to Cape Cod.

The name "Buzzards Bay" is a fluke. Folklore has it that early settlers mistook an indigenous flight of ospreys for buzzards, and the rest is history. The bay is not only a spectacularly beautiful natural resource but also a major channel of maritime commerce in southeastern Massachusetts. The combined environmental and commercial significance of the bay has sparked a pitched battle between federal and state sovereigns over the nature of preventative measures needed to safeguard against the risk of oil spills. These appeals mark the latest round in that battle.

The overarching question before us involves the Coast Guard's authority to promulgate regulations that preempt state environmental law with respect to tank vessels. But as the proverb teaches, there is many a slip twixt the cup and the lip. Discerning such a slip, we do not reach the preemption question but, rather, hold that, during the rulemaking process, the Coast Guard failed to comply with its obligations under the National Environmental Policy Act (NEPA), 42 U.S.C. §§ 4321–4347. Inasmuch as this bevue was not harmless, we reverse the district court's entry of summary judgment in favor of the Coast Guard, vacate the injunction against the enforcement of state law issued below, and remand for further proceedings.

I. Background

This case had its genesis in a particularly regrettable maritime misfortune. On April 27, 2003, the Bouchard Barge–120 struck an outcropping of rocks, spilling an estimated 98,000 gallons of oil into Buzzards Bay. Bad things sometimes can lead to good things and, spurred by this incident, the state legislature enacted the Massachusetts Oil Spill Prevention Act (MOSPA), codified as amended primarily at Mass. Gen. Laws ch. 21, §§ 42, 50B–50E; ch. 21M, §§ 1–8. The federal government saw this as a threat to its power to regulate commercial shipping on Buzzards Bay and sued to abrogate certain provisions of the MOSPA. The suit asserted that the challenged provisions of the state statutory scheme were preempted by the Ports and Waterways Safety Act, Pub.L. No. 92–340, 86 Stat. 424, as amended by the Port and Tanker Safety Act, Pub.L. No. 95–474, 92 Stat. 1471, codified at 33 U.S.C. §§ 1221–1232 and scattered sections of 46 U.S.C., and by Coast Guard regulations promulgated thereunder.

The district court (Tauro, J.) granted an injunction [to the U.S.]. United States v. Massachusetts, 440 F.Supp.2d 24, 48 (D. Mass. 2006). The Commonwealth appealed, seeking to reinstate the MOSPA's manning and tug escort requirements for vessels. We vacated the injunction because the district court had not applied the correct analytical model for resolving federal-state regulatory conflicts. United States v. Massachusetts, 493 F.3d 1, 4–5 (1st Cir.2007). The case was remanded for further development of the record. Id. at 4.

With the case pending before the district court, the Coast Guard changed the legal seascape by promulgating a final rule relating to navigation in Buzzards Bay (the 2007 Rule). This rule, unlike the version previously before this court, purported expressly to preempt the challenged provisions of the MOSPA. See 72 Fed. Reg. 50,052, 50,056–57 (Aug. 30,

2007). It established manning and escort requirements limited to Buzzards Bay. *See id.* at 50,052.

As part of the rulemaking process that culminated in the issuance of the 2007 Rule, the Coast Guard eschewed the preparation of either an environmental impact statement (EIS) or an environmental assessment (EA). It determined instead that its proposed action fell within a categorical exclusion that obviated any such analysis.

There are material differences between the protections afforded by the MOSPA and those afforded by the 2007 Rule. The MOSPA, with an exception not relevant here, requires a tugboat escort for all tank vessels transiting Buzzards Bay that carry 6,000 or more barrels of oil. Mass. Gen. Laws ch. 21M, § 6. The 2007 Rule has a variant tug escort provision, which does not apply at all to double-hulled barges. *See* 72 Fed. Reg. at 50,054, 50,059. Similar disparities exist as to manning requirements. The MOSPA demands that "[t]he navigation watch on all tow vessels transiting Buzzards bay and carrying 6,000 or more barrels of oil shall consist of at least 1 licensed deck officer or tow vessel operator, who shall serve exclusively as a lookout" and that "[t]hree licensed officers or tow vessel operators shall be on a tow vessel" when it is escorting a tank barge. Mass. Gen. Laws ch. 21M, § 4(a). The MOSPA also establishes crew requirements for tank barges. *Id.* § 4(b). Once again, the 2007 Rule takes a divergent approach; as to manning requirements, it is in some respects broader than the MOSPA and in some respects narrower. *See* 72 Fed. Reg. at 50,059.

Due to circumstances beyond the parties' control, the case below was passed from judge to judge to judge. On October 29, 2007, the Coast Guard renewed its motion for an injunction against the enforcement of the challenged MOSPA provisions. While that motion was pending, Judge Lindsay allowed the Commonwealth to file counterclaims alleging that the Coast Guard, in the process of promulgating the 2007 Rule, had violated both the Administrative Procedure Act (APA), 5 U.S.C. §§ 551–559, 701–706, and the NEPA.

In the fall of 2008, the district court (Young, J.), acting in conformity with a magistrate judge's recommendation, preliminarily enjoined the enforcement of the challenged MOSPA provisions. The parties subsequently cross-moved for summary judgment. The magistrate judge recommended that summary judgment enter for the Coast Guard on the ground that the 2007 Rule preempted the challenged MOSPA provisions.

On de novo review, the district court (Woodlock, J.) found a NEPA violation, but concluded that this violation was "essentially harmless" because "the substance of the Coast Guard's actual rulemaking analysis was the functional equivalent of what an environmental impact statement would have generated." United States v. Massachusetts, 724 F.Supp.2d

170, 174–75 (D.Mass.2010). The court proceeded to overrule the Commonwealth's other objections, found preemption appropriate, entered a declaratory judgment for the Coast Guard, and permanently enjoined enforcement of the controverted portions of the state statute. Id. at 175. These timely appeals followed.

II. NEPA Compliance

* * *

B. The Coast Guard's Supplemental Procedures

The CEQ [NEPA implementing] regulations are not meant to stand alone but, rather, contemplate that the agencies to which they apply adopt supplemental procedures, if and as needed. Id. § 1507.3(a). The Coast Guard has adopted such supplemental procedures and codified them in Commandant Instruction M16475.1D (Nov. 29, 2000). These supplemental procedures describe thirty-five categorical exclusions (CEs). COMDTINST M16475.1D, fig. 2–1. This compendium includes CEs that cover "[r]egulations establishing, disestablishing, or changing Regulated Navigation Areas and security or safety zones" and "[r]egulations in aid of navigation." Id. fig. 2–1, ¶ 34(g), (i). When promulgating the 2007 Rule, the Coast Guard asserted the applicability of both of these exclusions. 72 Fed. Reg. at 50,058. The Commonwealth does not dispute that the Coast Guard's proposed action fell within the compass of these CEs. But the applicability of a CE does not automatically relieve an agency of the obligation to prepare either an EIS or an EA.

The CEQ regulations recognize that even agency actions that are of a kind typically excluded from NEPA review by the operation of a CE "may have a significant environmental effect." 40 C.F.R. § 1508.4. In response to that concern, the Coast Guard, like many other agencies, has enumerated in its supplemental procedures various considerations to guide its assessment of whether a particular action, though nominally covered by a CE, involves "extraordinary circumstances" and, thus, requires the preparation of either an EIS or an EA. COMDTINST M16475.1D, ch. 2, § B.2.b. In effect, this constitutes a list of exceptions to the exclusions.

The Coast Guard has identified ten extraordinary circumstances exceptions which, if applicable, may trump a CE and require it to prepare an EIS or an EA. Id. By the same token, the Coast Guard may not rely upon a CE if its proposed action triggers any of the extraordinary circumstances exceptions limned in an incorporated Department of Transportation (DOT) order. Id. The incorporated order requires the preparation of an EIS or an EA for agency actions that are likely to involve any of four additional, albeit overlapping, extraordinary circumstances. Id. encl. 1 (DOT 5610.1C), § 20.b.(2).

The Coast Guard attempts to put a new gloss on the extraordinary circumstances described in its NEPA procedures. It claims the right to do so in consequence of its reassignment from the DOT to the Department of Homeland Security (DHS), which occurred in 2003. This reassignment, the Coast Guard implies, rendered its preexisting NEPA compliance procedures subject to creative interpretation (at least to the extent that they conflict with the DHS's own regulations). Under the guise of this creative interpretation, the Coast Guard rips out the heart of its own exceptions.

* * *

C. The Violation

The question that we must answer is whether the Coast Guard complied with the NEPA. In promulgating the 2007 Rule, it used a standard environmental checklist. This checklist included prompts corresponding to the extraordinary circumstances exceptions that might prevent the Coast Guard from relying on a CE. Each prompt received a simple "yes" or "no" answer.

The completed checklist contains a negative response to the prompt asking whether the proposed action is "likely to [have] a significant effect on public health or safety." Elaborating, the document explains that "[i]mplementation of the rule would have an indirect and beneficial impact on public health and safety" due to its anticipated prevention of future oil spills in Buzzards Bay. Negative responses also accompany prompts asking whether the proposed action presents the potential "to be highly controversial in terms of scientific validity or public opinion" or whether the proposed action would potentially violate state environmental law. There is no discussion of the reasoning behind these negative responses.

The checklist does contain a lone affirmative response. This affirmative response is to the prompt asking whether the proposed action is to take place "on or near a unique characteristic of the geographic area." The Coast Guard added, in a wholly conclusory fashion, that the proposed action "is projected to produce negligible adverse impacts on the environment from increased air and water emissions from the additional tugs."

In a bid to shut off further inquiry into the sufficiency of those responses, the Coast Guard says that the Commonwealth's failure to object during the notice-and-comment period to its proposed reliance on a CE amounts to a waiver. * * *

This brings us to the question of whether the Coast Guard, in relying on a CE as a means of sidestepping any meaningful environmental analysis, acted arbitrarily. In arguing for an affirmative answer to this question, the Commonwealth focuses on four extraordinary circumstances exceptions that, in its view, prevented the agency from relying on a CE.

These extraordinary circumstances exceptions relate to (i) agency actions affecting "[p]ublic health or safety," (ii) those touching upon a site including or "near a unique characteristic of the geographic area," (iii) those "likely to be highly controversial in terms of scientific validity or public opinion," and (iv) those creating "[a] potential or threatened violation of . . . state . . . law . . . imposed for the protection of the environment." COMDTINST M16475.1D, ch. 2, § B.2.b. If any one of these exceptions applies, then the Coast Guard was bound to determine whether further analysis was required based on the potential environmental effects of the proposed action. *Id.* And in that event, reliance on the CE would be inappropriate.

Here, we can limit our consideration to the extraordinary circumstances exception for proposed actions that are "likely to be highly controversial in terms of . . . public opinion" (to the extent that other exceptions might also apply, they are superfluous). Careful perscrutation of the record in this case persuades us that the Coast Guard's bareboned negative response—a simple "no"—to the prompt asking whether the proposed action was likely to be highly controversial was arbitrary and capricious.

Judicial review of the applicability of an extraordinary circumstances exception is informed by the agency's guidelines. [citations omitted] The Coast Guard's guidelines outline the considerations that should be factored into the decisionmaker's evaluative process. COMDTINST M16475.1D, encl. 2. As to the exception for "highly controversial" actions, they direct decisionmakers to "[c]onsider first whether [the] action is likely to be controversial in any way." If the decisionmaker concludes that it is, he is directed to "consider whether this controversy is likely to have an environmental element." The guidelines specifically caution decisionmakers to "be sure not to interpret the word 'environmental' too narrowly" to guard against "missing a controversial issue that should be addressed under NEPA."

We need not tarry. The record in this case belies the Coast Guard's conclusory determination that its proposed action was not likely to be highly controversial within the meaning of its own procedures and guidelines. During the rulemaking process, the Coast Guard received a plethora of worried comments from local officials, state legislators, and other representatives of state government. The state's principal environmental regulator, the Massachusetts Department of Environmental Protection (MDEP), expressed grave concerns about the potential environmental consequences of the proposed rule. The MDEP indicated that, in its strongly held view, tug escorts for *all* tank barges were necessary to reduce the risk of oil spills in Buzzards Bay. The MDEP specifically noted that escort requirements for double-hulled tank barges were enforced "in other environmentally sensitive waters" and should not be forsaken in Buzzards Bay. The Massachusetts congressional delegation urged the

Coast Guard to adopt broader tug escort standards parallel to those embedded in the MOSPA, so that both single and double-hulled barges would be covered. This coverage was essential, the solons wrote, in order to "provide[ ] crucial protection" for Buzzards Bay.

The Coast Guard shrugs off this tidal wave of comments as mere political opposition. Of course, many of the comments were submitted by "political" figures. But in a democracy, citizens may justifiably rely on political leaders to speak for them, and the fervent community concern expressed here went directly to potentially serious environmental effects of the Coast Guard's proposed action. This is the very type of controversy that the Coast Guard's guidelines direct decisionmakers to consider. At any rate, the public officials' comments were supplemented by submissions from private groups and individuals who believed that protections beyond those described in the proposed rule were needed to prevent environmental damage to Buzzards Bay.

What makes the Coast Guard's refusal to recognize the potential for controversy all the more difficult to fathom is that, during the notice-and-comment period, the Coast Guard was already embroiled in litigation that touched upon the environmental effects of a prior rule that affected Buzzards Bay. It made its decision to rely on a CE (and thereby avoid a more in-depth environmental analysis) while this litigation remained unresolved. At the very least, the pendency of that bitterly contested case should have alerted the Coast Guard to the existence of a serious disagreement about the wisdom of displacing the Commonwealth's regulatory regime and the environmental effects of the proposed federal action.

The short of it is that, during the time when rulemaking was underway, there was ferocious and widespread opposition to the Coast Guard's approach to the regulation of oil barges in Buzzards Bay. The Coast Guard knew of this opposition and also knew that much of it implicated the not implausible fear that environmental harm would ensue should the protections afforded by the MOSPA be eliminated and the proposed federal standards adopted. In the idiom of the Coast Guard's own procedures, "the potential significance of the proposed action's effects on the environment" was great. COMDTINST M16475.1D, ch. 2, § B.2.b. In the view of many, the proposed rule threatened to decrease materially the level of protection against oil spills in Buzzards Bay. Given these realities, we conclude, as did the district court, that the Coast Guard's eschewal of any meaningful environmental inquiry was arbitrary and capricious. *See Massachusetts,* 724 F.Supp.2d at 174 (characterizing Coast Guard's decision not to prepare an EIS as "an act of procedural hubris").

D. Harmless Error

This does not end our voyage. The Coast Guard contends that even if the existence of extraordinary circumstances foreclosed it from relying on a CE, its failure to prepare either an EIS or an EA was harmless. We turn to this contention.

Assuredly, NEPA violations are subject to harmless error review. *See* Save Our Heritage, Inc. v. FAA, 269 F.3d 49, 61 (1st Cir.2001); *see also* 5 U.S.C. § 706. "[T]he burden of showing that an error is harmful normally falls upon the party attacking the agency's determination." Shinseki v. Sanders, 556 U.S. 396 (2009). The circumstances of a particular case often will make clear whether the error was harmless or not. *Id.* In this case, the Coast Guard premises its harmless error argument on the notion that it conducted an analysis functionally equivalent to an EIS or an EA during the rulemaking process. The district court accepted this argument, relying heavily on our decision in *Save Our Heritage. See Massachusetts,* 724 F.Supp.2d at 175. That reliance was misplaced.

* * *

The case at hand is readily distinguishable from *Save Our Heritage.* Although the Coast Guard, in its advance notice of proposed rulemaking, mentioned two prior local studies (a 1996 regional risk assessment recommendation and a 2003 safety assessment), *see* 69 Fed. Reg. 62,427, 62,428 (Oct. 26, 2004), there is no indication that it took any steps to confirm the continued relevance of the information contained in those studies. The same is true of a 1999 regulatory assessment prepared for Puget Sound and included in the administrative record here.

In all events, these reports standing alone are neither sufficiently focused nor sufficiently detailed to serve, separately or in cumulation, as a proxy for the environmental analysis that the NEPA requires. The 1996 study recommended a Regulated Navigation Area, which, when adopted, would "impose [ ] certain requirements on single-hulled tank barges transiting New England waters, including Buzzards Bay." *Id.* The record offers no further information about this study. The 2003 report—a ports and waterways safety assessment—recognized "that the risk for oil or hazardous material discharge in Buzzards Bay is relatively high" and that one way of reducing this risk would be to "establish requirements for escort tugs." *Id.* But this report did not purpose to evaluate the merits (or relative merits) of any particular courses of action. Rather, its goal was to spur regional risk mitigation efforts by generating input from interested parties about ways to reduce the risks associated with a broad range of navigation concerns.

The last of the documents upon which the Coast Guard leans—the 1999 regulatory assessment for Puget Sound—goes into some depth in describing "the potential impact of oil spills on the environment." But this data is presented in the site-specific context of the topography and environmental characteristics of a body of water some 2,500 miles distant from Buzzards Bay. While this assessment could be relevant, the Coast Guard made no explanation of how it might apply to the presumably different topography and environmental characteristics of Buzzards Bay.

These shortcomings are troubling, but the sockdolager is that the Coast Guard did not perform any environmental analysis at all. Indeed, it made no site-specific appraisal of the potential environmental effects of its proposed action. For ought that appears, it took no "hard look" at the situation. It gave the matter the barest of glances and, in the parlance of the *Save Our Heritage* court, made no "reasoned finding." 269 F.3d at 61.

In a nutshell, this is not a case, like *Save Our Heritage,* in which an agency, while failing to carry out a formal EIS or EA, nevertheless performed a substantial environmental analysis. The absence of any such analysis is antithetic to a finding of harmlessness. *See* Wilderness Watch, 375 F.3d at 1096 (noting that courts "have only been willing to declare a NEPA violation harmless when the relevant decision makers actually engaged in significant environmental analysis prior to the decision but failed to comply with the exact procedures mandated"); *see also* Cal. Wilderness Coal. v. U.S. Dep't of Energy, 631 F.3d 1072, 1106 (9th Cir.2011) (finding error not harmless where agency had not shown that it had taken a "hard look" at the environmental consequences of its proposed action).

The Coast Guard suggests that the comments submitted during the rulemaking process compensate for the missing environmental analysis. We do not agree. Although these comments may have brought certain environmental concerns to the agency's attention, they did not bridge the gap between agency awareness of potentially detrimental environmental effects and agency analysis of those effects. It is precisely such an analysis that the NEPA requires. *See* 40 C.F.R. § 1508.9(b) (requiring an EA to include discussion "of the environmental impacts of the proposed action and alternatives").

At the expense of carting coal to Newcastle, we add that the NEPA framework is designed in part to stimulate public participation in the rulemaking process. *See Pub. Citizen,* 541 U.S. at 768 (describing an EIS as intended to "provid[e] a springboard for public comment" (alteration in original) (quoting Robertson, 490 U.S. at 349)); New Mexico ex rel. Richardson v. Bureau of Land Mgmt., 565 F.3d 683, 708 (10th Cir.2009) (finding failure to prepare a supplemental EIS not harmless and noting that "[a] public comment period is beneficial only to the extent the public has meaningful information on which to comment"). It would be Kafkaesque to deem the very comments submitted by the public, in and of themselves, a competent proxy for the NEPA determination that is meant to prompt and inform such comments.

What we have said to this point dictates what must be done. The error here was one of function, not merely of form. The administrative record, viewed as a whole, does not show that the Coast Guard ever analyzed, or even adequately studied, the environmental impact of its proposed action. Consequently, its failure to prepare either an EIS or an EA was not harmless.

B. REGULATION OF BALLAST WATERS DISCHARGES FROM SHIPS

NORTHWEST ENVIRONMENTAL ADVOCATES V. U.S. E.P.A.
U.S. Court of Appeals, Ninth Circuit, 2008
537 F.3d 1006

WILLIAM A. FLETCHER, CIRCUIT JUDGE.

Plaintiffs in this case are Northwest Environmental Advocates, San Francisco Baykeeper, and The Ocean Conservancy. Plaintiffs-intervenors are the States of Illinois, Michigan, Minnesota, New York, Pennsylvania, and Wisconsin. Plaintiffs and plaintiffs-intervenors challenge a regulation originally promulgated by the Environmental Protection Agency ("EPA") in 1973 exempting certain marine discharges from the permitting scheme of sections 301(a) and 402 of the Clean Water Act ("CWA"). That regulation, 40 C.F.R. § 122.3(a), provides that the following vessel discharges into the navigable waters of the United States do not require permits: discharge of effluent from properly functioning marine engines; discharge of laundry, shower, and galley sink wastes from vessels; and any other discharge incidental to the normal operation of a vessel, including the discharge of ballast water.

The district court concluded that the EPA had exceeded its authority under the CWA in exempting these discharges from permitting requirements. The district court vacated § 122.3(a), effective September 30, 2008. We affirm the decision of the district court.

I. Background

A. The CWA and 40 C.F.R. § 122.3(a)

In 1972, Congress enacted sweeping amendments to the Federal Water Pollution Control Act of 1948. After another round of substantial amendments in 1977, the statute became known as the Clean Water Act. The CWA declares a "national goal that the discharge of pollutants into the navigable waters be eliminated by 1985." 33 U.S.C. § 1251(a)(1).

Section 301(a) of the CWA provides that, subject to certain exceptions, "the discharge of any pollutant by any person shall be unlawful." *Id.* § 1311(a). One of these exceptions is for discharges authorized by a permit granted pursuant to the National Pollutant Discharge Elimination

System ("NPDES"), a system set forth in section 402 of the Act. *Id.* §§ 1311(a), 1342. The combined effect of sections 301(a) and 402 is that "[t]he CWA prohibits the discharge of any pollutant from a point source into navigable waters of the United States without an NPDES permit." *N. Plains Res. Council v. Fid. Exploration & Dev. Co.,* 325 F.3d 1155, 1160 (9th Cir.2003). The EPA administers the NPDES. 33 U.S.C. § 1251(d).

Obtaining a permit under the CWA need not be an onerous process. For example, in appropriate circumstances a discharge may be allowed under a "general permit" requiring only that the discharger submit a "notice of intent" to make the discharge. As we explained in *Natural Resources Defense Council v. U.S. EPA,* 279 F.3d 1180, 1183 (9th Cir.2002):

> NPDES permits come in two varieties: individual and general. An individual permit authorizes a specific entity to discharge a pollutant in a specific place and is issued after an informal agency adjudication process. *See* 40 C.F.R. §§ 122.21, 124.1–124.21, 124.51–124.66. General permits, on the other hand, are issued for an entire class of hypothetical dischargers in a given geographical region and are issued pursuant to administrative rulemaking procedures. *See id.* §§ 122.28, 124.19(a). General permits may appropriately be issued when the dischargers in the geographical area to be covered by the permit are relatively homogenous. *See id.* § 122.28(a)(2). After a general permit has been issued, an entity that believes it is covered by the general permit submits a "notice of intent" to discharge pursuant to the general permit. *Id.* § 122.28(b)(2). A general permit can allow discharging to commence upon receipt of the notice of intent, after a waiting period, or after the permit issuer sends out a response agreeing that the discharger is covered by the general permit. *Id.* § 122.28(b)(2)(iv).

In 1973, the EPA exempted by regulation several categories of vessel discharges from NPDES permitting requirements under the CWA. *See* NPDES, 38 Fed. Reg. 13,528, 13,530, § 125.4 (May 22, 1973). The regulation provides that "[t]he following discharges do not require NPDES permits":

> Any discharge of sewage from vessels, effluent from properly functioning marine engines, laundry, shower, and galley sink wastes, or any other discharge incidental to the normal operation of a vessel. This exclusion does not apply to rubbish, trash, garbage, or other such materials discharged overboard; nor to other discharges when the vessel is operating in a capacity other than as a means of transportation[.]

40 C.F.R. § 122.3(a). The CWA expressly exempts sewage discharges from vessels from the permitting process and regulates these discharges by other means. *See* 33 U.S.C. §§ 1362(6)(A), 1322. Because § 122.3(a) does not itself exempt sewage discharges but instead merely recognizes the

statute's exemption of sewage discharges, the sewage clause in § 122.3(a) is not subject to the *ultra vires* claim made here. *See also* Chevron U.S.A., Inc. v. Hammond, 726 F.2d 483, 493 n. 13 (9th Cir.1984) (contrasting the express statutory exemption of sewage with regulation relating to "deballasting" by ships). Therefore, three categories of discharges exempted by 40 C.F.R. § 122.3(a) are at issue in this case: (1) marine engine discharges; (2) graywater discharges ("laundry, shower, and galley sink wastes"); and (3) "any other discharge incidental to the normal operation of a vessel."

The first proposed draft of the regulation would have excluded only marine engine discharges. *See* NPDES, 38 Fed. Reg. 1362, 1363–64, § 125.4(c) (proposed Jan. 11, 1973). The EPA subsequently added the exclusions for graywater and other discharges incidental to normal vessel operations. When promulgating the final regulation in May 1973, the EPA explained its anticipated effect: "Most discharges from vessels to inland waters are now clearly excluded from the permit requirements." 38 Fed. Reg. at 13,528, (b)(13)(ii). The EPA stated that "[t]his type of discharge generally causes little pollution." *Id.* The EPA stated, further, that the "exclusion of vessel wastes from the permit requirements will reduce administrative costs drastically." *Id.* Decades later, an EPA administrator declared that in 1973:

> [W]e were faced with many, many other much higher priority situations such as raw sewage being discharged, municipal plants having to be built, very large paper mills or steel mills and the like discharging. At the time we thought that was not an important area to deal with. . . . Vessels were not important to the overall scheme of things at that time.

Craig Vogt, EPA, EPA Pub. Meeting #12227, Ocean Discharge Criteria (Sept. 12, 2000, 1 p.m.). The EPA amended the regulation in 1979 in minor respects that do not affect our analysis. *See* NPDES, Revision of Regulations, 44 Fed. Reg. 32,854, 32,902, § 122.4 (June 7, 1979); *see also* NPDES, Revision of Existing Regulations, 43 Fed. Reg. 37,078, 37,079, I(c)(2) (Aug. 21, 1978) (describing the proposed changes).

The text of the CWA does not exempt from NPDES requirements marine engine discharges, graywater discharges, or other discharges incidental to the normal operation of vessels. However, the EPA contended in 1973, and continues to contend, that it has the power to provide these exemptions by regulation. The Administrator of the EPA prefaced the draft January 1973 regulation with a statement that a discharger could discharge lawfully only if the discharger "possesses a valid permit or is excluded from coverage by law *or regulation*." NPDES, 38 Fed. Reg. at 1362 (emphasis added). The final rules similarly stated that "[a]ll discharges of pollutants . . . are unlawful . . . , unless the discharger has a permit or is specifically relieved by law *or regulation* from the obligation of obtaining a permit." NPDES, 38 Fed. Reg. at 13,531, § 125.11(a) (emphasis added).

The first category exempted by § 122.3(a), marine engine discharges, includes unburned fuel and various kinds of oil. The second category, graywater discharges, can include pathogens such as fecal coliform, *enterococci*, and *E. coli* and pollutants such as ammonia, arsenic, copper, lead, nickel, and zinc. . . . *Cf.* 33 U.S.C. § 1322(a)(12)(A)(i) (defining this broad "other discharge" category for purposes of a different CWA section).

Plaintiffs have made clear, both here and in the district court, that their primary environmental concern stems from the discharge of ballast water. We quote a passage from the district court's order granting plaintiffs' motion for permanent injunctive relief that describes the purpose of ballast water and the effects of its discharge:

> Ballast water is water that is taken on by cargo ships to compensate for changes in the ship's weight as cargo is loaded or unloaded, and as fuel and supplies are consumed. Ballast water may be used for a number of different purposes, such as maintaining stability, maintaining proper propeller and bow immersion, and to compensate for off-center weights. Thus, ballast water is essential to the proper functioning of cargo ships, as well as to the safety of its crew.

Because ballast water is primarily used to compensate for changes in cargo, it is generally taken in or pumped out at the ports along a ship's route. When a ship takes on ballast water, whether freshwater or saltwater, organisms found in that water are typically taken in as well. These organisms are carried in the ballast tanks of the ship until the ship arrives at its next port, where, due to changes in the distribution of the ship's cargo, they may be released into a new ecosystem. Due to the size of ballast tanks on modern cargo ships, and the speed with which these ships can reach their destinations, organisms are increasingly able to survive the journey to a new ecosystem. All told, "more than 10,000 marine species each day hitch rides around the globe in the ballast water of cargo ships." A number of these species are released into U.S. waters in the more than 21 billion gallons of ballast water released in the United States each year.

If these foreign organisms manage to survive and reproduce in the new ecosystem, they can cause severe problems in the natural and human environment. For example, zebra mussels, native to the Caspian Sea region of Asia, were brought into the Great Lakes in the ballast water of cargo ships. "Zebra mussels have clogged the water pipes of electric companies and other industries; infestations in the Midwest and Northeast have cost power plants and industrial facilities almost $70 million between 1989 and 1995." As another example, according to a 2001 EPA report,

> [a]n introduced strain of cholera bacteria, possibly released in the bilge water of a Chinese freighter, caused the deaths of 10,000 people in Latin America in 1991. This cholera strain was then imported into the United States from Latin America in the ballast tanks of ships that anchored in the port of Mobile, Alabama. Fortunately, cholera bacteria were detected in oyster and finfish samples in Mobile Bay . . . and no additional deaths occurred from exposure to this pathogen.

With a lack of natural predators, invasive species can multiply rapidly and quickly take over an ecosystem, threatening native species. Indeed, invasive species "are a major or contributing cause of declines for almost half the endangered species in the United States." Once established, invasive species become almost impossible to remove, leading "[s]cientists, industry officials, and land managers [to] recogniz[e] that invasive species are one of the most serious, yet least appreciated, environmental threats of the 21st century."

In economic terms, invasive species can also have a devastating effect. The Department of Agriculture spends millions of dollars per year to detect and prevent invasive species. One study cited by the [General Accounting Office] concluded that "total annual economic losses and associated control costs [are] about $137 billion a year-more than double the annual economic damage caused by all natural disasters in the United States."

Nw. Envtl. Advocates v. U.S. EPA ("Northwest Environmental Advocates II"), No. 03–05760, 2006 WL 2669042, at *3–4, 2006 U.S. Dist. LEXIS 69476, at *10–12 (N.D.Cal. Sept. 18, 2006) (citations omitted; sixth alteration added).

B. Procedural History

In January 1999, plaintiffs petitioned the EPA, asking that the agency repeal 40 C.F.R. § 122.3(a). *See* Petition for Repeal of 40 CFR § 122.3(a) (Jan.1999) ("Petition for Rulemaking"). Plaintiffs contended that the regulation was not authorized by the CWA and was thus *ultra vires*. Plaintiffs sued the EPA a year and a half later, alleging unreasonable delay in responding to their petition. The district court ordered the EPA to respond to the petition, but the EPA obtained a stay from this circuit. Under a subsequent consent decree, the EPA agreed to "grant, deny, or grant in part and deny any remaining part of NWEA's petition" by September 2,

2003. Nw. Envtl. Advocates v. U.S. EPA, 340 F.3d 853, 857 (9th Cir.2003). On the day of the deadline, the EPA denied plaintiffs' petition in its entirety. *See* EPA, Decision on Petition for Rulemaking To Repeal 40 C.F.R. 122.3(a) (Sept. 2, 2003) ("EPA Decision on Petition"); *see also* Availability of Decision on Petition for Rulemaking To Repeal Regulation Related to Ballast Water, 68 Fed. Reg. 53,165 (Sept. 9, 2003) (giving notice of the denial).

Plaintiffs brought suit against the EPA three months later, in December 2003. Their first cause of action alleged that 40 C.F.R. § 122.3(a) is not authorized by the CWA and is thus *ultra vires. See* 5 U.S.C. § 706(2)(C). Their second cause of action alleged, based on their *ultra vires* argument, that the 2003 EPA Decision on Petition was "not in accordance with law." *See* 5 U.S.C. § 706(2)(A). At the same time, as a protective measure in the event that the district court lacked jurisdiction, the plaintiffs filed directly with this court a petition for review of the EPA Decision on Petition, pursuant to jurisdictional provisions contained in 33 U.S.C. § 1369(b)(1).

In March 2005, the district court granted summary judgment to plaintiffs on their first cause of action and ordered the EPA to repeal § 122.3(a). Nw. Envtl. Advocates v. U.S. EPA ("Northwest Environmental Advocates I"), No. 03–05760, 2005 WL 756614, at *7, 2005 U.S. Dist. LEXIS 5373, at *40 (N.D.Cal. Mar. 30, 2005). It is unclear whether the district court reached plaintiffs' second cause of action. Given the court's holding on the plaintiffs' first cause of action, however, it did not need to do so. The district court ordered further proceedings to determine the appropriate remedy. *Id.* The six states intervened as plaintiffs at the remedy stage "to protect their sovereign, proprietary, regulatory, and economic interest in the States' waters." The Shipping Industry Ballast Water Coalition ("Shipping Coalition") intervened as a defendant. In September 2006, the district court vacated the challenged portions of 40 C.F.R. § 122.3(a) as of September 30, 2008. Nw. Envtl. Advocates II, 2006 WL 2669042, at *1, 2006 U.S. Dist. LEXIS 69476, at *2.

The EPA and the Shipping Coalition (collectively, "the EPA") appealed the district court's decision to this court. . . . We review the district court's remedial order for abuse of discretion. Biological Legal Found. v. Badgley, 309 F.3d 1166, 1176 (9th Cir.2002).

C. *Ultra Vires* Challenge

[P]laintiffs allege that the CWA does not authorize the exemptions of vessel discharges provided in 40 C.F.R. § 122.3(a). According to plaintiffs, the EPA acted *ultra vires* in promulgating § 122.3(a). *See* 5 U.S.C. § 706(2)(C) (covering agency actions "in excess of statutory jurisdiction, authority, or limitations, or short of statutory right"). If plaintiffs are right, the regulation is invalid. In their second cause of action, plaintiffs allege that the EPA did not act "in accordance with law" when the agency denied the 1999 Petition for Rulemaking asking the EPA to repeal § 122.3(a). *See* 5 U.S.C. § 706(2)(A). As in their first cause of action, the premise of the second cause of action is that the EPA acted *ultra vires* in promulgating § 122.3(a). Because both causes of action present a question of law, we start at step one of *Chevron* and apply the same standard of review. *See, e.g.,* Defenders of Wildlife v. Browner, 191 F.3d 1159, 1162 (9th Cir.1999) ("On questions of statutory interpretation, we follow the approach from *Chevron*.").

The EPA makes three arguments. The first is procedural; the second and third are substantive. First, the EPA argues that the 1999 Petition for Rulemaking challenged only the exclusion for ballast water provided by 40 C.F.R. § 122.3(a). Therefore, the EPA argues, plaintiffs are now limited to challenging only this exclusion. Second, the EPA argues that the CWA authorized the EPA to promulgate § 122.3(a), or that at least the statute is ambiguous and therefore this court should defer to the agency's interpretation of the statute. Third, the EPA argues that even if the CWA did not authorize the promulgation of § 122.3(a) when the CWA was enacted, Congress has now acquiesced in its promulgation. We consider these arguments in turn.

* * *

2. Text of the CWA

Our first substantive inquiry is whether § 122.3(a) is invalid under the plain meaning of the CWA. Our inquiry is guided by *Chevron*. The Court wrote:

> When a court reviews an agency's construction of the statute which it administers, it is confronted with two questions. First, always, is the question whether Congress has directly spoken to the precise question at issue. If the intent of Congress is clear, that is the end of the matter; for the court, as well as the agency, must give effect to the unambiguously expressed intent of Congress.

467 U.S. at 842–43, 104 S.Ct. 2778.

Section 301(a) of the CWA mandates that "the discharge of any pollutant by any person shall be unlawful." 33 U.S.C. § 1311(a). This prohibition is "[t]he 'cornerstone' and 'fundamental premise' of the Clean Water Act." *Se.* Alaska Conservation Council v. U.S. Army Corps of Eng'rs, 486 F.3d 638, 644 (9th Cir.2007) (citations omitted). Section 402 of the CWA provides that a "point source" can obtain a "permit for the discharge of any pollutant or combination of pollutants." 33 U.S.C. § 1342(a)(1). "[T]he Act categorically prohibits any discharge of a pollutant from a point source without a permit." Comm. to Save Mokelumne River v. E. Bay Mun. Util. Dist., 13 F.3d 305, 309 (9th Cir.1993).

The text of the statute clearly covers the discharges at issue here. A "discharge of any pollutant" is "any addition of any pollutant to navigable waters from any point source." 33 U.S.C. § 1362(12)(A). A "point source" is "any discernable, confined and discrete conveyance, including . . . [a] vessel or other floating craft, from which pollutants are or may be discharged." *Id.* § 1362(14). "[N]avigable waters" are "the waters of the United States, including the territorial seas," which begin near the coast and "extend[ ] seaward a distance of three miles." *Id.* §§ 1362(7), (8). "Pollutant" is defined as "dredged spoil, solid waste, incinerator residue, sewage, garbage, sewage sludge, munitions, chemical wastes, biological materials, radioactive materials, heat, wrecked or discarded equipment, rock, sand, cellar dirt and industrial, municipal, and agricultural waste discharged into water." 33 U.S.C. § 1362(6). The term "biological materials" includes invasive species. *See, e.g.,* Nat'l Wildlife Fed'n v. Consumers Power Co., 862 F.2d 580, 583 (6th Cir.1988).

* * *

3. Acquiescence by Congress

The EPA argues that even if the CWA as originally enacted did not authorize the EPA to promulgate § 122.3(a), Congress subsequently acquiesced in the agency's interpretation of the CWA. This is a heroic argument, for the standard for a judicial finding of congressional acquiescence is extremely high.

In *Solid Waste Agency of Northern Cook County v. U.S. Army Corps of Engineers* ("*SWANCC*"), Solid Waste Agency of Northern Cook County v. U.S. Army Corps of Engineers ("SWANCC"), 531 U.S. 159 (2001), the Court considered a challenge to an expansive definition of "navigable waters" under the CWA. The Army Corps of Engineers had promulgated a regulation containing that definition in 1977. The Corps argued that Congress had acquiesced in the regulation's definition. Id. at 168–69. The Court responded, "Although we have recognized congressional acquiescence to administrative interpretations of a statute in some situations, we have done so with extreme care." Id. at 169. . . .

The EPA points to a number of post–1973 statutes in which Congress has addressed the forms of pollution exempted by § 122.3(a), particularly ballast water. According to the EPA, those statutes satisfy the high standard for acquiescence set forth in *SWANCC*. For the reasons that follow, we disagree and hold that Congress has not acquiesced in § 122.3(a).

a. NDAA and DSHMRA

The EPA relies most heavily on two statutes. The first is the National Defense Authorization Act of 1996 ("NDAA"), Pub.L. No. 104–106, § 325, 110 Stat. 186, 254, *codified at* 33 U.S.C. §§ 1322(a), (j), (n), 1362(6). The second is the Deep Seabed Hard Mineral Resources Act of 1980

("DSHMRA"), Pub.L. No. 96–283, 94 Stat. 554, *codified at* 30 U.S.C. §§ 1419 *et seq.*

In the NDAA, Congress statutorily exempted discharges incidental to the normal operation of United States military vessels from CWA permitting requirements and established discharge controls specifically tailored to those vessels. Congress was well aware of 40 C.F.R. § 122.3(a) when it enacted the NDAA. Indeed, the statute cited the regulation as a partial aid in defining what the category "discharge incidental to the normal operation of a vessel" did not include. *See* 33 U.S.C. § 1322(a)(12)(B)(iii).

A Senate Report accompanying the Senate Bill explained that discharges from military vessels, like those from other vessels, already were exempted from NPDES permitting requirements by EPA regulation. But the report went on to explain why, nonetheless, a broader exemption was desirable:

> The Navy wishes to clarify the regulatory status of certain non-sewage discharges from Navy vessels. Vessels are point sources of pollution under the Clean Water Act. Any discharge of pollutants from a point source, including a vessel, into the waters of the United States is prohibited unless specifically permitted under section 402 or 404 of the Act. . . .

> Although EPA regulations generally exempt non-sewage discharges from vessels from the permit requirements of the Act, some coastal states have imposed regulations or inspection programs that may have application to these types of discharges. A series of events in the waters of several coastal states prompted concern at the Navy as to state authorities to regulate these discharges.

S.Rep. No. 104–113, at 1–2 (1995). The Senate Report explained that § 122.3(a) was the regulatory basis for the exemption of most "non-sewage discharges from vessels." Id. at 7. The report did not, however, endorse or otherwise indicate approval of regulatory exemptions for entire categories of marine discharges. If anything, the report may be read to suggest the contrary. The report indicated that, but for the statutory exemption contained in the NDAA, the CWA permitting process would have applied to marine discharges from military vessels: "The effect of [the NDAA] is to remove the statutory requirement for a permit for these point source discharges[.]" Id. at 3.

The most that can be said, based on the NDAA, is that Congress was well aware of § 122.3(a) and the exemptions it provided. Congress concluded that the existing statutory provisions and exemptions, including the exemptions provided in § 122.3(a), did not fully address the needs of military vessels. It therefore passed a new statute with provisions specifically tailored to military vessels. In so doing, the NDAA did nothing to endorse § 122.3(a). The NDAA only made § 122.3(a) irrelevant to military vessels except as a definitional tool.

In the DSHMRA, Congress required vessels engaged in deep sea mining and drilling operations to comply with the provisions of the CWA. Congress did so by explicitly extending the CWA's geographical reach over such vessels beyond the otherwise applicable three-mile limit. *See* 33 U.S.C. § 1362(9), (10), (12)(B). In pertinent part, the DSHMRA provided that:

> For purposes of this chapter, any vessel or other floating craft engaged in commercial recovery or exploration shall not be deemed to be "a vessel or other floating craft" under section 502(12)(B) of the Clean Water Act [33 U.S.C. § 1362(12)(B)] and any discharge of a pollutant from such vessel or other floating craft shall be subject to the Clean Water Act.

30 U.S.C. § 1419(e) (alterations in original).

When it enacted the DSHMRA, Congress noted with approval the final sentence of 40 C.F.R. § 122.3(a). This sentence provides that, despite the regulatory exemptions for three categories of marine discharges, CWA permitting requirements would apply to a range of vessels not being used for transportation:

> This exclusion does not apply to . . . discharges when the vessel is operating in a capacity other than as a means of transportation such as when used as an energy or mining facility, a storage facility or a seafood processing facility, or when secured to a storage facility or a seafood processing facility, or when secured to the bed of the ocean, contiguous zone or waters of the United States for the purpose of mineral or oil exploration or development.

40 C.F.R. § 122.3(a). Plaintiffs do not challenge this part of the regulation because it exempts nothing, but instead recognizes ongoing NPDES requirements. *See* Nw. Envtl. Advocates II, 2006 WL 2669042, at *1 nn. 1–2, 2006 U.S. Dist. LEXIS 69476, at *2–3 nn. 1–2.

The Senate Report accompanying the DSHMRA noted with approval the refusal of § 122.3(a) to exempt nontransportation vessels from NPDES:

> [T]he Environmental Protection Agency has concluded that the Congress did not intend to exempt pollutant discharges into ocean waters by vessels when engaged in such activities as mining or drilling for oil, etc. Relying on this interpretation [of the CWA], the Environmental Protection Agency amended [its regulations] to indicate that vessels engaged in ocean mineral exploration, extraction and processing activities are not exempt from permit requirements under section 402. The Committee concurs in this interpretation.

S.Rep. No. 96–360 at 2–3 (1979); *see also id.* at 3 (noting that the DSHMRA merely "clarif[ied] the application of section 402" to these vessels). Thus, the most that can be said of the DSHMRA is that Congress was aware of § 122.3(a) and explicitly approved of the EPA's decision *not* to exempt from the permitting process marine discharges from non-transportation vessels.

We conclude that neither the NDAA nor the DSHMRA comes close to satisfying the *SWANCC* standard of providing "overwhelming evidence of acquiescence" by Congress in § 122.3(a)'s exemption of three categories of marine discharges.

b. NANPCA, NISA, APPS, and Alaska Cruise Ship Legislation

The EPA also relies on four additional statutes. They are the Nonindigenous Aquatic Nuisance Prevention and Control Act of 1990 ("NANPCA"), Pub.L. No. 101–646, 104 Stat. 4761, *codified at* 16 U.S.C. §§ 4701 *et seq.;* the National Invasive Species Act of 1996 ("NISA"), Pub.L. No. 104–332, 110 Stat. 4073 (amending NANPCA); the Act to Prevent Pollution from Ships ("APPS"), Pub.L. No. 96–478, 94 Stat. 2297 (1980), *codified at* 33 U.S.C. §§ 1901 *et seq.;* and a statute regulating discharges by Alaska cruise ships, enacted as part of the Consolidated Appropriations Act of 2001, Pub.L. No. 106–554, § 1(a)(4), 114 Stat. 2763, 2763A–209 (enacting Title XIV of Division B of H.R. 5666, §§ 1401–1414, as introduced Dec. 15, 2000) (*see* 33 U.S.C. § 1901 Note for the text of the statute).

NANPCA and NISA address the problem of invasive species released in ballast-water-related discharges. For example, these statutes authorize the Coast Guard to develop voluntary guidelines and regulations for a Great Lakes ballast water program. *See* 16 U.S.C. § 4711(a)–(b). The statutes also require national guidelines for ballast-water-related discharges of nonindigenous species, *id.* § 4711(c), (f)(2)(A)(ii), and establish an Aquatic Nuisance Species Task Force, of which the EPA is a member, *id.* § 4721. Savings clauses provide that the Great Lakes regulations "shall. . . . not affect or supersede any requirements or prohibitions pertaining to the discharge of ballast water" under the CWA, and that the national guidelines "shall. . . . not affect or supersede any requirements or prohibitions pertaining to the discharge of ballast water" under the CWA. *Id.* § 4711(b)(2)(C), (c)(2)(J). These statutes do not demonstrate *SWANCC*'s "overwhelming evidence of [congressional] acquiescence" in the exemptions contained in § 122.3(a). They merely demonstrate a congressional intent to address the serious national problem of ballast water discharges of invasive species, and to do so on multiple, nonexclusive fronts. The Supreme Court recently came to similar conclusions regarding Congress's overlapping mandates to combat greenhouse gas emissions.

See Massachusetts v. EPA, 549 U.S. 497, 127 S.Ct. 1438, 1448–49, 1460–62, 1461 n. 27, 167 L.Ed.2d 248 (2007).

The APPS implemented the International Convention for the Prevention of Pollution from Ships of 1973 and the Protocol of 1978 (known collectively as "MARPOL 73/78"). The APPS applies to all U.S.-flagged ships worldwide and foreign-flagged ships in the navigable waters of the United States. 33 U.S.C. § 1902(a). The six annexes to MARPOL 73/ 78 address vessel discharges of oil, noxious bulk liquid substances, harmful packaged substances, sewage, garbage, and air pollution. The APPS's savings clause provides that "requirements of this [Act] supplement and neither amend nor repeal any other provisions of law, except as expressly provided in this [Act]." 33 U.S.C. § 1907(f). The APPS contains no indication of congressional intent to acquiesce in § 122.3(a).

Finally, the Alaska cruise ship legislation authorizes the EPA to regulate sewage and graywater discharges from cruise ships in specified Alaskan waters. A savings clause provides that "[n]othing in this title shall be construed as restricting, affecting, or amending any other law or the authority of any department, instrumentality, or agency of the Unites States." 33 U.S.C. § 1901 Note § 1411(a); *see* H.R. 5666, § 1411(a). This legislation, too, contains no indication of congressional intent to acquiesce in § 122.3(a).

D. Remedy

After finding that the EPA had acted *ultra vires* in promulgating § 122.3(a), the district court concluded that the best course was to vacate that regulation, effective September 30, 2008. This date gave the EPA a two-year period during which it could work to promulgate a new regulation. The district court also concluded that it would be best to leave the EPA free during this period to do its work in the manner the agency thought best. In so concluding, the district court did not provide to plaintiffs everything they had sought. Plaintiffs had asked the district court to provide only an eighteen-month period, and to engage in close supervision of the EPA's progress during that period. The district court explained its reasons in a careful twenty-one page order. It wrote, *inter alia:*

> [T]he Court is influenced by the fact that the regulation at issue has stood for the past 30 years, and by the fact that the effects of an immediate vacatur would be so dramatic as to make such an option a practical impossibility. Indeed, not even plaintiffs request an immediate vacatur of the challenged regulation. While the practical implications of the Court's order make the Court wary of imposing a deadline on EPA that is too ambitious, the potential harm that ballast waters represent to our nation's ecosystems leads the Court to conclude that there is an urgency to promulgating new regulations that EPA has not, to this point in the litigation, acknowledged. Thus, the

Court must decide upon a time frame for vacating the regulation that balances the need for prompt action against the need to allow EPA adequate freedom to address a complicated issue.

The most substantial question confronting the Court is whether to issue injunctive relief ordering EPA to act in accordance with the Court's order by a certain date. In light of the arguments the parties have presented, the Court finds that the preferable route is to give the agency a certain date on which the regulation will be vacated, and to allow the agency freedom to work around that date to find an appropriate solution to the problem of vessel discharges. Indeed, in considering the variety of technical arguments the parties have presented about the appropriate remedy, the Court has been reminded that EPA holds an expertise in this area that the Court cannot approach. Thus, the Court believes that EPA should be given wide latitude, within broad constraints, to address the problem of discharges from vessels. Accordingly, the Court rules as follows: the Court will GRANT plaintiffs' motion for a permanent injunction, and will set aside the challenged regulation as of September 30, 2008. Absent a compelling justification, the Court will not act further to supervise how EPA responds to this order.

Nw. Envtl. Advocates II, 2006 WL 2669042, at *10, 2006 U.S. Dist. LEXIS 69476, at *31–33 (footnotes omitted).

We affirm the district court's decision to vacate the regulation and to remand for further proceedings as a valid exercise of its remedial powers. *See, e.g., NRDC 9th. Cir.1992,* 966 F.2d at 1305. The district court's order requires the EPA to perform a substantial task-to bring the discharges previously exempted by § 122.3(a) within the permitting process of the CWA. Neither the district court nor this court underestimates the magnitude of the task. But "this ambitious statute is not hospitable to the concept that the appropriate response to a difficult pollution problem is not to try at all." *Costle,* 568 F.2d at 1380; *see also* Union Elec. Co. v. EPA, 427 U.S. 246, 268–69, 96 S.Ct. 2518, 49 L.Ed.2d 474 (1976) ("Allowing such [feasibility] claims to be raised . . . would frustrate congressional intent.").

The EPA informed this court at oral argument that it has been proceeding in accordance with the district court's order. We anticipate that in formulating a new regulation to replace § 122.3(a) the EPA will take advantage of the flexibility of the NPDES permitting process. For example, we take judicial notice of the fact that, in its request for comments, the EPA has indicated that "use of general permit(s) would appear to be an attractive possibility." Development of [NPDES] Permits for Discharges Incidental to the Normal Operation of Vessels, 72 Fed. Reg. 34,241, 34,247 (June 21, 2007).

On July 11, 2008, the Department of Justice informed us by letter that on June 17, 2008, the EPA published in the Federal Register draft "General Permits for Discharges Incidental to the Normal Operation of a Vessel," and that the public comment period on the draft is scheduled to close on August 1. *See* 73 Fed. Reg. 34,296 (June 17, 2008). The letter warns that a final version may not be ready by the September 30, 2008, deadline established by the district court, but the letter stops short of a request to extend the deadline. If the government chooses to request an extension of the deadline, that request should be addressed to the district court.

* * *

V. Conclusion

We hold that the district court had subject matter jurisdiction over plaintiffs' suit alleging that the EPA acted *ultra vires* in promulgating § 122.3(a). We affirm the district court, holding that the EPA acted *ultra vires* in promulgating § 122.3(a) and that EPA's denial of plaintiffs' 1999 petition requesting the repeal of § 122.3(a) was not in accordance with law. We affirm the district court's remedial order as a proper exercise of its discretion. Finally, we dismiss for lack of subject matter jurisdiction plaintiffs' petition for review filed directly with this court.

* * *

NOTES AND QUESTIONS

In Lake Carriers' Assoc. v. EPA, 652 F.3d 1 (D.C. Cir. 2011), the court upheld EPA's General NPDES permit for vessel intentional ballast water discharges despite its incorporation of 100 state conditions imposed through water quality certifications under Section 401(a) of the Clean Water Act, 33 U.S.C. § 1341(a). The court found that EPA's permit did not violate the uniformity principle of federal maritime law. On the shipping companies' claim that the conditions burdened interstate commerce in violation of the Commerce Clause, the court held that the Clean Water Act authorized such burdens in the certification provision of Section 401(a), stating:

> . . . we note that EPA's resolution of this matter does not leave the petitioners without recourse. If they believe that the certification conditions imposed by any particular state pose an inordinate burden on their operations, they may challenge those conditions in that state's courts. *See* Roosevelt Campobello Int'l Park Comm'n v. EPA, 684 F.2d 1041, 1056 (1st Cir.1982) (noting that "the courts have consistently agreed . . . that the proper forum to review the appropriateness of a state's certification is the state court"); *see also City of Tacoma,* 460 F.3d at 67. If they believe that a particular state's law imposes an unconstitutional burden on interstate commerce, they may challenge that law in federal (or state)

court. *See Am. Trucking Ass'n,* 600 F.3d at 628 n. 1. And if neither of these avenues proves adequate, they are free to ask Congress to amend the CWA, perhaps by reimposing the exemption for incidental vessel discharges. *See supra* note 1 (noting that, in response to the Ninth Circuit's decision vacating the exemption, Congress passed two acts that exempted small boats and recreational and commercial fishing vessels from the CWA's permitting requirements).

2. SHIP STRIKES, OCEAN NOISE, AND MILITARY READINESS

A. SHIP STRIKES AND SPEED LIMITS

DEFENDERS OF WILDLIFE V. GUTIERREZ
United States Court of Appeals, D.C. Circuit, 2008
532 F.3d 913

SENTELLE, CHIEF JUDGE.

I. Background

Right whales are mostly black in color, generally grow up to 45–55 feet in length, and can weigh up to 70 tons. *Proposed Endangered Status for North Atlantic Right Whales, 71 Fed. Reg. 77,704, 77,705 (Dec. 27, 2006)* ("Proposed Endangered Status"). Right whales are so named because, historically, they were considered the "right" (correct) whale to hunt due to their close proximity to coastlines, their relatively slow speed, the prized oils they contain, and the large volume of blubber that gives them a tendency to float when dead. U.S. Army Research Office, Endangered Species Act Biological Assessment for the U.S. Atlantic Coast, at 3–2 (Aug. 1, 1995) ("Biological Assessment"). By the early twentieth century, the right whale population was so depleted that both the League of Nations (in 1935) and the International Whaling Commission (in 1949) banned all whaling of them. NMFS, Final Environmental Impact Statement for Amending the Atlantic Large Whale Take Reduction Plan: Broad-Based Gear Modifications, Vol. I, at 9–6 & n.2 (Aug. 2007), *available at* NOAA Fisheries Service: 2007 Final ALWTRP Modifications, http://www.nero.noaa.gov/nero/hotnews/whalesfr/ (follow "9.0 Cumulative Effects Analysis" hyperlink) (last visited June 30, 2008).

Relatively recent population estimates show around 300 remaining right whales. *Proposed Endangered Status, 71 Fed. Reg. at 77,705.* The population does not reproduce rapidly; females are not mature reproductively until they reach the age of eight and even then reproduce at a rate of one calf every four years. Biological Assessment, at 3–6 to 3–7. Recent estimates show a mortality rate of at least four percent per year, which, combined with the low birth rate and already low population levels, "mak[e] it one of the most critically endangered large whale species in the world." Proposed Rule To Implement Speed Restrictions To Reduce the Threat of Ship Collisions with *North Atlantic Right Whales, 71 Fed. Reg. 36,299, 36,300 (June 26, 2006)* ("Proposed Rule"). Right whales were first listed as "endangered" under the Endangered Species Conservation Act of 1969, Pub. L. No. 91–135, 83 Stat. 275, the precursor to the Endangered Species Act of 1973 ("ESA"), *16 U.S.C. § 1531 et seq.,* which is the Act under which they are now listed. *See 50 C.F.R. § 17.11* (listing the North Atlantic right whale as endangered under the ESA); *see also 35 Fed. Reg. 8491, 8495 (June 2, 1970)* (listing the right whale as endangered pursuant to the Endangered Species Conservation Act). Right whales are also listed as "depleted" under the Marine Mammal Protection Act of 1972 ("MMPA"), *16 U.S.C. § 1361 et seq. See 38 Fed. Reg. 20,564, 20,570 (Aug. 1, 1973)* (listing the right whale as "depleted").

Right whales are migratory mammals. They generally spend spring, summer, and fall in New England waters near Massachusetts, Rhode Island, and Maine, but some whales have been spotted as far north as *Greenland. Proposed Endangered Status, 71 Fed. Reg. at 77,705.* Their only known wintering location is along the southeastern U.S. coastline near Georgia and Florida, which is where some females go to calve. *Id.* National Marine Fisheries Service designated these areas—the Great South Channel east of Cape Cod, Cape Cod and Massachusetts Bays, and the southeastern United States off the coasts of southern Georgia and northern Florida—as right whale "critical habitat." *50 C.F.R. § 226.203* (listing right whale critical habitat); *see 16 U.S.C. § 1533(a)(3)(A)* (giving the Secretary of Commerce authority to designate critical habitat); *id. § 1532(5)(A)* (defining "critical habitat").

Some of the areas labeled by NMFS as "critical habitat" for right whales are dense with shipping traffic. *See* Right Whale Ship Strike Reduction Strategy Notice of Intent To Prepare an *Environmental Impact Statement and Conduct Public Scoping, 70 Fed. Reg. 36,121, 36,121 (June 22, 2005)* ("Notice of Intent") ("Right whales are located in, or adjacent to, several major shipping corridors on the eastern U.S. and southeastern Canadian coasts."); Proposed Rule, 71 Fed. Reg. at 36,306 (describing shipping traffic in the bays and channels near Boston, Massachusetts). Ship strikes are "the greatest source of known deaths" of right whales. Proposed Rule, 71 Fed. Reg. at 36,300. They "are responsible for over 50 percent of known human-related right whale mortalities and are considered one of the principal causes for the lack of recovery in [the right whale population]." Notice of Intent, 70 Fed. Reg. at 36,121.

There are two primary agencies whose actions appellants challenge in this case. The first agency is National Marine Fisheries Service, which is an arm of the National Oceanic and Atmospheric Administration, which, in turn, falls within the Commerce Department. NMFS is one of the agencies to which the Endangered Species Act and Marine Mammal Protection Act delegate enforcement. *See 16 U.S.C. § 1533(a)(1)* and *id. § 1532(15)* (delegating to the Secretary of Commerce, of which NMFS is part, the duty to identify endangered species); *id. § 1362(12)(A)(i), (B)* (delegating to the Secretary of Commerce, and the National Oceanic and Atmospheric Administration within that agency, authority over the Marine Mammal Protection Act with respect to whales). The second agency is the United States Coast Guard, a part of the Department of Homeland Security. The Coast Guard is the main agency responsible for effectuating the Ports and Waterways Safety Act of 1972 ("PWSA"), *33 U.S.C. § 1221 et seq.,* under which it has the duty to designate vessel routing measures "to provide safe access routes for the movement of vessel traffic" coming in and out of ports, *id. § 1223(c)(1).*

On June 1, 2004, NMFS issued an Advance Notice of Proposed Rulemaking requesting comments on proposed regulations that aim to reduce the likelihood of right whale ship strike mortalities. *Advance Notice of Proposed Rulemaking (ANPR) for Right Whale Ship Strike Reduction, 69 Fed. Reg. 30,857 (June 1, 2004)* ("ANPR"). The agency noted that despite its efforts to notify mariners of right whale sightings and ship strikes, impose mandatory ship reporting systems, collaborate with the Coast Guard, and take other measures, "right whales continue to be killed as a result of collisions with vessels." *Id. at 30,858.* Because of these failings, the agency recognized "that this complex problem requires additional, more pro-active measures to reduce or eliminate the threat of ship strikes to right whales." *Id.* Without additional measures, the agency noted that "[r]ecent modeling exercises suggest that if current trends continue, the population could go extinct in less than 200 years" and that "the loss of even a single individual may contribute to the extinction of the species. . . . " *Id.* It further noted that "according to the models, preventing the mortality of one adult female a year alters the projected outcome." *Id.* The agency proposed, *inter alia,* to impose speed limits on vessels 65 feet and longer traveling in areas when right whales are present in significant numbers, and invited comments on its proposal. *Id. at 30,858, 30,861.*

On May 19, 2005, Defenders of Wildlife, The Humane Society of the United States, Ocean Conservancy, and others submitted a petition for emergency rulemaking to NMFS pursuant to *5 U.S.C. § 553(e).* Petition for Initiation of Emergency Rulemaking To Prevent the Extinction of the North Atlantic Right Whale to the Secretary of Commerce, the Administrator of the National Oceanic and Atmospheric Administration, and the Assistant Administrator for Fisheries at NMFS (May 19, 2005) ("Emergency Rulemaking Petition"); *see 5 U.S.C. § 553(e)* (requiring agencies to "give an interested person the right to petition for the issuance, amendment, or repeal of a rule"). The petition, among other things, requested "emergency regulations [that] require all ships entering and leaving all major East Coast ports to travel at speeds of 12 knots or less within 25 nautical miles of port entrances during expected right whale high use periods." Emergency Rulemaking Petition, at 3–4. Just over six months after the petitioners requested an emergency rule, NMFS published its denial. *Petition To Initiate Emergency Rulemaking To Prevent the Extinction of the North Atlantic Right Whale; Final Determination, 70 Fed. Reg. 56,884 (Sept. 29, 2005)* ("Denial of Emergency Rulemaking Petition").

At the same time the petitioners were pursuing an emergency rulemaking petition with NMFS, Defenders of Wildlife, The Humane Society of the United States, Ocean Conservancy, and Regina Asmutis–Silvia (together, "appellants") were challenging the Coast Guard about a series of purported omissions regarding its duties under the Endangered Species Act. On November 3, 2005, appellants sent a 60-day notice letter to the Coast Guard pursuant to the citizen-suit provision in the ESA, *16 U.S.C. § 1540(g)*, notifying the agency that it was violating ESA section 7(a)(2), *16 U.S.C. § 1536(a)(2)*, by failing to consult with NMFS about the impact its regulation of commercial shipping has on right whales, "and therefore failing to insure that this vessel traffic is not likely to jeopardize the continued existence of the species" and its habitat. The letter also maintained that the Coast Guard was violating its ESA section 7(a)(1), *16 U.S.C. § 1536(a)(1)*, obligation "to carry out programs for the conservation of the right whale." Appellants noted that the Coast Guard has authority to control vessel movement pursuant to *33 U.S.C. § 1223* and to take into account "environmental factors" while doing so, *id. § 1224(a)(6)*. They requested that the Coast Guard use this authority to protect the right whale. They also argued that the agency was violating ESA section 9, *16 U.S.C. § 1538*, by establishing and maintaining vessel shipping lanes in areas inhabited by right whales, effectuating the "take" of the marine mammals. The record contains no response to the notice letter.

* * *

On June 2, 2006, appellants moved for summary judgment, and on June 25, 2006, NMFS published its highly anticipated proposed ship strike rule. *Proposed Rule, 71 Fed. Reg. 36,299*. Approximately three weeks later, appellees filed a cross motion for summary judgment. On October 25, 2006, noting that NMFS had published its proposed ship strike rule, the district court ordered counsel for NMFS to "inform the Court within 10 days of the date of this Order when the final rule will issue." *Defenders of Wildlife,* No. 05–2191 (D.D.C. Oct. 25, 2006) (order). On November 13, 2006, appellees responded, explaining that NMFS must

> respond to over 10,000 public comments received on its proposed rule, consult with other Federal agencies affected by this rule, consult with itself for purposes of Section 7 of the ESA, finish a final environmental impact statement and record of decision, and wait 30

days prior to implementation of the proposed ship strike measures. . . .

Defendants' Response to the Court's October 25, 2006 Order at 1–2, *Defenders of Wildlife,* No. 05–2191 (D.D.C. Nov. 9, 2006). The agency estimated that it would "tak[e] final action on the proposed rule in June 2007." Id. at 2. In a hearing held on March 16, 2007, counsel stated to the district court that "the draft final rule has cleared the Department of Commerce and is currently with the Office of Management and Budget for review. . . . " Transcript of Hearing at 37, *Defenders of Wildlife,* No. 05–2191 (D.D.C. Mar. 16, 2007). Counsel also stated that the Office of Management and Budget received the draft final rule on February 20, 2007, and that pursuant to *Exec. Order No. 12866, 58 Fed. Reg. 51,735 (Oct. 4, 1993),* that office has 90 days to review the rule and return it to NMFS. Transcript of Hearing at 37.

On April 5, 2007, the district court granted appellees' cross motion for summary judgment and denied that of appellants. Defenders of Wildlife v. Gutierrez, 484 F. Supp. 2d 44 (D.D.C. 2007). The district court rejected appellants' challenge to the agency's denial of the rulemaking petition, explaining that

> [w]hile NMFS' explanation may have been lacking in detail, and may not represent the policy choices that the plaintiffs might make, the Court cannot conclude that NMFS "relied on factors which Congress has not intended it to consider, entirely failed to consider an important aspect of the problem, offered an explanation for its decision that runs counter to the evidence before the agency or [was] so implausible that it could not be ascribed to a difference in view or the product of agency expertise."

II. Analysis

A. Emergency Rulemaking

* * *

The explanations presented in the agency's denial represented reasoned decisionmaking. The agency's prediction that an emergency rule would detract agency resources from the promulgation of a final, comprehensive rule is based on facts found in the record. At the time of the denial of the petition for emergency rulemaking, NMFS was holding public meetings on the ANPR and preparing a draft environmental impact statement on proposed vessel speed restriction measures. Letter from William T. Hogarth, Assistant Administrator, NMFS, to Jonathan R. Lovvorn, Vice President, The Humane Society of the United States, at 1 (Sept. 14, 2005). Petitioners presented no evidence to rebut the agency's prediction that an emergency rule would curtail the public's notice-and-comment period and analysis of the rule's environmental impact. The agency made a policy decision to focus its resources on a comprehensive strategy, which in light of the information before the agency at the time, was reasoned and adequately supported by the record. We will not disturb it on appeal.

B. Coast Guard Action

Appellants' second claim is directed against the Coast Guard and its purported omissions while engaged in the process by which it promulgates, enforces, and alters vessel routing measures that coincide with right whale habitat. . . .

The Ports and Waterways Safety Act requires the Coast Guard to "designate necessary fairways and traffic separation schemes" to provide safe routes for boats traveling in and out of U.S. ports and other places subject to U.S. jurisdiction. *33 U.S.C. § 1223(c)(1)*. Traffic separation schemes ("TSSs") are similar to the markings on paved roads—they are "aimed at the separation of opposing streams of traffic . . . by the establishment of traffic lanes." *33 C.F.R. § 167.5(b)*. The Coast Guard's construction of "measures for controlling or supervising vessel traffic" is "[s]ubject to the requirements of *section 1224*," *33 U.S.C. § 1223(a)(1)*; *see also id. § 1223(c)(3)*, which, *inter alia,* requires the Coast Guard to "take into account all relevant factors concerning . . . protection of the marine environment, . . . including but not limited to . . . environmental factors," *id. § 1224(a)(6)*. Prior to designating a traffic separation scheme, the Coast Guard must, *inter alia,* (1) undertake a study, which the Coast Guard calls a port access route study ("PARS"), and publish notice of it in the Federal Register, *id. § 1223(c)(3)(A)*; (2) "take into account all other uses of the area under consideration," in consultation with the Secretary of Commerce and others, *id. § 1223(c)(3)(B)*; and (3) "to the extent practicable, reconcile the need for safe access routes with the needs of all other reasonable uses of the area involved," *id. § 1223(c)(3)(C)*. After completing the above tasks, the Coast Guard must issue a notice of proposed rulemaking of the contemplated route, or lack thereof, in the Federal Register, and state its reasons for the decision. *Id. § 1223(c)(4)*. The Coast Guard may later adjust the location or limits of these vessel shipping routes, *id. § 1223(c)(5)(C)*, and may also make them mandatory, *id. § 1223(c)(5)(B)*.

Since the enactment of the Ports and Waterways Safety Act, the Coast Guard has established numerous traffic separation schemes, some of which coincide with right whale habitat. In recent years, the Coast Guard has undertaken several port access route studies and modified traffic separation schemes in right whale-inhabited areas. *See, e.g., Port Access Routes: Approaches to Portland, ME and Casco Bay, 70 Fed. Reg. 7067 (Feb. 10, 2005)* (notice of PARS); *Port Access Routes Study: In the Approaches to Chesapeake Bay, VA, 69 Fed. Reg. 3869 (Jan. 27, 2004)* (notice of PARS results); *Port Access Routes Study: In the Approaches to Narragansett Bay and Buzzards Bay, Cleveland Ledge to the Race, Narragansett Bay East Passage, and the Areas Offshore of Connecticut, Rhode Island, and Massachusetts, 68 Fed. Reg. 74,199 (Dec. 23, 2003)* (notice of PARS); *TSS in the Approaches to Delaware Bay, 65 Fed. Reg. 12,944 (Mar. 10, 2000)*. There are at least six traffic separation schemes at issue in this case—namely, (1) In the Approaches to the Chesapeake Bay, (2) Off Delaware Bay, (3) Off New York, (4) In the Approaches to Narragansett Bay, R.I. and Buzzards Bay, Mass., (5) In the Approach to Boston, Mass., and (6) In the Approaches to Portland, Maine. *See* Defenders of Wildlife v. Gutierrez, 484 F. Supp. 2d 44, 55 n.9 (D.D.C. 2007) (listing the TSSs mentioned in the amended complaint).

The Endangered Species Act and the Marine Mammal Protection Act give the Coast Guard duties regarding the right whale. ESA section 7(a)(1) requires all federal agencies, "in consultation with and with the assistance of the Secretary, [to] utilize their authorities in furtherance of the purposes of this chapter by carrying out programs for the conservation of endangered species and threatened species. . . . " *16 U.S.C. § 1536(a)(1)*. And ESA section 9 prohibits any federal agency from "tak[ing]," *id. § 1538(a)(1)(B),* meaning, *inter alia,* harassing, harming, wounding, or killing, *id. § 1532(19),* "any endangered species of fish or wildlife" "within the United States or [its] territorial sea . . . [,]"*id. § 1538(a)(1)(B); see id. § 1532(13)* (including federal departments, instrumentalities, and agents in its definition of "person" for ESA purposes). The Marine Mammal Protection Act also prohibits the unauthorized "take" of all marine mammals, *id. § 1372(a)*, and requires the Secretary of Commerce to "prescribe such regulations as are necessary and appropriate to carry out the purposes of this subchapter," *id. § 1382(a)*.

The statutory provision most relevant to this dispute is ESA section 7(a)(2), *16 U.S.C. § 1536(a)(2)*. This provision requires "[e]ach Federal agency . . . in consultation with and with the assistance of the Secretary, [to] insure that any action authorized, funded, or carried out by such agency (hereinafter in this section referred to as an 'agency action') is not likely to jeopardize the continued existence of any endangered species or threatened species" or its habitat, unless the agency is granted an exemption. *Id.* No party disputes that the Coast Guard did not consult with NMFS about the potential effect of any of the above-listed traffic separation schemes on the right whale. They do argue, however, about the applicability of the ESA to the Coast Guard's role in the traffic separation scheme process.

* * *

Appellants challenge the Coast Guard's actions regarding the traffic separation scheme process as violations of ESA sections 7(a)(1), 7(a)(2), and 9. *16 U.S.C. §§ 1536(a)(1), (a)(2), 1538.* The district court dismissed this challenge, concluding that the International Maritime Organization, a multinational body, adopted the traffic separation schemes at issue, not the Coast Guard. *Defenders of Wildlife, 484 F. Supp. 2d at 55.* Because the district court held that there was no final agency action, the court concluded that it lacked jurisdiction to consider appellants' claims against the Coast Guard. Id. at 55–56.

The parties dispute whether "agency action" or *"final* agency action" is required in order to bring suit under the citizen-suit provision of the ESA, *16 U.S.C. § 1540(g),* based on a violation of ESA section 7(a)(2)'s consultation requirement. Appellants extract a simple "agency action" requirement from the text of ESA section 7(a)(2), which speaks only to "agency action." *16 U.S.C. § 1536(a)(2)* ("Each Federal agency shall, in consultation with and with the assistance of the Secretary, insure that any action authorized, funded, or carried out by such agency (hereinafter in this section referred to as an 'agency action') is not likely to jeopardize the continued existence" of endangered species or their habitats.). Appellees argue that the "final agency action" requirement in the second clause of the Administrative Procedure Act should be read into ESA section 7(a)(2). *See 5 U.S.C. § 704* ("Agency action made reviewable by statute and final agency action for which there is no other adequate remedy in a court are subject to judicial review."). We find it unnecessary to resolve this issue because we hold that appellants are challenging final agency action by the Coast Guard.

As they did in their standing arguments, appellees characterize the traffic separation scheme process as one controlled by an international organization with the State Department acting as an intermediary between the international body and the Coast Guard, leaving the Coast Guard with a minor and purely ministerial role. However, the record shows quite a different role for the Coast Guard in this process. Most significantly, the Coast Guard is the sole body charged with the duty of promulgating traffic separation schemes. *33 U.S.C. § 1223(c)(1); see 33 C.F.R. § 1.05–1.* Appellees point to no congressional authorization permitting the State Department to promulgate traffic separation schemes. Nor can they point to any provision that gives the International Maritime Organization, which was created as a "consultative and advisory" body, Convention on the Intergovernmental Maritime Consultative Organization, art. 2, Mar. 6, 1948, 9 U.S.T. 621, T.I.A.S. 4004, authority to promulgate regulations in U.S. waters. Treaties "are not domestic law unless Congress has either enacted implementing statutes or the treaty itself conveys an intention that it be self-executing and is ratified on these terms." Medellin v. Texas, 128 S. Ct. 1346, 1356 (2008) (internal quotation marks omitted). Appellees do not contend that Congress has enacted implementing statutes for the treaty at issue, International Convention for the Safety of Life at Sea ("SOLAS"), Nov. 1, 1974, 32 U.S.T. 47, T.I.A.S. 9700, or that the treaty is self-executing. In fact, the treaty relies on member nations to enforce its routing measures: "Contracting Governments will use their influence to secure the appropriate use of adopted routes and will do everything in their power to ensure adherence to the measures adopted by the Organization in conne[ct]ion with rout[ ]ing of ships." SOLAS, ch. 5, reg. 8(d).

By giving the Coast Guard authority to promulgate traffic separation schemes, Congress intended to make the Coast Guard accountable for them. *See 33 U.S.C. § 1223(c)(1)*. Were we to hold that the Coast Guard had delegated its duties under the Ports and Waterways Safety Act to the International Maritime Organization, and that this delegation relieved the Coast Guard of any responsibility for the final action, we would countermine this intent. Such an outcome would also undermine several other statutes that Congress enacted to give parties the ability to challenge unlawful agency action. A party harmed by the Coast Guard's failure to take into account "the safety and security of United States ports and waterways," *33 U.S.C. § 1224(a)*, or the "economic impact and effects," *id. § 1224(a)(7)*, of traffic separation schemes would normally have recourse under the citizen-suit provision of the Endangered Species Act, *16 U.S.C. § 1540(g)*, or the Administrative Procedure Act. But if the Coast Guard delegates its responsibility for traffic separation schemes to the International Maritime Organization, and if we accept this delegation as relieving the Coast Guard of any responsibility for them, no such recourse is available. The International Maritime Organization is not subject to the Administrative Procedure Act or the ESA. As we noted in U.S. Telecom Ass'n v. FCC, 360 U.S. App. D.C. 202, 359 F.3d 554 (D.C. Cir. 2004), "when an agency delegates power to outside parties, lines of accountability may blur, undermining an important democratic check on government decision-making." Id. at 565. Appellees point to no evidence showing that Congress intended to undermine the ability of injured parties to challenge unlawful agency action in the promulgation of traffic separation schemes. Just as the President cannot "unilaterally convert[ ] a non-self-executing treaty into a self-executing one," Medellin, 128 S. Ct. at 1368, the Coast Guard cannot convert the SOLAS treaty into domestic law by simply delegating its congressionally given authority under the Ports and Waterways Safety Act to the International Maritime Organization.

Even if the Coast Guard had delegated some or all of its decisionmaking authority under the Ports and Waterways Safety Act to an outside body not subordinate to it, such as the International Maritime Organization, the delegation would be unlawful absent affirmative evidence that Congress intended the delegation. "[W]hile federal agency officials may subdelegate their decision-making authority to subordinates absent evidence of contrary congressional intent, they may not subdelegate to outside entities—private or sovereign—absent affirmative evidence of authority to do so." *U.S. Telecom, 359 F.3d at 566.* Appellees do not argue that affirmative evidence of congressional intent to subdelegate the Coast Guard's decisionmaking authority to an outside party exists.

The simple fact that an agency possesses statutory authority is not a basis for finding final agency action if no evidence exists that the agency used it. However, appellants have presented evidence of final agency action in this case. The Coast Guard has conducted port access route studies, *see, e.g., Port Access Routes: Approaches to Portland, ME and Casco Bay, 70 Fed. Reg. 7067 (Feb. 10, 2005),* published notice of port access route study results, *see Port Access Routes: Approaches to Delaware Bay, 60 Fed. Reg. 49,237 (Sept. 22, 1995),* accepted comments on a proposed route, *see TSS in the Approaches to Delaware Bay, 65 Fed. Reg. 12,944 (Mar. 10, 2000),* and ensured that traffic separation schemes appear in the Code of Federal Regulations, *see, e.g., 33 C.F.R. § 167.170* (traffic separation scheme for the approach to the waters off Delaware Bay). These tasks are not merely ministerial; they require a significant amount of discretion. In promulgating traffic separation schemes, the Coast Guard must

> (a) take into account all relevant factors concerning navigation and vessel safety, protection of the marine environment, and the safety and security of United States ports and waterways, including but not limited to—(1) the scope and degree of the risk or hazard involved; (2) vessel traffic characteristics and trends . . . ; (3) port and waterway configurations and variations in local conditions of geography, climate, and other similar factors; (4) the need for granting exemptions for the installation and use of equipment or devices for use with vessel traffic services for certain classes of small vessels . . . ; (5) the proximity of fishing grounds, oil and gas drilling and production operations, or any other potential or actual conflicting activity; (6) environmental factors; (7) economic impact and effects; (8) existing vessel traffic services; and (9) local practices and customs, including voluntary arrangements and agreements within the maritime community; and (b) at the earliest possible time, consult with and receive and consider the views of representatives of the maritime community, ports and harbor authorities or associations, environmental groups, and other parties who may be affected by the proposed actions.

33 U.S.C. § 1224. The Coast Guard accepts and responds to public comment on all the above issues prior to codifying a traffic separation scheme in the Code of Federal Regulations. *See, e.g., Traffic Separation Scheme in the Approaches to Delaware Bay, 62 Fed. Reg. 25,576, 25,577 (May 9, 1997)* (stating, in the notice of proposed rulemaking, that changes may result from the notice-and-comment period). Accordingly, appellants have demonstrated final agency action, and the district court erred in granting summary judgment to appellees based on its conclusion that it lacked subject matter jurisdiction.

NOTES AND QUESTIONS

1. Although the principal defendant-appellee in this administrative law suit was the NMFS, the plaintiffs-appellants were also seeking regulatory action that falls under the U.S. Coast Guard's authority. The Coast Guard, however, argued that the International Maritime Organization was the lead "agency" controlling shipping lanes and vessel traffic in right whale habitat. Does the Gutierrez ruling put that argument to rest? To reprise a question posed following the U.S. v. Massachusetts case excerpt, why is the Coast Guard so reluctant to use its authorities to engage in environmental rule-making? Do its responsibilities for homeland security and navigational safety create internal conflicts of interest?

2. Final rules to implement the ship strike reduction strategy were published in October 2008. The voluntary mariners' awareness and speed reduction program failed to reduce the risk of ship-whale collisions, which by that time was widely acknowledged to be a leading source of mortality for Atlantic right whales. 73 Fed. Reg. 60173 (Oct. 10, 2008). The most important and most controversial measure was the 10-knot speed restriction on vessels 65 feet in length and greater in certain locations and at certain times of the year along the U.S. Atlantic seaboard. Under a dynamic management measure, where a concentration of three or more right whales is detected at anytime, speeds are reduced to 10 knots in a 15 nautical mile circle around the location for fifteen days. The rules apply to all vessels, except those owned or operated by the federal government, that are subject to the jurisdiction of the United States and to all vessels entering or departing a port or place under the jurisdiction of the United States. Due to lingering uncertainties in the role of speed in vessel strikes and to industry opposition, NMFS agreed to a 5-year expiration date for the rules. In June 2013, NMFS proposed to eliminate the rules' expiration date. 78 Fed. Reg. 34024 (June 6, 2013).

B. OCEAN NOISE AND MILITARY READINESS

WINTER V. NATURAL RESOURCES DEFENSE COUNCIL
Supreme Court of the United States, Nov. 12, 2008
555 U.S. 7

CHIEF JUSTICE ROBERTS delivered the opinion of the Court.

"To be prepared for war is one of the most effectual means of preserving peace." So said George Washington in his first Annual Address to Congress, 218 years ago. One of the most important ways the Navy prepares for war is through integrated training exercises at sea. These exercises include training in the use of modern sonar to detect and track enemy submarines, something the Navy has done for the past 40 years. The plaintiffs, respondents here, complained that the Navy's sonar-training program harmed marine mammals, and that the Navy should have prepared an environmental impact statement before commencing its latest round of training exercises. The Court of Appeals upheld a preliminary injunction imposing restrictions on the Navy's sonar training, even though that court acknowledged that "the record contains no evidence that marine mammals have been harmed" by the Navy's exercises. 518 F.3d 658, 696 (C.A.9 2008).

The Court of Appeals was wrong, and its decision is reversed.

* * *

The procedural history of this case is rather complicated. The Marine Mammal Protection Act of 1972 (MMPA) generally prohibits any individual from "taking" a marine mammal, defined as harassing, hunting, capturing, or killing it. 16 U.S.C. §§ 1362(13), 1372(a). The Secretary of Defense may "exempt any action or category of actions" from the MMPA if such actions are "necessary for national defense." § 1371(f)(1). In January 2007, the Deputy Secretary of Defense—acting for the Secretary—granted the Navy a 2-year exemption from the MMPA for the training exercises at issue in this case. The exemption was conditioned on the Navy adopting several mitigation procedures, including: (1) training lookouts and officers to watch for marine mammals; (2) requiring at least five lookouts with binoculars on each vessel to watch for anomalies on the water surface (including marine mammals); (3) requiring aircraft and sonar operators to report detected marine mammals in the vicinity of the training exercises; (4) requiring reduction of active sonar transmission levels by 6 dB if a marine mammal is detected within 1,000 yards of the bow of the vessel, or by 10 dB if detected within 500 yards; (5) requiring complete shutdown of active sonar transmission if a marine mammal is detected within 200 yards of the vessel; (6) requiring active sonar to be operated at the "lowest practicable level"; and (7) adopting coordination and reporting procedures.

The National Environmental Policy Act of 1969 (NEPA) requires federal agencies "to the fullest extent possible" to prepare an environmental impact statement (EIS) for "every . . . major Federal actio[n] significantly affecting the quality of the human environment." 42 U.S.C. § 4332(2)(C) (2000 ed.). An agency is not required to prepare a full EIS if it determines—based on a shorter environmental assessment (EA)—that the proposed action will not have a significant impact on the environment. 40 CFR §§ 1508.9(a), 1508.13 (2007).

In February 2007, the Navy issued an EA concluding that the 14 SOCAL training exercises scheduled through January 2009 would not have a significant impact on the environment. The EA divided potential injury to marine mammals into two categories: Level A harassment, defined as the potential destruction or loss of biological tissue (*i.e.,* physical injury), and Level B harassment, defined as temporary injury or disruption of behavioral patterns such as migration, feeding, surfacing, and breeding.

The Navy's computer models predicted that the SOCAL training exercises would cause only eight Level A harassments of common dolphins each year, and that even these injuries could be avoided through the Navy's voluntary mitigation measures, given that dolphins travel in large pods easily located by Navy lookouts. The EA also predicted 274 Level B harassments of beaked whales per year, none of which would result in permanent injury. Beaked whales spend little time at the surface, so the precise effect of active sonar on these mammals is unclear. Erring on the side of caution, the Navy classified all projected harassments of beaked whales as Level A . . In light of its conclusion that the SOCAL training exercises would not have a significant impact on the environment, the Navy determined that it was unnecessary to prepare a full EIS. See 40 CFR § 1508.13.

Shortly after the Navy released its EA, the plaintiffs sued the Navy, seeking declaratory and injunctive relief on the grounds that the Navy's SOCAL training exercises violated NEPA, the Endangered Species Act of 1973(ESA), and the Coastal Zone Management Act of 1972 (CZMA). The District Court granted plaintiffs' motion for a preliminary injunction and prohibited the Navy from using MFA sonar during its remaining training exercises. The court held that plaintiffs had "demonstrated a probability of success" on their claims under NEPA and the CZMA. The court also determined that equitable relief was appropriate because, under Ninth Circuit precedent, plaintiffs had established at least a " 'possibility' " of irreparable harm to the environment. Based on scientific studies, declarations from experts, and other evidence in the record, the District Court concluded that there was in fact a "near certainty" of irreparable injury to the environment, and that this injury outweighed any possible harm to the Navy.

The Navy filed an emergency appeal, and the Ninth Circuit stayed the injunction pending appeal. After hearing oral argument, the Court of Appeals agreed with the District Court that preliminary injunctive relief was appropriate. The appellate court concluded, however, that a blanket injunction prohibiting the Navy from using MFA sonar in SOCAL was overbroad, and remanded the case to the District Court "to narrow its injunction so as to provide mitigation conditions under which the Navy may conduct its training exercises." On remand, the District Court entered a new preliminary injunction allowing the Navy to use MFA sonar only as long as it implemented the following mitigation measures (in addition to the measures the Navy had adopted pursuant to its MMPA exemption):

(1) imposing a 12 nautical mile "exclusion zone" from the coastline; (2) using lookouts to conduct additional monitoring for marine mammals; (3) restricting the use of "helicopter-dipping" sonar; (4) limiting the use of MFA sonar in geographic "choke points"; (5) shutting down MFA sonar when a marine mammal is spotted within 2,200 yards of a vessel; and (6) powering down MFA sonar by 6 dB during significant surface ducting conditions, in which sound travels further than it otherwise would due to temperature differences in adjacent layers of water. 530 F.Supp.2d 1110, 1118–1121 (C.D.Cal.2008). The Navy filed a notice of appeal, challenging only the last two restrictions.

The Navy then sought relief from the Executive Branch. The President, pursuant to 16 U.S.C. § 1456(c)(1)(B), granted the Navy an exemption from the CZMA. Section 1456(c)(1)(B) permits such exemptions if the activity in question is "in the paramount interest of the United States." The President determined that continuation of the exercises as limited by the Navy was "essential to national security." He concluded that compliance with the District Court's injunction would "undermine the Navy's ability to conduct realistic training exercises that are necessary to ensure the combat effectiveness of . . . strike groups."

Simultaneously, the Council on Environmental Quality (CEQ) authorized the Navy to implement "alternative arrangements" to NEPA compliance in light of "emergency circumstances." See 40 CFR § 1506.11. The CEQ determined that alternative arrangements were appropriate because the District Court's injunction "create[s] a significant and unreasonable risk that Strike Groups will not be able to train and be certified as fully mission capable." Under the alternative arrangements, the Navy would be permitted to conduct its training exercises under the mitigation procedures adopted in conjunction with the exemption from the MMPA. The CEQ also imposed additional notice, research, and reporting requirements.

In light of these actions, the Navy then moved to vacate the District Court's injunction with respect to the 2,200-yard shutdown zone and the restrictions on training in surface ducting conditions. The District Court refused to do so, 527 F.Supp.2d 1216 (2008), and the Court of Appeals affirmed. The Ninth Circuit held that there was a serious question regarding whether the CEQ's interpretation of the "emergency circumstances" regulation was lawful. Specifically, the court questioned whether there was a true "emergency" in this case, given that the Navy has been on notice of its obligation to comply with NEPA from the moment it first planned the SOCAL training exercises. The Court of Appeals concluded that the preliminary injunction was entirely predictable in light of the parties' litigation history. The court also held that plaintiffs had established a likelihood of success on their claim that the Navy was required to prepare a full EIS for the SOCAL training exercises. The Ninth Circuit agreed with the District Court's holding that the Navy's EA—which resulted in a finding of no significant environmental impact—was "cursory, unsupported by cited evidence, or unconvincing."

The Court of Appeals further determined that plaintiffs had carried their burden of establishing a "possibility" of irreparable injury. Even under the Navy's own figures, the court concluded, the training exercises would cause 564 physical injuries to marine mammals, as well as 170,000 disturbances of marine mammals' behavior. Lastly, the Court of Appeals held that the balance of hardships and consideration of the public interest weighed in favor of the plaintiffs. The court emphasized that the negative impact on the Navy's training exercises was "speculative," since the Navy has never before operated under the procedures required by the District Court. In particular, the court determined that: (1) The 2,200-yard shutdown zone imposed by the District Court was unlikely to affect the Navy's operations, because the Navy often shuts down its MFA sonar systems during the course of training exercises; and (2) the power-down requirement during significant surface ducting conditions was not unreasonable because such conditions are rare, and the Navy has previously certified strike groups that had not trained under such conditions. The Ninth Circuit concluded that the District Court's preliminary injunction struck a proper balance between the competing interests at stake.

We granted certiorari, and now reverse and vacate the injunction.

III

A

* * *

The District Court and the Ninth Circuit concluded that plaintiffs have shown a likelihood of success on the merits of their NEPA claim. The Navy strongly disputes this determination, arguing that plaintiffs' likelihood of success is low because the CEQ reasonably concluded that "emergency circumstances" justified alternative arrangements to NEPA compliance. 40 CFR § 1506.11. Plaintiffs' briefs before this Court barely discuss the ground relied upon by the lower courts—that the plain meaning of "emergency circumstances" does not encompass a court order that was "entirely predictable" in light of the parties' litigation history. 518 F.3d, at 681. Instead, plaintiffs contend that the CEQ's actions violated the separation of powers by readjudicating a factual issue already decided by an Article III court. Moreover, they assert that the CEQ's interpretations of NEPA are not entitled to deference because the CEQ has not been given statutory authority to conduct adjudications.

The District Court and the Ninth Circuit also held that when a plaintiff demonstrates a strong likelihood of prevailing on the merits, a preliminary injunction may be entered based only on a "possibility" of irreparable harm. The lower courts held that plaintiffs had met this standard because the scientific studies, declarations, and other evidence in the record established to "a near certainty" that the Navy's training exercises would cause irreparable harm to the environment.

The Navy challenges these holdings, arguing that plaintiffs must demonstrate a likelihood of irreparable injury—not just a possibility—in order to obtain preliminary relief. On the facts of this case, the Navy contends that plaintiffs' alleged injuries are too speculative to give rise to irreparable injury, given that ever since the Navy's training program began 40 years ago, there has been no documented case of sonar-related injury to marine mammals in SOCAL. And even if MFA sonar does cause a limited number of injuries to individual *marine mammals,* the Navy asserts that plaintiffs have failed to offer evidence of species-level harm that would adversely affect *their* scientific, recreational, and ecological interests. For their part, plaintiffs assert that they would prevail under any formulation of the irreparable injury standard, because the District Court found that they had established a "near certainty" of irreparable harm.

We agree with the Navy that the Ninth Circuit's "possibility" standard is too lenient. Our frequently reiterated standard requires plaintiffs seeking preliminary relief to demonstrate that irreparable injury is *likely* in the absence of an injunction. [citations omitted] Issuing a preliminary injunction based only on a possibility of irreparable harm is inconsistent with our characterization of injunctive relief as an extraordinary remedy that may only be awarded upon a clear showing that the plaintiff is entitled to such relief.

It is not clear that articulating the incorrect standard affected the Ninth Circuit's analysis of irreparable harm. Although the court referred to the "possibility" standard, and cited Circuit precedent along the same lines, it affirmed the District Court's conclusion that plaintiffs had established a " 'near certainty' " of irreparable harm. At the same time, however, the nature of the District Court's conclusion is itself unclear. The District Court originally found irreparable harm from sonar-training exercises generally. But by the time of the District Court's final decision, the Navy challenged only two of six restrictions imposed by the court. The District Court did not reconsider the likelihood of irreparable harm in light of the four restrictions not challenged by the Navy. This failure is significant in light of the District Court's own statement that the 12 nautical mile exclusion zone from the coastline—one of the unchallenged mitigation restrictions—"would bar the use of MFA sonar in a significant portion of important marine mammal habitat."

We also find it pertinent that this is not a case in which the defendant is conducting a new type of activity with completely unknown effects on the environment. When the Government conducts an activity, "NEPA itself does not mandate particular results." Instead, NEPA imposes only procedural requirements to "ensur[e] that the agency, in reaching its decision, will have available, and will carefully consider, detailed information concerning significant environmental impacts." Part of the harm NEPA attempts to prevent in requiring an EIS is that, without one, there may be little if any information about prospective environmental harms and potential mitigating measures. Here, in contrast, the plaintiffs are seeking to enjoin—or substantially restrict—training exercises that have been taking place in SOCAL for the last 40 years. And the latest series of exercises were not approved until after the defendant took a "hard look at environmental consequences," as evidenced by the issuance of a detailed, 293-page EA.

As explained in the next section, even if plaintiffs have shown irreparable injury from the Navy's training exercises, any such injury is outweighed by the public interest and the Navy's interest in effective, realistic training of its sailors. A proper consideration of these factors alone requires denial of the requested injunctive relief. For the same reason, we do not address the lower courts' holding that plaintiffs have also established a likelihood of success on the merits.

B

A preliminary injunction is an extraordinary remedy never awarded as of right. In each case, courts "must balance the competing claims of injury and must consider the effect on each party of the granting or withholding of the requested relief." In this case, the District Court and the Ninth Circuit significantly understated the burden the preliminary injunction would impose on the Navy's ability to conduct realistic training exercises, and the injunction's consequent adverse impact on the public interest in national defense.

This case involves "complex, subtle, and professional decisions as to the composition, training, equipping, and control of a military force," which are "essentially professional military judgments." We "give great deference to the professional judgment of military authorities concerning the relative importance of a particular military interest." As the Court emphasized just last Term, "neither the Members of this Court nor most federal judges begin the day with briefings that may describe new and serious threats to our Nation and its people." [citations omitted] Here, the record contains declarations from some of the Navy's most senior officers, all of whom underscored the threat posed by enemy submarines and the need for extensive sonar training to counter this threat. Admiral Gary Roughead—the Chief of Naval Operations—stated that during training exercises:

"It is important to stress the ship crews in all dimensions of warfare simultaneously. If one of these training elements were impacted—for example, if effective sonar training were not possible—the training value of the other elements would also be degraded. . . . "

Captain Martin May—the Third Fleet's Assistant Chief of Staff for Training and Readiness—emphasized that the use of MFA sonar is "mission-critical." He described the ability to operate MFA sonar as a "highly perishable skill" that must be repeatedly practiced under realistic conditions. During training exercises, MFA sonar operators learn how to avoid sound-reducing "clutter" from ocean floor topography and environmental conditions; they also learn how to avoid interference and how to coordinate their efforts with other sonar operators in the strike group. Several Navy officers emphasized that realistic training cannot be accomplished under the two challenged restrictions imposed by the District Court—the 2,200-yard shutdown zone and the requirement that the Navy power down its sonar systems during significant surface ducting conditions (powering down in presence of surface ducting "unreasonably prevent[s] realistic training"); (shutdown zone would "result in a significant, adverse impact to realistic training"). We accept these officers' assertions that the use of MFA sonar under realistic conditions during training exercises is of the utmost importance to the Navy and the Nation.

These interests must be weighed against the possible harm to the ecological, scientific, and recreational interests that are legitimately before this Court. Plaintiffs have submitted declarations asserting that they take whale watching trips, observe marine mammals underwater, conduct scientific research on marine mammals, and photograph these animals in their natural habitats. Plaintiffs contend that the Navy's use of MFA sonar will injure marine mammals or alter their behavioral patterns, impairing plaintiffs' ability to study and observe the animals.

While we do not question the seriousness of these interests, we conclude that the balance of equities and consideration of the overall public interest in this case tip strongly in favor of the Navy. For the plaintiffs, the most serious possible injury would be harm to an unknown number of the marine mammals that they study and observe. In contrast, forcing the Navy to deploy an inadequately trained antisubmarine force jeopardizes the safety of the fleet. Active sonar is the only reliable technology for detecting and tracking enemy diesel-electric submarines, and the President—the Commander in Chief—has determined that training with active sonar is "essential to national security."

The public interest in conducting training exercises with active sonar under realistic conditions plainly outweighs the interests advanced by the plaintiffs. Of course, military interests do not always trump other considerations, and we have not held that they do. In this case, however, the proper determination of where the public interest lies does not strike us as a close question.

C

The Court of Appeals held that the balance of equities and the public interest favored the plaintiffs, largely based on its view that the preliminary injunction would not in fact impose a significant burden on the Navy's ability to conduct its training exercises and certify its strike groups. The court deemed the Navy's concerns about the preliminary injunction "speculative" because the Navy had not operated under similar procedures before. . . . The Court of Appeals also concluded that the 2,200-yard shutdown zone would not be overly burdensome because the Navy had shut down MFA sonar 27 times during its eight prior training exercises in SOCAL; in several of these cases, the Navy turned off its sonar when marine mammals were spotted well beyond the Navy's self-imposed 200-yard shutdown zone. Vice Admiral Samuel Locklear III—the Commander of the Navy's Third Fleet—stated that any shutdowns beyond the 200-yard zone were voluntary avoidance measures that likely took place at tactically insignificant times; the Ninth Circuit discounted this explanation as not supported by the record. In reaching this conclusion, the Court of Appeals ignored key portions of Vice Admiral Locklear's declaration, in which he stated unequivocally that commanding officers "would not shut down sonar until legally required to do so if in contact with a submarine." Similarly, if a commanding officer is in contact with a target submarine, "the CO will be expected to continue to use active sonar unless another ship or helicopter can gain contact or if regulatory reasons dictate otherwise." The record supports the Navy's contention that its shutdowns of MFA sonar during prior training exercises only occurred during tactically insignificant times; those voluntary shutdowns do not justify the District Court's imposition of a mandatory 2,200-yard shutdown zone.

* * *

The Court of Appeals concluded its opinion by stating that "the Navy may return to the district court to request relief on an emergency basis" if the preliminary injunction "actually result[s] in an inability to train and certify sufficient naval forces to provide for the national defense." 518 F.3d, at 703. This is cold comfort to the Navy. The Navy contends that the injunction will hinder efforts to train sonar operators under realistic conditions, ultimately leaving strike groups more vulnerable to enemy submarines. Unlike the Ninth Circuit, we do not think the Navy is required to wait until the injunction "actually result[s] in an inability to train . . . sufficient naval forces to provide for the national defense" before seeking its dissolution. By then it may be too late.

IV

As noted above, we do not address the underlying merits of plaintiffs' claims. While we have authority to proceed to such a decision at this point, doing so is not necessary here. In addition, reaching the merits is complicated by the fact that the lower courts addressed only one of several issues raised, and plaintiffs have largely chosen not to defend the decision below on that ground.[5]

* * *

President Theodore Roosevelt explained that "the only way in which a navy can ever be made efficient is by practice at sea, under all the conditions which would have to be met if war existed." President's Annual Message, 42 Cong. Rec. 67, 81 (1907). We do not discount the importance of plaintiffs' ecological, scientific, and recreational interests in marine mammals. Those interests, however, are plainly outweighed by the Navy's need to conduct realistic training exercises to ensure that it is able to neutralize the threat posed by enemy submarines. The District Court abused its discretion by imposing a 2,200-yard shutdown zone and by requiring the Navy to power down its MFA sonar during significant surface ducting conditions. The judgment of the Court of Appeals is reversed, and the preliminary injunction is vacated to the extent it has been challenged by the Navy.

It is so ordered.

* * *

JUSTICE GINSBURG, with whom JUSTICE SOUTER joins, dissenting.

The central question in this action under the National Environmental Policy Act of 1969 (NEPA) was whether the Navy must prepare an environmental impact statement (EIS). The Navy does not challenge its obligation to do so, and it represents that the EIS will be complete in January 2009—one month after the instant exercises conclude. If the Navy had completed the EIS before taking action, as NEPA instructs, the parties and the public could have benefited from the environmental analysis—and the Navy's training could have proceeded without interruption. Instead, the Navy acted first, and thus thwarted the very purpose an EIS is intended to serve. To justify its course, the Navy sought dispensation not from Congress, but from an executive council that lacks authority to countermand or revise NEPA's requirements. I would hold that, in imposing manageable measures to mitigate harm until completion of the EIS, the District Court conscientiously balanced the equities and did not abuse its discretion.

---

[5] The bulk of Justice GINSBURG's dissent is devoted to the merits. For the reasons stated, we find the injunctive relief granted in this case an abuse of discretion, even if plaintiffs are correct on the underlying merits. As to the injunction, the dissent barely mentions the Navy's interests. We find that those interests, and the documented risks to national security, clearly outweigh the harm on the other side of the balance.

* * *

II

NEPA "promotes its sweeping commitment" to environmental integrity "by focusing Government and public attention on the environmental effects of proposed agency action." "By so focusing agency attention, NEPA ensures that the agency will not act on incomplete information, only to regret its decision after it is too late to correct." The EIS is NEPA's core requirement. This Court has characterized the requirement as "action-forcing." Environmental concerns must be "integrated into the very process of agency decisionmaking" and "interwoven into the fabric of agency planning." In addition to discussing potential consequences, an EIS must describe potential mitigation measures and alternatives to the proposed course of action. The EIS requirement "ensures that important effects will not be overlooked or underestimated only to be discovered after resources have been committed or the die otherwise cast."

"Publication of an EIS . . . also serves a larger informational role." It demonstrates that an agency has indeed considered environmental concerns, and "perhaps more significantly, provides a springboard for public comment." At the same time, it affords other affected governmental bodies "notice of the expected consequences and the opportunity to plan and implement corrective measures in a timely manner."

* * *

The Navy's publication of its EIS in this case, scheduled to occur *after* the 14 exercises are completed, defeats NEPA's informational and participatory purposes. The Navy's inverted timing, it bears emphasis, is the very reason why the District Court had to confront the question of mitigation measures at all. Had the Navy prepared a legally sufficient EIS before beginning the SOCAL exercises, NEPA would have functioned as its drafters intended: The EIS process and associated public input might have convinced the Navy voluntarily to adopt mitigation measures, but NEPA itself would not have impeded the Navy's exercises.

The Navy had other options. Most importantly, it could have requested assistance from Congress. . . . Rather than resorting to Congress, the Navy "sought relief from the Executive Branch." On January 10, 2008, the Navy asked CEQ, adviser to the President, to approve alternative arrangements for NEPA compliance pursuant to 40 CFR § 1506.11 (1987). The next day, the Navy submitted supplementary material to CEQ, including the Navy's EA and after-action reports, the District Court's orders, and two analyses by the National Marine Fisheries Service (NMFS). Neither the Navy nor CEQ notified NRDC, and CEQ did not request or consider any of the materials underlying the District Court orders it addressed.

Four days later, on January 15, the Chairman of CEQ issued a letter to the Secretary of the Navy. Repeating the Navy's submissions with little independent analysis, the letter stated that the District Court's orders posed risks to the Navy's training exercises. ("You have explained that the training restrictions set forth in the . . . injunctive orders prevent the Navy from providing Strike Groups with adequate proficiency training and create a substantial risk of precluding certification of the Strike Groups as combat ready.").

The letter continued:

"Discussions between our staffs, your letter and supporting documents, and the classified declaration and briefings I have received, have clearly determined that the Navy cannot ensure the necessary training to certify strike groups for deployment under the terms of the injunctive orders. Based on the record supporting your request . . . CEQ has concluded that the Navy must be able to conduct the [exercises] . . . in a timeframe that does not provide sufficient time to complete an EIS. Therefore, emergency circumstances are present for the nine exercises and alternative arrangements for compliance with NEPA under CEQ regulation 40 C.F.R. § 1506.11 are warranted."

The alternative arrangements CEQ set forth do not vindicate NEPA's objectives. The arrangements provide for "public participation measures," which require the Navy to provide notices of the alternative arrangements. The notices must "seek input on the process for reviewing post-exercise assessments" and "include an offer to meet jointly with Navy representatives . . . and CEQ to discuss the alternative arrangements." The alternative arrangements also describe the Navy's existing research and mitigation efforts.

CEQ's hasty decision on a one-sided record is no substitute for the District Court's considered judgment based on a two-sided record. More fundamentally, even an exemplary CEQ review could not have effected the short circuit the Navy sought. CEQ lacks authority to absolve an agency of its statutory duty to prepare an EIS. NEPA established CEQ to assist and advise the President on environmental policy, 42 U.S.C. § 4342, and a 1977 Executive Order charged CEQ with issuing regulations to federal agencies for implementation of NEPA's procedural provisions, Exec. Order No. 11991, 3 CFR 123 (1977 Comp.). This Court has recognized that CEQ's regulations are entitled to "substantial deference," Robertson, 490 U.S., at 355, 109 S.Ct. 1835, and 40 CFR § 1506.11 indicates that CEQ may play an important consultative role in emergency circumstances, but we have never suggested that CEQ could eliminate the statute's command. If the Navy sought to avoid its NEPA obligations, its remedy lay in the Legislative Branch. The Navy's alternative course—rapid, self-serving resort to an office in the White House—is surely not what Congress had in mind when it instructed agencies to comply with NEPA "to the fullest extent possible." 42 U.S.C. § 4332.

NOTES AND QUESTIONS

1. Why was Chief Justice Roberts eager not to engage with the merits of the plaintiffs' NEPA claim?

2. Under the standards for injunctive relief articulate by the Court, are federal courts now obligated to give deference to the judgment of the military that readiness training takes priority over legally-mandated protections of marine wildlife and ecosystems under the ESA and the MMPA?

3. In the first paragraph of the Court's opinion, does Chief Justice Roberts fairly characterize the lower courts' decision as having acknowledged that "the record contains no evidence that marine mammals have been harmed" by the Navy's exercises? See generally, William H. Rodgers, Jr., Betty B. Fletcher: NEPA's Angel and Chief Editor of the Hard Look, 40 Envtl. L. Rep. News & Anal. 10268 (2010).

4. In Okinawa Dugong v. Gates, 543 F.Supp.2d 1082 (N.D. Cal. 2008), the court held that because the dugong is cultural property of the Okinawan people, the Defense Department had a duty to consult under the National Historic Preservation Act before building a new military base off the coast of Okinawa in grass flats inhabited by the dugong. Does this requirement interfere with the military's readiness for war? Does NEPA apply to decisions concerning the construction or relocation of offshore military bases? Does the Dugong decision constitute an emergency allowing the Department to exempt itself from NEPA?

3. INTENTIONAL POLLUTION

A. OCEAN DUMPING FROM VESSELS

National obligations under the 1982 Law of the Sea Convention to protect the marine environment include enforcement of global, regional, and national rules to control vessels transporting waste materials from land for disposal in the ocean. LOSC, article 210. According to J. Kindt, Ocean Dumping, 13 Denver J. Int'l & Pol'y 335, 336–337 (1984):

> Of the pollutants entering the world's oceans, approximately 10 percent are due to direct ocean dumping. * * * Of the 10 percent of ocean dumped materials, dredged spoils constitute 80 percent of this total. Approximately 1 to 10 percent of the dredged sediment taken from waterways and harbors has been contaminated to potentially unacceptable levels because of industrial, urban, and agricultural activities. Even non-toxic dredged spoils can physically damage marine organisms in ways ranging from inhibiting the penetration of light (due

to suspended sediments) to smothering organisms on the ocean floor when large quantities are dumped.

Sludge from onshore sewage treatment plants dumped in the ocean also may contain heavy metals and organic chemicals. Under Article 216, coastal nations can control, even prohibit, dumping within their territorial seas and exclusive economic zones seaward 200 nautical miles and on their continental shelves where they extend further.

In 1972, a group of nations was sufficiently concerned about ocean pollution problems that they negotiated the London Convention on the Prevention of Marine Pollution by Dumping of Wastes and Other Matter (London Dumping Convention). 11 I.L.M. 1294. The treaty came into force in 1975 and has been ratified by the United States. The Convention only applies to materials that are transported for the purpose of ocean disposal and does not cover the disposal of wastes derived from normal vessel operations. Restrictions on vessel disposal of plastics, garbage, and noxious liquids are provided by the MARPOL convention, which is briefly discussed below at p. 943.

The nations party to the convention originally agreed to prohibit the dumping of materials listed in Annex I of the Convention, unless they are "rapidly rendered harmless by physical, chemical, or biological processes in the sea." * * * (Annex I, No. 8, 26 U.S.T. At 2465). Dumping of material specifically listed in Annex II and other material was allowed only on the issuance of a prior permit. The Convention set forth a number of factors in Annex III to be considered in granting permits, including the characteristics of the waste and site, method of disposal, effect on marine organisms, other uses of the sea, and the availability of alternative methods of dumping. However, the Convention's 1996 Protocol, 36 I.L.M. 1, greatly restricts permissible dumping by prohibiting the ocean dumping of all wastes except those listed in revised Annex I. Revised Annex I only allows the dumping of dredged material, sewage sludge, fish wastes, inert geological materials, natural organic materials, abandoned vessels and platforms, and other bulky items made of iron, steel, concrete, and similar unharmful materials. Revised Annexes 2 and 3 to the 1996 Protocol deal with waste assessment and arbitral procedures. The 1996 Protocol entered into force in 2006. Nations have also adopted a number of multilateral treaties to control dumping in specific ocean regions such as the Mediterranean and Black Seas.

Although the oceans off the United States coast have been used as a disposal site for many years, generally only relatively small amounts of material were dumped, including the first known ocean disposal of radioactive waste done by the United States 50 miles off California in 1946. The annual amount of material (industrial wastes, sewage sludge, solid wastes, and construction and demolition debris) dumped in the early

1950s was approximately 1.7 million tons. By the mid-1960s, this figure rose to 7.4 million tons per year, a 335 percent increase. These figures do not include the amount of dredge spoil disposed; this is generally estimated to be four times, by weight, that of all other materials. Congressional Research Service, Library of Congress, Ocean Dumping Regulations: An Appraisal Of Implementation I (1976). Sources of waste material were identified as dredged material (680 million metric tons per year nationally, with 25 percent of it dumped into the ocean); sewage sludge (5.9 million wet metric tons were ocean dumped in 1979, and 2.8 million wet metric tons were discharged through the Los Angeles and Boston outfalls); industrial waste (2.6 million tons were ocean dumped in 1979); solid waste (570 million tons); nonpoint sources (vast amounts of wastes from urban runoff, mining wastes, and agriculture and silviculture runoff); and potential new sources. 12 Coastal Zone Management Newsletter No. 6, Feb. 11, 1981, at 2–3. Several probable causes of this drastic increase were identifiable:

1. There was a widely held perception, which to some degree continues today, that the ocean can serve as a vast ultimate sink for wastes. This view gave rise to the assumption that the ocean was a "safe" disposal site able to dilute and absorb otherwise harmful material.

2. Between 1930 and 1970 the population in coastal areas approximately doubled. This growth of population and associated land development led to the generation of tremendous amounts of solid waste. At the same time, this growth reduced the amount of land available for landfill disposal methods.

3. Since the late 1960s there have been growing numbers and types of controls upon air and water discharge. This has led to:

   a. A transfer of waste disposal processes to coastal and ocean dumping, transferring pollution from one medium to another rather than eliminating it; and

   b. Pollution controls have themselves expanded the amount of waste needing disposal. Sewage treatment has generated more sewage sludge and stack scrubbers collect large amounts of fly ash. Both of these are bulky wastes that require some type of disposal.

4. Until 1972 there was no federal regulation of ocean dumping. In many instances this encouraged use of ocean dumping over other methods of waste disposal.

   In response to this dramatic increase in ocean dumping, the President's Council on Environmental Quality took a deep look at the problem presented by unregulated ocean dumping. It recommended a "comprehensive national policy on ocean dumping of wastes to ban *unregulated* dumping of all materials and strictly limit ocean disposal of any materials harmful to the marine environment." Council on Environmental Quality, Ocean Dumping: A National Policy at *v* (1970) (emphasis added).

In response to the report's recommendations and to implement the London Convention, Congress passed the Marine Protection, Research and Sanctuaries Act (MPRSA) of 1972, 33 U.S.C. § 1401 et seq. Titles I and II pertain to ocean dumping and are commonly referred to as the Ocean Dumping Act; Title III concerns marine sanctuaries and is discussed later.

The Ocean Dumping Act adopts a national policy of regulating the dumping of all materials into ocean waters. "Material" is broadly defined in the Ocean Dumping Act to encompass just about any variety of waste, except for vessel sewage wastes regulated under the CWA. 33 U.S.C. § 1402(c). Unless within one of the limited exceptions, material is "dumped" if it is disposed of from a vessel or aircraft. 33 U.S.C. § 1402(f).

Title I of the MPRSA, the heart of the dumping regulatory scheme, prohibits, unless authorized by permit, (1) transportation from the United States of materials for the purpose of dumping them into ocean waters, and (2) dumping of materials transported from outside the United States within twelve nautical miles of the territorial sea baseline. 33 U.S.C. § 1411. The Corps of Engineers is authorized to issue permits with respect to dredged wastes only, see, e.g., Clean Ocean Action v. York, 57 F.3d 328 (3rd Cir. 1995), and the Environmental Protection Agency (EPA) has permit authority for all other wastes. 33 U.S.C. §§ 1412, 1412a, 1413. In addition, the EPA is authorized to designate recommended dumping sites and to limit or prohibit dumping of some items or dumping at specific sites if necessary to protect "critical areas." 33 U.S.C. § 1412(c); see National Wildlife Federation v. Costle, 629 F.2d 118 (d.C. Cir. 1980) (the EPA's designation of "interim" sites based on historical usage upheld). The act specifically bans the dumping of radiological, chemical, or biological warfare agents and high-level radioactive wastes. 33 U.S.C. § 1412(a).

The Ocean Dumping Act directs the EPA to promulgate criteria to be used both by the EPA and by the Corps in evaluating whether particular dumping proposals "will unreasonably degrade or endanger human health, welfare, or amenities, or the marine environment, ecological systems, or economic potentialities." 33 U.S.C. § 1412(a); see Clean Ocean Action v. York, 57 F.3d 328 (3rd Cir. 1995). See also 33 U.S.C. § 1412(a) (emergency permits). In developing these criteria, the Administrator must consider nine statutory factors, including the need for dumping, its effects, alternatives to the dumping, and alternative uses of the ocean areas, and must apply standards created by the London Convention "to the extent that he may do so without relaxing the [Act's] requirements." 33

U.S.C. § 1412. Pursuant to this directive, the EPA has promulgated regulations for site selection and permit application evaluation. 40 C.F.R. §§ 227–28; see City of New York v. U.S.A. EPA, 543 F. Supp. 1084 (S.D.N.Y. 1981) (lengthy discussion of the criteria structure).

The Corps, in evaluating permit applications for dumping "dredged material," must consider only those EPA-promulgated criteria that relate to the effects of the dumping. 33 U.S.C. § 1413(b). Adherence by the Corps to the EPA's criteria is assured by the EPA's veto power over the issuance of such permits. 33 U.S.C. § 1413(c). In the event that the EPA determines the granting of a permit by the Corps would not conform to the EPA's criteria, the Corps may request a waiver if the Corps finds "there is no economically feasible method or site available." 33 U.S.C. § 1413(d). A waiver must be granted unless the EPA concludes that the dumping will "result in an unacceptably adverse impact on municipal water supplies, shellfish beds, wildlife, fisheries (including spawning and breeding areas), or recreational activities." Id.; See Environmental Law Institute, Law of Environmental Protection 12–180—12–195. For comprehensive analyses of ocean dumping, see A. Courtney, S. Wildman & E. Merolli, Pollution, in D. Baur, T. Eichenberg, & M. Sutton, Ocean and Coastal Law and Policy 243–274 (2007); D. Squires, The Ocean Dumping Quandary (1983).

The Ocean Dumping Ban Act of 1988, Pub. L. No. 100–688, 102 Stat. 4139 (1988), provided a partial ban on ocean dumping. See M. Taylor, Ocean Dumping: A Light at the End of the Tunnel, 3 Hofstra Prop. L.J. 235 (1990). The Act prohibited the dumping of sewage sludge and industrial waste effective January 1, 1992. Regarding continued dredged material dumping, on October 31, 1992, President Bush signed H.R. 6167, the Water Resources Development Act of 1992, Pub. L. 102–580. Title V of that Act, entitled the "National Contamination Sediment Assessment and Management Act," amended the Ocean Dumping Act in a number of ways. First, Section 502 established a National Contaminated Sediment Task Force, composed of a variety of federal, state, and private interests, to review, inter alia, the extent and seriousness of aquatic sediment contamination and to report findings and recommendations to Congress. Next, the Act required the EPA, in consultation with NOAA and the Corps of Engineers, to conduct a comprehensive survey and monitoring program to assess and address aquatic sediment quality in the United States. Id. § 503. The Act also required the Corps to provide the EPA forty-five days to concur or object to Corps issuance of dredged material dumping permits. Id. § 504 (amending 33 U.S.C. § 1413(c)).

Significantly, section 505 preserved states' rights "to adopt or enforce any requirements respecting dumping of materials" into state ocean waters, except with regard to federal projects where the EPA makes specified findings (amending 33 U.S.C. § 1416(d)). The Act also required the EPA to designate sites and times for sediment disposal so as to mitigate environmental impacts while also giving the EPA authority to prohibit dumping when necessary (amending 33 U.S.C. § 1412(c)). Further, the EPA must develop site management plans to ensure environmental safety for existing and proposed disposal sites and after January 1, 1995, it may not officially designate any disposal site without completing such plans. Id. Additionally, section 507 of the act limits dumping permits to a period of seven years (amending 33 U.S.C. § 1414(a)). Finally, the act amended the criminal penalty provisions of 33 U.S.C. § 1415(b) to allow for the seizure and forfeiture of property or proceeds involved in or resulting from any knowing violation of the Act.

With regard to offshore disposal of dredged materials, the Corps of Engineers Ocean Dumping Act (ODA) permit authority geographically overlaps its Clean Water Act (CWA) section 404 permit authority to protect aquatic habitat in the zone extending three nautical miles seaward from the territorial sea baseline. As D. Christie and R. Hildreth, Coastal and Ocean Management Law in a Nutshell 323–324 (3d ed. 2007) explains:

> The ODA authorizes the Corps, with the concurrence of the EPA, to issue permits for the *dumping of dredged material*. 33 U.S.C. § 1413. Under Section 404 of the CWA, the Corps also has authority to permit the *discharge of dredged materials* into navigable waters. Id. § 1344(a). Because ODA jurisdiction includes waters seaward of the territorial sea baseline and because "navigable waters" under the CWA includes waters three nautical miles seaward of that baseline, the Corps' programs for disposal of dredged material overlap in the area three miles offshore. The Corps has published regulations addressing the issue of the overlapping jurisdiction of the CWA and the ODA in the territorial sea. All disposal in the ocean or territorial sea of material that has been excavated or dredged from navigable waters will be evaluated under the ODA. Only materials determined to be deposited primarily for the purpose of fill will be evaluated under section 404 of the CWA. See 33 C.F.R. § 336.0; see also 53 Fed. Reg. 14,902, 14,905 (1988).

> Whether a permit for dredged spoil disposal is evaluated under the CWA or the ODA can be significant. First, although the criteria for evaluation are virtually the same, the ODA requires that the Corps "make an independent determination as to the need for the dumping[,] * * * other possible methods of disposal[,] and * * * appropriate locations for the dumping." 33 U.S.C. § 1413(b). The CWA does not have a comparable requirement.

For comprehensive coverage of ocean dumping regulations, including the relationship between the Ocean Dumping Act and the London Dumping Convention, see A. Bakalian, Regulation and Control of United States

Ocean Dumping: A Decade of Progress, An Appraisal for the Future, 8 Harv. Envtl. L. Rev. 193 (1984); S. Moore, Troubles in the High Seas: A New Era in the Regulation of U.S. Ocean Dumping, 22 Envtl. L. 913 (1992).

NOTES AND QUESTIONS

1. An important question is whether the long-range goal of the Ocean Dumping Act is to phase out all ocean dumping of wastes or to continue ocean dumping as a feasible disposal alternative under adequate regulation and control at least for dredged materials.

2. Can ocean dumping of dredged materials affect the water quality or coastal zone of a state? If so, must the Corps' issuance of an ocean dumping permit or Corps' dumping of its own dredged materials be certified as complying with the state's water quality standards under Clean Water Act Section 401 or consistent with the state's federally approved coastal zone management program? See 33 U.S.C. § 1416(d).

3. Ocean incineration is regulated under the Ocean Dumping Act. The EPA denied Chemical Waste Management, Inc. (CWM) a permit to conduct a research burn at sea. 51 Fed. Reg. 20,344 (June 4, 1986). CWM proposed to burn 708,958 gallons of fuel oil containing 10–30% PCBs over a 19 day period at a site 104 miles east of the Delaware River. The EPA decided to deny the permit pending promulgation of final ocean incineration regulations which address issues such as the application of other federal statutes, including the Coastal Zone Management Act (CZMA), performance and operational standards, and liability and financial responsibilities. In March 1986, CWM filed suit in the U.S. District Court for the District of Columbia challenging various conditions imposed by New Jersey in its CZMA consistency determination regarding the proposed burn. CWM also charged that the Commerce Department violated the CZMA by permitting Maryland, in whose waters none of the proposed activities would take place, to review CWM's permit application for consistency with the Maryland state coastal zone management program. The EPA's permit denial was upheld in Waste Management, Inc. v. United States Environmental Protection Agency, 669 F. Supp. 536 (D.D.C. 1987). The EPA's interpretation of ocean incineration as dumping subject to regulation under the Ocean Dumping Act was upheld in Seaburn Inc. v. United States E.P.A, 712 F. Supp. 218 (D.D.C. 1989).

The 1993 amendments to the London Convention banned the ocean incineration and dumping of industrial wastes and the dumping of low-level radioactive wastes. These bans are continued in the Convention's 1996 Protocol described above.

4. The London Convention and U.S. Ocean Dumping Act also are relevant to proposals to sequester carbon dioxide including "fertilizing" the ocean with iron to increase its absorption of carbon dioxide. See P. Boyd, et al., A Mesocale Phytoplankton Bloom in the Polar Southern Ocean Stimulated by

Iron Fertilization, Nature 695–702 (Oct. 12, 2000); D. Freestone & E. Ray-fuse, Ocean Iron Fertilization and International Law, 364 Marine Ecology Progress Series 227 (2008); D. Hayes & J. Beauvais, Carbon Sequestration, in M. Gerrard, ed., Global Climate Changes and U.S. Law 714–715, 720–724 (2007); R. Purdy, The Legal Implications of Carbon Capture and Storage Under the Sea, VII Sustainable Development Law & Policy 22 (Fall 2006); R. Rayfuse, M. Lawrence, & K. Gjerde, Ocean Fertilization and Climate Change: The Need to Regulate Emerging High Seas Use, 23 Intl. J. of Marine & Coastal L. 297 (2008); P. Verlaan, Experimental Activities That Intentionally Perturb the Marine Environment: Implications for the Marine Environmental Protection and Marine Scientific Research Provisions of the 1982 United Nations Convention on the Law of the Sea, 31 Marine Policy 210 (2007); A. Weeks, Subsea Carbon Dioxide Sequestration as a Climate Mitigation Option for the Eastern United States: A Preliminary Assessment of Technology and Law, 12 Ocean & Coastal L.J. 245 (2007).

Underground injection of CO_2 has been used since the early 1970s to enhance recovery of oil and gas. For oil and gas fields leased from the federal government on the U.S. Outer Continental Shelf (OCS), section 354(a)(2)(B) of the 2005 Energy Policy Act, P.L. 109–58 (July 27, 2005), authorizes reductions in the royalties charged oil companies who increase their production by injecting CO_2 into their OCS wells. See 71 Fed. Reg. 11577 (March 8, 2006).

NOTE ON MARPOL ANNEX V

The United States Senate, in December 1987, unanimously approved MARPOL Annex V (regulations for the Prevention of Pollution by Garbage from Ships), which entered into force 12 months later. Annex V governs the disposal of garbage generated on board vessels into the sea. It prohibits the disposal of all plastics, including but not limited to synthetic ropes, synthetic fishing nets, and plastic garbage bags (regulation 3(1)(a)). It further regulates the disposal of garbage into the sea by limiting garbage disposal to 25 nautical miles for floatable dunnage, lining, and packing materials, 12 nautical miles for unground food wastes and other garbage (reg. 3 (1)(b)), and 3 nautical miles for ground non-plastic or food waste.

There are three exceptions to the discharge provisions: (1) disposal necessary for the purpose of securing the safety of the ship or saving life at sea; (2) escape resulting from damage to a ship or its equipment; and (3) accidental loss of synthetic fishing nets or synthetic material incidental to the repair of such nets (reg. 6).

The prohibitions apply to all ships and to fixed or floating platforms engaged in mineral exploration, exploitation, and associated offshore processing. Annex V also specifies that governments party to the convention "undertake to ensure the provision" for facilities at ports and terminals for the reception of garbage, "without causing undue delay to ships and according to the needs of the ships using them" (reg. 7 (1)). Special areas can be identified under Annex V which have more stringent regulations.

To implement MARPOL Annex V, the Marine Plastic Pollution Research and Control Act of 1987 (33 U.S.C. §§ 1901–1912) took effect on December 31, 1988. The Coast Guard has issued extensive regulations implementing Annex V and the act. The regulations apply to marine craft of any size and offshore platforms. Disposal of plastic wastes at sea is prohibited and other waste discharges are restricted. The National Oceanic and Atmospheric Administration has published a guidebook for ports in meeting their responsibilities under Annex V. See generally T. Brillat & M. Liffmann, The Implications of MARPOL Annex V on the Management of Ports and Coastal Communities, 19 Coastal Management 371 (1991); National Research Council, Clean Ships, Clean Ports, Clean Oceans: Controlling Garbage and Plastic Wastes at Sea (1995).

Aside from vessels, humans contribute large amounts of materials that can be categorized as persistent marine debris to ocean waters and beaches—oil tarballs, glass, metal—but over the last two decades, it has become clear that nondegradable plastics contribute the most significant threat to the marine environment. Much of this plastic debris, such as monofilament line, driftnets and other fishing nets, ropes, plastic sheeting, containers, and food packaging, is generated by vessels and offshore facilities. People incur direct economic and costs from marine debris on beaches and from debris that damages vessels. Perhaps more tragic, however, is the impact on marine wildlife. Inestimable numbers of fish, marine mammals, birds, and sea turtles die annually from entanglement with or ingestion of plastic debris. Under the London Convention plastics cannot be dumped at sea. The Convention only applies, however, to materials that are transported for the purpose of disposal in the ocean.

The multiple sources of debris have created the notorious Pacific Ocean "Garbage Patch" to which the 2011 Japan tsunami is expected to contribute significant debris. See H. Jacobson, The Pacific's Plastic Problem, Western Environmental Law Update 9 (Winter 2010); U. Karzarian, Islands of Garbage Continue to Grow in Pacific, Sustainable Development Law & Policy 63 (2009); Save the Plastic Bag Coalition v. Manhattan Beach (Cal. Sup. Ct. July 14, 2011); U.S. Marine Debris Research, Prevention, and Reduction Act, S. 362, 109th Congress (2006). For an analysis of U.S. and international legal standards for preventing plastic pollution, with a particular emphasis on drifting "fish aggregating devices" used to catch schools of tuna and composed of derelict fishing gear, see National Research Council, Tackling Marine Debris in the 21st Century (2009).

4. MARINE RESERVES AND SPATIAL PLANNING

A. MARINE AREA–BASED MANAGEMENT

Area-based management is commonly practiced on units of land such as parks, national forests, wilderness areas, and municipal zones, but only 1% of the global marine environment has been separated from surrounding waters into discrete management areas. Generally called "marine protected areas" or "marine sanctuaries," these spatial oceanic set-asides vary greatly in management and enforcement regimes, and even such basic parameters as definition, category (purpose), and scope. There is a national and international trend to expand the use of marine protected areas in ocean resources conservation. If established and implemented correctly, marine protected areas may prove to be powerful tools for achieving many important goals. Among those goals are pollution abatement, conservation of important habitats, fisheries and marine wildlife, preservation of biodiversity, protection of cultural and historic resources such as Native American artifacts and shipwrecks, and education of researchers and the public.

The many different categories of marine protected areas may correspond with the purposes set forth at the time of establishment or may relate to the entity in charge of managing the area. Often, the "purpose" categories are actually subcategories within a larger management infrastructure. For example, national marine sanctuaries, discussed below, are one type of marine protected area in the waters of the United States already existing under federal law. Zones within the borders of a national marine sanctuary may be created and regulated in different fashions; particular activities including fishing, biodiversity conservation, recreation, and oil and gas exploration may be assigned to different areas, and each area may then have its own rules and regulations attached. Some national parks are also considered marine protected areas; they may actually be located within the boundaries of a national marine sanctuary (e.g. Channel Islands National Park is within Channel Islands National Marine Sanctuary). State governments may establish marine protected areas within the 3-mile limit of the state ocean waters, and may work with the federal government to manage larger marine protected areas that span both federal and state waters. For state or territorial MPAs containing coral reefs, assistance in the development of management strategies may be available under the Coral Reef Conservation Act of 2000; Title II, Pub.L. 106–562. As of May 2012, about 8% of U.S. coastal and ocean waters at 1700 different sites were designated as MPAs.

A marine reserve is a more restrictive type of marine protected area, which can be as large as an entire marine protected area or may only be a zone within the larger area. Within a marine reserve, some or all of the biological resources are protected from removal or disturbance, virtually prohibiting all human activities. Marine reserves implemented for the purpose of protecting all living marine resources through various prohibitions on human activities are often called ecological reserves; for example, the Dry Tortugas and Western Sambos Ecological Reserves within the Florida Keys National Marine Sanctuary. Marine reserves implemented for the purpose of conserving fisheries, also called "no take" or fishery reserves, are often very controversial when proposed because stakeholders such as commercial fishermen and others who may follow more traditional notions of freedom of the seas view these no-take zones as "fencing off the ocean," infringements on rights to fish. See Donna Christie, Marine Reserves, the Public Trust Doctrine, and Intergenerational Equity, 19 J. Land Use & Envt'l. L. 427 (2004).

Some marine scientists consider the creation of marine reserves as necessary to ensure the survival of exploited marine species. Traditional fisheries quotas based on stock assessments have historically been set too high due to difficulties in population estimation and political pressure, especially considering the fact that there are significant problems with bycatch of non-target stocks closely associated with the target species. In theory, once a marine reserve is functioning well, a spillover effect occurs where catch levels outside the reserve increase in both quantity and quality. In short, marine reserves may create more and bigger fish because reproducing individuals within the reserve are left alone to replenish the population and young within reserves are able to grow to a larger size before being caught. This eventually translates into maintaining the range of sizes available in the genetic pool instead of causing a population to become smaller over time by constantly over-harvesting only the larger sized individuals. In the short term, marine reserves do impact some stakeholders such as commercial fishermen, accustomed to fishing everywhere, disproportionately. Programs such as license or gear buybacks and other economic incentives are in use in some regions to alleviate these socioeconomic effects. Several studies have suggested that despite their resistance to closing off fishing grounds, involving commercial and recreational fishermen in the marine reserve design and designation process is essential. Stakeholder cooperation is not only necessary for the eventual success of marine reserves because agency budgets for enforcement are usually limited, but also because people who have been fishing a particular area for several years have valuable knowledge that should not go unused when designing and implementing a marine reserve.

Successfully-run marine protected areas exist worldwide, including the marine protected areas of New Zealand and the Great Barrier Reef of Australia. Studying the relative successes and failures of other countries in establishing marine protected areas is important to designing and refining the marine protected areas in the waters of the United States, although U.S. ocean law and politics present unique challenges. See R. Hildreth, Place-Based Ocean Management: Emerging U.S. Law and Practice, 51 Ocean & Coastal Management 659 (2008). The lessons learned can then be incorporated into the U.S. Coastal and Marine Spatial Planning (CMSP) effort pursuant to President Obama's July 2010 Executive Order 13547 on Stewardship of the Ocean, Our Coasts, and the Great Lakes (75 Fed. Reg. 43023) (July 19, 2010). See also President Clinton's Executive

Order on Marine Protected Areas, E.O. No. 13158, 65 Fed. Reg. 34909 (May 26, 2000).

B. NATIONAL MARINE SANCTUARIES AND MARINE MONUMENTS

The National Marine Sanctuaries Program was created in 1972 as part of the Marine Protection, Research, and Sanctuaries Act. 16 U.S.C. § 1431 et seq. The purpose of the program is to identify marine areas of special national or international significance due to their resource or human-use values and to provide authority for comprehensive conservation and management of such areas where existing regulatory authority is inadequate to assure coordinated conservation and management. National or international significance is determined by assessment of:

> the area's natural resource and ecological qualities, including its contribution to biological productivity, maintenance of ecosystem structure, maintenance of ecologically or commercially important or threatened species or species assemblages, maintenance of critical habitat of endangered species, and the biogeographic representation of the site. * * *

Id. § 1433(b)(1)(A). The act stresses the importance of maintaining "natural biological communities * * * and to protect * * * natural habitats, populations, and ecological processes." Id. § 1431(b)(3). Designation of a marine area as a sanctuary, in itself, does not prohibit all development, but does require special use permits from the Department of Commerce (DOC) to authorize specific activities if compatible with the purposes of the sanctuary. Id. § 1440.

The United States has been slow to recognize the value of marine protected areas, and the National Marine Sanctuaries Program created in 1972 got off to a slow start. See Dave Owens, The Disappointing History of the National Marine Sanctuaries Act, 11 NYU Envt'l L.J. 711 (2003); W.J. Chandler and H. Gillelan, The History and Evolution of the National Marine Sanctuaries Act, 34 Envt'l L. Rep. 10505 (2004). The first sanctuary, the U.S.S. Monitor National Marine Sanctuary (NMS), was not designated by the Commerce Department until 1975. During this first phase of the NMS program, designation was a slow process and sanctuaries included relatively small areas of ocean space within their boundaries and were managed for narrowly defined purposes. Eight sanctuaries were designated during the period between 1975–88: the U.S.S. Monitor, Key Largo and Looe Key off Florida, Gray's Reef off Georgia, the Channel Islands, Gulf of Farallones, and Cordell Banks in California, and Fagatele Bay in the American Samoas. Criticism of the designation process and the effectiveness of the NMS program led to reassessment of the marine sanctuaries program.

In 1988 and 1992, the program was amended substantially. NOAA was given authority to review federal agency actions that may affect a sanctuary resource. Important provisions for enforcement and liability were added that give sanctuary designation and sanctuary management plans greater authority. The amendments provide that it is unlawful to:

(1) destroy, cause the loss of, or injure any sanctuary resource managed under law or regulations for that sanctuary;

(2) possess, sell, offer for sale, purchase, import, export, deliver, carry, transport, or ship by any means any sanctuary resource taken in violation of this section. * * *

Id. § 1436. A "sanctuary resource" is "any living or nonliving resource * * * that contributes to the * * * value of the sanctuary." Id. § 1432(8). The amendments create a rebuttable presumption that all sanctuary resources on board a vessel were taken in violation of the act or regulations. Id. § 1437(e)(4). Enforcement authorities are granted broad powers to board, search, and seize vessels, and impose penalties of up to $100,000 per violation per day. Id. § 1437. In addition, persons damaging or injuring any sanctuary resources are liable for response costs and damages, with retention of damage awards for restoration work. Id. § 1442. Damages from groundings, oil spills, and toxic pollution are covered. The 1984 grounding of the Cypriot M/V Wellwood in the Key Largo National Marine Sanctuary and the 1987 sinking of the oil tanker M/V Puerto Rican near the Gulf of Farallones National Marine Sanctuary had demonstrated the need for such a liability regime. See United States v. M/V Jacquelyn L., 100 F.3d 1520 (11th Cir. 1996); United States v. M/V Miss Beholden, 856 F. Supp. 668 (S.D. Fl. 1994); United States v. Great Lakes Dredge & Dock Co. 259 F.3d 1300 (11th Cir. 2001) (includes damages to state seabed within the sanctuary's boundaries). See also Tug Allie–B, Inc. v. United States, 273 F.3d 936 (11th Cir. 2001) (damages to coral reefs in Biscayne National Park collected under federal Park System Resources Protection Act).

The act also allows NOAA to review any federal agency action that might impact a sanctuary resource and requires NOAA to review and revise sanctuary management plans every five years. Id. §§ 1434(d),(e).

At times, Congress has accelerated the process by designating or ordering the designation of certain sanctuaries. During this second phase of sanctuary designation, the Florida Keys, Monterey Bay, Stellwagen Bank, the Hawaiian Islands Humpback Whale, the Flower Garden Banks, Olympic Coast, and Thunder Bay national marine sanctuaries have been created.

All these sanctuaries differ from those designated earlier in two ways: 1) their size, and 2) their management approach. The Stellwagen

Bank Sanctuary bans sand and gravel mining in the rich fisheries and whale calving grounds off the coast of Massachusetts, Pub. L. 102–587, while the Hawaiian Humpback Whale Sanctuary includes important breeding, calving, and nursing areas for the endangered humpback whale and requires development of a comprehensive management plan. Id. The Flower Garden Banks Sanctuary includes coral reefs and rich marine life 110 miles south of the Texas coast. Pub. L. 102–251. Furthermore, Congress finalized designation of the Monterey Bay Sanctuary, banning all oil and gas activities, Pub. L. 102–587; amended the Florida Keys Sanctuary Act to prioritize research needs, establish long-term ecological monitoring, and implement a water quality program, id.; prohibited oil and gas activities within the Olympic Coast Sanctuary off Washington State, id.; and authorized the President to establish the 100,000 square nautical mile Northwestern Hawaiian Islands Coral Reef Reserve pending its designation as a national marine sanctuary, Pub. L. 106–513.

President Clinton's executive orders creating the reserve restricted some activities throughout the reserve and established Reserve Preservation areas around certain islands, atolls, and banks in which all resource consumptive uses were restricted. See 66 Fed. Reg. 7395 (Jan. 18, 2001); 65 Fed. Reg. 76903 (Dec. 4, 2000). In 2005 the Hawaii Department of Land and Natural Resources issued a plan protecting the state islands, atolls, and their surrounding waters inside the reserve. In May 2006, state and federal officials signed an agreement to manage the area jointly. Then, to the surprise of many, in June 2006, rather than rely on the National Marine Sanctuaries Act to protect the coral reef ecosystems, President George W. Bush expanded and combined the reserve with two adjacent national wildlife refuges and declared them to be the 140,000 square mile (Northwestern Hawaiian Islands) Marine National Monument by proclamation under the Antiquities Act of 1906, 16 U.S.C. §§ 431–33. See 2006 WL 1646210 (June 15, 2006). Commercial fishing in the monument has been phased out (see 50 C.F.R. Part 665; 74 Fed. Reg. 15685 (April 7, 2009)) and other extractive resource uses are prohibited. Permits are required for all other activities. Based on nominations by the Bush Administration, the monument was subsequently designated a UNESCO World Heritage Site, and a Particularly Sensitive Sea Area (PSSA) by the International Maritime Organization (IMO) similar to the Florida Keys as discussed below. Res. MEPC. 171 (57), IMO Doc. MEPC 57/21, Annex 12 (2008). See Alison Rieser, The Unexpected Ark: The Blue Legacy of the Clinton and Bush Presidencies, 1993-2006, 28 J. Land Use & Envt'l L. ___ (2013).

When it was proclaimed a national monument in 2006, Papahanaumokuakea Marine National Monument was the world's largest MPA. Other nations were quick to follow suit and to establish other MPAs of comparable or even greater sizes. Alison Rieser, The Papahanaumokuakea Precedent: Ecosystem-scale Marine Protected Areas in the EEZ, 13 Asian-Pacific L. & Pol'y J. 210 (2011–12). In 2009 President Bush established three more marine national monuments in the Pacific totaling 195,274 square miles at the Marianas Trench, various remote coral atolls, and Rose Atoll in American Samoa.

The newest national marine sanctuaries and reserves encompass extensive ocean areas under both federal and state jurisdiction. Designation of large ocean areas allows management of more of the activities that affect sanctuary resources and provides the opportunity to develop an ecosystem approach to resource management. Management plans deal with direct and indirect, as well as primary and secondary, effects on sanctuary resources. For example, the management plan for the Monterey Bay sanctuary includes a Water Quality Protection Program. That program includes an Agriculture and Rural Lands Plan to help farmers in the bay's inland watershed minimize the runoff into the bay's waters of polluting sediments and nutrients from fields and rural roads.

International, as well as federal, state, and local cooperative programs are encouraged and advisory councils have become part of the management plan development process. For example, in May 2000, the International Maritime Organization (IMO) approved a Monterey Bay Vessel Traffic Plan designed to facilitate safe, efficient travel by large vessels through the Monterey Bay, Gulf of the Farallones, and Channel Islands national marine sanctuaries off California. In cooperation with the Stellwagen Bank National Marine Sanctuary, the IMO approved Atlantic coast traffic separation scheme changes and speed restricted areas designed to reduce ship collisions with whales.

Air quality in all North American coastal and offshore areas should be improved by the huge EEZ-wide Emission Control Area (ECA) approved by the IMO under MARPOL Annex VI in 2009. The ECA designation allows the U.S. to enforce U.S. air quality NO_x emission standards and fuel sulphur content limitations operating within 200 nautical miles off the U.S. coast, beginning in August 2012. The ECA covers the entire exclusive economic zones of Canada and the U.S., including Hawaii, but excluding U.S. flag Pacific Islands and Arctic areas of Canada and the U.S. north of 60°N latitude. See R. Hildreth & A. Torbitt, International Treaties and U.S. Laws as Tools to Regulate the Greenhouse Gas Emissions from Ships and Ports, 25 Int'l. J. of Marine & Coastal L. 347, 364–366 (2010).

In December 2002 the IMO approved a 3,000 square nautical mile Particularly Sensitive Sea Area (PSSA) in the Florida Keys, stretching from Biscayne National Park to the Tortugas, including all of the Florida Keys National Marine Sanctuary. Within the PSSA ships greater than 164 feet in length must avoid certain areas while in transit and when anchoring. Because designation of such large areas affects numerous user groups, conflict management is an important part of plan development and implementation as the following case illustrates.

PERSONAL WATERCRAFT INDUSTRY ASSOCIATION V. DEPARTMENT OF COMMERCE

United States Court of Appeals, District of Columbia Circuit, 1995
48 F.3d 540

RANDOLPH, CIRCUIT JUDGE.

These are cross-appeals from the District Court's judgment setting aside one of the regulations designed to protect and preserve the Monterey Bay National Marine Sanctuary off the central California coast. The regulation governs the use of "motorized personal watercraft"—jet skis, wet bikes, miniature speed boats, air boats, hovercraft, and the like—on the Sanctuary's waters. The District Court thought it arbitrary to regulate this sort of small craft without regulating other vessels. We reverse this portion of the Court's judgment.

I

The Monterey Bay National Marine Sanctuary encompasses 4000 square nautical miles of coastal and ocean waters, and the submerged lands thereunder. It is the nation's largest ocean sanctuary, spreading seaward as far as forty-six nautical miles, and extending along the California coast from the Gulf of Farallones in the north to San Simeon and Cambria Rock in the south. It encompasses the Monterey Peninsula, the "finest meeting of land and water in existence," so Robert Louis Stevenson believed. The area is home to thirty-one species of marine mammals, including the sea otter and twenty-one other threatened or endangered species protected under the Endangered Species Act, 16 U.S.C. §§ 1531–1544. There are large concentrations of whales, pinnipeds (e.g. seals) and seabirds. Fish stocks are substantial. Varieties of crustaceans and other invertebrates abound. Among the Sanctuary's diverse flora are forests of giant kelp growing from the seabed, with fronds towering to the surface as much as 175 feet above. Residents and visitors use the Sanctuary for kayaking, fishing, scuba diving, surfing, sailing, swimming, and other recreational activities.

Title III of the Marine Protection, Research, and Sanctuaries Act (the Act), as amended, 16 U.S.C. §§ 1431–1439, authorizes the Secretary of Commerce to designate as national marine sanctuaries discrete areas of the marine environment that are "of special national significance." 16 U.S.C. § 1433(a). In 1988, Congress directed the Secretary to issue a "notice of designation" under 16 U.S.C. § 1434(b)(1) for the waters in the vicinity of Monterey Bay "no later than December 31, 1989." Pub.L. No.

100–627, § 205(a)(3), 102 Stat. 3213, 3217 (1988). The National Oceanic and Atmospheric Administration (NOAA), to whom the Secretary had delegated authority, complied, but not until August 3, 1990, when it published in the Federal Register a notice of proposed designation, proposed implementing regulations, and a draft environmental impact statement discussing options for managing the proposed sanctuary. 55 Fed. Reg. 31,786 (Aug. 3, 1990). The agency requested comments within sixty days (by October 2, 1990).

In June 1992, after three public hearings and after receiving more than 1200 comments, NOAA issued its Final Environmental Impact Statement and, on September 18, 1992, its final regulations formalizing the designation of the Monterey Bay National Marine Sanctuary. 57 Fed. Reg. 43,310 (Sept. 18, 1992); 15 C.F.R. pt. 944.

One of the final regulations, 15 C.F.R. § 944.5(a)(8), limits the operation of "motorized personal water craft," also known as "thrill craft," in the Monterey Bay Sanctuary to four designated zones and access routes, an area of fourteen square nautical miles. The regulation defines "motorized personal watercraft" as:

> any motorized vessel that is less than fifteen feet in length as manufactured, is capable of exceeding a speed of fifteen knots, and has the capacity to carry not more than the operator and one other person while in operation. The term includes, but is not limited to, jet skis, wet bikes, surf jets, miniature speed boats, air boats and hovercraft.

15 C.F.R. § 944.3. NOAA's final regulations did not restrict the use of other types of vessels in the Monterey Bay Sanctuary. The agency stated that it was then working with the Coast Guard to determine whether such measures were needed. 57 Fed. Reg. at 43,311–12.

In July 1992, the Personal Watercraft Industry Association, an organization consisting of manufacturers and distributors, submitted comments to NOAA opposing the restrictions placed on personal watercraft. Thereafter the agency denied the Association's petition for rulemaking to rescind the "thrill craft" regulation. 58 Fed. Reg. 15,271 (Mar. 22, 1993).

* * *

On cross-motions for summary judgment, the district court held that the restriction on personal watercraft was arbitrary and capricious because NOAA had treated personal watercraft differently from all other vessels without providing a sufficient explanation. Personal Watercraft Indus. Ass'n v. Department of Commerce, No. 93–1381, at 3 (D.D.C. Aug. 24, 1993).

* * *

The Association complains about a "study" NOAA used in determining where personal watercraft would be allowed within the Sanctuary, but it is hard to tell exactly what the complaint is. Only two paragraphs of the Association's fifty-page brief are devoted to this topic; the summary of argument ignores it entirely. The two paragraphs are under the following heading, which does not talk directly about the study: the "personal watercraft restrictions were developed after the comment period closed and never made available for public scrutiny and comment." Appellees' Brief at 47. That of course is true with respect to NOAA's final regulations, and indeed would be true in any rulemaking proceeding in which an agency formulated its final rules in response to comments. If the heading is supposed to capture a colorable argument, we fail to see it. "Rulemaking proceedings would never end if the agency's response to comments must always be made the subject of additional comments." Community Nutrition Inst. v. Block, 749 F.2d 50, 58 (D.C.Cir. 1984).

* * *

NOAA retained Dr. James W. Rote, a marine biologist and former Director of the Office of Habitat Protection at NOAA. Dr. Rote was to "gather information about current restrictions and current areas of motorized personal watercraft use in the proposed Monterey Bay National Marine Sanctuary area" and "to develop recommended zones to which motorized personal watercraft use might be restricted." In June and October 1991, Dr. Rote delivered his recommendations. The four zones he suggested were designed to encompass the areas with the highest amount of personal watercraft use. The results of Dr. Rote's study were included in the final rulemaking. 57 Fed. Reg. at 43,328–29.

* * *

The District Court agreed with the Association that the regulation treated "personal watercraft (which are narrowly defined) differently from all other vessels, and that this disparate treatment is arbitrary and unsupported by the factual record." Personal Watercraft Industry Ass'n, No. 93–1381, at 2. It is worth keeping in mind that we are dealing with a marine sanctuary and measures an agency thought were needed to protect and preserve it. The regulations did indeed single out personal watercraft from other kinds of vessels. Maybe the presence of other vessels was a cause for concern; as we shall see, NOAA thought it might be. This scarcely means that NOAA had to regulate them if it was to do anything about thrill craft. An agency does not have to "make progress on every front before it can make progress on any front." United States v. Edge Broadcasting Co., 509 U.S. 418, ___ (1993). Agencies often must contend with matters of degree. Regulations, in other words, are not arbitrary just because they fail to regulate everything that could be thought to pose any sort of problem. Las Vegas v. Lujan, 891 F.2d 927, 935 (D.C.Cir. 1989); Louisiana v. Verity, 853 F.2d 322, 332 (5th Cir. 1988). This is a common principle, well known not only in administrative law cases but also in constitutional cases raising equal protection challenges to economic regulation. See Williamson v. Lee Optical of Oklahoma Inc., 348 U.S. 483, 489 (1955). To it, the district court here added a wrinkle—when an agency decides "to address several aspects of the problem itself in a single rulemaking, it must provide a reasoned basis for differential treatment of the various causes of the perceived problem." Personal Watercraft Industry Ass'n, No. 93–1381, at 4 n.2. This suggests that if an agency did a little, that would be permissible, but if it did more than a little, it had better have a good reason for not going all the way. We fail to see why it should matter whether the agency takes two steps instead of one, so long as it is heading in a proper direction. The patient has a headache, a sore throat and a hangnail. Are we to suppose that it would be arbitrary to treat only the headache and the sore throat in a single session, yet not be arbitrary to treat only the hangnail?

Before discussing this further, we ought to examine what made jet skis and other thrill craft the headache. The record is full of evidence that machines of this sort threatened the Monterey Bay National Marine Sanctuary. NOAA received written comments and testimony from marine scientists, researchers, federal agencies, state agencies, state and local governments, business organizations, and more than a hundred citizens on the issue of regulating these machines. Everyone agreed—personal watercraft interfered with the public's recreational safety and enjoyment of the Sanctuary and posed a serious threat to the Sanctuary's flora and fauna. The concept of a "sanctuary" entails elements of serenity, peace, and tranquility. Yet the commenters described instances of personal watercraft operators harassing sea otters and other marine mammals, disturbing harbor seals, damaging the Sanctuary's kelp forests, menacing swimmers, divers, kayakers, and other recreational users, and generally disrupting the esthetic enjoyment of the Sanctuary. All concerned recommended either prohibiting personal watercraft outright or restricting them to specific areas in the Sanctuary. No one urged NOAA to do nothing about the problem.

When NOAA acted, did it satisfactorily explain itself? The Administrative Procedure Act required it to give a "concise general statement" of the regulation's "basis and purpose." 5 U.S.C. § 553(c). Here is part of what NOAA said:

> The small size, maneuverability and high speed of these craft is what causes these craft to pose a threat to resources. Resources such as sea otters and seabirds are either unable to avoid these craft or are frequently alarmed enough to significantly modify their behavior such

as cessation of feeding or abandonment of young. Also other, more benign, uses of the Sanctuary such as sailing, kayaking, surfing and diving are interfered with during the operation of [personal water-craft].

* * *

This regulation is intended to provide enhanced resource protection by prohibiting operation of motorized personal watercraft in areas of high marine mammal and seabird concentrations, kelp forest areas, river mouths, estuaries, lagoons and other similar areas where sensitive marine resources are concentrated and most vulnerable to disturbance and other injury from personal watercraft.

57 Fed. Reg. at 43,314, 43,321. The first paragraph is the "basis," the second the "purpose." The statement is "concise" and it is "general."

Despite NOAA's evident compliance with the Administrative Procedure Act, the Association rails against "NOAA's unsupported and unexplained distinction between personal watercraft and other similar and larger vessels," Appellees' Brief at 32. The Association is very much mistaken and its citation of, for example, National Wildlife Federation v. Costle, 629 F.2d 118, 133–35 (D.C.Cir. 1980), is therefore off the mark. NOAA did explain and support the distinction. It said that personal watercraft were small, highly maneuverable, and fast, and it indicated that they operated close to shore, in areas of high concentrations of kelp forests, marine mammals and sea birds. That differentiated all larger craft, all slower craft, all less maneuverable craft, and all craft that did not tend to use the same areas in the same manner. As if this were not enough, NOAA also stated why it had decided not to regulate vessels other than personal watercraft *at this time*. NOAA said that it was working with the United States Coast Guard "to determine the need for additional measures to ensure protection of Sanctuary resources and qualities from vessel traffic," adding that:

These consultations aim to determine which resources are most at risk, which vessel traffic practices are most threatening and which regulations or restrictions would be most appropriate to alleviate potential threats, including those, if any, from foreign vessels.

57 Fed. Reg. at 43,311.

There for all who read the Federal Register are the reasons for NOAA's regulating personal watercraft and for not then regulating other vessels—the first category posed a clear problem, the rest needed further study, which the agency had undertaken.

The Act authorized NOAA to set down rules for the Sanctuary that it determined "may be necessary and reasonable." 16 U.S.C. § 1434(a)(1)(A).

The record amply supports NOAA's judgment of September 1992, that restricting thrill craft was then necessary and reasonable. It may turn out that regulating other vessels will also be necessary and reasonable. NOAA has yet to make that determination. But nothing in Title III of the Marine Protection, Research, and Sanctuaries Act, or in the Administrative Procedure Act, or in any judicial decision, forces an agency to refrain from solving one problem while it ponders what to do about others.

* * *

As NOAA pointed out in its Final Environmental Impact Statement, personal watercraft use was a relatively new phenomenon and local governments had only just begun issuing laws to minimize conflicts between this form of water sport, and other uses of marine resources. Many local officials urged NOAA to restrict jet skis; the towns of Capitola and Pacifica, and the County of Santa Cruz had their own restrictions, but these of course applied only within their jurisdictions. NOAA's regulatory jurisdiction—over 4000 square nautical miles—was considerably more comprehensive. As one would expect, the agency therefore determined that regulating personal watercraft throughout the Sanctuary was needed to fill what would otherwise have been a "major gap in the regulatory regime governing activities in the area."

* * *

NOAA's personal watercraft regulation is not arbitrary and capricious, and the district court's judgment is therefore reversed.

NOTES AND QUESTIONS

1. If the designation document for a national marine sanctuary is silent on the siting of floating nuclear power plants, would such energy facilities within the sanctuary be subject to regulation by the Secretary of Commerce?

2. Does authority to regulate activities occurring within a sanctuary include the power to meet threats from outside the sanctuary? For example, an oil spill from a source outside the sanctuary could drift across the sanctuary boundary. Or shipping could pose threats to whales designated as "sanctuary resources." How does the Secretary gain the cooperation of other agencies with authority to protect marine resources within marine sanctuaries?

3. What values is the marine sanctuary program intended to protect? The Act states that preserving aesthetic values is one reason for establishing marine sanctuaries. Could a marine sanctuary be used to protect an ocean vista from the impact of visible drilling platforms? In a dispute over oil and gas development in the Channel Islands National Marine Sanctuary, the California Coastal Commission's consistency objection to Union Oil's exploration plan to drill two new wells within the boundaries of the sanctuary was overruled by the Secretary of Commerce on appeal. The Secretary found the ex-

ploration plan to be consistent with the objectives of the CZMA and allowed federal agencies to approve exploration activities as described in the Union Oil exploration plan. 50 Fed. Reg. 872 (Jan. 7, 1985).

4. Could designation of a sanctuary ever result in restrictions on commercial and recreational fishing and diving activities? See Craft v. National Park Service, 34 F.3d 918 (9th Cir. 1994); United States v. Fisher, 22 F.3d 262 (11th Cir. 1994); United States v. Fisher, 977 F. Supp. 1193 (S.D. Fla. 1997) (injunctions and civil penalties imposed on divers and salvors for altering sanctuary seabed without permits). Final rules establishing requirements for fishing in the three Pacific marine national monuments created by proclamation in 2009 were published in 2013. 50 C.F.R. 665; 78 Fed. Reg. 32996 (June 3, 2013).

5. Which resource values should have priority in the designation of marine sanctuaries? Factors taken into account in the designation of marine sanctuaries have included the potential threat to the resources of the area, the significance of the area for research, the value of the area in complementing other areas or programs with similar objectives, the beauty of the area, the economic value of the area which might have to be forgone if designated a sanctuary, and the economic benefit to be derived from protecting the area.

6. In light of ocean warming and the loss of sea ice in the Arctic Ocean, could a U.S. president use the Antiquities Act of 1906 to create a "reverse Truman Proclamation" relinquishing the power to exploit the oil and gas resources of the continental shelf? Is the president's power under the Antiquities Act more durable than a congressional moratorium on oil and gas leasing?

C. STATE MARINE RESERVES AND PUBLIC ACCESS

As the brief history presented above demonstrates, Congress has been ambivalent at best about the Secretary of Commerce's authority to establish national marine reserves and sanctuaries. The Executive Branch has therefore resorted to using the Antiquities Act of 1906 to do so, as President George W. Bush's marine national monuments in 2006 and 2009 illustrate. The State of California has used state laws and private funding to plan for and then enact a network of marine protected areas in its waters. Despite extensive efforts to engage all stakeholders in the planning process, the process has been challenged on a number of grounds, including that the system deprives recreational users of access to public waters.

VENTURA COUNTY COMMERCIAL FISHERMEN'S ASS'N V. CAL. FISH & GAME COMM'N

Cal. Appellate Div., 2nd District, 2004
Not Reported in Cal.Rptr.3d, 2004 WL 293565

YEGAN, JUDGE.

Ventura County Commercial Fishermen's Association, United Anglers of Southern California, Pacific Coast Federation of Fishermen's Associations, Commercial Fishermen of Santa Barbara, Inc., Southern California Commercial Fishing Association, Sea Urchin Harvesters Association of California, California Lobster and Trap Fishermen's Association, Recreational Fishing Alliance/Southern California, and Sportfishing Association of California appeal from an order denying their motion for a temporary restraining order (TRO) to enjoin implementation of the Channel Islands Marine Protected Area Project (MPA). The MPA creates "no take" fish zones in the Channel Islands National Marine Sanctuary off the Santa Barbara Coast.[1] (Cal.Code Regs., tit. 14, § 632.)

Facts and Procedural History

On October 23, 2002, respondents California Department of Fish and Game and California Fish and Game Commission (Commission) adopted regulations to establish a network of Marine Protected Areas at the Channel Islands National Marine Sanctuary. (Cal.Code Regs., tit. 14, § 632.) Operative April 9, 2003, the regulations prohibit or restrict the "take of fish" and certain acquatic wildlife near Anacapa, Santa Cruz, San Miguel, Santa Rose, and Santa Barbara Islands. The MPA network closes 19 percent of the state waters around the islands to commercial and recreational fishing, and is designed to restore fish and aquatic resources.[2] In adopting the regulations, Commission certified a final environmental

---

[1] Although the Channel Islands National Marine Sanctuary is a national monument, the State of California has dominion over submerged lands and waters within one-mile belts around the islands. See, *United States v. California* (1978) 436 U.S. 32.

[2] The MPA Project is the culmination of three years of studies and a federal-state partnership to establish marine reserves in the Channel Islands National Marine Sanctuary. In 1999 the California Legislature enacted the Marine Life Protection Act (Fish & Game Code, § 2850 et seq), directing Commission to develop a master plan for the adoption and implementation of a network of MPAs to sustain, conserve, and protect marine life populations.

In 1999, the Channel Islands National Marine Sanctuary Advisory Council formed a stakeholder community-based group (Marine Reserves Working Group) to evaluate the establishment of MPAs around the Channel Islands. The group included state and federal agencies, recreational and commercial fishing groups, conservation interests, the public at large, and the California Sea Grant Program. The Channel Islands National Marine Sanctuary Advisory Council also created a Science Advisory Panel and a Socio-Economic Panel to develop MPA criteria, evaluate different marine reserve scenarios, collect baseline economic data, and study the socioeconomic effects of each marine reserve scenario.

Based on the recommendations of the Marine Reserve Working Group, the Channel Islands National Marine Sanctuary Advisor and its advisory panels, the Channel Islands National Marine Sanctuary Manager, and the California Department of Fish and Game, Commission drafted regulations for the MPA Project and undertook its own public and environmental review process.

document (FED), as required by the California Environmental Quality Act (CEQA; Pub. Resources Code, § 21000 et seq.).

Appellants, a group of nine commercial and sportfishing associations, filed a mandamus petition and complaint for declaratory relief. The first amended complaint alleged that (1) Commission violated the Administrative Procedure Act (Gov.Code, § 11340 et seq) in adopting the regulations, (2) that the final environmental document (FED) does not comply with CEQA, (3) that the regulations violate the California Constitution which guarantees the right to fish, (4) and Commission's approval of the MPA Project was invalid because the commissioner casting the definitive vote was appointed by the governor but the appointment was not yet approved by the Senate.

Discussion

Even though adoption of the MPA regulations was a quasi-legislative act, appellants assert that certification of the final environmental document (the FED) was a quasi-judicial act and subject to an administrative mandamus standard of review.In an administrative mandamus proceeding, the trial court may stay enforcement of the regulations pending trial based on a showing that the public will not be harmed.

Respondents correctly argue that the traditional mandamus standard of review applies where the plaintiff challenges an agency's quasi-legislative action and accompanying environmental decision. The dominant purpose of Commission's action was to adopt regulations for implementation of the MPA Project. As a traditional mandamus action, the trial court had no statutory authority to order a stay. (Kostka & Zichke, Practice Under the Cal. Environmental Quality Act (Cont.Ed.Bar 2003) § 23.83, p. 1003.) Before it could issue a TRO to enjoin enforcement of the regulations, the trial court was required to consider the likelihood that appellants would prevail at trial and balance the relative hardships.

Balancing of Harm

Appellants argue that the order denying the TRO is subject to de novo review because respondents submitted no evidence of comparative harm. They claim that there are no equities to balance. Appellants, however, seek injunctive relief by way of an ex parte temporary restraining order. The burden is on them to show interim harm and the likelihood of prevailing at trial.

Where the defendants are public agencies and the plaintiff seeks to restrain the performance of their duties, public policy considerations come into play. (Agricultural Labor Relations Bd. v. Superior Court (1976) 16 Cal.3d 392, 401.) "The codes, embodying a settled principle of equity jurisprudence, prohibit the granting of injunctive relief 'To prevent the execution of a public statute by officers of the law for the public benefit.'

(Code Civ. Proc., § 526, 2d subd. 4; Civ.Code, § 3423, subd. Fourth.) That rule is here applicable, inasmuch as a regulation adopted by a state administrative agency pursuant to a delegation of rulemaking authority by the Legislature has the force and effect of a statute. [Citations.]"

Although appellants predict irreparable economic harm, the declarations in support of the TRO are speculative, conclusory, and lack foundation. In a mandamus action challenging an agency's quasi-legislative administrative decision, evidence outside the administrative record is generally not admissible.

The record here refutes appellants' claim of dire economic harm to the fishing industry. It includes economic studiespredicting that the maximum annual loss to commercial fishing in state waters will be 16.5 percent or $3.3 million. The projected maximum loss of annual income for recreational fishing will be $3.28 million. The studies indicate that MPAs rapidly increase fish population and biomass and will rebuild stock in fish areas accessible to appellants. The spillover effect will offset appellants' projected losses. The administrative record states: "In the long term, the potential negative impacts are expected to be balanced by the positive impacts of sustainable fisheries, non-consumptive benefits, and ecosystem function in the reserve areas."

Substantial evidence supports the finding that the state will suffer great public harm if the MPA regulations are stayed pending trial. The Legislature has identified the public harm in declaring that "marine biological diversity is a vital asset to the state and nation. The diversity of species and ecosystems found in the state's ocean waters is important to public health and well-being, ecological health, and ocean-dependent industry. [¶] (c) Coastal development, water pollution, and other human activities threaten the health of marine habitat and the biological diversity found in California's ocean waters. New technologies and demands have encouraged the expansion of fishing and other activities to formerly inaccessible marine areas that once recharged nearby fisheries. As a result, ecosystems throughout the state's ocean waters are being altered, often at a rapid rate." (Fish & Game Code, 2851, subds. (b) & (c).)

The MPA Project was implemented because of a historic decline in fish stocks and degradation of marine habitats. The final environmental document (FED), which was certified by Commission, states that delays in implementing the project will result in a further decline of fish habitat and "could prevent rebuilding of overfished stocks and could lead to ESA [Endangered Species Act; 16 U.S.C. § 1531 et seq.] listings that would have dramatic negative consequences for the fisheries. There is no way to estimate or quantify those potential negative impacts."

We reject the argument that an ex parte TRO application may be used to reweigh evidence considered by Commission in adopting the MPA regulations. "The decisions do not sustain the [appellants'] contention that in determining the validity of the regulation this court should exercise its independent judgment and reweigh the proffered evidence. While such a test may apply to the review of the adjudicatory or quasi-judicial rulings of certain agencies (Code Civ. Proc., § 1094.5) it does not pertain to the review of regulations rendered by an agency in its quasi-legislative capacity."

Likelihood of Success

The trial court, in denying the TRO, found that appellants failed to show a reasonable likelihood of prevailing at trial. There was no abuse of discretion. "A trial court may not grant a [restraining order], regardless of the balance of interim harm, unless there is some possibility that the plaintiff would ultimately prevail on the merits of the claim. [Citation.]"

Appellants' action is based on the theory that Commission, in adopting the MPA regulations, violated certain notice provisions of the Administrative Procedure Act. (APA; Gov.Code, § 11340 et seq.) None of the APA claims are supported by the record.

* * *

California Constitution

Appellants argue that article 1, section 25 of the California Constitution establishes the right to fish and, by implication, prohibits "no take" fish reserves.[6] Our Supreme Court has held that "the right to fish under article I, section 25 is not an unqualified one. . . . [A]lthough the public has a constitutional right to fish, . . . this right is subject to reasonable regulation. . . . " (State of California v. San Luis Obispo Sportsman's Assn. (1978) 22 Cal.3d 440, 448; e.g., California Gillnetters Assn. v. Department of Fish & Game (1995) 39 Cal.App.4th 1145, 1154 ["right to fish" not a fundamental right].) Appellants have no constitutional right to deplete or destroy a fish preserve, in this instance, a marine sanctuary.

The Legislature, in the exercise of its regulatory powers, may protect and preserve fish and aquatic resources by imposing no-take zones. (People v. Zankich (1971) 20 Cal.App.3d 971, 980–981 [state may restrict taking of anchovies by closing fish area].) Article 4, section 20 of the California Constitution provides that the Legislature may delegate to the Fish and Game Commission "such powers relating to the protection and

---

[6] Article 1, section 25 of the California Constitution provides: "The people shall have the right to fish upon and from the public lands of the State and in the waters thereof, excepting upon lands set aside for fish hatcheries, and no land owned by the State shall ever be sold or transferred without reserving in the people the absolute right to fish thereupon; and no law shall ever be passed making it a crime for the people to enter upon the public lands within this State for the purpose of fishing in any water containing fish that may have been planted therein by the State; *provided, that the Legislature may by statute provide for the season when and the conditions under which the different species of fish may be taken.*" (Emphasis added.)

propagation of fish and game as the Legislature sees fit." In 1999, our Legislature enacted Fish and Game Code section 2860 which provides in pertinent part that "[t]he commission may regulate commercial and recreational fishing and any other taking of marine species in MPAs."

* * *

In the course of implementing the Marine Life Protection Act to create a network of marine reserves, the State of California was near bankruptcy. When the governor cancelled the funding for the program, a private foundation stepped forward to allow the program to continue. The following challenge ensued.

COASTSIDE FISHING CLUB V. CAL. RESOURCES AGENCY

Court of Appeal, First District, Division 2, California, 2008
158 Cal.App.4th 1183, 71 Cal.Rptr.3d 87

KLINE, P.J.

On August 27, 2004, respondents, the California Resources Agency (Agency) and the California Department of Fish and Game (DFG), which is supervised by the Agency, entered into a memorandum of understanding (MOU) with respondent Resources Legacy Fund Foundation (Foundation), a private nonprofit organization, for the purpose of facilitating implementation of the Marine Life Protection Act (MLPA). (Fish & G.Code, § 2850 et seq.) As later explained in detail, the Legislature failed to appropriate funds sufficient to support the new and substantial planning responsibilities the MLPA required DFG to complete within a specified period. The MOU was designed to rectify this problem through creation of a "public-private partnership" providing the resources necessary to comply with these mandates.

Appellants, Coastside Fishing Club, a nonprofit organization representing recreational fishermen, and Michael J. Nolan, a member of the Club residing in Del Norte County and a California taxpayer, claim that the MOU was not authorized by the MLPA; was improperly devised by the Agency and DFG to "appropriate" money in a manner other than that prescribed by the California Constitution (Cal. Const., art. XVI, § 7 ["Money may be drawn from the Treasury only through an appropriation made by law and upon a Controller's duly drawn warrant"]), and thereby also violated the constitutional doctrine of separation of powers (id., art. III, § 3 ["The powers of state government are legislative, executive, and judicial. Persons charged with the exercise of one power may not exercise either of the others except as permitted by this Constitution"]).

* * *

II

The Marine Life Protection Act

The MLPA declares that "California's marine protected areas (MPAs)[3] were established on a piecemeal basis rather than according to a coherent plan and sound scientific guidelines. Many of these MPAs lack clearly defined purposes, effective management measures and enforcement. As a result, the array of MPAs creates the illusion of protection while falling far short of its potential to protect and conserve living marine life and habitat." (§ 2851, subd. (a).) In order to improve the design and management of the MPA system, the MLPA directs the Fish and Game Commission (Commission)—which independently establishes the policies DFG must follow in administering programs and enforcing laws pertaining to fish, wildlife, and natural resources of the state—to adopt a "Marine Life Protection Program" designed to achieve legislatively specified goals. (§§ 2853, subd. (b)(1)–(6), 2859.) The Commission, which is not a party to this action, is also directed to "adopt a master plan that guides the adoption and implementation of the Marine Life Protection Program . . . and decisions regarding the siting of new MPAs and major modifications of existing MPAs." (§ 2855, subd. (a).) Like DFG, the Commission is located within the Agency; however, unlike the DFG or the Agency, the Commission is an independent constitutional body. (Cal. Const., art. IV. § 20.)

DFG's responsibilities under the MLPA are to prepare a draft master plan for consideration by the Commission, convene a "master plan team" to assist in that enterprise, and to carry out those duties in a specified manner (which is described, *post,* at pp. 105–09). The particular provision of the MLPA at issue, subdivision (b)(1) of section 2855, provides that in order to facilitate adoption of a master plan by the Commission, DFG "shall prepare, or *by contract shall cause to be prepared,* a [draft] master plan" compliant with the MLPA, and "shall convene a master plan team to advise and assist in the preparation of the master plan, or *hire a contractor* with relevant expertise to assist in convening such a team." (Italics added.) Appellants' chief claim is that the contracts authorized by this language are only those using public funds for the purpose of procuring expert assistance relating either to preparation of the draft master plan or the convening of a master plan team. Appellants maintain that the Foundation lacks the requisite expertise relevant to those matters and

---

[3] An MPA, which is "primarily intended to protect or conserve marine life and habitat," is "a named, discrete geographic marine or estuarine area seaward of the mean high tide line or the mouth of a coastal river . . . [which] includes marine life reserves and other areas that allow for specified commercial and recreational activities, including fishing for certain species but not others, fishing with certain practices but not others, and kelp harvesting, provided that these activities are consistent with the objectives of the area and the goals and guidelines of [the MLPA]." (§ 2852, subd. (c).)

that, in any case, it was not the purpose of the MOU to obtain such assistance. As appellants see it, the only and very different purpose of the MOU is simply to provide DFG private funds to defray the costs of implementing the MLPA. Appellants claim that neither the Agency nor DFG are statutorily authorized to solicit and employ private funds for that purpose, by means of contract or otherwise, and that implementation of the MLPA may be carried out only with public funds. According to appellants, the much broader interpretation of the statute adopted by the trial court cannot be reconciled with the doctrine of separation of powers embodied in article III, section 3, of the California Constitution.

* * *

IV

* * *

In the California Ocean Resources Stewardship Act of 2000 (Pub.Res.Code, §§ 36970–36973), which became law shortly after the MLPA was enacted, the Legislature noted that state agencies like DFG that have ocean and coastal management responsibilities "often lack basic information on which to base decisions," and that the "existing means for coordinating agency efforts need to be improved." (Pub.Res.Code, § 36971, subd. (e).) That act also stated that "[a]pproximately one hundred million dollars ($100,000,000) in *current, recent,* or planned marine science projects funded by the federal government, *foundations,* the University of California and California State University systems, and *private institutions* could be of great benefit to the state's coastal and ocean resource management agencies." (Pub.Res.Code, § 36971, subd. (f), italics added.) Aware of the importance of such assistance, the Legislature declared it the policy of the state to "encourage" the contribution of "nongovernmental resources" to supplement state resources devoted to ocean resource management. (Pub.Res.Code, § 36972, subd. (b).) The need for such supplemental funds is clear from the MLPA itself, because it requires the Commission to implement the California Marine Life Protection Program with regulations based on the final master plan on or before December 1, 2005 only "to the extent funds are [then] available." (§ 2859, subd. (b).) Finally, when it enacted the Marine Managed Areas Improvement Act (Pub.Res.Code, §§ 36601–36700), which is statutorily coordinated with the MLPA (§ 1591, subd. (a)), the Legislature explicitly endorsed the use of "public/private partnerships," such as the MOU, "to provide access to general information and data about ocean and coastal resources within California's [Marine Managed Areas]." (Pub.Res.Code, § 36601, subd. (a)(11).) Indeed, the Legislature has provided that "public-private partnerships, wherever practicable, shall be the primary means of achieving the objectives of the [California Wetlands Preservation Act]" (Pub.Res.Code, § 5811, subd. (c)), and has authorized DFG to "accept contributions to the Coastal Wetlands Fund . . . [from, among others] private individuals and organizations [and] nonprofit organizations. . . ." (Pub.Res.Code, § 5818.2, subd. (c).)

In 2004, during the session in which it appropriated $500,000 to provide the matching funds DFG needed to leverage private resources for MLPA implementation, the Legislature enacted the California Ocean Protection Act. (Pub. Res.Code, §§ 35500 et seq.) The purpose of that act, which relates to the MLPA, "is to integrate and coordinate the state's laws and institutions responsible for protecting and conserving ocean resources, including coastal waters and ocean ecosystems." (*Id.,* § 35515.) Significantly, one of the objectives of the measure is to "[u]se California's private and charitable resources more effectively in developing ocean protection and conservation strategies." (*Id.,* § 35515, subd. (d).)

The foregoing events and statutes may appropriately be taken into consideration in ascertaining the intent of the Legislature in enacting subdivision (b)(1) of section 2855.

* * *

We are also mindful that "[l]aws providing for the conservation of natural resources are of great remedial and public importance and thus should be construed liberally" so as to promote the general object sought to be accomplished. Because the narrow interpretation of subdivision (b)(1) of section 2855 urged by appellants would obstruct the purpose of the MLPA, we cannot accept it *unless,* as appellants maintain, the only competing interpretation would unconstitutionally delegate a legislative power to an executive branch agency, because "[a] statute should be construed whenever possible so as to preserve its constitutionality. [Citations.]" That is not, however, the case.

* * *

With the foregoing considerations in mind, we move to the central question whether, if the trial court's interpretation of subdivision (b)(1) of section 2855 were accepted, the MLPA would impermissibly delegate to DFG or those with whom it contracts the power to resolve "truly fundamental issues" constitutionally committed to the Legislature, because the MLPA fails to establish effective mechanisms, or safeguards, containing the discretion of DFG or its contractors, enabling them to distort or obstruct enforcement of the Legislature's policy decisions.

As we have seen, the fundamental issue the MLPA addresses is the need "to modify the existing collection of MPAs to ensure that they are designed and managed according to clear, conservation-based goals and guidelines that take full advantage of the multiple benefits that can be derived from the establishment of marine life reserves" (§ 2851, subd. (h)), through promulgation of a comprehensive Marine Life Protection Program. Delegating the power to adopt such a program and an implementing master plan to the Commission (§ 2853), the Legislature delegated to DFG the duty to prepare and submit to the Commission a draft master plan guiding adoption and implementation of the Marine Life Protection Program. (§ 2855, subds. (a), (b)(1).) We conclude that the delegation to DFG contains safeguards adequately ensuring that the draft master plan it prepares or causes to be prepared conforms to the legislative will.

First, by specifying the six "goals" of the Marine Life Protection Program and the five "elements" the program must contain (§ 2853, subds. (b), (c)), the Legislature has elaborately cabined the substance and scope of the master plan.[13] DFG's authority to prepare the draft master plan and convene the required "master plan team," and to obtain assistance in those efforts, is also statutorily constrained. DFG and the master plan team are mandated to "use the best readily available scientific information" and the draft plan must "use and build upon the findings of the Sea Grant survey of protected areas in California waters, entitled 'California's Marine Protected Areas,' the report of the State Interagency Marine Managed Areas Workgroup, the Department of Parks and Recreation's planning information and documents regarding existing and potential underwater parks and reserves, maps and other information from the department's marine nearshore ecosystem mapping project, and other relevant planning and scientific materials." (§ 2856, subd. (a)(1).)

The five elements the program must include are: "(1) An improved marine life reserve component consistent with the guidelines in subdivision (c) of Section 2857. (2) Specific identified objectives, and management and enforcement measures, for all MPAs in the system. (3) Provisions for monitoring, research, and evaluation at selected sites to facilitate adaptive management of MPAs and ensure that the system meets the goals stated in this chapter. (4) Provisions for educating the public about MPAs, and for administering and enforcing MPAs in a manner that encourages public participation. (5) A process for the establishment, modification, or abolishment of existing MPAs or new MPAs established pursuant to this program, that involves interested parties, consistent with paragraph (7) of subdivision (b) of Section 7050, and that facilitates the designation of

---

[13] The six goals are: "(1) To protect the natural diversity and abundance of marine life, and the structure, function, and integrity of marine ecosystems. 2) To help sustain, conserve, and protect marine life populations, including those of economic value, and rebuild those that are depleted. 3) To improve recreational, educational, and study opportunities provided by marine ecosystems that are subject to minimal human disturbance, and to manage these uses in a manner consistent with protecting biodiversity. (4) To protect marine natural heritage, including protection of representative and unique marine life habitats in California waters for their intrinsic value. (5) To ensure that California's MPAs have clearly defined objectives, effective management measures, and adequate enforcement, and are based on sound scientific guidelines. (6) To ensure that the state's MPAs are designed and managed, to the extent possible, as a network." (§ 2853, subd. (b)(1)–(6).)

MPAs consistent with the master plan adopted pursuant to Section 2855." (§ 2853, subd. (c)(1)–(5).)

The 11 "components" of the master plan are not only clearly identified but extraordinarily specific. (§ 2856, subd. (a)(2)(A)–(K).) To take just several of many possible examples, the MLPA not only requires the master plan to include "[r]ecommendations for the extent and types of habitat that should be represented in the MPA system and marine life reserves," but specifies that habitat types described on maps must include "rocky reefs, intertidal zones, sandy or soft ocean bottoms, underwater pinnacles, sea mounts, kelp forests, submarine canyons, and seagrass beds." (§ 2856, subd. (a)(2)(A).) The master plan must not only identify "species or groups of species likely to benefit from MPAs, and the extent of their marine habitat, with special attention to marine breeding and spawning grounds," but also provide relevant information pertaining to "oceanographic features, such as current patterns, upwelling zones, and other factors that significantly affect the distribution of those fish or shellfish and their larvae." (§ 2856, subd. (a)(2)(B).) Nor is it enough under the MLPA for the master plan to simply recommend a network of MPAs. Pursuant to section 2856, subdivision (a)(2)(D) and (F), the MPA siting alternatives recommended by the plan must be capable of achieving the statutorily-specified goals of the Marine Life Protection Program (§ 2853), and conform to five siting guidelines that are also statutorily specified (§ 2857, subd. (c)). The master plan must also include a "[a] simplified classification system" that is also consistent with specified goals and guidelines. (§ 2856, subd. (a)(2)(E).)

The impartiality and integrity of the draft master plan DFG or a contractor prepares, and the transparency of the preparation process, is ensured not only by the requirement that numerous "siting workshops" open to all interested persons be convened in each "biogeographical region" to review "alternatives for MPA networks and to provide advice on a preferred siting alternative" (§ 2857, subd. (a)), but as well by the requirement of "a process for external peer review of the scientific basis for the master plan" (§ 2858, see also § 7062). Before submitting a proposed final master plan to the Commission, DFG must make the draft master plan available for public review and conduct not less than three public meetings. (§ 2859, subd. (b).)

DFG's discretion to select the membership of the master plan team, and the derivative discretion of any contractor with whom DFG may contract for assistance in convening the team, is also severely limited. To begin with, members of the team are required to "have expertise in mrine life protection and shall be knowledgeable about the use of protected areas as a marine ecosystem management tool." (§ 2855, subd. (b)(2).) Members "shall also be familiar with underwater ecosystems found in California waters, with the biology and habitat requirements of major species groups in the state's marine waters, and with water quality and related issues." (*Ibid.*) The MLPA specifies that the team "shall be composed of . . . [A] [s]taff from [DFG], the Department of Parks and Recreation, and the State Water Resources Control Board, to be designated by each those departments, [B] [f]ive to seven members who shall be scientists, one of whom may have expertise in the economics and culture of California coastal communities [and] [C] [o]ne member, appointed from a list prepared by Sea Grant marine advisers, who shall have direct expertise with ocean habitat and sea life in California marine waters." (§ 2855, subd. (b)(3)(A), (B), (C).)

The MLPA also specifies other participants who must be involved in the planning process. The master plan must be prepared with the "advice, assistance and involvement of participants in the various fisheries and their representatives, marine conservationists, marine scientists, and other interested persons. In preparing the master plan, [DFG] shall [also] confer, to the extent feasible, with the commission, the Pacific Fishery Management Council, the National Marine Fisheries Service, the United States Navy, the United States Geological Survey's national biological survey, staff from national marine sanctuaries off California, Sea Grant researchers, marine advisers, and national parks personnel." (§ 2855, subd. (b)(4).) In carrying out its responsibilities, DFG "may engage other experts" (§ 2855, subd. (b)(5)), and "shall take into account relevant information from local communities, and shall solicit comment and advice for the master plan from [other] interested parties" on a nonexclusive list of specified issues. (§ 2855, subd. (c).)

The foregoing requirements of the MLPA demonstrate that the determination and formulation of legislative policy is not left in the hands of DFG, and certainly not in those of any private party with whom it may contract for assistance. Judicially enforceable standards identify the substantive issues required to be addressed in the master plan, ensure that those who prepare the draft master plan are scientifically qualified to do so, specify the transparent manner in which the plan is prepared, the persons and interest groups that must be invited to participate in the planning process, the experts who must be consulted, and the objectivity and quality of the scientific information relied upon. These many specifications significantly limit the discretionary authority of DFG and those with whom it contracts for assistance (including financial assistance) to produce a draft master plan that departs from the goals of the MLPA. . . . The trial court correctly determined that the MOU was authorized by subdivision (b)(1) of section 2855, and the result of that ruling does not compromise the doctrine of separation of powers and therefore does not violate article III, section 3 of the California Constitution.

NOTES AND QUESTIONS

1. Recalling Chief Justice Marshall's dissent in Alliance to Protect Nantucket Sound, supra Chapter 5, beginning on p. 502, would it violate the Massachusetts' public trust doctrine for the Commonwealth to contract with a private foundation to conduct a marine spatial planning process for Massachusetts' waters?

2. Could a private foundation give a gift to NOAA's National Marine Sanctuaries Program to fund a national planning process for establishing a network of marine reserves in the U.S. Exclusive Economic Zone?

INDEX

References are to Pages

*Figures and tables are indicated by "f" and "t"
following page numbers*